W9-BDN-444

PrincetonReview.com

THE BEST 295
BUSINESS SCHOOLS

2014 EDITION

The Staff
of The Princeton Review

Random House, Inc.
New York

TPR Education IP Holdings, LLC
111 Speen Street, Suite 550
Framingham, MA 01701
E-mail: editorialsupport@review.com

ISBN: 978-0-8041-2435-5
ISSN: 2161-5772

Senior VP, Publisher: Robert Franek
Production: Best Content Solutions, LLC
Production Editor: Melissa Duclos-Yourdon
Editor: Kristen O'Toole
Account Manager: David Soto

Printed in the United States of America on partially recycled paper.

9 8 7 6 5 4 3 2 1

2014 Edition

Editorial
Robert Franek, VP Test Prep Books, Publisher
Selena Coppock, Senior Editor
Calvin Cato, Editor
Meave Shelton, Editor
Kristen O'Toole, Editor
Alyssa Wolff, Editorial Assistant

Random House Publishing Team
Tom Russell, Publisher
Nicole Benhabib, Publishing Manager
Ellen L. Reed, Production Manager
Alison Stoltzfus, Managing Editor
Erika Pepe, Associate Production Manager
Kristin Lindner, Production Supervisor
Andrea Lau, Designer

ACKNOWLEDGMENTS

This book absolutely would not have been possible without the help of my husband, Paul. With each edition of this guide, his insights and support have been invaluable—this book continues to be as much his as it is mine. That said, I also need to thank my daughter, Kaela, and her little sister, Lexi, for enduring all the time I have spent immersed in this project.

A big thanks goes to Tom Meltzer and Anna Weinberg for their smart and savvy profile writing. The following people were also instrumental in the completion of this book: Scott Harris, Kristen O'Toole, Steve Koch, and David Soto for putting all the pieces together; and to Robert Franek and the folks at Random House, who helped this project reach fruition.

Thanks are also due to the business school folks who went far out of their way to provide essential information. They continue to make this book relevant and vital.

Linda Baldwin, Director of Admissions, The Anderson School, UCLA

Derek Bolton, Assistant Dean and Director of Admissions, Stanford University School of Business

Eileen Chang, former Associate Director of Admissions, Harvard Business School

Allan Friedman, Executive Director of Communications and Public Relations, University of Chicago

Wendy Hansen, Associate Director of Admissions, Stanford Business School

Stacey Kole, Deputy Dean for the full-time MBA Program and Clinical Professor of Economics, University of Chicago Graduate School of Business

Steven Lubrano, Assistant Dean and Director of the MBA Program, Tuck School of Business

Rose Martinelli, Director of Admissions and Financial Aid, The University of Chicago

Jon McLaughlin, Assistant MBA Admissions Director, Sloan School of Management, MIT

Julia Min, Executive Director of MBA Admissions, UC—Berkeley, Haas School of Business

Jeanne Wilt, Assistant Dean of Admissions and Career Development, University of Michigan

Linda Meehan, Assistant Dean for Admissions, Columbia University

CONTENTS

INTRODUCTION

A RETURN TO OUR ROOTS

Over the past 19 years, The Princeton Review has annually published a guide to business schools. For the early editions of the guide, we collected opinion surveys from thousands of students at a select group of graduate business schools as well as school statistics from school administrators that include enrollment and demographic figures, tuition, and the average GMAT scores of entering students. We used the students' opinions to craft descriptive narratives of the schools they attended and reported the statistics in the sidebars of those narrative profiles.

For the 2001–2004 editions of this guide, we discontinued collecting opinion surveys from students and writing narrative descriptions of the schools; instead, we focused solely on collecting and reporting school statistics. While we were able to report statistics for many more business schools in the new format, we learned over the next few years that readers are interested in more than just school-reported statistics. They want to read what the experts—current graduate business school students—have to say about the experiences of today's graduate business student. They want from-the-horse's-mouth accounts of what's great (*and* what's not) at each school.

So, in 2005, we decided to reintroduce the student survey-driven descriptive narrative, offering students a more intimate look at the inner workings of each school, and we've continued with this approach ever since.

We also brought back several top 10 lists that rank the profiled schools according to various metrics (more on the rankings later). You'll find these rankings in Part II of this book.

Taken together, we believe that these candid student opinions, school statistics, and rankings provide a unique and helpful resource to help you decide what business schools to apply to. But let us stress that we hope that this book will not be the *only* resource you turn to when making this expensive (both in terms of time and treasure) decision to enter a graduate business program. Do additional research on the Internet and in newspapers, magazines, and other periodicals. Talk to admissions officers and current students at the programs that interest you. If at all possible, visit the campuses you are seriously considering. But treat the advice of all these resources (including ours) as you would treat advice from anyone regarding any situation: as input that reflects the values and opinions of others as you *form your own opinion*.

TWO TYPES OF ENTRIES

For each of the 434 business programs in this book, you will find one of two possible types of entries: a two-page profile with lots of descriptive text and statistics, or a straight statistical listing. Our descriptive profiles are driven primarily by 1) comments business students provide in response to open-ended questions on our student survey, and 2) our own statistical analysis of student responses to the many multiple-choice questions on the survey. While many business students complete a survey unsolicited by us at http://survey.review.com, in the vast majority of cases we rely on business school administrators to get the word out about our survey to their students. In the ideal scenario, the business school administration sends a Princeton Review-authored e-mail to all business students with an embedded link to our survey website (again, http://survey.review.com). If for some reason there are restrictions that prevent the administration from contacting the entire graduate business school student body on behalf of an outside party, they often help us find other ways to notify students of the fact that we are seeking their opinions, such as advertising in business student publications or posting on business student community websites. In almost all cases, when the administration is cooperative, we are able to collect opinions from a sufficient number of students to produce an accurate descriptive profile and ratings of its business school.

There is a group of business school administrators, however, that doesn't agree with us that current business school student opinions presented in descriptive profile and rankings formats are useful to prospective business school students. Administrators at the many AACSB-accredited business schools not appearing with two-page descriptive profiles are a part of this group. They either ignored our multiple attempts to contact them in order to request their assistance in notifying their students about our survey, or they simply refused to work with us at all. While we would like to be able to write a descriptive profile about each of these many schools anyway, we won't do so with minimal business student opinion.

So if you are a prospective business school student and would like to read current business student opinion about schools that do not appear with a two-page descriptive profile, contact the schools and communicate this desire to them. (We include contact information in each of the business school data listings.) If you are a current business student at one of the many AACSB-accredited business schools without a two-page descriptive profile, please don't send us angry letters; instead, go to http://survey.review.com, complete a survey about your school, and tell all of your fellow students to do the same.

You will find statistics for business schools whose administrators were willing to report their school statistics to us but were unwilling to allow us to survey their students under the school's name in the section of the book entitled "Business School Data Listings."

One more thing to note about the different entries: The majority of our various rankings lists are based wholly or partly on student feedback to our survey. Only one top 10 ranking, The Toughest to Get Into, is based on school-reported statistics alone. So while *any* of the 434 programs listed in the book may appear on that list, *only those schools with two-page descriptive profiles will appear on all other rankings lists.*

BUT SOME THINGS NEVER CHANGE

Admission to the business school of your choice, especially if your choice is among the most selective programs, will require your absolute best shot. One way to improve your chances is to make sure you apply to schools that are a good fit—and the comments provided by students in our descriptive profiles will provide more insight into the personality of each school than does its glossy view book.

In addition, you'll find plenty of useful information in Part I of this book on how to get in to business school and what to expect once you arrive. You'll find out what criteria are used to evaluate applicants and who decides your fate. You will also hear directly from admissions officers on what dooms an application and how to ace the interview. We've even interviewed deans at several of the top schools to share with you their take on recent events, including trends in business, b-school applications, recruitment, and placement.

Again, it is our hope that you will consult our profiles as a resource when choosing a list of schools that suit your academic and social needs, and that our advice is helpful to you during the application process. Good luck!

HOW WE PRODUCE THIS BOOK

In August 1999, we published *The Best 80 Business Schools, 2000 Edition*. By the time the 2001 edition of the guide was published, we had shifted our focus from student opinion-driven profiles of a select number of schools to more data-driven profiles of every graduate business school accredited by the AACSB. Although we continue to present readers with data from 295 accredited graduate b-school programs, we have reintroduced the student survey-based descriptive profile. In order to clarify our position, intent, and methodology, we've created a series of questions and answers regarding the collection of data and the production of our descriptive profiles.

How do we choose which b-schools to survey and profile? And why do some competitive schools have only a data listing?

Any business school that is AACSB-accredited and offers a Master of Business Administration degree may have a data listing included in the book, as long as that school provides us with a sufficient amount of school-specific data. In addition, this year we offered each of those accredited schools in which the primary language of instruction is English an opportunity to assist us in collecting online business student surveys.

Some schools were unable to solicit surveys from their students via e-mail due to restrictive privacy policies; others simply chose not to participate. Schools that declined to work with us to survey their students remain in the book, although they do not have a descriptive profile. Listing only the data for a school does not suggest that the school is less competitive or compelling; we only separated these profile types into two sections for easier reference. If you're not sure where to find information on a school in which you're interested, you can refer to our alphabetical b-school listing in the back of the book.

There is no fee to be included in this book. If you're an administrator at an accredited business school and would like to have your school included, please send an e-mail to surveysupport@review.com.

What's the AACSB, and by what standards are schools accredited?

The AACSB stands for the Association to Advance Collegiate Schools of Business. In April 2003, the AACSB made some significant changes to its standards for accreditation. In fact, the actual number of standards went from 41 to 21. Some of the changes in accreditation included a shift from requiring a certain number of full-time faculty members with doctorates to a focus on teacher participation. Schools may employ more part-time faculty members if they are actively involved in the students' business education. The onus of both the development of a unique curriculum and the evaluation of the success of that curriculum will fall on each b-school, and schools will be reviewed by the association every five years instead of every ten. As a result of the changes in accreditation standards, a number of schools have been newly accredited or reaccredited.

How were the student surveys collected?

Back in fall 2012, we contacted Admissions Officers at all accredited graduate b-schools and requested that they help us survey their students by distributing our Princeton Review-authored survey message to the student body via e-mail. The survey message explained the purpose of the survey and contained a link to our online business student survey. We had a phenomenal response from students.

The surveys are made up of seventy-eight multiple-choice questions and seven free-response questions, covering five sections: About Yourself, Students, Academics, Careers, and Quality of Life. Students may complete the secure online survey at any time and may save their survey responses, returning later, until the survey is complete and ready for submission. Students sign in to the online survey using their school-issued .edu e-mail address to ensure that their response is attributed to the correct school, and the respondent certifies before submission that he or she is indeed a current student enrolled in said program. In addition, an automated message is sent to this address once the student has submitted the survey, and they must click on a link in the e-mail message in order to validate their survey.

We use the resulting responses to craft descriptive profiles that are representative of the respondents' feelings toward the b-school they attend. Although well-written and/or humorous comments are especially appreciated, they would never be used unless they best stated what numerous students had told us.

What about the ranking lists and ratings?

When we decided to bring the student opinion-driven resources back into the fold, we updated our online survey and reconsidered all ranking lists. You will find that only a few of the rankings in this year's book resemble our b-school rankings of yesteryear. We've done our best to include only those topics most vital to success in business school, and we have added a new ranking list to this edition, "Best Green MBA."

We offer several ranking lists on a variety of considerations, from academic experience to career expectations, to the atmosphere for women and minority students. It must be noted, however, that none of these lists purport to rank the business schools by their overall quality. Nor should any combination of the categories we've chosen be construed as representing the raw ingredients for such a ranking. We have made no attempt to gauge the "prestige" of these schools, and we wonder whether we could accurately do so even if we tried. What we have done, however, is presented a number of lists using information from two very large databases—one of statistical information collected from business schools and another of subjective data gathered via our survey of 21,000 business students at 295 AACSB-accredited business schools. We do believe that there is a right business school for you, and that our rankings, when used in conjunction with our profile of each school, will help you select the best schools to apply to.

Since the 2009 edition of this book, we have included "Best Classroom Experience" list, based on students' answers to survey questions concerning their professors' teaching ability and recognition in the field, the integration of new business trends and practices into course offerings, and the level of student engagement in the classroom.

What do the schools have to say about all this?

Our contact at each school is kept abreast of the profile's status throughout the production process. After establishing a contact through whom we are able to reach online student respondents, we get to work writing our profiles and crunching the data. Once this information has been poured into profile pages, we send a copy of the school's profile to our contact via e-mail. We request that the administrator review the data and comments included in the profile, and we invite their corrections to any inaccurate data, or text that may be misrepresentative of overall student opinion. With their suggestions in hand, we revisit survey responses and investigate any such claims of inaccuracy.

We are aware that a general distaste for rankings permeates the business school community, and that top schools have recently backed down from providing the data necessary for such calculations. We agree that overall rankings that purport to decide the "best" overall school are not so helpful to students, and that they may be tainted by the agendas of school administrators hoping to advance their schools' reputations, without taking the necessary measures to actually improve the quality of the school. This is why the meat of our book is the schools' descriptive profiles, which are meant to showcase each school's unique personality. The ranking lists are simply used as reference tools for students looking for a particular attribute in a prospective b-school. We don't claim to be the final word on what school has the best MBA program in the country—that's nearly impossible to determine. We simply relay the messages that the students at each school are sending us, and we are clear about how our rankings are determined.

HOW THIS BOOK IS ORGANIZED

This book is packed with information about business schools, and we want to make sure you know how to find what you're looking for. So here's a breakdown of how this book is organized.

Part I is comprised of several chapters that give you an idea of what to expect at business school and tell you how to put together a winning application.

Part II has our b-school ranking lists. Of the ten lists, six are based entirely on student survey responses; one is based solely on institutionally reported data, while four others are based on a combination of survey responses and statistical information. Along with each list, you will find information about which survey questions or statistical factors were used to calculate the rankings.

Part III contains profiles of all AACSB-accredited graduate schools with MBA programs divided into two sections: those with descriptive profiles based on student surveys, and those with only a statistical listing.

PART III-A: BUSINESS SCHOOL DESCRIPTIVE PROFILES

Please see the sample descriptive profile below.

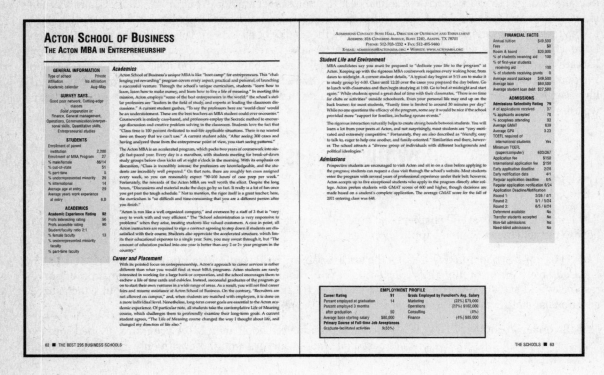

Each two-page spread is made up of eight major components. At the top of each page, you'll find the name of the business school, along with the name of an admissions contact and his or her address, phone number, fax number, if applicable, and e-mail address. This section also includes the b-school's website address. There are two sidebars (the narrow columns on the outer edge of each page) that contain information reported by the schools through the Business Data Set (BDS) and some student survey data as well. The Survey Says information reflects aspects of the school about which students feel the strongest; there are nine different possible results. We also offer an Employment Profile for each school, which is made up of statistical information from the BDS. The main body of the profile contains descriptive text discussing Academics, Placement and Recruiting, Student/Campus Life, and Admissions. Each description is based on student survey responses and may call upon statistical data where necessary.

The Sidebars

All information in the sidebars falls under the following categories: General Information, Academics, Financial Facts, and Admissions. Please note that not every category will appear for every school; in some cases the information is not reported or not applicable. These are the same data fields that are reported for those schools listed in Part III-B: Business School Data Listings, save for four of the five ratings, which appear only in the descriptive profiles.

Here is what each sidebar heading tells you.

General Information

Type of school

Public or private school.

Affiliation

Any religious order with which the school is affiliated.

Academic Calendar

Whether the school schedule runs according to trimesters, semesters, quarters, or another calendar type like a 4-1-4 (4-month semester, 1-month interim term, 4-month semester).

Survey Says

Survey Says gives you an at-a-glance look at what students are most in agreement about at their school. You'll find up to six results per school. Three will reflect the top three subject areas as indicated by responses to the following question:

How well has your school prepared you in the following areas:

Marketing	Presentation skills
Finance	Quantitative skills
Accounting	Computer skills
General management	Doing business in a global economy
Operations	Entrepreneurial studies
Teamwork	Environmental/Sustainability Issue Awareness
Communication/Interpersonal skills	Social Responsibility

In addition, Survey Says may include (up to) three things from the following list that students were most in agreement about:

- Students like Hometown, State. Based on level of agreement with the statement, "I like the town where my school is located."

- Friendly students. Based on level of agreement with the statement, "Your business school classmates are friendly."

- Good social scene. Based on level of agreement with the statement, "Your business school classmates have active social lives."

- Good peer network. Based on level of agreement with the statement, "Your business school classmates are the type of people you want to network with after graduation."

- Cutting-edge classes. Based on responses to the question, "How well has your school integrated new business trends and practices into course offerings?"

- Helpful alumni. Based on responses to the question, "How helpful have alumni been in assisting you in your job search?"

- Happy students. Based on level of agreement with the statement, "Overall, I am happy here."

Students

Enrollment of parent institution

Total number of undergraduate and graduate students enrolled in parent institution program.

Enrollment of MBA program

Total number of students enrolled in MBA programs at the business school, including both full- and part-time programs.

"% male/female" through "% international"

Items based on demographic information about full-time b-school students as reported by the schools.

Average age at entry

The average age of incoming first-year MBA students.

Average years work experience at entry

The average years of work experience for incoming first-year MBA students.

Academics

Academic Experience Rating

This rating measures the quality of the learning environment. Each school is given a score between 60 and 99. Factors taken into consideration include GMAT scores and undergraduate grades of enrolled students; percent accepted; percent enrolled; student/faculty ratio; and student survey questions pertaining to faculty, fellow students, and realization of academic expectations. This rating is intended to be used only to compare those schools within this edition of the book whose students completed our business student survey.

Please note that if a 60* Academic Experience Rating appears for any school, it means that the school didn't report all the rating's underlying data points by our deadline, so we were unable to calculate an accurate rating. In such cases, the reader is advised to follow up with the school about specific measures this rating takes into account.

Please also note that many foreign institutions use a grading system that is different from the standard U.S. GPA; as a result, we approximated their Admissions Selectivity and Academic Ratings, indicating this with a † following the rating.

Student/Faculty Ratio

The ratio of full-time graduate instructional faculty members to all enrolled MBA students.

Professors Interesting Rating

Based on the answers given by students to the survey question, "Overall, how good are your professors as teachers?" Ratings fall between 60 and 99. This rating is intended to be used to compare those schools within this edition of the book whose students completed our business student survey.

Professors Accessible Rating

Based on the answers given by students to the survey question, "How accessible are your professors outside of the classroom?" Ratings fall between 60 and 99. This rating is intended to be used to compare those schools within this edition of the book whose students completed our business student survey.

% female faculty

Percent of graduate business faculty in the 2011–2012 academic year who were women.

% minority faculty

Percent of graduate business faculty in the 2011–2012 academic year who were members of minority groups.

Joint Degrees

A list of joint degrees offered by the business school. See Decoding Degrees on page 733 for the full name of each degree.

Prominent Alumni

School administrators may submit the name, title, and company of up to five prominent alumni.

Financial Facts

Please note that we rely on foreign institutions to convert financial figures into U.S. dollars. Please check with any foreign schools you are considering for up-to-date figures and conversion rates.

"Tuition (in-state/out-of-state)" and "Fees (in-state/out-of-state)"

In-state and out-of-state tuition and fees per academic year. At state-supported public schools, in-state tuition and fees are likely to be significantly lower than out-of-state expenses.

Books and supplies

Estimated cost of books and supplies for one academic year.

Room and board

Cost of room and board on campus per academic year, and estimate of off-campus living expenses for this time period.

"% of students receiving aid" through "% of students receiving grants"

Percent of students receiving aid, then specifically those receiving grants and loans. These numbers reflect the percentage of all enrolled MBA students that receive financial aid, regardless of whether or not they applied for financial aid or for specific aid types. Likewise, the second figure, "% of first year students receiving aid" takes into account all first-year MBA students, regardless of whether they applied for financial aid or specific aid types.

Average award package

For students who received financial aid, this is the average award amount.

Average grant

For students who received grants, this is the average amount of grant money awarded.

Average student loan debt

The average dollar amount of outstanding educational MBA loans per graduate (class of 2010) at the time of graduation.

Admissions

Admissions Selectivity Rating

This rating measures the competitiveness of the school's admissions. Factors taken into consideration include the average GMAT score and undergraduate GPA of the first-year class, the percent of students accepted, and the percent of applicants who are accepted and ultimately enroll. No student survey data is used in this calculation. Ratings fall between 60 and 99. This rating is intended to be used to compare all schools within this edition of the book, regardless of whether their students completed our business student survey.

Please note that if a 60* Admissions Selectivity Rating appears for any school, it means that the school did not report all of the rating's underlying data points by our deadline, so we were unable to calculate an accurate rating. In such cases, the reader is advised to follow up with the school about specific measures this rating takes into account.

Please also note that many foreign institutions use a grading system that is different from the standard U.S. GPA; as a result, we approximated their Admissions Selectivity and Academic Ratings, indicating this with a † next to the rating.

of applications received

The total number of applications received for any and all MBA programs at the school.

% applicants accepted

The percentage of applicants to which the school offered admission.

% acceptees attending

Of those accepted students, the percentage of those who enrolled.

Average GMAT

The average GMAT score for the first-year class.

Average GPA

The average undergraduate GPA of the first year class, reported on a four-point scale.

TOEFL required of international applicants?

For those international students interested in applying, the b-school reports whether the Test of English as a Foreign Language (TOEFL) is required.

Minimum TOEFL (paper/computer/web)

The minimum TOEFL score necessary for consideration. We list acceptable scores for both the paper and computer versions of the test.

Application fee

The amount it costs to file an application with the school.

International Application Fee

The amount it costs an international student to file an application with the school if it is different from the cost of the regular application.

"Application deadline" and "Regular notification"

This regular application deadline reflects the date by which all materials must be postmarked; the notification date tells you when you can expect to hear back.

"Early decision program" and "ED deadline/notification"

If a school offers an early decision option, we'll tell you when early decision apps are due to be postmarked, and when you'll be notified of the school's decision.

"Deferment available?" and "Maximum length of deferment"

Some schools allow accepted students to defer enrollment for a year or more, while others require students who postpone attendance to reapply.

Transfer students accepted?

Whether or not students are accepted from other MBA programs.

Transfer Application Policy

Lets you know how transfer applications are reviewed and how many credits will be allowed to transfer from another program.

Non-fall admissions?

Some business schools may allow students to matriculate at the beginning of each semester, while for others, the invitation to attend stipulates that fall attendance is mandatory.

Need-blind admissions?

Whether or not the school considers applications without regard to the candidate's financial need.

Applicants also look at

The school reports that students applying to their school are also known to apply to a short list of other schools.

EMPLOYMENT PROFILE
Career Rating

Taking into account both student survey responses and statistical data, this rating measures the confidence students have in their school's ability to lead them to fruitful employment opportunities, as well as the school's own record of having done so. Factors taken into consideration include statistics on the average starting salary and percent of students employed within 3 months of graduation from the Business Data Set and comments from the student survey, assessing the efforts of the placement office, the quality of recruiting companies, level of preparation, and opportunities for off-campus projects, internships, and mentorships. Ratings fall between 60 and 99. This rating is intended to be used to compare only those schools within this edition of the book whose students completed our business student survey.

* Please note that if a 60* Career Rating appears for any school, it means that the school did not report all of the rating's underlying data points by our deadline, so we were unable to calculate an accurate rating. In such cases, the reader is advised to follow up with the school about the specific attributes this rating takes into account.

% grads employed within three months of graduation

This reflects the percentage of MBA grads who earned a job within three months of graduation.

Average starting salary

Average starting salary of all 2012 graduates.

Primary source of full-time job acceptances

This reflects the percentage of full-time job acceptances that are the result of school-facilitated, graduate-facilitated, or unknown activities.

Grads employed by field %: avg. salary

Reflects the distribution of 2011 graduates across many different industries and the average starting salary for each field.

Top five employers hiring grads

Reflects the top five employers who hired 2012 job seeking full-time MBA graduates, and the number of students they hired.

DESCRIPTIVE PROFILE

Each school's descriptive profile is made up of four sections which highlight those qualities that characterize the school as a unique institution. *Academics* covers students' opinions on the quality of professors, curriculum, special or noteworthy programs, the administration, and anything else academic in nature. *Career and Placement* deals with the school's efforts to secure internships and jobs for its current students and graduates; information about alumni assistance and popular recruiters of MBAs at the school may also be included. In *Student Life and Environment*, you'll find out how students balance work and play and whether they find it manageable to do so; often, you'll also find reviews of the school's facilities as well. Finally, the *Admissions* section describes what the Admissions Committee is looking for in potential students.

All quotes in these sections are taken from students' responses to our survey. We choose quotes that were consistent with the overall survey results.

PART III-B: BUSINESS SCHOOL DATA LISTINGS

This section contains all of the statistical info that is presented in the sidebars of the descriptive profile. Each school in this section will include an Admissions Selectivity rating but will not include the other three ratings, the Survey Says section, or a descriptive profile.

PART IV: SCHOOL SAYS

Part IV offers more detailed information about particular business schools authored by the schools themselves. The business schools included in this section pay a small fee for this space. These schools also have descriptive profiles or data listings in Part III.

EVERYTHING ELSE

Following Part IV, we offer a small section of profiles of b-schools who may pay a small fee for inclusion. Next is a section entitled *Decoding Degrees* that will help you make sense of the myriad degree abbreviations you'll see listed in the book. You'll then find the indexes—alphabetical by school name, and then by location. Finally, you'll have an opportunity to learn more about our author, Nedda Gilbert.

Enjoy and good luck!

PART I
ALL ABOUT BUSINESS SCHOOL

CHAPTER 1

THIS ISN'T YOUR FATHER'S (OR MOTHER'S) B-SCHOOL ANYMORE

THE NEW MBA CLASS: FEWER, YOUNGER, AND WORKING WHILE THEY LEARN

The MBA has always been seen as a golden passport; the trip ticket to romance and riches. The destination: career acceleration, power networks and recruiters, elite employers, and, of course, generous paychecks.

But not everyone wants to make the trip. Several factors will always impact on the popularity of the MBA: 1) the state of the economy—interest in getting the MBA has generally waxed and waned with economic times; 2) trends and favorable or unfavorable press—in the 1980s, a rash of insider trading scandals in which MBAs were ensnared made the degree look smarmy and other graduate programs, notably law and medicine, look more appealing; 3) the immediacy of good professional opportunities—the collapse of the dot-com boom, followed by the severe retrenchment of traditional MBA destinations (such as investment banks and consulting firms) in a depressed economy, has left many current MBAs stranded; and 4) recruiter demand for newly minted MBAs—do employers see the skill sets of today's MBAs bringing measurable value to their companies?

B-SCHOOL: INTEREST AND APPLICATIONS ON UPSWING

According to the 2012 GMAC Application Trends Survey, application volume to full-time MBA programs has increased slightly over the past year. After a spike in applications following the start of the recession in late 2007, most programs saw their application numbers decline slightly through 2011, but these numbers began to climb again in 2012. Part-time programs and executive MBA programs also saw small gains in applications.[1]

YOUNGER MINDS

Although lower application numbers can spell better fortunes for those currently applying to MBA programs, there are also some unrecognized opportunities for candidates with less than the traditional two to four years of work experience to make a strong case for admittance.

Admissions officers at large benchmark schools such as Stanford say that this trend pre-dates the economic downturn. Derek Bolton, director of admissions at Stanford notes, "The pendulum has gone too far in one direction in terms of the number of younger candidates applying to b-school. It has not kept pace with the overall pace of applicants. We want more young applicants applying. The goal is to bring the average age down in the next couple of years."

"What's driving this is the willingness on the part of the b-schools to not be rigidly fixed on what's right for someone. We may not always be the best judge of when the best time is for a candidate to go to b-school," continues Bolton.

Wharton's former Director of Admissions Rose Martinelli observed "a shift in that we became more tuned in to when students are ready in their leadership, professional, and personal development. We see so many nontraditional students that we don't want to have rules on when they can apply. We don't want to miss out on fabulous applicants because they don't think they can get in."

1. Graduate Management Admissions Council, 2011 Application Trends Survey Report, www.gmac.com/~/media/Files/gmac/Research/admissions-and-application-trends/2012-application-trends-survey-report.pdf (accessed June 21, 2013).

"When the applicant pool continues to get older and older, then we're closing out younger applicants who are on a fast track." Martinelli continues, "Why should we wait? Why should they wait? We want to catch the human element in the application process."

This perspective continues to hold true. As University of Chicago's Stacey Kole sums up, "The pendulum had swung too far in terms of the type of student who should be admitted and when. Now schools are correcting that and experimenting, taking less experienced candidates. We believe that this experimentation is a good thing."

There may be more to the story, too. Because they may be less likely to be in committed relationships or have families, younger students are more active, generous alumni, and b-schools can't afford to ignore the market that these younger students represent. Despite the heightened competition, candidates with less experience are increasingly being deemed worthy of a coveted b-school acceptance.

THE DRAW OF THE PART-TIME PROGRAM

Because part-time education programs continue to attract applicants, pundits say that the future of b-school may lie in programs that offer more flexible part-time opportunities, allowing students to get the degree without making a full-time commitment. In fact, Stacey Kole, Deputy Dean for the full-time MBA Program and Clinical Professor of Economics, University of Chicago Graduate School of Business states, "There is this tendency to think of the MBA as a full-time-only product. But schools like Chicago offer MBA programs in the evening, on weekends, and in executive program formats. For us, whether the student matriculates in our part-time or full-time program, the process is exactly the same. Ours is the same degree, only delivered in full-time, part-time, and weekend formats with different scheduling options. Chicago GSB offers individuals interested in an MBA considerable flexibility in how they pursue their education."

Kole continues, "Part-time and executive programs are now providing more of the outside-the-classroom, extracurricular experience that did not exist 10 years ago. For example, they are offering student-led clubs, speakers, and recruiter events that historically were the exclusive domain of full-time programs. This is one explanation for why part-time programs are looking like better substitutes for a full-time program."

PAYBACK TIME

The MBA, particularly at the top schools, continues to pay out high dividends to grads. That's a hefty return on investment. But the degree doesn't come with any promises. The world of business requires some risk, as many MBA wannabes found out several years go: You can enter a business school program at the height of the economy only to graduate when things are dismal. But you can also enter b-school at low tide then watch as the job market swells and employers are fighting over the newest and brightest MBA grads, including you. Indeed, the current economic climate has many MBA students and grads concerned about their job prospects, however, it's important to realize that with these financial challenges come opportunities for innovative and dedicated individuals.

MBA CONCENTRATIONS

The MBA has changed a lot over the years. Once upon a time, it was enough to simply earn your degree and enter the working world a more knowledgeable and employable individual for it. Nowadays, business represents an increasingly multi-faceted and diverse world, meaning that MBA students can't be jacks-of-all-trades—they need areas of specialization. When looking at potential business schools, it's imperative to know if they offer the concentration you're keen on. To help you decide what your concentration might be, we've added these helpful indexes to the back of our book (see page 753) along with brief explanations of what each entails below.

ACCOUNTING

As an accounting specialist, you'll become an expert in the gathering and interpretation of financial data, and the ways in which that data can affect a company.

ENTREPRENEURSHIP

A concentration in entrepreneurship offers you the chance to develop real business savvy, network with potential collaborators and investors, and try out new ideas with fewer risks than you'll encounter in the real world.

FINANCE

The finance concentration is about money: how to make it, manage it, and make more of it. A specialization in finance will prepare you to make smart financial decisions for individuals, institutions, and companies.

HEALTHCARE ADMINISTRATION

This specialization will teach you how the nation's healthcare system works, as well as the challenges facing healthcare organizations—from government agencies to hospitals to biotech, pharmaceutical, and medical technology companies.

HUMAN RESOURCES MANAGEMENT

In this concentration, you'll learn how to maximize human output in a business environment, from understanding individual behavior to designing effective management structures, training programs, and compensation schemes.

INTERNATIONAL MANAGEMENT

A concentration in international management will prepare you to succeed in today's global business environment. Many programs actually require students to spend a semester overseas, working at a company or studying at a partner university.

LEADERSHIP

This concentration is designed to help students develop skills that are essential to success in any field: critical thinking, problem-solving, communicating, negotiating, and acting ethically in professional situations.

MARKETING

Marketing professionals anticipate consumer demands, help to create products and services that consumers want, attract consumers to that product or service, and retain consumers over the long haul. They also have their hand in pricing and distribution; figuring out what products should cost and how they'll get to customers.

NON-PROFIT MANAGEMENT

Running a non-profit requires many of the same skills needed to run a business: raising capital, managing organization for maximum cost efficiency, and effectively delivering a service to your "clients."

SUPPLY CHAIN MANAGEMENT

A specialization in supply chain management will prepare you to create and manage the entire selling process for any company with a good or service to vend. In a world of global suppliers and tight profit margins, effective supply chain management can mean the difference between profitability and bankruptcy.

THE CONTINUING RELEVANCE OF BUSINESS SCHOOL

The MBA is such an attractive option because it *does* confer huge value on the recipient. Business schools know how to keep pace with the rapidly changing face of business. After all, that's *their* business, so you're never really out of the game. In fact, if you look at the nation's top business programs, you'll find exciting innovations in curriculum that reflect all that's new and relevant. This includes unique opportunities for teamwork, internships, and laboratory simulations that replicate real-world, real-time business scenarios.

The integration of these real-world experiences into the basics produces better-trained, more well-rounded managers, as graduates are more adept at discerning the correlation between principle and reality. Even so, programs and students in search of business knowledge that is more widely applicable and more relevant long-term has caused a strong return to fundamentals.

BACKPEDALING TO THE BASICS

Many top schools are reviving the old classics: It's back to basics. Both schools and students now have enough of a perspective to look back at the frenzy of the last business cycle and understand that enduring values are rooted in a solid foundation. Gone is the frothy demand for trendy courses on e-commerce and other hype-driven topics. Just five years ago, a class at Stanford on the principles of Internet marketing was oversubscribed. Last year, only a few people signed up for it.

So here's a sampler of the back-to-basics you'll get at b-school: An in-depth immersion in all of the key functional areas of an organization: marketing, management, sales, finance, operations, logistics, and so on. You'll look at these areas across dozens of industries and organizational types, from start-ups to *Fortune* 500 companies.

The renewed focus on basics doesn't mean that you'll find yourself shorted on current trends and events. Expect plenty of case study debate on corporate governance and the Enron debacle, and expect the themes of global perspective and technological competence to permeate many programs. You'll also find classes and seminars on leadership gaining popularity. "We're seeing a resurgence of leadership courses as students seek out professions and business models that are other-oriented," notes Stanford's Bolton. "This may be a new generation. But these are students who look at business as a positive force in the world, a more noble calling."

SURVIVOR POWER

Once you have your MBA, you can expect to hit the ground running. You'll start off your post b-school career with a load of contacts that you will periodically leverage over your career. Many graduates use the degree to embark on entirely new career paths than those that brought them to the school; consultants become bankers, entrepreneurs become consultants, marketers become financiers, and so on. The MBA has and will continue to be a terrific opportunity to reinvent oneself.

"An MBA is unlike any other professional degree because the breadth of knowledge poises you for a multitude of career choices," says Julia Min, Assistant Dean of MBA Admissions for NYU Stern School of Business. "You can be an investment banker, yet two years from that point, segue into nonprofit work. You can move from banking to corporate finance, to a venture-capital proposition, to ultimately having an entrepreneurial experience. So it's a credential that allows you the flexibility to explore different industries; it's a long-term investment that will give you the tools to transition if you want to."

"What's wonderful about the MBA is that it provides fundamental skills that you can use whenever and wherever you need them," champions Martinelli. "I'm a cheerleader for the nontraditional because I feel the MBA is such a fundamental tool. It offers an ability to enter the business world and link passion with functionality."

"For example, for folks who want to go into public service or nonprofit, even the arts industry, they're very narrow fields. You need the passion and vision to be successful in them. But often credibility is undermined when you don't understand the business world's perspective," states Martinelli.

"You've got to know that industry if you're going to make it viable for the future. But you have to be able to know how to talk to the business world in order to get those investments to make it happen. And that's one of the reasons why an MBA is so valuable. It bestows credibility in the marketplace and helps us maintain these organizations in a world that doesn't often respect passion over the bottom line," she continues.

Despite the nation's current financial woes, MBA grads still have plenty of prospects. Hundreds of companies continue to visit and recruit from business school campuses, with today's MBA candidates receiving two job offers on average. Recruiters exist in a symbiotic relationship with business schools. Employers like to maintain a strong presence on campus—even during an economic downturn—so that they'll have their top picks of MBA talent when the good times return. Thus, MBA programs remain one of the most effective means to get oneself in front of recruiters and senior managers from the most desirable companies. And while that may not grant you "immunity" from an economy characterized by up and downs, it will absolutely improve your survivor power.

COMPETITION HAS EASED UP

With an economic recovery seemingly underway, the chance to dive into any number of secure, well-paying jobs will lure a percentage of professionals away from the MBA. After years of struggling through economic hardship, a decent paycheck from the pocket of a much improved labor market may seem the best bet. There's no doubt that risk-averse individuals would prefer the stability of a secure job to what might-be, could-be, or should-be two years down the road—even with an MBA in hand. This may keep the applicant pool smaller.

Additionally, the continued decrease in the number of foreign applicants, who at many schools comprised more than 20 percent of students, will keep applications down, too. Other factors include the fact that there are currently smaller percentages of people in the country who are in the typical age bracket of business school applicants. Lastly, the increased interest in flexible and part-time MBA programs may continue to drive the decline in full-time business school applications.

What does all of this mean? Basically this: If you have a handsome application and you plan on applying to the most competitive programs this year, you may find yourself met with welcoming arms.

AS THE SONG GOES...MONEY, MONEY, MONEY, MONEY...

But don't go buying the flashy car to go with that flashy degree quite yet. It needs to be said that, after several years of a slump, there could actually be a surge in this upcoming applicant pool that would correspond with improvements in the economy. Recruiters are once again canvassing the top business schools as hiring slowly returns to healthy levels. At programs like Chicago, Harvard, and Stanford, six-figure salaries and signing bonuses of $15,000-plus are still the norm. That's why it's important to remember that the MBA from the right school can deliver an immediate and hefty return on investment. According to the GMAC 2013 Global Management Education Graduate Survey, Job Search: Class of 2013 Report, members of the class of 2012 reported that they expected salary increases of at least 57% over their pre-MBA pay.[2]

Another trend worth noting: Although applications have come down over the past 5 years, that doesn't mean the quality of applicants has suffered. Notes Chicago's Kole, "Our applications are of high quality, and applicants appear to be quite focused with regard to why they seek an advanced degree. Whether they are career switchers or planning to resume their career path, those applicants who present a compelling story for why they want to be here leave a stronger impression with the admissions committee."

Top schools are always going to have people knocking at their doors. The possibility that business school applications in general could once again rise means you'll still want to be competitive. The long application process starts with developing a solid application strategy and applying to a diverse portfolio of schools.

LET US HELP YOU DECIDE

There are many factors to consider when deciding whether or not to pursue an MBA, and we'll help you make that decision in the following chapters. We'll also tell you a bit about each school in our profiles and prepare you to do further research on the schools on your list. We've worked hard to provide you with thorough information on every aspect of the MBA, but you don't have to take our word for it—see for yourself. Stanford's Bolton advises future applicants, "Start early. Visit as many schools as you can, because it's very hard to differentiate among programs from websites, books, and marketing materials. You need to get a feeling from walking down the halls."

After you decide to go, finding the right program can be extremely difficult. Bolton explains, "Applicants really have to dig beneath the programs they're looking at to determine what's going to make them happy. A lot of people wind up going to the wrong school. A lot of external factors contribute to that. People shouldn't worry about justifying the decision to others, but to themselves."

MAKING THE DECISION TO GO

The next step for you may be b-school. Indeed, armed with an MBA you may journey far. But the success of your trip and the direction you take will depend on knowing exactly why you're going to b-school and just what you'll be getting out of it.

The most critical questions you need to ask yourself are the following: Do you really want a career in business? What do you want the MBA to do for you? Are you looking to gain credibility, accelerate your development, or move into a new job or industry? Perhaps you're looking to start your own business, in which case entrepreneurial study will be important.

2. Graduate Management Admissions Council, 2013 Global Management Education Graduate Survey Report, www.gmac.com/~/media/Files/gmac/Research/curriculum-insight/gmegs-2013-stats-brief.pdf (accessed June 21, 2013).

Knowing what you want doesn't just affect your decision to go, it also affects your candidacy; admissions committees favor applicants who have clear goals and objectives. Moreover, once at school, students who know what they want make the most of their two years. If you're uncertain about your goals, opportunities for career development—such as networking, mentoring, student clubs, and recruiter events—are squandered.

You also need to find a school that fits your individual needs. Consider the personal and financial costs. This may be the single biggest investment of your life. How much salary will you forego by leaving the workforce? What will the tuition be? How will you pay for it? If you have a family, spouse, or significant other, how will getting your MBA affect them?

If you do have a spouse, you may choose a program that involves partners in campus life. If status is your top priority, you should simply choose the most prestigious school you can get into.

The MBA presents many opportunities but no guarantees. As with any opportunity, you must make the most of it. Whether you go to a first-tier school or to a part-time program close to home, you'll acquire the skills that can jump-start your career. But your success will have more to do with you than with the piece of paper your MBA is printed on.

CHAPTER 2

SMART PHONES AND POWER LUNCHES: WHAT DOES AN MBA OFFER?

NUTS-AND-BOLTS BUSINESS SKILLS

Graduate business schools teach the applied science of business. The best business schools combine the latest academic theories with pragmatic concepts, hands-on experience, and real-world solutions.

B-schools also teach the analytical skills used to make complicated business decisions. You learn how to define the critical issues, apply analytical techniques, develop the criteria for decisions, and make decisions after evaluating their impact on other variables.

After two years, you're ready to market a box of cereal. Or prepare a valuation of the cereal company's worth. You'll speak the language of business. You'll know the tools of the trade. Your expertise will extend to many areas and industries. In short, you will have acquired the skills that open doors.

ACCESS TO RECRUITERS, ENTRÉE TO NEW FIELDS

Applicants tend to place great emphasis on "incoming" and "outgoing" statistics. First they ask, "Will I get in?" Then they ask, "Will I get a job?"

Obviously, the first is largely dependent on how selective the school is and the quality of your credentials. The latter question can almost assuredly be answered in the positive, "Yes, you will."

But the real question is: How many—and what kind—of offers will you receive? Again, that is dependent on the appeal of the school to recruiters (what companies recruit on campus and how often is a readily available statistic you can get from each school) and the particular industry you elect to pursue. For example, investment banks and consulting firms are always going to come to the schools for formal recruiting periods, whereas more off-the-beaten-path choices will possibly require you to go off campus in search of opportunity.

IT'S GOOD TO BE WANTED, IT'S GREAT TO BE PAID

According to the Graduate Management Council, MBA alumni typically recouped one third of their financial investment in their graduate degree within the first year after graduation, and 100 percent of their tuition and education expenses after four years.[3] Presumably, starting salaries will continue to increase as the economy improves.

The majority of top grads receive a generous relocation package too. Indeed, if you were fortunate enough to have spent the summer between your first and second year at a consulting company, then you will, in all likelihood, also receive a "rebate" on your tuition. These companies often pick up a student's second-year tuition bill. The best package, however, goes to those MBA students who worked at the firm before b-school. These lucky capitalists often get their whole tuition paid for.

3. Graduate Management Admissions Council, 2012 Alumni Perspectives Survey General Data Report, http://www.gmac.com/market-intelligence-and-research/market-research/why-your-school-should-participate-in-gmac-surveys/alumni-perspectives-survey.aspx (accessed June 21, 2013).

Getting the MBA for the Long Run

Despite its potential value, going to business school still requires you to take a bit of a gamble. Leaner years make business school a riskier proposition. The nation appears to be heading out of what has been a lingering recession, but economic factors are always unpredictable. Furthermore, the world has witnessed great political turmoil. All of these factors can quickly and negatively impact the job market for newly minted MBAs.

So as you make plans to go to b-school, you need to accept that there is some risk that the labor market won't greet you with open arms at graduation. Consider the plight of current MBAs: when they entered b-school, the economy was roaring ahead. The immediate future looked exceptionally bright. Most MBAs probably thought that once they got in, they had it made, and they looked forward to generous starting salaries and bonuses. Few probably anticipated that tough times could hit so dramatically.

But that's just the point. Good times and bad times cycle in and out. Many economic experts agree that the economy is starting to look up and the markets will continue to improve. This means traditional hirers of MBAs, such as the investment banks and consulting firms, may once again be wooing many a b-school grad. Still, it's hard to know when all of the recruiters who typically hire MBAs will feel comfortable again about bringing their hiring levels back up to what they were before the downturn.

The best way to consider the value of the degree is by focusing on its long-lasting benefits. "When people come here for their MBA, they talk about retooling for their life. They think about the long term and recognize that there are some short term hurdles," says Rose Martinelli, former director of admissions at the Wharton School. "Just out of business school, this is the very first job in a long career. This is really about building blocks and going for the long run. You may have to work harder to find a job now, but building your career is a lifelong process." The MBA gives you the tools, networking, and polish to meaningfully enhance your long-term prospects and earning potential.

"There is real opportunity here. The opportunity right now is to pursue your passion and perhaps not your wallet," continues Martinelli. "We're seeing more of an equalization in salary. Those high-paying jobs in finance, investment banking, and consulting are fewer and harder to find. So here you have an opportunity for a job with a true learning experience rather than one that just pays a lot. More people are going into nonprofit and government and making contributions back to the community."

Brand Power Counts

Of course, there is great variability with placement rates and starting salaries among schools. The MBA does not swap your tuition bill for a guarantee that you'll get rich quick. As we've noted, it is at the best schools—those that have the greatest prestige and global recognition—where the strongest recovery is taking place. It's brand power at work. Even in an uncertain economy, top schools will continue to produce in-demand MBAs for the marketplace.

Branded schools tend to have an extensive history with big recruiting companies because the schools are a steady source of exceptional talent. As the economy stabilizes and hiring creeps up again, recruiters are naturally going to orient themselves at the top-brand schools.

At the University of Chicago, Deputy Dean Stacey Kole notes: Hiring activity has really skyrocketed. . . . We had thousands of interviews available for our grads."

At less prominent schools, the picture may not be quite as optimistic. It is important to consider placement rates and the list of companies that typically recruit on campus at any school you are considering.

Getting a Job

For most would-be MBAs, b-school represents a fresh beginning—either in their current profession or in an entirely different industry. Whatever promise the degree holds for you, it's wise to question what the return on your investment will be.

Several factors affect job placement and starting salary. School reputation and ties to industries and employers are important. At the top programs, the lists of recruiters read like a "Who's Who" of American companies. These schools not only attract the greatest volume of recruiters, but consistently get the attention of those companies considered to be "blue chip."

Not to be overlooked are lesser-known, regional schools that often have the strongest relationships with local employers and industries. Some b-schools (many of them state universities) are regarded by both academicians and employers as number one in their respective regions. In other words, as far as the local business community is concerned, these programs offer as much prestige and pull as a nationally ranked program.

Student clubs also play a big part in getting a job because they extend the recruiting efforts at many schools. They host a variety of events that allow you to meet leading business people, so that you can learn about their industries and their specific companies. Most important, these clubs are very effective at bringing in recruiters and other interested parties that do not recruit through traditional mainstream channels. For example, the high-tech, international, and entertainment student clubs provide career opportunities not available through the front door.

Your background and experiences also affect your success in securing a position. Important factors are academic specialization, academic standing, prior work experience, and intangibles such as your personal fit with the company. These days, what you did before b-school is particularly important; it helps establish credibility and gives you an edge in competing for a position in a specific field. For those using b-school to switch careers to a new industry, it's helpful if something on your resume ties your interest to the new profession. It's also smart to secure a summer job in the new area.

Finally, persistence and initiative are critical factors in the job search. Many fast tracks have been narrowed since the beginning of the decade. Increasingly, even at the best schools, finding a job requires off-campus recruiting efforts and ferreting out the hidden jobs.

A RETURN ON YOUR INVESTMENT

Not everyone measures their return on investment from business school with a dollar amount. (See the interview at the end of this chapter as one example.) We've heard many b-school grads explain that the fundamental skills, the network of people, and the proper environment in which to formulate their long-term career path were the most valuable things they wanted to get back from their MBA programs—in doing so, they considered the experience a success, regardless of their starting salary at graduation.

But for those who are anxious to start paying back those school loans, it's important to note that the industry in which you are hired can strongly affect your job prospects. Traditionally heavy hirers such as investment banking and consulting companies continue to lead the salary pack. Historically these sectors have offered the highest starting salaries and sign-on bonuses, with recruiters gravitating to the name-brand schools. At Chicago, Kole notes, "We saw tremendous activity in consulting, investment banking, investment management, and in leadership development programs. We are up in all of these areas, but most significantly in management consulting."

Also impacting your placement outlook is the geographic location of the school. Regional powerhouses such as Rutgers University in New Jersey may hold great sway at nearby, national employers such as Johnson & Johnson and Warner Lambert/Pfizer, providing graduates of those programs a unique competitive advantage. Although these companies reach out far and wide to recruit everywhere, a homegrown MBA may catch their attention and hold greater appeal.

As always, prioritize your criteria for school selection. Research who the top hirers are at any school you are considering. If you know what field you are interested in, look at how strong a particular business school's track record is in finding jobs for their graduates in that industry. To cement the relationships between school and recruiter, companies often foster a partnership with the school that includes sponsoring academic projects and internships, and hosting school club functions and informational cocktail hour events.

You may indeed be accepted at one of the nation's most prestigious schools, but if they lack real access to the type of industry you desire to work in, you are better off elsewhere.

FRIENDS WHO ARE GOING PLACES, ALUMNI WHO ARE ALREADY THERE

Most students say that the best part about b-school is meeting classmates with whom they share common goals and interests. Many students claim that the "single greatest resource is each other." Not surprisingly, with so many bright and ambitious people cocooned in one place, b-school can be the time of your life. It presents numerous professional and social opportunities. It can be where you find future customers, business partners, and mentors. It can also be where you establish lifelong friendships. After graduation, these classmates form an enduring network of contacts and professional resources.

Alumni are also an important part of the b-school experience. While professors teach business theory and practice, alumni provide insight into the real business world. When you're ready to interview, they can provide advice on how to get hired by the companies recruiting at your school. In some cases, they help you secure the interview and shepherd you through the hiring process.

B-schools love to boast about the influence of their alumni network. To be sure, some are very powerful, but this varies from institution to institution. At the very least, alumni will help you get your foot in the door. A resume sent to an alum at a given company, instead of to "Sir or Madam" in the personnel department, has a much better chance of being noticed and acted on.

After you graduate, the network continues to grow. Regional alumni clubs and alumni publications keep you plugged in to the network with class notes detailing who's doing what, where, and with whom.

Throughout your career, an active alumni relations department can give you continued support. Post-MBA executive education series, fund-raising events, and continued job placement efforts are all resources you can draw on for years to come.

CHAPTER 3

ADMISSIONS

PREPARING TO BE A SUCCESSFUL APPLICANT

GET GOOD GRADES

If you're still in school, concentrate on getting good grades. A high GPA says you've got not only brains but also discipline. It shows the Admissions Committee you have what you need to make it through the program. If you're applying directly from college or have limited job experience, your grades will matter even more. The Admissions Committee will have little else on which to evaluate you.

It's especially important that you do well in courses such as economics, statistics, and calculus. Success in these courses is more meaningful than success in classes like "Monday Night at the Movies" film appreciation. Of course, English is also important; b-schools want students who communicate well.

STRENGTHEN MATH SKILLS

Number-crunching is an inescapable part of b-school. If your work experience has failed to develop your quantitative skills, take an accounting or statistics course for credit at a local college or b-school. If you have a liberal arts background and did poorly in math, or got a low GMAT Math score, this is especially important. Getting a decent grade will go a long way toward convincing the Admissions Committee you can manage the quantitative challenges of the program.

WORK FOR A FEW YEARS—BUT NOT TOO MANY

Business schools have traditionally favored applicants who have worked full-time for several years. There are three primary reasons for this:

1. With experience comes maturity.

2. You're more likely to know what you want out of the program.

3. Your experience enables you to bring real-work perspectives to the classroom. Because business school is designed for you to learn from your classmates, each student's contribution is important.

Until recently, b-schools preferred to admit only those students with two to five years of work experience. The rationale was that at two years you have worked enough to be able to make a solid contribution, while beyond four or five, you might be too advanced in your career to appreciate the program fully. However, as we noted earlier in this book, there is a new trend among top schools toward admitting "younger" applicants—that is, candidates with limited work experience as well as those straight from college.

Depending on the schools to which you're applying and the strength of your resume of accomplishments, you may not need full-time, professional work experience. Of course, there's a catch: The younger you are, the harder you'll have to work to supply supporting evidence for your case as a qualified applicant. Be prepared to convince Admissions Committees that you've already done some incredible things, especially if you're hailing straight from college.

If you've targeted top-flight schools like Wharton, Columbia, or Stanford, applying fresh out of college is still a long shot. While your chances of gaining admission with little work experience have improved, your best shot is still to err on the conservative side and get a year or two of some professional experience under your belt.

If you're not interested in the big league or you plan on attending a local program, the number of years you should work before applying may vary. Research the admissions requirements at your target school. There's no doubt the MBA will jumpstart your career and have long-lasting effects on your business (and perhaps personal) outlook. If you're not ready to face the real world after college, plenty of solid b-schools will welcome you to another two years of academia.

There is one caveat to this advice, however. If your grades are weak, consider working at least three years before applying. The more professional success you have, the greater the likelihood that Admissions Committees will overlook your GPA.

LET YOUR JOB WORK FOR YOU

Many companies encourage employees to go to b-school. Some of these companies have close ties to a favored b-school and produce well-qualified applicants. If their employees are going to the kinds of schools you want to get into, these may be smart places to work.

Other companies, such as investment banks, feature training programs, at the end of which trainees go to b-school or leave the company. These programs hire undergraduates right out of school. They're known for producing solid, highly skilled applicants. Moreover, they're full of well-connected alumni who may write influential letters of recommendation.

Happily, the opposite tactic—working in an industry that generates few applicants—can be equally effective. Admissions Officers look for students from underrepresented professions. Applicants from biotechnology, health care, not-for-profit, and even the Peace Corps are viewed favorably.

One way to set yourself apart is to have had two entirely different professional experiences before business school. For example, if you worked in finance, your next job might be in a different field, like marketing. Supplementing quantitative work with qualitative experiences demonstrates versatility.

Finally, what you do in your job is important. Seek out opportunities to distinguish yourself. Even if your responsibilities are limited, exceed the expectations of the position. B-schools are looking for leaders.

MARCH FROM THE MILITARY

A surprising number of b-school students hail from the military (although the armed forces probably had commanders in mind, not CEOs, when they designed their regimen). Military officers know how to be managers because they've held command positions. And they know how to lead a team under the most difficult of circumstances.

Because most have traveled all over the world, they also know how to work with people from different cultures. As a result, they're ideally suited to learn alongside students with diverse backgrounds and perspectives. B-schools with a global focus are particularly attracted to such experience.

The decision to enlist in the military is a very personal one. However, if you've thought of joining those few good men and women, this may be as effective a means of preparing for b-school as more traditional avenues.

Check Out Those Essay Questions Now

You're worried you don't have interesting stories to tell. Or you just don't know what to write. What do you do?

Ideally, several months before your application is due, you should read the essay questions and begin to think about your answers. Could you describe an ethical dilemma at work? Are you involved in anything outside the office (or classroom)? If not, now is the time to do something about it. While this may seem contrived, it's preferable to sitting down to write the application and finding you have to scrape for or, even worse, manufacture situations.

Use the essay questions as a framework for your personal and professional activities. Look back over your business calendar, and see if you can find some meaty experiences for the essays in your work life. Keep your eyes open for a situation that involves questionable ethics. If all you do is work, work, work, get involved in activities that round out your background. In other words, get a life.

Get involved in community-based activities. Some possibilities are being a big brother/big sister, tutoring in a literacy program, or initiating a green initiative on campus. Demonstrating a concern for others looks good to Admissions Committees, and hey, it's good for your soul, too.

It's also important to seek out leadership experiences. B-schools are looking for individuals who can manage groups. Volunteer to chair a professional committee or run for an office in a club. It's a wide-open world; you can pick from any number of activities. The bottom line is this: The extracurriculars you select can show that you are mature, multifaceted, and appealing.

We don't mean to sound cynical. Obviously, the best applications do nothing more than describe your true, heartfelt interests and show off your sparkling personality. We're not suggesting you try to guess which activity will win the hearts of admissions directors and then mold yourself accordingly. Instead, think of projects and activities you care about, that maybe you haven't gotten around to acting on, and act on them now!

Pick Your Recommenders Carefully

By the time you apply to business school, you shouldn't have to scramble for recommendations. Like the material for your essays, sources for recommendations should be considered long before the application is due.

How do you get great recommendations? Obviously, good work is a prerequisite. Whom you ask is equally important. Bosses who know you well will recommend you on both a personal and professional level. They can provide specific examples of your accomplishments, skills, and character. Additionally, they can convey a high level of interest in your candidacy.

There's also the issue of trust. B-school recommendations are made in confidence; you probably won't see exactly what's been written about you. Choose someone you can trust to deliver the kind of recommendation that will push you over the top. A casual acquaintance may fail you by writing an adequate, yet mostly humdrum letter.

Cultivate relationships that yield glowing recommendations. Former and current professors, employers, clients, and managers are all good choices. An equally impressive recommendation can come from someone who has observed you in a worthwhile extracurricular activity.

We said before you won't see *exactly* what's being written about you, but that doesn't mean you should just hand a blank piece of paper to your recommender. Left to their own devices, recommenders may create a portrait that leaves out your best features. You need to prep them on what to write. Remind them of those projects or activities in which you achieved some success. You might also discuss the total picture of yourself that you are trying to create. The recommendation should reinforce what you're saying about yourself in your essays.

About "big shot" recommendations: Don't bother. Getting some professional athlete who's a friend of your parent's to write you a recommendation will do you no good if he or she doesn't know you very well. Don't try to fudge your application; let people who really know you and your work tell the honest, believable, and impressive truth.

Prepare for the Graduate Management Admission Test (GMAT) or the Graduate Record Examinations (GRE)

Most b-schools require you to take the GMAT. The GMAT is now a three-and-a-half-hour computer adaptive test (CAT) with multiple-choice Math and Verbal sections as well as an essay section. Many schools will accept Graduate Record Examinations, or GRE, general test scores as a substitution for the GMAT. If you're interested in applying to both MBA and other master's programs, you may want to consider taking the GRE.

The GMAT begins with the Analytical Writing Assessment (AWA) containing one essay question. In the past, all questions that have appeared on the official GMAT have been drawn from a list of about 150 topics that appear in *The Official Guide to the GMAT* (published by the Educational Testing Service). Review that list and you'll have a pretty good idea of what to expect from the AWA. You will have 30 minutes to write your essay using a generic word processing program.

Next comes the multiple-choice section which has three parts: a 30-minute, 12-question Integrated Reasoning section (more on that below); a 75-minute Math section and a 75-minute Verbal section. The Math section includes problem-solving questions (e.g., "Train A leaves Baltimore at 6:32 A.M.") and data-sufficiency questions. Data-sufficiency questions require you to determine whether you have been given enough information to solve a particular math problem. The good news about these types of questions is that you don't actually have to solve the problem; the bad news is that these questions can be very tricky. The Verbal section tests reading skills (reading comprehension), grammar (sentence correction), and logic (critical reasoning).

The Integrated Reasoning section was introduced in June 2012 and replaced a second essay question. It combines verbal and quantitative reasoning skills. There are only 12 questions in this section, but each will have multiple parts. For the entire section, you'll actually need to select approximately 30 different responses. Unlike the Quantitative and Verbal sections, the Integrated Reasoning section is not adaptive.

For those unfamiliar with CAT exams, here's a brief overview of how they work: On multiple-choice sections, the computer starts by asking a question of medium difficulty. If you answer it correctly, the computer asks you a question that is slightly more difficult than the previous question. If you answer incorrectly, the computer asks a slightly easier question next. The test continues this way until you have answered enough questions that it can make an accurate (or so they say) assessment of your performance and assign you a score.

Most people feel they have no control over a standardized test. They dread it as the potential bomb in their application. Relax; you have more control than you think. Whether you choose to take the GMAT or the GRE, you can take a test-preparation course to review the material, learn test-taking strategies, and build your confidence. Test-prep courses can be highly effective. The Princeton Review offers what we think are the best GMAT and GRE courses available. Even better, it offers two options for online preparation in addition to the traditional classroom course and one-on-one tutoring. Another option is to use our books *Cracking the GMAT* and *Cracking the GRE* to prepare for the tests. Updated annually, they include access to full-length practice tests plus reviews of all the subjects you'll find on the tests and many of our proven techniques for raising your scores on these tests that you would learn in one of our courses.

How many times should you take the test of your choice? More than once if you didn't get your desired score on the first try. But watch out: Multiple scores that fall in the same range make you look unprepared. Don't take the test more than once if you don't expect a decent increase, and don't even think of taking it the first time without serious preparation. Limiting your attempts to two is best. Three tries are okay if there were unusual circumstances. If you take it more than three times, the Admissions committee will think you have an unhealthy obsession. A final note: If you submit more than one score, most schools will take the highest.

If you don't have math courses on your college transcript or numbers-oriented work experience, it's especially important to get a solid score on the quantitative section. There's a lot of math between you and the MBA.

HOW THE ADMISSIONS CRITERIA ARE WEIGHTED

Although admissions requirements vary among business schools, most rely on the following criteria: GMAT (or GRE) score, college GPA, work experience, your essays, letters of recommendation (academic and/or professional), an interview with an admissions representative, and your extracurriculars. The first four are generally the most heavily weighted. The more competitive the school, the less room there is for weakness in any area. Any component out of sync, such as a weak test score, is potentially harmful.

Happily, the admissions process at business school is one where great emphasis is placed on getting to know you as a person. The essay component is the element that allows the schools to do just that. Your essays can refute weaknesses, fill in gaps, and in general, charmingly persuade an admissions board you've got the right stuff. They are the single most important criteria in business school admissions.

But as we've just said, they're not the only criteria. All pieces of your application must come together to form a cohesive whole. It is the *entire application* that determines whether you win admission.

ANTICIPATE AND COORDINATE

The application process is very time-consuming, so anticipating what you need to accomplish within the admissions time frame is critical. To make the best use of our advice, you should first contact each of the programs on your personal list of schools. Their standards and criteria for admission may vary, and you'll need to follow their specific guidelines. Please note that the less competitive a school is, the more easily you may be able to breeze through (or completely omit) the rigorous requirements we identify as crucial in the application process for the top programs.

In addition, business school applicants are often overwhelmed by how much they have to do to complete not only one, but several applications. Proper management of the process is essential, since there are so many factors to coordinate in each application.

You'll have to prep for the GMAT and/or GRE, then actually take the test, round up some writers for your recommendations, follow up with those chosen to write recommendations, make sure the recommendations are mailed in on time, have your college transcript sent, and finally, write the essays. Of course, some schools require an interview as well. What makes all of this particularly challenging is that many applicants have to do all of this while balancing the demands of a full-time job.

We know that it takes a supreme force of will to complete even one application. As grad school applications go, a top business school's is pretty daunting. So if you don't stay focused on the details and deadlines, you may drop the ball.

There are many common and incredibly embarrassing mistakes you can avoid with prudent early planning. These include allowing your recommenders to miss the deadline, submitting an application full of typos and grammatical errors, sending one school an essay intended for another, or forgetting to change the school name when using the same essay for several applications. Applicants who wind up cramming for the GMAT (or GRE) or squeezing their essay writing into several all-nighters end up seriously shortchanging themselves.

Apply Early

The best advice is to plan early and apply early. The former diminishes the likelihood of an accidental omission or a missed deadline. The latter increases your chances of acceptance.

The filing period ranges anywhere from six to eight months. The earlier you apply, the better your chances. There are a number of reasons for this:

First, there's plenty of space available early on. Many b-schools have rolling admissions, and as the application deadline nears, spaces fill up. The majority of applicants don't apply until the later months because of procrastination or unavoidable delays. As the deadline draws close, the greatest number of applicants compete for the fewest number of spaces.

Second, in the beginning, Admissions Officers have little clue about how selective they can be. They haven't reviewed enough applications to determine the competitiveness of the pool. An early application may be judged more on its own merit than on how it stacks up against others. This is in your favor if the pool turns out to be unusually competitive. Above all, Admissions Officers like to lock their classes in early; they can't be certain they'll get their normal supply of applicants. Admissions decisions may be more generous at this time.

Third, by getting your application in early you're showing a strong interest. The Admissions Committee is likely to view you as someone keen on going to their school.

To be sure, some Admissions Officers report that the first batch of applications tend to be from candidates with strong qualifications, confident of acceptance. In this case, you might not be the very first one on line; but being closer to the front is still better than getting lost in the heap of last-minute hopefuls.

Rounds versus Rolling Admissions

Applications are processed in one of two ways: rounds or rolling admissions. Schools that use rounds divide the filing period into three or so timed cycles. Applications are batched into the round in which they are received and reviewed in competition with others in that round. A list of a b-school's round dates can be obtained by contacting its Admissions Office if it employs this method. Applications to schools with rolling admissions are reviewed on an ongoing basis as they are received.

GMAT or GRE and GPA

Test scores and GPA are used in two ways. First, they're "success indicators" for the academic work you'll have to slog through if admitted—will you have the brainpower to succeed in the program? Second, they're used as benchmarks to compare each applicant to other applicants within the pool. At the more selective schools, you'll need a higher score and average to stay in the game.

Research the schools to which you're planning to apply and identify which test makes the most sense for you. You'll need to register for the GMAT at www.mba.com or the GRE at "www.ets.org/gre. Many applicants take the exam more than once to improve their scores. Test preparation is also an option for boosting your numbers—visit PrincetonReview.com for more information about The Princeton Review's GMAT and GRE courses.

Your college transcript is a major factor in the strength of your candidacy. Some schools focus more closely on the junior- and senior-year grades than the overall GPA, and most consider the reputation of your college and the difficulty of your course selections. A transcript loaded with offerings like "Environmental Appreciation" and "The Child in You" won't be valued as highly as one packed with calculus and history classes.

The Essays

Admissions committees consider the essays the clincher, the swing vote on the admit/deny issue. Essays offer the most substantive information about who you really are. Your admissions test scores and GPA reveal little about you, only that you won't crash and burn. Your work history provides a record of performance and justifies your stated desire to study business. But the essays tie all the pieces of the application together and create a summary of your experiences, skills, background, and beliefs.

The essays do more than give answers to questions. They create thumbnail psychological profiles. Depending on how you answer a question or what you present, you reveal yourself in any number of ways—creative, witty, open-minded, articulate, mature, to name a few. On the other hand, your essay can also reveal a negative side, such as arrogance, sloppiness, or an inability to think and write clearly.

> **CHECK IT OUT:** Most top schools require multiple essays, and our popular book *Business School Essays that Made a Difference* lets you know how to ace them all. Including sample essays from successful applicants with comments from admissions officers on what worked and what didn't, *Business School Essays that Made a Difference* lets you know how to write the essays that will get you admitted. Pick it up at Princetonreview.com/bookstore.

Letters of Recommendation

Letters of recommendation function as a reality check. Admissions committees expect them to support and reinforce what they're seeing in the rest of your application. When the information doesn't match up with the picture you've painted, it makes you look bad. Because you won't see the recommendation (it's sent in "blind"), you won't even know there's a problem. This can mean the end of your candidacy.

That's why you need to take extreme care in selecting your references.

Scan each application for guidelines on choosing your references—business schools typically request an academic and a professional reference. The academic reference should be someone who can evaluate your performance in an academic environment. It's better to ask an instructor, teacher's aide, or mentor who knew you well than a famous professor who barely knew your name.

The same holds true for your professional reference. Seek out individuals who can evaluate your performance on many levels. The reference will be far more credible. Finding the right person to write your professional reference, however, can be trickier. You may not wish to reveal to your boss early on that you plan on leaving, and if the dynamics of your relationship are not ideal (hey, it happens once in a while), he or she might not make an appropriate reference. If this is the case, seek out a boss at a former job or someone who was your supervisor at your current job but has since moved to another organization. Avoid friends, colleagues, and clients as references unless the school explicitly says it's okay.

Advise your writers on themes and qualities you highlighted in your application. Suggest that they include real-life examples of your performance to illustrate their points. In other words, script the recommendation as best you can. Your boss, even if he or she is your biggest fan, may not know what your recommendation should include.

A great recommendation is rarely enough to save a weak application from doom. But it might push a borderline case over to the "admit" pile. Mediocre recommendations can be damaging; an application that is strong in all other areas now has a weakness, an inconsistency.

A final warning on this topic: Procrastination is common here. Micromanage your references so that each recommendation arrives on time! If need be, provide packaging for an overnight letter, have your reference seal it up, and then ship it out yourself.

THE INTERVIEW

Not all business schools attach equal value to the interview. For some, it's an essential screening tool. For others, it's used to make a final decision on those caught somewhere between "admit" and "reject." Some schools may encourage, but not require, the interview. Others make it informative, with little connection to the admissions decision.

Like the letters of recommendation, an interview may serve as a reality check to reinforce the total picture. It may also be used to fill in the blanks, particularly in borderline cases.

If an interview is offered, take it. In person, you may be a more compelling candidate. You can use the interview to further address weaknesses or bring dull essays to life. Most importantly, you can display the kinds of qualities—enthusiasm, sense of humor, maturity—that can positively sway an admissions decision.

Act quickly to schedule your interview. Admissions Departments often lack the time and staff to interview every candidate who walks through their doors. You don't want your application decision delayed by several months (and placed in a more competitive round or pool) because your interview was scheduled late in the filing period.

A great interview can tip the scale in the "admit" direction. How do you know if it was great? You were calm and focused. You expressed yourself and your ideas clearly. Your interviewer invited you to go rock climbing with him or her the following weekend. (Okay, let's just say you developed a solid personal rapport with the interviewer.)

A mediocre interview may not have much impact, unless your application is hanging on by a thread. In such a case, the person you're talking to (harsh as it may seem) is probably looking for a reason not to admit you, rather than a reason to let you in. If you feel your application may be in that hazy, marginal area, try to be extra-inspired in your interview.

Approach this meeting as you would a job interview. Remember, you're being sized up as a person in all of your dimensions. Here are a few tips to use during the interview.

- Dress and act the part of a professional but avoid being stiff or acting like a stuffed shirt.

- Limit your use of business jargon. Interviewers often hear a lot of the same generic answers. They are more interested in you being your witty, charming, natural self.

- Be personable and talk about your passions, such as hobbies or a recent trip you've taken. The idea is to get the interviewer thinking of you as someone who will contribute greatly to the quality of campus life.

Highlight your achievements and excellence, even in something like gourmet cooking, but avoid stunts, such as pulling out a platter of peppercorn pâté sautéed in anchovy sauce.

Chapter 4

Quotas, Recruitment, and Diversity

B-schools don't have to operate under quotas—governmental or otherwise. However, they probably try harder than most corporations to recruit diverse groups of people. Just as the modern business world has become global and multicultural, so too have b-schools. They must not only teach diversity in the classroom but also make it a reality in their campus population and, if possible, faculty.

Schools that have a diverse student body tend to be proud of it. They tout their success in profiles that demographically slice and dice the previous year's class by gender, race, and geographic and international residency. Prospective students can review this data and compare the diversity of the schools they've applied to.

However, such diversity doesn't come naturally from the demographics of the applicant pool. Admissions Committees have to work hard at it. In some cases, enrollment is encouraged with generous financial aid packages and scholarships.

While they don't have quotas per se, they do target groups for admission, seeking a demographic balance in many areas. Have they admitted enough women, minorities, foreign students, marketing strategists, and liberal arts majors? Are different parts of the country represented?

As we've said before, the best b-schools tend to attract top talent, students, and recruiters to their campus. Women and minorities are the most sought-after groups targeted for admission. So it's no surprise that programs that report higher-than-average female and minority enrollments tend to be among the very best.

INITIATIVES FOR MINORITIES

Some schools report higher minority enrollments than others, so our advice is consistent: You need to thoroughly research the program you've set your sights on. Consider your goals. Do you simply want to attend the most prestigious program? How will social factors impact your goals and experiences on campus?

Most business schools aspire to diversify their programs. It's the number of minorities applying to business school that has remained consistently low. The Graduate Management Admissions Council offers schools resources to diversify their recruitment efforts to reverse this trend and increase the number of underrepresented minorities pursuing a business career. GMAC has an extremely useful list of resources for prospective students, too, at www.gmac.com/reach-and-recruit-students/recruit-students-for-your-program/diversify-your-candidate-pool/diversity-resources-2.aspx. These organizations provide information on current opportunities for mentorships, internships, and financial assistance, services, and educational opportunities.

As you make up your mind about where you want to go for b-school, know that the scenario is positive and that new infrastructures exist to support your business career.

FEMALE APPLICANTS AND STUDENTS

If you've toured the campus and classrooms of a business school, you may have noticed something: On average, roughly 70 percent of any given MBA program's students are male. While this may make a nice pool of dating prospects for the women who are enrolled, it's not something business schools are happy with—far from it! In fact, it's something they are working to change as quickly as they can.

Beyond showing significantly higher application volume, MBA programs of all types are seeing female applications increase. About 64 percent of full-time MBA programs have seen applications from women rise since 2006; the figure is 47 percent for part-time-programs and 50 percent for executive programs. While these numbers may not match the 50 percent male-to-female ratio of other graduate programs, closing the b-school gender gap is only a matter of time.

SCHOOL INITIATIVES

How can we be sure that female enrollment will continue to increase? One reason is that getting women enthused about a career in business is a sky-high priority at business schools across the country these days. To wit, many business schools have launched their own women-only outreach and recruiting events. Columbia University hosts an annual "Women in Business" conference that brings together more than 700 alumnae, business leaders, students and prospective students to network and share ideas on achieving success in the marketplace. Linda Meehan, Assistant Dean for Admissions at Columbia Business School, knows that this outreach is working because "applicants walk away wowed by the extraordinary experience of being surrounded by so many intelligent, passionate, and successful women." Events like these aim to dispel myths, discuss the perceived lack of role models, and help women make informed decisions.

Stanford's events, says Wendy Hansen, Associate Director of Admissions at the Stanford Business School, "focus on the educational experience, but also on the unique types of issues women have, such as: how does getting the MBA fit in with having a family or having a spouse? How do I make this experience fit in with my life?" Julia Min, Executive Director of Admissions at UC Berkeley's Haas School of Business, says attendees often find comfort in numbers. "Seeing such a large presence of women is empowering. They realize they're not in this alone, that there are other women around like them."

If all this sounds like good public relations, it is. Schools want to get the word out: MBAs offer women viable opportunities. But if the business schools are talking the talk, they're also walking the walk. There's nothing superficial about this campaign. Bit by bit, the MBA landscape for women is changing.

Opportunities begin even before the first day of class. At Stanford, admitted women are treated to one-on-one admit-lunches with female alumni. Once an admit gets to campus, they find MBA life is chock-full of student-run women and management programs, support groups, retreats, executive conferences, mentoring programs, and other dedicated resources for women only.

For many years now, most business programs have had an on-campus Partners Club for spouses and significant others—a benefit to both female and male students. Newcomers to the business-school scene include groups like The Parents Club and Biz Kids where students can find family-oriented classmates and activities. Columbia University's Mother's Network is an initiative that provides a formal support network for new, current, and future b-school moms. Perhaps the most symbolic gesture of the increasing influence of women in business school is Stanford's provision of a private nursing room for MBA moms and their babies in its main classroom facility.

MORE FLEXIBILITY AND MAKING IT WORK

Of course, there's still room for improvement. A continuing problem at business schools is a lack of course work and case study material featuring women leaders. Likewise, there is an absence of female professors on the academic front.

Apart from these lingering issues, business schools continue to tackle the particular challenges female students face. For many women, the late starting age can be a turn-off. But even here, there are new options and opportunities to consider.

If you're stressed out from trying to have it all and have written off getting an MBA, new early-initiative programs might make you pause and reconsider your decision. Harvard and Stanford have developed an early career track that aims to minimize the impact of the biological clock on a prospective applicant's decision to pursue an MBA. Other schools are likely to follow suit.

The early career track offers a solution that is as simple as it is practical: Admit women (and men) to the MBA program either straight out of college or with just a few years of work experience. Business schools hope that the option to attain their MBA early on in their careers will prompt more women to apply to their programs. With a bigger window to accomplish their professional goals, more women will turn to the MBA as a viable option that won't require them to sacrifice their personal lives.

Beginning a business career earlier eliminates the immediate problem of timing. But what happens down the road? While it helps to remove one timing issue, it can't indefinitely postpone the balancing act that shadows many women's careers. It's hard to rationalize the opportunity costs of the MBA knowing that the investment might be forsaken when tough choices have to be made.

Business schools blame misconceptions about the utility of the MBA for women's reticence on this front. They feel that many women underestimate the broad reach of the degree. The MBA is not just for hard-core careers like banking and finance, but is also useful in not-for-profit work, less high-stress industries such as consumer goods, and leadership positions in a wide range of fields.

Further, says Hansen, "There is a tremendous amount of flexibility in a general management degree. The MBA positions you much more effectively to make an impact wherever you fall at different points in your life. It gives you the tools and framework to apply those skills at different levels and in different intensities. For example, women can rise to a partner level or a senior leadership position and then scale back to a different role within the organization. They can also scale back to part-time work." In other words, the investment doesn't have to be forsaken; it might instead be redirected.

There's no doubt the return on investment (that's ROI in business speak) for the MBA is high. Six-figure salaries and sign-on bonuses that pay you back for the cost of your MBA tuition are hard to beat (and unlike medical, veterinary, and law school grads, you won't have malpractice premiums eating into your take-home pay). If you've thought business school might be right for you, keep investigating—you might be right.

WHERE ARE THE WOMEN IN MBA PROGRAMS?

Are you a professional woman in her mid-to-late twenties? Do you see graduate school in your future? During these tough times, you might envision yourself back on campus sooner rather than later. Downturns do tend to fuel grad school applications. After all, what better place to wait out the economy and avoid the gaping pit of joblessness?

Grad school can be a cure-all for many ills: It can jump-start or redirect a stubbornly off-track career; it can give you a place to hang out while you figure out what you want to be when you grow up (law school, a three-year degree, offers an even longer alternative); and it can transform your personal life as you vault into a new career. Even in uncertain times there is certainty in knowing that after two years in school you can emerge reborn as a professional with a spanking new identity, prescribed career track, and a solid alumni network.

Despite the huge appeal of graduate school, be it as an escape from bad times or as your true, chosen path, MBA programs have remained a problematic choice for many women. Female enrollment at law, medical, and veterinary schools now hovers at, or near, the 50 percent mark. So what's up with business schools? Why has female enrollment at business schools stagnated at about 30 percent?

Even during the best of times, business schools have struggled to attract women. Is this due to the unique challenges women face in building and sustaining their careers over a lifetime of choices, both professional and personal, or is there another reason? Clearly an MBA presents many opportunities, but, for women, will these opportunities upset their already delicate balancing acts?

THINKING OF FAMILY

Let's start with biology—as in biological clocks. Since a prerequisite for admission to many business programs is prior work experience, first-year business school students are typically a bit older than their law or med school counterparts. In fact, the average age for entering full-time MBA students is 28. This means that by the time graduation rolls around, MBA students are heading into their thirties—a prime time for marriage and children. For some women, that timing couldn't be worse.

Newly minted MBAs in their early thirties are just starting to reap the rewards of their business school investments by scoring brand new, mid-to-senior level jobs. With these jobs come ever-greater demands and time pressures. But, for many, the pressure to have a personal life is just as great. Those kinds of competing priorities are the very headaches women hope to avoid. Making matters worse, MBA jobs at the senior level can vault women into a culture that may still be dominated by old-school thinking (translation: men) and a culture that may be less tolerant of efforts to balance work commitments with family.

These dilemmas begin long before business school graduation. Again, because MBA students tend to be older, many women have to factor a partner or child into their graduate school decision, especially if it involves relinquishing a paycheck and/or relocation. Many of these women encounter a potential double standard: Husbands and boyfriends, especially those with careers, are often less willing to relocate on their female partner's behalf than vice versa.

NO URGENT MATTER

Another reason business school enrollment for women may be low is that an MBA is not a barrier to entry nor is it a requirement for success in business. In addition, it isn't a rite of passage in many fields that appeal to high numbers of women: marketing, publishing, fashion, and teaching. By contrast, notes Eileen Chang, former Associate Director of Admissions at the Harvard Business School, "If your objective is to be a lawyer or doctor, you simply can't practice without the requisite degree. Business school is fundamentally different because the career path is one where the MBA can put you on any number of tracks—be it banking, accounting, or management—but doesn't require a credential." Between the lack of a required degree for entering business and the late starting age to enter a program, some women perceive a high opportunity cost for the MBA.

FEAR OF MATH?

Why more women aren't pursuing an MBA is a question that business schools have been asking themselves for years. Some hard answers came in the form of a recent study by the University of Michigan's Business School Center for the Education of Women and the Catalyst Foundation. The following issues were identified as key deterrents to business school for women: the MBA is still seen as a male domain; there is a lack of support from employers; a lack of career opportunity and flexibility; a lack of access to powerful business networks and role models; and a perception that b-school is overloaded with math.

According to many schools, math fears are just that—fears. Chang observes, "Maybe historically, math was considered a hurdle. But we see so many women who have strong skills coming from fields that are quantitative, such as banking and engineering, that I think the math fears are almost a myth. But this is a myth we want to work against. We want applicants to know they can handle the math."

Julia Min, Executive Director of Admissions at UC Berkeley's Haas School of Business, concurs, "The math phobia may be unfounded to a certain degree, and still it's a perception that has been long-lasting. Women [enter business school] and perform extremely well."

If you're frightened by math, you need to know that a business school education does require a basic command of the subject. "You do need to be comfortable with numbers," advises Wendy Hansen, Associate Director of Admissions at the Stanford Business School. "The strongest MBA programs are going to be rigorous in math. Knowing how to influence and lead an organization requires understanding the language of business, which includes accounting and finance."

Still, prospective MBAs with a math phobia need not panic; most programs will work with students who lack the necessary math background. "At Stanford, we have a pre-term program of courses before classes begin to get students up to speed," says Hansen, "We also encourage people to take quantitative courses before they come to our school to develop their skills."

If your math fears are not so easily assuaged, concerns about a persistent Old Boys Network might be. As Hansen notes, "Women may say, I don't see the masses of female role models doing what I want to do. That is going to change slowly. But it is going to change. We have to reach a point where those in school reach a place where they are out in the world having an impact."

OUR ADVICE

Look at the number of female MBA students attending your targeted school and evaluate whether you would feel comfortable there. Research the number and range of student organizations for women and speak with female MBAs about school life.

Chapter 5

Money Matters

HOW MUCH WILL IT COST?

The Truth

To say that business school is an expensive endeavor is an understatement. In fact, to really gauge how expensive business school is, you need to look not only at your tuition costs and living expenses, but also at the opportunity cost of foregoing a salary for the length of your program. Think about it: You'll have a net outflow of money.

But keep in mind that, unlike law school or medical school, business school is just a two-year program. Once those two years are over, you can expect to reap the rewards of your increased market value. Unfortunately, business school differs from law school and medical school in a much less desirable way as well—there are serious limitations on the amount of money available through scholarships and grants. Most business school students seeking financial aid will be limited to loans, and lots of them.

Try not to get too upset about borrowing the money for business school; think of it as an investment in yourself. But, like all investments, it should be carefully thought out and discussed with everyone (spouse, partner, etc.) concerned. This is especially important for those of you considering business school. You need a law degree to practice law, and a medical degree to practice medicine, but a business degree is not required to work in business. That said, certain professional opportunities may be tougher to pursue without an MBA on your resume.

The Cost of B-School

So get out some paper, a pencil, and a calculator, and figure out how much it will cost you to attend school. What should you include? Your opportunity cost (lost income) and your cost of attending b-school (tuition and fees). One more thing: For a more accurate assessment of your investment, you should figure taxes into the equation by dividing tuition cost by 0.65 (this assumes taxes of about 35 percent). Why? Because in order to pay tuition of $35,000, you would have to make a pre-tax income of about $54,000. If you are lucky enough to have a source of aid that does not require repayment, such as a grant, scholarship, or wealthy benefactor, subtract that amount from the cost of attending b-school.

For example, if you currently make $60,000 and plan to attend a business school that costs $35,000 per year, your investment would be approximately $228,000.

$(60,000 \times 2) + [(35,000 \times 2)/.65] = \$227,692.31$

Now say you receive an annual grant of $5,000. Your investment would now be approximately $212,300.

$(60,000 \times 2) + [(30,000 \times 2)/.65] = 212,307.69.$

How Long Will It Take You to Recoup Your Investment?

To estimate this figure, you first need to estimate your expected salary increase post-MBA. Check out the average starting salaries for graduates of the programs you are looking at and adjust upward/downward based on the industry you plan to enter. Subtract your current salary from your expected salary and you'll get your expected salary increase.

Once you complete the step above, divide your investment (tuition and fees plus lost income) by your expected salary increase, and then add 2 (the length of a full-time MBA program). If you are contemplating a one-year MBA program, just add 1.

Going back to the example above, if your pre-MBA salary is $60,000 and you expect to make $80,000 when you graduate, your expected salary increase is $20,000 (a 33 percent increase). Let's assume you did not receive a grant and that your investment will be about $228,000.

$(228,000/20,000) + 2 = 13.4$

It will take you approximately 13 years to earn back your investment.

Keep in mind, these are approximations and don't take into account annual raises, inflation, and so on. But it is interesting, isn't it?

While business school is an expensive proposition, the financial rewards of having your MBA can be immensely lucrative as we discussed before. You won't be forced into bankruptcy if you finance it correctly. There are tried-and-true ways to reduce your initial costs, finance the costs on the horizon, and manage the debt you'll leave school with—all without selling your soul to the highest bidder.

Comparison Shopping

While cost shouldn't be the first thing on your mind when you are choosing a school, depending on your goals in getting an MBA, it might be fairly high on your list. Private schools aren't the only business schools. Many state schools have fantastic reputations. Regional schools may be more generous with financial aid. Tuition costs will vary widely between public and private schools, especially if you qualify as an in-state student. Keep in mind, however, that salary gains tend to be less dramatic at more regional schools.

HOW DO I FUND MY MBA?

The short answer: loans. Unless your company is underwriting your MBA, or you're able to pay your way in cash, you'll be financing your two years of business school through a portfolio of loans. Loans typically come in one of two forms: federal and private. Only a few of you will be lucky enough to qualify for, and get, grants and scholarships.

Anyone with reasonably good credit, regardless of financial need, can borrow money for business school. If you have financial need, you will probably be eligible for some type of financial aid if you meet the following basic qualifications:

- You are a United States citizen or a permanent U.S. resident.

- You are registered for Selective Service if you are a male, or you have documentation to prove that you are exempt.

- You are not in default on student loans already.

- You don't have a horrendous credit history.

International applicants to business school should take note: Most U.S. business schools will require all international students to pay in full or show proof that they will be able to pay the entire cost of the MBA prior to beginning the MBA program.

FEDERAL LOANS

The federal government funds federal loan programs. Federal loans are usually the "first resort" for borrowers because many are subsidized by the federal government and offer generous interest rates. Some do not begin charging you interest until after you complete your degree. Most federal loans are need-based, but some higher interest federal loans are available regardless of financial circumstances. Your business school's Financial Aid Office will determine what your need is, if any.

PRIVATE LOANS

Private loans are funded by banks, foundations, corporations, and other associations. A number of private loans are targeted to aid particular segments of the population. You may have to do some investigating to identify private loans for which you might qualify. As always, contact your law school's Financial Aid Office to learn more.

ALTERNATIVE SOURCES OF FUNDING

We've already mentioned these in one form or other, but they are worthy of a bit more attention.

The first alternative is sponsorship of your employer or educational reimbursement. Not all companies treat this the same way, but if you are able to get your employer to kick in a portion of the cost, you are better off than before. But beware, this benefit also comes with strings attached. Most companies that pay for your MBA will require a commitment of several years upon graduation. If you renege, you could be liable for the full cost of your education. Others will require that you attend business school part-time, which you may or may not want to do. Often, part-time students are unable to participate in on-campus recruiting and networking efforts to the same extent as full-time students.

Educational reimbursement can come in another form as well. Some companies will provide sign-on bonuses to new MBAs that will cover the cost of a year's tuition. This is a fantastic development from the years of a robust economy, but it is by no means a guarantee during tougher times. Don't assume that you will have this option open to you just because it has been a common occurrence in past years.

The other "alternative" source of funding is a financial gift from family or another source. Either you have a resource that is willing and able to fund all or part of your MBA, or you don't. If you do, be thankful.

APPLYING FOR FINANCIAL AID

In order to become eligible for financial aid of any kind, you will need to complete the Free Application for Federal Student Aid, also known as the FAFSA. You complete and submit this form after January 1 of the year in which you plan to enter business school. You should aim to complete and submit this form as soon as possible after the first of the year to avoid any potential delays. The FAFSA is available from a school's Financial Aid Office. You can also download the form directly from the website of the U.S. Department of Education at FAFSA.ed.gov. A third option is to use the FAFSA Express software (also downloadable from the website) and transmit the application electronically.

It is important to note that the form requires information from your federal income tax returns. Plan to file your taxes early that year.

In addition to the FAFSA form, most schools will have their own financial aid form that you will be required to complete and submit. These often have their own deadlines, so it is wise to keep careful track of all the forms you must complete and all their respective deadlines. Yes, it's a lot of paperwork, but get over it. You'll be much happier when the tuition bill arrives.

LOAN SPECIFICS

Guide to Federal Loans

Stafford Loans

Stafford loans require you to complete the FAFSA form in order to qualify. These are very desirable loans because they offer low-interest rates fixed at 6.8 percent and are federally guaranteed. There is a limit to how much you can borrow in this program. The maximum amount per year you may borrow as a graduate student is $20,500. The maximum amount you may borrow in total is $138,500. The aggregate amount includes any Stafford loans you may have from your undergraduate or other graduate studies.

You may have borrowed Direct Subsidized or Unsubsidized Stafford loans as an undergraduate. It's important to remember that all direct loans for graduate students are unsubsidized. Unsubsidized loans are not need-based and do charge interest from the time of disbursement to the time of full repayment. You can pay the interest while you are in school or opt for capitalization, in which case the interest is added to the principal. You will pay more in the long run if you choose capitalization. Interest payments may be tax deductible, so be sure to check. The standard repayment period for both is 10 years.

You will pay a small origination and guarantee fee for each loan, but this is not an out-of-pocket expense. It is simply deducted from the loan amount. Some schools will allow you to borrow the money under the Stafford program directly from them, while others will require you to borrow from a bank. Direct federal loans are typically paid to the school to cover tuition, fees, and room and board (if you are living in campus housing). Any remaining balance will be paid to you by the school bursar. Repayment is handled by a loan servicer, which is a company that handles collection and administrative duties related to a loan. You will be contacted by your servicer upon receipt of your Direct loan. For more information on federal loans, call the Federal Student Aid Information Center at 800-433-3243 or visit studentaid.ed.gov.

Perkins Loans

Perkins loans are available to graduate students who demonstrate exceptional financial need. The financial aid office will determine your eligibility for a Perkins Loan. If you qualify for a Perkins Loan as part of your financial aid package, take it. The loans are made by the schools and are repaid to the schools, although the federal government provides a large portion of the funds. You can borrow up to $8,000 for each year of graduate study up to a total of $60,000 (this includes any money borrowed under this program during undergraduate study). The interest rates on this loan are low, currently 5 percent. There are no fees attached. The grace period is nine months upon graduation.

Direct PLUS Loans

Direct PLUS loans are made available through schools, though the U.S. Department of Education is actually the lender. You may borrow up to the full cost of attendance as determined by your school, less any other financial aid received. Like other federal loans, Direct PLUS loans have a small origination fee and a fixed interest rate, which is currently 7.9 percent. These funds are paid directly to your school to cover tuition, fees, and room and board. Any remaining balance will be refunded to you to cover other expenses associated with your education—when a school determines the cost of attendance, books, travel, and other expenses are typically included.

Private/Commercial Loans

This is expensive territory. Not only are interest rates high, but terms are also quite different from those found with federal loans. You may not be able to defer payment of interest or principal until after graduation. Origination and guarantee fees are also much higher since these loans are unsecured. After all, banks and other specialized lenders exist to loan money to folks like you, and unlike the federal government, want to make money doing it. If you go this route, shop around diligently. Think of it as good practice for your post-MBA executive career.

Scholarships and Grants

The usual sources for this type of funding are alumni groups and civic organizations. This funding is limited, and actual awards tend to be small. Even if you benefited from generous scholarship funding as an undergraduate, it would be unwise to assume you'll have the same experience as a graduate student. But do investigate. You never know what's out there. Schools will frequently list any scholarships and grants that are available at the back of their financial aid catalog.

For more information

Find out more about your financing options for business school education at PrincetonReview.com.

CHAPTER 6
WHAT B-SCHOOL IS REALLY LIKE

AN ACADEMIC PERSPECTIVE

The objective of all MBA programs is to prepare students for a professional career in business. One business school puts it this way:

Graduates should be all of the following:

1. Able to think and reason independently, creatively, and analytically.

2. Skilled in the use of quantitative techniques.

3. Literate in the use of software applications as management tools.

4. Knowledgeable about the world's management issues and problems.

5. Willing to work in and successfully cope with conditions of uncertainty, risk, and change.

6. Astute decision makers.

7. Ethically and socially responsible.

8. Able to manage in an increasingly global environment.

9. Proficient in utilizing technology as a mode of doing business.

Sound like a tall order? Possibly. But this level of expectation is what business school is all about.

Nearly all MBA programs feature a core curriculum that focuses on the major disciplines of business: finance, management, accounting, marketing, manufacturing, decision sciences, economics, and organizational behavior. Unless your school allows you to place out of them, these courses are mandatory. Core courses provide broad functional knowledge in one discipline. To illustrate, a core marketing course covers pricing, segmentation, communications, product-line planning, and implementation. Electives provide a narrow focus that deepen the area of study. For example, a marketing elective might be entirely devoted to pricing.

Students sometimes question the need for such a comprehensive core program, but the functional areas of a real business are not parallel lines. All departments of a business affect each other every day. For example, an MBA in a manufacturing job might be asked by a financial controller why the company's product has become unprofitable to produce. Without an understanding of how product costs are accounted for, this MBA wouldn't know how to respond to a critical and legitimate request.

At most schools, the first term or year is devoted to a rigid core curriculum. Some schools allow first-years to take core courses side by side with electives. Still others have come up with an entirely new way of covering the basics, integrating the core courses into one cross-functional learning experience, which may also include sessions on topics such as globalization, ethics, and managing diversity. Half-year to year-long courses are team-taught by professors who will see you through all disciplines.

TEACHING METHODOLOGY

Business schools employ two basic teaching methods: case study and lecture. Usually, they employ some combination of the two. The most popular is the case study approach. Students are presented with either real or hypothetical business scenarios and are asked to analyze them. This method provides concrete situations (rather than abstractions) that require mastery of a wide range of skills. Students often find case studies exciting because they can engage in spirited discussions about possible solutions to given business problems and because they get an opportunity to apply newly acquired business knowledge.

On the other hand, lecturing is a teaching method in which—you guessed it—the professor speaks to the class and the class listens. The efficacy of the lecture method depends entirely on the professor. If the professor is compelling, you'll probably get a lot out of the class. If the professor is boring, you probably won't listen, which isn't necessarily a big deal since many professors make their class notes available online.

THE CLASSROOM EXPERIENCE

Professors teaching case methodology often begin class with a "cold call." A randomly selected student opens the class with an analysis of the case and makes recommendations for solutions. The cold call forces you to be prepared and to think on your feet.

No doubt, a cold call can be intimidating. But unlike law school, b-school professors don't use the Socratic Method to torture you, testing your thinking with a pounding cross-examination. They're training managers, not trial lawyers. At worst, particularly if you're unprepared, a professor will abruptly dismiss your contribution.

Alternatively, professors ask for a volunteer to open a case, particularly someone who has had real industry experience with the issues. After the opening, the discussion is broadened to include the whole class. Everyone tries to get in a good comment, particularly if class participation counts heavily toward the grade. "Chip shots"—unenlightened, just-say-anything-to-get-credit comments—are common. So are "air hogs," students who go on and on because they like nothing more than to hear themselves pontificate.

Depending on the school, class discussions can degenerate into wars of ego rather than ideas. But for the most part, debates are kept constructive and civilized. Students are competitive, but not offensively so, and learn to make their points succinctly and persuasively.

A GLOSSARY OF INSIDER LINGO

B-school students, graduates, and professors—like most close-knit, somewhat solipsistic groups—seem to speak their own weird language. Here's a sampler of MBA jargon (with English translations):

Admissions Mistake: How each student perceives him or herself until getting first-year grades back from midterms.

Air Hogs: Students who monopolize classroom discussion and love to hear themselves speak.

B2B: "Business to Business"—a company that sells not to retail consumers, but to other enterprises. With the renewed focus on more traditional industries, this now stands for "Back to Basics."

B2C: "Business to Consumer"—a company that sells primarily to individual retail consumers. As with the above joke about B2B, business students occasionally say this really means "Back to Consulting."

Back of the Envelope: A quick analysis of numbers, as if scribbled on the back of an envelope.

Benchmarking: Comparing a company to others in the industry.

Burn Rate: Amount of cash a money-losing company consumes during a period of time.

Case Study Method: Popular teaching method that uses real-life business cases for analysis.

Cold Call: Unexpected, often dreaded request by the professor to open a case discussion.

Chip Shot: Vacant and often cheesy comments used not to truly benefit class discussion, but rather to get credit for participation.

Cycle Time: How fast you can turn something around.

Deliverable: Your end product.

Four P's: Elements of a marketing strategy: Price, Promotion, Place, Product.

Fume Date: Date the company will run out of cash reserves.

Functional Areas: The basic disciplines of business (e.g., finance, marketing, R&D).

HP12-C: A calculator that works nothing like a regular one, used by finance types when they don't have Excel handy.

Lingo Bingo: A furtive game of Bingo whereby he who "wins" must work a decided upon, often trite phrase (see "chip shot") into the class discussion. For example: "I didn't actually read the case last night, but the protagonist is *two beers short of a six-pack*." The winner also earns a prize and the admiration of classmates.

Low Hanging Fruit: Tasks or goals that are easiest to achieve (consultant jargon).

Monitize: To turn an idea into a moneymaking scheme.

Net Net: End result.

Power Nap: Quick, intense, in-class recharge for the continually sleep-deprived.

Power Tool: Someone who does all the work and sits in the front row of the class with his or her hand up.

Pre-enrollment Courses: Commonly known as MBA summer camp—quantitative courses to get the numerically challenged up to speed.

Pro Forma: Financial presentation of hypothetical events, such as projected earnings.

Quant Jock: A numerical athlete who is happiest crunching numbers.

Rule of Three: You should not talk more than three times in any given class, but you should participate at least once over the course of three classes.

Run the Numbers: Analyze quantitatively.

Shrimp Boy: A student who comes to a corporate event just to scarf down the food.

Skydeck: Refers to the back row of the classroom, usually when it's amphitheater style.

Slice and Dice: Running all kinds of quantitative analysis on a set of numbers.

Soft Skills: Conflict resolution, teamwork, negotiation, oral and written communication.

Take-aways: The key points of a lecture or meeting that participants should remember.

The Five Forces: Michael Porter's model for analyzing the strategic attractiveness of an industry.

Three C's: The primary forces considered in marketing: Customer, Competition, Company.

Value-Based Decision Making: Values and ethics as part of the practice of business.

YOUR FIRST YEAR

The first six months of b-school can be daunting. You're unfamiliar with the subjects. There's a tremendous amount of work to do. And when you least have the skills to do so, there's pressure to stay with the pack. All of this produces anxiety and a tendency to overprepare. Eventually, students learn shortcuts and settle into a routine, but until then, much of the first year is just plain tough. The programs usually pack more learning into the first term than they do into each of the remaining terms. For the schools to teach the core curriculum (which accounts for as much as 70 percent of learning) in a limited time, an intensive pace is considered necessary. Much of the second year will be spent on gaining proficiency in your area of expertise and on searching for a job.

The good news is that the schools recognize how tough the first year can be. During the early part of the program, they anchor students socially by placing them in small sections, sometimes called "cohorts." You take many or all of your classes with your section-mates. Sectioning encourages the formation of personal and working relationships and can help make a large program feel like a school within a school.

Because so much has to be accomplished in so little time, getting an MBA is like living in fast-forward. This is especially true of the job search. No sooner are you in the program than recruiters for summer jobs show up, which tends to divert students from their studies. First-years aggressively pursue summer positions, which are linked with the promise of a permanent job offer if the summer goes well. At some schools, the recruiting period begins as early as October, at others in January or February.

A DAY IN THE LIFE

MATT CAMP, FIRST YEAR
Tuck School of Business, Dartmouth College

7:00 A.M.: Get dressed. Out of the door by 7:45 A.M. to head to the campus dining hall for breakfast. If I have time, I'll scan both the *Financial Times* and *The Wall Street Journal*. Today, I have an informal get-to-know-you-better meeting with a marketing professor over breakfast.

8:30 A.M.: Core class in Corporate Finance. Grab any seat in a tiered classroom set-up. I'm usually in the middle toward the side. If possible, the front row stays empty.

10:00 A.M.: Check e-mail. Read the *Times*.

10:30 A.M.: Macroeconomics lecture/case study class. Again, no assigned seating. Expect cold calls on case. Cold calls are not terrifying. Professors are supportive, not out to embarrass you. Class discussion is lively, with a mix of people offering their views.

Noon: Back to the cafeteria. Tuck may be one of the few schools where everyone eats together at the same place. There isn't much in town, and you're tight on time, so it doesn't make sense to go back home or elsewhere. It's crowded, so I look for friends, but basically grab a seat anywhere at one of the large tables that seat six to seven. Professors, administrators, and students all eat at the same place. Food is above-average.

1:15 P.M.: Classes are over for the day. From this point, I begin to start homework; there's a lot of work to do. I can go to a study room on campus, but they get booked up pretty quickly for groups, so I head to the library. The majority of the people are doing work for tomorrow. It's rare to have someone working on a project that's due the following week. It's pretty much day-to-day.

4:00 P.M.: I head off to one of the scheduled sports I've signed up for. Today it's soccer, played about one mile from campus. I drive; friends hitch a ride with me. This is a big international scene, mostly men, but there's a small group of women too. It's definitely a game we play hard, but in a very congenial way.

6:00 P.M.: Head back to campus. I'm hungry. It's off to the dining hall again. Most first-years live in dorms, so home cooking is not an option. Almost all second-years live off-campus, so they head back for a home-cooked meal. Cafeteria is not crowded; I may eat alone.

7:00 P.M.: Head home for a quick shower and change. The night is just beginning.

7:30 P.M.: Meet with study group at school to flesh out rest of work that needs to be done in preparation for tomorrow's classes.

11:00 P.M.: Students and their wives/husbands or partners head out to play ice hockey at one of the two rinks here. Wives/husbands and partners play. There are different games going on for different skill levels. It's a lot of fun.

Midnight: Time to go and celebrate either a hard game or a sore butt, but everyone goes to get some wings and a beer. There are only two bars on campus, and they close at 1:00 A.M. so we head to one of them.

1:00 A.M.: After the bar closes, people head home.

1:15 A.M.: Exhausted, I go to bed. No TV. I've forgotten what that is.

YOUR SECOND YEAR

Relax, the second year is easier. By now, students know what's important and what's not. Second-years work more efficiently than first-years. Academic anxiety is no longer a factor. Having mastered the broad-based core curriculum, students now enjoy taking electives and developing an area of specialization.

Anxiety in the second year has more to do with the arduous task of finding a job. For some lucky students, a summer position has yielded a full-time offer. But even those students often go through the whole recruiting grind anyway because they don't want to cut off any opportunities prematurely.

Most MBAs leave school with a full-time offer. Sometimes it's their only offer. Sometimes it's not their dream job, which may be why most grads change jobs after just two years. One student summed up the whole two-year academic/recruiting process like this: "The first-year students collapse in the winter quarter because of on-campus recruiting. The second-years collapse academically in the first quarter of their second year because it's so competitive to get a good job. And when a second-year does get a job, he or she forgets about class entirely. That's why pass/fail was invented."

A DAY IN THE LIFE

Kristin Hansen, Second-Year
Tuck School of Business, Dartmouth College

9:00 A.M.: Wake-up (my first class is at 10:30 A.M.) and finish work for Monday classes.

10:15 A.M.: Ride my bike to campus for 10:30 A.M. class.

10:30 A.M.: Head to International Economics class, an elective. I have only three classes this semester, my last. Prior to this I had four and a half classes each term. I front-loaded so I would have a light last semester. Grab a yogurt and juice on way in. Eat in class. We discuss a currency crisis case.

Noon: Head to study room and check e-mail. Finish work for next class.

1:00 P.M.: Grab a quick lunch in the dining hall. Will bring it to eat during class.

1:15 P.M.: Managerial Decision Making class, another elective. Today is the very last class that second-years will have at Tuck; we're off to graduation! Our professor brings in strawberries and champagne to celebrate. We all hang out and toast each other. This obviously doesn't happen everyday, but this is just the kind of thing a Tuck professor would do.

2:45 P.M.: I'm one of four Tuck social chairpersons, so I use this time to send e-mails to my co-chairs about the upcoming chili cook-off and farm party. Then I send a message to the school regarding other social events for the weekend. I get an e-mail from the New York office of CS First Boston, with whom I've accepted a job offer, with a calendar of the dates for my private client-services training.

3:00 P.M.: Go for a run, swim, or bike ride.

5:00 P.M.: Head home to shower and change. Usually I'd make dinner at home and eat, but tonight, I'm heading out to a social event. So I relax a bit and do an hour of preparation for the next day. On Monday, Tuesday, and Wednesday nights, the workload is heavier.

7:00 P.M.: Off to a Turkey Fry Dinner. This is a meal that will be prepared by my two economics professors. They donated this "dinner" for the charity student auction. Friends of mine bid on it and won. Each of eight bidders gets to bring a guest, and I'm one of the guests. The professors are hosting this at one of their homes. Basically, they're taking three large turkeys and fry-o-lating them.

8:30 P.M.: We all head out to an open mic night, led by the same two economics professors that hosted the Turkey Fry. It's held at a local bar. Anyone in the audience can get onstage and perform. I'm a member of the Tuck band, so I get up on stage with my acoustic guitar and play various folk and bluegrass songs. This is a great warm-up for the open mic night at Tuck.

10:45 P.M.: We head out for Pub Night in downtown Hanover.

1:00 A.M.: The bar closes, so we head to "The End Zone," one of the second-year houses close to campus. All the second-year houses are named; these are names that have been passed down from generation to generation. On a typical Thursday night at Tuck, a small number of students will stay out until 3:00 A.M. I'm usually one of them.

3:00 A.M.: I walk home. My house, called "Girls in the Hood," is just a ten-minute stroll away. I may grab a 3:00 A.M. snack. Then, I quickly fall asleep, exhausted.

Life Outside of Class

Business school is more than academics and a big-bucks job. A spirited community provides ample opportunity for social interaction, extracurricular activity, and career development.

Much of campus life revolves around student-run clubs. There are groups for just about every career interest and social need—from MBAs for a Greener America to the Small Business Club. There's even a group for significant others on most campuses. The clubs are a great way to meet classmates with similar interests and to get in on the social scene. They might have a reputation for throwing the best black-tie balls, pizza-and-keg events, and professional mixers. During orientation week, these clubs aggressively market themselves to first-years.

Various socially responsible projects are also popular on campus. An emphasis on volunteer work is part of the overall trend toward good citizenship. Perhaps to counter the greed of the 1980s, "giving back" is the b-school style of the moment. There is usually a wide range of options—from tutoring in an inner-city school to working in a soup kitchen to renovating public buildings.

Still another way to get involved is to work on a school committee. Here you might serve on a task force designed to improve student quality of life, or you might work in the admissions office and interview prospective students.

For those with more creative urges there are always the old standbys: extracurriculars such as the school paper, yearbook, or school play. At some schools, the latter is a dramatization of "b-school follies" and is a highlight of the year. Like the student clubs, these are a great way to get to know your fellow students.

Finally, you can play on intramural sports teams or attend the numerous informal get-togethers, dinner parties, and group trips. There are also plenty of regularly scheduled pub nights, just in case you thought your beer-guzzling days were over.

Most former MBA students say that going to b-school was the best decision they ever made. That's primarily because of nonacademic experiences. Make the most of your classes, but take the time to get involved and enjoy yourself.

PART II
SCHOOLS RANKED BY CATEGORY

On the following pages you will find eleven top 10 lists of business schools ranked according to various metrics. As we noted earlier, none of these lists purports to rank the business schools by their overall quality. Nor should any combination of the categories we've chosen be construed as representing the raw ingredients for such a ranking. We have made no attempt to gauge the "prestige" of these schools, and we wonder whether we could accurately do so even if we tried. What we have done, however, is presented a number of lists using information from two very large databases—one of statistical information collected from business schools, and another of subjective data gathered via our survey of 19,000 business students at 296 business schools.

Ten of the ranking lists are based partly or wholly on opinions collected through our business student survey. The only schools that may appear in these lists are the 296 business schools from which we were able to collect a sufficient number of student surveys to accurately represent the student experience in our various ratings and descriptive profiles.

One of the rankings, "Toughest to Get Into," incorporates *only* admissions statistics reported to us by the business schools. Therefore, any business school appearing in this edition of the guide, whether we collected student surveys from it or not, may appear on this list.

Under the title of each list is an explanation of what criteria the ranking is based on. For explanations of many of the individual rankings components, turn to the "How This Book is Organized" section, on page 5.

It's worth repeating: There is no one best business school in America. There is a best business school for you. By using these rankings in conjunction with the descriptive profiles and data listings in subsequent sections of this book, we hope that you will begin to identify the attributes of a business school that are important to you, as well as those schools that can best help you to achieve your personal and professional goals.

The top schools in each category appear in descending order.

TOUGHEST TO GET INTO

BASED ON THE ADMISSIONS SELECTIVITY RATING (SEE PAGE 10 FOR EXPLANATION)

1. Stanford University
2. Massachusetts Institute of Technology
3. Harvard University
4. University of California—Berkeley
5. University of Pennsylvania
6. New York University
7. Columbia University
8. Dartmouth College
9. Yale University
10. Northwestern University

BEST CAREER PROSPECTS

BASED ON THE CAREER RATING (SEE PAGE 12 FOR EXPLANATION)

1. Stanford University
2. University of California—Berkeley
3. Dartmouth College
4. New York University
5. Columbia University
6. Harvard University
7. University of Pennsylvania
8. Carnegie Mellon University
9. Northwestern University
10. Massachusetts Institute of Technology

BEST CLASSROOM EXPERIENCE

BASED ON STUDENT ASSESSMENT OF PROFESSORS' TEACHING ABILITIES AND RECOGNITION IN THEIR FIELDS, THE INTEGRATION OF NEW BUSINESS TRENDS AND PRACTICES IN THE CURRICULA, AND THE INTELLECTUAL LEVEL OF CLASSMATES' CONTRIBUTIONS IN COURSE DISCUSSIONS

1. New York University
2. Stanford University
3. Harvard University
4. University of California—Berkeley
5. Yale University
6. Dartmouth College
7. University of Pennsylvania
8. Duke University
9. Georgia Institute of Technology
10. University of Massachusetts Amherst

BEST PROFESSORS

BASED ON THE PROFESSORS INTERESTING AND PROFESSORS ACCESSIBLE RATINGS (SEE PAGE 9 FOR EXPLANATION)

1. University of California—Berkeley
2. Harvard University
3. The University of Texas at Austin
4. Yale University
5. University of Virginia
6. Vanderbilt University
7. The Ohio State University
8. Rice University
9. Cornell University
10. Dartmouth College

MOST COMPETITIVE STUDENTS

Based on student assessment of how competitive classmates are, how heavy the workload is, and the perceived academic pressure

1. Acton School of Business
2. Purdue University
3. Texas A&M University—College Station
4. University of Pennsylvania
5. Bryant University
6. Howard University
7. University of Rochester
8. University of Miami
9. Texas Christian University
10. The University of Texas at Dallas

MOST FAMILY FRIENDLY

Based on student assessment of: how happy married students are, how many students have children, how helpful the business school is to students with children, and how much the school does for the spouses of students

1. Brigham Young University
2. Dartmouth College
3. Indiana University—Bloomington
4. The University of North Carolina at Chapel Hill
5. Pittsburg State University
6. Pennsylvania State University
7. The College of William & Mary
8. University of Notre Dame
9. Duke University
10. Cornell University

BEST CAMPUS ENVIRONMENT

Based on student assessment of the safety, attractiveness, and location of the school

1. Columbia University
2. University of California—Los Angeles
3. The University of North Carolina at Chapel Hill
4. Dartmouth College
5. Stanford University
6. The University of Texas at Austin
7. University of Illinois at Urbana-Champaign
8. Vanderbilt University
9. The University of Alabama at Tuscaloosa
10. Pennsylvania State University

BEST GREEN MBA

Based on students' assessments of how well their school is preparing them in environmental/sustainability and social responsibility issues, and for a career in a green job market

1. Yale University
2. University of California—Berkeley
3. University of Oregon
4. University of Denver
5. University of San Diego
6. Stanford University
7. The University of North Carolina at Chapel Hill
8. The George Washington University
9. University of Michigan—Ann Arbor
10. State University of New York— Binghamton University

BEST ADMINISTERED

BASED ON STUDENT ASSESSMENT OF HOW SMOOTHLY THE SCHOOL IS RUN, AND THE EASE WITH WHICH STUDENTS CAN GET INTO REQUIRED AND POPULAR COURSES

1. University of Florida
2. Elon University
3. Rice University
4. Vanderbilt University
5. Arizona State University
6. Colorado State University
7. Butler University
8. Babson College
9. University of Louisville
10. Illinois State University

GREATEST OPPORTUNITY FOR MINORITY STUDENTS

BASED ON THE PERCENT OF STUDENTS FROM MINORITIES, THE PERCENT OF FACULTY FROM MINORITIES, AND STUDENT ASSESSMENT OF RESOURCES FOR MINORITY STUDENTS, HOW SUPPORTIVE THE CULTURE IS OF MINORITY STUDENTS, AND WHETHER FELLOW STUDENTS ARE ETHNICALLY AND RACIALLY DIVERSE

1. Howard University
2. University of Houston—Victoria
3. Texas A & M International University
4. Florida International University
5. Mercer University—Atlanta
6. The University of Texas at San Antonio
7. University of San Francisco
8. Drexel University
9. Georgia State University
10. Carnegie Mellon University

GREATEST OPPORTUNITY FOR WOMEN

BASED ON THE PERCENT OF STUDENTS WHO ARE FEMALE, THE PERCENT OF FACULTY WHO ARE FEMALE, AND STUDENT ASSESSMENT OF: RESOURCES FOR FEMALE STUDENTS, HOW SUPPORTIVE THE CULTURE IS OF FEMALE STUDENTS, WHETHER THE BUSINESS SCHOOL OFFERS COURSEWORK FOR WOMEN ENTREPRENEURS, AND WHETHER CASE STUDY MATERIALS FOR CLASSES PROPORTIONATELY REFLECT WOMEN IN BUSINESS

1. Simmons School of Management
2. University of San Diego
3. Brandeis University
4. Pepperdine University
5. The George Washington University
6. University of California—Davis
7. University of California—Berkeley
8. University of Washington
9. University of California—Los Angeles
10. Babson College

PART III-A
BUSINESS SCHOOL
DESCRIPTIVE PROFILES

ACTON SCHOOL OF BUSINESS
THE ACTON MBA IN ENTREPRENEURSHIP

GENERAL INFORMATION

Type of school	Private
Affiliation	No Affiliation
Academic calendar	Aug–May

SURVEY SAYS...

Good peer network, Cutting-edge classes
Solid preparation in:
Finance, General management, Operations, Communication/interpersonal skills, Quantitative skills, Entrepreneurial studies

STUDENTS

Enrollment of parent institution	2,200
Enrollment of MBA Program	27
% male/female	86/14
% out-of-state	51
% part-time	0
% underrepresented minority	29
% international	14
Average age at entry	29
Average years work experience at entry	6.0

ACADEMICS

Academic Experience Rating	92
Profs interesting rating	96
Profs accesible rating	90
Student/faculty ratio	2:1
% female faculty	13

Academics

Acton School of Business's unique MBA is like "boot camp" for entrepreneurs. This "challenging yet rewarding" program covers every aspect, practical and personal, of launching a successful venture. Through the school's unique curriculum, students "learn how to learn, learn how to make money, and learn how to live a life of meaning." In meeting this mission, Acton employs "some of the best entrepreneurs in the world;" the school's stellar professors are "leaders in the field of study, and experts at leading the classroom discussions." A current student gushes, "To say the professors here are 'world-class' would be an understatement. These are the best teachers an MBA student could ever encounter." Coursework is entirely case-based, and professors employ the Socratic method to encourage discussion and creative problem solving in the classroom. Students love the fact that "Class time is 100 percent dedicated to real-life applicable situations. There is no wasted time on theory that we can't use." A current student adds, "After seeing 300 cases and having analyzed those from the entrepreneur point of view, you start seeing patterns."

The Acton MBA is an accelerated program, which packs two years of coursework into single fast-paced year. Every day is a marathon, with students meeting for break-of-dawn study groups before class kicks off at eight o'clock in the morning. With its emphasis on discussion, "Class is incredibly intense; the professors are knowledgeable, and the students are incredibly well prepared." On that note, there are roughly ten cases assigned every week, so you can reasonably expect "90-100 hours of case prep per week." Fortunately, the rewards of the Acton MBA are well worth the effort. Despite the long hours, "Discussions and material make the days go by so fast. It really is a lot of fun once you get past the tough schedule." Not to mention, the rigor itself is a great teacher; here, the curriculum is "so difficult and time-consuming that you are a different person after you finish."

"Acton is run like a well organized company," and overseen by a staff of 3 that is "very easy to work with and very efficient." The "School administration is very responsive to problems" when they arise, treating students like valued customers. A case in point, all Acton instructors are required to sign a contract agreeing to step down if students are dissatisfied with their course. Students also appreciate the accelerated structure, which limits their educational expenses to a single year. Sure, you may sweat through it, but "The amount of education packed into one year is better than any 2 or 2+ year program in the country."

Career and Placement

With its pointed focus on entrepreneurship, Acton's approach to career services is rather different than what you would find at most MBA programs. Acton students are rarely interested in working for a large bank or corporation, and the school encourages them to eschew a life of time cards and cubicles. Instead, successful graduates of the program go on to start their own ventures in a wide range of areas. As a result, you will not find career fairs and resume assistance at Acton School of Business. On the contrary, "Recruiters are not allowed on campus," and, when students are matched with employers, it is done on a more individual level. Nonetheless, long-term career goals are essential to the Acton academic experience. Of particular note, all students take the contemplative Life of Meaning course, which challenges them to profoundly examine their long-term goals. A current student agrees, "The Life of Meaning course changed the way I thought about life, and changed my direction of life also."

ADMISSIONS CONTACT: SUSIE HALL, DIRECTOR OF OUTREACH AND ENROLLMENT
ADDRESS: 816 CONGRESS AVENUE, SUITE 1240, AUSTIN, TX 78701
PHONE: 512-703-1232 • FAX: 512-495-9480
E-MAIL: ADMISSIONS@ACTONMBA.ORG • WEBSITE: WWW.ACTONMBA.ORG

Student Life and Environment

MBA candidates say you must be prepared to "dedicate your life to the program" at Acton. Keeping up with the rigorous MBA coursework requires every waking hour, from dawn to midnight. A current student details, "A typical day begins at 5:15 am to make it to study group by 6:00. Class until 12:20 over the cases you prepared the day before. Go to lunch with classmates and then begin studying at 1:00. Go to bed at midnight and start again." While students spend a great deal of time with their classmates, "There is no time for clubs or activities" outside schoolwork. Even your personal life may end up on the back burner; for most students, "Family time is limited to around 30 minutes per day." While no one questions the efficacy of the program, some say it would be nice if the school provided more "support for families, including spouse events."

The rigorous interaction naturally helps to create strong bonds between students. You will learn a lot from your peers at Acton, and not surprisingly, most students are "very motivated and extremely competitive." Fortunately, they are also described as "friendly, easy to talk to, eager to help one another, and family-oriented." Similarities end there, however. The school attracts a "diverse group of individuals with different backgrounds and political ideologies."

Admissions

Prospective students are encouraged to visit Acton and sit in on a class before applying to the program; students can request a class visit through the school's website. Most students enter the program with several years of professional experience under their belt; however, Acton accepts up to five exceptional students who apply to the program directly after college. Acton prefers students with GMAT scores of 600 and higher, though decisions are made based on a student's complete application. The average GMAT score for the fall of 2011 entering class was 648.

FINANCIAL FACTS

Annual tuition	$49,500
Fees	$0
Room & board	$20,000
% of students receiving aid	100
% of first-year students receiving aid	100
% of students receiving grants	0
Average award package	$49,500
Average loan	$69,500
Average student loan debt	$27,500

ADMISSIONS

Admissions Selectivity Rating	**79**
# of applications received	37
% applicants accepted	78
% acceptees attending	93
Average GMAT	639
Average GPA	3.23
TOEFL required of international students	Yes
Minimum TOEFL (paper/computer)	630/267
Application fee	$150
International application fee	$150
Early application deadline	2/28
Early notification date	4/1
Regular application deadline	6/5
Regular application notification	6/24
Application Deadline/Notification	
Round 1:	2/28 / 4/1
Round 2:	5/1 / 5/24
Round 3:	6/5 / 6/24
Deferment available	No
Transfer students accepted	No
Non-fall admissions	No
Need-blind admissions	No

EMPLOYMENT PROFILE

Career Rating	**91**	**Grads Employed by Function% Avg. Salary**	
Percent employed at graduation	14	Marketing	(22%) $75,000
Percent employed 3 months after graduation	50	Operations	(22%) $102,000
Average base starting salary	$80,000	Consulting	(4%)
Primary Source of Full-time Job Acceptances		Finance	(4%) $85,000
Graduate-facilitated activities	9(33%)		

ALFRED UNIVERSITY
SCHOOL OF BUSINESS

GENERAL INFORMATION

Type of school	Private
Affiliation	No Affiliation

SURVEY SAYS...

Good social scene, Cutting-edge classes
Solid preparation in:
Accounting

STUDENTS

Enrollment of parent institution	2,300
Enrollment of MBA Program	52
% male/female	71/29
% out-of-state	4
% part-time	40
% underrepresented minority	23
% international	8

ACADEMICS

Academic Experience Rating	**73**
Profs interesting rating	71
Profs accesible rating	69
Student/faculty ratio	8:1
% female faculty	25
% underrepresented minority faculty	37
% part-time faculty	12

Academics

If you're looking for an "intimate environment" for your MBA experience, Alfred University is well worth a look. This program serves a population of just a few dozen graduate students. The result is a "solid business school that's convenient," where "students are not just another number." As one student told us, "The greatest strength of Alfred University is its size." The classes are around 30 people, and "the interaction is incredible." The school recently added an MBA accounting program that qualifies accounting students to be able to obtain their CPA license (the teachers "are some of the strongest teachers in the business school"), and there are also graduate assistantships available to any full-time MBA students who are willing to assist graduate faculty members in their area of interest in exchange for a portion of their tuition. The school is especially strong in entrepreneurial studies.

Professors at Alfred have the time to go the extra mile for students, and they "work hard to make sure you understand what they are teaching, but they also expect you to do your share of the work." Students also appreciate that "professors here are very diverse" and "have a lot of experience in the business world." With no crowd to fight, Alfred students have a better chance to shine. Although, keep in mind, this also means there's no anonymity. "Professors know everyone in the program well." Another student writes, "One professor liked a paper I wrote for his class. He offered to co-author another paper with me and pursue getting it published. These opportunities are so valuable to me and something I would never have expected." This sense of support and enterprise doesn't end in the classroom. As one student explains, "one-on-ones outside of the classroom are extremely helpful, and I'm able to gain additional insight on my career path."

Of course, a small school can only offer students so much. Some students find that there are "few academic options within the program" and "concepts and theories are left at the basics," but "the new acting dean is also looking to change things around and improve elective options." Regardless, students appreciate that "most MBA classes are scheduled in the late afternoon and early evening, which is convenient for people who work." Students approve of the school's active learning strategies, which emphasize teamwork, case studies, simulations, and field experience (usually gained through an internship).

Career and Placement

All Alfred students receive career services through the Robert R. McComsey Career Development Center. The office provides one-on-one counseling sessions; workshops in interviewing, resume writing, and networking; a career library with online and conventional print resources; and annual job fairs. The school also boasts a 100-percent placement rate for its MBAs. Students point out, however, that Alfred's remote location complicates their search for jobs and internships. Many agree that "Alfred is a small community" and that "outside internships and projects are more difficult to obtain due to the University's rural location." However, over the past few years the administration has worked "to expand local and international opportunities with a particular focus on MBA students," and there is "the clear sense that the school, administrators and professors want you to succeed."

Prominent employers of Alfred MBAs include Alstom, AOL Communications, Avantt Consulting, Met Life/New England Financial, General Electric Company, Eli Lilly and Company, Citynet, Corning, Dresser Rand, Nestlé, NYSEG, Toro Energy, and Wal-Mart.

ADMISSIONS CONTACT: COREY FECTEAU, GRADUATE ADMISSIONS
ADDRESS: OFFICE OF GRADUATE ADMISSIONS, ALUMNI HALL, SAXON DRIVE, ALFRED, NY 14802
PHONE: 800-541-9229 • FAX: 607-871-2198
E-MAIL: GRADINQUIRY@ALFRED.EDU • WEBSITE: BUSINESS.ALFRED.EDU/MBA.HTML

Student Life and Environment

Alfred, New York, is a normal small town "with only the essentials in the village;" however, the campus provides plenty of entertainment, resources, and opportunities to keep students "engaged and happy." The University is "a fun-loving community" of about 2,000 students, including 210 business undergrads and a few dozen "competitive, ambitious, friendly, [and] hard working" MBAs, who comprise a "mix of recent grads and experienced professionals." The "wide variety of clubs and organizations offer great opportunity for individual growth," and if you want a club "all you have to do is ask." One student explains, "Alfred's clubs and activities are astounding. Diverse clubs and organizations regularly attend student senate to discuss concerns that are circulating the student population."

Alfred's infrastructure includes "plenty of computers and good Internet bandwidth;" however, "The recreational facilities aren't the best, and the library needs help." Fortunately, a "large renovation and expansion project" is underway, which could be "the largest project for the University within the last few decades." The renovations are expected to "address shortcomings of the university, greatly enhance the campus, and benefit students." Also, while the "huge" dorms get glowing reviews, "housing is really poor off campus."

Alfred's 16 Division-III intercollegiate teams provide entertainment, as does the popular intramural sports program. The school's divisions of music, theater, and dance frequently hold performances. Alfred also has an active visual-arts community; it houses one of the best ceramic arts programs in the country. The "peaceful and safe" village of Alfred has a year-round population of 1,000 and surrounding towns are not much larger. These "secluded" surroundings lessen "the chances of distractions from studies," though when students need a break from the books, Rochester is only 80 miles away, and Buffalo is only a little farther down the road—provided you have four-wheel drive in the winter.

Admissions

Applicants must provide the school with official copies of undergraduate transcripts, GMAT scores, TOEFL scores (for international students whose first language is not English), a statement of intent, professional resume, and two letters of recommendation (preferably from former employers or professors). Previous work experience is not required, and an interview, while always recommended, is optional.

FINANCIAL FACTS

Annual tuition	$36,736
Fees	$910
Cost of books	$1,500
Room & board	$10,000
% of students receiving aid	100
% of first-year students receiving aid	100
% of students receiving grants	100
Average award package	$17,321
Average grant	$17,321

ADMISSIONS

Admissions Selectivity Rating	71
# of applications received	35
% applicants accepted	91
% acceptees attending	81
Average GMAT	475
Range of GMAT	405–562
Average GPA	3.30
TOEFL required of international students	Yes
Minimum TOEFL (paper/computer)	590
International application fee	$60
Early application deadline	3/1
Early notification date	4/1
Regular application deadline	5/1
Regular application notification	6/1
Deferment available	Yes
Maximum length of deferment	1 year
Transfer students accepted	Yes
Transfer application policy: transfer a maximum of 6 credit hours from a comparable program	
Non-fall admissions	Yes
Need-blind admissions	Yes

EMPLOYMENT PROFILE

Career Rating	64	Grads Employed by Function	% Avg. Salary
		Marketing	(14%)
		Management	(28%)
		Finance	(28%)
		Other	(28%)

AMERICAN UNIVERSITY
KOGOD SCHOOL OF BUSINESS

GENERAL INFORMATION

Type of school	Private
Affiliation	Methodist
Academic calendar	Semester

SURVEY SAYS...

Students love Washington, D.C.
Solid preparation in:
Accounting, Doing business in a
global economy

STUDENTS

Enrollment of parent institution	13,165
Average age at entry	28
Average years work experience at entry	4.1

ACADEMICS

Academic Experience Rating	84
Profs interesting rating	85
Profs accesible rating	84

Joint Degrees

MBA/JD LLM/MBA MBA/MA

Prominent Alumni

Marvin Shanken, Chairman, M.
Shaken Communications; Loretta
Sanchez, United States Congress;
David Blumenthal, Senior Vice
President and COO, Lion Brand Yarn
Com; Mark Murphy, CEO and
President of the Green Bay Packers

Academics

The "small and friendly" MBA program at American University's Kogod School of Business offers a "solid academic program" that, like its namesake (Robert P. Kogod, Charles E. Smith Co.), excels in the area of real estate. American's Washington, D.C. location is ideally situated for a curricular focus on international matters, and the school exploits that opportunity well, interjecting "an international perspective in class discussions that is second to none. Almost all classes integrate an international component."

Kogod's strengths extend far beyond real estate and international business, however. The school boasts a finance faculty that is "internationally recognized for their research. They are great instructors too." Students praise the commercial banking concentration offered here and love the fact that the program "allows you to concentrate in two areas of expertise," which "lets you design your own MBA" and "is a great advantage in the job market." Kogod offers a diverse set of electives for their students to supplement their majors and some students even choose to design their own majors. Kogod recently "created the first LLM/MBA in the country, which is an excellent way to combine international law studies and business."

Kogod's pedagogical approach embraces a mixture of case studies and theory, combined with plenty of group work that acts as good practice for the real world. Professors "have a great reputation and have done interesting research." They are also easy to contact because of an "open-door policy." Faculty members "bring a lot of academic and professional experience" to the program—another plus. "We have former investment bankers, former consultants, former CFOs, and lifelong academics," brags one student. Small class sizes "give Kogod an advantage over the other D.C. schools like Georgetown and GW. I know everyone by name, and that's a nice feeling." As a result, the program "feels like being in a big family. Everyone knows you and does their best to help you."

Kogod's D.C. address "creates many opportunities for networking, internships, etc." As one student puts it, "The D.C. location gives Kogod a huge advantage. There are so many more opportunities to pursue when you are in a big city. It also helps Kogod draw "international students from very diverse countries," enhancing in-class and networking experiences. Perhaps best of all, this is a school that "is in the middle of overhauling its curriculum." In addition, the school recently completed a 21,000 square foot expansion which opened in 2009. The expansion which included 7 new class rooms, 3 student lounges, a financial services and information technology lab, a career center suite, a behavioral research lab, a mini-computer lab, and several breakout rooms. With these changes, one MBA predicts that "I think there will be some great changes" in the school's near future.

Career and Placement

Career Services at Kogod "does a great job in involving alumni in school life. There are lots of networking opportunities . . . [and] lots of on-site visits with direct interactions with alumni, both young and more experienced." A Wall Street trip includes visits to "all the major financial institutions with alumni as tour guides and a session for Q & A's and recruiting procedures and tips, concluded by an alumni networking dinner." Career Services Counselors also provide "constant information about new jobs/internship opportunities in the D.C. area and beyond."

Companies that have recently hired Kogod MBAs include: Accenture, Baker Tilly, Booz Allen Hamilton, Corporate Executive Board, CSC, Defense Logistics Agency, Deloitte Consulting, Discovery Communications, Ernst & Young, Fannie Mae, Hilton Hotels Corporation, IBM, Infastructure Management Group, Intelsat, National Geographic

ADMISSIONS CONTACT: SHANNON DEMKO, DIRECTOR OF ADMISSIONS
ADDRESS: 4400 MASSACHUSETTS AVENUE NW, WASHINGTON, DC 20016-8044
PHONE: 202-885-1913 • FAX: 202-885-1078
E-MAIL: KOGODGRAD@AMERICAN.EDU • WEBSITE: WWW.AMERICAN.EDU / KOGOD

FINANCIAL FACTS

Annual tuition	$33,014
Fees	$430
Room & board	$20,000

ADMISSIONS

Admissions Selectivity Rating	82
# of applications received	231
% applicants accepted	42
% acceptees attending	31
Average GMAT	550
Average GPA	3.18
TOEFL required of international students	Yes
Minimum TOEFL (paper/computer)	600
Application fee	$100
International application fee	$100
Application Deadline/Notification	
Round 1:	12/5 / 2/1
Round 2:	2/15 / 4/15
Round 3:	5/1 / 6/15
Round 4:	5/2 /
Deferment available	Yes
Maximum length of deferment	1 year
Transfer students accepted	Yes
Non-fall admissions	Yes
Need-blind admissions	Yes

Society, PricewaterhouseCoopers, Raytheon, Sunstar Strategic, Wells Fargo and The World Bank.

Student Life and Environment

The atmosphere in the Kogod MBA program "is low key, friendly, and accessible," with "a great learning environment. The students are all very friendly and socialize together regularly. The professors are very approachable and friendly, and have some impressive resumes. The academics are tough and the program is effective but not cut-throat." Kogod offers "many clubs and organizations in different fields," and students report that "involvement is highly encouraged."

Some here feel that "the program is not as social as others, and this is due in large part to the fact that the school is located in a relatively upscale neighborhood, and there are few restaurants or bars in the immediate area. Also, students tend to live all over Washington, D.C.," so "Getting large groups together can be difficult. However K-LAB provides co-curricular programs for grad students and students at Kogod are very involved with intramural sports. Further, most agree that "D.C. is one of the most exciting and fun cities in the country." As an added bonus, "There is so much work in D.C. that making $100K a year is almost automatic if you connect with the right government-related job."

Students here represent a variety of backgrounds. "I come from a military background," says one MBA, "and I really enjoy mingling and working with people from nonprofits, other government agencies, small companies, and large companies." The population includes a substantial international contingent.

Admissions

The Kogod Admissions Office requires the following from all applicants: a completed online application form; a personal statement of purpose in pursuing the MBA; a current resume; two letters of recommendation; an official transcript from all attended undergraduate and graduate institutions; and an official GMAT or GRE score report. International applicants whose first language is not English must also submit an official score report for other the TOEFL or the IELTS. An interview is required of all applicants.

EMPLOYMENT PROFILE			
Career Rating	86	Grads Employed by Function	% Avg. Salary
Percent employed at graduation	45	Marketing	(14%) $59,600
Percent employed 3 months after graduation	32	Operations	(3%)
		Consulting	(31%) $80,778
Average base starting salary	$68,540	Management	(%) $62,333
Primary Source of Full-time Job Acceptances		Finance	(%) $67,829
School-facilitated activities	13(36%)	HR	(8%) $57,497
Graduate-facilitated activities	11(31%)	MIS	(3%)
Unknown	12(33%)	Top 5 Employers Hiring Grads	
		Accenture, CSC, Discovery Communications	

Appalachian State University

Walker College of Business

GENERAL INFORMATION

Type of school	Public
Affiliation	No Affiliation
Academic calendar	Semester

SURVEY SAYS...

Good social scene, Happy students
Solid preparation in:
Accounting, Presentation skills,
Doing business in a global economy

STUDENTS

Enrollment of parent institution	17,589
Enrollment of MBA Program	85
% male/female	55/45
% out-of-state	11
% part-time	30
% underrepresented minority	0
% international	13
Average age at entry	31
Average years work experience at entry	8.0

ACADEMICS

Academic Experience Rating	79
Profs interesting rating	80
Profs accesible rating	77
Student/faculty ratio	20:1
% female faculty	20

Academics

Nested in the Blue Ridge Mountains of North Carolina, the Walker College of Business at Appalachian State University offers a small, efficient, and affordable MBA program to a largely local student population. For many, the fast-paced course schedule is a major benefit of this program. Here, the entire MBA—including an optional internship—can be completed in "only one year." (Prospective students should note that the one-year program is designed for students with an undergraduate degree in business. Before matriculation, the MBA requires up to 18 hours of prerequisite coursework.) Despite its speedy schedule, the MBA covers all functional areas of business, including accounting, economics, finance, management, marketing, operations, and information systems. In addition to the core curriculum, students have the option of tailoring their education through a concentration in one of four fields: sustainable business, international business, general management, or economics. There is a focus on international business throughout the curriculum, which helps students "gain the knowledge [they] will need to compete in today's global economy." Of particular note, all students participate in an International Seminar in the last semester of the MBA, which includes a trip overseas. Recent programs took students to China, Hong Kong, Turkey, Cuba, France, and Poland. While the program is scarcely large enough to support more variety, students feel, "the MBA program needs to add a computer information systems option" to the current offerings.

For full-time students, the schedule is rigorous and "the days are pretty packed." Throughout the program, "students spend about two hours in class each day, Monday through Thursday," while their afternoons are "spent working on group projects, homework, and or actually working at a job." Fortunately, the full-time MBA program is very small, with just over 20 students per class (in fact, the entering class size is capped at 24). The result is a caring, student-oriented atmosphere, and plenty of personal attention. Offering guidance and support, "The school has a great administration that is willing to work with the students in order to help the students achieve their goals." In addition, "The professors, on the whole, are easy to get along with and are always willing to help the students." Academically, the program is strong, but the teachers can be hit or miss. A student admits, "There have been some professors who have challenged me and were at the caliber that I expected, but there were also some who I felt were inadequate to be teaching graduate-level classes." Overall, Walker "teachers are knowledgeable and excited for students to learn."

In addition to the campus-based MBA program, ASU offers a part-time off-site MBA at a satellite facility in Hickory, North Carolina. In content, this program is similar to the Boone MBA, yet students learn through various delivery formats, including interactive audio-video sessions and web-based instruction, as well as in-person lectures from ASU faculty. No matter where you choose to study, the icing on the cake is the program's "low cost." This public school maintains a "very reasonable" tuition price, while also offering "scholarship and assistantship" programs, which can lower the price tag even further.

ADMISSIONS CONTACT: ANNA BASNIGHT
ADDRESS: ASU BOX 32068, BOONE, NC 28608-2068
PHONE: 828-262-2130 • FAX: 828-262-2709
E-MAIL: BASNIGHTAL@APPSTATE.EDU • WEBSITE: WWW.MBA.APPSTATE.EDU

Career and Placement

While the MBA program does not have its own career office, there is a career counselor assigned to the business school, who can help with career planning and placement. The program will also be hiring a career services director for the MBA program in the summer of 2013. In addition, the Career Development Center on the Appalachian State University campus serves the entire undergraduate and graduate student body, as well as ASU alumni. The Career Development Center assists students with cover letter and resume revisions, personalized career counseling, mock interviews, and myriad online resources. In addition, the Career Development Center organizes networking events and "career fairs that bring in companies that have positions all over the U.S. and around the world." With a strong local reputation, ASU "does well with helping the students find a job," but nothing's perfect and "there are still improvements that can be made."

Student Life and Environment

Located on a "beautiful campus" in Boone, North Carolina, "Life is fabulous" at ASU. On this pleasant, hilltop campus, "Students hang out as a collective most times and crime rates are relatively low." Not to mention, this Southern city boasts "terrific weather" and great outdoor activities, including hiking and fishing. MBA classes take place in Raleigh Hall, which boasts wireless Internet and graduate student lounges. On the larger campus, students have access to study labs and a large library system.

Bringing a positive attitude to the classroom, ASU students "are willing to learn, as well as willing to begin friendships that have lasted the length of the program." While the accelerated schedule keeps them busy, "Students find time to attend sporting events, concerts, and many other extra curricular activities. All of the students also find time to hang out with one another and with their friends." While there are some local student hangouts, students say "nightlife could be a little better," in Boone. Most students, however, feel that "Being in a small town has been wonderful for my school experience." A current student writes, "In general, I wouldn't have chosen anywhere else to go."

Admissions

Appalachian State University's small MBA program only enrolls about 20 to 25 students each year. Prospective students are evaluated based on their GMAT score, three letters of recommendation, undergraduate academic performance, and current resume. To be eligible for the program, students must have completed a series of prerequisite courses in marketing, finance, accounting, management information systems, economics, law, and calculus with a grade point average of B or better. Professional work experience is not required.

FINANCIAL FACTS

Annual tuition (in-state/ out-of-state)	$2,020/$7,926
Fees	$1,259
Cost of books	$1,200
Room & board (on/off-campus)	$4,400/$7,200
Average grant	$1,000
Average loan	$5,000

ADMISSIONS

Admissions Selectivity Rating	73
# of applications received	121
% applicants accepted	80
% acceptees attending	70
Average GMAT	539
Range of GMAT	460–620
Average GPA	3.40
TOEFL required of international students	Yes
Minimum TOEFL (paper/computer)	550/233
Application fee	$45
International application fee	$45
Regular application deadline	3/1
Regular application notification	3/31
Application Deadline/Notification	
Round 1:	2/1 /
Round 2:	4/1 /
Round 3:	7/1 /
Round 4:	11/1 /
Deferment available	Yes
Maximum length of deferment	1 year
Transfer students accepted	Yes
Transfer application policy: Up to six hours of graduate credit may be transferred for equivalent courses completed with at least grade of B.	
Non-fall admissions	Yes
Need-blind admissions	Yes

ARIZONA STATE UNIVERSITY
W.P. CAREY SCHOOL OF BUSINESS

GENERAL INFORMATION
Type of school	Public
Affiliation	No Affiliation
Academic calendar	Quarter

SURVEY SAYS...
Friendly students, Good peer network, Cutting-edge classes, Happy students
Solid preparation in:
General management, Teamwork

STUDENTS
Enrollment of parent institution	73,378
Enrollment of MBA Program	975
% male/female	76/24
% out-of-state	59
% part-time	8
% underrepresented minority	20
% international	12
Average age at entry	27
Average years work experience at entry	4.2

ACADEMICS
Academic Experience Rating	95
Profs interesting rating	90
Profs accesible rating	89
Student/faculty ratio	30:1
% female faculty	26
% underrepresented minority faculty	30
% part-time faculty	13

Joint Degrees
Two year programs: W. P. Carey MBA/Master of Science in Information Management; W. P. Carey MBA/Master of Accountancy; W. P. Carey MBA/Master of Taxation W. P. Carey MBA/MD with Mayo Medical School. Three to four year programs: W. P. Carey MBA/Juris Doctorate; W. P. Carey MBA/Master of Architecture

Prominent Alumni
Chris Cookson, President, Technologies, Sony Pictures; Mary Ann Miller, Senior Vice President and Chief Human Resource Officer, Avnet, Inc.

Academics

Using typical business parlance, MBA candidates feel that Arizona State's W.P. Carey School offers a "[fantastic] return on investment." And with "great scholarship offerings," a "great industry network," a top ranked program in supply-chain management and a fabulous location, it's easy to understand why. Moreover, W.P. Carey School places an emphasis on "small class sizes." In turn, this allows for a "very personal [MBA] experience" and courses with "more direct focus." The school operates on a quarter system which can sometimes make for a heavy workload. A first-year adds, "The quarter system allows exposure to more courses, but the drawback of this system is that courses are only seven and a half weeks long, and it is a challenge for the professors to cover the content in a meaningful way."

Students truly dig the fact that their professors are "question-askers." Indeed, they really "know how to teach application" and deftly weave lectures and conversations around "the most relevant topics of the day." More importantly, professors strive to make themselves readily "accessible." They are frequently "available outside of class time and take a personal interest in the success of the student." And they are "always challenging us to work up to and surpass our potential as students."

Student opinion on the administration is decidedly mixed. As one first-year candidate laments, "[It's] not clear who runs the joint." However, he does admit that "program coordinators do a good job with the day to day." And a second-year student counters, "The administration (deans, etc.) also involve themselves in student life by attending our meetings and asking us for our input." A fellow second-year enthusiastically adds that the, "majority of the school faculty are very receptive to students and incorporate our feedback into the course curriculum. [Indeed, they are] very willing to help students and also arrange guest lectures by industry leaders and tie in course material with them."

Career and Placement

For the most part, MBA students at Arizona State speak very highly of the career options and outreach available. Indeed, "One of the top highlights of ASU is the Career Management Center (CMC). The CMC team helps students prepare and search for internships and full-time employment. Nothing is a hand-out, but they help arm you with the tools and skills you need to be successful." Moreover, professors also generously "offer their networks to students looking for internships/jobs." Additionally, a first-year student quickly notes that ASU frequently, "sets up career events for us and encourages us to use eRecruiting, which is a very prosperous job and internship search engine."

Employers who frequently hire Arizona State MBAs include American Airlines, American Express, Williams-Sonoma, Goldman Sachs Group, Inc., PepsiCo, PetSmart, Sprint, US Airways, State of Arizona, Procter & Gamble, Raytheon, PricewaterhouseCoopers, Samsung Electronics, Honeywell, Black & Decker, Apple, Deloitte Consulting, Nestle, Intel Corporation, JPMorgan Chase and ChevronTexaco.

ADMISSIONS CONTACT: RUTHIE PYLES, DIRECTOR, ADMISSIONS, W. P. CAREY MBA
ADDRESS: P.O. BOX 874906, TEMPE, AZ 85287-4906
PHONE: 480-965-3332 • FAX: 480-965-8569
E-MAIL: WPCAREYMBA@ASU.EDU • WEBSITE: WPCAREY.ASU.EDU

Student Life and Environment

Though life at Arizona State is undoubtedly busy, students tell us that it's definitely possible to achieve a good work/life balance. Fortunately, "The class load allows for a focus on career search and time for social activities and family." And, of course, with over 60,000+ students university-wide, MBA candidates are part of a "bustling and lively community." Moreover, the "MBA program and its new McCord Hall are at the heart of campus and provide a convenient atmosphere for learning. The W.P. Carey program is located right next to the Memorial Union (activity center with restaurants) and the sports/fitness center. It's really the best location for a business school." Students also greatly appreciate that they're encouraged to "become part of clubs and organizations that span from professional, to cultural, to leisure." A second-year student shares, "I really enjoy spending time with my classmates outside of classroom settings. We have company sponsored tail gates during football season and program happy hours every Thursday to socialize after a long week of school work."

Admission

When it comes to assessing applicants, the admissions committee at Arizona State takes a holistic approach. All application facets, from undergraduate GPA and GMAT score to resume, work experience, letters of recommendations, essays and interviews are given thoughtful consideration. Fortunately, a bachelor's degree in business (or related discipline) is not required. Neither is previous coursework in math or statistics. Finally, applications to Arizona State are typically reviewed within two weeks of completion, interview or notification date (whichever is later).

FINANCIAL FACTS

Annual tuition (in-state/ out-of-state)	$10,001/$24,550
Fees	$13,516
Cost of books	$2,300
Room & board	$10,852
% of students receiving aid	98
% of first-year students receiving aid	99
% of students receiving grants	82
Average award package	$34,800
Average grant	$19,414
Average loan	$32,361
Average student loan debt	$51,975

ADMISSIONS

Admissions Selectivity Rating	94
# of applications received	383
% applicants accepted	36
% acceptees attending	49
Average GMAT	676
Range of GMAT	650–710
Average GPA	3.40
TOEFL required of international students	Yes
Minimum TOEFL (paper/computer)	550/250
Application fee	$70
International application fee	$90
Early application deadline	10/1
Early notification date	12/14
Regular application deadline	11/30
Regular application notification	2/15
Application Deadline/Notification	
Round 1:	10/1 / 12/14
Round 2:	11/30 / 12/15
Round 3:	2/1 / 4/15
Round 4:	4/1 / 5/15
Deferment available	No
Transfer students accepted	No
Non-fall admissions	Yes
Need-blind admissions	Yes

EMPLOYMENT PROFILE

Career Rating	97	**Grads Employed by Function% Avg. Salary**	
Percent employed at graduation	79	Marketing	(10%) $89,250
Percent employed 3 months		Operations	(54%) $97,481
after graduation	89	Consulting	(7%) $85,300
Average base starting salary	$92,556	Management	(14%) $94,378
Primary Source of Full-time Job Acceptances		Finance	(12%) $77,250
School-facilitated activities	30(51%)	MIS	(3%)
Graduate-facilitated activities	18(31%)	**Top 5 Employers Hiring Grads**	
Unknown	11(19%)	Dell(6), Cisco Systems (5), Johnson & Johnson (5), Intel Corporation (5), Bank of America (4)	

AUBURN UNIVERSITY
COLLEGE OF BUSINESS

GENERAL INFORMATION

Type of school	Public
Affiliation	No Affiliation
Academic calendar	Semester

SURVEY SAYS...
Good social scene
Solid preparation in:
Marketing

STUDENTS

Enrollment of parent institution	25,078
Enrollment of MBA Program	279
% male/female	59/41
% out-of-state	69
% part-time	86
% underrepresented minority	36
% international	36
Average age at entry	26
Average years work experience at entry	3.3

ACADEMICS

Academic Experience Rating	**87**
Profs interesting rating	85
Profs accesible rating	84
Student/faculty ratio	29:1
% female faculty	20
% underrepresented minority faculty	5
% part-time faculty	0

Joint Degrees
Dual degree program with Industrial and Systems Engineering (2 1/2 years). Other dual-degree options available with Masters in Information Systems and Finance, and on case-by-case basis with approval of AU Graduate School.

Prominent Alumni
Mohamed Mansour, CEO, Mansour Group in Egypt; Joanne P. McCallie, Head Coach, Duke University Women's Basketball; Wendell Starke, Past President of INVESCO

Academics

Auburn University offers one of the South's premiere business programs. Those interested in earning their MBA are often attracted to the school's great location and "reasonable price." Students at Auburn are quick to highlight the "small class [size] and student faculty ratio," which virtually guarantees "close relationships with professors." The curriculum allows students to master the fundamentals of business theory and focus on a particular area of interest, such as finance, agri-business management, project management, management of information technology, or marketing. Moreover, MBA candidates greatly appreciate the "flexibility" of the program and the "convenient weekend [class] schedule."

While opinions on professors do vary, by and large students are very happy with their teachers. The vast majority are "very helpful and resourceful" and extremely "knowledgeable." And one pleased student adds that professors are "always willing to help with your classes or even other ventures." Indeed they "care about students' progress in and outside of the classroom." They are also understanding and are often willing to work with students should "problems arise due to a work schedule and such."

Opinions are decidedly mixed when it comes to the administration. Some students complain that there is a lot "bureaucracy," which results in "administrative tasks [becoming] very slow and painstaking." However, other MBA students are thankful for the program's administrators, who are "a big help to students." Time and again the "staff members [show that they] care about the students and handle their problems on a timely basis."

The MBA candidates at Auburn really believe that the University offers "great and numerous opportunities for students to get involved and to find jobs. There are so many tools available to them to achieve success." As one content student sums up, "Overall, I think [Auburn] is a hidden gem in terms of an MBA program in Alabama."

Career and Placement

The Office of Professional and Career Development serves the Business school's entire undergraduate and graduate student population. The career specialists understand that job hunting is an in-depth process and provide the tools and techniques for success. They help students develop and implement an effective job search strategy, showing them how to create a marketing plan and craft a target list of potential companies. Additionally, they host numerous seminars and events, offering students everything from resume writing workshops to mock interviews. The office also hosts several career fairs each academic year. The College attracts companies hiring students into consulting roles such as Accenture, CapGemini, Deloitte, Ernst & Young, KPMG, and Quorum Business Solutions, as well as major companies focusing on supply chain management, including Exel Logistics, Home Depot, Lexmark, Target and Walmart. Financial services organizations including AFLAC, BB&T, BBVA, Regions Financial, and SunTrust, as well as the FDIC, Federal Reserve, OCC, the Alabama Securities Commission, and the Georgia Department of Banking and Finance also recruit Auburn's Business students.

Student Life and Environment

MBA candidates at Auburn speak very highly of their peers. Many are "busy [juggling] their work and family" so at times it can "be hard to connect with them outside of the classroom." Fortunately, they are still "very friendly" and are always "helpful when doing projects together." Students are also quick to report that their classmates are "easy going" and "highly intelligent." For the most part, they all seem to make a concerted effort "to contribute their opinions and share in class." This appears to be greatly appreciated as they often "provide [great] insight" and "bring great examples of real-time issues." Another student attempts to illuminate life at Auburn by stating, "There seem to be distinct groups: younger students, who participate in activities and clubs and hang out on campus vs. those like me, who come to school for class and then leave as quickly as possible." And while one graduating student claims that her peers are "interested in learning, but not overly involved in activities," another student delights in telling us that the school holds "an annual international festivity [and] several masquerade balls as well." Additionally, "tours and trips to different places are available."

Athletics play an important role in the social life on campus, particularly in the Fall, where SEC football reigns supreme. Auburn's football team won the BCS National Championship in January 2011, and tailgating activities before each game provide an opportunity to network with alumni and other students. Intramural sports are popular; outstanding golf courses are nearby, and the beaches of the Gulf of Mexico are 3 hours away by car. Since 2008, an International study trip of 10 days in length has been built into the cost of the program; each Spring groups of students and faculty travel to destinations to learn about doing business in those countries. Previous student groups have gone to Argentina, Brazil, China, France, Germany, South Africa, and many other countries. Students say that this trip is a highlight of their Auburn experience.

Atlanta is a 2 hour drive from Auburn, and provides a popular big-city weekend road trip destination, as well as permanent employment location for many students after graduation. Nearby Columbus, and Georgia, Alabama also offer plenty of entertainment options and distraction from schoolwork. Sports enthusiasts rejoiced when Auburn acquired the Biscuits, a minor league baseball team affiliated with the Tampa Bay Devil Rays, while the Columbus Cottonmouths provide an outlet for ice hockey enthusiasts. Columbus is also the home of Fort Benning, one of the Army's largest bases.

Admissions

Full-time MBA students interested in attending Auburn University's business school should submit their application materials by a priority admission date of March 1 prior to the start of the semester they wish to enter. Each applicant's undergraduate transcripts, GMAT scores, letters of recommendation, essays, and resume are closely examined. Admissions officers note that GMAT scores must be from within the last five years. After a review of academic records and standardized test scores, selected candidates will be interviewed by the admissions director.

FINANCIAL FACTS

Annual tuition (in-state/ out-of-state)	$7,866/$23,598
Fees	$6,374
Cost of books	$1,100
Room & board	$10,606
% of students receiving aid	98
% of first-year students receiving aid	97
% of students receiving grants	98
Average award package	$21,827
Average grant	$20,870
Average loan	$19,000
Average student loan debt	$19,000

ADMISSIONS

Admissions Selectivity Rating	**90**
# of applications received	109
% applicants accepted	45
% acceptees attending	80
Average GMAT	635
Range of GMAT	610–660
Average GPA	3.40
TOEFL required of international students	Yes
Minimum TOEFL (paper/computer)	550/213
Application fee	$70
International application fee	$70
Early application deadline	2/1
Regular application deadline	2/1
Deferment available	Yes
Maximum length of deferment	1 year
Transfer students accepted	Yes
Transfer application policy: AACSB schools only. Case-by-case basis and accepted in lieu of elective courses only. Limit of 12 credit hours.	
Non-fall admissions	No
Need-blind admissions	Yes

EMPLOYMENT PROFILE

Career Rating	82	Grads Employed by Function% Avg. Salary	
Percent employed at graduation	43	Marketing	(50%) $52,000
Average base starting salary	$52,000	Operations	(33%)
		Other	(17%)

AUBURN UNIVERSITY—MONTGOMERY
SCHOOL OF BUSINESS

GENERAL INFORMATION
Type of school	Public
Affiliation	No Affiliation

SURVEY SAYS...
Friendly students
Solid preparation in:
Communication/interpersonal skills,
Presentation skills, Quantitative skills

STUDENTS
Enrollment of parent institution	5,287
Enrollment of MBA Program	197
% male/female	60/40
% out-of-state	21
% part-time	57
% underrepresented minority	28
% international	12
Average age at entry	27
Average years work experience at entry	0.0

ACADEMICS
Academic Experience Rating	**69**
Profs interesting rating	77
Profs accesible rating	79
Student/faculty ratio	20:1
% female faculty	25
% underrepresented minority faculty	10
% part-time faculty	3

Academics

The AACSB-accredited MBA program at Auburn University Montgomery is "a great place to get your MBA at night," according to the program's locally-based student body. Students here also appreciate the "affordable" tuition as well as the school's "reputation for academic excellence" and "instructors who bring real-life business experiences to the classroom" and "have connections in the business world." The program is designed for part-time students; in fact, any student wishing to exceed a course load of nine hours per semester must first receive approval from the dean of the School of Business.

The MBA program at AUM is divided into three parts. The first is called the Basic Program, consisting of 11 half-term courses covering business concepts typically taught at the undergraduate level (accounting, management, marketing, business law, microeconomics, macroeconomics, operations management, statistics, MIS, and finance). Students who can demonstrate sufficient background in these areas may petition to be exempted from some or all of these requirements. The second part of the program is the Business Core, a seven-course set of classes covering such integrative concepts as managerial applications of accounting information and synergistic organizational strategy (the latter is a capstone course), as well as such essential functions as marketing, data analysis, and managing personnel. The program concludes with either three or four electives, depending on whether the student chooses a General MBA or a specialization. Specializations are offered in accounting, contract management, economics, finance, global business management, information systems, management of information technology, management, and marketing. Students earning a GPA below 3.25 must pass comprehensive exams at the end of the program in order to graduate. The program must be finished within five years of starting.

AUM MBAs brag that "Professors are extremely knowledgeable, helpful, and outstanding in their areas," and that they also "understand that most of the evening students are fully employed and try to incorporate their day-to-day activities" into the curriculum. Most here "would like to see the use of more technology in the classroom" and complain that the school needs "all classrooms to be enabled with things like wireless internet access." Classrooms could also be improved by making them "resemble the real world, i.e. u-shaped seating"; at the very least, the school "needs to upgrade classroom furniture to make it feel less like a high school/junior high," students tell us.

Career and Placement

The Career Development Center (CDC) at AUM serves all university students and alumni. The office maintains a library of career-related material, including documents tracking salary and hiring trends around the region, state, country, and world. Career counseling services are available, as are job fairs, and seminars and workshops in interviewing, job hunting, and resume and cover letter writing. The office arranges internships and recruiting events for qualifying MBA students.

ADMISSIONS CONTACT: SHARON JONES, ADMISSION SPECIALIST
ADDRESS: P. O. BOX 244023, MONTGOMERY, AL 36124-4023
PHONE: 334-244-3623 • FAX: 334-244-3927
E-MAIL: VJONES1@AUM.EDU • WEBSITE: WWW.AUM.EDU

Student Life and Environment

AUM MBAs are "mostly working students between their mid-20s and mid-30s in age, with some being older." Most "work full time and go to school at night" and, despite their busy schedules, find a way to remain "extremely focused on their class work and understanding of the material" while also being "extremely helpful, kind, open for conversation, and willing to do whatever it takes to see that everyone in class is successful." They "don't seem to have any specific clubs or organizations available to them, especially in the evening hours," but most agree that their extracurricular schedule wouldn't allow them time to participate.

Montgomery is a midsize southern city well known for its integral part in the civil rights movement. The population of the city is about evenly split between whites and blacks, with small Hispanic, Native American, and Asian populations accounting for a small minority. The city is home to the Alabama Shakespeare Festival, a year-round enterprise that mounts a dozen or more productions and attracts over 300,000 visitors annually. Another major attraction is the minor-league baseball Montgomery Biscuits, the AA affiliate of the Tampa Bay Devil Rays. And no Montgomery summer is complete without Jubilee CityFest, a three-day outdoor festival that in recent years has attracted such headlining musical acts as Taylor Swift, Erykah Badu, the Goo Goo Dolls, Ludacris, and Vince Gill.

Admissions

Applicants to the AUM MBA program must submit official transcripts for all previous post-secondary academic work, official GMAT score reports, and a completed application form. The screening committee may request an interview, typically in the case of borderline candidates; otherwise, interviews are not required. International applicants must meet all of the above requirements and must also provide certified English translations of any academic transcripts in a foreign language and a course-by-course evaluation of undergraduate work "by a recognized, expert service in the field of foreign credential evaluations and international admissions." Applicants whose first language is not English must submit TOEFL scores. Candidates may be admitted conditionally pending completion of prerequisite undergraduate-level classes in business.

FINANCIAL FACTS

Cost of books	$1,500
% of students receiving aid	60
% of first-year students receiving aid	65
% of students receiving grants	15
Average award package	$17,894

ADMISSIONS

Admissions Selectivity Rating	**68**
# of applications received	96
% applicants accepted	98
% acceptees attending	70
Average GMAT	473
Average GPA	2.92
TOEFL required of international students	Yes
Minimum TOEFL (paper/computer)	500
Application fee	$25
International Deferment available	No
Transfer students accepted	No
Non-fall admissions	Yes
Need-blind admissions	Yes

BABSON COLLEGE
F. W. OLIN GRADUATE SCHOOL OF BUSINESS

GENERAL INFORMATION

Type of school	Private
Affiliation	No Affiliation
Academic calendar	Semester

SURVEY SAYS...
Cutting-edge classes
Solid preparation in:
Doing business in a global economy,
Entrepreneurial studies

STUDENTS

Enrollment of parent institution	3,250
Enrollment of MBA Program	1,209
% male/female	72/28
% out-of-state	55
% part-time	66
% underrepresented minority	11
% international	55
Average age at entry	28
Average years work experience at entry	4.5

ACADEMICS

Academic Experience Rating	84
Profs interesting rating	89
Profs accesible rating	88
Student/faculty ratio	10:1
% female faculty	24
% underrepresented minority faculty	5
% part-time faculty	33

Prominent Alumni
J. Martin Carroll, President & CEO, Boehringer Ingelheim Corporation; Diane Sullivan, President and CEO, Brown Shoe Company; Akio Toyoda, President, Toyota Motor Corporation; Daniel Fireman, General Partner, Fireman Capital LLC; Geoffrey Molson, Owner, Montreal Canadiens

Academics

Consistently known as one of the most entrepreneurially-focused business programs in the country, the F.W. Olin Graduate School of Business at Babson College in Wellesley, MA offers students the "knowledge, support, flexibility and mentorship to enable students to exercise entrepreneurial thought and action." The word "action" in the Entrepreneurial Thought and Action® pedagogy should be stressed as practical application is a major component of the MBA curriculum, which incorporates experiential learning throughout (such as the first year consulting project). Additionally, the giant Arthur M. Blank Center for Entrepreneurship offers numerous cocurricular resources and services dedicated to supporting students in their entrepreneurial endeavors, as well as the largest entrepreneurship faculty in the world. "Babson prepares its students to make things happen and to discover the way to maintain an entrepreneurship mindset in big corporate companies, which is something that I think is absolutely relevant for future executives in this world," says a student.

There are four options for the "innovative" Babson MBA, presenting a unified curriculum and the same options for electives: the One-Year, Two-Year, Evening, and Fast Track Programs, the latter of which focuses on distance learning and is typically chosen by working professionals. The One- and Two-Year Programs are both full-time, and are composed of more than half international students. "Teamwork is a key element" of all Babson, and results in students "leaving with strong management skills" to bring to their positions.

Most who come to Babson are drawn in by the reputation for the entrepreneurial specializations, and a visit to the school usually seals the deal. "Everyone associated with Babson that I talked to prior to enrolling (alumni, faculty, current students) seemed very, very happy and satisfied in life," says a current student. Teachers are "highly qualified" and "outstanding," and challenge students to support their answers. "If you make a statement be prepared to offer your logic behind it," says one. The intellectual capital of the faculty never stops growing, as members remain fully dedicated to continuing researching and developing the field of study "without disregarding the needed time to help students."

The administration "has always been on top of their game." They are "flexible and change classes and professors if needs be (sickness)." Everyone ("including the Dean") has an open door policy and "always enjoy discussing ideas"; "the amount of support given to student initiatives is amazing."

Career and Placement

Babson's reputation within the Northeast is stellar, and the school often "teams up with BC, BU, Harvard, MIT, etc. to have events and network" (the national brand image is also "growing" at a nice clip, as helped by the San Francisco campus). There are plenty of meet and greets with different companies, info sessions, and CEO speeches that occur throughout the day for when one has time. However, many agree that the Babson Career Center "needs to do much more in ensuring that the international students who want jobs get placed with reputed companies."

In terms of application upon graduation, Babson does an excellent job at relating the entrepreneurial spirit to more than just a new business. "From growing a small business, M&A or large business expanding in a new market, the general business acumen is excellent at all levels." Students without jobs are encouraged to "take advantage of the powerful alumni network in every aspect possible!"

Top employers of Babson graduates include Athenahealth, CVS Caremark, EMC, Cognizant, and Credit Suisse.

ADMISSIONS CONTACT: BARBARA J. SELMO, DIRECTOR OF GRADUATE ADMISSIONS
ADDRESS: OLIN HALL, BABSON PARK (WELLESLEY), MA 02457-0310
PHONE: 781-239-5591 • FAX: 781-239-4194
E-MAIL: MBAADMISSION@BABSON.EDU • WEBSITE: WWW.BABSON.EDU/MBA

Student Life and Environment

While there is a common thread of entrepreneurship, the common entrepreneurial denominator draws a gumbo of a crowd, and Babson students come from "very, very diverse backgrounds, work experiences, [and] ethnicities"; another universal thread is that "everybody has a unique and exciting story and goals." In this "extremely driven" group, people are "competitive but not at the expense of others." "We all are friends and are involved in each other's family life. It has been a great place to make lifelong business contacts, as well as lifelong friends," says a student.

There are a lot of different cultural activities sponsored by different clubs and different ethnic groups to create cultural awareness. Students who live on campus (or nearby) can take advantage of the "countless events going on" ("more social activities than any one person could possibly attend"), ranging from academic, to business-related, to just-for-fun events such as ski trips, Class Olympics, and Red Sox games. Note that private transport is "essential" for commuting to Babson, but with MBA studies mostly concentrated in one building there is a lot of interaction with students, and "having on campus offices for work teams makes the campus very live at every time of day."

Admissions

Babson operates several rounds of admission for each graduate program—evening, Fast-Track, and full-time MBAs. You'll have the best chance of acceptance if you apply early in the admissions cycle. There is no minimum GMAT score required for admission, though the score range for accepted applicants ranges between 580 and 670 each year (25th and 75th percentile). All programs require an admissions interview.

FINANCIAL FACTS

Annual tuition	$58,884
Fees	$0
Cost of books	$1,300
Room & board	$17,076
% of students receiving aid	59
% of first-year students receiving aid	62
% of students receiving grants	55
Average award package	$21,152
Average grant	$19,967
Average loan	$40,960
Average student loan debt	$62,888

ADMISSIONS

Admissions Selectivity Rating	77
# of applications received	531
% applicants accepted	68
% acceptees attending	47
Average GMAT	618
Range of GMAT	580–670
Average GPA	3.23
TOEFL required of international students	Yes
Application fee	$100
International application fee	$100
Regular application deadline	4/1
Application Deadline/Notification	
Round 1:	11/1 / 12/15
Round 2:	1/15 / 2/15
Round 3:	2/15 / 3/15
Round 4:	4/1 /
Deferment available	Yes
Maximum length of deferment	1 year
Transfer students accepted	No
Transfer application policy: We do not accept transfer students to our full-time programs. However, we do accept transfer credit from AACSB accredited programs into our evening program.	
Non-fall admissions	Yes
Need-blind admissions	Yes

EMPLOYMENT PROFILE

Career Rating	95	**Grads Employed by Function% Avg. Salary**	
Percent employed at graduation	55	Marketing	(33%) $81,273
Percent employed 3 months		Operations	(8%) $77,625
after graduation	88	Consulting	(10%)$89,500
Average base starting salary	$89,742	Management	(19%) $110,526
Primary Source of Full-time Job Acceptances		Finance	(19%) $90,526
School-facilitated activities	58(43%)	MIS	(4%) $88,125
Graduate-facilitated activities	77(57%)	Other	(6%) $84,250
		Top 5 Employers Hiring Grads	
		Athenahealth(4), CVS Caremark (4), EMC (4), Cognizant (2), Credit Suisse (2)	

BALL STATE UNIVERSITY
MILLER COLLEGE OF BUSINESS

GENERAL INFORMATION
Type of school   Public
Affiliation   No Affiliation
Academic calendar   Semester

SURVEY SAYS...
Friendly students, Happy students
Solid preparation in:
General management, Teamwork

STUDENTS
Enrollment of parent institution	21,053
Enrollment of MBA Program	211
% male/female	65/35
% out-of-state	1
% part-time	69
% underrepresented minority	6
% international	23
Average age at entry	31
Average years work experience at entry	7.0

ACADEMICS
Academic Experience Rating	**83**
Profs interesting rating	81
Profs accesible rating	82
Student/faculty ratio	30:1
% female faculty	9
% part-time faculty	0

Prominent Alumni
E. Renae Conley, EVP-HR, Former
Pres & CEO-Energy

Academics

Long a pioneer in distance learning, the Miller College of Business at Ball State University in Muncie, Indiana offers an MBA program that is "broad and extensive, providing several different paths to earning your degree." The extraordinarily flexible (not to mention "very affordable") school offers numerous delivery options that can accommodate almost any student's situation, including full-time, part-time, on-campus, distance learning, and day or night classes (though classes are generally offered in the evenings), which "is very appealing to those who work full time or have to travel frequently." "I didn't know where I would be living before starting the program, and didn't want to start at a school only to have to not be able to attend anymore. Since most schools don't accept transfer MBA credit, I would have lost that time," reasons a student.

The greatest strengths of the school include "the professors and facilities"; professors have "extensive real world expertise" and "you can tell they LOVE what they do, which translates into excitement for the class, program and university." These "very engaging" teachers even communicate this to distance learning students through Skype, email and whiteboard, using "their professional experience to help us learn." "Everything is immersive," and the course work is certainly challenging. "I have to work really hard to achieve good grades," says one student. "Ball State provides immersive learning experiences to its students, [which] are difficult but necessary to understand the dynamic nature of the business world."

Uniquely, "there is a desire to get to know other distance learning students and collaborate in order to get more out of the taught materials." "I feel as though I am a traditional student even though I am connecting via the internet," says a student. The "cutting edge" technology and "access to the latest and greatest...software" truly makes for a "fantastic learning environment" that is "educating people of the future." The ease with which students can sign up for classes and complete their degree "is amazing." "Away with the old, go to Ball State, the way of the future universities!" says a student.

Career and Placement

The wide swath of backgrounds and experiences covered by each class is a blessing for all. "Everyone is interested in so many areas and has experience in a variety of jobs/internships to share with each class." The school does an excellent job of putting together job/internship fairs and attracting a variety of recruiters, and the fact that "you can graduate as quickly as you finish your coursework" in the distance learning program really benefits the working professionals that attend Ball State. The administration "focuses on helping you meet any academic needs you have."

ADMISSIONS CONTACT: REBECCA L. BAER
ADDRESS: WB 147, MUNCIE, IN 47306
PHONE: 765-285-5329 • FAX: 765-285-8818
E-MAIL: MBA@BSU.EDU • WEBSITE: WWW.BSU.EDU/MBA

Student Life and Environment

Many of the program's enrollees are also Ball State graduate assistants; perhaps it naturally follows that this "friendly," "outgoing" bunch is always "willing to offer assistance and advice." All in all, the student body here is very diverse, representing many countries, ages, and backgrounds. "From the recently laid off exec trying to better himself, to the house wife that wants to have a one up on the competition when re-entering the work force," all bases are covered. Although it is situated in the Midwest, "we seem to have a large amount of foreign students," as well.

While Muncie itself "is not a very nice city," the school is "heavily involved in the local community." Ball State has a strong reputation for maintaining high tech facilities especially in media, education, and business departments. A recent total overhaul of facilities has only further benefitted the school: "the entire campus has been updated including new buildings, roads, landscapes, etc." Everything is very student-friendly, "minus the parking." "Free internet EVERYWHERE on campus, all sporting events are free, most speakers and events on campus are also free." "I've had a VERY positive experience with BSU," says one student.

Admissions

Ball State is nothing if not amenable to all types of students, and the school's application reflects as much. The two primary criteria are your cumulative undergraduate GPA and GMAT scores; a minimum GPA of 2.75 is required (recent entering students had an average GPA of 3.21), as is a minimum GMAT of 450 (recent entering students had an average composite GMAT score of 550). Students must also submit a transcript, application, and a one- or two-page business resume or curriculum vita for use by the Admissions Selection Committee, in which they must portray their work and educational history in a professional style. Students must also submit GMAT or GRE scores from within the past six years; this requirement is waived for anyone who has a JD, PhD, PharmD, or MD. Students must be fully admitted and receive letters of acceptance from both the Graduate School and the MBA program before they can begin classes.

FINANCIAL FACTS

Annual tuition (in-state/ out-of-state)	$7,666/$19,114
Fees	$662
Cost of books	$1,020
Room & board (on/off-campus)	$8,870/$9,000
Average award package	$8,907
Average grant	$0
Average loan	$0

ADMISSIONS

Admissions Selectivity Rating	76
# of applications received	75
% applicants accepted	76
% acceptees attending	88
Average GMAT	531
Range of GMAT	400–740
Average GPA	3.28
TOEFL required of international students	Yes
Minimum TOEFL (paper/computer)	550
Application fee	$50
International application fee	$40
Deferment available	Yes
Maximum length of deferment	2 years
Transfer students accepted	Yes
Transfer application policy: Up to 9 credit hours may be considered for transfer from an accredited institution.	
Non-fall admissions	Yes
Need-blind admissions	Yes

EMPLOYMENT PROFILE

Career Rating	60*	Grads Employed by Function	% Avg. Salary
Percent employed at graduation	42	Marketing	(8%) $63,000
Percent employed 3 months after graduation	15	Operations	(12%) $43,167
		Consulting	(12%) $84,300
Average base starting salary	$48,500	Management	(19%) $58,667
Primary Source of Full-time Job Acceptances		Finance	(12%) $50,667
School-facilitated activities	5(5%)	HR	(4%) $45,000
Graduate-facilitated activities	22(24%)	MIS	(12%) $74,333
Unknown	64(70%)	Other	(23%) $88,667

BAYLOR UNIVERSITY
HANKAMER SCHOOL OF BUSINESS

GENERAL INFORMATION

Type of school	Private
Affiliation	Baptist
Academic calendar	Semester

SURVEY SAYS...

Friendly students, Good peer network, Smart classrooms
Solid preparation in:
Communication/interpersonal skills, Presentation skills

STUDENTS

Enrollment of parent institution	15,364
Enrollment of MBA Program	100
% male/female	70/30
% part-time	4
% underrepresented minority	24
% international	11
Average age at entry	26
Average years work experience at entry	2.2

ACADEMICS

Academic Experience Rating	**88**
Profs interesting rating	81
Profs accesible rating	88
Student/faculty ratio	14:1
% part-time faculty	0

Joint Degrees

MBA/MSIS is 2 years; MBA/Master of Engineering is 3 years for both degrees; JD/MBA, JD/MTax, and MBA/Master of Social Work are 4 years for both degrees.

Academics

Baylor University, a popular Southern institution located halfway between Dallas and Austin, appeals to those looking for "a small program" with "a cozy atmosphere" and "a lot of emphasis on ethics." With both a concentration and a dual degree program in healthcare administration, Baylor is also a strong draw for those looking to make their mark in the nation's transforming healthcare sector. By one student's tally, one-third of the full-time students at Hankamer were studying healthcare administration in 2009-2010. Those students have high praise for the program, asserting that "it will be ranked among the top programs" soon. "Hospital CEOs speak to our class approximately nine times per semester," writes one student, extolling the "incredible healthcare administration speaker series." The program includes a placement experience during which students "work directly with a CEO and become an actual hospital administrator for seven months."

There's more than healthcare to Baylor, though. MBAs call the strategy and organizational behavior courses here "some of the best in the country." Students also tell us that the program provides "the freedom and opportunity to engage in any activity that would benefit your personal development." "Whether it's spending an entire day with Warren Buffett, working in China for a semester with top global firms, traveling to Austin every Friday to learn and explore capital investment analysis, or going to a local prison to decrease the recidivism rate by going over business plans with inmates, you can do it at Baylor," one student writes. Another cites an MBA class devoted to inter-program case competition, for which Baylor not only offers a course but also pays participants' cost of participation, including "room, entry fee, flight, etc." (The team took third prize at the competition hosted by George Washington University in 2010.) Business education neophytes praise the Integrated Management Seminar, "a semester specifically designed for non-business undergrads to provide a fabulous foundation before the core MBA program begins."

Career and Placement

Baylor employs career placement professionals who work exclusively with the school's approximately 90 MBA students as well as with alumni. Students tell us that "The career professionals are planning to take the case to businesses more aggressively than bringing the businesses to Baylor (although…some of that will [still] take place)." Students say this strategy makes sense considering that "Baylor is not competing right now with Texas, Rice, and SMU" when it comes to on-campus recruiting, in part due to the small size of the program. Some complain that "The [placement office's] focus is on Texas, and if you're not looking in Texas, good luck!"

Employers who most frequently hire Baylor MBAs include: Accenture, American Express, Anadarko Petroleum, Bank of America, Baptist Health Center, Bearing Point, CITGO, CNA Insurance, Comerica, Community Bank And Trust, ConocoPhillips, Deloitte & Touche, Echostar Communications, Edward Jones, Ernst & Young, ExxonMobil, FBI, First City Financial, First Preference Mortgage, Hatteras Yachts, H.E.B. Grocery Company, Intecap, Internal Revenue Service, Johnson & Johnson, JP Morgan Chase Bank, Keller Williams, Kersher Trading, KPMG, Merck, Microsoft, Middleton, Burns & Davis, Occidental Services, Inc., Perot Systems, Perryman Consulting, PricewaterhouseCoopers, Protiviti, Quala-T, Steak 'n Shake Operations, Inc., Sterling Bank, Sungard Consulting, TXU, Texas Farm Bureau, U.S. Department of Labor, UBS Financial Services, Inc., and Wal-Mart.

Student Life and Environment

"Student life in the MBA program is excellent," with "ample opportunity to meet interesting business leaders outside of the classroom, attend case competitions, and participate in intramural sports. Additionally, many students find that there is a healthy work-life balance at Baylor's MBA program." The university "gives free tickets to all sporting events for graduate students, which is a big deal in the Big 12 Conference, and that includes football and basketball games. Business school students often attend the games together." Some students say Baylor is "a conservative Baptist school" that "does not encourage…drinking or partying," so those unaccustomed to a more conservative setting may find the extracurricular scene here "limited."

The Baylor campus features "several resources available for use [by] graduate students only, including a graduate lounge and breakout rooms with access restricted to grad students, which facilitates the ease of group work." When there are "breaks during the day, students usually hang out in the graduate lounge playing ping pong or talking and catching up on each other's weekend."

Admissions

Those seeking admission to Baylor's Hankamer School of Business must submit the following materials: a completed application (online application preferred); two letters of recommendation from individuals who know you professionally and can assess your skills and potential; official undergraduate transcripts (international students who attended a non-English-speaking school must provide professionally translated and interpreted academic records); a GMAT score report; a current resume; and personal essays detailing qualifications, experiences, and objectives in pursuing a Hankamer MBA. International students whose first language is not English must also submit a score report for the TOEFL or the IELS. Hankamer processes applications on a rolling basis; candidates are notified of their admission status as soon as a decision is made.

FINANCIAL FACTS

Annual tuition	$30,586
Fees	$5,530
Cost of books	$2,000
Room & board	$10,000
% of students receiving aid	75
% of first-year students receiving aid	75

ADMISSIONS

Admissions Selectivity Rating	90
# of applications received	181
% applicants accepted	39
% acceptees attending	73
Average GMAT	628
Range of GMAT	593–660
Average GPA	3.31
TOEFL required of international students	No
Minimum TOEFL (paper/computer)	600/250
International application fee	$50
Early application deadline	11/15
Early notification date	12/1
Regular application deadline	4/15
Regular application notification	5/1
Application Deadline/Notification	
Round 1:	11/15 / 12/1
Round 2:	2/15 / 3/1
Round 3:	4/15 / 5/1
Round 4:	6/15 / 7/1
Deferment available	Yes
Maximum length of deferment	1 year
Transfer students accepted	Yes

Transfer application policy: A student who has been admitted to a graduate program at another university, and who desires admission to Baylor, must present a transcript that presents the student's active, satisfactory work toward the same degree. Only 6 hrs may be transferred into the MBA program.

Non-fall admissions	Yes
Need-blind admissions	Yes

EMPLOYMENT PROFILE

Career Rating	90	Grads Employed by Function	% Avg. Salary
Percent employed at graduation	66	Marketing	(21%) $56,500
Percent employed 3 months after graduation	83	Operations	(10%) $66,050
		Consulting	(7%)
Average base starting salary	$66,426	Management	(28%) $71,000
Primary Source of Full-time Job Acceptances		Finance	(28%) $60,143
School-facilitated activities	2(7%)	MIS	(3%) $80,000
Graduate-facilitated activities	25(86%)	Other	(3%) $110,000
Unknown	2(7%)		

BELLARMINE UNIVERSITY
W. FIELDING RUBEL SCHOOL OF BUSINESS

GENERAL INFORMATION

Type of school   Private
Affiliation   Roman Catholic

SURVEY SAYS...

Friendly students, Cutting-edge
classes
Solid preparation in:
Teamwork, Communication/interpersonal skills, Presentation skills

STUDENTS

Enrollment of parent
  institution   3,200
Enrollment of MBA Program   195
% male/female   54/46
% part-time   53
% underrepresented minority   15
% international   1
Average age at entry   27

ACADEMICS

Academic Experience Rating   74
Profs interesting rating   83
Profs accesible rating   72
% female faculty   33
% underrepresented minority
  faculty   7

Prominent Alumni

Joseph P. Clayton, former CEO and
current Chairman of the Board of
Directors, Sirius Satellite Radio; Dr.
James Heck, inventor of the drug
Cancidas, honored by the National
Science Foundation for research;
Susan M. Ivey, Chairman,
President/CEO, Reynolds American
Inc.; Angela Mason, Co-founder, ITS
Services; Leonard P. Spalding,
Retired, CEO Chase Mutual Funds
Corp/Retired, Pres. & CEO Vista
Capital Mgmt.

ADMISSIONS

Admissions Selectivity Rating   71

Academics

A cozy business school in Louisville, Kentucky, Bellarmine University offers individual attention and personal growth within a practical MBA curriculum. The "small-school atmosphere and small classroom sizes" are a huge benefit of this program, allowing students to build close relationships with their professors and classmates. Academically, collaboration is a key aspect of the Bellarmine experience, and from the beginning of the program, "Everything is team based." To encourage group problem solving, networking, and interaction, "Bellarmine groups its students into cohorts of four or five," and they take all core courses together. In fact, the program is designed to help students round out their qualitative abilities, and the curriculum places a strong "emphasis on improving student's writing, speaking, presentation, and teamwork skills." In the classroom setting, professors are "good at facilitating meaningful class discussions," which bring each student's experience to light. A current student agrees, "The cohort design and grouping throughout the weekend program has increased my team-building skills."

Bellarmine's faculty comprises "published and scholarly professors," who have a strong understanding of business theory. Nonetheless, real world skills are emphasized over academic analysis, and students are pushed to "learn through case studies in a team-oriented environment." Don't expect to lean back and snooze through a lecture; courses are discussion based and, often, small groups "lead case study discussions for the entire class." Bellarmine has deep ties in the local metropolis. "One of Bellarmine's advantages is that a majority of its professors have great career experience, and some are still working in the Louisville area." A student recounts, "We have accounting teachers who have headed departments for Deloitte; IRS Tax Attorneys teaching tax and business law; and a lawyer/econ Ph.D. who teaches economics and how to do business in non-capitalistic countries." Although the school "could offer a wider variety of MBA electives," students appreciate the varied experience faculty members bring to the classroom. Class work is often augmented by the invitation of special "speakers and contributors, who are able to share more recent 'real world' experiences" with the student body.

For working professionals, the Bellarmine MBA program is flexible, allowing students to tailor coursework to fit their busy schedules. Depending on the pace in which you complete coursework, the MBA can take anywhere from two to five years to complete. Classes are held in the evenings and on weekends. "The convenience is great for someone looking to go to school part time." Overall, the program is "very well run, with minimal red tape." When it comes to planning your schedule or paying your bills, "The administration is wonderful to work with, very helpful, and makes things easier on students." A "personal touch" distinguishes the experience, and "staff, faculty, and administration care about the students and their success."

Career and Placement

Preparation for the real world begins in the Bellarmine classroom. Professors "know what is going on in the job market today and how it will affect us when we leave." As such, teaching is geared toward practical applications, which students can take directly back to their jobs. Those looking to make a career change after the MBA have access to the campus Career Center, which maintains online job and internship boards and hosts a series of job development events on campus. Though many of these events are directed at the undergraduate community, MBA students can benefit from campus-wide career fairs or make appointment with career counselors for a resume and cover letter review.

Working full-time as they attend the program, most students will stay at their current company after graduation. Therefore, career services aren't as robust at Bellarmine as

ADMISSIONS CONTACT: DR. SARA YOUNT PETTINGILL, DEAN OF GRADUATE ADMISSIONS
ADDRESS: 2001 NEWBURG ROAD, LOUISVILLE, KY 40205
PHONE: 502-272-8258 • FAX: 502-272-8002
E-MAIL: GRADADMISSIONS@BELLARMINE.EDU • WEBSITE: WWW.BELLARMINE.EDU

they are at other full-time MBA programs. There are "a lot of internship opportunities" offered through the career center, but an MBA student admits, "I have not seen a lot of recruiting, except for accounting or finance."

Student Life and Environment

Bellarmine students come from "a wide variety of race, social, and educational backgrounds," and join the program "experienced in various fields of business." In the classroom, students are "very supportive and collaborative," and most enjoy the heavy emphasis on group work. To facilitate student interaction, there is a "very nice computer lab and library study area" in the business school facilities. "Students normally gather at common areas on campus" before attending classes. Overall, "The facility is very safe and excellent," and comfortably located on a "beautiful" campus.

With laudable time management skills, most students at Bellarmine "can balance class loads with their professional duties quite well." Nonetheless, Bellarmine graduate students have a lot on their plates, and most are "not very social outside of class." A student explains, "Most all of us have full-time jobs, so we have limited time to spend at school." Socializing, when it happens, is mostly low-key. For example, "Many of us try to go out after Friday class to have fun for a couple of hours."

Admissions

To apply to Bellarmine's MBA program, students must submit a completed application form, personal essays, two letters of recommendation, academic transcripts from all college coursework, and official GMAT scores. Test scores and previous academic performance are the two most important factors in an admissions decision, though work experience is also weighted strongly. For last year's entering class, the average GMAT score was 501, and the average GPA was 3.2 on a 4.0 scale.

# of applications received	68
% applicants accepted	96
% acceptees attending	92
Average GMAT	495
Range of GMAT	430–570
Average GPA	3.20
TOEFL required of international students	Yes
Minimum TOEFL (paper/computer)	550/213
Application fee	$40
International application fee	$40
Deferment available	Yes
Maximum length of deferment	5 years
Transfer students accepted	Yes
Transfer application policy: Accept up to 12 graduate credits from an accredited university.	
Non-fall admissions	Yes
Need-blind admissions	No

BELMONT UNIVERSITY
THE JACK C. MASSEY GRADUATE SCHOOL OF BUSINESS

GENERAL INFORMATION

Type of school	Private
Affiliation	Christian
	(Nondenominational)
Academic calendar	Trimester

SURVEY SAYS...
Students love Nashville, TN, Good peer network, Cutting-edge classes
Solid preparation in:
Doing business in a global economy

STUDENTS

Enrollment of parent	
institution	6,647
Enrollment of MBA Program	140
% male/female	76/24
% out-of-state	36
% part-time	82
% underrepresented minority	4
% international	8
Average age at entry	26
Average years work experience	
at entry	5.0

ACADEMICS

Academic Experience Rating	**78**
Profs interesting rating	84
Profs accesible rating	79
Student/faculty ratio	6:1
% female faculty	35
% underrepresented minority	
faculty	8
% part-time faculty	15

Joint Degrees
Dual MBA/MACC, 2.5 to 3 years

Prominent Alumni
Damon Hininger, CEO, Correction Corporation of America; Richard Treadway, Founder, Psychiatric Solutions; Charles Hagood, CEO, Healthcare Performance Partners, Inc.; Nancy Leach, Founder/Owner, Facility Planners, Inc.; Helen Lane, Partner, C3 Consulting

Academics

For Nashville-area professionals looking to jump-start their career, Belmont University's graduate business programs offer a "great value." The professional MBA for working adults—Belmont's flagship program—offers a "great classroom-based education that is flexible enough for a working student." With all classes held at night, most Belmont students are juggling career and studies; fortunately, "educators understand [students'] work/life demands" and "are consistently flexible when [students need] to balance work and life with academics." Belmont's core curriculum covers a wide breadth of business areas, including basics like finance, business law, and technology, as well as more innovative topics in entrepreneurship and leadership. Neither highly qualitative nor quantitative, "The program is balanced between verbal, interpersonal, and mathematical reasoning abilities." Overall, the program is challenging, but "The pace is so fast that sometimes we are not able to cover some subjects in enough detail." If you do want to delve into details, the MBA offers the "flexibility to customize [your] degree" through areas of concentration in accounting, entrepreneurship, finance, general business, healthcare, marketing, or music business. Of particular note, every Belmont student must also participate in an international trip as a requirement of graduation; destinations range from Istanbul to Beijing to Amsterdam.

Working professionals want to learn skills they can apply in the workplace, and Belmont caters to that goal. Here, "The classes are focused on real world topics" and "the learning style is hands-on." In the classroom, "the program is largely case-based, encouraging students to use critical thinking skills and sharpen interpersonal skills," and across disciplines, "The professors encourage classroom discussion." The faculty further promotes Belmont's practical perspective by bringing their extensive business experience to the classroom. Like the students, most Belmont professors were "working professionals and therefore experts in the field they are teaching." At this friendly school, faculty members "give great practical advice" and are "truly interested in helping students learn and grow."

At Belmont, classes are uniformly small, with about 20 students in the average classroom. Students love the mix of big-name resources and intimate atmosphere, saying "Belmont has the feel of a small school with the professors and reputation of a top university." A student adds, "It is big enough to offer amenities and benefits of a large school, but small enough to still be a tight-knit group." On this community-oriented campus, "Fellow students, the professors, and the school staff seem to sincerely care about me and each other."

Career and Placement

The Massey College of Business Career Development Center serves undergraduate and graduate business students through individualized career coaching, interview training, resume preparation, and job and internship listings. After graduation, the vast majority of Massey graduates (about 85 percent) stay in the Middle Tennessee area, contributing to the school's strong alumni network in greater Nashville. While praising their school's deep ties in the region, students feel that "Belmont could improve more in getting more companies to recruit their students" and by drawing new employers from some of Nashville's largest industries, such as healthcare. In recent years, companies that have hired graduates of the Massey College of Business Administration, include AT&T, Dell, Deloitte & Touche, Ernst & Young, HCA, Pfizer, Morgan Stanley Smith Barney, Marriott, Sony/ATV, and WebMD.

ADMISSIONS CONTACT: TONYA HOLLIN, ADMISSIONS ASSISTANT
ADDRESS: 1900 BELMONT BOULEVARD, NASHVILLE, TN 37212
PHONE: 615-460-6480 • FAX: 615-460-6353
E-MAIL: MASSEYADMISSIONS@BELMONT.EDU • WEBSITE: MASSEY.BELMONT.EDU

Belmont MBA candidates are predominantly working professionals, and many aren't looking for a new position after graduation (rather, they are hoping to assume new responsibilities at their existing job with the help of an MBA). However, should they someday be looking to make a change, Massey graduates can count on lifelong loyalty: All alumni have access to services offered through Center for Career Development including a job posting site, career counseling, and various online tools.

Student Life and Environment

With its evening course schedule, accommodating staff, and practical approach to business, Belmont attracts many "young professionals up on current events and looking to advance their careers." At this school, "people are smart and hard workers, and have big, diverse goals [in] life," offering great opportunities to network in different industries. Between students, "the culture is professional but fun without being too rigid," and, though there is a mix of cultures and viewpoints, "Everyone feels comfortable and gets to express their personal views." "There are numerous activities and clubs to take part in" through the business school, including honor societies and volunteer work. Even if they don't participate in campus activities, "everyone is still very social and friendly," and networking opportunities abound. A student explains, "Courses are structured with many group work requirements, which somewhat supercedes the need for student activity groups, as we are all meeting together regularly."

Located on 75 acres in southeast Nashville, Belmont University has a "great urban location" and a comfortable campus environment, boasting modern classrooms and "beautiful flower gardens." Although most Belmont MBA students don't have extra time to take advantage of the resources on campus, they do appreciate the school's "convenient location." At the same time, Belmont has a growing reputation, and students say it's time to "significantly update some of [its] facilities and technologies to keep up with the expansion."

Admissions

To apply to Massey, students must submit an application, an undergraduate transcript, GMAT scores, a current resume, and at least two professional recommendations. In recent years, the average Belmont MBA candidate was about 28 years old, had over six years of professional work experience, and scored around 532 on the GMAT. To be eligible for the program, students must have an undergraduate degree in any field. For those without a degree in business, Belmont will help a student determine which basic business courses they should take before matriculation.

FINANCIAL FACTS

Annual tuition	$46,050
Fees	$780
% of students receiving aid	67
% of first-year students receiving aid	77
% of students receiving grants	24
Average award package	$29,000
Average grant	$3,000
Average loan	$15,000
Average student loan debt	$21,206

ADMISSIONS

Admissions Selectivity Rating	**70**
# of applications received	71
% applicants accepted	96
% acceptees attending	68
Average GMAT	536
Range of GMAT	500–580
Average GPA	3.23
TOEFL required of international students	Yes
Minimum TOEFL (paper/computer)	550/213
Application fee	$50
International application fee	$50
Regular application deadline	7/1
Deferment available	Yes
Maximum length of deferment	1 year
Transfer students accepted	Yes
Transfer application policy: Application process is the same for all students. May transfer up to 6 hours from an accredited university.	
Non-fall admissions	Yes
Need-blind admissions	Yes

BENTLEY UNIVERSITY
McCallum Graduate School of Business

GENERAL INFORMATION

Type of school	Private
Affiliation	No Affiliation
Academic calendar	Semester

SURVEY SAYS...
Cutting-edge classes, Happy students, Smart classrooms
Solid preparation in:
Teamwork, Computer skills, Doing business in a global economy

STUDENTS

Enrollment of parent institution	5,643
Enrollment of MBA Program	463
% male/female	65/35
% out-of-state	18
% part-time	61
% underrepresented minority	7
% international	54
Average age at entry	27
Average years work experience at entry	5.1

ACADEMICS

Academic Experience Rating	**77**
Profs interesting rating	79
Profs accesible rating	76
Student/faculty ratio	12:1
% female faculty	29
% underrepresented minority faculty	12
% part-time faculty	28

Joint Degrees
MBA with MS in Accountancy, Finance, Financial Planning, IT, Marketing Analytics or Taxation

Prominent Alumni
Chris Lynch '91 MBA, President and CEO Vertica Systems (now an HP Company); Amy Hunter '85 MBA, SVP, Investment Management, Boston Private Bank; S. Joseph Wickwire II '93 MBA, Portfolio Manager FMR/Fidelity Investments; Christine Freyermuth '98 MBA, Senior Associate PWC; Theresa Bresten '87 MBA, VP Treasurer HP Hood Inc.

Academics

Students in the McCallum MBA program at Bentley University brag that their program combines "the most modern technology available" with "real-world work experience" to provide "the best mix of price, location, and quality." Bentley's impressive resources include a 3,500-square-foot facility complete with a trading floor with two Trans-Lux data walls, 60 work stations, an adjacent business suite, and a marketing center that features numerous state-of-the-art research and analysis labs. "Some [of the technology] is accessible from home, too," a boon to the school's many commuting part-timers.

McCallum's cutting-edge approach extends to its academics. Students pursue "the most unique and interesting concentrations" in addition to "all the traditional areas of study." Unique offerings include Human Factors in Information Design, Business Analytics, and Marketing Analytics, programs that students argue "are in line with what is needed in the real world." Bentley's "accounting program is the best around," excelling in both general accounting and taxation. Information technology, unsurprisingly, is also an area of strength.

McCallum's many part-time students appreciate the program's flexibility ("You can take two courses in one night, and there are some online offerings," a student explains), but warn that "it is hard to connect with other students" because "there are no real cohorts." The full-time program, in contrast, "is comparatively small and becomes tight-knit over the two-year course." For all students, the program is "intense," but fortunately, "The professors and administration are very helpful." One student points out that "many workshops and information sessions exist outside of class," and as a result students enjoy "a very engaging academic experience." MBAs also appreciate that "professors teach course work in a practical manner. I always leave feeling like I have something I can use the next day."

Career and Placement

Bentley's Nathan R. Miller Center for Career Services (CCS) "offers a great deal of support in finding career opportunities" for the school's MBAs. Career Advisors receive a strong assist from Bentley's solid "reputation among Boston-area employers" as well as from professors who "use their networks" to help their students. Students here also benefit from the Job Search Skills (JSS), a program designed to help them better position themselves in the battle for top jobs. JSS programs vary by area of concentration, meaning students receive plenty of field-specific assistance. The CSS provides lifetime service to alumni, another huge plus.

Top employers of Bentley MBAs include: Boston Scientific, Converse Inc., Covidien, Deloitte Consulting, Federal Reserve Bank of Boston, Ernst & Young, Fidelity Investments, EMC, Genzyme Corporation, JPMorgan Chase & Company, KPMG, Morgan Stanley, PricewaterhouseCoopers, Microsoft, National Grid USA, Nuance Communications, Raytheon, Staples, and State Street Corporation.

Student Life and Environment

The majority of Bentley MBA students attend the part-time evening program. The full-time program is comprised of 10 percent of the student body. Bentley typically draws "academically capable people with many diverse backgrounds," although some here "wish there were fewer people coming straight out of a four-year program," even though such students "are still surprisingly able to contribute to conversations. However, they lack a certain perspective."

Bentley MBAs enjoy "a beautiful campus and buildings." Grad classes "are concentrated in a couple of buildings near each other," a blessing during the cold Massachusetts winters. So too are the "shuttles around campus." Even so, some feel that the space dedicated to graduate students needs to be expanded. One writes that the school "should have more options for dining on campus and more places suitable for graduate students to study either individual[ly] or in groups." Most part-time students must balance "a heavy course load" with work and family responsibilities, leaving little or no time for extracurricular and other campus activities. Those not so burdened report that "Campus activities are in abundance, from professional to entertainment. There is usually at least one club or association hosting an event open to the whole school body" at any time. Campus organizations "cater to different educational paths and cultures," with a number representing various international student constituencies.

Off-campus entertainment is also readily accessible, as Bentley is located in Waltham, a mere 10 miles from downtown Boston. Both Boston and Cambridge are easily accessible by train. The school also runs a regular shuttle between the Bentley campus and Harvard Square.

Admissions

Applicants to the Bentley MBA program must submit all of the following materials to the Admissions Committee: a completed application form; official copies of all transcripts for all post secondary academic work; an official GMAT score report; two letters of recommendation; essays (topics detailed in application); and a resume. Applicants to the full-time MBA program or the MS + MBA program must sit for an interview; interviews are optional for all other applicants. In addition to all of the above, international applicants must also submit an international student data form and confirmation of financial resources; a copy of their passport name page; and TOEFL score. International applicants are strongly encouraged to use a transcript evaluation service. Bentley admissions officers pride themselves on personalizing the admissions process by looking at the whole person when making admissions decisions. Work experience is strongly preferred but not required.

FINANCIAL FACTS

Annual tuition	$34,254
Fees	$404
Cost of books	$1,300
Room & board	$15,020
% of students receiving aid	51
% of first-year students receiving aid	79
% of students receiving grants	35
Average award package	$21,101
Average grant	$14,164
Average loan	$19,051
Average student loan debt	$36,063

ADMISSIONS

Admissions Selectivity Rating	75
# of applications received	424
% applicants accepted	76
% acceptees attending	60
Average GMAT	592
Range of GMAT	550–635
Average GPA	3.34
TOEFL required of international students	Yes
Minimum TOEFL (paper/computer)	600/250
Application fee	$50
International application fee	$50
Application Deadline/Notification	
Round 1:	12/1 / 1/15
Round 2:	1/20 / 3/15
Round 3:	3/15 / 5/1
Round 4:	5/1 /
Deferment available	Yes
Maximum length of deferment	Up to 1 year
Transfer students accepted	No
Non-fall admissions	Yes
Need-blind admissions	Yes

EMPLOYMENT PROFILE

		Grads Employed by Function	% Avg. Salary
Career Rating	94		
Percent employed at graduation	57	Marketing	(13%)
Percent employed 3 months after graduation	86	Operations	(7%)
		Consulting	(27%)$70,500
Average base starting salary	$75,616	Finance	(13%)
Primary Source of Full-time Job Acceptances		MIS	(27%) $87,310
School-facilitated activities	8(42%)	Other	(13%)
Graduate-facilitated activities	10(53%)	**Top 5 Employers Hiring Grads**	
Unknown	1(5%)	EMC(1), Deloitte & Touche (1), Biogen Idec (1), Epsilon (1), Hitachi Consulting (1)	

BERRY COLLEGE
CAMPBELL SCHOOL OF BUSINESS

GENERAL INFORMATION

Type of school	Private
Affiliation	
Academic calendar	August-July

SURVEY SAYS...
Friendly students
Solid preparation in:
General management, Teamwork,
Communication/interpersonal skills

STUDENTS

Enrollment of parent institution	2,093
Enrollment of MBA Program	26
% part-time	100
Average age at entry	26
Average years work experience at entry	4.5

ACADEMICS

Academic Experience Rating	**78**
Profs interesting rating	78
Profs accesible rating	82
Student/faculty ratio	12:1

Academics

Berry College is a small private school, located on a beautiful and expansive wooded campus in Rome, Georgia. This setting provides a unique backdrop for the Campbell School of Business, which unites a savvy MBA curriculum with a friendly and intimate atmosphere. Within the greater Rome area, Berry College is a "convenient and reputable" choice for an MBA, with all classes offered in the evenings (classes meet one night per week throughout the fall, spring, and summer terms). Located fewer than 100 miles from Atlanta and Chattanooga, the program is designed for working professionals, as well as early-career students. For full-time students, the school offers the opportunity to take on a graduate assistantship position, which offsets the cost of tuition in exchange for hours worked on campus.

Along with the master of education, the MBA is one of two graduate programs offered at Berry, and the atmosphere reflects the intimate atmosphere of the undergraduate college. With a low enrollment, the "small class sizes and the relationships students have with professors" are the best parts of the educational experience. Here, professors "are always willing to help and seem happy to be there, teaching the courses." Bringing strong educational and professional backgrounds to the program, "the faculty at Berry [is] surprisingly accomplished," and students note a "professional commitment to academic excellence" throughout the faculty and staff. Berry is an interactive environment where students are encouraged to participate in class discussions, and those who have already entered the workforce often "have interesting stories and work experience to contribute to class." While the benefits are manifold, the low enrollment also has some drawbacks. For example, course scheduling can be difficult because "the school does not offer all required classes at all times. Just once every two years." In addition, the elective offerings are more limited at Berry than at larger institutions; some feel it would be a benefit to have "more classes, more options" within the MBA curriculum.

Overseen by a competent administration, "the school is run well," and the curriculum is well-designed, emphasizing a holistic approach to business. The MBA begins with a series of proficiency requirements in accounting, marketing, statistics, economics, finance, and management—but these can be waived for students who have an undergraduate degree in business. Thereafter, all students must complete 21 credit hours of core courses and nine credit hours of business electives (students may also earn course credit for internships), which cover a range of topics including written and oral communication skills, leadership, and ethics. Typically, students complete the program in two years, though the college allows up to six years of study.

Career and Placement

The Berry College Career Center offers career counseling, resume and cover letter assistance, online job boards, and an online database of job tips and resources. These services are open to all undergraduates and graduate students, as well as alumni (alumni may even request login information to access online job boards); however, the Career Center's efforts are principally aimed at the undergraduate community.

Graduates of the Campbell School of Business, students have taken jobs with companies including CFA, Georgia Pacific, Walton Communications, Industrial Developments International, Wiser Wealth Management, and Anheuser Busch. While the school has a strong reputation in the region, students admit that, "Berry College could improve in connecting its grad students with jobs outside of the Rome metropolitan and Atlanta areas."

ADMISSIONS CONTACT: DR. GARY WATERS, ASSOCIATE VP OF ENROLLMENT MANAGEMENT
ADDRESS: 2277 MARTHA BERRY HWY NW, PO BOX 490159, MOUNT BERRY, GA 30149-0159
PHONE: 800-BERRY-GA • FAX: 706-290-2178
E-MAIL: ADMISSIONS@BERRY.EDU • WEBSITE: BERRY.EDU

Student Life and Environment

Taking a cue from Berry's pastoral campus environment, Berry students are "friendly and down-to-earth," yet also take their studies seriously. At Berry, students "work hard all day and work hard during their classes," and many are "goal-oriented" and "driven." A tribute to the Berry College's pleasant atmosphere and academic excellence, many MBA candidates are returning Berry students who also received their undergraduate degree from the school. In fact, many come to the graduate program directly after college. Therefore, "the majority of students are fairly young and inexperienced," with limited experience in the real world. As a result, the older, working students who "come from outside of the school add a great deal of value" to the program.

Berry is located on an enormous wooded campus (one of the world's biggest) on the outskirts of Rome, Georgia. If you would like to get involved in extracurricular pursuits, "the school has a great campus with many activities to participate in," and "there is always an activity or cultural event" at school. At the same time, students observe, "The graduate program isn't as active in the school community but the opportunity is there if the student wanted to be involved." Even so, "gym and library facility access is fully granted" to graduate students, and many take advantage of these resources.

Admissions

To apply to Berry College's MBA program, students must submit undergraduate transcripts, two letters of reference, official GMAT scores, a current resume, and a 500-word goals statement. To be eligible for the program, students must have a GMAT score of at least 400; an undergraduate GPA of 3.0 or better is preferred. To be considered for a position, students should submit their application materials at least 30 days before the start of a new semester.

ADMISSIONS

Admissions Selectivity Rating	**70**
# of applications received	17
% applicants accepted	94
% acceptees attending	81
Average GMAT	558
Range of GMAT	430–630
Average GPA	3.00
TOEFL required of	
international students	Yes
Minimum TOEFL	
(paper/computer)	550/213
Application fee	$0
International application fee	$0
Regular application deadline	7/1
Deferment available	Yes
Maximum length	
of deferment	One Semester
Transfer students accepted	Yes
Transfer application policy: The curriculum committee may grant transfer credit for appropriate graduate-level course work completed at other AACSB-accredited institutions to a maximum of two 3-Semester-hour courses, for a total of 6 Semester hours. Transfer credit is not granted for Strategies of World-Class Organizations (BUS 685).	
Non-fall admissions	Yes

BOSTON COLLEGE
CARROLL SCHOOL OF MANAGEMENT

GENERAL INFORMATION

Type of school   Private
Affiliation   Roman Catholic-Jesuit
Academic calendar   Semester

SURVEY SAYS...

Students love Chestnut Hill, MA,
Friendly students, Good social scene,
Good peer network
Solid preparation in:
Finance, General management,
Teamwork

STUDENTS

Enrollment of parent
   institution   14,359
Enrollment of MBA Program   602
% male/female   67/33
% part-time   68
Average age at entry   28
Average years work experience
   at entry   4.4

ACADEMICS

Academic Experience Rating   **92**
Profs interesting rating   86
Profs accesible rating   92
Student/faculty ratio   13:1
% female faculty   17
% underrepresented minority
   faculty   10
% part-time faculty   52

Joint Degrees

MBA/MSF; MBA/MSA; MBA/JD;
MBA/MSW; MBA/MSN; MBA/MEd.;
MBA/MS Biology, Chemistry,
Geology, Geophysics; MBA/MA
Math, Slavic Studies, Russian,
Linguistics; MBA/MA Pastoral
Studies

Prominent Alumni

Robert Manning, '87, Chairman,
President & CEO, MFS Investment
Management; Dennis J. O'Brien,
'82, Chairman, Digicel; Fay
Donohue, '80, CEO & President,
DeltaQuest (Delta Dental); David H.
Long, '89, CEO & President, Liberty
Mutual Insurance Co.

Academics

Boston College's Carroll School of Management's "brand reputation" is second to none, especially "in the Boston area." "People around here think that it's Harvard," one student proudly reports. Boston College has everything an MBA student could want, including "Boston location, small class size, great culture, strong alumni network, mix of theoretical and practical learning, affordable tuition, [and] good scholarships." "Boston College offered me the best combination of ranking and scholarship," an Oil and Energy student explains. "Additionally, Boston is a great city and the campus is awesome." The "opportunities provided by the city of Boston" are ample, and the Carroll School of Management has a "strong influence" in the city's thriving business community.

The "reputation and quality of professors" is a big draw for Boston College. Professors wield "a diverse array of learning tools (lecture, cases, group exercises, etc.)" and "make themselves entirely available and are supportive of personal goals in addition to classroom objectives." The "excellent" administration also gets high marks from students. "They work hard to get you registered and setup [and] support the learning experience." Basically, at Boston College the faculty "care about the student's success and the administration is there to make it happen." The school is responsive to student feedback too, taking it "very seriously and implement[ing] changes accordingly." Although some students did wish the school would "offer [more] online courses."

The "small class sizes" provide intimate learning environments of business students and an "emphasis on hands-on learning." However, being housed in Boston College means students at the Carroll School of Management get "the perfect blend of a small program with large resources from a major academic institution." A financial services student sums their decision to attend thusly: "After talking to alumni, the pride they had in BC was something I knew I wanted to be a part of."

Career and Placement

Boston College boasts "the best alumni network in Boston" and "influential alumni" abound in the area. The school's career placement office "really goes above and beyond to help students find their way." Although some students say that the school has a harder time finding student work outside of Boston, others say "there are MANY opportunities presented by career services for students looking for jobs outside of the Boston area." The school's award winning "TechTrek West" combines classroom learning on the BC campus with a week-long field study to Silicon Valley. It is "a perfect way to both study the industry and network with some great people in the [tech] industry." However, one student warns that you may need to be a full-time student to reap the full benefits of the Carroll School of Management's job placement. "We get weekly emails with job/interview postings, but they are separated by full time and part time students," the student explains. "Part timers don't even get access to view the jobs that are 'reserved' for full time students."

Last year's graduating class had an average total compensation (salary plus signing bonuses) of over $102,882. Seventy-five percent of those found placement in the Northeast. The top five employers from the most recent class were Liberty Mutual Insurance Co., State Street, EMC, Boston Consulting Group, and John Hancock/ManuLife.

ADMISSIONS CONTACT: SHELLEY BURT, DIRECTOR OF GRADUATE ENROLLMENT
ADDRESS: FULTON HALL 315, 140 COMMONWEALTH AVENUE, CHESTNUT HILL, MA 02467-3808
PHONE: 617-552-3920 • FAX: 617-552-8078
E-MAIL: BCMBA@BC.EDU • WEBSITE: WWW.BC.EDU/MBA

Student Life and Environment

Boston College boasts an "unbelievably beautiful" campus, and the location in the bustling city of Boston has many obvious benefits. Carroll School of Management's students tend to be "motivated and outgoing" men and women in their "late twenties to early thirties." The student body is "focused because they are balancing work and school, but are friendly and want to network." The nature of the business program can make some students "competitive," yet most students are "willing to help" and "interested in advancing their careers and those of their peers." The environment is unlike "the cutthroat and pretentious culture that is infamous at other schools." "Everyone knows one another because it is a small class," and there are always events going on both on campus and off.

Admissions

Admission to the Carroll School of Management's renowned program is understandably competitive. For the 2012 class, the average GPA was 3.41 and the average GMAT was 666. The school does pride itself on a diverse and accomplished student body, so other factors, such as work experience come into play. While the school only recommends two years of work experience before applying, the average student had 4.4 years of professional experience before beginning their MBA.

FINANCIAL FACTS

Annual tuition	$38,416
Fees	$150
Cost of books	$1,500
Room & board	$18,690
% of students receiving aid	80
% of students receiving grants	80
Average student loan debt	$61,400

ADMISSIONS

Admissions Selectivity Rating	**91**
# of applications received	759
% applicants accepted	35
% acceptees attending	39
Average GMAT	666
Range of GMAT	630–700
Average GPA	3.41
TOEFL required of international students	Yes
Minimum TOEFL (paper/computer)	600/250
International application fee	$100
Application Deadline/Notification	
Round 1:	11/15 / 1/15
Round 2:	1/15 / 3/15
Round 3:	3/15 / 5/1
Round 4:	4/15 / 6/1
Deferment available	No
Transfer students accepted	Yes
Transfer application policy: 4 courses are accepted (with a grade of B or higher) from other AACSB MBA Programs.	
Non-fall admissions	No
Need-blind admissions	Yes

EMPLOYMENT PROFILE

Career Rating	96	Grads Employed by Function	% Avg. Salary
Percent employed at graduation	58	Marketing	(19%) $88,895
Percent employed 3 months after graduation	85	Operations	(5%) $92,800
		Consulting	(8%)$97,453
Average base starting salary	$94,147	Management	(11%) $106,364
Primary Source of Full-time Job Acceptances		Finance	(14%) $89,071
School-facilitated activities	39(57%)	HR	(2%)
Graduate-facilitated activities	30(43%)	MIS	(1%)
		Other	(2%)

Top 5 Employers Hiring Grads
Liberty Mutual Insurance Co.(4), State Street (4), EMC (3), Boston Consulting Group (2), John Hancock / ManuLife (2)

BOSTON UNIVERSITY
SCHOOL OF MANAGEMENT

GENERAL INFORMATION

Type of school	Private
Affiliation	No Affiliation
Academic calendar	Semester

SURVEY SAYS...

Students love Boston, MA, Good peer network, Happy students
Solid preparation in:
Teamwork

STUDENTS

Enrollment of parent institution	33,683
Enrollment of MBA Program	1,004
% male/female	67/33
% part-time	70
% international	35
Average age at entry	28
Average years work experience at entry	5.3

ACADEMICS

Academic Experience Rating	93
Profs interesting rating	89
Profs accesible rating	90
Student/faculty ratio	18:1
% female faculty	32

Joint Degrees

MS/MBA (dual degree MS in Information Systems and traditional MBA), 84 credits in 21 months; MBA/MS Television Management; MBA/MA International Relations; MBA/MS Manufacturing Engineering; MBA/MA Economics; MBA/MA Medical Sciences, 80 credits; MBA/JD, 116 credits; MBA/MPH, 85 credits; MBA/MD, 114 credits.

Prominent Alumni

Christine Poon, Vice Chairman, Pharmacy Group, Johnson & Johnson; Millard S. (Mickey) Drexler, Chairman and CEO, J. Crew Group, Inc.; Edward J. Zander, Chairman, Motorola; Walter Skowronski, President, Boeing Capital; Donald McGrath, Chairman & CEO, Bank of the West

Academics

The "well-rounded and comprehensive" MBA program at Boston University's School of Management offers students the opportunity to tailor their MBA program experience to their life and their career.

In the two-year full-time MBA program (an "interactive learning experience addressing the dynamics of global business"), students spend their first year in a fifty or so person cohort (second year classes are generally held in the evenings with part time students); the school also offers a popular dual-degree MS-MBA program in which students can earn a traditional MBA with a concentration and a Master of Science in Information Systems, an "excellent" Health Sector MBA, and a Public & Nonprofit MBA. The Evening program, which takes longer to complete but is designed for working students, is taught by the same professors as found in the full-time two-year program and offers the same electives.

The traditional MBA courses are typically case-based and are partnered with additional seminars in Ethics and Business Law, as well as Executive Communications and Executive Presentations that help to "really refine students' 'soft' business skills." "The administration does a good job getting speakers and industry connections to come on campus," says a student. Some professors "are really good," others are "just so-so," but the top ones "bring out the best out of the student in the class discussions." There are a good number of team projects throughout the semester ("truly the strength of the school"), and students appreciate the "ample opportunities…to work collaboratively."

The administration (helmed by a well-liked new Dean) "really demonstrates their interest and commitment to the BU MBA student experience": "Daily through pre-term, and progressively throughout classes and individual lectures and projects, BU MBA administration and faculty consistently surveys students for feedback, ratings and potential changes." "I have compared it to friends in other graduate programs at other schools. It is remarkable how few headaches I have as a result of the well-managed administration," says one student.

Career and Placement

Students admit that despite the good hire rates and a "gigantic" and "active" alumni network, some of the "counselors [at the Career Center] are not very good," though they are "working on getting better." Students praise the interview readiness programs as top notch.

The company recruiters that the school draws "tend more toward finance, health care and consulting" (in particular health care), and "could be more diverse" to accommodate those students with other focuses. "If you, as a student, want to find a job at TOP companies, you need to make a lot of efforts on your own," says one student. "The few well-known recruiters on campus get their pick of the litter," says another.

Recent employers of BU students are PricewaterhouseCoopers, Cognizant, Liberty Mutual, AT&T, and Deloitte.

ADMISSIONS CONTACT: PATTI CUDNEY, ASSISTANT DEAN OF GRADUATE ADMISSION
ADDRESS: 595 COMMONWEALTH AVENUE, BOSTON, MA 02215
PHONE: 617-353-2670 • FAX: 617-353-7368
E-MAIL: MBA@BU.EDU • WEBSITE: MANAGEMENT.BU.EDU

Student Life and Environment

The "friendly and helpful" crew here is "antithetical to the expected cutthroat nature of business/business school." Life at BU is "incredibly social"; there are "school council dances, cohort parties, and classmates always putting together nights out to sporting events, bars, clubs, and fun places in Boston." From basketball tournaments to bake offs to bowling nights, the cohort competitions also "really bring the MBA class together." The student body has a large international component (particularly Asia).

BU is located centrally in an "amazing city," (also the epicenter of a healthcare hub), and does a great job of effectively leveraging the numerous surrounding schools. Students "have many places to meet and often participate in a lot of off-campus activities thanks to the incredible learning environment the city creates." Networking among Boston local professional groups is a huge benefit to getting a degree here.

Admissions

Admissions to BU's MBA programs are highly competitive, with only around 30 percent of applicants receiving an offer of admission each year. The mean GMAT score for last year's entering class was 680 (with a 50 percent mid-range of 640 to 720), the average GPA was 3.35, and students had an average of around five years of work experience.

FINANCIAL FACTS

Annual tuition	$42,400
Fees	$534
Cost of books	$4,310
Room & board	$12,070
% of students receiving aid	83
% of first-year students receiving aid	81
% of students receiving grants	71
Average award package	$39,662
Average grant	$22,617
Average loan	$38,534
Average student loan debt	$71,000

ADMISSIONS

Admissions Selectivity Rating	92
# of applications received	1,236
% applicants accepted	33
% acceptees attending	36
Average GMAT	680
Range of GMAT	640–720
Average GPA	3.35
TOEFL required of international students	Yes
Minimum TOEFL (paper/computer)	600/250
Application fee	$125
International application fee	$125
Regular application deadline	3/11
Regular application notification	4/12
Application Deadline/Notification	
Round 1:	10/29 / 12/14
Round 2:	1/7 / 2/15
Round 3:	3/11 / 4/12
Deferment available	No
Transfer students accepted	Yes
Transfer application policy: Classes must be from an AACSB-accredited institution.	
Non-fall admissions	Yes
Need-blind admissions	Yes

EMPLOYMENT PROFILE

Career Rating	95	**Grads Employed by Function% Avg. Salary**	
Percent employed 3 months		Marketing	(27%) $83,170
after graduation	87	Operations	(6%) $84,000
Average base starting salary	$93,591	Consulting	(23%) $107,335
Primary Source of Full-time Job Acceptances		Management	(14%) $87,346
School-facilitated activities	44(51%)	Finance	(17%) $102,912
Graduate-facilitated activities	33(40%)	HR	(4%)
Unknown	13(9%)	MIS	(9%) $91,029

Top 5 Employers Hiring Grads
PricewaterhouseCoopers(6), Cognizant (5), Liberty Mutual (3), AT&T (2), Deloitte (2)

BOWLING GREEN STATE UNIVERSITY
COLLEGE OF BUSINESS ADMINISTRATION

GENERAL INFORMATION
Type of school   Public
Affiliation   No Affiliation
Academic calendar   Semester

SURVEY SAYS...
Cutting-edge classes
Solid preparation in:
Doing business in a global economy

STUDENTS
Enrollment of parent
  institution   21,071
Enrollment of MBA Program   144
% male/female   70/30
% out-of-state   3
% part-time   76
% underrepresented minority   18
% international   33
Average age at entry   30
Average years work experience
  at entry   7.0

ACADEMICS
Academic Experience Rating   92
Profs interesting rating   85
Profs accesible rating   92
% female faculty   31
% underrepresented minority
  faculty   29
% part-time faculty   4

Joint Degrees
MBA (full-time) with specialization
in Accounting or Finance, 18
months

Prominent Alumni
William Ingram, CEO, White Castle
Systems; Cheryl Krueger, Founder,
Cheryl and Company; David May,
President, S.C. Johnson and
Company; Richard Stephens,
President (retired) Cooper Tire and
Rubber Company; John Meier, CEO
(retired), Libbey Glass

Academics

Whether you choose to enter the full-time, part-time, or Executive MBA program at Bowling Green State University you will experience efficient, practical, instruction at a great value. Offering a crash course in business, Bowling Green's full-time MBA "is only 12 months long," and is comprised of a series of foundation, core, and capstone courses. Tuition is reasonable and, for many students, graduate assistantships can cover "the cost of tuition, and [pay] an additional living stipend." Given the program's accelerated time frame, low cost, and scholarship options, students say, "It is probably [a] much better bang for the buck than most two-year programs (even at Ivy League schools.)" Similarly, the school's 23-month Professional MBA is "perfect for busy, working professionals." Designed for students with a minimum of three years in the workforce, "The location and times are extremely convenient and the cost is very reasonable," making it an affordable way to boost your career prospects in Bowling Green.

While convenience and value are large part of the equation, students assure us that practicality isn't the only reason they chose BGSU. For many, the school's small size and community atmosphere is a major draw. Here, the administration is accessible, and the school is "very well-run and very user-friendly." A current student shares: "I have had a very positive experience working with everyone in the college from the secretaries to the dean." Thanks to uniformly small class sizes, students are "encouraged to work with our fellow students through group projects and presentations." A current student adds, "We have a well-rounded cohort and the class spends a lot of time debating all kinds of issues relating to the material." No matter which program you enter, you'll benefit from friendly professors, who "share a love and enthusiasm for teaching as well as helping their students to [achieve] success." Providing both rigor and support, "The program is challenging (as it should be), but the professors are encouraging, treat us as professionals, and make themselves available outside of class and office hours to aid in our success." Successful in the real world—not just the ivory tower—Bowling Green's "knowledgeable and friendly" faculty "consistently incorporate[s] useful information and real-life scenarios into their instruction, making each class valuable to my future career." A student in the Professional MBA program agrees: "Even though I've been working for over 25 years, I have taken away a good deal of information to apply on the job." Despite the strength of the curriculum, some would like the school to offer "more areas of specialization" (currently, BGSU offers two areas of concentration in accounting, and finance".

In addition to the full-time and part-time programs at Bowling Green, the Executive MBA Program gets top marks from seasoned professionals, who say "the course work is very challenging and stimulating" and "professors are extremely knowledgeable and friendly." To make everything smooth and simple, "All course registration and book purchases are handled by the staff for the Executive MBA program, easing the burden on working professionals." While EMBA students "only spend Friday, Saturday and Sunday on campus once a month," they say, "Subjects are taught on task and time is used wisely."

Career and Placement

Most students in the Professional and Executive MBA programs are already working full time when they begin the program at Bowling Green, and therefore, many are not actively seeking employment. For full-time students, career planning is woven into the curriculum at Bowling Green State University through practical courses in leadership, technology, and other applied skills, as well as a series of professional development seminars. Through the business school, students may also contact career development specialists to help them with their job search.

In addition to the assistance they receive within the business school, the Bowling Green State University Career Center assists the undergraduate and graduate community with their job search through career counseling, job and internship fairs, campus recruiting and career development workshops.

Student Life and Environment

For Professional MBA students, "Classes are not held on the main campus, but rather at a newly renovated, state-of-the-art complex that is approximately 25 miles north of the main campus." This facility is "convenient, well-maintained," and offers "full access to all technology (wireless web access, software, printers, etc.) to ensure success." Even though they attend school off-site, part-time students say, "The administration office does a good job of keeping us informed of what is happening on campus." Unfortunately, most part-time students agree that between "working full time and going to school two nights a week, plus homework and reading, there is no time left for other club activities."

On the main campus, "The business school has made great strides in improving facilities," though some would like the school to improve the "building appearance and technology amenities" in the classrooms. Full-time students benefit from "an active student body" and "a diverse array of activities on campus such as sporting events that we can access for free." On campus and in the surrounding town, there are "a lot of students to socialize with." On that note, students say Bowling Green "is very much a college town, with a good bar scene" and an affordable cost of living.

Admissions

To apply to BGSU's graduate business programs, students must submit an application form, an official undergraduate transcript, GMAT scores, a resume, and two professional recommendations. The school also requests a personal statement, outlining the applicant's objectives in pursuing an MBA and explaining how they might contribute to the program. In some cases, applicants to the Executive MBA who have extensive work experience (10 years or more) may be exempt from submitting GMAT scores.

FINANCIAL FACTS

Annual tuition	$10,168
Fees	$1,414
Cost of books	$1,500
% of students receiving grants	88

ADMISSIONS

Admissions Selectivity Rating	**83**
# of applications received	108
% applicants accepted	79
% acceptees attending	89
Average GMAT	547
Range of GMAT	480–590
Average GPA	3.30
TOEFL required of international students	Yes
Minimum TOEFL (paper/computer)	550/213
Application fee	$45
International application fee	$75
Early application deadline	2/15
Regular application deadline	3/15
Deferment available	Yes
Maximum length of deferment	1 year
Transfer students accepted	Yes
Transfer application policy: Students in the MBA programs (full-time, professional, and executive) are limited to a maximum of nine graduate credit hours of transfer credit from AACSB accredited institutions.	
Non-fall admissions	Yes
Need-blind admissions	Yes

BRANDEIS UNIVERSITY
BRANDEIS INTERNATIONAL BUSINESS SCHOOL

GENERAL INFORMATION
Type of school   Private
Affiliation   nonsectarian
                Jewish-sponsored college
Academic calendar   Semester

SURVEY SAYS...
Cutting-edge classes
Solid preparation in:
Finance, Teamwork, Quantitative
skills, Doing business in a global
economy

STUDENTS
Enrollment of MBA Program	75
% male/female	60/40
% part-time	0
% underrepresented minority	1
% international	75
Average age at entry	27
Average years work experience at entry	3.9

ACADEMICS
Academic Experience Rating	**91**
Profs interesting rating	93
Profs accesible rating	84
Student/faculty ratio	8:1
% female faculty	43
% part-time faculty	17

Academics

At Brandeis International Business School, "learning is not limited to theoretical concepts. Keeping education connected to the real world of business and policy is an integral part of the IBS experience." The University offers students a "strong foundation in economics and finance." Moreover, Brandeis is renowned for its "global focus," and MBA candidates here are privy to "a truly global platform for professionals who seek advancement in international business." Indeed, many people here greatly appreciate that the school "has students from more than 70 countries." It provides an "excellent cultural mix" and "terrific exposure [to other] cultures." Overall, the "academic rigor can be quite high, but it, in part, depends on what course load you choose to take and how much you want to challenge yourself."

Importantly, Brandeis students are full of praise for their professors. Certainly, they "are well respected in their fields" and are "always available to provide further guidance." And one content second year student adds, "The professors are very friendly, extremely smart, and are concerned that we graduate with a great job. The open-door policy is very true." This admiration also extends to Brandeis' administration. As a first year student happily shares, "The administration is very proactive in organizing the events at the college and making sure that everyone participates in these events." And another second-year student quickly follows up stating, "Whatever you want to get done, the school's administration will help you achieve it."

Career and Placement

Brandeis' IBS Career Center strives to help their students land plum internships and employment opportunities. The office provides a number of services, from access to online libraries and databases to career education and advising. Students frequently take advantage of mock interview lessons, company information sessions, and panel presentations. Additionally, there are a handful of networking events, the culmination of which is the school's annual on-campus career fair. Of course, despite the Career Center's best efforts, many students wish they would be more proactive about attracting more companies. As one first-year student shared, "Although the Career Services Office does a great job, the possibilities to get paid internships are limited. From my point of view, most local and small companies recruit here." Additionally, a second-year student chimes in that he'd like to see "job placement increase for international students in the United States." However, an optimistic and hopeful student counters, "It is definitely a young school, but the rate that we are growing with the intelligent people graduating from here, in a few years we will have a larger alumni network of extremely successful professionals, who will carry the Brandeis IBS name throughout the world as a premier education in international business."

Employers that frequently hire Brandeis grads include BNP Paribas, Citibank, General Electric, Goldman Sachs, JP Morgan/Chase, Lehman Brothers, NERA Economic Consulting, United Airlines, and Watson Wyatt.

ADMISSIONS CONTACT: HOLLY L. CHASE, ASSISTANT DEAN OF ADMISSIONS AND FINANCIAL AID
ADDRESS: 415 SOUTH STREET, MS 032, WALTHAM, MA 02454
PHONE: 781-736-2252 • FAX: 781-736-2263
E-MAIL: ADMISSION@LEMBERG.BRANDEIS.EDU • WEBSITE: WWW.BRANDEIS.EDU/GLOBAL

Student Life and Environment

If pressed to describe their peers in one word, most MBA candidates at Brandeis would define their fellow students as "diverse." Indeed, the program is "hugely international," and "everyone here is open to new experiences." By and large, people find their classmates "cooperative" and "collaborative." And one second year breathes a sigh of relief explaining, "They are friendly, and the environment is encouraging as opposed to competitive." One slightly chagrined student does note that "the average student age is younger than I had expected." Another student concurs, adding that some classmates are "a bit too young and a bit too inexperienced to be in business school." Others disagree and quickly assert that their fellow students "bring interesting perspectives" and argue that there are plenty of "people with different professional backgrounds [to] enrich discussions." Perhaps this student sums up his peers best, "They are people I want to spend time with outside of the school."

Life at Brandeis moves "very fast." Students are "constantly multi-tasking between class work, group projects, and club events." Certainly there is much to participate in. As one MBA candidate highlights, "There are lots of clubs, and importantly, lots of opportunities of opening ones on your own. TGIFs and group activities at the International Graduate Business School are a good time to get together and relax after pretty stressful and hectic (although rewarding and energizing at the same time) study weeks at Brandeis." Additionally, students love to take advantage of Brandeis' proximity to Boston. As one student reveals, "Access to Boston is great. The school helps out on the weekend by providing busses, which run later than public transportation."

Admissions

Though Brandeis' MBA program is relatively new, competition for that coveted acceptance letter is still fierce. The admissions committee is on the hunt for applicants who can demonstrate both a keen analytical ability and proven leadership skills. Additionally, admissions officers will carefully assess your undergraduate record and expect strong GMAT or GRE scores. Further, given the curriculum and the makeup of the student body, it's important to display an interest in international issues. It is recommended that applicants have between two and five years of work experience. It is also expected that prospective students took intro micro- and macroeconomics and statistics while in undergrad. Finally, most international students will need to take the TOEFL exam. A score of 600 on the paper-based exam, 250 on the computer-based, or 100 on the IBT exam is usually required.

FINANCIAL FACTS

Annual tuition	$40,514
Cost of books	$12,000
Room & board	
(on/off-campus)	$6,000/$12,000
% of students receiving aid	84
% of first-year students	
receiving aid	80
% of students receiving grants	84
Average award package	$23,886
Average grant	$13,886
Average loan	$10,250
Average student loan debt	$20,500

ADMISSIONS

Admissions Selectivity Rating	90
# of applications received	191
Range of GMAT	520–640
TOEFL required of	
international students	Yes
Minimum TOEFL	
(paper/computer)	600/250
Application fee	$55
International application fee	$55
Early application deadline	11/15
Early notification date	12/20
Regular application deadline	2/15
Regular application notification	3/15
Deferment available	Yes
Maximum length	
of deferment	1 year
Transfer students accepted	Yes
Transfer application policy: We will accept transfer credit by waiving required courses.	
Non-fall admissions	Yes
Need-blind admissions	No

EMPLOYMENT PROFILE		
Career Rating	86	**Top 5 Employers Hiring Grads**
Percent employed at graduation	46	EMC(4), Observant LLC (consulting) (2), Knight
Percent employed 3 months		Libertas (part of Knight Capital Group) (2)
after graduation	72	
Average base starting salary	$66,962	

BRIGHAM YOUNG UNIVERSITY
MARRIOTT SCHOOL OF MANAGEMENT

GENERAL INFORMATION
Type of school   Private
Affiliation   Church of Jesus Christ
                of Latter-day Saints
Academic calendar   2 Semester

SURVEY SAYS...
Friendly students, Good peer network, Happy students
Solid preparation in:
Finance, Teamwork

STUDENTS
Enrollment of parent
  institution   32,947
Enrollment of MBA Program   329
% male/female   85/16
% out-of-state   4
% underrepresented minority   6
% international   14
Average age at entry   29
Average years work experience
  at entry   4.2

ACADEMICS
Academic Experience Rating   93
Profs interesting rating   95
Profs accesible rating   91
Student/faculty ratio   2:1
% female faculty   17
% underrepresented minority
  faculty   1
% part-time faculty   36

Joint Degrees
MBA/JD, 4 years; MBA/MS, IPD
Program with Engineering
Department, 3 years; MAcc/JD, 4
years; MPA/JD, 4 years.

Prominent Alumni
Andrea Thomas, Senior VP
Sustainability, Wal-mart; D. Fraser
Bullock, Founder/Managing Director,
Sorenson Capital; Robert Parsons,
Executive VP & CFO, Exclusive
Resorts; David W. Checketts,
Chairman, Sports Capital Partners;
Bill P. Benac Sr., Partner, Crescent
Equity, Inc.

Academics

The Marriott School of Management at Brigham Young University is a prestigious business school, known for its "focus on ethics, entrepreneurship, international business, and creative course work." Located on BYU's main campus in Provo, Utah, the MBA program recruits top-quality teaching staff, well versed in both academia and real-world business. "Some professors from Harvard push very hard on case," while others spend more time discussing business theory and ethics. Either way, critical thinking is emphasized, and "class materials and case studies are organized and presented in a method that solicits strong group discussions and forces students to think outside of their comfort zone in analyzing problems and complex business situations."

BYU students note that, "The dual emphasis on excellence in publishing and on effective teaching is very demanding on the faculty." Even so, professors take the time to build interesting lesson plans, and class "presentations are witty and memorable." You'll never snooze through a lecture, as BYU's "professors are absolutely outstanding and able to communicate ideas and to keep class engaging." Classes routinely incorporate discussion, and there is a "strong focus on group work" throughout the program. Additionally, "Experiential learning opportunities are excellent" at BYU. "Activities, field studies, cases, and opportunities to work with companies are really prevalent," giving students a chance to apply their studies outside the classroom. A student details, "I have participated in a student-run venture capital fund that provides opportunities to work on real deals and develop great analytical skills."

"Being an LDS-sponsored institution, ethics and honesty are a regular and critical part of class discussions," and faith ties the community together. Across the board, BYU professors have a "deep, vested interest in their students." A current student recounts, "I have had many professors meet with me to help with assignments, career advice, and job searches. I'm amazed at how caring the professors have been." Overseeing a large MBA program takes some brawn, and the "administration is extremely understaffed" at BYU, and therefore, "runs very lean." However, when it comes to overall attitude, students are pleased to report that, "The administration and professors are on the same page; they are innovative, well organized, and strive for continual improvement." Best of all, BYU won't break the bank. Savvy business students are pleased to point out that, "Tuition is subsidized by the Church of Jesus Christ of Latter Day Saints," making BYU a surprisingly affordable option.

Career and Placement

The Marriott School's Career Center offers a myriad of services to MBA candidates, including "top notch" career counselors, interview and resume preparation, and access to ongoing networking events. The school also manages a unique student-run job preparation program, through which "second-year MBA students are assigned four to five first-year students to guide them in their job search process." A massive boon to MBA candidates, "The alumni network is huge, very engaged, and eager to help students get into jobs they want." At the same time, the school is located in Provo, Utah, "far from big cities where, usually, big recruiters come in search of potential recruits." On top of that, "There are only two recruitment advisers for the entire program," so students have to do some legwork if they want to land a job.

BYU students benefit from a "great network and placement rate upon graduation." In fact, while the numbers depend on what industry you choose, the median base salary for BYU graduates hovers around $89,000. Marketing and sales, finance and accounting, and human resources are the most popular fields for graduates. Hewlett Packard, Ensign Group, Intel, and Cisco are among the biggest employers. In addition, thanks to the school's focus on entrepreneurship and innovation, "Many MBA students have gone on to work for these start-ups as opposed to the major corporations."

Student Life and Environment

BYU students are "very accomplished professionally and personally," and they bring an "optimistic, happy, and confident" vibe to campus. A close-knit community of students, MBA candidates are "genuinely concerned about the well being of others" and "There is a culture of helping each other through personal and career-related struggles." Due to the school's religious affiliation with the Church of Jesus Christ of Latter Day Saints, there is a "very strong religious culture" at BYU, and many students take a great interest in philanthropic projects. Between classmates, competition is minimized: "There is a feeling of wanting to be the best, but not at the expense of leaving others behind."

Students at BYU aptly balance academics with their personal lives. For MBA candidates, "BYU is rigorous but allows time for career exploration and club involvement." Helping to foster relationships between students, the school sponsors "rock climbing outings, intramural sports, women in business events, international student activities, ski days, singles retreats, case competitions, networking events, conferences, [and] job seeking trips to various cities." "The majority of students are married and have children" by the time they enter graduate school, and many gladly note that, "The spouse organization has lots of activities and strengthens the whole experience." As a result, "The program feels more like a family than a school program." Even so, single students note the "difficulty getting married students to work in the evenings on group projects."

Admissions

According to BYU's own data, a student's GMAT score is the most accurate predictor of "academic" success in the graduate program. Therefore, test scores, in addition to academic record, are very important. Currently, the average GMAT score is 673. All competitive applicants will also be invited to interview with the admissions staff. Undergraduate major is not important; however, "some incoming students may be required to take financial accounting and quantitative analysis courses online."

FINANCIAL FACTS

Annual tuition (in-state/ out-of-state)	$10,280/$20,560
Fees	$0
Cost of books	$1,600
Room & board	$10,600

ADMISSIONS

Admissions Selectivity Rating	95
# of applications received	474
% applicants accepted	42
% acceptees attending	80
Average GMAT	671
Range of GMAT	640–710
Average GPA	3.50
TOEFL required of international students	Yes
Minimum TOEFL (paper/computer)	590/240
Application fee	$50
International application fee	$50
Application Deadline/Notification	
Round 1:	12/1 / 2/1
Round 2:	1/15 / 3/15
Round 3:	3/1 / 5/1
Round 4:	5/1 / 7/1
Deferment available	Yes
Maximum length of deferment	2 years
Transfer students accepted	Yes
Transfer application policy: 15 credit hours of approved graduate-level courses, no pass/fail grades, and a minimum grade of B	
Non-fall admissions	No
Need-blind admissions	Yes

EMPLOYMENT PROFILE

Career Rating	95	Grads Employed by Function	% Avg. Salary
Percent employed at graduation	55	Marketing	(24%) $87,197
Percent employed 3 months after graduation	76	Operations	(6%) $89,333
		Consulting	(8%) $91,000
Average base starting salary	$87,573	Management	(8%) $79,125
Primary Source of Full-time Job Acceptances		Finance	(36%) $91,393
School-facilitated activities	70(70%)	HR	(12%) $82,222
Graduate-facilitated activities	30(30%)	MIS	(1%)
		Other	(5%) $75,380

Top 5 Employers Hiring Grads
Adobe Systems Inc.(8), PricewaterhouseCoopers (4), Exxon-Mobil (3), Symantec (3), Johnson & Johnson (3)

BROCK UNIVERSITY
FACULTY OF BUSINESS

GENERAL INFORMATION

Type of school	Public
Affiliation	No Affiliation
Academic calendar	Semester

SURVEY SAYS...
Friendly students, Students love St. Catharines, ON
Solid preparation in:
Accounting, Teamwork, Communication/interpersonal skills, Presentation skills

STUDENTS

Enrollment of parent institution	18,512
Enrollment of MBA Program	94
% part-time	36
% international	11
Average age at entry	26
Average years work experience at entry	4.0

ACADEMICS

Academic Experience Rating	**85**
Profs interesting rating	79
Profs accesible rating	89
Student/faculty ratio	1:1
% female faculty	24

Academics

Boasting "an excellent reputation for its business degree, especially in accounting," Ontario's Brock University offers "a great learning environment with many opportunities" to a youngish student body. Because it's a relatively new program, the Brock MBA is especially open to innovation; students praise the curriculum for "encouraging fresh ideas" and the faculty for its "innovative approaches to teaching."

MBAs also love Brock's "small class sizes, which enable professors to recognize students' strengths and weaknesses and permit students to approach professors when they need help. It is a relaxed learning environment" in which "an atmosphere of trust between students and school personnel" prevails. Brock profs "are knowledgeable and well-respected in their fields" and "do an exceptional job of presenting the material in an attention-grabbing style." Students appreciate how their instructors "always have time to talk outside of class and are extremely helpful."

The Brock MBA includes a sequence of required courses and an option for specialization in one of four "streams": accounting, finance, human resource management, and marketing. Students may also opt for a general MBA. Students may choose to replace up to three of their specialization courses with independent research projects; such projects are subject to the approval of the dean and the MBA Committee. Students may attend on a full-time or part-time basis. The full-time degree can be completed in two years; the part-time degree must be completed within six years. Part-timers who adhere to the suggested schedule—two courses during each of the Fall and Winter terms, one course during the Spring term—can finish the program in four years.

Career and Placement

The Faculty of Business at Brock University maintains a Business Career Development Office to serve all undergraduates and graduates enrolled at the faculty. The office manages the Graduate Recruitment Program for MBA students; through this program, students have access to employer information sessions and on-campus interviews. A Career Expo in the fall brings employers to campus for recruiting purposes. The office also offers resume review, interviewing and job search workshops, online job search tools, and assistance with international job placement. Brock offers a co-op MBA to students who are at the university for at least two semesters of study (beginning in the fall term) and who maintain at least a 75 average in the program. Co-op provides access to additional workshops, seminars, and a speaker series in addition to co-op placement. The program is open to international students.

Student Life and Environment

Brock's student body "is extremely diverse," with "many international students [who arrive] through the International Student Program and through exchanges." Students also bring "a diverse set of experiences" to the program: "Some students come to the program with many years of experience, while others bring a more academic perspective to the program." Some feel the balance needs to shift in this area, reporting that "way too many students have no work experience and are straight out of undergrad." Everyone agrees that "some here, especially the part-time students, have great work experience and input to contribute."

ADMISSIONS CONTACT: ANDREA JOHNSON, GRAD. MARKETING & COMMUNICATIONS COORDINATOR
ADDRESS: TARO HALL, 500 GLENRIDGE AVENUE, ST. CATHARINES, ON L2S 3A1 CANADA
PHONE: 888-528-0746 • FAX: 905-688-4286
E-MAIL: MBA@BROCKU.CA • WEBSITE: WWW.BROCKU.CA/BUSINESS

Brock's student-run Graduate Business Council "does an excellent job of giving us opportunities to connect outside of the classroom. They organize pub nights and socials as well as organize us to compete in business case competitions." Campus amenities include "state-of-the-art" gymnasiums, fitness centers, an Olympic size swimming pool, squash and tennis courts, outdoor fields, and a hiking trail system that runs through campus and beyond, leading to the Niagara Escarpment. Students report that school facilities "are great for athletics, food, and study areas."

Hometown St. Catharines, located a mere 12 miles from Niagara Falls and just 70 miles from Toronto, "has a great lifestyle," with "tons of trendy nightclubs in St. Catharines and Niagara Falls." Students describe the overall vibe as "easy-going" with "not too much hustle and bustle," which they ascribe to "the nature of being located in St. Catharines." The city is accommodating enough that "many students spend a lot of time off campus."

Admissions

Admission to the MBA program at Brock is based on five main criteria. The quality of one's undergraduate education is most important; Brock seeks students with at least a 3.0 undergraduate GPA. A minimum GMAT score of 550 is required, as are three letters of recommendation from professors and/or supervisors at work; a personal statement; and a resume. Applications are assessed holistically; strength in one area may be sufficient to compensate for weaknesses elsewhere, according to the school's website. Professional experience, though preferred, is not required. Those whose first language is not English must demonstrate English proficiency through the TOEFL or TWE; students with TOEFL scores between 570 and 620 may be admitted conditionally pending completion of an ELS program).

FINANCIAL FACTS

Annual tuition (in-state/ out-of-state)	$11,255/$21,978
Fees	$345
Cost of books	$1,000
Room & board	$10,000

ADMISSIONS

Admissions Selectivity Rating	**83**
# of applications received	133
% applicants accepted	60
% acceptees attending	63
Average GMAT	603
Range of GMAT	540–680
Average GPA	3.50
TOEFL required of international students	Yes
Minimum TOEFL (paper/computer)	620/260
Application fee	$125
International application fee	$125
Deferment available	Yes
Maximum length of deferment	1 year
Transfer students accepted	Yes
Transfer application policy: All transfer applications must submit the same documentation as regular applicants. Their transcripts are assessed for transfer credits (up to 10) during the admissions review process.	
Non-fall admissions	Yes
Need-blind admissions	Yes

EMPLOYMENT PROFILE

Career Rating	87	**Top 5 Employers Hiring Grads**
Percent employed at graduation	60	Royal Bank of Canada, CIBC, ScotiaBank,
Percent employed 3 months after graduation	93	Hydro One, Loblaw Co.
Average base starting salary	$78,500	

BRYANT UNIVERSITY
GRADUATE SCHOOL OF BUSINESS

Academics

Bryant University's MBA program is "designed with working professionals in mind," according to the school, and students report that the school definitely lives up to this reputation. The "structured part-time program [makes] it easy to balance the rigors of graduate study with the reality of maintaining a full-time job," one student explains.

The part-time MBA at Bryant is structured as a cohort program, "where students are accepted to the school as a class and move through the entire program together." Students complete all core courses as part of a single team (although "some professors allow teams to change members") before "becoming separated in electives." Most students find the cohort system a huge plus, saying it promotes "a lower dropout rate, better student interaction, and deeper relationships and networks with students." One writes, "The cohort approach is excellent. I have built great relationships with my fellow students, and teachers are in tune with where classes stand in the learning process, making the flow from semester to semester seamless."

Bryant recently added a full-time one-year program. The first class graduated in 2010, and some members say of their experience, " Being the first year there were some kinks, but they have tried to put together a program that is not only academically beneficial but also gives us some real-world exposure."

Students note that "Bryant has a very good reputation" in the region. Professors "have industry experience, they are not only theoretical or academic," and most "are enthusiastic...the passion they exude filters throughout the class." Administrators "are very open and approachable. We recently voted on electives, and there is one that wasn't selected. Instead of being stuck, the dean is setting aside time to consider how we might be able to add the course. I've been very pleased that this type of response has been the norm [for] any issues that arise and not just a glowing example." Academically, "the environment is challenging, yet fair, and [students are] well-supported. It is a great investment." As one student sums up, "Overall Bryant is probably the best value MBA in New England outside of Cambridge/Boston. The campus is very clean and safe, the professors are all gray hairs with decades of experience in the real world, and the library and gym facilities are exceptional."

Career and Placement

The Amica Center for Career Education serves the undergraduate students, graduate students, and alumni of Bryant University. The office provides counseling services, assessment instruments, and workshops on resume writing, interviewing, and job-search skills. The Center maintains a career services library and facilitates contact with alumni through the school's Alumni Career Network. It should be noted that the Bryant MBA is designed for working professionals, many of whom are looking to improve their positions with their current employers rather than seeking new jobs. The school draws students from a number of local employers, including Amgen, Amica Mutual Insurance, Citizens Bank, Davol, Fidelity Investments, Gilbane Building Company, Perot Systems, Rogers Corporation, Stanley Bostich, Tyco Healthcare, and Zebra Technologies.

ADMISSIONS CONTACT: KRISTOPHER SULLIVAN, ASSISTANT DEAN OF THE GRADUATE SCHOOL
ADDRESS: 1150 DOUGLAS PIKE, SMITHFIELD, RI 02917-1284
PHONE: 401-232-6230 • FAX: 401-232-6494
E-MAIL: GRADPROG@BRYANT.EDU • WEBSITE: WWW.BRYANT.EDU

Student Life and Environment

Located in "a safe rural setting," Bryant's campus is "beautiful and inviting, not too big but not too small." "All the buildings and grounds are maintained impeccably," one student reports. The campus is also "on the cutting edge of technology," with "every room completely equipped." Bryant has an active undergraduate campus life, but opinion is mixed on the extent to which Bryant MBAs take advantage. Some students observe that "Students in the graduate program are very removed from the undergraduate programs and students. For the most part, graduate students are not involved in campus life, although attendance is high at 'graduate only' events. Most graduate students do not get involved with campus organizations," though all this may change in coming years as the full-time, one-year MBA program expands. On the other hand, a student in the one-year program notes that "Life at Bryant is very community-focused. The school tries to involve all students in all activities, such as on-campus presenters, homecoming activities, etc."

Though the extent of graduate student involvement on campus might be up for debate, the on-campus diversity is not. There's "a really strong multicultural element" at Bryant. In the part-time program, "students range in age from early 20s to late 50s," and many have "more than 10 years of business experience. The diversity of professional backgrounds brings an added element to the class, as we have many engineers in the program." Students tend to be "competitive" and "like to challenge one another to promote and foster positive results. It's a very team-orientated program."

Admissions

Applicants to graduate programs at Bryant University must provide the Admissions Department with the following materials: a completed application form; a personal statement of objectives (no less than 500 words long); a current resume; one letter of recommendation from a professional who can evaluate your skills and potential; official transcripts for all previous undergraduate and graduate work (regardless of whether it resulted in a degree); and an official GMAT score report. In addition to the above, international students must also provide a statement of finances, professional translation and interpretation of any foreign language transcripts, and, for those whose first language is not English and who did not earn an undergraduate degree from an English-speaking institution, an official TOEFL score report. An interview is "strongly encouraged."

FINANCIAL FACTS

Annual tuition	$37,304
Cost of books	$1,200
Room & board	$13,200
% of students receiving aid	33
% of first-year students receiving aid	56
% of students receiving grants	3
Average award package	$29,093
Average grant	$9,624
Average loan	$19,501
Average student loan debt	$30,415

ADMISSIONS

Admissions Selectivity Rating	78
# of applications received	172
% applicants accepted	61
% acceptees attending	84
Average GMAT	519
Range of GMAT	470–557
Average GPA	3.15
TOEFL required of international students	Yes
Minimum TOEFL (paper/computer)	580/237
International application fee	$80
Early application deadline	4/15
Regular application deadline	7/15
Deferment available	Yes
Maximum length of deferment	1 year
Transfer students accepted	Yes
Transfer application policy: Transfer credits are limited to two courses taken within the last 3 years with a grade of B (3.0) or better from an AACSB-International accredited master's program.	
Non-fall admissions	Yes
Need-blind admissions	Yes

BUTLER UNIVERSITY
COLLEGE OF BUSINESS

GENERAL INFORMATION
Type of school   Private
Affiliation   No Affiliation
Academic calendar   Semester

SURVEY SAYS...
Students love Indianapolis, IN, Good peer network
Solid preparation in:
Doing business in a global economy

STUDENTS
Enrollment of parent institution	4,771
Enrollment of MBA Program	225
% male/female	70/30
% out-of-state	0
% part-time	97
% underrepresented minority	9
% international	3
Average age at entry	30
Average years work experience at entry	6.8

ACADEMICS
Academic Experience Rating	**79**
Profs interesting rating	81
Profs accesible rating	86
Student/faculty ratio	20:1
% female faculty	13
% underrepresented minority faculty	17
% part-time faculty	35

Joint Degrees
PharmD/MBA-6 years full-time to completion.

Prominent Alumni
Lynda Smirz, Chief Medical officer, IU Health-North; Hugh Lytle, President & CEO, Univita Health; Dennis Bassett, CEO, Indiana, Ohio & Kentucky region, JP Morgan Chase; Robert Postlethwait, Retired President, Ely Lilly & Co, Neuroscience Product Group; Jim Morris, President, Pacers Sports & Entertainment

Academics

Boasting a "broad program to introduce students to all business specialties," Butler's focus on "applying real world experiences to the classroom" provides an MBA experience that makes it "very popular" for residents of the region. Flexibility is key here. As one student notes, "If you want a concentration that is not offered, professors will work with you to tailor your education needs/wishes." Majors are offered in finance, international business, leadership, and marketing, though students must also take a core curriculum. This is launched by the Gateway Experience, a full day foray into the operations of a local business followed by student analysis. That sort of experience is typical of what students at Butler will enjoy; "executive mentors (are) provided," and professors "have been around the block a time or two," ensuring that this program "attracts a diversely experienced student body."

If flexibility is a hallmark of Butler's education, so is balance. Expect a "good balance of difficult and moderately easy classes." As one student noted, in some classes, "I didn't need to open the book but in some courses I read every page of the book." A helpful, "responsive" administration is a frequent target for praise among students. Administrators here "don't ignore you and always try to be helpful," ensuring they "work with students on every aspect. A large school wouldn't do that, but Butler does." This school's leadership "is very willing to make integrating the learning experience with busy careers and family lives" a priority, and it shows in the number of students who juggle active careers and busy class schedules. "They work with students to make sure they are successful while considering students' personal lives."

"Real life business application in the classroom is integral to learning at Butler," an approach led by "both adjunct and tenured professors who offer a balance of real world work experience as well as strong academic thought." Some students, whose comments largely focused on fill-in teachers, note that there are "one or two bad apples," but overall educators here "will really push you to learn stuff practical to the modern business world."

Career and Placement

For students in the Midwest in particular, Butler provides good inroads to a career. "Being in the program is helpful for networking with people in other companies (big and small) around Indianapolis," one student commented. When Forbes recently ranked the 200 largest metropolitan areas in the United States to determine which were the best places for business and careers, Indianapolis ranked in the top ten. That is a major help with job prospects. "There are thousands of top companies right in our backyard," a student noted. With opportunities to get hands-on experience with many of these companies and "guests that bring relevant speakers to class," Butler students enjoy good exposure to strong employers.

Butler's MBA graduates have gone on to work for companies such as Eli Lilly and

Company, Roche, M&I Bank, Regions Bank, Firestone, and the NCAA.

Student Life and Environment

Students who want to be surrounded by those with real life experience will find Butler to be a welcoming environment. Butler attendees are "generally about thirty years old and at the experienced or manager status in their careers," though they can "range from just out of undergrad to sixty years old." Working full-time while also attending classes is common. As one student noted, "Nearly all of my classmates had full time careers, so life at school was typically limited to class." Professions, ethnicities, and educational backgrounds vary, but a consistent trait is that students here are "committed, smart and friendly." Even though "most of the people have families and outside lives that are a priority when they aren't at work or in class," Butler students will still "get together for group projects, and occasionally socially." For those interested in connecting with their school in a way that extends beyond the classroom, "the MBA Association does a good job providing for opportunities to connect with peers, faculty, staff, business professionals and alumni."

Though there can be a competitive streak among some on campus—hardly unusual for an MBA program— "fellow students are more supportive than competitive; people are down to earth and have a good sense of humor." The "personable and great classmates" students work alongside come from "very different backgrounds and experiences, yet everyone has an incredibly strong work ethic." Students, especially those in the night programs, may have much to deal with outside the classroom, but in the classroom "we enjoy working in groups together." Some graduates say they "have developed some great lifelong friendships."

Admissions

Expect your undergraduate GPA, GMAT score, letters of recommendation, and work experience to be important when it comes to what the Admissions Committee for Butler's MBA program considers. What you have accomplished outside the classroom or work environment is not weighed at all; extracurricular activities are not taken into account in the admissions process. Residency is not a factor—Butler is a private institution—though most students are from the Midwest. The average GPA of recently admitted students was 3.33/4.0, and their GMAT score ranged from 560–650. Most students had seven or more years of work experience.

FINANCIAL FACTS

Fees	$0
Cost of books	$10,500
Room & board	$12,900
% of students receiving aid	0
% of first-year students receiving aid	0
% of students receiving grants	0
Average award package	$12,074
Average grant	$8,048
Average loan	$12,859
Average student loan debt	$22,310

ADMISSIONS

Admissions Selectivity Rating	76
# of applications received	85
% applicants accepted	81
% acceptees attending	75
Average GMAT	584
Range of GMAT	490–770
Average GPA	3.32
TOEFL required of international students	Yes
Minimum TOEFL (paper/computer)	550/213
Application fee	$0
International application fee	$0
Regular application deadline	7/1
Regular application notification	7/10
Deferment available	Yes
Maximum length of deferment	1 year
Transfer students accepted	Yes
Transfer application policy: Up to 9 credit hours may transfer; applicant must be transferring from an AACSB accredited intitution and with letter of good standing from program.	
Non-fall admissions	Yes
Need-blind admissions	Yes

CALIFORNIA POLYTECHNIC STATE UNIVERSITY—SAN LUIS OBISPO
ORFALEA COLLEGE OF BUSINESS

GENERAL INFORMATION
Type of school   Public
Affiliation   No Affiliation
Academic calendar   Quarter

SURVEY SAYS...
Students love San Luis Obispo, CA,
Good social scene
Solid preparation in:
General management, Teamwork

STUDENTS
Enrollment of parent
  institution   18,644
Enrollment of MBA Program   100
% male/female   65/35
% out-of-state   11
% part-time   15
% underrepresented minority   5
% international   5
Average age at entry   27
Average years work experience
  at entry   3.5

ACADEMICS
Academic Experience Rating   **95**
Profs interesting rating   82
Profs accesible rating   86
Student/faculty ratio   25:1
% female faculty   20
% underrepresented minority
  faculty   15
% part-time faculty   15

Joint Degrees
MBA/MS in Engineering Management;
MBA/MS in Computer Science
(MBA/MS); MBA/MS in Electrical
Engineering; MBA/MS in Mechanical
Engineering; MBA/MS in Industrial
and Technical Studies; MBA/MS in
Industrial Engineering; MBA/MS in
Civil and Environmental Engineering;
MBA/Master of Public Policy. Various
additional dual degree options are
available. In general, these options
take two years to complete.

Prominent Alumni
Robert Rowell, President, Golden
State Warriors; Linda Ozawa Olds,
Founder, Jamba Juice

Academics

Poised at the intersection of business and technology, California Polytechnic State University's graduate business programs are a great choice for students with a background in applied science or architecture. As a state school, Cal Poly is "less expensive" than comparable private institutions, yet its AACSB-accredited business programs are rigorous, current, and intimate, enrolling fewer than 50 students each year. The MBA comprises 60 to 64 total credits for graduation; depending on your schedule, availability, and academic goals, students have "the option for one- or two-year completion" of the MBA, with an academic focus in general management, agribusiness, or graphic communication document systems management. The chance to complete a specialized MBA in just one year—even without an undergraduate degree in business—is a huge advantage to this program. At the same time, students must be prepared to work hard: not only is coursework challenging and accelerated, "the program requires students [to] maintain a 3.0 GPA" throughout. For working students who want to pursue a degree part-time, or for those who'd like to explore concurrent employment or internship opportunities, Cal Poly also allows students to take fewer than the full-time 16 units per quarter, through a secondary MBA track.

For many, the major benefit of Cal Poly is its strength in technical fields, which students can exploit through technology-oriented electives, or through formal dual degree programs with other academic departments. Of particular note, the school offers joint MS and MBA degrees in engineering management and engineering fields (including aerospace, civil and environmental, computer science, and more). Almost 40 percent of current MBA candidates are concurrently enrolled in a master's program, telling us that, "the dual degree program is fantastic" at Cal Poly. A current student adds, "The MBA/EMP dual degree program they offer was exactly the type of program that I was looking for, and Cal Poly has a tremendous reputation in the world of engineering."

A hallmark of the Cal Poly MBA program is the "learning-by-doing teaching style," which encourages students to develop applicable skills through coursework. To that end, classes and assignments include teamwork, case studies, and presentations. Additionally, the "international business course"—a unique offering within an accelerated program—gives students the opportunity to study a foreign economy and business practices during a two-week trip overseas. In recent years, the program took students to India and China. Students can also tailor their education by pursuing research projects in conjunction with Cal Poly faculty, or by competing with other business students in national case study and strategy competitions. When it comes to Cal Poly's faculty and administration, it's a mixed bag. Here, "There are some professors that are outstanding, and some that are good in their field, but not good at teaching." A student summarizes, "It's a cliché, but the more effort you put into the program, the more you will get out of the program."

ADMISSIONS CONTACT: VICTORIA WALLS, ASSISTANT DIRECTOR OF GRADUATE PROGRAMS
ADDRESS: 1 GRAND AVENUE, OCOB, SAN LUIS OBISPO, CA 93407
PHONE: 805-756-2637 • FAX: 805-756-0110
E-MAIL: MBA@CALPOLY.EDU • WEBSITE: MBA.CALPOLY.EDU

FINANCIAL FACTS

Annual tuition (in-state/ out-of-state)	$7,356/$19,260
Fees	$9,897
Cost of books	$1,638
Room & board	$9,846
% of students receiving aid	40
% of first-year students receiving aid	40
% of students receiving grants	30
Average award package	$18,776
Average grant	$6,713
Average loan	$16,690

ADMISSIONS

Admissions Selectivity Rating	97
# of applications received	181
% applicants accepted	20
% acceptees attending	86
Average GMAT	640
Range of GMAT	580–750
Average GPA	3.36
TOEFL required of international students	Yes
Minimum TOEFL (paper/computer)	550/213
Application fee	$55
International application fee	$55
Regular application deadline	7/1
Deferment available	No
Transfer students accepted	Yes
Transfer application policy: Maximum of 8 units transfer	
Non-fall admissions	No
Need-blind admissions	Yes

Career and Placement

At Cal Poly, Career Services hosts career fairs and networking events for the entire school community. They also offer career preparation assistance, including resume revisions and interview skills workshops. While graduate students are free to participate in these offerings, "the career services are more geared towards undergrads" at Cal Poly. Fortunately, the school boasts an excellent reputation and strong ties to the local community. Even without extensive assistance, around 85 percent of Cal Poly students have accepted a job offer by graduation; three months out, 100 percent of MBA alumni are employed.

Top employers of Cal Poly MBA graduates include Northrup Grumman, Raytheon, Rantec, General Dynamics, Sun MicroSystems, Deloitte Consulting, Qualcomm, IBM, Agilent Technology, Amgen Inc., Lawrence Livermore Labs, Pacific Gas & Electric, USDA, Dept of Veterans Affairs, KPMG, Pratt & Whitney, Morgan Stanley, Boston Scientific, PriceWaterhouseCoopers, Sandia National Lab, Lam Research, Columbia Sportswear, Adelaida Cellars. The mean base salary for MBA graduates is $100,000.

Student Life and Environment

Life is good at Cal Poly. Located on a hilltop overlooking San Luis Obispo, "the college campus is gorgeous" and the surrounding town is beautiful, friendly, and student-oriented. No wonder many students say "the location" is among the Cal Poly's greatest assets. Graduate students have access to the school's excellent recreation center, health center, and library, and they may even choose to live on campus. Within the business school, the Graduate Students in Business Association (GSBA) organizes social gatherings for students and faculty, as well as fundraisers and professional development events.

Cal Poly offers just a few graduate programs; therefore "the undergrads overwhelmingly outnumber the graduate students" on campus. Fortunately, "the Graduate School of Business students have their own Room/Lounge with a fridge, microwave, tables, computers, and whiteboards"—a nice enclave for the more mature crowd. At Cal Poly, most MBA candidates are "young, career-driven" professionals, principally from technical or engineering backgrounds.

Admissions

To be eligible for admission to Cal Poly's Orfalea College of Business graduate programs, students must possess an undergraduate degree from an accredited university, and a competitive undergraduate GPA and GMAT scores. For accepted applicants, the mid-80 percent GPA range was 2.8 to 3.75; for GMAT scores, the mid-80 percent range was 580 to 750. To be eligible for dual degree programs, students must meet the eligibility requirements for both programs.

EMPLOYMENT PROFILE	
Career Rating	95
Percent employed at graduation	90
Percent employed 3 months after graduation	95
Average base starting salary	$95,000

CALIFORNIA STATE POLYTECHNIC UNIVERSITY—POMONA
COLLEGE OF BUSINESS ADMINISTRATION

GENERAL INFORMATION

Type of school	Public
Affiliation	No Affiliation
Academic calendar	Quarter

SURVEY SAYS...

Students love Pomona, CA
Solid preparation in:
General management, Teamwork,
Communication/interpersonal skills,
Presentation skills, Computer skills

STUDENTS

Enrollment of parent	
institution	22,156
Enrollment of MBA Program	131
% part-time	48

ACADEMICS

Academic Experience Rating	**92**
Profs interesting rating	84
Profs accesible rating	87

Academics

The College of Business Administration at California Poly Pomona parlays the university's strengths in engineering and technology into a unique MSBA in Information Systems Auditing, a program that prepares students for careers in computer forensics and information systems security. "It's a nationally-recognized program," students here remind us while insisting we feature it prominently in the school's profile. Consider it done.

Cal Poly also offers a more conventional MBA program, with concentrations available in accounting, finance, marketing, operations management, human resources, hospitality management, entrepreneurship, information management, and international business. Even in its more conventional pursuits, however, the school forges a unique tack. A Cal Poly MBA, students inform us, is a "hands on MBA" with "a technical emphasis" that encourages a "learning-by-doing philosophy." One student explains: "Very few professors will stand in the front of the room and lecture for four hours. Classes are very interactive and students are provided with plenty of opportunities to present their opinions and put learning points to use." Students also report that "All classes require students to work on group projects, which prepares you well to work in teams in real world." Cal Poly also offers a Professional MBA at its Metro in Downtown Los Angeles (minimum two years' supervisory work experience mandatory for entry).

Cal Poly is "one of the few state universities using the quarter system," which "makes things fly by. When you are starting the quarter, you already have to start studying for midterms; when mid-quarter arrives, you already have to start seeking for affordable books for the next quarter." Fortunately, the program has "exceptional instructors" who "are mostly young (in their forties) and provide access to modern management principles and practices while at the same timing give information about classical management principles." Good instruction helps ease the academic burden some, but students warn that many here "reduce their work responsibilities to cope with the heavy course load. It's not an easy place for full-time/part-time working professionals."

Career and Placement

Career services for MBAs here are provided by the Cal Poly Pomona Career Center (CPPCC), a central office serving all undergraduate and graduate students at the university. The CPPCC provides all standard counseling and placement services. Many students do not even use the service; they already have jobs that they hope to advance in by earning a graduate degree. One who does complains unequivocally: "The career placement is terrible at Cal Poly for MBA students. Ninety-five percent of companies come in looking for engineers, accountants and some hospitality, and most are only interested in undergrads for entry-level positions. I'm considering crashing a UCI career day just to get referrals." Employers who frequently recruit at Cal Poly include: Bank of America, Boeing, Deloitte, Disneyland Resort, Ernst and Young LLP, IBM, Kaiser Permanente, KPMG International, Merrill Lynch, PricewaterhouseCoopers, Proctor & Gamble, Southern California Edison, and Wells Fargo Bank.

ADMISSIONS CONTACT: HILARY BREEZE, GRADUATE PROGRAMS ADVISOR
ADDRESS: GRADUATE BUSINESS PROGRAM, 3801 WEST TEMPLE AVENUE, POMONA, CA 91768
PHONE: 909-869-2363 • FAX: 909-869-4559
E-MAIL: GBA@CSUPOMONA.EDU • WEBSITE: CBA.CSUPOMONA.EDU

Student Life and Environment

The Cal Poly student body consists of "smart working professionals" who are "very diverse both ethnically and professionally." Their professions "range anywhere from human resources managers to information technology managers to production line managers," and "several *Fortune* 500 companies" are represented here. Academically, the group includes "students who graduated with degrees in engineering, psychology, liberal arts, science, etc." The quality of students has "a significant impact on the class [because they] have plenty of experience to draw from" and "have a lot to say about the subjects that we are learning." Students "raise the bar [for each other] by being very competitive in studies and overall creativity and innovation."

Because most students are "full-time workers and commuters to classes," they typically "do not get too involved with on-campus activities." "MBA students here are more focused on their careers and families then on being connected to the school," one student explains. That's too bad, because the Cal Poly Pomona campus is "beautiful. It's nestled in between mountains and is full of trees," and students tell us that makes it a "good place to study and lead a stress-free life." Perhaps things will change in the years to come; some here already detect a campus that is "transferring from a commuter school to a school with a lot of campus activities. All of the events are getting bigger and better. The exposure of the campus is being seen in the size and popularity of the events."

Admissions

Cal Poly Pomona operates on a quarterly academic schedule; the school accepts MBA applications for each quarter. All of the following components of the application are carefully considered: complete post-secondary academic record as reflected in official transcripts; GMAT scores (must be no more than five years old); two letters of recommendation from current or former employers; and a resume. Applicants who attended an undergraduate institution at which English is not the primary language of instruction must provide official TOEFL scores. Applicants must meet the following criteria to be considered for admission: an overall undergraduate GPA of at least 3.0; a minimum GMAT score of 450; and, if required, TOEFL scores of at least 580 on the paper-and-pencil test, 237 on the computer-based test, or 92 on the Internet-based test. Meeting minimum requirements does not guarantee admission to the program.

FINANCIAL FACTS

Annual tuition (in-state/ out-of-state)	$11,464/$17,416
Room & board (on/off-campus)	$22,711/$14,171

ADMISSIONS

Admissions Selectivity Rating	90
# of applications received	281
% applicants accepted	22
% acceptees attending	65
Average GMAT	519
Range of GMAT	460–590
Average GPA	3.35
TOEFL required of international students	Yes
Minimum TOEFL (paper/computer)	580/237
Application fee	$55
International application fee	$55
Deferment available	No
Transfer students accepted	Yes
Transfer application policy: Candidates must meet our admission criteria.	
Non-fall admissions	Yes
Need-blind admissions	Yes

CALIFORNIA STATE UNIVERSITY, CHICO
COLLEGE OF BUSINESS

GENERAL INFORMATION
Type of school   Public
Affiliation   No Affiliation
Academic calendar   Semester

SURVEY SAYS...
Students love Chico, CA
Solid preparation in:
Social responsibility

STUDENTS
Enrollment of parent
  institution   16,470
Enrollment of MBA Program   58
% male/female   45/55
% out-of-state   33
% part-time   43
% underrepresented minority   2
% international   31
Average age at entry   25
Average years work experience
  at entry   4.3

ACADEMICS
Academic Experience Rating   76
Profs interesting rating   81
Profs accesible rating   72
Student/faculty ratio   25:1
% female faculty   40
% underrepresented minority
  faculty   10
% part-time faculty   10

Prominent Alumni
Steve Perricone, Entrepreneur;
Michael Polenski, Founder,
Blackbird Vineyard and Former
President/ CEO of Chase Manhattan
Corp's Global; Scott Hanson,
Founder/Principle Hanson McClain
Financial Advisors; Stephen Goodall,
Executive VP and Principle with
Outsell Inc. and Former President of
J. D. Power Associates (retired
2009); Prabhakar Kalavacherla, Full
time Member of International
Accounting Standards Board (IASB)

Academics

California State University, Chico offers a practical and personable MBA program, well suited to Northern California professionals. With a "great regional reputation," Chico students feel confident they can leverage their education in the workplace. Above all else, professors have "a lot of relevant industry experience" and offer "good insight into the business world." Across disciplines, Chico professors "keep up with current events," and class content is constantly "changing according to the news today." Chico distinguishes itself academically through a focus on information technology and business information systems. Chico State's innovative Center for Information Systems Research involves students in a variety of hands-on projects in the business technology sector, and the school has been "a member of the SAP alliance" since 1996.

While academics are strong, the environment is remarkably supportive, too. When a student needs extra assistance, professors are "easily accessible" and "always available outside of class." A current student shares, "I have met many professors through independent projects, and they have been very helpful and guided me to the right resources." Throughout the curriculum, there is an "emphasis on teamwork, interpersonal skills, and both qualitative and quantitative learning." Students are encouraged to engage with the work, and "most professors try to create an environment that promotes active discussions." The focus on group work, as well as real world applications, make for a "very practical learning experience," which is immediately applicable to the real world. A small business owner tells us, "Classes are at night, and my real-life laboratory is my business during the day."

Working students appreciate the balance at Chico, saying, "The atmosphere is focused, but there is not too much pressure on the students." "Overall, the program is consistent and organized," and the "staff is flexible and understanding" with students who work full-time. On the other hand, some feel the Chico experience "might be better if we had a more competitive environment," noting that there is a noticeable "lack of rigor in some classes." In addition to the value offered to professionals, Chico also offers a "3+2" program for business undergraduates from partner schools, which offers the "opportunity to get a masters degree one year after your bachelor degree." Several international universities also participate in the school's 3+2 program, which brings "a large number of international students" to campus. For many, the international community is an unexpected plus of a Chico education, helping them to develop "cultural skills in a business environment that is less cutthroat than the real business world."

Career and Placement

As a part of California State University, Chico, business students have access to the University's Career Center, where they can sign up for individual consultations with a career counselor. Students can also attend the Career Center's workshops and career development events throughout the year. Located in Northern California, Chico State maintains a "strong relationship with the San Francisco business community," and, every year, "CSU Chico brings in various companies at the career fair." International students, however, feel the school could do a better job helping them score internships and jobs, while locals say it is "very difficult to find employment" in surrounding Chico, which was affected by the economic downturn.

ADMISSIONS CONTACT: NEELAM BAHL, GRADUATE ADVISOR
ADDRESS: 121 GLENN HALL, CSU, CHICO, CA 95929-0041
PHONE: 530-898-6283 • FAX: 530-898-5889
E-MAIL: MBA@CSUCHICO.EDU • WEBSITE: WWW.CSUCHICO.EDU/COB

Around forty percent of Chico's MBA candidates are already employed when they begin the program, and most plan to stay at their current position after graduation. For those taking new positions, the mean base salary for graduates was $71,588 in 2010, with close to 80 percent of students remaining in the western United States. Chevron USA, IBM, and Deloitte are among the school's top employers.

Student Life and Environment

Chico State is a vibrant and bustling university, located in a pretty town in the Sierra Nevada foothills. The "beautiful campus" makes a wonderful backdrop to the business school, and "there are always people hanging out on campus" before and after class. There are "lots of things happening around campus" for those who want to partake, including "great cultural activities" and plenty of "volunteer opportunities" in the local community. While "most MBAs don't have time to participate in the many activities offered by the school," others say they make a concerted effort to get involved.

At this medium-sized public school, graduate students are "close-knit," yet diverse culturally, socially, and academically. Some students are "fresh out of undergraduate school with no experience" in the workplace, while others are seasoned professionals, who continue to work full-time throughout the duration of the program. Many students are "very passionate about learning," while "others are not very serious about the program." Because the school operates a partner program with several international universities, there are numerous students from overseas. With regards to the international community, a current student tells us, "Getting to know them on a collegial, friendly level during my MBA has been one of the most important experiences so far."

Admissions

To be eligible for a graduate program at Chico, prospective students must have an overall undergraduate GPA of 2.75, and a GPA of at least 3.0 for the final 30 hours of coursework. To apply to the MBA program, students must submit standardized test scores in addition to their academic transcripts, though the GRE may be substituted for the GMAT. The most recent entering class had an average GMAT score of 536 and an average GRE score of 1051. The average work experience for entering students is more than four years.

FINANCIAL FACTS

Annual tuition (in-state/ out-of-state)	$8,206/$14,902
Fees	$4,572
Cost of books	$1,000
Room & board (on/off-campus)	$0/$10,000
% of students receiving aid	40
% of first-year students receiving aid	40
% of students receiving grants	40
Average award package	$16,279
Average grant	$4,470
Average loan	$11,743
Average student loan debt	$17,473

ADMISSIONS

Admissions Selectivity Rating	76
# of applications received	54
% applicants accepted	65
% acceptees attending	49
Average GMAT	570
Range of GMAT	535–595
Average GPA	3.20
TOEFL required of international students	Yes
Minimum TOEFL (paper/computer)	550/213
Application fee	$55
International application fee	$55
Regular application deadline	3/1
Deferment available	No
Transfer students accepted	Yes
Transfer application policy: A maximum of 9 Semester units of post-baccalaureate transfer and /or CSU, Chico Open University coursework may be included in a master's degree program, provided that the courses are from an AACSB accredited institution.	
Non-fall admissions	Yes
Need-blind admissions	Yes

EMPLOYMENT PROFILE

Career Rating	75	Grads Employed by Function	% Avg. Salary
Average base starting salary	$71,588	Marketing	(15%) $41,000
Primary Source of Full-time Job Acceptances		Consulting	(15%) $65,000
School-facilitated activities	3(38%)	Management	(15%) $132,000
Unknown	5(63%)	Finance	(25%) $46,000
		MIS	(30%) $67,500

Top 5 Employers Hiring Grads
IGT Company, Cap Gemini, IBM, Deloitte, KPMG

CALIFORNIA STATE UNIVERSITY, EAST BAY
COLLEGE OF BUSINESS AND ECONOMICS

GENERAL INFORMATION
Type of school   Public
Affiliation   No Affiliation
Academic calendar   Quarter

SURVEY SAYS...
Happy students
Solid preparation in:
Quantitative skills, Computer skills

STUDENTS
Enrollment of parent
  institution   14,167
Enrollment of MBA Program   219
% part-time   100
Average age at entry   29
Average years work experience
  at entry   3.4

ACADEMICS
Academic Experience Rating   78
Profs interesting rating   79
Profs accesible rating   82
Student/faculty ratio   28:1
% female faculty   16
% underrepresented minority
  faculty   47
% part-time faculty   5

Prominent Alumni
Mark Mastov, Founder of 24 Hour Fitness; Bill Lockyer, State Treasurer of California; Mike Abary, Senior VP, Sony IT Products Division; Mahla Shagfi, Senior VP and Regional Director, Union Bank of California; Judy Belk, Senior VP Rockefeller Philanthropy Advisors

Academics

California State University—East Bay's College of Business and Economics offers a "convenient and affordable" MBA program, specially designed to accommodate working professionals in the greater San Francisco Bay Area. At this large public school, all "MBA classes are in the evenings," and the multi-year program's flexible schedule makes it easier for students to prioritize work and family while pursuing their degree. Core coursework comprises the majority of the MBA, with each student completing a series of required classes in management, marketing, economics, and finance. After the core, students can choose to specialize in one of seven business areas, and the program concludes with a capstone course in entrepreneurship or strategic management. Throughout disciplines, "Classes focus a great deal on working in teams and presentation skills," and "Almost every class requires at least one group project and at least one class presentation." Fortunately, students are generally "open to learning and contributing to team projects with enthusiasm," and the collaborative nature of the program teaches students "how to work with others, manage a team, and present to an important group of people, just as they will have to do in the business world."

Despite its low price tag, CSUEB does not skimp on quality. At this large public school, professors are "qualified and skilled professionals," who have "experience working as consultants to organizations around the world." Most instructors are "passionate about their subjects" and enjoy teaching, though the faculty is a "mixed bag," so you may not love every professor you get. Owing to the state of California's recent budget problems, you will run up against some burdensome bureaucracy at CSUEB. While red tape does not necessarily affect the quality of the MBA, "The administration can appear somewhat inept at times." A number of students are particularly frustrated that "The administration does not work with them to help them graduate on time." Following the school's recommendations, students should be able to complete the program in about three years, though scheduling conflicts can sometimes make the suggested schedule impossible to follow. On the flip side, those who reach out to administrators within the business school say the higher-ups can be friendly and helpful; a current student insists, "The head of the program and the program coordinator have been excellent to work with." All in all, the school strikes the right "balance between quality of education and price for education." With it's affordable tuition, "good reputation," and enviable location in the San Francisco Bay Area, "It's difficult to find a school that is a better value than California State University."

Career and Placement

As a part-time program, CSUEB principally attracts employed students who are not necessarily looking for a new position after graduation. Nonetheless, students think the school could do a better job offering "access to career advising for working students" and "promoting networking opportunities" within the local business community. On the whole, "It is up to the individual to find opportunities" at CSUEB. There is no dedicated career placement office for business students at CSUEB; however, MBA candidates can make an appointment at the university career center if they want help with the job search or need assistance with their resume and cover letter. The university at large also hosts career fairs and networking events. Not many MBA candidates take advantage of these offerings, though a current student explains, "The career fair that I attended did have companies that offer a wide range of internship opportunities."

ADMISSIONS CONTACT: DR. JOANNA LEE, DIRECTOR OF GRADUATE PROGRAMS
ADDRESS: 25800 CARLOS BEE BLVD, HAYWARD, CA 94542
PHONE: 510-885-2419 • FAX: 510-885-2176
E-MAIL: JOANNA.LEE@CSUEASTBAY.EDU • WEBSITE: CBEGRAD.CSUEASTBAY.EDU

The school's geographic location "near Silicon Valley" and San Francisco is an asset to anyone looking for work in the tech industry. According to the university's Success Report for 2008-2009, 91 percent of graduate business students were employed or pursuing further education after graduation. MBA graduates took jobs at many Bay Area companies, including Kaiser Permanente, Chevron, the City of San Jose, Ernst & Young, Genentech, PG&E, and SAP Labs Americas, among others.

Student Life and Environment

Cal State East Bay's large campus is known for its diversity, and the business school is no different. Here, students come "from different societies, educational and professional backgrounds, and age groups." There are also "a lot of students from overseas," which adds a unique flavor to an otherwise largely local student body. While their backgrounds vary, "There seems to be two groups: working professionals and younger students fresh out of college." Both younger and older students "take their classes seriously" at CSUEB.

Across departments, CSU is largely a "commuter school." Most students work during the day and take classes at night, describing their lifestyle as "hectic." Since few MBA candidates live on campus, "There's not much interaction among MBA students other than class- or project-related." When they do interact, students say their classmates are "friendly" and "easy to engage in conversation." Located in the suburban city of Hayward, California, the CSUEB campus is propitiously situated right between the city of San Francisco and Silicon Valley, offering easy access to a wide range of social and recreational opportunities, outdoor activities, and professional connections of the greater Bay Area.

Admissions

Students are admitted to CSUEB's graduate business programs based on an admissions index number, which is calculated with their GPA and GMAT scores. Therefore, a slightly lower GPA can be offset by slightly higher GMAT scores, and vice versa. Although the school does request a personal statement with your application materials, no recommendations or interviews are required. In recent entering classes, the average GPA and GMAT scores for incoming students was 3.23 and 560, respectively.

FINANCIAL FACTS

Fees	$11,871
Cost of books	$1,909
Room & board	
(on/off-campus)	$13,091/$15,000
% of students receiving aid	28
% of first-year students	
receiving aid	30
% of students receiving grants	19
Average award package	$15,064
Average grant	$5,530
Average loan	$13,419
Average student loan debt	$2,941

ADMISSIONS

Admissions Selectivity Rating	**75**
# of applications received	165
% applicants accepted	64
% acceptees attending	62
Average GMAT	519
Range of GMAT	470–560
Average GPA	3.10
TOEFL required of	
international students	Yes
Minimum TOEFL	
(paper/computer)	550/213
Application fee	$55
International application fee	$55
Regular application deadline	6/30
Regular application notification	8/30
Deferment available	No
Transfer students accepted	Yes
Transfer application policy: With the approval of the director of the program students can transfer up to 16 quarterly units (from AACSB accredited schools)	
Non-fall admissions	Yes
Need-blind admissions	No

CALIFORNIA STATE UNIVERSITY, FRESNO
CRAIG SCHOOL OF BUSINESS

GENERAL INFORMATION

Type of school	Public
Affiliation	No Affiliation
Academic calendar	Rotating spring and fall starts

SURVEY SAYS...

Friendly students, Good peer network, Happy students
Solid preparation in:
General management, Doing business in a global economy

STUDENTS

Enrollment of parent institution	20,100
Enrollment of MBA Program	126
% part-time	100
Average age at entry	30

ACADEMICS

Academic Experience Rating	**86**
Profs interesting rating	87
Profs accesible rating	85
Student/faculty ratio	20:1
% female faculty	30
% underrepresented minority faculty	18
% part-time faculty	0

Joint Degrees

Same as above

Academics

A member of the California State University System, California State University—Fresno's Craig School of Business offers "an education that rivals the top universities at a fraction of the cost." Many, if not most of those who attend Craig are working professionals, and the school's curriculum "works well with a full-time work schedule," including night and weekend classes. Fresno State employs world-class educators that have real world experience working with/managing companies, such as: HP, Rug Doctor and dozens more, and "many of the professors have owned their own companies and have experience outside of just their focus."

The "absolutely outstanding" faculty gives "consistently solid instruction" and brings "an incredible amount of work experience and knowledge in regards to their respective business fields." Many were "very successful business people who teach because they love it," and "it is wonderful to hear their life lessons shared with the students." "My experience has exceeded my expectations before I started the program," says one student. Everybody is willing to learn, "even the professors," whose genuine excitement about what they do rubs off on the student body. The "very astute" professors have "crystal clear and inspirational instructions" and leave memorable impressions on students. "I have encountered some professors I plan to keep in contact with for years to come," says one.

The "well-run" administration is more than understanding of how busy its students' lives are; at one point, "the program staff handled all of the paperwork so that we students didn't need to worry about them." Class sizes are small, so "you can get as much personal attention as you want," and it's "easy to get classes" of your choice. "I've learned a lot of interesting, applicable concepts at Fresno State," says a student.

Career and Placement

The prestige and recognition of the CSU Fresno name in the business world is a huge boon to graduates, and the school's "pay to tuition ratio is among the best." The Career Services Office "gives the students ample opportunity to find great jobs as well as overseas experience." Most already have jobs when they choose to attend Fresno State, but there are many group projects that are required, so students find that a great deal of natural networking occurs throughout the course of the program. Students are required to take three elective courses, and one of their internships may be used as an upper division elective towards their degrees. Specializations are available in agribusiness, entrepreneurship, finance, general management, human resource management, information systems, and marketing. Alumni are also especially useful to Craig graduates, and job offers are frequently posted for graduates via Craig's various social networking sites.

Student Life and Environment

Virtually every student here "is working full-time and going to school full-time," which "makes it easier to relate to one another." This "ethnically diverse" group is all "at different phases of their careers," and ranges from "professionals with young families up to people in their 40s with already established careers," including "VPs of companies, HR managers, entrepreneurs, stay at home moms, sales executives, and more." All are "willing to learn and want to learn along with you" and are "open to meeting new people and making new friends." Each "very eclectic" class represents "right, left and middle political points of view," making for a "fun mixture."

Life is "very busy" when classes are in session, with many local people swarming about and "a lot of activities available." A lot of the MBA students went to undergrad at CSU Fresno and live locally. There are "many social and health wellness fairs throughout the semester," and there is also "a pub that serves wine and beer" for students who "enjoy mingling socially with their classmates" over a drink.

Admissions

Applicants to the Craig MBA program must submit the following materials: official GMAT score report (minimum score of 550 with ranking at or above the first quartile on verbal and mathematics portions); a completed online application; two letters of recommendation; a statement of purpose/essay; and official transcripts for all post-secondary academic work. International non-English-speaking students who did not graduate from an English language institution must also submit an official TOEFL score report. Admissions decisions are based primarily on GMAT scores and academic performance over the last 60 semester credits of undergraduate work; applicants must have earned at least a 2.5 GPA over that period to merit consideration. Work experience, demonstrated management potential, and the applicant's statement of purpose are also considered.

FINANCIAL FACTS

Annual tuition (in-state/ out-of-state)	$12,114/$18,810

ADMISSIONS

Admissions Selectivity Rating	88
# of applications received	153
% applicants accepted	42
Average GMAT	602
Range of GMAT	500–770
Average GPA	3.40
TOEFL required of international students	Yes
Minimum TOEFL (paper/computer)	550/213
Application fee	$55
International application fee	$55
Regular application deadline	4/1
Application Deadline/Notification	
Round 1:	4/1
Round 2:	11/1
Deferment available	Yes
Maximum length of deferment	1 year
Transfer students accepted	Yes
Transfer application policy: Transfer must be from and AACSB accredited school, 9 units may be transfer on an approved basis and applicant must meet standard admittance requirements (same as a new applicant).	
Non-fall admissions	Yes

California State University, Fullerton
Mihaylo College of Business and Economics

GENERAL INFORMATION
Type of school	Public
Affiliation	No Affiliation
Academic calendar	Semester

SURVEY SAYS...
Friendly students, Happy students
Solid preparation in:
General management, Teamwork,
Computer skills

STUDENTS
Enrollment of parent institution	37,667
Enrollment of MBA Program	457
% male/female	38/62
% part-time	82
% underrepresented minority	17
% international	54
Average age at entry	26
Average years work experience at entry	0.0

ACADEMICS
Academic Experience Rating	**78**
Profs interesting rating	78
Profs accesible rating	78
Student/faculty ratio	24:1
% female faculty	17
% underrepresented minority faculty	14
% part-time faculty	15

Prominent Alumni
Steve Charton, President and CEO, Hospitality; Kevin Costner, Businessman and Actor; Steve G. Mihaylo, President & CEO, Telecommunications; Jim Woods, Chairman Emeritus & CEO (Retired), Aerospace; Richard Davis, President, CEO & Chairman, Banking

Academics

"A reputable state university with an excellent business school," Cal State Fullerton runs the largest accredited MBA program in the state of California. For current and future Southern California professionals, CSUF is a great way to get an edge in the business world, without breaking the bank. With a strong faculty and ties in the local business community, this school offers a "quality program at an affordable price." Whether you choose to go to school full-time or part-time, the Evening MBA is entirely "flexible and customizable," and "can be moderated in difficulty, depending on course choice and workload." Taking two classes per semester, evening students can complete the program in fewer than three years. Taking four classes per semester, full time students can complete the program in 16 months.

For both full-time and part-time students, the Mihaylo MBA program consists of ten foundation courses, four electives, and a capstone course. Through electives, students can pursue an academic concentration in one of 12 different fields; there is "great accounting faculty," as well as a strong finance department at CSUF. In addition to academic programs, the school operates 15 "centers for excellence," like the Small Business Institute, where faculty and students conduct research and case studies within a real business environment. Across departments, "professors are all very knowledgeable in terms of both theory and real world experience," and many "use their lifetime experiences to spice up the class discussions." While "most professors are outstanding and inspiring," students admit that the overall quality of the teaching staff can be "inconsistent," especially when it comes to tenured faculty.

Since many students are balancing work, school, and personal life, most CSUF professors are "sympathetic to the many demands facing graduate students, who have full-time jobs and families." Overall, CSUF is a "warm environment, with professors who care about students" and an administration that is "supportive and helpful" to its ample student body. At the same time, students note that the "school is facing heavy budget cuts," which can affect the smooth functioning of the administration. In the past few years, there have been "some admin mix-ups" with regards to books and scheduling. All things considered, an MBA at Cal State Fullerton is an "excellent value." Armed with both academic and practical experience, graduates leave the program "ready to work and lead in the workforce."

Career and Placement

For those who love the surf and sand in Southern California, "CSUF has excellent ties to the local Orange County business community." Throughout the program, "the professors and administration work as partners in helping us achieve our career goals." Students are encouraged to visit the Advising Center to meet with career path advisors, who help them choose a concentration, plan their education, and develop a career search strategy. In addition, students can make an appointment with the business career specialist at the university's Career Center, who helps place graduates in accounting, finance, international business, information systems, and marketing positions.

Though the programs are strong, career development could be improved with the addition of "more networking activities within the program, outside the program, and with other schools that have similar programs." Students would also like to see Cal State Fullerton build "relationships with higher quality employers and recruiters." A student explains, "We have a good program, but our career center is geared for undergraduates, and they do no have that much to offer for graduate students." The school has listened

ADMISSIONS CONTACT: PRE-ADMISSION ADVISOR
ADDRESS: 800 N. STATE COLLEGE BLVD, SGMH 4210, FULLERTON, CA 92831-3599
PHONE: 657-278-3622 • FAX: 657-278-7101
E-MAIL: MBA@FULLERTON.EDU • WEBSITE: MBA.FULLERTON.EDU

to its students, though, and an Associate Director of MBA Career Management has been hired for the Fall of 2011, and will create an MBA Career Center for full-time students.

After graduating from Cal State Fullerton, MBA candidates join a "large alumni network" of almost 50,000 former students in Southern California and beyond. Currently, Mihaylo graduates are employed at Ford Motor Company, Hewlett Packard, Merrill Lynch, Morgan Stanley, Nestlé, Fox Sports, KPMG, Warner Brothers, PricewaterhouseCoopers, Paramount, Boeing, Deloitte & Touche, US Bank, Verizon, Walt Disney Company, Kaiser Permanente, and Toshiba, among others. In recent years, the mean base salary reported by Cal State Fullerton MBA graduates was over $62,000 annually.

Student Life and Environment

CSUF is a large MBA program, which attracts a wide variety of students at any level of their career, but still brings the average class size to less than 30 students. Here, students are "very diverse in terms of ethnicity, race, ideas, background, and ages," though "most are in their mid- to late 20s and have 2-5 years of work experience." As a "very diverse and professional environment," CSUF caters to students "looking to move up in their careers." In the classroom, students keep the bar high, but competition low. Generally, students are "very sociable people," who are "pleasant to study with."

At the same time, "there isn't too much school spirit or ways to get involved with social activities on campus." Collegiate activities are generally "geared toward undergraduate students," so most MBA candidates are "only at the business school for class or to study." Nonetheless, CSF offers a nice school environment on their main campus, where the "new business school building" offers "plenty of nice, quiet, clean study areas." Caffeine-fueled students add, "The Starbucks in the business school is a definite plus," and there is a "state-of-the-art gym provided to students, free of charge." Most students are quick to praise their campus experience.

Admission

Admission to Cal State Fullerton is competitive. Incoming students in last year's class had an average GMAT score of 577 and a 3.2 GPA. To best prepare for admission, students should attend an information session on the Cal State Fullerton campus. These sessions regularly fill to capacity, so prospective students should register online in advance to secure a spot.

FINANCIAL FACTS

Annual tuition (in-state/ out-of-state)	$7,448/$14,144
Fees	$4,572
Cost of books	$4,624
Room & board	$12,708
Average award package	$4,000
Average grant	$4,000

ADMISSIONS

Admissions Selectivity Rating	74
# of applications received	382
% applicants accepted	67
% acceptees attending	53
Average GMAT	529
Range of GMAT	480–580
Average GPA	3.24
TOEFL required of international students	Yes
Minimum TOEFL (paper/computer)	570/230
Application fee	$55
International application fee	$55
Early application deadline	1/31
Regular application deadline	4/1
Deferment available	No
Transfer students accepted	Yes
Transfer application policy: Students must apply as a new student and courses will be evaluted. Students may transfer in up to 9 units.	
Non-fall admissions	Yes
Need-blind admissions	Yes

EMPLOYMENT PROFILE	
Career Rating	71
Average base starting salary	$62,666

CALIFORNIA STATE UNIVERSITY, LONG BEACH
COLLEGE OF BUSINESS ADMINISTRATION

GENERAL INFORMATION

Type of school	Public
Affiliation	No Affiliation
Academic calendar	Semester

SURVEY SAYS...

Happy students, Student love Long
Beach, CA
Solid preparation in:
General management, Teamwork

STUDENTS

Enrollment of parent institution	31,174
Enrollment of MBA Program	211
Average age at entry	28
Average years work experience at entry	4.0

ACADEMICS

Academic Experience Rating	**83**
Profs interesting rating	78
Profs accesible rating	77
Student/faculty ratio	25:1

Joint Degrees

The MFA/MBA is a three-year, full time program (including two summer sessions) offered jointly between the Theatre Arts Department and the Graduate School of Business.

Academics

Students looking for the biggest "bang for the buck" will appreciate California State University, Long Beach. Although "tuition and fees have gone up every semester, what we are getting in return is still a great deal," at least "compared to other universities." There are many reasons to choose Cal State in addition to its affordability. "The campus is conveniently located, parking is good and the resources (database subscriptions, computer equipment) provided are excellent." Also popular with students are the small program and class sizes, which make it "easy to get to know many of your classmates throughout your stay." At CSULB, "Classmates are invested in the education experience." "Fellow students are fun to work with and bring different experiences helping to enrich discussion." There are "many foreign students" in the graduate program who help to provide an "international business focus" during classroom discussions. International students appreciate the opportunity to "take advantage of their experiences" at Long Beach.

Finding a program that meets individual needs at CSULB is easy to do. There are "many options for working folk," including a "Saturday only program" which is a 23-month long lock-step cohort. The three basic options include the Saturday MBA, the Self-Paced Evening MBA, and the 13-month Daytime Accelerated MBA. A good majority of students fit into the part-time category, and these commuters appreciate the school's ample parking and location in the "convenient" city of Long Beach. A current student describes it as "one of the most beautiful and diverse cities in the country."

Generally, students attend CSULB for its "smaller classes, good choice of different programs, [and] great location." One student says the school and its programs are "definitely growing by leaps and bounds." Another student who is a military veteran says, "The VA program here is the best of any school I have seen." Overall, students should come away from the school with "strong academics" as well as a "great sense of a real life business experience."

Many students also find the cohort system as one of the school's "greatest strengths." Although at times it may create some "isolation" from the rest of the campus, it does a great job of unifying peers within one's group, allowing students "time to develop relationships and strengthen our network," which is "almost impossible when your classmates change every session."

Getting help on campus is a positive experience as well. "The administration and faculty are very accessible and diverse." Students say that administrators "are fantastic in keeping students informed and getting them involved." Students' opinions about the faculty vary, yet many feel that "professors are very helpful and always have open lines of communication." Some say that although their academic and professional knowledge is well respected, their ability to teach effectively covers a "wide range." Also, some students consider it a disadvantage that not all professors "have extensive real-world experience."

ADMISSIONS CONTACT: MARINA FREEMAN-GARVEY, GRADUATE PROGRAMS ADMISSIONS MANAGER
ADDRESS: 1250 BELLFLOWER BOULEVARD, LONG BEACH, CA 90840-8501
PHONE: 562-985-5565 • FAX: 562-985-5590
E-MAIL: MBA@CSULB.EDU • WEBSITE: WWW.CSULB.EDU/COLLEGES/CBA/MBA

Career and Placement

CSU's MBA Career Management Services "is very interactive and helpful with networking for future careers." Besides maintaining an MBA job board and hosting on-campus recruiting events in a variety of business disciplines, they also maintain contact with alumni to encourage networking opportunities. Attending one of the large, campus-wide career fairs hosted by the Career Development Center affords yet another opportunity to meet potential employers. In recent years, large companies have visited campus, including Alaska Airlines, Accountants Incorporated, American Capital Group, California National Bank, CVS/Carmark Pharmacy, First Investors, Kelly Scientific Resources, Ameriprise Financial, Boeing, Northrop Grumman, and Comerica Bank.

Student Life and Environment

The MBA program combines a mix of students from several different countries, some who come directly from an undergraduate program and others that have "15+ years of work experience." This "diverse, friendly" student body consists of a solid group of classmates who "are invested in the education experience."

Although the school provides "ample opportunities to get into clubs and programs," graduate students with busy lifestyles may not have the opportunity to be "as involved as [they] would like to be." They do say, however, that they appreciate the "beautiful" campus and the surrounding area is "very nice." Long Beach is a thriving community that "gives access to so many different activities and different cultures." Students feel "safe" in this environment. They welcome the comfortable surroundings that are not only motivating, but also provide "a great atmosphere to study."

Students looking for off-campus housing will find selections that are "organized" with "a lot of affordable options." Weekend students remark that Saturdays are "quiet and uneventful" and that "not all of the services are open that day." Having a full-time job means that they miss out on "attending training during the week."

Admission

GMATs, GREs and undergraduate GPAs carry the most weight when applying to CSU's graduate school. Work experience is a plus but is not required. Solid letters of recommendations and a strong personal statement can be helpful but involvement in extracurricular activities is not considered.

Applications are accepted on a rolling basis with deadlines for Fall admissions being 3/30 and Spring admissions being 10/30. Students enrolling in CSU's MBA program have an average age of 29 and with five years of work experience. Average GMAT scores were 555 and GPAs were 3.3, with a 2.75 minimum requirement.

FINANCIAL FACTS

Annual tuition (in-state/ out-of-state)	$11,358/$18,774
Average grant	$0
Average loan	$0

ADMISSIONS

Admissions Selectivity Rating	84
# of applications received	313
% applicants accepted	47
% acceptees attending	57
Average GMAT	570
Range of GMAT	470–660
Average GPA	3.30
TOEFL required of international students	Yes
Minimum TOEFL (paper/computer)	550/213
Application fee	$55
International application fee	$55
Deferment available	Yes
Maximum length of deferment	One Semester
Transfer students accepted	Yes
Transfer application policy: Must meet our admissions criteria	
Non-fall admissions	Yes
Need-blind admissions	Yes

CALIFORNIA STATE UNIVERSITY—NORTHRIDGE
COLLEGE OF BUSINESS AND ECONOMICS

GENERAL INFORMATION

Type of school	Public
Affiliation	No Affiliation
Academic calendar	Semester

SURVEY SAYS...
Friendly students, Good peer network
Solid preparation in:
Marketing, General management,
Teamwork, Communication/interpersonal skills, Presentation skills,
Quantitative skills

STUDENTS

Enrollment of parent institution	36,911
Enrollment of MBA Program	161
% male/female	41/39
% underrepresented minority	84
Average age at entry	29
Average years work experience at entry	7.0

ACADEMICS

Academic Experience Rating	**93**
Profs interesting rating	88
Profs accesible rating	88
Student/faculty ratio	22:1
% female faculty	18
% underrepresented minority faculty	6
% part-time faculty	3

Academics

For Golden State professionals, California State University, Northridge offers an affordable and convenient option for a graduate degree in business. Generally considered the "best school in the San Fernando Valley," Northridge is "comparable to other major business schools, such as USC and UCLA" but much easier on your pocketbook and personal life. "Prices are still a fraction of local private schools," and "the evening MBA program makes attending school while working full-time not only possible, but much easier than anticipated." This program is geared toward working professionals, and "All the classes are scheduled during the evening or on the weekends." While keeping up at work and school can certainly be challenging, faculty and staff are "sympathetic to the many demands facing graduate students, who have full-time jobs and families."

The Northridge MBA comprises core coursework and electives, which together offer a "good balance of academic and professional experience." As working professionals, CSUN students are looking to build knowledge and skills that they can immediately apply to their jobs. As such, they are pleased to report that the teaching staff is current and "well informed of the market trends." "Every course has applications to real-world business situations," and the program concludes with a mandatory 3-unit consulting project for a live business in the community. In addition, CSUN students can tailor their degrees though elective coursework. The school offers concentrations in international business, marketing, management, and information systems, among other disciplines. "The size of the program doesn't allow for all of the electives to be offered each semester," so students who wish to specialize must plan their schedules carefully.

For a public school, MBA enrollment is low. With only around 250 students in the program, "the small class sizes allow for you to ask questions and interact with the professors and fellow students." "Nearly every class involves small group work," which helps students improve their team-building skills while also benefiting from their classmates' expertise. Here, "The students are diverse in many ways, and each one has a wealth of knowledge that they gladly share." A current student enthuses, "The courses are solid, and the students really raise the bar. You know that most of the students will be reading, studying, memorizing, and applying the material." While all professors have great credentials, some are more effective than others. Among other differences, "The younger professors are very engaging, while many of the older ones can be a bit regimented." No matter what their teaching style, Northridge professors are generally "supportive" and "available to meet and discuss" business topics outside the classroom.

Career and Placement

Almost all MBA candidates at Cal State Northridge are working professionals hoping to advance in their current career. While the MBA program prepares them to take on professional challenges, many feel that the school needs "better career services for MBA" students looking to make a career change. There are no career resources dedicated exclusively to MBA students on campus, and there is "very little connection to the alumni network" in Southern California. With limited campus recruiting for graduate students and no career center in the business school, "Career placement is all but non-existent" for MBAs.

Students who attend the program full-time or who are considering a career change can visit CSUN's Career Center, which serves the entire undergraduate and graduate population at the school, including business students. The Career Center operates a series of career development workshops for the CSUN community, as well as numerous job fairs and employment expos throughout the year. Their services include events aimed at Northridge alumni and recent grads.

ADMISSIONS CONTACT: DEBORAH COURS, PH.D., DIRECTOR OF GRADUATE PROGRAMS
ADDRESS: NORTHRIDGE, CA 91330-8380
PHONE: 818-677-2467 • FAX: 818-677-3188
E-MAIL: MBA@CSUN.EDU • WEBSITE: CSUN.EDU/MBA

Student Life and Environment

All business classes are held at CSU Northridge's main campus, located in Los Angeles. The campus is well equipped and comfortable, and there is a "private MBA reading room" with computers, a printer, a presentation screen, a refrigerator, tables and chairs for students to get together, study, or relax. When getting together with other students, "The graduate lounge is great and is always available" for study meetings and casual chats. When schedules permit, "Sometimes, classmates go out to eat after class."

With active professional commitments outside of school, very few MBA students are actively involved in the community beyond "group meetings with classmates and study groups once a week." However, "Nearly every class involves small group work," so students at CSUN have an opportunity to get to know their colleagues outside the classroom setting. Drawing from the surrounding community in Los Angeles, "The students are diverse in many ways. In addition to representing a "mix of geographical, cultural, and work backgrounds," they "vary in experience, from recent college grads and young professionals to mid-career transitioners." On the whole, CSUN is a collaborative program, with "very little sense of academic competition" between students.

Admissions

CSUN is one of the most affordable programs in Southern California, but also rather small. Therefore, admission to the MBA program is competitive. To be eligible for graduate study, students must have at least a 3.0 GPA from their last 60 hours of undergraduate coursework and score within the 50th percentile on the GMAT. In reality, the average GPA for the most recent incoming class was 3.3, and the average GMAT score was 595. Two years of professional work experience is a requirement of the program, though the school favors applicants with three to five years in the workforce.

FINANCIAL FACTS

Annual tuition (in-state/ out-of-state)	$12,342/$15,690
Cost of books	$1,788
Room & board	$10,628
Average grant	$0
Average loan	$0

ADMISSIONS

Admissions Selectivity Rating	92
# of applications received	195
% applicants accepted	34
% acceptees attending	54
Average GMAT	586
Range of GMAT	510–740
Average GPA	3.39
TOEFL required of international students	Yes
Minimum TOEFL (paper/computer)	550/213
Application fee	$55
International application fee	$55
Regular application deadline	5/1
Regular application notification	Rolling
Transfer students accepted	Yes
Transfer application policy: 9 units max transfer credit	
Non-fall admissions	Yes
Need-blind admissions	Yes

CALIFORNIA STATE UNIVERSITY, SAN BERNARDINO
COLLEGE OF BUSINESS AND PUBLIC ADMINISTRATION

Academics

California State University of San Bernardino students attend for mostly two reasons: the reputation of the college and the value of the education. The school has numerous "highly ranked" MBA programs and possesses the coveted Association to Advance Collegiate Schools of Business (or AACSB) accreditation, which lends to the school's already sizeable esteem. The school not only offers an MBA program, but an MBA for Executives track that allows people who are currently working as "decision makers" to attend class for any number of subjects that affect the current workplace. Additionally, a majority of the classes take place at night, which allows working professionals to continue their education after they leave work for the day. The "convenience" and diversity of these classes and programs are appealing to "all age groups" and experience levels.

Students rave about the "experienced" faculty and explain that many teachers are "student-centric" and want to see their students learn and succeed. They are also "open and aware of new ideas in the business world and understand trends in the business market which [the students] need to be aware of when [they] leave school." While some professors may have a bit of trouble "captivating an audience" most are "outstanding" and "incredibly helpful." CSUSB tries to keep "small class sizes," which students feel is a strength because it allows for a greater "relationship you can have with your professors." While most schools can occasionally be mired in bureaucracy, many seem to agree that CSUSB's administration "is constantly seeking to improve [the] quality of the program by offering new coursework and enhancing current classes."

Career and Placement

Students at CSUSB consider the Career Development Center "really good" at finding placement for graduating students. The Center offers a wide-array of services including workshops, career counseling, career fairs, resume and interview preparation, an on-campus interview program and an online job board. Students love these programs and call the internships available "top-notch." The career fairs and on-campus interviews are also fantastic for job placement because the school has a "great connection" with local businesses and offers students plenty of opportunities to network with them. In fact, the school is so focused on helping their students with their careers that some exclaim that "professors sometimes cancel class so that [students] may participate in the job fairs."

The mean base salary for graduates of CSUSB's MBA program is about $47,500 annually. In recent years, 55 percent of students seeking employment have received a job offer by graduation. Some of the biggest employers of CSUSB graduates include the County of Riverside, Inland Empire Health Plan, Trans America Retirement, and Loma Linda Medical University.

Student Life and Environment

One of the large draws for many students includes the evening classes, which allow them to work during the day. Because of this, many students consider CSUSB a "commuter school" with students who tend to live off-campus and have lives outside of school. Many of the attendees are "middle-class, working adults" and are "honest, loyal, hard-working" people who are "open to new ideas" and are very open to working and networking with others. People praise the "diversity on campus" with a student body that relates to others with "various backgrounds." Students tend to stay fairly busy and say that they spend much of their time "studying, [completing] homework, coordinating teams, [and] checking emails," but they find generally enjoy a "well-rounded and fulfilling learning experience."

On the main campus, MBA classes are held at Jack H. Brown Hall, which includes a computer center with 400 machines. While the facilities are clean and modern, students would appreciate "longer hours of access to on-campus study areas" to help accommodate group work.

For those wishing to stay on-campus, CSUSB makes sure their students are never bored. The school is located by the San Bernardino Mountains and, though the area surrounding the campus may be in a somewhat "shady" area, the school and its facilities are "excellent" and the campus is "a safe place." Students rave about the library and facilities as well as the "brand new" gym. There are also "plenty of cultural group activities" as well that are within driving distance of the beautiful mountain range and the southern California beaches.

Admissions

For those looking for admission to CSUSB there are a few application requirements that you should be aware of beforehand. Students must have a GPA of at least 2.5 in the last 90 quarter (60 semester) units which may include post-baccalaureate work. The minimum GMAT score is 470 with 10% in both the verbal and quantitative sections OR a minimum GRE score is 293 with 10% in both the verbal and quantitative sections. The 250-word statement of purpose should state the reasons for pursuing a master's degree in Business Administration and choosing this university. Successfully completion of the Graduate Entrance Writing Requirement is mandatory, however if students do not meet the writing requirement prior to admission, students are allowed to enroll in an Expository Writing course concurrently with MBA-level coursework during their first quarter.

Anyone looking for scholarships or financial aid has a wealth of options at CSUSB. The Financial Aid Office allows students to apply online at their website between January 1 through March 3. However graduate students can still apply for loans after the March 3 deadline. Applicants only have to complete one application to be considered for all scholarships.

FINANCIAL FACTS

Annual tuition	$7,833
Fees	$8,112
Cost of books	$3,000
Room & board (on/off-campus)	$8,997/$18,000
% of students receiving aid	51
% of first-year students receiving aid	55
% of students receiving grants	41
Average award package	$11,775
Average grant	$4,158
Average loan	$15,841
Average student loan debt	$39,450

ADMISSIONS

Admissions Selectivity Rating	82
# of applications received	255
% applicants accepted	46
% acceptees attending	54
Average GMAT	540
Range of GMAT	500–570
Average GPA	3.20
TOEFL required of international students	Yes
Minimum TOEFL (paper/computer)	550/213
Application fee	$55
International application fee	$55
Early application deadline	2/1
Early notification date	3/1
Regular application deadline	7/15
Regular application notification	8/15
Application Deadline/Notification	
Round 1:	2/1 / 3/1
Round 2:	4/1 / 5/1
Round 3:	7/15 / 8/15
Deferment available	No
Transfer students accepted	Yes

Transfer application policy: Only three approved graduate courses may be transferred into our MBA Program from approved U.S. universities. All prospective students must apply to our MBA Program and meet all other admission requirements.

Non-fall admissions	Yes
Need-blind admissions	No

EMPLOYMENT PROFILE

Career Rating	70	**Grads Employed by Function% Avg. Salary**	
Percent employed at graduation	0	MIS	(1%) $60,000
Percent employed 3 months after graduation	2	**Top 5 Employers Hiring Grads**	
Average base starting salary	$62,500	ESRI(1), Sherwin Williams (1), U.S. Navy (1),	
Primary Source of Full-time Job Acceptances		Dept of Veteran's Affairs (1), BP Petroleum (1)	
School-facilitated activities	1(1%)		
Graduate-facilitated activities	1(1%)		
Unknown	86(98%)		

CARNEGIE MELLON UNIVERSITY
TEPPER SCHOOL OF BUSINESS

GENERAL INFORMATION
Type of school   Private
Affiliation   No Affiliation
Academic calendar   Mini Semester

SURVEY SAYS...
Smart classrooms
Solid preparation in:
Operations, Quantitative skills

STUDENTS
Enrollment of parent
   institution   12,569
Enrollment of MBA Program   590
% male/female   73/28
% part-time   29
% underrepresented minority   7
% international   33
Average age at entry   29
Average years work experience
   at entry   4.3

ACADEMICS
Academic Experience Rating   **96**
Profs interesting rating   93
Profs accesible rating   91
Student/faculty ratio   5:1
% female faculty   22
% underrepresented minority
   faculty   14
% part-time faculty   5

Joint Degrees
Computational Finance & MBA, 24
months; Software Engineering &
MBA, 3 years; Law & MBA, 4 years;
Environmental Engineering & MBA,
2.5 years; Civil Engineering & MBA,
2.5 years; MBA/Public Policy (Heinz),
2.5 years; MBA & Healthcare Policy
and Management, 2.5 years

Prominent Alumni
David A. Tepper, CEO & Founder,
Appaloosa Management; David
Coulter, Vice Chairman and
Managing Director, Warburg Pincus
LLC; Lewis Hay III, Chairman and
CEO, NextEra Energy, Inc.; Yoshiaki
Fujimori, President and CEO, JS
Group Corporation

Academics

The Carnegie Mellon name is synonymous with excellence in technology, math, and applied science, so it's no surprise that the Tepper School of Business is known for its "analytical rigor" and "tech focus." The school's unique MBA covers topics like finance, marketing, operations, entrepreneurship, and consulting in consecutive "six-and-a-half-week minis"—short, immersive courses, which are broken up by weeklong intensive seminars. What distinguishes the curriculum is that it "incorporates quantitative analysis into almost every class as a complement to the typical qualitative approach." Plus, for anyone interested in tech, Tepper will really give you the cutting edge: "Research and collaboration from across the entire campus is often implemented into lectures and readings." Business courses are further augmented by "fantastic interdisciplinary opportunities across campus," including joint degree programs in computational finance, software engineering, law, and health care policy, among other fields.

While analytics are the Tepper hallmark, soft skills are emphasized, too. Of particular note, classes almost all include a collaborative component, and "most professors assign work for groups of three to six students at a time." Through these projects, in addition to the academic focus on organizational behavior, the "skills that you learn at this school prepare you to manage and lead teams in organizations." "Coursework is tough, demanding, and challenging" (in fact, some would like to see the workload reduced), but the "outstanding faculty" makes the effort worthwhile. Plus, "The professors have an open door policy and are very accessible," so students are never left to fend for themselves while tackling hard material. A student exclaims, "I am quite surprised by how willing most of the professors can be to be helping outside of classes, even on Fridays!"

A model of efficiency, Tepper's administration is quick in implementing changes proposed by both students and faculty, and there is an effort to "constantly improve student experience and academic curriculum." For example, "A new class this semester was thought of by a professor, approved, and added to the offered courses list in under 48 hours." A student adds, "Administration is more than willing to help students with specific problems and due to the small size of our program, they're rarely overwhelmed with requests."

Career and Placement

Through both curricular and extracurricular offerings, Tepper "faculty and administration do a great job preparing students for future careers." In partnership with Carnegie Mellon's Career Opportunities Center, students have access to corporate presentations, on-campus interviews, career and internship counseling, and networking trips to cities like New York and Boston. The school maintains strong "relationships with specific tech and consulting firms" on the East Coast, yet recruiting comes from a range of sources: "Companies come here for all disciplines from all over the country/world," offering "quite a variety of opportunities." A current student shares, "I've had a great experience at Tepper. I was able to land a full-time offer at a prestigious consulting firm and I'm confident that I have learned the proper business tools to excel there once I graduate."

In recent years, Tepper students have taken diverse jobs at corporations including Deloitte, GlaxoSmithKline, Accenture, Booz and Company, McKinsey & Company, KPMG Consulting, PriceWaterHouseCoopers, General Mills, Amazon.com, Unilever, AOL, Google, Intel Corporation, Morgan Stanley, and Wachovia. The class of 2011 had a mean base salary of over $101,000, with almost 80 percent of the class receiving an additional signing bonus between $2,000 and $52,000. Financial services and consulting were the most popular industries, capturing almost 29 percent and 25 percent of the class, respectively, with technology coming in third, with about 20 percent of graduates.

Student Life and Environment

At this "very prestigious" business school, "Everyone is extremely career driven and most people really want to get value out of their education." At the same time, Tepper MBAs manage to be "ambitious without being obnoxious," balancing a dedication to their studies with a friendly and collaborative attitude. "There are no competitive undertones in classes or with career search" on this friendly campus. When interacting with their classmates, most students are "happy to help out with everything from careers to homework."

"Academic and social clubs and activities are diverse and well-funded" at Tepper, and most MBA candidates find time to get involved in extracurricular activities. One student tells us, "I spend at least as much time on extracurricular activities (case competitions, clubs, events, etc.) as I do on class work." Socially, "Most people will go out at least one or two nights a weekend, if they do not have families," often congregating at one of the "central watering holes within walking distance of where most students live." There are also "weekly social events on campus," which are particularly fun because "everyone knows each other" in this small program.

A great environment for graduate students professionals, and families, the Carnegie Mellon campus is located near downtown Pittsburgh, "a beautiful city and very affordable on a student budget." A student adds, "As someone with a family, there is definitely a lot in the Pittsburgh area to keep everyone busy and happy."

Admissions

Tepper evaluates prospective students on a range of factors, and the school encourages students to look beyond the medians and means when considering their eligibility for admission. That said, admission is selective. For the past three years, over 50 percent of the incoming class has submitted GMAT scores of 700 or higher. The average GPA for entering students was 3.26 for 2012.

FINANCIAL FACTS

Annual tuition	$55,800
Fees	$0
Cost of books	$8,554
Room & board	$14,612
% of students receiving aid	82
% of first-year students receiving aid	83
% of students receiving grants	68
Average award package	$77,000
Average grant	$17,724
Average loan	$47,476
Average student loan debt	$89,311

ADMISSIONS

Admissions Selectivity Rating	96
# of applications received	1,575
% applicants accepted	27
% acceptees attending	49
Average GMAT	693
Range of GMAT	660–720
Average GPA	3.26
TOEFL required of international students	Yes
Minimum TOEFL (paper/computer)	600/250
Application fee	$125
International application fee	$125
Application Deadline/Notification	
Round 1:	10/22 / 12/19
Round 2:	1/3 / 3/18
Round 3:	3/4 / 4/30
Round 4:	4/22 / 5/24
Deferment available	No
Transfer students accepted	No
Non-fall admissions	No
Need-blind admissions	Yes

EMPLOYMENT PROFILE

Career Rating		99
Percent employed at graduation		76
Percent employed 3 months after graduation		90
Average base starting salary		$107,700
Primary Source of Full-time Job Acceptances		
School-facilitated activities	125(75%)	
Graduate-facilitated activities	41(25%)	

Grads Employed by Function% Avg. Salary

Marketing	(23%)	$103,851
Operations	(5%)	$95,548
Consulting	(31%)	$122,353
Management	(12%)	$102,150
Finance	(25%)	$100,821
HR	(1%)	
MIS	(2%)	$88,333

Top 5 Employers Hiring Grads
Pricewaterhouse Coopers(18), Amazon.com (9), Deloitte & Touche (7), Deutsche Bank (5), Booz and Company (5)

CASE WESTERN RESERVE UNIVERSITY
WEATHERHEAD SCHOOL OF MANAGEMENT

GENERAL INFORMATION

Type of school	Private
Affiliation	No Affiliation
Academic calendar	Semester

SURVEY SAYS...
Good social scene, Cutting-edge classes, Smart classrooms
Solid preparation in:
General management, Teamwork, Communication/interpersonal skills, Environmental sustainability

STUDENTS

Enrollment of parent institution	10,029
Enrollment of MBA Program	100
% male/female	67/33
% out-of-state	19
% part-time	43
% underrepresented minority	11
% international	42
Average age at entry	27
Average years work experience at entry	4.3

ACADEMICS

Academic Experience Rating	86
Profs interesting rating	87
Profs accesible rating	85
Student/faculty ratio	9:1
% female faculty	24
% underrepresented minority faculty	3
% part-time faculty	27

Joint Degrees
MBA/JD; MBA/MD; MBA/MS in Social Administration; MBA/MPH; MBA/Master of Global Management; MSM Finance and Tongji University

Prominent Alumni
Mark Weinberger, Chairman & CEO-elect, Ernst & Young; Donald Washkewicz, President, Chairman & CEO, Parker-Hannifin Corporation; Andrew Gilchrist, President & Chief Commercia Officer, R.J. Reynolds Tobacco Company; Peter Hellman, President & CFO (retired), Nordson Corporation

Academics

One of the Midwest's finest business programs, Case Western's Weatherhead School of Management has a "great reputation" and "world class...faculty." The "relatively small" class sizes afford students the opportunity "to network with professors and staff." While students admit that, "core academics are probably not much different from those at other business schools," they staunchly assert that what sets Weatherhead apart is it emphasis on interpersonal skills, team building, leadership, design thinking and sustainability. Indeed, there "is no school like it when it comes to looking at the softer side of business." And students find this "forward-thinking curriculum" extremely beneficial and highly applicable to real world settings.

MBA candidates at Case are also quick to exclaim that "professors are without a doubt the strength of this program." As one ecstatic second-year student elaborates, "Across the board they are very accessible and giving of their time. It is easy to forge strong [a] personal relationships with them." And, "for the most part, they are highly engaging, professionals who are also great teachers."

Although the administration is currently in a bit of flux (a new dean was just appointed in 2013), students nonetheless give them fairly high marks as well. It's "clear from their activities that the administrators in Weatherhead are dedicated to constantly refining the program and improving the student experience year after year."

Career and Placement

Career opportunities are plentiful for Case MBAs. When on the job hunt, students eagerly turn towards Weatherhead's Career Management Office as they are great at "providing specific and one-on-one career service to every student." They excel at helping students leverage their talents and skills and expertly demonstrate how to maximize networking opportunities. Additionally, the office offers resume reviews, mock interviews, career coaching, dress-for-success workshops and host numerous career fairs.

A snapshot of employers who frequently hire Weatherhead grads might include Johnson & Johnson, American Greetings, IBM, Key Bank, McKinsey, Ohio Savings, General Electric, Ernst & Young, PNC Bank, Bristol West, Progressive, Eaton, National City and Deloitte Consulting.

ADMISSIONS CONTACT: DEBORAH BIBB, SENIOR DIRECTOR OF ADMISSIONS
ADDRESS: 150 PETER B. LEWIS BUILDING, 10900 EUCLID AVENUE, CLEVELAND, OH 44106-7235
PHONE: 216-368-2030 • FAX: 216-368-5548
E-MAIL: WSOMADMISSIONS@CASE.EDU • WEBSITE: WWW.WEATHERHEAD.CASE.EDU/DEGREES/MBA

Student Life and Environment

Students who attend Weatherhead should definitely be prepared to tackle an intense workload. As one overwhelmed student grumbles, "The course-load is heavy, perhaps too heavy at times. There are countless extracurricular competitions and events that often must be pushed aside in deference to the workload. Too often students at Weatherhead are hesitant to go to important networking events and club meetings due to the constant deluge of assignments."

However, when students do find a moment to catch their breath, they can easily take advantage of all Cleveland has to offer. "Case Western is closely intertwined with Cleveland's cultural centers in University circle. The Cleveland Museum of Art, the Museum of Contemporary Art, the Cleveland Botanical Gardens, the Cinematheque repertory theater, and the orchestra at Severance Hall are all just steps away from the campus. With such cultural wealth at your doorstep it can be a great place to clear your head for a few hours."

Admission

Gaining admission to Case's MBA program is certainly a competitive process and solid academic credentials are definitely required. The admissions office offers three application rounds—one with a November deadline, one with a January deadline and one with a March deadline. Applications received after the March deadline will be considered on a rolling basis (assuming space is still available). The school requires applicants to have an undergraduate degree from an accredited institution and a minimum of two years (preferred) of full-time work experience. Mandatory application materials include academic transcripts, GMAT (preferred) or GRE score, English proficiency exam for non-native speakers (minimum score of 100 on the IBT version of the TOEFL required), two essays, current resume, two letters of recommendation and, of course, an application fee.

FINANCIAL FACTS

Annual tuition	$44,000
Fees	$1,640
Cost of books	$1,392
Room & board	$17,530
% of students receiving aid	92
% of first-year students receiving aid	91
% of students receiving grants	84
Average award package	$34,880
Average grant	$21,871
Average loan	$35,014
Average student loan debt	$24,961

ADMISSIONS

Admissions Selectivity Rating	78
# of applications received	269
% applicants accepted	64
% acceptees attending	33
Average GMAT	631
Range of GMAT	580–690
Average GPA	3.30
TOEFL required of international students	Yes
Minimum TOEFL (paper/computer)	600/250
Application fee	$100
International application fee	$100
Application Deadline/Notification	
Round 1:	11/1 / 12/15
Round 2:	1/15 / 3/1
Round 3:	3/15 / 4/15
Deferment available	No
Transfer students accepted	Yes
Transfer application policy:	
Maximum number of transferable credits is 6 Semester hours from an AACSB-accredited program.	
Non-fall admissions	No
Need-blind admissions	Yes

EMPLOYMENT PROFILE

		Grads Employed by Function	% Avg. Salary
Career Rating	91		
Percent employed at graduation	64	Marketing	(20%) $80,500
Percent employed 3 months after graduation	86	Consulting	(24%) $87,227
		Finance	(26%) $72,630
Average base starting salary	$80,762	Other	(28%) $84,417
Primary Source of Full-time Job Acceptances		**Top 5 Employers Hiring Grads**	
School-facilitated activities	31 (57%)	Deloitte (5), KeyBank (2), Cleveland Clinic (2),	
Graduate-facilitated activities	8 (15%)	PricewaterhouseCoopers LLP (1), Ernst &	
Unknown	15 (28%)	Young (1)	

CENTRAL MICHIGAN UNIVERSITY
COLLEGE OF BUSINESS ADMINISTRATION

GENERAL INFORMATION
Type of school	Public
Affiliation	No Affiliation
Academic calendar	Semester

SURVEY SAYS...
Friendly students, Happy students
Solid preparation in:
General management, Teamwork,
Communication/interpersonal skills,
Quantitative skills, Doing business in
a global economy

STUDENTS
Enrollment of MBA Program	113
% male/female	64/36
% out-of-state	34
% part-time	49
% international	34
Average age at entry	28
Average years work experience at entry	3.0

ACADEMICS
Academic Experience Rating	**80**
Profs interesting rating	80
Profs accesible rating	87
Student/faculty ratio	23:1
% female faculty	20
% underrepresented minority faculty	10

Prominent Alumni
Roger L. Kesseler, Retired, VP &
Controller, The Dow Chemical
Company; Jerry D. Campbell, Pres.
& CEO, Community National Bank
of the South; Michael Fred
O'Donnell, Retired, Managing
Director, Protiviti Inc.; Robert I.
Noe, CEO, 1 Sync; Michael J.
Bowen, Chairman & CEO,
Westwood Development Group

Academics

Central Michigan University offers a comprehensive MBA program with a focus on general management. Students appreciate the fact that "The program is affordable, and offers flexible scheduling though weekend classes and night classes." CMU's "well-structured...flexible" curriculum begins with a set of foundational and core courses, taught in a series of quick, eight-week terms. While the core is "very broad," students can later pursue a concentration in one of many fields, including accounting, business economics, general management, management consulting, and management information systems. Emphasizing real-world business skills, CMU "allows students to learn through practical applications of techniques," including case studies, simulations, and consulting projects. "Faculty is the greatest strength" here. Well-versed in contemporary business topics, "The graduate level professors in the business school contribute well-researched concepts with real-world practices to provide students with a relevant, practical skill set."

CMU offers the complete full-time MBA on its main campus in Mount Pleasant, as well as at its auxiliary facilities in Midland, Michigan. "All MBA classes are in the evenings [and] some on weekends," which makes the program a "great fit for full-time employees." At the same time, the program is appropriate for early career professionals who want to make a move into management positions, and many complete the program on a full-time basis. No matter what your previous professional preparation, the small class size "fosters communication through insightful dialogue between students and faculty" and "really allow[s] students to become more involved in the learning process." In most classes, "Students are willing to engage in thoughtful conversation and challenge the view points of both other students and faculty." With a low graduate enrollment and a patently "friendly atmosphere," CMU's environment is student-centered and supportive. While the workload in some classes can be "very heavy," the teaching staff is "down-to-earth and easy to talk to," comprised of caring professors who "truly want what's best for the student." Similarly, "The administration at CMU is very competent and willing to help with an open-door policy to its students."

Career and Placement

Thanks to the school's flexible schedule and convenient evening classes, a large percentage of CMU students are working professionals—many of whom may not be looking for a new position after graduation. For those starting a new career (or those who want to make a career change), Central Michigan University's MBA program is designed to prepare students for a position in management, with numerous real world and practical experiences woven into the curriculum.

The university Career Services department maintains a job vacancy bulletin and hosts campus career fairs; however, students in the MBA program say the school could improve if they "spread more awareness of their programs." With such a strong academic program, students admit that, "CMU could improve how they market themselves as a business school. The quality of the MBA program is an aspect they should take greater steps to express to the nation."

ADMISSIONS CONTACT: PAMELA STAMBERSKY, MBA ADVISOR
ADDRESS: 252 ABSC-GRAWN HALL, MOUNT PLEASANT, MI 48859
PHONE: 989-774-3150 • FAX: 989-774-1320
E-MAIL: MBA@CMICH.EDU • WEBSITE: WWW.CBA.CMICH.EDU

Student Life and Environment

Attracting a mix of "international students, professionals, and full-time students," you might be "surprised at the diversity" on CMU's small, Midwestern campus. "There are a lot of foreign students and it is so cool to get to know people from around the world. You see many of the same faces as you move through the program so you are able to get to know people and make good friendships and networking connections." Across the board, students are "driven and striving for success in the program" and "willing to lend a hand."

"There is definitely a small-class, small-school feel" at CMU. The campus is "intimate, friendly, [and] safe," and "it is very easy to feel comfortable and welcome here." "People are very friendly, and good team players." While academics (and professional life) keep students on the go, there is more to CMU than classes and homework. "There are a multitude of clubs and activities for students to join," both through the business school, as well as the university at large. Juggling work and school, some part-timers don't have time to participate in extracurricular activities; others take full advantage of the school's lively atmosphere. A current MBA agrees, "As a married graduate student with a full-time career, I still find CMU to be engaging both in the classroom and on campus in general. There are plenty of student organizations, activities, and professional networking opportunities to take advantage of."

Most part-time students commute to school, while many full-time students live on campus. Unfortunately, campus residents without a car can feel a bit stranded. Happily, the CMU campus provides the necessary amenities, with "plenty of facilities like computer labs, libraries, [and a] student activity center." As its name implies, Mount Pleasant makes a nice backdrop to campus life; "The campus is located in a safe town, so students can freely walk around the beautiful campus and enjoy themselves." During the summer, students also enjoy "kayaking down the Chippewa River, bicycle trails, and events such as home shows and boat shows that are hosted on campus."

Admissions

To calculate a students' eligibility for admission, Central Michigan University multiplies their undergraduate GPA by 200, then adds that number to their GMAT score. Using this calculation, prospective students must achieve at least 1050 points to be considered for admission. Additionally, students cannot be admitted if their GMAT score is below 450, no matter what their GPA. International students must submit TOEFL scores; however, students with TOEFL scores that fall short of that minimum requirement may take additional English classes while they begin the MBA program.

FINANCIAL FACTS

Annual tuition (in-state/ out-of-state)	$13,303/$23,746
Cost of books	$1,600
Room & board	$7,947

ADMISSIONS

Admissions Selectivity Rating	**73**
# of applications received	93
% applicants accepted	86
% acceptees attending	89
Average GMAT	513
Average GPA	3.59
TOEFL required of international students	Yes
Minimum TOEFL (paper/computer)	550/213
International application fee	$45
Deferment available	Yes
Maximum length of deferment	one Semester
Transfer students accepted	Yes
Transfer application policy: Limit of 12 credit hours from an accredited institution	
Non-fall admissions	Yes
Need-blind admissions	No

CHAPMAN UNIVERSITY
THE GEORGE L. ARGYROS SCHOOL OF BUSINESS AND ECONOMICS

Academics

Chapman University, a "small," "beautiful" private university in Orange County, California, has a "very strong MBA program" that offers students a great education. But "It's not just about the classes," at Chapman. "It is about the relationships, the networking, and the experience. It is a comprehensive, 360-degree program." Chapman is "a research-intensive university" that offers "entrepreneurship incubators" and many other unique opportunities to its enthusiastic students. This is just one of the many reasons students are convinced that Chapman "will become one of the top business schools in the nation."

Chapman's distinguishing features include its programs in Entrepreneurship and Financial services, a dual MBA/MFA in Film and Television Producing, a "good study-abroad program" and its popular Flex MBA, which allows working students to attend full- or part-time during the evening. Chapman's traditional full-time MBA program has a strong focus on student career campaign. Students in both programs receive the majority of their credits from Chapman's core curriculum, which provides a solid foundation in business and finance. Electives include entrepreneurship, international business, corporate entrepreneurship, and marketing.

Students say they receive a "very personalized education" from the "outstanding faculty." Chapman's small classes are taught by "Ph.D.s and established professionals," who are "dedicated," "highly accessible," and "expect a lot." Academic and professional development is complimented by mentoring programs and contests run by the Ralph W. Leatherby Center for Entrepreneurship and Business Ethics, and research opportunities, conferences, and workshops hosted by the A. Gary Anderson Center for Economic Research, The Walter Schmidt Center for International Business, and Larry C. Hoag for Real Estate and Finance. Beyond the campus, the school has strong ties to the local business community, which gives students the chance to forge "lasting business relationships." Chapman students say the school does an excellent job preparing them to deal with "current economic conditions" and whatever else they may face in the future.

Career and Placement

Chapman's MBA program "has only become stronger with the addition of a highly visible office (Career Management Center) on campus," which employs "three full-time career placement specialists" to assist and support students in reaching their career goals. The center provides lots of specialized opportunities through individual career counseling and its many networking events, including the "Dinner for Eight" program, where eight students are selected to have an intimate dinner with a local business leader. One student says that the greatest strength of Chapman isn't the Career Management Center but "the people associated with the school," who provide "strong contacts, great jobs, networking, and lasting business relationships." The majority of graduates accepting new jobs took positions in the consumer products field, or in media or entertainment. The top five employers last year were Standard Pacific Homes, Ingram Micro, Experian, ADP, Commerce National Bank, Lanes Capital Partners.

ADMISSIONS CONTACT: DEBRA GONDA, ASSOCIATE DIRECTOR
ADDRESS: ASBE, ONE UNIVERSITY DR., ORANGE, CA 92866
PHONE: 714-997-6745 • FAX: 714-532-6081
E-MAIL: GONDA@CHAPMAN.EDU • WEBSITE: WWW.CHAPMAN.EDU/ARGYROS/MBA

Student Life and Environment

Life at Chapman is filled with opportunities for networking and academic enrichment. The Entrepreneur Speaker Series and the Distinguished Speaker series regularly host influential business leaders, and each of the four research institutes offer additional lectures, panel discussions, and even book signings. The MBA association, run by a group of students elected by their peers, organizes lots of social and professional events, such as "Pizza and Beer Night," which "gives students the opportunity to eat and have some drinks with a high profile executive in a relaxed, non-pretentious atmosphere."

Many Chapman students attend part-time, and students tend to be on the younger side, so there is a wide-range of work experience and perspectives in classrooms. Though many students come from work in business attire, others sport "flip-flops and board shorts," though they "clean up nice, when they have to." Students are "friendly" and "smart," and are "very willing to collaborate and help one another succeed." They're "not at all competitive about grades, so study groups are very common." "There are a lot of sports and community events" for students who need a break from homework or networking, and "plenty of nearby restaurants and bars that support a small community vibe."

Admissions

Students entering Chapman have three years of work experience on average, and though the school prefers students to have spent at least two years in a professional field, they do accept strong applicants with experience. The GMAT or GRE is required for all programs except the Executive MBA. In addition to GMAT scores, the application package must also include two recommendations from people who know the student "in either a professional or academic setting." Students must have a minimum undergraduate GPA of 2.5, but the average undergraduate GPA of the entering class is considerably higher. Interviews are required for the full-time and Executive MBA program, while interviews for the Flex program "are by request or invitation." International students must take the TOEFL and have minimum scores of 600 for the paper-based portion, 213 for the computer-based, and 87 for the Internet-based portion or IELTS with a minimum score of 7. Applications for the full-time and Executive MBA programs are accepted for the fall semester only. Applications for the Flex Program are accepted for the fall and spring.

FINANCIAL FACTS

Annual tuition	$34,500
Cost of books	$1,400
Room & board	$17,000
% of students receiving aid	78
% of first-year students receiving aid	73
% of students receiving grants	49
Average award package	$34,077
Average grant	$6,533
Average loan	$26,461
Average student loan debt	$53,989

ADMISSIONS

Admissions Selectivity Rating	87
# of applications received	113
% applicants accepted	46
% acceptees attending	58
Average GMAT	615
Range of GMAT	560–660
Average GPA	3.34
TOEFL required of international students	Yes
Minimum TOEFL (paper/computer)	600
International application fee	$60
Application Deadline/Notification	
Round 1:	11/1 /
Round 2:	2/1 /
Round 3:	5/1 /
Deferment available	Yes
Maximum length of deferment	1 year
Transfer students accepted	Yes
Transfer application policy: Transfer up to six units of course work	
Non-fall admissions	Yes
Need-blind admissions	Yes

EMPLOYMENT PROFILE

Career Rating	88	**Grads Employed by Function% Avg. Salary**	
Percent employed at graduation	45	Marketing	(60%) $58,188
Percent employed 3 months		Management	(7%)
after graduation	85	Finance	(20%) $84,000
Average base starting salary	$63,864	MIS	(7%)
Primary Source of Full-time Job Acceptances		Other	(13%) $56,333
School-facilitated activities	7(47%)	**Top 5 Employers Hiring Grads**	
Graduate-facilitated activities	5(33%)	GE(1), Ingram Micro (1), Experian (1), Deloitte	
Unknown	3(20%)	(1), Baxter (1)	

THE CHINESE UNIVERSITY OF HONG KONG
FACULTY OF BUSINESS ADMINISTRATION

GENERAL INFORMATION

Type of school	Public
Affiliation	No Affiliation

SURVEY SAYS...

Friendly students, Good social scene,
Good peer network,
Smart classrooms

STUDENTS

Enrollment of parent institution	14,817
Enrollment of MBA Program	344
% male/female	55/45
% part-time	64
% international	85
Average age at entry	28
Average years work experience at entry	5.0

ACADEMICS

Academic Experience Rating	82
Profs interesting rating	74
Profs accesible rating	76

Joint Degrees

CUHK MBA/ HEC Dual Degree
Program; CUHK MBA/ University of
Texas at Austin Dual Degree
Program; CUHK MBA/ RSM Dual
Degree Program

Academics

In 1966, The Chinese University of Hong Kong became the first school in China to offer a full-time MBA program. Today, the university boasts one of the most reputable business schools in Asia and the Pacific, attracting students for its "international recognition, good academic reputation, and diverse teacher and student pools." A great entryway for those seeking a professional position in Hong Kong, the school boasts a "strong alumni network" in the city and an excellent reputation in the region. In particular, the school is touted for its programs in finance and marketing, with a special emphasis on Chinese business. Through lecture, case studies, group work, directed research, and discussion, classes are a balance of "individual and group efforts that cultivate teamwork among students that is important for business." Group work is particularly gratifying at CUMBA, where students comprise "a very diverse group from just about every continent. Their combined work experience and life experiences has really contributed to the program."

Maintaining a working relationship with various universities in mainland China and Taiwan, the school's "administration is very dedicated and efficient." The school attracts faculty from all over the world, and the current teaching staff includes professors from Australia, Hong Kong, Europe, New Zealand, mainland China, Southeast Asia, Taiwan, and the United States. Despite their varied origins, CUMBA faculty are deeply engaged in the Hong Kong business culture. A student attests, "Teaching staff are actively involved in the business community in areas of research and consulting. So there are lots of first-hand findings and . . . information [on] local business trends." On the whole, students appreciate the school's progressive outlook, saying professors "stay abreast of the real-life market and keep up to date with their own knowledge."

While Cantonese is the dominant language spoken in Hong Kong, courses at CUMBA are taught in English, with the exception of a few elective courses whose unique nature demands instruction in Chinese. The 54-unit curriculum consists of required core course work, followed by electives. Through electives, students have the option to pursue a concentration in one of four areas: China business, finance, marketing, or entrepreneurship. The full-time curriculum can be completed in 16 months of study, including internships. Without an internship, the program can be completed as quickly as 12 months. Either way, the program is intense, with a "busy workload and no breaks in between terms." In addition to the traditional MBA programs offered through the school, students may choose to pursue a joint-degree with partner universities in Mainland China or the HEC School of Management in France or the University of Texas at Austin.

Career and Placement

As part of the MBA experience, students at The Chinese University of Hong Kong are expected to develop career goals and design a plan of action to meet those goals. The Career Management Centre facilitates students looking for summer internship placements, as well as students looking for permanent positions after graduation. The centre also hosts an executive development series on presentation, communication, and influencing skills project management, and a series of career talks and job search workshops.

The Asian market continues to be a popular work location for CUMBA graduates. An over-whelming 92% have taken up career opportunities in this region. The ever growing Greater China market has attracted 72% of the class to continue to pursue their career development (47% in Hong Kong, 21% in China and 4% in Taiwan). Twenty percent are spilt among other Asian countries including India, Singapore, Japan, Korea and Thailand – truly reflecting the diversity of the students in contributing to the growth of this ever important continent.

FINANCIAL FACTS

Annual tuition	$61,700
Room & board	
(on/off-campus)	$5,700/$11,500

ADMISSIONS

Admissions Selectivity Rating	85
Average GMAT	650
TOEFL required of	
international students	No
Application fee	$100
International application fee	$100
Early application deadline	10/31
Regular application deadline	3/31
Regular application notification	5/31
Application Deadline/Notification	
Round 1:	11/30 / 1/31
Round 2:	1/15 / 3/15
Round 3:	3/31 / 5/31
Deferment available	Yes
Maximum length	
of deferment	1 year
Transfer students accepted	No
Non-fall admissions	No
Need-blind admissions	Yes

Nearly 91% of these graduates have been successfully undergoing career changes, either in job function (86%) or work location (46%), or both (34%). The Chinese University of Hong Kong's comprehensive MBA curriculum with a strategic focus in China and Asia plays an essential part in equipping career changers in facing the challenges of transformation and enabling them to explore new ventures in their targeted industries and locations.

Graduates have successfully moved from non-business and/or technical background to front line business development, consulting, or finance function. These career changers have proved their abilities to bring transferrable skill sets and strategic insights to their new roles.

Student Life and Environment

CUMBA boasts a "beautiful campus" environment, and its daytime and weekend-mode students take classes on the main campus. Beginning from the early part of 2010, the business school will move into a state-of-the-art new teaching building near its main campus, and classes from then on will be given there. Evening-mode students attend classes in the school's MBA Town Centre, a modern and spacious 900-square-meter facility located in downtown. In addition to the extensive computer facilities available via the larger university, MBA students have access to over 100 microcomputers in the Town Centre, connected via LAN network. MBA students have the option of living on campus in the graduate residence halls; they also have access to the school's sports facilities, including three indoor gyms and an Olympic-sized swimming pool.

One of the major attractions of CUMBA is its diverse student population, who bring experience "from a variety of professions and cultures." Totally student-run, the MBA Student's Association sponsors a broad range of social and professional events, including executive seminars, company visits, and study tours to mainland China. The school also sponsors various social and recreational events, such as charity and fund-raising activities and sports teams, although some students say "Campus life is not adapted to international students at all." Even part-timers enjoy a sense of community. One says, "I am a part-time student. Fellow students usually have dinner gatherings after school."

Admissions

To be considered for admission to CUMBA, prospective students must hold an undergraduate degree (with at least a B average), have at least 3 years of relevant work experience post-graduation, and submit current GMAT scores. The average GMAT score for accepted applicants changes every year; however, the class average usually hovers between 620–640. Interviews are required for all short-listed applicants, either in person or via telephone, as determined by the selection committee.

EMPLOYMENT PROFILE

Career Rating	63	Grads Employed by Function% Avg. Salary	
Percent employed at graduation	66	Marketing	(36%)
Percent employed 3 months		Consulting	(13%)
after graduation	89	Management	(4%)
Primary Source of Full-time Job Acceptances		Finance	(27%)
School-facilitated activities	(34%)	**Top 5 Employers Hiring Grads**	
Graduate-facilitated activities	(66%)	Google, PricewaterhouseCoopers Consulting, Bank of China International, BlackRock, Bulgari	

THE CITADEL
SCHOOL OF BUSINESS ADMINISTRATION

GENERAL INFORMATION

Type of school	Public
Affiliation	No Affiliation
Academic calendar	Semester

SURVEY SAYS...

Students love Charleston, SC,
Friendly students, Good peer network
Solid preparation in:
Accounting

STUDENTS

Enrollment of parent institution	3,499
Enrollment of MBA Program	258
% male/female	76/24
% out-of-state	12
% part-time	90
% underrepresented minority	20
% international	12
Average age at entry	27

ACADEMICS

Academic Experience Rating	**74**
Profs interesting rating	79
Profs accesible rating	84
Student/faculty ratio	15:1
% female faculty	18
% underrepresented minority faculty	18
% part-time faculty	6

Joint Degrees

PharmD/MBA Program, 4 years;
MD/MBA, 1 year

Prominent Alumni

Pat Conroy, Author; Ernest Hollings, U.S. Senator, South Carolina; Lt. Col. Randy Bresnik, USMC, NASA Astronaut; CDR Greg McWherter, USN, Commander of the Blue Angels; Dr. Harvey W. Schiller, Former Executive Director, US Olympic Committee

Academics

If there is one word students at The School of Business Administration at The Citadel keep repeating, it's "reputation," "reputation," "reputation," with "location," "prestige" and "affordability" all coming in at a close second. The Citadel's long-standing record for "building leaders and sound decision-makers," educating "quality students," and having "by far the best MBA reputation in South Carolina" make the School a universally respected institution worldwide. What's more, just saying you go to The Citadel "gets a reaction from people." Students can also benefit from "in-state tuition" and "excellent professors"—41 in all—"with incredible work and academic histories," most of whom "are working professionals, some with military backgrounds." According to one sales management major, the "administration and professors are flexible, encouraging, and easily accessible. The MBA program has challenged me in many ways, and the overall educational experience has been very rewarding." Another like-minded student tells us, "All professors consider the global perspective and tailor their classes" accordingly.

The MBA program at The Citadel is roughly a two to six year program, depending on students' work status and class load, totaling 36 credit hours. Other dual-degree programs, such as the PharmD/MBA and MD/MBA will often require the same amount of time from students. Candidates have the option to pursue areas of study in sports management, financial services, supply chain management, and project management. In their course of study, all enrolled students are required to take classes that specifically emphasize cooperative learning and experiential learning, while internships and entrepreneurship courses are both offered but not required.

One unique co-curricular offering at The Citadel is the Mentors Program, which matches MBA students with leaders in the local business community. Students who choose to participate in this program will be matched with a prominent business leader based on common interest and career path. Students also have the option to pursue study abroad, which offers programs in Ireland, Spain, France, and the UK.

Career and Placement

The Citadel's Career Services Center maintains an online job and resume database for current students and alumni. The Center also has working relationships with several online job boards, which give students a wide breadth of places to begin their job hunts. In addition, the Center organizes several career fairs, which are open to the entire school community. As one "of the most highly recognized business schools" in the area, recruiters and companies will be on the lookout for recent graduates, but overall "career training and placement" are areas in need of attention from the administration. One student enrolled in a dual-degree PharmD/MBA pointed out that, "Boeing is expanding into Charleston, and a lot of opportunities are passed along to the Citadel MBA students." Another student, a childcare administration major, tells us, "There is a very active MBA Association that is always organizing activities." Additionally, the School will often receive "many interesting speakers," and "alumni visit often," all of which offer unique and abundant networking opportunities for MBA candidates on the job-hunt.

Student Life and Environment

Among the reasons many students give for wanting to earn their MBA at The Citadel, it's often as simple as, "It's in Charleston." Much celebrated for its relaxed pace, friendly residents, and pristine ocean-front locale, Charleston, South Carolina, is a major draw for just about anyone. Thanks to the city's bucolic setting and old world charm, some students have cited the School's "old world study environment," consisting of leather couches and chairs, high ceilings, and old paintings." For prospective MBA students, The Citadel's status as a military academy can be somewhat misleading. One student reminds us that, while there "a lot of ex- or current military students, which is kind of to be expected at a military school, I was actually surprised at the number of non-military affiliated classmates." Another student touches on a similar point, offering that The Citadel is "much more diverse than one would expect at a conservative Southern military school."

On par with this sentiment, The Citadel does offer a wide range of activities for students, in addition to increasingly flexible scheduling options for commuters and part-time students with full-time jobs. "I'm very happy that the School is introducing more and more online courses," says a music business major. Many other students are taking advantage of The Citadel's night school program, which accommodates those who "work all day, then come straight to school" and will often take only "two classes per semester."

Admissions

Applicants to the MBA program at The Citadel must submit the following materials: GMAT scores, essay/personal statement, official undergrad transcript, resume, and at least two letters of recommendation. Other materials, such as proof of state residency, list of extracurricular activities, and an interview, are all optional but recommended. GRE scores will be taken into consideration, and proof of US residency or immigration form if an international student.. Interestingly enough, while GMAT scores are given due attention, The Citadel places greater emphasis on an applicant's undergraduate GPA and essay/personal statement, indicating the school's vested interest in working with students who show exceptional aptitude, work ethic, and sincere desire to attend The Citadel.

FINANCIAL FACTS

Cost of books	$500
% of students receiving aid	38
% of first-year students receiving aid	26
% of students receiving grants	3

ADMISSIONS

Admissions Selectivity Rating	79
# of applications received	117
% applicants accepted	54
% acceptees attending	67
Average GMAT	500
Range of GMAT	320–710
Average GPA	3.13
TOEFL required of international students	Yes
Minimum TOEFL (paper/computer)	550/213
Application fee	$30
International application fee	$30
Regular application deadline	6/15
Regular application notification	6/15
Application Deadline/Notification	
Deferment available	Yes
Maximum length of deferment	12 months
Transfer students accepted	Yes

Transfer application policy: A maximum of six hours credit for graduate courses from an AACSB-accredited institutions may be approved for transfer (except BADM 740), provided: (1) that those courses are determined to be equivalent to one of the advanced or elective courses at The Citadel, (2) that grades of "B" or better were received in the courses being considered for transfer credit, and (3) that credit for the courses was earned within the five years prior to admission into The Citadel MBA program.

Non-fall admissions	Yes
Need-blind admissions	Yes

CITY UNIVERSITY OF NEW YORK—BARUCH COLLEGE

ZICKLIN SCHOOL OF BUSINESS

GENERAL INFORMATION

Type of school	Public
Affiliation	No Affiliation
Academic calendar	Semester

SURVEY SAYS...

Students love New York, NY, Cutting-edge classes, Smart classrooms
Solid preparation in:
Accounting

STUDENTS

Enrollment of parent institution	16,500
Enrollment of MBA Program	1,531
% male/female	60/40
% part-time	87
% underrepresented minority	11
% international	22
Average age at entry	28
Average years work experience at entry	5.1

ACADEMICS

Academic Experience Rating	**84**
Profs interesting rating	78
Profs accesible rating	76
Student/faculty ratio	35:1
% female faculty	23
% underrepresented minority faculty	5
% part-time faculty	27

Joint Degrees

JD/MBA, 4.5 years (full-time)

Prominent Alumni

Larry Zicklin, Former Managing Partner, Neuberger Berman; Marcel Legrand, Sr. Vice President, Monster.com; JoAnn Ryan, President, ConEdison Solutions; William Newman, Founder & Chairman New Plan Excel Realty Trust; Hugh Panero, President & CEO, XM Satellite Radio

Academics

The City University of New York, Baruch College is an excellent choice for New York residents looking for "extremely affordable" in-state tuition rates. This public school offers "heavily discounted tuition" and is considered a "best value among business schools in NYC." "While there are some minor headaches (broken escalators) they are worth the affordable tuition and the quality and variety of educational offerings found at Baruch."

Location is another factor. Many students chose the Zicklin School of Business "because it was in New York," in close "proximity to Wall Street," "at the center of the world of finance." Although there are more prestigious graduate schools, some students prefer being "the underdog in NYC. We don't have as much pressure to 'succeed' the way that the Columbia and NYU students have, so we focus on becoming the best that we can. It's a very positive environment, which allows us to learn a lot."

The availability of a flexible program is popular among students who hold full-time jobs. This option allows students to "switch between full-time and part-time" employment. As one student currently working in the entertainment field explains, "I have a fluid but predictable schedule. I needed a program that allowed me to shift between full-time and part-time class dependent upon my workload." The school is also "well regarded in the tax and accounting fields," and has a "highly competitive MBA in Accountancy program."

Opinions vary on the quality of professors at Baruch. "Many of the professors bring in experiences from outside of the classroom that are extremely relevant to our learning. A textbook can only stay up-to-date for so long and that's why non-classroom experience plays such a big role in our learning. For the amount of money I've paid (relatively inexpensive compared to other good B-schools) I've been pleasantly surprised by the professors and their ability to teach at such a high level." Another student comments, "They are extremely intelligent however they do not always explain the material in an easy-to-understand manner."

Many students expressed dissatisfaction with the school's administration. Understaffing, as well as "budget constraints, and size of the academic class" were listed as possible reasons for the administration's "slow" response to students' concerns. Registration tends to go smoothly as this student notes, "Required classes are all registered for us automatically. We select electives, relay them to the MBA administration, and they register them for us. It's very simple."

Career and Placement

Location definitely helps Baruch students with their job search with many graduates finding positions in the financial sector. "Being in New York is very helpful." There are "a lot of alums in New York who are helpful resources for information." "The network of alumni…is extremely active in helping students find employment and build connections with the community." Equally appealing is "the proximity to recruiters from all of New York City and surrounding areas."

The school regularly hosts events "to promote awareness and networking." Many of these occur during the day when it is difficult for some part-time graduate students to attend. However, networking with fellow students can be done anytime, as a second-semester student points out. "I see many familiar faces in my classes and have been able to develop a network among students without attending club meetings or other events." The school has a "positive environment. Students help each other. Career advisory is great!"

ADMISSIONS CONTACT: THOMAS LO, ASSOCIATE DIRECTOR OF GRADUATE ADMISSIONS
ADDRESS: ONE BERNARD BARUCH WAY, BOX H-0820, NEW YORK, NY 10010
PHONE: 646-312-1300 • FAX: 646-312-1301
E-MAIL: ZICKLINGRADADMISSIONS@BARUCH.CUNY.EDU
WEBSITE: WWW.BARUCH.CUNY.EDU/ZICKLIN

Student Life and Environment

Everyone agrees: Baruch's "city campus" is in a "great location in NYC." There are "plenty of places on campus to study or meet with class groups. Student organizations are highly active and cover the spectrum of professional, academic, and extracurricular interests." Social clubs are popular, "particularly mentoring and other professional related program[s]." Although it "could use a cosmetic make-over," the "campus is very accessible." "The school's library is great, and…they have a swimming pool." Full-time MBA students have the added bonus of a dedicated lounge "which provides a nice place to be, study, and socialize."

Social life at Zicklin School of Business is plentiful. "Numerous social gatherings are organized by the graduate students and also include social gatherings co-hosted with other schools such as with NYU, Fordham, and Pace." "Everyone is extremely friendly and approachable." "In class there's a general sense of togetherness. We have study sessions together before big exams. Everyone is very smart, so it's challenging and exciting to get scores above the mean." Cohorts prove valuable. "My cohort spends a lot of time together whether it is preparing for projects or letting loose on a Thursday night. We are all hard-workers and try to utilize the resources provided by our counselors and mentors." The few complaints about student life mostly come from part-time students with full-time jobs, who just don't have the time to partake in all that is available, like this student who says, "I work full time and don't spend time on campus or doing many activities. Many grad students seem to be in the same boat."

Admissions

An accredited bachelor's degree with official transcripts must be submitted along with GMAT scores, letters of recommendation, undergraduate GPA, and a personal statement describing career goals and your reasons for obtaining a graduate degree is required. A resume of work experience is required as are TOEFL scores for international students. Students enter Baruch at the average age of 28, with an average 3.3 GPA, and an average GMAT score of 501. The first round of applications is due 1/15; the second round is due 4/15.

FINANCIAL FACTS

Annual tuition (in-state/ out-of-state)	$12,770/$24,795
Fees	$2,269
Cost of books	$1,337
Room & board	$21,450
% of students receiving aid	80
% of first-year students receiving aid	95
% of students receiving grants	60
Average grant	$4,000
Average loan	$16,300
Average student loan debt	$30,000

ADMISSIONS

Admissions Selectivity Rating	86
# of applications received	1,146
% applicants accepted	47
% acceptees attending	62
Average GMAT	591
Range of GMAT	550–640
Average GPA	3.30
TOEFL required of international students	Yes
Minimum TOEFL (paper/computer)	610/243
Application fee	$135
International application fee	$135
Early application deadline	1/15
Early notification date	3/31
Regular application deadline	5/31
Application Deadline/Notification	
Round 1:	1/15 / 3/31
Round 2:	4/15 / 6/30
Deferment available	Yes
Maximum length of deferment	1 year
Transfer students accepted	Yes
Transfer application policy: Same application process as all applicants; up to 12 credits from an AACSB-accredited institution may be transferred.	
Non-fall admissions	Yes
Need-blind admissions	Yes

EMPLOYMENT PROFILE

Career Rating	86	Grads Employed by Function	% Avg. Salary
Percent employed at graduation	39	Marketing	(7%)
Percent employed 3 months after graduation	13	Operations	(11%) $83,833
		Consulting	(14%) $105,000
Average base starting salary	$81,678	Management	(4%)
Primary Source of Full-time Job Acceptances		Finance	(50%) $84,615
School-facilitated activities	12(43%)	HR	(4%)
Graduate-facilitated activities	15(54%)	MIS	(4%)
Unknown	1(4%)	Other	(7%)
		Top 5 Employers Hiring Grads	
		PwC(5), Ernst & Young (3), JPMorgan Chase (2)	

CLAREMONT GRADUATE UNIVERSITY
THE PETER F. DRUCKER AND MASATOSHI ITO GRADUATE SCHOOL OF MANAGEMENT

GENERAL INFORMATION

Type of school	Private
Affiliation	No Affiliation
Academic calendar	Semester

SURVEY SAYS...

Students love Claremont, CA, Friendly students, Good peer network, Happy students
Solid preparation in:
General management, Teamwork

STUDENTS

Enrollment of parent institution	2,200
Enrollment of MBA Program	123
% male/female	67/33
% part-time	31
% underrepresented minority	28
% international	41
Average age at entry	27
Average years work experience at entry	3.0

ACADEMICS

Academic Experience Rating	**83**
Profs interesting rating	90
Profs accesible rating	87
Student/faculty ratio	3:1
% female faculty	27
% underrepresented minority faculty	27
% part-time faculty	58

Joint Degrees

Dual-degree programs in human resources, biosciences, information sciences, economics, cultural management, education, psychology, public policy, and by special arrangement in other disciplines.

Prominent Alumni

Rajiv Dutta, President, Skype Technologies SA; Ming-Hsun Chen, Chairwom, China Development Finincial Holding Corp; Stephen Rountree, President & COO, Music & Performing Art Ctr of LA Cnty; Colin Forkner, CEO & Vice Chairman, Pacific Coast National Bank

Academics

The Peter F. Drucker and Masatoshi Ito Graduate School of Management operates a distinctive MBA program in general management, which "embeds both business and social values into its curriculum." The school's "unique management philosophy" is largely inspired by the eponymous Peter F. Drucker, a pioneer writer and thinker in the field of management theory and practice. Particularly interesting is the school's Drucker-inspired concept of "management as a liberal art," which "gives students the opportunity to gain insights into management from various perspectives." In addition to "classes that focus on leadership, sustainability, organizational development, and effective management," every student must "take a class solely based on Drucker's philosophies as a core requirement." Of particular note, the Drucker MBA focuses on "developing ethical leaders," with class materials constantly emphasizing "the importance of social responsibility in business."

Drucker offers a number of graduate-level business degrees, including an MA in Arts Management as well as three options for the MBA: a full-time MBA in the day, a fully employed MBA for working professionals, and an executive MBA in the evenings and weekends. Students in all three programs have access to intensive overseas courses, offered during semester breaks, as well as semester-long exchange programs. While students are not required to complete an internship, "There are plenty of opportunities for students to get access to various companies through the many extracurricular clubs offered like the Entrepreneur & Venture Capital Club that visits businesses and entrepreneurs in Southern California." Most Drucker instructors are "excellent teachers," who are "very talented [and] well trained in their fields." While most have PhDs in business, the program is not overly academic; "Material feels very up to date and applicable." While some students would like to see more academic rigor, they also appreciate the school's "good reputation" as a member of the Claremont Consortium of Colleges, which includes such well-known institutions as Pomona College and Claremont McKenna.

A "boutique" school with intimate class sizes, Drucker students benefit from "small classes and extremely close and personal interaction with professors." In addition to office hours, "It's not uncommon to be invited to lunch or coffee with a professor." When it comes to participating in this management-focused school, students are not let down: "The MBA Administration at Claremont Graduate University is amazing," consistently demonstrating accessibility, as well as "a willingness to accommodate the various needs of students." Despite incorporating a number of distinct degree programs, "There is a very good culture of communication between the administration, professors and students."

Career and Placement

The Career Management office at Drucker works with students on career planning, skills development, and networking. They also oversee an alumni mentor program, which connects current students with graduates of the MBA. Nonetheless, students would like to see "better relations with alumni" across the board. Unlike at larger business programs, "recruiters do not come on campus" for interviews, though students notice that there has been a recent push to bring more companies to Drucker for interviews and networking events. Though still slightly beleaguered, "Recruitment has increased and the effort is noticeable, but [it is] a work in progress."

For the class of 2011, at least 73 percent of graduates were employed within three months of graduation, with an average starting salary of almost $73,000. There are Drucker graduates living in all 50 states, and recent graduates have accepted positions at a range of

ADMISSIONS CONTACT: BRANDON TUCK, DIRECTOR OF ADMISSIONS AND RECRUITING
ADDRESS: 1021 NORTH DARTMOUTH AVENUE, CLAREMONT, CA 91711
PHONE: 909-607-7811 • FAX: 909-607-9104
E-MAIL: DRUCKER@CGU.EDU • WEBSITE: WWW.DRUCKER.CGU.EDU

companies, including Bank of NY Mellon, Barclays Capital, Northwest Airlines, Ernst & Young, Deutsche Bank, General Motors, Goldman Sachs, International Monetary Fund, KPMG, Mattel, and Risk Management Solutions, among many others.

Student Life and Environment

Maybe it's all that Southern California sunshine, but students at Drucker say the school's "atmosphere is light and harmonious." Attracting MBA candidates from across the country, as well as internationally, "The student body is very diverse." In the full-time program, students "generally skew younger and less experienced," but they are nonetheless "friendly and eager to learn." Friendships blossom easily, and collaboration is more common than competition among classmates. A student explains, "We are competitive on a friendly level, for example in case competitions we get very competitive, yet we can also go grab a beer at the end of the day and have a good time."

When they are not hitting the books, Drucker students are eager to socialize with their colleagues. Among other campus events, the school hosts "regular student mixers," of which the biweekly Thursdays on Drucker Way are particularly popular. It's hard to dispute the fact that "Beer, food, and table tennis is a nice way to end the week." Located in the small town of Claremont, just north of Pomona, California, and east of Los Angeles, "Claremont is known as the city of trees and PhDs." Around the business school, "The landscape is beautiful," and it is located "close to the village (downtown) so we can easily walk there if we need anything that isn't on campus." A current student enthuses, "I'm having the time of my life here!"

Admissions

To apply to Claremont Graduate University, prospective MBA candidates must submit a completed application, academic transcripts from all college-level coursework, current GMAT or GRE scores, three letters of recommendation, a personal statement, and a resume. Qualified candidates are invited to interview on campus; a current student warns, "The interviewing process to be admitted to the program was not easy." Students entering the full-time program had an average undergraduate GPA of 3.32 and an average GMAT score of 633, with a range of 590-680. Students applying to the EMBA must have at least five years of experience in a senior-level position.

FINANCIAL FACTS

Annual tuition	$47,456
Fees	$500
Cost of books	$1,500
Room & board (on/off-campus)	$12,500/$15,000
% of students receiving aid	71
% of first-year students receiving aid	76
% of students receiving grants	56
Average grant	$10,361
Average loan	$20,500
Average student loan debt	$45,515

ADMISSIONS

Admissions Selectivity Rating	80
# of applications received	131
% applicants accepted	60
% acceptees attending	37
Average GMAT	614
Range of GMAT	580–660
Average GPA	3.29
TOEFL required of international students	Yes
Minimum TOEFL (paper/computer)	600/250
Application fee	$70
International application fee	$70
Early application deadline	11/1
Early notification date	12/1
Regular application deadline	2/1
Regular application notification	3/1
Application Deadline/Notification	
Round 1:	11/1 / 12/1
Round 2:	12/1 / 1/1
Round 3:	2/1 / 3/1
Round 4:	4/1 / 5/15
Deferment available	No
Transfer students accepted	Yes
Transfer application policy: The maximum number of transferable credits is 10 units.	
Non-fall admissions	Yes
Need-blind admissions	Yes

EMPLOYMENT PROFILE

Career Rating	85	Grads Employed by Function	% Avg. Salary
Percent employed at graduation	64	Marketing	(28%) $77,800
Percent employed 3 months after graduation	62	Operations	(6%) $95,000
		Consulting	(17%) $63,333
Average base starting salary	$70,361	Management	(11%) $80,500
Primary Source of Full-time Job Acceptances		Finance	(22%) $67,875
School-facilitated activities	7(39%)	HR	(11%) $49,000
Graduate-facilitated activities	8(44%)	MIS	(5%) $62,000
Unknown	3(17%)		

CLARK UNIVERSITY
GRADUATE SCHOOL OF MANAGEMENT

GENERAL INFORMATION

Type of school	Private
Affiliation	No Affiliation
Academic calendar	Semester

SURVEY SAYS...
Friendly students, Cutting-edge classes, Smart Classrooms
Solid preparation in:
General management, Teamwork, Doing business in a global economy

STUDENTS

Enrollment of parent institution	3,232
Enrollment of MBA Program	210
% male/female	53/47
% out-of-state	8
% part-time	47
% underrepresented minority	4
% international	59
Average age at entry	25
Average years work experience at entry	2.0

ACADEMICS

Academic Experience Rating	**84**
Profs interesting rating	77
Profs accesible rating	84
Student/faculty ratio	18:1
% female faculty	32
% part-time faculty	36

Joint Degrees
MBA/MA in Community Development & Planning, 3 years; MBA/MS in Environmental Science & Policy, 3 years; MBA/MS in Finance, 3 years.

Prominent Alumni
Wolfgang Hammes, Managing Director, Deutsche Bank; Lawrence Norman, Vice President Global Basketball, adidas; Ralph D. Crowley, President, Polar Beverages; Matt Goldman, Co-founder, Blue Man Group; Bonnie Keefe-Layden, CEO, Rehabilitative Resources, Inc.

Academics

A small graduate business program strong in finance (so strong, in fact, that it offers both an MBA with a finance concentration and a Master of Science in Finance), the Graduate School of Management at Clark University provides a "collaborative atmosphere" to a student body drawn from both the immediate region and halfway around the globe. As a result, Clark is "very diversified, which brings many different perspectives to the classroom."

Finance and accounting are standout disciplines here ("Many of the finance professors have impressive concurrent careers, running hedge funds by day and teaching courses by night; they typically have highly recognized professional certifications in addition to their PhDs," one student notes), but MBAs report other curricular strengths as well, including a "recently added concentration in social change, which allows students to take elective courses in the International Development, Community and Environment (IDCE) Department at Clark....There is also a three-year dual-degree program (MBA/MA in CD or ESP) between these two departments." Clark's forward-looking, green-leaning proclivities are further revealed in "the dual-degree program offered in environmental science and policy and the MBA." The School of Management recently added a Master of Science in Accounting.

Clark's professors are "demanding but fair." Some "are outstanding. They come from experienced fields and they help you live the experience of the new material in all its aspects. Suddenly statistics and finance become easy and enjoyable with them." Others, however, "are dull and give you tedious work that takes hours but is not interesting." Students appreciate that "The school makes sure to take the student's opinion into account when re-enlisting a professor to teach for the upcoming semesters." The program also offers "many opportunities to help real businesses in the city" in order to gain "real life experience." More of this sort of thing could be on the way; as one student observes, "I have seen a steady progression in Clark's course offerings that indicates that they understand the 'real-world' challenges facing students and are adapting appropriately. I am particularly encouraged by the apparent increase in courses addressing innovation, social sustainability, entrepreneurship, and management leadership."

Career and Placement

Many Clark students say the Stevenish Career Management Center at Clark's GSOM "does a good job of helping students prepare for their career search. They edit resumes and cover letters, provide interview coaching, and give students information on nearby career fairs."

The Center provides a range of services including individual advising, resume and cover letter assistance, workshops, career fairs, on-campus recruiting events, alumni networking events, alumni professional seminars, internship placement, and job and internship postings. Although internships are required of students with fewer than three years of professional experience, some students consider that "it shouldn't be a requirement to attain an internship as a graduate student." Others state the office does "not do a sufficient job of getting employers interested in Clark's students." Employers who have recently hired Clark GSOM graduates include Johnson & Johnson, Deloitte, Aetna Insurance, Public Consulting Group, JP Morgan, AMCOR, and Bristol-Myers Squibb.

Student Life and Environment

Clark University's location in the urban setting of Worcester, Massachusetts, provides the same opportunities and challenges of any urban campus. Clark's University Park Partnership brings together the University and Main South communities to help create a safe and vibrant neighborhood for all. However, students must take the usual safety precautions. Some report that there are "no real student bars and the like in the Clark area and that the neighborhoods surrounding the school have been allowed to fall into poverty by the town of Worcester." Students quickly note that "Clark has a world-class police force whose mission to protect the students is paramount" and that policing on campus includes a "good and very, very helpful" escort service though "there have been cases of students being mugged from time to time."

About half of Clark's MBAs are full-time students. Many spend a lot of time on and around campus. While "undergraduate student groups are closed to graduate students," MBAs enjoy "fun social events that the business school's student council puts on, and an interesting stock market activity that happens each semester." Some report that graduate student life "feels very disconnected from the rest of the school" and that it can "get boring at times because we are a very small community." Others state that the school "provides some networking alumni activities to help us to search jobs, and for international students, they organize some specific activities, such as Asian New Year, to make students (come) together and feel (at) home."

Clark's part-time students "are mostly native[s of] Worcester or Massachusetts, with different ages and backgrounds." Full-timers typically "come from different Asian countries," with India and China especially well-represented. International students "add a richness in perspective," although some "are weak in English."

Admissions

Clark requires the following of applicants: a completed admissions application; a personal essay; a current resume; two letters of recommendation; an official score report for either the GMAT or the GRE (an uncommon option); and official transcripts from all undergraduate and graduate programs previously attended. Interviews are optional. International applicants must submit all of the above as well as an official score report for the TOEFL or IELTS (if their native language is other than English) and proof of the financial support while attending the program. The school strongly encourages, but does not require, an online application.

FINANCIAL FACTS

Annual tuition	$28,800
Fees	$1,690
Cost of books	$2,100
Room & board	$10,000
% of students receiving grants	48
Average grant	$13,824

ADMISSIONS

Admissions Selectivity Rating	83
# of applications received	353
% applicants accepted	44
% acceptees attending	28
Average GMAT	566
Range of GMAT	530–640
Average GPA	3.30
TOEFL required of international students	Yes
Minimum TOEFL (paper/computer)	577/233
International application fee	$50
Early application deadline	4/1
Regular application deadline	6/1
Deferment available	Yes
Maximum length of deferment	12 months
Transfer students accepted	Yes

Transfer application policy: A maximum of two graduate courses from an AACSB accredited school can be transferred into the program. Foundation courses can be waived for undergraduate business majors.

Non-fall admissions	Yes
Need-blind admissions	Yes

EMPLOYMENT PROFILE

Career Rating	73	Grads Employed by Function	% Avg. Salary
Percent employed at graduation	41	Operations	(10%) $36,000
Percent employed 3 months after graduation	47	Consulting	(10%) $65,000
		Management	(10%) $39,000
Average base starting salary	$49,000	Finance	(50%) $46,720
		MIS	(10%) $45,000

Top 5 Employers Hiring Grads

Epsilon (2), Commerce Bank (2), Ernst & Young (1), Staples (1), Tommy Hilfiger (1)

CLARKSON UNIVERSITY
SCHOOL OF BUSINESS

GENERAL INFORMATION
Type of school	Private
Affiliation	No Affiliation
Academic calendar	August-May

SURVEY SAYS...
Smart classrooms
Solid preparation in:
General management, Operations,
Quantitative skills, Computer skills

STUDENTS
Enrollment of parent institution	2,901
Enrollment of MBA Program	40
% male/female	53/47
% out-of-state	19
% part-time	20
% underrepresented minority	3
% international	19
Average age at entry	26
Average years work experience at entry	2.0

ACADEMICS
Academic Experience Rating	**81**
Profs interesting rating	80
Profs accesible rating	78
Student/faculty ratio	3:1
% female faculty	29
% underrepresented minority faculty	5
% part-time faculty	0

Joint Degrees
Master of Engineering/Master of
Business Administration (2 years)

Prominent Alumni
William Harlow, VP Corporate
Development; Paul Hoeft, President
and CEO; Elizabeth Fessenden,
President, Flexible Packaging; David
Fisher, President; Vickie Cole,
President and CEO

Academics

Clarkson University, located in Potsdam New York, is a private university known "first and foremost as an undergrad engineering school"; however, many students look to its burgeoning business program to help them get a foothold in the business world. Its MBA program allows many of its students to finish in less than 12 months, even though many believe they could receive their degree in around "nine months." The "speed and reputation" of the program are just two of the good aspects of the program that many students enjoy. The school tends to use its engineering acumen to teach students about innovations in the engineering sector that may affect business and its own Institute for a Sustainable Environment, which helps to foster "green business."

The main focus of the curriculum, however, is the use of the "supply chain" style of management. While many find this especially "helpful" in the workplace, some students wish the curriculum were a little broader and that the school "cater a little more to marketing and sales students." One thing all students can agree on is that they love the size of the school and praise that, "[it] is very small [and] gives each student a very personalized experience." The faculty are a huge part of the experience and each takes "the time to get to know" the students. Those enrolled in the program think that most professors are "absolutely wonderful" and have taught them a great deal about various facets of business, yet the professors are occasionally hindered by an administration that is not exactly "unified," leaving some to re-teach material that students have already learned. Some subjects may also be under taught. Despite this, they say that the faculty is more than "willing to help students with schoolwork and find jobs." If the faculty is not available, many students love the team-oriented courses and say they "love working at school as [their] fellow students are always available if [they] need help."

Career and Placement

Clarkson University boasts 1-6 former graduates that have become CEO, president, or vice-president of a company. A large reason for this owes to the Graduate Career Services office, which helps all students find jobs after graduation. While some would like "more opportunities to network for jobs," all agree that the Career Services office is invaluable to students with assets like KnightLink which allows prospects to find job, co-op and internship listings, as well as career workshops. Students also take advantage of the alumni-mentoring program, which allows them to connect with graduates who will help and guide them through the process of finding a job.

Clarkson MBAs most frequently find work with IBM, Accenture, Lockheed Martin, GE, Cooper Industries, Frito-Lay, HSBC, Knowledge Systems and Research, Texas Instruments, and Whiting Turner. While the majority of graduates remain in the Northeast, students are placed throughout the country.

ADMISSIONS CONTACT: JOSHUA LAFAVE, ASSOCIATE DIRECTOR, GRADUATE BUSINESS PROGRAMS
ADDRESS: 8 CLARKSON AVE., CU BOX 5770, POTSDAM, NY 13699
PHONE: 315-268-6613 • FAX: 315-268-3810
E-MAIL: BUSGRAD@CLARKSON.EDU • WEBSITE: WWW.CLARKSON.EDU/GRADUATE

Student Life and Environment

Potsdam is located in rural New York, so "there isn't a whole lot to do unless you knowwhere to find activities." The upside of an isolated campus is that students have fewer distractions: "You learn that business work is not always going to be a 40 hour work week;" weekends are often "straight work days where most group meetings and homework for the next week are done." Though some students note problems with "administration not always taking care of small issues immediately," "because it is a one-year program…problems are not an issue for very long before a new class comes in."

"Almost all [students] are what you'd traditionally picture as 'MBA' students: white, upper middle class, financially and socially moderate to slightly conservative," and "they are very good at quantitative analysis." "Everyone is accepting of what you believe. They may disagree but it is done in a way that allows for intelligent and thought-provoking conversation." And some students note "the pleasure to meet, interact with and become friends with students from other countries."

Admissions

The admissions department at Clarkson University requires that applicants submit an undergraduate transcript, GMAT or GRE scores, TOEFL scores (if necessary), and a Test of Spoken English (TSE) (for international students whose native language is not English; the TSE can be administered via telephone), a detailed resume, two one-page personal essays, and three letters of reference. Awards of merit-based scholarships are determined during the admissions process; no separate application is required. Those requiring foundation course work prior to commencing their MBAs "may enroll in the courses at Clarkson during the summer Business Concepts Program before entering the advanced MBA program. For students doing graduate work at another university, they may be allowed to transfer in nine credit hours of graduate work."

FINANCIAL FACTS

Annual tuition	$37,590
Fees	$440
Cost of books	$2,000
Room & board	$7,500
% of students receiving aid	85
% of first-year students receiving aid	85
% of students receiving grants	85
Average award package	$26,476
Average grant	$6,500
Average loan	$34,000
Average student loan debt	$31,932

ADMISSIONS

Admissions Selectivity Rating	78
# of applications received	121
% applicants accepted	60
% acceptees attending	55
Average GMAT	525
Range of GMAT	480–580
Average GPA	3.58
TOEFL required of international students	Yes
Minimum TOEFL (paper/computer)	550/213
International application fee	$35
Deferment available	Yes
Maximum length of deferment	1 year
Transfer students accepted	Yes

Transfer application policy: Graduate students who need to complete foundation coursework may enroll in the summer business concepts program at Clarkson before entering the advanced MBA program. For students doing graduate work at another university, they are allowed to transfer in up to 9 credit hours of graduate work from another AACSB accredited institution.

Non-fall admissions	Yes
Need-blind admissions	Yes

EMPLOYMENT PROFILE

		Grads Employed by Function	% Avg. Salary
Career Rating	84		
Percent employed at graduation	36	Operations	(50%) $58,833
Percent employed 3 months after graduation	75	Consulting	(17%) $50,000
		Management	(8%) $58,000
Average base starting salary	$57,000	Finance	(17%) $55,000
Primary Source of Full-time Job Acceptances		MIS	(8%) $50,000
School-facilitated activities	12(44%)	**Top 5 Employers Hiring Grads**	
Graduate-facilitated activities	4(14%)	IBM (3), Frito Lay (1), Cooper Industries (1),	
Unknown	11(42%)	Bechtel (1), J&J/Duracell (1)	

CLEMSON UNIVERSITY
COLLEGE OF BUSINESS AND BEHAVIORAL SCIENCE

GENERAL INFORMATION

Type of school	Public
Affiliation	No Affiliation
Academic calendar	Aug-May

SURVEY SAYS...

Students love Clemson, SC, Friendly students, Good peer network, Smart classrooms
Solid preparation in:
General management

STUDENTS

Enrollment of parent institution	20,768
Enrollment of MBA Program	301
% male/female	69/31
% out-of-state	1
% part-time	71
% underrepresented minority	0
% international	40
Average age at entry	31
Average years work experience at entry	18.6

ACADEMICS

Academic Experience Rating	**80**
Profs interesting rating	80
Profs accesible rating	77
Student/faculty ratio	5:1
% female faculty	34
% underrepresented minority faculty	10
% part-time faculty	11

Joint Degrees

Dual Clemson MBA and MIB (Masters in International Business) at the IESEG business school in France. Students must be accepted by both institutions.

Prominent Alumni

J. Strom Thurmond, U.S. Senator (died 2003); Kristie A. Kenney, U.S. Ambassador to the Phillipines; Robert H. Brooks, President, Naturally Fresh Foods; Nancy Humprhies O'Dell, Access Hollywood co-anchor

Academics

The College of Business & Behavioral Science at Clemson University offers a combination of daytime and evening classes to its full-time MBAs as well as a full slate of evening classes to part-timers at the school's satellite campus in Greenville. Clemson MBAs tout the program's "rigorous curriculum" and excellent value; "The value of this degree vs. the cost of the degree appears to be very high," one student tells us.

Clemson's MBA offers concentrations in innovation and entrepreneurship, services science, supply chain management, health services, and marketing analysis. Full-timers are enthusiastic about "the entrepreneurial focus of the program." One writes, "It is rare to find relevant assistantships in an MBA program, and Clemson University provides some [of the] best opportunities for entrepreneurs to learn necessary business skills while working closely with start-up companies in South Carolina. They also do a marvelous job of bringing technologies developed by Clemson's Research Institutes to a forefront and finding their commercial value."

The program boasts "some very good professors and interesting class topics," and students praise professors for "their willingness to help outside of class" and for being "generally reasonable when it comes to grades and making changes if the general class population is not grasping the material well." Students also note that "The administration here at Clemson University is very helpful. Any time I have asked for help regarding admission, enrollment, or financial aid they have always been able to answer my questions." Finally, they report that "Clemson's study abroad programs are attractive and meaningful."

Career and Placement

Clemson University maintains an Office of MBA Career Development dedicated to its business graduates. For those who seek out the service, the Office of Career Development office offers career placement support including one-on-one professional coaching and personalized placement assistance as well as a range of self-assessment instruments, job-search counseling, interviewing and resume-writing workshops, and recruiting and networking events. Students also report that "the alumni base and networking opportunities" here are "a great strength." Companies hiring recent Clemson MBAs include Blackbaud, Bausch & Lomb, CapGemini, Colonial Life, Disney, GE, Home Depot, Lockheed Martin, Michelin, Milliken, Nestle, Northwestern Mutual, Resurgent Capital Service, Schneider, and Target. About one-third of Clemson MBAs wind up in marketing and sales; about as many find work in general management.

Student Life and Environment

The full-time and part-time degree programs are now located in downtown Greenville, South Carolina, about 45 minutes away from the main university campus. The Greenville campus, known as Clemson at the Falls, is located at Falls Park—an urban park featuring hiking and jogging paths, landscaped gardens, and an architecturally distinctive suspension bridge linking the Clemson campus building to Main Street. Students tell us that life here involves "hectic course work with case studies, quizzes, midterms, discussions, presentations and projects. Apart from the course work, we have regular MBA Student association meetings . . . to discuss and organize events related to community work, organizing events with alumni, etc. Then we have regular discussions and talks by guest speakers, which are compulsory to attend as part of our course work. We have regular social gathering with MBA alumni and with faculty also." Reflecting upon all this

ADMISSIONS CONTACT: ADMISSIONS DIRECTOR, MBA PROGRAMS
ADDRESS: 55 E. CAMPERDOWN WAY, GREENVILLE, SC 29601
PHONE: 864-656-3975 • FAX: 864-656-0947
E-MAIL: MBA@CLEMSON.EDU • WEBSITE: WWW.CLEMSON.EDU/MBA

activity, one student observes that "Clemson has a great tradition of merging academia with life. You feel like you're a part of the school and the community."

Beyond the classroom, the new location strategically places college faculty and students at the center of the Greenville business community, allowing full-time students to attend classes and simultaneously hold internships or part-time positions in local businesses.

The Clemson MBA program attracts students who "are very competitive in most facets of life: sports, academics, job-search, etc. However, this competitive spirit does not manifest itself in pettiness, but rather in a collective effort to elevate the performances of both ourselves and our peers."

Admissions

Applicants to the MBA program at Clemson must submit a current resume (two years of work experience is required for students w/undergraduate degree in business); one official transcripts representing all undergraduate work; two letters of recommendation; a one- to two-page personal statement; interview (full-time applicants only); and, an official GMAT score report (score of at least 600 preferred for applicants to the full-time program). Non-native English speakers applying to the full-time program must also submit TOEFL scores (score of 600 paper-based or 237 computer based preferred), an International Student Financial Certification Form, and translations of transcripts not in English.

FINANCIAL FACTS

Annual tuition (in-state/ out-of-state)	$9,744/$19,426
Fees	$7,248
Room & board	$13,152
% of students receiving aid	51
% of students receiving grants	0

ADMISSIONS

Admissions Selectivity Rating	74
# of applications received	207
% applicants accepted	84
% acceptees attending	74
Average GMAT	588
Range of GMAT	545–630
Average GPA	3.14
TOEFL required of international students	Yes
Minimum TOEFL (paper/computer)	600/250
Application fee	$80
International application fee	$90
Regular application deadline	6/1
Regular application notification	6/30
Deferment available	Yes
Maximum length of deferment	1 year
Transfer students accepted	Yes
Transfer application policy: Must meet all admission requirements. Can transfer a maximum of 12 Semester hours of acceptable coursework.	
Non-fall admissions	Yes
Need-blind admissions	Yes

EMPLOYMENT PROFILE

		Grads Employed by Function	% Avg. Salary
Career Rating	84		
Percent employed at graduation	37	Marketing	(22%) $48,000
Percent employed 3 months		Operations	(11%) $50,000
after graduation	47	Management	(22%) $58,000
Average base starting salary	$53,370	Finance	(33%) $60,900
Primary Source of Full-time Job Acceptances		Other	(11%) $48,000
School-facilitated activities	7(41%)	**Top 5 Employers Hiring Grads**	
Unknown	10(59%)	Fluor (2), Lowes (1), Desoutter (1), UHS-Pruitt (1), US Army Corps of Engineers (1)	

THE COLLEGE OF WILLIAM & MARY
MASON SCHOOL OF BUSINESS

GENERAL INFORMATION

Type of school	Public
Affiliation	No Affiliation
Academic calendar	Semester

SURVEY SAYS...
Good peer network, Smart classrooms
Solid preparation in:
Accounting

STUDENTS

Enrollment of parent institution	7,874
Enrollment of MBA Program	396
% male/female	63/37
% out-of-state	63
% part-time	48
% underrepresented minority	17
% international	37
Average age at entry	27
Average years work experience at entry	4.0

ACADEMICS

Academic Experience Rating	87
Profs interesting rating	93
Profs accesible rating	90
Student/faculty ratio	11:1
% female faculty	24
% underrepresented minority faculty	14
% part-time faculty	17

Joint Degrees
MBA/ Master of Accounting, 2.5 years; JD/MBA, 4 years; MBA/MPP, 3 years; MBA/ Master of Global Management: A joint degree program with Thunderbird School of Global Management (Glendale, AZ).

Prominent Alumni
Donald Lee Lowman, MBA '82, Managing Director, Strategic Growth, Towers Perrin (consulting); Amy C. McPherson, MBA '85, President & Managing Director, European Lodging - Marriott International, Inc. (hospitality)

Academics

MBAs love the "personalized approach to teaching" at the Mason School of Business at the College of William & Mary. This approach results in part from the program's "smaller class sizes" and dedicated "professors who want to teach and who care about students' success." Mason's professors utilize a "holistic approach to teaching both in terms of content (challenging academics, but also specific classes on communication and leadership skills) and form (case studies, hands-on projects, traditional)." It is also the result of several value-added features of the program that many students feel are Mason's greatest assets.

Chief among these is Mason's Executive Partner Program, "a fantastic resource that pairs us up with leaders in business who live in Williamsburg (coincidently, a lot of people retire from Wall Street and move to Williamsburg)." Through the program, "Each student gets a mentor who meets with him or her on a regular basis. These executive partners are readily available to students for career advice, interview guidance, and feedback on projects and presentations." "The Executive Partner program really brought it home that [the program is] committed to teaching us the soft skills…. The aim is to teach MBAs to think and not just do," one student explains. Other unique features of the program include the "immersive Career Acceleration Modules," which "allow for you to actually work with clients and provide solutions" in such areas as real estate "corporate finance, financial markets, entrepreneurship, healthcare, B2B and B2C marketing, and consulting." Finally, there is Mason's "capstone course, a field consultancy program that allows us to consult with real companies to solve real problems."

Students report that the Mason curriculum places an "emphasis on both qualitative and quantitative skills, presentations, and teamwork to create a well-rounded education that has helped students to excel in the business world." Students also appreciate that the program "offers many opportunities to develop as a leader. There are so many options to get involved with and the cross-program bonds are stronger than any other MBA school that I have asked people about. It is commonplace to socialize with a law student just as much as a business student." Mason's administration "is open to doing things better, and if you have an idea or project, they encourage you to do it….For example, we now have green-belt six sigma certification and a project with the Department of Defense because a student took the initiative to get it started. This is just one of many examples. Students play a very active part in the school and have a large say in what happens here."

Career and Placement

Placement and recruiting services at the Mason School of Business receive mixed reviews from students. Some praise the "high quality of jobs and high job placement" and conclude that the "program is exceedingly strong," others are less complimentary. A common complaint focuses on the fact that Mason "is a small school" in a location that isn't "ideally placed to attract MNC's and conglomerates to recruit here," putting the school "at a disadvantage when it comes to on-campus recruiting. Most companies focus on larger schools. Therefore, we need a more robust career services department to help mitigate the disadvantages that go along with that." To boost prospects, the school recently rolled out two new career services programs, MBA CareerPrep and Corporate Relations, which incorporate career development and employer contact into the business school curriculum. The programs include regional "recons' where MBA students are connected with corporate recruiters in a variety of regions.

ADMISSIONS CONTACT: AMANDA BARTH, DIRECTOR OF MBA ADMISSIONS
ADDRESS: ALAN B. MILLER HALL, 101 UKROP WAY, P. O. BOX 8795, WILLIAMSBURG, VA 23187
PHONE: 757-221-2900 • FAX: 757-221-2958
E-MAIL: ADMISSIONS@MASON.WM.EDU • WEBSITE: MASON.WM.EDU

Top employers of Mason MBAs in recent years include: Booz Allen Hamilton, Capital One, Dominion Resources, Ernst & Young, Target, Amazon, AT&T, Bank of America, Deutsche Bank, Genworth Financial, Deloitte Consulting, Saatchi & Saatchi X, and Wachovia. One in four 2010 MBAs found work with the government; 15 percent took jobs in the finance sector; and 27 percent entered the consulting business.

Student Life and Environment

Mason recently moved into a "new 166,000 square foot facility" that students say is "fantastic." "The study rooms or the conference rooms are comparable to the offices in any high-tech company," one student writes. Within the building's confines, "students are heavily involved in projects that originate in the classroom but often move to the weekends and off time. This is balanced with social events, intramural sports, clubs, committee involvement, and community service." Clubs "ranging from community service to marketing" are "student-run and all give us experience trying out real-world situations." The student body forms a "small community...with a high level of cooperation and teamwork and very little of the competitiveness rumored at other business schools."

William and Mary is located in Williamsburg, Virginia, a "historic, safe, and picturesque" town "small enough that you go out and see your classmates and enjoy getting to know them in a non-professional setting" but with "great access to both large cities within an hour-and-a-half drive or a great oceanfront within an hour-and-a-half drive." Regardless of where they are, "students find a way to make it fun. Whether having mug night at the Greenleaf, or celebrating Diwali with the Indian students (with professors dancing!), or the Chinese New Year with the Chinese students, or random intramurals, hanging out at Miller Hall, or just having a conversation, I am thoroughly enjoying my experience here," one student writes.

Admissions

Applicants to Mason must submit: official academic transcripts for all undergraduate and graduate work; an official GMAT or GRE score report; letters of recommendation; three personal essays; and a resume. Interviews are required and are by invitation of the school only. International applicants whose first language is not English must submit official score reports for the TOEFL, the IELTS, or the PTE (applicants scoring in at least the 60th percentile on the verbal section of the GMAT and at least a 5.0 on the AWA section of the GMAT are exempted from this requirement).

FINANCIAL FACTS

Annual tuition (in-state/ out-of-state)	$29,350/$39,750
Fees	$1,000
Cost of books	$1,500
Room & board	$8,300
% of students receiving aid	81
% of first-year students receiving aid	83
% of students receiving grants	73
Average award package	$28,296
Average grant	$14,989
Average loan	$35,383
Average student loan debt	$72,506

ADMISSIONS

Admissions Selectivity Rating	83
# of applications received	304
% applicants accepted	58
% acceptees attending	52
Average GMAT	610
Range of GMAT	570–650
Average GPA	3.30
TOEFL required of international students	No
Minimum TOEFL (paper/computer)	600/250
Application fee	$100
International application fee	$100
Application Deadline/Notification	
Round 1:	11/3 / 1/10
Round 2:	1/12 / 3/07
Round 3:	3/09 / 4/18
Round 4:	5/11 / 6/06
Deferment available	Yes
Maximum length of deferment	1 year
Transfer students accepted	No
Transfer application policy: Transfer credits are not accepted.	
Non-fall admissions	No
Need-blind admissions	Yes

EMPLOYMENT PROFILE

Career Rating	91	**Grads Employed by Function% Avg. Salary**	
Percent employed at graduation	57	Marketing	(24%) $68,092
Percent employed 3 months after graduation	83	Operations	(7%)
		Consulting	(21%)$90,944
Average base starting salary	$75,674	Management	(11%) $73,250
Primary Source of Full-time Job Acceptances		Finance	(22%) $71,045
School-facilitated activities	45(63%)	HR	(2%)
Graduate-facilitated activities	22(31%)	MIS	(4%)
		Other	(9%) $67,911

Top 5 Employers Hiring Grads
Deloitte Consulting (3), Booz Allen Hamilton (2), IBM (2), Citi (1), Amazon (1)

COLORADO STATE UNIVERSITY
COLLEGE OF BUSINESS

GENERAL INFORMATION

Type of school   Public
Affiliation   No Affiliation
Academic calendar   August-July

SURVEY SAYS...
Good peer network,
Cutting-edge classes
Solid preparation in:
Accounting, General management

STUDENTS
Enrollment of parent
  institution   28,547
Enrollment of MBA Program   1,450
% part-time   87
Average age at entry   33
Average years work experience
  at entry   8.0

ACADEMICS
Academic Experience Rating   84
Profs interesting rating   86
Profs accesible rating   87
Student/faculty ratio   35:1
% female faculty   10
% underrepresented minority
  faculty   12

Joint Degrees
DVM/MBA, 5 years

Academics

Convenience and affordability define the MBA experience at Colorado State University, whether you choose to attend classes at the school's scenic Fort Collins campus, or from your home computer 1,000 miles away. Operating one of the longest-running distance MBAs in the country, CSU has online education down to a science. What makes the CSU distance MBA unique is that it runs concurrently with the Professional MBA program on the CSU campus. Together, distance and campus-based students complete the MBA simultaneously—viewing lectures, completing group projects, and turning in assignments in tandem. "The in-class lectures are recorded and made available to distance students within 24 hours of each class ending" via the Internet, and "DVDs are mailed to you" within the week. As a result, distance students literally watch "the same lecture that is delivered to the on-campus students" and even "hear questions that the ground students have." "Technology is top-notch" and students can easily meet for group work via the school's web-based platforms. With absolutely no residency requirements or in-person orientation programs, CSU's program is "completely online and affordable," attracting professional students from every corner of the country—and the globe. While many students consider other low-residency MBAs before deciding where to apply, they say Colorado State offers the "best combination of course content, reputation, accreditation, cost, and flexibility for distance learners."

Whether taking place in the lecture hall or on the small screen, CSU classes are a "good balance of practical and theoretical ideas" and "the material is current and in-depth." Here, you'll get all the MBA essentials, with a touch of innovation; at CSU, "they continue to push the envelope academically but not at the expense of what is real and proven in the field." Professors "are knowledgeable, engaging, and bring excellent guest speakers to the lectures." Most faculty members "have real-world business experience, not just theory" to share. Classes are "demanding," yet both online and on-campus students benefit from the excellent personal relationships they build with CSU professors. As one online student explains, "The professors are responsive and really care for the success of the students." "They know my name, even though I am one of 1,200 students."

Coordinating such a large program is a feat, but the CSU administration is a well-oiled machine. Students praise the remarkable "ability of the administration and staff to assemble an impressive collection of students from around the globe, and then to effectively manage such a diverse group." A current student attests, "I cannot say enough about how much assistance I receive from professors, the distance coordinator, and administrators. I have a very unique job that requires me to be in remote areas with little or no Internet access, and my professors are more than accommodating in working with me during these times." Adds another, "Even though I am a distance student, I feel as connected as I would be if I were on campus."

Career and Placement

The Office of Career Services at the College of Business offers individual career counseling, resume critiques, and networking events for undergraduate and graduate business students. The emphasis, however, is on undergraduate students looking to start a career, rather than MBA candidates. In recent years, undergraduate and graduate students at CSU have gone on to jobs at Accenture, Oppenheimer, Target, EnCana Oil & Gas, and Ernest and Julio Gallo Winery.

For online students, career development is a different story. Most of CSU's distance students "are looking to move their careers forward, are dedicated employees, and want to gain more knowledge to make them better employees and managers." To that end, most are not seeking new career opportunities—and most, it should be added, do not live in the Colorado area. As a result, graduate student career services are not particularly robust at CSU, and "career center resources are non-existent for distance students." Fortunately, Colorado State University "has a great reputation around the country and the world," which is an asset to any career or job search.

Student Life and Environment

Drawing students from far and wide, CSU brings together a "great mix of people, from diverse work environments, from all around the world, each bringing their piece of diversity to the mix." The program is well suited to busy professionals, and distance students are "mostly mid-career with backgrounds ranging from engineering to veterinary." Needless to say, "Personal interactions are limited due to the distance format," though students are still expected to participate in group projects through the university's technology platforms. It might sound like a bit of a headache, but current students assure us that, "All the online students are courteous and willing to help."

Those who study on campus say that CSU's business school, located on "a safe and friendly campus" in the pretty town of Fort Collins, Colorado, "offers a great environment in which to learn and grow personally and professionally." With spectacular recreational opportunities in the surrounding Rocky Mountains, affordable cost-of-living, and a laid-back social scene, students ask us, "How can you complain?"

Admissions

To be eligible for admission to CSU, students must have maintained a 3.0 GPA or better from an accredited undergraduate college, or they must have completed a graduate degree and have at least four years of professional work experience. Students with a lower GPA must include a statement explaining their academic performance. Students with significant professional work experience may apply for a GMAT waiver. Applicants are advised of their admission status within three weeks of the application deadline.

FINANCIAL FACTS

Annual tuition (in-state/ out-of-state)	$21,000/$24,000
Fees	$40
Cost of books	$400
% of students receiving aid	32
% of first-year students receiving aid	36
% of students receiving grants	2

ADMISSIONS

Admissions Selectivity Rating	78
# of applications received	57
% applicants accepted	63
% acceptees attending	78
Average GMAT	543
Range of GMAT	495–590
Average GPA	3.19
TOEFL required of international students	Yes
Minimum TOEFL (paper/computer)	565/227
Application fee	$50
International application fee	$50
Regular application deadline	5/1
Regular application notification	6/1
Deferment available	Yes
Maximum length of deferment	1 year
Transfer students accepted	No
Non-fall admissions	No
Need-blind admissions	Yes

COLUMBIA UNIVERSITY
COLUMBIA BUSINESS SCHOOL

Academics

Quite literally, few top MBA programs are as perfectly positioned as Columbia Business School. Columbia's enviable New York City location is one of its major selling points, offering "immense exposure to U.S. economy and the corporate industry." Through academics, internships, campus programs, speakers, and an active alumni network, the school's "ability to draw from New York City resources and people is incomparable."

As a member of the Ivy League, Columbia maintains an "excellent academic reputation" across disciplines, though it is particularly noted for finance and investment management, consulting, real estate, and social enterprise. Here again, the local community plays a role in the strength of these programs; for example, "The access to 'Wall Street-savvy' professors gives the finance program a wonderful balance between strong academic content and applicability of knowledge." Even if you don't see yourself managing stock portfolios, "Most NGOs are located in NYC, which gives Columbia students a unique access to internship and advisory opportunities."

At CBS, "The core is really well organized," running through all business essentials; at the same time, some feel there are "too many academics teaching core courses," making them less relevant to real world business. Those anxious to begin electives with "rock star" professors will be happy to hear that "Columbia now has placed an emphasis on the ability to place out of these core courses through exemption exams." While Columbia is known for research, "Students who want a practical approach to teaching as opposed to one that is purely academic and theory-based will feel much more at home here." In fact, Columbia excels at "preparing students with strong analytical skills needed to succeed in any field." Most professors are "excellent at merging academic theoretical concepts with real-world applications," offering a solid perspective on how business works in the real world. When it comes to faculty, the school recruits professors directly from the New York business community, with the "amazing adjunct selection" spicing up the tenured staff.

When Columbia students say their school is "run like a business," they mean it as a compliment. Seeing students as the first priority, "The administration is very responsive, from dealing with minor administrative issues to making the deans accessible regularly to students." Students feel valued, and "administrators do respond to student feedback on classroom management or issues with professors."

Career and Placement

With a top name and a rock solid education to back them up, Columbia graduates enjoy "excellent career opportunities" in New York City and beyond. Through the Career Management Center (CMC), "recruiting does start day one, and it will be intense throughout the two years." However, students are incredibly impressed with "how hard the CMC will work with you as an individual to ensure placement." To help counteract the madness of the job hunt, the CMC offers a four-session job strategy series for first-year students, as well as individual advising sessions. In addition, there are "tons of alumni and professional mentors available for coaching" throughout the graduate program. Competition is minimized, and "while recruiting is an extremely rigorous process, particularly in finance and consulting, students are extremely supportive of each other and work together to accomplish mutual goals."

"All the best companies are a stone's throw away from you" at Columbia, and graduates consistently score plum positions in New York. The school's top employers include Amazon, American Express Company, Bain & Company, Barclays, Boston Consulting Group, Booz & Company, Citigroup, Credit Suisse, Deloitte Consulting, Deutsche Bank,

ADMISSIONS CONTACT: AMANDA CARLSON, ASSISTANT DEAN, ADMISSIONS
ADDRESS: 3022 BROADWAY, URIS HALL, ROOM 216, NEW YORK, NY 10027
PHONE: 212-854-1961 • FAX: 212-662-6754
E-MAIL: APPLY@GSB.COLUMBIA.EDU • WEBSITE: WWW.GSB.COLUMBIA.EDU

FINANCIAL FACTS	
Annual tuition	$58,384
Fees	$2,512
Cost of books	$900
Room & board	$20,700

Goldman, Sachs & Co., Google, IBM Corporation, JPMorgan Chase, McKinsey & Company, Microsoft, Bank of America Merrill Lynch, Morgan Stanley, and Unilever. More than 40 percent of graduates work in finance, while another 30 percent take jobs in consulting. The average starting salary for Columbia graduates is well over $100,000 annually.

Student Life and Environment

Surrounded by fascinating classmates and a vibrant metropolis, Columbia students enjoy a "very active social scene" both on and off campus. "During the first semester, there's a lot to juggle between schoolwork, meeting new people, and recruiting," but "life becomes exponentially better each semester." From happy hours to speaker events, students could "attend at least one social event every single day of the two-year program without having to plan or organize anything." Among the most popular events, "On-campus happy hour on Thursday is a highlight of everyone's week."

Despite an enrollment of more than 1,000, "Columbia has a strong and tight-knit community," comprised of students who "are very fun but also driven to succeed." On this diverse campus, "students are generally great people to hang out with socially and in the classroom." Despite the demands of coursework, "Most everyone is involved in the social life, from people with families to single folks." Without a doubt, "Being in New York also makes for an amazing experience, since we are always going to new places in the city, and it seriously never sleeps." If CBS students have one minor complaint about their environment, it's the lack of a "better library and student studying spaces" on campus. However, the school is currently planning its move to the University's newly developed Manhattanville campus, which will address the shortcomings of the current space.

Admissions

A serious record of leadership and achievement is what distinguishes Columbia MBA candidates from other graduate business students. To determine a candidate's eligibility for the program, the admissions committee reviews academic transcripts, test scores, recommendations, personal essays, and background. Admission to Columbia is highly competitive, with only about 15 percent of applicants receiving an offer of admission. In recent years, incoming students had an average GMAT score of 714, with the middle 80 percent ranging from 680 to 760.

ADMISSIONS	
Admissions Selectivity Rating	99
# of applications received	5,409
% applicants accepted	21
% acceptees attending	66
Average GMAT	714
Range of GMAT	690–730
Average GPA	3.50
TOEFL required of international students	Yes
Application fee	$250
International application fee	$250
Early application deadline	10/2
Regular application deadline	4/9
Deferment available	No
Transfer students accepted	No
Non-fall admissions	Yes
Need-blind admissions	Yes

EMPLOYMENT PROFILE			
Career Rating	99	**Grads Employed by Function**	**% Avg. Salary**
Percent employed at graduation	77	Marketing	(9%) $99,286
Percent employed 3 months		Operations	(3%) $108,667
after graduation	92	Consulting	(28%) $124,125
Average base starting salary	$112,728	Management	(7%) $106,210
Primary Source of Full-time Job Acceptances		Finance	(50%) $111,193
School-facilitated activities	276(57%)	HR	(0%) $95,000
Graduate-facilitated activities	78(16%)	MIS	(0%) $95,000
Unknown	128(27%)	Other	(2%) $89,000
		Top 5 Employers Hiring Grads	
		McKinsey & Company (60), Bain & Company	
		(24), Deloitte (17), Goldman, Sachs & Co.	
		(15), JP Morgan Chase (15)	

CORNELL UNIVERSITY
JOHNSON GRADUATE SCHOOL OF MANAGEMENT

Academics

Even in the midst of numerous top-notch graduate programs, Cornell University's reputation for producing strong business leaders stands out. The school's strong brand name ("especially in Asia"), varied approach to teaching and learning, and the "wealth of interdisciplinary course offerings" are just some of the many things that students love, not to mention the "regular opportunities to collaborate closely with students from other prestigious graduate departments, located just steps from the business school." Johnson has a "fantastic, collaborative culture" that draws people in from the get-go and turns them into helpful alumni. "My academic experience at Johnson has encouraged me to refer other colleagues to this program," says a student.

Professors here go the extra mile for students and are "engaged and enthusiastic inside the classroom and extremely available for outside meetings with students." They're "obviously experts in their respective fields," and "they will push you, and sometimes frustrate you, but they care most about helping you succeed." Other unique aspects of Johnson include: a dual degree program between with the top HR program in the country, a strong focus on sustainability, and the student-run hedge fund (currently valued at $10 million), where "students pitch stocks and vote to decide whether or not to invest in a stock." The school's immersion program, which many students cite as their main reason for attending, is an intense, hands-on semester of integrated course and field work in a specific industry or career interest.

The administration is "pretty responsive to student needs," and it thinks of the little things that make students happy "like having bagels and coffee for finals." It "goes out of its way to garner feedback from students and constantly improves the curriculum." Most core subjects are condensed into the first semester, creating "occasional strains," but "the school works hard to schedule exams and deliverables to avoid overwhelming students." Being part of Cornell also "creates opportunities in multiple related disciplines, from engineering to city planning to agriculture."

Career and Placement

The recruiting opportunities at Johnson are "incredible," and the teaching and professional staff encourages students to challenge themselves, providing support "every step of the way." A "superior international network" means that alumni are "happy to speak with you and many take on the role of career coach, connecting you to unusual internship and job opportunities or helping with interview prep." "If you ever reach out to a Johnson alum, they will always get back to you," says a student. There is no cutthroat mentality here: "We work together to compete with students from other schools for jobs, not students within our school."

Career Services stands out "as a place that will go out of their way to help any student." The school has "the best system to prepare students for the summer internships, which is arguably the most important aspect of career switching." Its "tremendous" track record of placement in consulting internships and careers allows students "to gain hands-on experience in [their] field of interest as well as leadership impact."

ADMISSIONS CONTACT: MR. RANDALL SAWYER, ASSISTANT DEAN OF ADMISSIONS
FINANCIAL AID, AND INCLUSION • ADDRESS: 111 SAGE HALL, ITHACA, NY 14853
PHONE: 607-255-4660 • FAX: 607-255-0065
E-MAIL: MBA@JOHNSON.CORNELL.EDU • WEBSITE: WWW.JOHNSON.CORNELL.EDU

Student Life and Environment

One student calls the Johnson crowd "some of the most intelligent, driven, passionate people I have ever been around." Each class brings "diverse perspectives from past work experiences and cultural backgrounds," and "there is a strong environment of collaboration"; despite "healthy competition," the majority of students "study together in Sage" and "informally tutor others for exams." When free time can be found, students enjoy spending it with each other" at local bars, playing on one of our many intramural teams, participating in a club event or going to hockey games," such as those of the Frozen Assets, the women's ice hockey team.

The community is "as tightly knit as can be," partly "because we're so far from a major city, but also because faculty and second-year students stress mutual support and collaboration." The somewhat remote location in Ithaca is "a gift," as "it forces you create new social circles with your classmates." Johnson students have access to the entire Cornell campus, including its facilities and other student clubs and activities. With so much to do, some life planning can be in order. One student advises, "Choose one to two professionally-focused club(s), one socially-focused club, and one sports-focused club. I find most students follow this 2-1-1 approach and are incredibly invested in their activities." Every Thursday, the whole Johnson community comes together for the "well-attended" Sage Social (which provides food and drinks for everyone, and sometimes themed events); social circles are "fluid," with many activities attended by students of all backgrounds and interests. The best way to describe a Johnson student is this: "they take their work seriously but not themselves."

Admissions

The Johnson application is online only and includes four 400-word essays – three mandatory, one optional. Mandatory topics cover professional achievement and career goals, and the optional essay may be used to detail extenuating circumstances or provide additional bolstering information. Johnson initially reviews applicants through a two-reader system; those who make the cut receive an interview, and only disputed files go to committee. As with other systems, this simply means that it pays to present an extremely strong case for admission. Last year's entering class reported a median GPA of 3.33, average GMAT score of 700, and 5 years of work experience.

FINANCIAL FACTS

Annual tuition	$55,948

ADMISSIONS

Admissions Selectivity Rating	95
# of applications received	2,105
% applicants accepted	28
Average GMAT	694
Average GPA	3.29
TOEFL required of international students	Yes
Minimum TOEFL (paper/computer)	600/250
International application fee	$200
Application Deadline/Notification	
Round 1:	10/17
Round 2:	11/28
Round 3:	1/30
Round 4:	3/27
Deferment available	No
Transfer students accepted	No
Non-fall admissions	Yes
Need-blind admissions	Yes

EMPLOYMENT PROFILE

Career Rating	92	**Grads Employed by Function% Avg. Salary**	
Percent employed at graduation	82	Marketing	(13%) $95,700
Percent employed 3 months		Consulting	(26%)$121,800
after graduation	8	Management	(16%) $100,400
Average base starting salary	$106,500	Finance	(43%) $101,800
Primary Source of Full-time Job Acceptances		HR	(1%)
School-facilitated activities	169(74%)	MIS	(1%)
Graduate-facilitated activities	52(23%)	Other	(1%)
Unknown	6(3%)	**Top 5 Employers Hiring Grads**	
		Citi(19), Accenture (9), Deloitte Consulting (9), JP Morgan Chase & Co. (8), Samsung (6)	

DARTMOUTH COLLEGE
TUCK SCHOOL OF BUSINESS

GENERAL INFORMATION
Type of school   Private
Affiliation   No Affiliation
Academic calendar   Quarters

SURVEY SAYS...
Friendly students, Good social scene,
Good peer network, Helpful alumni
Solid preparation in:
General management

STUDENTS
Enrollment of parent
   institution   6,100
Enrollment of MBA Program   549
% male/female   67/33
% underrepresented minority   10
% international   33
Average age at entry   28
Average years work experience
   at entry   5.0

ACADEMICS
Academic Experience Rating   **99**
Profs interesting rating   96
Profs accesible rating   93
Student/faculty ratio   9:1
% female faculty   26
% underrepresented minority
   faculty   17

Joint Degrees
MD/MBA; MPH/MBA; MBA/MALD
with Tufts Fletcher School of Law
and Diplomacy; MBA/MPA with the
Kennedy School of Government at
Harvard; MBA/MELP with Vermont
Law School; and MBA/MA with the
Paul H. Nitze School of Advanced
International Studies at Johns
Hopkins University.

Prominent Alumni
Carlos Rodriguez-Pàstor, Jr.,
Chairman of the Board, Interbank;
Elyse Allan, President & CEO,
General Electric Canada; Roger
McNamee, Co-Founder & Advisory
Director, Elevation Partners; Eric
Spiegel, President & CEO, Siemens
Corporation

Academics

There is no rest for the weary at Tuck, where the "intensive academic core for first-years is accelerated and rigorous." During the elongated (32-week) school year, students take 18 courses, two of which are electives. One of these is Tuck's trademark First-Year Project, a course in which student teams develop new business ventures or act as consultants in existing ventures, and in which grades rest on the final presentation and other outcomes. This method reflects Tuck's emphasis on "academic deliverables, such as group papers, projects, and presentations." The second year consists of 12 elective courses, which may reflect well-rounded interests or a specialization. For example, Tuck recommends that a student interested in nonprofit and sustainability management take Corporate Social Responsibility, Entrepreneurship in the Social Sector I and II, Ethics in Action, the Tuck Global Consultancy international field study, and Strategic Responses to Market Failure. One student reports, "I feel completely prepared to take on my career post-Tuck. The school does a fantastic job of working students hard in the first year, teaching them the core fundamentals of business, and letting them craft their own paths during the second year." One student notes, "Tuck could update its core curriculum and case study assignments to reflect the current business environment, i.e., more standard courses to better understand the private-market investment climate, corporate ethics, digital media/entertainment, and emerging economies."

Tuck operates through "full immersion." Students "do a lot of work in study groups, which are assigned and required for first-years." Mandatory team rotation forces each student to work closely with a wide swath of his or her peers during the first year. The small class size and rural location reinforces class cohesiveness and fosters intimacy between MBA students and Tuck faculty and staff. Professors host social "gatherings at their homes and get involved with student organizations." "I have had lunches, dinners, or drinks with the majority of my professors," reports one second-year, "and I am treated with a respect that goes beyond [typical] teacher-student interactions." Administrators are "the nicest people on Earth." Some have even been known to "come in on a Sunday evening and bring food and coffee for us when we have exams." The overall "quality" of faculty and administration alike is "extraordinary."

Career and Placement

Tuck is "very focused on helping students land the jobs they came here to get." "The Career Development Office works tirelessly on behalf of students," though this benefit is most useful for students pursuing "traditional career paths (i.e., consulting, finance, general management)." However, "students interested in other opportunities (i.e., marketing, retail) may need to do more work outside the Career Development Office." Dartmouth is a magnet for recruiters, and "one of the best parts of Tuck is that visiting executives spend meaningful time with us. They don't stop by on their way to another meeting; rather, they have lunch and/or dinner with us, hold individual office hours, and make an effort to share their experiences with members of the class." Recruitment is Northeast focused, but the career office "is continually trying to reach out to West Coast firms"—the ones who often "recruit locally at Stanford and UCLA"—"and does a couple of treks for students interested in returning to the West." The tides may be turning; one student reports seeing "Google, Microsoft, and PG&E on campus this year," a possible "indication that a more diverse lineup of firms [is] coming to Tuck."

ADMISSIONS CONTACT: DAWNA CLARKE, DIRECTOR OF ADMISSIONS
ADDRESS: 100 TUCK HALL, HANOVER, NH 03755
PHONE: 603-646-3162 • FAX: 603-646-1441
E-MAIL: TUCK.ADMISSIONS@DARTMOUTH.EDU • WEBSITE: WWW.TUCK.DARTMOUTH.EDU

Students seeking jobs in "nontraditional" vocations and regions will have better luck with Tuck's extremely strong, supportive alumni network. One student told this story of success: "I emailed a Tuck alum who is a managing director at a bulge-bracket investment bank in London, and he called me 5 minutes later to talk. He arranged a personal office visit…and actually talked HR into sending me straight to second round interviews, because the firm's London office didn't recruit on campus…all because I put 'Tuck' in the subject line."

Tuck's most recent graduating class reports a median total annual compensation of $179,000.

Student Life and Environment

Students call posh, pretty Hanover "the quintessential small, New England, Ivy League town," "within a short drive of many great ski resorts" and far removed "from the hustle and bustle of a big city." Unlike at many schools, most first-years live on campus. Couples and families live in the Dartmouth-owned Sachem Village housing complex or elsewhere off-campus. The environment is extremely "intimate" and "supportive." Tuckies consider their school very family-friendly, telling us that partners are an integral part of the social scene, and note that "classmates who have children while at Tuck" are surrounded by a "phenomenal support network." Tuck is very inclusive of gay and lesbian students and partners.

The isolated location and clustered housing contribute to "a great deal of school spirit" and "strong camaraderie" in a "work-hard, play-hard environment." "Tuck students really transplant their lives to be here…we make friends quickly here and socialize a lot with our classmates." Students belong to more than 60 clubs, teams, and publications, and attend numerous social functions every week. "The end of the week is typically characterized by social mixers (Tuck Tails), small group dinners…and the occasional full-blown party (winter and spring formals, Tuck Vegas, beach party)." Students report that "sports are very much a part of life at Tuck."

No one gripes about the intimacy, which results in great friendships and means close business ties in the future. "I have had a substantive conversation with each of my 240 classmates and will feel very comfortable calling any of them after graduation for career advice and/or business counsel," reports one Tuckie. The class of 2013 is 34 percent international and an additional 14 percent minority, however, sometimes students note they wish there was a bit more diversity.

Admissions

Like many other schools, Tuck wants to know that you love it for what it is, not only for what it can do for you; show that you have researched the school thoroughly. The class of 2013 reports an average GPA of 3.5 and GMAT score of 717.

FINANCIAL FACTS

Annual tuition	$58,935
Fees	$4,350
Cost of books	$1,280
Room & board	$12,375
% of students receiving aid	70
% of first-year students receiving aid	72
% of students receiving grants	44
Average award package	$56,859
Average grant	$23,847

ADMISSIONS

Admissions Selectivity Rating	99
# of applications received	2,502
% applicants accepted	20
% acceptees attending	55
Average GMAT	717
Range of GMAT	680–760
Average GPA	3.5
TOEFL required of international students	Yes
International application fee	$225
Application Deadline/Notification	
Round 1:	10/12 / 12/16
Round 2:	11/9 / 2/10
Round 3:	1/4 / 3/16
Round 4:	4/2 / 5/11
Deferment available	Yes
Maximum length of deferment	case by case basis
Transfer students accepted	No
Non-fall admissions	No
Need-blind admissions	Yes

EMPLOYMENT PROFILE

Career Rating	99
Percent employed at graduation	86
Percent employed 3 months after graduation	93
Average base starting salary	$115,302

DELAWARE STATE UNIVERSITY
COLLEGE OF BUSINESS

GENERAL INFORMATION

Type of school	Public
Affiliation	No Affiliation
Academic calendar	Rolling Basis

SURVEY SAYS...
Good peer network
Solid preparation in:
Operations, Teamwork,
Communication/interpersonal skills,
Presentation skills, Quantitative skills,
Doing business in a global economy

STUDENTS

Enrollment of MBA Program	70
% male/female	53/47
% out-of-state	40
% underrepresented minority	31
% international	64
Average age at entry	29
Average years work experience at entry	4.0

ACADEMICS

Academic Experience Rating	**75**
Profs interesting rating	73
Profs accesible rating	73
Student/faculty ratio	8:1
% female faculty	30
% underrepresented minority faculty	60
% part-time faculty	20

Academics

Most of the students enrolled in the MBA program at Delaware State University's College of Business choose the program for its "convenient location" and for its attention to the needs of the "working professionals and aspiring managers" who attend here (classes are held exclusively during evening hours and weekends). The school describes its MBA as "an accelerated program geared towards working adults" that can be completed in 18 months by those taking two courses per eight-week term and in just 12 months by those taking three courses per term. Even those shouldering a lighter workload can complete the program in two years by attending at least one summer session.

The DSU MBA program is designed to promote integrative learning in a functional context so that students can build important managerial and organizational skills. The program requires students to complete 21 credit hours of core courses, one capstone course, and nine credit hours of electives, which can be used to pursue a concentration in a single subject. Students lacking corresponding undergraduate coursework may be required to take some or all of 18 credit hours in foundation courses. Foundation courses cover the following subjects: accounting, economics, finance, management information systems, marketing, and quantitative methods. Students may attempt to place out of any of these courses by passing a comprehensive exam, developed by the College of Business faculty, in the subject.

DSU's required core courses cover advanced economics, marketing management, business law and ethics, financial management, organizational leadership and behavior, operations analysis and management, and information and technology management. The capstone course is entitled Applied Strategic Management. Electives are offered in finance, information systems, and general management; concentrations are available in finance and information systems. Students may also participate in a case project in order to fulfill one of their elective requirements. According to the school's website, the case project "tests the student's strategic thinking and analytic skills" by requiring students either to (1) assess a company's income statement, balance sheet, annual reports, and other such documentation and provide recommendations; (2) manage an investment portfolio; or, (3) analyze "a series of general management cases that cover a broad range of strategic issues facing companies."

In order to graduate, students must earn a minimum grade point average of 3.0 with no more than six credit hours with a grade of C. Students who receive a grade of D or F during a course will be dismissed from the program; the school has procedures in place for students to appeal dismissal and/or academic probation. Students are required to complete the program in no more than five years.

Career and Placement

According to the school's website, the DSU Career Services office provides "technological and practical resources to provide students with the talent to conduct job searches, to become proficient in effective interviewing and presentation, and understanding the fit between their competencies and occupational requirements. Students also gain marketable experience through on- and off-campus collegiate activities, campus and community service, research projects, cooperative education, and internships to prepare them to manage their careers pre- and post-graduation." The service is designed primarily for the benefit of undergraduates, although graduate students and recent alumni may also utilize it.

ADMISSIONS CONTACT: KISHOR SHETH, MBA DIRECTOR
ADDRESS: 1200 N. DUPONT HIGHWAY, ROOM 106C, BANK OF AMERICA BUILDING, DOVER, DE 19901
PHONE: 302-857-6906 • FAX: 302-857-6945
E-MAIL: KSHETH@DESU.EDU • WEBSITE: WWW.DESU.EDU

Student Life and Environment

Students in the DSU MBA program form "a very culturally and ethnically diverse" group. Most are "hard-working students with full-time jobs" and "many have families to support," but there are also "some fresh college grads" in the mix. These "dedicated and helpful" students contribute to an intellectually challenging atmosphere."

DSU is located in Dover, the state capital. The state government and the United States Air Force are among the area's top employers; others include Playtex, Procter & Gamble, and General Mills, all of which have manufacturing facilities in or around Dover. The city is conveniently located, with fairly easy access to Philadelphia, Washington D.C., and Baltimore.

Admissions

Applicants to the Delaware State MBA program must submit the following documentation to the Admissions Committee: a completed application; official transcripts for all previous undergraduate and graduate work; an official score report for the GMAT; two letters of recommendation from individuals capable of assessing the candidate's ability to succeed in a graduate business program; a resume; and, a personal statement of career objectives and personal philosophy. In order to earn unconditional admission, applicants must have completed all foundations courses at the undergraduate level, and they must show an undergraduate GPA of at least 2.75, a minimum GMAT score of 400, and earn a score of at least 975 under the formula [(undergraduate GPA x 200) + GMAT score]. Applicants failing to meet these requirements may be admitted conditionally if they have an undergraduate GPA of at least 2.5 and a minimum GMAT score of 400; or, have an undergraduate GPA of at least 3.0 or an upper-division GPA of at least 3.25; or, meet all requirements except for the foundations requirement. Students admitted conditionally will have their status changed to 'unconditional admission' once they have completed three MBA-level courses with a grade of at least B; they must submit a satisfactory GMAT score before being allowed to register for a fourth MBA-level course. Applicants with significant work experience (at least five years) in management may apply for admission as non-traditional students; the school may waive GPA and GMAT requirements for such applicants.

FINANCIAL FACTS

Annual tuition (in-state/out-of-state)	$12,000/$24,000
Fees	$400
Cost of books	$1,200
Room & board (on/off-campus)	$7,500/$4,800
% of students receiving aid	20
% of first-year students receiving aid	40
% of students receiving grants	20
Average award package	$5,000
Average grant	$6,000

ADMISSIONS

Admissions Selectivity Rating	**70**
# of applications received	48
% applicants accepted	92
% acceptees attending	100
Average GMAT	450
Average GPA	3.00
TOEFL required of international students	Yes
Application fee	$50
International application fee	$50
Deferment available	Yes
Maximum length of deferment	unlimited
Transfer students accepted	Yes
Transfer application policy: They must complete the application process and provide the official transcripts.	
Non-fall admissions	Yes
Need-blind admissions	No

EMPLOYMENT PROFILE			
Career Rating	**69**	**Grads Employed by Function**	**% Avg. Salary**
Percent employed at graduation	2	Marketing	(20%)
Percent employed 3 months after graduation	3	Operations	(5%)
		Management	(20%)
Average base starting salary	$55,000	Finance	(20%)
Primary Source of Full-time Job Acceptances		**Top 5 Employers Hiring Grads**	
School-facilitated activities	(40%)	Bank of America (13), Chase (15), JP	
Graduate-facilitated activities	(20%)	Morgan (25)	
Unknown	(40%)		

DREXEL UNIVERSITY
LeBow College of Business

GENERAL INFORMATION

Type of school	Private
Affiliation	No Affiliation
Academic calendar	September–June

SURVEY SAYS...

Students love Philadelphia, PA,
Smart classrooms
Solid preparation in:
Accounting

STUDENTS

Enrollment of parent institution	23,637
Enrollment of MBA Program	711
% male/female	65/35
% out-of-state	60
% part-time	80
% underrepresented minority	45
% international	44
Average age at entry	29
Average years work experience at entry	6.0

ACADEMICS

Academic Experience Rating	93
Profs interesting rating	77
Profs accesible rating	82
Student/faculty ratio	26:1
% female faculty	33
% underrepresented minority faculty	30
% part-time faculty	4

Joint Degrees

MBA/MS in Accounting, MBA/MS in Finance, MD/MBA: 5 years; JD/MBA, 4 years; MBA/MS in Television Management, 3 years.

Prominent Alumni

Bennett S. LeBow, Chairman Vector group; Chairman and CEO Borders Group; Gary Bernstein, Vice President, IBM; Nicholas DeBenedictis, Chairman, AquaAmerica; Raj Gupta, Former Chairman and CEO, Rohm & Haas; Dominic J. Frederico, Chairman, President and CEO, Assured Guaranty

Academics

Academics at Drexel University encompass a breadth of Colleges and Schools whose programs are designed to provide the foundation of study coupled with cooperative education experiences to produce the next generation of scholars, professionals, and leaders. LeBow College fits squarely into that tradition. Noted strengths of the MBA program include "a pragmatic approach to real-world application." Offering a "strong and dynamic curriculum" that "stresses practical education," LeBow offers "a solid emphasis on business analysis processes with a strong technology background as well." Practical application is delivered through "case studies and other real-life simulations" that "help in applying concepts and attaining a better understanding of how to approach a given situation." Students in the two-year full-time MBA program also benefit from a co-op program that provides hands-on experience while "helping students learn more about the industries in which they might wish to pursue a career."

Part-time and full-time students will find numerous options at LeBow. The school offers a one-year full-time MBA as well as the aforementioned two-year program. Those unable to attend daytime classes will likely prefer the two-year evening cohort MBA (called the LEAD MBA, for LeBow Evening Accelerated Drexel MBA). LeBow also offers a more traditional part-time Professional MBA and two online part-time MBAs. The first, called MBA Anywhere, is a conventional part-time cohort MBA delivered primarily online over 24 months (three on-campus residencies are required). The other is the Corporate MBA in Pharmaceutical Management, whose curriculum was designed in collaboration with Johnson & Johnson. All programs operate on a fast-paced quarterly academic calendar that allows "more chances to take courses during a year," and all programs place "a strong emphasis on leadership."

Students praise the LeBow administration, reporting that the school "appears to be pouring a lot of money into the marketing of the LeBow brand. That will likely produce more of a return for [us] upon graduation." One MBA happily tells us that "The administration could not make the process any easier to prevent any type of potential distraction from your academics. If you wish to pursue further study in a discipline or make local contacts in a discipline they are always there to help." Likewise, professors "are really open to meeting with students and discussing classroom ideas in a different context. They enjoy getting to know their students and sharing their own experiences." Faculty members "bring real-world issues to classroom for discussions and potential problem solutions. Some even share their consultancy experiences with the students. Overall, it is highly stimulating and excellent learning experience."

Career and Placement

LeBow's Office of MBA Career Services offers "excellent career services," according to students. Through "various career service events and networking opportunities," career counselors "really make an effort to involve as many students as possible and showcase their events in a professional way. Just in the last few months I have attended several Employer of the Week sessions that have [piqued] my interest in industries I had not previously considered. Also the Mentor Match program has been pivotal in honing my networking skills and [giving me the opportunity to interact] with alumni in both formal and informal settings." Drexel's alumni network represents another "great opportunity to see how Drexel positively impacted the careers of so many professionals who were once in our position years ago." Finally, "regular job fairs...are often good opportunities for networking."

ADMISSIONS CONTACT: JOHN ADAMSKI, DIRECTOR GRADUATE ADMISSIONS
ADDRESS: 3141 CHESTNUT STREET, MATHESON HALL 207, PHILADELPHIA, PA 19104
PHONE: 215-895-6804 • FAX: 215-895-1725
E-MAIL: MBA@DREXEL.EDU • WEBSITE: WWW.LEBOW.DREXEL.EDU/

Top employers of recently graduated Drexel MBAs include: Deloitte & Touche, PricewaterhouseCoopers, Prudential Bank of America, PNC Bank, Wachovia Securities, TIAA CREF, Campbell Soup Company, Siemens, Sungard, and Exelon Corporation.

Student Life and Environment

"Drexel provides plenty of professional and social networking opportunities" for its MBAs, although full-time students benefit the most (since they are on campus most frequently). Full-timers report "an overwhelming range of opportunities available," with "clubs and competitions for every interest" that include "networking events for women in business, video game clubs, consulting groups, music labels, etc. Academics are always number one priority, but there are plenty of outside opportunities for fun." Philadelphia is an asset in that regard. It's "a city that has a ton of opportunities" and provides a "great local business and government network." Overall, students enjoy a "good life/school/work balance," with "plenty of opportunities to pursue other school-related activities without having to overcommit yourself."

LeBow has a diverse population in its MBA programs with one-third of the students coming with undergraduate degrees in business, one-third in the sciences including engineering, and one-third having liberal arts degree. Students say this mix results in "a nice balance between very intelligent and a lot of fun." The different programs draw different types of students, of course. The full-time program tends to be younger and less experienced, while the Executive MBA draws students who "have extensive work experience and understand the importance of a business graduate degree."

Admissions

Applicants to the Drexel MBA program must submit all of the following: transcripts for all undergraduate work and for any graduate study; an official GMAT score report; letters of recommendation; a personal essay; and a resume. Applicants are assessed based on academic performance, professional experience, career goals, extracurricular record, and potential to contribute positively to the Drexel MBA program. International applicants must also submit an official score report for the TOEFL if English is not their first language, unless they hold an undergraduate degree from an institution at which instruction is in English.

FINANCIAL FACTS

Annual tuition	$25,000
Fees	$800
Cost of books	$1,200
Room & board	$15,000
% of students receiving aid	76
% of first-year students receiving aid	76
% of students receiving grants	42
Average award package	$29,890
Average grant	$16,246
Average loan	$21,050
Average student loan debt	$48,981

ADMISSIONS

Admissions Selectivity Rating	92
# of applications received	1,370
% applicants accepted	29
% acceptees attending	54
Average GMAT	620
Range of GMAT	580–680
Average GPA	3.20
TOEFL required of international students	Yes
Minimum TOEFL (paper/computer)	600/250
Application fee	$50
International application fee	$50
Early application deadline	10/15
Regular application deadline	8/1
Deferment available	Yes
Maximum length of deferment	12 months
Transfer students accepted	Yes
Transfer application policy: Completed application and all supporting materials to be reviewed by Admissions Committee. Only non-cohorted programs allow for transfer credits from an AACSB accredited school.	
Non-fall admissions	Yes
Need-blind admissions	Yes

EMPLOYMENT PROFILE

Career Rating	87	Grads Employed by Function	% Avg. Salary
Percent employed at graduation	26	Marketing	(15%) $87,400
Percent employed 3 months after graduation	59	Operations	(12%) $53,250
		Consulting	(24%) $55,875
Average base starting salary	$63,691	Management	(12%) $82,000
		Finance	(29%) $61,402
		Other	(6%)

Top 5 Employers Hiring Grads
TYCO Electronics, PNC, Deliotte, Campbell's Soup, South Jersey Industries

DUKE UNIVERSITY
THE FUQUA SCHOOL OF BUSINESS

GENERAL INFORMATION
Type of school	Private
Affiliation	No Affiliation
Academic calendar	Terms

SURVEY SAYS...
Good social scene, Good peer network, Happy students, Smart classrooms
Solid preparation in:
Teamwork, Communication/interpersonal skills

STUDENTS
Enrollment of parent institution	14,248
Enrollment of MBA Program	900
% male/female	70/30
% part-time	0
% underrepresented minority	10
% international	39
Average age at entry	29
Average years work experience at entry	5.0

ACADEMICS
Academic Experience Rating	**98**
Profs interesting rating	96
Profs accesible rating	91
Student/faculty ratio	8:1
% female faculty	17
% underrepresented minority faculty	5
% part-time faculty	8

Joint Degrees
MBA/JD; MBA/Master of Public Policy; MBA/Master of Forestry; MBA/Master of Environmental Management; MBA/MS Engineering; MBA/MD; MBA/MSN in Nursing

Prominent Alumni
Melinda French Gates, Co-chair and Trustee, Bill & Melinda Gates Foundation; Timothy D. Cook, Acting CEO, Apple Inc.; Michael W. Lamach, Chariman, President and CEO, Ingersoll Rand; L. Kevin Kelly, CEO, Heidrick & Struggles

Academics

Students come to Duke University's Fuqua School of Business for many reasons. For some, "the opportunity to be associated with one of the premier universities in the world" is an obvious advantage, while others cite the school's "strong social entrepreneurship program." The "culture of diversity," "international programs," and "focus on developing global business leaders," are other highly attractive qualities of a Fuqua education, as are the school's many institutes and abundant areas of study. Across the board, however, almost everyone agrees that the "incredible atmosphere of collaboration" and "emphasis on teamwork" make Fuqua stand out. Both inside and outside the classroom, Fuqua maintains "an environment that highly values (and teaches) principles of communication and inter-connection between people." Coursework is collaborative, teamwork is integrated throughout the curriculum, and students are encouraged to take leadership roles in the school community. In fact, "The challenge from the administration to be leaders of consequence is woven throughout our activities, not just a trite phrase mentioned during orientation." A student details, "The administration gives students the freedom to shape much of our experience, and has an open-door policy when we need to confront any situations that might arise, even for items as small as thermostat settings in classrooms." In fact, "Much of the day-to-day activities of the school are student-run," and even "core functions of the school, such as admissions and career management, have great leadership opportunities for current students." With such an active and robust student experience, many feel that Duke offers "the best blend of academics and atmosphere of any of the top business schools."

The Duke MBA–Daytime begins with a four-week term called the "Global Institute," designed to develop international business and leadership skills. Thereafter, Duke's curriculum is organized into a series of six-week terms, during which students take a blend of electives and required core courses. "Taught by seasoned, senior faculty," "the core classes truly prepare you for every aspect of business." There is also a "plentiful" selection of electives (more than 100, at present), which adds "a great blend of breadth and depth" to the program. As a part of an internationally renowned university, Duke's "phenomenal" faculty is "widely recognized for its prolific research output," yet "very devoted to classes they teach." Each class crams "a full semester of material into a six week term." Therefore, you'll "learn a lot in a short period of time"—and be amply challenged, at that. A dazzled student exclaims, "The academic experience is the best one can get in the world; I have learned more in these two years than in my five years of college and 10 years of experience combined."

Career and Placement

With an excellent reputation and accomplished student body, there is "a wide breadth of companies for each discipline" who recruit on the Duke campus. In recent years, top recruiters included Apple, Bain & Company, Boston Consulting Group, Citi, Deloitte, Golman Sachs, Google, Johnson & Johnson, McKinsey, and Microsoft. While some students hail the Career Management Center's ample contacts and recruiters, other say they would like to continue to see the school work toward implementing a "better off-campus strategy for students," a goal that the Center has recently addressed with a new, proprietary model for organizing and implementing an off-campus search. Most students note that given the current trouble in the economy, the school has responded adequately; "They have added additional sessions throughout the week to make sure students have the resources they need to have a successful job search." Further, "50 to 60 students formally assist—via Career Management Center—other students to critique resume, cover letter, and interview skills." Others relay the desire for the Center to continue to "improve in building relationships with international employers." Though, as the school notes, with more than 9 out of 10 students citing the U.S. as their pre-

ADMISSIONS CONTACT: LIZ RILEY HARGROVE, ASSOCIATE DEAN FOR ADMISSIONS
ADDRESS: 100 FUQUA DRIVE, DURHAM, NC 27708-0120
PHONE: 919-660-7705 • FAX: 919-681-8026
E-MAIL: ADMISSIONS-INFO@FUQUA.DUKE.EDU • WEBSITE: WWW.FUQUA.DUKE.EDU

ferred destination post-graduation, student employment interests have traditionally been focused in the U.S. despite the fact that Fuqua's student population is very global.

Student Life and Environment

Student leadership is a key component of the Fuqua experience, and "The business school activities and clubs are solely student-run." As a result, "Day-to-day life is very busy between classes, career search, clubs, and social activity." A student shares, "The workload (class, career search, club related) is very challenging and prepares you well for the busy life of an executive." But, with 24 hours in the day, there is even time for fun. A student marvels, "I work at 100% capacity but somehow still manage to enjoy a dynamic social life." In fact, "Team Fuqua"—as the business school community is fondly called—is a "friendly" and "tight-knit" group. As "most people come to Durham just for business school," you'll find "an instant community whose members bond very quickly and socialize very often." A popular event is the weekly "Fuqua Friday," a happy hour during which "students, partners, children, professors and administrators can decompress and have some fun." In addition, students get together for "lots of parties and barbecues at apartment complexes." For married students (which comprise about a third of the population), "The school also has a great community of spouses and partners who meet regularly which makes it easier for those who are married or in relationships."

On campus, "The facilities are amazing. There is a new building with high end technology, a top library, and 58 team rooms." When it comes to surrounding Durham, most students praise the school's comfortable "suburban location" in a city that "affords a good quality of life." Among other benefits, there is "a plethora of affordable housing," and "the weather is nice for most of the year."

Admissions

Admission to Fuqua is highly competitive; you will have the best chance of acceptance if you apply as early in the admissions cycle as possible. The admissions committee does not have any minimum GMAT scores or GPA requirements. However, for the class of 2012, the GMAT range for students in the 25th to 75th percentile was 640–750, while the average GPA range was 3.02 to 3.80.

FINANCIAL FACTS

Annual tuition	$47,960
Fees	$1,786
Cost of books	$6,530
Room & board	$10,610
% of students receiving aid	79
% of first-year students receiving aid	77
% of students receiving grants	43
Average student loan debt	$92,828

ADMISSIONS

Admissions Selectivity Rating	97
# of applications received	3,506
% applicants accepted	24
% acceptees attending	53
Average GMAT	697
Range of GMAT	640–750
Average GPA	3.42
TOEFL required of international students	Yes
Application fee	$200
International application fee	$200
Application Deadline/Notification	
Round 1:	9/30 / 12/3
Round 2:	11/1 / 1/31
Round 3:	1/5 / 3/25
Round 4:	3/8 / 5/9
Deferment available	Yes
Maximum length of deferment	Considered on a case-by-case basis after May 1
Transfer students accepted	No
Non-fall admissions	No
Need-blind admissions	Yes

EMPLOYMENT PROFILE

Career Rating	97	Grads Employed by Function	% Avg. Salary
Percent employed at graduation	64	Marketing	(29%) $97,647
Percent employed 3 months after graduation	77	Operations	(4%) $106,700
		Consulting	(28%) $111,907
Average base starting salary	$102,056	Management	(13%) $103,310
Primary Source of Full-time Job Acceptances		Finance	(23%) $94,728
School-facilitated activities	211(71%)	Other	(3%) $100,286
Graduate-facilitated activities	78(26%)	**Top 5 Employers Hiring Grads**	
Unknown	9(3%)	Deloitte Consulting (18), Johnson & Johnson (12), Bank of America (11), Boston Consulting Group (8), Samsung (8)	

DUQUESNE UNIVERSITY
JOHN F. DONAHUE GRADUATE SCHOOL OF BUSINESS

GENERAL INFORMATION

Type of school	Private
Affiliation	Roman Catholic
Academic calendar	Semester

SURVEY SAYS...

Cutting-edge classes, Happy students
Solid preparation in:
Doing business in a global economy,
Social responsibility

STUDENTS

Enrollment of parent institution	10,011
Enrollment of MBA Program	332
% male/female	60/40
% part-time	70
% international	12
Average age at entry	29
Average years work experience at entry	6.0

ACADEMICS

Academic Experience Rating	82
Profs interesting rating	81
Profs accesible rating	85
Student/faculty ratio	6:1
% female faculty	26
% underrepresented minority faculty	12

Joint Degrees

MBA/JD; MBA/MS – Information
Management, Environmental
Science Management, Health
Management Systems, Industrial
Pharmacy or Pharmacy Doctorate
MBA/MA – Corporate
Communication, Public Policy

Prominent Alumni

Nicholas Deluliis, President and
COO, Consol Energy; Gail Gerono,
Vice President, Calgon Carbon
Corporation; Richard Hoerner, CFA &
Managing Director, BlackRock; Jack
Ouellette, Chief Executive Officer,
American Textile Corporation ;
Stephan Schenk, Operational Risk
Executive, TD Bank

Academics

Duquesne University's Donahue School of Business is unique because of its emphasis on sustainability and business ethics. Duquesne's award-winning, full-time, one-year MBA in sustainability is its star program, drawing students who believe sustainability will soon be "a global business imperative." One student in this "outstanding" program says it will "open a lot of doors as the business world continues to evolve." Duquesne's other MBA programs are also strong. Its part-time and full-time evening MBA allows students to work and participate in various academic and professional enrichment activities. All students are required to take a foundational core of classes but can take electives or add a concentration in the following areas: Business Ethics, Finance, Health Care Management, Human Resource Management, Information Systems Management, International Business, Management, Marketing, and Supply Chain Management. The school also offers masters programs, and joint MBA/JD and MBA/MS-Information Systems Management degrees, such as an MS in Accountancy and an MBA/MS in Accountancy.

Duquesne is devoted to teaching and supporting ethical business practices, and all students are required to take an "Applied Business Ethics" course. The Beard Institute promotes "business ethics, responsible financial management, and sustainability in the global marketplace," and hosts the Distinguished Ethics Speaker Series. Students looking to broaden their professional experiences can spend a semester abroad in France, Colombia, Mexico, Japan, China, Belgium, or Germany. However, students don't need to go abroad to gain diverse or international perspectives. The "varied work backgrounds of [my fellow] students" and the presence of international students ensure everyone is exposed to global viewpoints.

Teamwork is a big part of academic life at Duquesne, where "small class sizes" allow students to work with each other on rewarding projects "that collaborate across all classes." Professors are "enthusiastic" and "knowledgeable in their respective fields," and bring "real-world application to the material." They are "friendly" and "accessible," and "show a genuine interest in the success of their students." Students looking to enrich their academic experience or become more involved in the school can apply for a graduate assistantship. These competitive appointments employ students in one of three areas: assisting with faculty research; tutoring in accounting, economics, finance, or statistics; or working in administrative offices. Students are not eligible for these positions until they are accepted, and they must maintain a 3.5 GPA while holding them.

Career and Placement

The Donahue School of Business does not have its own student career office, so students use the University's Career Services Center, which serves the rest of the school. The center hosts career fairs, networking events, and on-campus interviews for students at all levels. It also provides resume help and career counseling. However, some students would like to see "better alumni networking and career services for graduate students."

Duquesne's "excellent reputation" means it is able to attract a wide range of companies to its events. Employers who recently visited campus include Allegheny Technologies, Alcoa, Bank of New York Mellon, Deloitte, PNC Bank, Price Waterhouse Coopers, T. Rowe Price, US Steel, Westinghouse.

ADMISSIONS CONTACT: PATRICIA MOORE, MANAGING DIRECTOR OF GRADUATE PROGRAMS
ADDRESS: 600 FORBES AVENUE, PITTSBURGH, PA 15282
PHONE: 412-396-6276 • FAX: 412-396-1726
E-MAIL: GRAD-BUS@DUQ.EDU • WEBSITE: WWW.BUSINESS.DUQ.EDU/GRAD

Student Life and Environment

"The greatest strengths of Duquesne are the students," who are "enthusiastic, innovative, hard working, competitive and very smart." One student described his peers as "young professionals" who want to take their careers "to the next level."

Many students commute and work part- or full-time, which means classes are filled with people with "interesting and diverse" professional experience. "I appreciate the varied work backgrounds of my fellow students," one student says. "It helps to provide insight to other industries and fields."

Despite its large commuter population, the school still manages to provide a "close-knit community" and a "personal" educational experience. One commuter says that even students who live off campus feel like they live on campus because they're "constantly in the buildings." Students love Duquesne's location in downtown Pittsburgh, which makes the school "convenient for working professionals" and puts students in "close proximity to downtown Pittsburgh's business and professional climate." The school is also "close to some of the most popular entertainment districts" of Pittsburgh "as well as within a 5-mile radius of four other colleges," so there are lots of opportunities for socializing and meeting people.

Admissions

All students applying to Duquesne's MBA programs must take the GMAT, and international students must also take the TOEFL. The full- and part-time MBA program admits students for the fall and spring semesters, but students in the Sustainability MBA program may only enter in the fall. Applications require official transcripts, letters of recommendation, a resume, and a personal statement on what strengths you will bring to the program. Students seeking admission to the Sustainability program have different personal essay options. Interviews are not required, but personal or phone interviews can positively supplement applications. Four-year bachelor degrees are required for admission, and international students who received a degree after three years of study may enroll in Duquesne's MBA Bridge Program, which allows them to take the necessary year of classes at the undergraduate level and apply those credits toward their MBA.

FINANCIAL FACTS

Annual tuition	$49,083
Cost of books	$2,550
Room & board	$9,806
% of students receiving aid	50
Average award package	$12,000

ADMISSIONS

Admissions Selectivity Rating	87
Average GMAT	590
Average GPA	3.20
TOEFL required of international students	Yes
Early application deadline	2/1
Early notification date	3/1
Regular application deadline	7/1
Regular application notification	Rolling
Application Deadline/Notification PT	
Round 1:	7/1 / Rolling
Round 2:	11/1
Round 3:	4/1
Deferment available	Yes
Maximum length of deferment	1 year
Transfer students accepted	Yes
Transfer application policy: The Donahue School will accept up to 15 transfer credits from an accredited college or university (evening programs only).	
Non-fall admissions	Yes
Need-blind admissions	Yes

EAST CAROLINA UNIVERSITY
COLLEGE OF BUSINESS

GENERAL INFORMATION
Type of school	Public
Affiliation	No Affiliation
Academic calendar	Semester

SURVEY SAYS...
Friendly students, Good social scene,
Cutting-edge classes
Solid preparation in:
Teamwork, Communication/interpersonal skills, Quantitative skills,
Computer skills

STUDENTS
Enrollment of MBA Program	797
% part-time	75
Average age at entry	31

ACADEMICS
Academic Experience Rating	69
Profs interesting rating	77
Profs accesible rating	74

Joint Degrees
MD/MBA, full-time, part-time; 42
credits; must be enrolled in an
accredited medical school, be a
medical resident; 12 months.

Academics

East Carolina is a medium-sized public school, but it seems like a smaller, more expensive one. Its MBA program provides students with lots of "individual attention" and allows them to tailor the program to their needs. "ECU has an intimate feel," one student says. "Professors know students' names," and the campus has a "friendly atmosphere." Students can take classes on campus, online, or both. It's common for distance education programs to feel alienating, but students say "very little of the East Carolina spirit is lost over the Internet." "There is still a lot of communication that goes on" in the online program, and the interactive media "makes up for the lack of face time" and means students still "get a chance to know people pretty well." Students may attend full or part time, and can change the number of classes they take and the method through which they take them every semester. One student explains, the school "is set up to meet students' needs, not the students having to work around the school."

East Carolina requires a number of core classes, such as Financial and Managerial Accounting and Financial Management, but students who studied business as an undergraduate can have these requirements waived if they took similar courses and received a B or higher. All students must take seven breadth-level courses that provide a solid foundation in business and three elective courses that allow them to focus on areas of their choice. Students may use the three elective requirements toward a certificate in an area they want to specialize in. Current offerings include Health Care Management, Finance and Management Information Systems.

Professors at East Carolina get high marks. The "strong" and "challenging" faculty members are "genuinely concerned with their students' success in the program." "Professors know students' names" and really "push them to get better." They are accessible outside of class, and students can "build real relationships with them." One student explains that a "professor put me in touch with professional networking organizations. Another put me in touch with a professor outside my program, who had insight into an aspect of business I am interested in." Professors definitely "expect hard work and high professionalism from each student," and those interested in East Carolina should be prepared to devote themselves to their studies. One online student who also works full time says, "My life revolves around class assignments, cases, group work, and other obligations. This program is not for the faint of heart!" East Carolina's combination of a demanding, but flexible academic program, dedicated professors, and enthusiastic students make for a great experience and is why so many people think the school offers a great "bang for the buck."

Career and Placement

East Carolina University's Center for Student Success offers students a wide-range of individualized support for their academic and professional needs. Career Services assists students with internship and job searches, conducts mock interviews, and provides help with resumes. In addition to providing networking opportunities, the Center hosts career fairs and on-campus interviews. Companies that visited campus in the past year include Credit Suisse, BB&T bank, Ferguson/ Wolseley, PIE Event, Sinclair Broadcasting, and McGladrey & Pullen.

ADMISSIONS CONTACT: TINA WILLIAMS, DIRECTOR OF GRADUATE PROGRAMS
ADDRESS: 3203 BATE BUILDING, GREENVILLE, NC 27858-4353
PHONE: 252-328-6970 • FAX: 252-328-2106
E-MAIL: GRADBUS@ECU.EDU • WEBSITE: WWW.BUSINESS.ECU.EDU

FINANCIAL FACTS

Annual tuition (in-state/ out-of-state)	$7,920/$19,752
Cost of books	$800

ADMISSIONS

Admissions Selectivity Rating	67
# of applications received	205
% applicants accepted	83
TOEFL required of international students	Yes
Minimum TOEFL (paper/computer)	550/213
Application fee	$70
International application fee	$70
Deferment available	Yes
Maximum length of deferment	1 year
Transfer students accepted	Yes
Transfer application policy: Maximum of 9 Semester credit hours from AACSB accredited institution accepted.	
Non-fall admissions	Yes
Need-blind admissions	Yes

Student Life and Environment

The flexibility offered by East Carolina attracts a wide-range of students. You'll find students, who are "young and old, single and married, career changers, and professionals seeking to enhance their status within their current career tracks." Though people may be different, one student says "everybody is here to learn." Students are "excited about learning, and this energy comes through." Students who have "been in the professional world for several years, bring a wealth of knowledge and experience" into classroom discussions. The large number of distance learners does not diminish the school's spirit; in fact, the online students are some of the program's biggest champions.

The campus itself is nice and has "great places to study and to wind down" and offers lots of "great extracurricular activities." The football games are popular and "always a whole lot of fun." However, as many students work full time and have family obligations, not everyone has time to participate in campus life, so those looking to actively socialize may have to look beyond the MBA program. Luckily, the Graduate Business Association organizes a lot of activities, such as networking programs with local business leaders and recruiters, as well as professional development seminars and social nights. Many certificate programs, such as Accounting, Finance, and Management, have their own student organizations, and the school also has chapters of two national business honor societies, Beta Gamma Sigma and Phi Kappa Phi.

Admissions

East Carolina University does not require applicants to have previous professional experience and does not ask for recommendations or a personal statement. To be eligible for admission, students must have a degree from an accredited institution. Admissions for all programs are on a rolling basis, and students may begin classes in the fall, spring, or summer. Admission is based off of a student's "admission index number," which is calculated from the student's GMAT score (students must have a score greater than 450) and undergraduate GPA. International students must take the TOEFL and score at least 550 on the written exam, 213 on the computer exam, and 80 on the Internet portion of the exam.

EAST TENNESSEE STATE UNIVERSITY
COLLEGE OF BUSINESS AND TECHNOLOGY

Academics

There aren't many choices at the College of Business and Technology at East Tennessee State University—the small program maintains only three business and three technology departments (accounting, economics/finance, management/marketing)—but for those who are interested in a general purpose business degree, ETSU delivers.

In addition to the traditional MBA, the school also offers an MAcc (master's of accounting), and a graduate certificate in business administration for "those who seek a basic understanding of business administration but who may not be able to make the commitment of time, effort, and money required to seek a master's degree."

MBAs at ETSU feel that "The administration and faculty here are very student-oriented. Most have set times when they are available outside of class; others excel and really go the extra mile both in class presentation and in their availability to those students that require extra instruction." Overall, "The program is very well-organized and runs smoothly. The program has been staffed administratively to be a success. Everyone is focused on their customer—the student." Professors are regarded as "very knowledgeable in their fields, and many of them are widely recognized as great scholars." One student writes, "Most of them have a work background that can lead to some very good discussions in class, and [the professors present] the applications of the concepts in the real world through their stories." Faculty members are also "easy to work with and understanding about personal matters that can arise." ETSU students are "a very diverse and accepting group. All of us have different ideals and political and social backgrounds." Another student concurs: "We are like a family at ETSU. You go through the same classes with pretty much the same group of students. We are all interested in each other's success. There is low competition." Most students agree that the school does "a very good job of getting the student prepared with the knowledge that is needed in the workplace, but there is just so much that can be taught in the classroom setting." Many students have full-time jobs, and say "true learning from the classroom is applied to the jobs that are obtained after school." Across the board, students love that "The school is large enough to offer remote-learning facilities, and classes are generally available at convenient times for working adults." Most of all, however, students appreciate that professors "show a major interest in students' ability to understand the work."

Career and Placement

The Career Placement and Internship Services Office at East Tennessee University serves the school's entire undergraduate and graduate student body. The office hosts recruitment visits from various companies, sponsors and participates in career fairs, maintains online job boards and resume books, and offers counseling in interview skills, job search, career match, and resume writing. Recent on-campus recruiters included New York Life, Norfolk Southern, Wachovia, and Wells Fargo. Students are aware that "Johnson City is a small town, which limits the amount of recruiting that is done on campus." Even so, many "believe that [the] school could improve by really showing students what is available out there and helping them find jobs when they get done. It is there right now [at the Career Placement and Internship Services Office], but a student really has to push to find it."

ADMISSIONS CONTACT: DR. MARTHA POINTER, DIRECTOR OF GRADUATE STUDIES
ADDRESS: PO BOX 70699, JOHNSON CITY, TN 37614
PHONE: 423-439-5314 • FAX: 423-439-5274
E-MAIL: BUSINESS@BUSINESS.ETSU.EDU • WEBSITE: WWW.ETSU.EDU/CBAT

Student Life and Environment

East Tennessee State University is located in Johnson City, a small Appalachian city close to both the North Carolina and Virginia borders. The surrounding area, dubbed the Tri-Cities region, also includes Bristol and Kingsport; the charming town of Abingdon, Virginia, is also not too far afield. The area is an outdoor enthusiast's paradise, offering plenty of opportunities for hiking, climbing, skiing, and nature walks. The Tri-Cities area is a rising force in the health care industry, with a developing biotech industry that could bring big players to the region.

With more than 14,000 students (about 2,200 of whom are graduate students), the ETSU campus has the population to support a busy social scene. MBAs report, "There is a very good social scene, with Thursday nights being the night that most students go out to the clubs. There are not a lot of clubs in the area, but there are many places that one can go and have a beer if they so choose." Students try to find time to support their men's basketball team, the ETSU Bucs.

ETSU has expanded in recent years, adding several new buildings, including a fitness center (students love the "fully-equipped athletic facility"). Not all MBAs take the time to enjoy the ETSU campus, however; they note that "the school is a high commuter school. This leads to a low participation level in on-campus clubs" and other activities. Those who do participate recommend the school's several national honor societies. One student touts "the university organization called 'President's Pride.' Through this organization, I am able to socialize with other students, faculty, administrators, and [members of the] community by volunteering for university/community functions."

Through its Adult, Commuter, and Transfer Services (ACTS) Office, ETSU assists its many nontraditional students in adapting to student life. ACTS staff advises students on the nuts and bolts of registration, direct them to the campus's various tutoring services, and help parents find child-care services. This last one can be a problem for MBAs, who typically attend evening classes.

Admissions

Applications to the College of Business and Technology at East Tennessee State University are considered on a rolling basis. Applicants must submit the following to the Graduate Admissions Office: official copies of transcripts for all undergraduate and graduate work; standardized test scores (GMAT for the MBA or MAcc; TOEFL scores (where applicable); a personal statement; and a resume. All applicants are presumed to be competent with computers and math literate through calculus.

FINANCIAL FACTS

Annual tuition (in-state/ out-of-state)	$5,446/$15,722
Fees	$1,100
Cost of books	$1,000
Room & board (on/off-campus)	$5,000/$6,000
% of students receiving aid	25
% of first-year students receiving aid	25
% of students receiving grants	25
Average award package	$6,000
Average grant	$6,000
Average loan	$4,000
Average student loan debt	$10,000

ADMISSIONS

Admissions Selectivity Rating	76
# of applications received	70
% applicants accepted	77
% acceptees attending	85
Average GMAT	535
Range of GMAT	450–700
Average GPA	3.30
TOEFL required of international students	Yes
Minimum TOEFL (paper/computer)	550/213
Application fee	$25
International application fee	$35
Regular application deadline	6/1
Deferment available	Yes
Maximum length of deferment	1 year
Transfer students accepted	Yes
Transfer application policy: Up to 9 approved hours may be accepted.	
Non-fall admissions	Yes
Need-blind admissions	Yes

EMPLOYMENT PROFILE

Career Rating	73	Grads Employed by Function	%	Avg. Salary
Average base starting salary	$38,000	Marketing	(10%)	$38,000
		Management	(50%)	$30,000
		HR	(10%)	$30,000

Top 5 Employers Hiring Grads
Eastman Chemical (2)

EASTERN MICHIGAN UNIVERSITY
COLLEGE OF BUSINESS

Academics

With its convenient location, "experienced professors," and "low tuition," the MBA program at Eastern Michigan University's College of Business offers a great return on investment. "Designed for working professionals," EMU's courses are offered in the evenings, on the weekends, via the Internet, and through hybrid online/classroom delivery. The format is totally flexible, and students can take as little as one class per semester and up to a full course load. While balancing a career and an education can be tricky business, students say EMU "provides great support for students and overall great atmosphere of learning."

At EMU, "Most of the professors are amazing," with close to 100 percent of the school's faculty holding the highest degree available in their field. Students admit that, "You get a couple bad professors/classmates along the way, but there is little if anything to complain about." Graduate class sizes average fewer than twenty, which gives students the opportunity to "work directly with professors who provide PhD-level class time, rather than having to work through a teaching assistant." The result is a dynamic classroom environment, in which discussion is encouraged and "professors challenge you to develop your own opinions regarding global business and economies." In addition to the professors, there is "lots of diverse work experience among the students," adding even more depth to the academic environment. Real-world applications are stressed in the classroom, though students would like to see coursework incorporate "more up-to-date case studies" and hands-on instruction. One student suggests, "EMU needs to strengthen their program with real business partnerships where students can apply what they learn and gain real job experience."

The MBA curriculum is comprised of foundation coursework (which can be waived for students with previous education in business), core coursework, electives, and an area of specialization, which combine for a program of study between 36–34 credit hours. Catering to its diverse student body, EMU offers specializations in a variety of business fields, including e-business, entrepreneurship, internal auditing, international business, management, and nonprofit management, as well as the opportunity to pursue a general MBA with no particular specialization (in that case, students can take a range of elective coursework to meet the units required for graduation). While the program runs smoothly, students would like to see the school "upgrade technology," as well as the infrastructure: "Stairwells, classrooms, and presentation areas sorely need updates." College of Business classes are being relocated in late summer 2013 to accommodate planned classroom technology upgrades.

Career and Placement

EMU students love the fact that their school caters to full-time working professionals. Unfortunately, the flip side of this arrangement is that there is more limited career support and recruiting programs at EMU than you'd find at a traditional full-time MBA. For those looking to expand their network in Detroit and Ann Arbor, "There are several clubs that have outstanding connections to our alumni and important people in the area." In addition, the College of Business maintains updated listings of internships and full-time jobs available in the area, and occasionally invites recruiters to campus to meet with current students and alumni.

ADMISSIONS CONTACT: MICHELLE HENRY, DIRECTOR ACADEMIC SERVICES, GRADUATE PROGRAMS
ADDRESS: 300 W. MICHIGAN AVENUE, STE. 404, YPSILANTI, MI 48197
PHONE: 734-487-4444 • FAX: 734-483-1316
E-MAIL: COB.GRADUATE@EMICH.EDU • WEBSITE: WWW.COB.EMICH.EDU

In complement to the resources at the business school, the University Advising and Career Development Center has a COB office that can assist with career planning and job-search skills. They also organize on-campus recruiting events with local companies. Prospective students should note, however, that the Career Development Center's services are chiefly directed at undergraduates, and "many of the recruiting companies are hiring retail managers, rather than looking for candidates for higher-quality positions." A student adds, "Our Career Services Center has little help for those outside of accounting and finance."

Student Life and Environment

Eastern Michigan University is a large public school with more than 20,000 students, a vibrant athletics program, and more than 300 active student organizations on campus. In the business school's sizable graduate programs, most students "work full-time and enroll in school part-time," making it difficult to also get involved with extracurricular campus activities. Nonetheless, students say it's "great to interact with other professionals" at the College of Business, describing their classmates as "career-oriented" and ambitious, yet "easy to get along with." For students on the main campus who'd like to branch out socially, there are "a number of clubs available for those who have time," including an MBA Association.

Located in the suburban community of Ypsilanti, the EMU campus is "very convenient" to both Ann Arbor and Detroit, and theses two cities provides endless cultural, entertainment, food, and nightlife options. Drawing from the greater metropolitan area, EMU's College of Business is incredibly "multicultural," with students from a range of backgrounds and levels of experience.

Admissions

To be considered for admission to Eastern Michigan University's MBA program, students must have a minimum undergraduate GPA of 2.75, and a score of at least 450 on the GMAT (with a score of 20 or better in the verbal section and 24 or better in the quantitative section). The school will also accept the GRE in lieu of the GMAT; a score of 297 or higher is required for admission. Prospective students must also submit a personal statement detailing their educational goals and professional experience, a résumé, and, for students whose first language isn't English, TOEFL or IELTS scores.

FINANCIAL FACTS

Annual tuition (in-state/ out-of-state)	$8,082/$15,931
Fees	$2,000
Cost of books	$675
Room & board	$8,709
% of students receiving aid	84
% of first-year students receiving aid	92
% of students receiving grants	23
Average award package	$10,572
Average grant	$4,209
Average loan	$11,906

ADMISSIONS

Admissions Selectivity Rating	**84**
# of applications received	147
% applicants accepted	46
% acceptees attending	78
Average GMAT	509
Range of GMAT	450–570
Average GPA	3.25
TOEFL required of international students	Yes
Minimum TOEFL (paper/computer)	550/213
Application fee	$35
International application fee	$35
Regular application deadline	5/15
Regular application notification	6/15
Application Deadline/Notification	
Round 1:	5/15 /
Round 2:	10/15 /
Round 3:	4/15 /
Deferment available	Yes
Maximum length of deferment	1 year
Transfer students accepted	Yes
Transfer application policy: 6 credits may be accepted for the core and 6 credits for electives upon approval	
Non-fall admissions	Yes
Need-blind admissions	Yes

EASTERN WASHINGTON UNIVERSITY
COLLEGE OF BUSINESS AND PUBLIC ADMINISTRATION

GENERAL INFORMATION

Type of school	Public
Affiliation	No Affiliation
Academic calendar	Quarter

SURVEY SAYS...

Students love Cheney, WA, Good
peer network
Solid preparation in:
Marketing, Communication/
interpersonal skills, Computer skills

STUDENTS

Enrollment of parent institution	12,130
Enrollment of MBA Program	78
% male/female	89/11
% out-of-state	20
% part-time	61
% underrepresented minority	2
% international	17
Average age at entry	31
Average years work experience at entry	6.0

ACADEMICS

Academic Experience Rating	**75**
Profs interesting rating	72
Profs accesible rating	73
Student/faculty ratio	25:1
% female faculty	46
% underrepresented minority faculty	2
% part-time faculty	0

Joint Degrees
MBA/MPA 80 Credits 2 Years;
MBA/HSAD Certificate 70 Credits 1
1/2 Years

Academics

Current and future Spokane professionals choose Eastern Washington University's MBA program for its blend of affordability, convenience, and quality. The curriculum consists of 50 credit hours, with elective concentrations in information technology or finance. In addition to the traditional MBA, the school offers "a dual master (MBA/MPA) option" for those interested in the public or nonprofit sector. Taking a full course load, the MBA "program can be finished within one year," though the flexible schedule is highly accommodating to working professionals too. "Night classes fit well within a typical 8-5 working schedule," and the campus in central Spokane is "easily accessible from in or slightly out of town." Most importantly, the school's instructors are "very understanding when you have personal circumstances interfering with class, and will do everything they can to work with you while still maintaining the highest academic standards for their students."

At this small public school, students speak highly of the MBA faculty, describing their professors as "knowledgeable, professional, personable, down-to-earth, accessible, and reasonable." Many instructors are "very highly regarded in the academic community," staying active in business research and regularly publishing scholarly articles. They are not only academics though. With strong ties to the local business community, professors "bring significant professional experience to the classroom, which helps tremendously in understanding and applying models and theories taught in class." Plus, with students ranging in age from 21 to 59, "The diversity of students and faculty significantly enhances the learning environment and challenges you to think more critically." Nonetheless, some students would like to see the program take an even more practical approach, saying the coursework contains "very few case studies" and skips over some essential skills, like business-plan writing.

While rigor varies by course, most "Professors are tough" and classes are time-consuming. According to a current student, "We all work our tails off together to get through this program." Fortunately, professors are "all very accessible outside the classroom, even when you don't come knocking during office hours," and most "go out of their way to explain things in a way that you can understand." Likewise, "The administration is very helpful and patient" and the "easy enrollment process" makes it easier for working students to consider a degree. In addition to kindness and convenience, cost is a major reason students choose the program; EWU is "considerably less expensive than its neighboring competitors, yet it has the same AACSB accreditation."

Career and Placement

Eastern Washington University's Office of Career Services provides counseling and job placement assistance to the entire student body. The office organizes occasional career fairs, on-campus interviews, and other recruitment events, in addition to maintaining an online career management system, which matches potential employers with current students and alumni. Career Services is mostly focused on the school's large undergraduate population, so recent graduates in the MBA program are the most likely to benefit from their services.

Within the business school, students would like to see more contact with the local community: "The MBA program director does what she can as far as generating job leads for us, but it would really help if the business school were to develop partnerships with businesses." The good news is: no matter what your career plans, counting yourself among the many EWU alumni is a huge benefit in the real world. At EWU, "The network you gain access to is by itself worth the cost of the program."

ADMISSIONS CONTACT: CYNTHIA PARKER, PROGRAM COORDINATOR
ADDRESS: 668 NORTH RIVERPOINT BLVD., SPOKANE, WA 99202-1677
PHONE: 509-358-2248 • FAX: 509-358-2267
E-MAIL: CPARKER@MAIL.EWU.EDU • WEBSITE: WWW.EWU.EDU/MBA

Student Life and Environment

Though it is a small program, there is quite a bit of diversity within Eastern Washington University's MBA class. The affordable in-state price tag draws many locals, but the program also attracts "students from all over the world, so there is a high percentage of international people" on campus. In terms of life experience, "Many students come straight from undergraduate into [the] MBA program," while others enroll mid-career. Overall, the mix of people and personalities creates a positive learning environment wherein "Each student brings a wealth of personal and professional experiences" to the classroom.

Eastern Washington University's main campus is located in the small town of Cheney, Washington, whereas MBA classes are taught on a satellite campus in downtown Spokane. With no direct link to the school's large undergraduate community, there is not much action at the small business school facility. A student admits, "The campus I am on does not have many student activities; it would be nice if some could be added." Nevertheless, there is "a very positive, supportive atmosphere" throughout the business school as well as "an increasing sense of students working together to achieve similar goals." Up-to-date facilities, including a 200-seat auditorium, create a great learning environment, and there is plenty of nearby parking in addition to numerous public transportation options for commuters.

Admissions

To be eligible for admission to Eastern Washington University's MBA program, students must have a GPA of at least 3.0 from the last 60 semester hours of undergraduate coursework and a GMAT score of at least 450. In-person interviews are also required for admission to the program. Applications are accepted on a rolling basis; for domestic applicants, there are no application deadlines for any semester. Prospective students can attend one of the evening information sessions if they would like more information about the program, the facility, and admissions.

FINANCIAL FACTS

Annual tuition	$22,500
Fees	$165
Cost of books	$1,500
Room & board	
(on/off-campus)	$6,900/$12,000
% of students receiving aid	25
% of first-year students	
receiving aid	25
% of students receiving grants	5
Average grant	$0
Average loan	$0

ADMISSIONS

Admissions Selectivity Rating	72
# of applications received	120
% applicants accepted	86
% acceptees attending	76
Average GMAT	502
Range of GMAT	460–550
Average GPA	3.29
TOEFL required of	
international students	Yes
Minimum TOEFL	
(paper/computer)	580/237
Application fee	$100
International application fee	$100
Regular application deadline	1/1
Regular application notification	1/1
Deferment available	Yes
Maximum length	
of deferment	1 Year
Transfer students accepted	Yes
Transfer application policy: We will accept up to 12 transfer credits.	
Non-fall admissions	Yes
Need-blind admissions	Yes

Elon University
Martha and Spencer Love School of Business

GENERAL INFORMATION
Type of school	Private
Affiliation	No Affiliation
Academic calendar	Trimester

SURVEY SAYS...
Cutting-edge classes
Solid preparation in:
Communication/interpersonal skills,
Presentation skills, Doing business in
a global economy

STUDENTS
Enrollment of parent institution	6,029
Enrollment of MBA Program	137
% part-time	100
Average age at entry	32
Average years work experience at entry	8.9

ACADEMICS
Academic Experience Rating	**79**
Profs interesting rating	83
Profs accesible rating	76
Student/faculty ratio	21:1
% female faculty	38
% underrepresented minority faculty	24
% part-time faculty	10

Prominent Alumni
Danielle Hoversten, Executive VP & CFO, Senn Dunn Insurance; Michael Levy, Vice Chair of Administration at U of Miami, Miller School of Medicine; Allan Davis, CEO, AllFab Solutions; Kathleen Galbraith, Chief Hospital Ops & Bus. Dev. Officer, Durham Reg. Hosp.; Bernadette Spong, Executive VP & CFO, Rex Health Care

Academics

For a business education with a "personal touch," the Elon MBA is an excellent choice. This smaller North Carolina program enrolls 60 new students each semester, offering a surprisingly flexible education for professionals in every stage in their career. With uniformly small class sizes and an emphasis on group work, professors "really take the time to know everyone personally," and students get "lots of personal attention" from faculty and staff. A current student tells us, "The professors have worked with me to help find projects I can apply directly to my career. This has enhanced my learning experience and my work experience at the same time."

With classes held during the evenings, this program particularly appeals to working professionals. Depending on your availability, courses can be completed through an aggressive 21-month schedule, or more slowly over the course of 33 months. Elon's MBA provides "a well-rounded, general management education," covering advanced business topics in finance, economics, operations, and marketing. Within the curriculum, there is an "international perspective" incorporated into many classes, as well as strong focus on leadership and business ethics. Students are encouraged to participate in class discussions, and group assignments are common throughout the curriculum. "Collaboration is the essence of getting things done in the real world, and Elon places substantial focus on preparing us in that area." Students universally praise Elon's tiny size and flexible schedule; however, some would also appreciate access to "more diverse courses," as well as the opportunity "to concentrate in certain areas, rather than just focus on a general management MBA, including Operations, Human Resources Management, Management and Marketing, Organizational Analytics, and Entrepreneurship."

Uniting theory and practice, most Elon professors have "both advanced degrees and significant experience in private and non-profit companies." Some students would like to see the tenured staff augmented by a team of "younger, more relevant faculty," though most agree that the professors are "top notch" overall. Academically, "Some classes are challenging, and some are merely time intensive." Fortunately, "Faculty are acutely aware of the work and family demands that students face and make appropriate accommodations" in their classes. Likewise, students dole out praise for the school's "seamless" administration, telling us that, "everything runs extremely smoothly." "From the admissions process to scheduling classes, the administration is responsive and proactive" at Elon. When solicited by students, staff "will reply to any email—even the smallest scheduling detail—within an hour or two."

Career and Placement

The majority of Elon students are working professionals, and the school is dedicated to helping them get ahead in their careers, conduct salary negotiations, or make a career change, if desired. Students note that, "the Elon MBA program is always working to keep the current students and alumni together by creating lots of activities and networking events." On the larger campus, the Student Professional Development Center hosts frequent career development activities and speakers, open to the entire Elon community, and the Office of Employer and Corporate Relations collaborates with the nation's top employers to bring recruiters to campus in order to hire Elon graduates. In addition, there is an Associate Director of Career Services located in the Koury Business Center. Students can schedule an individual appointment with the Associate Director, who can help students research their options and prepare for interviews. Despite these services, some students feel the school could still offer "more guidance with career development and placement."

ADMISSIONS CONTACT: ARTHUR W. FADDE, DIRECTOR OF GRADUATE ADMISSIONS
ADDRESS: 2750 CAMPUS BOX, ELON, NC 27244
PHONE: 800-334-8448 EXT. 3 • FAX: (336)-278-7699
E-MAIL: GRADADM@ELON.EDU • WEBSITE: WWW.ELON.EDU/MBA

Current Elon students and employees work at top companies in the region, including Cisco, Dow Corning, Fresh Market, General Dynamics, Glen Raven, Henredon Furniture Industries, Johnson Controls, LabCorp, Merck, Novartis, Oracle, Procter & Gamble, Ralph Lauren, RF Micro Devices, SAS Institute, Inc., Siemens Industry, Inc., VF Corporation, Volvo, and Wells Fargo Bank.

Student Life and Environment

At this small school, your fellow students may be the "most valuable part" of the MBA experience. Elon students are "fun, friendly, committed to their degrees," and always "helpful in group projects." Professionally, they come from a range of backgrounds, and "everyone brings different experiences and stories to the table." While there are a number of younger faces among the group, "most are in their late 30s to early 40s and have a good deal of work experience." In fact, the average work experience for incoming students is approximately 10 years.

Although group work is one of the most fundamental parts of the program, it doesn't necessarily translate into lots of extra face time with your classmates. When called on to work together, most students "have full-time jobs, and many have children, so we do a lot of work via conference calls and email." However, "The school helps to foster a strong sense of community through formal gatherings and informal events, like a mid-semester pizza break." Those looking for more interaction say you can get involved in "social events, such as football tailgating, dinner and a play, and a ropes course" offered through the school, as well as "family friendly" events offered for both current students and alumni. On campus, students appreciate "state-of-the-art facilities" and an excellent location in Elon, North Carolina, a small city not far from both Greensboro and Raleigh.

Admissions

Elon is looking for students with a past record of achievement and the capacity to excel as managers. Students are evaluated on their academic transcripts, GMAT scores (the school will also accept the GRE), past leadership experience, professional experience and credentials, and letters of recommendation. To be considered for admission to Elon, students must have a minimum undergraduate GPA of 2.5 and GMAT scores of 500 or GRE scores of 297 or better. Admitted students usually exceed these minimums. For the fall class of 2011, students had an average GPA of 3.3 and average GMAT scores of 563.

FINANCIAL FACTS

Annual tuition (in-state/ out-of-state)	$13,806/$13,806
Fees	$0
Cost of books	$570
% of students receiving aid	36
% of first-year students receiving aid	30
% of students receiving grants	10
Average award package	$11,653
Average grant	$8,861.
Average loan	$12,202
Average student loan debt	$30,971

ADMISSIONS

Admissions Selectivity Rating	76
# of applications received	95
% applicants accepted	74
% acceptees attending	80
Average GMAT	563
Range of GMAT	510–600
Average GPA	3.30
TOEFL required of international students	Yes
Minimum TOEFL (paper/computer)	550/213
International application fee	$50
Deferment available	Yes
Maximum length of deferment	1 year
Transfer students accepted	Yes
Transfer application policy: A student may transfer up to 9 Semester hours of credit from another AACSB accredited school	
Non-fall admissions	Yes
Need-blind admissions	Yes

EMORY UNIVERSITY
GOIZUETA BUSINESS SCHOOL

GENERAL INFORMATION

Type of school	Private
Affiliation	No Affiliation
Academic calendar	Semester

SURVEY SAYS...

Friendly students, Good social scene, Good peer network, Helpful alumni
Solid preparation in:
Communication/interpersonal skills, Doing business in a global economy

STUDENTS

Enrollment of parent institution	14,236
Enrollment of MBA Program	596
% male/female	72/28
% part-time	43
% underrepresented minority	18
% international	35
Average age at entry	32
Average years work experience at entry	8.0

ACADEMICS

Academic Experience Rating	**96**
Profs interesting rating	95
Profs accesible rating	90
Student/faculty ratio	6:1
% female faculty	24
% part-time faculty	25

Joint Degrees

Master of Business Administration/Doctor of jurisprudence(MBA/JD), Master of Business Administration/Master of Public Health (MBA/MPH), Master of Business Administration/Master of Divinity (MBA/MDIV)

Prominent Alumni

Alan Lacy, MBA '77, CEO, Sears; Michael Golden, EMBA '84, Vice Chairman & SVP, New York Times Company; Charles Jenkins Jr., BBA '64, MBA '65, CEO, Publix Super Markets, Inc.; C. Scott Mayfield, EMBA '86, President, Mayfield Dairy Farms, Inc.; Andrew Conway, MBA '92, Managing Director, Credit Suisse First Boston

Academics

"The community is the greatest strength" of the Goizueta Business School at Emory, where "there are 200 other [students] happy to help with any project or connect [you] to their network." And it's not just the student body that personifies the "culture of collaboration over severe competition" that presides here. "The community outside the current students is also phenomenal," we're told. "Alumni are happy to mentor, connect you to networks, and help you find directed study [opportunities], jobs, or internships."

Collaboration is encouraged in part through Goizueta's "lack of a hard-lined grading system" (grades are evaluative and do not correspond to GPA). It "definitely helps the community atmosphere," although students "still feel pressured to do well personally." The size of the program also helps; "the smaller school size makes Goizueta thrive on the ambition, creativity and curiosity of its students," one student writes.

Given the communal vibe, some might find it ironic that Goizueta's primary curricular emphasis is leadership. Regardless, the school offers "wonderful leadership courses with guest speakers and applied learning." It's all part of a "flexible" curriculum to which "new and relevant courses are frequently added (e.g., e-marketing, globalization, and illiquid assets in times of financial crisis)," and which provides ample opportunities for students to pursue their unique interests through electives. As one MBA student explains, "Emory's curriculum is very customizable, which comes from having a small class size."

Despite the laid-back atmosphere, academics are demanding at Goizueta. As one student puts it, "you genuinely need to push yourself hard and are challenged to reach the top of any class, but the focus is on really internalizing and learning the basics and foundations well. It's not an insanely competitive environment; it's one where you can truly learn and if you want to excel with grades and recognition, you can without feeling as though such things [are] easy or commonplace." Goizueta's location in Atlanta, a major metropolis home to many *Fortune* 500 companies, provides plenty of networking opportunities and a steady stream of well-connected professors and guest lecturers. Faculty members "are leaders in their fields, passionate about the material, and very accessible." "Every one of them brings great work experience as well as academic credentials to the classroom. They are willing to bring in current business-related events into the classroom and are eager for students to bring in their work experience into class discussions," students tell us.

Career and Placement

Student perspective on the Goizueta Career Management Center is mixed. "Career services could use some love," is how one student puts it. "No one seems to be able to pinpoint what exactly goes wrong there, but in general people seem less than satisfied with their help. Placement seems to be good, though, so something is working." Several voiced the feeling that the office "struggles with attracting large companies to recruit here. Despite our name, we are not a feeder school for Coke nor do we see much of the other major companies in the Atlanta area. On the other hand, we have many alumni at all those companies who through the power of networking are happy to help students find jobs and placements."

ADMISSIONS CONTACT: JULIE R. BAREFOOT, ASSOCIATE DEAN AND DIRECTOR OF MBA ADMISSIONS
ADDRESS: 1300 CLIFTON ROAD, ATLANTA, GA 30322
PHONE: 404-727-6311 • FAX: 404-727-4612
E-MAIL: ADMISSIONS@BUS.EMORY.EDU • WEBSITE: WWW.GOIZUETA.EMORY.EDU

Despite the fact that many Atlanta companies have been on a hiring freeze in recent years, over 150 companies have visited Goizueta for on-campus recruitment. Employers who most frequently hire Emory MBAs include: Accenture, AT Kearney, AT&T, Bank of America, Citigroup, Chevron, Delta Air Lines, Ernst & Young, General Electric, Georgia-Pacific, Humana, IBM, JP Morgan, Kimberly-Clark Corporation, Kurt Salmon Associates, PricewaterhouseCoopers, SunTrust, The Coca-Cola Company, and Wipro.

Student Life and Environment

Because of the small size of the program, Goizueta MBAs form a "very close group" that participates in "lots of social activities, both formal and informal." Student life "is very busy, but we learn so much in such a short time. Our networking opportunities are extensive as well, with Thursday afternoon networking activities, our mentor program, and very accessible alumni. Social activities and clubs are numerous," so much so that "it is difficult to decide which clubs to become involved in and which social activities to attend." As one student puts it, "The quality of life is great." The city of Atlanta helps in that regard; not only is it "a great place to live," it also "provides a wealth of business opportunities."

Goizueta students "are very collaborative." "We all want to see each other succeed, so although we are very competitive (all business school students are), we all want to help each other out," one student explains. Another adds, "This is not a cut-throat environment, but rather one in which everyone wants everyone else to succeed." The prevailing attitude is "nice, professional, and polished (this is the South and it does show through)."

Admissions

Applicants to the Goizueta MBA program must submit the following materials: a completed online application; official transcripts for all undergraduate and graduate schools attended; an official GMAT score report; and two letters of recommendation (the first is a narrative resume; the second offers a choice of subjects that center on your sources of inspiration or your career and life aspirations). An interview, while not required, is "strongly recommended." International students whose first language is not English must also submit official score reports for the TOEFL, PTE, or IELTS. Candidates for the one-year program must have an undergraduate degree in a business-related discipline or a strong quantitative background and "solid business experience."

FINANCIAL FACTS

Annual tuition	$44,600
Fees	$514
Cost of books	$2,000
Room & board	$18,128

ADMISSIONS

Admissions Selectivity Rating	95
# of applications received	1,104
% applicants accepted	32
% acceptees attending	42
Average GMAT	677
Range of GMAT	640–710
Average GPA	3.38
TOEFL required of international students	Yes
Minimum TOEFL (paper/computer)	600/100
Application fee	$150
International application fee	$150
Early application deadline	10/5
Early notification date	11/28
Regular application deadline	3/8
Regular application notification	4/24
Application Deadline/Notification	
Round 1:	10/5 / 11/28
Round 2:	11/30 / 1/25
Round 3:	1/18 / 3/15
Round 4:	3/8 / 4/24
Deferment available	Yes
Maximum length of deferment	1 year
Transfer students accepted	No
Non-fall admissions	No
Need-blind admissions	Yes

EMPLOYMENT PROFILE

Career Rating	97	**Grads Employed by Function% Avg. Salary**	
Percent employed at graduation	86	Marketing	(28%) $94,579
Percent employed 3 months		Operations	(1%)
after graduation	93	Consulting	(36%)$9117,818
Average base starting salary	$89,225	Management	(6%) $100,000
Primary Source of Full-time Job Acceptances		Finance	(26%) $98,091
School-facilitated activities	88 (89%)	HR	(2%)
Graduate-facilitated activities	11 (11%)	Other	(1%)

Top 5 Employers Hiring Grads
Deloitte (9), Accenture (6), Bank of America (3), Delta Air Lines (3), General Electric (3).

ESSEC BUSINESS SCHOOL
THE ESSEC MBA PROGRAM

GENERAL INFORMATION

Type of school	Private
Affiliation	No Affiliation
Academic calendar	Trimester

SURVEY SAYS...
Good social scene
Solid preparation in:
Finance, General management,
Teamwork

STUDENTS

% male/female	51/49
% international	20
Average age at entry	24
Average years work experience	
at entry	1.0

ACADEMICS

Academic Experience Rating	**71**
Profs interesting rating	69
Profs accesible rating	77
% female faculty	23

Joint Degrees
China: Peking University; Germany: Mannheim University; Korea: Seoul National University (2); Singapore: Nanyang Technological University; Mexico: EGADE–Tec de Monterrey; India: IIM Ahmedabad; Japan: Keio University

Prominent Alumni
Christian Balmes, President Director General, Shell France; Charles Bouaziz, General Manager, Pepsico Europe; Emmanuelle Mignon, President Sarkozy's Chief of Staff; Dominique Reiniche, President Europe, The Coca Cola Company; Serge Villepelet, President, PriceWaterHouseCoopers

Academics

If you're looking for a "flexible" MBA at "a major player on the international level among European business schools" and one of "the top business schools in France," ESSEC is a school you should consider. After completing eight management fundamentals courses, ESSEC MBAs fashion their own curricula, choosing from more than "200 electives" each semester. Students love the freedom, telling us that "each quarter, we can basically choose to take classes at ESSEC Business School in Paris or Singapore, do an internship with a company in France or abroad, or go on an exchange program abroad with one of ESSEC MBA's 80 academic partners," whose ranks include many prestigious names in the United States and around the world. The school's administration "does a great job of managing this 'a la carte' system," allowing students to "choose almost any courses we want in order to create our specialization and formation."

Because ESSEC believes that students should make "a constant connection between work and the classroom," all students must have at least 18 months of validated professional experience prior to graduation. These internships are easy to find thanks to ESSEC's "great relationship with the business world." The school "has strong links with international finance and consulting companies;" and a campus in Singapore means that opportunities to intern in Southeast Asia are constantly developing. ESSEC's practical philosophy permeates the classroom as well; here "Courses are not just theory. We have a lot of business cases given by corporate partners, and we have a lot of work every week to prepare other business cases in groups (teamwork is very important here)." Throughout the program, there is a "prominent international dimension" bolstered by "the school's ever-increasing partnerships overseas."

The faculty includes "outstanding professors recognized in their fields of specialization, people who publish a lot. They help us get most prepared for our chosen profession and they are also very available and most willing to give us useful insights." Part-time faculty are drawn from "top-notch businesswomen and men and successful entrepreneurs. In any case, they always have a great experience and very useful insights to share."

Career and Placement

Students report that "ESSEC is the best passport to great job opportunities in France and worldwide. The school administration and students are really eager to keep in very close contact with firms. There is a constant exchange between the academic, student, and business world. Companies are often involved in student projects too." The school's "excellent relations with European businesses" help students procure the internships required to complete their MBAs. While ESSEC's connections are strongest in France, "Many foreign companies also recruit (largely for their French subsidies), such as the consulting companies McKinsey, BCG, etc. ESSEC is part of their main target schools for recruiting."

Employers most likely to hire ESSEC MBAs include: PricewaterhouseCoopers, L'Oréal, Renault, Societe Generale, Deloitte Touche Tohmatsu, Danone, Michelin, BNP Paribas, Capgemini, Accenture, EDF-GDF, Pinault Printemps Redoute, Procter & Gamble, Deutsche Bank, 3 Suisses International, Pfizer, LVMH, Ernst & Young, Boston Consulting Group, A.T. Kearney, SC Johnson, and Bain.

Student Life and Environment

ESSEC encourages students to participate in extracurricular life, and students respond, forming "about 80 different clubs" that encompass not only business activities but also "theater, a choir, painting, photography, sports, and social groups." The area surrounding ESSEC, Cergy Pontoise, is "Parisian suburb" located "about an hour from the center of the city by commuter train." Some describe it as "a modern city with very good amenities, including an artificial lake for sailing or rowing and other water sports, a nearby skating rink, and very good town libraries." Others tell us that "living in Cergy can be a little bit disappointing for those who would prefer the dense atmosphere of Paris to ESSEC school life." Local housing "is pretty easy to find" and "not too expensive."

ESSEC is "undergoing immense changes," students tell us, reporting that new professors are being recruited at an international level. The school is going global and will become internationally known very soon." Some here tell us that "you can stay all day long at ESSEC, and there's always something to do and somewhere to go." Though in the past students have noted that "facilities here could improve." Recent renovations have been completed including several new buildings."

Admissions

Students are admitted to ESSEC either as traditional MBAs (this is the way international students enter the program), French MBAs, or as "grande école" students (French students who have attended 2 years of postsecondary school and are now ready for intensive, focused study in a discipline such as business). Students applying to the traditional MBA program must provide the school with an official GMAT or TAGE-MAGE score report, official transcripts for all postsecondary academic work, an interview, and a resume. Applicants must be under the age of 32; 1 or 2 years of professional experience is highly recommended. French MBA students follow the "French MBA" admissions path. "Grande école" applicants must meet a variety of requirements, including completion of the undergraduate period and completion of at least one six-month internship.

FINANCIAL FACTS

Annual tuition (in-state/ out-of-state)	$32,500/$45,500
Cost of books	$500
Room & board	$10,000

ADMISSIONS

Admissions Selectivity Rating	76
# of applications received	5,117
Average GMAT	675
Range of GMAT	600–730
TOEFL required of international students	Yes
Minimum TOEFL (paper/computer)	600/250
Deadline/Notification	
Round 1:	10/10 / 12/5
Round 2:	1/26 / 3/23
Round 3:	4/29 / 6/9
Deferment available	Yes
Maximum length of deferment	1 year
Transfer students accepted	No
Non-fall admissions	No
Need-blind admissions	Yes

EMPLOYMENT PROFILE

Career Rating	65	Grads Employed by Function% Avg. Salary	
Average base starting salary	$67,000	Marketing	(21%)
Primary Source of Full-time Job Acceptances		Operations	(5%)
School-facilitated activities	(50%)	Consulting	(36%)
Graduate-facilitated activities	(4%)	Management	(5%)
Unknown	(46%)	Finance	(20%)
		HR	(1%)
		Other	(12%)
		Top 5 Employers Hiring Grads	
		Cap Gemini (10), BNP Paribas (6), Ernst & Young (5), KPMG (5), McKinsey & Company (5)	

FAIRFIELD UNIVERSITY
CHARLES F. DOLAN SCHOOL OF BUSINESS

GENERAL INFORMATION
Type of school   Private
Affiliation   Roman Catholic-Jesuit
Academic calendar   Semester

SURVEY SAYS...
Students love Fairfield, CT, Good peer
network
Solid preparation in:
Finance, Accounting

STUDENTS
Enrollment of parent
  institution   5,000
Enrollment of MBA Program   143
% part-time   74
Average age at entry   28
Average years work experience
  at entry   3.0

ACADEMICS
Academic Experience Rating   88
Profs interesting rating   87
Profs accesible rating   85
Student/faculty ratio   20:1
% female faculty   40

Prominent Alumni
Dr. E. Gerald Corrigan, Managing
Director, Goldman Sachs & Co.;
Robert Murphy, Jr., Senior VP, The
Walt Disney Company Foundation;
Christopher McCormick, President
& CEO, LL Bean, Inc.; Dr. Francis
Tedesco, President, Medical College
of Georgia

Academics

Armed with a "strong reputation" coupled with a "strong commitment to the Jesuit ideals of serving others," it's no surprise that students flock to attend Fairfield University's MBA program. Students here greatly appreciate that the school "caters to people who work full time." Moreover, Fairfield offers "small class sizes," "an extensive alumni network," and "great business contacts." Although the school offers a "challenging curriculum," some students feel that it is time for an overhaul or update. As one slightly chagrined student explains, "The University should take the time to conduct a thorough overview of its curriculum and concentrations. It could use some refreshing."

Fortunately, students are ebullient when it comes to describing their professors. They are truly "dedicated and experienced professionals" who are "very knowledgeable, accessible and open-minded." They "encourage students to think for themselves, even if that means challenging the professors in class." Additionally, they are highly accessible. Another highly content student shares, "many of them will go out to lunch or coffee and explain concepts or help with networking." Though the vast "majority of the school's professors care a lot about the quality of their teaching" some students feel that there's room for improvement. A second-year student clarifies, "Newer, younger professors with more current experience would be a welcome improvement to the program. I would like to have more women professors, as well." However, she does conclude by stating, "Overall I am very happy with my academic experience at Fairfield University and have learned a lot."

Career and Placement

Fairfield University's Career Center is truly focused on helping students find coveted internship and employment opportunities. The office endeavors to take advantage of the school's prime location between Boston and New York, developing relationships and connections with companies in both cities. Of course, some students wish they would also focus on opportunities within their own backyard. As one graduating student shares, "Fairfield should actively seek to build relationships with financial institutions based in Stamford (RBS, UBS, etc)." The career center continually offers resume workshops and practice interview sessions. It also provides access to a number of local career fairs. Another student adds that Fairfield has "an extensive alumni network and great business contacts." However, some begrudge the fact that the office serves the entire university and feel this detracts from specific MBA prospects. As one student states, "It seems to me career placement is geared more toward undergraduates than graduate students; while Fairfield has addressed the career needs of graduate students lately, I think the efforts should be on par with the undergraduates."

Employers that frequently hire Fairfield graduates include General Electric, People's Bank, American Skandia, United Technologies, Pitney Bowes, The Common Fund, Bayer Corporation, UBS Warburg, Gartner, Unilever, and Pfizer.

ADMISSIONS CONTACT: DR. MARK LIGAS, ASSOCIATE DEAN/DIRECTOR OF GRADUATE PROGRAMS
ADDRESS: 1073 NORTH BENSON ROAD, FAIRFIELD, CT 06824
PHONE: 203-254-4000 • FAX: 203-254-4029
E-MAIL: MLIGAS@FAIRFIELD.EDU • WEBSITE: WWW.FAIRFIELD.EDU/MBA

Student Life and Environment

Fairfield University manages to attract a "wide variety of student," ensuring the MBA program is an eye-opening experience. While students do admit that their peers can be "competitive," they quickly stress that they are also incredibly "friendly." Moreover, they are "hardworking," "creative," and "dedicated." There is also a healthy mix of students in their 20s, 30s, and 40s. The older MBA candidates tend to "work full-time, have families, and go to school at night." These students tend to limit their interaction to "night and weekend classes" and "don't spend much time on campus other than for class." However, the younger MBA crowd is eager to move the discussion outside of the classroom. As one student says, "The social atmosphere is one of my favorite parts of the school. Group discussions and projects are obviously very fun, but so is grabbing a drink with a few students after class and even having professors tag along! We all have a great time talking about our current jobs, and grabbing tips from each other. I cannot say enough about how much I have loved getting to know the other students and professors." Another student continues, "The University has formed an office of graduate students, which has been doing a much better job of offering specific programs and services for graduate students of all schools." By and large, students appreciate Fairfield's "great" location, which is "not too rural, but not too urban either." They also enjoy the fact that it is "close enough to some of the major metro NY companies (IBM and Pepsi) without being in the hustle and bustle of it all." When students want to unwind, they frequently take advantage of downtown Fairfield "for dinner, drinks, and hanging out."

Admissions

Admission to Fairfield University's business school is certainly competitive. All facets of the application, from professional resume and personal statement to transcripts and GMAT scores, are thoroughly considered and evaluated. Applicants must have successfully completed undergraduate coursework in college-level mathematics, microeconomics, macroeconomics, and statistics. Typically, accepted students have at least a 3.0 GPA and earned a GMAT score of 500, at minimum. Additionally, students from non-English speaking countries must take the TOEFL. To secure admission, it is strongly recommended that applicants earn a composite score of 550 for the paper test, 213 for the computer-based, or 80 on the Internet-based test. Applications are accepted on a rolling basis. Those candidates supremely interested in attending Fairfield should submit their application as early as possible.

FINANCIAL FACTS

Annual tuition	$18,720
Fees	$280
Cost of books	$1,000

ADMISSIONS

Admissions Selectivity Rating	87
# of applications received	79
% applicants accepted	52
% acceptees attending	90
Average GMAT	530
Range of GMAT	500–650
Average GPA	3.45
TOEFL required of international students	Yes
Minimum TOEFL (paper/computer)	550/213
Application fee	$60
International application fee	$60
Deferment available	Yes
Maximum length of deferment	1 year
Transfer students accepted	Yes
Transfer application policy: Up to 6 credits from another graduate program. We also have a reciprocity agreement with the other Jesuit institutions.	
Non-fall admissions	Yes
Need-blind admissions	No

FAIRLEIGH DICKINSON UNIVERSITY
SILBERMAN COLLEGE OF BUSINESS

GENERAL INFORMATION

Type of school	Private
Affiliation	No Affiliation

SURVEY SAYS...

Cutting-edge classes
Solid preparation in:
Communication/interpersonal skills,
Doing business in a global economy

STUDENTS

Enrollment of parent institution	12,247
Enrollment of MBA Program	704
% male/female	60/41
% out-of-state	39
% part-time	51
% underrepresented minority	18
% international	28
Average age at entry	29

ACADEMICS

Academic Experience Rating	74
Profs interesting rating	82
Profs accesible rating	78
Student/faculty ratio	20:1
% female faculty	21
% underrepresented minority faculty	41
% part-time faculty	40

Joint Degrees

MBA in Management/MA in Corporate and Organizational Communications, 72 credit program.

Prominent Alumni

Cheryl Beebe, VP & CFO, Corn Products International, Inc.; Dennis Strigl, President & COO, Verizon Communications (retired); Robert Huth, President & CEO, David's Bridal; Joseph Mahady, President, Wyeth Pharmaceuticals; Dick Sweeney, VP, Keurig

Academics

Fairleigh Dickinson University, or FDU, attracts students from around the world, especially those looking for a strong faculty and a vicinity to New York City. Another highlight for the University is its AACSB accreditation, which many students cite as another factor in their decision to attend the school. FDU offers MBAs with nine different specializations including accounting, finance, international business, and marketing, among others. Another option for those looking to speed up their education is the Accelerated MBA that allows their liberal arts or business undergraduate students a chance to earn an MBA in 15 months. They also have a shortened study abroad program that allows their busier students to travel to another country for two weeks in the summer, giving them a taste of what international business is like.

This kind of drive is prevalent throughout the student body with many saying that both "competition" and an "eagerness to learn" are the norms. Many say that "work and studies tend to be heavy," but that the experience is worth it with most raving that the "classroom atmosphere is spectacular." Many find that they learn how to "prioritize time very quickly." The school tries to keep each class small and the students realize this fact explaining that they feel like they are getting "individual attention." While a small minority wishes there was "more emphasis" on teacher evaluations, most students are more than happy with their teachers raving that the school's professors are its "greatest strength," and that the students are "proud" to have them as instructors.

The majority of the faculty is "a mix of global businessmen and local success stories" but have earned a great reputation with the students and are considered "very attentive and helpful." This mix helps give classes "every possible view of business and provides students with insight from different points of view." The diversity is much appreciated as participants feel it gives them "a strong global business education." Students have a desire to be involved in their classes through the teachers "encouraging class participation [and] linking new events with class materials." They are known for their willingness to offer an abundance of support in that they "spend an extraordinary amount of time outside of the classroom helping and guiding students."

Career and Placement

The Career Development Services Center helps students in a variety of ways by providing different help such as assessment testing, career fairs, workshops, internship opportunities, on-campus recruiting, and an online job search website, among others. Occasionally students say they wish there was "more focus on internships" from the University, but that they find the "proximity to companies and New York" to be a "distinct advantage," when looking for job opportunities. The professor's experience does not hurt either, with many of them having "strong ties to local businesses."

Graduates have a average base starting salary of $70k per year with the top five employers being Verizon, Deloitte, Johnson & Johnson, ADP, and Credit Suisse.

ADMISSIONS CONTACT: SUSAN BROOMAN, DIRECTOR OF GRADUATE RECRUITMENT & MARKETING
ADDRESS: FAIRLEIGH DICKINSON UNIVERSITY GRADUATE ADMISSIONS, METROPOLITAN CAMPUS
1000 RIVER ROAD (T-KB1-01), TEANECK, NJ 07666 • PHONE: 201-692-2554
FAX: 201-692-2560 • E-MAIL: GRAD@FDU.EDU • WEBSITE: WWW.FDU.EDU

Student Life and Environment

FDU has two campuses in New Jersey, one in Teaneck and one in Madison. One of the things that many students love about both campuses is the fact that the college "attracts a number of different students with highly diverse backgrounds." A significant portion of the student body includes international students who describe FDU as a "truly global school." In fact some think it's wonderful that "in a room of ten to twelve people … no two people [might] be from the same country." Despite any cultural differences, the students show great respect and label each other "helpful, enthusiastic, [and] smart." The student body is also "fairly young" for those seeking an MBA, but part of that may be the aforementioned ability for undergraduates to gain an MBA as well.

FDU succeeds in striking "a balance between academic, social and recreational aspects of student life." Many students bond not only in the classroom, but also in one of the many activities the campus puts together. The school often "organizes various trips outside the classroom to get [us] acquainted with various places" and with New York City nearby, there is no shortage of things for students to see and do. And, unlike a lot of other schools, students have no issues with the administration saying they find it "very helpful," to their learning experience and course registration.

Admissions

Those seeking to apply can do so in two ways, online or via printed out form. Applications are accepted on a rolling basis. Those applying online will have the forty dollar application fee waived. Domestic students need to make sure to send proof of their bachelor's degree, official college transcripts, their official score report for the GMAT taken within the last five years, and a current resume. International students will also need to send in their TOEFL, IELTS, or Pearsons PTE-A as well as two letters of recommendation and a completed and notarized affidavit of financial support if they are applying for a student visa.

Those looking for help on the GMAT can enroll in the Sexton Preparation Course. Upon completion of the course, a full credit will be applied to the student's tuition charge.

FINANCIAL FACTS

Annual tuition	$20,340
Fees	$225
Cost of books	$1,000
Room & board	$8,000
% of students receiving aid	75
% of students receiving grants	25
Average award package	$13,500
Average grant	$5,225
Average loan	$14,670

ADMISSIONS

Admissions Selectivity Rating	68
# of applications received	642
% applicants accepted	57
% acceptees attending	34
Average GPA	3.40
TOEFL required of international students	Yes
Minimum TOEFL (paper/computer)	550/213
Application fee	$40
International application fee	$40
Deferment available	Yes
Transfer students accepted	Yes
Transfer application policy: Foundation courses can be waived by meeting FDU waiver policy. 6 graduate level credits can be transferred from other AACSB schools.	
Non-fall admissions	Yes
Need-blind admissions	Yes

EMPLOYMENT PROFILE

Career Rating	77	Top 5 Employers Hiring Grads
		Verizon, Deloitte, Johnson & Johnson, ADP, Credit Suisse

FAYETTEVILLE STATE UNIVERSITY
SCHOOL OF BUSINESS AND ECONOMICS MBA PROGRAM

GENERAL INFORMATION
Type of school	Public
Affiliation	No Affiliation
Academic calendar	Aug - May

SURVEY SAYS...
Friendly students, Good peer network
Solid preparation in:
Accounting, General management,
Quantitative skills

STUDENTS
Enrollment of parent institution	6,060
Enrollment of MBA Program	107
% male/female	41/59
% out-of-state	1
% part-time	100
% underrepresented minority	50
% international	10
Average age at entry	33
Average years work experience at entry	5.0

ACADEMICS
Academic Experience Rating	85
Profs interesting rating	88
Profs accesible rating	80
Student/faculty ratio	12:1
% female faculty	25
% underrepresented minority faculty	30
% part-time faculty	10

Prominent Alumni
Dr. Ashok Jain, Founder, Pediatrics Assoc. Franchise; J. Bagley, Vice President, Banking; V. King, Vice President, Hospital System; Dr. R. Benedicktus, Professor of Marketing; S. Hu, Sr. Strategy Manager, WalMart

Academics

Fayetteville State University's Business School offers students the unbeatable combination of "low cost" coupled with a "great reputation." Students here truly appreciate that the "core curriculum is not repetitive and boring" and that the "small class sizes make learning easy and interactive." The program caters to individuals who are employed full-time and promises a "flexible" course schedule. Moreover, students can opt to either take classes online or on campus, and many courses are offered in the evening or on weekends.

Students at Fayetteville are full of admiration for their professors. An impressed first-year student shares, "All my professors are top notch. Not only are they proficient in their fields, they have a true desire to see each and every student succeed." Additionally, students here truly appreciate the unparalleled access professors seem to grant them. As one MBA candidate reveals, "Professors are also extremely helpful. They are willing to give you their cell phone numbers, so that you can call anytime with questions, and they make themselves available on weekends, throughout the day." Perhaps almost as impressive is that "e-mails for the most part are answered immediately. Professors also ensure that each class is recorded via Panopto, so if you are unable to attend you can still see them lecture on blackboard."

Praise is also extended to the "outstanding" administration. As another student shares, "They are all tremendously helpful and quick to assist students with anything from advising to outside competitions, opportunities, and internships." "The MBA office's open-door policy created an atmosphere of nurturing support for its students. My experience in the MBA program not only taught me the necessary skills to be successful in the business world, but also how to think logically in a stringently growing global enterprise."

Career and Placement

Fayetteville State's Career Services Center works diligently to ensure that students and alumni have a myriad of employment opportunities. Advocating on behalf of its students, Career Services has partnered with a number of organizations and services to guarantee that students have access to a variety resources. The office provides a number of workshops, and MBA candidates can receive help honing their resume, practice with mock interviews, and learn tips about refining their job search. The University also hosts several career fairs throughout the year. These events attract a wide variety of companies and organizations, such as Rite Aid, The Hershey Company, Lowe's, WalMart, Internal Revenue Service, Social Security Administration, BB&T, and Altria. While the Career Services Center does offer assistance, some MBA students feel as though the office could do more. As one student states, "From my experience, the career placement is more geared to undergrads. Specific emphasis should be placed on MBA students."

ADMISSIONS CONTACT: DR. ASSAD TAVAKOLI, DEAN, MBA PROGRAM
ADDRESS: MBA PROGRAM, SCHOOL OF BUSINESS & ECONOMICS, FAYETTEVILLE STATE UNIVERSITY,
FAYETTEVILLE NC 28301 • PHONE: 910-672-1197 • FAX: 910-672-1849
E-MAIL: MBAPROGRAM@UNCFSU.EDU • WEBSITE: WWW.UNCFSU.EDU/MBA

Student Life and Environment

MBA candidates at Fayetteville State definitely agree that their fellow students truly enrich their academic experience. They are "very friendly" and "concerned with grasping the material verses simply going through the motions." As one student elaborates, "My fellow classmates are excited to learn new and interesting things, and they are always willing to work together to make sure that everyone is on the same page." Indeed, despite sometimes letting their "competitive" natures shine through, most students are "helpful and promote teamwork and team building." Fortunately, Fayetteville's Business School manages to attract a "diverse" group of students. As one graduating student shares, "My fellow classmates are a diverse group from all walks of life. I enjoy each class because of the stimulating class discussions and rigorous debate. I look forward to building a valuable network, because they all are leaders within their respective fields."

While some students occasionally grumble that "parking is not always easy," most agree that life at Fayetteville is "great." And though a number of students enroll in online or evening classes, many find the campus "full of life." A large number of students are busy with families and full-time jobs, so socializing is often kept to a minimum. However, there are opportunities for extracurricular activities. As another student recounts, "There are several organizations available that give students an opportunity for national recognition. FSU has provided opportunities for me to compete in national business plan competitions, where I have won cash prizes and gained powerful connections."

Admissions

Admissions officers at Fayetteville State take a holistic approach to their evaluation process, assessing undergraduate transcripts, GMAT scores, and letters of recommendation. Additionally, international applicants hailing from non-English speaking countries are required to take the TOEFL exam. It should be noted that students who have not yet taken the GMAT will be allowed to enroll in a maximum of 12 credit hours before gaining full admission to the program. If the student earns a minimum of a "B" in each course, the classes will count toward fulfilling requirements upon full admission. Further, current Fayetteville undergraduates studying accounting, business administration, or economics, and finance may apply for admission during their junior year. Upon acceptance, they can begin taking graduate level courses as a senior. The remaining MBA courses can be completed in one additional year.

FINANCIAL FACTS

Annual tuition (in-state/ out-of-state)	$3,190/$14,039
Fees	$3,288
Room & board (on/off-campus)	$5,300/$8,000

ADMISSIONS

Admissions Selectivity Rating	86
# of applications received	115
% applicants accepted	36
% acceptees attending	83
Average GMAT	493
Range of GMAT	450–570
Average GPA	3.26
TOEFL required of international students	Yes
Minimum TOEFL (paper/computer)	550/213
Application fee	$35
International application fee	$35
Regular application deadline	4/15
Deferment available	Yes
Maximum length of deferment	Normally one year
Transfer students accepted	Yes
Transfer application policy: Up to six credit hours can be transferred from an AACSB accredited program.	
Non-fall admissions	Yes
Need-blind admissions	Yes

FLORIDA GULF COAST UNIVERSITY
LUTGERT COLLEGE OF BUSINESS

Academics

Opened in 1997, the Lutgert College of Business at Florida Gulf Coast University offers a part- or full-time traditional MBA and executive MBA program, as well as an MS in accounting and taxation and an MS in computer information systems. Students may attend the traditional MBA on campus or online, but the other programs require on-campus and full-time attendance. The traditional MBA requires all students to take 24 hours of foundation courses and 21 hours of core courses; those who studied business as an undergraduate and earned good grades may find that they can waive many or all of the foundation requirements. Students in the traditional MBA program must choose a concentration in Finance, General Management, Information Systems, or Marketing, though students may opt for an interdisciplinary concentration with the approval of their academic advisor. Those taking courses online may only do an interdisciplinary concentration from the above areas. All of FGCU's MBAs receive solid training in systems orientation and relevant technology. Additionally, students in all programs leave with strong analytical and creative thinking skills, communication, and interpersonal skills. They appreciate that the program is newer than most and that they are a part of a "growing institution" and "community," with a "beautiful" and "expanding campus" and "state-of-the-art infrastructure and classrooms with highly integrated technology."

The program's strengths are its "flexibility and the professors," as well as the small classes that allow people to know their "professors and other classmates on a more personal level." The faculty has lots of "real-world work experience," and "draw from their experience and teach you real-world applications of the academics." They're "engaging, accessible, and interested in your personal and professional development." Classes range from "exceedingly demanding" to "easy," but either way it can be tough for those working full time or who've been out of school for a while to "adjust to the course load." Students report that "course selection and availability is somewhat limited," which can make it difficult to get all the classes needed to complete a degree in a shortened timeframe." Electives are also offered less consistently than students would like.

FGCU has forged relationships with many international business schools and has an international student exchange program known as the "Second Circle." The program allows students from universities in China, France, Germany, Mexico, New Zealand, and Sweden to study at FGCU for up to two semesters. FGCU students with a GPA of 3.0 or higher may spend up to two semesters at designated partner universities in these countries. Second Circle is an impressive and rewarding program for students seeking to deepen their understanding of international business and who want to gain experience abroad and work on their language skills.

Career and Placement

FGCU's Career Development Services office serves the entire undergraduate and graduate population, and some students in the MBA program would like to see "more resources for graduating MBA students for professional/career positions and internship opportunities." However, the office does host career fairs and on-campus recruiting events, as well as workshops and seminars. Students can also receive help with their job searches, resumes, and business etiquette. Employers who will visit the campus in 2011 include General Electric, Northwestern Mutual Financial Network, Marathon Engineering Corp, Prudential, Primerica Financial Services, Scotlynn Commodities, Target, and Algenol Biofuels, though these companies are not necessarily looking to hire graduates of the MBA program.

ADMISSIONS CONTACT: ANA HILL, ADMISSIONS-REGISTRAR OFFICER-GRADUATE ADMISSIONS
ADDRESS: 10501 FGCU BOULEVARD SOUTH, FORT MYERS, FL 33965
PHONE: 239-590-7408 • FAX: 239-590-7843
E-MAIL: GRADUATE@FGCU.EDU • WEBSITE: WWW.FGCU.EDU

Student Life and Environment

Students at FGCU are busy. Many who attend on campus work full time, and many of them also have families, so their ability to enjoy the campus or extracurricular activities is limited, if it exists at all. FGCU undergrads who entered the program directly and international students tend to have far fewer obligations and, therefore, have a larger presence outside of class. People at FGCU say their peers are "dedicated, hard-working, knowledge driven, enjoyable to work with, and dependable." Many students "have had professional work experience, which translates into richer class discussions that help to make material covered in class more practical, rather than theoretical."

The Graduate Business Association coordinates many different professional growth opportunities for students. It arranges for local business people to speak on campus or meet with students and provide strong connections to alumni. Additionally, the Graduate Business Association hosts social events for students, such as happy hours, family picnics, and an annual golf tournament.

Admissions

Applicants to FGCU's MBA program do not need to have professional experience. The admission committee focuses on student's undergraduate GPA and GMAT scores when evaluating applications. Students must have either a minimum GPA of 3.0 for their final 60 credit hours of undergraduate work or a minimum GMAT score of 500; and a formula score of at least 1,050 under the formula [(undergraduate GPA X 200) + GMAT score], with a minimum GMAT score of at least 450. International students from countries where English is not the primary language must also submit TOEFL scores. The school requires a minimum of 550 for the written portion of the test, 213 for the computer based, and 79 for the Internet-based portion.

FINANCIAL FACTS

Annual tuition (in-state/ out-of-state)	$6,458/$26,083
Fees	$1,831
Cost of books	$1,200
Room & board	$8,250
% of students receiving aid	67
% of first-year students receiving aid	51
% of students receiving grants	31
Average award package	$10,083
Average grant	$2,516
Average student loan debt	$21,465

ADMISSIONS

Admissions Selectivity Rating	**78**
# of applications received	92
% applicants accepted	57
% acceptees attending	79
Average GMAT	499
Average GPA	3.10
TOEFL required of international students	Yes
Minimum TOEFL (paper/computer)	550/213
Application fee	$30
International application fee	$30
Early application deadline	5/1
Regular application deadline	6/1
Regular application notification	7/1
Deferment available	Yes
Maximum length of deferment	1 Semester
Transfer students accepted	Yes
Transfer application policy: 6 credits of approved graduate-level coursework may be transferred from a regionally accredited institution.	
Non-fall admissions	Yes
Need-blind admissions	Yes

FLORIDA INTERNATIONAL UNIVERSITY
ALVIN H. CHAPMAN GRADUATE SCHOOL OF BUSINESS

Academics

As its moniker suggests, Florida International University offers MBAs that are "more internationally-oriented" than your standard graduate business program. This emphasis is especially pronounced in the school's one-year International Business program, but it applies to all the graduate degrees offered here. The school parlays its location in Miami, "the gateway to the Americas," to focus particular attention on Latin America and the Caribbean, regions well-represented on the faculty and among the student body.

No matter your academic interests and scheduling needs, FIU probably has an MBA program to suit you. Its 20-month Executive MBA "is an excellent program for managers with over 12 years of work experience." For less experienced professionals, the 18-month Downtown MBA or the Evening MBA on FIU's campus may be good fits. For those unable to get away from the office, the Corporate MBA delivers the program to the workplace. And if you're looking for a specialized MBA in healthcare, FIU offers that as well.

Students praise FIU's "excellent reputation in the south Florida business community," its affordability, and the "top-notch" professors and administration. Students report approvingly that "The school has a team of administrators assigned to the MBA program. They handle everything for us, and I mean everything: enrollment, books, materials, copies, meals, etc." One MBA notes, "It is especially appealing that the business program is run somewhat independently from the rest of the university to ensure higher quality services and resources." Overall, students find the program "very well-organized," led by "extremely competitive and prepared" professors who "are all known leaders in their field and have great experiences to share with us." "The faculty have provided real insight into their industry[ies] and created stimulating learning environments for the most part," one student explains. Classroom discussion is enhanced by a "very international" and diverse student body. "You get investment bankers [and people in] rank and file jobs trying to get ahead, all working together" here. With all these assets, no wonder students call an FIU MBA "a superb investment at a very low price."

Career and Placement

Chapman's Career Management Services office provides graduate students and alumni with counseling and placement assistance. The office works closely with the university's general Career Services Office to coordinate career fairs, on-campus interviews, and other career-related events. Students tell us that FIU's alumni network is large and very helpful.

Top employers of FIU MBAs (including currently employed students attending one of the part-time programs) include: PricewaterhouseCoopers, B/E Aerospace, Commerce Bank, P&G, FPL, Fitch Ratings, Brightstar Corporation, Bank of America, Caterpillar, GE, and Choice Hotels International.

Student Life and Environment

FIU's MBA program is housed "in a brand-new building with extremely comfortable and high-technology resources," with "many locations for classmates to gather and work in a comfortable environment." "The resources you need for research and completing assignments are readily available" here, and the school even "makes ample provision for students who are without computers; for example, access to computers whether in the computer room or the library." Full-time students report that they experience "a fast-paced environment" driven by classes, extracurriculars, and an active Student Government Association. They also tell us that "The sports program is up and coming, so the students are very excited and try hard to get the rest of us motivated to cheer for the Golden Panthers!" Part-timers tend to visit campus only for classes and schoolwork, and as a result are less engaged in campus life.

The FIU MBA program is "like the United Nations. We come from many nations: Germany, France, [United States], Central America, and South America. When they say 'Florida International University'—they mean it." Students are drawn from an equally impressive array of industries "including banking, healthcare, pharmaceutical, automotive, logistics, insurance, etc." There are a lot of "strong A-type personalities, which in my book means we 'Ace' in everything we do, be it group assignments, weekly tests, heated arguments over project submissions, or a chilled beer to commemorate the end of a quarter."

Admissions

Admissions requirements to FIU's MBA programs vary somewhat from program to program. As a general rule, students with the best combination of grade point average, applicable test scores, and pertinent work experience who also meet specific program requirements will have the first opportunity to enter the programs, according to the school's website. Applicants to the school's popular International MBA program must submit the following materials: an official copy of an undergraduate transcript, with a GPA of at least 3.0 in upper-division course work strongly preferred; official proof of undergraduate degree; a current resume; a personal statement; and an official GMAT or GRE score report. In addition to the above documents, international students whose primary language is not English must also provide an official score report for the TOEFL or the IELTS. They must also submit their transcripts to a translation agency to be forwarded to FIU, and they must provide the following documents: Declaration of Certification of Finances (DCF); a bank letter; a sponsor letter if applicable; and an F-1 transfer if they already have an F-1 Visa.

FINANCIAL FACTS

Annual tuition (in-state/ out-of-state)	$34,000/$39,000
Cost of books	$2,000
Room & board (on/off-campus)	$12,000/$18,000
% of students receiving aid	79
% of first-year students receiving aid	82
% of students receiving grants	4
Average award package	$21,080
Average grant	$5,000
Average loan	$8,000
Average student loan debt	$40,000

ADMISSIONS

Admissions Selectivity Rating	80
# of applications received	1,094
% applicants accepted	56
% acceptees attending	69
Average GMAT	551
Range of GMAT	510–580
Average GPA	3.28
TOEFL required of international students	Yes
Minimum TOEFL (paper/computer)	550/213
Application fee	$30
International application fee	$30
Deferment available	Yes
Maximum length of deferment	1 year
Transfer students accepted	Yes
Transfer application policy: A student may receive permission to transfer up to six Semester hours of graduate credit towards his or her degree program, if specific criteria are met.	
Non-fall admissions	Yes
Need-blind admissions	Yes

EMPLOYMENT PROFILE

		Grads Employed by Function	% Avg. Salary
Career Rating	73		
Percent employed at graduation	11	Marketing	(14%) $46,000
Percent employed 3 months after graduation	2	Operations	(14%) $60,000
		Management	(14%) $70,000
Average base starting salary	$45,571	Finance	(43%) $37,000
Primary Source of Full-time Job Acceptances		HR	(0%) $49,250
School-facilitated activities	3(43%)	MIS	(0%) $52,000
Graduate-facilitated activities	4(57%)	Other	(14%) $60,000

Top 5 Employers Hiring Grads
Price Waterhouse Coopers (13), Burger King Corp. (11), Grant Thornton (4), Cherry Bekaert & Holland CPA's (2), Marriot International (1)

FLORIDA STATE UNIVERSITY
COLLEGE OF BUSINESS

Academics

The College of Business at Florida State University offers a variety of options to suit the diverse needs of its MBA student body. Students straight out of college and anxious to earn a graduate degree typically find their way to the school's one-year full-time MBA program. Busy professionals can choose between an on-campus part-time program and an online program with "an asynchronous, totally web-based curriculum." The super-ambitious can pursue joint degrees in business and law or business and social work. In all programs, the reasonable tuition ("It's a prestigious school at a great value," writes one student) and "the growing reputation of the business school" are compelling factors in bringing students aboard.

Florida's full-time MBA is a cohort-based lockstep curriculum, with students remaining in the same work group throughout the twelve-month program. Students in the program may concentrate in finance or marketing and supply chain management, or they may earn a general MBA. Part-time students complete the same core courses and study with the same professors as do their full-time counterparts; however, they are not divided into cohorts and they cannot pursue a concentration. The online MBA can be completed in its entirety remotely. Again, students complete the same core courses with the same professors as do other FSU MBAs. The online MBA allows for concentrations in real estate and analysis or hospital administration. Students may also complete a general MBA.

FSU faculty members receive strong grades overall. Students tell us, "The professors in the business department are amazing. They are very congenial and well-spoken. They are helpful at all times. Most teachers are older and contain a strong sense of experience. They know how to teach a class that is entertaining, interactive, and fun." Some warn that "There are quite a few professors here with heavy accents that may take a little concentration to understand," but even they concede that "their willingness to help you outside the classroom and brilliance far outweigh this drawback." Teachers also "do a very good job of keeping class interesting by incorporating technology, group assignments, etc."

Career and Placement

Because FSU's MBA program is small and largely part time, the school does not maintain a separate career services office for graduate students in business. It does, however, sponsor an MBA Internship Program in which "carefully structured project work" allows both students and employers to "realize the benefits of this program." The school also offers coaching and career-related resources in order to help students plan their job search and marketing of their skills. The school hosts semi-annual MBA Networking Night events and on-campus and videoconference interviews. It also provides students access to a host of job-posting resources. Students report, "Our career center is great about creating internship opportunities. However, as far as full-time positions after graduation, the focus is more on undergrads. There are few recruiters [who] come specifically for MBAs." In the plus column, "Networking seems to be one of the biggest strengths of Florida State. Through the College of Business, my sorority, and all the amazing staff, the opportunities are endless."

Employers most likely to hire FSU MBAs include BB&T, CSX, Harris, JP Morgan, Protiviti, and Wachovia Bank.

ADMISSIONS CONTACT: LISA BEVERLY, ADMISSIONS DIRECTOR
ADDRESS: GRADUATE PROGRAMS, COLLEGE OF BUSINESS, FSU, TALLAHASSEE, FL 32306-1110
PHONE: 850-644-6458 • FAX: 850-644-0588
E-MAIL: GRADPROG@COB.FSU.EDU • WEBSITE: WWW.COB.FSU.EDU/GRAD

FINANCIAL FACTS

Cost of books	$8,000
Room & board	
(on/off-campus)	$23,838/$24,082

ADMISSIONS

Admissions Selectivity Rating	**95**
# of applications received	377
% applicants accepted	25
% acceptees attending	74
Average GMAT	558
Range of GMAT	500–610
Average GPA	3.35
TOEFL required of	
international students	Yes
Minimum TOEFL	
(paper/computer)	550
Application fee	$30
International application fee	$30
Regular application deadline	2/1
Deferment available	Yes
Maximum length	
of deferment	12 months
Transfer students accepted	Yes
Transfer application policy: Transfer applicants must complete the same application process as all other applicants.	
Non-fall admissions	Yes
Need-blind admissions	Yes

Student Life and Environment

Full-timers at FSU basically get to extend their college years by one, albeit with a heavier workload. Students tell us: "Life is relaxed and challenging. We have a lot of work but ample time to complete it. Everyone wants to have a good time, but it's about priorities. If you go to class, you will succeed." Campus life offers "the perfect balance of challenging schoolwork, amazing social groups, and fun nightlife," and "the School of Dance and Music puts on (sometimes free) performances for the community. FSU energizes Tallahassee," a city that is "a great place to be" although "it is a small town and can get boring quick." One student suggests "picking up a hobby that you can do around town in all the parks and woods—Frisbee, mountain biking, kayaking, football, whatever—just stay involved in a physical activity."

Part-time students engage mostly in class and study groups. One observes: "It's nice being able to see the same people semester after semester. That gives us all a sense of warmth when we get into new classes. Life here is pretty busy, people running around trying to get things done on time...not much different from in the real world." Part-timers regard themselves as "more adaptable and friendly" than their full-time peers, whom they regard as "still a bit immature."

Admissions

The Admissions Office at Florida State University requires all of the following from applicants to its MBA program: two official copies of transcripts for all post-secondary academic work; an official GMAT score report; three letters of recommendation from former professors and/or employers; a current resume; a personal statement; and a Florida Residency affidavit, if appropriate. Students must have proficiency working with PCs. International students whose first language is not English must also submit an official score report for the TOEFL (minimum score: 600 paper-based test, 250 computer-based test, or 100 Internet-based test). All test scores must be no more than five years old. The school lists the following programs designed to increase recruitment of underrepresented and disadvantaged students: the FAMU Feeder Program, FAMU Graduate & Professional Days, GradQuest, MBA Advantage, Minority Student Orientation Program, Leslie Wilson Assistantships, the Delores Auzenne Minority Fellowship, and the University Fellowship.

EMPLOYMENT PROFILE

Career Rating	80	**Top 5 Employers Hiring Grads**
Percent employed at graduation	63	Ernst & Young, KPMG LLP, Deloitte and
Average base starting salary	$67,132	Touche Tomatsu, Walt Disney, Ameraprise
		Financial Services

FORDHAM UNIVERSITY
GRADUATE SCHOOL OF BUSINESS ADMINISTRATION

Academics

With a "phenomenal location" in the heart of the financial capital of the world, "Fordham University's Graduate School of Business Administration is well-positioned for both full-time students and working professionals to take advantage of furthering their education." For part-time students the "flexibility of scheduling" is a major plus. Not only is there the "ability to switch from part time to full time if necessary," but the interaction between the two groups in the classroom "allows great student mix...and adds to networking opportunities." With an abundance of students having "great jobs in NYC," these individuals can help assist "anyone [who may be] switching careers or looking for advancement at different companies." The "networking potential in the student body" alone is difficult for other schools to match.

Students benefit from the "international diversity within the student body, which provides a global perspective in classroom discussions and projects." Classmates bring "with them knowledge of different markets and cultures. Classes are more interesting with these different viewpoints." This diversity in the classroom is especially valuable since "the majority of classes are highly interactive, where professors are looking for feedback from students to drive the discussion, rather than constantly lecturing them." Adding to the "engaging atmosphere" present in the classroom is the abundance of part-time students who "bring significant work experience to class discussions and case studies."

Understanding the social responsibility of business is another reason students choose Fordham University. "As a Jesuit university, the academic environment is more of a holistic achievement approach versus a competitive 'everyone for him/herself' attitude. One student explains the Jesuit concept as "educating the whole person" by sensitizing students to the importance of promoting corporate ethics and social justice." Many students appreciate this emphasis upon "the ethics of doing business, and [on] social and environmental responsibility."

The professors have "diverse backgrounds" and bring real-world experience and insight into the classroom, which keeps lessons interesting and relevant. "Most professors are career professionals and not career academics. That lends a lot more credibility to their courses than those taught by those with mostly academic backgrounds." They are "very knowledgeable of the current course topic/market/industry they are discussing in class" and "[seem] to stay on top of trends and developments." Overall, classes are "friendly" yet "competitive." "It's an environment where you feel like studying hard and...the professors will make you work hard."

Career and Placement

Networking is key to taking advantage of the endless employment opportunities that New York City has to offer, and Fordham's alumni offer a "vast network," holding positions "all over the place in the city." To fully utilize these valuable resources, there are "several programs that the school has launched to connect alumni to the current community." Students who participate in groups such as Fordham Women in Business, the Finance Society, and the Graduate Marketing Society are sure to increase their network. "These organizations are constantly spearheading events with industry topics and guest speakers and offer workshops to build specific skills in these areas."

ADMISSIONS CONTACT: PATRICIA CAFFREY, DIRECTOR OF ADMISSIONS AND ENROLLMENT
ADDRESS: 113 WEST 60TH STREET, 6TH FLOOR, NEW YORK, NY 10023
PHONE: 212-636-6200 • FAX: 212-636-7076
E-MAIL: ADMISSIONSGB@FORDHAM.EDU • WEBSITE: WWW.BNET.FORDHAM.EDU

The school also provides "lots of student groups and weekly social events [where] you can socialize and network to your heart's desire." Career Management also "provides students with plenty of opportunities for mock interviews" as well as helps with "resume writing, navigating career fairs, [and] networking workshops." In addition, "There are weekly social networking nights with other school members and other universities. Weekly panel discussions occur as well regarding current events and relevant themes."

With so many students seeking jobs in a somewhat unsteady economy, students stress that there is still a need for "more career placement assistance." Specifically, some students feel that "the quality of companies that recruit on campus" could be improved. The program has answered theses concerns with the establishment of the Alumni-Student Career Alliance and the Professional Development Program.

Student Life and Environment

The Fordham campus offers a lot, but not all students appear to take advantage of these opportunities. "Student life is mixed between people who commit a lot of their time socially... and those who come to campus for classes and go home afterward. Part of that is the cultural mix of part-time and full-time students." For students who can commit the time, "There are a variety of student organizations that are good for meeting new people, and it is through these specific organizations that the best networking at Fordham can be done." A student attests, "Weekly happy hours are the best way to meet new people. These are usually conducted by various student clubs and the way I have made several long-term connections."

At Fordham, environment is everything. "There is nothing like the experience of New York City. The campus is located right next to Lincoln Center and the activities around are endless. You could go to school here for years and still have vast amounts of shops, restaurants, and entertainment to explore."

Admissions

Students looking to enroll in Fordham's Graduate School of Business Administration MBA program will need to have an up-to-date resume of their work experience. Most average about 6 years of previous work. Although test scores are important, they are not the deciding factor. The admissions office looks more closely at undergraduate GPA, good letters of recommendations, and a well-written essay. Ninety countries are represented at Fordham; 40% of full-time graduate students are international. The average age at enrollment is 27, average GPA is 3.3, and average GMAT is 620. Rolling applications need to be received by 6/01 (5/01 for international students).

FINANCIAL FACTS

Annual tuition (in-state/ out-of-state)	$41,365/$41,365
Fees	$546
Cost of books	$1,500
Room & board (on/off-campus)	$14,926
% of students receiving aid	92
% of first-year students receiving aid	46
% of students receiving grants	25
Average award package	$25,468
Average grant	$7,537
Average loan	$28,370
Average student loan debt	$57,406

ADMISSIONS

Admissions Selectivity Rating	80
# of applications received	577
% applicants accepted	60
% acceptees attending	45
Average GMAT	620
Range of GMAT	570–660
Average GPA	3.30
TOEFL required of international students	Yes
Minimum TOEFL (paper/computer)	600/250
Application fee	$130
International application fee	$130
Regular application deadline	6/1
Deferment available	Yes
Maximum length of deferment	1 Year
Transfer students accepted	No
Non-fall admissions	Yes
Need-blind admissions	Yes

EMPLOYMENT PROFILE

		Grads Employed by Function	% Avg. Salary
Career Rating	87		
Percent employed at graduation	33	Marketing	(31%) $86,381
Percent employed 3 months after graduation	10	Operations	(3%) $65,000
		Consulting	(11%) $92,625
Average base starting salary	$91,028	Management	(4%) $80,667
Primary Source of Full-time Job Acceptances		Finance	(45%) $97,130
School-facilitated activities	33 (37%)	Other	(6%) $88,000
Graduate-facilitated activities	46 (52%)	**Top 5 Employers Hiring Grads**	
Unknown	10 (11%)	Deloitte (5), KPMG (3), Quest Diagnostics (3), Accenture (2), Barclays (2)	

FRANCIS MARION UNIVERSITY
SCHOOL OF BUSINESS

Academics

The School of Business at South Carolina's Francis Marion University offers "excellent preparation for real-world business decision-making" in a "convenient" MBA program "scheduled in the evening to accommodate working students." Since FMU is a state school, it does so at a price that doesn't break the bank.

This small school—one of the smallest state universities to earn AACSB accreditation, according to the university's public relations materials—offers a "challenging learning environment" in which "professors are easy to approach" and, consequently, the almost exclusively part-time student body "gets to know professors one on one." FMU offers a general MBA that is designed to serve the general business population of the Pee Dee region and beyond.

All FMU MBAs must complete courses in accounting for management control, managerial economics, financial theory and applications, strategic management, management science and statistics, and marketing theory and application. Students in the general MBA program must also complete classes in financial accounting, information systems, international business, management theory and applications, production management, and entrepreneurship.

MBAs praise the program's faculty, noting that "professors with real-world experience are integrated into active businesses and graduate programs." Primarily, they appreciate the convenience afforded by the school's location and scheduling, as well as the low cost of attending to Palmetto State natives.

Career and Placement

FMU's MBA program is too small to support career services dedicated exclusively to its students. MBAs receive career assistance from the university's Office of Career Development, which serves undergraduates and graduates in all divisions. Students here also benefit from an active Alumni Association, whose newest chapter is the MBA Alumni Chapter.

ADMISSIONS CONTACT: BEN KYER, DIRECTOR
ADDRESS: BOX 100547, FLORENCE, SC 29501-0547
PHONE: 843-661-1436 • FAX: 843-661-1432
E-MAIL: ALPHA1@FMARION.EDU • WEBSITE: ALPHA1.FMARION.EDU/~MBA

Student Life and Environment

FMU draws a "driven and goal-oriented" student body that is "culturally diverse and career diverse." Life here is hectic, with most students juggling career and family obligations in addition to school responsibilities. Because of the many demands on their time, most students have little inclination to join in extracurricular activities. The program offers "many organizations" to those interested, but students warn that "they aren't as organized or publicized as well as they should be."

The school does a better job with its cultural and entertainment offerings to the general student population, hosting a wide range of performances, exhibits, and lecture series. The school houses an art gallery that displays student and faculty work as well as traveling exhibitions, film series, a planetarium and observatory, concerts, and festivals. FMU's Patriots are successful enough that the school plans to move its entire athletic program to Division I in the coming years; two teams already compete at that level, with the other ten currently competing in Division II.

FMU is located just outside of Florence, SC, a city with nearly 70,000 residents within its borders and its suburbs. Florence offers a number of movie theaters, malls, restaurants, a symphony orchestra, and professional hockey (the Pee Dee Pride skate in the East Coast Hockey League). The city is located at the intersections of I-95 and I-20, making travel in all four cardinal directions a snap. Columbia, Charleston, Myrtle Beach, and Fayetteville, NC, are all within 100 miles.

Admissions

Applicants to the FMU MBA program must submit a completed application; official transcripts for all postsecondary academic work, in a sealed envelope addressed to the applicant from the awarding school; official GMAT scores; two letters of recommendation; and a personal statement of purpose. All materials must be delivered to the school in a single envelope or package. In addition, international applicants must submit official TOEFL scores and a Confidential Financial Statement form demonstrating their ability to pay all expenses related to an FMU MBA. All successful applicants meet the following minimum guidelines: a score greater than 950 under the formula [(undergraduate GPA x 200) + GMAT score] or a score greater than 1000 under the formula [(GPA for final 60 hours of undergraduates work x 200) + GMAT score]. Also, they must earn at least a score of 400 on the GMAT. Applicants with non-business undergraduate degrees are generally required to complete the business foundation sequence prior to beginning work on their MBA. The sequence is 3-course curriculum covering the basics of information systems, finance, and marketing. Students with undergraduate business degrees typically have this requirement waived.

FINANCIAL FACTS

Annual tuition (in-state/ out-of-state)	$3,500/$7,000
Fees	$60
Cost of books	$750
% of students receiving aid	8
Average grant	$1,000
Average loan	$1,000

ADMISSIONS

Admissions Selectivity Rating	69
# of applications received	33
% applicants accepted	85
% acceptees attending	93
Average GMAT	400
Average GPA	3.00
TOEFL required of international students	Yes
Minimum TOEFL (paper/computer)	550/213
Application fee	$30
Deferment available	Yes
Maximum length of deferment	9999
Transfer students accepted	No
Non-fall admissions	No
Need-blind admissions	No

THE GEORGE WASHINGTON UNIVERSITY
SCHOOL OF BUSINESS

GENERAL INFORMATION

Type of school	Private
Affiliation	No Affiliation
Academic calendar	Semester

SURVEY SAYS...

Students love Washington, D.C.,
Good social scene
Solid preparation in:
Accounting, Doing business in a
global economy, Environmental
sustainability

STUDENTS

Enrollment of parent institution	25,653
Enrollment of MBA Program	240
% male/female	64/36
% part-time	0
% underrepresented minority	8
% international	32
Average age at entry	27
Average years work experience at entry	4.0

ACADEMICS

Academic Experience Rating	**87**
Profs interesting rating	81
Profs accesible rating	85
Student/faculty ratio	15:1
% female faculty	42
% underrepresented minority faculty	28
% part-time faculty	44

Joint Degrees

MBA/JD degree; MBA/MA in
International Affairs; MBA/MS
Finance; MBA/Project Management;
MBA/Information Systems
Technology.

Prominent Alumni

Colin Powell, MBA, Former US
Secretary of State; Henry Duques,
BBA & MBA, Former President &
CEO, First Data Corp.; Edward M.
Liddy, MBA, Chairman & CEO,
Allstate Insurance; Michael Enzi,
BBA, US Senator; Clarence B.
Rogers, Jr., MBA, Chairman,
President & CEO, Equifax, Inc.

Academics

A new breed of business school, The George Washington University's Global MBA program brings ethical leadership and international savvy into the classroom. Having recently redesigned its MBA program, the school's "bold new curriculum" (combined with its historic strength in real estate, sports management, and other fields) has attracted many enthusiastic and socially-minded students to the program. At GWU's School of Business, core coursework has a heavy focus on entrepreneurship and global business, as well as an emphasis on "ethics, corporate social responsibility, and sustainability." During the first two semesters, students complete a "full-time compressed curriculum with fixed cohorts"—a series of interdisciplinary courses taught by teams of professors. A "relatively small MBA program," the GWU MBA allows more personal interaction in the classroom, and throughout the program, "Schoolwork is extremely team-based, which empowers students to develop essential teamwork skills." After completing the core, students can "tailor their second-year curriculum to their interests" through one of 17 areas of concentration.

A long-standing D.C. institution, GWU's stellar location adds incredible value to students educational experience, providing "many opportunities to supplement classroom learning with out-of-class experiences, such as seeing the treasury secretary and other politicians discuss important legislation." A student agrees, "While the academic experience is vital (and excellent), I would say it's all the opportunities outside the classroom that are most valuable to me." To supplement the academic curriculum with real-world know-how, GWU students pursue summer internships, attend lectures in the MBA speaker series, participate in school-sponsored co-curricular activities in the Washington, D.C., area, or volunteer through the "active Net Impact chapter." Of particular note, every GWU student gets hands-on experience through the "international consulting project"—a three-course sequence, which concludes with a real-world consulting experience overseas (recent destinations include Rwanda, Istanbul, and Peru.)

At GWU, professors and administrators are "all very professional and very competent"—as well as student-oriented. In fact, students say, "The most impressive thing about GWU's professors is their accessibility outside of class…. Most professors display a genuine interest in the students, which is very refreshing." Even so, many think the school needs to invest more time and energy in recruiting better faculty, as "the professors are very hit or miss" in the classroom. "Some of them are very effective instructors and go out of their way to help students succeed in learning the subject matter," while others "may be better researchers than educators." Students also admit that there have been a few hiccups as the school implements its new curriculum, but "the administration is working hard to smooth out all the wrinkles." Overall, the school "functions exceptionally well" and administrators are always "very responsive to student feedback."

Career and Placement

The F. David Fowler Career Center (FDFCC) at the School of Business distinguishes itself from other MBA placement programs through its partnership with Meridian Resources, Inc, a career management consulting firm, which augments the campus program with expanded career planning and job placement resources. Students begin working with the FDFCC before they arrive on campus, and they continue to prepare for their career throughout the program through one-on-one career counseling, career development workshops, career fairs, and networking events. GWU has "a strong alumni network in the Washington, D.C., area and elsewhere," and "There are a number of programs that link students with alumni." However, given the school's global focus, many feel that "More of an effort should be made to engage international alumni."

ADMISSIONS CONTACT: CHRISTOPHER STORER, EXECUTIVE DIRECTOR, MBA ADMISSIONS
ADDRESS: 2201 G ST. NW, SUITE 550, WASHINGTON, DC 20052
PHONE: 202-994-1212 • FAX: 202-994-3571
E-MAIL: GWMBA@GWU.EDU • WEBSITE: WWW.BUSINESS.GWU.EDU/GRAD

For recent MBA classes, the mean salary upon graduation was $84,208, with 32 percent of students receiving an additional signing bonus. Students took jobs at companies including AARP, AE Strategies, Booz Allen Hamilton, General Electric, Metro Associates, Samsung Securities, SAP, U.S. Department of Commerce, and U.S. Department of Health and Human Services.

Student Life and Environment

At The George Washington University, extracurricular, networking, and social activities are just as vital to the student experience as the academic program. With an emphasis on teamwork and cooperation, GWU "values the balance of networking and social relationships in conjunction with demanding academics." Taking advantage of the urban environment, the school offers "organized events around sightseeing and community service initiatives." In addition, "There are tons of ways to be involved, and nearly every student keeps exceptionally busy, through a combo of classes, internship(s), part-time work, and student clubs/activities." There really is something for everyone, and, "If you don't see a club you like, it's easy to start your own."

With its small class sizes, "The atmosphere at GWU is definitely collegial—in contrast to other schools which get fairly competitive, GWU students are happy to work together and help each other out." Socially, members of study groups often become close friends, and students say, "We go out at least once a week to socialize with each other and with other business school students as well." With its campus located in "the center of Washington D.C.," students say it is "very easy to get around in this city, and there is always a lot going on at the business school, around campus, and elsewhere." Thanks to the urban environs, "There is access to great speakers, events, and museums all the time and often for free;" however, some students complain that campus safety can be spotty, and there are "not many places to study on campus or near campus."

Admissions

To apply to The George Washington University, prospective students must submit a completed application, a resume, two letters of recommendation, essays, official transcripts from all higher education institutions attended, and official GMAT or GRE scores. In recent years, the entering class had an average 4.0 years of professional work experience, an average GMAT score of 635, and an average undergraduate GPA of 3.3.

FINANCIAL FACTS

Annual tuition (in-state/ out-of-state)	$40,470/$40,470
Fees	$23
Cost of books	$3,200
Room & board (on/off-campus)	$26,957/$26,957
% of students receiving aid	68
% of first-year students receiving aid	69
% of students receiving grants	48
Average award package	$42,057
Average grant	$23,200
Average loan	$42,122
Average student loan debt	$83,112

ADMISSIONS

Admissions Selectivity Rating	85
# of applications received	599
% applicants accepted	49
% acceptees attending	39
Average GMAT	635
Range of GMAT	590–690
Average GPA	3.3
TOEFL required of international students	Yes
Minimum TOEFL (paper/computer)	600/250
Application fee	$75
International application fee	$75
Application Deadline/Notification	
Round 1:	11/1 / 12/19
Round 2:	1/10 / 3/8
Round 3:	3/15 / 5/3
Deferment available	No
Transfer students accepted	Yes
Transfer application policy: Standard Application Procedures. Transfer credits accepted only from AACSB accredited schools.	
Non-fall admissions	Yes
Need-blind admissions	Yes

EMPLOYMENT PROFILE

Career Rating	95	Grads Employed by Function	% Avg. Salary
Percent employed at graduation	56	Marketing	(13%) $78,056
Percent employed 3 months after graduation	85	Operations	(4%)
		Consulting	(28%) $87,906
Average base starting salary	$84,208	Management	(11%) $96,214
Primary Source of Full-time Job Acceptances		Finance	(24%) $82,245
School-facilitated activities	36(48%)	HR	(4%) $98,000
Graduate-facilitated activities	30(40%)	MIS	(4%)
Unknown	9(12%)	Other	(12%) $77,350

Top 5 Employers Hiring Grads

General Electric (6), The World Bank (3), Deloitte (2), IBM (2), International Finance Corporation (IFC) (2)

GEORGETOWN UNIVERSITY
McDonough School of Business

GENERAL INFORMATION
Type of school   Private
Affiliation   Roman Catholic-Jesuit
Academic calendar Semesters and modules

SURVEY SAYS...
Students love Washington, D.C.,
Friendly students, Good peer network, Helpful alumni
Solid preparation in:
Doing business in a global economy

STUDENTS
Enrollment of parent institution	17,357
Enrollment of MBA Program	879
% male/female	71/29
% part-time	43
% underrepresented minority	5
% international	31
Average age at entry	28
Average years work experience at entry	5.1

ACADEMICS
Academic Experience Rating	**94**
Profs interesting rating	83
Profs accesible rating	91
Student/faculty ratio	8:1
% female faculty	19
% underrepresented minority faculty	15
% part-time faculty	46

Joint Degrees
MBA/MSFS - 3 years; MBA/JD - 4 years; MBA/MPP - 3 years; MBA/MD - 5 years

Prominent Alumni
Michael Chasen, Co-Founder, Blackboard Inc.; Ann Sarnoff, COO, BBC Worldwide America; Eric Bauer, COO, The Children's Place; Laurence Tosi, CFO, Blackstone; Kaya Henderson, Chancellor, DC Public Schools

Academics

Located in Washington, D.C., Georgetown's access to international interests in both business and policy make it a desirable choice for career-minded students. The school offers an MBA with "a global approach," with the second year ending in a 9-day international consulting experience. Due to this and other factors, students are "impressed with their global focus and their emphasis on using business to help society." Because the business program "is not focused on any one particular aspect of business," Georgetown "gives its students a true understanding of business from many points of view around the world, allowing for international opportunities for growth."

Those hoping for a foundation in ruthless business practices will not find it here. McDonough fosters a "collaborative spirit when it comes to both learning and practicing business." In fact, "the Georgetown MBA program was the first institution to implement a business ethics course as a requirement for graduation." The school "pushes integrity across all levels," the result being a "high caliber of business professionals" among the graduates. Some students hope to see more "emphasis on sustainability/green trends in coursework."

Georgetown has "an excellent reputation for being academically rigorous, diverse, and high quality," and regarding the business school specifically, students consider McDonough the "highest caliber school in the region," a school that will "afford me better opportunities than other programs in this area." Students enjoy that the "smaller program size is more intimate compared to other large business schools."

A newly designed MBA Curriculum launched in the Fall of 2012 to replace the former modular system; it is filled with both classroom and experiential learning, and provides greater rigor, greater emphasis on quantitative and analytical skills, and a focus on principled leadership. One student in particular recognizes this fact yet remarks that "at the end of a course, I still come out learning more than what I bargained for."

Career and Placement

Career-minded students should find no shortage of post-school opportunities thanks to a "strong alumni network," "great networking connections," and "good access to recruiters." Some suggest that "due to its smaller size (compared to other business schools), some employers do not spend as much time as they might at other institutions," but because McDonough boasts "proximity to power sources in D.C.," hard-working graduates can expect a "great upward trajectory" provided they take advantage of the "great recruiting sessions" and "strong career connections in the business world." Though "the administration is relatively new," students say they are "dedicated to improving the school." An integral part of that is a new Director of Career Management, who works to be "extremely helpful in providing advice and consultation."

Employers who have hired McDonough graduates include: Citigroup, Booz Allen Hamilton, Credit Suisse, Merrill Lynch, AES, America Online, International Finance Corporation (IFC), 3M, American Express Company, Avaya, Bank of New York, Deloitte Touche Tohmatsu, Ford Motor Company, and JPMorgan Chase.

ADMISSIONS CONTACT: KELLY WILSON, ASST DEAN & DIRECTOR OF ADMISSIONS
ADDRESS: RAFIK B. HARIRI BUILDING, 37TH & O STREET, NW, WASHINGTON, DC 20057
PHONE: 202-687-4200 • FAX: 202-687-7809
E-MAIL: GEORGETOWNMBA@GEORGETOWN.EDU • WEBSITE: MSB.GEORGETOWN.EDU

Student Life and Environment

Life at the McDonough School of Business at Georgetown University is one of constant challenge, with academics the focus of most days. "Georgetown's MBA is all-consuming," students say, but "in a good way." Indeed, "It is often difficult to find a group study room or classroom not filled with students studying on an evening or weekend." Students feel they are encouraged to work hard, "especially when [they] see my peers working just as hard." The school's collaborative, often non-competitive environment helps foster an atmosphere in which the "intense" workload is not overwhelming; it is just a fact of life. "Life at McDonough is rigorous and community-driven," attendees insist. "Students work extremely hard and take great pride in the Georgetown brand."

However, McDonough students do find time to relax. There is a "very social atmosphere with many social activities planned for students." "Post-class happy hours" take place, though most say that school activities are preferred, including "clubs, student government associations, and community service projects." Living in or around the D.C. Metro area offers ample things to do outside of school. "Wine tours, sports and activities on Capitol Hill" and more are regularly on the agenda, as well as volunteering with school and local organizations, music clubs, museums, and more. Even with all those opportunities, the "intense school spirit" present throughout the Georgetown student body means that for many it is school first, even when it comes to leisure time.

One student sums it up: "Students are engaged in campus life, however [they are] mostly focused on business school events and activities."

Admissions

If you do not have a minimum of 2 years of post-collegiate professional experience, do not apply. At least 2 years, with 3 or more preferred, is required prior to admission. Prospective students should be prepared with the including documents: an online application form (required), a resume, four essays (required), official transcripts for all postsecondary academic work, at least two recommendations from professional relationships, and an official GMAT score report. International students take note: an official score report for the TOEFL, IELTS, or Pearson Test of English is required in addition to the above materials. Interviews are invitation-only and come after the first application deadline; accepting interview invitations is strongly encouraged.

FINANCIAL FACTS

Annual tuition (in-state/ out-of-state)	$49,440/$49,440
Fees	$2,485
Cost of books	$2,600
Room & board (on/off-campus)	/$19,894
% of students receiving aid	71
% of first-year students receiving aid	73
% of students receiving grants	27
Average award package	$54,449
Average grant	$22,092
Average loan	$57,640
Average student loan debt	$50,318

ADMISSIONS

Admissions Selectivity Rating	95
# of applications received	1,458
Average GMAT	683
Range of GMAT	640–730
Average GPA	3.34
TOEFL required of international students	Yes
Minimum TOEFL (paper/computer)	600/250
Application fee	$175
International application fee	$175
Application Deadline/Notification	
Round 1:	10/15 / 12/15
Round 2:	1/5 / 3/15
Round 3:	4/1 / 5/15
Deferment available	No
Transfer students accepted	No
Non-fall admissions	No
Need-blind admissions	Yes

EMPLOYMENT PROFILE

Career Rating	96	Grads Employed by Function	% Avg. Salary
Percent employed at graduation	68	Marketing	(11%) $94,346
Percent employed 3 months after graduation	89	Operations	(3%) $98,000
		Consulting	(27%) $110,142
Average base starting salary	$99,799	Management	(9%) $104,460
Primary Source of Full-time Job Acceptances		Finance	(28%) $97,957
School-facilitated activities	112 (56%)	Other	(15%) $86,436
Graduate-facilitated activities	82 (41%)	**Top 5 Employers Hiring Grads**	
Unknown	5 (3%)	Deloitte Consulting (13),	
		PricewaterhouseCoopers (8), Citi (6),	
		American Express (5), Bank of America/Merrill Lynch (5)	

GEORGIA INSTITUTE OF TECHNOLOGY
SCHELLER COLLEGE OF BUSINESS

Academics

No doubt Georgia Tech boasts "a great brand name," but that's hardly all this school has to offer its MBAs. With a "curriculum designed to integrate management and technology," Georgia Tech positions its grads well in the increasingly technologically-focused world of business. Furthermore, the school's Atlanta location means access to some of the best business minds—and some of the top business employers—in the Southeast. In addition, the school "provides great value for the money."

Students find Georgia Tech's many assets in surprising places. One writes, "Before coming to school, I would have said our greatest strength was our technology focus and proximity to one of the premier engineering schools in the world. Now…I would say that our professors and career services are tied for greatest strengths. I will put either up against any top-ten business school any day." MBAs here report that Georgia Tech has "a great faculty in accounting, IT, and operations," and identify entrepreneurship, finance, and international management as other standout areas. Across disciplines, an "innovative curriculum keeps pace with the rapidly changing business and technology environment."

Georgia Tech's full-time program is limited to 75 students, which results in "strong networks and personal attention." "Small class sizes mean that students can have a high degree of impact in clubs, research assistantships, and special, self-initiated projects," one student observes (Of course, it also means that "not all electives that you may want will be offered.") The program places "an emphasis on teamwork and collaborative relationships" that students embrace, describing "a positive yet challenging work environment." The "workload can be overwhelming at times," but "the heavy emphasis on group projects means we have strong and reliable classmates to lean on if we need it."

Career and Placement

The Jones MBA Career Center provides "outstanding" support to assist students in developing a successful career strategy and plan. Each student is assigned a career advisor "who helps us find internships and jobs in our preferred fields," a service students deem "invaluable." Other resources include an in-depth career course, job search tools, and individual career coaching.

Atlanta's big-city locale is a plus for students in their job search, because the school "can get business heads and leaders from the city of Atlanta" to visit campus, meet with and mentor students, assist in networking, and provide internships and jobs. As one student sums up, "The program is very much oriented toward the job market, and the school is known to get 100 percent job placement. From the time you are accepted, you begin evaluating employers and job hunting. You are given exceptional tools and resources (however, you are also under a great deal of pressure to secure a high-paying job)."

Among the top employers of Georgia Tech MBAs are North Highland, Bank of America, Emerson, Delta Airlines, KPMG, Capgemini Consulting, Booz & Company, Verizon Wireless, and Deloitte Consulting.

Student Life and Environment

There's a "friendly atmosphere" in the Georgia Tech MBA program, where "social networking events and clubs are an integral part of [the] business school experience." The b-school facility "has several common areas, comfortable lobbies, and group work areas," so "no one is ever by himself. Even if working diligently on different homework assignments, we tend to cluster together and have a social environment." Classrooms

ADMISSIONS CONTACT: AMY LARRABEE, MBA RECRUITING MANAGER
ADDRESS: 800 WEST PEACHTREE ST., NW, SUITE 302, ATLANTA, GA 30308
PHONE: 404-894-8722 • FAX: 404-894-4199
E-MAIL: MBA@SCHELLER.GATECH.EDU • WEBSITE: WWW.SCHELLER.GATECH.EDU/MBA

"are all equipped with a computer-managed multimedia system, which includes double projectors and screens, document camera, laptop hookups and DVD," and "Faculty offices are easily accessible in the building. The facilities are very clean and updated."

Because the program holds "no classes on Fridays," Thursday night is a time for socializing. "Every Thursday there is a social event either at a restaurant, atrium in the academic building, or elsewhere where current students, alumni, and professors interact in a relaxed environment," students tell us. Fridays aren't for hangovers, though; students "have two or three group meetings every Friday." The "Fridays off" policy, students explain, "is the only thing that makes group work possible" in this busy program.

Georgia Tech's "midtown Atlanta location" "offers numerous educational, professional, and social opportunities," although some warn that the surrounding neighborhood "has some safety issues." Most everyone agrees that the Atlanta location is a huge advantage overall, both in terms of "keeping outside 'real world' connections with professionals in our industry of choice" and culturally. "It is an exciting and vibrant life at Georgia Tech," one student reports.

Georgia Tech "attracts many people from the engineering fields, but also from financial services as well. This makes for a strong competition between teams in case reports and presentations." The program is home to lots of "Type-A driven people who are very engaging in class discussion and projects." Even so, "The culture is not over-competitive or cut-throat. We are like a family pushing each other to learn and to accomplish great things."

Admissions

GMAT or GRE scores, undergraduate GPA, work experience, and the results of a personal interview (scheduled by invitation only) are the factors that weigh most heavily with those who evaluate applicants for Georgia Tech's MBA program. Personal essays and recommendations are also important. A satisfactory grade in a college-level calculus course is a required prerequisite for enrollment. TOEFL scores are required of applicants whose first language is not English or who have not successfully completed a year of college/university level study in the United States or another English-speaking country. Applications are processed on a rolling basis, a system that typically favors those who apply early.

FINANCIAL FACTS

Annual tuition (in-state/ out-of-state)	$26,466/$37,322
Fees	$2,392
Cost of books	$1,200
Room & board (on/off-campus)	$7,778/$7,778
% of students receiving aid	80
Average award package	$26,250
Average grant	$3,842
Average student loan debt	$39,294

ADMISSIONS

Admissions Selectivity Rating	95
# of applications received	347
% applicants accepted	35
% acceptees attending	59
Average GMAT	678
Range of GMAT	650–730
Average GPA	3.38
TOEFL required of international students	Yes
Minimum TOEFL (paper/computer)	600/250
Application fee	$50
International application fee	$50
Early application deadline	11/1
Regular application deadline	3/15
Deferment available	Yes
Maximum length of deferment	1 year
Transfer students accepted	No
Non-fall admissions	No
Need-blind admissions	Yes

EMPLOYMENT PROFILE

Career Rating	97	Grads Employed by Function	% Avg. Salary
Percent employed at graduation	78%	Marketing	(15%) $88,438
Percent employed 3 months after graduation	95	Operations	(9%) $86,400
		Consulting	(37%) $96,395
Average base starting salary	$92,138	Management	(5%) $92,000
Primary Source of Full-time Job Acceptances		Finance	(15%) $76,438
School-facilitated activities	41(70%)	HR	(2%)
Graduate-facilitated activities	12(20%)	MIS	(14%) $111,429
Unknown	6(10%)	Other	(3%)

Top 5 Employers Hiring Grads
North Highland, Bank of America, Emerson, Delta Airlines, KPMG

GEORGIA REGENTS UNIVERSITY (FORMERLY AUGUSTA STATE UNIVERSITY)
HULL COLLEGE OF BUSINESS

GENERAL INFORMATION
Type of school — Public
Affiliation — No Affiliation
Academic calendar — Trimester

SURVEY SAYS...
Happy students, Students love Augusta, GA
Solid preparation in:
Accounting, General Management

STUDENTS
Enrollment of parent
  institution — 9,557
Enrollment of MBA Program — 115
% male/female — 45/55
% out-of-state — 38
% part-time — 65
% underrepresented minority — 38
% international — 28
Average age at entry — 27
Average years work experience
  at entry — 5.0

ACADEMICS
Academic Experience Rating — 80
Profs interesting rating — 82
Profs accesible rating — 81
Student/faculty ratio 25:1
% female faculty — 7
% underrepresented minority
  faculty — 1
% part-time faculty — 1

Academics

Convenience and cost are the two main reasons students cite for choosing the MBA program at Georgia Regents University (which formed in 2013 when Augusta State University merged with Georgia Health Sciences University). Many students here tell us that they attended the school as undergraduates and saw no reason to leave.

At GRU's MBA program, "Personal attention and career development are a given. Students have to actively work at not being known by the administration and faculty of the business school." Service is key; despite its relatively small MBA enrollment, "[GRU] has a dedicated educational professional to usher graduate students through the program." One student notes, "The school is the perfect size. It is small enough to allow for more personal relations between the student and the teacher but is big enough to enjoy all the aspects of attending a college." A "low teacher/student ratio" and "professors who are approachable and willing to help students" are among the other perks of attending. GRU works hard to accommodate its students' schedules by offering "almost every needed subject in the program" during the fall and spring semesters.

MBAs at GRU must complete a twelve-course sequence that includes two electives and ten required courses in human resources management, marketing, finance, accounting, economics, production management, leadership, management information systems, business research methods, and an integrating course in strategic management. Students tell us that the school has traditionally been recognized for strengths for economics, finance, and accounting, as well as in "certain quantitative-based courses like market research." In addition, GRU has taken steps in order to better prepare the students for information-based knowledge. Those steps include "recently naming an information technology professor to chair the program."

Career and Placement

The GRU Career Center serves all undergraduates and graduate students at the university. Services are geared primarily toward undergraduates, in part because the school's graduate divisions are so small and in part because many graduate students—including many MBAs—attend while continuing in jobs they intend to keep post-graduation. The office sponsors an annual Career Fair and offers the standard battery of career services: job posting, counseling, mock interviews, on-campus recruiting, and more.

Student Life and Environment

Most GRU MBAs "work full-time during the day and attend classes at night," which means they have limited time to devote to extracurricular activities. Students tell us that "many professors acknowledge the average students' work/demand schedule and design their courses to allow students to catch up on the weekends." MBAs also appreciate how the small-school environment creates "the opportunity to get to know the students and faculty on a greater than superficial level," an opportunity students take advantage of by "congregating in a small centralized area of the building before classes." With so many chances to bond with peers and professors, it's no wonder students tell us that "the school feels like a family."

Full-time students—consisting primarily of international students and undergraduates proceeding directly from their BA program to the MBA—tell us that "there is an active campus life at [GRU] even though few students actually live on campus. There are so many groups to be involved with and [there are] always activities going on. The school spirit at [GRU] is so alive, and the students there really love their campus. Most of the MBA students are graduates of [Augusta State], so I believe they feel the same as well." Clubs "are very active on campus." Phi Beta Lambda is one of the major ones for business students. MBAs tell us that the school has worked hard to beautify and improve this campus, which, they note, "was an arsenal during the Civil War. The school has done a great job of keeping that heritage intact" while simultaneously adding such assets as a "beautiful new student center" that "provides study areas, gym equipment, billiards, and a host of other activities for students that help to release school stress." Commuters warn that "parking is limited during morning hours, but afternoon and evening parking is very good."

The GRU student body is "broadly diverse in age, occupation, race, and educational background, but [they are] uniformly goal oriented, serious, and competitive, [while also] capable or working in a team environment." Students seem to appreciate this diversity. One student says, "I have come in contact with people from many different cultures, and it gives me a different outlook on business." Even though there are "so many international students," most "seem to be regular people with careers who have felt a need to improve themselves."

Admissions

Applicants to the Hull College of Business MBA program must submit all of the following: official transcripts for all undergraduate and graduate work; an official score report for the GMAT (test score can be no more than five years old); and a completed application form. In addition, international students whose first language is not English must submit an official score for the TOEFL and a financial responsibility statement. International transcripts must be submitted via Educational Credential Evaluators, Inc., a company that matches international course work to its American equivalent. The admissions committee looks for students with significant and diverse work experience, varied educational backgrounds, and sound academic achievement. Incoming students must be able to run word processing, spreadsheet, and database programs.

FINANCIAL FACTS

Annual tuition (in-state/ out-of-state)	$4,296/$15,960
Fees	$1,665
Cost of books	$1,675
Room & board	$9,145

ADMISSIONS

Admissions Selectivity Rating	76
# of applications received	54
% applicants accepted	56
% acceptees attending	53
Average GMAT	490
Range of GMAT	470–560
Average GPA	3.07
TOEFL required of international students	Yes
Minimum TOEFL (paper/computer)	550/213
Application fee	$50
International application fee	$50
Deferment available	Yes
Maximum length of deferment	1 year
Transfer students accepted	Yes
Transfer application policy Must meet regular MBA admission standards. Up to nine Semester credit hours from a regionally accredited institution may be accepted for transfer.	
Non-fall admissions	Yes
Need-blind admissions	Yes

GEORGIA SOUTHERN UNIVERSITY
COLLEGE OF BUSINESS ADMINISTRATION

GENERAL INFORMATION
Type of school	Public
Affiliation	No Affiliation
Academic calendar	Semester

SURVEY SAYS...
Friendly students
Solid preparation in:
Accounting, Communication/
interpersonal skills, Presentation
skills

STUDENTS
Enrollment of parent institution	20,574
Enrollment of MBA Program	207
% male/female	63/37
% out-of-state	12
% part-time	76
% underrepresented minority	37
% international	12
Average age at entry	31
Average years work experience at entry	0.0

ACADEMICS
Academic Experience Rating	**76**
Profs interesting rating	77
Profs accesible rating	83
Student/faculty ratio	30:1
% female faculty	37
% underrepresented minority faculty	19
% part-time faculty	8

Joint Degrees
MBA with a concentration in Health
Services Administration,
Information Systems, or
International Business - 2 years
evening/part time

Prominent Alumni
Dan Cathy, President/CEO,Chick-fil-
A; James Kennedy, Director,NASA
John F. Kennedy Space Flight
Center; Karl Peace,
President,Biopharmaceutical
Research Consultants; Steven
Cowan, Novelist; Tony Arata,
Singer/Songwriter

Academics

Uniting an "excellent academic reputation" with a "reasonable cost," Georgia Southern University has been conferring graduate business degrees for more than 40 years. Today, a Georgia Southern MBA isn't only for those in the Savannah-Statesboro region. In addition to the school's long-standing MBA program for professionals, Georgia Southern's popular "WebMBA program has a good reputation," as well as AACSB accreditation. Students who need the convenience of an online diploma choose Georgia Southern because the "flexible online format" makes it easy for students to complete their courses from anywhere in the country. For those seeking a more traditional MBA experience, Georgia Southern is also a "well known, brick-and-mortar school," which specifically caters to part-time students.

Whether you choose to attend in person or online, there is a "heavy workload" throughout the program. Live classes are generally interactive, and "you have to stay on your toes" during discussions. Fortunately, "Professors genuinely want to see students learn and succeed." If you need extra assistance, "the majority of professors are very accessible," and "willing to answer questions and address concerns" during office hours or via email. As instructors, Georgia Southern professors are "helpful and knowledgeable" about the topics they teach, and always "stay on top of current business trends." In fact, "Many of them are actively researching in their field," while others bring strong real-world credentials to the classroom. Of particular note, "Many of the professors are professionals and consultants, so their experience is invaluable to classroom instruction." At the same time, students say the program would be improved if the curriculum included "more real-life classes, such as entrepreneurship and negotiation," as well as "more managerial applications" in coursework.

Currently, there are three official MBA specialties at Georgia Southern—health services administration, information systems, and international business—as well as a SAP certification. For students who choose to concentrate their studies in health services administration, the school "just opened a new College of Public Health building." The administration is efficient and generally "runs things in the background without any problems." "The faculty and staff at GSU are very helpful and available to answer any questions" students have. Student concerns are listened to and addressed. For example, in the past, there were problems with regards to taking required classes, but "the school is already taking steps to streamline the enrollment process." As a part of Georgia's public school system, the MBA is offered at a "very reasonable price." Overall, for convenience, quality, and cost, this program is "worth every penny."

Career and Placement

Students in Georgia Southern's part-time and web-based programs are generally working in a professional capacity at the time they start their MBA. As a result, there are rather limited career services for these students. In fact, many web students have very little interaction with the Georgia Southern campus or administration.

ADMISSIONS CONTACT: DR. GORDON N. SMITH, MBA DIRECTOR
ADDRESS: P. O. BOX 8050, STATESBORO, GA 30460-8050
PHONE: 912-478-5767 • FAX: 912-478-7480
E-MAIL: GRADSCHOOL@GEORGIASOUTHERN.EDU • WEBSITE: COBA.GEORGIASOUTHERN.EDU/MBA

For students considering a career change, there is a dedicated career counselor assigned to the College of Business through the University's Office of Career Services. Students can meet with the counselor for help creating a job search strategy. Students and alumni from the College of Business also have access to all the services offered by the greater Office of Career Services, which include conferences, career development seminars, campus recruiting programs, and internship placements. For those with limited career experience, "Many of the programs offered have internships and co-ops built into the curriculum." Overall, "The University does an excellent job of making resources available to students, particularly given the anemic job market." However, students would still love to see "more job opportunities at career services."

Student Life and Environment

The largest higher-learning institution in the Savannah area, "Georgia Southern is a wonderful school located in a great, slow-paced part of Georgia." The charming campus is situated in the small town of Statesboro, and the school's "proximity to Savannah" makes it easy for students to commute to work, while also offering access to all the rich cultural life of Georgia's coastal city. The vast majority of GSU students are "working professionals with diverse backgrounds and busy lives outside of school." They join the program "from all walks of life" but share a passion for their career and education. Academically, the program can get "competitive among classmates," yet students are "very cooperative" when working together on group projects.

Web students have little to no contact with life at Georgia Southern, and "students who use the satellite campus aren't able to enjoy GSU's beautiful campus." Fortunately, those who crave camaraderie will find a "strong network of alumni and student organizations," which host "ongoing activities" on the larger campus, from athletics to performances. On occasion, the business school will also host special events "for graduate students to mingle." Some students would welcome the addition of family-friendly activities on campus, while younger MBA candidates would like to see "more activities on the graduate student level" in general. A student laments, "There are some of us who do not have families and would like to socialize in an adult atmosphere in our free time."

Admissions

To be considered for a spot at Georgia Southern University, students must submit a completed application, transcripts from their undergraduate college, and official GMAT scores. Admissions are determined using a "standard formula," which combines test scores and GPA to calculate a student's eligibility for the program. Using this formula, a slightly lower GPA can be balanced out by strong GMAT scores, or vice versa. In recent years, incoming MBA students had an average undergraduate GPA of 3.27 and average GMAT scores of 510. Students are enrolled three times annually for the fall, spring, and summer semesters.

FINANCIAL FACTS

Annual tuition (in-state/ out-of-state)	$9,300/$28,174
Fees	$1,872
Cost of books	$3,750
Room & board (on/off-campus)	$9,290/$9,290
% of students receiving aid	77
% of first-year students receiving aid	64
% of students receiving grants	57
Average award package	$13,929
Average grant	$9,989
Average loan	$12,681

ADMISSIONS

Admissions Selectivity Rating	76
# of applications received	112
% applicants accepted	69
% acceptees attending	100
Average GMAT	495
Range of GMAT	453–538
Average GPA	3.11
TOEFL required of international students	Yes
Minimum TOEFL (paper/computer)	/530
Application fee	$50
International application fee	$50
Regular application deadline	7/1
Deferment available	Yes
Maximum length of deferment	1 year
Transfer students accepted	Yes

Transfer application policy: No more than 6 Semester hours of graduate credit may be transferred to a graduate program at Georgia Southern. Only grades of "B" or higher will be accepted for transfer.

Non-fall admissions	Yes
Need-blind admissions	Yes

GEORGIA STATE UNIVERSITY
J. MACK ROBINSON COLLEGE OF BUSINESS

Academics

"One of the top business schools in Atlanta," Georgia State University offers a cosmopolitan MBA to a diverse student body. Catering to a range of urban professionals, the school offers several distinct MBA tracks. For those with busy careers, the Flexible MBA is an evening and weekend program, which allows up to five years for completion. Another popular choice, the PMBA, is also designed for working professionals; however, this program is a two-year cohort-based degree, which moves quickly and maximizes networking opportunities with classmates. In addition to these two programs, the school offers an Executive MBA for seasoned managers, as well as a full-time program with major overseas components, called the Global Partners MBA. With evening classes at "multiple locations" in Atlanta, the majority of Georgia State's MBA programs give students "the flexibility to remain employed full time throughout the curriculum."

Georgia State's MBA provides a "strong background in general business areas, while allowing you to focus on your area of interest" through electives and study abroad. "Professors are a mix of experienced professionals and long-tenured educators," who are "extremely knowledgeable" and able to "make complicated concepts understandable and relevant." Teaching working professionals, professors excel at "staying up to date with current business trends, from global to local." Just as importantly, "The business school learning environment depends heavily on your classmates' experiences." Since "many of the students have ten-plus years of relevant work experience," students are pleased to find that their "classmates bring good industry knowledge to discussions."

Keeping up with classes and professional life is definitely a challenge for many MBA students, as "the program moves at a very fast pace." At the same time, the "PMBA isn't as intense or competitive as some full-time programs because everyone is working full time." Helping to streamline the experience, "the administration is very involved" with students, and it "has perfected making the process easy" on busy working professionals. Staff handles most of the paperwork, so "students don't have to do any of the 'administrative' tasks, like registering or ordering books." "PMBA facilities are top notch," located on a number of convenient satellite campuses in Atlanta.

Career and Placement

Throughout Georgia State, there is a strong "focus on getting the MBA student where they want to go" in their career. While many part-time students aren't necessarily seeking a new job after graduation, they are nonetheless pleased that "the school leverages its location in a vibrant business city and its connections to business leaders to give students access to reputable companies for academic and career purposes." "Individual career counseling is made available as part of the program," and students have access to myriad services through the Robinson Career Management Center in the business school. There are frequent career development workshops on campus, as well as a few recruiting events. At the same time, "The job selection through the career placement center is limited," as the program lacks a large community of job seekers. A student explains, "We don't have a full-time program, so companies don't recruit at GSU like they do at Emory and GT."

ADMISSIONS CONTACT: TOBY MCCHESNEY, ASSISTANT DEAN
GRADUATE RECRUITING AND STUDENT SERVICES
ADDRESS: SUITE 625, 35 BROAD STREET, ATLANTA, GA 30302-3988
PHONE: 404-413-7167 • FAX: 404-413-7162
E-MAIL: MASTERSADMISSIONS@GSU.EDU • WEBSITE: WWW.ROBINSON.GSU.EDU

In recent years, many important companies have hired MBA grads from Georgia State, including Hewitt Associates, Tauber & Balser PC, KPMG LLP, Coca-Cola Enterprises, Deloitte Consulting, Towers Perrin, Federal Reserve Bank of New York, McKesson Corporation, UPS, Wells Fargo, GE Healthcare, KPMG UNUM Corporation, Frazier & Deeter LLC, Ernst & Young LLP, and Wachovia Securities. The average starting salary for PMBA graduates is $75,000, with a range between $45,000 and $150,000 annually. Flexible MBA students earn an average salary of about $65,000.

Student Life and Environment

Drawing from Atlanta's large urban population, the MBA program at GSU is "very diverse." One of the program's major benefits is making connections and networking with "student peers from major corporations." Fortunately, social interactions are, to some extent, built into the curriculum. Group work is included in most classes, and students say you should expect to attend "team meetings and phone conferences at least two hours weekly." On the whole, students are "competitive in their work lives but more collaborative in the academic environment."

Georgia State students are "surrounded by countless opportunities in downtown Atlanta," and, when time permits, "Students enjoy each other's company in and out of the classroom." Spread across several satellite facilities, many students rarely come to the main campus downtown. However, "the program tries to host mixers" for business students, and "the Graduate Business Association puts on a Leadership Speaker Series and several networking/happy hours throughout the year." As expected for marketing mavens, "events are generally held at trendy, popular venues and executed flawlessly." In addition to blowing off steam, these events are "excellent opportunities for networking and making new friends." At the same time, students with families note that most student activities are "geared at single, younger students."

Admissions

Admissions requirements vary for each of Georgia State's MBA programs, specifically with regards to work experience. For the executive MBA, students should have at least seven years of experience (with five in a management position), while the PMBA is designed for students with a minimum of four years full-time in the workforce. The Flexible MBA requires at least one year of work experience. Georgia State prefers that students have spent two or three years in the real world before beginning the program. For fall 2012, the average GMAT score for the entering class was 611.

FINANCIAL FACTS

Annual tuition (in-state/ out-of-state)	$7,866/$22,482
Fees	$2,128
Cost of books	$2,000
Room & board (on/off-campus)	$13,148/$11,195

ADMISSIONS

Admissions Selectivity Rating	81
# of applications received	444
% applicants accepted	64
% acceptees attending	69
Average GMAT	611
Range of GMAT	570–650
Average GPA	3.32
TOEFL required of international students	Yes
Minimum TOEFL (paper/computer)	610/255
Application fee	$50
International application fee	$50
Early application deadline	2/1
Early notification date	3/15
Regular application deadline	4/1
Regular application notification	6/15
Deferment available	Yes
Maximum length of deferment	Two Semesters
Transfer students accepted	No
Non-fall admissions	Yes
Need-blind admissions	Yes

GONZAGA UNIVERSITY
GRADUATE SCHOOL OF BUSINESS

Academics

Gonzaga University is about "teaching students life lessons through a Jesuit education," which appeals to the MBA students in its Graduate School of Business. A "great reputation in the business community," especially for its "accounting program," and an "awesome flexible curriculum structure" that "is designed with working individuals in mind (with evening and online classes)" also draw area business grads to the program, which can be completed in three semesters (including summer, fall, and spring).

Gonzaga's MBA curriculum consists of 22 credits in core courses (11 two-credit classes) and 11 credits in electives, and students are given the option for a "core-trailer," which gives them "a very unique opportunity to focus in on a subject that they enjoyed during the core part of the semester." Students report that the curriculum is "broad and covers many aspects of the modern business environment" and is "a tough workload that stresses excellence. Classes may run from 7:30 a.m. to 8:00 p.m. at night," with break hours in between. Professors "integrate course material throughout the program" and "rarely present contradicting information" as "the material in the program is well-planned," though "some tenured professors don't seem to care about updating their courses anymore." Students also appreciate that the program allows for a "flexibility of coursework." Some, however, believe the program would benefit from "more course-end teamwork projects." "Students need to have more opportunities to simulate complex projects and the teamwork needed to solve them," one student notes. Luckily, "Gonzaga's School of Business is always looking for students' input to make those improvements."

At Gonzaga, both faculty and the business administration "stress the importance of personal connections. As a result, students are able to easily build a strong alumni network." This close-knit culture "really adds to the MBA experience." "For those who are entrepreneurial, the Hogan Center offers hands-on experience, as do other business classes, such as business consulting, which enables students to try their hand at consulting for a local business." "I learned more practical skills in Gonzaga's MBA program than I ever expected in an academic setting," says one student.

Career and Placement

The Gonzaga Career Center and the School of Business Administration staff and faculty "do a great job of trying to provide students with as much planning help and advice that they can possibly give," including: Career 301 Seminars covering self-assessment, career planning, resume writing, and conducting a successful job search; mock interviews and interview critiques; on-campus recruiting and interviewing; a career-resources library; alumni events; and internship placement assistance. Students complain, "Despite its great instructors and faculty, the school needs to do a better job in connecting students with careers." Due to the small size of both the city of Spokane and the University, not a lot of major companies recruit at Gonzaga, and "a lot more legwork is needed on behalf of the student to find his or her post-graduation path." Thus, despite its "great reputation" in the Northwest, "the MBA program may best benefit those who already know where they want to go after they graduate."

Employers of Gonzaga business graduates include Avista, Bank of America, Boeing, Deloitte, Ernst & Young, Honeywell, Itron, KPMG, Microsoft, PricewaterhouseCoopers, and Starbucks. Fifty percent of Gonzaga MBAs go into finance and accounting.

ADMISSIONS CONTACT: STACEY CHATMAN, ASSISTANT DIRECTOR FOR GRADUATE ADMISSIONS
ADDRESS: 502 EAST BOONE AVENUE, SPOKANE, WA 99528-0009
PHONE: 509-313-4622 • FAX: 509-313-5811
E-MAIL: CHATMAN@GONZAGA.EDU • WEBSITE: WWW.GONZAGA.EDU/MBA

Student Life and Environment

Gonzaga's MBA candidates are broken down to recent undergrad graduates who immediately started their MBAs and working individuals who are returning to get an MBA after starting a career. Some feel that many students "have little to no work experience, which makes getting an MBA a real disservice to themselves." The culture is "more collaborative than competitive," and students tend to be "friendly and willing to help their peers," down-to-earth, "dependable" and "can pull their own weight." "Being taught from the Jesuit perspective and a student population in which you get to know most of the other students quite well" is a positive at Gonzaga, one student says.

Students are "fairly isolated from the campus in that our classes start at the end of the traditional day, and our building is on one edge of the campus," though you "can tell that administration has made great efforts to try to improve the camaraderie of all students." Luckily, the building is "amazing, has everything in one place, and the lounge has a fantastic view of a lake beneath and downtown in the distance." Evening classes "allow working professionals to attend classes." One student notes, "I cannot say enough about the flexibility and responsiveness of the MBA program team. From professors to the administrative staff, this experience has been outstanding."

Those who choose to engage in campus life tell us that it is "full of opportunities to get involved in fun activities and helpful charities," though not many of these apply to the family-oriented. "A few attempts have been made to encourage students to socialize, but nothing really applies to families, so I do not participate," says one student. The basketball games are free for students and are "full of excitement" and, as an added bonus, revenue "generated by the basketball team is used to improve the school and the school's reputation." Local charities "love the help from grad students and rely on them for help in creating business plans, conducting market research, and planning marketing activities." Hometown Spokane is in eastern Washington, is "cold during the winter, and not all that exciting compared to Seattle, which is four hours away."

Admissions

Applicants to the MBA program at Gonzaga must submit one official copy of all postsecondary academic transcripts, official GMAT scores (minimum score of 500 required), resume, two letters of recommendation, and a completed application (which includes three short essays). International students must also submit official TOEFL scores (if English is not their first language) and a financial declaration form. An interview may be required of some international applicants. Work experience is not required, "but is strongly encouraged," and "the majority of students who enter the program have four or five years of prior work experience."

FINANCIAL FACTS

Annual tuition	$27,720
Fees	$250
Cost of books	$600
Room & board	$4,500
% of students receiving aid	80
% of first-year students receiving aid	80
% of students receiving grants	40
Average award package	$14,000
Average grant	$2,000
Average loan	$12,100
Average student loan debt	$12,000

ADMISSIONS

Admissions Selectivity Rating	85
# of applications received	128
% applicants accepted	52
% acceptees attending	83
Average GMAT	550
Range of GMAT	480–650
Average GPA	3.38
TOEFL required of international students	Yes
Minimum TOEFL (paper/computer)	570/230
Application fee	$50
International application fee	$50
Deferment available	Yes
Maximum length of deferment	4 years
Transfer students accepted	Yes
Transfer application policy: Transcripts are evaluated to ensure that desired learning objectives have been fulfilled. Up to 6 credits can be transferred in from an AACSB accredited MBA program if the grade of a B or higher has been achieved in the coursework.	
Non-fall admissions	Yes
Need-blind admissions	Yes

EMPLOYMENT PROFILE

Career Rating	80	Grads Employed by Function	% Avg. Salary
Average base starting salary	$66,500	Marketing	(7%)
		Operations	(13%)
		Consulting	(5%)
		Management	(5%)
		Finance	(35%)
		HR	(5%)
		MIS	(5%)
		Other	(25%)

Top 5 Employers Hiring Grads
Itron, Boeing, WA Trust Bank, Providence Health, Avista

GRAND VALLEY STATE UNIVERSITY
SEIDMAN COLLEGE OF BUSINESS

GENERAL INFORMATION
Type of school   Public
Affiliation   No Affiliation
Academic calendar   Semester

SURVEY SAYS...
Cutting-edge classes
Solid preparation in:
General management

STUDENTS
Enrollment of parent
  institution   24,662
Enrollment of MBA Program   214
% male/female   73/27
% part-time   79
% underrepresented minority   18
% international   18
Average age at entry   29
Average years work experience
  at entry   6.0

ACADEMICS
Academic Experience Rating   **81**
Profs interesting rating   76
Profs accesible rating   83
Student/faculty ratio   25:1
% female faculty   20
% underrepresented minority
  faculty   30
% part-time faculty   0

Joint Degrees
Dual JD/MBA with MSU Law, 4 years

Prominent Alumni
Laurie Beard, Pres/CEO, Founders Trust Personal Bank; John Bultema, Pres., Fifth Third Bank Western Michigan; Curt Pullen, EVP Herman Miller, Pres Herman Miller NA; Robert Bockheim, Pres/COO, Nucraft Furniture; Mark Olesnavage, Pres, Hopen Therapeutics

Academics

Tucked away in western Michigan, Grand Valley State University promises both "afford-ability" and a celebrated reputation. Indeed, the MBA program at Grand Valley offers "a great education in a great location." Students can either enroll in the traditional MBA program (geared toward working professionals) or the full-time integrated (FIMBA) MBA.

The traditional MBA offers a balance of both business theory and practical application. There is a heavy emphasis on applied research and group projects, helping students hone their problem-solving abilities. Moreover, MBA candidates are required to take a large number of core courses, ensuring they have a breadth of knowledge and a strong foundation in business fundamentals. These courses range from Contemporary Managerial Accounting and Marketing Management to Global Competitiveness, Strategy and Operations, and Supply Chain Management. Additionally, traditional MBA students may choose to focus in finance, innovation and technology management, or health sector management.

The full-time integrated MBA (FIMBA) is an accelerated program aimed at students who studied business as an undergraduate. FIMBA students complete their MBA in a mere 14 months. The curriculum takes a holistic approach to business, and candidates have the opportunity to participate in an 11-month paid business fellowship. Students also partake in a weeklong trip to Washington, D.C., in the fall semester and travel to an international destination for two weeks during the winter semester.

MBA students at Grand Valley truly appreciate their "smart" and "efficient" professors. They work diligently to "instill real-world principles" in their students and know how to demonstrate "solutions to everyday business problems." A pleased student shares, "Professors all have real-world experience, which makes a very big difference in the quality of education. They aren't just talking about what they think it is like in the business world; they can honestly say 'when I worked on a project like this' or 'when I was Project Manager/CFO.' It makes a big difference not only in quality but the amount of respect they are given from the student body." Students are also full of praise for the "incredible" administration, which "seems to run fairly smoothly." They always appear "well prepared," and it is very clear that they "truly care about the students."

Careers and Placement

The Seidman Traditional MBA is a program primarily for working professionals, as opposed to a full-time MBA program. Most students are employed when they begin their MBA studies and remain employed by the same firms when they graduate. However, there are a handful of students interested in pursuing new career options and professional opportunities, and they do feel that Grand Valley's career services can be lacking. Many would appreciate if the office became "more visible and helpful." As one somewhat frustrated student expounds, "Career Services should help expose students to jobs and internships and to business people in the community in order to help us get better jobs. They need to foster introductions with those companies that strongly value a MBA from GVSU."

ADMISSIONS CONTACT: CLAUDIA BAJEMA, GRADUATE BUSINESS PROGRAMS DIRECTOR
ADDRESS: 401 W. FULTON, GRAND RAPIDS, MI 49504
PHONE: 616-331-7400 • FAX: 616-331-7389
E-MAIL: GO2GVMBA@GVSU.EDU • WEBSITE: WWW.GVSU.EDU/BUSINESS

Student Life and Environment

Grand Valley manages at attract a "great mix of personalities" who hail "from different backgrounds." Most agree that their peers are "friendly and easy to approach." Moreover, they are "intelligent" and quite focused on "pursuing success inside and outside of the classroom." A graduating student adds that she has found her fellow students to be "encouraging and supportive and always willing to lend a hand to a friend." Further, the vast majority of Grand Valley MBA students maintain full-time employment while enrolled, and they manage to successfully incorporate their work experience into class discussions. Many students truly appreciate this facet and find it adds to their "market knowledge" and certainly "helps to expand horizons."

Though many MBA candidates are busy juggling their jobs and families, they are quick to assert that "there is always something fun to do" around campus. Students also love hometown Grand Rapids, Michigan's second largest city. Located between Detroit and Chicago, Grand Rapids is a vibrant city in its own right. Students can take advantage of a myriad of cultural events and opportunities. Entertainment options include the Grand Rapids Symphony, Broadway Theater Guild, Grand Rapids Ballet, and Opera Grand Rapids. Sports enthusiasts will also find their appetite satiated. Grand Rapids features several professional sports teams including the Griffins (AHL hockey), the Rampage (arena football), and the Whitecaps (baseball).

Admissions

The admissions officers at Grand Valley State are looking for applicants who want to strengthen their business acumen and learn how to tackle today's business challenges. Successful candidates demonstrate that they have keen analytical skills, strong problem-solving abilities, and proven leadership experience. Applicants' academic records, GMAT scores, and work history are all thoroughly evaluated. The admissions committee does not require or request any particular undergraduate major with the exception of those students applying to the FIMBA (Full-time Integrated MBA) program. FIMBA students are required to have an undergraduate degree in business. Additionally, they must answer specific essay prompts and participate in a personal interview before gaining admission. Lastly, applicants who are not native English speakers must also submit scores for the TOEFL.

FINANCIAL FACTS

Annual tuition (in-state/ out-of-state)	$9,846/$13,140
Cost of books	$1,500
Room & board (on/off-campus)	$7,600/$6,000
% of students receiving aid	26
% of students receiving grants	14
Average award package	$12,734

ADMISSIONS

Admissions Selectivity Rating	79
# of applications received	100
% applicants accepted	83
% acceptees attending	89
Average GMAT	571
Range of GMAT	470–720
Average GPA	3.40
TOEFL required of international students	Yes
Minimum TOEFL (paper/computer)	550/213
Application fee	$30
International application fee	$30
Regular application deadline	8/01
Regular application notification	8/10
Deferment available	Yes
Maximum length of deferment	1 year
Transfer students accepted	Yes
Transfer application policy: Up to 9 credits of MBA equivalent course work from another AACSB-accredited university, grade of B or better, and course(s) taken within past 5 years.	
Non-fall admissions	Yes
Need-blind admissions	Yes

EMPLOYMENT PROFILE

Career Rating	64	**Top 5 Employers Hiring Grads** Amway Corporation, Steelcase Corporation, Gordon Food Service, Mercantile Bank, X-Rite Corporation

HARVARD UNIVERSITY
HARVARD BUSINESS SCHOOL

GENERAL INFORMATION

Type of school	Private
Affiliation	No Affiliation
Academic calendar	Sept-May

SURVEY SAYS...

Good social scene, Good peer network, Cutting-edge classes
Solid preparation in:
General management, Doing business in a global economy, Entrepreneurial studies

STUDENTS

Enrollment of MBA Program	1,822
% male/female	60/40
% part-time	0
% underrepresented minority	22
% international	34
Average age at entry	27
Average years work experience at entry	4.0

ACADEMICS

Academic Experience Rating	99
Profs interesting rating	97
Profs accesible rating	96
% female faculty	22
% underrepresented minority faculty	25
% part-time faculty	17

Joint Degrees

JD/MBA, 4 years; MPP/MPA/MBA, 3 years; MD/MBA, 5 years; DMD/MBA, 5 years

Prominent Alumni

Michael Bloomberg, Mayor of New York City, Founded Bloomberg L.P.; Jamie Dimon, Chairman & CEO, J.P. Morgan Chase & Co.; Alex Maybank and Alexandra Wilson, Founders, Gilt Groupe, Inc.; Sheryl Kara Sandberg, Chief Operating Officer, Facebook; Jason Kilar, CEO, Hulu

Academics

A "tried-and-true General Management focus with no concentrations or majors and no published GPAs," a "pedagogical approach that relies strongly on the case method," and most of all "a reputation as the best business program in the country" make Harvard Business School one of the top prizes in the MBA admissions sweepstakes. Applicants lucky enough to gain admission here rarely decide to go elsewhere.

The school's full-time-only program is relatively large; approximately 900 students enter the program each year. Students tell us, "Despite its large size, the school feels surprisingly small" thanks to a combination of factors. First is an administration that "could be a role model for any enterprise. This place is very well-run." Second is the subdivision of classes into smaller sections of 90 students, who together attack approximately 500 case studies during their two years here. Finally, there's a faculty that "is obviously committed to excelling at teaching and developing relationships with the students. Each faculty member loves being here, regardless of whether they are a superstar or not, and that makes a difference. Faculty guide discussion well and enliven the classroom."

The case method predominates at Harvard; explains one student, "I sit in my section of 90 students every day and debate business topics. My section mates come from all walks of life and all of them are incredibly successful. I prepare my 13 cases per week so that I can contribute to this environment." Students love the approach, although they point out that "the case method is not as great for quantitative courses such as finance." Numerous field-study classes supplement the program, especially during the second year, which is devoted to elective study. School-wide initiatives—combinations of interdisciplinary classes, field study, contests, and club work—encourage research and provide added focus in the areas of social enterprise, entrepreneurship, global issues, and leadership.

Ultimately, though, HBS' strength resides in the quality of its instructors. One student notes, "HBS is one of the few schools where a large part of the professor's evaluation is based on classroom teaching. The professors at HBS are wonderful teachers and take great interest in their students." As one first-year puts it, "If first semester is representative of the whole experience, I'll be a happy grad. My accounting professor managed to make accounting my favorite class (seems unimaginable!), and I'll definitely take whatever he teaches during the second year of elective courses."

Career and Placement

Harvard Business School maintains a robust career services office all the same, providing a full range of counseling and internship- and career-placement services, with more than 40 career coaches seen by more than 80 percent of the class. There are more than 800 recruiting events on campus each year; of those, 400 focus on full-time employment and the other 400 focus on summer internships. Nearly half of all MBAs remain on the East Coast after graduation, about a quarter of whom take jobs in New York City. Nineteen percent find international placements; 10 percent of the class work in Europe and 6 percent work in Asia.

Student Life and Environment

Life at HBS "is as hectic as you want it to be." One student writes, "My life is pretty much moving along at breakneck speed. I wouldn't want it any other way because the school offers an incredible amount and array of activities, from volunteer consulting to running conferences." Because Harvard University is a magnet for innovative and prestigious thinkers in all disciplines, "This place is like a candy store for a five-year-old; you want

ADMISSIONS CONTACT: MBA ADMISSIONS
ADDRESS: SOLDIERS FIELD, DILLON HOUSE, BOSTON, MA 02163
PHONE: 617-495-6128 • FAX: 617-496-8137
E-MAIL: ADMISSIONS@HBS.EDU • WEBSITE: WWW.HBS.EDU

FINANCIAL FACTS

Annual tuition	$53,500
Fees	$9,788
% of students receiving aid	62
% of first-year students receiving aid	61
% of students receiving grants	46
Average award package	$63,660
Average grant	$30,689
Average student loan debt	$70,731

ADMISSIONS

Admissions Selectivity Rating	99
# of applications received	8,963
% applicants accepted	11
% acceptees attending	89
Range of GMAT	570–790
TOEFL required of international students	Yes
Application fee	$250
International application fee	$250
Application Deadline/Notification	
Round 1:	9/24 / 12/12
Round 2:	1/7 / 3/27
Round 3:	4/8 / 5/15
Deferment available	No
Transfer students accepted	No
Non-fall admissions	No
Need-blind admissions	Yes

to eat a lot more than what's good for you. You can spend all your time on studies, lectures from academics/politicians from all over the world, visiting business leaders, conferences, sports, or the nightlife. A 60-hour day would be appropriate."

Students generally manage to find the time to enjoy "a very social and outgoing environment" at HBS. One married student writes, "Most weekends my husband and I have a choice: the 'college scene' where we can hit up the Harvard or Central Square bars with the singles, or the 'married scene' where we have dinner, play goofy board games, and drink with our 'couple friends.' Either can be a great escape from the other, and both are always a lot of fun!" Close relationships are easy to forge here, as "the section system means you have 89 close friends in the program, which makes learning and being here fun. It also means in the business world there will always be 89 incredibly smart, connected people who will go to bat for me no matter what."

The population of this program is, unsurprisingly, exceptional. As one MBA explains, "The quality of people here is unlike anything I've experienced. For the first time in my adult life, I'm surrounded by people whose interests and abilities fascinate and inspire me. All religions, nationalities, cultures, and sexual orientations exist here, happily, and together. I think Boston cultivates this kind of 'meshing of all thoughts' in such a way that everyone is comfortable, and everyone learns. The city and the school are both comfortable in their own skins, and the students take on that characteristic here."

Admissions

Applicants to Harvard Business School must submit a "complete HBS application portfolio, including personal essays, academics transcripts, and three letters of recommendation." In addition, students must provide scores from the GMAT or GRE, and applicants from non-English-speaking countries must submit scores for either the TOEFL or the IELTS (scores must be no more than two years old). Applications must be submitted online. Academic ability, leadership experience, and unique personal characteristics all figure prominently into the admissions decision. The school notes that "because our MBA curriculum is fast-paced and rigorously analytical, we strongly encourage all applicants to complete introductory courses in quantitative subjects such as accounting, finance, and economics before coming to HBS. For some candidates, we may make admission contingent upon their completing such courses before they enroll." HBS has opened its doors to an innovative new program for college juniors. It's called HBS 2+2: two years of work, then two years of immersion in the Harvard Business School MBA program.

EMPLOYMENT PROFILE

Career Rating	99	Grads Employed by Function	% Avg. Salary
Percent employed at graduation	77	Marketing	(15%) $110,035
Percent employed 3 months after graduation	89	Operations	(1%) $104,400
		Consulting	(32%) $125,923
Average base starting salary	$124,085	Management	(12%) $111,919
		Finance	(34%) $136,982
		Other	(3%) $100,344

HEC MONTRÉAL
MBA PROGRAM

GENERAL INFORMATION

Type of school	Public
Affiliation	No Affiliation
Academic calendar	Aug–Sept

SURVEY SAYS...

Students love Montreal, Quebec,
Cutting-edge classes
Solid preparation in:
General management

STUDENTS

Enrollment of MBA Program	167
% male/female	68/32
% out-of-state	45
% part-time	38
% international	45
Average age at entry	31
Average years work experience at entry	7.0

ACADEMICS

Academic Experience Rating	69
Profs interesting rating	75
Profs accesible rating	77
Student/faculty ratio	2:1
% female faculty	36
% part-time faculty	20

Joint Degrees

Business Law-MBA

Prominent Alumni

Mr. Louis Couillard, MBA 91, President, Pfizer France; Mr. Thierry Vandal, MBA 95, President, Hydro-Quebec; Mr. Jianwei Zhang, MBA 90, President, Bombardier China; Mr. Luc Sicotte, MBA 80, President, Canderel; Mr. Yannis Mallat, MBA 99, President and CEO, Ubisoft

Academics

HEC Montréal is an internationally recognized business school that offers two program options: a renowned one-year full-time program in English or French, or a three-year part-time evening program in French only (though students may take some electives in English in order to improve their language capacity). Many permanent residents take advantage of the intense, cost-effective full-time program to get the "best bang for the buck" and then re-enter the work force with a HEC degree under their belts and a network of alumni to tap into.

This being an "extremely strenuous" one-year intensive program, "life is hectic"; classes are broken down into 6-week periods (followed by exams) and large course projects to be completely almost exclusively in groups. "With only two and a half days of class, I find myself in school at least four days a week and sometimes even seven days a week, needing to do group work or attend information sessions," says a student. Still, the school makes "excellent use of available slots to schedule seminars, meetings and workshops." The administration is "very available, well-run and supportive of student life." They are very clearly "there to make things easier for us," according to a student. Professors are similarly outstanding; faculty members are "almost 100 percent PhDs, with solid work experience" to boot, and are "very accessible and have a lot of business experience."

Career and Placement

A HEC Montréal is a highly visible degree to have (particularly in the international business world), and 88% of graduates find employment within six months of graduation. The school's ties with leading companies make for excellent recruiting options, and there are many opportunities to take part in networking events and clubs—it's just a matter of "finding time around class and other work to do all the activities desired." "It is do-able, it just requires a lot of motivation and time," says an exhausted student. Top recent employers of HEC Montréal graduates include Bombardier, Deloitte, RBC Financial Group, Fidelity investment, and Telefilm Canada.

ADMISSIONS CONTACT: JULIE BENOIT, ADMINISTRATIVE DIRECTOR, MBA PROGRAM
ADDRESS: 3000, CHEMIN DE LA CÔTE-SAINTE-CATHERINE, MONTREAL, QC H3T 2A7
PHONE: 514-340-6957 • FAX: 514-340-7327
E-MAIL: MBA@HEC.CA • WEBSITE: WWW.HEC.CA

Student Life and Environment

This is a highly international group that "comes from all the continents." "I believe we do speak…more that fifteen to twenty different languages," says a student. People are "friendly" and "their experiences are very relevant," so "contribution is very important" and people always "work together and help each other." The life stages of each "very culturally diverse" class runs the gamut—some are married and well-entrenched in careers, some are single and just starting out—but there is "a great social life" and a "collegial atmosphere amongst fellow students and the facilities." The cafeteria, library, and classrooms are "very high quality," which "makes day-to-day life as comfortable as possible," and Montréal is "a great place to live" and spend time in the few free hours a student can squeak out.

Admissions

Admission to the MBA program at HEC Montréal is competitive; the school reports that it is "unable to accept all eligible candidates who apply" because class space is limited. Admissions decisions are based on academic record, professional experience (three years minimum required), standardized test scores (TAGE-MAGE or GMAT), letters of recommendation, interviews and candidates' career objectives. Applicants must provide the school with official transcripts for all post-secondary academic work, a curriculum vitae, and an official score report for standardized tests. The application includes supplementary questions, to be answered in essay form. Applicants to the English-language fulltime intensive program must demonstrate English proficiency via testing (TOEFL, IELTS, or HEC Montréal's own HECTOPE) if their native language is not English. Non-native French speakers applying to the French-only program must complete the Test de français international (an ETS-administered exam). Applicants who are not citizens of Canada must obtain a certificat d'acceptation du Québec (C.A.Q.) and a document attesting to their right to reside in Canada (Student Authorization or Ministerial Permit). The school recommends that accepted students apply for these documents as soon as they receive confirmation of their admission to the program.

FINANCIAL FACTS

Annual tuition (in-state/ out-of-state)	$7,920/$34,100
Cost of books	$2,750
Room & board (on/off-campus)	$20,900
% of students receiving aid	50
% of first-year students receiving aid	50
% of students receiving grants	50
Average award package	$33,000
Average grant	$4,900

ADMISSIONS

Admissions Selectivity Rating	**74**
# of applications received	472
% applicants accepted	53
% acceptees attending	67
TOEFL required of international students	Yes
Application fee	$282
International application fee	$282
Early application deadline	2/1
Early notification date	3/15
Regular application deadline	3/15
Regular application notification	4/15
Deferment available	Yes
Maximum length of deferment	1 year
Transfer students accepted	No
Non-fall admissions	No
Need-blind admissions	Yes

EMPLOYMENT PROFILE			
Career Rating	87	**Grads Employed by Function% Avg. Salary**	
Percent employed at graduation	39	Marketing	(21%) $72,710
Percent employed 3 months after graduation	38	Operations	(5%)
		Consulting	(15%)$78,735
Average base starting salary	$87,980	Management	(16%) $80,805
Primary Source of Full-time Job Acceptances		Finance	(17%) $73,205
School-facilitated activities	(61%)	MIS	(17%) $75,760
Graduate-facilitated activities	(31%)	Other	(9%) $80,500
Unknown	(8%)	**Top 5 Employers Hiring Grads**	
		Bombardier (12), Deloitte (3), RBC Financial Group (2), Fidelity investment (2), Telefilm Canada (2)	

HEC PARIS
HEC MBA PROGRAM

GENERAL INFORMATION
Type of school   Public
Affiliation   No Affiliation

SURVEY SAYS...
Friendly students, Good peer network
Solid preparation in:
Marketing, Accounting,
Presentation skills

STUDENTS
Enrollment of parent
  institution   4,000
Enrollment of MBA Program   214
% male/female   67/33
% part-time   13
% international   86
Average age at entry   30
Average years work experience
  at entry   6.0

ACADEMICS
Academic Experience Rating   **76**
Profs interesting rating   77
Profs accesible rating   80
% female faculty   30

Prominent Alumni
Francois Hollande, President of the
French Republic; Paul Agon, CEO,
L'Oreal; Mercedes Erra, Executive
President, Havas Worldwide; Wayne
Wang, Chairman and CEO of CDP
Group Limited; Hubert Joly, CEO,
Best Buy

Academics

With a reputation in Europe that is "second to none," HEC Paris (located just outside the city) boasts a "stellar" faculty, a world class reputation, a double degree option, and a significant presence in niche areas such as Luxury and Sustainable Business that is not commonly found in other MBA programs. Following a recent curriculum overhall a truly "global and well-rounded view" of business is presented, and the "amazing" method of teaching by case studies and group work is admirably cited by many who go here.

The full-time HEC MBA lasts for sixteen months and is divided into two phases. During the fundamental phase, students gain a solid foundation in the core business subjects; in the customized phase, students choose to complete either a specialization or an international exchange (based upon their personal MBA needs), and either a fieldwork project or "a wide range" of electives. HEC also offers other degrees and programs, and "the entire campus is well integrated," with an interconnection between Masters, MBAs, and Grande École students via the sharing of "a lot of activities" such as sports, festivities, and parties.

The MBA administration team is drawn from various nationalities and "reflects the school's international character"; it is "unlike usual french administrations" in that it is "quick, effective and listens to demands promptly." The school helps students in making visa and other travel arrangements, and "class representatives meet the administration on a regular basis." The dean's office is also "wide open," with specific time slots made available for students.

Career and Placement

The administration has "excellent outreach" to the "vast alumni network" (more than 45,000 graduates), calling upon them to meet with current students and act as guest speakers. Companies come "from all over" to recruit at HEC, and the school has "one of the most widespread and global networks available." "I have contacted lots of alumni with an 80%+ response rate and willingness to help," says a student. Soft skills are highly stressed here, and "professors are very talented at ingraining the skills into the pupils," and there are also career management activities every Friday, which include presentation skills, mock interviews, and CV writing sessions.

A large number of students go on to work outside of France; many students are "multilingual, not just bi-lingual," but english is the only language required to attend HEC, as students say that "with intermediate French you can work almost everywhere." "You need French just to joke around with colleagues. Business is all English," says one. The much-appreciated duration of the program is "the perfect timing for a career change," and many students here have taken a pause from a former job in order to gain international exposure before going back into the work force.

Recent employers of HEC Paris graduates include AT Kearney, McKinsey, Credit Suisse, GE, and Amazon.

ADMISSIONS CONTACT: ADMISSIONS OFFICE
ADDRESS: 1, RUE DE LA RUE DE LA LIBÉRATION, F-78351 JOUY-EN-JOSAS CEDEX, FRANCE
PHONE: +33 (0) 1 39 67 95 63 • FAX: +33 (0)1 39 67 74 65
E-MAIL: ADMISSIONMBA@HEC.FR • WEBSITE: WWW.MBA.HEC.EDU

Student Life and Environment

This is a "very serious and career oriented" group, but the overall climate is "very friendly" and "the level of respect is very high among the participants in the program." Program participants are divided into "intakes" (read: season of admission), and with fifty countries represented at the school, the student body is "very diverse in experience and ethnicity." "The term minority doesn't apply at this school since students from every country/region are a minority." "It is really amazing how much we learn from other students by the simple fact the work teams are made, on purpose, of people whose background have nothing to do with each other's," says another.

The campus is located near the foothills of Jouy-en-Josas and has "a very large green area, a lake and plenty of playgrounds." Coupled with "good and affordable" family housing, the school is a "great place to raise kids in a quiet and healthy environment." "Overall the quality of life here is outstanding if you enjoy living in a 'student bubble' type environment," says a student of the campus that is "somewhat cut off from the city of Paris." Perhaps this accounts for the "great social life" between students, many of whom take weekend trips to other European destinations.

Admissions

HEC admissions process is rigorous. First, each candidate is evaluated based on their standardized test scores and undergraduate performance, as well as quantitative factors as evidenced in their personal recommendations and work experience. After candidates have passed the first stage of review, they must attend two in-person interviews with HEC alumni, HEC professors, or other HEC community members. Each of these interviews begins with a ten-minute presentation by the MBA candidate, followed by a question- and-answer session. Last year's entering class had an average GMAT score of 685, with a range between 650 and 720.

FINANCIAL FACTS

Annual tuition	$62,516
Room & board	
(on/off-campus)	$8,908/$12,503
% of students receiving grants	58
Average grant	$14,717

ADMISSIONS

Admissions Selectivity Rating	86
# of applications received	1,856
% applicants accepted	19
% acceptees attending	61
Average GMAT	685
Range of GMAT	650–720
TOEFL required of	
international students	Yes
Minimum TOEFL	
(paper/computer)	600/250
Application fee	$169
International application fee	$169
Deferment available	Yes
Maximum length	
of deferment	Case-by-case basis
Transfer students accepted	No
Non-fall admissions	Yes
Need-blind admissions	Yes

EMPLOYMENT PROFILE

Career Rating	94	Grads Employed by Function% Avg. Salary	
Percent employed at graduation	67	Marketing	(13%)
Percent employed 3 months		Operations	(3%)
after graduation	90	Consulting	(27%)
Average base starting salary	$109,880	Management	(33%)
Primary Source of Full-time Job Acceptances		Finance	(21%)
School-facilitated activities	(48%)	HR	(0%)
Graduate-facilitated activities	(35%)	MIS	(1%)
Unknown	(17%)	Other	(2%)

Top 5 Employers Hiring Grads
AT Kearney (4), McKinsey (3), Credit Suisse (3), GE (3), Amazon (3)

HHL Leipzig Graduate School of Management

GENERAL INFORMATION

Type of school   Private
Affiliation
Academic calendar   Sept–Mar

SURVEY SAYS...

Friendly students
Solid preparation in:
Finance, Accounting, General
management

STUDENTS

Enrollment of MBA Program	71
% male/female	81/19
% part-time	55
% international	84
Average age at entry	32
Average years work experience at entry	7.0

ACADEMICS

Academic Experience Rating	**80**
Profs interesting rating	78
Profs accesible rating	77
Student/faculty ratio	5:1
% female faculty	15

Prominent Alumni

Eugen Schmalenbach, Professor.
Father of German Cost Accounting;
Stefan Niemeier, Doctor. Partner at
McKinsey & Co.; Andre Schaebel,
Associate Manager, Google; Jack
Artman, Director of M&A Infineon
Technologies; Lukasz Gadowski,
Founder & CEO Spreadshirt

Academics

According to the ecstatic students we spoke with, HHL Leipzig is "the best business school in Germany." While "best" might be difficult to qualify, the school certainly offers a stellar reputation along with an affordable price tag. MBA candidates here greatly appreciate the program's entrepreneurial focus and are also quick to highlight the "great strategy and finance departments." While the vast majority of professors are German, one graduating student assures us that he has "had visiting professors from all over the world." Students also find their teachers "very friendly, helpful, and competent." Additionally, many assert that professors are "flexible" and very "student oriented."

The HHL curriculum is interdisciplinary, focusing on leadership and global experience and takes an integrated management approach. Students must complete a core group of courses to gain a foundation in basic management concepts. They then select a number of electives of their choosing, ensuring expertise in a field of interest. Their education is capped by a master's thesis. Finally, students can either opt to complete the program in 15 months or 18 months.

Career and Placement

Graduates of HHL's MBA program find themselves privy to a great number of career opportunities. Many land employment with a myriad of prominent international consulting, commercial, industrial, and financial firms. A large range of companies regularly recruit at HHL for both internships and permanent positions. Impressively, 100 percent of German students find employment within six months of graduation, and 95 percent of international applicants gain employment. The Career Services Office helps to facilitate this process by providing a variety of resources to their MBA candidates. Students can attend company presentations, interview training, and CV and cover letter writing workshops. They can also take assessment tests and receive assistance with career path modeling. There are also a handful of on-campus recruiting events, along with career fairs. However, despite this, some students still feel that Career Services could "improve helping international students to find jobs in and outside of Germany."

Employers that frequently hire HHL Leipzig graduates include Allianz AG, Amazon, Arthur D. Little, Bain & Company, Barclays Capital, BASF, Bayer AG, Bertelsmann, BMW, Booz & Co., Bosch, Citigroup, Deutsche Bahn AG, Ernst & Young, Henkel KgaA, Horváth & Partner, JP Morgan, KPMG, Lufthansa Cargo, McKinsey, Mercedez Benz, Morgan Stanley, Nestlé, OC & C Strategy Consultants, Porsche, Procter & Gamble, PwC, Roland Berger, SMC, Stern Stewart, The Boston Consulting Group, Axel Springer, Hitachi, arvato, Deloitte, Infosys, eBay, adidas.

Student Life and Environment

MBA students at HHL are generally fairly impressed with their classmates. Although they can be "competitive," they show a high level of "intellectual curiosity" and are "eager to contribute to team work." Not surprisingly, the school manages to net a "diverse" student body and one that is "open to different people and cultures." Additionally, students define their peers as "motivated" and "flexible" and people who "seek a challenge." The program yields a wide age range, and students are generally anywhere from 24 to 40 years old. However, the average age is 29, and most have around five years of work experience. Despite the diversity, most agree that a "family environment" permeates the campus.

ADMISSIONS CONTACT: MARGARITA SETSKA, ADMISSIONS OFFICER
ADDRESS: JAHNALLEE 59, LEIPZIG, GERMANY 04109
PHONE: +49 341~ 9851 734 • FAX: +49 341 - 9851 731
E-MAIL: MARGARITA.SETSKA@HHL.DE • WEBSITE: WWW.HHL.DE

Academics at HHL are demanding, and students "spend many hours at school." If they aren't in class, students can often be found attending "lectures, networking in the cafeteria, or slaving over group work." Of course, even these industrious souls need to kick back every now and again, and many classmates frequently "gather to have some drinks and share thoughts on business, economics, and politics."

Beautiful Leipzig also provides great distractions from business theory. A mere hour from Berlin by train, Leipzig is a cosmopolitan city in its own right. Considering that Bach, Mendelssohn, Wagner, and Goethe all lived there, it's no surprise that there is still a thriving arts scene. The city is home to the Gewandhaus Orchestra; the world famous St. Thomas Choir; and a variety of museums, cafes, restaurants, and nightclubs. And with more than 30,000 students, it's no wonder that this is a great place to study.

Admissions

Admissions officers at HHL Leipzig Graduate School of Management are on the hunt for applicants who demonstrate a global outlook and international experience. Exposure to other cultures will be paramount for any successful candidate. Applicants should have an undergraduate degree or the equivalent academic qualification and a minimum of two years of professional experience prior to starting the program. In addition to transcripts, the admissions committee also closely examines GMAT scores, curriculum vitae (maximum three pages), documents confirming employment, a motivation letter, and two letters of recommendation. Applicants who reside in countries that do not offer the GMAT may instead submit GRE scores as a substitute. Further, students who hail from non-English speaking countries must prove proficiency through either the TOEFL or IELTS. However, there are exceptions. Non-native English speakers do not have to submit test scores if they either earned an undergraduate or postgraduate degree from an English-speaking program or if they have lived or worked in an English speaking country for the last two years. Finally, it should be noted that some non-EU residents face an earlier application deadline due to visa requirements. This does not affect applicants from Australia, Israel, Japan, the United States, Canada, and New Zealand.

FINANCIAL FACTS

Annual tuition	$23,400
Fees	$277
Cost of books	$150
Room & board	$6,500
% of students receiving aid	30
% of first-year students receiving aid	45
% of students receiving grants	15
Average award package	$30,000
Average grant	$10,000
Average loan	$30,000

ADMISSIONS

Admissions Selectivity Rating	82
# of applications received	124
% applicants accepted	52
% acceptees attending	49
Average GMAT	610
Range of GMAT	510–720
TOEFL required of international students	Yes
Minimum TOEFL (paper/computer)	580/250
Application fee	$0
International application fee	$0
Regular application deadline	6/30
Regular application notification	7/20
Deferment available	Yes
Maximum length of deferment	1 year
Transfer students accepted	Yes
Transfer application policy: Double Degree agreements with international partners	
Non-fall admissions	Yes
Need-blind admissions	Yes

EMPLOYMENT PROFILE

Career Rating	70	Grads Employed by Function% Avg. Salary	
Percent employed at graduation	20	Consulting	(24%)
Percent employed 3 months after graduation	40	Management	(34%)
		Finance	(7%)
Average base starting salary	$93	MIS	(14%)
Primary Source of Full-time Job Acceptances		Other	(21%)
School-facilitated activities	(76%)	**Top 5 Employers Hiring Grads**	
Graduate-facilitated activities	(33%)	Robert Bosch (1), eBay (1), Porsche (1), Vodafone (1), Deloitte (1)	

HOFSTRA UNIVERSITY
FRANK G. ZARB SCHOOL OF BUSINESS

Academics

"Located on Long Island...near New York City," Hofstra University is "a growing school that is ever improving its facilities and academic standing." This location "is perfect" and provides "a quiet learning condition" for business students. The proximity to America's largest city provides students with easy access to internships and post-MBA work connections. The Frank G. Zarb School of Business "has a good reputation, especially in marketing field," and is well-known in the tri-state area. Like nearby NYC, Hofstra's student body is very "diverse" with a large number of international students, especially from China. Academics are focused on post-school success. "Teamwork, networking, and mentorships are encouraged and integral parts of the MBA program," one student explains. A Retail major reports that "professors encourage all of us to bring WSJ articles that we think are related to the course topic and we [talk] about real world examples."

While the "administration is doing its best to improve the program and enter the top 100 rankings," by far the most common student complaint was the "terrible" administration. "It is impossible to get a hold of any advisors and when you do it takes another two weeks to get answers," one student opines. "Registering for classes is difficult," and "the main office is not staffed properly to support all the students." On the other hand, students give high marks to the "friendly, rigorous, and professional" faculty. Hofstra professors are "obviously subject matter experts" with "strong background[s] in their professional fields." Most are "accessible outside of class for further help." "The professors here tend to have extensive industry experience, and many are based out of NYC," giving students a direct connection to the gigantic business community in America's greatest city. "My academic experience has been above expectations," one happy student says. "Overall, Hofstra University administration and professors show an active interest in the success of each student," another explains.

Career and Placement

Like most things in life, business success is all about location, location, location. Students report there is no better location for MBAs than NYC. "Having the NYC network with the lower cost of living in suburban Long Island is a boon for students starting their career path," one student explains. "[The] Frank G. Zarb School of Business has a great reputation with numerous connections to companies as well as great location and proximity to NYC." The "access to industry leaders as teachers in their given field" is a great benefit for students after graduation. "Many of my professors are in prominent positions with local employers and government," a Hospital Finance major proclaims. "This is very helpful in relating real-world experience as well as being a valuable networking tool." "Hofstra has a strong affiliation with my hospital system" and an especially "strong connection to North Shore-LIJ Health system." This is huge help to "the Healthcare Administration MBA program as well as the MHA program."

Hofstra's career center "really cares about the future career plan of every MBA student." In 2012, the average mean base salary was around $67,000. Eighty-eight percent of graduates found work nearby in the Northeast region. By far the most common landing spot was Financial Services, with nearly 60 percent of graduates finding work in that industry.

ADMISSIONS CONTACT: CAROL DRUMMER, DEAN FOR GRADUATE ADMISSIONS
ADDRESS: 126 HOFSTRA UNIVERSITY, 105 MEMORIAL HALL, HEMPSTEAD, NY 11549
PHONE: 800-463-7672 • FAX: 516-463-4664
E-MAIL: GRADSTUDENT@HOFSTRA.EDU • WEBSITE: WWW.HOFSTRA.EDU/BUSINESS

Student Life and Environment

"Located on 240 acres of land," Hofstra's campus is a "quiet place. Not like a school in Manhattan." However, the student body does "represent the melting pot that is New York." "Our MBA program is very international," students say, even reporting that "international students outnumber domestic students" with "fully 50 percent [coming] from China." The student body is "friendly, but competitive" and students find their peers to be "smart, driven individuals who have clear career goals." Campus life is "pretty vibrant" as "Hofstra is big enough to provide a lot of activities and resources for students." "The utilities at school are really useful, and students can access to these utilities easily and free," one student explains. "Besides, there are many activities for students to attend" and overall campus life is "flexible and interesting."

Admissions

Most of Hofstra's graduate business programs begin accepting applications in the fall or spring term. Students are evaluated based on their undergraduate academic performance, professional experience, leadership potential, letters of recommendation, and GMAT or GRE scores. The average GPA for the 2012 class was 3.23, and the average GMAT score was 584. High-achieving students have the option of applying as an Honors Scholar, a title that will be conferred at graduation.

FINANCIAL FACTS

Annual tuition	$19,440
Fees	$970
Cost of books	$4,165
Room & board (on/off-campus)	$16,270/$16,760
% of students receiving aid	75
% of first-year students receiving aid	76
% of students receiving grants	62
Average award package	$15,141
Average grant	$5,608

ADMISSIONS

Admissions Selectivity Rating	74
# of applications received	2,136
% applicants accepted	68
% acceptees attending	30
Average GMAT	584
Range of GMAT	530–640
Average GPA	3.23
TOEFL required of international students	Yes
Minimum TOEFL (paper/computer)	550/213
International application fee	$75
Deferment available	Yes
Maximum length of deferment	1 year
Transfer students accepted	Yes
Transfer application policy: Number of transferable credits is limited to a maximum of 9 credits.	
Non-fall admissions	Yes
Need-blind admissions	Yes

EMPLOYMENT PROFILE

Career Rating	85		
Percent employed at graduation	33		
Percent employed 3 months after graduation	47		
Average base starting salary	$66,938		

Primary Source of Full-time Job Acceptances

School-facilitated activities	9(43%)
Graduate-facilitated activities	12(57%)

Grads Employed by Function% Avg. Salary

Marketing	(12%) $47,000
Operations	(6%) $70,000
Consulting	(6%)$68,000
Management	(12%) $76,976
Finance	(53%) $73,000
MIS	(6%) $50,000
Other	(6%) $45,000

Top 5 Employers Hiring Grads

Openlink (4), Pricewaterhouse Coopers (4), Northshore LIJ Health Systems (3), Ernst & Young (2), Bank of America / Merrill Lynch (1)

HONG KONG U. OF SCIENCE AND TECHNOLOGY
HKUST BUSINESS SCHOOL

Academics

Business students looking to catch a ride on the Asian economic boom would do well to consider The Hong Kong University of Science and Technology (HKUST), the "top MBA school in Asia" with a "strategic location at the heart of Asia." "The focus of the program is on the region," and the program is in "a perfect location to leverage Asia's booming economy." "Ever since my studies, I have had the ambition to prepare myself for a career in the Asian region," one student says, explaining the decision to attend HKUST. HKUST employs a "very strong teaching facility in finance" and an "intense academic atmosphere." "The MBA office has some major gaps to cover, but it is clearly trying to improve itself to better serve the MBA students."

Academics at HKUST can be intense, and the "workload is a killer." "We need 100+ hours a week" to complete homework, classes, group projects, discussion, and club activities, according to one student. Although students also note that "the school is very supportive." The Administration "must be the friendliest and helpful bunch of people I have ever met." On the other hand, "the MBA office is not very efficient."

Despite the problems students have with the MBA office, they are much happier with the professors. "Overall the school has brilliant teachers that are balanced between academia and business experience," offering a "nice blend of practitioners from the East, business professionals from the West, and academics." "I was initially worried about joining a business school based in Hong Kong because of perceived language barriers," one student explains. "Thankfully, I never faced such a challenge because all the professors were educated from the top business schools in the United States, and as a result, their communication skills are exceptionally good." Some of the "business leaders in Asia" who the school boasts as faculty include WalMart China's former president, PepsiCo Asia's former president, and the GM of Hutchinson Whampoa's Investment and Head Legal Counsel.

Career and Placement

"Hong Kong is the best transition point to the China market," and HKUST provides lots of help for students to get in on the action. "As a European with work experience in North America, I wanted to become part of the Asian growth story," one student says. "What better place could there be than the leading Asian business school!" HKUST takes students on trips to different cities and even countries in the region, such as Beijing or Singapore, to get students acquainted with the Asian style of business. The business school also stations representatives in Beijing, Shanghai, and Shenzhen. The HKUST career team constantly offers workshops, networking opportunities, one-on-one career coaching sessions, and many other services to help students begin careers.

HKUST is best "known for finance," and 46 percent of graduates accept a job in finance or accounting. Some students say HKUST "needs to improve on other career tracks." For example, there are "very few courses on marketing." Students also wish the school had a better brand recognition outside of Asia. "I really think the key for the school is to build a stronger brand," one student says. "I heard from exchange students from U.S. top schools that our classes are comparable." Ninety-seven percent of students found employment within three months of graduation, and their average base salary was $93,974 in U.S. dollars. Some companies that have recruited from HKUST include ANZ, Banco Santander, Barclays, Cisco, Citi, DuPont, Google, IMS Healthcare, J.P. Morgan, Li & Fung, LinkedIN, Microsoft, Nomura, Samsung, and Walmart.

ADDRESS: CLEARWATER BAY, HKUST KOWLOON, HONG KONG
PHONE: 852-2358-7539 • FAX: 852-2705-9596
E-MAIL: MBA@UST.HK • WEBSITE: WWW.MBA.UST.HK

FINANCIAL FACTS

Annual tuition	$69,900
Cost of books	$1,300
Room & board	$5,800

ADMISSIONS

Admissions Selectivity Rating	**76**
Average GMAT	647
Range of GMAT	600–700
TOEFL required of international students	Yes
Minimum TOEFL (paper/computer)	600/250
Deadline/Notification	
Round 1:	11/13 / 2/8
Round 2:	1/13 / 4/11
Round 3:	3/13 / 6/6
Deferment available	Yes
Maximum length of deferment	1 year
Transfer students accepted	No
Non-fall admissions	No

Student Life and Environment

HKUST boasts a very diverse student body, as the school "attracts students from all over the world. On any given day, we have at least around 15 to 20 nationalities represented in class." "Ninety-eight percent of students are from overseas," and the school is a veritable "United Nations." This means students approach school in different ways. "Westerners are very liberal" at HKUST, while "there are many students from China, who have a somewhat more conservative approach." The school has "more than ten clubs and often has different activities," which makes "life at HKUST really interesting and fascinating." Students like to "participate in different social events, like doing charity work, mingling with students of other schools, and having dinner with alumni." "Half of the students are more into social networking, and half are not very sociable," suggests one student. Students spend most of their time doing work, and "sleeping fewer than five hours is common" in the fall.

"The campus is amazing" and "located next to the bay," offering great views from dorm room windows. "Sports facilities available are great, including soccer pitch, track, in/outdoor pools, in/outdoor basketball, tennis, ping pong, squash, weight lifting, wall climbing, volleyball, and badminton." Some students say dorm "facilities are worn out," and business students should try to live off campus. "The student housing is meant for undergraduates. There are only two bathrooms shared by the whole floor." Living quarters are usually small and austere, so "all students should live off campus."

Admissions

Students applying to HKUST need to have an undergraduate degree and at least two years of work experience. The average GMAT score for accepted students is between 610 and 736. Having an interest in Asian culture and Asian business markets doesn't hurt either.

EMPLOYMENT PROFILE

Career Rating	77	Grads Employed by Function	% Avg. Salary
Percent employed 3 months after graduation	97	Marketing	(4%)
		Operations	(4%)
		Consulting	(16%)
		Management	(11%)
		Finance	(50%)
		Other	(10%)

HOWARD UNIVERSITY
SCHOOL OF BUSINESS

GENERAL INFORMATION
Type of school   Private
Affiliation   No Affiliation
Academic calendar   Semester

SURVEY SAYS...
Students love Washington, D.C.,
Friendly students, Good social scene,
Good peer network
Solid preparation in:
Operations, Communication/
interpersonal skills,
Presentation skills

STUDENTS
Enrollment of parent
  institution   11,115
Enrollment of MBA Program   95
% male/female   42/58
% out-of-state   90
% part-time   32
% underrepresented minority   80
% international   20
Average age at entry   26
Average years work experience
  at entry   3.9

ACADEMICS
Academic Experience Rating   **84**
Profs interesting rating   77
Profs accesible rating   84
Student/faculty ratio   3:1
% female faculty   28
% underrepresented minority
  faculty   89
% part-time faculty   8

Joint Degrees
JD/MBA, 4 years; MDiv/MBA;
MD/MBA, 5 years; DDS/MBA;
PharmD/MBA; BBA/MBA
Accounting; BSE/MBA Engineering

Prominent Alumni
Van Andrew Ewing II, Managing
Partner, New York Life Insurance
Company; Sheila Morgan-Johnson,
Chief Investment Officer and Chief
Operating Officer, District of
Columbia Retirement Board

Academics

Students at Howard University School of Business feel confident that their degree will earn them the right position after graduation. Job placement is one of the school's greatest strengths, and "with the economy in the state that it is, it is imperative that you attend a university that will help you get employment." An education at Howard provides students with "access to top-level managers within the business world and...out-of-class preparedness for the real world of business." "The school has a far-reaching network and reputation, and also provides opportunities to its students that are on par with top 20 MBA programs."

Many know Howard University as the "most prestigious African American University in the country." Being a part of the school's "strong legacy" is important to many and also a source of pride to carry the Howard "brand name." The School of Business "provides a wealth of opportunities to students," and perhaps some of the "best opportunities for minority students." "From CEO lectures, Fortune 500 companies recruiting daily on campus, and various opportunities abroad, the program is able to provide a well-rounded MBA experience."

"Howard University School of Business is a very unique learning environment." "Everyone in the program is striving for excellence." A student explains the value of her classmate's energy and excitement towards learning. "I look forward to every class because it's...intellectually stimulating." Intimate classes add to the quality of learning and overall strength of the program. "Due to the size of the program the students are extremely close and supportive." High quality learning is possible thanks to professors that are "extremely personable and more than willing to go out of their way to assist students." Outside of classes, professors "are always approachable and are actively interested in how their subject directly relates to the students internships and future career goals so they can do their best to prepare students for their bright futures."

Thankfully, the obstacle of cost is surpassed for many here as "Howard provides a significant amount of financial assistance to its students." "When you consider that some high-performing students are able to earn half or full tuition coverage, there is even more value added to the degree." "The academic experience can be difficult to balance at times as most students are involved in some form of extracurricular activities." What makes all the hard work and money Howard students spend worthwhile are the "high returns expected from the investment." With all the "access to networks and recruiters, and global travel opportunities, the program does deliver considerable value for an MBA."

Although students would mostly agree that "school administration have an invested interest in our success," several opined that they "could be more efficient." Other areas that students thought could use improvement include, "technology capabilities of classroom[s] and aging buildings."

Career and Placement

Many students appreciate career services for their "outstanding program" and "great networking opportunities." One student says these services are "the best I've seen around, they create opportunities after opportunities." Not only do they do "a fantastic job placing their students with internships and careers," they also have in place a "strong alumni network." Students receive "tons of emails from the University staff about internship and full-time employment opportunities." They report "plenty of social and networking opportunities," and appreciate the "several programs [organized] by the school to develop [their] leadership skills." These include required monthly leadership

ADMISSIONS CONTACT: MBA ADMISSIONS, OFFICE OF GRADUATE PROGRAMS
ADDRESS: 2600 SIXTH STREET, NW, SUITE 236, WASHINGTON, DC 20059
PHONE: 202-806-1725 • FAX: 202-986-4435
E-MAIL: MBA_BSCHOOL@HOWARD.EDU • WEBSITE: WWW.BSCHOOL.HOWARD.EDU

development workshops "that help with job preparation, search, placement, and achievement," as well as "an executive lecture series every semester where the CEOs of large corporations come and speak with us and we are able to network with them."

Besides Howard's "corporate connections" and "resources available in Washington, D.C.," students are "impressed with the variety of recruiters that visit the school with a sincere interest in the MBA students (particularly in the Supply Chain Management program)." Top Businesses recently hiring Howard graduate students include Intel, Dell, AT&T,WW Grainger, Inc., and Bank of America Merrill Lynch. "The recruitment here for minority talent is unparalleled." This student definitely agrees and declares, "I am confident that I will secure the job that want when I graduate."

Student Life and Environment

"The life as a graduate student in Howard University is filled with work as well as fun." The school offers a good amount of "student activities and community involvement." The student body consists of a "creative, organized, and motivated" bunch who are eager to "change the future of business." This dedication shows by their commitment to serve "on Boards and associations throughout DC, MD and VA"; and even though, "there is a healthy competition among classmates," it does not deter from the "family" environment that exists around the school. "We are all focused on being successful but just as interested in doing what we can to ensure our classmates are making the right connections and prepared to succeed as well. We all want our class to continue Howard's legacy of producing competent and successful minority students."

Admissions

Along with an application, prospective students must submit GMAT scores, official transcripts for all undergraduate and graduate course work, three letters of recommendation from at least one academic and one professional supervisor, a personal statement describing the applicant's abilities, experiences, and goals in pursuing the MBA, undergraduate GPA, and proof of at least two years of significant post-collegiate professional or managerial experience. Applicants must have completed business or applied calculus at the undergraduate college level in order to be admitted. International applicants must also submit a Statement of Financial Resources.

FINANCIAL FACTS

Annual tuition	$31,290
Fees	$1,233
Cost of books	$4,045
Room & board (on/off-campus)	$21,223/$21,266
% of students receiving aid	95
% of first-year students receiving aid	90
% of students receiving grants	63
Average award package	$34,653
Average grant	$21,935
Average loan	$29,459
Average student loan debt	$34,993

ADMISSIONS

Admissions Selectivity Rating	84
# of applications received	115
% applicants accepted	44
% acceptees attending	69
Average GMAT	542
Range of GMAT	460–630
Average GPA	3.05
TOEFL required of international students	Yes
Minimum TOEFL (paper/computer)	550/213
Application fee	$65
International application fee	$65
Early application deadline	11/15
Early notification date	1/1
Regular application deadline	4/1
Regular application notification	5/1

Application Deadline/Notification

Round 1:	11/15 / 1/1
Round 2:	2/1 / 3/1
Round 3:	4/1 / 5/1
Round 4:	5/15 / 6/1
Deferment available	Yes
Maximum length of deferment	2 Semesters
Transfer students accepted	Yes

Transfer application policy: Must meet Howard's MBA Program Admission Criteria; can only transfer a maximum of 6.0 credit hours from an AACSB-accredited Graduate Business Program.

Non-fall admissions	Yes
Need-blind admissions	Yes

EMPLOYMENT PROFILE

Career Rating	94	Grads Employed by Function% Avg. Salary		
Percent employed at graduation	55	Marketing	(9%)	$91,500
Percent employed 3 months after graduation	77	Operations	(26%)	$87,333
		Consulting	(22%)	$93,000
Average base starting salary	$92,452	Management	(9%)	$110,000
Primary Source of Full-time Job Acceptances		Finance	(34%)	$94,000
School-facilitated activities	18(75%)	Top 5 Employers Hiring Grads		
Graduate-facilitated activities	6(25%)	Department of Treasury(2), JPMorgan Chase (2), Marsh & McLennan (2), Alcoa (1), Unilever (1)		

IAE Business School
Management and Business School

Academics

Located in Pilar, Argentina, IAE Business School's intensive MBA programs maintain an "excellent reputation in Argentina and throughout Latin America," a strong global focus throughout the curriculum, and "regionally-related" course material for those interested in Latin American business. The rigorous, efficient, bilingual program (classes are taught in Spanish and English) has been honed over time to provide a quality education to its students. As the school's website states, the one-year MBA program "is the result of the 25-year experience IAE has acquired in providing part-time Executive MBA programs and the contributions of many years of delivering full-time programs supplied by the Harvard Business School and the IESE of Barcelona." IAE's "intensive" program combines 1800 hours of campus study, with a daily schedule that "runs from 9:00 A.M. to 6:00 P.M., with only a two-hour break in the middle of the day (from 12:30 P.M. to 2.30 P.M.) for sports and eating." The program begins with a computer-based "leveling course," during which students are reacquainted with fundamental quantitative skills in statistics, mathematics, and accounting. After completing these basic proficiencies, students begin the extensive core curriculum, which focuses on three areas: "technical skills in marketing, finance, etc.; critical thinking skills that teach you new ways to approach both professional problems and personal problems; and teamwork skills." While required material is extensive, the school also offers several elective courses, as well as a Team Building and Outdoor Activities module, designed to promote problem-solving skills in a playful environment. Throughout the MBA, international business is emphasized, and the school's highly international student body adds depth and perspective to the school's global focus.

Students speak highly of the program, describing their professors as "excellent." Friendly and student-oriented, "Most of them have PhDs, and they have a lot of patience. They always are able to help you inside and outside the class." A student adds, "They are always available to answer the questions or [have] meetings to study some specific and interesting topics." The program runs smoothly, and this ease is especially important given the amount of work piled on students; no one here has time to wade through bureaucratic red tape. As one MBA notes, "The administration provides exceptional service. It is well prepared for the needs of its classmates: Everything we need is available for us." And perhaps most important, "IAE has very good contacts with businesses in Latin America, and a very important aspect is that it provides us with internal and external mentors."

Career and Placement

The Career Services Department at IAE works with students and companies to facilitate recruitment and placement. Among other services, they offer mentoring programs, on-campus interviews, individual and group career counseling, and career development workshops. Despite the school's international focus, students report that "the department is underdeveloped, especially in the international job market." The alumni network, on the other hand, "is unbelievable," according to students; one reports, "I could speak to many important executives from the best companies of my country because they were alumni." Today, IAE graduates are working in diverse countries, including Germany, Malaysia, the United States, Mexico, and Puerto Rico. Employers who have worked with IAE include Alto Parana SA, Hewlett Packard Argentina, Banco Galicia, Belise & Asociados, Bodegas Lagarde, CCBASA, Citibank NA, Fiat Argentina, Ernst & Young, Google, GE Capital Cia, Global Praxis, Hart Casares, Johnson & Johnson Medical SA, KPMG Consultores, Kraft Food Argentina, McKinsey & Company, Nestlé Argentina SA, Novartis Argentina SA, and The Walt Disney Company.

Address: Casilla de Correo no. 49 - Mariano Acosta s/n y Ruta Nac. 8 (B162WWA) Pilar
Buenos Aires, Argentina
Phone: 011 54.2322.48.1000 • Fax: 011 54.2322.48.1050
E-mail: mba@iae.edu.ar • Website: www.iae.edu.ar

FINANCIAL FACTS

Annual tuition	$17,000

ADMISSIONS

Admissions Selectivity Rating	**84**
# of applications received	111
% applicants accepted	57
% acceptees attending	76
Average GMAT	618
TOEFL required of international students	Yes
Minimum TOEFL	230

Student Life and Environment

IAE's campus "is located in Pilar, 50 kilometers from the capital" of Argentina, in a beautiful setting "with a lot of trees, grass, and greenery everywhere." The "campus building and facilities are incredible," and, in the surrounding community, "you can find everything near the campus: a mall, restaurants, supermarkets, movies, gas stations, etc." Campus facilities include areas where students "can play soccer, tennis, and rugby during the two-hour lunch break." Big-city life isn't too far off, as "the campus is one hour away from Buenos Aires." Students note, however, that "since IAE's program is a one-year MBA, the workload is so heavy that there is very little time to do activities outside the classroom." Classes convene from 9:00 A.M. to 6:00 P.M.; most students "study until 9:00 P.M., then have some dinner with friends," and then call it a day. Despite the rigors of the program, "the nice environment, people, and landscape make you enjoy every moment."

Drawing a largely international student body, only about 54 percent of IAE's MBA students are Argentine; the remaining 46 percent of students come from other parts of Latin America, Europe, and the United States. Students are drawn from all sectors, including marketing, banking, consulting, engineering, services, and even agriculture. Students are "very different but open-minded," and universally described as "very supportive" of their classmates. In addition to their professional prowess, most "have great senses of humor, don't hesitate to help one another, and enjoy hanging out."

Admissions

Experience is very important to IAE Austral Universidad. Applicants to the full-time MBA program at IAE must have at least three years of post-undergraduate work experience and be at least 25 years old. The admissions department requires all of the following materials: official transcripts for all postsecondary academic work; an official GMAT score report with a minimum score of 550; a resume; personal essays; letters of recommendation; a completed application form; and, for students whose first language is not English, a minimum TOEFL score of 570 (paper-based test) or 230 (computer-based test). IAE also offers its own skills exam which can be taken in lieu of the GMAT and which can be taken by appointment in Buenos Aires.

EMPLOYMENT PROFILE			
Career Rating	72	**Grads Employed by Function**	**% Avg. Salary**
Average base starting salary	$17,000	Marketing	(13%)
		Operations	(6%)
		Consulting	(11%)
		Finance	(4%)
		HR	(4%)

IDAHO STATE UNIVERSITY
COLLEGE OF BUSINESS

GENERAL INFORMATION

Type of school	Public
Affiliation	No Affiliation
Academic calendar	Semester

SURVEY SAYS...
Friendly students, Happy students
Solid preparation in:
Accounting, General management

STUDENTS

Enrollment of parent institution	13,977
Enrollment of MBA Program	110
% male/female	74/26
% part-time	52
% underrepresented minority	8
% international	15
Average age at entry	30
Average years work experience at entry	0.0

ACADEMICS

Academic Experience Rating	**78**
Profs interesting rating	82
Profs accesible rating	83
Student/faculty ratio	23:1
% female faculty	20
% underrepresented minority faculty	2
% part-time faculty	0

Academics

The College of Business at Idaho State University offers MBA classes in two locations: on its main campus in Pocatello and at a satellite location in Idaho Falls. Students love the convenience and the cost of the program; many laud the "great return on investment" represented by an ISU MBA. One student notes that the Idaho Falls location is "very convenient for professionals working for or with Idaho National Laboratory." Evening-only classes at the location make the program even more convenient (the school notes that some emphasis areas require students to take some daytime classes).

"Class sizes are small and the professors are always available outside of class" at ISU, where "Everyone is on a first-name basis with the professors and the atmosphere is laid back yet still professional." One student writes, "I have been pleasantly surprised with the quality of teachers and students that are a part of this program. I feel that the teachers genuinely care about the success of the students and their understanding and application of the material. The students come with years of experience and willingly and beneficially contribute to the material taught." The curriculum here, while "challenging, is backed by a supportive network of professors and students. Relying on help outside of class in the way of face-to-face meetings and study groups makes the experience much more successful."

ISU offers a general MBA as well as MBAs with emphasis areas in accounting, computer information systems, management, marketing, finance, and health care administration. Students tell us that "finance and accounting are very strong at Idaho State University." As for the future, students report that the administration is "doing a good job of moving the university towards a good goal—a medical school—which is what they were hired to do." Look for the health care administration segment of this program to grow as the school continues in this direction.

Career and Placement

MBAs at Idaho State University receive career services from the Career Development Center, which serves all undergraduates, graduates, and alumni at ISU. The office provides career counseling, career testing, internship referrals, student employment opportunities, alumni connections, workshops in job search skills, resume review, on-campus interviews, and job fairs. Students tell us that the school needs to "attract recruiters from world-class companies for all areas of emphasis. It seems like the accounting department does well but that other areas of emphasis are lacking these contacts." One MBA observes: "There are not that many recruiters from outside of southeast Idaho at job fairs. This is especially a problem for the MBA students who most likely will be looking for jobs prior to and immediately after graduation."

Student Life and Environment

Idaho State University's main campus is located in Pocatello, a city with a population of about 50,000. ON Semiconductor, Alliance Title and Escrow, and the university are among the city's largest employers. Students tout the "small-town feel of the town," noting the "low crime rate and conservative values." The location provides easy access to outdoor recreation, and "most people enjoy outdoor activities on the weekend such as skiing, snowmobiling, hiking, etc." The school also offers MBA classes in Idaho Falls, a city whose motto "Where Great Adventures Begin" highlights its proximity to such attractions as Grand Teton National Park and Yellowstone National Park. Idaho National Laboratory is by far the city's biggest employer with about 7,500 employees. Healthcare, education, government, and retail are the city's other primary employers.

ADMISSIONS CONTACT: SAM PETERSON, MBA DIRECTOR
ADDRESS: STOP 8020, 921 S 8TH AVE, POCATELLO, ID 83209
PHONE: 208-282-2966 • FAX: 208-236-4367
E-MAIL: PETESAM@ISU.EDU • WEBSITE: COB.ISU.EDU

Students appreciate that "ISU is very facilitating to married families," with "an incredibly family-friendly campus. There's plenty of family housing on campus and a huge day care center." Their only complaint is that "facilities are outdated." "The building is slightly in need of renovation," one student explains. Another points out that "The university has taken steps to modernize the college's building and its miscellaneous resources such as computer labs and information networks," but even she concedes that a facilities overhaul is in order.

"Most students are non-traditional students" here. This "is true of the undergraduate classes and the graduate ones. Since most students have spouses and children, college life is not as exciting as one may expect." MBA candidates "generally have at least two or three years of work experience since receiving their undergraduate degree" and are "focused and serious about learning." They tend to be typically conservative Idahoans, but "a politically liberal transplant from a West Coast city" in their midst assures that "it was easy to form great relationships with my conservative classmates."

Admissions

Applicants to the CoB MBA program at Idaho State University must apply for admission to the university Graduate School and must also meet additional CoB admissions requirements. A completed application includes: official transcripts for all post-secondary academic work; an official GMAT score report; a current resume; and two letters of recommendation. A score of at least 1150 under the formula [(200 x GPA for final 60 semester hours of undergraduate work) + GMAT score] is required for consideration; those meeting this requirement are not guaranteed admission. Applicants holding a master's degree from an accredited institution may have the GMAT requirement waived. International applicants must also submit a statement of financial support and an official score report for either the TOEFL or the IELTS. Minimum required scores: 80, Internet-based test; 213 with a 21 on Section 1, computer-based test; 550 with a score of at least 55 on Section 1, paper-based test; or 6.5, IELTS.

FINANCIAL FACTS

Annual tuition (in-state/ out-of-state)	$5,848/$15,650
Cost of books	$1,000
Room & board	$7,500
Average grant	$0
Average loan	$0

ADMISSIONS

Admissions Selectivity Rating	74
# of applications received	73
% applicants accepted	75
% acceptees attending	60
Average GMAT	540
Range of GMAT	480–580
Average GPA	3.46
TOEFL required of international students	Yes
Minimum TOEFL (paper/computer)	550/213
International application fee	$55
Regular application deadline	7/1
Regular application notification	7/7
Deferment available	Yes
Maximum length of deferment	2 yrs
Transfer students accepted	Yes
Transfer application policy: 9 credits max, from an AACSB program.	
Non-fall admissions	Yes
Need-blind admissions	No

EMPLOYMENT PROFILE	
Career Rating	77
Percent employed at graduation	47
Average base starting salary	$59,000

ILLINOIS INSTITUTE OF TECHNOLOGY
STUART SCHOOL OF BUSINESS

GENERAL INFORMATION
Type of school	Private
Affiliation	No Affiliation
Academic calendar	Semester

SURVEY SAYS...
Students love Chicago, IL, Smart classrooms
Solid preparation in:
Finance

STUDENTS
Enrollment of parent institution	7,787
Enrollment of MBA Program	132
% male/female	63/37
% out-of-state	0
% part-time	24
% underrepresented minority	4
% international	90
Average age at entry	24

ACADEMICS
Academic Experience Rating	**78**
Profs interesting rating	79
Profs accesible rating	77
Student/faculty ratio	19:1
% female faculty	18
% underrepresented minority faculty	11
% part-time faculty	24

Joint Degrees
MBA/JD, 4–6 years; MBA/MS, 3–4 years; MBA/MPA, 3–4 years; MBA/MSF, 3–4 years; MDes/MBA, 3–4 years; JD/MS, 4–6 years; JD/MPA, 4–6 years

Prominent Alumni
John Calamos, President/Chief Investment Officer/Founder, Calamos Asset Management; Ellen Jordan Reidy, President/Founder, America's Food Technologies, Inc. (AMFOTEK); Robert Growney, Former President/COO, Motorola; Frank Brod, Corporate Vice President/Chief Accounting Officer, Microsoft Corporation

Academics

The Stuart School of Business at Chicago's Illinois Institute of Technology (IIT) recognizes the diverse needs of its students and "focuses on innovation" in order to accommodate them all. Those looking to expedite their MBAs, for example, can enroll in the school's full-time program. About three quarters of the students here do just that. Those who want to pursue their degrees contemporaneously with their careers have a number of part-time options." Classes are scheduled during weekdays, evenings, and weekends for the convenience of all of Stuart's students. All MBA programs consist of a minimum of 16 classes.

IIT is a world-class research institution, and, not surprisingly, Stuart MBAs benefit from the presence of the high-powered academics here and the "excellent research opportunities." Three research centers—the Center for Financial Markets, the Center for Strategic Competitiveness, and the Center for Sustainable Enterprise—offer unique options to adventurous MBAs. There is even an optional specialization in sustainable enterprise that trains students "to identify, develop, communicate, and help implement practical and equitable business strategies that advance the ecological sustainability of the Chicago area, while fostering current and future economic viability." Stuart was recently ranked among the world's leaders in incorporating environmental management.

Many here, however, prefer more traditional fare. Stuart MBAs laud the School's entrepreneurship program, as well as offerings in finance and marketing. Quite a few full-time students take advantage of dual-degree programs in law, design, finance, or public administration. Throughout the curriculum, students praise the use of technology and real-life examples, and the fact that "presentation skills and teamwork are highly celebrated and nurtured." The "superb" Stuart professors "are always willing to help and provide out-of-the-classroom tutorials and further explanations." Plus, they always "challenge students to do their best." "I have never met another group so willing to teach," says a student. However, at this level, "there is no 'spoon feeding'; students have to do their research on their own and learn the skills to do so." Similarly, administrators "are extremely helpful and go out of their way to get to know each student personally and help anyone."

With IIT's small cohorts, there is no crowding in the school's computer labs or the "vast library," which offers a "very huge online research library and article access and excellent infrastructure." For many, though, "the school's greatest strength is its strategic location," as downtown Chicago is "an amazing place to study and grants access to businesses around the school and access to socialize, not only with fellow students, but with professionals in the vicinity." About the only weakness here, students tell us, is that "the school should do more marketing of itself, and Career Services should do more on its networking with employers."

Career and Placement

The Office of Career Services at the Stuart MBA program provides students with one-on-one career counseling, workshops in interviewing, and resume preparation, and research on companies and opportunities appropriate to each student's goals. A self-assessment, conducted as students enter the program, helps the office tailor its services to the individual needs of each MBA, and for the part-timers, "the course work flows very easily with full-time work obligations." The university at large conducts career fairs through its Career Development Center.

Employers who most frequently hire Stuart MBAs include Bank One, Northern Trust, Bank of America, ABN-Amro, Lucent Technologies, JPMorgan, Navistar, Johnson &

Johnson, Capitol One, Vankampen, US EPA, Reuters, Cantor Fitzgerald, McLagan Partners, Motorola, Inc., and Akamal Trading. About half of all Stuart MBAs remain in the Midwest after graduation; most of the rest head to one of the two coasts.

Student Life and Environment

IIT's main MBA programs are located "in a separate building in downtown Chicago. That building houses law and business school students only, so there isn't much activity there really, just serious-looking students walking to and fro." Still, "the open-space lay-out of the building and the open-minded students allow for students to be able to talk, ask questions or even ask one another to watch their stuff while they go use the rest-room." The main campus has more life, including "amenities for kids and spouses," and there is a free shuttle to transport students between campuses. MBA students participate in "lots of study groups, there are socials many Wednesdays and "there is plenty of time for students to be involved in extracurricular activities." The way that Stuart is designed, there are also "many opportunities to network both inside and out of school through events," and a "high level of trust, cooperation, and communication among students."

The student body includes many "young, hardworking, and individualistic" students, who have considerable work experience, and it is "highly diverse," meaning that students are "very accepting of different cultures and backgrounds." One student observes, "The diverse population aids in creating a learning experience unlike any other. Students learn as much (if not more) outside the classroom than in the classroom, just by interacting with everyone around them." When they can find the time, students love to take advantage of "the world's biggest financial city," which also offers plenty in the way of culture, entertainment, fine dining, and nightlife. Again, it comes back to location. "Stuart is located near the Chicago Loop in the midst of big-name business companies, allowing for excellent networking and job opportunities. It's also very close to public transportation."

Admissions

The IIT Stuart School of Business requires applicants to submit GMAT scores (the School's minimum is 500, though a few exceptions are allowed), official undergraduate transcripts for all schools attended, two letters of recommendation from individuals "who are able to assess your academic and/or career achievements and potential," three required essays (personal statements and career goals) with the option to submit an additional essay that offers details that you feel would assist the admission committee in evaluating your application, and a resume. International students must also submit TOEFL scores no more than two years old. Undergraduate transcripts in languages other than English must be accompanied by an English translation.

FINANCIAL FACTS

Annual tuition	$26,784
Fees	$805
Cost of books	$844
Room & board	$5,622
% of students receiving aid	37
% of first-year students receiving aid	36
% of students receiving grants	37
Average award package	$9,658
Average grant	$5,477
Average loan	$20,905
Average student loan debt	$6,000

ADMISSIONS

Admissions Selectivity Rating	72
# of applications received	277
% applicants accepted	78
% acceptees attending	23
Average GMAT	596
Range of GMAT	560–620
Average GPA	3.18
TOEFL required of international students	Yes
Minimum TOEFL (paper/computer)	600
Application fee	$75
International application fee	$75
Regular application deadline	7/10
Deferment available	Yes
Maximum length of deferment	1 year
Transfer students accepted	Yes
Transfer application policy: With advisor approval, may transfer up to 6 Semester credits hours or equivalent.	
Non-fall admissions	Yes
Need-blind admissions	Yes

EMPLOYMENT PROFILE

Career Rating	79	Grads Employed by Function	% Avg. Salary	
Percent employed at graduation	53	Marketing	(20%)	$54,500
Percent employed 3 months after graduation	58	Operations	(10%)	$64,500
		Consulting	(20%)	$64,500
Average base starting salary	$66,167	Finance	(10%)	$84,500
Primary Source of Full-time Job Acceptances		MIS	(10%)	$64,500
School-facilitated activities	(20%)	Other	(30%)	$64,500
Graduate-facilitated activities	(50%)			
Unknown	(30%)			

ILLINOIS STATE UNIVERSITY
COLLEGE OF BUSINESS

Academics

Price, flexibility, and reputation are the cornerstones of Illinois State University's College of Business. Led by professors who "provide the students with learning experiences that effectively prepare us for the business world" and an administration which gives students "a strong foundation for the program by frequently communicating school objectives, supplying valuable resources, and assisting students outside the classroom," this is a school that offers "big school resources and ranking at a budget price."

The MBA program at ISU is geared towards flexibility to meet the needs of both full and part-time students. One student is glad to be provided with "the flexibility to increase or decrease my workload as best fits my situation." Professors here are "willing to go the extra mile to help out" and accommodate a student's work schedule. Some students complain that "research is not a large priority," indicating that "finding sponsorship for optional thesis study is nearly impossible." Others say the College of Business should invest in new technology in order to keep pace with changes in the business world. "Direct application to corporate (and public sector) business settings should be a focus in the classroom. This will better prepare students for their next job."

Students say ISU has "the right combination of location, cost, reputation, and challenging coursework," making it so that they feel "there was no other choice for me in terms of graduate schools." The five academic departments of ISU's College of Business and the highly-focused centers of study within each – the Institute for Entrepreneurial Studies and the International Business Institute within the department of Management and Quantitative Methods, for instance – allow students to refine job skills relevant to their field. The "challenging coursework" here is offset by professors who "challenge students to critically think and are genuinely enthusiastic to teach us."

Career and Placement

Along with eRecruiting and other services provided by ISU's Career Center, "corporate partnerships" and general networking help move students into the next phase of their life in the business world. "Strong cooperation between companies and the business school through internships and classroom instruction from practitioners in various fields of business," along with large job fairs, places students in close contact with companies such as State Farm, Financial, Mitsubishi Motors North America, Caterpillar, Growmark, Sprint, Archer Daniels Midland, Country Financial, and Sherwin-Williams Company.

Student Life and Environment

At ISU's College of Business, full-time students will work side-by-side with "older individuals with families and 20-plus years of full-time professional experience." As many as half the attendees are part-time students, juggling the burdens of work, home, and family on top of a challenging body of academics. According to one student, "Coming to school is a quiet break from reality where I get to interact with many diverse and interesting people." One might think this mix would divide classrooms, but "the atmosphere... promotes interaction amongst all the sections of students," with both longtime professionals and younger students learning from one another. The small size of ISU's MBA program means it has "a close-knit student population," a group of "friendly, helpful" classmates who make sure "the atmosphere is always positive."

Diversity among the student population extends to the student body's place of origin. A large portion of the student population "are either international or have a strong international background." The positive atmosphere extends to this portion of the student body, too. "The students are friendly and there is a shared culture of learning for growth opportunity – professionally and personally – not just to acquire the degree."

For those whose primary daily responsibilities revolve around school, there is no shortage of things to do when class is over. "There is always something going on over the weekend, especially during the summer," students enthuse, indicating that "overall, quality of life is good and a good stress-buster from the hectic study schedules." Athletics, a wealth of student organizations, and a campus with easily accessible facilities make filling downtime simple.

Admissions

Applications to ISU's MBA program must go through the Graduate School. Fall semester applications are due by July 1; spring semester applications by December 1; and summer semester applications by April 1. Though work experience is not required, it is considered beneficial and is "strongly encouraged." Ensure all applications include two official copies of transcripts for all academic work completed beyond high school, along with GMAT scores, a resume, and personal essays. All must be attached to the online Graduate School application. The two letters of reference should also be included; send them directly to the MBA Program office. Applicants will want a strong GPA for their final 60 credit hours of undergraduate work and excellent GMAT scores, as those are the biggest factors in admissions decisions. Successful applicants have posted an average GPA of 3.45 and an average GMAT score of 570. TOEFL or IELTS scores are required for international students whose first language is not English. Be prepared to meet a minimum score of 600 on the paper-and-pencil TOEFL, 250 on the computer-based TOEFL, 83 in the Internet-based TOEFL, or 6.5 on the IELTS. Prospective students interested in Graduate Assistantship appointments must apply for a position prior to March 1st. The application is separate from the Program application and can be found via the "employment" link on the university's homepage. The benefits include a tuition waiver and monthly stipend.

FINANCIAL FACTS

Annual tuition (in-state/ out-of-state)	$7,108/$13,066
Fees	$1,150
Cost of books	$954
Room & board (on/off-campus)	$9,364/$7,699
% of students receiving aid	42
% of first-year students receiving aid	40
% of students receiving grants	37
Average award package	$4,281
Average grant	$2,989
Average loan	$7,083
Average student loan debt	$4,763

ADMISSIONS

Admissions Selectivity Rating	80
# of applications received	43
% applicants accepted	70
% acceptees attending	87
Average GMAT	570
Range of GMAT	520–670
Average GPA	3.43
TOEFL-required of international students	Yes
Minimum TOEFL (paper/computer)	600/250
Application fee	$40
International application fee	$40
Regular application deadline	7/1
Regular application notification	8/1
Deferment available	Yes
Maximum length of deferment	1 year
Transfer students accepted	Yes
Transfer application policy: Must be in good academic standing and complete all regular application requirements, maximum 9 hours transfer credit accepted	
Non-fall admissions	Yes
Need-blind admissions	Yes

EMPLOYMENT PROFILE

Career Rating		90
Percent employed at graduation		58
Percent employed 3 months after graduation		74
Average base starting salary		$63,490

Grads Employed by Function	%	Avg. Salary
Marketing	(10%)	$60,125
Operations	(20%)	$68,800
Management	(8%)	$53,452
Finance	(22%)	$73,487
HR	(10%)	$49,580
MIS	(15%)	$62,950
Other	(10%)	$57,258

Top 5 Employers Hiring Grads

State Farm Insurance, Country Financial, Archer Daniels Midland, Caterpillar, Heritage Enterprises

IMD INTERNATIONAL
INTERNATIONAL INSTITUTE FOR MANAGEMENT DEVELOPMENT

Academics

The International Institute for Management Development, located in Lausanne, Switzerland, is "one of the best MBAs for general management" with a "strong and unique focus on leadership development." Nearly all students mention the strength of the leadership program, one calling it one of the best "in the world." The curriculum "integrates all courses seamlessly" and is "covered from different angles in different courses, which helps facilitate learning in a very effective way." The whole program is only eleven months long and has a student body of exactly 90. This creates close bonds between students and faculty. "Students develop personal relationships with most of them that extend beyond the MBA term." Also, the small class size means each student is given a great deal of attention. "The program is extremely personalized and tailored to our needs." The teaching method, described as "real world, real learning," begins in the first month. "We start working on a consulting project for a start-up company, and two more consulting projects are lined up: one in South Africa for two weeks, and another with an international firm after the summer break." Students praise "the balance between academic work and real life implementation." They appreciate the school's "focus on introspection and leadership." Understanding yourself is integral in "learning how to lead others." Such a diverse student body helps with this. "Our interactions are intellectually challenging and personally enriching. We have a genuine understanding of the potential of a group to achieve great results."

Professors have "deep industry know-how," due to a unique balance of teaching, research, and real company consulting. They "spend all breaks and after class answering questions," have an open-door policy, and still find time to consult "with companies around the world." "The academic program covers all relevant world developments, whether in finance or global political economy. When a new development warrants extra attention, IMD brings in guest speakers." In addition to sensitivity to global concerns, the faculty specializes in entrepreneurship and executive leadership.

"This school runs like a Swiss watch," with "efficiency, precision, and effectiveness." "The only way this can happen without any glitches is the professionalism, sensitivity, and excellent organization of the MBA office." There is an office dedicated solely to students in the MBA program and a very high student-to-administration ratio. "The level of infrastructure (computer network, stationary, lunch, etc.) is excellent." The staff even helps students with mobile phones and setting up bank accounts. "The administration is incredibly responsive to feedback and suggestions and incorporates any necessary adjustments almost immediately."

Career and Placement

IMD does an outstanding job getting its students jobs. For example, 70 percent of students say they were employed through a school-related activity, and 88 percent had a job offer by graduation; 95 percent had job offers three months after graduation, and 93 percent have jobs internationally. Alumni work all over the globe, from the Ukraine to Belgium to Brazil. At IMD students work with career coaches to define clear goals, and the Career Services Office offers "individual strategy sessions" and workshops on everything from "networking" to "negotiating salary." Also, the students themselves are marketed. The school sends out student profiles to more than 5,000 companies and managers worldwide. They also distribute "resume portfolios" to "more than 250 organizations." Additionally, there is a "super strong, though small, MBA alumni network" and "an opportunity to network with executives who come to IMD for shorter training courses."

ADMISSIONS CONTACT: MBA OFFICE
ADDRESS: CH DE BELLERIVE 23, PO BOX 915 LAUSANNE, SWITZERLAND 01001
PHONE: 011 41 21 618 0298 • FAX: 011 41 21 618 0615
E-MAIL: MBAINFO@IMD.CH • WEBSITE: WWW.IMD.CH/MBA

The top five companies who hired graduates last year were BCG. Shell, Nestle, Samsung, and Schindler.

Student Life and Environment

"Life at IMD is all about intensity." Students agree, "The work is fascinating, but there is not much time for a social life." However, most "study work happens in groups," which results in "life-long, lasting friendships." Students describe one another as "inspiring," and "mature, open, ambitious, fun, and friendly." More than a few use the word "humble." There is a "strong sense of community" and a wonderful diversity. Forty-five nationalities are represented in a class comprised of only ninety students. Not only are they diverse, but "they have a true respect for diversity." This variety extends to vocational backgrounds, as well. Students are "extremely intelligent" with "different points of view, but with the same mentality." "Despite a very intense workload, we have several class committees that work closely with the program management and class participants to enhance the health, social, and intellectual well being of the student body."

IMD is located in Lausanne, Switzerland, which is "a lovely town. People are friendly and competent, and the support for families and spouses is fantastic." The town sits on the shores of Lake Geneva, roughly forty miles from Geneva itself. Lausanne is in the French speaking part of the country and has roughly 130,000 inhabitants. It has been a Celtic settlement, a Roman military camp, a place of refuge for French Huguenots, and now houses a multitude of museums, music and film festivals, several universities, as well as nearby vineyards.

Admissions

When considering students for admission, the committee requests the following from its applicants: an official GMAT score, personal essay, undergraduate GPA (from an accredited institution), letters of recommendation, an interview, and official transcripts. The committee values letters of recommendation and personal essays most, along with work experience. Most students have at least three years experience, while the average is seven. Other factors considered are leadership potential, international outlook, interpersonal skills, and demonstrated career progression. Fluency or near fluency in English is required, and 97 percent of the student body is international. The average student age is 31. Roughly one in four applicants are admitted.

FINANCIAL FACTS

Annual tuition	$63,894
Fees	$26,622
Cost of books	$0
Room & board	$38,336
% of first-year students receiving aid	38
Average award package	$49,456
Average grant	$33,722
Average loan	$47,289

ADMISSIONS

Admissions Selectivity Rating	94
# of applications received	
Average GMAT	676
Range of GMAT	630–710
TOEFL required of international students	No
Application fee	$371
International application fee	$371
Early application deadline	2/1
Regular application deadline	9/1
Application Deadline/Notification	
Round 1:	2/1 /
Round 2:	4/1 /
Round 3:	6/1 /
Round 4:	8/1 /
Deferment available	No
Transfer students accepted	No
Non-fall admissions	Yes
Need-blind admissions	Yes

EMPLOYMENT PROFILE

Career Rating	97	Grads Employed by Function	% Avg. Salary
Percent employed at graduation	57	Marketing	(21%) $153,435
Percent employed 3 months after graduation	89	Operations	(10%) $153,143
		Consulting	(25%) $128,312
Average base starting salary	$142,412	Management	(14%) $126,353
Primary Source of Full-time Job Acceptances		Finance	(16%) $157,733
School-facilitated activities	47(74%)	Other	(14%) $145,989
Graduate-facilitated activities	17(27%)	**Top 5 Employers Hiring Grads**	
		BCG (4), Shell (3), Nestle (3), Samsung (3), Schindler (3)	

INDIANA STATE UNIVERSITY
COLLEGE OF BUSINESS

GENERAL INFORMATION
Type of school   Public
Affiliation   No Affiliation
Academic calendar   Trimester

SURVEY SAYS...
Friendly students, Happy students
Solid preparation in:
General management, Teamwork,
Doing business in a global economy

STUDENTS
Enrollment of parent
  institution   12,066
Enrollment of MBA Program   56
% male/female   76/24
% out-of-state   37
% part-time   35
% underrepresented minority   1
% international   7
Average age at entry   25
Average years work experience
  at entry   4.0

ACADEMICS
Academic Experience Rating   **79**
Profs interesting rating   79
Profs accesible rating   76
Student/faculty ratio   18:1
% female faculty   15
% underrepresented minority
 faculty   7
% part-time faculty   6

Prominent Alumni
Paul Lo, Pres.CEO SinoPac

Academics

Designed primarily for students early in their business careers, the MBA program at Indiana State University offers graduate-level preparation to aspiring managers and business professionals. "Small classes, great teachers, good assistantships" and an affordable tuition add up to excellent value for students here.

Size is both a major asset and an occasional drawback at ISU. With fewer than 60 students in the entire program, students enjoy "individual attention that better prepares the students in a hands-on manner." Small class sizes also mean great faculty accessibility; one student points out, "All of my classes have been taught by senior professors, department chairs, etc. The mentors and connections I'm gaining are fantastic." The size of the program also helps foster a "friendly environment inside and outside the classroom." On the downside, "Class scheduling can be difficult since limited classes are offered each semester." Also, small programs often suffer from neglect in some areas, and ISU's is no exception. For example, ISU "needs to continually update case studies," an area in which students say the program is deficient. "Especially during these economic times, we need very current cases."

The Indiana State MBA consists of 33 semester units (plus foundational course work for students who did not study business as an undergraduate; students seeking a specialized concentration must complete an additional 3 semester units), which can be completed in one year and four months of full-time study. Students wishing to continue to work while they earn their MBAs may also choose to study part-time. Through core course work and electives, the program emphasizes strategic thinking, problem-solving skills, organizational change, international business, and group dynamics. Hands-on learning occurs through opportunities to assist faculty in real-world research projects in programs such as the Small Business Development Center (SBDC), which provides business planning assistance to start-up companies, and through consulting services to existing small businesses.

Career and Placement

Since 2004 when the College of Business opened the Career Experience Center (CEC), where students have had a dedicated facility where they can research positions using the Sycamore CareerLink electronic database, attend career-building workshops, and prepare for interviews. One student writes the following: "My experience with the Career Center is that they only provide the website for assistance in job searches and two career fairs per year. The staff does not provide any other help." Employers interviewing on the ISU campus during a recent recruiting year included: AFLAC, AmSouth, Caterpillar, Dauby O'Connor & Zaleski CPA, Federated Mutual Insurance Company, Marathon Oil, Travelers, and West Point Financial/Mass Mutual.

ADMISSIONS CONTACT: JEFF HARPER, DIRECTOR, MBA PROGRAM
ADDRESS: INDIANA STATE UNIVERSITY, 800 SYCAMORE STREET, TERRE HAUTE, IN 47809-BUS
PHONE: 812-237-2002 • FAX: 812-237-8720
E-MAIL: ISU-MBA@MAIL.INDSTATE.EDU • WEBSITE: WEB.INDSTATE.EDU/SCHBUS/MBA.HTML

Student Life and Environment

"There is always something to be involved in for anyone who wants to get involved" in ISU's MBA community, students tell us. "Whether they are activities organized by the MBA Association (MBAA) or seminars and conferences hosted by leaders of industries, the ISU business school contributes positively towards a student's personality and mentality," a student observes. Students are particularly impressed with MBAA, whose events "allows students from all cultures to come together." Students also appreciate "a lounge for MBA students to study, eat, socialize, and plan." While students complain that "the classrooms need to be upgraded," they also point out that "they are already working on a new business building for us."

Hometown Terre Haute "has the most amazing public parks," facilitating "all [sorts] of outdoor activities. We are also very close to Indianapolis, Chicago, Louisville, and St. Louis, so we have been to Pacers games, Rams games etc. There is so much to do in this area and the cost of living is so low that you have money to enjoy life, even while in b-school."

The ISU MBA program attracts a mix of full timers—typically "young and busy," with some continuing directly from undergraduate study—and part timers adding school to a busy calendar that also includes a full-time job and family obligations. There is a large international contingent here, which makes for a "culturally diverse" campus. Students are "friendly and helpful," even when there are language barriers, and "work together on projects to make sure everyone understands." One writes: "As an international student I have never felt like a foreigner at ISU...[My classmates] always contribute positively in the classroom environment as well as outside." Academically, students describe their peers as "moderately competitive, with the occasional outstanding scholar."

Admissions

In considering applicants for the MBA program, Indiana State University considers the following criteria: acceptance to the School of Graduate Studies; successful completion of undergraduate degree; GPA of at least 2.7, or a GPA of at least 3.0 over the final 60 semester hours of undergraduate study; basic computing skills; GMAT scores; and prerequisite competency. Prerequisite course work for the program includes micro- and macroeconomics, financial accounting, finance, and US business law; additionally, marketing and production and operation management are "strongly recommended." Potential students must earn a GMAT-GPA admissions index of 1050 or higher (the admissions index numbers are calculated by multiplying GPA by 200 and adding GMAT scores), with scores ranking in at least the 50th percentile in both the math and verbal portions of the GMAT. Students failing to meet this requirement may be granted conditional admission to the program.

FINANCIAL FACTS

Annual tuition (in-state/ out-of-state)	$8,000/$15,000
Fees	$129
Cost of books	$900
Room & board	$7,800
% of students receiving aid	30
% of first-year students receiving aid	30
% of students receiving grants	30
Average award package	$12,210
Average grant	$6,210
Average loan	$0

ADMISSIONS

Admissions Selectivity Rating	79
# of applications received	37
% applicants accepted	54
% acceptees attending	40
Average GMAT	520
Range of GMAT	430–750
Average GPA	3.00
TOEFL required of international students	Yes
Minimum TOEFL (paper/computer)	550/213
Application fee	$35
International application fee	$35
Deferment available	Yes
Maximum length of deferment	2 years
Transfer students accepted	Yes
Transfer application policy: Will only accept 6 credit hours from AACSB accredited Universities.	
Non-fall admissions	Yes
Need-blind admissions	No

EMPLOYMENT PROFILE			
Career Rating	64	**Grads Employed by Function**	**% Avg. Salary**
		Marketing	(10%)
		Management	(30%)
		HR	(10%)
		MIS	(10%)

INDIANA UNIVERSITY—BLOOMINGTON
KELLEY SCHOOL OF BUSINESS

Academics

An administration that is "extremely student-focused and works hard to enhance (their) experience" is a hallmark of Indiana University—Bloomington's Kelley School of Business. This "well run" school "responds very quickly to the problems of students," with an administration and educators who "do all that they can to enhance students' experiences." While some students call the administration at the parent school, IU, "out of touch," the administrators at Kelley are "on par with any top ten program."

Part of that comes from teachers who are "are incredible at making textbook problems become real-world applicable." The "incredibly qualified and smart" professors "are passionate about making our experience a positive one." There is no question that "academics are taken seriously at Kelley. Professors care about students learning—not just about grades, but understanding concepts." The "rigorous curriculum" here "prepares a student to compete with the best," key to helping students "grow personally and professionally." Faculty recognize that the world of business is not a solo sport, and the education here reflects that. "Students become very dynamic in team settings because of it."

Students here will begin with an integrated fifteen-week core curriculum before plunging into an education that will ask you to "continuously strive to keep up with change and improvement." Even with challenging academics, few students will find roadblocks at Kelley, in large part thanks to the "excellent faculty" being on hand to help. "The administration and faculty of the Kelley School are second to none. Any administration issues are dealt with quickly and the professors are very interested in preparing you for success by making themselves available after class."

Career and Placement

The Academy structure at Kelley "leads to better interview preparation and therefore more companies being interested in coming to campus." Couple that with the "broad Hoosier network" and a "top marketing program with fantastic companies coming on campus" and it's easy to see why Kelley has "unrivaled exposure to best-in-class CPG companies (Kraft, General Mills, P&G, Nestle, ConAgra)." Add to that a "strong entrepreneurship program and international experience opportunities," as well as faculty who will "bend over backwards to help you land that job/internship," and opportunities abound. Students don't need to rely solely on the faculty, either. They can also rely on one another. "Many students find internships and full time offers because their classmates helped them make the right connections."

The biggest recruiters of students here include Cummins, Deloitte, 3M, Ernst & Young, and General Electric, and those MBAs went on to a wide range of positions: In 2011, about one-fifth wound up in consumer products; 13 percent took positions in technology; 18 percent were in manufacturing; 13 percent found financial services gigs; and 18 percent were hired for consulting.

ADMISSIONS CONTACT: JAMES HOLMEN, DIRECTOR OF ADMISSIONS AND FINANCIAL AID
ADDRESS: 1275 EAST TENTH STREET, SUITE 2010, BLOOMINGTON, IN 47405-1703
PHONE: 812-855-8006 • FAX: 812-855-9039
E-MAIL: MBAOFFICE@INDIANA.EDU • WEBSITE: WWW.KELLEY.INDIANA.EDU/MBA

Student Life and Environment

If you want an opportunity to slow down, you won't get it here. "Life at the Kelley School is very busy, but it is very gratifying because you are able to apply what you're learning to projects that the professors have spent time developing." Students here tend to be "busy with lot of learning," but expect "inclusion and collaboration" rather than classmates who only look out for themselves. "Graduate school is difficult enough without having a cut-throat culture or a miserable environment. The Kelley environment supports students to achieve and to help one another." Just be ready to remain motivated. "The pace is fast, and you feel like a slacker if you are not actively involved with activities and projects keeping you busy all the time. It's a great environment for staying sharp and competitive."

That is not to say there aren't opportunities for fun. "Bloomington offers a lot for a smaller town - great restaurants, museums and shows. At the same time, things are easy to get to and relatively cheap, which is a great combination for a busy student." You'll be on your feet most of the time, as students "often walk to school, walk to the gym and walk to go out," but that only serves to enhance the "one big family" atmosphere at Kelley. If you don't want to hit the town, "there are many clubs and groups for different interest groups which are all student-led under the student-elected MBA Association," as well as "many weekend social/networking opportunities."

Admissions

Many hope to be part of the Kelley MBA program, but because it is highly selective, competition to get in is fierce. Expect the Admissions Office to consider your academic record, including cumulative grade point average; area of concentration; balance of electives and trend of grades; GMAT scores; work experience (two or more years strongly recommended); evidence of leadership ability; two letters of reference; and personal essays. You don't need to have majored in business as an undergraduate, but you should understand algebra and statistics and have some facility with spreadsheets. There are separate screenings for each of the program's four separate application deadlines. Regardless, your chances are better if you apply early; however, it is better to wait for a later deadline if doing so will improve your application. If you are seeking merit scholarships, try to apply by the January 5th deadline.

FINANCIAL FACTS

Annual tuition (in-state/ out-of-state)	$24,478/$43,460
Fees	$2,084
Cost of books	$1,900
Room & board	$8,750
% of students receiving aid	92
% of first-year students receiving aid	92
% of students receiving grants	64
Average award package	$41,035
Average grant	$24,690
Average loan	$35,170
Average student loan debt	$76,685

ADMISSIONS

Admissions Selectivity Rating	90
# of applications received	935
% applicants accepted	39
% acceptees attending	49
Average GMAT	664
Range of GMAT	620–710
Average GPA	3.34
TOEFL required of international students	Yes
Minimum TOEFL (paper/computer)	600/250
Application fee	$75
International application fee	$75
Application Deadline/Notification	
Round 1:	10/15 / 12/30
Round 2:	1/5 / 3/15
Round 3:	3/1 / 4/30
Round 4:	4/15 / 5/30
Deferment available	Yes
Maximum length of deferment	1 year
Transfer students accepted	No
Non-fall admissions	No
Need-blind admissions	Yes

EMPLOYMENT PROFILE

Career Rating	94	Grads Employed by Function	%	Avg. Salary
Percent employed at graduation	76	Marketing	(32%)	$97,239
Percent employed 3 months after graduation	89	Operations	(7%)	$94,600
		Consulting	(17%)	$106,143
Average base starting salary	$97,489	Management	(11%)	$93,528
Primary Source of Full-time Job Acceptances		Finance	(27%)	$94,727
School-facilitated activities	125(74%)	HR	(1%)	
Graduate-facilitated activities	39(23%)	MIS	(2%)	$96,667
Unknown	5(3%)	Other	(4%)	$97,167

Top 5 Employers Hiring Grads
Cummins (7), Proctor & Gamble (5), Deloitte (4), Ernst & Young (4), Abbott Labs (4)

INDIANA UNIVERSITY—KOKOMO
SCHOOL OF BUSINESS

GENERAL INFORMATION
Type of school	Public
Academic calendar	Semester

SURVEY SAYS...
Friendly students, Happy students
Solid preparation in:
Accounting, General management, Operations, Communication/interpersonal skills, Quantitative skills, Computer skills

STUDENTS
Enrollment of parent institution	3,712
Enrollment of MBA Program	49
% male/female	77/23
% out-of-state	2
% part-time	63
% underrepresented minority	2
% international	2
Average age at entry	32

ACADEMICS
Academic Experience Rating	72
Profs interesting rating	72
Profs accesible rating	74
Student/faculty ratio	3:1
% female faculty	31
% underrepresented minority faculty	1
% part-time faculty	0

Academics

The School of Business at Indiana University—Kokomo (IU Kokomo) capably serves area professionals seeking to advance their careers through an MBA degree, offering a "great education at an affordable price." Students praise the program's "excellent reputation" with area employers, as well as its "convenient location" and small class sizes that "make for an intimate setting." "Students are people, not numbers here." A public school that is one of only a dozen AACSB-accredited MBA programs in the state of Indiana, Kokomo provides a compelling option to business people seeking an affordable career-advancement opportunity in and around this city of 50,000.

IU Kokomo's program is "attuned to the regional industry base" of north-central Indiana, but is also flexible enough to "foster effective management of resources in diverse organizational units and settings," according to the school's promotional material. Because nearly all its students work full time, the program offers flexible scheduling. All required classes are held during the week in the evening hours; electives are offered either during the day or in the evenings. Classes are alternately offered in eight- and sixteen-week formats, accommodating both those in a hurry to complete course work and those who wish to learn at a less frantic pace. Except for a capstone course, classes may be taken in any order, another accommodation for the convenience of IU's busy students. Such convenience comes with a tradeoff, however, making it impossible for the school to fully integrate the curriculum, and some wish that there were "more electives" and more real-world learning experiences "where we actually get to use what the professor is stressing in lectures." For example, it would be helpful to have, "an integrated case study that encompasses at least two courses per semester," an impossibility under the current system. Some think that a few of the professors overcompensate for this lack of opportunities for practical demonstration by developing trickier and more "complex exams."

Part-time students typically complete Kokomo's 30-credit MBA program in four years. The program is small, facilitating student-teacher interaction, and professors here are accessible, willing, and "brilliant, for the most part." The downside of the school's size is that it limits options. Some students complain that some courses are not offered frequently enough.

Career and Placement

IU Kokomo does not aggressively promote its career services for MBA students. Because most students in the program "are employed full time in positions of responsibility," few actually require placement services or career counseling, and those who do generally rely on the assistance of their professors. MBAs may take advantage of the University's Office of Career Services, which maintains job boards, a Career Library and Resource Center, and online career-related databases.

Top employers in Kokomo include Delphi Electronics & Safety, Howard Regional Health, Saint Joseph Hospital, Haynes International, Meijer, and the University.

ADMISSIONS CONTACT: LINDA FICHT, ASSISTANT DEAN AND MBA DIRECTOR
ADDRESS: PO BOX 9003, KOKOMO, IN 46904-9003
PHONE: 765-455-9465 • FAX: 765-455-9348
E-MAIL: LFICHT@IUK.EDU • WEBSITE: WWW.IUK.EDU/MBA

Student Life and Environment

IU Kokomo attracts a "larger population of older students" of "all forms and fashions," with "many women and minorities" filling out the ranks. MBAs here tend to be "normal, everyday people trying to better themselves in tough economic times," and most often have a full-time job. They have "multiple demands on their time" in addition to school, including careers and, quite often, family obligations, so the school is usually "close to home" for all who attend. "My teammates for group work have been strong contributors, leaving no one person with a disproportionate work load. Our work groups are committed to getting as much done as possible just before or just after classes meet, as we are all busy otherwise, and that works well for everyone." Though most are "very friendly and helpful," some "tend to stick together with fellow students from the same employer" and are "not always welcoming to outsiders."

IU Kokomo is "strictly a commuter campus" where students "come in, go to class, and leave," so "there are relatively few gatherings as with other traditional campuses." Despite the lack of socializing, there are few complaints, as this is specifically what most students are here for. "The format of the classes is set up in a way that it's possible to have a life while earning your degree. The value of the program is amazing." It is worth highlighting the efforts of the MBA Association (MBAA), which organizes social and intellectual events for those students who do spend time on campus. The school invites business leaders as part of its distinguished lecture series, enabling students to learn from some of the business world's top players. Some here feel that "the safety of students attending night classes is an issue. I never see security at night, and the lighting could be better." Statistics indicate that the city of Kokomo has a below average rate of crimes, such as assault, robbery, and automobile theft.

Admissions

Admission to the MBA program at IU Kokomo requires a bachelor's degree from an accredited college or university (business major not required), a completed application to the program, a personal statement of career goals, and official transcripts for all post-secondary academic work. Most applicants must also submit GMAT scores; those already holding graduate degrees from accredited institutions, however, are exempted from this requirement. A formula score of at least 1,000 under the formula [(undergraduate GPA + 200) + GMAT score] is required of all applicants who submit GMAT scores. Successful completion of undergraduate-level courses in calculus, statistics, and composition, and a background in microcomputer applications are prerequisites to beginning the MBA program. These courses can be completed after admission to the program, however. Some qualified applicants may be denied admission due to space and resource constraints. Admissions decisions are made on a rolling basis, so it pays to apply as early as possible. International applicants must meet the aforementioned requirements and must also submit TOEFL scores (minimum score 550). The MBA program admits students for fall, spring, and summer semesters. IU Kokomo accepts students with deficiencies in their business education background, but these students are required to complete up to 18 credit hours of foundation courses in business.

FINANCIAL FACTS

Annual tuition (in-state/ out-of-state)	$8,700/$19,770
Fees	$535
Cost of books	$2,000
Room & board	$10,000
Average grant	$0

ADMISSIONS

Admissions Selectivity Rating	71
# of applications received	17
% applicants accepted	94
% acceptees attending	94
Average GMAT	504
Average GPA	3.25
TOEFL required of international students	Yes
Minimum TOEFL (paper/computer)	550/213
Application fee	$40
International application fee	$60
Regular application deadline	8/1
Deferment available	Yes
Maximum length of deferment	NR
Transfer students accepted	Yes
Transfer application policy: 6 credits from AACSB accredited schools	
Non-fall admissions	Yes
Need-blind admissions	Yes

INDIANA UNIVERSITY OF PENNSYLVANIA
EBERLY COLLEGE OF BUSINESS AND INFORMATION TECHNOLOGY

GENERAL INFORMATION

Type of school	Public
Affiliation	No Affiliation
Academic calendar	Semester

SURVEY SAYS...

Friendly students, Good social scene
Solid preparation in:
Marketing, General management,
Communication/interpersonal skills,
Doing business in a global economy

STUDENTS

Enrollment of parent institution	15,379
Enrollment of MBA Program	269
% male/female	59/41
% out-of-state	55
% part-time	15
% underrepresented minority	7
% international	53
Average age at entry	27
Average years work experience at entry	0.0

ACADEMICS

Academic Experience Rating	**86**
Profs interesting rating	85
Profs accesible rating	84
Student/faculty ratio	8:1
% female faculty	21
% underrepresented minority faculty	36
% part-time faculty	0

Prominent Alumni

Richard B. Clark, '80, President & CEO, Brookfield Financial Properties LP; Terry L. Dunlap, '81, General Manager, Allegheny Ludlum; Florence Mauchant, '85, Partner, HT Capital Advisors LLC; Timothy W. Wallace, '79, CEO, FullTilt Solutions; Jeffrey R. DeMarco, '81, Partner, KPMG LLP

Academics

With a broad-based curriculum, affordable in-state tuition, and uniformly small class sizes, the MBA program at Indiana University of Pennsylvania is suitable to both recent graduates and mid-career professionals. With many courses taught in the evenings, the program can be tailored to fit your schedule, as well as your educational goals. For those who want to complete the degree quickly, the school offers "a fast-paced one-year completion opportunity" (open to students with an undergraduate degree in business). However, there are also "options for doing concentrations/ specialization for those who want a longer program," or for those who wish to concentrate their studies on a field like international business, human resources, supply chain management, marketing, finance, and accounting. Offering a great return on investment, this public school "is not expensive compared to another MBA programs, and the quality is still very good." Despite the attractive price tag, the curriculum is well-designed, the administration is efficient, and "Everything is done to allow students to work as smoothly as possible, [and] we have easy access to all resources needed."

Eberly's MBA curriculum strives to stay current with business trends, and practical business applications are constantly incorporated into class work. Drawing on their real-world credentials, "Professors are constantly reinforcing what is being taught with real life experiences or with what is going on in the world today." The school has made strides in integrating industry trends into the business curriculum. For example, it has recently introduced an elective in social media marketing to augment traditional marketing coursework. Another feature that stands out about the Eberly MBA is its focus on international business. This focus is reflected in both the staff and the students, as Eberly recruits "professors and students who are from all different parts of the world, as well as who have been to all different parts of the world." Here, "It is a pleasure to work in an intercultural group and we learn more about other cultures and our globalized world economy!"

Uniting intimacy with opportunity, "The greatest strength of the school is the small campus feel mixed with a big college feeling." Thanks to the relatively small graduate enrollment, Eberly students enjoy "small class sizes" and the opportunity to work directly with their professors, while still benefiting from the larger campus environment as well as the big, state-of-the-art Eberly College of Business complex. Within the business school, "Professors are always willing to give an extra hand, and are always available during office hours." Likewise, the "School administration is very helpful and reacts very quickly to all our inquiries and demands!"

Career and Placement

The Indiana University of Pennsylvania Career Development Center assists all undergraduates, graduate students, and alumni with career preparation, internships, and job placement. The Career Development Center offers help with resume writing, interviewing skills, and job-hunting techniques, and it offers one-on-one counseling by appointment. In addition, the Career Development Center organizes job fairs and campus recruiting programs, while also maintaining an updated list of job opportunities online. While their services are open to MBA candidates, some say the Center "could use some overhauling," with a greater focus on "attracting good companies for internships and placements."

ADMISSIONS CONTACT: KRISH KRISHNAN, DIRECTOR MBA PROGRAM
ADDRESS: 664 PRATT DRIVE, RM 301, INDIANA, PA 15705-1081
PHONE: 724-357-2522 • FAX: 724-357-6232
E-MAIL: IUP-MBA@IUP.EDU • WEBSITE: WWW.EBERLY.IUP.EDU/MBA

In recent years, the mean base salary for IUP graduates was over $50,000, and over 70 percent of students had accepted a job within three months of graduation. Companies that recruit on the IUP campus include American Express, Bristol-Myers Squibb Co., Cigna, DuPont Company, EDS, Exxon Company, Federated Investors, General Motors, Georgia Pacific, Deloitte & Touche LLP; Ernst & Young LLP; PriceWaterhouseCoopers LLP, Sun Microsystems, Inc., Wal-Mart, Walt Disney World Company, and Westinghouse.

Student Life and Environment

A "very diverse" student body, over 30 percent of Eberly students are international, with more than 20 countries represented on campus. This diversity is a blessing to the academic experience, as "everyone comes to class with a clear mind, ready to share their background [and] experiences" and most "find it very interesting to learn about their cultures and societies."

Despite their different backgrounds, students at this program get along well. In fact, "Being in the MBA school at IUP is like having a small group of friends…. It's easy to get together with fellow students to study and go over things or just hang out." A student exclaims, "I've always enjoyed IUP for the vast social networking I'm able to do. Even though the town is small, I always have something to do, whether it's participating in a club, or just relaxing on weekends." An hour northeast of Pittsburgh, IUP is near a major city, yet the small-town atmosphere makes it a "peaceful place for studying" and ensures "affordable" cost of living. On that note, hometown Indiana, Pennsylvania isn't everybody's cup of tea. In fact, Indiana "is a very tiny town, so you can either enjoy it or hate it."

Admissions

To be eligible for admission to IUP, students must have a minimum undergraduate GPA of at least 2.6 (for those who graduated from college fewer than five years ago) or 2.4 (for those who graduated from college more than five years ago.) Prospective students must also present GMAT scores of 450 or better. In addition to test scores and undergraduate transcripts, students must also submit a one-page personal statement, at least two letters of recommendation, and an updated resume. High-achieving national and international applicants are eligible to apply for graduate assistantships after completing the first part of the core curriculum.

FINANCIAL FACTS

Annual tuition (in-state/ out-of-state)	$8,136/$12,204
Fees	$2,232
Cost of books	$1,100
Room & board	$10,166
% of students receiving aid	92
% of first-year students receiving aid	93
Average award package	$13,550
Average grant	$7,015
Average loan	$15,851

ADMISSIONS

Admissions Selectivity Rating	86
# of applications received	279
% applicants accepted	51
% acceptees attending	79
Average GMAT	542
Range of GMAT	450–720
Average GPA	3.40
TOEFL required of international students	Yes
Minimum TOEFL (paper/computer)	540/207
Application fee	$50
International application fee	$50
Regular application deadline	8/1
Deferment available	Yes
Maximum length of deferment	1 year
Transfer students accepted	Yes
Transfer application policy: Written request for transfer required of transfer applicants. Maximum of six credits transfer. Credits requested for transfer must carry a grade of "B" or its equivalent or better and must have been completed within the last five years.	
Non-fall admissions	Yes
Need-blind admissions	Yes

EMPLOYMENT PROFILE

Career Rating	79	Grads Employed by Function% Avg. Salary	
Percent employed 3 months		Other	(41%) $54,210
after graduation	51	Top 5 Employers Hiring Grads	
Average base starting salary	$54,210	BNY Mellon, IBM, Prudential, BNP Paribas, Ernst & Young	

INDIANA UNIVERSITY SOUTH BEND
JUDD LEIGHTON SCHOOL OF BUSINESS AND ECONOMICS

GENERAL INFORMATION

Type of school	Public
Affiliation	No Affiliation
Academic calendar	Semester

SURVEY SAYS...
Happy students
Solid preparation in:
Computer skills

STUDENTS

Enrollment of parent institution	8,400
Enrollment of MBA Program	257
Average age at entry	27
Average years work experience at entry	2.0

ACADEMICS

Academic Experience Rating	74
Profs interesting rating	76
Profs accesible rating	74
Student/faculty ratio	17:1
% female faculty	8
% underrepresented minority faculty	23
% part-time faculty	10

Academics

Indiana University South Bend's Leighton School of Business and Economics is a "value provider" when it comes to getting an exceptional business education. The school offers working professionals a "cost effective" and convenient means to advance their careers or switch industries. The flexible schedule (including night classes), "great business school credentials," and the part-time MBA program make for a "good reputation," and "the in-state-residence tuition is attractive."

Most of the professors "know present and past students by name," and are "engaged" and accessible to students. "I am able to get questions answered expeditiously," says one. The cultural and ethnic diversity of professors is a huge plus, and though "some are better than others," all are "extremely well-versed in the subjects they teach." There is an "ease of contact" with teachers, and "all professors have a sincere interest in working with students." The administration is also well run, and "when we contact the Dean of the program directly, he is very responsive."

Students who have taken specific business classes within the last five years may qualify for automatic exemption from the first level of prerequisite classes to save time and money. MBA candidates have three concentrations from which to choose: General Business, Finance, and Marketing. As most people here have already tasted the world of full-time employment, the commitment to work is high, and these students "always turn in their assignments and give really impressive presentations."

Career and Placement

Since the majority of those who attend IU South Bend are currently employed and whose degrees are frequently paid for by their employers, Career Services is not as necessary as at some other business schools; the typical candidate enters the program because their present or future position requires increased managerial competence. The one exception includes younger students or those who are looking to change their careers. A few students say that IU South Bend "needs more connections to businesses" so that graduates can have more ease to "transition from [an] MBA program into a job that requires the specific concentration of the MBA." Most who attend apply for the business degree and are normally not disappointed by the program or their results. "The experience has been everything I expected," says one student.

ADMISSIONS CONTACT: TRACY P. WHITE, GRADUATE BUSINESS RECORDS REPRESENTATIVE
ADDRESS: 1700 MISHAWAKA AVENUE, P O BOX 7111, SOUTH BEND, IN 46634-7111
PHONE: 574-520-4138 • FAX: 574-520-4866
E-MAIL: GRADBUS@IUSB.EDU • WEBSITE: GRADUATEBUSINESS.IUSB.EDU

Student Life and Environment

The business school is "well laid out," most of the buildings are close together, and parking is not overly difficult. IU South Bend is mostly a commuter school composed of "local people wanting to get their MBA while at a full-time job," so the school "doesn't offer many outside activities," and "there is limited student-student interaction." Though most interactions do center on classes and professional organizations, students are always "social and eager to exchange ideas." One student comments, "They have helped me see different sides of issues and solutions." This "friendly and down to earth, intelligent and unpretentious" group is "evenly split between males and females," and made up of mostly "older students…with families," and "younger students [who] are international." All around, students are "very motivating and inspiring." "Everyone has interesting side stories and business ventures," says a student.

Admissions

The MBA program at requires applicants to submit all of the following: an online application; official transcripts of all postsecondary academic work; two recommendations (completed online); a personal statement; current resume; and an official GMAT score report. International students whose native language is not English must submit all of the above as well as an official score report for the TOEFL; minimum required score for consideration is 550 (paper-based test), 213 (computer- based test) or 79 (internet-based test). Applications are accepted for Fall, Spring, or Summer semesters. IU South Bend admits students at two levels: full admission and probationary admission. Full admission requires a minimum GMAT score of 450 and an undergraduate business degree with a minimum GPA of 2.75. Probationary admission is granted to applicants "whose GPA does not quite meet minimum standards." All students must maintain a cumulative GPA of at least 2.75 to remain in, and to graduate from the program.

FINANCIAL FACTS

Average grant	$0
Average loan	$0

ADMISSIONS

Admissions Selectivity Rating	71
# of applications received	74
% applicants accepted	93
% acceptees attending	65
Average GMAT	542
Range of GMAT	450–700
Average GPA	3.20
TOEFL required of international students	Yes
Minimum TOEFL (paper/computer)	550/213
Application fee	$40
International application fee	$60
Regular application deadline	7/1
Deferment available	Yes
Maximum length of deferment	1 year
Transfer students accepted	Yes
Transfer application policy: Contact the office for a determination of which classes might transfer. In general, max is 12 credits from AACSB school only with min course grade of B	
Non-fall admissions	Yes
Need-blind admissions	No

INDIANA UNIVERSITY—SOUTHEAST
SCHOOL OF BUSINESS

GENERAL INFORMATION

Type of school	Public
Affiliation	No Affiliation
Academic calendar	Semester

SURVEY SAYS...
Cutting-edge classes
Solid preparation in:
Computer skills

STUDENTS

Enrollment of parent institution	6,910
Enrollment of MBA Program	207
% male/female	68/32
% part-time	97
Average age at entry	31
Average years work experience at entry	7.0

ACADEMICS

Academic Experience Rating	**75**
Profs interesting rating	85
Profs accesible rating	79
Student/faculty ratio	7:1
% female faculty	32
% underrepresented minority faculty	18
% part-time faculty	18

Joint Degrees
Both degree plans (MBA and MSSF) can be completed by taking 54 graduate credit hours (plus any necessary foundation course work)

Academics

With a strong local reputation and a low in-state price tag, savvy business students say Indiana University Southeast is an "excellent value" for an MBA. The combination of "reasonable tuition rates and a flexible part-time program" makes IUS particularly attractive to working professionals. Plus, some "classes are offered at satellite locations for the convenience of students." There are more than 200 MBA candidates in the program, and IUS maintains a surprisingly intimate academic environment. Believe it or not, "the Director of Graduate Business Programs makes personal phone calls to each student upon enrollment and throughout their academic careers." "Navigating the program is very easy," and the administration is generally responsive to student concerns. For example, "when classes are full, they can add a couple of openings to keep from disrupting an entire schedule or add additional times or nights."

Consummate professionals, "professors are outstanding and treat students with respect." Students enjoy almost every class they take at IUS, as the professors "truly love the subjects they teach, and their enthusiasm is contagious." The school recruits faculty from the local business community, and many "professors come with a track record of professional success in their respective business fields." Perfect for current professionals, "materials are relevant to an evolving job market," and the school excels at "making the newest technologies and software available to students." While Indiana University offers a "well-rounded MBA" in advanced business topics, some feel "IUS could offer more variety in its elective choices."

Those balancing academic, professional, and personal pursuits are happy to report that "classes are challenging but not overwhelming" at IUS, and professors are there to support their students every step of the way. A student explains, "Once challenging expectations are set, instructors work with students on reaching them." "Class sizes are small," and professors "care about their students' success." Most will "bend over backward to help you out," when work or scheduling difficulties interfere with school. They are also "available outside of class time" if students need additional help with the material. Most students of this program "appear to be five or more years out from undergraduate studies and bring a wealth of experience from the real world into the classroom." Drawing on this wealth of wisdom, professors promote classroom discussion, and "there are a lot of group projects" required within the curriculum.

Career and Placement

Indiana University Southeast is located in the Louisville metropolitan area, close to Indianapolis, so students have access to a couple of major job markets. While a few students are actively looking to make a career change, most plan to leverage the graduate education at their current job. IUS students are generally "young professionals looking to obtain skills and knowledge to help them move into management positions." Looking toward their future, students note that the school's "alumni are successful," and many continue to maintain contact with the business program after graduation.

ADMISSIONS CONTACT: LISA BOOK, DIRECTOR OF GRADUATE BUSINESS PROGRAMS
ADDRESS: HILLSIDE HALL 214, 4201 GRANT LINE ROAD, NEW ALBANY, IN 47150
PHONE: 812-941-2364 • FAX: 812-941-2581
E-MAIL: IUSMBA@IUS.EDU • WEBSITE: WWW.IUS.EDU/GRADUATEBUSINESS

Those looking for a new position can take advantage of the Indiana University Southeast Career Services office, which offers online job boards, career counseling, and resume and cover letter revisions. They also host several University-wide job fairs on campus. Graduate students note that, "The career development office tends to focus on the undergrads." Plus, "most of the trainings they hold are during the day, so those of us who work aren't able to attend." No matter what their future plans, students agree that, "more career days or networking opportunities would be advantageous" to the entire MBA program.

Student Life and Environment

Ninety-seven percent of students are enrolled part time at IUS. About half the students have both full-time jobs and families, while "the other half are a younger group that are working full-time but finishing education goals before starting families." No matter what their age and background, students are "career oriented" and "passionate about the learning experience" at IUS. While competitive in the workplace, students are "friendly and interested in networking" with their classmates. Here, students "come together and complete group projects and presentations."

"Most students work full time and lead busy lives outside of school," so they "don't take part or really have much interest in any on-campus activities." Even coursework can be a juggling act for some students. A current MBA candidate admits, "Group work is difficult for students like me who work 45-50 hours a week and have a family." While "there aren't a lot of school activities to get involved in," students occasionally stick around campus for professional development or networking events. For example, "internationally acclaimed business speakers regularly speak at our campus."

Admissions

For the IUS admissions committee, the most important factors in an admissions decision are a student's previous academic performance, the quality of his or her undergraduate degree program, standardized test scores, and previous work experience. The average GMAT score for this year's class was 544, with a range between 490–590 for the 25th to 75th percentile. Students generally receive a response from the University within three weeks of the application deadline. Any applications post-marked after the deadline will be considered on a space-available basis.

FINANCIAL FACTS

% of students receiving aid	27
% of students receiving grants	7
Average award package	$9,260
Average grant	$1,678
Average loan	$11,051
Average student loan debt	$29,388

ADMISSIONS

Admissions Selectivity Rating	**73**
# of applications received	56
% applicants accepted	84
% acceptees attending	81
Average GMAT	544
Range of GMAT	490–590
Average GPA	3.27
TOEFL required of international students	Yes
Minimum TOEFL (paper/computer)	550/213
Application fee	$35
International application fee	$35
Early application deadline	6/15
Early notification date	7/15
Regular application deadline	7/20
Regular application notification	8/15
Deferment available	Yes
Maximum length of deferment	1 Semester
Transfer students accepted	Yes

Transfer application policy: Students may transfer a maximum of 6 graduate credit hours (with no grades below B) from another AACSB-accredited MBA program to count toward the 36 credit hour MBA curriculum at IU Southeast. Students may request that graduate credit not meeting this criterion be reviewed for transfer approval. The final disposition of all transfer course work is determined by the Director.

Non-fall admissions	Yes
Need-blind admissions	Yes

INSEAD

Academics

INSEAD brands itself as "the business school for the world," and it can provide hard facts to support its claim. Students tell us the program is "is incredibly international, unrivaled by any other school," with a broad international student population and campuses in both France and Singapore. One student observes: "My fellow students come from 70 countries. My study group is an epitome of globalization: a Mexican investment banker, a Taiwanese accountant, a French Navy officer, an American diplomat, and a Bulgarian marketer, all exchanging knowledge in INSEAD. How much better could it be?" Further driving the point home is the fact that INSEAD is "the only prestigious MBA program that requires three languages upon exit."

Students, grateful for a program that "is not only US-centric," love the international focus at INSEAD. At the same time, students may augment their time in Asia or Europe with a semester in the United States through the school's partnership with the Wharton School at University of Pennsylvania and the Kellogg School of Management at Northwestern University. They also appreciate the fact that it's a 10-month program that "gives quicker return on investment" than longer, more expensive MBA programs. INSEAD has "a strong reputation in consulting and general management" that translates into "placement success with top-tier consulting firms." The school also offers "exceptional private equity and investment courses (private equity, realizing entrepreneurial potential, leveraged buyouts, etc.)." Perhaps the school's greatest strength, though, is the quality of its student body; one MBA tells us, "The work experience of all candidates is extremely high, which creates in-depth, dynamic discussions and learning in the classroom." Another adds: "At this point, any question I have about any country or industry can be solved by simply asking the right classmate."

As in most accelerated programs, "academics are extremely challenging" at INSEAD, especially "for someone completely new to business or on topics for which you have no knowledge. " However, "At the same time there is a stress toward making sure that students understand the basics and all that is necessary for business. What's more, other students who have had experience or who studied business in undergrad are always open to help and encourage each other." The large size of the program, coupled with the speed at which it is completed, "sometimes makes it feel as though you are passing through an MBA factory." Even so, "The administration is generally prompt and receptive, especially with regards to clubs, network and career activities," and is also very efficient.

Career and Placement

INSEAD maintains Career Services offices on both its campuses in France and Singapore. The offices promote students to employers around the globe while providing MBAs with one-on-one counseling and coaching, job search strategies, and on-campus recruiting events. Some students complain that Career Services counselors are "used to a specific way of working and don't think outside the box. The focus is all on consulting, finance, and maybe a little industry." Others say, "Career Services is doing a good job, but there is room for improvement, as the school has a lot to offer on the job market." Nearly all agree that the school's substantial alumni network is "very helpful and intent on seeing current graduates succeed."

The diversity of the student body is reflected in the global career prospects; in 2011, INSEAD graduates took jobs at more than 370 companies in 68 different countries. Employers most likely to hire INSEAD MBAs include McKinsey & Company, Google, LVMH, Credit Suisse, The Boston Consulting Group, Samsung, Barclays Capital, Bain & Company, Amazon,

ADMISSIONS CONTACT: KARA KEENAN, ASSISTANT DIRECTOR OF MARKETING FOR THE AMERICAS
ADDRESS: BOULEVARD DE CONSTANCE, 77305 FONTAINEBLEAU, CEDEX, FRANCE
PHONE: +1-856-375-9002 OR +33 (0)1 60 72 40 05 • FAX: +33 (0)1 60 74 55 30
E-MAIL: MBA.INFO@INSEAD.EDU • WEBSITE: WWW.INSEAD.EDU

FINANCIAL FACTS

Annual tuition	$70,808
Cost of books	$1,008
Room & board	$26,000
% of students receiving grants	20

ADMISSIONS

Admissions Selectivity Rating	81
Average GMAT	704
TOEFL required of international students	Yes
Minimum TOEFL (paper/computer)	620/260
Deadline/Notification	
Round 1:	3/10 / 4/16
Round 2:	6/9 / 7/16
Round 3:	7/28 / 9/10
Deferment available	No
Transfer students accepted	No
Non-fall admissions	Yes

Microsoft, Standard Chartered Bank, Rocket Internet/Groupon, Shell, and Siemens. Nearly 40 percent of INSEAD MBAs wind up in consulting functions, 23 percent take jobs in financial services, and 38 percent take jobs in industry.

Student Life and Environment

"The INSEAD year is a very intense period," students tell us, noting, "As there are classes every day, we have to study just like in high school and more or less all the time. There is a lot of group work...But, we all understand the quality of the people around us and the need for social interaction," and most here find time for fun.

INSEAD's Fontainebleau campus "is extremely dynamic. There's always something going on, but at the same time depends on the intake. At the end of the day, activities are driven by students. Sometimes, the one-year nature of the program makes keeping activities and clubs continuous a bit challenging." Weekends often feature "fantastic parties at chateaus in the French countryside. The school even provides shuttle buses. Can you beat that?" The Singapore campus "is superb" and "quite relaxed because of the setting."

Admissions

INSEAD has two intake points, in September and January. Students may apply to begin the program at either time; application is online only. All applicants must provide a personal profile, five personal essays (with a sixth optional essay), two recommendations attesting to leadership potential and management capacity, a photograph, a statement of integrity, an official GMAT or GRE score report, and official transcripts for all post-secondary academic work. In addition, all students must enter the program with proficiency in English and a second language. Non-native English speakers may submit results from the TOEFL, TOEIC, PTE Academic, CPE, or IELTS; English speakers must provide certification of a second language. A third commercially useful language (sorry, no Latin!) is required to graduate; while language instruction is available through INSEAD, the intensity of the MBA program is such that the school recommends students get a start on their third language before the program begins. The applicant's choice of campus is not taken into account in the admission decision. However, if the program at their first-choice campus is full, candidates will be offered a spot at the other campus or on the wait list.

IONA COLLEGE
HAGAN SCHOOL OF BUSINESS

Academics

"Iona has a good reputation in the Tri-state area," students tell us when explaining why they chose the MBA program at Iona's Hagan School of Business. Convenience is another major factor: "The proximity to Stamford, New York City, and its location in Westchester County…makes it ideal for job searches," one student writes. Familiarity with the program is a third contributing factor; many of the students in our survey attended Iona as undergraduates and "had a great experience." For them, the only question is why they wouldn't continue at Iona for their graduate degrees.

Hagan's relatively small MBA programs offer a surprising number of options to students, most of whom attend part time while working at full-time jobs. A fast-track MBA hustles students through the program in as little as 13 months. Classes are offered in a traditional classroom setting, online, or in a hybrid format that mixes on-campus and online study. Concentrations in financial management, information systems, general management, human resources management, marketing, public and general accounting, public accounting, and healthcare management are all available. Students speak especially highly of the HR program; many note approvingly of the entire MBA program's international focus, and several appreciate the "Christian influence" at this Christian Brothers-affiliated school.

Most of all, students love Hagan's faculty, which they describe as "outstanding." The faculty includes "some seasoned professionals with previous illustrious business careers" and teachers who "have owned companies or currently own companies, [and] who have provided a wealth of knowledge for future perspective entrepreneurs." Professors "are always available to help the students," "genuinely care about educating their students, and go the extra mile to help. They are accommodating, fair, and highly knowledgeable in their fields." The "excellent" administration "will reach out to you" as well. Campus resources, including the library and "up-to-date" technology, also earn accolades.

Career and Placement

The Gerri Ripp Center for Career Development handles counseling and placement services for all Iona students and alumni. Online job searches are facilitated by GAELlink, Iona's proprietary job database. The school also holds a career and internship fair in the spring and welcomes on campus recruiters. Students tell us it's not enough, wishing that the school did more in the way of "helping us network and bringing more recognized companies onto campus." The situation is complicated by the fact that many students attend at the expense of their current employers, who presumably do not want the school to assist students in finding better opportunities elsewhere. Professors, who "aid in networking," are considered a more dependable source of career assistance. Students tell us that the school is also beginning to reach out to its considerable alumni network on behalf of MBAs, "which should help the graduating students entering the labor market."

ADMISSIONS CONTACT: BEN FAN, DIRECTOR OF MBA ADMISSIONS
ADDRESS: 715 NORTH AVENUE, NEW ROCHELLE, NY 10801
PHONE: 914-633-2256 • FAX: 914-637-7720
E-MAIL: SFAN@IONA.EDU • WEBSITE: WWW.IONA.EDU/HAGAN

Student Life and Environment

Iona's campus "is beautifully maintained and manicured," making it a welcome respite from the hectic and cluttered New York metropolitan area beyond its walls. Undergraduates will tell you it's an "active campus" with plenty of "events, entertainment, guest speakers, and sporting events." These events "are well-planned and publicized both on campus and via the web and emails," one MBA explains. The result of all this extracurricular activity is a solid community that engenders plenty of school pride, and even the MBAs feel it, even though they are mostly too busy to participate. As one explains, "Life at school is all about the classroom. Students do not hang out around school. They show up to class, then go home."

Hagan attracts a lot of young professionals as well as a substantial number of Iona undergraduates, some of whom proceed directly from undergraduate work to the MBA program. Older students include those "returning to further develop skill sets (as a result of the economy)" who "work for a diversity of companies from small organizations to large ones like Morgan Stanley." These older students sometimes complain that their younger classmates "do not care about education but [only] the title," but even they concede that "there are a great number of smart, dedicated, and committed students [in the program] that make you want to be smarter."

Admissions

Applicants to the Hagan MBA program must submit the following materials: a completed Hagan School of Business application form, along with a $50 application fee; copies of official transcripts from each undergraduate and graduate institution attended; two letters of recommendation; and an official score report for the GMAT reflecting a score no more than five years old (the GMAT requirement may be waived for applicants with at least seven years of post-undergraduate professional experience). Interviews are optional. International applicants must submit all of the materials listed above, as well as an official score report for the TOEFL, WES, and a cash support affidavit. Transcripts in languages other than English must be translated and interpreted by an approved service. Applications are processed on a rolling basis and are valid for one full year from the day they are received by the school. Applicants may request an interview, which the school recommends but does not require.

FINANCIAL FACTS

Annual tuition	$24,624
Fees	$450
Cost of books	$1,500
% of students receiving aid	81
% of first-year students receiving aid	83
% of students receiving grants	56
Average award package	$21,516
Average grant	$7,056
Average loan	$22,497
Average student loan debt	$30,663

ADMISSIONS

Admissions Selectivity Rating	**68**
# of applications received	118
% applicants accepted	100
% acceptees attending	85
Average GMAT	420
Range of GMAT	340–500
Average GPA	3.18
TOEFL required of international students	Yes
Minimum TOEFL (paper/computer)	580/213
Application fee	$50
International application fee	$50
Deferment available	Yes
Maximum length of deferment	1 year
Transfer students accepted	Yes
Transfer application policy: Max of 6 upper-level credits accepted. 30 credit minimum required to earn a degree at Iona.	
Non-fall admissions	Yes
Need-blind admissions	Yes

ITHACA COLLEGE
SCHOOL OF BUSINESS

GENERAL INFORMATION
Type of school	Private
Affiliation	No Affiliation

SURVEY SAYS...
Students love Ithaca, NY
Solid preparation in:
Finance, Presentation skills,
Quantitative skills, Doing business in
a global economy

STUDENTS
Enrollment of parent institution	6,448
Enrollment of MBA Program	29
% male/female	69/31
% out-of-state	35
% part-time	21
% underrepresented minority	14
% international	20
Average age at entry	24
Average years work experience at entry	1.0

ACADEMICS
Academic Experience Rating	74
Profs interesting rating	78
Profs accesible rating	82
Student/faculty ratio	1:1
% female faculty	26
% underrepresented minority faculty	26
% part-time faculty	0

Academics

MBA students in Ithaca College's small graduate program may choose between an MBA in business administration and an MBA in professional accountancy. Both degrees require 36 credit hours and can be completed by full-time students in 12 months—and this is the selling point of the program. As one student explains, "A one-year program offered me a faster track to my post-MBA life."

The curriculum for Ithaca's Business Administration MBA includes 8 required courses, which build up to a comprehensive capstone experience. In addition, students choose four elective courses. Classes emphasize "a balance between building technical and interpersonal skills," and students praise professors for their "hands-on teaching philosophy." "The faculty is always willing to bend over backwards to meet students' academic and professional needs," says one student. "While the professors remain rather rigid in their expectations of students, most will work tirelessly with students to ensure they succeed." Another student notes, "The school does a good job offering elective courses that are in line with students' career aspirations. Since the program is small, faculty surveys students prior to each semester. The result is a course offering that honestly reflects the interests of students. I see this adaptability as Ithaca's greatest strength because it can help overcome the obstacles often associated with a smaller business school."

Ithaca's Professional Accountancy MBA primarily functions as the culmination of a 5-year undergraduate/graduate program for students in the college's undergraduate accounting program, although candidates from other schools can gain admission. Most here agree that although "many students that graduated from Ithaca as undergrads" are now part of the MBA program, there are also "older" or "married" students in attendance.

The curriculum includes a thorough review of principles of business administration as well as advanced instruction in financial accounting and reporting, managerial and cost accounting, auditing, taxation, and principles of business law. Students in both programs are full of praise for the school. "Overall, I think the school is really starting to take off. Ithaca worked hard to receive AACSB accreditation, [and] since that happened the school has retained high standards for both students and faculty." Another adds, "Tuition is high, but you can definitely see where the money went. Everything from the smart boards in the classrooms—which help make articulating difficult accounting concepts much easier—to the trading room is state-of-the-art."

Students note that the one-year duration of the program helps offset the relatively high cost of attending. That said, while it had been a "little pricey" in the past, "Prices have come down." They also appreciate the fact that the business school administration "welcome(s) comments and suggestions from the grad students on what could help better the program. If you have any problems, they do their best to help you solve the issues." The future's looking bright here, so bring your shades.

ADDRESS: OFFICE OF GRADUATE STUDIES, ITHACA COLLEGE
101 TERRACE CONCOURSE ITHACA, NY 14850-7020
PHONE: 607-274-3527 • FAX: -607-274-1263
E-MAIL: MBA@ITHACA.EDU • WEBSITE: WWW.ITHACA.EDU/BUSINESS/MBA

Career and Placement

The Ithaca College Career Services Office provides self-assessment inventories, e-Recruiting tools, one-on-one advising, mock interviews, workshops, a library, and on-campus recruiting. The school also hosts a graduate school job fair and other special recruiting events. Though despite all this, some students find that "Ithaca could do a better job attracting recruiters from upper-tier businesses." While they appreciate the "many local recruiters on campus" and "ample alumni network and mentoring program," some still find a dearth of businesses at which they're "trying to get [their] foot in the door."

Employers who recruit on the Ithaca campus include Lockheed-Martin, Merrill Lynch, PricewaterhouseCoopers, Ernst & Young, Deloitte, KPMG International, and an active alumni recruiting network.

Student Life and Environment

MBA students at Ithaca College enjoy "a great community atmosphere" at a school that "is just the right size, so that you can go anywhere and know somebody, and meet somebody new." One student writes, "All students are easygoing and approachable. The small size of the program means that many people have identical course schedules. This makes for a tight-knit group of students and strong, long-lasting friendships."

The demands of the program keep MBA students "pretty detached from the rest of the campus. You never deal with grad students from any of the other programs (unless they happen to take a business elective)." However, "Students work hard and play hard" when their schedule allows. "Most weekends I find myself in one or more bars or restaurants eating and drinking with classmates," says one student. Ultimately, "Life at Ithaca is good."

Admissions

Applicants to Ithaca's MBA program must have completed either a bachelor's program in business or accounting, or a bachelor's program in any field along with having taken Ithaca's Pre-MBA Modules. Post-undergraduate work experience is not required; in fact, many students enter the program immediately after completing work on their bachelor's degree. Successful applicants typically have "an undergraduate GPA of 3.0 or higher and a minimum GMAT score of 500." All applications must include official undergraduate transcripts, official GMAT scores, and two letters of recommendation in addition to the essay. Merit-based academic scholarships are also available from the program.

FINANCIAL FACTS

Annual tuition	$24,444
Cost of books	$1,500
% of students receiving grants	21
Average grant	$5,100

ADMISSIONS

Admissions Selectivity Rating	70
# of applications received	47
% applicants accepted	91
% acceptees attending	56
Average GMAT	542
Range of GMAT	460–590
Average GPA	3.21
TOEFL required of international students	Yes
Minimum TOEFL (paper/computer)	550/213
Application fee	$40
International application fee	$40
Early application deadline	4/1
Early notification date	5/1
Regular application deadline	6/1
Regular application notification	6/20
Deferment available	Yes
Maximum length of deferment	NR
Transfer students accepted	Yes
Transfer application policy: Transfer credits from AACSB-accredited institutions accepted on case-by-case basis.	
Non-fall admissions	Yes
Need-blind admissions	Yes

JOHN CARROLL UNIVERSITY
THE BOLER SCHOOL OF BUSINESS

GENERAL INFORMATION
Type of school   Private
Affiliation   Roman Catholic-Jesuit
Academic calendar   Semesters

SURVEY SAYS...
Good peer network
Solid preparation in:
Marketing, General management,
Social responsibility

STUDENTS
Enrollment of parent institution	3,583
Enrollment of MBA Program	107
% male/female	60/40
% out-of-state	9
% part-time	49
% underrepresented minority	4
% international	2
Average age at entry	25
Average years work experience at entry	3.0

ACADEMICS
Academic Experience Rating	**78**
Profs interesting rating	81
Profs accesible rating	75
Student/faculty ratio	14:1
% female faculty	33
% underrepresented minority faculty	19
% part-time faculty	31

Prominent Alumni
Don Shula, Former NFL Coach;
John Boler, Chairman & Founder of
The Boler Company; Richard
Kramer, President & CEO of
Goodyear Tire; John Breen, Retired
CEO of Sherwin Williams; Carter F.
Ham, General, U.S. Army

Academics

The Boler School of Business at John Carroll University offers a part-time MBA program for working professionals with at least two years of work experience and a full-time one year accelerated program(5th-year) for recent graduates. Unlike traditional MBA programs, the part-time "MBA is focused around solving real business problems" and learning about the decisions business leaders have to make. Every class starts with a real problem, posed by a regional company, and "over the semester, students learn tools to help solve the company's problem." These unique courses "are designed to challenge students to leverage all business disciplines" and learn about project management, leadership, innovation, and resource allocation, instead of separating knowledge fields by theme or topic. This helps students "absorb relevant knowledge" and learn "to solve problems from a multi-discipline perspective" and approach them "from a holistic point of view." This is particularly helpful to "those who work full time" because they can "immediately put into practice theories they've learned in their current profession."

Students think the majority of professors are great and appreciate that they "are connected to community business leaders." Professors "tend to have real-world experience" and are "knowledgeable in their fields." Additionally, they are "friendly" and "helpful," and are willing to "go the extra mile to ensure a great education and comprehension of material." Students appreciate the flexibility of the program and the "convenient scheduling" that allows them to vary the number of classes they take each semester. John Carroll is really about putting students first, and with its affordable tuition and "stellar" local reputation, it's no surprise students are so "impressed" with the program.

Career and Placement

The Boler School of Business does not have its own career office, so students must rely on the Center for Career Services that is used by all graduate and undergraduate students. The Center hosts career fairs and on-campus interviews that are well attended thanks to Boler's strong reputation for producing excellent students. "Career Services does a great job bringing companies to campus for interviews and helping students find jobs," one student says. The Center also provides career coaching and help with fundamentals like resumes. Boler does offer a lot of networking events, and local business leaders are always speaking on campus. One student says that "John Carroll business students are viewed as extremely competent, hard-working, and ethical. With many Fortune-500 firms located in Cleveland, John Carroll students are strong contenders for any position within them." A dedicated internship coordinator provides assistance to 5th year MBA students to complete their professional development requirement.

Still, students think there is "room for improvement" in the school's career programming. One of Boler's best resources is its professors, who "move in the spheres of influence and can be a catalyst to professional growth." Additionally, other students in the program are "invaluable resources and serve as internal referral sources to help students in search of new careers get a foot in the door." Organizations that recently visited the campus include GE Capital, Avery Dennison, Ernst & Young LLP, Progressive, PricewaterhouseCoopers LLP, PolyOne Corporation, and Sherwin Williams, although these organizations were not specifically looking for MBA grads.

ADMISSIONS CONTACT: GAYLE BRUNO-GANNON, ASSISTANT TO DEAN FOR
GRADUATE BUSINESS PROGRAMS
ADDRESS: 20700 NORTH PARK BOULEVARD, UNIVERSITY HEIGHTS, OH 44118-4581
PHONE: 216-397-4524 • FAX: 216-397-1827
E-MAIL: GGANNON@JCU.EDU • WEBSITE: WWW.JCU.EDU/MBA

Student Life and Environment

Like many universities with a large commuter and online student population, student life at Boler is a little lacking. But while some wish there were more activities or options for socializing, others say "there is no reason any John Carroll student should ever be bored." "John Carroll's sports teams are always competing on campus and provide high-level sports entertainment." Additionally, "there is plenty to do in the area socially," and "downtown is within 15 minutes of campus." Perhaps some of the 5th year MBA students find themselves with time to socialize, but plenty of part-time students say that between their jobs, classes, schoolwork, and families, they don't have time for anything else anyway. Students say that despite this, they've "formed several relationships within their cohort" and are in "constant e-mail communication" with other students. There is a lot of "camaraderie" among students, who describe their peers as "friendly," "supportive," "professional," and "intelligent." Students are competitive but are still "very open and willing to help each other."

Admissions

Boler requires a minimum of two years of professional experience to be admitted to the part-time MBA program. No work experience is required for students applying to the 5th-year MBA program. Students applying to Boler must submit official transcripts from all colleges attended, GMAT scores, one letter of recommendation, a resume, and a personal statement entitled "Graduate Business Education: Enabling Me to Achieve My Personal Goals and Become a Leader." The MBA program requires a minimum GPA of 2.8 and a GMAT score of 500. The average GPA of the entering class is 3.30 and an average GMAT score of 540. International applicants, whose primary language is not English must take the TOEFL and score a minimum of 550 on the paper portion, 215 on the computer portion and 79 on the Internet portion. They must also have their "non-US credentials" evaluated by an independent organization.

FINANCIAL FACTS

Annual tuition	$15,390
Fees	$0
Cost of books	$1,000
% of students receiving aid	58
% of first-year students receiving aid	76
% of students receiving grants	14
Average award package	$15,616
Average grant	$4,200
Average loan	$10,409
Average student loan debt	$15,679

ADMISSIONS

Admissions Selectivity Rating	73
# of applications received	78
% applicants accepted	74
% acceptees attending	53
Average GMAT	540
Range of GMAT	500–560
Average GPA	3.30
TOEFL required of international students	Yes
Minimum TOEFL (paper/computer)	550/215
Application fee	$0
International application fee	$0
Deferment available	Yes
Maximum length of deferment	1 year
Transfer students accepted	Yes
Transfer application policy: Applicants from members of the Network of MBA Programs at Jesuit Universities and Colleges, will have all MBA credits transferred. Otherwise, applicants are reviewed on a case-by-case basis.	
Non-fall admissions	Yes
Need-blind admissions	Yes

EMPLOYMENT PROFILE

Career Rating	73	Grads Employed by Function	% Avg. Salary
Percent employed at graduation	62	Marketing	(15%)
Primary Source of Full-time Job Acceptances		Operations	(0%)
School-facilitated activities	4(31%)	Consulting	(0%)
Graduate-facilitated activities	4(31%)	Finance	(77%)
Unknown	5(38%)	Other	(8%)

Top 5 Employers Hiring Grads
PricewaterhouseCoopers (5), Ernst & Young (1), Fastenal (1), Grant Thornton (1), Park Place Technologies (1)

KENNESAW STATE UNIVERSITY
MICHAEL J. COLES COLLEGE OF BUSINESS

GENERAL INFORMATION
Type of school   Public
Affiliation   No Affiliation
Academic calendar   Semester

SURVEY SAYS...
Cutting-edge classes
Solid preparation in:
General management, Teamwork

STUDENTS
Enrollment of parent institution	24,502
Enrollment of MBA Program	455
% male/female	100/0
% out-of-state	0
% part-time	71
% underrepresented minority	0
% international	0
Average age at entry	33
Average years work experience at entry	9.0

ACADEMICS
Academic Experience Rating	**84**
Profs interesting rating	88
Profs accesible rating	89
Student/faculty ratio	8:1
% female faculty	35
% underrepresented minority faculty	20
% part-time faculty	5

Prominent Alumni
Gregory Simone, President and Chief Executive Officer of WellStar Health Systems,Inc.; Wiliam Hayes, Chief Exedcutive Officer of Northside Hospital-Cherokee; Lawrence Wallace, principal accountant at Price-Waterhouse-Coopers; Kerstin Valdes, Vice President and Chief Internal auditor at Earthlink; Carl Johnson, Principal Accountant at Coca-Cola company

Academics

The second largest business program in the state of Georgia, Coles College of Business at Kennesaw State University has a "strong reputation in the Southeast" and deep ties in the Atlanta business community. This school's efficient MBA program is specifically designed for working professionals, offering a "flexible class schedule" and business facilities in "different locations in and around Atlanta." Students who want to pursue an aggressive schedule can get their degree in as few as 18 months, though the school allows up to six years to complete an MBA.

No matter which pace you pursue, the MBA program is "academically challenging and rewarding," kicking off with a seven-course core curriculum in management, finance, accounting, marketing, and other business fundamentals. After completing the core, there is "a lot of flexibility with upper-level electives to help shape your degree." In addition to topics like marketing, finance, accounting, and systems administration, the school offers a range of interesting electives in international business topics. Outside the classroom, there are ample opportunities to augment coursework with "networking and outside class experiences," from overseas service projects to national recruiting events. One student tells us, "As a part of Operation Management class, we are carrying out a project of improving the University's warehouse and asset handling system."

Courses are "fast paced, modern, and focused on entrepreneurship." Striking a good balance, "professors are experts in their fields and passionate about teaching others." Often, they teach from "their experiences rather than from a textbook." In addition, the majority of faculty is "approachable, easy to get along with, and professional." The school maintains an excellent faculty-student ratio, and professors really "make themselves accessible to students" outside the classroom.

Throughout coursework, "classmates are very involved in class discussions and bring real-world examples and experiences into the classroom." A student relates, "I am so impressed with the diverse backgrounds and experiences of my classmates. I have learned so much, not only from the class material, but also from the discussions in class." Rigor, however, can be lacking, and some think the school would benefit from "tougher courses or stronger requirements to succeed in existing courses." Like the teaching staff, "the administration puts a lot of effort into communicating" with students. Despite the size and affordable tuition, students never feel like a number at Kennesaw State.

Career and Placement

To assist graduate students in their job searches, Coles has partnered with the independent job services website, CareerBeam. This virtual career services portal assists students with everything from resume and cover letter preparation to building a job search strategy and conducting industry research. MBA candidates may also solicit help at the University's Career Services Center, which operates on-campus recruiting programs for both jobs and internships. Students would love to see "better job placement opportunities" aimed specifically at the MBA program, as well as larger career fairs with big Atlanta companies. Students admit that, at the Kennesaw career fairs, "The number of companies represented is few and poor." In addition to the resources available at the Career Services Center, there is a dedicated career counselor in the Coles Business School, available to help both undergraduate and graduate students.

ADMISSIONS CONTACT: DAVID BAUGHER, DIRECTOR OF ADMISSIONS
ADDRESS: 1000 CHASTAIN ROAD, #9109, KENNESAW, GA 30144
PHONE: 770-420-4470 • FAX: 770-423-6141
E-MAIL: KSUGRAD@KENNESAW.EDU • WEBSITE: WWW.COLESMBA.COM

The majority of students are already working when they enter the program, and they are not actively pursuing new positions after graduation. However, they continue to leverage their business school education after graduation through increased career opportunities and the large Atlanta alumni network. After graduation, alumni can continue to visit the college and make contacts through ongoing networking events at the business school.

Student Life and Environment

Kennesaw recruits students with diverse backgrounds, admitting qualified students from overseas or through its unique program for former Peace Corps volunteers. In the classroom, there is a "wide range of views, industries, experience, and personality" among the student body. In fact, the atmosphere can feel "like a good family reunion—crazy Uncle Bob, nerdy Aunt Susan, hard-working cousin Mike, fun-living sister Sally... all wildly different, but all happy to see you and willing to help out like family." "A good sense of camaraderie exists among students," who are "sociable and helpful when it comes to class work." Even as they balance demanding careers, students "are all willing to work together to get projects done and willing to spend the necessary time to do a quality job."

Although the Coles MBA program is "great for professionals," it tends to attract busy young adults with little time for campus life. For graduate students, Kennesaw is predominantly a "commuter school," and there is "not a lively graduate student presence on campus." However, those who'd like to get involved in the school community say, "There are plenty of academic and professional clubs," as well as numerous volunteer activities at the business school and through the larger University. It's up to each student to determine the time and energy they want to invest.

Admissions

To apply to Kennesaw State's MBA programs, prospective students must submit three items: a professional resume, official academic transcripts, and GMAT scores. Although interviews are not required, students may also request an interview with admissions staff. In recent years, the average GMAT score for incoming graduate students was 556. The class had an average undergraduate GPA of 3.1. Anyone who submits an online application to the University can enroll in free GMAT prep courses at the Kennesaw campus.

FINANCIAL FACTS

Room & board	
(on/off-campus)	$7,500/$10,000
Average loan	$10,250
Average student loan debt	$20,500

ADMISSIONS

Admissions Selectivity Rating	82
# of applications received	418
% applicants accepted	65
% acceptees attending	76
Average GMAT	592
Range of GMAT	550–700
Average GPA	3.27
TOEFL required of	
international students	Yes
Minimum TOEFL	
(paper/computer)	550/213
Application fee	$60
International application fee	$60
Early application deadline	6/1
Regular application deadline	8/1
Deferment available	Yes
Maximum length	
of deferment	1 year
Transfer students accepted	Yes
Transfer application policy: Transfer credit from AACSB International accredited universities is possible. Limits and restrictions apply.	
Non-fall admissions	Yes
Need-blind admissions	Yes

KENT STATE UNIVERSITY

THE COLLEGE OF BUSINESS ADMINISTRATION AND GRADUATE SCHOOL OF MANAGEMENT

Academics

A big name in Ohio education, Kent State University serves the Midwest with a range of high-quality MBA programs. Here, young professionals can jump-start their careers through an "enjoyable and enlightening" academic curriculum, offered at "a value price." Catering to students at every stage of life, the school operates a full-time MBA on the main campus and part-time professional programs at various satellite campuses, including "distance learning for students at the Lorain County Community College and Kent State Stark campus." Seasoned managers can apply for the fast-paced Executive MBA, and "Kent is one of a few schools in the nation that has a dual-masters degree with architecture and business." Cost effective and convenient, "Kent State is in the heart of northeast Ohio, which makes it possible to have a career in one of the surrounding cities, while going to graduate school part-time."

Kent State maintains an accomplished team of business professors, who often come to the college from impressive executive and managerial positions. On the whole, "professors are extremely knowledgeable and eager to teach," and they usually "stay up-to-date on current events and issues related to their fields in business." At the same time, the classroom experience can be "hit and miss," with students often noting that, "tenured staff tends not to be as good as younger staff." In less popular classes, "the coursework is outdated" or too academic to feel applicable. To encourage networking and build soft skills, the program "promotes group work," and classroom discussions are encouraged. A current student adds, "In the professional MBA program, everyone is working, so we are able to share real-world experiences in the classroom. There is something every night in class that I can take and apply to my job."

Whether they attend in the evenings or full-time, MBA students can expect a "fairly heavy workload" throughout the program. Fortunately, they'll receive plenty of support from the faculty and staff. At Kent State, "the professors are incredibly interested in the students' success," and they are "almost always available for individual consultation on topics not necessarily related to class work." A student shares, "I am very comfortable meeting with professors during office hours, even when I am not enrolled in one of their courses." Administrators are also "very helpful," and make it clear that they "really care about your future success as an individual." Finally, Kent State is an excellent value. As a state school, "the tuition is relatively low," while the regional reputation is excellent.

Career and Placement

Most students in the Professional MBA are already employed when they enter the program, and may even be receiving tuition reimbursement from their employer. As a result, the majority of these students are not actively seeking employment. However, Kent State makes an "effort to prepare students for life after graduation," even if they aren't looking for a new job. Across the curriculum, "the classes are well integrated into real-world business careers," and practical applications are emphasized.

While completing an MBA, students have access to various professional development opportunities, including networking events, career planning workshops, and a mentorship program, through which students are paired with executives in their field of interest. Students can also "consult advisors and a career manager to know more about how to draft a career plan and get fully prepared." With a strong reputation throughout the state, the school maintains "good contacts with potential employers" in the region. However, students feel Kent State could improve job prospects by "increasing the availability of career fairs and resume-builder nights" aimed at MBA candidates. After

ADMISSIONS CONTACT: LOUISE DITCHEY, ADMINISTRATIVE DIRECTOR
ADDRESS: P.O. BOX 5190, 475 TERRACE DRIVE, KENT, OH 44242-0001
PHONE: 330-672-2282 • FAX: 330-672-7303
E-MAIL: GRADBUS@KENT.EDU • WEBSITE: WWW.KENT.EDU/BUSINESS/GRAD

completing the MBA program, Kent State graduates earn anywhere between $30,000 and $72,500 annually.

Student Life and Environment

On the main campus, as well as the auxiliary facilities, Kent State offers a "great atmosphere and learning environment for its students." Students are able to maintain a balanced lifestyle, as "the workload is enough to keep busy, but not so busy that you cannot have a life outside of school and work." Plus, "the business school encourages students to stay involved with extracurricular activities," like case competition and academic clubs. "Full-time students are more apt to be involved" in campus life than busy part-time students. Nonetheless, "The camaraderie among professional students is very strong" at Kent State. Drawing students from across the globe, the business program benefits from "rich diversity in student culture and ethnicity." Classroom discussion can become rather lively, and "even if we don't agree on political or social issues, there is always room for intellectual debate."

Beyond the business school, the greater Kent State University is "large enough to offer any club or activity students are interested in." Off campus, Kent is "a college town" that offers "opportunities for community service and professional practice," as well as good old-fashioned fun.

Admissions

If you are considering Kent State for your MBA, you'll get your first taste of the college's charms through the "friendliness of the recruiting staff." Full-time students can only apply for fall admission, and there are several priority application deadlines during the winter and spring. The school also offers graduate assistantship programs to help full-time students pay for their education. To be considered for an assistantship or scholarship, students must submit an additional application form and should apply as early as possible. The average test scores, work experience, and GPA of incoming students vary by program. However, the average GPA and GMAT scores for the entire program were 3.4 and 565, respectively.

FINANCIAL FACTS

Annual tuition (in-state/ out-of-state)	$10,290/$17,806
Fees	$1,200
Cost of books	$1,200
Room & board (on/off-campus)	$9,744/$8,500
% of students receiving aid	15
% of first-year students receiving aid	7
% of students receiving grants	0
Average award package	$19,354
Average grant	$0
Average loan	$0

ADMISSIONS

Admissions Selectivity Rating	84
# of applications received	86
% applicants accepted	43
% acceptees attending	43
Average GMAT	569
Range of GMAT	520–620
Average GPA	3.27
TOEFL required of international students	Yes
Minimum TOEFL (paper/computer)	550/213
Application fee	$30
International application fee	$60
Regular application deadline	4/1
Regular application notification	4/15
Deferment available	Yes
Maximum length of deferment	two years
Transfer students accepted	Yes
Transfer application policy: AASCB accredited program, less than 6 years old by the time Kent degree is conferred, 12 credit hours maximum, approved by graduate committee and dean.	
Non-fall admissions	Yes
Need-blind admissions	Yes

EMPLOYMENT PROFILE

Career Rating	68	Grads Employed by Function	% Avg. Salary
Average base starting salary	$35,750	Finance	(50%) $40,000
		MIS	(25%)
		Other	(25%)

LAMAR UNIVERSITY
COLLEGE OF BUSINESS

GENERAL INFORMATION
Type of school	Public
Affiliation	No Affiliation
Academic calendar	Semester

SURVEY SAYS...
Friendly students, Happy students
Solid preparation in:
General management, Teamwork,
Communication/interpersonal skills,
Presentation skills

STUDENTS
Enrollment of parent institution	14,675
Enrollment of MBA Program	117
% male/female	79/21
% part-time	32
Average age at entry	28

ACADEMICS
Academic Experience Rating	**80**
Profs interesting rating	78
Profs accesible rating	81
Student/faculty ratio	3:1
% female faculty	26
% underrepresented minority faculty	40
% part-time faculty	9

Joint Degrees
MSN/MBA in 61 hours MBA/MSA

Academics

"They are constantly trying to improve and innovate the program" at Lamar University, where students love being part of an "an outstanding university that is growing almost exponentially." Not that it needs much in the way of improvement; even as it currently stands, Lamar is seen by its students as "a great school with well-educated professors and a good learning environment." A student body drawn largely from Beaumont and the surrounding area chooses the Lamar MBA for its convenience, its low cost, its reputation, and its unwillingness to settle for "good enough."

Lamar offers a 5 year BBA/MBA, a full-time evening program that includes several experiential learning opportunities. The program is intense: Classes meet four nights a week, and the curriculum goes pretty much nonstop for 16 months, but those who tough it out are rewarded with an MBA earned in a relatively short time for relatively little money. The school also offers a traditional MBA, which also meets in the evenings, but it allows for part-time attendance. The traditional MBA program is open to all college graduates; those who lack the requisite academic business background must complete a series of leveling courses before commencing the MBA proper.

Students report that the programs have more of a cooperative than competitive feel. They appreciate the "relaxed classroom settings" and "the ability to meet with faculty and students without pressure and [to discuss] issues related to business." "Smaller classes" make it "easy to obtain one-on-one time with a professor" and also ensure that students aren't just a number or name on a list to administrators. In fact, "every student is required to be advised, which means the people in MBA office know who you are and what you are doing when you walk into the office." "The administration for the MBA program is well-organized."

Lamar professors "keep current with the latest business developments and they constantly work on outside research projects. They often present papers at conferences and work to expand their professional knowledge base. We have several professors that work as marketers or business owners so they bring their practical experience to class." The faculty consists of a "small core group of professors," which "builds relationships [between students and teachers] throughout the years."

Career and Placement

The Career and Testing Center at Lamar provides services for all undergraduates, graduate students, and alumni of the university. Services include counseling, workshops, online job database access, and recruitment events. The majority of Lamar MBAs work full time while attending the program. Many do not plan to leave their employers during or after the program.

Employers who most frequently hire graduates include: Ernst and Young, Melton and Melton, Merrill Lynch, Smith Barney, JP Morgan Chase, Medical Center of Southeast Texas, Wells Fargo, and Verizon.

ADMISSIONS CONTACT: MELISSA GALLIEN, GRADUATE ADMISSIONS OFFICE
ADDRESS: P. O. BOX 10009, BEAUMONT, TX 77710
PHONE: 409-880-8356 • FAX: 409-880-8414
E-MAIL: GRADMISSIONS@LAMAR.EDU • WEBSITE: MBA.LAMAR.EDU

Student Life and Environment

"Lamar has traditionally been a commuter [school]," and while "that is changing," for the most part it's still the case that "students come to class and go home afterwards even when activities are planned." There are some "active on-campus organizations" for MBAs, but they "tend to be geared towards those living on-campus, which mainly consist of international students and those receiving full scholarships."

Lamar's business facility is "dated, and some classrooms have equipment and maps that are falling apart," which understandably rankles some. Students also complain that "more business-specific applications could be available on our college's computers, [as well as] more labs with larger work stations to accommodate groups. Much of the MBA program is centered around group work, and it is difficult to cram into a narrow row of computers set up traditional classroom-style to spread out and collaborate."

Lamar's "friendly, yet competitive" MBAs mostly "work full time, and they bring plenty of real-world experience to the class." The program creates "quite a diverse setting with many international students as well as local commuters. Lamar is very well-rounded and diverse for its size."

Admissions

Lamar University requires all applicants to provide GMAT scores, undergraduate transcripts, essays, and TOEFL scores (for students whose native language is not English). An interview, letters of recommendation, personal statement, resume, and evidence of computer experience are all recommended but not required; all are taken into account in rendering an admissions decision. Applicants must earn a score of at least 950 under the formula (200 multiplied by GPA plus GMAT score) or a score of 1000 under the formula (200 multiplied by GPA for final 60 semester hours of undergraduate work plus GMAT score). In both cases, a minimum GMAT score of 450 is required for unconditional admission; students with scores between 400 and 450 qualify for conditional admission. International applicants must provide proof of financial support.

FINANCIAL FACTS

Annual tuition (in-state/ out-of-state)	$8,046/$18,873
Fees	$3,345
Cost of books	$1,741
Room & board	$9,980
% of students receiving aid	99
% of first-year students receiving aid	100
% of students receiving grants	84
Average award package	$3,537
Average grant	$932
Average loan	$2,605
Average student loan debt	$27,319

ADMISSIONS

Admissions Selectivity Rating	83
# of applications received	93
% applicants accepted	44
% acceptees attending	76
Average GMAT	507
Range of GMAT	460–558
Average GPA	3.05
TOEFL required of international students	Yes
Minimum TOEFL (paper/computer)	550/212
Application fee	$25
International application fee	$75
Early application deadline	4/15
Regular application deadline	7/1
Deferment available	Yes
Maximum length of deferment	1 year
Transfer students accepted	Yes
Transfer application policy: Accept 6 hours from another AACSB MBA program	
Non-fall admissions	Yes
Need-blind admissions	Yes

EMPLOYMENT PROFILE

Career Rating	68	Grads Employed by Function	% Avg. Salary
Primary Source of Full-time Job Acceptances		Management	(13%) $28,500
School-facilitated activities	1(7%)	Finance	(33%) $71,200
Graduate-facilitated activities	1(7%)	HR	(13%) $54,600
Unknown	12(86%)	MIS	(7%)
		Other	(33%) $48,562

LONG ISLAND UNIVERSITY—C.W. POST CAMPUS
COLLEGE OF MANAGEMENT

GENERAL INFORMATION

Type of school	Private
Affiliation	No Affiliation
Academic calendar	Trimester

SURVEY SAYS...

Students love Brookville, NY, Cutting-edge classes
Solid preparation in:
General management, Doing business in a global economy

STUDENTS

Enrollment of parent institution	16,695
Enrollment of MBA Program	228
% male/female	56/44
% out-of-state	2
% part-time	30
% underrepresented minority	6
% international	53
Average age at entry	26
Average years work experience at entry	4.5

ACADEMICS

Academic Experience Rating	**72**
Profs interesting rating	73
Profs accesible rating	73
Student/faculty ratio	15:1
% female faculty	34
% underrepresented minority faculty	17
% part-time faculty	10

Joint Degrees

JD/MBA, JD-3 years, MBA 1.5 years; BS/MBA, BS-4 years, MBA 1 year

Academics

Long Island University's C.W. Post Campus offers an AACSB-accredited MBA through "the flexibility of a Saturday program" or through a series of night classes, which occur weekly, Monday through Thursday. The Saturday program takes anywhere from 15 to 23 months to complete and features all-day classes held only on Saturdays. Additionally, those who opt for weekly night classes may supplement them with Saturday classes, as well. There is also an advanced certification program in which students may opt to specialize in one of six areas, including finance and international business. The requirement for this program is four additional electives. Most students choose a part-time schedule because it allows them to comfortably continue leading lives off campus. "I attend night classes, which do not interfere with my daily schedule. As a full-time student I am enrolled in three courses of study, which are highly relevant and have real-world applications." Another student says, "I would truly recommend others for this program. Flexibility is key when you have a full-time job."

Enrolled students come from various business backgrounds, such as medical communications, construction, and wedding planning. "The differing perspectives at Post help to broaden the overall attitude of students and faculty alike. You learn something new every day." Some "students are looking to kick start their own careers and help contribute to Long Island communities," while others have little or no experience. Students who attended LIU for their undergraduate studies say they have no problem adapting to the graduate curriculum. And of those with no prior training, one claims to have quickly gained an "excellent" grasp on the material because of the program's professors. "They are always willing to clarify content and go the extra mile." "The faculty are all Ph.D. holders from prestigious business schools." "Most or all have considerable real-world experience" as well. Students are pleased with the professors' ability to follow current global events and economic shifts. One student says the program "makes you become more creative and competitive. I can see the big difference between my friends in other colleges. I feel gifted for being educated in this school." Some students feel differently, suggesting that not all professors measure up. They also argue that there aren't enough options. "The range of courses could be a lot better and wider." Some classes that are listed are not offered every year.

ADMISSIONS CONTACT: CAROL ZERÁH, DIRECTOR OF GRADUATE AND INTERNATIONAL ADMISSIONS
ADDRESS: 720 NORTHERN BOULEVARD, BROOKVILLE, NY 11548
PHONE: 516-299-3952 • FAX: 516-299-2418
E-MAIL: CAROL.ZERÁH@LIU.EDU • WEBSITE: WWW.LIU.EDU/CWPOST

As far as the administration is concerned, students had little to say. One complimented the librarians who help with projects and papers, and another says, "All the departments have very good employees and are always willing to help you." The B. Davis Schwartz Memorial Library houses 2.3 million volumes.

Career and Placement

The Office of Career Services offers a variety of services to the students at LIU including the following: career counseling, mock interviews, recruiting events, and self-assessment diagnostics. Students, however, find real job assistance lacking. One describes it as "nonexistent," while another suggests, "Get better companies to come to job fairs." However, many students at LIU are professionals already working in the field, and the student services do not apply to them. As of 2013, LIU has a Placement Director exclusively for College of Management students.

Student Life and Environment

Students praise each other as "smart" and "dedicated." "There is a good mix ranging in age, ethnic background, educational background, and career background. All are friendly and we work well together." They also describe each other as "intelligent," "ambitious," "outgoing," and "cooperative." Students "bring a lot of ideas to class discussion," probably because they are a part of a "very diverse population." LIU has many international students. There is a high percentage of locals in the student body as well. They choose the school precisely for that reason—it's close to home.

C.W. Post's "breathtaking campus" spans a few hundred acres of green lawns and dense woods. It's near the beaches on the North Shore of Long Island, and students "love the location," as well as its proximity to New York City. Most are commuters and find that aside from academics, there isn't much to keep them on campus. They do mention, however, that "class times are set up to provide ample time for commuters." One thing they do complain about is the lack of parking on campus, although a few students suggest it's nicer to have the trees and a longer walk, than sacrifice the natural beauty. As far as balancing home and work life with a part-time MBA, one student says confidently, "I am very busy with work and a family, and I have been able to accomplish everything that will ensure my success."

Admissions

The admissions committee at LIU requires candidates to submit official GMAT scores, undergraduate GPA, two letters of recommendation, a personal essay, and a resume. Other elements the committee takes into consideration are extracurricular activities, work experience, and an interview. Students must also be competent in business communications, mathematics, and computers and be able to pass a waiver exam. TOEFL scores are necessary for those students whose first language is not English. The average GMAT score of admitted students is 465, and the average GPA is 3.24.

FINANCIAL FACTS

Annual tuition $19,224	
Fees	$1,266
Cost of books	$2,100
Room & board	
(on/off-campus)	$15,620/$17,650
Average grant	$3,000

ADMISSIONS

Admissions Selectivity Rating	71
# of applications received	152
% applicants accepted	78
% acceptees attending	51
Average GMAT	470
Range of GMAT	430–490
Average GPA	3.21
TOEFL required of international students	Yes
Minimum TOEFL (paper/computer)	563/223
Application fee	$40
International application fee	$40
Regular application deadline	8/15
Regular application notification	8/15
Deferment available	Yes
Maximum length of deferment	1 year
Transfer students accepted	Yes
Transfer application policy: Maximum of 6 credits within the last five years, grades of "B" or better. AACSB accredited School.	
Non-fall admissions	Yes
Need-blind admissions	Yes

LOUISIANA STATE UNIVERSITY
E. J. OURSO COLLEGE OF BUSINESS

GENERAL INFORMATION
Type of school   Public
Affiliation   No Affiliation
Academic calendar   Fall/Spring/
                                       Summer

SURVEY SAYS...
Friendly students, Good social scene
Solid preparation in:
Teamwork

STUDENTS
Enrollment of parent
  institution   28,810
Enrollment of MBA Program   207
% male/female   56/44
% out-of-state   10
% part-time   55
% underrepresented minority   4
% international   22
Average age at entry   23
Average years work experience
  at entry   1.4

ACADEMICS
Academic Experience Rating   92
Profs interesting rating   85
Profs accesible rating   83
Student/faculty ratio   20:1
% female faculty   27
% underrepresented minority
  faculty   3
% part-time faculty   0

Joint Degrees
JD/MBA, also awards a Bachelor of
Science in Civil Law, 4 years

Prominent Alumni
James C. Flores, Chairman, Chief
Executive Officer and President,
Plains Exploration & Production
Company; Joseph Herring,
CEO/Chairman of the
Board/Director, Covance, Inc.; David
P. Steiner, President and Chief
Executive Officer, Waste
Management; Emmet Stephenson,
Chief Executive Officer of
Stephenson and Company and
Stephenson Ventures.

Academics

Louisiana State University's E. J. Ourso College of Business unites "a great quality curriculum, impressive career placement, and low tuition costs" in a single prestigious program. This large public school serves the needs of a diverse business community by offering full-time, Professional MBA (part-time), and Executive MBAs, while maintaining an "outstanding reputation on a national level." For students in all three programs, the MBA begins with a core curriculum in business fundamentals, including accounting, marketing, and finance. After completing the core, "students get a lot of freedom in choosing their electives," which range from entrepreneurship to IT management. Of particular note, the school distinguishes itself with "one of the best internal audit programs in the country." Special academic programs further compliment coursework; for example, the entrepreneurship programs offers "real-world coursework that allows students to work with local business upstarts in obtaining venture capital."

At LSU, the classroom experience is top notch. "Classes are well structured and academically challenging," and "the small class size makes getting access to professors easy." Professors are generally "well accomplished in their careers," but never look down their noses at students. On the contrary, they are "open to new ideas and shape lectures based on student input, student interest, and current events." Incorporating lots of discussion and group work, classes are "structured in a way that resembles a work environment rather than a normal classroom." Through case studies and presentations, students are called upon to "discuss real-world applications in all classes instead of just learning the theories behind the topics." By encouraging a deeper involvement with the material, professors "really create a learning and participatory environment that encourages thinking."

The real world is never far from the classroom, and LSU makes a point of "connecting us with area business leaders and exposing us to opportunities with local companies." As a result, "LSU is known around the South for having one of the best MBA programs," as well as a loyal alumni base. While students don't dispute the school's great reputation, they have mixed feelings about the school's operation. Some say the "administration could use some work," but the school has recently undergone a drastic change in administration as well as opened a brand new MBA facility in 2012.

Career and Placement

LSU Flores knows that MBA candidates want to land choice jobs after graduation, and "all levels of administration are focused on placing students into their jobs of choice by rigorous career management and a high level of academics." Real-world skills are taught throughout the program, and students "get lessons on everything from dinner etiquette to attire and interviewing." "The fact that LSU has such a strong connection with Louisiana companies and businesses from the surrounding local areas, really provides benefit to students." LSU also connects students with "a vast network of alumni that come back to the school to speak and recruit." For full-time students, "the internship program is remarkable," offering the opportunity to get their feet wet in the real world. In addition to business school programs, graduate students can make use of LSU's Career Services Office. There is an annual career fair, which serves the entire campus, as well as a special career reception for just the business school.

ADMISSIONS CONTACT: DANA C. HART, ASSISTANT DIRECTOR OF ENROLLMENT & STUDENT SERVICES
ADDRESS: E. J. OURSO COLLEGE OF BUSINESS, 3176 PATRICK F. TAYLOR HALL, BATON ROUGE, LA 70803
PHONE: 225-578-8867 • FAX: 225-578-2421
E-MAIL: BUSMBA@LSU.EDU • WEBSITE: MBA.LSU.EDU

Finance and accounting are the two most popular fields for LSU graduates, capturing more than 35 percent of the student body. Operations and marketing follow, together comprising more than a third of the students. The average salary for LSU graduates is about $55,000, with offers ranging from $45,000 to $75,000, depending on a student's field and industry. Shaw Group, Capital One, Altria, Schering-Plough, ExxonMobil, AmSouth Bank, Eli Lilly and Company, Entergy Corporation, Cameron, and Chevron are among LSU's recent employers. By graduation, 62 percent of MBA students had already accepted an offer, and another 12 percent joined them three months later.

Student Life and Environment

For LSU Flores MBA candidates, the lifestyle at LSU is well-rounded and rewarding. Coursework is very time consuming, but "there is a strong sense of camaraderie among students, which is fueled by long hours spent working on group projects." Plus, "the curriculum is challenging, but is beautifully balanced by constant social opportunities." Among the many options within the business school, "The LSU Flores MBA Association has made great efforts to sponsor social events, so students get a chance to meet their classmates." In addition, students are involved in numerous philanthropic projects around Baton Rouge, and "regularly partner with Toys for Tots, Habitat for Humanity, and Boys Hope Girls Hope." Even those who rarely participate in campus activities are quick to admit that, "LSU athletic events are the experience of a lifetime, especially football games at Tiger Stadium."

"Baton Rouge is easily one of the top college towns in the country," offering a plethora of inexpensive, student-oriented fun. In their free time, classmates "get together to participate in amateur sports leagues, foreign movie night, charity events, Mardi Gras, Baton Rouge Arts Melt, and marathons." Those who love the South are particularly happy here, noting that, "Louisiana State University is fueled by deep southern traditions, rooted in cultures and customs that cannot be duplicated anywhere else in the nation."

Admissions

Admission to the LSU Flores MBA Pprogram is competitive. To be considered eligible for the program, students must have a GPA of at least 3.0 from undergraduate coursework. Although there is no minimum GMAT score required for admission, the school favors applicants with scores in the 600s, or better. In 2010, the average GMAT score was 609. LSU encourages students seeking scholarships to apply early in the admissions cycle.

FINANCIAL FACTS

Annual tuition	$7,200
Fees	$6,000
Cost of books	$1,500
Room & board (on/off-campus)	$7,000/$8,500
% of students receiving aid	60
% of students receiving grants	21
Average award package	$18,645
Average grant	$16,139
Average loan	$17,265
Average student loan debt	$8,181

ADMISSIONS

Admissions Selectivity Rating	90
# of applications received	151
% applicants accepted	37
% acceptees attending	64
Average GMAT	632
Range of GMAT	500–740
Average GPA	3.40
TOEFL required of international students	Yes
Minimum TOEFL (paper/computer)	550/213
Application fee	$50
International application fee	$70
Early application deadline	12/3
Early notification date	12/17
Regular application deadline	5/15
Regular application notification	6/1

Application Deadline/Notification	
Round 1:	12/3 / 12/17
Round 2:	2/4 / 2/25
Round 3:	4/8 / 4/29
Round 4:	5/15 / 6/1
Deferment available	Yes
Maximum length of deferment	1 year
Transfer students accepted	Yes

Transfer application policy: Applicants must have attended an AACSB accredited school and meet the entrance requirements for the Flores MBA Program. Core course transfers may not be approved. Limited transfer credit may be approved on an individual basis. LSU Professional MBA students may transfer under certain circumstances.

Non-fall admissions	No
Need-blind admissions	Yes

EMPLOYMENT PROFILE

Career Rating	87		
Percent employed at graduation	84		
Percent employed 3 months after graduation	92		
Average base starting salary	$59,762		
Primary Source of Full-time Job Acceptances			
School-facilitated activities	29(50%)		
Graduate-facilitated activities	29(50%)		

Grads Employed by Function	%	Avg. Salary
Marketing	(12%)	$53,350
Operations	(7%)	$65,000
Consulting	(14%)	$68,500
Management	(20%)	$49,262
Finance	(22%)	$62,778
HR	(2%)	$93,000
Other	(23%)	$61,017

Top 5 Employers Hiring Grads
Exxon (1), Deloitte (2), Baker Hughes (2), Ernst & Young (2), KPMG (1)

LOYOLA MARYMOUNT UNIVERSITY
COLLEGE OF BUSINESS ADMINISTRATION

GENERAL INFORMATION

Type of school   Private
Affiliation   Roman Catholic-Jesuit
Academic calendar   Semester

SURVEY SAYS...

Friendly students, Good peer network, Good social scene, Happy students, Students love Los Angeles, CA
Solid preparation in:
Entrepreneurial studies, Social responsibility

STUDENTS

Enrollment of parent institution	9,369
Enrollment of MBA Program	242
% part-time	100
Average age at entry	27
Average years work experience at entry	5.0

ACADEMICS

Academic Experience Rating	**85**
Profs interesting rating	87
Profs accesible rating	86
Student/faculty ratio	3:1
% female faculty	20
% underrepresented minority faculty	29
% part-time faculty	38

Joint Degrees

JD/MBA, 4 years; SELP/MBA, 4 years

Academics

Students rule the school at Loyola Marymount University. At this private Southern California institution, each MBA candidate can pursue an education that uniquely fits his or her lifestyle, professional commitments, and educational goals. Offering both full-time and part-time programs, Loyola offers the "flexibility of á la carte course selection as opposed to traditional cohort or 'lock-step' study." The "versatile and flexible schedule" even allows students to "switch between being part-time or full-time fairly easily." While 30 percent of students attend full-time, everything is designed with the busy student in mind; for example, the school offers "shorter two-week international classes, which are ideal for fully employed students who want to study abroad." "Getting required courses is always easy," and students appreciate "the ability to waive core courses" if you have equivalent academic or work experience. If students aren't sure exactly how to shape their experience, Loyola will help. Throughout the program, "professors and advisers will work with students to craft a program that meets their needs without taking over their life."

Loyola maintains a "very challenging and well-rounded curriculum," consisting of core coursework in ten key areas, an area of concentration, and five breadth electives. Loyola is a Jesuit school, and, as a result, "social entrepreneurship and ethics are hot topics throughout all the classes." The school is also "a leader in green business and has very strong connections to technology, aerospace, and defense industries." The academic experience is defined by "small class sizes and personal attention." When students need extra assistance with coursework—or even just to chat—"professors are easily accessible via phone, email, or during office hours." "Professors publish work regularly" and "are tremendously knowledgeable and up to date" on the business world. While a number of classes are extremely current, some students feel that "the school could do a much better job integrating current business and economic trends into the coursework."

Business students are keen to evaluate an organization's efficiency, and most give high marks to Loyola's operations. From class registration to scheduling, "the school's administration is a well-oiled machine that keeps everything running very smoothly and efficiently." "The new library is exceptional and helps facilitate on-campus studies and group work." The school even employs a "business librarian, who can help us do research." Unlike most commuter campuses, "parking on campus is a breeze, with free valet service during peak hours." Although Loyola maintains a reputation as "one of the best schools in the Los Angeles area," it continues to improve its rank and services. Among other factors, "The competitiveness and caliber of student has also increased significantly in just the past few years, improving the overall value of the experience."

Career and Placement

Current LMU students and alumni have full access to the MBA Career Services Office (CSO). The CSO provides access to several online job boards, provides resume and interview preparation advice, and offers individual career counseling. Students praise the career services staff that is "willing to provide extensive one-on-one time to students and will connect them with alumni across the nation." On that note, "Alumni have been extremely helpful in career advice, opportunities, and placement."

Students love Loyola's fabulous Los Angeles location, which keeps them close to a plethora of great job opportunities. While they have L.A. at their fingertips, students "would like to see more networking events and employers on campus" and more aggressive career placement. Fortunately, Loyola Marymount is constantly bettering its servic-

ADMISSIONS CONTACT: ELYNAR MORENO, MBA COORDINATOR
ADDRESS: ONE LMU DRIVE, MS 8387, LOS ANGELES, CA 90045-2659
PHONE: 310-338-2848 • FAX: 310-338-2899
E-MAIL: MBAPC@LMU.EDU • WEBSITE: MBA.LMU.EDU

es in response to student requests. Many note that, "The CSO has improved drastically over the past year with an increase in staff and response to student feedback." During the last few semesters, the "frequency of seminars and workshops has increased," while "job postings specifically recruiting LMU students have begun to rise." There is also a new push to create "joint programming with the Alumni Association."

Student Life and Environment

"Perched atop the bluff overlooking Marina Del Rey, the LMU campus is lush and beautiful," boasting an excellent environment and great resources for students. "The library is state of the art with phenomenal technology," and there is an "excellent gym and pool facility, which is also open to spouses." In the business school, students can take advantage of "an amazing new library, more computer and study rooms, an on-campus bar, and lounges and restaurants."

At Loyola, the year kicks off with the "Annual Welcome Back BBQ to bring current students and new students together." Thereafter, full-time students spend the most time on campus, "with part-time students often joining for study groups or networking mixers." For those who want to get involved in campus life, "the Student Association is very active and plans many events and volunteering programs throughout the year." Community service is popular with the business school, as are "happy hours, soccer matches, softball games, BBQs, and tailgating at University sports events." Since many students attend classes part-time, "Grad students mostly just come and go and don't really stay on campus between classes." However, "LMU has started organizing activities for married students with families," which may attract a new group of participants.

Admissions

Applicants are accepted to Loyola Marymount's MBA program on a rolling basis. Once all materials have been submitted, the admissions committee will render a decision in just two weeks. With limited space in the program, early applicants will have an advantage over those who apply late in the admissions cycle. Students are evaluated on their previous academic performance, work experience, GMAT scores, personal essay, and recommendations. The average GMAT for last year's entering class was 616, but the school accepted students with a wide range of test scores.

FINANCIAL FACTS
% of students receiving aid	74
% of students receiving grants	74
Average award package	$19,103

ADMISSIONS
Admissions Selectivity Rating	83
# of applications received	278
% applicants accepted	48
% acceptees attending	45
Average GMAT	582
Range of GMAT	550–622
Average GPA	3.26
TOEFL required of international students	Yes
Minimum TOEFL (paper/computer)	600/250
Application fee	$50
International application fee	$50
Deferment available	Yes
Maximum length of deferment	1 year
Transfer students accepted	Yes

Transfer application policy: Students from other Jesuit MBA Programs may transfer core and electives through the Jesuit Transfer Network. Students who attend an AACSB accredited MBA Program (non-Jesuit) with equivalent course work of B or better may ONLY transfer in 6 units of upper division course credit but may be elgibile for core course waivers.

Non-fall admissions	Yes
Need-blind admissions	Yes

EMPLOYMENT PROFILE
Career Rating	65	**Top 5 Employers Hiring Grads**
		Northrop Grumman (30), Boeing (9),
		Raytheon (7), Sony (5), B of A (4)

LOYOLA UNIVERSITY CHICAGO
GRADUATE SCHOOL OF BUSINESS

Academics

A university founded in the Jesuit tradition, "Loyola is a school that is focused on developing the entire individual," and business ethics is a mainstay of the MBA program. While MBA course content resembles other graduate business programs, Loyola distinguishes itself in a number of ways. In particular, "Success is not measured in dollars, but rather [in] how one can contribute to society in a meaningful and productive way." To that end, "Every class incorporates ethics and ethical situations and relates them to real-world business issues." At the same time, the curriculum focuses on practical business, and "is very relevant and applicable." Through coursework, students work in teams, analyze case studies, or work on live projects in cooperation with a partner business or organization. A current student enthuses, "I take advantage of student organizations and outside consulting projects, and often feel that these have more value than my classes." To add an international perspective to the MBA, "The study abroad program is fantastic," offering numerous two-week summer courses overseas. A current student enthuses, "I will be afforded wonderful study abroad opportunities through this program and will be traveling to China, India, and Rome."

Combining expertise with excellence, the majority of Loyola professors are "highly experienced and make the learning experience worthwhile." While there are some "pure academics" on staff, they are outnumbered by current and former business leaders, who bring real-world content to the coursework. In fact, Loyola's adjunct professors "are among the best at bringing a 'real-world' perspective into the classroom." Most importantly, professors are "very enthusiastic about their subject and classes, and they all very much love teaching." As a result, "The classroom experience is dynamic and engaging," and the "thought-provoking course content" inspires discussion and critical thinking. A student enthuses, "I have enjoyed many of my classes so much, I am actually somewhat disappointed when the quarter comes to an end!" At the same time, Loyola is a large school, so it's easier to get lost in the crowds. A current student admits, "It's difficult to have good, thoughtful discussions in classes with 50 people in attendance."

Loyola's "flexible class schedule" is great for part-time students, and "the course load is perfect for a professional who has a full-time job." In addition, the "ability to switch between full-time and part-time status" gives students the opportunity to complete their degree at their own pace. Full-timers, on the other hand, sometimes feel "the course work doesn't seem as challenging as it could be." A school on the move, "The GSB has grown considerably just within the last year," and students admit, "The administration seems a little overwhelmed by the number of students currently enrolled." Fortunately, a student writes, "The school is committed to providing students with an exceptional experience. When there are hurdles to overcome, the administration is quick to identify how things might improve."

Career and Placement

Loyola's downtown "location in a world class city" brings students within a stone's throw of many reputable employers. This private university maintains a great local reputation, and the focus on practical skills throughout the MBA curriculum helps to prepare students for the workplace. A current student agrees, "In this time of economic crisis, I feel incredibly prepared and optimistic that my MBA degree will make me stand out from the competition."

ADMISSIONS CONTACT: OLIVIA HEATH, ENROLLMENT ADVISOR
ADDRESS: 1 E. PEARSON, CHICAGO, IL 60611
PHONE: 312-915-6124 • FAX: 312-915-7207
E-MAIL: GSB@LUC.EDU • WEBSITE: WWW.LUC.EDU/GSB

Loyola University's Career Management Services assists job seekers through resume critiques, career workshops, and advising. They also operate an online recruiting program, which allows students to research employers, post their resumes, and sign up for campus interviews via the web. Despite these services, "The school could do a much better job attracting more quality employers to recruit at Loyola." A current MBA candidate laments, "The school is in a sweet spot for business in the country but doesn't take full advantage of the networking possibilities." On the other hand, "There are students who have found great jobs through Career Management and have received excellent coaching from the staff....It all depends on what a person expects."

Student Life and Environment

Loyola is a large, urban university, which attracts "all different backgrounds, ages, interests, career paths (if working), intelligence levels, and points of life." While some students are too busy to participate in extracurricular activities, others find time to "belong to a number of clubs that meet before class once or twice a month." More informally, there are "plenty of opportunities to mingle after class and on weekends," and students attend "social events at bars or restaurants after class every month." Still, you won't get the social atmosphere you'd find on a residential campus: "Although the social life is improving, the school definitely feels like a commuter school."

"Located in the heart of downtown Chicago," Loyola's well-placed campus is a major benefit of the program. Academic resources are good, and "The library is excellent." "Getting information from any source at the school has been easy." Unfortunately, many business school classrooms lack modern technology and suffer from "a poor layout, not conducive to class discussion." A student adds, "More than 30 percent of assignments are group related, yet less than 5 percent of computers in the library cater toward group work. Options like LCD projectors (or mounted televisions with a monitor input) in group rooms would be greatly appreciated."

Admissions

At Loyola, the academic calendar is divided into quarters. Accordingly, there are four start dates each year, so the school is continuously accepting and enrolling new students. To apply, prospective students must submit an application form, two letters of recommendation, a statement of purpose, a current resume, undergraduate transcripts, and official GMAT test scores.

FINANCIAL FACTS

Fees	$816
Cost of books	$1,200
Room & board	$15,930
% of students receiving aid	57
% of first-year students receiving aid	58
% of students receiving grants	7
Average award package	$26,863
Average grant	$11,628
Average loan	$27,780

ADMISSIONS

Admissions Selectivity Rating	74
# of applications received	401
% applicants accepted	71
% acceptees attending	50
Average GMAT	547
Range of GMAT	500–590
Average GPA	3.27
TOEFL required of international students	Yes
Minimum TOEFL (paper/computer)	577/233
Application fee	$50
International application fee	$50
Regular application deadline	7/15
Deferment available	Yes
Maximum length of deferment	1 year
Transfer students accepted	Yes

Transfer application policy: Up to 9 hours of B or better coursework can transfer from AACSB-accredited institutions. In order to assist students who are transferred to other cities before graduation, the MBA program at Loyola University Chicago participates in the Multilateral Jesuit MBA Agreement with a number of other MBA programs at Jesuit universities. The Jesuit Business School Network (JEBNET) transfer program allows special accommodations for students transferring from most Jesuit schools of business.

Non-fall admissions	Yes
Need-blind admissions	Yes

EMPLOYMENT PROFILE

Career Rating	79	**Grads Employed by Function% Avg. Salary**	
Percent employed at graduation	90	Marketing	(27%) $70,000
Percent employed 3 months after graduation	6	Operations	(8%) $70,000
		Consulting	(7%) $90,000
Average base starting salary	$70,000	Management	(12%) $60,000
Primary Source of Full-time Job Acceptances		Finance	(20%) $70,000
School-facilitated activities	30(20%)	HR	(4%) $60,000
Graduate-facilitated activities	102(68%)	MIS	(6%) $90,000
Unknown	17(12%)	Other	(17%) $50,000

Top 5 Employers Hiring Grads

Aon (2), Baxter Healthcare Corporation (2), Nokia (2), Deloitte (2), PepsiCo (2)

LOYOLA UNIVERSITY MARYLAND
SELLINGER SCHOOL OF BUSINESS AND MANAGEMENT

Academics

Loyola's Sellinger School of Business and Management is anchored by core Jesuit beliefs. It offers a "value-based" education that emphasizes "reflective learning" and the importance of ethical behavior and leadership skills. All students must take two courses in the Law and Social Responsibility department: one on legal and regulatory compliance and another on ethics and social responsibility. The department also offers electives, such as legal and managerial issues in not-for-profit organizations and intersections among power, privilege, and professional identity for those wanting to further specialize in the area. Students say they "appreciate the Jesuit influence" and name the Jesuit "commitment to excellence" and "strong belief in business ethics" as reasons for picking the school.

Loyola is dedicated to its students and offers four different MBA programs, at two locations, with varying delivery methods. This ensures that students' needs are met, and that they are not forced into a cookie-cutter program. The most popular program is the part-time Professional MBA, which offers evening classes and the freedom to vary the number of credits students take each semester. The MBA Fellows program is designed for professionals with managerial experience and has Saturday classes only. The Executive MBA is a cohort program for seasoned professionals that meets all day Friday and Saturday every other weekend. Loyola's Emerging Leaders MBA is a full-time, 12-month accelerated program for early career students. The school also offers an MS in finance and a certificate in accounting and cyber security. All of these programs have a "great reputation" and a reasonable price.

Loyola's part-time programs "cater to working individuals" and give them "flexibility and greater control" over the curriculum. Classes are offered at convenient times in locations close to the Baltimore area. All programs require a set of core classes to ensure students have a wide and strong understanding of the business world, but some professional MBA students may find requirements waived if they graduated from college in the past few years and received high grades in similar courses. After completing these courses, professional MBA students may concentrate in accounting, finance, information systems, international business, management, or marketing. Classes are challenging and require group projects. While theory is taught, the program emphasizes "where business and the country are headed, and how to be a part of that." One student loves that "many of the concepts taught can be applied as both an entrepreneur and corporate executive." Loyola's professors fall at "both ends of the spectrum." Students find the full-time faculty is "incredible" and "very effective and encouraging." Some of the adjunct professors, however, should "simply stick with their day jobs." The administration also gets mixed reviews, but most find them "fantastic to work with." When you consider Loyola's "great reputation," price, and willingness to support student success, it's no wonder students say going there is a "great experience."

Career and Placement

The Sellinger School of Business does not have its own career office, so students must use the Career Center that serves the rest of the undergraduate and graduate students. Loyola's Career Center is still able to provide personal and relevant help to graduate business students, however. Experienced advisors offer career counseling, and the center holds various workshops, mock interviews, and resume critiques. Sellinger has a very strong alumni network that provides valuable networking and mentoring opportunities for students. Career fairs and on-campus recruiting events help students make connections to future employers. Businesses that attended the most recent career fair include ING Financial Partners, Liberty Mutual, State Farm, Primerica, The Central Intelligence Agency, Financial Management Service, Morgan Stanley, and The Neilson Corporation.

Student Life and Environment

All of Sellinger's programs attract high-caliber individuals. Students are "very motivated and intelligent," and while they can sometimes be "competitive," almost everyone is "helpful and friendly." Most students work full time, and many are married and have families. Students say their peers' different personal and professional backgrounds really "add to the learning environment." "Everyone brings something unique," one student explains, and this creates an "innovative, challenging, and intellectually stimulating culture." Students are "opinionated and interested in the topics covered in classes," which makes for "engaging" and "active discussions."

Most students at Loyola are incredibly busy and generally don't have time to socialize with other students. Some students would like to see "more opportunities for socializing and networking outside of the classroom," as "it would help strengthen the program and build upon the teamwork and morale already present."

Admissions

Students applying to Loyola must submit their undergraduate transcript, GMAT scores, recommendations, resume, and personal statement. Students applying to all programs except the Emerging Leaders MBA and the Accounting Certificate Program must have previous work experience. The average undergraduate GPA for the entering class was 3.3, and the average GMAT score was 557. Applicants with a 3.25 undergraduate GPA and five years of work experience may request a waiver for the GMAT requirement, as may students with an advanced degree in another discipline. International students whose first language is not English must submit TOEFL scores. Additionally, applicants who hold degrees from non-U.S. institutions must have their academic record evaluated by an independent service.

FINANCIAL FACTS

Annual tuition (in-state/ out-of-state)	$58,000/$62,000
Fees	$50
Cost of books	$2,800
Room & board	$16,650
% of students receiving aid	30
% of first-year students receiving aid	33
% of students receiving grants	15
Average award package	$10,219
Average grant	$5,270
Average loan	$18,612
Average student loan debt	$37,406

ADMISSIONS

Admissions Selectivity Rating	71
# of applications received	163
% applicants accepted	85
% acceptees attending	40
Average GMAT	536
Range of GMAT	468–600
Average GPA	3.28
TOEFL required of international students	Yes
Minimum TOEFL (paper/computer)	550/213
Application fee	$50
International application fee	$50
Deferment available	Yes
Maximum length of deferment	1 year
Transfer students accepted	Yes
Transfer application policy: Only classes from another AACSB accredited school will be counted, total 6 credits.	
Non-fall admissions	Yes
Need-blind admissions	Yes

EMPLOYMENT PROFILE

Career Rating	75	Grads Employed by Function	%	Avg. Salary
Percent employed at graduation	15	Marketing	(33%)	$50,000
Percent employed 3 months after graduation	60	Management	(17%)	$49,000
		Finance	(25%)	$54,333
Average base starting salary	$52,125	Other	(25%)	$51,667
Primary Source of Full-time Job Acceptances		**Top 5 Employers Hiring Grads**		
School-facilitated activities	5(25%)	CareFirst BlueCross Blue Shield (1), Dunbar		
Graduate-facilitated activities	13(65%)	Armored (1), CohnReznick (1), McGladrey (1),		
Unknown	2(10%)	Vocus (1)		

LOYOLA UNIVERSITY NEW ORLEANS
JOSEPH A. BUTT, S.J. COLLEGE OF BUSINESS

GENERAL INFORMATION

Type of school	Private
Affiliation	Roman Catholic-Jesuit
Academic calendar	Semester

SURVEY SAYS...
Students love New Orleans, LA
Solid preparation in:
General management, Teamwork,
Presentation skills

STUDENTS

Enrollment of parent institution	4,982
Enrollment of MBA Program	79
% male/female	67/33
% out-of-state	22
% part-time	58
% underrepresented minority	12
% international	15
Average age at entry	27
Average years work experience at entry	3.0

ACADEMICS

Academic Experience Rating	90
Profs interesting rating	83
Profs accesible rating	88
Student/faculty ratio	5:1
% female faculty	19
% underrepresented minority faculty	19
% part-time faculty	43

Joint Degrees
MBA/JD, 4–5 years; MBA/Master of
Pastoral Studies, 3–7 years

Academics

Loyola's "small, flexible MBA program" "really caters to each and every student," a fact appreciated by the predominantly part-time student body in the College of Business' graduate programs. MBAs here also love the "Jesuit tradition," which encourages "involvement in the New Orleans community." "I appreciate being at a place that not only educates my mind, but gives me social awareness as well," one student writes.

Loyola offers a general MBA as well as a combined MBA/JD and a combined MBA/MPS. The school does not offer concentrations, but it does offer "strands," sets of pre-selected electives in a particular discipline that function a lot like concentrations. Students may pursue a strand in finance, leadership, marketing, or supply chains, or they may use their electives to pursue other interests, including forensic accounting, international business, entrepreneurship, negotiations, or sustainability. The MBA culminates in a capstone course called Total Global Strategy, which emphasizes case study and integrative analysis.

Loyola professors "are very involved with the students. The classes are small and the faculty care about the students' well being and learning." One student writes, "I was shocked to learn how easily accessible my professors were. They really are interested in your education and your life and they want you to succeed! In fact, they will put in extra hours to make sure you do just that. The business school here is more like a family, which makes it that much easier to learn." Administrators are "excellent." One student reports, "There are a few classes the administration is trying to reorganize because of complaints from last semester. I think this is a good thing that the administration is listening to the students." Indeed, the administration seems intent on exploring all opportunities to improve the program. "The quality and experience of the new students has improved each year as admission standards have become tougher," MBAs here report approvingly.

Career and Placement

Loyola maintains a Career Development Center to serve all undergraduate and graduate students of the university. Services include self-assessment instruments, career counseling, internship and job placement services, and guidance in resume writing, interviewing, job search, and salary negotiation skills. The office organizes on-campus recruiting events. One student "is not sure how much other students utilize" the CDC, but she does use the office's service and finds it "extremely helpful, especially because I recently moved to the area." The MBA Association also contributes by organizing networking events.

In recent years, Loyola MBAs have been placed with Chevron, Cox Communications, Deloitte, Entergy, Ernst & Young, Harrah's Entertainment, JPMorgan, Northwestern Mutual, the Ochsner Health System, Shell, Prudential Financial, and the Target Corporation.

ADMISSIONS CONTACT: STEPHANIE MANSFIELD, MBA DIRECTOR
ADDRESS: 6363 ST. CHARLES AVENUE, CAMPUS BOX 15, NEW ORLEANS, LA 70118
PHONE: 504-864-7965 • FAX: 504-864-7970
E-MAIL: SMANS@LOYNO.EDU • WEBSITE: BUSINESS.LOYNO.EDU/MBA

Student Life and Environment

Designed to "keep your attention," "classes are interactive and fun" at Loyola, where "professors expect your best and highest quality work, but go above and beyond to provide the support you need in order to succeed. Coming to class is like meeting with friends and family every night." Students tell us that "life at school is stressful" but worth the hard work. "I do feel like I am learning more then I ever have," one writes.

Loyola classes meet once a week on weekday evenings. While most students are part-timers with full-time jobs, "there are [also] many full-time students that have part-time jobs. Everybody knows everyone. You have many of the same classes with the same people." "Significant effort has been made recently to improve the cohesiveness among students" at Loyola, with "MBA functions almost every week to bring the students closer together." One student reports, "The MBA program does a good job of organizing social events within as well as outside of the school."

Loyola is located in the fashionable uptown section of New Orleans, just down the road from Tulane University. The area is known for its fine restaurants and upscale shopping. The city's Central Business District, Garden District, and French Quarter are all easily accessible from campus via the city's picturesque streetcar line.

Most MBAs at Loyola "are just out of [their] four-year degree [programs], but there are some that have been in the workforce for a while." It's not just locals in attendance here. One student told us he was "very surprised to discover how many students are from every part of the country and so many different backgrounds." Across the board, students tend to be "very friendly and willing to help each other out. The MBA association facilitates this atmosphere by scheduling meet and greets and other social events throughout the semester."

Admissions

Loyola requires the following of applicants to its MBA program: official transcripts for all past postsecondary academic work; an official score report for the GMAT; two letters of recommendation; a 400-word personal statement of purpose; and a resume. International students whose first language is not English must also submit TOEFL scores; all international students must provide an affidavit demonstrating sufficient financial resources to support themselves during their tenure at the university. Interviews and letters of recommendations are optional, and letters of recommendations are required. Work experience, though not required, is strongly recommended.

FINANCIAL FACTS

Annual tuition	$17,244
Fees	$1,036
Cost of books	$1,500
Room & board	
(on/off-campus)	$9,960
Average grant	$5,000
Average loan	$21,610

ADMISSIONS

Admissions Selectivity Rating	84
# of applications received	98
% applicants accepted	47
% acceptees attending	67
Average GMAT	560
Range of GMAT	530–580
Average GPA	3.19
TOEFL required of	
international students	Yes
Minimum TOEFL	
(paper/computer)	580/237
Application fee	$50
International application fee	$50
Regular application deadline	6/30
Deferment available	Yes
Maximum length	
of deferment	1 academic year
Transfer students accepted	Yes

Transfer application policy: If applicant comes from an accredited program, the foundation work may apply to our program. Also, a maximum of 6 credit hours may be applied to the core/elective level. Only B's (3.0) or better are accepted.

Non-fall admissions	Yes
Need-blind admissions	Yes

MARIST COLLEGE
SCHOOL OF MANAGEMENT

GENERAL INFORMATION
Type of school	Private
Affiliation	No Affiliation
Academic calendar	Semester

SURVEY SAYS...
Solid preparation in:
General management, Operations, Computer skills, Doing business in a global economy

STUDENTS
Enrollment of parent institution	6,377
Enrollment of MBA Program	165
% male/female	59/41
% out-of-state	27
% part-time	100
% underrepresented minority	19
% international	1
Average age at entry	29

ACADEMICS
Academic Experience Rating	83
Profs interesting rating	75
Profs accesible rating	76
Student/faculty ratio	9:1
% female faculty	50
% underrepresented minority faculty	11
% part-time faculty	22

Prominent Alumni
Marsha Gordon, Pres./CEO Business Council of Westchester Chamber; Karen Sieverding, Healthcare; Jeff Clark, Telecommunications; Christopher McCann, President, 1-800-FLOW-ERS; Timothy G. Brier, Co-founder-price.com

Academics

For more than 30 years, Marist College has offered working professionals the opportunity to pursue an MBA degree on a part-time basis. Today, the school continues to operate a part-time, campus-based program, while also distinguishing itself as "one of the few AACSB-accredited graduate schools that offered an MBA program fully online, while being affordable." While part-time students in other MBA programs complain about the difficulties of balancing home life, work, and school, the Marist "program [is] tailored to those working long hours and still offer[s] a strong reputation with a decent curriculum." The flexibility of the program is perhaps its most attractive feature, allowing students to take traditional or online courses, or a blend of the two. Indeed, students tell us that "being able to mix online courses as well as traditional in-class courses is very beneficial for students who also work full time."

The curriculum at Marist is divided into foundation courses, core courses, concentrations and electives; however, foundation courses may be waived for students who have an undergraduate degree in business. Taking two courses per semester and one course in the summer, many students are able to earn their MBA in just 2 years. To accommodate the schedule of working professionals, traditional classroom courses are scheduled one evening per week, Monday through Thursday, at the Fishkill campus as well as in off-site classrooms. Online classes are available 24 hours a day, 7 days a week, and have no on-campus requirement whatsoever. "The high quality of the program and professors" draws many students to the school, and online students are welcome to meet with faculty in person while taking the course. Students say Marist professors are, on the whole, "accessible and very helpful."

The school is technologically and organizationally equipped to help online students plan and execute a quality educational program. A student shares, "Enrollment is a breeze, and the Associate Dean who works with online students is very helpful." Another adds, "The administration was very helpful in getting [me] access to courses to meet my academic plan." Online classes are very similar to classroom courses in that students must be prepared to turn in assignments, take exams, participate in class, and meet deadlines. Course work is fully multimedia and includes group projects, case studies, computer simulations, and presentations. Students insist that they build a sense of community via the Internet, and "Group projects illuminate personalities pretty well even over the web." A current student enthuses, "I completed my program completely online. I have found many students to be actively engaged and willing to collaborate via online chat, e-mail, and over the phone."

Whether online or in the classroom, students say the program is high quality and challenging. One shares, "I started here after moving away from Chicago, where I attended a top-10 MBA program (Kellogg). I find the classes to be rigorous and academically competitive. I was worried that the courses would seem much easier than Kellogg['s], but my fears were misplaced." The program is structured to allow students to concentrate in one of four areas: ethical leadership, financial management, healthcare administration, or international business.

Career and Placement

Ninety-five percent of Marist students work full-time while completing their MBA. Ranging from relatively young professionals to senior managers, most students plan to stay with their current company upon termination of the program. For those who are looking for a new position, MBA students do have access to the Marist College Career Services Office. Additionally, Marist has long standing relationships with many employers, including: Affinity Group/Mass Mutual, Aldi, CVS Pharmacy, First Investors Corporation, Gap, Gunn Allen Financial Corporation, Household Finance, IBM, MetLife, Morgan Stanley, Northwestern Mutual Financial Network, Ryder Transportation, Target, United Parcel Service, Wells Fargo, and Worldwide Express.

Student Life and Environment

Because a large percentage of Marist courses are taught via the Internet, the student community is largely virtual. Even so, Marist students have the opportunity to get to know their classmates through the phone and Internet, describing them as "hardworking, intelligent [people], with work and family obligations." Those who attend classes on campus tell us the school promotes a "good sense of community" and "attracts people who are just plain nice and helpful both to work and teach and as students." While the business school is located on Marist's lively undergraduate campus, there aren't many social or recreational activities targeted at business students. Indeed, some would like to see "more opportunities for socializing, networking, out-of-classroom learning (speakers, etc.)."

Marist is located in Poughkeepsie, New York, a small city about 90 minutes from both New York City and Albany. A picturesque campus environment, the school is located near the Catskill Mountains, and the surrounding area is a paradise for hiking, cross-country skiing, mountain biking, and other outdoor activities. There are also a number of attractions in the town of Poughkeepsie, including the historic Barbadon Theater and Mid-Hudson Civic Center, which show opera, ballet, Broadway shows, and popular performers.

Admission

To apply to the graduate program at the Marist School of Management, students must possess an undergraduate degree in any discipline. Whether applying to the online or on-campus program, all applicants must submit a completed graduate school application, an application fee, two letters of recommendation, responses to the essay questions, official GMAT scores, and official transcripts from undergraduate study.

FINANCIAL FACTS

Cost of books	$1,350
Room & board	$11,430
% of students receiving aid	44
% of first-year students receiving aid	62
% of students receiving grants	37
Average award package	$17,750
Average grant	$2,797
Average loan	$19,056
Average student loan debt	$26,524

ADMISSIONS

Admissions Selectivity Rating	81
# of applications received	120
% applicants accepted	50
% acceptees attending	67
Average GMAT	524
Range of GMAT	460–570
Average GPA	3.30
TOEFL required of international students	Yes
Minimum TOEFL (paper/computer)	550/213
Application fee	$50
International application fee	$50
Regular application deadline	8/1
Regular application notification	8/15
Deferment available	Yes
Maximum length of deferment	1 year
Transfer students accepted	Yes
Transfer application policy: No more than six credit hours of core courses.	
Non-fall admissions	Yes
Need-blind admissions	Yes

MARQUETTE UNIVERSITY
COLLEGE OF BUSINESS ADMINISTRATION

GENERAL INFORMATION
Type of school	Private
Affiliation	Jesuit
Academic calendar	Semester

SURVEY SAYS...
Cutting-edge classes, Happy students
Solid preparation in:
Teamwork, Quantitative skills

STUDENTS
Enrollment of parent institution	11,749
Enrollment of MBA Program	371
% part-time	86
Average age at entry	29
Average years work experience at entry	5.3

ACADEMICS
Academic Experience Rating	**80**
Profs interesting rating	81
Profs accesible rating	82
Student/faculty ratio	6:1
% female faculty	17
% underrepresented minority faculty	9
% part-time faculty	36

Joint Degrees
MBA-JD 4 years; MBA-JD in sport business 4 years; MBA-MSN 4-6 years; MBA-MS Political Science 3-6 years

Academics

A respected MBA program in downtown Milwaukee, Marquette University provides a balanced perspective on business education. The strength of the program stems from the top-quality teaching staff, comprised of experienced academics with long careers in the classroom. Many have distinguished themselves through "very good published research and a strong reputation for teaching modern theories of economics." At the same time, "the academic experience is a good mix of high-level thinking and actual financial, economic, and accounting knowledge." Tenured staff is augmented with adjunct faculty, so you get a good "mixture of full-time professors and working professors." The school furthers real-world instruction by regularly "inviting guest speakers from prominent local businesses" to address classes or speak to the MBA community.

Designed for working professionals, Marquette classes are held in the evenings and weekends on three campuses in metropolitan Milwaukee. One thing that separates Marquette from other graduate business programs is that "it is not a program that is split between full-time and half-time students, but rather, its night classes cater to anyone and everyone." "Smaller class sizes allow for more discussion and interaction," so Marquette students really benefit from the fact that the "best and brightest young professionals in Milwaukee are sitting next to you in class." It can even be a great way to network, as "classes are full of students who work for Fortune-500 companies." Across disciplines, the education is "consistent in quality" with "good professors throughout the program." Beyond the core, however, "class offerings may be a bit light," making it more difficult to specialize your coursework through electives. Some would love to see a concentration in public health, while others say, "a larger selection of finance classes would be nice."

While Marquette is "very accommodating to part-time students," MBA candidates are quick to remind us that "classes are rigorous" and the program is time-consuming. If the workload gets overwhelming, "professors are always welcoming and willing to spend time during office hours and after class to help." Likewise, the administration is highly accessible and helpful. A current student shares, "I can easily schedule time with my advisor, there have been no billing or schedule mistakes, and when I call with questions, the people are knowledgeable and quick to respond."

Career and Placement

For current and future Midwest professionals, "a Marquette MBA makes a statement in the Milwaukee, Madison, Chicago, and Minneapolis areas." Most students plan to leverage this excellent reputation at their current positions. However, some students attend the program full-time or plan to make a career change after completing graduate school. For these students, Marquette operates the Business Career Center, where students can seek individual career counseling, resume and interview preparation, and help with networking strategies. The Career Center can also help career changers set up informational interviews and research local companies.

ADMISSIONS CONTACT: DR. JEANNE SIMMONS, ASSOCIATE DEAN
ADDRESS: PO BOX 1881, STRAZ HALL SUITE 275, MILWAUKEE, WI 53201-1881
PHONE: 414-288-7145 • FAX: 414-288-8078
E-MAIL: MBA@MARQUETTE.EDU • WEBSITE: WWW.MARQUETTE.EDU/GSM

In addition to the Business Career Center, graduate students have access to Marquette University's online job boards and are welcome to attend campus-wide career fairs and networking events. Since few students are actively applying for a new position after the MBA, job seekers feel that the school could "improve job search counseling" for those who want to start a new career, and ramp up its "internship placement for full-time students."

Student Life and Environment

The MBA program at Marquette attracts students from a range of backgrounds: "Some students are liberal, some conservative, some entrepreneurial, some corporate." Nonetheless, there is a strong community on campus, and even new students feel well-integrated into the program. A current MBA relates, "As a full-time student [who] entered the MBA program straight from my undergrad career, I never felt like I have been treated differently by the more experienced students and professors." In class, students are commendably "hardworking, task-oriented, and committed to contributing to class and group work." Outside the classroom, group projects usually go smoothly and "everyone is helpful and accommodating" to each other's ideas and schedules.

Although the school operates two satellite facilities, "the downtown campus is part of what defines the Marquette experience" for many students. Not only are they "close to the business center of the city," Milwaukee is "a nice place to live and work." Convenience is also a large factor, as "the proximity of Marquette's campus to downtown Milwaukee, where many students live and work, allows for a quick and easy commute." When feeling social, Marquette students might "meet for a drink after class or after a test to talk about school, work, and life." However, because the program is largely part-time, most students admit that, "school life is limited to attending class, team project activities, and the occasional MU basketball game."

Admission

To be considered for admission to Marquette, students must have a minimum GPA of 3.0 from their undergraduate coursework, and a total score of 580 or better on the GMAT. Students who fall below these guidelines may be admitted provisionally to the graduate program. Though work experience is not a requirement, an applicant's resume is also strongly weighed; currently, the average Marquette student has over seven years of professional experience. Students can apply to begin their coursework any semester. There are special deadlines for those who want to study on the satellite campuses in Waukesha or Kohler.

FINANCIAL FACTS

Annual tuition	$17,730
Fees	$0
Cost of books	$1,200

ADMISSIONS

Admissions Selectivity Rating	77
# of applications received	178
% applicants accepted	71
% acceptees attending	71
Average GMAT	590
Average GPA	3.27
TOEFL required of international students	Yes
Minimum TOEFL (paper/computer)	580/220
Application fee	$50
International application fee	$50
Deferment available	Yes
Maximum length of deferment	usually one year
Transfer students accepted	Yes
Transfer application policy: We accept transfers from other Jesuit Schools (JEBNET agreement; see www.jesuitmba.org). We will also accept up to 6 approved credits from AACSB schools.	
Non-fall admissions	Yes
Need-blind admissions	No

MASSACHUSETTS INSTITUTE OF TECHNOLOGY
SLOAN SCHOOL OF MANAGEMENT

Academics

The MIT Sloan MBA Program has "both the best entrepreneurial program of any business school in the world and the most fantastic technology available," students insist. And that's hardly all the school offers; on the contrary, students tell us that MIT Sloan is "the best all-around program in allowing students to learn about innovative endeavors while still teaching and offering the most academically challenging traditional MBA curriculum of all schools."

MIT expertly exploits the synergies of its location in a great city and its affiliation with a great university. Students brag about "Sloan's ties to the real business world. In the last week alone, I listened to three *Fortune* 500 CEOs speak on campus and had dinner with a partner from a local VC firm and a partner from a local law firm. Many of the professors have incredibly deep experience and connections to industry and bring great insight along those dimensions." They are especially impressed with "how connected MIT Sloan is with companies in a non-recruiting season," which they justly see as "a real point of differentiation" for the program. MIT's Herculean status in the worlds of math, engineering, and science contribute substantially to the MBA program. "There are very low barriers between schools; interdisciplinary work and entrepreneurship are actively encouraged between business and engineering," one student writes. MIT's many strengths make possible such programs as the Leaders for Global Operations Program—"an operations and logistics-focused program" that students call "the best dual-degree program in business and engineering in the country."

Throughout the program, MIT Sloan emphasizes "a strong hands-on approach to learning" and cooperative work. "At MIT Sloan, practically everything is done in teams," students tell us. The workload "is what you expect of MIT: rigorous and quantitative." Most don't mind the challenge; as one explains, "Although the workload is heavy, people actually want to prepare just for the opportunity to participate in discussions in where faculty are posing questions to the most pressing business issues. A place like MIT Sloan is a reason why people want to continue their education." The cherry on the sundae is global travel; "Everyone travels on trips or treks, both foreign and domestic. I am headed to Japan for 10 days with 200 of my classmates. These are student-planned trips that are excellent ways to get to see other cultures and get business exposure around the world."

Career and Placement

MIT Sloan's Career Development Office provides MBAs with a range of career management resources, including seminars, self-assessment tools, library materials, and online databases and services. Students tell us that "the CDO is great for traditional MBA jobs such as banking, [and] consulting and the major corporations and tech companies." Some report the office is "not as good with smaller and tougher markets such as private equity and venture capital," although students interested in those fields can make use of the "career trek" program, which offers trips around the globe to job-hunt and learn about a variety of industries. "The focus on entrepreneurship means that a lot of MIT Sloan students are starting companies or working at early-stage startups right after school," and are thus less inclined to make use of the CDO. Supplementing the CDO, "Clubs have a huge impact on career choices, setting up relationships, bringing in speakers, etc. Alumni are also a great resource, and a fantastic channel for connecting. Many Sloanies are looking to work for startups, tech, or smaller firms without traditional recruiting seasons, and alumni are very helpful in this regard."

ADMISSIONS CONTACT: ROD GARCIA, ADMISSIONS DIRECTOR
ADDRESS: 50 MEMORIAL DRIVE, SUITE 126, CAMBRIDGE, MA 02139
PHONE: 617-258-5434 • FAX: 617-253-6405
E-MAIL: MBAADMISSIONS@SLOAN.MIT.EDU • WEBSITE: MITSLOAN.MIT.EDU/MBA

Employers most likely to hire MIT Sloan MBAs include Bain & Company, Booz & Co., The Boston Consulting Group, Citi, Amazon.com, Fidelity, Goldman Sachs, Google, IBM, and McKinsey & Company.

Student Life and Environment

MIT Sloan keeps students plenty busy with work, but they still somehow find time to "participate in clubs and set up the many conferences we host. For example, the Sports Analytics Conference this spring had general managers from each of the top four professional sports (basketball, hockey, baseball, and football) sit on a panel. How cool is that?" Students tell us that MIT Sloan "provides more opportunities than anyone could expect. I find that I spend about 50 percent of my time on academics and the other 50 percent working with clubs and local companies, a perfect balance that allows me to take what I've learned in the classroom and apply it in a real-world setting." It's easy to get overwhelmed; according to one student, "School is a blur with so many classes, activities, guest speakers, etc. In terms of social activities, I think you have to pick your spots. Otherwise you will fall behind in your coursework and job search, but the options are pretty limitless here."

Admissions

Completed applications to the MIT Sloan MBA program include two letters of recommendation, post-secondary transcripts (self-reported prior to interview; if called for an interview, applicants must provide official transcripts), a current resumé, two personal essays, supplemental information, and GMAT or GRE scores. The school requires additional materials from applicants to the Leaders for Global Operations Program (LGO). The nature of the program favors candidates with strong quantitative and analytical skills, as well as those with strong personal attributes including leadership, teamwork, and ability to make decisions and pursue goals.

Prominent Alumni

Rafael del Pino, Chairman, Groupo Ferrovial SA; Jeff Wilke, Sr VP North American Retail, Amazon.com; Robin Chase, Founder and CEO, Meadow Networks; Ron (Ronald) A. Williams, Chairman and CEO, Aetna, Inc.; Michael Kaiser, President, Kennedy Center

FINANCIAL FACTS

Annual tuition	$61,440
Fees	$272
Cost of books	$2,107
Room & board	$19,137
% of students receiving aid	82
% of first-year students receiving aid	82
% of students receiving grants	4
Average award package	$66,355
Average grant	$25,502
Average loan	$60,061
Average student loan debt	$92,937

ADMISSIONS

Admissions Selectivity Rating	99
# of applications received	4,113
Average GMAT	710
Range of GMAT	660–760
Average GPA	3.60
TOEFL required of international students	No
Application fee	$250
International application fee	$250
Application Deadline/Notification	
Round 1:	9/24 / 12/20
Round 2:	1/7 / 4/1
Deferment available	No
Transfer students accepted	No
Non-fall admissions	No
Need-blind admissions	Yes

EMPLOYMENT PROFILE

		Grads Employed by Function	%	Avg. Salary
Career Rating	99			
Percent employed at graduation	92	Marketing	(6%)	$106,646
Percent employed 3 months after graduation	96	Operations	(10%)	$118,996
		Consulting	(35%)	$126,537
Average base starting salary	$118,406	Management	(10%)	$112,366
Primary Source of Full-time Job Acceptances		Finance	(24%)	$110,980
School-facilitated activities	(81%)	Other	(1%)	$0
Graduate-facilitated activities	(18%)			
Unknown	(1%)			

Top 5 Employers Hiring Grads

McKinsey & Company (30), Bain & Company (10), Boston Consulting Group (16), Deloitte Consulting (7)

MERCER UNIVERSITY—ATLANTA
EUGENE W. STETSON SCHOOL OF BUSINESS AND ECONOMICS

Academics

One of Georgia's premiere higher-learning institutions, Mercer University offers several business degree options on its graduate-focused Atlanta campus: a flexible evening MBA, an Executive MBA, professional MBA, virtual MBA, a master of accountancy (MAcc), and a one-year full-time MBA (the only of Mercer's various campuses that offers a full-time option). The school is also home to "one of the only pharmacy programs in the country to offer a dual MBA/PharmD degree." Mercer's flexible MBA is popular with local professionals, who call it "Atlanta's most accommodating MBA program for working students." For part-timers, "Classes meet one night a week for eight weeks, so it's possible to take classes even when you have a full-time job and other commitments." On top of that, professors "understand we work full-time and have family obligations, so the workload is moderate but challenging." How challenging is up to the student: "Some take their time with one class per session, others overload to finish early." The full-time MBA is likewise efficient, covering business fundamentals in an intense, cohort-based program that spans less than one calendar year (though students who did not study business as an undergraduate must take additional four-week Business Foundations courses before matriculation).

Known for "academic excellence in finance and accounting," Mercer's curriculum covers business fundamentals from economics to communications. After completing the core, students take electives, including a required international business class or an overseas trip. Throughout disciplines, Mercer employs "strong professors with real-world experience," who are able to offer an "in-depth understanding of what we were learning in class and how it applied to the business world." On top of that, Mercer's "small class size" lends itself to "team-oriented projects and a lot of class interaction," giving students a chance to collaborate, network, and develop their communication skills. Students dole out praise for Mercer's "extremely dedicated professors," who balance top-notch business skills with a true desire "to help students succeed." In fact, "Everyone at Mercer is committed to enhancing the student's experience." Like the faculty, "The administrative offices are also helpful," ensuring the program runs smoothly.

Career and Placement

Many MBA candidates at Mercer are attending the program part-time and are not looking for a new job after graduation. Instead, they plan to leverage the practical skills they've acquired in the classroom to gain a better position and higher salary at their current job. To that end, a Mercer education is effective. One student attests, "I was able to secure my current position prior to graduation as a direct result of my then-current graduate enrollment at Mercer. I graduated in December, have earned an 18 percent increase in salary and am currently searching for a more significant managerial position within my firm and outside."

Those in the full-time program (or looking to make a career change after completing the degree part-time) have access to the university's Office of Career Services, which offers career counseling and workshops on résumé preparation and interviewing, in addition to hosting career fairs on campus. (Note that career fairs are often aimed at a certain industry, like pharmacy.) While students certainly benefit from Mercer's "good reputation" in Atlanta, they say their school could improve its career-development offerings by promoting "more involvement from alumni," as well as "a stronger link to the Atlanta business community."

ADMISSIONS CONTACT: KELLY HOLLOWAY, DIRECTOR OF ADMISSIONS
ADDRESS: MERCER UNIVERSITY, 3001 MERCER UNIVERSITY DRIVE, ATLANTA, GA 30341-4155
PHONE: 678-547-6159 • FAX: 678-547-6160
E-MAIL: HOLLOWAY_KL@MERCER.EDU • WEBSITE: WWW.MERCER.EDU/BUSINESS

Student Life and Environment

Mercer's Atlanta campus is focused on graduate programs, with advanced students of medicine, education, and theology, among other disciplines, sharing 300 tree-filled acres inside the Atlanta Perimeter. The business school attracts students from "diverse age ranges and backgrounds," as well as at different points in their careers. In the evening programs, "MBA students are mostly part-time students with full-time jobs (and some are effectively full-time students with full-time jobs)." As a result, there is "little emphasis on social or extracurricular activities"; for most, "school life consists of classes, group project meetings and studying." Nonetheless, Mercer's emphasis on collaboration means students frequently work together and build relationships, even if they don't socialize outside of class.

For full-timers, "Mercer is a thriving campus during the day," offering students access to myriad clubs and activities, as well as recreational facilities and fitness classes. At the business school, there are frequent career-related special events, like guest speakers and alumni networking events, as well as "festivities such as a "cook outs" (free to students) to celebrate the end of the semester." "The library and the library's website are also great resources for research," and students appreciate the "nice meeting rooms available for students to reserve in order to study, work on projects, [and] have meetings." Plus, the school's "suburban campus" offers a central Atlanta location that is both "outstanding and safe."

Admissions

For Mercer's flexible and day MBA programs and the MAcc, a prospective student's GRE or GMAT scores and previous academic record are the most important factors in an admissions decision. A résumé is also required as a part of the application package. Though no work experience is required for the full-time program, the average student has three years of professional experience before matriculation. For full consideration, applications should be submitted to the full-time program by May 15; there are five entry points for part-time students, who are admitted on a rolling basis.

FINANCIAL FACTS

Annual tuition	$17,235
Fees	$400
Cost of books	$1,600
Room & board	$13,365
% of students receiving aid	61
% of first-year students receiving aid	66
% of students receiving grants	0
Average award package	$17,024
Average grant	$0
Average loan	$17,024
Average student loan debt	$35,055

ADMISSIONS

Admissions Selectivity Rating	71
# of applications received	61
% applicants accepted	87
% acceptees attending	77
Average GMAT	506
Range of GMAT	460–540
Average GPA	2.96
TOEFL required of international students	Yes
Minimum TOEFL (paper/computer)	550/213
International application fee	$100
Early application deadline	7/1
Early notification date	7/15
Regular application deadline	7/15
Deferment available	Yes
Maximum length of deferment	Five years past GMAT
Transfer students accepted	Yes
Transfer application policy: Will consider up to two courses (6 sem. hrs.)in transfer within past five years, from AACSB accredited institutions.	
Non-fall admissions	Yes
Need-blind admissions	Yes

EMPLOYMENT PROFILE

Career Rating	76	Grads Employed by Function	% Avg. Salary
Average base starting salary	$73,100	Marketing	(7%) $65,500
		Operations	(48%) $110,000
		Management	(17%) $118,166
		Finance	(22%) $75,600
		HR	(5%) $92,250
		MIS	(5%) $55,000
		Other	(7%) $25,000

MERCER UNIVERSITY—MACON
EUGENE W. STETSON SCHOOL OF BUSINESS AND ECONOMICS

GENERAL INFORMATION

Type of school	Private
Affiliation	Baptist

SURVEY SAYS...

Good peer network
Solid preparation in:
Marketing, Accounting,
Communication/interpersonal skills

STUDENTS

Enrollment of parent institution	40
Enrollment of MBA Program	40
% male/female	45/55
% out-of-state	0
% part-time	99
% underrepresented minority	0
% international	0
Average years work experience at entry	4.0

ACADEMICS

Academic Experience Rating	73
Profs interesting rating	82
Profs accesible rating	78
Student/faculty ratio	20:1
% female faculty	55
% part-time faculty	0

Joint Degrees

JD/MBA 3 YEARS

Academics

A long-standing Georgia institution with a "great reputation" and a strong "community feeling," Mercer University offers a friendly and convenient evening MBA program, specially designed for working professionals. Based at the school's main campus in Macon (though the university also operates several MBA programs in other Georgia cities, including Atlanta), this program is divided into two parts: foundational courses and core courses. For those with previous academic experience in business, the foundation courses may be waived. All students, however, must complete the core, a series of advanced courses in business fundamentals, including applied microeconomic analysis, management and leadership, and business ethics. With a focus on the relationship between business and society, the Mercer curriculum is current and contemporary. According to current students, "The administration goes to great lengths to offer courses relevant to our career goals and interests." An "outstanding offering of seminars and lecture series" augment the core, and students can take advantage of "faculty-led study abroad opportunities each year." While students generally praise the academic program, some say the school should offer a greater variety of electives, as well as coursework that is "more applicable to small business and entrepreneurs."

Mercer maintains a "low student-to-faculty ratio" and "optimal" class sizes, encouraging interaction and discussion between students and teachers. In the classroom, "Lectures are loosely structured to provide ample opportunities to contribute and share real-world perspectives." A student details, "Everyone has different educational, ethnic, and social backgrounds. Everyone likes to add to classroom discussion where they can." Fortunately, collaboration is more common than competition, and "most people work toward each person succeeding as oppose to the "cut-throat" environment some business students experience." Since most Mercer students are balancing their education with a career (and personal lives), it can definitely be challenging to keep pace with the program. Fortunately, the school is known for its decidedly "friendly atmosphere." If schoolwork proves challenging, "professors are willing to take extra time for those who need it and to lend advice in projects inside the classroom or in work life outside the classroom." Like the faculty, "The administration generally cares about students, and there is an overall open-door policy for students." Exclaims a student, "My academic experience has been hard work and time consuming, but it is worth every moment!" Another agrees, "There is a lot of work involved, but it's not impossible to get everything done. The administration is very helpful. The majority of the professors are easily accessible."

Career and Placement

The Office of Career Services at Macon serves the undergraduate and graduate communities of the main Macon campus, as well as the Eastman Center. Among other student services, the Office of Career Services hosts career fairs and campus recruiting events. At a recent career fair, Frito Lay, GEICO, Geotechnical & Environmental Consultants, Honeywell Technology Solutions, Inc, Support Systems Associates, Inc., and Universal Avionics Systems Corp. were among the employers that came to interview MBA candidates. However, for those hoping to change careers, Mercer students admit that, "Because most students are employed, emphasis on career services is not present. More energy towards helping students with career decisions would be appreciated." A current student adds, "As an MBA student, I would definitely like to see the Career Placement services improve for MBA students. The school currently tailors this program to mainly

ADMISSIONS CONTACT: ROBERT HOLLAND JR, DIRECTOR OF ACADEMIC ADMINISTRATION
ADDRESS: 1400 COLEMAN AVENUE, SSBE, MACON, GA 31207
PHONE: 478-301-2835 • FAX: 478-301-2635
E-MAIL: HOLLAND_R@MERCER.EDU • WEBSITE: WWW.MERCER.EDU

ADMISSIONS	
Admissions Selectivity Rating	**69**
# of applications received	12
% applicants accepted	100
% acceptees attending	100
Average GMAT	530
TOEFL required of international students	Yes
Minimum TOEFL (paper/computer)	550/213
Application fee	$50
International application fee	$100
Deferment available	Yes
Maximum length of deferment	1 year
Transfer students accepted	Yes
Transfer application policy: Can't transfer more than 6 hours from an AACSB accredited program	
Non-fall admissions	Yes

undergraduate students." Nonetheless, students know that they will be able to cash in on the Mercer name during their career, as well as benefit from the school's "established network with leaders in many fields of business and economics." A student agrees, "I chose Mercer because it has a great reputation."

Student Life and Environment

According to most MBA students, it's strictly business at Mercer University. While Mercer's undergraduate college is lively and social, most MBA students "work and live off campus" and "don't seem to be involved in other organizations on campus." A current MBA candidate (and undergraduate alumni) laments, "There was a lot more to do while I was getting my undergraduate degree." At the same time, some note that the MBA student population is beginning to change as the school admits younger students, especially through the school's joint degree and work-study programs. A student explains, "There is a good mix of full-time working adults from the community, and young adult graduate assistants and law students." No matter what their age, experience, or career goals, most Mercer MBAs are "Driven individuals pursuing skills that will increase their performance in their current career or make them more marketable for a future career."

Located in downtown Macon, "The campus is quiet and safe-feeling and fosters an environment for learning." However, some say they'd like to see "More parking and more convenient food options for night class students." Others mention that, "Campus security could be better." A current student elaborates, "Students live in what they call the Mercer Bubble, protected by patrolling campus police, who do a very good job, but can't stop everything."

Admissions

Students are accepted to Mercer University based on a combination of their GMAT scores, prior academic performance, and, in some cases, previous professional experience in a management position. Mercer admits students three times a year for the fall, spring, and summer terms. In recent years, the average student was 29 years old, and 15 percent of the student body was international.

MIAMI UNIVERSITY (OH)
RICHARD T. FARMER SCHOOL OF BUSINESS

GENERAL INFORMATION

Type of school	Public
Affiliation	No Affiliation
Academic calendar	Semesters

SURVEY SAYS...
Friendly students, Good peer network
Solid preparation in:
Marketing, General management,
Teamwork, Presentation skills, Doing
business in a global economy

STUDENTS

Enrollment of MBA Program	34
% part-time	100
Average age at entry	33
Average years work experience at entry	10.0

ACADEMICS

Academic Experience Rating	**88**
Profs interesting rating	89
Profs accesible rating	87
Student/faculty ratio	4:1
% female faculty	17
% underrepresented minority faculty	3
% part-time faculty	11

Academics

Students at Miami University's Farmer School of Business say their efficient program is "the best option in the Cincinnati area for working professionals with families to get their MBA." Before they even enroll, Farmer makes it easy for fully employed professionals to consider a graduate degree, offering prerequisite coursework online (as well as proficiency exams for students who want to test out of foundational classes) and a GMAT prep course right on the Farmer campus. Once they have been accepted, students find the MBA program is "designed to be convenient for the working professional," with classes offered two evenings per week over the course of two years. The school's administration makes every effort to streamline the experience, offering "concierge-level" services for students. Among other conveniences, the all-inclusive tuition includes all fees and materials; at the beginning of each semester, the administration will "register you for class" and "buy all your books." They even have dinner service for evening classes, which "is a significant help to make the day easier." A current student enthuses, "They understand that we are working full time and make every effort to cater to us so all we have to do is study and attend class."

"A very focused professional MBA," the Farmer curriculum includes 36 credit hours of upper-level business courses, of which 27 are core courses in economics, accounting, marketing, management, and other key business areas. With the remaining 9 elective credits, students may choose to pursue a concentration in marketing or finance. Throughout the curriculum, there is an emphasis on collaboration, with a "cohort-based" program that maintains students within the same small academic community during the full MBA. Note that the program does not allow flexibility in the academic calendar; "The classes are prescheduled to keep the cohort together." Throughout the program, Farmer professors rely on case-based instruction, encouraging students to use critical thinking skills and real-world experience to solve business problems in the classroom. This interactive approach to education is particularly effective at Miami University, as students are "extremely intelligent with a lot of work experience," making them valuable contributors to class discussion. In fact, students range from "very early in their career to executives that have owned multiple companies." Staying on top of the coursework is not always a breeze, but it is rewarding: "Academically, the work is a challenge to keep up with, but it is that challenge that keeps it engaging."

Many students choose the Farmer School of Business for its excellent regional reputation, telling us that the school lives up to its strong credentials: The professors are "all very smart and challenge students to excel." In the classroom, "Some teachers are outstanding and some are not so great." However, the vast majority are "approachable and seem to care about doing a good job." Plus, any time the program falls short, students feel they have the full attention of the school's administration and staff. As they continue developing the part-time MBA, "The administration is open to suggestions on how the program or any given course can be improved."

Career and Placement

The Farmer School's MBA program is specifically designed for working professionals, with a curriculum focused on increasing business acumen and problem-solving skills. To that end, the program is effective in promoting a student's long-term career goals. A current student attests, "I received my undergraduate degree from Miami University's Farmer School of Business and was well-prepared to enter the workforce. I knew that this program would afford that same high-caliber education."

ADMISSIONS CONTACT: C. BRAD BAYS, DIRECTOR, MBA PROGRAMS
ADDRESS: 1038 FARMER SCHOOL OF BUSINESS, OXFORD, OH 45056
PHONE: 513-529-6643 • FAX: 513-529-6488
E-MAIL: MIAMIMBA@MUOHIO.EDU • WEBSITE: MBA.MUOHIO.EDU

While they are looking to advance their career, most Farmer students aren't actively looking for a new job after graduation. At the same time, "Miami is well known in the Cincinnati area," so the degree is a good investment in the future.

Student Life and Environment

The Miami University graduate business program is located in the Voice of America Learning Center (VALC) a special satellite campus located just off the I-75 in West Chester, Ohio. "The facility is state of the art," with classrooms specially designed for business instruction and discussion. The VALC is also "centrally located and close to Cincinnati and Dayton," making it convenient for students in either city to get to campus in the evenings. Several of Miami's undergraduate programs, as well as the graduate education department, share the VALC campus with the MBA.

There are no residential facilities on the Farmer campus; "Everyone in the program lives in the greater Cincinnati Area" and commutes to school in the evenings. As a result, "The concept of student life in a classical sense does not apply" to the Farmer experience. Nonetheless, the atmosphere at the business school is consistently friendly and professional. Most Miami students are "highly motivated professionals," who are always "intelligent, professional, and pleasant" in dealing with their classmates. The cohort structure encourages networking and relationships among MBA candidates, to good effect. A current student tells us, "The 40 people that are in my class are like family to me now after two years."

Admissions

Applications for the fall semester are accepted through June 15. Once you have submitted all your application materials, including GMAT scores and undergraduate transcripts, the admissions committee will make a decision within two to three weeks. The class of 2010 had an average GMAT score of 562 and an average undergraduate GPA of 3.15, as well as an average of ten years professional work experience before matriculation. While almost half of incoming students hold an undergraduate degree in business, the other half join the program from liberal arts or technical fields.

FINANCIAL FACTS

% of students receiving aid	17
% of first-year students receiving aid	24
Average loan	$15,846
Average student loan debt	$15,846

ADMISSIONS

Admissions Selectivity Rating	**86**
# of applications received	83
% applicants accepted	48
% acceptees attending	85
Average GMAT	567
Range of GMAT	510–625
Average GPA	3.29
TOEFL required of international students	Yes
Deferment available	Yes
Maximum length of deferment	2 years
Transfer students accepted	Yes

Transfer application policy: Miami courses (ACC 221, ECO 201, and STAT 261 or DSC 205) are used as the standard for each of three topics. If you completed these courses (or higher level course/s) at Miami, you meet the requirements. If you have completed a similar course/s at another school, Transfer.Org will be used to evaluate whether your coursework is equivalent to the standard.

Non-fall admissions	Yes
Need-blind admissions	Yes

MILLSAPS COLLEGE
ELSE SCHOOL OF MANAGEMENT

GENERAL INFORMATION

Type of school	Private
Affiliation	Methodist
Academic calendar	Semester

SURVEY SAYS...

Friendly students, Good peer network, Good social scene
Solid preparation in:
Communication/interpersonal skills

STUDENTS

Enrollment of parent institution	1,100
Enrollment of MBA Program	65
% male/female	63/37
% part-time	45
Average age at entry	28
Average years work experience at entry	4.0

ACADEMICS

Academic Experience Rating	**81**
Profs interesting rating	88
Profs accesible rating	87
Student/faculty ratio	12:1
% female faculty	40
% underrepresented minority faculty	0
% part-time faculty	1

Prominent Alumni

Bo Chastain, CEO, MS State Hospital; John Stupka, former CEO Skytel; Richard H. Mills, Jr., CEO, Tellus Operating Group; Will Flatt, CFO Parkway Properties; Sharon O'Shea, president and CEO, e-Triage

Academics

A cozy place to get an MBA, Else School of Management at Millsaps College maintains a friendly "small-college feel" alongside a "strong reputation for academic excellence" throughout the South. With its pleasant, liberal arts atmosphere, "You feel welcome no matter where you are on campus, and the size gives you a warmth you wouldn't expect" from a top-rated business program. The intimate environment really distinguishes the Else School experience, in which "Faculty and staff always take a personal interest in helping students reach their goals." Thanks to the low MBA enrollment, students can also count on having "smaller class sizes" throughout the graduate business program, giving them a chance to interact closely with their professors, as well as their classmates. From economics to marketing, "The atmosphere of class is always full of discussion and open-minded conversation."

The only Millsaps department to confer graduate-level degrees, Else offers a Masters in accounting, as well as a full-time MBA program for traditional students and an Executive MBA for mid-career managers. The full-time MBA is comprised of foundation, core, and elective courses; foundation courses may be waived for students with an undergraduate degree in business. Depending on their previous preparation, students entering the program post-college can finish the MBA in anywhere between one to three years, though "There is a fast track" for current Millsaps undergraduates, which allows them to obtain an MBA with just one additional year of study. For EMBA students, it can be a challenge to balance work; family life, and academics. Fortunately, busy part-timers feel supported by the school's faculty, and say the "Administration is very personal and helpful" in response to student concerns.

Boasting both real-world know-how and a genuine dedication to teaching, Else School professors are "insightful, experienced, and entertaining." Throughout the program, professors "do all they can to make the classroom experience worthwhile," and the academic experience is "engaging and very interactive." Most importantly, students feel their education has immediate real-world applicability. The professors are "experts in their fields "and" stay on top of current events and trends. Academically, "Courses are tough, but you will definitely learn through rigorous application of theory." Plus, "Instructors that take time to make sure the students understand the material," and they are very "approachable" outside of class. Not only do they maintain office hours, professors "enthusiastically give their time to support students, even after the semester is over."

Career and Placement

The Else School Career Center assists undergraduate and graduate business students in their internship or job search; they are also available to Else School alumni. The Career Center organizes networking events and career fairs on campus, offers resume and interview assistance, and runs career-related workshops throughout the year. Through the Career Center, business students also have access to numerous online job boards. While students say their career prospects look good, they also say the school could "make sure that working students (older students) are aware of career fairs, career opportunities," which are generally directed at recent graduates.

Not only is a Millsaps education "highly regarded in the region," it is the "only accredited MBA in Jackson," so students have a serious advantage in the local job market. Plus, the school's faculty has strong ties in the local area, so "Communication and networking are easily facilitated here." Outside the Jackson area, there may be fewer opportunities to translate a Millsaps MBA into a top-notch job offer. Almost all of Millsaps business graduates take positions in the South.

ADMISSIONS CONTACT: MELISSA MEACHAM, DIRECTOR OF GRADUATE BUSINESS ADMISSIONS
ADDRESS: 1701 NORTH STATE STREET, JACKSON, MS 39210
PHONE: 601-974-1253 • FAX: 601-974-1260
E-MAIL: MBAMACC@MILLSAPS.EDU • WEBSITE: WWW.MBA.MILLSAPS.EDU

Student Life and Environment

A "warm and welcoming" environment permeates the business school at Millsaps, where students say, "It's very easy to make friends" and get involved in the campus community. Most MBA candidates are "very intelligent but also have great social skills," making them ideal companions both inside and outside the classroom. Within this "close-knit" community, the "business school clubs always have different activities that keep a strong cohesiveness within the student body throughout the semesters." Millsaps is a residential college, where "Most undergraduates live on campus, while most MBAs live off campus." Even if they don't shack up in the dorms, full-time MBA candidates may still be highly involved with the school community. Here, both undergrads and graduate students "are able to participate in IM activities and other functions the school puts on (plays, concerts, varsity games etc.)"

By contrast, there is "not a great deal of campus life" for part-time MBA candidates. Balancing schoolwork with professional and family commitments, older students would love to see "more resources for parents with children." At the same time, "Millsaps has gone to lengths to make the EMBA students feel welcome and as much a part of other Business School activities as we are able to or wish to participate in." A part-time student assures us, "Even with our really busy schedules with work and school, we are still able to enjoy every aspect of life."

Admissions

To apply to Millsaps, prospective MBA candidates must submit undergraduate transcripts, GMAT scores, an admissions essay, and two letters of recommendation. In addition to regular application materials, applicants to the graduate business programs are also required to interview with the Director or Associate Director of Graduate Admissions. The fall 2011 entering class had an average undergraduate GPA of 3.4 and an average GMAT score of 560. The GMAT is not required for EMBA applicants.

FINANCIAL FACTS

Annual tuition	$26,400
Cost of books	$550
% of students receiving aid	85
% of first-year students receiving aid	100
% of students receiving grants	90

ADMISSIONS

Admissions Selectivity Rating	76
# of applications received	48
% applicants accepted	85
% acceptees attending	90
Average GMAT	560
Range of GMAT	500–730
Average GPA	3.40
TOEFL required of international students	Yes
Minimum TOEFL (paper/computer)	550/230
International application fee	$25
Early application deadline	4/1
Application Deadline/Notification	
Round 1:	4/1 / 4/25
Deferment available	Yes
Maximum length of deferment	1 year
Transfer students accepted	Yes
Transfer application policy: Student in Good Standing. 6 hours from a non-AACSB program; 12 hours from a AACSB accredited program	
Non-fall admissions	Yes
Need-blind admissions	Yes

EMPLOYMENT PROFILE

Career Rating	66	Grads Employed by Function	% Avg. Salary
Percent employed at graduation	5	Marketing	(2%)
Percent employed 3 months after graduation	8	Finance	(2%)
		MIS	(2%)

Minnesota State University—Mankato
College of Business

GENERAL INFORMATION
Type of school	Public
Affiliation	No Affiliation
Academic calendar	Semester

SURVEY SAYS...
Friendly students, Good peer network, Cutting-edge classes, Happy students, Smart classrooms
Solid preparation in:
General management

STUDENTS
Enrollment of parent institution	15,000
Enrollment of MBA Program	56
% male/female	75/25
% underrepresented minority	12
% international	12
Average years work experience at entry	6.0

ACADEMICS
Academic Experience Rating	**78**
Profs interesting rating	80
Profs accesible rating	79
Student/faculty ratio	14:1
% female faculty	33
% underrepresented minority faculty	10
% part-time faculty	6

Academics

A completely affordable price tag, a Twin City area satellite campus located in Edina, and a "powerful track record for delivering quality education," not to mention one of the few accredited MBA programs in the state make the College of Business at Minnesota State University—Mankato "a big part of the community as a whole, and held in high regard." There have been recent capital improvements to the "beautiful campus," including "great visual and technological facilities."

The program is "quite well run," especially considering "it is naturally difficult to balance each course's difficulty considering the different background experiences of the students." The activities that accompany the academic work are "up to date, current, and not from the old books," giving students something they "can see and work with in…real life." The statistics/financial courses in particular are "beneficial and challenging," as are "innovative courses like the Executive seminar and Strategic Management."

Though the "excellent" professors get mostly high marks all around – a few "put only a small amount of work into class or are unprepared" – some would like to see more "come from business and not academia," so they might bring more practical applications to the classrooms. "I feel like those of us who are currently working have much more relevant experience to share than the instructors," says a student. The majority of the professors who are adjunct are "awesome and have great real world experience."

The difficulty and workload differs greatly from course to course, but the "flexible program structure" allows students to match their workload with their personal responsibilities and time. Courses are "more hands-on than theoretical," "very content and knowledge driven, and are updated real time based on the trends." Classes usually "use case analysis and team-based projects to present the course work," and many students meet on weekends. "The knowledge gained from my course mates cannot be overemphasized," says one student. Evening classes are a plus and a two-month semester is also "a plus." Some students do wish there were more courses available and "more options with regards to MBA concentrations."

Career and Placement

The MNSU MBA is "definitely directed toward people who are working full-time." The huge international student and full-time working population reduces the burden on the Career Development Center, which offers "very little help" for those who are looking for jobs after graduation, but "this is not a big issue as most students are employed." "The value of MSU-Mankato's MBA program is higher than that of most programs because costs are relatively cheap," and most students are mainly looking for the degree rather than the placement. There are plenty of experience opportunities as well as excellent career networking for international students, and "the way the program is designed makes it easy…to learn and understand the concepts in a better way." Students also benefit from "a strong focus on leadership throughout the program."

Student Life and Environment

This "friendly, social" group is "overall pretty great." "We all get along and work together to solve problems that arise," says a student, "[we're] a great group of new friends." One student says that "there are not as many working students as I expected, so much of the work situation discussion comes from a small number of us," but "many of them are very engaging with worldly views and experience." This is still "a good mix of students. There are people fresh out of college, people looking for a career change, and people looking to advance in their current career." Minnesota also draws a sizeable international student population.

Life at school is pretty "stress free." "I go twice a week, meet with classmates before class for supper, then go to class," says one student. Many will also meet with classmates on weekends to study. The campus is in "a great area that showcases the school—housing is close, businesses are nearby and support students, public transportation is available, but it is also a ped/bike friendly area too." There is a "well set up" daycare available (although a long waitlist exists) for working parents to use during the day.

Admissions

Applicants to the MBA program at MSU Mankato's College of Business must submit all of the following materials to the College of Graduate Studies: a completed application form; two official transcripts from one's degree-granting institution(s); a completed immunization form; and official score reports for the GMAT and, if applicable, the TOEFL. International applicants must also complete a Financial Statement Form demonstrating that they have sufficient funds to pay for the program. Most international applicants are required to have their undergraduate transcripts evaluated by a well-regarded credential evaluation service. All applicants must submit a resume, and two letters of reference to the College of Business. Admission to the MBA program is competitive. Students earning a score of 1000 or higher under the formula [(200 × undergraduate GPA) + GMAT score] and scoring at least 500 on the GMAT will be admitted to the program.

FINANCIAL FACTS

Annual tuition	$9,265
Fees	$610
Cost of books	$1,000

ADMISSIONS

Admissions Selectivity Rating	76
# of applications received	28
% applicants accepted	20
% acceptees attending	28
Average GMAT	543
Range of GMAT	480–650
Average GPA	3.27
TOEFL required of international students	Yes
Minimum TOEFL (paper/computer)	500/173
Application fee	$40
International application fee	$40
Deferment available	Yes
Maximum length of deferment	1 year
Transfer students accepted	Yes
Transfer application policy: Upon evaluation, would accept a maximum of 8 credits from another MBA or graduate program.	
Non-fall admissions	Yes
Need-blind admissions	Yes

MONMOUTH UNIVERSITY
LEON HESS BUSINESS SCHOOL

GENERAL INFORMATION
Type of school	Private
Affiliation	No Affiliation
Academic calendar	Semester

SURVEY SAYS...
Students love West Long Branch, NJ
Solid preparation in:
Finance, Teamwork,
General management

STUDENTS
Enrollment of parent institution	6,472
Enrollment of MBA Program	232
% male/female	55/45
% out-of-state	11
% part-time	57
% underrepresented minority	14
% international	8
Average age at entry	25
Average years work experience at entry	2.0

ACADEMICS
Academic Experience Rating	75
Profs interesting rating	74
Profs accesible rating	82
Student/faculty ratio	6:1
% female faculty	28
% underrepresented minority faculty	18
% part-time faculty	15

Prominent Alumni
Linda C Deutsch, Legal Affairs Correspondent; Noel L Hillman, Federal Judge; Christie Pearce Rampone, Olympic Gold Medalist; Herbert Butler, R & D first televised weather satellite; Robert Santelli, Executive Director GRAMMY Museum

Academics

A small school in West Long Branch, New Jersey, Monmouth University operates an MBA program suitable to students at every phase of their careers. All Monmouth MBA candidates complete the same core curriculum, with the opportunity to tailor their education through a concentration in health administration, or by completing a series of courses in the finance track, the accounting track, or the commercial real estate track. Students may also elect a general MBA program, choosing from assorted electives to complete their post-core course credits. In addition to being "one of the very few schools with a concentration in healthcare management," Monmouth's curriculum has a strong focus on international business and ethics.

With all classes held mainly in the evenings with a few on Saturday, Monmouth's "scheduling offers flexibility for those who are working full time or have families." Some would like to see "more hybrid and online classes" to better accommodate their busy schedules, though there is an "emphasis on group work in the classroom," which would be difficult to replicate electronically. In addition to their long-standing, part-time MBA program (which classically catered to working professionals), Monmouth has recently introduced an accelerated full-time MBA, which can be completed in just a year. Students say the program runs smoothly, and "the administration is very willing and available to talk about any questions or concerns." Whether it's financial aid or scheduling, the "school's administration is helpful in solving day-to-day issues, especially for international students." Beyond the availability of the faculty and staff, students also praise Monmouth's "affordability," saying tuition is lower than at regional public schools.

Academically, "professors are a diverse group," running the gamut from lifetime academics to real-world professionals. Instructors with business credentials usually emphasize the "application of principles to real-world situations" and often incorporate "personal experiences to enrich the course and make it easy to understand." Others "just teach from slides," offering little class discussion or interaction with students. Even so, Monmouth generally offers its students more personalized attention than they would get at a larger program. Many classes are discussion based, allowing "close interaction with the professors," as well as classmates. Classes are "focused on helping students learn the material and not just memorizing facts in order to pass the exams." If a student is struggling academically, "the professors always show concern for students' progress and are available to answer questions whether it's over the phone, by email, or by appointment during office hours." With few exceptions, "professors are available outside of the classroom for help or review."

Career and Placement

Monmouth's MBA program was traditionally geared toward working professionals, who are "getting their MBA to advance their careers." These students are rarely looking to leave their current jobs, and some are even receiving tuition assistance from their employers. In recent years, the school has added a full-time program, and is working to keep pace with the growing need for strong career services. Students note that, "Monmouth has a great placement program for MBA honors accounting students," saying "it would be wonderful to see this type of service extended to all business concentration areas, as it is so very successful."

All graduate business students have access to the Career Services department at Monmouth University's Center for Student Success. Career Services staff can offer career counseling, job search strategies, and resume reviews. They also maintain an online job board and host an annual career fair. While these events present some opportunities, students feel that the school "needs to be more involved with the business community" in the region.

Student Life and Environment

With a total MBA enrollment of approximately 200, "students are a small community, so everybody knows everybody." Close to several major cities, "the school's location allows for a good mix of students to attend," and Monmouth students join the program "from a variety of professions" and life experiences. While a good number of students come "right after undergrad," others are "older professionals" or young adults who "have worked for several years." "Many students work during the day," and spend little time on campus beyond classes. However, group assignments encourage students to work together and network. On the whole, Monmouth graduate students say their classmates are "friendly, sociable, and open-minded."

For those who like extracurricular experiences, "there are some interesting activities" within the business school, including international student organizations and a series of guest speakers. Students also take advantage of the greater campus environment, which offers a wonderful collegiate culture. "One of the many wonderful things about Monmouth is the Woods Theatre, which features adorable 'cozy' productions in a quaint little theatre right on campus." Monmouth's "stunning campus" is located "a mile to the beach and hour to NYC or Philly." In addition to the obvious benefits of the Jersey Shore, students appreciate the school's "geographic convenience to all of Monmouth and Ocean County."

Admissions

Prospective students appreciate Monmouth's "fast and easy admissions process." Students with a GMAT score over 500 or equivalent GRE score are admitted with less consideration to their GPA. Students with a minimum GMAT score of 450 are considered for the program with additional emphasis on their GPA. Prospective students with a CPA or CFA license or master's degree may waive the admissions tests altogether. Graduate Fellowships are available through the Office of Graduate Admission to matriculated students in a master's degree program, based on a variety of factors, and are renewable throughout enrollment assuming preset academic minimums.

FINANCIAL FACTS

Annual tuition	$17,334
Fees	$628
Cost of books	$660
Room & board	$16,443
% of students receiving aid	78
% of first-year students receiving aid	84
% of students receiving grants	68
Average award package	$12,256
Average grant	$4,869
Average loan	$15,262
Average student loan debt	$31,561

ADMISSIONS

Admissions Selectivity Rating	**75**
# of applications received	201
% applicants accepted	61
% acceptees attending	60
Average GMAT	467
Range of GMAT	420–530
Average GPA	3.28
TOEFL required of international students	Yes
Minimum TOEFL (paper/computer)	550/213
International application fee	$50
Regular application deadline	7/15
Deferment available	Yes
Maximum length of deferment	1 year
Transfer students accepted	Yes
Transfer application policy: must complete at least 30 cr at Monmouth Transfer crds must be within 7yrs and with acceptable grade	
Non-fall admissions	Yes
Need-blind admissions	Yes

MONTCLAIR STATE UNIVERSITY
SCHOOL OF BUSINESS

GENERAL INFORMATION

Type of school	Public
Affiliation	No Affiliation
Academic calendar	Year-round

SURVEY SAYS...

Students love Upper Montclair, NJ,
Friendly students, Good social scene,
Happy students, Smart classrooms
Solid preparation in:
Accounting, General management,
Presentation skills

STUDENTS

Enrollment of parent institution	18,382
Enrollment of MBA Program	292
% male/female	54/46
% out-of-state	3
% part-time	76
% underrepresented minority	31
% international	27
Average age at entry	27

ACADEMICS

Academic Experience Rating	74
Profs interesting rating	73
Profs accesible rating	77
Student/faculty ratio	25:1
% female faculty	26
% underrepresented minority faculty	36
% part-time faculty	20

Prominent Alumni

Dr. Steve Adubato, Anchor, WNET
NY, PBS; Dr. Paul Weber, Senior
Director, Medical Affairs at Enzon
Pharmaceuticals; Annette Catino,
President & CEO, QualCare, Inc.;
Thomas P. Zucosky, CIO, Discovery
Capital Management; A. J. Khubani,
President & CEO, Telebrands

Academics

Graduate students get a good return on their investment at Montclair State University, an "affordable" public school with an "up-and-coming business program" near New York City. Having recently reworked their graduate curriculum, Montclair School of Business offers several distinct MBA options on three New Jersey campuses: an evening program on the main Montclair campus, a weekend Executive Style MBA on the Meadowlands campus of Bergen Community College in Lyndhurst, and a hybrid accelerated Saturday program held at Brookdale Community College in Monmouth County. For all three programs, the school has introduced a "redesigned cohort-based MBA," through which students complete a comprehensive core curriculum in tandem with a small group of classmates. The new structure encourages greater interaction and networking between MBA candidates—a huge asset to the experience, given that "fellow students are competent, pleasant to work with, and provide an engaging atmosphere in the classroom."

Beyond classroom instruction, the new Montclair curriculum provides a "complete educational experience," from the ongoing executive speaker series to the "foundations toolbox," an online resource to help students prepare for the MBA. Among other interesting innovations, "The program integrates technology (iPad2) into the curriculum," using iPads like "electronic book bags" that contain some MBA class materials. For a global perspective, students participate in a seven to ten day "international [study] trip," an intensive course taught overseas, which focuses on the political and cultural aspects of global business. While the program offers a range of excellent resources, prospective students should carefully review the course offerings before enrolling, to ensure a cohort structured program is the correct fit for them. On the whole, "the administration for the new MBA has been very receptive to students." Whenever a problem arises, "The MBA office is very quick in their responses and follow up."

Thanks to the small class size, "You do not get lost in the crowd" at Montclair, and "The professors do seem to offer a lot of assistance outside of class." The majority of the "professors are outstanding," though students admit that while there are "rock stars", a few professors can be lacking. In particular, finance and accounting professors get good marks from students, and "The economics professors are above average." Essential to working adults, practical education is a focus in the coursework; in the classroom, professors "use their real life experiences to teach us and get us up to date."

Career and Placement

The majority of Montclair students are already employed when they begin the program, using the MBA to advance in their current position. Those looking for new jobs will benefit from the school's proximity to New York City, one of the largest and most diverse job markets in the world. Currently, graduates of Montclair School of Business hold jobs at companies including Northwestern Mutual, Market Analytics, Enterprise RAC, Disney World, New York Life, Deloitte, Citigroup, CH Robinson, Estee Lauder, Merrill Lynch, KPMG, MTV, Prudential, The Hampton Inn, Bayer Healthcare, Party City, Target, Ernst & Young, and others.

ADMISSIONS CONTACT: MS. JENNIFER O'SULLIVAN, ADMISSIONS COORDINATOR
ADDRESS: COLLEGE HALL, ROOM 203, ONE NORMAL AVENUE, MONTCLAIR, NJ 07043
PHONE: 973-655-5147 • FAX: 973-655-7869
E-MAIL: GRADUATE.SCHOOL@MONTCLAIR.EDU • WEBSITE: WWW.MONTCLAIR.EDU/MBA

The School of Business Career Services office is available to help undergraduate and graduate students explore careers and prepare for the job hunt through workshops, speakers, Internet resources, and individual career counseling sessions. With regards to the assistance offered by Career Services, a current student explains, "You basically post your resume, which they pass on to employers involved in in-campus recruiting. They call you for interviews, when they feel you are a match for a position." While this system does produce opportunities, students would love to see more networking events on campus.

Student Life and Environment

Montclair's graduate business programs principally attract students from the local area, in addition to a smaller population of international students. Within the student body, there is a "very diverse mix ethnically, and many different professions represented." No matter what their background, students are generally "hard-working professionals that are attending the MBA program at night." A student in the Saturday program attests, "My fellow students within the cohort are very intelligent, hard working, reliable, and goal oriented."

Outside the classroom, the business school hosts networking events and frequent business speakers for the benefit of the MBA program, and it recently began hosting case competitions as well. While most students cannot find the time for extracurricular activities, others take advantage of the collegial atmosphere. "On campus, life is pretty rich. You get to meet lots of people, interact, network and have fun." A current student adds, "I have always been a commuter in my studies. Montclair is the first school that I felt truly encouraged [to have] an on campus social life."

Students admit that "The business school building is rather run down," but overall, the school's 250-acre campus is "very nice with many improvements in the past few years." Only 14 miles from New York, it's easy to take advantage of the big city's recreational, professional, and entertainment options, while enjoying the more tranquil, suburban atmosphere in Montclair and the surrounding cities.

Admissions

Applications for Montclair's MBA programs are accepted on a rolling basis year-round. Usually, an admissions decision will be rendered within two to three weeks after the school receives a completed application packet. To be considered, students must submit undergraduate transcripts, official GMAT or GRE scores, a personal essay, and two letters of recommendations. Students may be eligible for admissions without taking the GMAT or GRE if they have a recent BS in business administration from Montclair State or an AACSB accredited institution with a 3.5 GPA or higher, 10 or more years of full time work experience, a MS degree in a quantitative or technical area, or if they have an MD, JD, or PhD in any discipline. Successful applicants to the weekend program usually have at least five years of full-time work experience before matriculation.

FINANCIAL FACTS

Annual tuition	$11,424
Fees	$4,848
Cost of books	$1,500
Room & board	$18,000
% of students receiving aid	41
% of first-year students receiving aid	53
% of students receiving grants	1
Average award package	$15,827
Average grant	$10,723
Average loan	$15,794
Average student loan debt	$32,472

ADMISSIONS

Admissions Selectivity Rating	67
# of applications received	146
% applicants accepted	70
% acceptees attending	67
Average GPA	3.25
TOEFL required of international students	Yes
Minimum TOEFL (paper/computer)	380/207
Application fee	$60
International application fee	$60
Deferment available	Yes
Maximum length of deferment	1 year
Transfer students accepted	Yes
Transfer application policy: Students who have completed prior academic coursework in business, may be waived from up to 12 credits of foundation courses.	
Non-fall admissions	Yes
Need-blind admissions	Yes

MONTEREY INSTITUTE OF INTERNATIONAL STUDIES
FISHER INTERNATIONAL MBA PROGRAM

GENERAL INFORMATION
Type of school	Private
Affiliation	No Affiliation
Academic calendar	Semester

SURVEY SAYS...
Friendly students, Good social scene
Solid preparation in:
Teamwork, Doing business in a
global economy, Social responsibility

STUDENTS
Enrollment of parent institution	780
Enrollment of MBA Program	73
% male/female	61/39
% out-of-state	14
% part-time	12
% underrepresented minority	16
% international	39
Average age at entry	27
Average years work experience at entry	4.0

ACADEMICS
Academic Experience Rating	**77**
Profs interesting rating	81
Profs accesible rating	82
Student/faculty ratio	7:1
% female faculty	21
% underrepresented minority faculty	18
% part-time faculty	71

Joint Degrees
MBA/MA International
Environmental Policy, 3 years;
MBA/MA International Policy
Studies with focus on Trade,
Investment and Development, or
Human Security and Development,
3 years; MBA/MPA Non-rofit
Management, 3 years; MBA/MA
Translation, 3 years; MBA/MA
Translation & Localization
Management, 3 years

Prominent Alumni
Fumio Matsushima, Head of Private
Banking, HSBC Japan; Laurent-
Gabriel Vinay, CEO/President, Hugo
Boss Japan

Academics

The Fisher International MBA program at MIIS offers students just what it says it does, an MBA in international business. Not only that, but the campus itself, located in central California, has an international feel. "Half the students in every class are international students," and all are required to be proficient in a second language. Students are also "encouraged to study abroad." "I came here to avoid being around the traditional business school student wanting to go make millions and maximize profit without caring about social or environmental impact." There is an emphasis on green business strategies, as well as an understanding of what the future of business will actually look like. "The school itself is entrepreneurial. This year, it launched an innovative program in partnership with social impact investment firms to send students out to emerging countries like Vietnam, India, Nigeria, and Tanzania. The students work with the venture firms directly." The program's focus is on language studies, environmental issues, corporate responsibility, and cross-cultural negotiation. "Last year as a part of the sustainability lecture series, business leaders from interesting new ventures like Revolution Foods and Numi Tea came to lecture weekly." Students appreciate the "cross-sector focus, specifically international development and environmental policy." They also like the "accessibility to other disciplines." At MIIS students have the opportunity to specialize or opt for a dual degree. They can work toward an MBA, as well as an MA in fields, such as environmental policy, public administration, and translation.

Students love "the international perspective, the size (for its adaptability, personal attention, etc.), the innovative nature of the curriculum, and the focus on sustainability." "The school is small but packs a punch. In the same week, students could see guest lecturers on Nuclear Proliferation in Iran, and representatives from Denmark talk about how the country achieved a 100 percent growth rate without an increase in petroleum use." Because of its small size, "everything is personalized. The administration has designed the program, so that no two students' experience is the same, each being custom tailored to the student's professional goals." "If we want to see something happen, we can make it happen." "The administration is forward-thinking and proactive in finding new and exciting directions for the school; there is an ability to adapt quickly to new trends in education and business." Some professors are "excellent" and "frequently engage with students" outside of class. Students say professors are on a first-name basis with many students. One suggests "the academic rigor could be more standardized. Some courses are highly rigorous, while others are not." Others worry that "a couple really good professors retired this term." They hope they will be replaced "with equally talented professors."

Career and Placement

The Center for Advising and Career Services (CACS) for the Fisher International MBA program "acts as an 'executive search firm'," helping students "target potential employers and enhance their value." Students are assigned advisors during the admissions process, and career planning starts from day one. They offer personal consultations, as well as a multitude of workshops covering topics, such as salary negotiation, how to interview, and networking. Students admit the office "is slowly pulling things together." What hampers this process is the school's size and location. Not many recruiters are coming to campus, and one student reports you can "expect to get a job and an internship on your own." However, there is an online job resource for both students and alumni, and the school hosts an annual career fair, which draws more than 100 employers to campus.

ADMISSIONS CONTACT: CAROLINE LaTORRE, ENROLLMENT MANAGER
ADDRESS: 460 PIERCE STREET, MONTEREY, CA 93940
PHONE: 831-647-4123 • FAX: 831-647-6405
E-MAIL: ADMIT@MIIS.EDU • WEBSITE: FISHER.MIIS.EDU

The top five employers who hired graduates last year were the following companies: PriceWaterhouse Coopers, Veritas Wealth Advisors, Ernst & Young, LeCroy Corp, Foundation for Community Development.

Student Life and Environment

At MIIS "students are responsible, well rounded, and honest." They are also "aware of international issues," "socially conscious," and "culturally sensitive." Students are "motivated by new and creative ideas" and "have a desire to operate outside of their comfort zones." They have "a great combination of international experience and curiosity. Many students have been in the Peace Corps or are going. Many are bilingual or multilingual." Most have lived and worked abroad or are international students visiting from other countries.

"You can't ask for a more beautiful area than the Monterey Bay peninsula." Monterey is located on the coast in central California about two hours south of San Francisco. It has a population of about 30,000 residents, making it "fairly quiet." There are "wonderful restaurants in town and in surrounding areas." However, there is "not much variety in night life." The school sponsors a monthly happy hour during which students mingle with faculty and staff, and students also interact with students in other programs through various activities. There is a scuba club, a golf club, as well as a Women in Business club, just to name a few. There are also "many opportunities for outdoor activities in the surrounding area."

Admissions

The committee requires from its applicants the following materials for admission: an official GMAT score report; a personal essay; undergraduate GPA and transcripts from all post-secondary institutions previously attended; letters of recommendation; work experience; and two years of foreign language study. Most students average three to four years of work experience. A GRE score will suffice in lieu of the GMAT. Second language proficiency (which is also required), can be acquired through an intensive language immersion program offered by the school the summer prior to entrance.

FINANCIAL FACTS

Annual tuition	$32,800
Fees	$56
Cost of books	$900
Room & board	$27,565
% of students receiving aid	85
% of first-year students receiving aid	95
% of students receiving grants	85
Average award package	$23,665
Average grant	$10,394
Average loan	$28,985

ADMISSIONS

Admissions Selectivity Rating	75
# of applications received	101
% applicants accepted	74
% acceptees attending	63
Average GMAT	572
Range of GMAT	520–650
Average GPA	3.35
TOEFL required of international students	Yes
Minimum TOEFL (paper/computer)	550/213
Application fee	$50
International application fee	$50
Early application deadline	12/1
Early notification date	12/15
Regular application deadline	3/15
Regular application notification	5/1
Deferment available	No
Transfer students accepted	Yes

Transfer application policy: Credits must be from an AACSB accredited college or university, must be with a B or better. Possible to transfer up to 25% of total program. Dean makes final determination.

Non-fall admissions	Yes
Need-blind admissions	Yes

EMPLOYMENT PROFILE

Career Rating	77	**Grads Employed by Function% Avg. Salary**	
Percent employed at graduation	30	Marketing	(13%) $68,000
Percent employed 3 months after graduation	45	Consulting	(40%)$59,333
		Finance	(20%) $67,500
Average base starting salary	$57,500	HR	(13%) $30,000
Primary Source of Full-time Job Acceptances		MIS	(7%) $80,000
School-facilitated activities	4(27%)	Other	(7%) $38,000
Graduate-facilitated activities	9(60%)	**Top 5 Employers Hiring Grads**	
Unknown	2(13%)		

Top 5 Employers Hiring Grads
PriceWaterhouse Coopers (3), Veritas Wealth Advisors (1), Ernst & Young (1), LeCroy Corp (1), Foundation for Community Development (1)

NATIONAL UNIVERSITY OF SINGAPORE

BUSINESS SCHOOL

GENERAL INFORMATION

Type of school	Public
Affiliation	No Affiliation

SURVEY SAYS...

Students love Singapore, Smart classrooms
Solid preparation in:
Accounting, General management, Quantitative skills

STUDENTS

Enrollment of MBA Program	185
% male/female	76/24
% out-of-state	90
% part-time	44
% international	90
Average age at entry	28
Average years work experience at entry	6.0

ACADEMICS

Academic Experience Rating	88
Profs interesting rating	79
Profs accesible rating	86
% female faculty	42

Joint Degrees

NUS-Peking University IMBA (24 months); UCLA-NUS Executive MBA (15 months) The NUS MBA Double Degree Masters in Public Policy with Lee Kuan Yew School of Public Policy (24-36 months full-time); The NUS MBA Double Degree Masters in Public Administration with Lee Kuan Yew School of Public Policy (24-36 months full-time); S3 Asia MBA (18 months); NUS-HEC MBA (23 months)

Prominent Alumni

Ms Janet Ang, Vice President, Lenovo; Mr Wong Ah Long, CEO,Pacific Star Investments & Development Pte Ltd; Mr Hsieh Fu Hua, CEO, Singapore Exchange Ltd; Mr Peter Seah, Chairman, Singapore Technologies Engineering Ltd; Mr Pratap Nambiar, Regional Partner, KPMG Asia Pacific

Academics

Located in the heart of bustling Asia in one of the most globalized cities in the world, the NUS MBA program offer an "astoundingly great" academic experience, providing comprehensive coverage of global academia with an excellent focus on regional issues and activities. Academically, the school "prepares you for all major general management tasks in global enterprises and provides you with a fair range of specialization fields." As part of the largest university in the country, MBA students also have the option of obtaining a double-degree from Peking University, HEC Paris, the Lee Kuan Yew School of Public Policy, or the Asia-focused S3 Asia MBA, in which students spend semesters in Shanghai, Seoul, and Singapore.

Although the workload is heavy, students "do learn a lot form the academic process here." Most professors have a strong academic background in their specific teaching field, and professors teaching electives all have "extensive industry background." A few teachers do have problems engaging an audience (especially those subjects that are considered "dry"), but for the most part students are pleased with the quality of instruction. Frequent interactions with classmates from over thirty countries "[helps] broaden your perspective and analytical thinking," and in the end, the school "imparts a lot of skills on its students, preparing [you] for real-world challenges in the workplace." "With all the focus on team-based work and discussion based learning, [the] academics seem to prepare me for today's multi-cultural collaborative work environment," says a business-ready student.

The administration is "well organized in several major departments covering research and coursework academia" and "[keeps] in regular touch with students to update on current issues." "We continue to have one talk after another talk and loads of networking session," says a student.

Career and Placement

Students of the flagship university of Singapore have access to the massive network of 196,000 alumni, many of whom are hold prominent opportunities globally. A location in the "hub and center of a global growth region" (and headquarters for numerous Fortune 500 MNCs) means that many well-known companies come to campus for recruitment, but "exclusive events for MBA-only are rare." "[Much] of the time they combine an event for undergrad and MBA into one, [and] the effect in turn becomes diluted," says a student of the efforts of the MBA Career Center, which quite a few would like to see more involved. Still, the future is bright for NUS grads: "So much economic growth will take place in Asia, so this is a great place to be to further learn about the region and immerse yourself in the culture."

Top employers of recent NUS graduates include CapitaLand, DBS, Google, Mapletree Investment, and Credit Suisse.

ADMISSIONS CONTACT: MS. CHUA NAN SZE, MARIE-ANTONIE, DIRECTOR (GRADUATE STUDIES)
ADDRESS: MOCHTAR RIADY BUILDING, 15 KENT RIDGE DRIVE, LEVEL, 4 SINGAPORE, 119245
PHONE: 011-65-651-8763 • FAX: 011-65-68724423
E-MAIL: MBA@NUS.EDU.SG • WEBSITE: MBA.NUS.EDU

Student Life and Environment

The student body itself hails from all over the world (with a high percentage from India), and is "extremely diversified in terms of cultural and professional background." The "fun loving and smart" individuals here are "easy going by nature and competitive in school," and grow close with classmates (called "batchmates") through a school life that is "full of exciting events" like the Holi Celebration, Chinese New Year Celebration, and semester-ending gatherings. The per-semester study trips are also "very worthwhile" (or even "one of the best elements of the curriculum"), enabling students to "visit companies in other countries, meet with NUS MBA alumni who reside/work there, visit partner schools, and do some cultural exploration."

Students benefit from excellent facilities (such as "very modern libraries, student houses, research and sports facilities, [and] class rooms"), and have easy access to the city center. "The new business school building is modern and compact. It is easy to move around between classes, library and the MBA lounge," says a student.

Admissions

NUS seeks applicants who "have leadership capabilities and the strong desire and drive for academic and management excellence" and who are "motivated, mature, focused and have a desire to make a positive impact on business and society," according to the school's website. Applicants to the NUS School of Business must provide the Admissions Office with transcripts for all undergraduate and graduate work, GMAT scores, TOEFL or IELTS scores (for non-native English speakers), answers to essay questions, two letters of recommendation, and a resume demonstrating at least two years of professional experience after obtaining their first degree or equivalent. Shortlisted applicants will be interviewed and may be required to take further evaluation tests. Interviews are conducted face-to-face or via phone for candidates located overseas.

FINANCIAL FACTS

Annual tuition	$40,000
Cost of books	$800
Room & board	
(on/off-campus)	$9,171/$9,000
% of students receiving aid	46
% of first-year students	
receiving aid	46
% of students receiving grants	10
Average award package	$30,400
Average grant	$19,539
Average loan	$0
Average student loan debt	$0

ADMISSIONS

Admissions Selectivity Rating	90
# of applications received	1,174
% applicants accepted	19
% acceptees attending	82
Average GMAT	662
Range of GMAT	590–720
TOEFL required of	
international students	Yes
Minimum TOEFL	
(paper/computer)	620/260
International Early application deadline	1/31
Early notification date	3/1
Regular application deadline	3/31
Regular application notification	5/31
Application Deadline/Notification	
Round 1:	1/31 / 3/1
Round 2:	3/31 / 5/31
Deferment available	Yes
Maximum length	
of deferment	1 year
Transfer students accepted	Yes
Transfer application policy:	
Admission and credit transfer applications are evaluated on a case-by-case basis, and depend on the student's record and performance within the MBA program, and the quality of the program and School.	
Non-fall admissions	No
Need-blind admissions	Yes

EMPLOYMENT PROFILE

Career Rating	87	Grads Employed by Function	% Avg. Salary
Percent employed at graduation	46	Marketing	(22%) $68,516
Percent employed 3 months		Operations	(11%) $71,775
after graduation	43	Consulting	(14%)$68,538
Average base starting salary	$65,613	Management	(14%) $64,888
Primary Source of Full-time Job Acceptances		Finance	(28%) $66,595
School-facilitated activities	(80%)	Other	(11%) $63,522
Graduate-facilitated activities	(20%)	**Top 5 Employers Hiring Grads**	
		CapitaLand (3), DBS (2), Google (2),	
		Mapletree Investment (2), Credit Suisse (1)	

New Jersey Institute of Technology

School of Management

Academics

One of the things that really sets the New Jersey Institute of Technology, or NJIT, apart from other schools is its emphasis on understanding how technology and science intersect within the business sector. The school promotes the notion that business is not a "separate entity" from technology and that the two are more intertwined than ever. A great number of students say they chose to attend NJIT for their MBA so that they, having received a degree in an area such as Technology Management, could be "unique" among their colleagues in the business sector. The school also boasts an impressive Executive MBA, or EMBA, program and most classes take place on weekends or Fridays allowing the "flexibility [they] require to work and obtain an MBA at the same time." The EMBA takes it's philosophy of "relevance, practicality, and innovation" to heart and this "the curriculum is geared towards the job market." The program focuses on knowledge that can be directly applied in the workplace, which many of the students find not only helpful, but also "very interesting." This focus on practical knowledge is refreshing, and most students say that it's a "more valuable emphasis" than if the school were only "focused on finance" or other areas of a similar ilk. There are also online courses, in addition to weekend courses, for those that may still have trouble getting to and from each class.

The school has also built up quite a "strong reputation in the Northeast region." With its AACSB accreditation for both its graduate and undergraduate programs, and the fact that the MBA program costs "considerably less than other programs" of its kind, it is no wonder that so many students are singing its praise.

The classes at the NJIT School of Management tend to be "very small," which is fine for most students as they find the faculty to be "excellent." The school has 30 faculty members and approximately 700 students. While there are, of course, issues with the occasional professor, such as prolonged responses "to emails or requests for office hours," most of the professors are said to be "very accessible and willing to help," and they come to the classroom with "good field experience [from] corporate America."

Career and Placement

The Career Resource Center of NJIT helps students through a variety of ways, including resume review, job search, students write resumes, search for jobs, find career fairs, and locate online job postings. They also have a section that assists students in finding jobs with "Green" companies. In keeping with their focus on technology, the center also has a career podcast that keeps students up-to-date with career tips and thoughts on the job market. Employers seeking MBAs during a recent NJIT Career Fair included the Air Force, Alcatel-Lucent, Apex Technology, Associated Press, AT&T, Broadridge Financial Solutions, Census 2010, CIGNA, Makro Technologies, Maquet Cardiovascular, McKesson, MMC Systems, New York State Department of Transportation, Public Service Enterprise Group, QPharma, Schindler Elevator Corporation, Softnice, Verizon, and Vonage.

ADMISSIONS CONTACT: OFFICE OF UNIVERSITY ADMISSIONS
ADDRESS: FENSTER HALL - ROOM 100, UNIVERSITY HEIGHTS, NEWARK, NJ 07102
PHONE: 973-596-3300 • FAX: 973-596-3461
E-MAIL: ADMISSIONS@NJIT.EDU • WEBSITE: WWW.NJIT.EDU

Student Life and Environment

One of the first things that students seem to mention is the school's location. Located in New Jersey, the campus is "conveniently close" to New York City. While the school, located in downtown Newark, is in the middle of "museums [with] plenty of restaurants in the area," most tend to focus on the proximity of New York due to the "quick access by public transportation." This quick access is also helpful since NJIT is largely a commuter school, and many of the students have jobs during the day. For those who have time, trips to places like Washington D.C. and other various locales are available, which provide "educational value" and allow students to expand their knowledge and visit various companies and landmarks in each city.

People get along with their fellow classmates and identify the student body as being "very diverse and friendly." Since many of those attending classes have jobs, they "all contribute their work experiences" to each classroom and team function, which gives everyone a chance to learn from each other's unique experience set. This type of shared understanding helps students learn to respect each another's views and to hold each other "in great esteem and with great affection." In fact, even in the distance-learning program, students say their fellow classmates are, "more helpful and supportive than [they] would have expected from a distance learning program." The administration maintains this mutual respect as well. Some say that there are "miscommunications" at the administrative level, but the majority believes that "student feedback is truly listened to and evaluated carefully," and that level of attention helps students. They believe the administration is both "accommodating and helpful."

Admissions

As with most MBA programs, applicants must provide proof of their earned bachelor's degree and submit their Graduate Management Admissions Test or GRE; although, applicants who already hold a master's or doctoral degree from an accredited university are exempt from the GMAT/GRE requirement. International students may submit their TOEFL score in addition to the GMAT. Students can also submit a personal statement, a resume of their work experience and up to three letters of recommendation. although optional, these submissions are recommended by the school.

FINANCIAL FACTS

Annual tuition (in-state/ out-of-state)	$16,836/$24,370
Fees	$2,318
Cost of books	$2,000
Room & board	$11,750
% of students receiving aid	60
% of first-year students receiving aid	27
% of students receiving grants	15
Average award package	$14,695
Average grant	$3,839
Average loan	$22,704
Average student loan debt	$38,012

ADMISSIONS

Admissions Selectivity Rating	**75**
# of applications received	267
% applicants accepted	60
% acceptees attending	35
Average GMAT	547
Range of GMAT	520–590
Average GPA	3.63
TOEFL required of international students	Yes
Minimum TOEFL (paper/computer)	550/213
Application fee	$65
International application fee	$65
Deferment available	No
Transfer students accepted	No
Non-fall admissions	Yes
Need-blind admissions	No

NEW MEXICO STATE UNIVERSITY
COLLEGE OF BUSINESS

GENERAL INFORMATION

Type of school   Public
Affiliation   No Affiliation
Academic calendar   Semester

SURVEY SAYS...

Cutting-edge classes, Happy students
Solid preparation in:
Accounting, General management

STUDENTS

Enrollment of parent
  institution   16,660
Enrollment of MBA Program   160
% male/female   51/49
% underrepresented minority   36
% international   11
Average age at entry   27
Average years work experience
  at entry   4.0

ACADEMICS

Academic Experience Rating   **75**
Profs interesting rating   70
Profs accesible rating   81
% female faculty   32
% underrepresented minority
  faculty   14
% part-time faculty   0

Joint Degrees

Joint B Sc Engr/MBA, 5 yrs.

Prominent Alumni

John J. Chavez, Former Cabinet
Secty, Dept of Tax & Revenue;
Robert D. Chelberg, Retired, U.S.
Army Lt. General; John M. Cordova,
Former Dir. of Mktg-Milwaukee
Brewers Baseball; Andres Gutierrez,
Founder/Mgr Dir of New Co
Production; James Hawkins, Exec.
Vice President/Ranchers Bank

Academics

The College of Business at New Mexico State University is "extremely technologically savvy," a quality that serves it well in a state that is home to several air force bases, major NASA operations, two national laboratories, Spaceport America, and several big tech players (Intel, for one, has a large manufacturing plant in Albuquerque). The tech sector is, in fact, the fastest-growing employer in the Las Cruces area.

NMSU incorporates technology in all disciplines, and has developed several specialized degrees. The school also "concentrates on entrepreneurs because of its abundant resources. It's planning new ways to convert these resources into products." NMSU is a participant in the Space Alliance Technology Outreach Program (SATOP), "which creates interactions between students and the corporate people and gives a very good exposure to the aerospace industry."

Many students simply appreciate the convenience of the program, praising its "wonderfully-located campus with a very unique and culturally-diverse academic program." The school serves both full-time and part-time MBAs, and fully understands and meets the needs of traditional and nontraditional students when it comes to education. NMSU has even "created an MBA cohort program for the Los Alamos National Laboratory. Every other weekend a NMSU professor comes to Los Alamos. We are enrolled in two classes per semester and each class meets once a month for two 5-hour sessions. This schedule is wonderfully convenient, and communication is ongoing throughout the months." A school that comes to you—you can't beat that for convenience.

Instructors at NMSU "are well-respected in their fields and apply real-world applications to their lectures and assignments," while "The administration is always very responsive whenever a conflict arises." A "socially and ethnically diverse student population" informs class discussion. One student sums up, "I have had a very positive overall academic experience. Every single administrator and faculty member has treated me with the utmost respect and professional courtesy."

Career and Placement

NMSU's Placement and Career Services Office provides university students with on-campus employment, internship listings, career listings, workshops, advising, job fairs, and online research tools. The school holds a number of job fairs and other recruiting events throughout the year, but all are primarily targeted toward undergraduates. As a result, relatively few of the many companies that visit campus seek MBAs.

Recent employers of NMSU MBAs include: Accenture, ElPaso Electric, Ernst & Young, Agilent Technologies, ConocoPhilips Company, General Motors, Hewlett-Packard, IBM, Intel, KPMG International, NASA, Los Alamos National Laboratories, Sandia National Laboratory, TXU Energy, and Wells Fargo.

Student Life and Environment

NMSU "is a great place to continue your education and the Las Cruces area is second to none," students report, adding that "Las Cruces is a very slow-paced, small-town type environment. It is, however, slowly changing due to this area being designated as one of the top-10 places to retire in the nation." The school is located "in its own private corner of the city, and it is very safe, clean, and spirit-oriented."

ADMISSIONS CONTACT: JOHN SHONK, ADVISOR, MBA PROGRAM
ADDRESS: 114 GUTHRIE HALL, MSC 3GSP, LAS CRUCES, NM 88003-8001
PHONE: 505-646-8003 • FAX: 505-646-7977
E-MAIL: MBA@NMSU.EDU • WEBSITE: BUSINESS.NMSU.EDU/MBA

Many who attend the MBA program work part time as well; one such student writes, "This is a focused and relevant MBA that meets my needs as a nontraditional student who holds down a full-time civil engineering job." When they can manage to take a break from their responsibilities, they "enjoy attending college sporting events and special events at the Pan American Center on campus. The campus is also a nice place to take a long walk for exercise or leisure, strolling from pond to pond." The campus includes excellent facilities for workouts and for study. Some here point out that "NMSU could definitely improve in how it caters to students with families. Child care is only available to students with very low incomes, or at the standard child care rates in this city." There are a number of activities for children at the NMSU Museum, the Las Cruces Natural History Museum, the Farm and Ranch Heritage Museum, as well as youth sports teams.

The NMSU MBA population includes "a large portion of international students, who come because of the affordability and friendly environment. [Students] with widely diversified cultures and nations contribute to the discussions related to international trade and global business management." Students "have diverse work experience, which makes interaction between students interesting and useful" and results in "a very professional approach to problem-solving case studies or application of curriculum covered in course material."

Admissions

Applicants to the NMSU MBA program must apply for admission to the university's graduate school before they can be admitted to the MBA program. Admission to the graduate school requires that the applicant hold a 4-year undergraduate degree from an accredited institution with a GPA of at least 3.0 (some exceptions to the GPA requirement are possible; contact school for details). International applicants must earn at least a 550 on the paper-based TOEFL or a 79 on the IBT; NMSU also accepts the IELTS with a 6.5 score. Applicants to the MBA program must meet one of the following criteria: an undergraduate GPA of at least 3.5 from an institution with a business program accredited by AACSB or ACBSP; a minimum GMAT score of 400 and a minimum score of 1050 under the formula (GPA multiplied by 200 plus GMAT); possession of a graduate degree from a U.S. regionally accredited institution; or completion of at least 4 years of full-time professional work and an undergraduate GPA of at least 3.25 from an institution with a business program accredited by AACSB or ACBSP..

FINANCIAL FACTS

Annual tuition (in-state/ out-of-state)	$4,885/$14,656
Cost of books	$1,000
Room & board (on/off-campus)	$6,914/$8,550

ADMISSIONS

Admissions Selectivity Rating	75
# of applications received	75
% applicants accepted	68
% acceptees attending	73
TOEFL required of international students	Yes
Minimum TOEFL (paper/computer)	550
Application fee	$40
International application fee	$50
Regular application deadline	7/15
Regular application notification	8/4
Deferment available	Yes
Maximum length of deferment	1 year
Transfer students accepted	Yes
Transfer application policy: A maximum of 9 Semester credits from AACSB International accredited schools.	
Non-fall admissions	Yes
Need-blind admissions	Yes

NEW YORK UNIVERSITY
LEONARD N. STERN SCHOOL OF BUSINESS

GENERAL INFORMATION
Type of school   Private
Affiliation   No Affiliation
Academic calendar   Semester

SURVEY SAYS...
Students love New York, NY, Good
social scene, Good peer network,
Cutting-edge classes, Happy students
Solid preparation in:
Finance

STUDENTS
Enrollment of parent
  institution   44,516
Enrollment of MBA Program   2,811
% male/female   65/35
% out-of-state   56
% part-time   72
% underrepresented minority   14
% international   31
Average age at entry   28
Average years work experience
  at entry   4.8

ACADEMICS
Academic Experience Rating   **99**
Profs interesting rating   94
Profs accesible rating   86
Student/faculty ratio   8:1
% female faculty   16
% underrepresented minority
  faculty   16

Joint Degrees
MD/MBA, with the School of
Medicine; JD/MBA, with the School
of Law; MA/MBA, with the Institute of
French Studies (GSAS); MA/MBA,
with the Department of Politics
(GSAS); MPA/MBA, with the Wagner
School of Public Service; MBA/MFA,
with the Tisch School; MBA/MS in
Mathematics in Finance; MS in
Biology/MBA; Dual MBA with HEC
School of Management

Prominent Alumni
John Paulson, Paulson & Co., Inc.;
Ken Langone, Founder, Chairman
and Chief Executive Officer, Invemed
Associated LLC

Academics

Smack dab in the middle of New York City, NYU's Stern School of Business couldn't have a better location, location, location. From finance to the arts, "New York delivers every opportunity imaginable," and Stern is "well integrated into NYC, both physically and in the people it brings in as faculty, guest speakers, and partners." Best suited to ambitious students with well-honed career goals, "You can do anything you want to do at Stern." Over half of the credit hours required for the MBA are electives, and "Stern is able to offer a very broad range of courses and activities for students with any business interest." A dream school for future bankers, Stern has deep ties on Wall Street and is ranked "among the top schools in the world for people working or hoping to work in finance." At the same time, it is known for its excellent programs in luxury retail, marketing, technology, and media and entertainment; those with an interest in nonprofit work or creative fields also note that "Stern has a great support system for alternative career goals," including partnerships with the Wagner School of Public Service and Tisch School of the Arts. In fact, Stern "is fully integrated within the university," and business students can take up to a quarter of their classes at other NYU schools, allowing for a truly individualized education. To top it all off, "Most students take advantage of opportunities to study abroad" through Stern's one- and two-week "Doing Business In..." international program, spring-break trips, or semester-long exchange programs.

Despite Stern's historic strength in the finance, there's "less corporate/institutional mindset" here; instead you'll find "an emphasis on thinking creatively," as well as a "dedication to solving real world problems through business." On campus, "The culture is extremely collaborative," and "students don't just care about their own success; they care about their classmates' as well." Likewise, "Professors make it a point to be accessible and often make it mandatory to meet students one-on-one." In the classroom, "The faculty is exceptional," including a number of well-known business personalities. Though there are some academics on staff, most instructors "have vast real-world experience in the fields they teach," bringing a practical perspective into the classroom. While students admit there is "some bureaucracy at the administrative level," administrators are "always addressing our needs, eager for our feedback and putting that feedback into action."

Career and Placement

Thanks to its stellar reputation, wide-ranging career-development opportunities, and aggressive campus recruitment programs, Stern boasts an impressive track record for placing MBA candidates in prestigious, high-paying positions. Through the Office of Career Development, students have access to myriad services, from career panels to résumé reviews, as well as industry-specific training. The school maintains deep ties with many companies and "incredible access to recruiters"; plus, the "location in the heart of New York makes networking with alumni and companies all the easier." With so much in their favor, Stern graduates hit the ground running—in fact, most have made major strides long before graduation day. A current student enthuses, "With no finance experience, I have already secured my summer internship offer at a top investment bank."

In recent years, the following companies hired multiple Stern graduates: Accenture, Bain & Company, Booz & Company, IBM Consulting, PricewaterhouseCoopers, McKinsey & Company, Colgate-Palmolive, Estée Lauder, Kraft, L'Oréal, PepsiCo, Disney, Google, Sony, Yahoo!, JPMorgan, Citi, Goldman Sachs, Credit Suisse, Deutsche Bank, Barclays Capital, Morgan Stanley, Amazon.com, Bayer Healthcare, and UBS. The class of 2012 had a salary range of $50,000-$160,000, with an average base salary of over $107,000 (the average signing bonus was an additional $32,000). Impressively, more than 87 percent of the class found

ADMISSIONS CONTACT: PAULA STEISEL GOLDFARB, EXECUTIVE DIRECTOR, MBA AND EXECUTIVE
MBA ADMISSIONS AND FINANCIAL AID
ADDRESS: 44 WEST 4TH STREET, SUITE 6-70, NEW YORK, NY 10012 • PHONE: 212-998-0600
FAX: 212-995-4231 • E-MAIL: STERNMBA@STERN.NYU.EDU • WEBSITE: WWW.STERN.NYU.EDU

their position through on-campus recruiting and interviews, or other Stern-supported professional development activities.

Student Life and Environment

"There is a strong sense of community" at Stern, where students are hard working and competitive, but also "very outgoing, collaborative, and inquisitive." As soon as you step on
campus, "you have a great support network in all parts of your life, and it's easy to make
friendships that will last long past graduation." There's never a dull moment on this
"vibrant" campus, where "everyone is on their hustle, all the time, with incredibly varied
interests." Every day, there are "an abundance of social activities and networking opportunities" at the school, from club meetings and "guest speakers" to the well-attended weekly
Beer Blasts. A current student exclaims, "The hardest part is knowing how to pick one activity over another! There are frequently too many enticing conferences, programs, and activities going on to make an easy decision."

"Located in one of the most exciting cities in the country," Stern is a great place to go to
school "both because of the opportunities and activities available here and the wide range
of people you meet." A reflection of the city that surrounds it, Stern draws students from
many backgrounds and industries; the "professional diversity" among students enriches
the academic experience, while "high percentage of international students" brings a global
perspective to the community. Without exception, everyone loves the urban location, saying, "You can't beat New York City." However, they do mention one well-advertised detrac-
tor: "Cost of living overall is very high in New York."

Admissions

Admission to Stern is highly selective. For the 2012–2013 entering class, the school received
close to 4,000 applications for fewer than 400 spots in the entering class. Entering students
had an average undergraduate GPA of 3.51 and an average GMAT score of 720. Note that
Stern accepts either the GRE or the GMAT; there is no minimum test score needed to apply.
Close to 40 percent of the class is international or a dual-citizen.

FINANCIAL FACTS

Annual tuition	$52,828
Fees	$2,326
Cost of books	$1,960
Room & board	$24,472
Average award package	$68,443
Average student loan debt	$87,342

ADMISSIONS

Admissions Selectivity Rating	99
# of applications received	3,907
% applicants accepted	16
% acceptees attending	52
Average GMAT	720
Range of GMAT	700–740
Average GPA	3.51
TOEFL required of international students	Yes
Application fee	$225
International application fee	$225
Application Deadline/Notification	
Round 1:	11/15 / 2/15
Round 2:	1/15 / 4/1
Round 3:	3/15 / 6/1
Transfer students accepted	No
Non-fall admissions	No
Need-blind admissions	Yes

EMPLOYMENT PROFILE

Career Rating	99	Grads Employed by Function% Avg. Salary	
Percent employed at graduation	79	Marketing	(18%) $100,627
Percent employed 3 months		Consulting	(33%) $118,956
after graduation	90	Management	(5%) $102,885
Average base starting salary	$107,875	Finance	(42%) $104,405
Primary Source of Full-time Job Acceptances		Other	(2%) $82,000
School-facilitated activities	218(72%)	**Top 5 Employers Hiring Grads**	
Graduate-facilitated activities	47(15%)	American Express, CITI, Credit Suisse,	
Unknown	38(13%)	Deloitte, JPMorgan	

NORTH CAROLINA STATE UNIVERSITY
POOLE COLLEGE OF MANAGEMENT

GENERAL INFORMATION
Type of school	Public
Affiliation	No Affiliation
Academic calendar	Semester

SURVEY SAYS...
Students love Raleigh, NC, Friendly students
Solid preparation in:
Teamwork

STUDENTS
Enrollment of parent institution	34,340
Enrollment of MBA Program	403
% male/female	72/28
% out-of-state	10
% part-time	63
% underrepresented minority	7
% international	15
Average age at entry	26
Average years work experience at entry	3.8

ACADEMICS
Academic Experience Rating	**80**
Profs interesting rating	80
Profs accesible rating	80
Student/faculty ratio	10:1
% female faculty	9
% underrepresented minority faculty	8
% part-time faculty	16

Joint Degrees
Joint Masters of Microbial Biotechnology and MBA; Joint Degree in Doctor of Veterinary Medicine (DVM) and MBA; Joint Master of Accounting (MAC) and MBA; Joint Master of Global Innovation Management (MGIM) and MBA; Joint Master of Biomanufacturing (BIOM) and MBA; Joint Juris Doctor (JD) and MBA; Joint Master of Industrial Engineering (MIE)and MBA

Prominent Alumni
Tony O'Driscoll, Duke, Fuqua School of Business, Professor of the Practice

Academics

Programs at North Carolina State University's College of Management place a large emphasis on skills that will tie directly into the strengths of the region. With the university located in the state capital of Raleigh (a satellite program is also located in Durham), expect "a focus on technology and innovation" with "a strong emphasis on hands-on experiences." For future-oriented students, the "emphasis on real world projects and technology focus in many classes" makes NCSU "one of the best values for a full-time MBA in the country." This "emphasis on real world, hands-on learning differentiates it from the other programs in the area," especially the "focus on technology and innovation." Indeed, one student notes, "This is a program for people who want to lead teams and stay on the cutting edge of technology."

A discipline helping this MBA program "dramatically increase in ranking and reputation" despite the program being new is its Supply Chain program. "They are able to provide real projects with real companies allowing students to apply knowledge they learn to real life situations." Other programs of note include a lauded Biosciences Management program, which fits well with Durham's self-proclaimed distinction as "The City of Medicine" and the regional presence of several major pharmaceutical and bioengineering corporations.

Though high achievement is expected, cutthroat academics are not. Here the "atmosphere is congenial but focused," and "teamwork is highly emphasized." Because most classes take place in the same building, "there is a great deal of interaction with other students." Students who are "focused on career success and money" may be disappointed that "that is not the case at NC State," but others will be pleased to find that educators here "care a lot about sustainability" and showcasing how business fits into the larger world. School administration shows "an almost fanatical focus on improvement and a willingness to experiment." The result is that despite its relative newness, "some elements of the program are already receiving national attention (Supply Chain, the TEC Program) and some will soon (the new Consumer Behavior initiative)."

Career and Placement

"The promise of working on real world projects for companies in co-ordination with normal academic activities" is not only a major draw for students here, it gives them an opportunity to get hands-on experience with many of the same corporations that may later recruit them. There is a "long-term culture of industry partnerships that is expanding to startups" at NCSU which helps the school "stay abreast of events and networking opportunities." MBAs will benefit from the services of an MBA-dedicated Career Resources Center which not only aids in networking and recruitment, but which also provides workshops on resume writing and cover letters, interviewing skills, and job search strategies.

During the course of their study, students can expect to work hand-in-hand with entities such as CAT, Lenovo, IBM, Bank of America and Lenovo. Graduates from NCSU's Jenkin's Graduate School of Management have in recent years been recruited by firms such as American Airlines, BB&T, Chevron, Cisco Systems, Deloitte, Eaton Corporation, Ericcson, Glaxo Smith Kline, Lab Corp, Net App, Novartis Animal Health, Novozymes, Progress Energy, Red Hat, Research Triangle Institute, SAS, and Siemens Medical.

Student Life and Environment

Those accepted to NCSU should expect to find an "extremely diverse" group of "intelligent, friendly people who work hard during the day and still have energy and enthusiasm to continue learning and make class fun in the evenings." Those hoping to immerse themselves in ambition will find it among the student body. Attendees say it is "great to work with other students committed to their goals and aspirations." Students at NCSU are in the business of learning about business, and they are serious about it. "They push us in our studies, and encourage us to work hard."

Life here centers around a "very collaborative environment," one in which objectives, either within or outside of the classroom, are "based centrally around team activities." Those who see business as a ruthless, individual pursuit will instead find a "program … trying to develop a different mindset from traditional MBA programs." This is aided by the MBA Student Association, which "works to provide social activities and community service projects for the students outside of class." The goal is to provide both full-time and part-time students an opportunity "to network with each other, as well as providing opportunities to positively impact the community."

Outside of class and class projects, MBA students spend a lot of time brainstorming. One student explains, "There's always a few of us throwing plans at each other. These aren't all Silicon Valley plans either - we've got fashion designers, textile inventors and others all listening to each other. It's a very stimulating environment." There are also many clubs, cultural activities, and of course Raleigh's nightlife to distract from the relentless pursuit of knowledge and experience typical among those in the MBA program.

Admissions

Academic record, GMAT scores, essays, letters of reference all come into play, as do work and volunteer experience, when weighing one's application to NCSU's MBA Program. The highly competitive admissions process will take into account your management potential, as well as prior employment, or volunteer and/or military experience. Though not required of full-time students, two years of full-time employment is "strongly recommended." Such experience is, however, required of part-time students. One's background should include coursework in either calculus or statistics. Applicants whose primary language is not English must submit TOEFL or IELTS scores; a minimum TOEFL score of 250 on the computer-based test or 100 on the Internet-based test or a minimum IELTS score of 7.5 is required. Interviews are also required, and potential candidates will be contacted directly once all of their documents are reviewed and accepted.

FINANCIAL FACTS

Annual tuition (in-state/ out-of-state)	$16,608/$29,141
Fees	$2,051
Cost of books	$1,000
Room & board (on/off-campus)	$7,000/$12,348
% of students receiving aid	89
% of first-year students receiving aid	90
% of students receiving grants	85
Average award package	$24,722
Average grant	$16,441
Average loan	$19,097
Average student loan debt	$19,630

ADMISSIONS

Admissions Selectivity Rating	75
# of applications received	153
% applicants accepted	73
% acceptees attending	42
Average GMAT	600
Range of GMAT	550–640
Average GPA	3.33
TOEFL required of international students	Yes
Minimum TOEFL (paper/computer)	600/250
Application fee	$65
International application fee	$75
Early application deadline	10/15
Early notification date	11/15
Regular application deadline	3/1
Regular application notification	4/1
Application Deadline/Notification	
Round 1:	10/15 / 11/15
Round 2:	1/15 / 2/15
Round 3:	3/1 / 4/1
Deferment available	Yes
Maximum length of deferment	1 year
Transfer students accepted	Yes
Transfer application policy: The NC State MBA Program can accept up to 12 hours of transfer credit from another AACSB-accredited MBA program The grade received for a transfer class must be a "B" or better, and the class must have been taken no more than 6 years prior to the applicants projected graduation date from the MBA program at NC State's College of Management.	
Non-fall admissions	No
Need-blind admissions	Yes

EMPLOYMENT PROFILE

Career Rating	85	Grads Employed by Function	% Avg. Salary
Percent employed at graduation	53	Marketing	(21%) $63,857
Percent employed 3 months after graduation	83	Operations	(18%) $76,570
		Consulting	(6%) $73,000
Average base starting salary	$70,053	Management	(9%) $70,000
Primary Source of Full-time Job Acceptances		Finance	(18%) $67,142
School-facilitated activities	14(42%)	HR	(3%) $60,000
Graduate-facilitated activities	19(58%)	MIS	(6%) $61,000
		Other	(18%) $82,667

Top 5 Employers Hiring Grads
Lenovo (2), Red Hat (2), American Air (1), BCBS (1), Caterpillar (1)

NORTHEASTERN UNIVERSITY
COLLEGE OF BUSINESS ADMINISTRATION

GENERAL INFORMATION

Type of school	Private
Affiliation	No Affiliation
Academic calendar	Semester

SURVEY SAYS...

Students love Boston, MA, Cutting-edge classes
Solid preparation in:
Accounting

STUDENTS

Enrollment of parent institution	30,731
Enrollment of MBA Program	619
% male/female	67/33
% out-of-state	56
% part-time	65
% underrepresented minority	11
% international	22
Average age at entry	27
Average years work experience at entry	4.0

ACADEMICS

Academic Experience Rating	**92**
Profs interesting rating	88
Profs accesible rating	81
Student/faculty ratio	7:1
% female faculty	26
% underrepresented minority faculty	7
% part-time faculty	29

Joint Degrees

MSA/MBA, 15 months; MSF/MBA, 2.5 years; MSN/MBA, 3 years; and JD/MBA,45 months

Prominent Alumni

Alan McKim, Chairman and CEO, Clean Harbors, Inc.; Richard D'Amore, Partner, North Bridge Venture Management; Bob Davis, Founder of Lycos; Manuel Henriquez, Founder, Chairman and CEO, Hercules Technology Growth Capital; Nikesh Arora, Chief Business Officer, Google

Academics

Northeastern offers both full-time and part-time MBA tracks, as well as online MBA options. The part-time program has three options: an Evening MBA, an Executive MBA, and a High Tech MBA. The biggest perk of a part-time MBA is "flexibility." Students can keep their full-time jobs and organize their class schedules around them. The full-time program is two years long and includes the famous "Corporate Residency" in which students are given paid internships for six months with a business in the Boston area. Most students admit this is why they chose Northeastern for their MBA. "The opportunity to work with a company for six months will allow me to learn more about the company, be involved in a project from start to finish, and impress hiring managers." Also, the program "has a great reputation." Students who enter the school hoping for a career change find the internship indispensable. In addition to the opportunity to gain tangible field experience and get paid for it, many mention "Northeastern also provided more scholarship funds than any other school." Other highlights of the program are "the required international field study" and the "manageable class sizes of around 35 students." Also, "the quality of professors is very high." "Northeastern has done an excellent job recruiting professors from top-tier schools." "All of them have Ph.D.s, and the Boston area has such an academic wealth that many teachers are of very high quality." Professors are "easy to approach" and incorporate a "great teaching style" in their classrooms. "Courses are designed to allow students to understand each discipline in a managerial/decision-making way." Professors also "coordinate projects and exams with each other" and are "very available outside of class."

Students do notice that some courses aren't as engaging as others. "There is a noticeable difference in energy between the first-year, full-time classes and the second-year, evening classes (not nearly as strong)." Still, most students feel the school "deserves a better ranking."

Career and Placement

"There is a great deal of emphasis placed on each student's career development. The career center team makes sure that every student has the opportunity to get placed in a six-month paid corporate residency position." Students also praise the "variety of businesses" participating in the program. "You are given an executive-level mentor and even participate in six executive networking lunches during your first year." The luncheons are limited to six students, so each gets "individual attention" from the executives, who are from "top companies." In addition to the Executive Luncheon Series, there are "Insider Insight Sessions, guest speakers, and an alumni database." These opportunities are why most students say they chose Northeastern. The career center doesn't stop at internships; it also places students in full-time positions. Students say Northeastern has "high placement rates."

Of the past year's graduating class, 66 percent had accepted job offers by graduation, and 95 percent had accepted offers three months after graduation. Students were hired by the following companies: IBM Corporation, Raytheon, Staples, Inc., W.R. Grace & Co., and Ernst & Young.

Admissions Contact: Evelyn Tate, Director, Recruitment and Admissions
Address: 350 Dodge Hall, 360 Huntington Avenue, Boston, MA 02115
Phone: 617-373-5992 • Fax: 617-373-8564
E-mail: gsba@neu.edu • Website: www.mba.neu.edu

Student Life and Environment

"The NEU MBA program is very social." "There is a sense of friendly competition, but at the end of the day, everyone wants to see each other succeed." "The students in my program opened up quickly to each other." "Our class became one large group of friends by the end of the first year." Students describe each other as "easy going, intelligent, spirited, inspirational, and fun." Another says fellow classmates are "outgoing, realistic, pragmatic, and down to earth." Some students did mention a social gap between those entering fresh from undergrad and more experienced students. However, they all tend to be "supportive of each other." The small class size "leads to very strong bonds."

Most students mention location as one of the main reasons why they chose Northeastern. "The location of the school within Boston cannot be better. It is next to the Museum of Fine Arts. It has its own stop on the subway and is connected to the greater Boston area via public transportation." "Most students stay on campus all day." The school is located in what is known as the Fenway Cultural District. Even though it's in an urban setting, it has trees, green quads, and is a beautiful space.

Admissions

The admissions committee at Northeastern University requires the following materials from its applicants: copies of official transcripts from all post-secondary schools attended; a current resume; three essays; two letters of recommendation; an official GMAT score report; and the online application form. An interview is also important, as is work experience. The school prefers its entrants to have at least two years of professional work experience. International students whose first language is not English must send TOEFL or IELTS scores. Roughly one in four candidates is selected.

FINANCIAL FACTS

Annual tuition	$40,350
Fees	$634
Cost of books	$1,700
Room & board (on/off-campus)	$15,000
% of students receiving aid	71
% of first-year students receiving aid	89
% of students receiving grants	55
Average award package	$30,702
Average grant	$23,005
Average loan	$22,445

ADMISSIONS

Admissions Selectivity Rating	95
# of applications received	401
% applicants accepted	28
% acceptees attending	58
Average GMAT	643
Range of GMAT	605–680
Average GPA	3.27
TOEFL required of international students	Yes
Minimum TOEFL (paper/computer)	600/250
Application fee	$100
International application fee	$100
Early application deadline	11/30
Early notification date	1/15
Regular application deadline	4/15
Regular application notification	5/15
Application Deadline/Notification	
Round 1:	11/30 / 1/15
Round 2:	2/1 / 3/30
Round 3:	3/15 / 4/15
Round 4:	4/15 / 5/15
Deferment available	No
Transfer students accepted	Yes
Transfer application policy: We may award a limited number of transfer credits for MBA courses taken at AACSB-accredited institutions.	
Non-fall admissions	No
Need-blind admissions	Yes

EMPLOYMENT PROFILE

Career Rating	97	**Grads Employed by Function% Avg. Salary**	
Percent employed at graduation	59	Marketing	(21%) $68,220
Percent employed 3 months after graduation	95	Operations	(9%) $73,750
		Consulting	(7%)$82,500
Average base starting salary	$72,191	Management	(9%) $90,000
Primary Source of Full-time Job Acceptances		Finance	(41%) $70,664
School-facilitated activities	31(53%)	MIS	(3%) $70,000
Graduate-facilitated activities	22(38%)	Other	(10%) $65,000
Unknown	5(9%)	**Top 5 Employers Hiring Grads**	
		Raytheon Company (4), Wellington Management (4), State Street Corporation (4), IBM Corporation (3), Deloitte (2)	

NORTHERN ARIZONA UNIVERSITY
THE W.A. FRANKE COLLEGE OF BUSINESS

GENERAL INFORMATION

Type of school	Public
Affiliation	No Affiliation
Academic calendar	August-May

SURVEY SAYS...

Friendly students, Smart classrooms
Solid preparation in:
Accounting, Teamwork,
Communication/interpersonal skills,
Presentation skills

STUDENTS

Enrollment of parent institution	26,002
Enrollment of MBA Program	31
% male/female	65/35
% out-of-state	52
% part-time	0
% underrepresented minority	22
% international	16
Average age at entry	24
Average years work experience at entry	2.5

ACADEMICS

Academic Experience Rating	**79**
Profs interesting rating	75
Profs accesible rating	84
Student/faculty ratio	3:1
% female faculty	42
% underrepresented minority faculty	0
% part-time faculty	0

Joint Degrees

Master of Business Administration-Accounting (MBA-ACC): for graduates with an undergraduate degree in accounting; Full-time, 30 total credits required; 10 months to complete program.

Academics

Efficiency is the name of the game at the Franke College of Business at Northern Arizona University. This school's AACSB accelerated MBA program is just "10 months from start to finish," cramming a full MBA curriculum into less than a year of coursework. Not surprisingly, the result is an "intense course load," tons of homework, and a "fast-paced, invigorating environment." A current student admits, "I'm lucky if I get more than a couple of hours on the weekends to go grocery shopping. This place will get you in and out in a hurry, but you certainly won't have time for anything else while you're doing it." At the same time, the breakneck format affords students a number of important benefits. In particular, it's a great deal: Here, students only leave the workforce for a year and tuition is "significantly lower" than at a traditional two-year program. In addition, for students who plan to take the CPA exam, NAU offers the opportunity to complete their accounting courses and earn an MBA in just two years. A popular choice, "Over half the program is enrolled in the MBA-ACC offering, while the other half navigates the traditional MBA." On that note, accounting classes get top marks, while students say "the management and finance courses add value and the principles learned will be handy going forward."

Despite the program's rigor, the Franke College of Business is a surprisingly cooperative and down-to-earth place. Throughout the business school, "The environment is one of learning and collaboration where the majority of teachers are interested in helping students achieve success." With few exceptions, "the teachers are extremely approachable," and, due to the limited graduate enrollment, "The small class sizes means we receive more individual attention from professors." Teamwork is encouraged across the curriculum, which builds soft skills while also helping to ease the stress of coursework. A student agrees, "The academic experience at NAU is demanding and high-pressured, although the group nature of a lot of our work allows students to use their best skills when contributing within this environment." Like the faculty, "the school's administration goes that extra mile" to assist students, and it truly works "to make the MBA program as stress-free as possible." The school generally runs smoothly and the curriculum is well-designed; however, some students tell us, "There does not appear to be a lot of communication between the professors" when it comes to planning and evaluating courses.

Career and Placement

The 10 month program allows students to enter the workforce sooner. In some cases, students don't even need to look for a new job after graduation. A current student explains, "I left my job to be in this program, but given that I will be applying back with them within a year, I don't need to go through the same hiring process." For those students looking for a new position, the Career Development Office provides undergraduate and graduate students with various career and professional development programs. Through the Career Development Center, employers recruit students for entry-level and full-time positions, as well as for internships. Companies that recently participated in one of the Career Development Office's recruiting events include Vanguard, Equity Methods, McGladrey, Grant Thornton, PFSweb, CliftonLarsonAllen, Target, Lohman Company, Deloitte & Touche, KPMG, Eide Bailly, and Ernst & Young. Still, students feel the MBA would improve with the addition of "more job placement opportunities." In particular, students would like to see more recruiting companies from Phoenix and other big cities.

ADMISSIONS CONTACT: KATIE POINDEXTER, COORDINATOR
ADDRESS: BUSINESS GRADUATE PROGRAMS, P.O. BOX 15066, FLAGSTAFF, AZ 86011-5066
PHONE: 928-523-7387 • FAX: 928-523-7996
E-MAIL: FCB-GRADPROG@NAU.EDU • WEBSITE: WWW.FRANKE.NAU.EDU/GRADUATEPROGRAMS

Student Life and Environment

Located in the beautiful mountain town of Flagstaff, NAU offers "outstanding" facilities, a professional atmosphere, and a scenic backdrop. Recently constructed, "The W.A. Franke College of Business is one of the newest buildings on campus and is LEED-certified." All classrooms "overlook a green retention area" where students can be seen "playing Frisbee, sitting and reading under the perimeter trees, or just relaxing." In addition, students have access to a "great MBA lounge that offers students a place to complete course work as well as eat lunch and socialize." "Most students are laid-back and easy-going" with their classmates, though "hardworking" and competitive in the classroom. A younger crowd, many MBA candidates are "recent graduates with no actual work experience," though you'll also meet some mid-career professionals in class.

While the atmosphere is laid-back, MBA students are definitely busy. One admits, "Honestly, in a 10-month accelerated program, I haven't much of an opportunity to have much of a life outside of school." When they want to relax, there are plenty of "outdoor activities" in the surrounding area, from local hikes and skiing, to the nearby Grand Canyon. On campus, the larger university also offers social, recreational, and cultural events. MBA students can be as involved in the school as they'd like; "Some students take full advantage of everything NAU has to offer, while others do not."

Admissions

Students who have completed foundation business coursework can complete the accelerated MBA in ten months. Those lacking one or more foundation courses can complete needed coursework at NAU in the summer before the MBA program begins. To apply, prospective students must submit their undergraduate transcripts, official GMAT or GRE scores, a current resume, two references, and a set of personal essays. After submitting their application materials, prospective students are invited to interview. Interviews begin in the fall and students are admitted on a rolling basis. Complete applications are accepted until July 10, or until the class reaches capacity of fifty students.

FINANCIAL FACTS

Annual tuition (in-state/ out-of-state)	$10,023/$21,117
Fees	$7,000
Cost of books	$750
% of students receiving aid	94
% of first-year students receiving aid	94
Average award package	$12,628

ADMISSIONS

Admissions Selectivity Rating	**76**
# of applications received	57
% applicants accepted	72
% acceptees attending	76
Average GMAT	531
Range of GMAT	450–670
Average GPA	3.40
TOEFL required of international students	Yes
Minimum TOEFL (paper/computer)	550/213
Application fee	$65
International application fee	$65
Deferment available	Yes
Maximum length of deferment	1 year
Transfer students accepted	No

EMPLOYMENT PROFILE	
Career Rating	72
Percent employed at graduation	55

NORTHERN KENTUCKY UNIVERSITY
HAILE/US BANK COLLEGE OF BUSINESS

GENERAL INFORMATION
Type of school	Public
Affiliation	No Affiliation
Academic calendar	Semester

SURVEY SAYS...
Good peer network
Solid preparation in:
Finance

STUDENTS
Enrollment of parent institution	15,000
Enrollment of MBA Program	200
% part-time	90
Average age at entry	28
Average years work experience at entry	5.0

ACADEMICS
Academic Experience Rating	77
Profs interesting rating	74
Profs accesible rating	83
Student/faculty ratio	22:1
% female faculty	27
% underrepresented minority faculty	13
% part-time faculty	33

Joint Degrees
Juris Doctor/Master of Business Administration - minimum 5 years

Academics

Its location "10 minutes from downtown Cincinnati, Ohio" and "affordable [overall cost] relative to other AACSB-accredited schools in the area" draws enthusiastic students to Northern Kentucky University's College of Business. About 85 percent of the students here attend part-time, and those who do appreciate that "classes are offered in the evenings"—most courses meet from 6:00 to 9:00 P.M. once a week—"so that [students] can attend all required classes without cutting into [their] work schedules." NKU also offers two 7-week summer sessions that run on accelerated evening schedules. While class times are convenient, students say that NKU's "greatest strength" is "the course work itself. NKU is very challenging and very strict with academics. Although it is not so easy to prepare for class at times, this has helped prepare me well for my professional career by pushing me to the limit." Class sizes are "small," and professors are "passionate about their subject areas" and "always willing to stay [after class] with you and meet whenever you need to." They're also, for the most part, "flexible and understand that most graduate students also work full time and have a family." Many have "very relevant real-life experience to impart," and their ranks "include the former director of human resources of a major public utility, a consultant who specializes in turning businesses around, and a finance professor who works as a Certified Financial Planner on the side. No, Jack Welch does not teach here, but those [who] do are knowledgeable and do a good job." Students love that NKU "allows specialization of the MBA" and cite its Entrepreneurship Institute, International Business Center, and finance programs as major strengths.

Overall, students find NKU to be a place where "The student is the top priority." "The staff has always been quick [when] answering my questions and available when I need them," a student writes.

Career and Placement

"There is a wonderful Career Center on campus, but it is primarily focused on meeting the needs of undergraduates," NKU business students tell us. That being said, students admit that, for the most part, they "already have jobs, so career placement is not a large need." Most are looking to move up the ranks with their current employer; those looking to jump ship turn to their fellow students for job leads. Which isn't to say there aren't those who'd like a little more help in the area of job placement: "I think we need more career counselors within the MBA program for those of us who do not come from a traditional business background," one student tells us. Another would like NKU to "improve job [placement] opportunities through alumni relations."

Student Life and Environment

Many at NKU are "on the 'slow' track to finish because of the demands of family and jobs." As such, the school differs from institutions that "have the same students begin and end the program together"; most here "meet different students each semester." Despite this, students report that their "classmates are great people who, through this MBA program, have become real friends." Such friendships are forged largely without the assistance of clubs or activities geared toward graduate students: "I'm a commuter, so most of my time at school is in class, in the library, or meeting to do group work," a typical student writes. While NKU's campus "has food/coffee stands in almost every building" and "computers everywhere with free printing," drawbacks include a "mostly concrete" aesthetic and difficult parking "at certain times of the day."

ADMISSIONS CONTACT: JIM BAST, DIRECTOR, MBA PROGRAM
ADDRESS: 363 BC, NUNN DRIVE, HIGHLAND HEIGHTS, KY 41099
PHONE: 895-572-7695 • FAX: 859-572-7694
E-MAIL: MBUSINESS@NKU.EDU • WEBSITE: WWW.NKU.EDU/~COB/GRADUATE/MBA

Students describe their "hardworking" peers as "friendly" but "competitive." NKU strongly recommends that potential applicants obtain two years of work experience before applying, and, by all accounts, its student body is "very diverse" in employment backgrounds. "Most [students here] are mid-20s to mid-30s," but "age ranges from 20 to 50." "Quite a few are married with children" and "Most have significant work experience." When students seek common ground, they need look no further than their objective: "We are all here for the same reason: to get an MBA," one student writes. That being said, most students are "eager to learn and get the most from their MBA experience, not just a credential."

Admissions

To gain admission to NKU, applicants must obtain a bachelor's degree from a regionally accredited institution and possess a cumulative undergraduate GPA of at least 2.50 on a 4.00 scale; he or she must also obtain a score of at least 450 on a GMAT taken within the last 5 years and, if applicable, obtain a score of at least 550 on the paper version of the TOEFL (or at least 213 on the computer version of the test). Applicants will be admitted if he or she obtains at least 1,000 points via the formula 200 multiplied by GPA plus GMAT score. In lieu of admission via the formula above, a student will be admitted if he or she obtains at least 1,050 points via the formula 200 multiplied by GPA for student's last 60 semester hours plus GMAT score. Exceptions to the GMAT include: GRE score within the last 5 years, possession of a Master degree, MD, or PhD, or similar advanced degree.

FINANCIAL FACTS	
Cost of books	$0

ADMISSIONS	
Admissions Selectivity Rating	**71**
# of applications received	84
% applicants accepted	88
% acceptees attending	59
Average GMAT	513
Range of GMAT	440–630
Average GPA	3.23
TOEFL required of international students	Yes
International Regular application deadline	6/1
Application Deadline/Notification Round 1:	6/1 /
Deferment available	Yes
Maximum length of deferment	1 year
Transfer students accepted	Yes
Non-fall admissions	No
Need-blind admissions	Yes

NORTHWESTERN UNIVERSITY
KELLOGG SCHOOL OF MANAGEMENT

GENERAL INFORMATION

Type of school	Private
Affiliation	No Affiliation
Academic calendar	Quarter

SURVEY SAYS...
Friendly students, Good social scene, Good peer network, Cutting-edge classes
Solid preparation in:
Teamwork

STUDENTS

Enrollment of MBA Program	1,973
% male/female	66/34
% part-time	41
Average age at entry	28
Average years work experience at entry	5.0

ACADEMICS

Academic Experience Rating	86
Profs interesting rating	88
Profs accesible rating	86
Student/faculty ratio	10:1
% part-time faculty	22

Joint Degrees
MBA/JD - law school, 3 years; and MMM (MEM/MBA)- engineering school, 2 years

Prominent Alumni
Peter Tan, CEO, Burger King Asia Pacific; Gloria Guevara, Secretary of Tourism, Country of Mexico; Joe De Pinto, President and CEO, 7-Eleven; Gregg Steinhafel, Chairman, President, and CEO, Target; Roslyn Brock, Chairman of the Board, NAACP

Academics

At the Kellogg School of Management at Northwestern University, you can almost feel the cooperation in the air. "It's the kind of atmosphere that even if you don't know people, you will say 'hi' in the halls," reports one student. This "collaborative," "collegial," and "student-led environment" at Kellogg means that students' input is always sought, and their voices and desires have a huge impact on the course the school takes both academically and socially. Students agree that this crash-course in democracy is "the best way to train tomorrow's business leaders" and note that it also lends the school "a certain energy around the campus that brings excitement to each and every day."

One facet of the collaborative spirit is that professors receive regular performance evaluations. However, it seems the results are rarely negative as the majority of students here praise them as "bright, accomplished, fair, and engaging."

Another major draw to the program is the school's One-Year MBA Program that allows students to earn their MBAs in just 12 months. "Kellogg's One-Year Program is one-of-a-kind," one student says. "It's the best return on investment and offers great flexibility combined with small classes and highest quality students." There is, of course, the traditional Two-Year Program available as well. In addition to the One-Year MBA Program, another unique facet at Kellogg is the MMM Program, a dual-degree in conjunction with the McCormick School of Engineering at Northwestern University and designed to aid students who wish to pursue "management roles in product and/or service driven companies." In addition, the MMM program integrates management, operations, and design.

Kellogg offers a lengthy list of majors in which students can specialize, from biotechnology management to social enterprise. Conversely, students single out the "breadth of the marketing, strategy, and finance departments."

Overridingly, students feel confident in regards to their prospective futures thanks to the Kellogg School's "overall atmosphere, solid reputation and ranking, [and] strength across academic disciplines."

Career and Placement

Recent recruiters with a presence at Kellogg include Abbott, McKinsey & Company; Microsoft Corporation, Google and Target; most students are confident that their school has a "sterling reputation among corporate recruiters." It helps, too, that professors are "student-focused" and fellow students are "willing to go out on a limb to help . . . with recruiting, career advice, and schoolwork." Students agree that the team-focused environment ensures that "networking at Kellogg is tremendous."

ADDRESS: DONALD P. JACOBS CENTER, 2001 SHERIDAN ROAD, EVANSTON, IL 60208
PHONE: 847-491-3308 • FAX: 847-491-4960
E-MAIL: MBAADMISSIONS@KELLOGG.NORTHWESTERN.EDU
WEBSITE: WWW.KELLOGG.NORTHWESTERN.EDU

Student Life and Environment

Kellogg is situated in Evanston, Illinois, along the shores of Lake Michigan, with only a short commute on the El (elevated train) to downtown Chicago. While most here appreciate the city's proximity to campus "There is [also] a lot going on [at] school." One student explains, "There are dozens, maybe hundreds of clubs at school—special interest, sports, academic, career, spouse/children, politics and government, nonprofit, gay and lesbian, etc." The student body on the whole is "alive and energetic."

In addition, the Kellogg School plans to build a new facility on its Evanston campus. It will be the first educational building of its kind for the 21st century – a one-of-a-kind lakeside structure designed to maximize flexibility in teaching, leverage the use of technology, foster creativity and community building, convene conversations that matter and inspire global interconnections.

Admissions

Admissions Officers at Kellogg have the unenviable job of whittling a pile of approximately 5,000 applications down to an admitted class of about 550. During this process, they look for work experience, academic excellence, and personality. The school's Admissions Board conducts thousands of interviews each fall. For the entering class of 2011, the average GMAT score was 714. In addition, 32 percent of Kellogg students hail from outside of the United States, and for those applicants, TOEFL scores are required. The average TOEFL score for enrolled students is 109 on the internet-based exam.

FINANCIAL FACTS

Annual tuition	$56,550
Cost of books	$2,472
Room & board	
(on/off-campus)	$13,950/$15,714
% of students receiving aid	69
% of first-year students	
receiving aid	69
Average student loan debt	$88,740

ADMISSIONS

Admissions Selectivity Rating	98
# of applications received	4,930
% applicants accepted	23
% acceptees attending	55
Average GMAT	707
Range of GMAT	690–730
TOEFL required of	
international students	Yes
Application fee	$250
International application fee	$250
Application Deadline/Notification	
Round 1:	10/16 / 12/17
Round 2:	1/3 / 3/21
Round 3:	4/10 / 5/15
Deferment available	Yes
Maximum length	
of deferment	case by case
Transfer students accepted	No
Non-fall admissions	Yes
Need-blind admissions	Yes

EMPLOYMENT PROFILE

Career Rating	99	**Top 5 Employers Hiring Grads**
Average base starting salary	$116,864	McKinsey & Company, The Boston Consulting
Primary Source of Full-time Job Acceptances		Group, Bain & Company
School-facilitated activities	(60%)	

THE OHIO STATE UNIVERSITY
MAX M. FISHER COLLEGE OF BUSINESS

GENERAL INFORMATION
Type of school — Public
Affiliation — No Affiliation
Academic calendar — Semester

SURVEY SAYS...
Good peer network
Solid preparation in:
Finance, Teamwork

STUDENTS
Enrollment of parent institution	63,511
Enrollment of MBA Program	536
% male/female	73/27
% out-of-state	21
% part-time	57
% underrepresented minority	6
% international	19
Average age at entry	28
Average years work experience at entry	4.9

ACADEMICS
Academic Experience Rating	**97**
Profs interesting rating	93
Profs accesible rating	97
Student/faculty ratio	3:1
% female faculty	30
% underrepresented minority faculty	16
% part-time faculty	37

Joint Degrees
MBA/JD (four years); MBA/MHA (three years); MBA/MD (five years); MBA/PharmD (five years); MLHR/HESA in Education (three years); MBA/MENR (three years); MBA/MS Ag Dev (three years); MBA/MPA (three years); MAcc/BSBA (five years)

Prominent Alumni
Mr. Jesse J. Tyson, Acting President, National Black MBA Association; Mr. Leslie Wexner, Chair, CEO and Founder of Limited, Inc.; Mr. Lionel Louis Nowell, Senior Vice President and Treasurer (Retired), PepsiCo, Inc.

Academics

Despite being a part of a large sports and research university, the intentionally small size of the Fisher College of Business allows the school to create a high quality and personalized program focused on results and excellence. The school offers an Executive MBA, an MBA for Working Professionals, and a full-time program of about 120 students per year, and boasts top-notch Operations and Logistics and Marketing programs that attract recruiters from top companies each year. Students in in the Working Professional program can customize a specialized niche of study to complement their general MBA degree, and students from all programs can cull from more than 100 elective courses to create an individualized degree.

"Everyone is willing to support the student experience," and "learning takes place on many levels, from in the class, to around the pizza box, to having a lunch appointment with a local business executive that serves as your mentor." "The administration, professors, and academic experience exceed the high expectations I set," says a student. "I have been blown away by the quality of the professors," says another. Most come from top-rated business schools and offer "an outstanding mix of industry experience and academic integrity." "I wake up every day excited to attend school," says a student. The administration tries very hard to offer students as many options for electives as possible,

Most of the assignments are dynamic group projects which "equates to many hours with fellow students," and "the pace is quick and often times we'll have a VERY heavy case/work load in a short period of time." This "frustrates many students, but keeps them sharp." The work load "strikes a good balance of class work with external networking events and social functions."

Career and Placement

"Career Services are excellent" at Fisher, which attracts top national employers with ease and "will work hard to help you get a job with a company with whom they already have connections." "They will help you land a job at your dream company but they won't do it for you." The thorough business education provided by the school has given it a leading reputation across the country, and students are even able to take on "real consulting projects with paying clients" during their program. "The mix of industry executives with high profile academics as well as the extraordinarily wide breadth of resources that comes with the Ohio State and Big Ten creates the perfect mixture for an MBA student to become a future industry executive," says a student. "Although we technically compete for the same jobs everyone is extremely friendly and helpful," says a student of the annual job hunt frenzy. "Fisher students can enjoy all the resources from OSU."

Recent top employers of Fisher graduates include Deloitte, Ernst & Young, Nationwide Insurance, Emerson, and Amazon.

ADMISSIONS CONTACT: ALISON MERZEL, DIRECTOR, MBA ADMISSIONS
ADDRESS: 100 GERLACH HALL, 2108 NEIL AVENUE, COLUMBUS, OH 43210-1144
PHONE: 614-292-8511 • FAX: 614-292-9006
E-MAIL: MBA@FISHER.OSU.EDU • WEBSITE: FISHER.OSU.EDU

Student Life and Environment

"We all know each other, and everyone is willing to help others out for the sake of individual and group success," says a student of this highly collaborative group, who are "around one another frequently." Columbus is "a very live city," and is a "fun environment for married or single students." There is a good community of people who regularly socialize outside of school either at bars, restaurants, houses or events. Every Thursday or Friday, the class social chairs host "some sort of End Of The Week [EOTW] activity for the entire business school," and of course, everyone is "actively engaged in the Ohio State sports culture."

As for the logistics of life, "off campus housing is outstanding," there is an "excellent…day care" for those with kids, leisure activities are available to spouses, and "the best part is, you can live well on a student budget." The facilities at Fisher are only ten years old and "are extremely well maintained," so "if you are going to spend hours studying or working on group projects, Gerlach Hall is a great place to do it."

Admissions

The Admissions Office at Fisher requires applicants to provide two official copies of transcripts for all undergraduate and graduate institutions attended, GMAT scores, two letters of recommendation, essays, and a resume of work experience (work experience is preferred but not required). In addition to the above, international applicants whose first language is not English must provide proof of English proficiency (the school accepts several standardized tests, including the TOEFL, MELAB, and IELTS) and admitted international students must provide an affidavit of financial support. Admissions interviews are conducted only at the request of the Admissions Department.

FINANCIAL FACTS

Annual tuition (in-state/ out-of-state)	$26,968/$44,280
Fees	$1,387
Cost of books	$1,602
Room & board	$9,360
% of students receiving aid	88
% of first-year students receiving aid	85
% of students receiving grants	72
Average award package	$33,413
Average grant	$6,873
Average loan	$24,517
Average student loan debt	$50,656

ADMISSIONS

Admissions Selectivity Rating	**96**
# of applications received	507
% applicants accepted	32
% acceptees attending	71
Average GMAT	668
Range of GMAT	640–710
Average GPA	3.38
TOEFL required of international students	Yes
Minimum TOEFL (paper/computer)	600/100
Application fee	$60
International application fee	$70
Early application deadline	12/15
Deferment available	Yes
Maximum length of deferment	1 year
Transfer students accepted	No
Non-fall admissions	No
Need-blind admissions	Yes

EMPLOYMENT PROFILE

Career Rating	**97**	**Grads Employed by Function**	**% Avg. Salary**
Percent employed at graduation	77	Marketing	(24%) $83,080
Percent employed 3 months after graduation	20	Operations	(18%) $84,038
Average base starting salary	$91,311	Consulting	(22%) $107,729
		Management	(8%) $100,857
		Finance	(17%) $80,000
		HR	(1%)
		Other	(4%) $78,447

Top 5 Employers Hiring Grads
Deloitte (6), Ernst & Young (6), Nationwide Insurance (4), Emerson (3), Amazon (2)

OLD DOMINION UNIVERSITY
COLLEGE OF BUSINESS AND PUBLIC ADMINISTRATION

GENERAL INFORMATION

Type of school — Public
Affiliation — No Affiliation
Academic calendar — Semester

SURVEY SAYS...

Friendly students, Cutting-edge classes, Smart Classrooms
Solid preparation in:
Accounting, General management, Doing business in a global economy

STUDENTS

Enrollment of parent institution	24,466
Enrollment of MBA Program	219
% male/female	51/49
% out-of-state	22
% part-time	69
% underrepresented minority	39
% international	22
Average age at entry	31
Average years work experience at entry	4.9

ACADEMICS

Academic Experience Rating	**85**
Profs interesting rating	83
Profs accesible rating	87
Student/faculty ratio	5:1
% female faculty	17
% underrepresented minority faculty	10

Joint Degrees

Students may pursure dual degrees with nearly any degree offered at Old Dominion University with varying degrees of course overlap.

Prominent Alumni

Elizabeth Duke, Federal Reserve Board Member; Linda Middleton, Senior VP; John Sanderson, President; Larry Kittelberger, Senior VP & CIO; Bruce Bradley, President

Academics

Old Dominion University's College of Business and Public Administration in Virginia is a cost-effective program with "a very good reputation and…a robust international business program," designed specifically to meet the needs of "active professionals seeking advanced degrees to increase competitive advantage." Classes are offered in the evenings, late afternoons and Saturdays, and the curriculum features a set of one-hour module classes that are often taught by local business professionals.

The "demanding" curriculum consists of nine core courses that provide a foundation in business theory and decision making skills, and then student-selected electives that meet specific professional needs or fall under the available concentrations: Port and Maritime Management, International Business, Information Technology, Financial Analysis and Valuation, Health Sciences Administration, Public Administration and Business and Economic Forecasting. The international business focus means that students are "exposed to a large number of international faculty and students, which has really helped me to expand my global business knowledge and perspective."

The faculty is "very solid, always accessible, and [has] great real world experience." Class sizes are small, and the "extremely knowledgeable" professors use "innovative teaching methodologies and case studies." "Nearly all my professors have an excellent academic background and years of business or consulting experience that lends itself to the course material," says a student.

Career and Placement

The university offers a lot of "freebies" to students in the way of luncheons and opportunities to network, and the MBA administrative staff is "attentive and very helpful with the process." This is a "fairly close-knit" student body; the commuter nature of the school isn't naturally the most conducive to outside of class interactions, but the administration "does a good job trying to supplement this with plenty of structured networking opportunities." There are also "numerous clubs that offer networking opportunities in every field, as well for minorities and veterans." As a mostly regional (but growing) school, the alumni base in the area is "up-and-coming as a strong group."

ADMISSIONS CONTACT: MS. SHANNA WOOD, MBA ASSOCIATE DIRECTOR
ADDRESS: 1026 CONSTANT HALL, NORFOLK, VA 23529
PHONE: 757-683-3585 • FAX: 757-683-5750
E-MAIL: MBAINFO@ODU.EDU • WEBSITE: HTTP://ODU.EDU/MBA

Student Life and Environment

The majority of students here are married and holding down full-time jobs, and the program is populated with "hard-working individuals who are constantly challenged to balance their work, family, and school commitments." "People are here to learn as much as they possibly can about business from not only the courses, but also from each other," says a student. Many come to campus before class to "study, work on group projects, hang out and network with other students, or to attend speakers and other school sponsored events."

Thanks to ODU's close proximity to the nearby naval base, the school is "military-friendly" and "the school caters very much towards full-time working students," though some full-time students would like the option to attend daytime classes. Students are "a good blend" of full-time students and working professionals, and "the students who work are mostly full-time workers, while most of the students are full time students." "As a working professional, I still get to feel like an undergrad again with access to the rising football team or participate in intramurals," says one. The safety of the surrounding community is "an issue," however the ODU community "has done a terrific job at keeping the campus safe."

Admissions

All applicants to the MBA program at ODU must submit the following materials: a completed application (online) including a statement of personal objectives and resume; an official GMAT score report; official transcripts for all undergraduate and graduate work; a letter of recommendation (from a professor if you are currently a student; from a supervisor if you are currently employed); and a tuition-rate-determination form (to determine eligibility for in-state tuition). International students whose first language is not English must also submit an official score report for the TOEFL. Incoming students who have not completed college-level calculus are required to complete an equivalent undergraduate course during their first semester of MBA work. ODU considers the trend of undergraduate grades as well as overall cumulative GPA; those who showed marked improvement in junior and senior years can overcome poor performance as underclassmen.

FINANCIAL FACTS

Annual tuition (in-state/ out-of-state)	$9,432/$23,928
Fees	$210
Cost of books	$1,200
Room & board (on/off-campus)	$8,200/$9,200
% of students receiving aid	10
% of first-year students receiving aid	10
% of students receiving grants	1
Average award package	$400,000
Average grant	$20,000

ADMISSIONS

Admissions Selectivity Rating	88
# of applications received	139
% applicants accepted	39
% acceptees attending	87
Average GMAT	555
Range of GMAT	510–590
Average GPA	3.28
TOEFL required of international students	Yes
Minimum TOEFL (paper/computer)	550/213
Application fee	$50
International application fee	$50
Deferment available	Yes
Maximum length of deferment	1 year
Transfer students accepted	Yes
Transfer application policy: We accept up to 12 credit hours from AACSB accredited MBA programs only.	
Non-fall admissions	Yes
Need-blind admissions	Yes

PACIFIC LUTHERAN UNIVERSITY
SCHOOL OF BUSINESS

Academics

Offering a "globally-focused program" that's "well-known in the area," the School of Business at Pacific Lutheran University satisfies South Puget Sound area locals, who appreciate "the convenience offered to working professionals" here. With "small class sizes" facilitating plenty of "one-on-one interactions," the PLU MBA program employs a "customer service approach" that keeps students happy. This part-time program, "designed for working professionals," can be completed in less than two years.

Standout features of the PLU MBA include an emphasis in technology and innovation management, mentioned by several students as the main draw to the school; PLU also offers areas of emphasis in entrepreneurship and closely-held enterprises, as well as in health care management. A general MBA without concentration is also available. All students must complete a "ten-day international trip requirement," which grateful MBAs note is "included in the cost of tuition." Recent destinations include France, Spain, China, Taiwan, Germany, Switzerland, Ireland, and Peru. Students describe the experience as "amazing" and cite it as a major asset to the program.

Most agree, however, that the faculty and program administrators are PLU's primary selling points. The "excellent professors" at the School of Business are "experienced, flexible, always available, and professional." They go out of their way to utilize their students' professional experiences in class. As one student explains, "Professors try very hard to learn about each student and cater lessons/lectures to our professional backgrounds." Small classes mean lots of student participation. "As a student you are challenged to learn, and you are a part of the class. It's expected that the students are active in the classes," one MBA warns. The administration of PLU's MBA program "is handled almost exclusively by the program administrator/director," a great arrangement for students, who report that administrative services in their program are among the best on campus.

Career and Placement

The Career Development Office at PLU provides placement and counseling services for all undergraduates, graduate students and alumni. The office assists students with internship and career placement. The PLU Business Network is an alumni group who schedules networking events to help alumni and current BBA and MBA students connect. A significant networking opportunity open to PLU MBAs is the State Farm MBA Executive Leadership Series, a series of addresses delivered by area executives. Recent speakers have included the President and CEO of Esterline, President and COO of Miligard Windows, and the CFO of 5.11 Tactical. But a "strong alumni network" is probably PLU's greatest placement service. Students note the "sustained good reputation of [PLU] graduates," and benefit from "having a larger number of them in key companies and industries, serving in positions of great importance and responsibility."

Employers who most frequently hire Pacific Lutheran MBAs include Boeing, Microsoft, Weyerhaeuser, State Farm Insurance, Intel, and Starbucks.

Student Life and Environment

A "new business building" and a "beautiful campus" are among the top amenities of the PLU MBA experience. The building boasts "state-of-the-art facilities [that] cater to the unique [challenges] of working students," including "Wi-Fi available throughout the entire building." Opportunities to connect with classmates are limited as a result of the part-time nature of the program and the busy schedules most students maintain. However, students have the opportunity to connect at monthly networking events for students and alumni as well as frequently interact though, "classroom-related team project activities" that one student describes as "exciting and promising, as well as offering distinct challenges." Despite the fact that many students' schedules prevent them from spending a lot of time on campus, a "very collegial atmosphere" still manages to pervade the program.

Students in the PLU MBA program bring "very diverse backgrounds and professional experiences" to the classroom. A great many are "hardworking, family-oriented professionals with a lot going on in their lives," ranging "from stay-at-home moms and dads to army surgeons and city managers." One student reports that "when working together, I felt in all cases that we were peers, that never did one person's experience make them better than another, that everyone was able to contribute."

Admissions

At PLU, applicants are "evaluated individually based on a presentation of factors indicating equivalence to admission standards, a promise of success in graduate school, qualities of good character, and potential contributions to the educational mission of the graduate program and university." Applicants must provide the school with the following materials: official transcripts covering all undergraduate and graduate work; an official GMAT or GRE score report; a current resume; a completed application form; two letters of recommendation; and a 300-word statement of personal goals. Candidates whose native language is other than English must also submit an official TOEFL or IELTS score report. International transcripts must be submitted to the Educational Perspectives transcript translation agency for evaluation. All international applicants are required to submit a Declaration of Finances prior to issuance of an I-20.

FINANCIAL FACTS

Annual tuition	$24,332
Fees	$0
Cost of books	$1,800
Room & board (on/off-campus)	$9,230/$9,130
% of students receiving aid	62
% of first-year students receiving aid	66
% of students receiving grants	26
Average award package	$12,756
Average grant	$5,819
Average loan	$19,646
Average student loan debt	$45,243

ADMISSIONS

Admissions Selectivity Rating	**85**
# of applications received	44
% applicants accepted	50
% acceptees attending	82
Average GMAT	556
Range of GMAT	470–640
Average GPA	3.33
TOEFL required of international students	Yes
Minimum TOEFL (paper/computer)	573/88
Application fee	$40
International application fee	$40
Deferment available	Yes
Maximum length of deferment	1 year
Transfer students accepted	Yes
Transfer application policy: In order to graduate, a student must complete a minimum of 24 Semester hours in residence at PLU.	
Non-fall admissions	Yes
Need-blind admissions	Yes

EMPLOYMENT PROFILE

Career Rating	77	Top 5 Employers Hiring Grads
Average base starting salary	$75,000	Boeing, Intel, Russell Investments, Weyerhaeuser, Microsoft

PENNSYLVANIA STATE UNIVERSITY
SMEAL COLLEGE OF BUSINESS

GENERAL INFORMATION

Type of school   Public
Affiliation   No Affiliation
Academic calendar   Semester
                     7-week modules

SURVEY SAYS...

Smart classrooms
Solid preparation in:
Teamwork, Communication/interpersonal skills, Presentation skills

STUDENTS

Enrollment of parent
  institution   45,351
Enrollment of MBA Program   159
% male/female   72/28
% out-of-state   70
% part-time   0
% underrepresented minority   6
% international   37
Average age at entry   28
Average years work experience
  at entry   4.5

ACADEMICS

Academic Experience Rating	**92**
Profs interesting rating	93
Profs accesible rating	89
Student/faculty ratio	2:1
% female faculty	21
% underrepresented minority faculty	17
% part-time faculty	0

Joint Degrees

JD/MBA 4 years; BS/MBA 5-6 years; MD/MBA 5 years

Prominent Alumni

John Surma, Chairman and CEO, U.S. Steel; J. David Rogers, CEO, JD Capital Management; Stephen Sheetz, Chairman of the Board, Sheetz, Inc.; Karen Quintos, Senior Vice President and Chief Marketing Officer, Dell; Patricia Woertz, President and CEO, Archer Daniels Midland Company

Academics

Students entering Penn State's Smeal MBA program should "Expect to be challenged!" Here, conversations are "intellectually stimulating" and people are "not afraid to roll up their sleeves and get to work." Students have high opinions of themselves and their classmates. As one student attests, "There are only strong candidates here; no weakest links among us." Students appreciate small classes that deliver a "high quality education," laced with "personal attention" as well as "great access to professors." Students do not feel they are missing out by going here instead of a larger school, saying that Smeal offers this close, "tight-knit community" feel without missing out on the great wealth of resources of a big school. Students point out that although their school may be small when you look at its numbers, it is large in other ways, such as its cultural diversity. "As a result of that, class discussion is very rich." Topics of discussion and materials presented continually change with the times as the Smeal MBA program "prides itself on keeping its academics as current as possible." An "attention to professionalism" is evident throughout the school.

"Exceptional professors are the cornerstones of student success both inside and outside of class. They are "well regarded in their respective fields and have a way of making complex concepts digestible." Students find the ease of accessing professors outside of class as "remarkable." They go "above and beyond to place a student in their dream internship or open the door to a dream company." An equally qualified and "very dedicated" administrative staff backs the strong faculty. Students appreciate how the administration "constantly improves the system throughout the semester based on student feedback and ensures a smooth transition for the incoming classes."

Career and Placement

Getting recruiters to notice a small school is always a challenge. Students understand this and appreciate that recently career services "has made tremendous strides to get recruiters into Smeal. They are constantly devising new programs to support students." This school is well-known for its strong "supply chain" and Smeal students take full advantage of this proven and successful system. "Whether it's through one of the many career fairs held on campus or in the Business Building, or through an alumni contact, you can get connected to any company in the world."

Smeal's "big alumni network" provides an "extensive, passionate alumni base" for internship and job possibilities close to home as well as "around the world." Students may "challenge, conflict with, and motivate each other," in class but their actions only serve to benefit each other. A student explains, "My classmates are an invaluable resource. We all want to see each other succeed because we want to have a great grad network."

ADMISSIONS: STACEY DORANG PEELER, ADMISSIONS DIRECTOR
ADDRESS: 220 BUSINESS BUILDING, UNIVERSITY PARK, PA 16802
PHONE: 814-863-0474 • FAX: 814-863-8072
E-MAIL: SMEALMBA@PSU.EDU • WEBSITE: WWW.SMEAL.PSU.EDU/MBA

Student Life and Environment

As one might expect at such a high-powered place, life at Smeal is "heavily focused on schoolwork and finding a job," but most students are also "able to make time for social and community activities." Bonds of friendship are quickly and easily formed within this "relatively small program," which offers a "friendly environment." During the program, there is a "coffee buzz" between morning classes "where students gather with administrators and professors to talk about anything." This helps foster and perpetuate the "great sense of community" students describe within their program.

Embracing the diverse cultures of the large international population on campus is another way to learn and grow as an individual. At Smeal, students "celebrate almost every possible event from all nations and religions." There are "numerous events throughout the year to celebrate other cultures such as Chinese New Year, Diwali and Diversity Days, where international students bring in artifacts/food and give a brief overview of their home country." One student boasts, "We are extremely proud of anything our classmates do."

Admissions

Although Penn State undergrads do sometimes enter directly in the MBA program, most students have an average of four years professional experience. The admissions office seeks diversity of background and life experiences for incoming classes to keep in line with the school's existing classroom experience that enlightens and enriches on a global perspective. Applicants to the program must submit the following materials: a completed online application form; 2 official copies of all transcripts for all postsecondary academic work; an official GMAT or GRE score report; two letters of recommendation from individuals who can assess your past professional performance; personal essays; a resume; and an interview. A video submission is optional. In addition, international applicants must also submit an official score report for the TOEFL or IELTS in addition to evidence of sufficient funds to cover at least one year's expenses while in the program, which approximates $55,000.

FINANCIAL FACTS

Annual tuition (in-state/ out-of-state)	$21,676/$34,886
Fees	$1,082
Cost of books	$3,500
Room & board	$17,400
% of students receiving aid	88
% of first-year students receiving aid	95
% of students receiving grants	79
Average award package	$24,450
Average grant	$14,830
Average loan	$25,750
Average student loan debt	$51,330

ADMISSIONS

Admissions Selectivity Rating	92
# of applications received	544
% applicants accepted	29
% acceptees attending	50
Average GMAT	643
Range of GMAT	590–710
Average GPA	3.20
TOEFL required of international students	Yes
Minimum TOEFL (paper/computer)	600/250
Application fee	$65
International application fee	$65
Early application deadline	11/9
Early notification date	1/10
Regular application deadline	4/12
Regular application notification	5/31
Application Deadline/Notification	
Round 1:	11/9 / 1/10
Round 2:	1/11 / 3/29
Round 3:	4/12 / 5/31
Deferment available	Yes
Maximum length of deferment	1 year
Transfer students accepted	Yes
Transfer application policy: A maximum of six elective credits can be transferred. All core courses must be taken.	
Non-fall admissions	No
Need-blind admissions	Yes

EMPLOYMENT PROFILE

Career Rating	93	Grads Employed by Function	% Avg. Salary
Percent employed at graduation	54	Marketing	(15%) $79,667
Percent employed 3 months after graduation	80	Operations	(45%) $86,513
		Consulting	(8%) $101,400
Average base starting salary	$84,345	Management	(3%)
Primary Source of Full-time Job Acceptances		Finance	(21%) $82,077
School-facilitated activities	62(79%)	HR	(2%)
Graduate-facilitated activities	13(17%)	MIS	(3%)
Unknown	3(4%)	Other	(3%)

Top 5 Employers Hiring Grads
Apple (6), Baker Hughes (3), Dell (3), Deloitte Consulting (3), VWR International (3)

PENNSYLVANIA STATE UNIVERSITY—ERIE, THE BEHREND COLLEGE
SAM AND IRENE BLACK SCHOOL OF BUSINESS

GENERAL INFORMATION
Type of school   Public
Affiliation   No Affiliation
Academic calendar   Semester

SURVEY SAYS...
Smart classrooms
Solid preparation in:
General management

STUDENTS
Enrollment of parent
  institution   4,607
Enrollment of MBA Program   88
% male/female   76/24
% out-of-state   20
% part-time   72
% underrepresented minority   1
Average age at entry   25
Average years work experience
  at entry   4.0

ACADEMICS
Academic Experience Rating   76
Profs interesting rating   76
Profs accesible rating   75
Student/faculty ratio   5:1
% female faculty   23
% underrepresented minority
  faculty   26
% part-time faculty   0

Joint Degrees
none

Prominent Alumni
Ann Scott, Vice President and
Director of Diversity and
Community Outreach, Erie
Insurance Group; Scott Mitchell,
President and CEO, Erie Zoo; Nancy
Anderson, CIO and Quality Leader,
GE Transportation Systems; Dennis
Prischak, President, Plastek US;
James Fetzner, CEO, Comfort Care
& Resources

Academics

The Black School of Business at Penn State Behrend College "provides the best value for a working student in the local area," one MBA here explains, adding, "You get the Penn State name, an outstanding general MBA education, and student-work flexibility." Behrend enjoys "an outstanding reputation" in the region, making it an excellent choice for students looking to build their careers in and around Erie.

A general degree that aims to develop the critical-thinking skills necessary for a career in mid- and upper-level management, the Behrend MBA curriculum consists of 48 units, or 13 courses. Of these, 18 units form the foundational core courses, which are comprised of three introductory classes: Costs, Competition, and Market Performance; Demand, Operations, and Firm Performance; and Integrated Business Analysis. After completing these courses, students must complete 21 credits of required advanced courses and 9 credits of elective course work. For those who have already taken business courses, the program can be streamlined through the omission of certain foundation courses. Depending on their previous academic preparation, full-time students can usually complete the MBA curriculum in three semesters; part-time students usually require two to four years to complete the program.

Behrend works hard to keep its MBA program student-friendly with an "attractive and clean" campus (that includes "a new facility for the business school"), "small classes" and "accessible professors." Most faculty members "have extensive real-world experience that greatly adds to their lessons. Additionally, many are locals and have experience at the major companies in the area and understand the general job situation of the area." Students describe the curriculum as challenging, citing "tough courses" that "equate to well-educated students." Another reports, "The professors expect a lot. No class was easy. I consider myself to be an intelligent person, but have felt less so at times because of the difficulty of the work." Among the drawbacks of a Behrend MBA, "some courses are only offered one semester each year," making it "very difficult to have a consistent workload. Some semesters are much heavier than others due to course offerings." Even so, students here agree that Behrend is "the best school, academically, for the region."

Career and Placement

A high percentage of Penn State Behrend students are currently employed in professional positions and are pursuing an MBA with the intention of improving their career opportunities at their current companies. In fact, a considerable number of Penn State Behrend students receive tuition assistance from their employers. Some, however, see their MBAs as a stepping stone to a new career (or, for students pursuing MBAs straight out of college, simply a career). For those, the Penn State Behrend Academic Advising and Career Development Center serves both the undergraduate and graduate population at the college, including students in the MBA program. The CDC hosts career fairs, on-campus recruiting and interview events, seminars, and workshops. A growing number of organizations participate in Penn State Behrend career fairs each year. Employers who frequently hire Behrend MBAs include: Deloitte Consulting, Paradigm Wave, Ingentor, GE Infrastructure-Transportation Systems, IBM, Erie Insurance Group, National City Corporation, Graham Packaging, HealthAmerica, and the Pennsylvania State University.

ADMISSIONS CONTACT: ANN M. BURBULES, GRADUATE ADMISSIONS COUNSELOR
ADDRESS: 4851 COLLEGE DRIVE, ERIE, PA 16563
PHONE: 814-898-7255 • FAX: 814-898-6044
E-MAIL: PSBEHRENDMBA@PSU.EDU • WEBSITE: WWW.BEHREND.PSU.EDU

Student Life and Environment

Behrend MBAs enjoy "state-of-the-art" classrooms that "allow us to utilize multimedia learning," which they very much appreciate. The campus itself is "very clean, safe, and attractive," "not so large that it is overwhelming but still offering most [of the] opportunities of a large school." And here's something you rarely hear at any school, much less a state institution: there's "plenty of parking" here.

Campus life offers "a number of clubs and organizations for students," and "the school also hosts a very wide array of speakers, and events," but most of these events seem planned primarily for undergraduates. "There are no solely business school programs of any kind. The most activity available is an unofficial happy hour at the end of the semester," one student writes.

There's a clear divide among the Behrend MBA population. "The morning sessions of class are more geared toward the younger generation," while "the evening sessions [consist] more of your business professionals who take things more seriously." The student body includes "a large number of engineers due to the engineering school at the Behrend School." Several full-time students reported that they were only attending full time as a result of the down economy; otherwise, they'd be working and attending part time.

Admissions

Students may apply to begin study at Penn State Behrend's Black College of Business in the fall, spring, or summer semester. Admissions decisions are made on a rolling basis. To apply, students must submit two official transcripts, official GMAT scores, a statement of purpose, an application fee, and three recommendation forms. Candidates with the highest GMAT scores and GPA are given priority in admissions. Candidates are evaluated based on the strength of their combined GMAT score and GPA; therefore, a lower GMAT score can be compensated for by a higher GPA, or vice versa. International applicants whose first language is not English must meet all of the above requirements and must also submit an official score report for the TOEFL or IELTS.

FINANCIAL FACTS

Annual tuition (in-state/ out-of-state)	$13,914/$21,564
Fees	$1,020
Cost of books	$1,548
Room & board (on/off-campus)	$0/$11,718
% of students receiving aid	63
% of first-year students receiving aid	67
% of students receiving grants	47
Average award package	$20,320
Average grant	$16,079
Average loan	$13,598
Average student loan debt	$28,552

ADMISSIONS

Admissions Selectivity Rating	**73**
# of applications received	46
% applicants accepted	83
% acceptees attending	71
Average GMAT	561
Range of GMAT	498–595
Average GPA	3.30
TOEFL required of international students	Yes
Minimum TOEFL (paper/computer)	550/213
Application fee	$65
International application fee	$65
Regular application deadline	7/1
Application Deadline/Notification	
Deferment available	Yes
Maximum length of deferment	two years
Transfer students accepted	Yes

Transfer application policy: Up to 10 credits of relevant graduate work completed at an accredited institution. Credits earned to complete a previous graduate degree may not be used to fulfill MBA degree requirements. Transferred graduate work must have been completed no more than five years before the student is fully admitted as a degree candidate at Penn State Behrend. Course work must be of at least a B quality and appear on the graduate transcript of a regionally- accredited institution. Pass/Fail grades are not transferable.

Non-fall admissions	Yes
Need-blind admissions	Yes

EMPLOYMENT PROFILE

Career Rating	89	**Grads Employed by Function% Avg. Salary**	
Percent employed at graduation	60	Management	(33%) $85,000
Average base starting salary	$71,667	Finance	(33%) $85,000
Primary Source of Full-time Job Acceptances		**Top 5 Employers Hiring Grads**	
Unknown	3(%)	GE Transportation Services (1), Jameson Publishing (1), Addvetco (1),,	

PEPPERDINE UNIVERSITY
GRAZIADIO SCHOOL OF BUSINESS AND MANAGEMENT

GENERAL INFORMATION

Type of school   Private
Affiliation   Church of Christ
Academic calendar   Trimester

SURVEY SAYS...

Students love Malibu, CA, Friendly
students
Solid preparation in:
Teamwork, Social responsibility

STUDENTS

Enrollment of parent
  institution   7,604
Enrollment of MBA Program 1,286
% male/female   62/38
% part-time   71
% underrepresented minority 38
% international   24
Average age at entry   27
Average years work experience
  at entry   4.0

ACADEMICS

Academic Experience Rating 83
Profs interesting rating   86
Profs accesible rating   81
Student/faculty ratio   16:1
% female faculty   33
% underrepresented minority
  faculty   25
% part-time faculty   41

Joint Degrees

Five-Year Bachelor of Science and
Master of Business Administration -
5 years; Bachelor of Science and
International Master of Business
Administration - 5 years; Joint Juris
Doctor and Master of Business
Administration - 4 years; Joint
Master of Business Administration
and Master of Public Policy - 4
years

Prominent Alumni

Victor Tsao, Founder, Vice
President and General Manager,
Linksys; John Figueroa, President,
McKesson U.S. Pharmaceutical;
Christos M. Cotsakos, CEO and
President, Mainstream Holdings

Academics

Armed with a "gorgeous campus," "great alumni network" and "relaxed" atmosphere, it's obvious why MBA candidates are attracted to Pepperdine. The "small class sizes" virtually guarantee a lot of "personal attention from professors." Additionally, many students are drawn to Graziadio for its "SEER Program (Socially, Environmentally, and Ethically Responsible Business Practices) and its focus on sustainability." Students also love that the Pepperdine "provides multiple opportunities to get real-world consulting experiences within courses called E2B (education to business)."

Further, Graziadio MBAs find that their professors certainly run the gamut. Indeed, there "are some absolutely fantastic professors in each department, plenty of just average professors, and a handful of professors who make you wonder how they are possibly still picking up a paycheck." Overall, students definitely "appreciate that all of our professors are much more experienced in the professional world than the academic world." A second year student speaks glowingly of his "excellent" professors sharing that they "challenge(d) me and force me to think critically. They require team work and foster great environments for collaboration and strong work ethics." And a pleased first year chimes in, "I do not feel like teaching is just an income generator for them, I feel like they actually care and really want to see me succeed in the future."

Finally, Graziadio's administration gets fairly high marks as well. Granted some students feel that "the administration doesn't interact with us all that much." However, the staff does appear to be comprised of "interesting, competent people" who are "more than willing to help you network if they get to know you."

Career and Placement

Students at Graziadio are decidedly mixed when it comes to the career services, opportunities and insight available. On the one hand, professors certainly "bring valuable career experience into the classroom" which many find "extremely beneficial." Additionally, the "E2B...is a great way to get hands-on experience consulting for companies in the LA area." Indeed, it's a "great program that applies practical application to coursework." However, some find the actual career services office to be a bit lacking. As one second year student laments, "I wish [they] would set up more on campus interviews." Another classmate agrees sharing, "Career services could use some work, but proactive approaches from the students alleviates most problems in that area." Of course, that's not to say that career services is without merit. MBA candidates can take advantage of one-on-one, short term coaching sessions. During these meetings, students receive guidance on salary negotiation, career planning, resumes and interviews. And the office hosts a number of industry panels, career panels, webinars and career workshops throughout the year.

Though you can definitely find Graziadio graduates scattered across the country and the globe, the majority of students find employment on the west coast. Typical companies that hire Pepperdine MBAs include Google, Starbucks, Herbalife, Countrywide, Merrill Lynch, AT&T, Citibank, Yahoo!, Technicolor, IBM, Northrop Grumman and RSM Equico.

ADMISSIONS CONTACT: DARRELL ERIKSEN, PREADMISSION ADVISOR
ADDRESS: 6100 CENTER DRIVE, STE. 400, LOS ANGELES, CA 90045
PHONE: 310-568-5555 • FAX: 310-568-5727
E-MAIL: MBABSM@PEPPERDINE.EDU • WEBSITE: BSCHOOL.PEPPERDINE.EDU

Student Life and Environment

A congenial atmosphere permeates Pepperdine's campus. And students happily report that there "aren't many arrogant, cutthroat students." Additionally, "friendliness" abounds. A second-year affirms this sharing, "Almost all students are willing to help if someone does not understand a particular subject or topic." And considering these MBAs find their peers "intelligent and hardworking," their helpful nature definitely comes in handy.

Outside of academics and campus events, students also love to take advantage of Pepperdine's amazing location. As a second year student brags, "Quality of life here is second to none. We live in Malibu. The beach is within walking distance. The nightlife in LA has everything from world champion sports to modern art. The mountains are nearby. The recreational opportunities outside of class are endless."

Admission

The admissions process for Pepperdine's MBA program is fairly by the book. The committee seeks successful professionals looking to enhance or develop their management skills. Applicants must have earned a bachelor's degree (complete with a solid GPA) from an accredited university. Further, they are required to have a minimum of two years work experience. Pepperdine's application also calls for a professional recommendation, either from an immediate supervisor or an individual qualified to assess a candidate's abilities. Finally, applicants must submit an undergraduate transcript as well as GMAT (preferred) or GRE scores earned within the last five years.

FINANCIAL FACTS

Annual tuition	$38,734
Fees	$80
Cost of books	$2,000
Room & board	$15,000
% of students receiving aid	76
% of first-year students receiving aid	58
% of students receiving grants	48
Average award package	$30,191
Average grant	$17,790
Average loan	$41,801
Average student loan debt	$75,550

ADMISSIONS

Admissions Selectivity Rating	81
# of applications received	391
% applicants accepted	64
% acceptees attending	63
Average GMAT	643
Range of GMAT	605–657
Average GPA	3.21
TOEFL required of international students	Yes
Minimum TOEFL (paper/computer)	600/250
Application fee	$100
International application fee	$100
Early application deadline	12/15
Early notification date	1/15
Regular application deadline	5/1
Deferment available	Yes
Maximum length of deferment	1 year
Transfer students accepted	Yes
Transfer application policy: No more than 2 courses may be transferred, contingent upon policy committee approval	
Non-fall admissions	No
Need-blind admissions	Yes

EMPLOYMENT PROFILE

Career Rating	79	**Grads Employed by Function% Avg. Salary**	
Percent employed at graduation	40	Marketing	(13%) $72,637
Percent employed 3 months		Operations	(5%) $83,000
after graduation	23	Consulting	(3%)$75,000
Average base starting salary	$69,167	Management	(9%) $84,375
Primary Source of Full-time Job Acceptances		Finance	(10%) $55,640
School-facilitated activities	22(37%)	HR	(4%) $68,500
Graduate-facilitated activities	30(50%)	Other	(1%) $45,000
Unknown	7(13%)	**Top 5 Employers Hiring Grads**	
		AT&T(4), Bank of America (3), Deloitte & Touche (2), Cooking.com (2), Disney (2)	

PITTSBURG STATE UNIVERSITY

GLADYS A. KELCE COLLEGE OF BUSINESS

Academics

For a "high-quality education at an affordable price," Kansas professionals recommend Pittsburg State University's graduate business program. At this affordable public school, the "atmosphere is very conducive to learning and interacting with people," thanks to small class sizes, low enrollment, and a patently student-friendly attitude. Taking an active interest in their students' education, "the faculty does a great job pushing students to excel and make contributions to the school and community." Small class sizes ensure that "students can develop a very personal relationship with professors" and "actively engage in learning." Administration, like faculty, is "professional and efficient," always willing to "bend over backwards to try to meet students' needs and make everything run as smoothly as possible." With so many friendly faces, some students regard the Pitt State campus as a "second home."

Depending on a student's previous preparation, the MBA consists of anywhere between 34 and 64 hours of upper-division coursework. Students with an undergraduate degree in business may be eligible to skip courses in the 20-unit foundation series, which covers key topics like marketing, finance, and accounting. With foundation courses taken or waived, full-time students can complete the entire MBA curriculum in just a year. Students may also choose to study part-time, while continuing to work professionally, spacing out courses over several years. Juggling work and school can be a challenge, but Pitt State makes it easy for students to meet their goals. While professors "have high expectations for students," they are "willing to offer extra support as needed" and will often "go above and beyond to help students succeed." When dealing with the faculty, "you can ask any question without hesitation, and they are always ready to help you."

Currently, Pitt State students may pursue an MBA in general management, or tailor their degree with a concentration in international business or accounting. Students at Pitt say the education is modern and progressive, often covering the newest trends in the marketplace. Faculty members are "extremely aware and knowledgeable about the current business world," and are always "willing to implement new concepts that have been introduced to the business world in the past year or two." Particularly relevant to today's business climate, "Pitt State is dedicated to teaching corporate citizenship and the need for green business technique." In the classroom, "the technology available is top notch and prepares students for a career where technology is becoming more and more important." In this and other ways, "PSU is always working on improving."

Career and Placement

Pitt State students can get professional development assistance at the University's Office of Career Services. The office provides reference materials, career counseling, and resume preparation services, while also coordinating on-campus interviews and recruiting events. They host several large career expos annually, as well as smaller events, like workshops and speakers. While these career events are aimed at the entire Pitt State population, "there are diverse companies at the career fairs," many of which are interested in business students. A recent career fair included representatives from Cessna, Verizon, Farmers Insurance Group, General Electric, Northwestern Mutual, Sherwin-Williams, Toyota Financial Services, Walmart, and more. Despite the line-up, business students would like to see a few more big names on the roster.

ADMISSIONS CONTACT: JAIME VANDERBECK, ADMINISTRATIVE OFFICER–GRADUATE STUDIES
ADDRESS: 1701 SOUTH BROADWAY, PITTSBURG, KS 66762-7540
PHONE: 620-235-4223 • FAX: 620-235-4219
E-MAIL: CGS@PITTSTATE.EDU • WEBSITE: WWW.PITTSTATE.EDU/KELCE

About half of Pitt State's MBA graduates take jobs in general management, with another quarter heading to marketing or sales positions. The average base salary for MBA graduates is $46,000 annually. The school's biggest employers include Deloitte, Sprint, Walmart, and Allstate. In recent years, anywhere between 75 and 95 percent of students were employed by graduation.

Student Life and Environment

"There is an incredible sense of student spirit and pride" on the Pitt State campus, and a "strong diversity of cultures" within the business school. In addition to attracting a fairly large international population, the School's "proximity to the borders of Missouri and Oklahoma makes it a viable and excellent choice for students in these neighboring states." Together, students get a nice mix of regional culture and international perspectives. "Teamwork and presentation skills" are stressed throughout the curriculum, so students have many opportunities to work together during the program. While the atmosphere is comfortable and collegial, the physical environment is less appealing. Pitt students admit, "the business school could use newer facilities."

Beyond coursework, "it is very easy to get involved and meet other students" in the MBA program. In the evenings, "there are always social events on campus with a variety of clubs and organizations." Student clubs provide "great networking opportunities, as well as opportunities for teamwork and leadership" outside the classroom. To compliment the academic programs, "Every week, there is some sort of guest speaker" on campus, and the administration organizes "special seminars and other events every Friday." From Big Brothers/Big Sisters to political groups, "there are a lot of school-run clubs and student organizations" on the larger Pitt State campus, and many of the younger students get involved with collegiate activities." The surrounding community of Pittsburg, Kansas is "somewhat small, isolated, and conservative," but the atmosphere is "very friendly" and highly supportive of the University and its students.

Admissions

To be eligible for the MBA program, applicants must hold a four-year degree in any field from an accredited college or university. Students are evaluated via an admissions formula, which calculates a student's GPA and GMAT scores to determine their eligibility for admission. Therefore, you can balance out a lower GPA with strong performance on the GMAT, or vice versa. No matter what your GPA, a minimum GMAT score of 400 is necessary for unconditional admission to the program. Around 40 percent of incoming students do not have undergraduate degrees in business. Starting fall 2011, equivalent GRE scores are accepted in lieu of GMAT.

FINANCIAL FACTS

Annual tuition (in-state/ out-of-state)	$6,164/$14,518
Cost of books	$1,000
Room & board	$6,288
% of students receiving aid	50
% of first-year students receiving aid	25
% of students receiving grants	15
Average award package	$8,500
Average grant	$3,500
Average loan	$8,500

ADMISSIONS

Admissions Selectivity Rating	75
# of applications received	305
% applicants accepted	71
% acceptees attending	72
Average GMAT	540
Range of GMAT	400–740
Average GPA	3.25
TOEFL required of international students	Yes
Minimum TOEFL (paper/computer)	550/213
Application fee	$60
International application fee	$60
Regular application deadline	7/15
Regular application notification	8/1
Application Deadline/Notification	
Round 1:	6/1 / 6/15
Round 2:	10/15 / 10/30
Round 3:	4/1 / 4/15
Round 4:	5/1 / 5/15
Deferment available	Yes
Maximum length of deferment	1 year
Transfer students accepted	Yes
Transfer application policy: Up to 9 Semester hours may be transferred from another MBA accredited program.	
Non-fall admissions	Yes
Need-blind admissions	Yes

EMPLOYMENT PROFILE

Career Rating	73	Grads Employed by Function% Avg. Salary	
Percent employed at graduation	60	Marketing	(24%) $54,000
Percent employed 3 months after graduation	25	Management	(54%) $50,000
		MIS	(22%) $52,000
Average base starting salary	$50,000	**Top 5 Employers Hiring Grads**	
Primary Source of Full-time Job Acceptances		Deloitte & Touche (2), Sprint (4), Kock\h (2),	
School-facilitated activities	43(72%)	Walmart (2), AllState (2)	
Unknown	17(28%)		

PORTLAND STATE UNIVERSITY
SCHOOL OF BUSINESS ADMINISTRATION

GENERAL INFORMATION

Type of school	Public
Affiliation	No Affiliation

SURVEY SAYS...

Students love Portland, OR, Friendly students, Good peer network
Solid preparation in:
Marketing, Accounting, General management, Teamwork, Social responsibility

STUDENTS

Enrollment of parent institution	30,000
Enrollment of MBA Program	246
% male/female	55/45
% out-of-state	55
% part-time	70
% underrepresented minority	28
% international	31
Average age at entry	33
Average years work experience at entry	8.8

ACADEMICS

Academic Experience Rating	**84**
Profs interesting rating	79
Profs accesible rating	82
Student/faculty ratio	35:1
% female faculty	31
% part-time faculty	61

Prominent Alumni

Gary Ames, former President/CEO, U.S. West; Gerry Cameron, retired Chairman of the Board, U.S. Bancorp; Scott Davis, Chief Executive Officer, UPS; Larry Huget, President/COO, ESCO Corp; J. Greg Ness, President/COO, StanCorp Financial Group

Academics

Taking a cue from its progressive environs in Portland, Oregon, Portland State University offers an MBA program with a "focus on sustainability" and an emphasis on "personal development as a leader." Offering more than your standard MBA, "This school is committed to the whole student," and "creativity, along with sustainable, equitable solutions, are promoted, even prized." Throughout the hefty 74-credit curriculum, you'll never lose sight of the school's core values: "PSU also works hard to integrate sustainability into most aspects of the curriculum, from core classes to elective offerings." The MBA includes plenty of required coursework (as well as required hands-on projects), yet electives give students the opportunity to tailor their education. In fact, "the wide latitude given to students to pursue their studies in a multi-disciplinary manner" is a trademark of PSU's graduate program. One student, for example, chose to take "public policy classes through the school of Public Administration, an environmental economics course through the School of Liberal Arts and Sciences (Economics), and a two-term seminar on the Smart Grid, also through the school of Public Administration."

Thanks to its strong reputation and enviable Portland location, PSU can "attract and retain an extremely high-quality faculty roster." On the whole, "Professors are informed, enlightened educators as well as experts in their respective fields." Despite overall excellence, students say there are a few instructors who "seem unprepared, disorganized, and unclear on what they're supposed to be teaching us." The local community also plays an important role in the PSU experience. "Portland is truly at the center of this nation's move toward sustainability," and therefore, "Being in Portland is a huge plus—there's so much sustainable business thinking and practice here that it's easy to see in the field what I learn in school." A student adds, "I have been introduced to and met with many people that are driving regional and national movements on the cutting edge of sustainability."

PSU is a large school, but you won't get lost in the crowd. Despite its 600-plus enrollment, "The SBA manages by breaking up [its] graduate studies into discrete cohorts and providing a concrete plan of study for each. There's never much doubt what you should be doing, yet there is flexibility should you need it." Depending on your schedule, the school offers several program options. For full-time students, "MBA cohort classes are four hours long one day a week from about [noon] until four," while part-time students "typically go to class two to three evenings a week." The school also operates a "well-regarded online program," which participants describe as "very smooth and very accessible." Though students say the business school's classrooms could use a refresh, "The academic resources are great." For example, "The library has done a lot of work to make research as easy as possible, even for those of us who are only on campus a couple times a week."

Career and Placement

The largest school in the state, PSU maintains "powerful connections to the Portland-area business community." Within the business school itself, faculty and administrators are "are ultra-accessible and always willing to provide career advice or introduce you to people they know in the business community." In addition, PSU has "a good alumni network" throughout the state of Oregon. Drawing on its deep ties in the Portland community, the academic experience at PSU is augmented by various professional development activities, like expert panel discussions, alumni networking events, and a mentorship program. At the same time, students note that career services are not as robust as they'd like. While the school affords them many opportunities, "Students are expected to leverage other offerings, such as mentoring programs, informational interviews, etc." Companies that have partnered with PSU through the mentor program, as student project partners, or as employers include Columbia Forest Products, Columbia Sportswear, Costco, Ernst & Young, Intel, Nestle, Nike, PepsiCo, and WebTrends. The average starting salary for full-time PSU students is about $65,320.

Student Life and Environment

Friendly and down-to-earth, PSU students "defy the typical business school stereotype of sharkish students dying to get ahead." A current student observes, "While I expected to enter B-school with a bunch of traders and bankers, I was surprised to find a group of students that shared my, and Portland's, sensibilities regarding the world, and who are looking forward to showing the world that businesspeople are not only out to bring down the financial system en route to earning billions." Although there is a general interest in sustainability and ethics, at PSU you'll meet students from a "wide range" of backgrounds. As such, there are "a variety of activities to participate in regardless of your industry," and, on campus, there are lots of resources for a diverse student body—including "several childcare centers."

In both the full-time and part-time MBA program, many "people come to class and then go home," without making time for clubs or student groups. However, most students are involved in school-related activities outside of class, such as "internships, networking opportunities, and even…regular community service." In addition, many students are "open to meet after class or on weekends to socialize." Thanks to PSU's "vibrant urban location" in downtown Portland, students enjoy everything the Pacific Northwest has to offer, including plenty of "good food and coffee locations close by."

Admissions

To be considered for the full-time MBA program, students must have a minimum undergraduate GPA of 2.75, or, alternately, 3.0 in nine units of graduate-level coursework. Prospective students must also have at least two years of professional work experience before entering the program. In the class of 2010, the average GMAT score was 615 and the mean undergraduate GPA was 3.37.

FINANCIAL FACTS

Annual tuition (in-state/ out-of-state)	$20,590/$24,732
Fees	$1,263
Cost of books	$2,028
Room & board	$11,019

ADMISSIONS

Admissions Selectivity Rating	84
# of applications received	276
% applicants accepted	55
% acceptees attending	63
Average GMAT	623
Range of GMAT	580–660
Average GPA	3.30
TOEFL required of international students	Yes
Minimum TOEFL (paper/computer)	550/213
Application fee	$50
International application fee	$50
Application Deadline/Notification	
Round 1:	11/1 / 12/15
Round 2:	2/1 / 4/1
Round 3:	5/1 / 7/1
Deferment available	No
Transfer students accepted	Yes
Transfer application policy:	
Maximum of 1/3 of the total number of PSU credits may transfer from a US accredited university.	
Non-fall admissions	No
Need-blind admissions	Yes

EMPLOYMENT PROFILE

Career Rating	89	Grads Employed by Function	% Avg. Salary
Percent employed at graduation	33	Marketing	(38%) $61,000
Percent employed 3 months after graduation	73	Operations	(17%) $72,750
		Consulting	(20%) $74,667
Average base starting salary	$66,409	Management	(4%) $45,000
Primary Source of Full-time Job Acceptances		Finance	(17%) $48,000
School-facilitated activities	6(25%)	Other	(4%) $85,000
Graduate-facilitated activities	10(42%)	**Top 5 Employers Hiring Grads**	
Unknown	8(33%)	The Standard Insurance (1), Slalom Consulting (1), Dupont (1), Amazon (1), Pacific Natural Foods (1)	

PURDUE UNIVERSITY
KRANNERT SCHOOL OF MANAGEMENT

GENERAL INFORMATION

Type of school	Public
Affiliation	No Affiliation
Academic calendar	Semester

SURVEY SAYS...
Smart classrooms
Solid preparation in:
Finance, Operations, Quantitative
skills

STUDENTS

Enrollment of parent institution	69,030
Enrollment of MBA Program	103
% male/female	77/23
% out-of-state	79
% part-time	0
% underrepresented minority	12
% international	58
Average age at entry	28
Average years work experience at entry	4.1

ACADEMICS

Academic Experience Rating	**90**
Profs interesting rating	92
Profs accesible rating	87
Student/faculty ratio	2:1
% female faculty	26
% underrepresented minority faculty	2
% part-time faculty	20

Joint Degrees
BS Management/MBA(5 years), BS
Industrial Engineering/MBA (5
years), BS Mechanical
Engineering/MBA (5 years),

Prominent Alumni
Joseph Forehand, Retired
Chairman, Accenture; Marshall
Larsen, Chairman, President, CEO,
Goodrich Corp.; Marjorie Magner,
Managing Partner, Brysam Global
Partners, listed among Most
Powerful Women in Business
(Forbes); Venu Srinivasan,
Chairman and Managing Director,
TVS Motor Co.; Jerry Rawls,
President and CEO, Finisar

Academics

Purdue University's Krannert School of Management is a heavyweight in the MBA universe, especially when it comes to its "areas of strength: quantitative methods, operations, finance, and economics." Those looking to develop a "strong analytical and quantitative background" can hardly go wrong with a Krannert MBA. Best of all, at state school prices, Krannert "provides a great return on investment." But it's not just the school's low tuition that lends Krannert a kinder bottom line. As one student explains, "Many of us are actually doing this program at almost no cost thanks to the number of scholarships and assistantships [on offer]. This is very unique for a top MBA program. My friends at Wharton, MIT, Tepper, etc. are paying way more!"

Krannert excels even outside its quantitatively-focused standout disciplines. Students encounter a faculty experienced "in every aspect of management, from operations and finance to marketing and HR" here. But Krannert's academic excellence comes with high expectations. Academics are tough; there's a "'no BS' atmosphere here. Here you are expected to 'work hard, work right, and work together.'" MBAs assure us that Krannert "will push everyone to the limits, truly creating upending experiences that develop the individual along several dimensions." This is true not merely in terms of in-class work; the program "also provides several experiential learning opportunities through [its] consulting projects and study abroad programs." "The experiential learning projects give us good exposure to real-world work before we actually take the plunge," students tell us.

In terms of size, Krannert is just right. The program "is small enough for each student to stand out and become a leader if they would like to," yet "large enough and diverse enough to really learn a lot from your classmates." Krannert keeps class sizes small, which "means that students have greater one-on-one time with professors and they remain closely knit even years after graduation." Krannert professors "work to continue to contribute to research and stay involved in their respective fields," yet remain "genuinely interested in helping their students and are open and available to them any time we need."

Career and Placement

Students can prepare for interviews, contact employers, research companies, and complete career counseling through the Krannert Graduate Career Services office. The office receives mixed reviews. Some praise career services staff as attentive and "very committed to the students." Others demur, complaining that "The school should do a better job at alumni networking and improve its career services." This problem is particularly acute, we're told, when it comes to career services for international students, no small issue at a school with a 43 percent international student enrollment.

Recent employers of Krannert MBAs include: Bank of America, Citibank, Cummins, Discover Financial, General Electric, Guidant, IBM, Intel, Pratt & Whitney, Procter & Gamble, Raytheon, Samsung, United Technologies, and Wyeth. Manufacturers claimed 19 percent of Krannert's MBAs from 2007 to 2009; in that same period, 18 percent found work in consumer products, 16 percent in pharma/biotech, and 15 percent in each of technology and financial services.

ADMISSIONS CONTACT: BRENDA KNEBEL, DIRECTOR OF ADMISSIONS
ADDRESS: RAWLS HALL, SUITE 2020, 100 S. GRANT STREET, WEST LAFAYETTE, IN 47907-2076
PHONE: 765-494-0773 • FAX: 765-494-9841
E-MAIL: KRANNERTMASTERS@PURDUE.EDU • WEBSITE: KRANNERT.PURDUE.EDU

Student Life and Environment

Krannert "had the best building of any school I visited," one student notes, referring to the "well-equipped facilities in the recently completed Rawls Hall," which "is consistently rated the best building on campus (inaugurated in 2003). It is in the best location on campus, next to the student union building, and the main hill where all the shops and stores are, and only literally ten steps from the most popular bar in town." The building is a nexus of activity, hosting "classes, student club activities, social gatherings, coffee [houses], call outs, company presentations, guest speakers, team assignments, study groups, etc."

The school "really tries to make a community for all of its students," through campus "organizations that help new students, international students, and families become accustomed to life in West Lafayette. They host many cultural events to show the diversity of its student body and educate everyone [on the different] cultural background[s]." Campus life offers "a huge number of activities that one can take part in or lead. Be it clubs, the entrepreneurship center (Burton D. Morgan), international trips, club trips, case competitions, taskforces, GCSMI (Supply Chain Initiative), social activities, etc." Hometown West Lafayette has "plenty of restaurants to choose from and cost of living is very affordable." Purdue athletics is another big attraction, of course.

The student body includes "a truly international population that provides for diversity in culture, thoughts, and work styles." "It has truly been a melting pot experience," one student writes. Students are also diverse in age: "There are a number of students who are married [and some with] kids," while "at the same time, there are quite a few students that graduated from undergrad within a year of starting the MBA program."

Admissions

To apply to the Krannert School of Management, all candidates must submit an official undergraduate transcript, GMAT scores, a resume, letters of recommendation, and several admissions essays. The most recent entering class had a mean GPA of about 3.3 on a 4.0 scale, and an average GMAT score in the 640s. Women comprised 34 percent of the entering class. Approximately one-third of the entering class arrived with undergraduate degrees in business; almost as many majored in engineering at the undergraduate level.

FINANCIAL FACTS

Annual tuition (in-state/ out-of-state)	$21,624/$41,390
Fees	$693
Cost of books	$3,460
Room & board	$12,170
% of first-year students receiving aid	72
Average award package	$21,553
Average grant	$8,432
Average loan	$18,573
Average student loan debt	$38,975

ADMISSIONS

Admissions Selectivity Rating	88
# of applications received	679
% applicants accepted	35
% acceptees attending	43
Average GMAT	635
Range of GMAT	560–680
Average GPA	3.32
TOEFL required of international students	Yes
Minimum TOEFL (paper/computer)	575/235
Application fee	$60
International application fee	$75
Early application deadline	11/1
Early notification date	12/15
Regular application deadline	1/10
Regular application notification	2/20
Application Deadline/Notification	
Round 1:	11/1 / 12/15
Round 2:	1/10 / 2/20
Round 3:	2/1 / 3/20
Round 4:	3/1 / 4/1
Deferment available	Yes
Maximum length of deferment	1 year
Transfer students accepted	No
Non-fall admissions	No
Need-blind admissions	Yes

EMPLOYMENT PROFILE

Career Rating	94	**Grads Employed by Function% Avg. Salary**		
Percent employed at graduation	77	Marketing	(14%)	$76,240
Percent employed 3 months after graduation	91	Operations	(26%)	$80,728
		Consulting	(14%)	$83,000
Average base starting salary	$80,022	Management	(12%)	$80,409
Primary Source of Full-time Job Acceptances		Finance	(24%)	$78,250
School-facilitated activities	63(%)	Other	(3%)	$89,667
Graduate-facilitated activities	27(%)	**Top 5 Employers Hiring Grads**		

Top 5 Employers Hiring Grads
Amazon.com (8), Samsung Electronics (6), Bank of America (4), Cummins (4), Sears Holding and Proctor & Gamble Co. (4 each)

QUINNIPIAC UNIVERSITY
SCHOOL OF BUSINESS

GENERAL INFORMATION
Type of school	Private
Affiliation	No Affiliation

SURVEY SAYS...
Cutting-edge classes
Solid preparation in:
Teamwork

STUDENTS
Enrollment of parent institution	8,614
Enrollment of MBA Program	307
% male/female	48/52
% out-of-state	39
% part-time	66
% underrepresented minority	10
% international	21
Average age at entry	28
Average years work experience at entry	5.0

ACADEMICS
Academic Experience Rating	76
Profs interesting rating	81
Profs accesible rating	85
Student/faculty ratio	17:1
% female faculty	36
% underrepresented minority faculty	15
% part-time faculty	21

Joint Degrees
JD/MBA - 4 years

Prominent Alumni
Murray Lender '50, Co-Founder Lender's Bagels; Bruce Dumelin '71, CFO (retired) Bank of America; Joseph Onorato '71, CFO (retired) Echlin, Inc.; Terry Goodwin '67, VP & Mgr./Equity Trading (retired) Goldman Sachs

Academics

At Quinnipiac University, located in Hamden, Connecticut, a conventional MBA is offered along with options to specialize in Healthcare Management and Supply Chain Management. Students may also choose to pursue a CFA (Chartered Financial Analyst) certification. Quinnipiac also offers Internet classes to help students achieve these goals, as well as full online MBA program. The school of business is comprised of part-time professionals, as well as full-time students pursuing a joint BA/MBA or a joint BS/MBA. Part-time students can choose from evening classes or accelerated online courses, while the full-time program offers classes in the afternoons and evenings.

Students choose Quinnipiac because it's "strong in finance and accounting." It has an "excellent reputation," "hybrid MBA" program, and a "good teacher-student ratio." Students enjoy the small class sizes, claiming "the professors know all their students." Small class sizes translate into a "more personalized" educational experience. "Professors are very visible and very willing to help. They really invest their time in the students and understand the real-life issues (work, family obligations, etc.) that we face." Professors also bring "real-world experience" into the classroom, and "the courses keep up with current trends." Professors are "smart," "challenging," and "available." Students are often given group assignments, which culminate in a presentation. "This prepares you for presentations in the real world, as well as building your skills to work with others." Students emphasize the "practical" education they receive. Professors also take the time to "speak with students about their particular fields." Most agree they've had a "great experience" with Quinnipiac faculty.

The "classroom facilities are some of the best I've seen." The program has "high-tech equipment for presentations, a Financial Technology Center for real-time trading, and HD video monitors that constantly keep us up-to-date on current news." One student admits the facilities are what made Quinnipiac a top choice. "The administration has a solid strategy of how to make Quinnipiac a major university with many opportunities. Unfortunately, the MBA Director position has seen high turnover in recent years." Quinnipiac students admit its reputation is slowly growing. Still, they praise the administration's flexibility.

Career and Placement

Career services at the School of Business, include individual career counseling appointments, career fairs, on-campus recruiting, and mock interviews. If students need help writing resumes and cover letters, that is also provided. Additionally, there is an online tool called QU Career Connections where students can view job listings, add their resume, and sign up for interviews. The School of Business "has an extremely devoted team that works diligently to host network receptions, maintain the career website, assist with resumes, and regularly communicate with students." Also, there is "a new director of the business school who has worked very hard to make QU more competitive and to bring new employers to recruit." QU "has been great at providing work opportunities for all the students in many diverse fields in the business world." Part-time students are concurrently employed by some of the following organizations: Bayer, Yale New Haven Hospital, and United Technologies.

ADMISSIONS CONTACT: JENNIFER BOUTIN, ASSOCIATE DIRECTOR OF GRADUATE ADMISSIONS
ADDRESS: 275 MOUNT CARMEL AVE, N1-GRD, HAMDEN, CT 06518-1940
PHONE: 203-582-8672 • FAX: 203-582-3443
E-MAIL: GRADUATE@QUINNIPIAC.EDU • WEBSITE: WWW.QUINNIPIAC.EDU

Student Life and Environment

Quinnipiac is located in Hamden, Connecticut, a suburb of the city of New Haven. It has a population of just under 60,000 and is two hours north of New York City. Quinnipiac is "a beautiful campus located right outside of Sleeping Giant State Park." It's "safe and offers a great environment for learning and social life." Another student claims that "when you step foot on QU grounds, you just want to grab a book and start studying." The academic environment at Quinnipiac is described as "friendly, yet challenging" and "culturally diverse." "When working on a team project, students are very professional and contribute equally to the work." Students' ages vary somewhat. "There are older students, such as myself enrolled in the program (age 40+), but the majority are just starting their careers." They have a chance to mix by joining one of the "limited number of graduate clubs" available, but, "the graduate population is not very interested in participating in additional activities or socials." This may be because many older students have work and families. Due to their myriad obligations, "there is no time for life at school." However, some suggest that "all the students are connected and stay so through a variety of ways, like going out for dinners, meeting for classes, etc." Of those "'older students'" some hope for "more programs and options."

Admissions

In addition to the application, the admissions committee requires the following from its applicants: official transcripts for all post-secondary academic work; an official GMAT or GRE score report; a personal essay; undergraduate GPA; two letters of recommendation; and a current resume. The GMAT score and the undergraduate GPA are most important in the process. Also considered are work experience, extracurricular activities, and an interview. TOEFL scores are required for those whose native language is not English. The average GPA for admitted students is 3.25, and the average GMAT score is 530. There is a high acceptance rate at Quinnipiac, and the admissions process is rolling. The five-year BS/MBA program is open to Quinnipiac undergraduates only.

FINANCIAL FACTS

Annual tuition	$24,000
Fees	$666
Cost of books	$4,320
Room & board	
(on/off-campus)	$12,990/$14,830
% of students receiving aid	49
% of first-year students	
receiving aid	58
% of students receiving grants	10
Average award package	$19,753
Average grant	$8,142
Average loan	$19,781
Average student loan debt	$41,406

ADMISSIONS

Admissions Selectivity Rating	73
# of applications received	225
% applicants accepted	80
% acceptees attending	81
Average GMAT	530
Range of GMAT	460–630
Average GPA	3.36
TOEFL required of	
international students	Yes
Minimum TOEFL	
(paper/computer)	575/233
Application fee	$45
International application fee	$45
Deferment available	Yes
Maximum length	
of deferment	1 year
Transfer students accepted	Yes
Transfer application policy: up to 9 graduate transfer credits allowed from regionally accredited schools. The grades must be a B or better.	
Non-fall admissions	Yes
Need-blind admissions	Yes

RADFORD UNIVERSITY
COLLEGE OF BUSINESS AND ECONOMICS

Academics

Repeat business is one of the telltale signs of success in retail, and by that standard Radford University must be doing a pretty good job; a considerable number of students in our survey self-identified as former Radford undergrads, and nearly all cited their satisfaction during their first go-around as the reason for pursuing an MBA here. With an undergraduate population consisting of approximately 25 percent business majors, Radford has a large customer base from which to draw graduate students. You could say that business is booming at Radford's College of Business and Economics.

Radford now offers two MBA programs: a full-time program on the Radford campus and the Professional Part-time program on the Roanoke and Radford campuses. Radford MBAs tell us that their program "is general in nature" and that "students wanting to specialize in a specific segment of business, e.g., marketing, may be well-served to look elsewhere." They are quick to add, however, that the program "does prepare you for work in many areas of business and does not skimp on content or focus in doing so" and that "Those who want the knowledge and skills to run an organization, even a global one, will be hard-pressed to find a better school, especially for the price." Part-time students also appreciate the way the program is "geared toward people who work full-time jobs." While describing the Radford MBA as "a challenging part-time program," they note that convenient scheduling and professors who will "work with your work schedule to [help you] get through the MBA program" make it "easy for a working professional to get an MBA" here.

Radford's 36 credit hour curriculum is divided in a two-thirds, one-third split between required courses and electives (which constitute 12 hours). The program utilizes "a face-to-face presentation format" and includes a substantial writing component. "Small class sizes" and a faculty that "is very student-oriented (rather than concentrating on writing professional papers and books, they concentrate on teaching, which is a good thing)" make this a very student-friendly program. Professors "do an excellent job of tying in current events and international matters of interest," although some "don't seem to have much experience in the professional corporate world. Many seem to have spent most of their time in academia." MBA courses are offered in two locations: the main campus in Radford, Virginia, and the Roanoke Higher Education Center in Roanoke, Virginia. A distance learning option is also available. The RU MBA Program is moving towards differentiating its full-time and professional part-time programs. Full-time students have classes during the day and professional part-time classes will be held in the evenings in both Roanoke and Radford. Additional program support services will be provided for each of these groups.

Career and Placement

The Career Services Office at Radford University offers a variety of resources to undergraduates, graduates, and alumni. These include a virtual resume, internship, and a jobs database "where students and employers come together to post and view resumes and position openings," as well as workshops in resume and portfolio development, career fairs, and career-assessment tools. On-campus recruiters include Ameriprise Financial, DMG Securities, Ferguson Enterprises, Northwestern Mutual, State Farm, Wachovia, and the federal government.

ADMISSIONS CONTACT: MR. CHRISTOPHER H. NILES, DIRECTOR, RU MBA PROGRAM
ADDRESS: RU MBA OFFFICE, P.O. BOX 6956, RADFORD, VA 24142
PHONE: 540-831-6905 • FAX: 540-831-6655
E-MAIL: RUMBA@RADFORD.EDU. • WEBSITE: RUMBA.ASP.RADFORD.EDU

Student Life and Environment

The RU MBA program is "a mix of adult and young adult students." The latter group includes nearly all of the full-time students, a combination of recently minted American undergraduates and international students. The student body tends to be "young, eager to get into a professional setting, worried about the job market," "friendly, hard-working, and intelligent." Working professionals constitute a substantial minority whose experience and insights are welcomed by their younger peers.

Full-timers describe campus life as being "like any typical college student's life," with the "majority of time spent studying and preparing for class." Part-time students typically don't have time for the "many activities, clubs, and organizations that are at this school." Those who attend classes at the Roanoke Higher Education Center tell us that "the RHEC is a newly remodeled, high tech, and comfortable facility more suited to providing an appropriate atmosphere for educating older MBA students."

Hometown Radford is a small town in the Blue Ridge Mountains; Roanoke is about 45 miles away. The area is most amenable to outdoor enthusiasts, as it provides easy access to the Appalachian Trail, the New River, and Claytor Lake. Shopping, restaurants, nightlife, and such are not in great supply, students warn, although the proximity of Roanoke helps to make up for this deficiency. Charleston, West Virginia, and Greensboro, North Carolina, are also within a reasonable driving distance.

Admissions

Admission to Radford's MBA program is considered via a full portfolio review. Application requires successful completion of an undergraduate degree with a preferred minimum GPA of 2.75. Applicants must also submit an official report of GMAT or GRE scores (applicants with five or more years of work experience can apply for a waiver of the GMAT or GRE requirement); two letters of recommendation; a resume of work experience; and statement of intent. Also, applicants must demonstrate business proficiency through accredited collegiate preparation in the following foundation areas or equivalents: economics, accounting, finance, and statistics. Students can earn credit for some of these foundation areas through CLEP testing. In addition to meeting the above requirements, international students must also provide a certified letter of sponsorship and a bank statement proving sufficient finances to cover their first year of study. Those whose first language is not English must submit TOEFL scores.

FINANCIAL FACTS

Annual tuition (in-state/ out-of-state)	$6,482/$15,050
Fees	$2,888
Cost of books	$1,100
Room & board	$7,498
% of students receiving aid	39
% of first-year students receiving aid	48
% of students receiving grants	8
Average award package	$7,800
Average grant	$2,390

ADMISSIONS

Admissions Selectivity Rating	72
# of applications received	48
% applicants accepted	79
% acceptees attending	63
Average GMAT	506
Range of GMAT	440–570
Average GPA	3.24
TOEFL required of international students	No
Minimum TOEFL (paper/computer)	550/213
Application fee	$50
International application fee	$50
Deferment available	Yes
Maximum length of deferment	1 year
Transfer students accepted	Yes

Transfer application policy: Transfer students complete the same application process as other students. They may transfer in a maximum of twelve credit hours. Individual decisions on transferability of credits are made based on a syllabus review.

Non-fall admissions	Yes
Need-blind admissions	Yes

RENSSELAER POLYTECHNIC INSTITUTE
LALLY SCHOOL OF MANAGEMENT AND TECHNOLOGY

Academics

Rensselaer Polytechnic Institute's Lally School of Management and Technology offers numerous graduate business programs with a strong focus on technology and close ties to the Northeast business community. For hard-working students, Lally's MBA is fast-paced and efficient: taking a full course load, required credit hours can be completed in a mere 12 months. Those who want to tailor their degree or make a career change can pursue a specialization module in addition to core courses, but they'll still have a diploma within 17 to 24 months. (Currently, the school offers optional specializations in entrepreneurship, finance, information systems, marketing, and new product development, business analytics, supply chain management, and global enterprise management.) For local professionals, Lally also offers a flexible full-time MBA. In addition, the school operates numerous master's programs in related business fields, such as an MS in financial engineering and risk analytics, and an MS in Technology Commercialization and Entrepreneurship. These specialized programs "raise the level of the MBA program by exposing MBA students to other advanced disciplines and specializations so that MBA students, upon graduation, are already familiar with working with field specialists such as financial engineers."

While the delivery format differs, MBA programs at Lally comprise 45 credit hours of coursework, with the option of extending the degree to 60 credits. The core curriculum takes a cross-disciplinary approach to business, and several courses are taught by teams of professors from different disciplines. As students point out, Rensselaer is a "world-class research institution," and the MBA program draws on the school's historic strength in technology and applied science. Here, students benefit from a "very good mix of technology management classes with traditional finance, marketing, and operations management classes." Business issues in fields like information technology or nanotechnology are often discussed in the classroom, and "many of the MBA students are working on commercializing technologies." A student elaborates, "The greatest strength of RPI is the interdisciplinary nature of all of the degree programs. For the Lally School specifically, its strength is the integration of technology into the classroom, preparing students to work in the high-tech 21st century workplace."

"The faculty is fantastic" at Rensselaer, and "small class sizes help [students] take advantage of their experience and research." While "Professors and classes get an A-plus," students say Rensselaer's "administration gets a C-plus." Overseen by "a multi-layer bureaucracy," there can be plenty of red tape. Fortunately, the personnel at the business school are approachable and friendly. "The administrators understand the issues that students have and are very patient and understanding, and go above and beyond to help students."

Career and Placement

Lally's Career Services Team manages a comprehensive suite of workshops, professional development tools, and a portfolio of employment opportunities. The Career Team also oversees employer information sessions, MBA career panels, and trips to New York City and Boston to meet with alumni and provide career shadowing opportunities. Lally has a strong reputation in the local region, and students find that the "alumni [were] extremely helpful during my career search!"

ADMISSIONS CONTACT: GINA O'CONNOR, ASSOCIATE DEAN OF ACADEMIC AFFAIRS
ADDRESS: 110 EIGHTH STREET–PITTSBURGH BUILDING, TROY, NY 12180-3590
PHONE: 518-276-6565 • FAX: 518-276-8190
E-MAIL: LALLYMBA@RPI.EDU • WEBSITE: LALLYSCHOOL.RPI.EDU

FINANCIAL FACTS

Annual tuition	$43,350
Fees	$1,949
Cost of books	$2,545
Room & board	
(on/off-campus)	$11,795/$11,795

ADMISSIONS

Admissions Selectivity Rating	81
# of applications received	199
% applicants accepted	64
% acceptees attending	52
Average GMAT	652
Range of GMAT	608–700
Average GPA	3.22
TOEFL required of	
international students	Yes
Minimum TOEFL	
(paper/computer)	577/230
International application fee	$75
Early application deadline	12/15
Regular application deadline	6/15
Deferment available	Yes
Maximum length	
of deferment	1 year, must reapply
Transfer students accepted	No
Non-fall admissions	No
Need-blind admissions	Yes

Companies that have recently recruited at Lally include Accenture, American Express, Albany Molecular Research Corporation, Bank of America, Blue Slate Solutions, Boeing, Citigroup, Clorox, Deloitte, ECG Consulting Group, Foster Miller, General Electric, Honeywell, IBM, Microsoft, Mimeo.com, Phillips, Proctor & Gamble, United Technologies, and Xerox. More than 40 percent of graduates stay in the Northeast region.

Student Life and Environment

The full-time MBA program at Lally comprises "roughly 15 hours per week in class," plus another 20–25 hours per week doing homework, projects, and readings. Stimulated by the team-oriented curriculum, "Study groups emerge between students, and project teams learn to work with each other and spend time together outside of the classroom." Beyond academics, students also might get together for mingling and career development opportunities. In particular, "The Graduate Management Student Association does a great job organizing social and networking events."

The MBA program is targeted at those with work experience. For those coming direct from RPI or other undergraduate programs, there is an International Scholars Program that includes visits to several companies in Rome and Shanghai as part of the Global Enterprise Management Concentration. It is easy to participate in the multitude of activities on the larger Rensselaer campus. For example, a current MBA candidate tells us, "I am involved in multiple performing arts groups, including Sheer Idiocy, the improvisational comedy troupe; WRPI, the college radio station; and The Players, the traditional theater organization. I am also the Student Outreach Coordinator for the Admissions Office." Not everyone, however, gets so involved in campus life. At Lally, "Some students are detached from the program, but others are very engaged and make the experience very good."

Admissions

To apply to Lally's graduate business programs, students must submit a completed application form, two personal essays, standardized scores, undergraduate transcripts, two letters of recommendation, and, if applicable, TOEFL scores. Candidates are also encouraged to schedule an interview with the admissions department. The school accepts both the GMAT and the GRE. A recent incoming class had a mean GMAT score of 653 and an average undergraduate GPA of 3.34, and more than 50 percent majored in a technical field as an undergraduate. Those far removed from school or a test-taking setting can submit the ETS Personal Potential Index(PPI) to supplement their application.

EMPLOYMENT PROFILE

		Grads Employed by Function% Avg. Salary	
Career Rating	88		
Percent employed at graduation	33	Marketing	(35%) $64,200
Percent employed 3 months		Operations	(10%) $61,000
after graduation	66	Consulting	(5%)$85,000
Average base starting salary	$65,133	Management	(10%) $67,000
Primary Source of Full-time Job Acceptances		Finance	(15%) $67,000
School-facilitated activities	8(40%)	Other	(25%) $62,000
Graduate-facilitated activities	6(30%)	**Top 5 Employers Hiring Grads**	
Unknown	6(30%)	Deloitte Consulting (1), Proctor & Gamble (1), GE (1), TIAA-CREF (1), Bank of America (1)	

RICE UNIVERSITY
JESSE H. JONES GRADUATE SCHOOL OF BUSINESS

GENERAL INFORMATION

Type of school	Private
Affiliation	No Affiliation
Academic calendar	Semester

SURVEY SAYS...
Good peer network
Solid preparation in:
Finance, Accounting, Presentation
skills, Quantitative skills

STUDENTS

Enrollment of parent institution	6,082
Enrollment of MBA Program	696
% male/female	72/28
% out-of-state	28
% part-time	44
% underrepresented minority	14
% international	25
Average age at entry	28
Average years work experience at entry	5.0

ACADEMICS

Academic Experience Rating	95
Profs interesting rating	94
Profs accesible rating	95
Student/faculty ratio	6:1
% female faculty	20
% underrepresented minority faculty	20
% part-time faculty	49

Joint Degrees

MBA/MD (with Baylor College of
Medicine); MBA/Master of
Bioengineering; MBA/Master of
Chemical Engineering; MBA/Master of
Civil Engineering; MBA/Master of
Computational and Applied
Mathematics; MBA/Master of
Computer Science; MBA/Master of
Electrical Engineering; MBA/Master of
Environmental Engineering;
MBA/Master of Materials Science;
MBA/Master of Mechanical
Engineering; MBA/Master of Statistics;
MBA/Professional Science Master

Academics

Learning at the Jones School at Rice University is a collaborative effort. So much so that students may feel they are "learning just as much from [their] classmates as from [their] teachers." The diversity of the student body in ethnicity, background, and thought lends to a broad range of topics and discussions in the classroom and a vast array of "different ideas" to consider. The small program and small class size means "everybody is on a first-name basis with each other," and creates a family-like environment.

The state of Texas is a selling point for many pursuing the finance and energy fields. The school's "convenient" Houston location offers "the greatest exposure to the energy industry" and the school's "reputation is the best in town." Students will have to work hard to earn their degrees here. "The first semester of first year is extremely competitive, but eases as the program progresses." Upon being accepted to Rice, one must be well organized. "The work load is very heavy, which teach[es] the students how to multi-task, prioritize, and be efficient with time."

The success of the Jones School program can in part be attributed to continual improvements by administration. "The school is constantly looking for feedback and addressing issues on an ongoing basis." The school really is what each student makes of it. "Every student has the opportunity to make a positive impact, improve the program, and contribute to the overall experience." A high-quality and "accessible" teaching staff is also a hallmark at Jones School. "The professors are very approachable and willing to discuss numerous topics. Overall the academics have been challenging but rewarding." Professors provide a perfect mix of academia and research for an enriching classroom experience, and they are also keenly aware of the content that each colleague is teaching at any given time. "This creates a holistic program wherein each class complements the others."

Campus facilities are described as "very nice" and "new," and the environment is remarkably "clean." Although course offerings and networking opportunities are rich in the finance and energy fields, some would like to see this carry over to other areas of study. "National recognition" was also mentioned as an area of potential weakness. Although the school's graduates are well received in the immediate areas of internships and job placement, Rice could still stand to "Build [a] better national brand."

Career and Placement

The "dynamic" metropolitan city of Houston is "a great location to look for a new career." The school is "well connected with Houston's energy community" and "energy and financial firms are strong here and come to Rice often." Additionally, Rice alumni are "tremendously helpful."

Networking on campus is a common occurrence. "Partio," Party on the Patio, is a popular way to spend Thursday nights. Representatives from various companies attend, and students have a chance to spend time with them in a casual setting." At this event, "students get together to talk about their week, job search, and also network with alumni and current recruiters." Among other programs, Rice also has "a strong chapter" of MBA Women International and a highly-regarded Action Learning Project which is "an incredibly rich and rewarding experience to put our skills into action."

ADMISSIONS CONTACT: MELISSA BLAKESLEE, DIRECTOR OF ADMISSIONS
ADDRESS: MBA ADMISSIONS, PO BOX 2932-MS 531, JONES SCHOOL, HOUSTON, TX 77252-2932
PHONE: 888-844-4773 • FAX: 713-348-6147
E-MAIL: RICEMBA@RICE.EDU • WEBSITE: WWW.BUSINESS.RICE.EDU/

Student Life and Environment

The gym is a popular place for busy students to "vent stress and keep healthy while taking on a rigorous course load." Its location "right in front of the business building" provides ample opportunity for a quick "Ping-Pong game break" or even a "squash game" to invigorate students during study sessions. Many students praise the school's administration, which "works very hard to create a fun community for both academic and social events." Administrators are even known to send emails to students "whenever there is free food after an event." "Facilities and amenities are second to none at Rice."

The campus is full of students who are "goal driven, smart, [and] diverse," and who "are always willing to lend a helping hand." When students are not visiting the "tons of clubs" or bars and restaurants on campus, they venture into Houston where people "are incredibly welcoming and friendly."

Admissions

Rice looks for well-rounded students with a proven track record. The admissions office seeks for students who have a high level of preparedness. One must possess a minimum 3.0 undergraduate GPA to be considered for acceptance. Most students accepted have an average GMAT score of 673 and an average GPA of 3.4. Work experience, resume, and interview skills are equally important with students averaging four years of work upon enrollment. Letters of recommendations and well-written essays can serve to bolster one's application. Students should also be ready to submit samples of writing or portfolios if they are asked. Admission applications to Jesse H. Jones Graduate School of Business are accepted in four rounds: 11/7, 1/9, 2/20, and 4/2.

Prominent Alumni

James S. Turley, Chairman and CEO, Ernst & Young LLP

FINANCIAL FACTS

Annual tuition	$48,500
Fees	$2,972
Cost of books	$1,500
Room & board (on/off-campus)	$10,350/$11,700
% of students receiving grants	89
Average award package	$43,393
Average grant	$28,865
Average loan	$37,390
Average student loan debt	$55,291

ADMISSIONS

Admissions Selectivity Rating	96
# of applications received	705
% applicants accepted	27
% acceptees attending	62
Average GMAT	673
Range of GMAT	640–720
Average GPA	3.40
TOEFL required of international students	Yes
Minimum TOEFL (paper/computer)	600/250
Application fee	$125
International application fee	$125
Application Deadline/Notification	
Round 1:	10/29 / 12/7
Round 2:	1/7 / 3/1
Round 3:	2/25 / 4/5
Round 4:	4/8 / 5/10
Deferment available	Yes
Maximum length of deferment	varies depending on student's situation
Transfer students accepted	No
Non-fall admissions	No
Need-blind admissions	Yes

EMPLOYMENT PROFILE

Career Rating	98	**Grads Employed by Function% Avg. Salary**	
Percent employed at graduation	77	Marketing	(10%) $97,543
Percent employed 3 months		Operations	(7%) $91,933
after graduation	94	Consulting	(22%)$110,030
Average base starting salary	$99,506	Management	(14%) $97,364
Primary Source of Full-time Job Acceptances		Finance	(34%) $97,607
School-facilitated activities	59(66%)	HR	(4%) $95,000
Graduate-facilitated activities	13(14%)	MIS	(3%) $89,500
Unknown	18(20%)	Other	(4%) $90,667

Top 5 Employers Hiring Grads
ExxonMobil (5), Ernst&Young (5), Cameron (3), FMC Technologies (3), ConocoPhillips (2)

ROCHESTER INSTITUTE OF TECHNOLOGY
E. PHILIP SAUNDERS COLLEGE OF BUSINESS

GENERAL INFORMATION

Type of school	Private
Affiliation	No Affiliation
Academic calendar	Semester

SURVEY SAYS...
Cutting-edge classes
Solid preparation in:
General management, Teamwork,
Communication/interpersonal skills,
Doing business in a global economy

STUDENTS

Enrollment of parent institution	17,950
Enrollment of MBA Program	191
% male/female	70/30
% out-of-state	50
% part-time	42
% underrepresented minority	15
% international	43
Average age at entry	26
Average years work experience at entry	3.1

ACADEMICS

Academic Experience Rating	**81**
Profs interesting rating	82
Profs accesible rating	.85
Student/faculty ratio	8:1
% female faculty	28
% underrepresented minority faculty	13
% part-time faculty	9

Prominent Alumni
James Richard Salzano, President, Clarks Companies North America; Sean R.H. Bratches, EVP, Sales and Marketing, ESPN; Donald James Truesdale, Partner, Managing Director, Goldman Sachs; Frank S. Sklarsky, EVP and CFO, Tyco International Ltd.; Kathleen A. McNulty, Sr. VP and CIO, Schwan Food

Academics

Located in upstate New York, Rochester Institute of Technology is known for its academic excellence in technology and applied science. Accordingly, RIT's MBA programs provide a "great blend of management and technical education," preparing students for the realities of the workplace through practical instruction, teamwork, and applied learning. Within the MBA curriculum, "Courses are updated frequently to allow for new events, technologies, and information." (In recent years, "green sustainability is growing in importance," as is entrepreneurship.) A major benefit of the program is the "the wide array of concentrations offered," including such unique offerings as digital marketing, quality and applied statistics, and environmentally sustainable management—as well as more traditional business fields like accounting and supply chain management. In addition to established concentrations, students can tailor their education through elective courses in other RIT departments, like public policy or web programming.

The MBA can be completed on a full-time or part-time basis, with classes offered in the daytime and the evening, as well as online. Course work is "fast-paced" and challenging, yet students like the school's academic calendar, saying the "quarter system is great because it keeps things moving at a fast pace." Despite the "vigorous schedule," "Professors are extremely flexible if students need to miss class for work." On that note, most RIT instructors "know students' names and take interest in the students' personal lives." With an average class size of just 25 students, "Professors go out of their way to be sure concepts are well understood and topics are relevant and beneficial to us." Even in the classroom, RIT emphasizes practical skills, and most professors "have significant corporate experience and tie it well with the academics to offer an enriched experience." In fact, many RIT instructors "still work as consultants for major companies."

Students who received an undergraduate business degree from RIT can "waive some classes" in the MBA program, or, if they are currently enrolled, complete a BS and MBA through on accelerated five-year schedule. Taking advantage of this attractive opportunity, many "students seem to come directly from undergrad," though "Each class tends to have at least some students who have been in the workplace." Furthermore, RIT undergraduates "are required to have a good deal of co-op (internship) experience before they graduate (usually between six months to one year or more.)" For those who want to build on their real-world credentials, RIT offers plenty of "hands-on, experiential, practical learning" experiences. Here, students can participate in optional internships or co-op work experiences, business plan and case competitions, and team-based projects both on and off campus. Among other offerings, the school's "Innovation Center is a new-business incubator, and they are always asking for the business students to come and consult for them."

Career and Placement

Serving the undergraduate and graduate community, RIT's Cooperative Education and Career Services offers robust career preparation services, including an executive-in-residence program, mentorship program, online job resources, career fairs, and networking events. While the campus maintains a robust recruiting program, "the greatest weakness is the lack of opportunities for business majors at the career fairs." Based on the school's strength in engineering, technology, and science, "Most of the companies at the career fair are looking to hire tech students with very few hiring management students." As such, "The campus is still trying to get more interest from the business community to send companies here for new talent."

ADMISSIONS CONTACT: DIANE ELLISON, DIRECTOR, PART-TIME & GRADUATE ENROLLMENT
ADDRESS: 105 LOMB MEMORIAL DRIVE, ROCHESTER, NY 14623
PHONE: 585-475-7284 • FAX: 585-475-5476
E-MAIL: GRADINFO@RIT.EDU • WEBSITE: WWW.RITMBA.COM

In recent years, full-time MBA candidates reported a median starting salary of more than $52,000, with a range between $30,000 and $90,000. They took jobs at Alstom Signaling, Bausch & Lomb, Carrier Corporation, Citibank, Coopers & Lybrand, Deloitte & Touche, Eastman Kodak, Global Crossing, Harris Corporation, IBM, JP Morgan Chase, Johnson & Johnson, M&T Bank, Merck & Company Inc., Paychex, Toyota, Unisys Corp., Wegmans, and Xerox.

Student Life and Environment

Part of a large, private, comprehensive university, Saunders College of Business offers a well-rounded student experience, which appeals to both part-time and full-time students. Here, "the facilities are good and campus activities are diversified," and there are plenty of "great resources available"—including an "outstanding" gym. As you'd expect from a technical school, business students enjoy contemporary technology in the classroom and "have access to amazing equipment" to prepare their "group presentations." In fact, "The whole campus has Wi-Fi, and you can even find plugs near picnic tables and other outdoor locations for your laptop!"

On this large campus, students "come from about 20 different countries," creating a "very diverse and global environment." All totaled, you'll probably meet "more part-time, employed MBA students" than full-time students at RIT, though there are also plenty of recent graduates who are completing the MBA full-time. While they enthusiastically participate in class, "It is hard for graduate students to be more involved due to the late night classes and other obligations." Still, even these students acknowledge that "There are lots of opportunities on campus for fun and Rochester is a great place to live." Among full-timers, "The students are friendly and very focused when it comes to school, but don't shy away from playing the occasional poker game now and then."

Admissions

To be considered for admission to RIT's graduate business programs, students must have a minimum undergraduate GPA of 3.0 and a GMAT score of 520 or higher. In addition to a student's academic record and test scores, RIT evaluates a student based on his or her letters of recommendation, resume, and personal statement. While many full-time students join the program directly after undergraduate work, most part-time students have three to five years of professional experience before starting the program.

FINANCIAL FACTS

Annual tuition	$34,659
Fees	$228
Cost of books	$1,950
Room & board (on/off-campus)	$10,413
% of students receiving aid	75
% of first-year students receiving aid	75
% of students receiving grants	65
Average award package	$24,000
Average grant	$10,398
Average loan	$25,000
Average student loan debt	$40,000

ADMISSIONS

Admissions Selectivity Rating	79
# of applications received	256
% applicants accepted	58
% acceptees attending	42
Average GMAT	575
Range of GMAT	530–630
Average GPA	3.34
TOEFL required of international students	Yes
Minimum TOEFL (paper/computer)	580/237
Application fee	$60
International application fee	$60
Regular application deadline	8/1
Deferment available	Yes
Maximum length of deferment	1 year
Transfer students accepted	Yes

Transfer application policy: Transfer up to 3 courses if relevant to program. Grade of B or better. Credits must be earned within 5 years of transferring to RIT.

Non-fall admissions	Yes
Need-blind admissions	Yes

EMPLOYMENT PROFILE

Career Rating	87	Grads Employed by Function	% Avg. Salary
Percent employed at graduation	40	Marketing	(18%) $52,400
Percent employed 3 months after graduation	73	Operations	(7%) $43,833
		Consulting	(2%)
Average base starting salary	$54,264	Management	(17%) $45,875
Primary Source of Full-time Job Acceptances		Finance	(34%) $57,777
School-facilitated activities	57(65%)	HR	(3%)
Graduate-facilitated activities	19(21%)	MIS	(17%) $50,167
Unknown	12(14%)	Other	(1%)

Top 5 Employers Hiring Grads
Epic Systems (3), Pricewaterhouse Cooper (2), Wegmans (2), Bausch and Lomb (2), Garlock Sealing Technoloogy (2)

ROLLINS COLLEGE
CRUMMER GRADUATE SCHOOL OF BUSINESS

GENERAL INFORMATION

Type of school	Private
Affiliation	No Affiliation
Academic calendar	Semester

SURVEY SAYS...
Students love Winter Park, FL
Solid preparation in:
Communication/interpersonal skills,
Presentation skills

STUDENTS

Enrollment of parent institution	3,237
Enrollment of MBA Program	317
% male/female	56/44
% out-of-state	24
% part-time	60
% underrepresented minority	10
% international	13
Average age at entry	26
Average years work experience at entry	5.0

ACADEMICS

Academic Experience Rating	92
Profs interesting rating	92
Profs accesible rating	89
Student/faculty ratio	13:1
% female faculty	13
% underrepresented minority faculty	13
% part-time faculty	0

Prominent Alumni
Allen E. Keen, Chairman & CEO;
Tom McEvoy, President-operations;
Stan Gale, Chairman-operations;
Erin Wallace, Executive Vice
President-operations; F. Duane
Ackerman, Chairman Emeritus

Academics

The Rollins College Crummer School of Business is a small school that offers personalized attention and a growing national reputation that "will only get stronger in the coming years." The school offers a "top entrepreneurship and career development center," Six Sigma certification, and has a strong international business offering that is particularly germane to its Florida location, which is "quickly becoming a hub for international business, especially with Latin America." Teaching is socratic, and "the level of inclusion and the depth of the courses" mean that students are constantly "learning at a rapid rate."

Rollins uses a team-based approach and experiential learning in order to increase the practicality of the degree, and the "very challenging and intense" first year cohort component sees the creation of student teams that last the entire the entire year. There is a good balance between reading, research, teamwork ("an integral part of the MBA program") and exams, and "students need to be proficient in many types of communication including verbal, written, and non-verbal." The school pressures students "to prioritize acquisition of knowledge over grades," although the relationship between them is also well-recognized and acknowledged.

Rollins offers three MBA programs: the Early Advantage MBA, which is a full-time day program for recent college graduates and career changers; the Professional MBA, for people with more work experience (and who often continue working throughout); and the Executive MBA, for mid- to senior-level professionals. The "always available" faculty are former or current business professionals "[who] have had very impressive careers in their respective fields" and are "quick to offer advice based on their own personal experience." They "clearly have a vested interest in the success of their students," and "contribute impressive and diverse backgrounds to their different areas of focus."

Career and Placement

"Rollins is run like a professional business," and challenging coursework by day is complimented by "social and networking events by night." The lauded career center is "absolutely essential" in helping students to find internships and jobs, and there are "ample networking opportunities" in this regionally prestigious program. Many agree that quite a few events and resources seem "geared for young, just-graduated students," and the school could stand to recognize "that there are a lot of returning students. even in the early advantage program."

Because students are not graded on a curve, "there is a strong feeling of camaraderie." In addition, the alumni network is "small but very strong": "Most executives in Florida have graduated from Rollins and all are willing to network with students." Top employers of Rollins grads include The Walt Disney Co., SAP, Siemens Energy, Fidelity Investments, and CNL Financial Group, Inc.

ADMISSIONS CONTACT: JACQUELINE BRITO, ASSISTANT DEAN
ADDRESS: 1000 HOLT AVE. - 2722, WINTER PARK, FL 32789-4499
PHONE: 407-646-2405 • FAX: 407-646-2522
E-MAIL: MBAADMISSIONS@ROLLINS.EDU • WEBSITE: WWW.ROLLINS.EDU/MBA

Student Life and Environment

The location of the "beautiful" campus (not far from Orlando) is "fabulous," and the school's reach into the community is "unparalleled," as well. The small size (cohorts are typically 30-50 students) creates "a familial atmosphere," and "you can enjoy your free time near the lake or at swimming pool or just sit and chat with your friends." Students tend to be focused on class, but "try hard to not let the course load take over their lives." "Everyone has other things going on outside of school," says one. Rollins tends to cater to students a few years out of undergrad, so "one of the defining qualities of the school is our youth." Along with that comes "a bevy of bright ideas, high energy, and a very competitive environment." There "really is room for anything that a student wants to do," and the administration is happy to assist with club organizations and encourages the formation of new groups. "My overall academic experience has been tough, fair, and very rewarding," says a student.

Admissions

Applicants to Crummer's EAMBA program must provide the school with the following: official transcripts for all undergraduate, graduate, and professional schoolwork; an official GMAT score report; statement of purpose; two confidential evaluations; and a resume. Interviews are conducted only at the school's invitation. Applicants to the Executive MBA program must meet all of the above requirements (though GMAT scores are only needed conditionally for some), in addition to a required interview and a strongly encouraged proof of support from their employer. PMBA applicants must interview as part of the application process as well.

FINANCIAL FACTS

Annual tuition	$33,000
Fees	$220
Cost of books	$2,400
Room & board	$15,000
% of students receiving aid	52
% of first-year students receiving aid	41
% of students receiving grants	52
Average award package	$47,176
Average grant	$47,176
Average loan	$29,584
Average student loan debt	$59,169

ADMISSIONS

Admissions Selectivity Rating	89
# of applications received	170
% applicants accepted	37
% acceptees attending	67
Average GMAT	580
Range of GMAT	500–670
Average GPA	3.44
TOEFL required of international students	Yes
Application fee	$50
International application fee	$50
Application Deadline/Notification	
Round 1:	2/1 /
Round 2:	5/1 /
Round 3:	8/1 /
Deferment available	Yes
Maximum length of deferment	1 year
Transfer students accepted	Yes

Transfer application policy: The school accepts up to 6 credits transferred from an MBA program that is accredited by the AACSB.

Non-fall admissions	Yes
Need-blind admissions	Yes

EMPLOYMENT PROFILE

Career Rating	80	**Grads Employed by Function% Avg. Salary**	
Percent employed at graduation	49	Marketing	(3325%) $46,429
Percent employed 3 months		Operations	(6%) $44,000
after graduation	29	Consulting	(12%) $50,833
Average base starting salary	$48,253	Finance	(25%) $54,938
Primary Source of Full-time Job Acceptances		HR	(3%) $50,000
School-facilitated activities	2228(43%)	MIS	(3%) $41,600
Graduate-facilitated activities	28(43%)	Other	(18%) $37,500
Unknown	9(14%)	**Top 5 Employers Hiring Grads**	

Top 5 Employers Hiring Grads
The Walt Disney Co. (4), SAP (2), Siemens Energy (2), Fidelity Investments (2), CNL Financial Group, Inc. (2)

ROTTERDAM SCHOOL OF MANAGEMENT
ERASMUS UNIVERSITY

GENERAL INFORMATION

Type of school	Public
Affiliation	No Affiliation

SURVEY SAYS...

Students love Rotterdam, Netherlands
Solid preparation in:
Finance, Teamwork, Quantitative skills

STUDENTS

Enrollment of MBA Program	140
% male/female	67/33
% international	94
Average age at entry	29
Average years work experience at entry	6.0

ACADEMICS

Academic Experience Rating	**69**
Profs interesting rating	65
Profs accesible rating	65
Student/faculty ratio	1:1
% female faculty	16
% part-time faculty	12

Joint Degrees

MBA Dual Degree Programme with CUHK-12 months

Academics

Future international business moguls choose Rotterdam School of Mangement, Erasmus University (RSM) for two simple reasons: The school provides "the most international MBA" experience in the world, and Rotterdam is in the heart of the EEC, with "easy access" to Germany and the "EU labor market." RSM provides a "very challenging, positive learning environment," but its intensive 12-month MBA program is not for the faint of heart. The "workload is heavy," and the curriculum is front-loaded (students take 11 general management courses in the first two semesters). During this period, the day "starts at 9:30 A.M. with classes and ends at 7:00 P.M. with some group work or . . . [an] assignment." Overworked students take comfort in the fact that their professors are "excellent! They clearly enjoy teaching their subject matters, and because they are from all over the world, we get different perspectives in class." Students also point out that "the small class size means we have more opportunities to form close relationships with the program staff." During the third semester, students choose an advanced course from one of four areas of specialization (finance, marketing, or strategy). The final semester is an elective curriculum. All academic work in residency at RSM is conducted in English.

With one eye trained on the executive job market and the other on skill development and business knowledge, Rotterdam is what "b-school should be"; that is, "practical and academic at the same time." The Personal Leadership Development program, a mandatory 12-month experiential course, adds additional value. One student sums it up: "In hindsight I would not have gone to any other business school. RSM offers the right balance of soft and hard skills." "The school [also] has a strong sense of social responsibility." "I am now equipped to be a stronger and more sensitive businessperson," writes one satisfied student.

Career and Placement

RSM MBAs can look forward to bright and lucrative careers. While the school is responsible for connecting students with optional internships and half of post-MBA jobs, students also find significant career opportunities within an ever growing alumni network and elsewhere. Companies recruiting at RSM include ING Ban, ABN Amro, Johnson & Johnson, Deloitte, Amazon, AT Kearney. Top recruiters of 2012 are Philips, Infosys, PwC Consulting, Aligntech. The main goal of career services is to facilitate progress towards the best suitable job after graduation.

Student Life and Environment

RSM "Students form a strong and very connected group," students say. "Everyone is automatically a member of every club. It's your responsibility to contribute as much or as little to the events. For example, though you may not be in any entrepreneurial courses, you are automatically invited to [hear] every entrepreneurial speaker on campus. And once you arrive, you are welcome in the room." The collegial atmosphere is "perfect and wonderful," says one MBA candidate. "I'd like to go back to the first semester and to start again." Even so, students are "extremely driven." "Almost half want to be entrepreneurs or have owned businesses." RSM's "inspiring and challenging" students don't shrink from competition or from giving "positive and constructive criticism."

Diversity is no afterthought here—it's the reason MBA candidates choose RSM. Students say that the "international perspective was a big draw. Several other [schools] claimed to be international, but mostly had over 50 percent from one or two backgrounds." RSM, on the other hand, "has 50 nationalities and only small clusters from the same backgrounds." This means that students learn "a lot from classmates," and "There is no ruling racial group in our class." "It is just great!" enthuses one student. "A mix of cultures brings so many good things out of each student that it is almost like magic. The amount of kindness that I've experienced is just overwhelming." Demographically speaking, a preponderance of the students are European and Asian, with large Indian and Taiwanese communities; the average student is in his or her late 20s, with an undergraduate background in business or economics and more than five years of pre-MBA work experience. A quarter of MBA candidates are women. Partners and spouses "have banded together" to form "a supportive network," "and routinely have nights out on the town."

Admissions

RSM follows a personal approach to admissions which means they only encourage candidate with potential to apply—good news to the self-selected pool of MBA candidates whose passion for international business and culture brings them to RSM. Admission is no cakewalk—successful applicants report an average GMAT score of 640 and a minimum of three years' work experience—but the numbers give good reason for optimism. The most recent application requires essays on career goals, hobbies and interests, and difficult decisions—slightly more personal topics than appear on American applications. Submit translations of your academic transcripts if they are written in languages other than English, and prepare for an interview if you make the first cut. Admission is rolling.

FINANCIAL FACTS

Annual tuition	$50,750
Fees	$65
Cost of books	$1,600
Room & board	$18,000
% of first-year students receiving aid	17
Average award package	$20,356
Average grant	$9,744
Average loan	$54,316
Average student loan debt	$59,225

ADMISSIONS

Admissions Selectivity Rating	73
Average GMAT	650
TOEFL required of international students	No
Application fee	50 euros
International application fee	50 euros
Regular application deadline	11/5
Deferment available	No
Transfer students accepted	No
Non-fall admissions	Yes
Need-blind admissions	Yes

EMPLOYMENT PROFILE

Career Rating	85	Grads Employed by Function% Avg. Salary	
Percent employed at graduation	55	Marketing	(32%)
Percent employed 3 months after graduation	26	Operations	(8%)
		Consulting	(16%)
Average base starting salary	$86,163	Management	(11%)
Primary Source of Full-time Job Acceptances		Finance	(24%)
School-facilitated activities	62(63%)	HR	(0%)
Graduate-facilitated activities	37(38%)	MIS	(4%)
Unknown	1(1%)	Other	(5%)
		Top 5 Employers Hiring Grads	
		Philips (7), Shell (3), KPMG (3), Samsung (3), Nike (2)	

ROWAN UNIVERSITY
THE ROHRER COLLEGE OF BUSINESS

Academics

Offering "a good location, good tuition, and good environment" in the Philadelphia area (and, thanks to the recent addition of online classes, beyond), Rowan University's Rohrer College of Business MBA program delivers what local students want. As one such student explains, "The school has a good ranking within schools in the Northeast and has a tuition rate that could not be matched by comparably ranked schools. Short of someone else paying for my education, it was the best value, period."

Part-time students love the flexible scheduling at Rowan. Classes meet for three hours once a week (typically on a weeknight, although some courses meet on Saturday mornings). The program is available online, further enhancing the convenience of the program. The curriculum commences with 27 hours of required core courses covering fundamental general management skills. The curriculum also leaves room for nine hours of electives; students may choose to take a variety of courses that match their career needs or may use these courses to specialize in finance, accounting, management, marketing, supply chain and logistical systems, or management information systems. Part-time students typically take between three to six years to complete their MBAs here. Those enrolled full-time have the option of completing the program in a single year.

Students love "the small size" of Rowan's MBA program, reporting that it increases "the accessibility of the professors." As one student tells us, "Every professor I have had you could email them a question about the course, and get a solid answer within a day usually." Administrators earn similarly high marks. One student notes, "I have had nothing but a pleasant experience at Rowan, even when I had a family emergency. The faculty and staff were very understanding and accommodating and allowed me to work around the days I needed to provide care for a relative."

Career and Placement

Rowan maintains a Career Management Center "to provide developmental advising" to all students in their pursuit of academic and professional goals. The CMC serves the entire school; there is no office dedicated specifically to MBAs or to business students on the undergraduate and graduate levels. CMC Services include one-on-one counseling, workshops, online self-assessment and job databases (like Experience), career publications, and employer directories. Services are available to alumni as well as to current students. It should be noted that most current students are full-time workers looking to advance within their current places of work; relatively few students seeking MBAs at Rowan are actively searching for new jobs. Those in the job market tell us that Rowan's small size "is a strength" when it comes to academics, "while at the same time it is a weakness when it comes to companies that recruit at the school."

ADMISSIONS CONTACT: JAMES JORDAN, MBA PROGRAM DIRECTOR
ADDRESS: BUNCE HALL, 201 MULLICA HILL ROAD, GLASSBORO, NJ 08028
PHONE: 856-256-4024 • FAX: 856-256-4439
E-MAIL: CGCEADMISSIONS@ROWAN.EDU • WEBSITE: WWW.ROWAN.EDU/MBA

Student Life and Environment

Rowan's MBA program "is meant for both part-time and full-time students," with the majority attending part time, usually while also managing full-time jobs. On-campus activities "are meant for people who live on campus," which means that they are directed at undergraduates. "On-campus stuff [does not apply] to most MBAs at Rowan, since they are for the most part commuters or from the South Jersey area." Residents and non-residents alike warn that parking on or near campus can be a challenge.

Rowan's suburban New Jersey hometown of Glassboro is a mere half-hour's drive from Philadelphia; the Jersey shore is less than an hour to the east, and Atlantic City is only 50 miles away. New York, Washington, D.C., and the Chesapeake are all within easy commuting distances. All of this adds up to opportunity. To prove it, the Rowan campus is in the midst of an ambitious expansion program, with makeovers planned for most facilities and several new buildings going up. Students praise the new athletic center and enjoy watching Rowan's excellent Division III men's and women's basketball teams.

Most Rowan MBAs "are in their upper 20s to upper 30s with very diverse backgrounds and experience[s]." Rowan's considerable international population includes a large group from China. American students enjoy the international student body, whom they describe as "a pleasure to work with."

Admissions

Rowan's graduate business school students are required to complete nine foundation courses in accounting, statistics, principles of finance, principles of marketing, calculus, operations management, and economics. Students who have successfully completed equivalent courses at the undergraduate level may place out of these foundation classes. Applicants to the MBA program must submit official transcripts for all undergraduate work (with a minimum GPA of 2.5 overall), GMAT or GRE scores, two letters of recommendation, a personal statement of career objectives, and a resume. International students whose first language is not English must also provide TOEFL scores (minimum required score: 79 iBT, 550 written exam, 213 computer-based exam).

FINANCIAL FACTS
Annual tuition	$14,614
Cost of books	$2,000

ADMISSIONS
Admissions Selectivity Rating	88
# of applications received	80
% applicants accepted	35
% acceptees attending	82
Average GMAT	510
Range of GMAT	478–553
Average GPA	3.23
TOEFL required of international students	Yes
Minimum TOEFL (paper/computer)	550/213
Application fee	$65
International application fee	$65
Deferment available	Yes
Transfer students accepted	Yes
Transfer application policy: Students may transfer up to 9 credit hours.	
Non-fall admissions	Yes
Need-blind admissions	Yes

RUTGERS, THE STATE UNIVERSITY OF NEW JERSEY
RUTGERS BUSINESS SCHOOL—NEWARK AND NEW BRUNSWICK

GENERAL INFORMATION

Type of school	Public
Affiliation	No Affiliation
Academic calendar	Trimester

SURVEY SAYS...
Cutting-edge classes
Solid preparation in:
Teamwork, Communication/interpersonal skills, Presentation skills

STUDENTS

Enrollment of parent institution	50,000
Enrollment of MBA Program	1,220
% male/female	65/35
% out-of-state	17
% part-time	80
% underrepresented minority	16
% international	18
Average age at entry	27
Average years work experience at entry	4.3

ACADEMICS

Academic Experience Rating	94
Profs interesting rating	84
Profs accesible rating	84
Student/faculty ratio	2:1
% female faculty	27
% underrepresented minority faculty	28
% part-time faculty	87

Joint Degrees
BA/MBA, BS/MBA, MPH/MBA, MD/MBA, JD/MBA, MS/MBA in Biomedical Sciences, MPP/MBA, MCRP/MBA

Prominent Alumni
Thomas A. Renyi (MBA '68), Chairman & CEO, The Bank of New York Mellon; Gary M. Cohen (MBA '83), President, BD Medical (Becton, Dickinson and Co.); Irwin M. Lerner, Retired Chairman of the Board, Hoffmann-La Roche; Nicholas J. Valeriani, Worldwide Chairman, Johnson & Johnson; Ralph Izzo, President & CEO, PSEG

Academics

With campuses in New Brunswick and Newark, many choose Rutgers Business School because it offers "the very best combination of quality and cost." The fact that it is "more affordable than private schools in the NY area" makes it attractive to many when coupled with its "solid reputation." Strengths include the top ranked Supply Chain Management and Pharmaceutical Management programs (the pharmaceutical industry is thriving in New Jersey, so job prospects abound), as well as strong Marketing and Finance programs. "Some Finance professors are even better than those at Ivy Leagues," one student enthused. "I'm pleasantly surprised and thankful not to get into any Ivy League, where the cost-benefit tradeoff would have been negative."

Professors are described as "hit or miss," but most agree that their teachers fall under the category of "hit," with students praising their "engaging, challenging, and thought provoking curriculum." They are happy to find their professors "have real hands-on experience in the class they teach and are very interested in educating us on their material" and describe them as educators who "do not simply teach, [but also] mentor, offer career advice, and share career opportunities that match with students interests." However, while professors are generally praised, many students complain about a "sorely understaffed" administration, which "can be a red tape nightmare." Overall though, students find them to be "accessible and genuinely concerned with [their] success"

Career and Placement

The MBA program is seen as offering strong inroads to a post-school career. The Supply Chain Management and Pharmaceutical Management programs at Rutgers not only win high praise; they draw in "guest speakers from the pharmaceutical industry" among many others. It is "pretty well known and a lot of companies do recruit from the school, such as Johnson and Johnson," as well as Newark-based Prudential. Some students suggest the school "should make more connections with the large financial institutions in the New York City area," claiming a lack of strong recruitment. The same criticism is aired about opportunities coming out of their marketing department.

Students will not have to work alone in making connections. An "excellent" career services department will "help you with resumes, cover letters and mock interviews," along with soliciting feedback from companies after your interviews. The Office of Career Management will "go to great lengths to bring top companies to recruit on campus and readily go to bat for students who seek positions at companies that would normally only recruit from Ivy League schools." Add to that a "strong alumni network" and a Small Business Development Center, which "helps entrepreneurs prepare business plans and start their own businesses," and students are given excellent preparation for post-school success.

Student Life and Environment

Campus life is rarely relevant for MBA students; for them, "it's a commuter's lifestyle." Though Rutgers boasts "a very large campus with a lot of activities," offering "many clubs and organizations to join and … a lot of career fairs where companies will recruit," MBA students will find that the commuter lifestyle "doesn't lend well to a strong social network, because people tend to be on campus only for classes." That said, for those on campus, "Rutgers Business School has a congenial environment where everyone is very approachable." Even part-time students "still feel a part of the community." Whether full-time or part-time, "both groups are professional and competitive," a group who are "very driven and are very inspired academically." Working students come from varied career backgrounds – and that is seen as a positive. "As we have different professional backgrounds the contributions made during class are very informative." That said, some complain that the school's curved grading policy "does not encourage the sharing of ideas and help" since "everyone is competing for the same grade of A and the rest of just placed on the curve."

Part-time students are "usually focused on their current careers and applying classroom learning to work situations (and vice versa)," while full-time students "have more time to socialize and to network." This gives the latter "more opportunities to meet people from the industry or recruiters, and to apply for internships, Leadership Development Programs etc." Some say students here "do not team well, they are only concerned with collecting a grade and degree," but that is a minority opinion. Most suggest the student body is "respectful" and "friendly," even "when we have disagreement within class discussions. We respect each other."

Admissions

Two different admissions offices handle applicants to the business programs at the Newark and New Brunswick campuses. Students must apply to the campus at which they hope to attend – but take note that the full-time program is available only at the Newark campus. There are no minimum GMAT score requirements or GPA requirements, and a specific academic background is not required, but at least two years of professional work experience is strongly recommended. Interviews are not always part of the admissions process, but they may be requested of MBA candidates.

FINANCIAL FACTS

Annual tuition	$22,274
Fees	$2,451
Cost of books	$5,000
Room & board (on/off-campus)	$26,000/$27,000
% of students receiving aid	82
% of first-year students receiving aid	82
% of students receiving grants	27
Average award package	$46,140
Average grant	$10,000
Average student loan debt	$46,000

ADMISSIONS

Admissions Selectivity Rating	93
# of applications received	349
Average GMAT	638
Range of GMAT	590–700
Average GPA	3.30
TOEFL required of international students	Yes
Minimum TOEFL (paper/computer)	600/250
Application fee	$73
International application fee	$73
Application Deadline/Notification	
Round 1:	1/20 / 2/20
Round 2:	3/15 / 4/15
Round 3:	5/18 / 6/18
Deferment available	Yes
Maximum length of deferment	1 Year
Transfer students accepted	Yes
Transfer application policy: Flex students may transfer a maximum of 12 applicable core (Full-time 6 transfer credits)credits earned at an AACSB-accredited MBA program, with a grade of "B" or better, taken within 5 years.	
Non-fall admissions	Yes
Need-blind admissions	Yes

EMPLOYMENT PROFILE

Career Rating		84	**Grads Employed by Function% Avg. Salary**	
Percent employed at graduation		60	Marketing	(45%) $86,871
Percent employed 3 months after graduation		30	Operations	(27%) $79,625
			Consulting	(7%)$110,000
Average base starting salary		$85,053	Management	(0%) $0
Primary Source of Full-time Job Acceptances			Finance	(21%) $79,934
School-facilitated activities	32(67%)		**Top 5 Employers Hiring Grads**	
Graduate-facilitated activities	16(33%)		Bristol-Myers Squibb (4), Johnson & Johnson Family of Companies (4), Novartis (2), LifeCell (2), Bloomberg (1)	

RUTGERS, THE STATE UNIVERSITY OF NEW JERSEY—CAMDEN

SCHOOL OF BUSINESS

GENERAL INFORMATION

Type of school	Public
Affiliation	No Affiliation
Academic calendar	Semester

SURVEY SAYS...

Cutting-edge classes, Happy students
Solid preparation in:
Quantitative skills, Doing business in
a global economy

STUDENTS

Enrollment of parent institution	6,500
Enrollment of MBA Program	281
% male/female	67/33
% part-time	88
% international	12
Average age at entry	26
Average years work experience at entry	4.8

ACADEMICS

Academic Experience Rating	**78**
Profs interesting rating	83
Profs accesible rating	84
Student/faculty ratio	9:1
% female faculty	26
% underrepresented minority faculty	3
% part-time faculty	18

Joint Degrees

MBA/JD - 117 credits (4 to 7 years);
MBA/MD: 5-6 years

Prominent Alumni

Tony D'Alessandro, Vive President/
CIO, Avantor Performance; Thomas
Cellucci, Chief Commericalization
Officer, Dep tof Homeland Security;
David Tilton, President, Atlantic
Care Regional Medical center;
Arthur Hicks, President, Cybex
International; Stuart Hill, Vice
President, Hill International

Academics

Rutgers, The State University of New Jersey-Camden, or "Rutgers-Camden," boasts a "strong brand name through research literature," and "caters to part-time returning students" who benefit from, among other things, "in-state discounts." In addition to enjoying a "good reputation," students at this business school repeatedly cite Rutgers-Camden's "location, location, location," owing to the school's "close proximity" to nearby cities like Philadelphia, New York, and Washington, D.C., not to mention its "proximity to home" for many working, part-time students. "This school has a good mix of students," one MBA student informs us. "Some are older and in professional careers—physicians, CPAs, lawyers, and engineers. Some are analysts looking to move into management, and some students are in the MBA/JD program going to school full-time." Among those students enrolled in the joint MBA/JD program, the general consensus is that Rutgers-Camden is "a respected institution in the legal community."

For students enrolled in the MBA program alone, they can expect to complete their 54 required credits within two to four years, while dual-degree students in the MBA/JD and MBA/MD joint programs can expect longer stints to accommodate the greater class load of 117 credits. Degree programs and concentrations in the following are offered: finance, international business and operations, management, marketing, and entrepreneurs. Study-abroad programs in France, Brazil, and South Africa are also offered. The school also offers two new Masters programs: the Professional Master of Business Administration (PMBA), an accelerated 21-month lock-step, cohort-based program for working professionals; and the Professional Master of Accountancy (PMAc) program, an accelerated 16-month lock-step, cohort-based program for participants with a broad background in accounting and business who want to develop their careers in other areas.

The 34 faculty members at Rutgers-Camden are described as "knowledgeable," "flexible," and "responsive" to students' needs. Additionally, the professors "bring interesting life and work experiences to the classroom." One procurement specialist informs us that, "I attended Rutgers for my undergrad degree in Business Management," and "the professors are what brought me back" for the MBA program. As one student notes, "they are very good at using different teaching methods—group projects, in-class discussions, and resources beyond the text book." Considering that many students arrive at Rutgers-Camden with a solid resume in hand, it's particularly beneficial that, according to one accounting major, the professors "value your work experience." However, some students have informed us when it comes to the overall quality of faculty, it can be "hit or miss." While on the one hand, "some are engaging and have worked in the private sector before teaching, others are bookworms with no teaching ability or private sector experience." But this same student concedes, "I guess in a way it is good to have both types." According to one recent MBA graduate, "The caliber of this School's professors and administration help to make Rutgers-Camden an absolutely amazing value considering its relatively low tuition."

Career and Placement

The Career Services office at Rutgers-Camden, like that of any reputable business school, offers a wide array of resources for graduating students, in addition to the 20 or so companies who regularly recruit summer interns each year. According to recent data, full-time students who found employment within 3 months of graduating enjoy a mean base salary of nearly $59,000. Although Rutgers-Camden has a favorable reputation among business schools, it very much remains a "local" institution, and "close to home" for most of its students. This is evidenced by the fact that approximately 80 percent of full-time MBA graduates accepted employment in the Northeast, and the remaining 20 percent went to Mid-Atlantic states. A vocal minority informs us that "Career Services are awful." However, not many students second this sentiment. More than adequate "job placement resources" are used by the student body, and as one satisfied student specializing in marketing research tells us, "marketing and database marketing are superior classes that offer hands-on learning and focus on the job market."

Student Life and Environment

The student body at Rutgers-Camden has been described as a "multicultural mix of both recent undergrads and very seasoned professionals." But one important thing for prospective students of Rutgers-Camden to keep in mind is that "many students enrolled in the MBA program are working professionals, and take classes part time." This factors in to how Rutgers-Camden caters to its student body. As one corporate communications major tells us, "classes are offered in the evenings, and occasionally on weekends or online," although the MBA program itself is not offered online. She continues, "I find that there is a lack of camaraderie among students, because many of us are only on campus one-two nights a week, have full-time jobs, and some also have families." By and large, "it is difficult for most of the MBA population to dedicate a lot of time to extracurricular activities," although "some students do socialize at a weekly 'Thirsty Thursday' event," and generally speaking, "there is availability to participate in clubs." Rutgers-Camden also happens to be situated in the heart of Camden, right "next to public transportation, so you have the option to drive or take the train," whether you are commuting to and from home, or looking to enjoy some of the night life in Philadelphia, which is just across the river from Camden.

Above all, students have informed us that this is a place to work and to be among "friendly, hard-working people trying to advance their careers and knowledge." Camden is a comfortable environment in which to do this, but for most students at Rutgers-Camden, clearly the work comes first. Diversity in the classroom is also important to many students, as they feel this translates well into the professional realm. As one JD-MBA student tells us, "My fellow students are a very a very diverse group, who run the gamut from single, foreign-exchange students, to single parents working full-time, to reservist, to the older married family-oriented types, employed and unemployed alike."

Admissions

Applicants to the Rutgers-Camden MBA program must submit the following: an online application (via the school's website), academic transcripts from undergrad and graduate (if applicable) institutions, essay/personal statement, two letters of recommendation, GMAT scores (this requirement is waived for applicants with a Ph.D., JD, or MD degree from an accredited U.S. institution), and a current resume (optional, but highly recommended for those applicants with work experience). Prospective students should keep in mind that, among the admissions requirements, Rutgers-Camden places great emphasis on GMAT scores, undergraduate GPA, and work experience. International applicants are required to submit a TOEFL score of 230 (computer based test) or 550 (written test). These applicants must also submit a Financial Statement Documentation (available on the school's website).

FINANCIAL FACTS

Annual tuition (in-state/ out-of-state)	$20,306/$3,227,600
Fees	$1,800
Cost of books	$1,800
Room & board	$7,494

ADMISSIONS

Admissions Selectivity Rating	**77**
# of applications received	206
% applicants accepted	60
% acceptees attending	61
Average GMAT	548
Average GPA	3.20
TOEFL required of international students	Yes
Minimum TOEFL (paper/computer)	550/230
Application fee	$65
Deferment available	Yes
Maximum length of deferment	1 Semester
Transfer students accepted	Yes
Transfer application policy: Students must complete at least 36 credits in our program. We will transfer courses from AACSB-accredited schools with a grade of B or better.	
Non-fall admissions	Yes
Need-blind admissions	Yes

EMPLOYMENT PROFILE		
Career Rating	**74**	**Top 5 Employers Hiring Grads**
Average base starting salary	$58,812	Lockheed Martin (1), Campbells Soup (3), Deloitte & Touche (1), JP Morgan Chase (1), Computer Sciences Coporation (1)

SACRED HEART UNIVERSITY
JOHN F. WELCH COLLEGE OF BUSINESS

GENERAL INFORMATION

Type of school	Private
Affiliation	Roman Catholic
Academic calendar	Trimester

SURVEY SAYS...

Cutting-edge classes
Solid preparation in:
General management, Teamwork

STUDENTS

Enrollment of parent institution	6,347
Enrollment of MBA Program	146
% male/female	58/42
% part-time	77
Average age at entry	29
Average years work experience at entry	7.0

ACADEMICS

Academic Experience Rating	82
Profs interesting rating	81
Profs accesible rating	85
Student/faculty ratio	5:1
% female faculty	44
% underrepresented minority faculty	5
% part-time faculty	11

Academics

The imprimatur of Jack Welch, former CEO of General Electric, impresses many MBAs at Sacred Heart University. "I'm a big fan of Jack Welch," one current student tells us; "the name Welch being attached to the school will hopefully bring much more recognition," another adds hopefully. The GE connection isn't lost on students either; the fact that the program "is held in high regard by GE in Connecticut," where many of these graduates will eventually seek employment, is a key factor in their decision to pursue the Welch MBA.

Sacred Heart is not merely relying on a famous name to attract and satisfy students. In 2009, the school introduced a new curriculum that begins with a fixed integrated core curriculum that "is very applicable to the real world" and culminates in concentration work in accounting, finance, marketing, or management. Students note that "the new Welch MBA format has been a monumental task to get rolling" and commend "the staff and professors[, who] go above and beyond to make sure each student is heard and prepared for the tasks at hand." They call the new curriculum "an interesting and exciting new take on the traditional MBA" with a "dynamic new format [that] is very interesting and keeps us on our toes!" The program "fully embraces the fast-paced changes of the modern world" and "trains students to be more than analytical" in order to produce "effective leaders and decision makers, ready to go."

Students commend "the breadth and depth of knowledge of the faculty" at Welch, calling their teachers an "outstanding group of professors with diverse backgrounds to teach various aspects of the business world. Their skills and knowledge in their particular subject is outstanding and…[set within] today's business world." Because "the school is not too large," students benefit from "the opportunity to get to know one another" and their teachers in the classroom. Through an international MBA in Luxembourg offering concentrations in finance and general management, Welch students have the opportunity to undertake internships in finance, marketing, international business and information technology in Luxembourg.

Career and Placement

SHU's Office of Career Development offers a range of services to MBA students. Staff members provide assistance with resume creation and critique; conduct seminars on interview skills; maintain online job postings; and organize on-campus job fairs and interview sessions. The office hired a full-time Assistant Director whose primary focus is on MBA student internships and job placement. During a recent academic school year, 105 employers attended the school's annual career fair and 19 employers interviewed on campus, including PricewaterhouseCoopers, General Electric, Target, Ernst & Young, Sikorsky, KPMG, and Legg Mason.

Student Life and Environment

"Most students are commuters who hold jobs during the day" at Welch, although "The students who come directly from undergraduate work appear to do a lot together." MBAs agree that in its current manifestation, the school's extracurricular life "is mainly geared towards the full-time undergraduates (concerts, clubs, student activities, sports). The graduate schools tend to just focus on classes and not student life." However, they also note that "The business school is just starting to survey its students about how we want help: network with alumni and other community leaders [versus] speakers, etc." That bodes well for the future. For now, though, "If you are not already a part of the university via undergrad work or currently working at the school, there is a major gap between the university and its graduate students."

The student body is a mix of seasoned professionals and freshly minted BAs. The older students "are personable and knowledgeable without being 'know-it-alls.'" All students in the program enjoy a "strong sense of collegiality and collaboration."

Admissions

Applicants to the MBA program at SHU's Welch College of Business must submit the following materials: a completed online application; official transcripts from all undergraduate institutions attended (showing a minimum 3.0 cumulative GPA); a personal statement of career and academic goals and a summary of relevant business experience; two letters of recommendation; a current professional resume; and an official GMAT score report (applicants with at least two years professional work experience must score a minimum of 400; for all others, the minimum score is 500). International applicants, including applicants to the MBA program in Luxembourg, must submit transcripts in English; foreign language transcripts must be translated and analyzed by an approved professional service. Applicants whose first language is not English (except those with a degree from an English-language institution) must submit an official score report for the TOEFL or IELTS. Students should anticipate at least a three month wait in the issuance of student visas for the Luxembourg program. The Luxembourg program runs approximately nine six-week sessions per year; students may apply for admission and begin the program during any session. The Fairfield campus operates on a trimester calendar.

FINANCIAL FACTS

Annual tuition	$20,250
Fees	$141
Cost of books	$2,000

ADMISSIONS

Admissions Selectivity Rating	85
# of applications received	111
% applicants accepted	49
% acceptees attending	87
Average GMAT	520
Range of GMAT	470–570
Average GPA	3.41
TOEFL required of international students	Yes
Minimum TOEFL (paper/computer)	570
Application fee	$60
International application fee	$60
Deferment available	Yes
Maximum length of deferment	1 year
Transfer students accepted	Yes
Transfer application policy: Transferred credits are reviewed by the Program Director.	
Non-fall admissions	Yes
Need-blind admissions	Yes

SAGINAW VALLEY STATE UNIVERSITY
COLLEGE OF BUSINESS AND MANAGEMENT

GENERAL INFORMATION

Type of school	Public
Affiliation	No Affiliation

SURVEY SAYS...

Cutting-edge classes
Solid preparation in:
General management, Doing business in a global economy, Entrepreneurial studies

STUDENTS

Enrollment of parent institution	10,552
Enrollment of MBA Program	136
% male/female	62/38
% out-of-state	0
% part-time	49
% underrepresented minority	0
% international	100
Average age at entry	26
Average years work experience at entry	2.6

ACADEMICS

Academic Experience Rating	**71**
Profs interesting rating	72
Profs accesible rating	75
Student/faculty ratio	12:1
% female faculty	17
% underrepresented minority faculty	8
% part-time faculty	0

Academics

Saginaw Valley State University, located in University City, Michigan, just outside of Saginaw, appeals to many prospective students because of its "good reputation," "large number of international students," "fair tuition," and "accredited program." Factors such as "small class size" and the fact that SVSU is "close to home" are also received well by a large portion of the student body. According to one student majoring in public education and government service, "I was looking for a different perspective than the one I received while getting my BBA at the University of Michigan—one that considers small business." A solid faculty and administrative staff help provide these different perspectives. Like any other accredited graduate institution, students' feedback indicates that some professors are "great," while "others are horrible." But as one sales and marketing students tells us, "the professors and administration staff continue to teach and learn business practices that shape the students of the MBA program. They have consistently encouraged effective teamwork, communication, entrepreneurialism, and globalization." "Administration has made things very easy for most MBA candidates," another student assures us, and overall are "pretty supportive when you have other work requirements," such as a full-time job in addition to your studies.

The online component, in combination with onsite classes (or "hybrid format"), is something many students consider beneficial for their learning needs. While SVSU has a "surrounding environment that is good for studying," the offering of "eight-week courses in hybrid format" is an "affordable" and "convenient" option for students who cannot commit to full-time, on-campus study. Additionally, all core courses are offered in the hybrid format. The hybrid format, however, is something several students have expressed hesitation toward. According to one healthcare major, "ninety-five percent of your time must be on campus." Another student has suggested that, "maybe weekend classes could be offered, and more fully online courses, as well."

SVSU offers degree programs and concentrations in accounting, economics, entrepreneurship, finance, international business, leadership/management, and marketing. An optional course in sustainability practices is also offered, which explores and analyzes the use, development, and implementation of alternate energy strategies for sustainable business projects.

Cost-effectiveness is also something many SVSU students praise and makes the school particularly appealing for recent undergrads looking to pursue graduate work without the hassle of relocating. One newly enrolled MBA candidate tells us, "I completed my undergraduate degree in electrical engineering at SVSU and had a good experience while there. Furthermore, the cost of the MBA at SVSU is significantly cheaper than elsewhere." Compared to the estimated "$80,000 to complete your degree at U of Michigan," a similar degree from SVSU will run you about "$20,000," and "both degrees are accredited."

Admissions Contact: Jill Wetmore, Dean
Address: 7400 Bay Road, University Center, MI 48710
Phone: 989-964-4064 • Fax: 989-964-7497
E-mail: CBMDEAN@SVSU.EDU • Website: WWW.SVSU.EDU/CBM

Career and Placement

SVSU's Career Planning and Placement Office regularly hosts on-campus interviews, career fairs, and resume building workshops. A bevy of internships, available to Saginaw students and graduates, are also coordinated through the Office. Among the provided services, students have noted the Office's concern with testing students' aptitude to gauge proper career placement, but as one science research major tells us, this practice should be lessened, and the administration should be more focused on "finding you gainful employment." The general consensus among the students who provided feedback is that career services at SVSU could do with significant improvement. Both "alumni relations and job placement" are particular areas that students have expressed concern over, and according to one student, the career fairs are attended by "companies that aren't hiring, or they won't talk to you and just direct you to their websites."

Student Life and Environment

As a relatively new school within the Michigan state college system, SVSU has a decent-sized campus (750 acres) and a surrounding area with much to offer. As one sales and marketing major puts it, SVSU has a "small-town feel mixed with big-town academics and accreditation." This does help cultivate an "atmosphere that is ideal for learning and developing professional business skills." On the whole, the school and its administration appear most concerned with catering to a working and career-oriented student body. One satisfied student informs us that, "SVSU MBA students are all working students; even the international students for the most part have jobs." While this type of environment is beneficial for most looking to juggle responsibilities and advance their careers, "this offers a challenge for group activities." But for those students with the time and inclination, the school "provides an excellent gym with lots of extracurricular activities. There are also several clubs, such as the International Student Club, Chess Club, and Math Club."

For MBA candidates seeking a place where they can supplement their working lives with night classes, SVSU is very "accommodating." Some students have expressed a need for improvement when it comes to international students. One student in particular had this to say: "They should have a specific officer to help us international students to be easier involved in the University culture." On-campus support offices are also available for various students groups, including minorities, international students, women, and LGBT groups.

Admissions

Applicants to the MBA program at Saginaw Valley State University must submit the following: official undergraduate transcript, essay/personal statement, and two letters of recommendation. Both GMAT and GRE scores are optional, but GMAT scores, in particular, will carry more weight, and the higher the score (450 minimum), the better your chances. A resume is optional as well, but for those applicants with significant work experience and less than stellar test scores should consider off-setting one with the other. International students are required to submit TOEFL scores, with the following minimum scores: 550 for written test, 213 for computer-based test, and 79 for web-based test.

FINANCIAL FACTS

Annual tuition (in-state/ out-of-state)	$8,348/$15,936
Fees	$261
Cost of books	$2,000
Room & board	$9,050
% of students receiving aid	43
% of first-year students receiving aid	59
% of students receiving grants	26
Average award package	$8,860
Average grant	$4,250
Average loan	$12,620
Average student loan debt	$0

ADMISSIONS

Admissions Selectivity Rating	**69**
# of applications received	111
% applicants accepted	88
% acceptees attending	39
Average GMAT	470
Range of GMAT	460–480
Average GPA	3.20
TOEFL required of international students	Yes
Minimum TOEFL (paper/computer)	550/213
Application fee	$30
International application fee	$80
Deferment available	Yes
Maximum length of deferment	7 Semesters
Transfer students accepted	Yes
Transfer application policy: may transfer 6 credits	
Non-fall admissions	Yes
Need-blind admissions	Yes

SAINT JOSEPH'S UNIVERSITY
ERIVAN K. HAUB SCHOOL OF BUSINESS

GENERAL INFORMATION

Type of school   Private
Affiliation   Roman Catholic-Jesuit
Academic calendar   Semesters

SURVEY SAYS...

Friendly students, Happy students, Students love Philadelphia, PA
Solid preparation in:
General management, Teamwork, Communication/interpersonal skills, Presentation skills

STUDENTS

Average years work experience
   at entry   7.2

ACADEMICS

Academic Experience Rating   **80**
Profs interesting rating   83
Profs accesible rating   76
Student/faculty ratio   35:1

Joint Degrees

DO/MBA Program with Philadelphia College of Osteopathic Medicine (2 years for MBA component)

Academics

Saint Joseph University's proud "Jesuit tradition" challenges students "intellectual abilities" while providing "a holistic business education." "Saint Joseph's University has a solid academic reputation and offers scheduling flexibility for working students." The Finance program in particular has a "great reputation" especially in the Philadelphia area. SJU has "strong alumni ties in the region" and students love the location in one of America's most famous Eastern cities. Students are very pleased with the "fairly priced" and "reasonable" tuition. "The part time MBA is flexible and recognized," and the school offers the "freedom to attend classes online or on campus." The Jesuit tradition is infused in SJU, something many students love. "The idea of social responsibility and teaching individuals for the greater good of society is a real focal point," one student declares, "and I think that is something our country needs at the moment."

"Course offerings have been plentiful and variable (allowing the available times to easily fit your work/home schedules)," one Project Management student reports. "Professors and Faculty are excellent," although some complain the administration "sometimes makes questionable decisions related to the quality of students accepted into the program." Others say "the administration is extremely helpful particularly regarding picking classes." "Almost everyone is helpful and informative" and "you can tell the faculty and staff really care and are passionate about the school." Courses at SJU "[integrate] past and present business techniques and concepts." As at many schools, your academic experience "really comes down to which professors you have that make or break your experience." Still, "generally the Professors are well rounded" and "very supportive of students." "So far so good," reports a Business and Finance student. "I am about to begin my third semester and have only great things to say about Saint Joseph's University." Another likens SJU to "the picture of a well-oiled machine" and says "from the moment I showed up at an information session until now, my 9th week of my first semester, every experience has been a positive one."

Career and Placement

"SJU has a great reputation in the Philadelphia area and a strong alumni base," and does a great job of helping students find work in the area. The professors, who "have more than twenty years of industry experience," help create "a good base for a breadth of careers in business." The career development center "serves the entire university and has no department specifically for graduate students" and some students suggest they do not put enough work into placement. Still between the large alumni network, the location in Philadelphia, and "companies recruiting on campus," SJU students tend to find great work in Philadelphia and elsewhere.

ADMISSIONS CONTACT: JANINE N. GUERRA, JD, MBA, ASSOCIATE DIRECTOR OF PROFESSIONAL MBA
ADDRESS: 5600 CITY AVENUE, MANDEVILLE 284, PHILADELPHIA, PA 19131
PHONE: 888-SJU-MBA-1 • FAX: 610-660-1599
EMAIL: SJUMBA@SJU.EDU • WEBSITE: WWW.SJU.EDU/MBA

Student Life and Environment

SJU "is a warm friendly community" of "mainly working professionals that take class at night. Though some full-time younger students are also involved." Students are "kind," "friendly," "ambitious, and eager to learn something new." Because of this, "conflicts during 'group' projects have been minimal." "As a foreign student with some trouble to understand the US culture and language," one international student says, "I get a lot of help with my patient fellow classmates and professors." The SJU experience will vary depending on if you are a full-time, part-time, or online student. "Life at school allows students to network however due to the part-time nature of the program students try to be as efficient as possible with their time on campus," one student reports. Although the "neighborhood is a little rough, and there is a history of crime around West Philadelphia," students generally feel safe on campus. One student sums the SJU experience up thusly: "I find that I am comfortable on campus, I feel welcomed, and I absolutely enjoy studying at the library and Post Learning Commons."

Admissions

Saint Joseph's accepts rolling submissions and admits MBA students for spring, fall, and summer terms. Applicants will need to submit the following materials to the school: an official transcript from each undergraduate and graduate institution at which credits were earned; an official GMAT score report (not more than five years old), GRE is also accepted; two letters of recommendation; a current resume; and a personal statement of 250 to 500 words outlining career objectives and the value of an MBA in reaching those objectives. International applicants must submit all of the following as well as a statement of financial support.

FINANCIAL FACTS

Annual tuition	$16,056
Fees	$0
Cost of books	$800

ADMISSIONS

Admissions Selectivity Rating	74
# of applications received	297
% applicants accepted	70
% acceptees attending	65
Average GMAT	528
Range of GMAT	470–580
Average GPA	3.20
TOEFL required of international students	Yes
Minimum TOEFL (paper/computer)	550/213
Application fee	$35
International application fee	$35
Deferment available	Yes
Maximum length of deferment	1 year
Transfer students accepted	Yes
Transfer application policy: They must provide a completed application including original test scores. A total of 6 credits may be transferred into the Core Course requirement provided that they receive a C or better and the school is AACSB accredited	
Non-fall admissions	Yes
Need-blind admissions	Yes

SAINT LOUIS UNIVERSITY
JOHN COOK SCHOOL OF BUSINESS

GENERAL INFORMATION
Type of school	Private
Affiliation	Roman Catholic
Academic calendar	Semester

SURVEY SAYS...
Good peer network, Cutting-edge classes
Solid preparation in:
Doing business in a global economy

STUDENTS
Enrollment of parent institution	14,073
Enrollment of MBA Program	387
% male/female	65/35
% out-of-state	50
% part-time	85
% underrepresented minority	9
% international	11
Average age at entry	27
Average years work experience at entry	4.5

ACADEMICS
Academic Experience Rating	**74**
Profs interesting rating	80
Profs accesible rating	81
Student/faculty ratio	22:1
% female faculty	15
% underrepresented minority faculty	4
% part-time faculty	27

Joint Degrees
Doctor of Jurisprudence/Master of Business Administration, 3.5 years. Master of Health Administration/Master of Business Administration, 2 years. Medical Doctor/Master of Business Administration, 5 Years. Master of Arts (Education)/Master of Business Adminisitration, 2 years.

Prominent Alumni
August A. Busch, IV, President, Anheuser-Busch, Inc; Mark Lamping, CEO of New Meadowlands Stadium Company; Robert Ciapciak, General Partner, Edward Jones; Alison Talbot, VP of Operations, Miss Elaine

Academics

If there's one pervasive reason that students choose Saint Louis University for their MBAs, it's the school's "impeccable reputation" in the local business community. In practice, students say the program lives up to its solid gold credentials. "The overall academic experience is both challenging and rewarding," combining business theory and real-world practice with a refreshing "ethical consciousness" for the modern workplace. Depending on a student's professional goals, SLU offers two different MBA options, as well as dual-degree programs in law, health administration, medicine, and education. Those who want a quick but professional degree can pursue an MBA through the school's new "full-time, one-year timeline," which runs students through a rigorous interdisciplinary business program over the course of one calendar year. For working professionals, the part-time MBA is "flexible enough to accommodate students with active careers," allowing them to "shape the classes to better fit their needs and interests." "Professors understand the difficulties in working full-time while pursuing an MBA," and administrators "provide outstanding services to part-time MBA students."

Both part-time and full-time students must complete a series of foundation, breadth, and required courses in advanced business topics. After that, the curriculum "allows students to choose an area of emphasis for their MBA" through elective coursework in accounting, economics, entrepreneurship, finance, international business, health industries, nonprofit organizations, real estate, management, information technology management, marketing, project management, or supply chain management. Business trends and world events are integrated into the curriculum, and students can expect to "spend a lot of time learning about current (and therefore extremely relevant) business issues." A student enthuses, "The John Cook School of Business at Saint Louis University has challenged me to think domestically and globally, both quantitatively and qualitatively, and with a sense of social responsibility, ethics, and morals." Even while attending the program part time, MBA candidates benefit from "the flexibility to customize the program," along with the "the opportunity to study abroad for a week or two."

SLU's business program is "competitive and academically challenging," but well balanced. Within the faculty, students find "a combination of full-time professors who are very knowledgeable in their fields, as well as adjunct, who are actually doing what they are teaching." At the same time, students admit that "faculty members are inconsistent in quality." Researching professors before signing up for classes can vastly improve the experience. The total graduate enrollment at the Cook School of Business is fewer than 400 students, making the school feel rather small and manageable. Students feel comfortable expressing their opinions, and "the administration is very approachable and willing to listen to feedback." A current student attests, "Everyone I have interacted with in the Graduate Business School office is friendly, knowledgeable, and quick to help resolve any question or problem you might have."

Career and Placement

The John Cook School of Business has its own dedicated Career Resource Center, which serves both undergraduate and graduate business students through one-on-one career counseling, job search strategies, and resume revisions. "The Career Resources Center is top-notch," and it "frequently holds seminars and networking sessions" for MBA candidates. Among other programs, the School hosts company information sessions and casual meet-and-greet events with local businesses. In addition, SLU has done "a great job integrating with the local business community and in connecting with alumni." However, students in the part-time program mention that the school might improve the process of "mentoring and advising those of us looking to change careers," though those who want individual attention can seek out the dedicated graduate career advisers.

Saint Louis University graduates work at companies that include Anheuser-Busch/InBev, The Boeing Company, Express Scripts, Wells Fargo, Cintas Corp, Monsanto, and Emerson. Graduates have a mean base salary of $57,450, with a range from $40,000 to $82,000. Marketing and sales are the two most popular career fields for SLU graduates.

Student Life and Environment

No matter whether a student is in the part-time, full-time, or joint degree programs at SLU, the curriculum is challenging and time-consuming. At the same time, "the culture is very welcoming," and students in the business school enjoy a surprisingly "laid-back environment" amid group work and case studies. "There is a real sense of camaraderie" between students and a surprisingly bustling atmosphere around the business school building, where there are frequent regional, national, and international speakers. "There are a variety of study areas in the business school," and "there are always students hanging out in the common areas studying and eating." While the environment is comfortable, students say it isn't always functional. Fortunately, the University Library, located right next to the business school, is undergoing a large-scale renovation.

Unlike most professional or executive programs, "SLU makes the extra effort to make commuter and part-time students really feel at home on campus." For example, "the last week of every month, the Graduate Business office provides dinner each night during the part-time MBA courses." Students also point out the value of "the social events that are planned for the business school," through which "full-time and part-time students can meet and socialize."

Admissions

To apply to Saint Louis University, prospective students must submit official academic transcripts from undergraduate coursework, a current resume, GMAT scores, two letters of recommendation, a personal statement, and a completed application form and related fee. The full-time program enrolls students once a year, in May. Part-time students are reviewed and accepted on a rolling basis, all year long. In recent years, the average GMAT score for entering students was 570.

FINANCIAL FACTS

Annual tuition	$52,035
Fees	$440
Cost of books	$1,500
Room & board	
(on/off-campus)	$0/$12,000
% of students receiving aid	90
% of first-year students	
receiving aid	90
% of students receiving grants	90
Average grant	$11,840

ADMISSIONS

Admissions Selectivity Rating	73
# of applications received	184
% applicants accepted	85
% acceptees attending	70
Average GMAT	581
Range of GMAT	520–620
Average GPA	3.20
TOEFL required of	
international students	Yes
Minimum TOEFL	
(paper/computer)	570/230
Application fee	$90
International application fee	$90
Deferment available	Yes
Maximum length	
of deferment	1 year
Transfer students accepted	Yes
Transfer application policy: Part-time MBA only; 6 credit hours from another AACSB accredited school. Also, member of Jesuit MBA Consortium.	
Non-fall admissions	Yes
Need-blind admissions	Yes

EMPLOYMENT PROFILE

Career Rating	**80**	**Grads Employed by Function**	**% Avg. Salary**
Percent employed at graduation	39	Marketing	(30%) $56,943
Percent employed 3 months		Operations	(13%) $60,000
after graduation	69	Consulting	(26%) $62,567
Average base starting salary	$57,435	Finance	(13%) $43,667
Primary Source of Full-time Job Acceptances		Other	(17%) $59,000
School-facilitated activities	8(32%)	**Top 5 Employers Hiring Grads**	
Graduate-facilitated activities	17(68%)	Anheuser Busch (1), The Boeing Company (1), Emerson (1), Monsanto (1), Cintas Corp (1)	

SAN DIEGO STATE UNIVERSITY
GRADUATE SCHOOL OF BUSINESS

GENERAL INFORMATION
Type of school	Public
Affiliation	No Affiliation
Academic calendar	Semester

SURVEY SAYS...
Students love San Diego, CA, Good
Social scene, Happy students
Solid preparation in:
Teamwork, Doing business in a global economy

STUDENTS
Enrollment of parent institution	30,843
Enrollment of MBA Program	595
% male/female	57/43
% out-of-state	3
% part-time	48
Average age at entry	27
Average years work experience at entry	4.5

ACADEMICS
Academic Experience Rating	88
Profs interesting rating	83
Profs accesible rating	81
Student/faculty ratio	28:1
% female faculty	20
% underrepresented minority faculty	20
% part-time faculty	18

Joint Degrees
Master of Business
Administration/Master of Arts in
Latin American Studies (MBA/MA)3-
4 yrs. Joint MBA/JD 4 yrs to complete

Prominent Alumni
Linda Lang, Chairman & CEO Jack
in the Box; Jim Sinegal, Co-founder;
Costco; Zane Rowe, Exec VP, CFO;
United Continental Holdings; Rick
Hamada, CEO; Avnet; Dennis
Gilmore, CEO, President; 1st
American Financial Corp

Academics

It is not difficult to sum up the qualities that draw students to San Diego State University's Graduate School of Business. One student explains, "[It's a] nice location for me, good class times, a competitive curriculum, and a good solid reputation for a great up-and-coming business program and full and part time MBA programs." Those views are consistent throughout the comments about this "quite affordable" local school that has "a great business reputation." Though some air complaints about a few "mostly uninterested" professors, the consensus is that SDSU's business program is the "best quality for the money." Couple a "flexible program" with a "large networking base" and attendees will find "a community with numerous opportunities to give back and share [one's] new skills in constructive ways."

What students walk away with will depend on their own focus and drive, since the "quality of professors is highly volatile and you can't be sure how well they will teach or lecture." However, when the professors are good, the classroom experience is very worthwhile. Business students are glad that "professors with long work experience are common." For example, one student boasts, "The two courses in my last semester consisted of a senior director and a CEO from Qualcomm (a Fortune 500) and biotech firm, respectively." That "large depth of experience and knowledge" these educators share with their students suggests "professors promote critical thinking in class, as opposed to just lecturing. More emphasis is placed on in-depth analysis than on test taking." One student without a strong background in business was glad to note, "This school made my transition from a non-business background to a business program very smooth."

Such experience extends to the students. "Fifty percent of people have their own business in my classes," one student notes. Even for those without a wealth of previous business experience, SDSU offers a "consistently [top] ranked" entrepreneurship program and a Sports MBA program that boasts "access to many higher-ups in the sports industry in the San Diego and Southern California area," It also takes part in a Venture Capital Investment Competition that gains big exposure for participants. Some students worry that "ridiculous budget cuts" will mar the MBA program, but for others the future looks bright. Current administrators are "transforming the program," and the school is "integrating lecturers into the courses," all of which indicates a program that is sometimes "flying by the seat of its pants" but is generally on the upswing.

Career and Placement

A "large alumni network," strong "career services assistance ... helpful MBA advisors, and the flexibility of the program" are the strengths of the program here. There are "excellent career counselors and job matching," along with "lots of alumni in the community" that make for good post-school career opportunities. With more than 60 years in operation, the school has amassed "a huge alumni base" which, some students note, "The program needs to utilize [more fully]." "The systems are in place, and as long as students tap into it," one student writes, "the resources the school provides are amazing."

ADMISSIONS CONTACT: NIKHIL VARAIYA, DIRECTOR, GRADUATE BUSINESS PROGRAMS
ADDRESS: 5500 CAMPANILE DRIVE, SAN DIEGO, CA 92182-8228
PHONE: 619-594-8073 • FAX: 619-594-1863
E-MAIL: GRADBUSINESS@SDSU.EDU • WEBSITE: WWW.SDSU.EDU/BUSINESS

Student Life and Environment

"The San Diego State Campus is full of life and activity," bustling with concerts, shows, and more. The San Diego area offers sports, a huge array of restaurants catering to every culinary desire, and of course, the students of SDSU. No matter your focus, and no matter whether full-or part-time, "there are many places where you can find your niche and be happy." The common ground for SDSU Graduate School of Business students is, unsurprisingly, San Diego itself. One student notes, "It is a beautiful location, with beautiful weather and happy people. It has the feel of a big city, with many small communities making up that big city, so you get the best of both worlds." Despite its cozy feel, San Diego is indeed a city – and urban areas often mean opportunities for education, recreation, and more. "The closer to campus you live, the more involved you can get, which ultimately leads to success in classes or building lasting relationships that will serve you into life beyond graduation."

Like the surrounding city itself, students here are "very outgoing and easy to interact and work with," a group of "high achievers with a strong competitive drive and interest in furthering their careers." SDSU keeps students "very busy with work," while the city offers ample opportunities for entertainment. Whether full-time students who are "hardworking, motivated individuals who want to improve their future career possibilities" or part-time students who are "busy, working professionals, mostly young in their careers," students here tend to be "diverse, friendly, knowledgeable, and very helpful."

Admissions

Prepare to compete against almost 1,500 other applicants to SDSU's MBA program. Taken into consideration will be your GMAT score; GPA or undergraduate academic work (a minimum of 2.85 for American students, 3.0 for international students is required, with an average GPA for admitted students of 3.3); letters of recommendation, a resume (work experience is not required but is preferred); and personal statement. The final three "can enhance an application" but are not required. Expect to submit official TOEFL scores if you are an international student whose first language is not English. Such students should expect to meet a minimum paper-and-pencil test score of 550, computer-based score of 213, or an Internet-based score of 80. Apply as early as possible; whether for the fall or spring terms, applications are processed on a rolling basis.

FINANCIAL FACTS

Annual tuition (in-state/ out-of-state)	$8,462/$17,390
Fees	$6,672
Cost of books	$1,717
Room & board (on/off-campus)	$13,052/$12,091
% of students receiving aid	46
Average award package	$18,100
Average loan	$8,800

ADMISSIONS

Admissions Selectivity Rating	78
# of applications received	675
% applicants accepted	63
% acceptees attending	55
Average GMAT	590
Range of GMAT	550–620
Average GPA	3.25
TOEFL required of international students	Yes
Minimum TOEFL (paper/computer)	550/213
Application fee	$55
International application fee	$55
Deferment available	No
Transfer students accepted	Yes
Transfer application policy: Transfer applicants apply through the normal admissions process. A limited number of transfer credits may be accepted based on an evaluation of the applicant's transcripts.	
Non-fall admissions	No
Need-blind admissions	Yes

EMPLOYMENT PROFILE

Career Rating	78	Grads Employed by Function	% Avg. Salary
Percent employed at graduation	48	Marketing	(11%) $46,376
Percent employed 3 months after graduation	5	Operations	(11%) $96,600
		Finance	(48%) $65,909
Average base starting salary	$75,106	MIS	(11%) $106,800
Primary Source of Full-time Job Acceptances		Other	(13%) $10,583
School-facilitated activities	19(20%)	**Top 5 Employers Hiring Grads**	
Graduate-facilitated activities	26(28%)	Deloitte (3), Grant Thornton (3), KPMG (3),	
Unknown	48(52%)	PricewaterhouseCoopers (2), Qualcomm (2)	

SAN FRANCISCO STATE UNIVERSITY
COLLEGE OF BUSINESS

Academics

San Francisco State University's College of Business offers a contemporary MBA program, right in the middle of the Bay Area's business community. While SFSU's main campus is located in a residential neighborhood, the business school has its own building in "the heart of San Francisco's financial district." The curriculum is high quality and progressive, and the "flexible schedule and very convenient location" make this school a top choice for San Francisco professionals. "The opportunity to individually tailor an MBA to a specific job market is key," and many students choose SFSU to participate in the school's popular "sustainable business emphasis." In fact, there is a "focus on corporate responsibility and sustainability" throughout the program, which is well aligned with the Bay Area's forward-thinking business climate.

The faculty takes a varied approach to teaching, with mixed results. "There are some that read directly from slides and others that are extremely engaging. They take book concepts and translate them into real-life situations." Students admit that, "you need to be a little selective in the professors you choose," but reassure us that, "If you do your research, there are enough accomplished professors here to get a solid education." No matter who oversees classes, the curriculum is time consuming, as "courses require a lot of group work, a lot of reading, and several presentations." However, the rewards are worth the effort, and students benefit from "engaging classroom discussion" in their classes. Always current, SFSU "professors are teaching the latest trends" through contemporary case studies.

Due to "the state of California budget constraints," the program has experienced some recent limitations. For example, "they aren't always able to offer elective classes consistently." Fortunately, "the administration has done an excellent job communicating potentialities and schedule changes to the student body." In fact, the administration gets high marks all around, and the "program advisers and program coordinator are very easy to talk to and helpful." Both full-time and part-time students assure us, "If you plan out your schedule right, you won't really have any trouble getting the classes you need." And, even as the state raises student tuition and fees, an MBA from San Francisco State still comes at a "fairly low cost" for its quality.

Career and Placement

According to SFSU's happy grad students, "San Francisco is an amazing city to get an MBA in because so many companies are headquartered nearby, especially if you have an interest in entrepreneurship." On top of that, the school's close "proximity to Silicon Valley" opens up a world of options in high tech and computing. While there are several top-rated business schools in the greater Bay Area, SFSU students say you can't write off their strong, yet affordable public program. A current student elaborates, "a lot of students feel that SFSU doesn't have a name like Stanford or UC Berkeley, but the connections are there. We have people who work for Google and Yahoo! and, like myself, at Genentech, who, if you reach out, are connected and can help students."

Within the business school, students have access to ongoing career workshops and personalized career counseling. There is an annual career fair, as well as ongoing recruiting events at the business school and the main SFSU campus. MBA candidates may also take advantage of the online job boards managed by the University's Career Center. The mean base salary for last year's San Francisco State MBA graduates was about $85,000 annually, with 90 percent of students accepting a position within three months of graduation. Some of the biggest employers of SFSU graduates are Wells Fargo Bank, Genentech, PG&E, Autodesk, and Bank of America.

Student Life and Environment

The student body at SFSU reflects the Bay Area's interesting local culture, and "because nearly 50 percent of the school's students are international, the school ranks very high in diversity." Group projects tend to go well, and "most everyone is laid back," despite the pressures of business school. Some complain that students who "come straight from undergrad" are "uninterested and inexperienced" when compared to their older counterparts, but San Francisco's MBA candidates are "generally thoughtful, professional, and engaged" throughout the program.

Located downtown, the petite SFSU "campus is brand new and very nice," and "the surrounding area is, of course, awesome." Not only is the campus convenient for downtown professionals, there are "tons of restaurants and shops around" the neighborhood. On campus, the school augments the curriculum through "interesting events and presentations outside regular classes," and administrators "constantly send out emails about networking events and clubs." Among the more popular activities, "every Thursday, the social club meets at a bar after night class." Even so, "there is not a strong community aspect among SFSU students," as most maintain an active personal and professional life outside of school.

Admissions

Prospective SFSU students are evaluated on their undergraduate academic records, GMAT scores, current resumes, statements of purpose, and letters of recommendation. To be eligible for admission, students must have a 3.0 GPA and an undergraduate degree from an accredited university. While there is no minimum requirement, the University recommends at least three years of full-time work experience before matriculation. For more information about programs or to get help deciding which MBA is right for you, the business school hosts periodic open houses for prospective students.

FINANCIAL FACTS

Annual tuition (in-state/ out-of-state)	$14,200/$23,128
Cost of books	$1,500
Room & board (on/off-campus)	$1,300/$18,000
Average grant	$0
Average loan	$0

ADMISSIONS

Admissions Selectivity Rating	88
# of applications received	569
% applicants accepted	37
% acceptees attending	49
Average GMAT	581
Range of GMAT	540–620
Average GPA	3.40
TOEFL required of international students	Yes
Minimum TOEFL (paper/computer)	590/243
Application fee	$55
International application fee	$55
Regular application deadline	5/1
Regular application notification	5/20
Deferment available	No
Transfer students accepted	Yes
Transfer application policy: Applicants need to apply to the program waive foundation requirements or transfer program courses.	
Non-fall admissions	Yes
Need-blind admissions	No

EMPLOYMENT PROFILE

Career Rating	90	Top 5 Employers Hiring Grads
Percent employed at graduation	75	Wells Fargo Bank, Bank of America, Pacific
Percent employed 3 months after graduation	90	Gas and Electric (PG&E), Genentech, Autodesk
Average base starting salary	$85,000	

SAN JOSE STATE UNIVERSITY
LUCAS GRADUATE SCHOOL OF BUSINESS

Academics

Located smack dab in the middle of the Silicon Valley, San Jose State University's business programs benefit from the energy and innovation of their famous surroundings. "No place on earth is more entrepreneurial or technology-centric" than SJSU, where the MBA programs boast an "innovative syllabus," a "global mindset," and a top-notch faculty from the region's prominent industries. For MBA candidates, SJSU offers several program options: the traditional two-year MBA program on the main SJSU campus, the MBA One (a full-time, cohort-based program that can be completed in just a year), and the Executive-Style MBA, a "flexible program for working students," offering year-round classes on the weekends and in the evenings. With accommodating teachers and a flexible schedule, the Executive-Style MBA "is an ideal program for anyone who wants an MBA, but needs to keep working full-time while getting it." A current student attests, "When I needed to be out of town for work the week of a final, the professor was very willing to reschedule the test for me so it wouldn't interfere with my business trip."

Delivered by a team of "world-class teachers" and an "accommodating" administration, the "academic experience is positive, effective, and worthwhile" at San Jose State. Academically, the program balances "a good mix of lectures, case studies, and assignment[s]." On that note, you'll get a blend of theory and practice in the classroom, as "professors are very knowledgeable and have experience in both academics and industry." "Teachers here are experienced in Silicon Valley trends and do their best to incorporate them into class work." Coursework is interactive, and "discussions in class are lively, [and] periodically include [the] latest news and trends." Friendly as well as experienced, "Professors are very easily approachable and always try to correlate classroom learning with real-world problems as closely as possible."

"Value" is another important factor in many students' decisions to attend SJSU. A state school, SJSU has a much lower price tag than other local programs, giving prospective MBA candidates an "affordable option at a respected school," without leaving the Bay Area. Unfortunately, like many public schools, budget cuts have affected San Jose State and there has been "an increase in tuition" in response. Within the business school, the "administration is struggling with budget issues beyond [its] control," and course availability isn't always what it should be. "The courses aren't offered often enough, there is usually a wait list, so it's a lottery to see if you will even get into the classes you need." Despite limitations, "the administration has been wonderful and very responsive to all concerns," and students say the program runs efficiently.

Career and Placement

The business school at San Jose State University is propitiously located "right in the middle of Silicon Valley, with access to all [the] big-shot companies, and their executives." In addition, "the majority of students in the program come from great high-tech companies," which makes networking as easy as attending class. The Career Center at SJSU helps the undergraduate and graduate student community make connections in the local job market through recruiting events and job fairs. While most SJSU grads score great post-grad positions, some full-time students would like to see Career Services provide "better help finding jobs after graduation," through the addition of new events like "job fairs specifically designed for MBA students." Many students in the part-time program

ADMISSIONS CONTACT: MARGARET FARMER, ADMISSIONS COORDINATOR
ADDRESS: ONE WASHINGTON SQUARE, BUSINESS TOWER 350, SAN JOSE, CA 95192-0162
PHONE: 408-924-3420 • FAX: 408-924-3426
E-MAIL: MBA@COB.SJSU.EDU • WEBSITE: WWW.COB.SJSU.EDU/GRADUATE

receive tuition assistance from their current companies and therefore aren't looking for new jobs after graduation. Currently, you'll find recent SJSU business school graduates working at diverse companies like Charles Schwab, City Bank, Apple, Applied Materials, Chevron Corporation, Cisco Systems, Ebay, E*TRADE, HSBC Group Holdings, IBM, Lockheed Martin, Intel Corporation, Hewlett-Packard, Sprint, Nortel, Genentech, Microsoft, Pepsico, Google, Starbucks Coffee, NASA, Texas Instruments, and Xerox.

Student Life and Environment

Students in SJSU's full-time MBA programs love life on their well-equipped urban campus. The school is located right in the middle of downtown San Jose, and "Food at the Student Union is great and the campus is gorgeous." Diversity is a trademark of this large public school, and within the business program, "a lot of the students speak more than one language and have lived abroad." Despite cultural, ethnic, professional, and political diversity, "Everybody makes an effort to get along, get to know each other. The teamwork required for projects is very good as it encourages intercultural interaction."

In the Executive-Style program, "Classes are taught off campus" so many part-timers "feel very disconnected from the SJSU student body." Fortunately, the auxiliary facility is "centrally-located and well-equipped," and there is plenty of parking for commuters. While full-time cohorts are tight, socializing is more limited among part-timers, who are "very busy outside of class (since we are in an evening program, almost all of my classmates also have full-time jobs)." For most, that means a "get-in and get-out" attitude about school, and "Class work outside of class is usually handled via teleconferences or face-to-face meetings when possible."

Admissions

For those considering SJSU's graduate business programs, the school offers the unique opportunity to schedule a pre-qualification interview, which allows prospective students to discuss their eligibility for the MBA program with admissions officials. In all cases, students must have an undergraduate degree with a GPA of at least 2.5 to be considered for the program. Competitive candidates will have a GPA of 3.3 or better and GMAT scores of 550 or above.

FINANCIAL FACTS

Annual tuition (in-state/ out-of-state)	$12,927/$16,275
Cost of books	$1,754
Room & board (on/off-campus)	$11,730/$12,404

ADMISSIONS

Admissions Selectivity Rating	86
# of applications received	268
% applicants accepted	36
% acceptees attending	53
Average GMAT	551
Range of GMAT	490–605
Average GPA	3.23
TOEFL required of international students	Yes
Minimum TOEFL (paper/computer)	550/213
Application fee	$55
International application fee	$55
Regular application deadline	5/1
Regular application notification	7/1
Deferment available	No
Transfer students accepted	Yes
Transfer application policy: Applicant must meet admission requirements. Up to 20% of units can be transferred from a regionally accredited institution.	
Non-fall admissions	Yes
Need-blind admissions	Yes

Santa Clara University

Leavey School of Business

GENERAL INFORMATION

Type of school	Private
Affiliation	Roman Catholic-Jesuit
Academic calendar	Quarters

SURVEY SAYS...

Cutting-edge classes
Solid preparation in:
Finance, General management,
Teamwork, Doing business in a
global economy, Entrepreneurial
studies

STUDENTS

Enrollment of parent institution	8,800
Enrollment of MBA Program	792
% male/female	67/33
% part-time	82
% underrepresented minority	28
% international	22
Average age at entry	28
Average years work experience at entry	6.0

ACADEMICS

Academic Experience Rating	**80**
Profs interesting rating	84
Profs accesible rating	88
Student/faculty ratio	16:1
% female faculty	18
% underrepresented minority faculty	10
% part-time faculty	30

Joint Degrees

JD/MBA - 4 years; JD/MSIS - 4 years

Academics

The Leavey School of Business at Santa Clara University combines "Jesuit values, primarily in the quality of education and the emphasis on high integrity," with a Silicon Valley location that draws "the cream of the crop to the faculty, such as the former 3Com CEO." The result is a unique MBA program—available in either an evening, accelerated, or Executive MBA format—that "caters to part-time students," but also has plenty to offer full-timers, all within the confines of an "environment that is very supportive." Depending on the MBA track, classes are either offered in cohort or regular class format and on evenings or weekends, which allows students to maintain their current positions in the workplace.

Customer service is the name of the game at Leavey, where administrators "do everything they can to keep up with the changing trends in business and business schools." For example, recently they introduced international exposure for the student (required for those in the Accelerated MBA program). Every summer, one or two student groups visit another country to meet with business leaders and financial institutions to understand how business is done in that country. Students recently went to China, and next year will visit places such as Brazil and Germany. Professors all "know the subject of their teachings and are very professional" and take a similar student-first approach as the administration. They are "eager to help students in the classroom and to introduce them to colleagues for future employment opportunities. They are always available for personal/professional consultation."

Leavey's curriculum employs "a great case-study approach" that "is structured to maximize teamwork abilities." Students find this pedagogical approach immediately applicable to their professional lives. MBAs also "love the 'experimental' classes that students can choose as electives, such as Spirituality and Leadership, which really gets you to focus on your inner self and become a better, less stressed person." Students tell us the school excels in accounting, general management, and marketing. Asked where the school should improve, one student comments, "For some reason, the school is not as well-recognized as other schools in the area, namely Stanford and Berkeley. I think the school will stand to gain if marketed better." Another adds, "I wanted something that was going to challenge me as well as help me get a jump start in the business world. As of so far, the business school has surpassed all expectations."

Career and Placement

Students appreciate the "great Bay-Area network" connected to SCU. MBAs benefit from "a terrific level of interaction with leaders and innovators in Silicon Valley." The Graduate Business Career Management Office capitalizes on these connections to help students procure internships. "The quarter system allows for some interesting internship opportunities in the area because local employers know some students can be available part-time or full-time for a quarter or two," explains one student. Though the Office does offer recruitment events, individual consulting services, and workshops exploring topics—such as personal branding and business etiquette—students feel the service isn't all it could be. As one observes, "Since most students are working, there are limited resources devoted to the internship/career placement program. Also, SCU does not do enough promotion of the program out in the business community. Its reputation is only good regionally, despite its high ranking as a part-time business program." However, many changes have been implemented in career management in the past few years.

FINANCIAL FACTS

Fees	$150
Room & board	$17,000
Average grant	$4,164
Average student loan debt	$19,000

ADMISSIONS

Admissions Selectivity Rating	77
# of applications received	288
% applicants accepted	73
% acceptees attending	76
Average GMAT	611
Average GPA	3.25
TOEFL required of international students	Yes
Minimum TOEFL (paper/computer)	600/250
Application fee	$100
International application fee	$150
Early application deadline	4/1
Regular application deadline	6/1
Application Deadline/Notification	
Round 1:	4/1 /
Round 2:	6/1 /
Deferment available	Yes
Maximum length of deferment	2 Quarters
Transfer students accepted	Yes
Transfer application policy: Apply as all others; must be in good standing in the program they are transferring from.	
Non-fall admissions	Yes
Need-blind admissions	Yes

Employers of graduates are Cisco, Deloitte & Touche, Wells Fargo, Lockheed Martin, Johnson & Johnson, Hewlett-Packard, VMWare, and Intel.

Student Life and Environment

MBAs report that SCU "provides a safe, clean study environment coupled with a very caring and personal staff. The school really treats students as 'customers' and caters to their needs, offering extended library hours during exams. The staff wants the students to succeed." Part-time students appreciate that "the schedule is really terrific and works for working folks as well as commuters." In addition, the school opened a new facility in 2008.

SCU's "gorgeous and safe campus" offers a number of top amenities, including "a state-of-the-art gym and pool, great recreation areas, and a late-night venue called The Bronco with a pool table, a large television, and several couches." Also available are campus-wide wireless access, breakout rooms for private meetings/study, and case-style and collaborative classrooms. Although most students are part-time with numerous other commitments outside school, MBAs here do occasionally socialize. "It's easy to spot people you know everywhere; unfamiliar faces never stay that way." Another student points out that "life at school can be great for those who do the work to get involved. It can be a commuter school if that is all a student wants to get out of it. But there is always something social to do on the weekends, either sponsored by the school or just going out with other MBA students."

"Many students here have jobs," which "provides the best opportunity for networking and recruiting after graduation, as you have gained so many resources at numerous organizations," students tell us. MBAs range from the mid 20s to the mid 40s. Their "backgrounds are extremely diverse; they come from such areas as financial services, banking, semiconductors, software, technology management, finance, and human resources, to name a few." Engineers from the Silicon Valley are the single most visible contingent.

Admissions

Applicants to Leavey MBA programs at SCU must provide the Admissions Office with all of the following: Official transcripts for all postsecondary academic work; official GMAT/GRE score reports reflecting scores no more than five years old; a completed online application; two letters of recommendation from individuals "who can speak directly to your professional strengths and areas of growth;" and personal essays. A third essay is optional, and candidates will be contacted for interviews once all application materials are submitted. Candidates whose first language is not English must also submit official score reports for the TOEFL (minimum required score: 600 paper-based test, 100 on the new IBT test). Leavey also accepts Pearson and IELTS to demonstrate English proficiency. Work experience is not a prerequisite to admission, although a minimum of two years of experience is recommended; on average, admitted students have between five and seven years of post-undergraduate professional experience.

SEATTLE PACIFIC UNIVERSITY
SCHOOL OF BUSINESS AND ECONOMICS

GENERAL INFORMATION
Type of school	Private
Affiliation	Free Methodist
Academic calendar	Quarters

SURVEY SAYS...
Students love Seattle, WA
Solid preparation in:
General management, Operations,
Communication/interpersonal skills

STUDENTS
Enrollment of parent	
institution	3,902
Enrollment of MBA Program	92
% male/female	70/30
% out-of-state	5
% part-time	94
% underrepresented minority	10
% international	14
Average age at entry	33
Average years work experience	
at entry	6.0

ACADEMICS
Academic Experience Rating	**78**
Profs interesting rating	77
Profs accesible rating	78
Student/faculty ratio	17:1
% female faculty	30
% underrepresented minority	
faculty	10
% part-time faculty	5

Academics

A small, Christian-affiliated college in a progressive Northwest city, Seattle Pacific University offers an MBA and Masters in Information Systems Management that considers "another way of doing business." At SPU, business education "really isn't just about the bottom line, but about sustainable, ethical business practices." "Christian values" are fundamental to the school's mission, and students note a "dedication to social issues" through the curricular and extracurricular offerings. In addition, the school's Center for Integrity in Business explores the intersection of faith and business, bringing plenty of experts, new research, and special events to campus. As a result, this MBA doesn't just introduce skills; it focuses on "building character to stand in the face of obstacles." A current student enthuses, "I believe there are some great leaders that come from the school, and will go on to affect their communities and the world in a powerful way."

The MBA at Seattle Pacific is a comprehensive general management degree comprising nine core courses, 10 required advanced courses, and five elective courses. Teamwork and communication skills are emphasized throughout the curriculum, and there is a "focus on social ventures" in the coursework. To tailor the MBA, the school recently introduced another area of concentration in social and sustainable enterprise. In addition, SPU "offers a MS-ISM degree," which "incorporates the best of the technical IT world and the business world to create leaders who can excel, and most importantly, communicate in both worlds." Despite the emphasis on technology, students feel the curriculum could include "better teaching of quantitative subjects and less reliance on qualitative." While small in size, Seattle Pacific University boasts great "connections to [the] business community" and an active "mentorship program" with local business partners through the Center for Applied Learning. In addition, the school frequently invites "community leaders into class[es]...for live demonstration."

For working professionals, "flexibility" is a major advantage of SPU's programs, which include MBA classes in the evenings. Professional students also appreciate "the willingness of the staff and faculty to work with you to accommodate a busy work life." On that note, the atmosphere at SPU is very supportive, and "most of the professors are very receptive to extending help and want feedback on their classes." The program is small, so class sizes are reduced. In the MBA program, there are rarely more than 30 students in a class (and the average class size is just 13 to 15 students.) In addition to provoking students' comments and discussion, "The small class sizes have allowed us good access to our professors." Employing both adjunct and full-time faculty, "Most of the professors are very good" and students, on the whole, are "very satisfied with the classes, professors, and classmates." Students are split on the administration, however. Some say the top brass should "be more responsive to their customers," while others assure us that "The administration is solid, wants the best for us, and works hard to get the best."

FINANCIAL FACTS

Fees	$0
Cost of books	$1,320
Room & board	$12,800
% of students receiving grants	2
Average grant	$1,200

ADMISSIONS

Admissions Selectivity Rating	**75**
# of applications received	42
% applicants accepted	69
% acceptees attending	66
Average GMAT	547
Range of GMAT	430–660
Average GPA	3.27
TOEFL required of international students	Yes
Application fee	$50
International application fee	$50
Regular application deadline	8/1
Regular application notification	8/31
Deferment available	Yes
Maximum length of deferment	2 quarters
Transfer students accepted	Yes
Transfer application policy: Regular Admission Process	
Non-fall admissions	Yes
Need-blind admissions	Yes

Career and Placement

At SPU, students are prepared for the workplace throughout their studies. Practical business applications are emphasized in MBA coursework, and the school's mentorship program is active and appreciated. At the same time, "There aren't very many internship opportunities for graduate business students" at Seattle Pacific University, as many students are already working when they start the program. Those who enter the MBA with more limited business experience say the program would improve if the "Internships program integrated with the grad business program, so we can get some experience before graduating with a new degree."

Open to all MBA candidates, Seattle Pacific University serves the undergraduate, graduate, and alumni communities at the school. Through this office, graduate students can schedule one free career counseling appointment and one resume review, and also gain access to online job boards and research tools. Top employers of Seattle Pacific MBA candidates include Boeing, Microsoft, Starbucks, and Safeco.

Student Life and Environment

Seattle Pacific University is a small, private school, located on a 40-acre campus just 10 minutes from downtown Seattle. Within the graduate business programs, SPU attracts a small but engaging student body. For many, "What has made the classroom so interesting [is] the diverse backgrounds and experiences of...student[s]." Teamwork is a mainstay of the program, and most students are "able to work well on small group projects, have good communication skills, [and] are inclusive." Overall, students are "friendly and helpful," and "the school has a great, positive atmosphere."

Thanks to the flexible course schedule, most MBA candidates are working "professionals with full-time jobs" in Seattle. For busy evening students, life consists of "work all day, school all night, and then homework the rest of the week."

Admissions

Prospective students with an undergraduate GPA of 3.0 and one year of full-time work experience can take up to three MBA courses or two ISM courses before officially applying to the program. SPU accepts applicants for the autumn, winter, spring, and summer terms. To be eligible for the MBA and MS-ISM programs, students must have an undergraduate degree with a 3.0 GPA and substantive work experience (at least one full year of post-undergraduate work experience.) A GMAT score over 500 is preferred.

SEATTLE UNIVERSITY
ALBERS SCHOOL OF BUSINESS AND ECONOMICS

GENERAL INFORMATION

Type of school	Private
Affiliation	Roman Catholic-Jesuit
Academic calendar	Quarter

SURVEY SAYS...
Cutting-edge classes
Solid preparation in:
Teamwork

STUDENTS

Enrollment of parent institution	7,847
Enrollment of MBA Program	498
% male/female	63/37
% part-time	87
% international	23
Average age at entry	30
Average years work experience at entry	7.0

ACADEMICS

Academic Experience Rating	**77**
Profs interesting rating	78
Profs accesible rating	79
Student/faculty ratio	14:1
% female faculty	35
% underrepresented minority faculty	24
% part-time faculty	15

Joint Degrees
JDMBA, 4 years; JD/MSF, 4 years; JD/MIB, 4 years; JD/MPAC, 4 Years

Prominent Alumni
Mohamed Ali Alabbar, Chairman, Emaar Properties; William Foley, Jr., Chairman and CEO, Fidelity National Financial; Gary Brinson, President, G.P. Brinson Investments; Allan Golston, President U.S. Programs Bill and Melinda Gates Foundation; Michelle Burris, Executive VP, CFO, COO OncoGenex

Academics

The Albers School of Business and Economics at Seattle University "is focused entirely on the working professional, so the evening program receives [its] full effort and is not a watered-down version of a day program," students here happily report. The program caters almost exclusively to part-timers (a small number of students attend full time), offering "an extremely flexible part-time MBA program" that "you can complete at your own pace." "You can enroll during any term" and enjoy "the ability to take a quarter off if necessary," MBAs here point out.

Albers' location in Seattle positions it to capitalize on some major international businesses headquartered nearby, and students say the school does just that. "Albers has a great reputation with local businesses, including Microsoft, Boeing, Amazon, Costco, Starbucks, and T-Mobile," one MBA explains. Another reports, "My IT class was taught by the CTO of Alaska Air, which pioneered online ticket sales and kiosk check-in." Seattle businesses feed Albers' "excellent mentor program" and provide valuable internship opportunities for those seeking them (most here already have full-time jobs).

Seattle University is a Jesuit school, and Albers honors that tradition by "really emphasizing personal development in addition to technical skills." The "Jesuit philosophy of social responsibility" manifests itself in a curricular "emphasis on being a good citizen and giving back to the community." As one student explains, Albers seeks to "develop ethical team players who are tuned into workplace dynamics. The basis of this program is that you can learn accounting, finance, etc., anywhere. What sets a university apart is its ability to develop students' leadership and communication skills. The school does an excellent job in this arena while never neglecting the basics."

Students praise Albers' "great resources," "diverse student body," and "wonderful" "small classroom size." Professors here "are passionate about their fields. Many have run businesses themselves and have practical, relevant knowledge. They are easy to talk to and fun to learn from." Perhaps even better, they are "great [at] recognizing that most of the students are working professionals and bringing their experiences into the educational setting." Administrators "respond well to student needs and appear to be interested in improving the school's reputation in the academic and professional worlds."

Career and Placement

The Albers Placement Center provides the expected complement of career counseling, internship and career placement services, job search tools, workshops, and networking events. The school's location in a major business center helps; even so, students here generally yearn for "better placement opportunities and networking." "Increasing the number of companies affiliated for careers and internships" would be a critical improvement, according to one MBA.

Top employers of Seattle University MBAs include: Amazon.com, The Boeing Company, CB Richard Ellis, Clark Nuber, Collier International, Deloitte & Touche, Ernst & Young, Expeditors, GMI, KPMG, Microsoft, Moss Adams, PACCAR, Russell Investment Group, Starbucks, and T-Mobile.

ADMISSIONS CONTACT: JANET SHANDLEY, DIRECTOR, GRADUATE ADMISSIONS
ADDRESS: 901 12TH AVENUE, PO BOX 222000, SEATTLE, WA 98122-1090
PHONE: 206-296-2000 • FAX: 206-296-5656
E-MAIL: GRAD-ADMISSIONS@SEATTLEU.EDU • WEBSITE: WWW.SEATTLEU.EDU/ALBERS

Student Life and Environment

"The courses are all in the evening" at Albers and "most students live away from campus and commute to class," "so graduate student life is not a strong focus" here. Even so, "social/networking activities are planned at least monthly and seem fairly well-attended." Because they commute, students "are very efficient with study groups," and there is "lots of teamwork in the program." For those who can spare the time, campus life provides "lots of organizations doing all sorts of events. There is no lack of opportunity to get involved." Popular extracurricular events include "a valuable executive speaker series."

The campus, conveniently located downtown, "is full of life when the weather is nice, with people playing with their dogs on campus or having a picnic on the grass, or playing with their children." Commuters can hang in the collegium, "which is divided up by major and/or level of education, so the grad students are separate from the undergrad students. They have a kitchen, food available on an honor system, computer access, a living room-like atmosphere, music, games, activities. It really is wonderful." "A coffee stand on the main floor of the business school…stays open into the evening for the grad students." This is Seattle, after all.

Albers' student body consists primarily of "working professionals. Many are in their late 20s to early 30s and a good number are married." They "take their studies very seriously, even while juggling full-time work schedules and personal lives" and "bring a diverse range of experience to the classroom that is very helpful to furthering class discussions."

Admissions

Applicants must submit an official undergraduate transcript; transcripts reflecting any post-baccalaureate academic work (regardless of whether it led to a degree); an official GMAT score report; a current resume; and a completed application form. International students whose first language is not English must also submit an official TOEFL score report (students with low scores may be admitted but must complete the Culture Language Bridge Program). Evidence of two years continuous full-time work experience is required for the MBA, Master of Science in Finance, and Master of International Business programs; work experience is not required for the Master of Professional Accounting program. Personal statements and letters of reference are not required but may be included, especially if there is information an applicant feels is important for the committee to take into consideration in its decision.

FINANCIAL FACTS

Annual tuition	$20,196
Cost of books	$846
Room & board	$12,123
% of students receiving aid	65
% of first-year students receiving aid	65
% of students receiving grants	28
Average award package	$16,484
Average grant	$10,041
Average loan	$19,630
Average student loan debt	$19,442

ADMISSIONS

Admissions Selectivity Rating	75
# of applications received	171
% applicants accepted	75
% acceptees attending	59
Average GMAT	577
Range of GMAT	460–720
Average GPA	3.32
TOEFL required of international students	Yes
Minimum TOEFL (paper/computer)	580/237
International application fee	$55
Regular application deadline	8/20
Deferment available	Yes
Maximum length of deferment	1 year
Transfer students accepted	Yes

Transfer application policy: Applicants must meet standard admission requirements. University will accept 9 quarter credits from AACSB accredited schools. Students transferring from an accredited Jesuit MBA program (JEBNET) may transfer up to 50% of credits.

Non-fall admissions	Yes
Need-blind admissions	Yes

SETON HALL UNIVERSITY
STILLMAN SCHOOL OF BUSINESS

GENERAL INFORMATION

Type of school	Private
Affiliation	Roman Catholic
Academic calendar	Semester

SURVEY SAYS...
Friendly students, Happy students
Solid preparation in:
Communication/interpersonal skills,
Presentation skills, Doing business in
a global economy

STUDENTS

Enrollment of parent institution	10,000
Enrollment of MBA Program	273
Average age at entry	28
Average years work experience at entry	8.0

ACADEMICS

Academic Experience Rating	79
Profs interesting rating	81
Profs accesible rating	83
Student/faculty ratio	7:1
% female faculty	18
% underrepresented minority faculty	24
% part-time faculty	36

Joint Degrees
MBA/JD (open to full-time students only) - 115/118 credits (3.5 to 5 years); MBA/MSN - 54 credits (2.5 - 5 years); MBA/MA Diplomacy & International Relations - 60 credits (2.5-5 years)

Prominent Alumni
James O'Brien, CEO Napier Park Global Capital; Gerald P. Buccino, Chairman and CEO of Buccino & Associates; David B. Gerstein, President Thermwell Products Co., Inc.; Martin Tuchman, CEO Kingstone Capital V and the Tuchman Grou; Steve Waldis, Founder, President & CEO of Synchronoss

Academics

Located just outside the hustle and bustle of New York City, Seton Hall University offers a convenient, suburban alternative for city professionals looking to pursue an MBA. At Seton Hall, "the MBA program is designed for students who work full time," and features evening classes and a "convenient location" near major New Jersey roadways. (In addition to the campus-based program, the school offers "classes off campus at the Hackensack University Medical Center.") Coining its program "The Practical MBA," efficiency is a key advantage of Seton Hall, which offers "a streamlined program of 42 credits, compared to other schools with 60 credits." Even with lower credit requirements, the program can be "taxing" and students warn, "The commitment, perseverance, and dedication one has to make while working a demanding job in NYC or on the NJ business coastline across from NYC must not be underestimated." Fortunately, Seton Hall makes every effort to accommodate busy professionals. Here, professors are highly accommodating and accessible, and "Even if they can't meet for special office hours, personal cell phone calls or emails are not uncommon."

"Seton Hall University is one of the most prestigious universities in the area," and the MBA program lives up to the school's strong reputation. Throughout the MBA core curriculum, the "subject material is made very relevant to modern business," with a focus on accounting, economics, and behavioral and quantitative sciences. After the core, students can tailor their coursework through academic concentrations in fields like accounting, information technology management, and sports management. The academic experience is hands-on, so be prepared to roll up your sleeves and get busy: "Presentations, in-class discussions, and group assignments are [a] vital part of every course." In addition, every student must conceive and complete a service project before graduation. Students really appreciate the fact that Seton Hall "incorporates core values in its program: integrity, diversity, social responsibility."

In the classroom, "Professors can be hit or miss but, for the most part, they are good at what they do and teach well." A current student enthuses, "I am very impressed with how lively my professors are...even the ones teaching stats and heavy quants." In addition to tenured staff, Seton Hall can "attract excellent adjunct professors from nearby corporations in New York City and Northern New Jersey." Most are "demonstrated leaders in the field," ranging from the "CEO of a public company" to a "lawyer for the Vatican." Things run smoothly at Seton Hall and, throughout the business school, "The offices are always well-staffed with knowledgeable employees." An important compliment to the academic experience, students appreciate that "The facilities are modern and the use of technology aids with learning during a full-time work lifestyle." For example, "The trading room is equipped with a Bloomberg terminal which is also a nice touch."

Career and Placement

The Seton Hall University Career Center assists both undergraduate and graduate students with their job search through career assessment and career counseling, mock interviews, online job boards, and networking events. For MBA candidates, the Career Center maintains several counselors who are specially designated to help graduate business students find a job or internship. While many Seton Hall students are already working when they enter the program, they say, "The school has been working towards providing more support for career transition, such as networking events and career fairs."

ADMISSIONS CONTACT: CATHERINE BIANCHI, DIRECTOR OF GRADUATE ADMISSIONS
ADDRESS: GRADUATE ADMISSIONS - STILLMAN SCHOOL OF BUSINESS, 400 SOUTH ORANGE AVENUE
SOUTH ORANGE, NJ 07079-2692 • PHONE: 973-761-9262 • FAX: 973-761-9208
E-MAIL: MBA@SHU.EDU • WEBSITE: WWW.BUSINESS.SHU.EDU

Seton Hall alumni work at a wide range of companies, including Johnson & Johnson, Deloitte, Ernst & Young, Merrill Lynch, New York Life Insurance Company, Booz Allen Hamilton, New Jersey Nets, New York Mets, New York Yankees, Madison Square Garden, Masterfoods USA, Mercedes-Benz, Prudential Financial, PricewaterhouseCoopers, and Tiffany & Co.

Student Life and Environment

Located on a "very safe and clean" campus "just 10 miles from New York City," Seton Hall University offers a pleasant environment with excellent facilities. The MBA program is largely part-time, so most students "drive in for class and leave" directly afterwards. However, others tell us that they "love spending time on the green terrace anytime between or after classes," or often "grab food at the dining hall/food court, which has a diverse selection of restaurants." Housed in Jubilee Hall—"the new business building with numerous resources inside it for class"—business students enjoy a comfortable and modern facility, with "state-of-the art" resources, wireless Internet, and web-based classroom technology.

The largely part-time student population can "create difficulties in creating and sustaining clubs on the school campus;" however, the upshot is that you get a "great mix of industry experience among students" which contributes to class discussion and "creates a stimulating learning environment." Most students have work experience before entering the program, but "The age range and experience is dramatic—from fifth years to [those seeking] career transitions, as well as dual-degree students from the Whitehead School of Diplomacy." Despite their differences, "Everyone is eager to learn and help out the others around them," and, in general, group work goes smoothly and everyone pulls their weight.

Admissions

To apply to Seton Hall's Stillman School of Business, prospective graduate students must submit transcripts from their undergraduate studies, GMAT scores, a resume of work experience and credentials, a two-paragraph personal statement, and a letter of recommendation. Every applicant is evaluated individually; however, Seton Hall generally requires admits to have a minimum undergraduate GPA of 3.0 on a 4.0 scale, and a minimum GMAT score of 500. Applications are reviewed and admissions decisions are rendered on a rolling basis.

FINANCIAL FACTS

Annual tuition	$26,664
Fees	$610
Cost of books	$1,200
Room & board	$12,000
% of students receiving grants	3
Average grant	$23,036

ADMISSIONS

Admissions Selectivity Rating	78
# of applications received	255
% applicants accepted	58
% acceptees attending	60
Average GMAT	547
Range of GMAT	490–600
Average GPA	3.17
TOEFL required of international students	Yes
Minimum TOEFL (paper/computer)	607/254
Application fee	$75
International application fee	$75
Regular application deadline	5/31
Deferment available	Yes
Maximum length of deferment	1 academic year
Transfer students accepted	Yes

Transfer application policy: Students must submit a formal application and satisfy all requirements for admission. In addition to graduate transcripts, it is suggested that the student also submit a course description and syllabus for the courses he/she intends to transfer. Upon gaining admission to the MBA program, the Associate Dean for Academic Services will review the student's transcripts to determine which graduate courses may be transferred. Students are eligible to transfer/waive up to a maximum of 12 credits.

Non-fall admissions	Yes
Need-blind admissions	Yes

SHIPPENSBURG UNIVERSITY
JOHN L. GROVE COLLEGE OF BUSINESS

Academics

Founded in 1971, Shippensburg University's John L. Grove College of Business is one of the premier business schools in the Mid-Atlantic, offering three different options for its MBA program: a part-time night program for working professionals, a full-time cohort program for recent college graduates and young professionals, and an entirely online program. The school's numerous satellite campuses in Harrisburg, York, and East Stroudsburg offer the convenience and proximity that many of those who attend Shippensburg rank highest on their list of priorities, and the administration is "very flexible with class scheduling and seem to try and accommodate everyone within the three different branch campuses." "From what I know, they are doing a good job running the program," says a student.

Overall, students come here because "Shippensburg offers a great curriculum for the cost." Though the student body is "sometimes challenged with students lacking 'real-world' experience," the conversation and discussion is "animated and good when properly facilitated and creates a great learning environment." The faculty are "good - some are great," but their grading standards are sometimes too forgiving: "they pass everyone," according to one student. One plus that students commend is the faculty's willingness "to be available for contact almost all the time." Small class sizes and a "good use of technology" also facilitate "an intimate learning experience between professor and student."

Career and Placement

The lax grading means "there are people [who] will get an MBA [who] don't deserve it." Still, the school's reputation proceeds it within the central Pennsylvania area, and a Shippensburg MBA usually serves the intended purpose of the student, which is to receive an accredited MBA; whether they are trying to switch careers or advance within a current one, most students will take care of their professional development goals on their own. There are no options for students to focus on one area in the MBA program, which a few do regret, but students agree that they "would highly recommend the program to prospective students." "I have been impressed and thoroughly pleased," says one.

Student Life and Environment

It's a busy life for most of those who attend Shippensburg, who are often "older, non-traditional students" who come to campus just for classes – the part-time program is two classes a night, one night a week – and then duck out to attend to personal responsibilities. "I work 9-10 hrs a day, then take two classes away from the main campus. I don't have time to become involved in much else," says a student, who is one of many who prefer to keep their experience "simple and basic." Students are "accepting, caring, and helpful" and range from fresh-out-of-school grads to veterans of the working world, with a fair number of "mid-level employees of government or local companies" enrolling in the part-time program.

Those who attend classes at the satellite campuses, mainly "working professionals from a diverse range of businesses," "do not have the interactions that people from the main campus do." Most clubs and activities meet in the late afternoon and so are reserved for full-time students, and part-time students do wish that the school was better at "making the business clubs more accessible to working professionals." Within class, people find a "very good camaraderie" and fellow students that are "open-minded in group situations and overall supportive and collaborative."

Admissions

The Admissions Office at Shippensburg University requires applicants to submit official copies of transcripts for all undergraduate work and a current resume. GMAT scores are required for applicants that have less than 5 years of work experience from the date of their undergraduate degree; students required to take the GMAT must submit an official GMAT score report of 450 or higher. In addition, applicants must either have work experience or undergraduate credits in computer usage, oral and written communication, and quantitative analysis. A personal statement and letters of recommendation are both optional. International applicants must not only meet all of the above requirements but must also submit: an international student application; an evaluation of their transcripts by a professional evaluating service (either Educational Credential Evaluators (ECE) or World Education Services (WES)); an official score report for the TOEFL; and an affidavit of support accompanied by a current bank statement. Applicants who do not meet Shippensburg's admissions requirements may seek special consideration. Some such students do receive provisional admissions status, which allows them to enter the program and continue contingent upon success in their initial MBA course work.

FINANCIAL FACTS

Annual tuition (in-state/ out-of-state)	$7,488/$11,232
Fees	$1,071
Cost of books	$1,000
% of students receiving aid	51
% of first-year students receiving aid	59
% of students receiving grants	25
Average grant	$8,394
Average loan	$14,495

ADMISSIONS

Admissions Selectivity Rating	**77**
# of applications received	231
% applicants accepted	66
% acceptees attending	99
Average GMAT	531
Range of GMAT	465–560
Average GPA	3.15
TOEFL required of international students	Yes
Minimum TOEFL (paper/computer)	570/230
Application fee	$40
International application fee	$40
Deferment available	Yes
Maximum length of deferment	Up to one year
Transfer students accepted	Yes
Transfer application policy: If applicable can transfer up to nine credits.	
Non-fall admissions	Yes
Need-blind admissions	Yes

SIMMONS COLLEGE
SCHOOL OF MANAGEMENT

Academics

Business-focused women will find many reasons to be drawn to the School of Management at Simmons College, a school "known for empowering and motivating women." Foundations of Business, a week-long symposium, kicks off the MBA program, leading directly into courses on decision-making, marketing, accounting, leadership, and other fundamentals of business. Borrowing from the case-based learning style developed at Harvard Business School, Simmons boasts a "strong track record of success" with its "focus on women in business and sustainability." These efforts make Simmons "a leader in the business world in helping women achieve their full potential."

Giving credence to "the reputation it has as a great program for women," there is an "emphasis placed on principled leadership and giving voice to values." A "highly supportive and accessible" administration, along with "extremely dedicated, energetic and passionate" professors, help ensure that despite an "intense" work load students "are learning volumes every week." However, some students say an "understaffed" administration "makes it difficult to do alternate course pathways," while others suggest there exists "an unwillingness to share information or allow student participation ... We are not involved in curriculum or scheduling decisions except for general surveying."

Most in the MBA program are part-time students, and professors "recognize that most of us work full time and cannot make traditional office hours." Teachers are teaching from experience. Professors "typically had a wealth of business (or non-academic) experience that they draw upon in class, which has been very helpful to solidify course concepts." These "very accessible" instructors share "stories and experiences that help us learn." Because "the coursework applies to real concepts" students find it is "easy to see how the assignments hone in certain concepts." Indeed, "as a woman in the business world, Simmons has given me the voice and confidence to stand up for what I believe and to create change."

Career and Placement

Women seek a business education at Simmons because "the network is incredibly strong and wide, and every alum I talked to said that the network has been integral in her success." Indeed, the view is that the opportunities offered here "couldn't even be approached by any other business school." Students need only "find a professor, work with them constantly, and prove to them your abilities and then you will find plenty of opportunities to seize," opportunities which will "undoubtedly help me secure a great position after school." Staff here "have made it their mission to ensure that each of us is known and seen and has access to the resources that we need."

Entrepreneurship opportunities, career symposiums, employer luncheons, industry panels, company presentations and more are among the benefits offered by the Career Services Office. Individualized career counseling and networking is also available. The strengths of the Simmons network are most noticeable locally, where "employers inevitably make favorable comments about the SOM." Graduates from Simmons have ended up at companies like American Express, Bank of America, Blue Cross Blue Shield, Deloitte, Digitas, Four Seasons Resort, The Gap, Genzyme, Harvard University, Hewlett Packard, JP Morgan, Kraft Food, Monster Worldwide, MOMA, Partners Healthcare, Pfizer, PricewaterhouseCoopers, Sun Microsystems, Time Warner, Turner Construction, and Unisys.

ADMISSIONS CONTACT: MELISSA TERRIO, DIRECTOR OF ADMISSION
ADDRESS: 300 THE FENWAY, BOSTON, MA 02115
PHONE: 617-521-3840 • FAX: 617-521-3880
E-MAIL: SOMADM@SIMMONS.EDU • WEBSITE: WWW.SIMMONS.EDU/SOM

Student Life and Environment

Part-time MBA students will find many others who share their varied burdens. "I'm an evening student," one student writes, "so most of my cohort is employed full time and is juggling the demands of work, school, and family. We tend to be respectful of one another and supportive in our struggles to attain this degree." The "intelligent, driven, diverse, hard-working, goal-oriented, inspiring" student body is glad that "Simmons makes it as easy as possible for me to balance everything while not relaxing for a moment their high academic standards." The mutual sense of admiration is not merely strong on a personal level – "my fellow students are amazing, smart, accomplished, and interesting women," another student proclaims – it also extends to the education itself, where those same students "consistently bring new insights to the classroom."

Evening students regret having "so little time outside of study groups to get to know these fascinating, professional women even better," but those with an opportunity to get more involved at the school will find no shortage of ways in which to do it. Many clubs and activities offer more than a mere diversion from the classroom; they also offer ways to further one's education and network. These include Net Impact GOLD, Women on Boards, the Entrepreneur Connect club, the Student Ambassador teams (Recruitment, Admissions, and Marketing), career services events, company presentations, the Simmons Leadership Conference, and more. Net Impact in particular "is very active in offering students opportunities to learn about green jobs, environmental hot topics, and other responsible business practices." Still, some students admit that "it is hard to participate heavily in the activities due to work load," while others complain that since the otherwise "very strong" part-time program is "meant for the commuter student … not much is done to enrich the part-time experience."

Admissions

Admissions are based on aptitude and promise; candidates are evaluated on an individual basis. Applicants are required to submit an application and essays, two letters of recommendation, official transcripts from all post-secondary education, a current resume, and official GMAT or GRE scores. International applicants must submit TOEFL scores.

FINANCIAL FACTS

Annual tuition	$1,280 per credit
Fees	$100 per semester
Cost of books	$2,500
Room & board	$7,500
% of students receiving aid	83
% of first-year students receiving aid	75
% of students receiving grants	60
Average award package	$22,417
Average grant	$7,903
Average loan	$19,986
Average student loan debt	$39,432

ADMISSIONS

Admissions Selectivity Rating	**78**
# of applications received	153
% applicants accepted	63
% acceptees attending	64
Average GMAT	550
Range of GMAT	477–632
Average GPA	3.34
TOEFL required of international students	Yes
Minimum TOEFL (paper/computer)	550/213
Application fee	$75
International application fee	$75
Application Deadline/Notification	
Round 1:	2/15 / 3/15
Round 2:	3/15 / 4/15
Round 3:	4/15 / 5/15
Deferment available	Yes
Maximum length of deferment	1 year
Transfer students accepted	Yes
Transfer application policy: Transfer credit reviewed on a case by case basis	
Non-fall admissions	Yes
Need-blind admissions	Yes

EMPLOYMENT PROFILE

Career Rating	92	Grads Employed by Function% Avg. Salary	
Percent employed at graduation	72	Marketing	(20%) $78,750
Percent employed 3 months after graduation	81	Operations	(10%) $66,500
		Consulting	(6%) $82,500
Average base starting salary	$75,714	Management	(10%) $87,500
		Finance	(8%) $79,167
		Other	(45%) $72,857
		Top 5 Employers Hiring Grads	
		BNY Mellon, Harvard University, Vanguard, EMC, Ocean Spray	

SOUTHEAST MISSOURI STATE UNIVERSITY
DONALD L. HARRISON COLLEGE OF BUSINESS

GENERAL INFORMATION

Type of school	Public
Affiliation	No Affiliation
Academic calendar	Semester

SURVEY SAYS...
Friendly students
Solid preparation in:
General management,
Communication/interpersonal skills,
Presentation skills, Computer skills

STUDENTS

Enrollment of parent	
institution	11,000
Enrollment of MBA Program	132
% male/female	53/47
% out-of-state	7
% part-time	68
% underrepresented minority	2
% international	27
Average age at entry	26
Average years work experience	
at entry	5.0

ACADEMICS

Academic Experience Rating	75
Profs interesting rating	76
Profs accesible rating	79
Student/faculty ratio	19:1
% female faculty	40
% underrepresented minority	
faculty	10

Joint Degrees
Joint MBA and Masters in
International Business and
Economics offered with University
of Applied Sciences, Schmalkalden,
Germany.

Academics

For a "top-notch education at an affordable price," Missouri residents recommend the business school at Southeast Missouri State University. An inexpensive public school, "The university provides an excellent bang for your buck," yet doesn't skimp on a quality education. Catering to current and soon-to-be professionals in the Cape Giradeau area, all classes are held in the evenings. However, SEMO's MBA programs can be completed either part time or full time (the former is the more popular option), and the school operates an entirely online program for students whose schedules do not accommodate classroom work. The program begins with the common core, which covers key business areas ranging from accounting and finance to quantitative and qualitative research methods. After completing the core, students can focus their studies in a single business area, such as finance, industrial management, health administration, or sports management. In addition to coursework, full-time students often augment their coursework with for-credit internships, with teaching assistant positions through the ample "graduate assistantship opportunities" (which also include tuition assistance), or through one of the school's numerous short-term overseas programs. As one appreciative student exclaims, "Their international programs were the best experience of my life!"

Appealing to mature students, "The class environment is unique, in that is very professional, as if you were going to work." Likewise, "The teachers expect all students to come prepared and [they] develop helpful but strenuous assignments." A current student adds, "They give us the responsibility to learn and take on the role as a facilitator of learning rather than keeping it very structured, letting the students do a lot on their own." The teaching staff gets strong reviews from current students, who say their instructors add "very helpful and relevant insight into what we are studying." A current student enthuses, "The professors at Southeast are wonderful. Not only are they experienced in their field, but their teaching styles are excellent."

Despite the emphasis on professionalism, the environment at SEMO is incredibly down-to-earth and friendly. Here, "class sizes are small, so professors get to know you pretty well" and in-class discussions are encouraged. For those who need extra guidance, "The teachers do a great job of making themselves available to the students outside of the classroom for one-on-one help." The small size also facilitates networking between students; "having a smaller campus helps you connect with a wide variety of people in a variety of fields," which makes "classroom discussions very interesting and relevant to the real world."

Career and Placement

As a graduate student enrolled in the MBA program, SEMO students may take advantage of the various services offered through the university's Career Services office. Career Services offers free career advising, salary projections, resume and cover letter revisions, career testing, and interview preparation by appointment. The Career Services office also organizes both job fairs and campus recruiting programs, free of charge. For a fee, students may also access a list of current job opening listings in the region. Because their efforts serve the entire school community, MBA candidates feel, "The Career Center could be greatly improved in order to better serve graduate students."

FINANCIAL FACTS

Cost of books	$500
Room & board	$5,200
Average award package	$11,200
Average grant	$11,200

ADMISSIONS

Admissions Selectivity Rating	**72**
# of applications received	118
% applicants accepted	78
% acceptees attending	62
Average GMAT	504
Range of GMAT	440–545
Average GPA	3.28
TOEFL required of international students	Yes
Minimum TOEFL (paper/computer)	550/213
Application fee	$30
International application fee	$40
Deferment available	Yes
Maximum length of deferment	1 year
Transfer students accepted	Yes
Transfer application policy: may transfer 9 hours authorized by Director of MBA Program	
Non-fall admissions	Yes
Need-blind admissions	Yes

While Career Service does not work exclusively with graduate business students, students say "The MBA office does a great job of making MBA students aware of job opportunities that come to its attention." In fact, many students say, "The school puts a great deal of effort [into helping] students get jobs after graduation and organizes various networking events throughout the semester." Students enrolled in the program full-time can also lay the foundation for their career through for-credit internships.

Student Life and Environment

Located in the riverside city of Cape Giradeau, the SEMO campus is a "peaceful and safe place" to work and study. Just over 100 miles from St. Louis, Cape Giradeau is a small city of 35,000, yet provides "everything that we need as students, and…is a great place to live as well." With classes held in the evenings, most SEMO students work during the day and commute to school in the evenings; therefore, they aren't actively involved in campus life. However, if you're interested in some campus camaraderie, students assure us that "There are a ton of things going on all the time, if people just look around."

On the whole, "Students at SEMO are very diverse and intelligent" joining the business program "from many different work environments." The atmosphere is more collaborative than competitive, and, for group assignments, everyone is "very helpful and work great together." Students say "The moderately-sized student body is also a strength." At this school, "It's big enough that you can meet plenty of new people, but small enough that you can walk across campus and run into several people you know on the way."

Admissions

To be eligible for admission to Southeast Missouri State University's graduate business program, students must have an undergraduate degree in business from an accredited college or university. Students who do not have an undergraduate degree in business must take a series of prerequisite coursework before they can begin the MBA. Successful applicants will generally have a minimum GMAT score of over 400 and a minimum GPA in foundational (prerequisite) coursework of a C or better. To be considered for a graduate assistantship position, applicants must have a minimum undergraduate grade point average of 2.7.

SOUTHERN ILLINOIS UNIVERSITY CARBONDALE
COLLEGE OF BUSINESS

Academics

With its affordable tuition and strong academic programs, Southern Illinois University is a smart pick for professionals from the Midwest. Through the College of Business, SIU offers a traditional MBA, a masters of accountancy, and a PhD in business administration, as well as an AACSB-accredited online MBA. Students in the campus program dole out praise for the business school. "The MBA program is outstanding and the professors are well-educated in their particular fields." Students are also quick to point out that the faculty boasts "a lot of well-established names," including a number of professors who are "recognized worldwide for their research." Small class sizes and a friendly atmosphere ensure that students have close contact with their talented professors. Coming from a "wide variety of academic and professional backgrounds," professors not only offer deep "insight and knowledge" in their subject area, they also encourage debate and discussion between students. Classes are "full of intellectual conversation," and students "contribute valuable information to class discussion and always make you strive to outperform your peers." A current student enthuses, "Classes can actually be enjoyable because I know I'm going to learn something each day." Outside the classroom, collaboration is encouraged, and frequent "group work is also time consuming, but very educational."

Speaking to the quality of the program, a large number of current MBA candidates received their undergraduate degree from SIU's College of Business and decided to stay on or return to the school for the graduate program. Particularly attractive to early-career MBA candidates, the school offers the opportunity to apply for a graduate assistantship, which pays a monthly stipend in return for twenty hours a week of work with a full-time faculty member. These positions are valuable, but challenging; a current student with a graduate assistantship explains, "Most of the day is spent on campus, with some days lasting from 8 a.m. to 10 p.m." On that note, the MBA workload is intense, "but not impossible," and students "are encouraged to learn how to work more efficiently" in order to keep up with the demands of the curriculum. While instructors are often "very strict and demanding," they "typically have an open door policy for students." When you take the time to visit professors in their offices, "They are really good at answering questions and make sure that you have a full understanding of everything before leaving."

SIU offers "very competitive tuition rates for an excellent program." Regardless of affordability, students are pleased to report that the school maintains a "very professional environment" with "efficient operations" and "good communication" with the student body. At SIU, "weekly if not daily emails are sent to business students informing them of upcoming events." SIU attracts many recent grads and early-career professionals, who would like to see "more interaction with employers (Internships, recruiting, projects)" to prepare them for the real world. At the same time, the school offers a number of programs "that help prepare students for the real world. For example, "Saluki Student Investment Fund manages the SIU foundation portfolio worth over 1 million dollars." SIU also offers a month-long overseas program for students who would like to add an international focus to their studies.

ADMISSIONS CONTACT: DR. SUZANNE ALTOBELLO, MBA PROGRAMS DIRECTOR
ADDRESS: REHN HALL 133, 1025 LINCOLN DRIVE, MAIL CODE 4625, CARBONDALE, IL 62901
PHONE: 618-453-3030 • FAX: 618-453-2832
E-MAIL: COBGP@BUSINESS.SIU.EDU • WEBSITE: MBA.BUSINESS.SIU.EDU

Career and Placement

The College of Business Placement Center at Southern Illinois University serves undergraduate and graduate students, alumni, and online MBA candidates. The center provides individual career counseling services and conducts mock interviews, maintains online job listings, and organizes campus career fairs. Through the center, students also have access to a number of online job boards, as well as the "Digital Kiosk," a collection of career-related articles and resources for job seekers. Those who have attended career events say, "The employers at career fairs are substantial, including CAT, Boeing, etc." At the same time, graduate students feel "career development is a little weak" for MBA graduates. The Placement Center does "have contacts with the big four accounting firms," but most hiring managers come to campus in search of undergraduate students and accounting majors.

Student Life and Environment

While there are more than 20,000 students on the greater SIUC campus, there is a collegial atmosphere within the business school. Enrolling around 100 graduate students, "The College of Business is not huge and we quickly get to know everyone." Students at SIU are "mostly from the Midwest"; however, the school attracts a number of international students, bringing "very diverse cultures" to the small campus environment. Students are "high achievers for the most part," who take their studies seriously. When the semester is thoroughly underway, MBA candidates are "slightly insane from [a] lack of sleep." Fortunately, most manage to be both "friendly and competitive at the same time." Some say they "like to catch drinks together after class."

Nestled within the Shawnee National Forest, "Carbondale is a college town, hence life here is very peaceful." Students really appreciate "the small town feel that normally doesn't go along with such a large university." In their free time, Carbondale residents can "go to the wineries, hike in the beautiful state parks, or just enjoy the beautiful weather." When in search of more cosmopolitan pleasures (as well as a larger job market), the city of St. Louis is fewer than 100 miles to the west of SIUC's campus; both Chicago and Kansas City are also within striking distance, fewer than 300 miles away.

Admissions

To be eligible for admission to SIU's graduate programs, students must have a minimum GMAT score of 550 and a GPA of at least 2.7 for the last two years of undergraduate coursework. While these are the required minimums, the median GPA for students admitted MBA program was much higher, at 3.5. Students with a business-related degree from an AACSB-accredited school and a GPA of 3.5 or higher may qualify for a GMAT waiver.

FINANCIAL FACTS

Annual tuition (in-state/ out-of-state)	$7,767/$17,897
Fees	$2,798
Cost of books	$1,100
Room & board (on/off-campus)	$12,712/$0
% of students receiving aid	72
% of first-year students receiving aid	74
% of students receiving grants	37
Average award package	$22,283
Average grant	$8,233
Average loan	$25,559
Average student loan debt	$21,045

ADMISSIONS

Admissions Selectivity Rating	74
# of applications received	118
% applicants accepted	86
% acceptees attending	87
Average GMAT	594
Range of GMAT	550–628
Average GPA	3.35
TOEFL required of international students	Yes
Minimum TOEFL (paper/computer)	550/213
Application fee	$50
International application fee	$50
Early application deadline	3/1
Early notification date	3/15
Regular application deadline	6/15
Regular application notification	6/30
Deferment available	Yes
Maximum length of deferment	1 year
Transfer students accepted	Yes
Transfer application policy: We will accept a maximum of 6 hours of transfer credit from an AACSB-accredited school. Courses that meet our foundation requirements are not transferred, they are merely accepted. as fulfilling the requirement.	
Non-fall admissions	Yes
Need-blind admissions	No

SOUTHERN ILLINOIS UNIVERSITY EDWARDSVILLE
SCHOOL OF BUSINESS

Academics

Located just thirty minutes away from downtown St. Louis, the School of Business at Southern Illinois University Edwardsville offers an "exceptional and...convenient" MBA program with courses in evening and weekend formats on the Edwardsville campus. This "up and coming school" offers "a well-rounded program" that is "taught by professors with real world experience." The school's curriculum, which includes condensed ten week courses, tends to be more general, meaning that students "take a wide variety of classes" and follow a pretty standard structure. Though some wish that there were "more possible concentrations" and the program was less geared towards "non-business undergrads," most are quite pleased with the degree they obtain here since the school is "in the midst of an expansion."

Students love most of their "exceptional" professors and feel that "they relate the coursework to everyday life." They "seem to truly care about students learning and being able to apply information in the real world," and "know how to communicate their information to their students effectively." "Their ability to answer questions from their experience in the field has earned my respect," says one admiring student. "Most of my professors still consult in their respective industries. They are very current on business trends and developments," says a student.

Though the overall satisfaction level is quite high, people agree that the school could stand to "weed out some of the less effective professors"; while most "are readily available for appointments or have preset office times," a handful "could not be inconvenienced with meeting with students outside normal class time." The school's administration is known for being "easily accessible and friendly," "has made planning classes easy," and has "a great concept of real-world work life [that they] implement . . . in the classroom." Classes here place a great deal of emphasis on group work, which is furthered by the "ease of communication through online resources (great e-presence)."

Career and Placement

Most students at SIUE "seem to be working professionals pursuing their MBA in order to enhance their income or receive a promotion," and "SIUE has the best value for the level of accreditation of all St. Louis area schools." Some wish that the school would "align coursework with skills needed for upper management"; the more experienced students are pretty much in agreement that classes are a breeze. "The instructors are good, but anyone who breathes gets a B," says one. A couple of students who are looking to get placed into a new job directly after graduation wish that the school would "add more networking and recruiting efforts aimed specifically at MBA students," but others have lauded the school for its "helpfulness when acquiring an assistantship," among other things. Its base efforts are also appreciated: "I went to a mock interview at the CDC, and I was treated seriously and went away from the experience pleased that I'd spent the time. Plus, they've always offered (organized) career fairs, resume services, and other professional events to the MBA students, as well as the undergraduate students."

ADMISSIONS CONTACT: SCHOOL OF BUSINESS STUDENT SERVICES, ADMISSIONS OFFICER
ADDRESS: CAMPUS BOX 1186, EDWARDSVILLE, IL 62026
PHONE: 618-650-3840 • FAX: 618-650-3979
E-MAIL: MBA@SIUE.EDU • WEBSITE: WWW.SIUE.EDU/BUSINESS/MBA

Student Life and Environment

The students at SIUE are "a near equal mix of recent undergraduate graduates and returning adults," all of whom are "very competitive, yet helpful and friendly." Everybody "is nice," and "it helps that everybody is working on their MBA for similar reasons." Though many in the MBA program just drop in for classes (one student says that "social life is not existent among MBA students"), there are "many various clubs, sports, Greek life, and volunteer options at SIUE" on this "vibrant and active campus" for those who do choose to participate.

Aside from its extremely convenient location near St. Louis, the campus is located on its own 2600 acres, "making it non-commercialized, which is another plus." Furthermore, "the size is perfect and the accommodations are excellent."

Admissions

Applicants to the SIUE MBA program must apply for admission to the university Graduate School, which includes submitting official transcripts for all post-secondary academic work and an official GMAT score report (applicants holding a PhD, MD, or equivalent degree need not submit GMAT scores, and graduates of SIUE do not need to have official transcripts sent). Admissions decisions are based primarily on undergraduate performance and GMAT scores (recent entering class had an average GPA of 3.2 and average GMAT score of 520). The school recommends at least two years of work experience prior to entering the program. Entering students must demonstrate proficiency (typically through undergraduates coursework) in statistics and computer software; students lacking these proficiencies will be required to complete non-degree courses in the subjects in order to gain proficiency. International applicants must meet all the above criteria and submit an official TOEFL score report (minimum score of 550 paper-based test or 213 computer-based test). Rejected applicants may appeal the admissions decision to the MBA program manager. Applicants with undergraduate GPAs of at least 2.8 may be admitted conditionally, pending subsequent successful completion of six credit hours of coursework in the program.

FINANCIAL FACTS

Annual tuition (in-state/ out-of-state)	$6,504/$16,260
Fees	$2,820
Cost of books	$2,500
Room & board (on/off-campus)	$10,000
% of students receiving aid	47
% of first-year students receiving aid	75
% of students receiving grants	26
Average award package	$11,899
Average grant	$1,585
Average loan	$4,042
Average student loan debt	$16,000

ADMISSIONS

Admissions Selectivity Rating	74
# of applications received	126
% applicants accepted	72
% acceptees attending	85
Average GMAT	495
Range of GMAT	400–620
Average GPA	3.15
TOEFL required of international students	Yes
Minimum TOEFL (paper/computer)	550/213
Application fee	$30
International application fee	$30
Deferment available	Yes
Maximum length of deferment	1 year
Transfer students accepted	Yes
Transfer application policy: From an AACSB accredited school and up to 9 hours.	
Non-fall admissions	Yes
Need-blind admissions	Yes

SOUTHERN METHODIST UNIVERSITY
COX SCHOOL OF BUSINESS

GENERAL INFORMATION

Type of school	Private
Affiliation	Methodist
Academic calendar	Mod/Semester

SURVEY SAYS...
Friendly students, Smart classrooms
Solid preparation in:
Accounting

STUDENTS

Enrollment of parent institution	10,982
Enrollment of MBA Program	560
% male/female	76/24
% part-time	61
% underrepresented minority	17
% international	19
Average age at entry	28
Average years work experience at entry	4.8

ACADEMICS

Academic Experience Rating	**92**
Profs interesting rating	91
Profs accesible rating	92
Student/faculty ratio	39:1
% female faculty	20
% underrepresented minority faculty	2
% part-time faculty	15

Joint Degrees
JD/MBA, 4 years; MA Arts
Administration/MBA, 21 months

Prominent Alumni
Beth E. Mooney, Chair and CEO - KeyCorp; Thomas Horton, Chair and CEO - American Airlines; Martin L. Flanagan, President and CEO - Invesco; Hugh Jones, CEO - Travelocity; William J. O'Neil, Chairman and CEO - Investor's Business Daily

Academics

Southern Methodist University provides its students with an "exceptional academic business community that you can't find anywhere outside of the coasts." Located in Dallas, "a great business city," the school has "a great reputation in the Southwest" and may just be "the premier school in the entire Southwest, not just the DFW area." Dallas is a major draw for students as, in addition to being "a very attractive and livable city," it is a "thriving and growing economic area" with "no state income tax" and "one of the strongest economies in the country." SMU fosters "a competitive environment where fellow students challenge one another in the classroom, but also encourage each other to excel through leveraging one another's work experience." The campus is "beautiful" as are the "new graduate business school facilities, including the Collins Center."

Although the administration "needs some work" and is "a little overwhelmed/understaffed," it is "working hard to make SMU the best business school it can be." "The administration is always ready and willing to help with anything," one student says. "I think being such a small school makes this a little easier to accomplish than if we were a big school." Another says, "I have not had any trouble whatsoever finding someone to talk to in resolving any problems I have had over the last two years." The SMU program has several unique properties, such as sending "all full-time students on a two-week trip abroad in May." "If you have a business undergrad degree," the curriculum the first year may be redundant. "The first semester is a complete waste of time," one student says. "With approximately 10 percent of full-time MBA students also working on an MA or a JD, the dual-degree programs are an important part of the academic life at SMU Cox," a student says.

Professors at SMU "challenge students constantly" and "have real-world experience and provide valuable insight from their professional experiences." These "excellent professors" are "extremely smart, well-regarded in their industries, and easily accessible." "Professors are not afraid to bring new concepts into the school or adjust curriculum based on what the outside world needs in terms of trained graduating students." "Because the school doesn't have a Ph.D. program, you get faculty who actually want to teach," one student says. "Most of the faculty works in their chosen fields, so you get a lot of real-world teaching, as opposed to theory."

Career and Placement

SMU has a "strong connection to the Dallas business community" and "a stand-out capability to prepare its students for the working world." SMU provides many services to help students find a career. For example, "the Business Leadership Center hosts optional late night workshops with high-profile local executives to teach soft skills like negotiation, sales, etc." However, the career center "is currently reorganizing" and re-staffing. "While undergoing significant improvement is the only component of the Cox School keeping it from assuring itself a seat at the table of elite business schools."

About 67 percent of graduates find employment within three months of graduation, and more than 87 percent of those who do find it in the growing Southwest economy. The mean base salary of recent graduates is around $80,000. Some companies that have recently recruited out of SMU include Deloitte, Eatzi's, Hilton Hotels, Turnberry Advisers, and Wells Fargo.

Student Life and Environment

The student body at SMU is "ethnically and age diverse" as well as "diverse culturally and geographically." "Most students come from financial backgrounds, but all industries are represented here as well." This "diverse work background" creates a place where everyone "is very willing to contribute their experiences with the group." "Cox is mainly a conservative school, but the students here have diverse thought," so liberal students will feel welcome as well. "There is a little bit of an alpha-male culture in the case of some people, but that's business school in general," one student says. "These students know how and when to study but are not bookworms" and have fun doing non-academic activities, such as "intramural sports." "Life revolves around studies and networking," and some students say the school can develop cliques. "There is an active social life, but a select 'elite' group of students seems to have formed," one student says. "There are frequent happy hours where students get together with spouses and have a great time," and "SMU offers numerous opportunities to be involved in school through clubs, case studies, and networking activities." "Students are competitive, but in a healthy way," meaning that "no one is above helping out fellow classmates at any point." Students enjoy the city life of Dallas, and "the surrounding area has tons of housing that is relatively affordable."

Admissions

Successful applicants to SMU have leadership experience, a strong academic record, and competitive scores on the GMAT. Last year, the average GMAT score for accepted applicants was 643, and the average undergraduate GPA was 3.22. Personal qualities are also heavily weighed, and Cox admits students with a history of professional and personal growth, demonstrated achievements, proven academic abilities, and leadership potential. Although an academic background in business is not a requirement for admission, SMU recommends students enter the program with a working knowledge of calculus, accounting, statistics, and microeconomics.

FINANCIAL FACTS

Annual tuition	$43,036
Fees	$5,630
Cost of books	$2,500
Room & board	$15,000
% of students receiving aid	76
% of first-year students receiving aid	75
% of students receiving grants	69
Average award package	$45,257
Average grant	$36,735
Average loan	$39,303
Average student loan debt	$75,179

ADMISSIONS

Admissions Selectivity Rating	94
# of applications received	455
Average GMAT	639
Range of GMAT	605–675
Average GPA	3.40
TOEFL required of international students	Yes
Minimum TOEFL (paper/computer)	600/250
Application fee	$0
Deadline/Notification	
Round 1:	11/15 / 12/20
Round 2:	1/15 / 2/25
Round 3:	3/1 / 4/10
Round 4:	5/1 / 5/31
Deferment available	Yes
Maximum length of deferment	1 year
Transfer students accepted	No
Non-fall admissions	No
Need-blind admissions	Yes

EMPLOYMENT PROFILE

Career Rating	92	**Grads Employed by Function% Avg. Salary**	
Percent employed at graduation	52	Marketing	(16%) $85,250
Percent employed 3 months		Operations	(5%) $88,175
after graduation	76	Consulting	(15%)$100,083
Average base starting salary	$87,694	Management	(3%)
Primary Source of Full-time Job Acceptances		Finance	(39%) $83,342
School-facilitated activities	28(28%)	MIS	(5%) $86,200
Graduate-facilitated activities	33(33%)	Other	(16%) $90,844
Unknown	38(38%)	**Top 5 Employers Hiring Grads**	

Top 5 Employers Hiring Grads
American Airlines (7), PwC (4), Hunt Oil Company (3), ExxonMobil (2), Samsung Telecommunications (2)

ST. JOHN'S UNIVERSITY
THE PETER J. TOBIN COLLEGE OF BUSINESS

GENERAL INFORMATION
Type of school   Private
Affiliation   Roman Catholic
Academic calendar   Semester

SURVEY SAYS...
Students love Jamaica, NY, Happy
students, Smart classrooms
Solid preparation in:
Presentation skills

STUDENTS
Enrollment of parent
institution   21,087
Enrollment of MBA Program   351
% male/female   49/51
% out-of-state   57
% part-time   34
% underrepresented minority   8
% international   50
Average age at entry   25

ACADEMICS
Academic Experience Rating   76
Profs interesting rating   73
Profs accesible rating   77
Student/faculty ratio   21:1
% female faculty   20
% underrepresented minority
faculty   27
% part-time faculty   33

Joint Degrees
JD/MBA in Accounting: 4 years —
full-time enrollment required;
JD/MS in Accounting: 4 years —
full time enrollment required

Prominent Alumni
Diane D'Erasmo, EVP, HSBC Bank
USA; Kathryn Morrissey, President,
Global Wholesale Markets, AT&T;
Vincent Coleman, Vice Chairman,
Pricewaterhousecoopers; Pascal
Desroches, SVP and Controller,
Time Warner, Inc.; Thomas
Anderson, SVP/Chairman, American
Express

Academics

St. John's University's business school, the Peter J. Tobin College of Business, enjoys quite a reputation, and deservedly so. Many students say they applied to the school on its "good reputation," let alone the fact that it offers students many unique perks throughout its program. One of the main academic draws to the school is its Risk Management Program. The School of Risk Management is a 10-story campus located in one building in downtown Manhattan. In addition to their "very strong curriculum," the School of Risk Management building also houses the Center for Professional Education, the division of the School of Risk Management that provides custom and non-degree granting programs, the Insurance Hall of Fame and the world famous Kathryn and Shelby Cullom Davis Library.

One of the true hallmarks of any good university includes its professors, and St. John's follows this precedent. While there are some teachers at SJU that the occasional student identifies as, "not helpful and stressful," the vast majority of professors here "convey a true commitment and investment in the university and the students," and provide "excellent lectures." Many teachers are "experienced in the fields they teach or oversee," which allows them to "provide the latest information" from the business world and "apply [the] concepts in class [to] real world examples." This kind of teaching provides "valuable insight" into the business world, which is useful since most students either work full-time or are looking for a job. By offering real world experience, instead of only tests, the school demonstrates that it is "more focused on [the] growth of its students than it is on what grade they get at the end of the year."

Career and Placement

St. John's Career Center helps students in a variety of ways: it offers them assistance in writing a resume, searching for jobs, selecting appropriate courses, and evaluating potential job offers. In addition, St. John's promotes an on-campus group called Career Peers, which connects students to a group of other students their own age who are trained to answer any job search questions they might have. The school personalizes the center so students do not have to search through an answer database for help. There are two major campuses: one in Rome and one in New York City, and students find ample job opportunities in both. There are "good connections" in New York, "specifically in finance," and in Rome many students intern with the UN'S World Food Program, which "offers an incredible resume boost." Indeed the university is "very up-to-date with the job market," and it helps it students make themselves some of the "most marketable" graduates in the tri-state area.

ADMISSIONS CONTACT: SHEILA RUSSELL, ASSISTANT DIRECTOR OF MBA ADMISSIONS
ADDRESS: 8000 UTOPIA PARKWAY, 111 BENT HALL, QUEENS, NY 11439
PHONE: 718-990-1345 • FAX: 718-990-5242
E-MAIL: MBAADMISSIONS@STJOHNS.EDU • WEBSITE: WWW.STJOHNS.EDU/TOBIN

Student Life and Environment

As with most MBA programs, many people commute to class since they have full-time jobs, but since the two campuses are located in major cities those who do attend find the commute "very convenient." In New York there are campuses in both Manhattan and Queens and students love that they can choose classes in either borough. This option makes it "easier to fit [in] trips to campus" in students' schedules. There are also plenty of opportunities to study abroad and students can sign up to visit, or even attend classes, at the Rome campus as well. Many find this opportunity to be "a truly amazing experience." It is easier for students studying abroad as well since all of the classes are taught in English, but foreign students still get the flavor of living in a new city with other students who have "come from all over the world." Both campuses have plenty to do for those living on campus, or just looking to hang around after class since there are "lots of different kinds of organizations." In addition, the "random activities that take place here are great ways to battle the stress of an MBA."

Students tend to be a fairly mixed group of people; their personalities and backgrounds are all quite unique. "Some students are extremely competitive, while others are a bit more relaxed," but the mixing of different groups really makes class discussions "vibrant." Despite any differences, students still greatly respect one another and define the student body as "independent, hard-working, and smart." As far as school administration goes, there seems to be a "requisite amount of difficulty when it comes to doing basically anything," but the "administrators are accessible and generally helpful" as well as "very accommodating" to many of the students' needs. With the convenient locations and "hard-working" students, many find a "very fulfilled life" at SJU.

Admissions

For those looking to apply, keep in mind that Fall semester applications are usually due at the beginning of May and Spring semester applications are usually due near the beginning of November. Applicants must submit evidence of a baccalaureate degree, two letters of recommendation, and their official GMAT score. GPA is not "exclusively" taken in to consideration, but the current average GPA of accepted students is 3.2 on a 4.0 scale. Students looking for financial aid can apply for FAFSA at the beginning of the calendar year.

FINANCIAL FACTS

Annual tuition	$25,440/$25,440
Fees	$340
Cost of books	$1,045
Room & board (on/off-campus)	$17,270/$17,365
% of students receiving aid	55
% of first-year students receiving aid	55
% of students receiving grants	31
Average award package	$31,965
Average grant	$16,010
Average loan	$28,101
Average student loan debt	$46,110

ADMISSIONS

Admissions Selectivity Rating	69
# of applications received	382
% applicants accepted	81
% acceptees attending	41
Average GMAT	538
Range of GMAT	490–580
TOEFL required of international students	Yes
Minimum TOEFL (paper/computer)	600/100
Application fee	$50
International application fee	$50
Regular application deadline	5/1
Deferment available	Yes
Maximum length of deferment	1 year
Transfer students accepted	Yes
Transfer application policy: Must use regular application. Individual review of transfer credits. Maximum of six credits from another AACSB accredited program.	
Non-fall admissions	Yes
Need-blind admissions	Yes

EMPLOYMENT PROFILE

Career Rating	78	Grads Employed by Function	% Avg. Salary
Percent employed at graduation	16	Marketing	(18%)
Percent employed 3 months after graduation	11	Consulting	(16%)
		Management	(5%)
Average base starting salary	$59,296	Finance	(47%)
Primary Source of Full-time Job Acceptances		MIS	(8%)
School-facilitated activities	24(%)	Other	(5%)
Graduate-facilitated activities	12(%)	**Top 5 Employers Hiring Grads**	
Unknown	86(%)	Pricewaterhousecoopers (4), Deloitte (3), Grant Thornton (2), Ernst & Young (1), KPMB (1)	

ST. MARY'S UNIVERSITY
BILL GREEHEY SCHOOL OF BUSINESS

GENERAL INFORMATION

Type of school   Private
Affiliation   Roman Catholic
Academic calendar   Semester

SURVEY SAYS...

Friendly students
Solid preparation in:
Marketing, Communication/
interpersonal skills, Doing business
in a global economy

STUDENTS

Enrollment of parent
  institution   4,700
Enrollment of MBA Program   53
% male/female   75/25
% part-time   36
% international   15
Average age at entry   28
Average years work experience
  at entry   3.0

ACADEMICS

Academic Experience Rating   83
Profs interesting rating   88
Profs accesible rating   81
Student/faculty ratio   10:1
% female faculty   36
% underrepresented minority
  faculty   4
% part-time faculty   5

Joint Degrees

JD/MBA 108 hours; JD/24 hours;
MBA. 3 years.

Prominent Alumni

Bill Greehey, CEO, Nustar

Academics

The MBA program at St. Mary's University's Bill Greehey School of Business offers innovative programs designed to graduate conscientious global business leaders. The program includes a JD/M.B.A. dual degree option, as well as an additional dual degree with The University of Applied Sciences in Schmalkalden, Germany. The MBA program, which is the only AACSB-accredited program at a Catholic university in the state, advances the University's Marianist tradition of community service through "a wealth of classes" in ethical leadership, corporate social responsibility, sustainability, and social entrepreneurship. It is also home to a unique host of real-world experiential learning opportunities, such as the chance to be a volunteer federal income tax preparer for area residents through St. Mary's Volunteer Income Tax Assistance (VITA) program or to study abroad in places like Dubai, Mongolia, and Russia. In addition, the curriculum is based on a Marianist focus on the education and development of the total person. This includes modules on Advanced Behavioral Skills including conflict resolution, innovation and creativity, interpersonal communication and other skills that differentiate top performers at work.

Prerequisites to MBA study at Greehey begin with the completion of nine undergraduate-level fundamentals courses. Typically, students arriving with undergraduate degrees in business have already completed most, if not all, of these courses, or otherwise demonstrated proficiency through CLEP and DSST examinations or other means approved by the program director. After completing or placing out of these fundamentals courses. Students must complete a 30 semester-hour program that includes ten courses which include an employment internship, consultative practicum, or Three-Day Startup, an International Field Study, and a capstone course. The program requires three full semesters and a summer to complete and new cohorts are launched each fall. With the help of "the friendly administration," students are also able to tailor their degrees by mapping out a personalized track, in order "to choose a plan that ideally fits the industry they are wishing to move into or get a step ahead in."

Students praise faculty for "focusing on teaching and understanding" and providing "real-life cases that the professors experienced in their former occupations," including the wisdom of "some exceptional standouts, who are nationally competitive." St. Mary's has always been known for its personal touches and small class sizes, and students confirm that faculty "spend a lot of time working with students on the nuances that can't be conveyed in an hour" and help "mentor them on career decisions." Students appreciate that this small program is not overly bureaucratic, which is derived from an administration-faculty union that "works hand-in-hand to ensure that students receive the best education and support both inside and outside the classroom as possible."

Career and Placement

The Career Services Center at St. Mary's University provides one-on-one career counseling to both students and alumni; a library of career-related materials, including hardcopy and online job-search databases; special events (Resume Drive, Business Etiquette Dinner, Mock Interview Day); a career fair; and connections to an alumni mentoring program. Many wish that the Center engaged in more than just "passive marketing" and had "more connections to different industries," and most agree that St. Mary's is "primarily a San Antonio school." "Many of the students are from the area and intend to stay in the area following graduation." For this reason, students tell us that "the strong alumni network" is one of the biggest attractions of a St. Mary's degree. Employers interviewing on the St. Mary's campus include such organizations as USAA; HEB; The San

ADMISSIONS CONTACT: EARNEST BROUGHTON, DIRECTOR, MBA & EXECUTIVE EDUCATION PROGRAMS
ADDRESS: ONE CAMINO SANTA MARIA, SAN ANTONIO, TX 78228-8507
PHONE: 210-436-3101 • FAX: 210-431-2220
E-MAIL: GRADSCH@STMARYTX.EDU • WEBSITE: WWW.STMARYTX.EDU/MBA

Antonio Spurs; Union Pacific; CIA; Fisher, Herbst &Kemble; Enterprise Rent-A-Car; The American Red Cross; Tesoro Corporation; Valero; and NuStar Energy.

Student Life and Environment

St. Mary's student body is "extremely varied in terms of background, education, and experience," and most are there "to further their career or gain a competitive edge in their respective industries." The school has traditionally served the Hispanic community well; over half of all undergraduates here are Hispanic. On the whole, students "are clearly proud of this university," and this shows in the "strong interaction between undergraduate and graduate students." Most "usually work full-time" or have a family. Classmates describe each other as a "team-oriented, hard-working, and friendly" group that "converges on campus and brings a wealth of information and context to class discussions and group projects," providing a "'been-there' context, which solidifies the theory taught in class." This willingness to share is also demonstrated through the numerous "clubs, activities, festivals and academic events," as "there is always something taking place on campus for students, athletes, and the community."

With over one million residents within city limits and almost as many living in the metropolitan area, San Antonio is the second-largest city in Texas and one of the larger cities in the country. The military and petroleum industries both have major presences here. With nearly 20 million visitors every year, San Antonio (and its "excellent weather") is also a major player in the nation's tourism trade. Students speak highly of the city, although they warn that "the school is located in a very rough part of town."

Admissions

Applicants to the M.B.A. program at St. Mary's must apply to the graduate school for admission. There is no cost associated with the application process. Applications are reviewed by the M.B.A. program director, who makes recommendations to the Office of the Graduate Dean. Candidates must submit the following materials to the graduate admissions office: a completed on-line application form; an official score report for the GMAT or the GRE (contact the program director for minimum acceptable scores); an LSAT score for students pursuing the JD/M.B.A. option; two sets of official transcripts for all postsecondary academic work; two letters of recommendation from individuals well acquainted with the applicant's academic/professional ability; and a completed health form (required by Texas State Law). A telephone or on-campus interview is required. International applicants must provide all of the above materials, as well as a signed financial statement, and an official score report for the TOEFL (minimum acceptable score: 570 paper-based, 230 computer-based, 80 Internet or a minimum score of 6.5 on the IELTS English-language proficiency test (Academic or General); students with lower TOEFL or IELTS scores may be allowed to attend an English language program or classes at St. Mary's in order to meet minimum language proficiency requirements. Students may receive regular admission, which is unconditional. Conditional admission under certain circumstances is permitted, allowing students to enroll in no more than nine hours of classes after which their admission status is reappraised. International students are not eligible for conditional admission.

In addition, students may receive special admission as non-degree seeking students for the M.B.A. Professional Accountancy track or under other special circumstances approved by the Program Director.

FINANCIAL FACTS

Annual tuition	$18,204
Fees	$3,140
Cost of books	$1,300
Room & board	
(on/off-campus)	$6,000/$7,500
% of students receiving grants	1
Average grant	$5,375

ADMISSIONS

Admissions Selectivity Rating	76
# of applications received	69
% applicants accepted	71
% acceptees attending	78
Average GMAT	553
Range of GMAT	508–590
Average GPA	3.29
TOEFL required of	
international students	Yes
Minimum TOEFL	
(paper/computer)	570/230
Application fee	$0
International application fee	$0
Early application deadline	6/1
Early notification date	6/30
Deferment available	Yes
Maximum length	
of deferment	1 year
Transfer students accepted	Yes
Transfer application policy: On recommendation of the Graduate program director may accept a maximum of 6 Semester hours for the those seeking an MBA with a concentration in Professional Accountancy from AACSB-accredited programs. However, no transfer hours are accepted into the lockstep Greehey MBA.	
Non-fall admissions	Yes
Need-blind admissions	Yes

STANFORD UNIVERSITY
STANFORD GRADUATE SCHOOL OF BUSINESS

GENERAL INFORMATION

Type of school	Private
Affiliation	No Affiliation
Academic calendar	Quarter

SURVEY SAYS...

Good social scene, Good peer network
Solid preparation in:
General management,
Communication/interpersonal skills,
Entrepreneurial studies

STUDENTS

Enrollment of MBA Program	803
% male/female	65/35
% part-time	0
% underrepresented minority	20
% international	42
Average years work experience at entry	4.2

ACADEMICS

Academic Experience Rating	**99**
Profs interesting rating	85
Profs accesible rating	88
Student/faculty ratio	6:1
% female faculty	18
% underrepresented minority faculty	9
% part-time faculty	46

Joint Degrees

It is possible to earn dual degrees with any other Stanford University department. Joint degrees offered for JD/MBA, MBA/MA in Education, MBA/MS in Environment and Resources, and MBA/MPP (public policy).

Prominent Alumni

Phil Knight, Founder and Chairman, Nike Inc.; John Donahoe, President and CEO, eBay Inc.; Charles Schwab, Founder and Chairman, Charles Schwab & Co.; Jacqueline Novogratz, Founder and CEO, Acumen Fund; Jeffrey Bewkes, CEO and Chairman, Time Warner

Academics

Stanford boasts one of the most sought after business programs in the country for a reason: "Alongside Harvard, it is the best business school in the world." This is an environment in which "you are surrounded by exceptionally smart and driven classmates, and the professors ensure that the rigorous courses are challenging." Stanford's "incredible curriculum" begins with Management Perspectives, a series of courses completed during the first year. After that, choices abound. Students can choose from over 100 electives within the business school alone, and they can even take classes in other graduate departments at Stanford. "At Stanford, students are encouraged to innovate and to take risks. The school is known for pushing you to dream and to develop your own audacious career goals."

While pursuing those goals, you will be supported by a staff and fellow students who will help you attain those goals. "Your classmates, professors, and academic advisors are available to you every step of the way to ensure that you are continuing to learn and grow." Students find that "the administration cares about each student, and it is extremely responsive to student needs." Their goal is to make you "a better, more informed, more self-aware and thoughtful person." This would be impossible were it not for the staff. "Everything is incredibly well-run, and professors are not only excellent at teaching but also have amazing backgrounds/experience."

In order to further its mission, Stanford has continued to evolve. In 2007 and in the years since, the MBA curriculum was redesigned and continues to change as the school strives to perfect its program. Indeed, "the administration knows the customers are the students. We learn about the centrality of the customer in class and the administration understands this." Educators are "responsive to student needs," as well as "obsessive about constant feedback and making quick adjustments," ensuring they are adept at adapting on the fly to a changing world, business climate, and student population. It is "extremely easy to have lunch with a professor that you have not even taken a class with yet." Perhaps this is because the professors at Stanford are "very passionate about their courses, and they make classes extremely entertaining, engaging, and intellectually stimulating."

Career and Placement

It should come as no surprise that career placement from Stanford is strong. With "accessibility to innovative companies" and "an alumni network that will respond to any outreach effort (you) make," plus "job opportunities in many sectors," the prospects are broad and deep. This is helped by Stanford GSB's robust Career Management Center, which offers personal career advising, resume and cover letter preparation, as well as alumni mentoring and networking opportunities, company presentations, career workshops, and job fairs. Perhaps that's why many consider it "the best business school in the country for a general management degree."

The list of organizations that recruit MBAs from Stanford is 2,100 strong, pulling from the pool via career fairs, job postings, and online resume services. The employers make up a laundry list of the best in their field: Amazon.com, Apple, Bain & Company, Booz & Company, Boston Consulting Group, Cisco Systems, Dell, Education Pioneers, Genentech, General Mills, Goldman Sachs, Johnson & Johnson, Intel, Google, Hulu, IDEO, NBC Universal (GE), U.S. Government, Nike, VMware, Warner Bros., and many more. Salaries have been equally inviting, with the median base salary for graduating MBAs standing at $125,000, with a range between $20,000 and $260,000.

ADMISSIONS CONTACT: DERRICK BOLTON, DIRECTOR OF MBA ADMISSIONS
ADDRESS: 518 MEMORIAL WAY, STANFORD, CA 94305-5015
PHONE: 650-723-2766 • FAX: 650-725-7831
WEBSITE: WWW.GSB.STANFORD.EDU

Student Life and Environment

Community and networking is key at Stanford. "All students are there to learn from each other, help each other grown and not brag about their accomplishments." While "there is undoubtedly diversity among student personalities within any given class," at Stanford you have not only "the intelligence and incredible accomplishments of Stanford GSB students," you have a group who "have consistently stood out as being unusually caring and supportive of others, even in difficult work environments and trying circumstances."

Students tend to have an influence on one another here. As one student says, "Stanford is the only place where I felt I wanted to become more like the alumni and current students. So many of the people I've met are incredibly competent and self-possessed, yet also genuinely caring and interested in others." The Northern California climate and attitude mean students here enjoy "mood-alteringly gorgeous weather" on a campus located a stone's throw from Stanford's world-class schools of law, medicine, engineering, education, and sciences. "Students really tend to customize their experiences, with some students focusing more heavily on schoolwork and others on start-ups, consulting projects, and outdoor activities."

There is no question of enjoying yourself here. "Stanford is basically a paradise. The weather is beautiful, the vegetables in California are amazing, the people are wonderful." It's hard for most students not to be impressed. "Life at Stanford is amazing - academic environment is challenging, quality of life in California is out of this world. I love studying and living here." The "smart, humble, ambitious, down-to-earth, funny, well-traveled" students here will challenge you to be the best person you can be. "They take Stanford's motto seriously, and they are investing in themselves with a goal to positively change lives, change organizations, and change the world."

Admissions

Stanford being Stanford, admission is selective. Applicants will be evaluated in three areas: intellectual vitality, demonstrated leadership potential, and personal qualities and contributions. That means grades are not enough. Stanford is looking for outstanding candidates who will fit into the school's history of accomplishment and innovation. Admissions, according to school officials, is an art, not a science. There are no minimum GMAT score or GPA requirements. Current students have a GMAT range from 580–790, with a median score of 740. In other words, there is no magic formula. Excel, succeed, and stand out from the crowd in all aspects of your life to improve your chances.

FINANCIAL FACTS

Annual tuition	$57,300
Fees	$0
Cost of books	$3,894
Room & board (on/off-campus)	$23,391/$27,486
% of students receiving aid	73
% of first-year students receiving aid	70
% of students receiving grants	55
Average award package	$61,083
Average grant	$24,913
Average loan	$40,407
Average student loan debt	$79,049

ADMISSIONS

Admissions Selectivity Rating	99
# of applications received	6,716
Average GMAT	729
Average GPA	3.69
TOEFL required of international students	Yes
Minimum TOEFL (paper/computer)	600/250
Application fee	$265
International application fee	$265
Application Deadline/Notification	
Round 1:	10/2 / 12/11
Round 2:	1/9 / 3/27
Round 3:	4/3 / 5/15
Deferment available	Yes
Maximum length of deferment	very limited
Transfer students accepted	No
Non-fall admissions	No
Need-blind admissions	Yes

EMPLOYMENT PROFILE

Career Rating	99	Grads Employed by Function	% Avg. Salary
Percent employed at graduation	71	Marketing	(20%) $113,977
Percent employed 3 months after graduation	88	Operations	(3%) $117,500
		Consulting	(22%) $129,015
Average base starting salary	$129,652	Management	(13%) $112,054
Primary Source of Full-time Job Acceptances		Finance	(33%) $153,022
School-facilitated activities	95(44%)	MIS	(3%) $117,500
Graduate-facilitated activities	120(55%)	Other	(8%) $112,971
Unknown	2(1%)		

STATE UNIVERSITY OF NEW YORK AT BINGHAMTON
SCHOOL OF MANAGEMENT

GENERAL INFORMATION

Type of school	Public
Affiliation	No Affiliation
Academic calendar	2 Semester

SURVEY SAYS...

Smart classrooms
Solid preparation in:
General management, Teamwork,
Presentation skills, Computer skills

STUDENTS

Enrollment of parent institution	15,308
Enrollment of MBA Program	58
% male/female	55/46
% out-of-state	29
% part-time	5
% underrepresented minority	17
% international	27
Average age at entry	23
Average years work experience at entry	3.8

ACADEMICS

Academic Experience Rating	89
Profs interesting rating	86
Profs accesible rating	89
Student/faculty ratio	6:1
% female faculty	19
% underrepresented minority faculty	20
% part-time faculty	34

Joint Degrees

Watson (School of Engineering)/MBA Fast Track-5 years (Bachelors+MBA); Harpur (College of Arts & Sciences)/MBA Fast Track-5 years (Bachelors+MBA)

Prominent Alumni

Mark Deutsch, Partner/Private Equity; Matthew Singer, Partner/Accounting; Gary Meltzer, US Advisory Leader/Investment Mgmt & Real Estate; Howard Eisen, Managing Director/Business Development; Allen Zwickler, Managing Director/Finance

Academics

"Close proximity to New York City," an excellent "reputation for quality" (particularly in New York), "one of the best accounting programs in the nation," and a small program size that ensures students won't get lost in the crowd, are among the top reasons students give for choosing the MBA program at Binghamton University. It also doesn't hurt that it "all comes with an extremely reasonable price tag," with "cheap tuition" even for out-of-state students.

The four-semester MBA program at Binghamton University (BU) employs "an extremely team-based approach" to education "that replicates real-world business in a way many other business programs do not," students inform us. This is especially true in the first year, during which the program covers core essentials. One student explains, "The first year of the program requires students to stick with a set group of students to work on projects, presentations, papers, and cases. It can be difficult at times, but the lessons learned are crucial for the real world." Full-time MBA students are also required to obtain an internship during the course of the program, which may be used toward fulfilling an elective course requirement. The school also offers a Fast Track Professional MBA in New York City (with classes taking place on Saturdays over the course of a year), and a Fast Track MBA to Binghamton undergraduates. The program allows them to earn both a BA and an MBA in five years, no small feat considering that a Binghamton MBA requires 69 credits, "more than any other university."

For a state school, BU provides excellent service and a "smart organizational system." Students tell us that "the school really tries to adapt to the latest management concepts and ideals" and that administrators are "are diligent and available to help students with interviews and networking opportunities." Most of the professors have been practitioners in their respective fields at one point or another, which means "the tone of the course matches the tone of the discipline and serves to address the gap between theory and practice that plagues weaker business programs." The only knock on teachers is that "many are foreign," so that "sometimes it is difficult to understand what is being said due to accents." Most often, however, instructors "can communicate easily with the students." Another asset to the program is that "the alumni that are in highly respected companies are great, and everyone really tries to pull for other Binghamton students." "I have also interfaced with alumni on many occasions, gaining insights into investment banking and asset management," says one student.

Career and Placement

For a small program, Binghamton does a good job of bringing some major recruiters to its relatively remote location. One student informs us that "we have powerhouse recruiters from Credit Suisse, Goldman Sachs, the big four accounting, all the engineering firms, as well as many others. Without question, the recruiting at this school is on an incredible climb upwards. More and more powerhouse companies are coming to Binghamton." Still, those here would like to see the school's reputation grow at a faster rate, as "most rankings underestimate the potential on campus." The Career Development Center offers counseling services, career workshops, resume-development services, resume-referral services, a career-resource library, and access to the alumni network.

Top employers of Binghamton MBAs include Ernst & Young, Deloitte, KPMG, Lockheed Martin, and Target.

ADMISSIONS CONTACT: ALESIA WHEELER-WADE, ASSISTANT DIRECTOR MBA/MS PROGRAMS
ADDRESS: SCHOOL OF MANAGEMENT, P.O. BOX 6000, BINGHAMTON, NY 13902-6000
PHONE: 607-777-2317 • FAX: 607-777-4872
E-MAIL: SOMADVIS@BINGHAMTON.EDU • WEBSITE: SOM.BINGHAMTON.EDU

Student Life and Environment

Many classes for the fall are held in the evenings at Binghamton's "centralized campus," which "leads to very long days, especially for those who also have part-time jobs" and hampers extracurricular involvement. As these "motivated" students progress through the program, however, the school offers "plenty opportunities to get involved on campus," from the Finance Society to stock pitch and M&A competitions that allow students to "apply coursework to real-world topics and compete with fellow students in a constructive manner." The latter "implements various activities throughout the year including coffee hours, open bars, networking events," "horseback riding, bowling, etc." There is also a wide range of work experience among students, which benefits those at all stages of their careers. "The breadth of industry knowledge in the program is very impressive and fosters meaningful class discussions that drive home course material," says a student.

The city of Binghamton "has lots of things going for it besides the downtown bar scene. For one thing, there is a hometown hockey team and baseball team, an opera house, numerous playhouses, and theaters, too. We are also the carousel capital of the United States. Binghamton is ethnically diverse as well, and there are often ethnic festivals going on throughout the Southern Tier." Also, "living expenses here are not much," especially when compared to the cost of living in much of the rest of the state. The university also "has a great Division-I athletic department that provides exciting competitions for the students to attend," and many do.

Admissions

Applicants to the Binghamton MBA program must submit two copies of official undergraduate transcripts for all college work, two letters of recommendation, a personal statement, a resume, and GMAT scores. Work experience, while preferred, is not required. Additionally, international students must submit a certified statement of financial responsibility and TOEFL scores (minimum acceptable score is 590 for the paper version, 243 for the computer version, or 96 for the internet version). A basic understanding of calculus is "strongly recommended" for all incoming students; strong calculus skills are necessary for those interested in studying finance or operations management.

FINANCIAL FACTS

Annual tuition (in-state/ out-of-state)	$11,130/$18,320
Fees	$1,695
Cost of books	$750
Room & board (on/off-campus)	$0/$6,800
% of students receiving aid	48
% of first-year students receiving aid	53
% of students receiving grants	8
Average award package	$18,282
Average grant	$6,509
Average loan	$18,985
Average student loan debt	$11,563

ADMISSIONS

Admissions Selectivity Rating	89
# of applications received	245
% applicants accepted	37
% acceptees attending	49
Average GMAT	614
Range of GMAT	580–640
Average GPA	3.48
TOEFL required of international students	Yes
Minimum TOEFL (paper/computer)	590/243
Application fee	$75
International application fee	$75
Regular application deadline	3/1
Deferment available	Yes
Maximum length of deferment	1 year
Transfer students accepted	No
Non-fall admissions	No
Need-blind admissions	Yes

EMPLOYMENT PROFILE

Career Rating	87	Grads Employed by Function	% Avg. Salary
Percent employed at graduation	71	Marketing	(18%) $50,000
Percent employed 3 months after graduation	82	Operations	(5%)
		Consulting	(23%) $61,200
Average base starting salary	$57,500	Management	(18%) $50,667
Primary Source of Full-time Job Acceptances		Finance	(14%) $62,000
School-facilitated activities	9(41%)	MIS	(23%) $60,000
Graduate-facilitated activities	13(59%)	**Top 5 Employers Hiring Grads**	

Top 5 Employers Hiring Grads
Epic Systems(3), Binghamton University (2),
Ernst and Young (2), NBT Bank (2), Protiviti (1)

STATE UNIVERSITY OF NEW YORK—OSWEGO

SCHOOL OF BUSINESS

GENERAL INFORMATION

Type of school	Public
Affiliation	No Affiliation
Academic calendar	Semester/ Year Round

SURVEY SAYS...

Good peer network, Cutting-edge classes
Solid preparation in:
Accounting, General management

STUDENTS

Enrollment of parent institution	7,921
Enrollment of MBA Program	117
% male/female	58/42
% out-of-state	7
% part-time	54
% underrepresented minority	13
% international	7
Average age at entry	26

ACADEMICS

Academic Experience Rating	**78**
Profs interesting rating	82
Profs accesible rating	81
Student/faculty ratio	20:1
% female faculty	17
% underrepresented minority faculty	33
% part-time faculty	22

Joint Degrees

5 Year BS-Accounting/MBA, 5 Year BA-Psychology/MBA, 5 Year BA-Broadcasting and Mass Communications/MBA: 1 year full-time (for graduate work).

Prominent Alumni

Al Roker, NBC Today Show weather anchor; Alice McDermott, National Book Award Winner and best-selling novelist; Ken Auletta, New Yorker Columnist & critically acclaimed author; Harold Morse, Founder of The Learning Channel and Ovation TV Network; Heraldo Munoz, Assistant Secretary-General of the United Nations

Academics

Students who enroll in the School of Business at SUNY Oswego can expect several things: excellent value for their money, intimate classes, knowledgeable professors, state-of-the-art facilities, and an excellent hockey team. As one student puts it, "In most areas, the school of business is at the top of its class. The classes are challenging and worthwhile. Most professors are really good at their areas. They are also widely available to help students both inside and out of class," and "really want to see the students succeed." According to most of the students, the "very small classes promote learning and student-professor interaction." The program "provides a lot of hands-on work and team activities to help form a strong work ethic" among students.

Designed as a degree in general management, an MBA from SUNY Oswego provides a solid grounding in the basics of modern business organization. The school says that "this program is intended to be equally applicable to private, public, and governmental sectors of management." The foundation subjects required of students include management, accounting, marketing, organization, law, and finance. In addition, students can choose to specialize in a specific field such as international management, manufacturing management, organizational leadership, or financial services. Foundation course requirements include management information systems, managerial finance, marketing management, management science I, international business, global perspectives on organizational management, and management policy. Students have a choice of taking classes at the Oswego Campus, at the Metro Center in downtown Syracuse, and online. In addition to general management electives, students can also specialize in accounting. Students in the accounting track can gain professional experience by participating in the Volunteer Income Tax Assistance (VITA) program. Students interested in finance can spend a semester at the Levin Institute's International Finance and Global Banking in New York City.

Students find their coursework both rigorous and exciting. As one puts it, "the professors are excellent and the classes are fun and challenging." Another says, "the course load is challenging, requiring solid communication and organization skills." Fortunately, the student body as a whole is "reliable and helpful." "We help each other out in our classes. I think the students in the graduate program really create a bond with one another."

ADMISSIONS CONTACT: DAVID W. KING, DEAN GRADUATE STUDIES
ADDRESS: 606 CULKIN HALL, SUNY OSWEGO, OSWEGO, NY 13126
PHONE: 315-312-3692 • FAX: 315-312-3577
E-MAIL: MBA@OSWEGO.EDU • WEBSITE: WWW.OSWEGO.EDU/BUSINESS/MBA

Career and Placement

Although Oswego has a lot to offer—lovely campus, low cost, quality education, intimate program—most students wish it would go further in strengthening its Career Services department. There is little aid specifically for prospective MBAs, and the job search is often directed almost entirely by the student. As one puts it, "Connecting with employers is a difficult task. Linking up with quality employers looking for graduates with postgraduate degrees needs to be addressed." The exception is accounting, which has numerous national and regional public accounting firms actively recruiting throughout the year.

Student Life and Environment

Students say their "classmates are very intelligent. They provide a lot of feedback to one another, work well together, and create a competitive environment which prepares people for the job market." All rave about their "beautiful campus," which, they proudly point out, is also extremely "technologically-advanced and mostly wireless." The typical MBA's social life is strong, and there are "plenty of bars around for an active nightlife." As one student says, "At Oswego, I had the opportunity to make new friends from all over the world. The social life is active and I consider myself lucky." For the most part, students claim to be "very active on campus. There is a multitude of clubs and organizations to choose from." Students enjoy their "great gyms to work out in or play a game of racquetball." Plus—as is typical in upstate New York—the school's athletic life centers on their "excellent hockey team, instead of football." As one student puts it, "what's excellent about living on campus here is that there is every resource that you could possibly need available on campus. There are new buildings and renovations, from a new student center to the newly renovated freshman residence hall and new business center with technology classrooms."

Admissions

To be considered for admission to the small MBA program at the School of Business at SUNY Oswego, a candidate must have a minimum GPA of 2.6 out of 4.0. The minimum required score for the GMAT is 490. Taking the TOEFL test is also required for students whose native language is not English.

FINANCIAL FACTS

Annual tuition (in-state/ out-of-state)	$11,130/$18,320
Fees	$890
Cost of books	$800
Room & board	$12,410
% of students receiving aid	72
% of first-year students receiving aid	74
% of students receiving grants	5
Average award package	$17,402
Average grant	$1,250
Average loan	$17,628
Average student loan debt	$17,048

ADMISSIONS

Admissions Selectivity Rating	69
# of applications received	97
% applicants accepted	95
% acceptees attending	35
Average GMAT	518
Range of GMAT	470–570
Average GPA	3.21
TOEFL required of international students	Yes
Minimum TOEFL (paper/computer)	560/220
Application fee	$50
International application fee	$50
Deferment available	Yes
Maximum length of deferment	1 year
Transfer students accepted	Yes
Transfer application policy: Two courses may be accepted for transfer into the program.	
Non-fall admissions	Yes
Need-blind admissions	Yes

STATE UNIVERSITY OF NEW YORK—UNIVERSITY AT ALBANY
SCHOOL OF BUSINESS

GENERAL INFORMATION
Type of school   Public
Affiliation   No Affiliation
Academic calendar   September-May

SURVEY SAYS...
Friendly students
Solid preparation in:
General management, Teamwork

STUDENTS
Enrollment of MBA Program   283
% male/female   59/41
% out-of-state   12
% part-time   77
% underrepresented minority   2
% international   11
Average age at entry   27
Average years work experience
   at entry   3.0

ACADEMICS
Academic Experience Rating   79
Profs interesting rating   78
Profs accesible rating   80
Student/faculty ratio   28:1
% female faculty   27
% underrepresented minority
   faculty   0
% part-time faculty   20

Joint Degrees
JD/MBA (5 years); BA/MBA (5 years)

Prominent Alumni
Kimberly Welsh, Managing Director, Morgan Stanley; Dale Carleton, Vice Chairman, Retired, State Street Corporation; Steve Rotella, President and CEO, Chase Manhattan Mortgage Corp.; Harold Cramer, VP, Exxon Mobil Fuels; Anthony McCarthy, Global CIO-Investment Banking, Deutsche Bank

Academics

Since 1970, the School of Business at the University at Albany has "the best combination of education quality and value." Many who attend, having already been undergrads, are familiar with the State University of New York system, and it is well known that the School of Business offers solid academics at an incredibly affordable price. Even though the University at Albany is a larger research institution, the "small size of the school dictates easy accessibility to the administration and instructors," so "graduate students are treated well here."

The "great professors" of UA really "know their subjects" and are "available outside of class to discuss class and other materials." Class sizes are small, yet the projects are "challenging but not impossible." Currently the full-time program offers only two concentration paths: Information Technology Management and Human Resources Information Systems. A few students wish there were options for "a more generalized degree, or more common concentrations like Finance and Marketing," which "would assist students with ambitions beyond the scope of these concentrations." Each student takes part in a cornerstone, integrative project at the end of their first year called "G3"; it applies the various functional aspects of business learned throughout the first year to the sustainability issues facing a real organization in today's competitive, global economy.

The school's administration "provides support to students who need resources for business plan competitions and the like"; students are also easily able to gain experience through internships in the school's Small Business Development Center, which supports small startup companies, family-owned enterprises, entrepreneurial ventures, among others, by offering free personal counseling in developing strategic business plans, identifying appropriate sources of funding, and providing market research, management information, and financial analysis. Other experience building opportunities can be found through the Center for Institutional Investment Management, which actively promotes institutional investment management research among faculty and students through research grants, travel support, and the acquisition of relevant academic and practitioner databases – not to mention the Center's dedicated Bloomberg terminal.

Career and Placement

As already mentioned, the greatest strength of the School of Business is its small size. "This drives the administration and faculty to go out of their way to try to place students in jobs, "even if students are not able to land their first choice of a position and must start lower on the totem pole. For those who work hard, the school's name and reputation for "an incredibly competitive education" bring in enough recognition and recruitment to land top jobs (the school has a particularly strong relationship with the Big 4 accounting firms). "I have been able to land a job in a Fortune 500 company due to the excellent career placement services," says one. One intangible quality that students gain from UA's many projects includes the invaluable practice of presenting themselves "without fear," and the school is very good at putting students "into the organizations that will hire them."

Student Life and Environment

Students here "tend to be younger and less experienced than [students at] other schools, and this is reflected in their behavior and thoughts," says one member of the student body. "They are bright and willing to learn, but I was surprised by the lack of work experience," says another. The "diverse range of backgrounds makes it hard to generalize," but overall students here "are outgoing, smart, and socially active." "Very few" are married or have children. "Everyone is friends, and there is shared camaraderie with the entire class," according to one. "They will help when needed and are always available to help [one] another out."

Coursework typically fills up the week, and "after class, we usually meet with our teams to work on assigned projects" or business plan competition entries. As for extracurricular fun, there are plenty of friends to be found in the school's other graduate programs, and the state capital of Albany "has a lot to offer in terms of restaurants, parks, and museums if you know where to look."

Admissions

Applicants to the MBA program at the State University of New York at Albany School of Business must provide the graduate admissions department with all of the following: official copies of transcripts for all postsecondary academic work, an official score report for the GMAT, a resume, three letters of recommendation, a personal statement of purpose, and a completed application. International applicants whose undergraduate degrees were earned at non-English language institutions must provide all of the above plus an official score report for the TOEFL (minimum acceptable score: 580 paper-based; 450 computer-based); a financial affidavit accompanied by appropriate supporting documentation to demonstrate the applicant's "ability to meet all educational and living expenses for the entire period of intended study"; and they must past a SPEAK test during orientation. Furthermore, international academic transcripts in languages other than English must be accompanied by a certified English translation.

FINANCIAL FACTS

Annual tuition (in-state/ out-of-state)	$11,130/$18,320
Fees	$1,284
Cost of books	$1,600
Room & board	$10,808

ADMISSIONS

Admissions Selectivity Rating	80
# of applications received	244
% applicants accepted	69
% acceptees attending	79
Average GMAT	560
Range of GMAT	510–700
Average GPA	3.37
TOEFL required of international students	Yes
Minimum TOEFL (paper/computer)	600/250
Application fee	$75
International application fee	$75
Early application deadline	3/1
Early notification date	4/1
Regular application deadline	5/1
Regular application notification	6/1
Deferment available	Yes
Maximum length of deferment	1 Year
Transfer students accepted	Yes
Transfer application policy: We accept up to 50% transfer credit in each program of study.	
Non-fall admissions	Yes
Need-blind admissions	Yes

STATE UNIVERSITY OF NEW YORK—UNIVERSITY AT BUFFALO
SCHOOL OF MANAGEMENT

GENERAL INFORMATION

Type of school	Public
Affiliation	No Affiliation
Academic calendar	Semester

SURVEY SAYS...
Happy students, Students love
Buffalo, NY
Solid preparation in:
Teamwork, Communication/
interpersonal skills, Presentation
skills, Quantitative skills

STUDENTS

Enrollment of parent institution	28,952
Enrollment of MBA Program	465
% male/female	65/35
% out-of-state	4
% part-time	40
% underrepresented minority	5
% international	35
Average age at entry	24
Average years work experience at entry	2.0

ACADEMICS

Academic Experience Rating	**89**
Profs interesting rating	80
Profs accesible rating	90
% female faculty	28
% underrepresented minority faculty	3
% part-time faculty	9

Joint Degrees
JD/MBA; MD/MBA;
Architecture/MBA; Pharmacy/MBA;
Geography/MBA; BS/MBA Business
or Engineering; MBA/MSW;
AuD/MBA; MBA/MPH; DDS/MBA

Prominent Alumni
Millard S. Drexler, Chairman and
CEO, J.Crew Group, Inc.; John R.
Alm, Retired President & CEO Coca
Cola Enterprises; Mitchell S. Klipper,
CEO, Barnes & Noble Retail Group;
James P. Lederer, Executive Vice
President, QUALCOMM Incorporated;
Marvin J. Herb, Chairman, President
& CEO, Herbco Investments LLC

Academics

Offering AACSB-accredited graduate programs since the 1930s, the University at Buffalo School of Management has a long history of excellence, operating both a full-time and part-time MBA, as well as a 22-month executive MBA for seasoned professionals. The academic programs are "very well-organized" and "the school does a great job of emphasizing 'management' as an underlying factor in each course" in the core curriculum. While covering business fundamentals like finance and marketing, the curriculum moves ahead with the times, and "Courses are constantly updated and altered to reflect real-world experience based on current events," and integrated ethics. Getting a strong practical perspective isn't a problem: UB complements the academic offerings with "great opportunities outside the classroom," including "professional speakers, networking events, country forums, [and] community service," as well as case competitions and special offerings, like "marketing projects with GM or Smart Car USA." To further augment the curriculum, UB operates several formal exchange programs with business schools overseas, as well as shorter "trips to China for international business classes."

Despite the affordable tuition and high enrollment, UB offers a "smaller, more intimate MBA experience" with an "emphasis on teamwork and leadership skills" throughout the curriculum. Within each incoming class, full-time students are divided into fixed cohorts then assigned to a fixed study group of five to six students. "Group meetings outside of class require a lot of time and commitment" and can be among the most challenging aspects of the program. A student elaborates, "The curriculum is difficult and pushes students to their limits in all realms, especially in regards to working in a team environment with people you may not know to start out or who have very different perspectives than you." Despite the challenges, the focus on teamwork "simulates the real world" and "provides for a great learning environment." A student admits, "I have created a great network here, both with the students, professors, alums and other community members." Adds another, "The students are all very close and the faculty and administration are extremely involved." While the environment is friendly, the teaching staff can be "hit and miss" in the classroom, and some professors are universally disliked. Fortunately, "professors are very good overall" and "many are leaders in [their] fields." Even more importantly, "The professors have been great and are always accessible if needed, whether...after class, during weekly office hours, or by setting up a special time to meet."

Career and Placement

At UB, career planning begins—quite literally—before you even step on campus. As a requirement of graduation, all students must complete MBA Advantage, a comprehensive professional development program in August before your first year (with additional sessions in January and September). In addition to MBA Advantage, the Frank L. Ciminelli Family Career Resource Center (CRC) helps students prepare for the job hunt through career development workshops, practice interviews, career advising and more. The CRC also hosts various networking and recruiting events to link current students with local employers and alumni. UB is "very well-known in Western New York," and students benefit from the school's "great reputation and strong regional recruiting" program. For those who plan to stay in the area, UB has a "strong alumni network, especially locally."

ADMISSIONS CONTACT: JAIMIE FALZARANO, INTERIM DIRECTOR OF GRADUATE PROGRAMS
ADDRESS: 203 ALFIERO CENTER, BUFFALO, NY 14260
PHONE: 716-645-3204 • FAX: 716-645-2341
E-MAIL: SOM-APPS@BUFFALO.EDU • WEBSITE: MGT.BUFFALO.EDU

In recent years, MBA graduates report an average base salary of more than $58,000, with a range between $16,500 and $100,000. Eighty-two percent of students were employed within three months of graduation. More than half the class took positions in Western New York, with another 8 percent landing jobs in downstate New York. Over the past few years, the top employers of MBA graduates have included M&T Bank, Citigroup, Deloitte & Touche, Toys R Us, IBM, Fisher-Price, Rich Products, PriceWaterhouseCoopers, Ernst & Young, New Era Cap, and Xerox.

Student Life and Environment

Group work is an integral part of the UB curriculum and for many, "the variety of students from varying backgrounds/majors" and "The great presence of international students from all around the world make this academic experience tremendous both in and out of class." While teamwork can be challenging, "Everybody gets along well and builds great relationships." Throughout the MBA, "classes are all in one building," a recently completed facility, complete with high-tech classrooms, conference rooms, breakout rooms, and a cafe. With everything concentrated into one space, "it has become like a family atmosphere." While MBAs share facilities with the undergraduate population, a new graduate lounge was opened in 2013 to provide them with their own exclusive space.

Outside of course work, many full-time students are involved in extracurricular activities, like case competitions, student clubs, and special programs like "alternative spring break events." The most active campus club, the Graduate Management Association hosts happy hours and daytrips, among other activities. On campus, "Frequent student-focused events are held, including a formal dinner with students and faculty [at] the end of each semester, in addition to charity drives and social events." A great place to call home, "Buffalo is a small city, but many of the students are from the area and know where the hangouts are."

Admissions

In 2007, The University at Buffalo School of Management reduced [its] MBA class size by almost a third, limiting enrollment to 100 and imposing more stringent admissions standards on the incoming class. There are no minimum GMAT score requirements for entry into UB's MBA program; a student's full background is considered when making an admission's decision.

FINANCIAL FACTS

Annual tuition (in-state/ out-of-state)	$11,130/$18,320
Fees	$2,977
Cost of books	$1,627
Room & board	$9,300
% of students receiving aid	25
% of first-year students receiving aid	20
% of students receiving grants	25
Average award package	$14,000
Average grant	$5,000
Average student loan debt	$21,220

ADMISSIONS

Admissions Selectivity Rating	86
# of applications received	375
% applicants accepted	47
% acceptees attending	54
Average GMAT	613
Range of GMAT	530–680
Average GPA	3.40
TOEFL required of international students	Yes
Minimum TOEFL (paper/computer)	573/230
Application fee	$75
International application fee	$75
Application Deadline/Notification	
Round 1:	11/15 / 12/19
Round 2:	2/15 / 3/17
Round 3:	3/1 / 3/31
Round 4:	6/1 / 6/12
Deferment available	Yes
Maximum length of deferment	1 year
Transfer students accepted	No
Non-fall admissions	No
Need-blind admissions	Yes

EMPLOYMENT PROFILE

Career Rating	91	Grads Employed by Function	% Avg. Salary
Percent employed at graduation	50	Marketing	(13%) $59,900
Percent employed 3 months after graduation	82	Operations	(8%) $60,000
		Consulting	(13%) $58,500
Average base starting salary	$58,209	Management	(11%) $66,600
Primary Source of Full-time Job Acceptances		Finance	(34%) $53,417
School-facilitated activities	33(62%)	HR	(4%)
Graduate-facilitated activities	20(38%)	MIS	(11%) $61,000
		Other	(6%) $61,667

Top 5 Employers Hiring Grads
M&T Bank (5), Citi (4), Ernst & Young (3), PricewaterhouseCoopers (3), BlueCross BlueShield (2)

STETSON UNIVERSITY
SCHOOL OF BUSINESS ADMINISTRATION

GENERAL INFORMATION
Type of school	Private
Affiliation	No Affiliation
Academic calendar	Semesters

SURVEY SAYS...
Happy students
Solid preparation in:
Finance, Accounting, Doing business
in a global economy

STUDENTS
Enrollment of parent institution	3,961
Enrollment of MBA Program	145
% male/female	49/51
% out-of-state	10
% part-time	23
% underrepresented minority	19
% international	14
Average age at entry	28
Average years work experience at entry	2.0

ACADEMICS
Academic Experience Rating	83
Profs interesting rating	86
Profs accesible rating	87
Student/faculty ratio	15:1
% female faculty	19
% underrepresented minority faculty	14
% part-time faculty	24

Joint Degrees
MBA/JD - 3 Years; MSP/MBA - 8
Semesters

Prominent Alumni
Bill Davis, President & COO,
Universal Orlando

Academics

Stetson University offers fast-paced MBA programs for working professionals on three of its four central Florida campuses. In broad strokes, the Stetson MBA is divided into the following areas: foundational course work (or prerequisite courses), advanced course work, and electives. Stetson's is a general MBA, so students do not have the option of selecting an area of concentration; however, they can tailor their education through elective courses in fields like decision science, finance, management, information technology, and marketing. In addition, the MBA International Summer Program gives students the opportunity to spend two or four weeks overseas, where they tour local companies, meet with executives, and learn about the culture (current destinations include Austria, Italy, Germany, or China). Throughout the MBA course work, professors emphasize case studies and real world applications, giving students important skills they can take back to the workplace.

Stetson offers the MBA degree on their main campus in DeLand, as well as on their campuses in Celebration (Orlando) and Gulfport. In all locations, the school offers a "great class schedule" for working professionals, with MBA courses offered once a week in the evenings. While Stetson's Professional MBA allows students to take as many courses as fit their schedule, the Accelerated MBA is both fast and efficient. Students who have already fulfilled the prerequisites can complete the program in just over a year by attending full-time. Even part-time students often finish the entire MBA in just two years of study. (Stetson will review an applicant's undergraduate transcript to estimate how many prerequisite courses are required; often, students with an undergraduate degree in business are required to complete fewer courses.) In addition to the traditional MBA, Stetson offers a challenging, cohort-based, 51-credit hour Executive MBA (more than four years of work experience is required for this program) on the school's Celebration campus. The school also offers a joint MBA/JD at Gulfport, which can be completed at lightening speed: just three years for both degrees, start to finish.

A recommendation in itself, many students come to Stetson's graduate business program after completing their undergraduate degree at the college. Indeed, Stetson's graduate programs retain many of the qualities—like intimacy and friendliness—that define the undergraduate experience. A particular advantage, the Stetson MBA is a relatively small program, giving students excellent access to their professors, and an emphasis on "one-on-one discussions." Even more importantly, "the professors are excellent and outstanding mentors on campus," providing insight and support to their students. While many professors are accomplished professionals, they are "dedicated to the educational services, not busy with their own research." Course delivery is in-person (not online), but professors incorporate technology, using Blackboard software to post syllabi, assignments, grades, and, occasionally, discussion forums online.

ADMISSIONS CONTACT: JOHN F. MOORE, ASSISTANT DIRECTOR OF GRADUATE ADMISSIONS
ADDRESS: 421 NORTH WOODLAND BOULEVARD, UNIT 8398, DELAND, FL 32723
PHONE: 386-822-7410 • FAX: 386-822-7413
E-MAIL: GRADADMISSIONS@STETSON.EDU • WEBSITE: WWW.STETSON.EDU/PORTAL/GRADUATE

Career and Placement

Stetson's campuses are located throughout central Florida, keeping students close to the job markets in Orlando, Daytona Beach, and St. Petersburg. The university operates a Career Services Office on the main campus, open to current students and alumni. Students can sign up for individual counseling appointments, or they may attend career-related events, such as skills presentations, expert speakers, or on-campus interviews. Most services are directed towards the undergraduate community. All things considered, Stetson's placement programs aren't as robust as at other MBA programs; however, Stetson's MBA is designed for working professionals who are hoping to advance in their current positions, rather than those looking for a new position.

Student Life and Environment

With a convenient evening course schedule and several campus locations, Stetson attracts many "working professionals who are striving to advance their careers." On the whole, these students comprise a "very driven group," who are "goal-oriented" and "serious about academics." At the same time, the atmosphere is collaborative, as most students are also "interested in diversifying their skills in both business and networking." For professionals the atmosphere is supportive, and students find they "can relate with classmates, since many also have full-time jobs."

Located in central Florida, students at Stetson enjoy proximity to both local businesses and the beach—and everyone loves Florida's year-round sunny weather. On the main campus, the Lynn Business Center is equipped with high-speed Internet and numerous computer terminals. Despite the nice campus environment, prospective students should be aware that Stetson's MBA is principally designed for working professionals, so most students come to campus for class—and nothing more. Accordingly, some students would like to see "more of a sense of community" at Stetson, as "the campus is a ghost town on the weekends." However, the school has placed great emphasis on student life and student activities in recent years.

Admissions

Stetson accepts new students to the MBA program on a rolling basis. Generally speaking, students must apply at least 45 days before the start of the new term; once all application materials are received, students can expect a reply from the university immediately. To be considered for the joint MBA/JD on the Gulfport campus, students must first meet the requirements of the Stetson School of Law. Undergraduate GPA and GMAT scores are typically the two most important factors in an admissions decision.

FINANCIAL FACTS

Annual tuition	$25,050
Fees	$0
Cost of books	$1,400
% of students receiving aid	72
% of first-year students receiving aid	57
% of students receiving grants	14
Average award package	$20,584
Average grant	$7,417
Average loan	$20,562

ADMISSIONS

Admissions Selectivity Rating	85
Average GMAT	550
Range of GMAT	490–620
Average GPA	3.30
TOEFL required of international students	Yes
Minimum TOEFL (paper/computer)	550/213
Application fee	$50
International application fee	$50
Regular application deadline	5/31
Regular application notification	6/30
Deferment available	Yes
Maximum length of deferment	1 year
Transfer students accepted	Yes

Transfer application policy: The graduate business programs require a basic foundation in business administration courses. Foundation requirements may be satisfied by courses taken at institutions accredited by the appropriate regional association. Coursework taken by applicants as part of their undergraduate curriculum may be applied to the foundation requirements if the coursework is comparable and if the applicant earned a course grade of a C or higher. After admission to a graduate program at Stetson, any foundation course may be satisfied by completion of a comparable course credit from an institution accredited by the appropriate regional association. Advanced course requirements are ordinarily to be taken at Stetson.

Non-fall admissions	Yes
Need-blind admissions	Yes

SUFFOLK UNIVERSITY
SAWYER BUSINESS SCHOOL

GENERAL INFORMATION
Type of school · Private
Affiliation · No Affiliation
Academic calendar · Semester

SURVEY SAYS...
Students love Boston, MA
Solid preparation in:
Communication/interpersonal skills,
Doing business in a global economy

STUDENTS
Enrollment of parent
  institution · 7,911
Enrollment of MBA Program · 692
% male/female · 62/38
% out-of-state · 9
% part-time · 81
% underrepresented minority · 8
% international · 57
Average age at entry · 27
Average years work experience
  at entry · 4.1

ACADEMICS
Academic Experience Rating · **80**
Profs interesting rating · 77
Profs accesible rating · 77
Student/faculty ratio · 15:1
% female faculty · 30
% underrepresented minority
  faculty · 16
% part-time faculty · 36

Joint Degrees
MBA/MS Accounting - 18 to 24
months full-time; 20-32 months
part-time. MBA/MS Finance - 18 to
24 months full-time; 20 - 32
months part-time. MBA/MS Taxation
- 18 to 24 months full-time; 20-32
months part-time. JD/MBA - 4 years
full-time; 5 years part-time.
JD/Masters in Public Administration
-4 years total full-time; 5 years part-
time. JD/Masters in Finance - 4
years full-time; 5 years part-time.

Prominent Alumni
Robert Mudge, New England Region
President, Verizon; Tara Taylor, VP,
State Street Global Advisors

Academics

Boston's Suffolk University offers a conventional MBA as well as specialized MBAs in health administration, and nonprofit management. The school also offers a Global MBA in which students combine upper-level course work focused on international finance and marketing with a required international internship. Students laud the "diversity [of] hands-on learning experiences through global travel seminars" in the Global MBA program. One reports, "I will be going to Brazil and London for week-long seminars this year." Another adds, "The company that currently employs me does business throughout the world. This program would allow me to advance within this organization."

Suffolk "caters to the working professionals" who make up the majority of its MBA student body with "great scheduling" and "program flexibility" that "allow us to balance both work and school." "Classes are offered at night, on the weekends, online, and through the summer" to maximize students' opportunities to complete needed classes. A convenient "urban setting close to work" is another boon for those who work in and around the Financial District.

To many though, "Suffolk's greatest strength is the professors' holistic approach to management." Suffolk professors are "working professionals teaching relevant courses" emphasizing "a balance of quantitative management skills while recognizing the importance of interpersonal qualitative skills." "Many professors have a 'This is your class' mentality, where they are open to student input on the structure of the class," one student writes approvingly, adding "I have learned a tremendous amount."

Career and Placement

Suffolk prides itself on preparing students for the real world, and effective, long-term career planning is a major piece of the puzzle. In fact, every student at Suffolk must take an introductory course aptly named Effective Career Planning, designed to help students evaluate their professional skills and career paths and to make a solid plan for what they wish to accomplish with an MBA. In addition, the Suffolk MBA EDGE offers professional development events throughout the academic year. These events run the gamut from seminars on power lunches and the professional image to MBA Networking Week and Technology Day. MBA EDGE also hosts a number of career services events such as workshops on resume writing and salary negotiations. Students tell us that these "programs and classes required for new students have been great. They really push us to develop career plans and help us develop many different skills that will help us in planning and pursuing our careers."

Student opinion of Suffolk's career services office is mixed, with a number of supporters observing that recruiting and placement disappointments "may be a product of the poor economy and lack of jobs due to the recession" rather than shortcomings in the placement office. Top employers of Suffolk MBAs include: Bank of America, Fidelity Investments, Investors Bank & Trust, KPMG, PricewaterhouseCoopers, and State Street Bank.

Student Life and Environment

Over 80 percent of Suffolk MBAs are part-time students, and the university designs its program to accommodate their schedules. "Classes are [almost] always offered during evenings," with "very few day classes for full-time students." The downside is that the system necessitates a very long day for some. "When you are taking two classes back to back from 4:30 P.M. to 10 P.M., it is tough," one student explains, adding "I worked full time this last semester and went to school full time. It was tough but doable." Overall,

ADMISSIONS CONTACT: DIRECTOR OF GRADUATE ADMISSIONS
ADDRESS: 8 ASHBURTON PLACE, BOSTON, MA 02108
PHONE: 617-573-8302 • FAX: 617-305-1733
E-MAIL: GRAD.ADMISSION@SUFFOLK.EDU • WEBSITE: WWW.SUFFOLK.EDU/BUSINESS

however, students appreciate the lengths to which Suffolk goes to serve its evening students. The school "has amazing networking events and an exceptional 'Meet the Firms Night,'" and is also "very active in promoting networking and helping to improve social interactions in preparation of interviews." As one student observes, "As a full-time professional, work, school, and life are a balancing act. I would say that Suffolk caters to my needs, extends my breadth of knowledge, and positions me well for future success."

The school is not without its shortcomings, however. "The gym is awful," says one. Worse, "The actual b-school building is old and resembles a high school in some regards. They need a dedicated facility for the business school." Fortunately, the building is equipped with wireless Internet and most classrooms have multimedia capacities. Students wish there were "more resources for graduate students. There is a graduate student lounge, but it only accommodates about seven people. The computer lab is always full. The dining options in the graduate school are nothing special."

Suffolk MBAs are "a very diverse group," with many part-time students who are "mid- to upper-20-somethings in their second or third jobs" and "full time students from India, the Middle East, and Eastern Europe" as well as from the United States (the majority of full-timers are international students who "add a global perspective"). Part-timers note that "Everyone is at a different point in the program, so it is hard to foster and maintain friendships since everyone has busy and changing schedules."

Admissions

To apply to the Suffolk University Sawyer Business School, students must submit undergraduate transcripts, a resume, and a completed application, including essays. Those applying to the full-time program must have at least one year of work experience; however, the average admit has logged three years in a professional position. Part-time applicants are expected to have spent more time in the professional world and average five to seven years of work experience. For the Global MBA, students must have at least three years of full-time work experience to be considered. Applicants must also submit GMAT or GRE scores, though exceptions may be made for practicing CPAs and attorneys. In addition to the requirements above, international applicants must submit TOEFL or IELTS scores.

FINANCIAL FACTS

Annual tuition	$36,260
Fees	$20
Cost of books	$1,200
Room & board	$16,396
% of students receiving aid	51
% of first-year students receiving aid	51
% of students receiving grants	28
Average award package	$35,609
Average grant	$16,366
Average loan	$30,497
Average student loan debt	$52,538

ADMISSIONS

Admissions Selectivity Rating	**79**
# of applications received	364
% applicants accepted	52
% acceptees attending	64
Average GMAT	499
Range of GMAT	450–560
Average GPA	3.12
TOEFL required of international students	Yes
Minimum TOEFL (paper/computer)	550/213
International application fee	$50
Early application deadline	3/15
Regular application deadline	6/15
Deferment available	Yes
Maximum length of deferment	1 year
Transfer students accepted	Yes
Transfer application policy: same as for regular applicants	
Non-fall admissions	Yes
Need-blind admissions	Yes

EMPLOYMENT PROFILE

Career Rating	**78**	**Grads Employed by Function% Avg. Salary**	
Percent employed at graduation	53	Marketing	(40%) $57,700
Percent employed 3 months		Operations	(7%) $75,000
after graduation	47	Management	(7%) $103,000
Average base starting salary	$60,500	Finance	(21%) $52,300
Primary Source of Full-time Job Acceptances		HR	(7%) $45,000
School-facilitated activities	4(29%)	MIS	(7%) $62,000
Graduate-facilitated activities	10(71%)	Other	(2%) $57,500

Top 5 Employers Hiring Grads
State Street Global Advisors(1), Deloitte (1), Johnson & Johnson (1), Partners Health Care (1), Dreambridge Partners, Experian (1)

SYRACUSE UNIVERSITY
MARTIN J. WHITMAN SCHOOL OF MANAGEMENT

GENERAL INFORMATION

Type of school	Private
Academic calendar	Semester

SURVEY SAYS...
Smart classrooms
Solid preparation in:
Operations, Entrepreneurial studies

STUDENTS

Enrollment of parent institution	20,407
Enrollment of MBA Program	98
% male/female	64/36
% underrepresented minority	4
% international	52
Average age at entry	24
Average years work experience at entry	2.0

ACADEMICS

Academic Experience Rating	85
Profs interesting rating	75
Profs accesible rating	84
Student/faculty ratio	4:1
% female faculty	19
% underrepresented minority faculty	7
% part-time faculty	24

Joint Degrees
MBA/Juris Doctorate (4 years); MBA/Master of Public Administration (3 years); With any other degree-bearing graduate program offered at Syracuse University

Prominent Alumni
Martin J. Whitman, Founder of Third Avenue Value Fund; Dick Clark, Chairman and CEO of Dick Clark Productions; Dan D'Aniello, Founding Partner of the Carlyle Group; The Honorable Alfonse D'Amato, former U.S. Senator; Arthur Rock, venture capitalist, Arthur Rock & Company

Academics

The small MBA program at Syracuse University's Whitman School of Management is a good fit for early- and mid-career professionals hoping to ramp up their business acumen and gain valuable experience in the real world. Academically, the MBA curriculum is well rounded, covering a wide breadth of subject areas, while also placing "emphasis on finance, supply chain, and entrepreneurship." A great place to get your feet wet in the world of business, there is an "experiential component featured in many of the classes," as well as myriad "opportunities given to MBA students to participate within different organizations, whether as an intern or as a consultant to a large reputable firm." A current student adds, "These academic consulting engagements added depth to many of the courses through projects that provided and often required innovative and hands-on approaches."

Whitman professors are generally "productive and efficient," with "excellent academic backgrounds" in their field of specialization. When it comes to leading a class, however, students say their skill set varies: "There are professors who are great, know their fields, and can quickly apply lessons to what is going on around the world." On the other hand, "Many of the older faculty lacks presentation skills. Lectures can be very dry." The upshot is that, across the board, professors are supportive and "willing to help on projects outside of the classroom." In fact, thanks to the "very small class size," "you can get to know your classmates and your professors on a personal level." At the same time, students love the fact that Syracuse offers all the "resources of a large institution," including a "beautiful new building" for business students, replete with "up-to-date technology."

In addition to the traditional MBA, busy professionals have the option of enrolling in the well-regarded iMBA at Syracuse, "which combines actual on-campus learning via week-long residencies, along with online course work." According to those in the program, "The iMBA program provides the same educational experience as the full-time MBA (same curriculum, professors, etc.), but has a much more flexible format." In addition, the school offers a "great JD/MBA program with lots of connections in NYC," as well as a joint masters program in conjunction with the U.S. Army.

Career and Placement

Whitman's emphasis on experiential learning is a boon to students looking to jump-start their career after the MBA. Plus, the school's individualized focus makes it easier to prep for a successful job hunt. Here, faculty and staff "go above and beyond to ensure you are well prepared for your career, and customize plans to place you in your dream company." Specifically, via the Whitman Career Center, students have access to professional-development workshops, personal coaching, and "strong networking events" with local companies. Particularly advantageous for those looking locally, "Alumni is set on creating successful opportunities for current students."

While everyone agrees that "Syracuse's MBA program is on the rise," students would like to see more on-campus recruitment opportunities for MBA candidates, suggesting the school could improve by opening a "career center focused specifically and only on graduate students, (MBAs, master's, and PhD students)." Fortunately, improvement is already in the works: students note that, this year, the school is "doing a great deal to bring more business recruiters and alumni onto campus for networking opportunities." In 2014, Syracuse graduates had an average base salary of $72,119, with a range between $45,000 and $110,000. Top hiring companies include the Federal Reserve, Chrysler, Pfizer, KPMG, Ernst & Young, JPMorgan Chase, Intuit, and Lockheed Martin.

ADMISSIONS CONTACT: JOSHUA LaFAVE, DIRECTOR OF RECRUITING
ADDRESS: 721 UNIVERSITY AVENUE - SUITE 315, SYRACUSE, NY 13244-2450
PHONE: 315-443-3497 • FAX: 315-443-9517
E-MAIL: BUSGRAD@SYR.EDU • WEBSITE: WHITMAN.SYR.EDU

Student Life and Environment

Students at Whitman are a "very diverse group" of people, who "all come from different industries," as well as varying academic backgrounds. With long-term goals and plenty of ambition, these "highly intelligent" students are "competitive and driven" when it comes to coursework and careers. Fortunately, that competitiveness does not negatively affect the academic environment. On the contrary, the atmosphere at Whitman is "very collegial and collaborative," and students are "friendly, extremely helpful, and supportive" of their classmates.

"Syracuse's full-time MBA group is very close," described by some as "one big extended family." On campus, "There is hardly ever a day that goes by when there isn't an event, speaker, or sports activity that students can attend," and "there are plenty of clubs and groups to join where you can mentor, lead, participate in the community and more." In addition to events at the business school, MBA candidates can also take advantage of the resources on the greater campus, like "attending sold-out sports games and events featuring figures such as Hillary Clinton or the Dalai Lama." Though "winter is long" and very cold, the medium-sized city of Syracuse is a comfortable hometown, with plenty of recreation and cultural events for students. For example, "The city of Syracuse has different events going on every weekend in the summer. They have blues festivals, Irish festival, and several others." On top of that, the school is "near New York City," allowing students to take advantage of the many social and professional opportunities in the Big Apple.

Admissions

To apply to both the full-time and iMBA programs, students must submit academic transcripts, GMAT scores, two essays, and two letters of recommendation. In 2014, incoming students had an average GMAT score of 627 and average pre-MBA work experience of thirty months. More than 65 percent of incoming student had undergraduate degrees in fields other than business.

FINANCIAL FACTS

Annual tuition	$34,860
Fees	$1,332
Cost of books	$1,308
Room & board	$12,850
% of students receiving aid	96
% of first-year students receiving aid	93
% of students receiving grants	96
Average award package	$30,453
Average grant	$23,218
Average loan	$23,150
Average student loan debt	$48,546

ADMISSIONS

Admissions Selectivity Rating	85
# of applications received	187
% applicants accepted	45
% acceptees attending	48
Average GMAT	636
Range of GMAT	580–650
Average GPA	3.24
TOEFL required of international students	Yes
Minimum TOEFL (paper/computer)	600/250
Application fee	$75
International application fee	$75
Early application deadline	11/30
Early notification date	12/21
Regular application deadline	4/19
Regular application notification	5/17
Application Deadline/Notification	
Round 1:	11/30 / 12/21
Round 2:	1/1 / 2/1
Round 3:	2/15 / 3/15
Round 4:	4/19 / 5/17
Deferment available	Yes
Maximum length of deferment	1 year
Transfer students accepted	No
Non-fall admissions	Yes
Need-blind admissions	Yes

EMPLOYMENT PROFILE

		Grads Employed by Function	% Avg. Salary
Career Rating	86		
Percent employed at graduation	52	Marketing	(29%) $51,650
Percent employed 3 months after graduation	75	Operations	(29%) $57,800
		Consulting	(12%) $77,500
Average base starting salary	$60,640	Finance	(29%) $53,000
Primary Source of Full-time Job Acceptances		Other	(6%)
School-facilitated activities	10(67%)	**Top 5 Employers Hiring Grads**	
Graduate-facilitated activities	5(33%)	Win-Holt (2), Ayco Corporation (1), Morgan Stanley (1), Ernst & Young (1), Care Stream (1)	

TEMPLE UNIVERSITY
THE FOX SCHOOL OF BUSINESS AND MANAGEMENT

GENERAL INFORMATION

Type of school	Public
Affiliation	No Affiliation

SURVEY SAYS...

Smart classrooms
Solid preparation in:
Accounting, Doing business in a
global economy

STUDENTS

Enrollment of parent institution	38,648
Enrollment of MBA Program	494
% male/female	70/30
% out-of-state	60
% part-time	50
% international	33
Average age at entry	28
Average years work experience at entry	5.3

ACADEMICS

Academic Experience Rating	94
Profs interesting rating	87
Profs accesible rating	93
Student/faculty ratio	15:1
% female faculty	29
% underrepresented minority faculty	31
% part-time faculty	12

Joint Degrees

JD/MBA 4 years; DMD/MBA 4
years; MD/MBA 4-5 years; JD/MBA
3 years

Prominent Alumni

Harry J. Mullany III, CEO The
Service Master Company; Mallipudi
Raju Pallam Mangapati, Ministerfor
Education, India; Brenton Saunders,
Esq, CEO Bausch + Lomb New York,
NY; David Schoch, Chair and CEO of
Ford Motor China; Stanley Wang,
CEO of Pantronix Corporation for
Griffiths

Academics

Temple University's reputation has been growing exponentially in the business world. Naturally, this notion is certainly not lost on current students who praise the school's "high-end new facilities, rising rankings, and strong brand equity." Additionally, Temple's Philadelphia location guarantees "proximity to major companies;" companies with whom the school has forged strong relationships. Students also benefit from "small class sizes" which "provide a one-on-one experience with the opportunity to collaborate with award-winning faculty." However, opinion on academic rigor is definitely divided. While some students find the caliber to be "world class," others think some classes "seem tailored more toward an undergrad population."

For the most part, professors "truly care about each individual student and keep classes fresh with ideas and topics that are timely in today's business world." Students also eagerly report that they are great at fostering "meaningful discussion." Just as essential, it's apparent that Temple professors are "dedicated to teaching" and they really do their utmost to make themselves "accessible."

Moreover, the administration makes a concerted effort to "seek student input." They frequently ask MBA candidates to "evaluate [their] classes, courses and overall experience." And the school truly utilizes this feedback to ensure the program "constantly stays up on trends." Indeed, "The Fox School is on the road to continuous improvement; the program is continually evolving to help meet student needs."

Career and Placement

The Fox School of Business provides students with many avenues for job placement. For starters, Temple MBAs truly value that they can turn to their teachers for career advice and assistance. As a second-year student proudly shares, "With some exception, most professors have fantastic real-world experience and are happy to share themselves and their networks with any willing student." Additionally, MBA candidates can take advantage of Temple's "strong...web application[s] that help students find internships and jobs." Though a demoralized second-year laments that "job postings are not always indicative of the industries students are looking to enter." Fortunately, due to Temple's growing stature, students have noticed "more prominent recruiters showing up at career fairs."

The vast majority of Temple MBAs seek employment within the Northeast and Mid-Atlantic regions. Of course, the program does attract an international crowd and graduates can be found around the globe from England and France to Nigeria and India. Employers who frequently hire Fox students include Accenture, Ernst & Young, Campbells Soup, Vanguard, GlaxoSmithKline, KPMG, G.E., Comcast, and Boenning and Scattergood.

ADMISSIONS CONTACT: PHYLLIS TUTORA, DIRECTOR GRADUATE ENROLLMENT MANAGEMENT
ADDRESS: 1801 LIACOURAS WALK, ALTER HALL, SUITE 701, PHILADELPHIA, PA 19122-6083
PHONE: 215-204-5890 • FAX: 215-204-1632
E-MAIL: FOXINFO@TEMPLE.EDU • WEBSITE: FOX.TEMPLE.EDU/GRAD

Student Life and Environment

Temple MBAs speak quite highly of their peers. Indeed, "My fellow students are what I love most about Temple—they are cooperatively competitive. Students are there to help one another with class work, internship/job searches, networking, etc. This has been one of the most collaborative environments I've enjoyed thus far." Moreover, many also describe their fellow students as "wonderful, interesting, intelligent people." And a content first-year further explains, "My fellow students are a diverse mix of both domestic and international students with a variety of professional backgrounds. We have a great sense of community and associate with the members of our cohort both inside and outside of the classroom."

"With few exceptions," Temple MBAs are "busy from 7:00 AM to midnight." Of course, that's completely understandable considering "there is always something to do here, and there is always somebody to do it with." The school "consistently offers speakers and events that we can attend for free—these include C-Suite individuals, athletic coaches, various politicians, etc." And when students are looking to unwind in a less academic manner, they can "always go out to bars and house-parties in Philadelphia." All in all, "It is a work hard play hard environment and the learning experience is outstanding."

Admissions

We won't mince words; gaining admission to Temple's MBA program is competitive. When assessing applicants, admissions officers look for individuals with solid business exposure, strong interpersonal skills, academic aptitude and potential. A candidate's personal goals are also considered. To apply, you'll be required to submit college transcripts, a current resume, two letters of recommendation, two essays (and an optional statement) and a GMAT score from within the last five years. Non-native English speakers will also be required to submit a TOEFFL score from within the last two years (unless a previous degree was acquired from an English speaking university). Finally, admission interviews are conducted on an invitation only basis.

FINANCIAL FACTS

Annual tuition	$25,137
Fees	$965
Cost of books	$1,000
Room & board (on/off-campus)	$16,520/$17,375
% of students receiving aid	55
% of first-year students receiving aid	86
% of students receiving grants	39
Average award package	$32,270
Average grant	$32,232
Average loan	$39,966
Average student loan debt	$31,113

ADMISSIONS

Admissions Selectivity Rating	95
# of applications received	376
% applicants accepted	28
% acceptees attending	94
Average GMAT	643
Range of GMAT	580–680
Average GPA	3.42
TOEFL required of international students	Yes
Minimum TOEFL (paper/computer)	600/250
Application fee	$60
International application fee	$60
Early application deadline	12/10
Early notification date	1/15
Regular application deadline	3/1
Regular application notification	3/31
Application Deadline/Notification	
Round 1:	12/10 / 1/15
Round 2:	3/1 / 3/31
Round 3:	5/31 / 6/15
Round 4:	6/30 / 7/15
Deferment available	Yes
Maximum length of deferment	1 Calendar year
Transfer students accepted	Yes
Transfer application policy:	
Reviewed on a case by case basis.	
Non-fall admissions	Yes
Need-blind admissions	Yes

EMPLOYMENT PROFILE

Career Rating	93	**Grads Employed by Function% Avg. Salary**	
Percent employed at graduation	74	Marketing	(23%) $80,917
Percent employed 3 months after graduation	98	Operations	(8%) $86,000
		Consulting	(15%)$74,500
Average base starting salary	$79,078	Management	(12%) $93,333
Primary Source of Full-time Job Acceptances		Finance	(12%) $69,167
School-facilitated activities	16(40%)	HR	(4%) $85,000
Graduate-facilitated activities	26(60%)	MIS	(12%) $88,333
		Other	(15%) $65,760

Top 5 Employers Hiring Grads
FMC Corporation (3), Bridge-X Technologies, Inc. (2), Hersha Hospitality Trust (2), JP Morgan Chase (2), Schindler Elevator Corporation (2)

TEXAS A&M INTERNATIONAL UNIVERSITY
A.R. SANCHEZ, JR. SCHOOL OF BUSINESS

GENERAL INFORMATION
Type of school	Public
Affiliation	No Affiliation
Academic calendar	Semester

SURVEY SAYS...
Friendly students, Cutting-edge classes, Happy students
Solid preparation in:
Finance, General management, Teamwork

STUDENTS
Enrollment of parent institution	7,213
Enrollment of MBA Program	148
% male/female	71/29
% out-of-state	0
% part-time	84
% underrepresented minority	50
% international	46
Average age at entry	30
Average years work experience at entry	7.0

ACADEMICS
Academic Experience Rating	**71**
Profs interesting rating	75
Profs accesible rating	76
Student/faculty ratio	23:1
% female faculty	14
% underrepresented minority faculty	76
% part-time faculty	17

Academics

Texas A&M International University (TAMIU) is conveniently "located in an area with a strong international trade industry" and offers a "normal work environment" that has "grown much" in recent years. TAMIU's Sanchez School of Business has, according to one student concentrating in international trade, "a strong international business focus and a faculty from diverse educational, professional, and cultural backgrounds." The school's "relatively small classes" also help cultivate "an excellent learning environment" in which to earn an accredited MBA. The course load has been described as "intense and demanding," and even "too much if you are a student who works full-time." But overall, as one student tells us, "The effort gone into this coursework is greatly compensated by the knowledge attained. It takes practice and hands-on projects to learn what is expected of my career."

In addition to a diverse faculty of 36, who specialize in international taxation, accounting, banking and finance, and trade theory, among other disciplines, TAMIU's student body also covers a broad spectrum of experience and background. "Most of my fellow classmates," one student notes, "are older and wiser with experience from different business backgrounds. It is very interesting to learn about their experiences. We get to hear about real-life scenarios and how they are handled or should have been handled." TAMIU also benefits from a "relaxed" and "peaceful" learning environment, which complements the school's intense academic workload. There are also "great computer labs and library," and the "food retailers are excellent."

Among the advanced degrees offered by TAMIU, the list includes an onsite MBA, an online MBA, as well as MPACC, MC-IS and a Ph.D. in International Business Administration. On average, the approximate length of each master's program for full-time students is one and a half years of study. Specific degree programs and concentrations at TAMIU include international banking and finance, international business, and management. Given the impressive offerings at TAMIU, not many students find cause for complaint, but some students have expressed concern that members of the local business community are unable to audit classes.

Career and Placement

The Texas A&M International Career Services Office provides counseling and placement services to the entire undergraduate and graduate student body. The office organizes on-campus recruiting events, career expos, and job fairs. It also offers one-on-one counseling, workshops, library services, and resume review. Many TAMIU students have professed a need for improvement in some areas of career placement. For instance, the complete lack of available internships and scarce opportunities for "job networking" and "training" are areas of concern, while other students have noted the need for greater recruiting services and better "alumni relations."

ADMISSIONS CONTACT: IMELDA LOPEZ, GRADUATE ADMISSIONS ADVISOR
ADDRESS: 5201 UNIVERSITY BLVD., LAREDO, TX 78041
PHONE: 956-326-2485 • FAX: 956-326-2479
E-MAIL: LOPEZ@TAMIU.EDU • WEBSITE: WWW.TAMIU.EDU/ARSSB

Student Life and Environment

Campus life at TAMIU has been described as "very diverse," comprised of "dedicated individuals who help promote and improve clubs and organizations." Among the more popular organizations, and in particular those active in assisting students "figure out a future career," are the "Students in Free Enterprise (SIFE), Association of International Students (AIS), and Student Government." These organizations are instrumental in coordinating timely lecture series, so that students can remain up to date on current practices and concerns in the business community. Adding to the diverse flavor of campus life at TAMIU, the student body is made up of a vast international body, including students from "China, India, Russia, Spain, Italy, Mexico, Kenya, Jordan, Nepal," and several other countries.

"Life here is awesome," says one student. "I have great communities like AIS, and the recreational center helps me" release the stress of an "exhaustive and hectic" course load. Another student majoring in business administration had this to offer: "The student body is a close family group. TAMIU is my school family, from professors to the students." Another noted perk for much of the student body, particularly those with full-time jobs, is the availability of evening courses. "I am able to take courses in the evening and work full-time during the day," says one student attending school part-time.

Located in the southern Texas town of Laredo, also known as "The Gateway City" due to a shared border with Mexico, the city's location makes it a hub for international trade and manufacturing, and thus in many respects, an ideal place for business students. On the TAMIU campus itself, extracurricular activities are available but by no means abundant. As one student puts it, "While school life is somewhat budding, the school does little to promote campus life in general; most of the 'campus life' exists off campus."

Admissions

Applying to the TAMIU MBA program is a two-step process, as applicants must be admitted to both the University and the A.R. Sanchez, Jr. School of Business in order to enroll in the MBA program. All applicants to the MBA program must submit the following materials: GMAT or GRE scores, essay/personal statement, official undergraduate transcript, two letters of recommendation, and resume/CV, all of which will be given great and equal consideration by the Graduate Admissions Committee. TOEFL scores are required from all international applicants, with minimum scores of 550 for the written test, 213 for the computer-based test or 79 for the internet-based test. An IELTS score of 6.5 or higher may be used in lieu of the TOEFL. Eligible Mexican students can benefit from in-state tuition fees, which are much lower than those paid by other international students.

FINANCIAL FACTS

Annual tuition (in-state/ out-of-state)	$1,386/$7,704
Fees	$3,612
Cost of books	$4,227
Room & board (on/off-campus)	$7,313/$6,275
% of students receiving aid	41
% of first-year students receiving aid	45
% of students receiving grants	24
Average award package	$6,987
Average grant	$1,599
Average loan	$8,122
Average student loan debt	$17,333

ADMISSIONS

Admissions Selectivity Rating	**68**
# of applications received	35
% applicants accepted	100
% acceptees attending	83
Average GMAT	443
Average GPA	3.25
TOEFL required of international students	Yes
Minimum TOEFL (paper/computer)	550/213
Application fee	$50
International application fee	$50
Regular application deadline	4/30
Deferment available	Yes
Maximum length of deferment	1 YEAR
Transfer students accepted	Yes
Transfer application policy: Application process is the same as new applicants; transfer students may request to transfer up to six hours of graduate credit	
Non-fall admissions	Yes
Need-blind admissions	Yes

TEXAS A&M UNIVERSITY—COLLEGE STATION
MAYS BUSINESS SCHOOL

GENERAL INFORMATION

Type of school	Public
Affiliation	No Affiliation
Academic calendar	Semester

SURVEY SAYS...

Good peer network, Smart class-
rooms
Solid preparation in:
Accounting, General management,
Operations

STUDENTS

Enrollment of parent institution	53,187
Enrollment of MBA Program	132
% male/female	76/24
% out-of-state	23
% part-time	0
% underrepresented minority	15
% international	33
Average age at entry	28
Average years work experience at entry	5.0

ACADEMICS

Academic Experience Rating	96
Profs interesting rating	93
Profs accesible rating	91
Student/faculty ratio	7:1
% female faculty	17
% underrepresented minority faculty	6
% part-time faculty	0

Joint Degrees

MBA/MS Management Information
Systems - 24 months. MBA/MS-
Finance - 24 months

Academics

Business-minded MBA candidates say you get a "great return on investment" at Texas A&M. While tuition at this public university is "relatively inexpensive," the business school offers a "high-quality education," spearheaded by an "unmatched teaching staff." The "academically-challenging and quantitatively-focused" curriculum is incredibly intense, compressing the equivalent of a two-year fulltime MBA into just sixteen months. Students praise the efficiency of the school's accelerated schedule, which reduces costs and career interruption while nonetheless providing "well-rounded" business training. In fact, "The ability of the professors and the program to crunch so much information into that time is outstanding." On the flip side, some students feel the program's speed isn't necessarily an advantage, as "we never have to time to prepare sufficiently and then discuss it in depth." Fortunately, those who'd like to extend their education may decide to stay at Texas A&M for an extra semester, during which time they can specialize in accounting, consulting, e-commerce, finance, marketing, and real estate, among others.

Teaching is taken seriously Texas A&M, and the school's "excellent" faculty are truly involved with the educational process. In class, "The teachers are engaging and concerned about student learning," and "try hard to make sure everybody understands the course material." Outside of class, "Professors and administration are extremely helpful. They have open-door policies and are easily accessible." In addition, the school's administration is friendly and student-oriented. From top to bottom, "Everybody in the MBA office goes out of their way to make sure we have great opportunities to learn outside the classroom, hear great speakers, and succeed in the program."

Every Texas A&M business school class is small, allowing plenty of individual attention while simultaneously encouraging interaction and discussion in (and outside) the classroom. Explains a student, "The classes are a perfect size to harness great discussions—a lot of opinions and viewpoints, but not so many that it's difficult to be heard in a single class period." At the same time, the intimate classroom environment means no one can slack off or slip through the cracks; "The classes are discussion-intensive, so every day requires a good bit of preparation." On the whole, students admit that Mays is a "very, very competitive environment," and, to keep up with the program's demands, students "often spend weekends studying and preparing for the upcoming week."

If Mays students didn't already have enough on their plate, the program includes a plethora of curricular and extracurricular activities that are designed to add depth and practical experience to the program. Of particular note, the MBA includes a required consulting project, which gives students the opportunity to apply classroom principals to a real-world business environment. Students can also sharpen their investment acumen through the Reliant Energy Securities & Commodities Trading Center, where Bloomberg terminals keep finance students in touch with the market. Beyond curricular offerings, the program incorporates enrichment features like the "MBA Venture Challenge" case competition, a "Dean's Leadership Speaker Series" and opportunities for executive coaching and leadership development and training.

Career and Placement

With an excellent 94 percent job placement rate, it's no surprise that students sing the praises of the Graduate Business Career Services Office. The Career Services staff is "professional, respectful, and wonderful to work with," and is lauded for coming up with "creative ideas in a challenging internship/job market." Another unique advantage of the school's sixteen-month format is that A&M students graduate in December, making them "available for that recruiting period when there is not a large supply of MBA students attempting to be recruited."

ADMISSIONS CONTACT: CHRIS REED, DIRECTOR OF MBA ADMISSIONS
ADDRESS: 4117 TAMU, COLLEGE STATION, TX 77843-4117
PHONE: 979-845-4714 • FAX: 979-862-2393
E-MAIL: FTMBA@TAMU.EDU • WEBSITE: FTMBA.TAMU.EDU

In addition to the business school's job placement services, the school's active alumni network is another benefit of attending Texas A&M. With graduates all over Texas and beyond, "the Aggie network is famous for how in-touch alumni are to students." In a recent academic year, the majority of Texas A&M graduates (almost 76 percent) took jobs in the southwest, and most students went on to work in consulting, finance, management, or marketing. Last year, the mean starting salary was $93,511.

Student Life and Environment

Between classes, homework, lectures, and social life, there is "never a dull moment" at Texas A&M. Though most MBA candidates say their coursework keeps them supremely occupied, they also appreciate the openness and camaraderie that exists between the students at Mays Business School. While students are "determined to succeed," "everybody in the class is very social and works together." Within the Mays community, "Friendliness and professionalism abound."

The business school is located on Texas A&M's main campus, home to 48,000 students. Politically and socially, "A&M is a very conservative school and the students, for the most part, are very conservative" in the business school as well. As a part of a large, research university, "It is very easy to get involved in Texas A&M's culture. Football games and other outside activities are a "must see" and current students make it a point to take new students to these events." School spirit surges—even in the graduate programs—and students tell us, "The Aggie Spirit is something one ought to experience." Surrounding College Station is a "quiet, largely safe" town of 125,000, which grew alongside the university. If you're craving something a little more urban, the campus is just a few hours drive from Austin, Dallas/Fort Worth, Houston, and San Antonio.

Admissions

Texas A&M deliberately limits the size of each incoming class, and admissions are competitive. Prospective students must have fulltime post-baccalaureate work experience to be considered for the program; however, Peace Corps, missionary work, or military service is counted as work experience, even if it took place before the college degree. Select applicants may be invited to interview with the Admissions Committee.

FINANCIAL FACTS

Annual tuition (in-state/ out-of-state)	$8,156/$20,792
Fees	$14,057
Cost of books	$2,114
Room & board	$9,900
Average award package	$22,619
Average student loan debt	$32,278

ADMISSIONS

Admissions Selectivity Rating	95
# of applications received	557
% applicants accepted	23
% acceptees attending	51
Average GMAT	649
Range of GMAT	610–690
Average GPA	3.40
TOEFL required of international students	Yes
Minimum TOEFL (paper/computer)	600/250
Application fee	$175
International application fee	$200
Early application deadline	9/17
Application Deadline/Notification	
Round 1:	11/1 /
Round 2:	1/15 /
Round 3:	3/15 /
Round 4:	4/15 /
Deferment available	Yes
Maximum length of deferment	1 year
Transfer students accepted	No
Non-fall admissions	No
Need-blind admissions	Yes

EMPLOYMENT PROFILE

Career Rating	96	Grads Employed by Function	% Avg. Salary
Percent employed at graduation	73	Marketing	(22%) $85,000
Percent employed 3 months after graduation	94	Operations	(11%) $91,500
		Consulting	(17%)$100,875
Average base starting salary	$93,511	Management	(22%) $95,125
Primary Source of Full-time Job Acceptances		Finance	(24%) $93,364
School-facilitated activities	25(54%)	MIS	(4%) $103,500
Graduate-facilitated activities	21(46%)	**Top 5 Employers Hiring Grads**	
		HP (4), Dell (4), Deloitte (4), ExxonMobil (3), Amazon (1)	

TEXAS A&M UNIVERSITY—CORPUS CHRISTI
COLLEGE OF BUSINESS

GENERAL INFORMATION

Type of school	Public
Affiliation	No Affiliation
Academic calendar	Semester

SURVEY SAYS...

Happy students, Smart classrooms
Solid preparation in:
Teamwork

STUDENTS

Enrollment of parent institution	10,510
Enrollment of MBA Program	163
% male/female	52/48
% part-time	38
% underrepresented minority	21
% international	61
Average age at entry	27

ACADEMICS

Academic Experience Rating	**74**
Profs interesting rating	74
Profs accesible rating	80
% female faculty	34
% underrepresented minority faculty	25

Academics

Students at Texas A&M University—Corpus Christi (TAMUCC) say that in order to truly appreciate their school's stellar MBA programs, you must first put them in proper geographical perspective. TAMUCC "is a regional school, so comparing it with the experience of [students] at Top-25 schools is not fair," one such student points. However, "Given its status as a regional school and the mission of the university as it relates to the regional approach, the TAMUCC MBA program is excellent." Indeed, most here want a program that is first and foremost convenient, affordable, and flexible enough to accommodate students with full-time jobs. In these areas and more, students here tell us, TAMUCC delivers.

Point in case: TAMUCC "has a great core foundation and the potential to become a great public university." MBAs here benefit from the "wide variety of students [from] different countries" which broadens their educational experience. There is a particularly strong Hispanic student presence and a concurrent focus on business matters of interest to the American-Hispanic community. And then, of course, there's the "affordable tuition," the "small size of most classes"—the program is "not...too congested while still being large enough to have good facilities"—and the "easy-to-deal-with university administration," which works hard to ease the burdens of the school's overtaxed students. One student took special note of the program's "flexibility for working parents. I'm a single parent and have felt supported and encouraged by all of my professors and my advisor."

Similarly, professors "take the students' welfare into consideration" and "will always create extra time outside the class to answer questions to help make the learning process easy." Most instructors here "are very passionate about their work and it shows in their lecturing. They have relevant experience in their disciplines that they can relate to students showing real-life applications of the material." As one student explains, "I believe that the professors are the greatest strengths [of the program]. The passion and experience that they bring to the classroom is great. There are a couple who are not so great, but the majority are fantastic. Their enthusiasm makes you want to learn, and the material is challenging." TAMUCC offers its MBAs two areas of concentration: international business, and health care management.

Career and Placement

The TAMUCC Career Services office provides counseling and placement services for all undergraduates, graduate students, and alumni of the university. Frequent seminars and presentations are offered on such topics as "How to Job Search in the 'Hidden Market,'" "The Second Interview and Salary Negotiation," and "How to Get a Federal Job." The office also provides career counseling, computer-based self-assessments, job search advisement, online and hard-copy job postings, a career resource library and computer lab, videotaped mock interviews, and job fairs and on-campus recruiting events.

Top employers in the area include the Naval Air Station Corpus Christi, Christus Spohn Health System, the Corpus Christi Army Depot, H-E-B Grocery Co., Bay Limited, SSP Partners/Circle K, Driscoll Children's Hospital, APAC, First Data, and Gulf Marine Fabricators.

ADMISSIONS CONTACT: SHARON POLANSKY, DIRECTOR OF MASTERS PROGRAMS
ADDRESS: 6300 OCEAN DRIVE UNIT 5808, CORPUS CHRISTI, TX 78412-5808
PHONE: 361-825-2655 • FAX: 361-825-2725
E-MAIL: SHARON.POLANSKY@TAMUCC.EDU • WEBSITE: WWW.COB.TAMUCC.EDU

Student Life and Environment

"There is a very diverse population from a multitude of cultures" within the TAMUCC MBA program, and "this is very important…in South Texas, [where] the majority of the population is either Hispanic or white." Students here are "very ambitious and amiable," and while "discussions in class are heated, there is a mutual respect." The student body "is about 30 percent international," "which gives a very diverse, unique experience in the classroom." A sizeable group of military personnel further adds to the diverse backgrounds and perspectives. Except for the international students, most here are "balancing a full work load, course load, family life and other extracurricular activities."

TAMUCC's "attractive campus by the ocean" engenders a "laid-back, casual, 'feels like island time'" atmosphere. "Don't let people wearing flip flops fool you," though; these are "very hardworking/studying individuals." The program forces them to be actively involved in class, as the classroom "is very participation-oriented rather than the professor only lecturing." Fortunately TAMUCC students are up to the challenge.

Admissions

All applicants to the TAMUCC MBA program must submit the following materials: official transcripts for all undergraduate and graduate work; an official score report for the GMAT (test score can be no more than five years old); two letters or recommendation; a current resume or curriculum vitae; a personal essay stating your reasons for pursuing the MBA; and a completed application form. In addition, international students whose first language is not English must submit an official score for the TOEFL and an evaluation of non-English language transcripts executed by Education Credential Evaluators, Inc., International Education Research Foundation, Inc., or World Education Services. All international applicants must submit an I-34 form or other notarized confirmation of adequate financial support, a copy of their current visa, and proof of medical insurance.

FINANCIAL FACTS

Annual tuition (in-state/ out-of-state)	$3,522/$9,840
Fees	$2,110
Cost of books	$792
Room & board (on/off-campus)	$11,448/$10,087

ADMISSIONS

Admissions Selectivity Rating	73
# of applications received	55
% applicants accepted	78
% acceptees attending	88
Average GMAT	484
Range of GMAT	438–523
Average GPA	3.28
TOEFL required of international students	Yes
Minimum TOEFL (paper/computer)	550/213
Application fee	$50
International application fee	$70
Regular application deadline	7/15
Deferment available	Yes
Maximum length of deferment	1 year
Transfer students accepted	Yes
Transfer application policy: Possibility of transferring in 6 credits from accredited school with grade of B or above.	
Non-fall admissions	Yes
Need-blind admissions	Yes

TEXAS CHRISTIAN UNIVERSITY
NEELEY SCHOOL OF BUSINESS

GENERAL INFORMATION
Type of school   Private
Affiliation   Disciples of Christ
Academic calendar   Semester

SURVEY SAYS...
Good peer network
Solid preparation in:
Operations, Communication/
interpersonal skills

STUDENTS
Enrollment of parent institution	9,725
Enrollment of MBA Program	209
%.male/female	68/32
% out-of-state	22
% part-time	61
% underrepresented minority	15
% international	33
Average age at entry	27
Average years work experience at entry	5.0

ACADEMICS
Academic Experience Rating	**87**
Profs interesting rating	91
Profs accesible rating	84
Student/faculty ratio	8:1
% female faculty	27
% underrepresented minority faculty	6
% part-time faculty	12

Joint Degrees
Educational Leadership, MBA/Ed.D,
two years (MBA)three-five years
(Ed.D); Divinity MBA combined with
one of three graduate degrees in
Divinity, two years MBA plus two to
three years Divinity

Prominent Alumni
Bob McCann, CEO, Group Americas
at UBS; Luther King, Jr., President,
Luther King Capital Management
Corp.; Lorna Donatone, COO and
Education Market President at
Sodexho; Chris Kleinert, CEO &
President, Hunt Consolidated
Investments; Laurent Attias,
President EMEA, Alcon Labs, Inc.

Academics

Texas Christian University's Neeley School of Business offers the best of both worlds, uniting a "small-school atmosphere with big business ties." Located in the heart of the Dallas–Forth Worth metropolitan area, the school has "access to and relationships with many top companies." "Networking opportunities are second to none," and career and internship prospects look particularly positive in this vibrant business-oriented city. At the same time, "personalized attention" is a hallmark of the TCU program. With just fifty to sixty students in each incoming class, the "small and accessible size" of the school guarantees that students benefit from plenty of interaction with the "world-class faculty." Here, "It is easy to reach professors and ask questions." In addition to the faculty, "Every TCU employee involved with the MBA program has a clear and unwavering passion for growing the program and graduating successful students." Administrators are "very accommodating, know all of the students well, and are very accessible."

Depending on your needs and your career experience to date, Neeley offers a range of MBA options, including a part-time evening program, an executive MBA, a twenty-one-month full-time program, and an accelerated twelve-month full-time program. In the full-time program, students are assigned to small project teams during the first year, a great way to get to know your classmates. While the atmosphere is close-knit, the curriculum is rigorous. There is an "extremely heavy workload in the beginning" of the full-time MBA, and "All of the students in the program hold each other to a high standard." Described as "outstanding," Neeley professors bring "a ton of practical industry experience" to the classroom. Students point out that "the professors in supply chain are really good," and the school offers the opportunity to pursue a functional concentration in that field, as well as in marketing, finance, and accounting. MBA candidates may further tailor their studies through elective courses in a specific industry, like health care or real estate; the school's "up-and-coming" MBA for Energy Professionals is particularly suited to its Texas location.

A Neeley education "focuses more on experiential learning" than strict academics. In this "applicable career-focused program," there is an emphasis on developing a practical perspective, and professors are committed to "pushing our limits and growing our skills in communication, presentations, etc. from the moment classes begin." Throughout the MBA, class work is "supplemented with a great deal of real-world work experiences, though programs like Neeley & Associates Consulting," a specialized class in which students review and evaluate real-world clients under the supervision of faculty experts. Students can further augment their education through study abroad, frequent "networking events," and special trips and events, like "going to meet Warren Buffet."

Career and Placement

In addition to the many real-world projects incorporated into the Neeley MBA curriculum, the school offers a robust suite of job-related resources for MBA candidates, including individualized career coaching, internship placement, interview prep, and an annual New York City trip. There are also ample networking events on campus, including roundtables and special dinners with regional business leaders. Students say the school has deep ties in the local business community, and "The alumni are fiercely loyal to their own and most will go out of their way to help."

Eighty-seven percent of students graduating from TCU in May 2012 had a job within three months of graduation, with starting salaries averaging $81,331 (an average 102 percent salary increase after completing the program) and other guaranteed compensation totaling over $10,000. Students recently took jobs or internships at Accenture, AT&T,

FINANCIAL FACTS

Annual tuition	$36,000
Fees	$5,800
Cost of books	$1,600
Room & board	$13,000
% of students receiving aid	97
% of first-year students receiving aid	98
% of students receiving grants	95
Average award package	$38,456
Average grant	$28,987
Average loan	$24,760
Average student loan debt	$32,107

ADMISSIONS

Admissions Selectivity Rating	83
# of applications received	147
% applicants accepted	56
% acceptees attending	50
Average GMAT	641
Range of GMAT	580–700
Average GPA	3.18
TOEFL required of international students	Yes
Minimum TOEFL (paper/computer)	600/250
Application fee	$100
International application fee	$100
Early application deadline	11/1
Early notification date	12/15
Regular application deadline	3/1
Regular application notification	4/1

Application Deadline/Notification

Round 1:	11/1 / 12/15
Round 2:	1/15 / 2/15
Round 3:	3/1 / 4/1
Round 4:	4/15 / 5/15
Deferment available	Yes
Maximum length of deferment	1 year
Transfer students accepted	Yes

Transfer application policy:
Maximum transferable credits are six Semester hours of elective credit from an AACSB accredited institution.

Non-fall admissions	Yes
Need-blind admissions	Yes

Deloitte Consulting, Ericsson, Ernst & Young, Frito-Lay, Galderma, Halliburton, Healthpoint LTD, Hewlett-Packard, Intel Corp., JCPenney, Johnson & Johnson, Kellogg's, Kimberly-Clark, Merrill Lynch, Sherwin Williams, Texas Instruments, and Verizon. The school has a "great reputation in DFW," but students do note that the school "tends to place best at companies in DFW. For students looking for jobs elsewhere, that can be difficult."

Student Life and Environment

Despite its modest size, you'll find plenty of diversity on the TCU campus. The school attracts a unique group of students whose collective "experience crosses the globe and many different industries." An ambitious and "capable" group, MBA students are also collaborative: Here, "students are often found working and studying together" as they try to keep up with group projects and assignments. Despite the program's demands, TCU is a "welcoming" environment, where "People know each other well and easily become friends."

"The community is very vibrant" at TCU, with ongoing extracurricular activities and social events taking place on campus. For example, "There are multiple networking opportunities every week," as well as "free movies, speeches from famous professors from other schools, festivals for minority communities," and more. In addition to school-related activities, students hook up for "happy hours, meals, working out at the Rec, or other fun activities as the occasion arises." Students can also take advantage of the multitude of recreational activities, arts, and entertainment in the Dallas–Fort Worth area, where they'll find everything from "honky-tonk" to "golfing" to world-class museums.

Admissions

Neeley seeks to admit highly motivated and academically talented students who will succeed in a graduate-level program. That said, there is no minimum GPA nor minimum test scores required for admission; the range of GMAT scores for admitted students is usually very broad, spanning from the mid 500s to the mid 700s. (If they want to edge up their numbers, applicants to the program can take a free GMAT prep course via the Neeley website.) In the full-time program, students typically have about four to five years of professional experience before starting the MBA. In the professional MBA, five to seven years is the norm.

EMPLOYMENT PROFILE

		Grads Employed by Function	% Avg. Salary
Career Rating	95		
Percent employed at graduation	62	Marketing	(23%) $83,063
Percent employed 3 months after graduation	87	Operations	(21%) $79,971
		Consulting	(18%) $79,500
Average base starting salary	$81,331	Management	(5%) $0
Primary Source of Full-time Job Acceptances		Finance	(18%) $82,857
School-facilitated activities	24(62%)	HR	(5%) $0
Graduate-facilitated activities	10(26%)	MIS	(3%) $0
Unknown	5(13%)	Other	(8%) $88,333

Top 5 Employers Hiring Grads
Stage 3 Separation, LLC (3), Alcon Laboratories (3), Sabre Holdings (3), American Airlines (2), Fidelity Investments (2)

TEXAS SOUTHERN UNIVERSITY
JESSE H. JONES SCHOOL OF BUSINESS

GENERAL INFORMATION

Type of school   Public
Affiliation   No Affiliation
Academic calendar   Trimester

SURVEY SAYS...
Solid preparation in:
Finance, General management,
Operations, Entrepreneurial studies

STUDENTS

Enrollment of parent
  institution   9,646
Enrollment of MBA Program   179
% male/female   51/49
% out-of-state   10
% part-time   50
% underrepresented minority   87
% international   6
Average age at entry   27
Average years work experience
  at entry   2

ACADEMICS

Academic Experience Rating   77
Profs interesting rating   69
Profs accesible rating   72
Student/faculty ratio   19:1

Joint Degrees
JD/MBA, 5 years

Prominent Alumni
Gerald B. Smith, Finance &
Investment; Kase Lawal, Oil & Gas

Academics

Students at the Texas Southern University's Jesse H. Jones School of Business have a lot of great things to say about their program, not the least of which is the school's focus on "diversity and entrepreneurship." Students enrolled in graduate programs in business at this historically black college can choose from the following degree programs: MBA in general business with concentrations available in Accounting, Health Care Administration or Management Information Systems (MIS), an online Executive MBA (EMBA) in general business with a concentration available in Energy Finance, a dual JD/MBA degree, or, the Master of Science in Management Information Systems (MMIS). Whatever degree program they ultimately choose, students across the board speak of a "very intense program with very friendly and accessible staff members" and a "challenging" curriculum. "Professors are awesome," students say, and they "love the relationship between students and professors." In fact, one of the most common reasons that students choose Texas Southern is because of the school's visionary and "awesome" professors. Of these luminaries, students say, "They are highly competitive and knowledgeable about their professions," and students appreciate the "quality of their experience and expertise." Also, as one student points out, the professors show a distinct "ability to steer students' creativity and innovation." Despite these accolades, a few students commented that there could be "more professors" and that the "administration needs major work."

Beyond the "convenience" and "academic excellence" along with "a unique perspective" that Texas Southern offers, other strengths cited by students were the school's "location, cost, [and] small classes." "My MBA class is like a small family," one student said. While the small class sizes are a boon when it comes to gaining access to faculty, students say it can also be a limitation, especially when it comes to course selection. "We need more marketing courses," one student says. One student believes the problem is that "the business school does not fully challenge the academic potential of the students." Another adds that the school needs to "broaden the curriculum and course offerings," and that the administration should "design classes around the application of curriculum." But on the whole, however, student comments lean more toward the positive. "My overall academic experience has been great," one student says. "It's a good school," another sums up.

Career and Placement

According to the school, Texas Southern is a "major historically black college and university located in a leading international business environment." Located in Houston, Texas, the school prides itself—and students enjoy the benefits of—its "location, location, location," which any business student knows is a key component to landing the right job post-graduation. Hometown Houston offers "good career and placement" according to students. The largest city in Texas and the fourth largest city in the United States, Houston and its "booming economy" attract "31,000 new jobs among the 18 *Fortune* 500 companies and thousands of energy-related firms headquartered here," according to the school's website.

The Cooperative Education and Placement Services Center at Texas Southern University works every year to capitalize on the school's great location, and bring more companies on campus to recruiting events. The center hosts information sessions throughout the year where students can meet with company representatives to learn more about opportunities with their firm. Some of the companies that have conducted sessions recently are: Black & Decker, CITGO, Continental Airlines, Shell Oil Company, Target, Pfizer, and Kraft Foods. Other companies have visited the campus as part of a career development series, and they include: Merrill Lynch, ING, Enterprise, and US Airways..

Student Life and Environment

When it comes to student life at Texas Southern, it's literally all about the students. Given Texas Southern's small class size and "intimate" learning environment, it's no wonder that student life at the school is characterized by a sense of "community" and a "welcoming" atmosphere. In fact, the "intimacy of the students in the program" is a common theme running throughout student comments about Texas Southern. Students say the class is like a "tight-knit family," characterized by "supportive instructors" and "diverse," "open communications." Students here appreciate the "unique perspective" their peers bring to the campus, and note that they "cut across every strata—social, economic, business experience, [and] age." Despite their differences, these "talented," and "career-oriented" students "have similar goals and objectives," commonalities that are bolstered by the school's "encouragement of teamwork" and "smart, competitive, and fun" learning environment. It helps that students in the program are "nice and professional" and "encouraging and compassionate about education." It's clear that Texas Southern's "professional, career-focused, results-driven, friendly, and down-to-earth" MBAs feel they are in good company.

Admissions

Students seeking admission to any of Texas Southern University's graduate degree programs in business will need to apply online.

For admission consideration all applicants need to submit a complete application online along with the application fee; official transcripts from all colleges and universities previously attended; a personal statement; a current resume; and two letters of recommendation. Applicants for the MBA or MMIS graduate degree programs also need to submit GMAT scores with an analytical writing score of 3.5 or higher (English Proficiency requirement). Applicants for the online Executive MBA (EMBA) graduate degree program are not required to submit GMAT scores but must have the requisite work experience: five years of progressive and significant work experience at the management or supervisory level. International applicants need to submit TOEFL scores. Applicants are admitted to the business graduate degree programs for the Fall and Spring semesters.

FINANCIAL FACTS

Annual tuition (in-state/ out-of-state)	$3,561/$6,161
Cost of books	$744
Room & board (on/off-campus)	$5,283/$6,487

ADMISSIONS

Admissions Selectivity Rating	83
# of applications received	189
% applicants accepted	45
% acceptees attending	97
Average GMAT	375
Range of GMAT	300–500
Average GPA	3.12
TOEFL required of international students	Yes
Minimum TOEFL (paper/computer)	550/213
Application fee	$50
International application fee	$75
Early application deadline	4/30
Early notification date	6/15
Regular application deadline	7/15
Regular application notification	8/15
Deferment available	Yes
Maximum length of deferment	1 year
Transfer students accepted	Yes
Transfer application policy: Apply similar to regular applicants	
Non-fall admissions	Yes
Need-blind admissions	Yes

EMPLOYMENT PROFILE

Career Rating	69	**Grads Employed by Function% Avg. Salary**	
Average base starting salary	$98	Marketing	(35%)
Primary Source of Full-time Job Acceptances		Finance	(20%)
School-facilitated activities	59(62%)	HR	(10%)
Unknown	22(23%)	MIS	(20%)
		Other	(15%)

Top 5 Employers Hiring Grads
Sysco, Citgo, City of Houston, Accenture, State of Texas

TEXAS TECH UNIVERSITY
JERRY S. RAWLS COLLEGE OF BUSINESS ADMINISTRATION

GENERAL INFORMATION
Type of school   Public
Affiliation   No Affiliation
Academic calendar   Rolling

SURVEY SAYS...
Good social scene, Happy students
Solid preparation in:
Finance

STUDENTS
Enrollment of parent
  institution   32,480
Enrollment of MBA Program   426
% male/female   66/32
% out-of-state   20
% part-time   65
% underrepresented minority   10
% international   10
Average age at entry   26
Average years work experience
  at entry   5.0

ACADEMICS
Academic Experience Rating   **82**
Profs interesting rating   85
Profs accesible rating   88
Student/faculty ratio   13:1
% female faculty   17
% underrepresented minority
  faculty   6
% part-time faculty   3

Joint Degrees
MD/MBA 7 years; JD/MBA 3 years;
PharmD/MBA 3 years. Dual Foreign
Degree: Universidad
Anahuac/Mexico 2 years; Sup de Co
Montpellier; MA Architecture/MBA 2
years; MA foreign language/MBA 2
years

Prominent Alumni
Gary Peterson, EnCap Investments
Jerry Smith, JV Smith PC; Carrol R.
McGinnis, McGinnis Investments;
Frank M. Burke, Jr., Burke,
Maybourne Co.; R. Cannon
Clements, J. Henry Schroder
Banking Corp.

Academics

Busy West Texas professionals seeking an MBA program with "affordable tuition, friendly professors, and a broad curriculum" may find a home at the Rawls College of Business at Texas Tech. Rawls' MBA program offers evening courses to part-time and full-time students. In addition, Executive-style MBA programs offer the option of a convenient block scheduling system that students like ("We meet twice a year for seven days straight, eight hours a day") or a one-weekend-a-month calendar. Rawls has custom designed a number of combined degrees and Executive-style MBA programs to fit the needs of professionals of all stripes. A combined MD/MBA "is a unique opportunity providing the experience and preparation for a future in healthcare administration or private practice." Dual business degrees are also available in architecture, foreign languages, law, personal financial planning, and environmental toxicology.

Students praise the Rawls MBA for "the flexibility it offers to working professionals" and for a "benefit/cost ratio much greater than similar programs" in the area. They are especially effusive about the administration, which "takes care of everything for the students. They register us for classes, feed us, and provide us with all of the materials and resources needed for our classes." As one student puts it, "The administration is a joy to work with. If you have any questions about courses, registration, etc. they respond quickly to emails and have an open-door policy." Likewise, students are "especially impressed by the willingness of the professors to accommodate students with full-time jobs and families. As a group, they have been very helpful in making sure that my workload is effective in the curriculum and works with my schedule."

Tech, one student observes, is "not so large and accomplished that everyone has a sense of entitlement and arrogance, yet it's not small and struggling to keep its head above water." It is large enough to offer a broad selection of specialties, including agribusiness, entrepreneurship, health organization management, MIS, real estate, and international business. Instructors in these disciplines "are beyond knowledgeable in their fields and are also easy to access for questions about course work or the job market in their particular field. I have never met anyone within the program that was not willing to help the students succeed," one student writes.

Career and Placement

Texas Tech serves a full-time and part-time student body. Many of the students in the Executive-style MBA program attend at the expense of their employers and intend to remain with those employers after graduation. Companies likely to employ Texas Tech MBAs include Accenture, Amegy Bank, Bank of America, BNSF Railway, C.H. Robinson Worldwide, CB Richard Ellis, Comerica, Conoco Phillips, Deloitte, Enterprise Rent-a-Car, Ernst & Young, Exxon Mobil , FDIC, Frito Lay, Frost Bank, Geico, General Motors, Goldman Sachs, ISNetworld, JPMorgan Chase, KPMG, Lockheed Martin, National Instruments, Northrop Gruman, ORIX USA, PlainsCapital, PricewaterhouseCoopers, Ryan, Pioneer Natural Resources, Protiviti, Sherwin-Williams, Target, USAA, WalMart, and Wells Fargo Bank.

ADMISSIONS CONTACT: MARY FRANCES WEATHERLY, DIRECTOR, GRADUATE & PROFESSIONAL PROGRAMS
ADDRESS: RAWLS COLLEGE OF BUSINESS, GRADUATE SERVICES CENTER, LUBBOCK, TX 79409-2101
PHONE: 806-742-3184 • FAX: 806-742-3958
E-MAIL: RAWLS@TTU.EDU-EMAIL • WEBSITE: TEXASTECHMBA.COM

Student Life and Environment

The Texas Tech campus "has excellent facilities overall," and while the b-school facilities themselves "need to be improved," the school is in the process of effecting those improvements. The Rawls Building, which was completed in December 2011, achieved LEED Gold certification for energy use, lighting, water and material use. The classrooms are state of the art with billboard size projection and sophisticated wi-fi.

The rest of the "beautiful" Tech campus is "filled with art from around the world," and "its Spanish-style architecture is unique and beautiful." Campus amenities include "a gym [that] has outstanding equipment and a library [that] has an extensive availability of resources, including media resources and things through interlibrary loan (the staff is very helpful with this)." It's a welcoming atmosphere on campus, according to one student: "I have always felt comfortable on Tech campus, especially walking around at night." It's a busy place; "there are always sporting events to attend on the weekends and the Center for Campus Life and Student Government Association [is] always hosting free events for students. The graduate association also makes sure students are involved with monthly socials, philanthropy events (especially during the holidays), and campus-wide events, like tailgating before football games. The Rawls Graduate Association works especially hard to connect students in the program together, making classes more comfortable and provides more networking overall."

Admissions

Texas Tech requires applicants to submit undergraduate transcripts, GMAT scores, and a resume. Other optional elements of the application considered by the school include research experience, awards, leadership positions held in college and/or industry, civic and volunteer activities, motivation, evidence of past success, letters of recommendation, and the admissions office's assessment of the applicant's potential to provide a unique perspective within the program. To boost minority recruitment, the school advertises in minority magazines, recruits on minority college campuses in New Mexico and Texas, and attends and recruits at minority forums and at conferences such as the National Black Graduate Student Conference.

FINANCIAL FACTS

Annual tuition (in-state/ out-of-state)	$9,448/$15,485
Fees	$435
Cost of books	$1,500
Room & board	$8,802
% of students receiving aid	100
% of first-year students receiving aid	100
% of students receiving grants	100
Average grant	$2,000
Average loan	$8,500
Average student loan debt	$12,638

ADMISSIONS

Admissions Selectivity Rating	81
# of applications received	155
% applicants accepted	63
% acceptees attending	72
Average GMAT	545
Range of GMAT	520–690
Average GPA	3.29
TOEFL required of international students	Yes
Minimum TOEFL (paper/computer)	550/213
Application fee	$60
International application fee	$100
Early application deadline	3/1
Deferment available	Yes
Maximum length of deferment	1 year
Transfer students accepted	Yes
Transfer application policy: up to six hours may transfer	
Non-fall admissions	Yes
Need-blind admissions	Yes

EMPLOYMENT PROFILE

Career Rating	78	Grads Employed by Function	% Avg. Salary
Percent employed 3 months after graduation	77	Marketing	(6%) $62,500
		Operations	(8%) $51,500
Average base starting salary	$50,124	Consulting	(19%)$53,333
		Management	(30%) $49,017
		Finance	(17%) $64,325
		MIS	(3%) $62,000
		Other	(17%) $41,000

Top 5 Employers Hiring Grads
BNSF Railway, Lockheed Martin, ConocoPhillips, Pioneer Natural Resources, Wells Fargo

THUNDERBIRD
SCHOOL OF GLOBAL MANAGEMENT

GENERAL INFORMATION

Type of school	Private
Affiliation	No Affiliation
Academic calendar	Trimesters

SURVEY SAYS...

Friendly students, Good social scene,
Good peer network
Solid preparation in:
General management, Teamwork,
Communication/interpersonal skills,
Doing business in a global economy

STUDENTS

Enrollment of parent institution	1,216
Enrollment of MBA Program	380
% male/female	71/29
% underrepresented minority	19
% international	52
Average age at entry	28
Average years work experience at entry	4.4

ACADEMICS

Academic Experience Rating	90
Profs interesting rating	85
Profs accesible rating	89
Student/faculty ratio	26:1
% female faculty	29
% underrepresented minority faculty	21

Joint Degrees

Online Dual Degree with Indiana
University (MBA and Master of
Global Management): 28 months.
Full-time MBA + Master of Global
Management Dual Degree with part-
ner institution: 12-18 months.
Thunderbird MBA, Master of Arts or
Master of Science + Vermont Law
School JD or Master of
Environmental Law and Policy: 19-
40 months, depending on degree
combination chosen.

Prominent Alumni

Luis Moreno, President, Inter-
American Development Bank; Bob
Dudley, CEO, BP Group

Academics

As the "#1 International Business School," Thunderbird has a "global emphasis, collabo-rative student body, world-class professors, and a fantastic alumni network." "Thunderbird is a very special business school with what we like to call the 'Thunderbird mystique,'" one student explains. "The international experience is the best in the field," which is a major draw for students who are interested in the global community. "In our current world, where nationalist fences are falling and globalization is rising, we need more global leaders," says one student. "That's why I came to Thunderbird." The school heavily emphasizes the "international component of the curriculum," allowing students opportunities to "spend several semesters abroad, consult for a business in a developing country, and learn from professors that on average speak 3 languages."

If there is a downside in students eyes, it is the administration which is "very bureaucrat-ic" and "seems disorganized." "I love Thunderbird, but it has more insane bureaucracy and hypocrisy than any other organization I have seen," an IT Senior Management stu-dent says. On the other hand, the professors are quite literally "world-class," having "global work experiences" and being "distinguished members of the academic and busi-ness world internationally." Professors care about students and "are willing to help stu-dents out in any way possible." Thunderbird's "values most closely aligned with mine," an International Education student says of their decision to attend. "It valued my previ-ous experience, which was all international, and provided a context where I could devel-op as a truly 'global' leader." Another simply declares "I love Thunderbird!!!!!!!!"

Career and Placement

Thunderbird is all about preparing students for work in the global economy. "My class-mates, professors, and curriculum are the best preparation that I am aware of for a career in international business," one student explains. "Thunderbird consulting and emerging market practicums are amazing" and there are "many great opportunities to learn about where business is going in the world today that other schools aren't able to match." However, while the alumni network is "world-class" students say they "have almost no engagement with current students" and students think that "job placement" could be improved. However, alumni around the world host "First Tuesday" networking events every month and current students are encouraged to engage with other T-birds at these events.

The average base salary for graduates in 2012 was $83,000. Technology, Consumer Products, and Financial Services were the most common industries that students found work in. The top five employers were Eli Lilly, Deloitte Consulting, L'Oreal, Intel, and US Airways.

ADMISSIONS CONTACT: JAY BRYANT, ASSISTANT VICE PRESIDENT OF ADMISSIONS
ADDRESS: 1 GLOBAL PLACE, GLENDALE, AZ 85306-6000
PHONE: 602-978-7100 • FAX: 602-439-5432
E-MAIL: ADMISSIONS@THUNDERBIRD.EDU • WEBSITE: WWW.THUNDERBIRD.EDU

Student Life and Environment

With its global focus, it is no surprise that the school has an "international mystique" from its "diverse student body" that offers a "priceless" "cross-cultural perspective." "I am still learning from my fellow students every day," one happy student says. The "intelligent, hardworking" students "come from everywhere." "We are 60% international here" and "the three largest minority groups are Indians, Chinese, and Mormons"

"There are forty-five different professional, regional, and sports clubs for a school with only about 500 students," meaning there is plenty to do for students who want to get involved. Most students "are very active and organize lots of cultural and professional events. I am always confused which one should I go to, because most of them are really good," one happy student says. "Students are addicted to travel, so with nowhere to go nearby we travel mostly abroad." Thunderbird students "spend a lot of time together outside of school," for example going to "'regional nights' where the students celebrate different global cultures." This creates a "very tight and very involved" student community.

Admissions

Students looking to apply to Thunderbird will need to compile three personal essays, a completed online application, two letters of recommendation, GMAT scores (and TOEFL scores for international students), any official transcripts, and a resume. GREs are not required. For the accelerated program, applicants must have the above requirements and the following additional requirements: an undergraduate degree in business or completed course work in statistics, accounting, finance and management, or a minimum of five years work experience with managerial and budget responsibilities. For the 2012 class, the average GPA was 3.31 and the average GMAT score was 602. Requirements vary for different programs so prospective students should consult the Thunderbird website for specific programs.

FINANCIAL FACTS

Annual tuition	$43,080
Cost of books	$1,900
Room & board	
(on/off-campus)	$6,270/$13,580
% of students receiving aid	71
% of first-year students	
receiving aid	81
% of students receiving grants	55
Average award package	$28,390
Average grant	$16,703
Average loan	$38,884
Average student loan debt	$49,564

ADMISSIONS

Admissions Selectivity Rating	89
# of applications received	378
% applicants accepted	78
% acceptees attending	48
Average GMAT	602
Range of GMAT	490–760
Average GPA	3.31
TOEFL required of	
international students	Yes
Minimum TOEFL	
(paper/computer)	610/250
Application fee	$125
Deadline/Notification	
Round 1:	11/30 /
Round 2:	1/30 /
Round 3:	3/30 /
Round 4:	5/10 /
Deferment available	Yes
Maximum length	
of deferment	1 year
Transfer students accepted	
Non-fall admissions	Yes
Need-blind admissions	Yes

EMPLOYMENT PROFILE

Career Rating	91	**Grads Employed by Function% Avg. Salary**	
Percent employed at graduation	24	Marketing	(31%) $94,211
Percent employed 3 months		Operations	(9%) $63,286
after graduation	46	Consulting	(13%)$83,438
Average base starting salary	$83,034	Management	(7%) $86,489
Primary Source of Full-time Job Acceptances		Finance	(19%) $70,533
School-facilitated activities	31(31%)	HR	(4%) $93,002
Graduate-facilitated activities	22(22%)	MIS	(2%)
Unknown	46(47%)	Other	(14%) $100,625

Top 5 Employers Hiring Grads
Eli Lilly (5), Deloitte Consulting (3), L'Oreal (3), Intel (3), US Airways (3)

TULANE UNIVERSITY
FREEMAN SCHOOL OF BUSINESS

GENERAL INFORMATION

Type of school	Private
Affiliation	No Affiliation
Academic calendar	Semester

SURVEY SAYS...

Good social scene, Smart
classrooms
Solid preparation in:
Finance, Doing business in a global
economy, Entrepreneurial studies

STUDENTS

Enrollment of parent institution	13,486
Enrollment of MBA Program	315
% male/female	64/36
% part-time	49
% underrepresented minority	18
% international	33
Average age at entry	27
Average years work experience at entry	3.8

ACADEMICS

Academic Experience Rating	88
Profs interesting rating	85
Profs accesible rating	90
Student/faculty ratio	15:1
% female faculty	22
% underrepresented minority faculty	24
% part-time faculty	12

Joint Degrees

MBA/MD; MBA/JD; MBA/Master of
Arts in Latin American Studies;
MBA/Master of Health
Administration; MACCT/MBA;
MACCT/JD; MBA/ MGM; MBA/
MNRG

Prominent Alumni

Ricardo Salinas Pliego, President and
CEO of Grupo Salinas and Grupo
Elektra; Regina Benjamin, Surgeon
General of the United States; Mark
Bostick, President, Comcar Industries;
Larry Gordon, Film Producer, former
President of 20th Century Fox; Haibo
Dai, Exec. Director, Shanghai Lingang
New Town

Academics

A number of outstanding features distinguish the Freeman School of Business at Tulane University, particularly in the area of finance, where enrolled students enjoy "one of the best finance programs in the country." The program is equipped with an "unmatched" trading floor; a portfolio management program (Fenner Fund) where students manage over $2.5 million in real funds; and an investment analysis program (Burkenroad Reports) where students capture stocks-under-rocks.

Finance has such a "well-deserved great reputation" at Freeman that other strengths of the program are sometimes overlooked. Marketing "continues to grow here, while the energy specialization "is very smart for this area of the country." Freeman also excels in entrepreneurial studies; as one student explains, "I chose Tulane because of the ability to focus on entrepreneurship and the school's access to successful entrepreneurs, through whom I could learn to be a more effective business owner." Finally, the school recognizes the speed at which all business is becoming international through its "strong experiential Global Management program," which "sends the entire class on three trips abroad," thereby "emphasizing the global business curriculum in a truly hands-on environment."

The sum is greater than the considerable parts at Freeman, students tell us. One writes, "The greatest strengths of Tulane are its abilities to integrate the different segments of business and make them relevant, not just to corporate America, but also to small business and global business. Tulane also facilitates discussion on how your business or company can align its operations to take into consideration all stakeholders, thus becoming an organization that creates both profit and social good." An "excellent" relationship with the local community means that "business leaders around the community are accessible and supportive." Students also appreciate how the "school administration has done a great job in the recovery efforts since Katrina." Be forewarned that the program operates on seven-week terms that can fly by; "the first is by far the most intense, and they get gradually easier," one student explains.

Career and Placement

Tulane's Career Management Center earns mixed reviews from students. Several complain that "On campus recruiting is weak. We miss almost all of the big companies due to our location. We only get energy companies or a few other random companies based in Texas or the rest of the South to come to Tulane." Some simply wish the office would be "more proactive," but some go further, calling it the school's "weakest area" and asserting that "Students are practically on their own when it comes to acquiring an internship or employment." Several acknowledged that the down economy was certainly a factor in the Center's disappointing outcomes.

Companies most likely to hire Freeman MBAs include BearingPoint, Capital One, Citibank, Daymon Worldwide, Deloitte & Touche, Entergy, Federal Express, First Albany Capital, Hibernia, Johnson & Rice, JPMorgan Chase, Latitram, Piper Jaffray & Co., RBC, Simmons & Company, Teracore Consulting, Tidewater Marine, TXU, Verizon, and Wachovia.

ADMISSIONS CONTACT: PATRICK FORAN, DIRECTOR OF GRADUATE ADMISSIONS AND FINANCIAL AID
ADDRESS: 7 MCALISTER DRIVE, SUITE 401, NEW ORLEANS, LA 70118
PHONE: 504-865-5410 • FAX: 504-865-6770
E-MAIL: FREEMAN.ADMISSIONS@TULANE.EDU • WEBSITE: FREEMAN.TULANE.EDU

FINANCIAL FACTS

Annual tuition	$46,147
Fees	$5,144
Cost of books	$1,600
Room & board	$15,900
% of students receiving aid	80
% of first-year students receiving aid	80
% of students receiving grants	68
Average award package	$33,565
Average grant	$18,768
Average loan	$22,711

ADMISSIONS

Admissions Selectivity Rating	**82**
# of applications received	216
% applicants accepted	83
% acceptees attending	50
Average GMAT	629
Range of GMAT	570–690
Average GPA	3.24
TOEFL required of international students	Yes
Minimum TOEFL (paper/computer)	600/240
International application fee	$125
Application Deadline/Notification	
Round 1:	11/1 / 12/1
Round 2:	1/1 / 2/1
Round 3:	3/1 / 4/1
Round 4:	5/1 / 6/1
Deferment available	No
Transfer students accepted	No
Non-fall admissions	No
Need-blind admissions	Yes

Student Life and Environment

Tulane is in New Orleans, so it should come as no surprise that life here can be "a lot of fun." "Many people socialize heavily on the weekends (we go out a lot). New Orleans literally has events every weekend. If you can't find something to do here, you're not looking at all," is how one student sums things up. The city is so focused on socializing that "school slows down during busy periods, such as Mardi Gras." Accordingly, many here enjoy a "very good mix of school and entertainment. New Orleans is the best place to go to school. Mardi Gras, Jazz Fest, and the food [all add up to] a once-in-a-lifetime experience."

Within the program, "the numerous clubs are mostly strong. The strongest is [the] entrepreneurship club, [which] is very good with matching people [with] local small business owners who can be mentors/potential employers." The local business community "truly embraces the MBA students, with leaders often speaking on campus and offering to meet with us individually on our own time. People are simply friendly here and take an interest in Tulane students. It makes networking locally incredibly easy." Freeman classes "are hard but not impossible," and for many, "juggling so many opportunities…is probably the hardest part of attending grad school [at Tulane]."

Tulane MBAs "are a diverse group from all over the world, many with different political views and worldviews." "One-third of our class is made up of international students, so it makes everything—discussion, group work, assignments—much more interesting," one student tells us.

Admissions

Freeman reviews applications to its graduate programs in three separate rounds, and the school encourages students to apply as early as possible to maximize their chances of gaining admission. The following is required to apply: an undergraduate transcript, an affidavit of support, an official GMAT score report, TOEFL scores (for international students whose first language is not English), two letters of recommendation, a current resume, personal statement, and interview. Minority recruitment efforts include Destination MBA, the National Black MBA Association Career Fair, targeted GMASS searches, and minority fellowships. For the incoming class of 2011, entering students earned a median GMAT score of 674 and boasted a median 3.3 undergraduate GPA.

EMPLOYMENT PROFILE

Career Rating	92	**Grads Employed by Function% Avg. Salary**	
Percent employed at graduation	53	Marketing	(25%) $74,000
Percent employed 3 months after graduation	86	Consulting	(11%)$84,000
		Management	(11%) $80,000
Average base starting salary	$75,000	Finance	(46%) $71,300
Primary Source of Full-time Job Acceptances		Other	(7%) $0
School-facilitated activities	24(55%)	**Top 5 Employers Hiring Grads**	
Graduate-facilitated activities	18(41%)	APTIFY (7), Laitram / Intralox (4), Eli Lilli &	
Unknown	2(4%)	Co (1), BP (1), Sun Trust Bank, Inc (1)	

THE UNIVERSITY OF AKRON
COLLEGE OF BUSINESS ADMINISTRATION

GENERAL INFORMATION

Type of school	Public
Affiliation	No Affiliation
Academic calendar	Fall

SURVEY SAYS...
Cutting-edge classes
Solid preparation in:
Finance, Accounting, General management, Operations, Communication/interpersonal skills, Presentation skills, Quantitative skills, Doing business in a global economy, Entrepreneurial studies

STUDENTS

Enrollment of parent institution	28,711
Enrollment of MBA Program	290
% male/female	70/30
% out-of-state	4
% part-time	63
% underrepresented minority	8
% international	50
Average age at entry	28
Average years work experience at entry	4.0

ACADEMICS

Academic Experience Rating	85
Profs interesting rating	87
Profs accesible rating	75
Student/faculty ratio	7:1
% female faculty	14
% underrepresented minority faculty	34
% part-time faculty	32

Joint Degrees
MBA/Juris Doctor 3-4 years; M. Tax/Juris Doctor 3-4 years

Prominent Alumni
Mary Taylor, Lieutenant Governor State of Ohio; Anthony Alexander, President and CEO, FirstEnergy Corp.; Don Misheff, Managing partner, Ernst & Young, LLP; John Costello III, Chief Global Customer & Marketing Officer, Dunkin Brands; Russell C. Holmes, Sr. VP District Retail Leader, Key Bank

Academics

The University of Akron's College of Business Administration offers both full-time and part-time programs, including an evening MBA program which qualifying students can complete in as few as 12 months if they meet the required undergraduate course work. An orientation session at the start of the first semester will allow students to get acquainted with the program. From there, it is on to a program devoted to "preparing you for your future." Concentrations include finance, international business, international finance, management, management and global technological innovation, strategic marketing, supply-chain management, health care, interdisciplinary, leadership of organizational change, global technological innovation, and direct interactive marketing.

Through a diverse student body, "high competition" among classmates, and an administration willing to "change curriculum to better serve students," the University of Akron "really prepare[s] its students to excel in the marketplace." However, one student believes the work is "much less difficult than I had anticipated." Still others say that "some professors are difficult to approach and to schedule time with," with the most disgruntled of students claiming a few professors are "arrogant and really don't want to help students." This is in sharp contrast to those who find educators at Akron to be "friendly and accessible" and a group that "make[s] sure that we learn through discussions and active participation."

In fact, many students are "amazed" at the qualifications of the "fantastic" MBA professors here and are pleased to find "an outstanding staff and members of faculty that know what is best for their students to be the future cadres of the worldwide village." Educators who "bring real world, practical knowledge that is second to none" not only help provide a "rewarding" educational experience, they also "inform you of job opportunities, workshops, internships, clinics, etc." But do not expect your hand to be held. "It is up to you to follow up. If you do follow up you have all of their resources at your disposal."

Career and Placement

Akron is located near Cleveland's job market, which is an immediate plus, as is the school's "local connections with reputable companies." The school's Center for Career Management offers career services for all undergraduates, graduate students, and alumni. Through this office, students and alumni will have access to help with career planning, summer internships, job searching, interviewing, and resume writing. With Akron's "strong network," and "companies in both public accounting and industry heavily recruiting here, it helps make it very easy to land a job in whichever area you prefer." School-organized career fairs give students a "chance to meet some prominent businesses" and "build [their] professional network." Employers who have hired from the Akron MBA pool include Goodyear Tire & Rubber Company, Delloite & Touche, Babcock & Wilcox, Dominion, FirstEnergy, Enterprise, Progressive, National City Bank, and J.M. Smuckers.

Student Life and Environment

As is typical with MBA programs, Akron's program is peopled with a mix of full-time and part-time students, along with the "vast array of career backgrounds" one expects from such a mix. "Some have just finished undergraduate school," one student writes, "and some are returning to school after 20 years of work experience." The group is "as intellectually diverse as we are ethnically. For every one of our students who are truly interested in learning this material and gaining these experiences, there are an equal number who are clearly trying to put in as little work as possible to achieve a passing grade." Overall, most are "hard-working" and "friendly" students interested in "obtaining a degree to enhance their career."

ADMISSIONS CONTACT: MYRA WEAKLAND, ASSISTANT DIRECTOR
ADDRESS: THE UNIVERSITY OF AKRON, CBA 412, AKRON, OH 44325-4805
PHONE: 330-972-7043 • FAX: 330-972-6588
E-MAIL: GRADCBA@UAKRON.EDU • WEBSITE: MBA.UAKRON.EDU

There is no great divide between full-time and part-time students. "Even though the majority of the students are part-time, they are interested in working with and giving back to the university. This provides for an interactive environment that sparks interesting discussion both inside and outside of the classroom." Those accepted to Akron's MBA program will find that their classmates "are strong academically with important experience that contributes to classroom discussion." Most students here "honestly enjoy the process of learning and take pride in what we accomplish, regardless of what letter winds up on our transcripts." In addition to students with diverse work backgrounds, "we also have students from different countries that bring an interesting perspective to discussions."

Outside the classroom "there is always something fruitful that you can hook yourself up with." When not utilizing the library or the resources of the Center for Career Management, students can check on weekly emails sent to Zipline that "update us on the events that will happen the week to come." The urban setting of Akron may not compare to a major city's – students admit, "the surrounding areas are not that great" – but "there is a pretty good nightlife." The school itself features athletics, a free bowling alley, recreation center, and other amenities, along with the clubs and students organizations one expects from a major college. As one student sums it up, "The bottom line is you can do a lot of useful things every day. The only thing that keeps us from contributing to these activities is our classes."

Admissions

While weighing your application Akron's admissions committee will consider your undergraduate GPA (minimum GPA of 2.75 required), GMAT scores (minimum score of 500 required), and TOEFL scores (international applicants). In addition, they will seek two letters of recommendation; a letter of purpose; a resume; a review of graduate and post-baccalaureate performance; and professional association and student organization memberships. International applicants must apply at least three months prior to their intended date of entry into the program. The school also sponsors a diversity program to enhance minority recruitment to the MBA program.

FINANCIAL FACTS

Room & board	$12,000
% of students receiving aid	33
% of students receiving grants	14
Average award package	$9,372
Average grant	$26,171
Average loan	$7,333
Average student loan debt	$9,080

ADMISSIONS

Admissions Selectivity Rating	87
# of applications received	290
% applicants accepted	44
% acceptees attending	67
Average GMAT	582
Range of GMAT	530–620
Average GPA	3.39
TOEFL required of international students	Yes
Minimum TOEFL (paper/computer)	550/213
Application fee	$40
International application fee	$60
Regular application deadline	7/15
Regular application notification	8/15
Deferment available	Yes
Maximum length of deferment	1 year
Transfer students accepted	Yes
Transfer application policy: Gateway courses may be waived based on comparable coursework or proficiency testing. Nine credits of advanced course work may transfer from AACSB accredited schools if approved by the Director.	
Non-fall admissions	Yes
Need-blind admissions	Yes

EMPLOYMENT PROFILE

		Grads Employed by Function	%	Avg. Salary
Career Rating	68			
		Operations	(20%)	$62,500
		Finance	(40%)	$53,563
		MIS	(20%)	$68,320
		Other	(20%)	$42,000

THE UNIVERSITY OF ALABAMA AT BIRMINGHAM
SCHOOL OF BUSINESS

GENERAL INFORMATION
Type of school   Public
Affiliation   No Affiliation
Academic calendar   Semester

SURVEY SAYS...
Cutting-edge classes
Solid preparation in:
Teamwork, Presentation skills

STUDENTS
Enrollment of parent institution	16,000
Enrollment of MBA Program	398
% male/female	56/44
% out-of-state	5
% part-time	66
% underrepresented minority	5
% international	17
Average age at entry	27
Average years work experience at entry	4.0

ACADEMICS
Academic Experience Rating	76
Profs interesting rating	76
Profs accesible rating	83
Student/faculty ratio	30:1
% female faculty	18
% underrepresented minority faculty	9
% part-time faculty	0

Joint Degrees
Master of Business Administration/Master of Public Health (MBA/MPH): Full-time, part-time; 72 total credits required. Master of Business Administration/Master of Science in Health Administration (MBA/MS): Full-time; 72 total credits required. Master of Business Administration/Master of Science in Nursing.

Prominent Alumni
John Bakane, CEO, Mills; Daryl Byrd, CEO and President, Iberia Bank; Susan Story, CEO and President, Gulf Power Company

Academics

Offering a "strong curriculum" in an "urban location with close ties to local business," the Graduate School of Management serves a primarily part-time student body looking to advance their careers for a "reasonable" tuition. Through evening classes offered on a "flexible schedule," students at UAB can earn an MBA with a concentration in finance, information technology management, or healthcare management. Healthcare is a standout discipline at the university, and UAB exploits that by offering not only a concentration in the field but also a combined MBA/Master of Public Health, MBA/Master of Science in health administration, and MBA/Master of Science in nursing.

MBA students at UAB who lack an undergraduate business background are required to take foundational courses. The MBA curriculum at UAB has been streamlined for the academic year 2013/14. All MBA students at UAB are required to take 36 credit hours for graduation. There are four courses of tools and perspectives on business, five functional core courses, two elective course options and one capstone course in Strategic Management. Classes are offered in sequence to allow for a cohort experience that enhances networking opportunities for all students.

UAB professors and administration "are, for the most part, knowledgeable and willing to help." Professors "have had experience in the corporate environment (which is helpful for relating the material and applying it)." "I liked the fact that UAB professors all had much field experience and had been in the workplace several years before coming to teach at UAB," one student explains, adding "as a student, that makes a huge difference because one can see that they know what they are talking about, even [down] to the specific details." Across the board, teachers are "solid instructors, and most of them are very approachable after class. They were all very flexible and willing to work with us when a work conflict came up, even if sometimes it meant extra work."

Career and Placement

The Career Services Office is located in the School of Business building at UAB, which offers career counseling, coaching, practical workshops on areas such as resume writing and job searching, and an online database of jobs as well as a database to which students may upload their resumes. The office hosts recruiting visits from employers, coordinates career fairs, maintains job bulletin boards, and does resume referral. In addition, the School of Business works to arrange internships for MBAs who seek them; however, most MBAs at UAB are currently employed.

Employers who frequently hire UAB graduates include Regions Bank, Southern Company, Southern Progress, UAB, and Wells Fargo.

ADMISSIONS CONTACT: CHRISTY MANNING, MBA PROGRAM COORDINATOR
ADDRESS: 1530 3RD AVENUE SOUTH BEC 210, BIRMINGHAM, AL 35294-4460
PHONE: 205-934-8815 • FAX: 205-934-9200
E-MAIL: CMANNING@UAB.EDU • WEBSITE: WWW.UAB.EDU/MBA

Student Life and Environment

UAB "is well-suited for both the traditional full-time student as well as students that are getting a degree around a full-time job." Most fall into the latter category; they "work full time, then attend classes at night" and consequently have "little interaction with on-campus life and activities." They barely have time "to meet outside of class multiple times a week" to complete group work. "The level of group work required does not fit the student body of the MBA school," one student tells us.

UAB is located "in an urban setting with all of the advantages and disadvantages that come with being in an urban environment: traffic, occasional crimes, easy access to cultural centers, unique restaurants, and entertainment venues." One student feels the positives outweigh the negatives, telling us that she "loves walking out the front door of the school and seeing downtown Birmingham! The campus comes alive in the evening with grad students pouring in after they get off work." Campus amenities include "a great, free student activity center" and "good computer rooms."

UAB hosts a "very diverse student body [that] provides a unique and real-life view of the conditions that are encountered in the business world," which "allows for many unique perspectives which contribute to a more practical learning environment." They "range from straight out of undergrad to retired and looking for new opportunities," and "they come from a wide variety of jobs and bring a lot of different experiences to the classroom." The banking industry is well-represented.

Admissions

Work experience, academic GPA, and scores on the GMAT are considered very important by those making admissions decisions for the graduate business programs at UAB. Personal essays, and letters of recommendation also receive consideration. Applicants to the program must submit an official GMAT score report, official transcripts from all colleges and universities attended, two letters of reference, a current resume, and a 500 word statement of purpose. Students must demonstrate aptitude in calculus with a grade of C or better in a calculus course completed within the previous five years. The admissions committee may request an interview, but otherwise interviews are not required. Non-native English speakers must score at least 550 on the TOEFL and provide an ECE report to accompany their transcripts. It is recommended that international applicants apply six months in advance of the application deadline to ensure adequate time to process appropriate visas.

ADMISSIONS

Admissions Selectivity Rating	74
# of applications received	276
% applicants accepted	81
% acceptees attending	77
Average GMAT	553
Range of GMAT	510–600
Average GPA	3.20
TOEFL required of international students	Yes
Minimum TOEFL (paper/computer)	550/213
Application fee	$50
International application fee	$75
Regular application deadline	7/1
Regular application notification	8/1
Deferment available	Yes
Maximum length of deferment	1 year
Transfer students accepted	Yes

Transfer application policy: Must meet UAB MBA admission requirements, transfer courses must be from AACSB accredited program and equivalent to our required courses. We will accept up to 25% of the degree program in transfer work with a minimum "B" grade.

Non-fall admissions	Yes
Need-blind admissions	Yes

THE UNIVERSITY OF ALABAMA AT TUSCALOOSA
MANDERSON GRADUATE SCHOOL OF BUSINESS

GENERAL INFORMATION
Type of school   Public
Affiliation   No Affiliation
Academic calendar   Semester

SURVEY SAYS...
Friendly students, Good peer network
Solid preparation in:
Operations, Communication/
interpersonal skills, Computer skills

STUDENTS
Enrollment of parent institution	33,602
Enrollment of MBA Program	73
% male/female	70/30
% out-of-state	41
% part-time	0
% underrepresented minority	5
% international	11
Average age at entry	24
Average years work experience at entry	1.3

ACADEMICS
Academic Experience Rating	**89**
Profs interesting rating	92
Profs accesible rating	84

Joint Degrees
JD/MBA Program: 3-year or 4-year options; MBA/MS-Mechnical Engineering: 2 calendar years (5 Semesters) MBA/MS-Civil Engineering: 2 calendar years (5 Semesters); MBA/MFA-Theater Management: Three years

Prominent Alumni
Sam DiPiazza, Jr, CEO PriceWaterhouseCoopers; Gary Fayard, Sr. VP & CFO Coca-Cola; Richard Anthony, Chairman and CEO, Synovus Financial Corp; Don James, Chairman and CEO, Vulcan Materials Company; Clyde Anderson, Executive Chairman of the Board, Books-A-Million

Academics

With collaborative learning a mandatory part of the curriculum, students at Manderson will find that they will rarely be facing the challenges of this small business program alone. That spirit of collaboration extends to the staff, too. Here "administration is very involved and helpful," working to "send out daily emails relating to various business related activities including career fairs, job/internship offers, and helpful hints/tools for interviews, resumes, and cover letters." What difficulties students face are overcome through "easy to access professors who foster individual relationships with students both in and outside of the classroom." Another student notes that "the MBA Administration has faced some turnover as far as personnel," but these changes "did not keep the MBA Administration from focusing on students."

Manderson graduates say they have "had the honor to learn from some of the best teachers I have ever had here in the program," a group who are also "great mentors" who "love for the students to come meet with them and ask them for advice, even if it has nothing to do with class." Drawing from their real world experiences allows professors here to equip students for the challenges they will face. "They want students to do well, and don't just preach from a textbook. The professors at Alabama use everyday examples and demonstrate how integrity is the most important." Some students say professors can be "a mixed bag," but overall they are seen as "very experienced and knowledgeable, so they have a lot to offer to the students and expect students to be prepared, dedicated, and ambitious throughout their education in the program."

Evolution is part of the process here. "The administration inside the MBA program has been going through major changes through our first year, but they have done everything in their power to make the transition as smooth as possible." The "helpful administration, good professors, and a tough but fair academic experience" show that educators here "work hard and honestly care about helping the students reach their goals." As one student says, "Entering the MBA/MSCE program here at The University of Alabama was one of the best things to happen for my life and hopefully my career."

Career and Placement

Manderson students have ample opportunities for career advancement, and those opportunities are rich in part "because of a strong department of finance with excellent faculty and opportunities to network with alumni." The "well-developed entrepreneurship and innovation program" will sway many Manderson's way, especially since the school has "great relationships with large companies for internship and employment opportunities." For outgoing students, those shots at great positions won't take long to arise. "The Manderson staff has great corporate connections and the teachers try to make class assignments as similar as possible to real life situations."

In a recent year, 77 percent of the graduating class had accepted a job offer by the time of graduation. Some 91 percent accepted an offer within three months of graduation. The median base salary was about $65,000, with a range between $22,500 and $120,000. The career coordinators that are part of the Manderson Graduate School of Business program arrange individual advising sessions, resume revisions, skills workshops, alumni career panels, and on-campus recruiting programs for both jobs and internships. There are countless opportunities. Over the last few years, students here took internships at companies like Alabama Power, Compass Bank, Sterne Agee, PriceWaterhouseCoopers, Chesapeake Consulting, BMW, Red Cross, Wal-Mart, Hewlett Packard, Procter &

Gamble, and St. Vincent Hospital.

Student Life and Environment

"Life at school is essentially super-undergraduate," with a workload that is "intense but manageable." The collaborative environment means "there is a lot of interaction with teams and groups." Indeed, "you can often find many students in the lounge provided for MBA students. It also usually involves a panel or information session from a company or business." What downtime students get is often used for career advancement, "researching internships and jobs and filling out many applications. Additionally, there's also constant work to be done on one's resume and cover letter, etc."

None of this is to say that students are working twenty-four hours a day. Both students and the school work together to create meaningful distractions from your studies. "Outside of class, there are plenty of opportunities to get involved with groups that involve your interests as well as social groups that meet once a week," and "organizations within the MBA program also provide opportunities to gather with fellow classmates for a variety of activities." The "unique and pretty cool atmosphere" and attractive location mean that "outside of school and work activities, the campus is full of things to do to add a little fun when you need a break." Indeed, "Tuscaloosa is a great city that affords the small college feel with the amenities of a larger city," offering plenty to do on weekends. Happy hours, intramural games, community service projects, outdoor activities, and more provide ways to wind down from the "very busy" week.

Admissions

Less than 100 students are admitted to the program each year, with classes beginning in the fall. To apply, students must submit a current resume, GMAT or GRE scores, three letters of recommendation, and official undergraduate transcripts. Decisions on admissions are made on a rolling basis; those seeking financial assistance should apply by the priority deadlines. About 40 percent of those in the program enter directly from college; applicants are not required to have significant professional experience before matriculation.

FINANCIAL FACTS

Annual tuition (in-state/ out-of-state)	$9,200/$22,950
Fees	$2,500
Cost of books	$950
Room & board	$6,000
% of students receiving aid	54
% of first-year students receiving aid	48
% of students receiving grants	40
Average award package	$9,211
Average grant	$7,850

ADMISSIONS

Admissions Selectivity Rating	88
# of applications received	198
% applicants accepted	54
% acceptees attending	69
Average GMAT	642
Range of GMAT	600–700
Average GPA	3.55
TOEFL required of international students	Yes
Minimum TOEFL (paper/computer)	550/213
Application fee	$50
International application fee	$60
Early application deadline	1/5
Early notification date	1/15
Regular application deadline	3/15
Regular application notification	3/25
Deferment available	Yes
Maximum length of deferment	1 year
Transfer students accepted	Yes
Transfer application policy: Applicants may be able to transfer up to 12 hours of elective credit from another AACSB-accredited graduate program. However, the MBA core must be taken in our program.	
Non-fall admissions	No
Need-blind admissions	Yes

EMPLOYMENT PROFILE

Career Rating	88	Grads Employed by Function	% Avg. Salary
Percent employed at graduation	77	Marketing	(6%) $79,000
Percent employed 3 months after graduation	91	Operations	(16%) $66,027
		Consulting	(8%) $49,375
Average base starting salary	$66,069	Management	(10%) $68,656
Primary Source of Full-time Job Acceptances		Finance	(20%) $60,303
School-facilitated activities	43(63%)	MIS	(5%) $79,000
Graduate-facilitated activities	24(35%)	Other	(3%)
Unknown	1(2%)		

Top 5 Employers Hiring Grads

Mercedes-Benz (3), Walmart (2), International Paper (2), PriceWaterhouseCoopers (2), Procter & Gamble (2)

UNIVERSITY OF ALBERTA
SCHOOL OF BUSINESS

GENERAL INFORMATION

Type of school — Public
Affiliation — No Affiliation

SURVEY SAYS...

Good peer network, Smart classrooms
Solid preparation in:
Doing business in a global economy

STUDENTS

Enrollment of parent institution	37,000
% male/female	57/43
% part-time	44
% international	59
Average age at entry	27
Average years work experience at entry	4.6

ACADEMICS

Academic Experience Rating	**86**
Profs interesting rating	79
Profs accesible rating	86
Student/faculty ratio	4:1
% female faculty	25

Joint Degrees

MBA/JD (Master of Business Admin./Bachelor of Law) (4 years); MBA/MEng (Master of Business Admin./Master of Engineering)(2 years); MBA/MAg (Master of Business Admin./Master of Agriculture) (2 years); MBA/MF (Master of Business Admin./Master of Forestry) (2 years)

Prominent Alumni

Brain Vassjo, CEO, Capital Power Corporation; Gay Mitchell, Executive Vice-President-Ontario / RBC; Guy Turcotte, Past-Chairman / Western Oil Sands; Eric Morgan, CEO / Capgemini; Michael Lang, Chairman / Stonebridge Merchant Capital

Academics

The first business school in Canada to receive accreditation from the American Assembly of Collegiate Schools of Business, University of Alberta operates a full-time and part-time MBA on its Edmonton campus, an accelerated executive MBA, and a part-time program in Ft. McMurray. Integrating quantitative know-how with important qualitative skills, University of Alberta offers a "well-balanced education" through a mix of core course work and electives. Lectures are enhanced by "up-to-date case analyses," and throughout the curriculum there is a "focus on interpersonal skills and relationships." "There is a lot of group work in the MBA program," and therefore, "who you choose to work with, identifying your working style, and how to work with others are all vital components of a success strategy for the MBA." In complement to course work, students can participate in co-curricular opportunities, like the annual International Study Tour and MBA mentorship program. Students also note that the school's excellent lecture series is "worth attending" and "case competitions are fantastic."

"Since it's a research university, most professors have PhDs;" however, the Alberta faculty comprises a "good mix of academics and professionals." The classroom experience is generally rewarding, and "Most professors are well-prepared and appropriate for their specific classes." At the same time, some professors "deliver a better course than others and who you get is simply the luck of the draw." Fortunately, the administration is receptive to student input, and "feedback is given from students to professors at the end of each term regarding the class and their teaching." A current student assures us, "They truly care and listen to suggestions on how to make things better."

When it comes to the nuts and bolts, things run smoothly at Alberta. "The MBA Programs Office does a great job behind the scenes," and, for the most part, the "registration process for class is well-run, smooth, and easy." At the same time, there is a bit of a divide between full-time students and their part-time counterparts. In many cases, "the part-timers do not feel as connected to the administration as the full-timers as we are not at school during the day." On the flipside, part-timers praise the fact that the "part-time program is excellent—flexible around work schedules and amenable to work-life balance." When it comes to the bottom line, students agree that the University of Alberta is an "excellent value." "Highly-regarded" in the Edmonton area, tuition is inexpensive, the area offers an "affordable cost of living," and the program is efficient (the full-time program can even be completed in as little as 16 months).

Career and Placement

Through the MBA Career Services Office, students have access to professional career coaching and myriad career management resources. For first-year students, Career Services also offers the workshops, "Business 504," a crash course in career management. With 20,000 Alberta alumni, the school maintains a strong local network, and many corporate speakers, recruiters, and representatives visit campus. In fact, some students say "the network[ing] opportunities that are made available" are the program's greatest strength. Unfortunately, part-time students often feel they weren't invited to the party. A part-time student complains, "If there are company info sessions they are held during the day, so it is hard for part-time students to attend a lot of the sessions."

Over the past five years, 90 percent of Alberta graduates had accepted a position within three months of graduation. Alberta graduates have been hired by Accenture, Alberta Economic Development, ATB Financial, Bell, Bearing Point, CEMEX, China Zheshang Bank, Deloitte, Ernst & Young, Edmonton Airports, Direct Energy, HSBC Bank Canada,

ADMISSIONS CONTACT: JOAN WHITE, ASSOCIATE DEAN, MBA PROGRAMS
ADDRESS: 2-30 BUSINESS BUILDING, UNIVERSITY OF ALBERTA, EDMONTON, AB T6G 2R6
PHONE: 780-492-3946 • FAX: 780-492-7825
E-MAIL: MBA@UALBERTA.CA • WEBSITE: WWW.MBA.NET

Intuit, KPMG, Newell Rubbermaid, Parks Canada, Saudi Aramco, Sierra Systems, TD Canada Trust, and TEC Edmonton, among many others. Full-time graduates had an average starting salary of over $75,000 annually, and part-time students reported an average salary of over $95,000.

Student Life and Environment

With a broad-based core and numerous areas of specialization, Alberta attracts students from "many different business and non-business backgrounds"—as well as from many countries across the world. While students are "very diverse in every aspect," most agree that Alberta students are generally "knowledgeable, hard-working, respectful, and intelligent." In the part-time program, "most classmates are busy people, majority married and working," and they rarely have time to participate in extracurricular activities on campus. Spare time is squeezed even tighter because "all collaboration [has] to take place outside of normal business hours and outside of class time." (Fortunately, the business school is well equipped, and "there is an MBA specific lounge and study area that is very useful for group work and activities.")

Full-time students have a different take on life at Alberta. For them, "School life is filled with a multitude of opportunities, movies, social events, case competitions, [and] athletics." In the evenings, "there are numerous social events put on by the MBA association, which includes high-ranking guest speakers, free food, and great information." A second-year student tells us, "Life at school is a lot of fun. I spend more time in group meetings and extra-curricular activities (e.g., case competitions) than in class." Another student chimes in: "From the courses offered to the students in the program (55 percent international) to the social events and clubs to join, there is truly something here for everyone."

Admissions

To be considered for admission to the University of Alberta, students must have a minimum undergraduate GPA of 3.0, a minimum GMAT score of 550, and at least two years of professional work experience. Students must also submit two letters of recommendation and a personal statement. In the part-time and full-time programs, the recent incoming class had an average undergraduate GPA of 3.4 and average work experience of more than five years.

FINANCIAL FACTS

Annual tuition (in-state/ out-of-state)	$12,000/$23,500
Fees	$1,000
Cost of books	$1,300
Room & board (on/off-campus)	$7,000/$9,500
% of students receiving grants	100
Average grant	$5,000

ADMISSIONS

Admissions Selectivity Rating	86
# of applications received	220
% applicants accepted	48
% acceptees attending	58
Average GMAT	596
Range of GMAT	550–645
Average GPA	3.40
TOEFL required of international students	Yes
Minimum TOEFL (paper/computer)	600
Application fee	$100
International application fee	$100
Regular application deadline	4/30
Deferment available	Yes
Maximum length of deferment	1 year
Transfer students accepted	Yes
Transfer application policy: Transfer students are reviewed on an individual basis. Transfer credit is normally limited to 18-credits and must be from an AACSB accredited school.	
Non-fall admissions	No
Need-blind admissions	Yes

EMPLOYMENT PROFILE

Career Rating	91	**Grads Employed by Function**	**% Avg. Salary**
Percent employed at graduation	41	Marketing	(13%) $70,000
Percent employed 3 months after graduation	93	Operations	(4%) $57,400
		Consulting	(22%) $69,500
Average base starting salary	$73,300	Management	(4%) $81,300
Primary Source of Full-time Job Acceptances		Finance	(27%) $80,700
School-facilitated activities	(35%)	HR	(2%)
Graduate-facilitated activities	(56%)	MIS	(13%) $65,800
		Other	(16%) $76,200

Top 5 Employers Hiring Grads
Ernst & Young (3), Finning (3), Government of Alberta (3), Deloitte (2), RBC (2)

UNIVERSITY OF ARIZONA
ELLER COLLEGE OF MANAGEMENT

GENERAL INFORMATION

Type of school	Public
Affiliation	No Affiliation
Academic calendar	Semester

SURVEY SAYS...
Friendly students
Solid preparation in:
Teamwork, Communication/interpersonal skills, Presentation skills

STUDENTS

Enrollment of parent institution	39,806
Enrollment of MBA Program	52
% male/female	75/25
% out-of-state	34
% part-time	0
% underrepresented minority	15
% international	38
Average age at entry	27
Average years work experience at entry	4.5

ACADEMICS

Academic Experience Rating	**90**
Profs interesting rating	85
Profs accesible rating	86
Student/faculty ratio	1:1
% female faculty	33
% underrepresented minority faculty	30
% part-time faculty	0

Joint Degrees
JD/MBA-4 years; MD/MBA- 5 years; MBA/Master in Global Management- 3 years; MS MIS/MBA- 3 years; MBA/PharmD- 5 years; MBA/MMF-2-3 years; MBA/MS in Engineering and Optical Science: 3 years; MBA/MPH: 3 years

Prominent Alumni
Gregory Boyce, CEO, Peabody Energy; Brian Gentile, CEO, Jaspersoft; Terry Lundgren, CEO, Macy's; Richard Carmona, President, Canyon Ranch; Charles Nelson, Owner, Sprinkles Cupcakes

Academics

The Eller College of Management at the University of Arizona is "recognized as one of the nation's leading business schools" in MIS and entrepreneurship, many students here report. And "the weather doesn't hurt, either" adds one happy student.

Experiential learning plays an important part in the Eller curriculum; students identify this as "one of the greatest strengths" of the program. One MBA explains how it works: "In the spring semester, MBAs work in teams with local businesses to assess real-world problems, make strategic recommendations, and ultimately assist the businesses in solving those problems." Another tells us that "The experiential learning is more than just a resume builder. It's a very real, very challenging experience, designed to prepare students for future leadership positions." The school's strong "relationship with key businesses" in the area plays a key role in making the experiential learning component a success.

Students also appreciate that class sizes at Eller "are small enough that the students have easy access to professors.... Students are able to develop relationships and personal bonds with professors." These personal touches permeate the program's administration as well. One student reports that "The administrative staff adds great value to the student experience...[and] goes out of its way to help students find whatever they need. Cross-discipline courses, job opportunities, highly tailored informational interviews— the administration works hard to provide students with any resources they need." At the other end of the size spectrum is the university-at-large. It is huge, and this too is seen as an asset; "With a large campus, the business students can take advantage of wonderful resources for the entire school," one student explains.

Eller professors "are very engaging and add significant value. The tenured staff places a strong emphasis on real-world experiences, ranging from case competitions judged by working professionals to company site visits." Instructors "are also very available for office hours and discussion outside of class. This creates an atmosphere of '24-hour learning.'"

Career and Placement

The Office of Career Management aims to provide highly personalized service to each individual student, in the process of helping them plan and achieve their career goals. The office organizes five annual job fairs on campus, networking events with alumni, company visits, and financial support for students who want to go to national MBA job fairs. The office further supports students in their job search through professional development workshops, interview preparation, resume preparation, and professional mentoring.

Companies most likely to hire Eller MBAs include Emerson, Deloitte, Discover, AT&T, Intel, Henkel, Bard, Roche, PetSmart, US Airways, Raytheon, Sandia National Labs, APS, Solon, PricewaterhouseCoopers, and WalMart.

Student Life and Environment

"Great weather and a very nice campus" soften the edges of Eller's intense program in graduate business study. So too does the perception that "no one in the MBA program needs to kill themselves to pass." Those who want to do better than scrape by will need to exert themselves, however; "excelling in all classes and electives requires an intense work week," students report. Program cohesion is enhanced through group work (the program requires "continuous case competitions, group projects, and presentations") and "lots of networking activities (e.g., happy hours, philanthropy, coed intramural sports teams)." Eller hosts "numerous guest speakers and [provides] chances to learn more with outside class activities." Students "work very hard but play hard as well. Everyone knows everyone else and there is a standing invite to any social events."

ADMISSIONS CONTACT: JIM DERANEK, DIRECTOR OF MBA ADMISSIONS
ADDRESS: MCCLELLAND HALL, BUILDING 108, RM 210, P.O. BOX 210108, TUCSON,
AZ 85721-0108
PHONE: 520-621-4008 • FAX: 520-621-6227
E-MAIL: MBA_ADMISSIONS@ELLER.ARIZONA.EDU • WEBSITE: ELLERMBA.ARIZONA.EDU

Eller's "friendly, conservative, helpful, hard-working, social, busy" students form "a small group" who as a result are "very close. Everyone works together and helps others succeed while remaining competitive with people from other schools (instead of walking over people from the same program)." It's "a very diverse [group] with backgrounds ranging from Peace Corps workers to former hedge fund traders. We have military officers and students with private consulting backgrounds."

Admissions

Eller admissions officers seek candidates with a strong academic background, professional experience that demonstrates progress and the desire for challenges, leadership potential, and integrity. All applicants must submit one copy of unofficial transcripts for all post-secondary academic work, an official GMAT score report, a professional resume, two professional letters of recommendation, and two comprehensive personal essays (and a third for scholarship applicants). Interviews are required but are scheduled at the request of the school only; in other words, only those who make the first cut are asked to interview. International applicants must meet all the criteria above and submit TOEFL scores (if English is not their first language), official transcripts and two copies of their diploma(s) (translated by a recognized service if not granted by an English-language institution), and a statement of financial self-sufficiency.

In its efforts to maximize the presence of underrepresented groups, the Eller MBA Program attends regional and national job/recruiting fairs organized by National Society of Hispanic MBAs (NSHMBA), Society of Hispanic Professional Engineers (SHPE) and National Society of Black Engineers (NSBE). In addition, the Eller MBA program is listed in Hobsons' Black MBA and Hispanic MBA Students' Guides and maintains partnerships with the Association of Latino Professionals in Finance and Accounting (ALPFA). It also participates in on-campus recruitment fairs geared toward underrepresented minority students.

FINANCIAL FACTS

Annual tuition (in-state/ out-of-state)	$20,630/$36,042
Fees	$4,500
Cost of books	$4,000
Room & board	$8,400
% of students receiving aid	99
% of first-year students receiving aid	100
% of students receiving grants	98
Average award package	$20,014
Average grant	$11,194
Average loan	$22,079
Average student loan debt	$47,327

ADMISSIONS

Admissions Selectivity Rating	88
# of applications received	197
% applicants accepted	42
% acceptees attending	63
Average GMAT	634
Range of GMAT	600–660
Average GPA	3.28
TOEFL required of international students	Yes
Minimum TOEFL (paper/computer)	600/250
Application fee	$100
International application fee	$100
Application Deadline/Notification	
Round 1:	12/1 / 1/15
Round 2:	1/15 / 2/15
Round 3:	3/15 / 4/15
Round 4:	5/1 / 6/1
Deferment available	Yes
Maximum length of deferment	1 year
Transfer students accepted	No
Non-fall admissions	No
Need-blind admissions	Yes

EMPLOYMENT PROFILE

Career Rating	90	**Grads Employed by Function**	**% Avg. Salary**
Percent employed at graduation	68	Marketing	(10%) $92,333
Percent employed 3 months after graduation	88	Operations	(10%) $79,333
		Consulting	(27%) $95,000
Average base starting salary	$86,388	Management	(10%) $111,667
Primary Source of Full-time Job Acceptances		Finance	(27%) $64,839
School-facilitated activities	24(80%)	MIS	(6%)
Graduate-facilitated activities	6(20%)	Other	(10%) $85,000

Top 5 Employers Hiring Grads
Deloitte Consulting (3), IBM (2), Intel (3), Dial/ Henkel (2), Liberty Mutual (2)

UNIVERSITY OF ARKANSAS—FAYETTEVILLE
SAM M. WALTON COLLEGE OF BUSINESS

Academics

Just thirty miles from Walmart headquarters, the "top-ranked public business college" at the University of Arkansas—Fayetteville gets more than just its name from the world-famous retailer. "Walmart's extensive involvement" in the school pays off in a thousand different ways, from fantastic internship opportunities to the "cutting edge" supply chain and retail management program—not to mention, the world-class business environment in Fayetteville. Thanks to the school's famous benefactor, "Northwest Arkansas is a business epicenter," with "over 1,500 suppliers based locally." Without jetting off to New York or Tokyo, "Students are given opportunities to interact with Fortune 500 CEOs on a regular basis"—often without leaving campus. Here, "You'll rarely find a day when there is not a CEO or other successful alumni coming back to contribute."

Walton operates two MBAs: a traditional full-time program and a part-time Executive MBA. With classes held "once a month on Saturdays," the part-time program "offers a lot of flexibility for working professionals." Students praise the "blended delivery," which "incorporates both in-class and distance learning." On top of that, "The administration ensures that the students lives are easy when it comes to enrollment and degree requirements"—they even provide all the materials (and meals!) on class day. For full-timers, the experience is likewise fast-paced, packing a full academic program—including an internship or overseas trip, independent projects, and case competitions—into just sixteen months of study.

Students in both full-time and part-time programs are bowled over by the quality of the academic experience. With a name like Walton, it's hardly a surprise that "the retail and supply chain management is highly recognized," drawing many students already working in the field. Yet professors across departments are "experienced professionals with real-world knowledge," who are "incredibly gifted in their field of research" and "truly excited about the material they teach." Professors are also willing to provide "additional instruction beyond class time," both to help with class material and to "answer any questions we have related to application of learned material in the workplace."

The MBA is "very, very well run," overseen by an administration that is "second to none." A boon to busy students, "The administration ensures that the students lives are easy when it comes to enrollment and degree requirements." They also "take steps to "improve the MBA program every year according to students' feedback." Icing on the cake, "The cost of the program is relatively inexpensive compared to their national rankings," making a Walton education a rather savvy venture.

Career and Placement

The future looks bright for Walton graduates. Not only are there "a huge amount of new jobs in this area per capita," students say they "have a leg-up" with local employers through the school's corporate partnerships. Walton offers a host of "great resources, like the career center, the writing center, and professional development classes," which all contribute to the school's excellent placement rate. One student raves, "The career services office has to be one of the best in the nation." Not only do they provide career advice but they "will happily make calls on your behalf and are constantly engaging you in the process of finding a job." For full-timers, "The Walton school does a great job of setting students up with internships," and better yet, it's "extremely easy to get a job after graduation at a great company."

ADMISSIONS CONTACT: MARION DUNAGAN, ASSISTANT DEAN
ADDRESS: 310 WILLARD J. WALKER HALL, UNIVERSITY OF ARKANSAS, FAYETTEVILLE, AR 72701
PHONE: 479-575-2851 • FAX: 479-575-8721
E-MAIL: GSB@WALTON.UARK.EDU • WEBSITE: GSB.UARK.EDU

In recent years, over 130 companies recruited on the Walton campus, with students taking jobs at companies including Axion Corporation, Deloitte & Touche, General Mills, IBM, KPMG, J.B. Hunt Transport Services, NBC Universal, Newell Rubbermaid, Tyson Foods, Shell Oil, Spectrum Brands, USA Truck, and, of course, Walmart. The 2012 graduating class had an average starting salary of $60,555, with a range between $35,000 and $82,000.

Student Life and Environment

University of Arkansas—Fayetteville provides a "rich cultural and academic atmosphere" in which to study, including "excellent facilities for MBA students." Full-timers usually "spend a significant amount of time on campus," studying, hanging out with friends, or, on game day, cheering on the Razorbacks; "As a part of the SEC, sports are a major event on campus." Students in the EMBA program admit that they are "not that involved in school activities," but they do make some time for networking: "A majority of the first and second year executive MBA students will all gather together at a local bar for food and drinks after our Saturday classes."

The school draws students from "very diverse backgrounds," though "the majority of us work with or for Walmart in some fashion." Walton does an excellent job fostering friendships and networking between MBA candidates. A student shares, "By the end of orientation, I knew my way around the town, fun places to go, and the names and backgrounds of my entire class as well as my faculty/administration." Of the warm atmosphere, another student adds, "As a woman, I feel incredibly welcomed into this business environment. Our class is 50/50—a huge reason I chose U of A."

Overall, "Northwest Arkansas is a very nice area to live and work." With a population of around 75,000, "Fayetteville is the perfect size for a college town. It offers everything a student needs with reasonable costs."

Admissions

For students applying to Walton's full-time MBA, GMAT scores and academic record are the most important factors in an admissions decision, though previous work experience is also recommended. The school prefers a score of 600 or better on the GMAT and an undergraduate grade point average of 3.3 or above. For part-time students, GMAT scores and previous work experience are the two most important factors in evaluating an application, with a minimum of two years' professional experience required to apply. GMAT waivers are available to Executive MBA applicants with exceptional work experience.

FINANCIAL FACTS

Annual tuition (in-state/ out-of-state)	$14,442/$34,394
Fees	$1,804
Cost of books	$1,750
% of students receiving aid	78
% of first-year students receiving aid	74
% of students receiving grants	40
Average award package	$30,000
Average grant	$7,500

ADMISSIONS

Admissions Selectivity Rating	95
# of applications received	355
% applicants accepted	34
% acceptees attending	85
Average GMAT	601
Range of GMAT	570–710
Average GPA	3.21
TOEFL required of international students	Yes
Minimum TOEFL (paper/computer)	550/213
Application fee	$40
International application fee	$50
Early application deadline	4/1
Early notification date	5/1
Regular application deadline	9/15
Regular application notification	10/15
Deferment available	No
Transfer students accepted	Yes
Transfer application policy: 6 hours may transfer from AACSB Institutions	
Non-fall admissions	Yes
Need-blind admissions	Yes

EMPLOYMENT PROFILE

Career Rating	90	**Grads Employed by Function**	**% Avg. Salary**	
Percent employed at graduation	91	Marketing	(50%)	$64,333
Percent employed 3 months after graduation	96	Operations	(25%)	$52,000
		Consulting	(5%)	
Average base starting salary	$60,555	Finance	(5%)	$53,000
Primary Source of Full-time Job Acceptances		MIS	(10%)	$60,125
School-facilitated activities	17(89%)	Other	(5%)	
Graduate-facilitated activities	2(11%)	**Top 5 Employers Hiring Grads**		
		Kellogg's (2), Walmart (2), FedEx (2), JB Hunt (2), Henkel (1)		

THE UNIVERSITY OF BRITISH COLUMBIA
SAUDER SCHOOL OF BUSINESS

GENERAL INFORMATION

Type of school	Public
Affiliation	No Affiliation
Academic calendar	Unique

SURVEY SAYS...

Students love Vancouver, BC,
Friendly students, Good peer network
Solid preparation in:
Accounting, Teamwork

STUDENTS

Enrollment of parent institution	50,000
% male/female	74/26
% international	55
Average age at entry	30
Average years work experience at entry	6.0

ACADEMICS

Academic Experience Rating	**85**
Profs interesting rating	80
Profs accesible rating	82
Student/faculty ratio	20:1
% female faculty	17

Joint Degrees

Joint MBA/JD: 4 years; Joint
MBA/MAPPS (Master of Arts, Asia
Pacific Policy Studies): 2 years;
Combined MBA/CMA: approx. 2
years

Academics

The Sauder School of Business at the University of British Columbia offers both a 15-month full-time and 28-month part-time MBA in the Robert H. Lee Graduate School. The full-time program convenes at the school's 100-acre campus west of Vancouver's downtown core; the part-time program meets at the school's downtown campus in Robson Square.

Sauder's full-time program commences with a fully integrated core curriculum that "integrates 11 subjects to create one hectic but excellent learning environment." Students describe this intensive 13-week sequence, which imposes a heavy workload and requires a high level of complex analysis, as a boot camp-like experience. The remainder of the program is devoted primarily to specialization electives and professional development. Students tell us that finance is one of the school's strongest areas, although supply chain management, entrepreneurship, and international business also earn praise. An "option to partake in international exchange and an internship" during the final six months of the program means students can leave UBC with two unique and valuable experiences; the former reinforces the international focus of the curriculum as a whole.

Part-time students at Sauder experience the same faculty and curriculum as do full-timers, including the rigorous Integrated Core. The chief difference is scheduling; the part-time program is offered on Friday evenings and on weekends to accommodate students' work schedules. Students in both the full-time and part-time programs describe professors as "a mixed bag. Some are excellent scholars, some are accomplished business leaders, but others don't seem fit to teach master's level courses. Thankfully this last group is a minority." They also tell us that "The support the MBAs receive from the dean, the library staff, the career center, and the MBA office is unbelievable" and that "UBC also has excellent research facilities."

Career and Placement

UBC's Hari B. Varshney Business Career Centre offers "both personal consultation and a structured program" to help students identify goals and develop strategies to meet those goals. Self-assessment, coaching sessions, skills-training programs in resume-writing, interviewing, and networking, recruiting events that bring "corporate recruiters from prominent companies" to campus to interview job candidates, and job postings all figure into the mix here. Some here tell us that "The career center is also very helpful when it comes to finding internships, preparing for interviews or just researching industries," while others complain that the office still needs to improve its performance "if the school wants to be taken seriously at a global level."

Employers likely to hire UBC MBAs include Accenture, BC Hydro, Bell Mobility, Best Buy/Future Shop, BP, Business Objects, Cadbury, Elecronic Arts, Elli Lilly, Fraser Health Authority, GE, Health Canada, Hilti, Honeywell, HSBC, Intrawest, Kodak, Kraft, L'Oreal, Lululemon Athletica, Nike Inc, Nokia, Pepsi Bottling Group, Pivotal Corporation, PMC-Sierra, PricewaterhouseCoopers, Royal Bank Canada, Teekay Shipping Corporation, Telus, Terasen, Vancity, Vancouver Coastal Health, Vancouver International Airport Authority, Vancouver Port Authority, VANOC, and Weyerhauser.

ADMISSIONS CONTACT: MBA & ECM PROGRAMS OFFICE
ADDRESS: #111 - 2053 MAIN MALL, VANCOUVER, BC V6T 1Z2
PHONE: 604-822-8422 • FAX: 604-822-9030
E-MAIL: MBA@SAUDER.UBC.CA • WEBSITE: WWW.SAUDER.UBC.CA/MBA

Student Life and Environment

The Sauder School "treats the MBA students extremely well. We're spoiled, in fact," with loads of opportunities for career-building extracurricular clubs, recreation, and study-related travel. One student reports: "I have traveled to Nashville and Hamilton, and before this degree is completed I will have been to London (Ontario), Harvard, Philadelphia, and Porto Fino, Italy. Each of these trips is heavily subsidized by our dean. It is his mission to get as many students involved in activities that help promote the Sauder name." The full-time program also has "an excellent social rep who is constantly creating new excuses for us to take a night off from studying." Hometown Vancouver "is amazing," students tell us. "There is always a group of students going for a run, a bike, a hike or a sail," and skiing is accessible during much of the year, thanks to the proximity of Whistler Mountain.

The full-time program at Sauder draws "a very diverse group" that is "nearly 60 percent international, bringing to the classroom "diverse backgrounds of experience and culture." While "quite competitive," students here are quite willing to "help each other with course issues." The school has "a great MBA office to assist students with any problems. It also has a language center to help international students edit their papers and improve their proficiency in English."

Admissions

Admission to the Sauder MBA program is extremely competitive. All applicants must submit official transcripts for undergraduate work (students who attended schools where English was not the primary language must arrange for a certified translation of their transcripts to be delivered to UBC), official GMAT score reports, evidence of English proficiency (TOEFL scores for students whose first language is not English) essays, a resume, and three letters of reference. Interviews are by invitation only; the school interviews roughly half its applicant pool. The school's brochure notes, "Competitive applicants generally have more than two years of full-time post-baccalaureate work experience for admission to the program." On average, students enter the program with six years' full-time professional experience. Applications are processed on a rolling basis; the process favors those who apply early. Admitted students may not defer admission.

FINANCIAL FACTS

Annual tuition	$32,450
Cost of books	$2,200

ADMISSIONS

Admissions Selectivity Rating	87
# of applications received	512
% applicants accepted	48
% acceptees attending	51
Average GMAT	642
Range of GMAT	570–730
Average GPA	3.30
TOEFL required of international students	Yes
Minimum TOEFL (paper/computer)	600/250
Application fee	$125
International application fee	$125
Regular application deadline	4/30
Application Deadline/Notification	
Round 1:	12/15 /
Round 2:	2/28 /
Round 3:	4/30 /
Deferment available	No
Transfer students accepted	No
Non-fall admissions	No
Need-blind admissions	Yes

EMPLOYMENT PROFILE

Career Rating	92	Grads Employed by Function	% Avg. Salary
Percent employed 3 months after graduation	83	Marketing	(20%) $78,700
		Operations	(9%) $73,000
Average base starting salary	$77,500	Consulting	(20%) $98,000
		Management	(15%) $66,100
		Finance	(20%) $75,500

UNIVERSITY OF CALGARY
HASKAYNE SCHOOL OF BUSINESS

GENERAL INFORMATION

Type of school	Public
Affiliation	No Affiliation
Academic calendar	Semester

SURVEY SAYS...
Good peer network
Solid preparation in:
Accounting

STUDENTS

Enrollment of parent institution	28,200
Enrollment of MBA Program	106
% male/female	61/39
% out-of-state	10
% part-time	55
% underrepresented minority	19
% international	27
Average age at entry	28
Average years work experience at entry	6.0

ACADEMICS

Academic Experience Rating	**85**
Profs interesting rating	78
Profs accesible rating	84
Student/faculty ratio	3:1
% female faculty	29
% part-time faculty	3

Joint Degrees
MSC in Sustainable Energy Development - 16 months; MBA/JD - 4 years MBA/MSW - 2 full calendar years (year-round); MBA/MD - 5 full calendar years; MBA/MBT - 2 full calendar years

Prominent Alumni
Al Duerr, President and CEO, Al Duerr & Associates; Charlie Fisher, President and CEO, Nexen; Hal Kvisle, President & CEO, Trans Canada; Brett Wilson, Managing Director/First Energy Capital; Byron Osing, Chairman, Launchworks Inc.

Academics

Located in Canada's "second business center (behind Toronto)," University of Calgary's Haskayne School of Business "has close connections with local business." That's a big deal when you're in "the heart of the energy sector of Canada" and those connections forge a "link to the oil and gas business environment and high-level executives." Students note that "the integration into the oil and gas community is very evident here (e.g., speaker panels with oil execs, etc)." With an eye toward the future, Haskayne's energy-related specialization is in "energy management and sustainable development."

Energy isn't the sole focus of a Haskayne MBA, though; on the contrary, "there is a good emphasis on bringing in execs from a wide range of industries," with finance and accounting among the program's other strengths. Across the curriculum, Haskayne employs "a mix of both…cases and structured lectures…and methods even beyond the two…to provide all the learning that's essential to make good leaders for tomorrow." "In some courses, the guest speakers alone provided the ROI in the course," one student exclaims. "Really, really interesting" electives include "entrepreneurship and new venture courses that are so much fun." "Leadership panel discussions and other networking and learning events for students" add further value. Speaking of value, "the cost of living as well as the tuition rates are reasonable" here, meaning that Haskayne "offers an outstanding graduate education at a fairly affordable price." Students also see, and appreciate, the program's "willingness to be innovative and [administrators'] willingness to receive student input." Haskayne offers a twenty-month full-time daytime MBA, an evening MBA, an executive MBA, an early evening MBA at its new downtown campus, a Global Energy Executive MBA offered in 5 locations around the world, and a thesis-based MBA for those interested in pursuing business research.

Career and Placement

Students are very enthusiastic about the career opportunities afforded by Haskayne's "close connections with local businesses," and the Career Center earns praise for "providing access to new job opportunities." In surveys, the school's location is consistently listed as one of its major benefits. As one student explains, the program "takes advantage of being located in an energy industry hub to provide relevant courses of study and integrat[ion] with the local business community." Some feel there's too much focus on the energy sector; one student tells us that "the Career Center is great, but a lot of the companies they bring in are oil- and gas-focused. It would be nice if they also engaged other industries."

Companies that frequently hire graduates include Enmax Corporation, Nexen Inc., Enbridge Inc., Suncor Energy, Bell Canada, CIBC World Markets Inc., Scotia Bank, SMART Technologies Inc., TransCanada, TELUS Communications Ltd., Devon Canada, Shell Canada, Imperial Oil LTD, ATB Financial, Mercer Management, and Deloitte Consulting.

Student Life and Environment

Life at Haskayne "allows each student to be as involved or uninvolved as we want to be. Those who want to get involved can join the MBA Society. Those who don't have time to get involved...simply go to classes and that's it." Involvement is strongest among full-time students, one of whom reports "that following great classes and group meetings there is a large proportion of students that get together and go out for drinks. We have great networking and social events planned throughout the year such as 'Iron Chef MBA,' curling, ski trips, etc. Just a great relaxing break from the busy schoolwork." Those in the part-time program, on the other hand, usually "do not get the benefit of experiencing school life to its fullest." School, work, and family obligations typically leave them little time for networking events.

Haskayne MBAs "range in age from 22 to 42, single to married and having five kids, limited experience to amazing experience. Despite my classmates coming from different regions of the planet and different regions of Canada, we have a strong sense of camaraderie and good communication." The program includes "a lot of creative people and well-rounded people...just the kind of people that you wouldn't expect to run into in an MBA program." Students represent "a broad range of industries...but many are experienced professionals from the oil and gas sector."

Admissions

Applicants to Haskayne must submit the following materials: two sets of official transcripts for all post-secondary work (minimum undergraduate GPA of 3.0 over final two years of course work required), an official GMAT score report, two letters of reference, two copies of a current resume (three years appropriate professional experience is preferred), and two copies of a personal statement explaining their purpose in pursuing a Haskayne MBA and detailing any special attributes they can contribute to the program. College transcripts in a language other than English must be translated by a recognized translation service. Applicants for whom English is a second language must submit an official score report for either the TOEFL or IELTS.

FINANCIAL FACTS

Annual tuition (in-state/ out-of-state)	$12,666/$22,260
Fees	$1,170
Cost of books	$2,000
Room & board	$12,000
% of students receiving grants	40
Average grant	$5,000
Average loan	$0

ADMISSIONS

Admissions Selectivity Rating	**85**
# of applications received	271
% applicants accepted	54
% acceptees attending	73
Average GMAT	610
Range of GMAT	550–680
Average GPA	3.25
TOEFL required of international students	Yes
Minimum TOEFL (paper/computer)	600/250
Application fee	$100
International application fee	$130
Regular application deadline	5/1
Application Deadline/Notification	
Round 1:	11/15 / 1/15
Round 2:	1/15 / 3/1
Round 3:	3/1 / 5/1
Round 4:	5/1 / 6/15
Deferment available	Yes
Maximum length of deferment	1 year
Transfer students accepted	Yes
Transfer application policy: We can accept up to nine courses (5 exemptions and 4 higher standing).	
Non-fall admissions	Yes
Need-blind admissions	Yes

EMPLOYMENT PROFILE

Career Rating	**94**	**Grads Employed by Function%**	**Avg. Salary**
Percent employed 3 months		Marketing	(11%)
after graduation	93	Operations	(36%)
Average base starting salary	$95,351	Consulting	(14%)
Primary Source of Full-time Job Acceptances		Finance	(31%)
School-facilitated activities	(44%)	HR	(3%)
Graduate-facilitated activities	(56%)	MIS	(3%)
		Other	(2%)

UNIVERSITY OF CALIFORNIA—BERKELEY
HAAS SCHOOL OF BUSINESS

GENERAL INFORMATION

Type of school	Public
Affiliation	No Affiliation
Academic calendar	Semester

SURVEY SAYS...

Friendly students, Good social scene,
Good peer network, Happy students
Solid preparation in:
Teamwork, Entrepreneurial studies,
Environmental sustainability

STUDENTS

Enrollment of parent institution	36,142
Enrollment of MBA Program	1,293
% male/female	69/31
% out-of-state	33
% part-time	62
% underrepresented minority	9
% international	37
Average age at entry	29
Average years work experience at entry	5.0

ACADEMICS

Academic Experience Rating	99
Profs interesting rating	97
Profs accesible rating	97
% female faculty	22
% part-time faculty	64

Joint Degrees

MBA/MPH in Public Health: 5
Semesters; MBA/JD: 8 Semesters
(3-4 academic years); MBA/MIAS:
(3 years)

Academics

The Haas School of Business at the University of California—Berkeley is a "top school for academics and recruitment opportunities," especially "on the West Coast." Students here note that the MBA program is "Outstanding on all levels: professionally, academically, and socially." Thanks to an environment that encourages student involvement and input, most here "feel like they have a real role in shaping their own academic experiences." As one student explains, there are "a million ways to get involved and really make a difference. Experiential learning opportunities everywhere you turn." Things "move fast here" thanks to the structure of the courses, but students find themselves supported by "fantastic" and "accessible" professors who "sincerely care" about these future entrepreneurs. "We learn from professors who not only are recognized as top academics in their respective fields, but also professionals who shape the direction of the industry," explains one student. Additionally, Haas' administration "seems to have a singular focus on improving the experience for students." According to students, "They go to great lengths to take in, process, and change the program per student recommendations."

Students praise the "small, intimate program" for being exactly that: "small" and "intimate." "We only have 240 students per class (at least officially...sometimes one or two more get added)," says one student. This "tight-knit" environment creates a distinctly "collaborative culture" that forges lasting connections (which come in handy after graduation). The "caliber of students, faculty, administration, and career services staff" are all "top-notch," which provides a solid base for development. "Haas excels at entrepreneurship (not just social entrepreneurship)," explains one student. "Its heavy involvement and leadership in the Berkeley Energy Resources Collaborative (BERC) provides great opportunities in alternative/green energy entrepreneurship." The school also offers a "health care and international business focus." Another key component of the program is its "close ties" and proximity "to Silicon Valley." Students also single out their "excellent" dean, Richard Lyons, for praise. As one student says, "He's an energetic, reputable professor who spent time in the real world on Wall Street."

Career and Placement

After graduation, Berkeley MBAs breathe easy knowing that their program's high profile and sound reputation go a long way in providing job opportunities for them—not to mention that it also has "an alumni network that spans the globe." As is often the case at such schools, the Haas Career Center provides a broad range of excellent services. Students here benefit from one-on-one advisement, access to numerous online job databases, industry clubs, workshops, seminars, and a mentoring program in which second-year students counsel first years in their search for internships. Employers most likely to hire Berkeley MBAs include Google, Amazon, Apple, Bain & Company, Deloitte Consulting LLP, Pacific Gas and Electric, McKinsey, Genentech.

Student Life and Environment

According to students, life at Haas is "extremely busy and involved." "Beyond schoolwork—which is the focus—almost every student is involved in at least one if not two or three extracurricular activities, most of which are student-run," says one student. "There are often symposiums, speakers, new clubs forming, and conferences to attend." The extracurricular activities, just like the school, are largely "student-driven," meaning that "If a student can dream of an activity, club, or academic venture...it can be done, and in fairly easy fashion." "Life at school is a whirlwind," explains one student. "There are so many clubs, speakers, and events to check out—but never enough time in the day. Last

ADMISSIONS CONTACT: STEPHANIE FUJII, EXECUTIVE DIRECTOR OF ADMISSIONS, FULL-TIME MBA PROG.
ADDRESS: 430 STUDENT SERVICES BUILDING #1902, BERKELEY, CA 94720-1902
PHONE: 510-642-1405 • FAX: 510-643-6659
E-MAIL: MBAADM@HAAS.BERKELEY.EDU • WEBSITE: WWW.HAAS.BERKELEY.EDU

week, I was involved in organizing a panel on sustainable design with speakers from IDEO, Patagonia, and Nike, while also participating in a chili cook-off!"

Needless to say, "Life at Haas is rich and very intensive." Despite being "very active and busy between academic and social opportunities," students find time for the "important things in life." "Dodgeball on Mondays, softball on Tuesdays, and bar of the week on Thursdays—I love b-school!" says one student. Berkeley is "a great college town" with "amazing access to San Francisco, Napa Valley, and Lake Tahoe" (no surprise that the student body reports an "overall appreciation for the outdoors). In addition, the location in the Bay Area "provides a wealth of opportunity for networking."

Thanks to the school's "small class size" Haas has "a very strong sense of community." "People are trustworthy and helpful," says one student. "Friendly," "easygoing," and "international" are all words that could be used to describe the student body here. The "collaborative" environment means that there "isn't the typical cutthroat competition apparent at other business schools." The "diverse" and "welcoming" students here are "keen to support each other." As one student explains, "Life at Haas is unique to every individual, and yet there are so many opportunities for shared experiences."

Admissions

Applicants to Haas graduate programs must submit all the following materials to the admissions department: official copies of transcripts for all postsecondary academic work; an official GMAT score report, letters of recommendation, a personal statement, and a resume. Interviews are conducted on an invitation-only basis. In addition to the above materials, international applicants whose first language is not English must also submit official score reports for the TOEFL or IELTS. The school considers all of the following in determining admissions status: "demonstration of quantitative ability; quality of work experience, including depth and breadth of responsibilities; opportunities to demonstrate leadership, etc.; strength of letters of recommendation; depth and breadth of extracurricular and community involvement; and strength of short answer and essays, including articulation of clear focus and goals."

FINANCIAL FACTS

Annual tuition (in-state/ out-of-state)	$0/$12,245
Fees (in-state/ out-of-state)	$51,422/$53,969
Cost of books	$2,500
Room & board	$20,870
% of students receiving aid	69
% of first-year students receiving aid	60
% of students receiving grants	50
Average award package	$41,698
Average grant	$22,228
Average loan	$41,800
Average student loan debt	$63,652

ADMISSIONS

Admissions Selectivity Rating	99
# of applications received	3,329
% acceptees attending	52
Average GMAT	715
Range of GMAT	700–740
Average GPA	3.61
TOEFL required of international students	Yes
Minimum TOEFL (paper/computer)	570/230
Application fee	$200
International application fee	$200
Application Deadline/Notification	
Round 1:	10/17 / 1/10
Round 2:	11/29 / 2/21
Round 3:	1/16 / 4/11
Round 4:	3/12 / 5/16
Deferment available	No
Transfer students accepted	No
Non-fall admissions	No
Need-blind admissions	Yes

EMPLOYMENT PROFILE

Career Rating		99
Percent employed at graduation		74
Percent employed 3 months after graduation		18
Average base starting salary		$116,045

Primary Source of Full-time Job Acceptances

School-facilitated activities	131(65%)
Graduate-facilitated activities	72(36%)

Grads Employed by Function	% Avg. Salary
Marketing	(26%) $114,390
Operations	(1%)
Consulting	(22%) $122,229
Management	(26%) $114,594
Finance	(19%) $112,764
MIS	(1%)
Other	(5%) $120,375

Top 5 Employers Hiring Grads
Deloitte Consulting (10), McKinsey & Co. (9), Boston Consulting Group (8), PayPal (6), Google (6)

UNIVERSITY OF CALIFORNIA—DAVIS
GRADUATE SCHOOL OF MANAGEMENT

Academics

The Graduate School of Management at University of California—Davis "maintains the perfect balance between size and quality of institution," students here report. The smaller scale of operations here means that students enjoy "amazing professors who we are in constant contact with and have easy access to" and an administration that "is responsive to student needs. Most students are on a first-name basis with staff." In short, Davis' "small program with good course options" results in a "personal nature of education [that] is amazing compared to many similarly ranked schools."

The Davis MBA program exploits its presence within a greater university—one that excels in the sciences, among other fields—to create more opportunities than would typically be available in a program of this size. A "thriving interdisciplinary environment" encourages students to seek these opportunities. One student pursuing "degrees in economics and transportation technology while earning the MBA" notes "close collaboration in these programs with industry and government sponsors (auto and energy, state and federal agencies), [which] has positioned me well for my desired career at the intersection of energy and transportation." Other survey respondents identify business opportunities springing from the university's work in biotech, viticulture (the school has "good ties to the wine industry"), and sustainability and clean energy industries. Students note approvingly the emphasis on social responsibility throughout the Davis curriculum.

Davis attracts an "excellent faculty" whose members "are not just academics; they are board members and former CEOs, which makes class work a lot more relevant." Teaching "focuses on case curricula" and professors "integrate a lot of material that is currently happening around us whenever they can." The "very qualified, effective, and communicative" administration "bends over backwards to help the students," helping to ease the stress that invariably accompanies graduate study. On the downside, the relatively small size of the program means that "getting into popular classes can be difficult due to faculty size and course offerings."

Career and Placement

Students report that Davis' cozy size is a drawback when it comes to job-hunting season. "Even though our small size is one of our greatest strengths, it also hinders us from making an impact with recruiters," a student warns. A "tightly knit alumni network" helps ease the pain a bit. Although that alumni network is relatively small, its members are committed to helping fellow alums find their place in the business world

Employers that most frequently hire Davis MBAs include: CalPERS; Blue Shield; Wells Fargo; CalSTRS; Hewlett Packard Company; Agilent Technologies; Intel Corporation; Kaiser Permanente; AT&T; Brocade; Elite Capitol; Ernst & Young; KPMG; PricewaterhouseCoopers; Rabobank International; Deloitte, LLP; and PG&E. Approximately 26% of the class of 2010 found work in consulting (median starting salary $95,000); 24% took jobs in finance/accounting ($92,070); and about 15% entered general management. Most graduates remain in the area; two in five find work in San Francisco or the surrounding Bay Area, one in five finds a job in the greater Sacramento region, and the rest are split between Silicon Valley and destinations farther afield.

ADMISSIONS CONTACT: JAMES STEVENS, ASSISTANT DEAN, STUDENT AFFAIRS
ADDRESS: GRADUATE SCHOOL OF MANAGEMENT, ONE SHIELDS AVE, GALLAGHER HALL,
DAVIS, CA 95616 • PHONE: 530-752-7658 • FAX: 530-754-9355
E-MAIL: ADMISSIONS@GSM.UCDAVIS.EDU • WEBSITE: WWW.GSM.UCDAVIS.EDU

Student Life and Environment

The Davis MBA program operates out of a "brand new state-of-the-art building" on a "new campus that is clean and high tech." "There are plenty of places to study and I can find access to any needed resource," one student reports. The school's proximity to San Francisco and Sacramento creates opportunities for connections in business and government. Hometown Davis "is a growing midsize city. It is called 'bike town U.S.A.' because there is no need to own a car (this is rare in California).... There is a diverse mix of restaurants, including Thai, Chinese, Japanese, Mexican, Czech, Bavarian, French, European, Indian, American fare, and others."

The Davis campus engenders "a good sense of community," according to students. While "full-time students have opportunities to participate in clubs," those who attend part time either "work or have classes during club meetings." Either way, their participation is limited, which suits them. As one explains, "As working professionals, we all have established lives. We have homes. Most of us are married and many of us have children. Because of this school is less central in our lives."

Davis MBAs are "great team players" and "friendly people" "with a diverse array of skill sets and career aspirations." Many "care about the environment and the impact they make on the world." "Many are very liberal," which is not that common in graduate business programs, but "then you have about half who are more stereotypical business-minded people."

Admissions

Admissions Officers for the full-time MBA program at UC Davis consider the following factors in assessing candidates: academic potential, professional potential, and personal qualities. Full-time work experience is not required for admission, but most students have at least a few years of work experience. Applicants must submit the following materials: a completed application form (online or hard copy); a current resume; a list of outside activities and honors; three short personal essays; official transcripts from each undergraduate and graduate institution attended; two letters of recommendation; and an official GMAT score report. Applicants whose native language is not English must submit an official TOEFL score report or IELTS reflecting a score no more than two years old. Applications to the full-time program are accepted for the fall semester only.

FINANCIAL FACTS

Annual tuition (in-state/ out-of-state)	$34,560/$46,805
Fees	$1,887
Cost of books	$1,753
Room & board	$14,335
% of students receiving aid	78
% of first-year students receiving aid	79
% of students receiving grants	73
Average award package	$30,590
Average grant	$13,284
Average loan	$34,038
Average student loan debt	$46,411

ADMISSIONS

Admissions Selectivity Rating	97
# of applications received	361
% applicants accepted	19
% acceptees attending	68
Average GMAT	680
Range of GMAT	640–710
Average GPA	3.30
TOEFL required of international students	Yes
Minimum TOEFL (paper/computer)	600/250
Application fee	$125
International application fee	$125
Early application deadline	11/7
Early notification date	12/26
Regular application deadline	3/6
Regular application notification	4/24
Application Deadline/Notification	
Round 1:	11/7 / 12/26
Round 2:	1/9 / 2/27
Round 3:	3/6 / 4/24
Round 4:	5/15 / 6/26
Deferment available	Yes
Maximum length of deferment	1 year
Transfer students accepted	Yes
Transfer application policy: A maximum of 12 quarter units from a University of California campus or 6 quarter units from another university can be applied toward the fulfillment of our elective requirement.	
Non-fall admissions	No
Need-blind admissions	Yes

EMPLOYMENT PROFILE

Career Rating	96	Grads Employed by Function	% Avg. Salary
Percent employed at graduation	63	Marketing	(36%) $87,000
Percent employed 3 months after graduation	93	Operations	(3%)
		Consulting	(18%) $89,000
Average base starting salary	$91,569	Management	(5%)
Primary Source of Full-time Job Acceptances		Finance	(30%) $94,057
School-facilitated activities	19(50%)	MIS	(5%)
Graduate-facilitated activities	19(50%)	Other	(3%)

Top 5 Employers Hiring Grads
Gartner, Inc. (3), PG&E (3), AT&T (2), HP (2), Tesla (2)

UNIVERSITY OF CALIFORNIA—IRVINE
THE PAUL MERAGE SCHOOL OF BUSINESS

GENERAL INFORMATION
Type of school   Public
Affiliation   No Affiliation

SURVEY SAYS...
Friendly students, Good social scene,
Good peer network, Smart
classrooms
Solid preparation in:
Teamwork, Presentation skills

STUDENTS
Enrollment of parent
  institution   28,000
Enrollment of MBA Program   635
% male/female   65/35
% out-of-state   10
% part-time   66
% international   40
Average age at entry   28
Average years work experience
  at entry   5.0

ACADEMICS
Academic Experience Rating   89
Profs interesting rating   82
Profs accesible rating   87
% female faculty   29
% underrepresented minority
  faculty   21
% part-time faculty   61

Joint Degrees
MD/MBA: Five or Six year program
JD/MBA: Four year program

Prominent Alumni
Lisa Locklear, Vice President,
Ingram Micro; Darcy Kopcho,
Executive Vice President, Capital
Group Companies; George
Kessinger, Pres. and CEO, Goodwill
Industries International; Norman
Witt, Vice President Community
Development, The Irvine C

Academics

The combination of academic innovation, strong industry ties, and a relaxed California environment make UC Irvine's Paul Merage School of Business a top pick for future SoCal professionals. The school's first-year MBA curriculum covers business fundamentals like finance and marketing while maintaining "a strong emphasis on innovation and international business" throughout disciplines. In the second year, students tailor their education through an impressive selection of elective courses in areas ranging from brand management to new product development. A student tells us, "I started with an interest in finance, and gradually discovered an affinity for strategy and technology. Because Merage does not put you on a track, I had the chance to get exposure to finance but the freedom to switch my focus late in my first year." Class work is augmented by ample hands-on "opportunities outside of the classroom," including business-plan competitions and nonprofit consulting projects, as well as the ten-week field project course, through which students consult for a regional company. Study abroad programs also receive top marks. A current MBA candidate attests, "My four months living in Budapest, Hungary was life changing and gave me an incredible perspective on international business and cultural differences in the workplace."

With only 100 students in each incoming class, the "intimate learning environment" is a signature of the Merage program. The small class size makes it easy to "build personal relationships with everyone at the school, including professors and staff." At Merage, "The professors really want to see us succeed and make themselves available to all students to answer questions or talk about their research." The staff and administration is also "world-class": "The career center and programming support staff are excellent and always available to meet," and administrators are "extremely quick to respond and act to just about anything." Of particular note, the dean is "outstanding," "communicating his vision for our school and supporting students through has vast connections and experience in business." Between students, "The program requires a lot of group work," which encourages networking both in and out of the classroom. Fortunately, Merage maintains an unwaveringly "cooperative environment." Here, "Students want to see each other succeed, as evidenced by the large groups that study together prior to tests, or the peer feedback we receive in preparing for group presentations."

Career and Placement

"The major business program in all of Orange County," Merage has the edge in the local job market, where students benefit from direct "access to some of the top companies in the country: Taco Bell, Blizzard, Pimco, the list goes on and on." In addition to the old standbys, "There are a lot of new companies moving to the area and have established recruiting efforts with the school." On top of that, "The school has a very strong alumni base which is very interested in helping current students in their search for employment." Merage may not be as famous as some of L.A.'s big business schools, but students assure us that the "companies that know our school love us."

Merage's "excellent career center" makes the most of the school's strong local connections, maintaining a "great track record" with graduating MBAs. Career Center programs start right at the beginning of the MBA, guiding student through every step in the career-search process, from defining their career goals to landing a choice internship. Top hiring companies at Merage include AT&T, Deloitte, AERS, Deloitte Consulting, Experian, General Electric, IBM, Johnson & Johnson, JP Morgan, KPMG, Niagara Bottling, Pacific Life, Roth Capital Partners, and the Walt Disney Company, among many others. Finance and accounting, consulting, and sales and marketing were the most popular job functions for the class of 2012.

ADMISSIONS CONTACT: ELISA LEE, ASSISTANT DIRECTOR, RECRUITMENT AND ADMISSIONS
ADDRESS: SB 220, IRVINE, CA 92697-3125
PHONE: 949-824-4622 • FAX: 949-824-2235
E-MAIL: MBA@MERAGE.UCI.EDU • WEBSITE: MBA.MERAGE.UCI.EDU

Student Life and Environment

"Life at Merage is very dynamic." Beyond the classroom, there are frequent "networking events, volunteer events, interviewing, seminars, academic group meetings, and many other opportunities for professional and personal growth." Though the administration creates a lot of these opportunities, you'll also find that student-run "clubs are very active and organize a mix of social and career focused events like executive panels, mixers, trips, speaker series, and tours." Socially, "There is a business school student mixer at a nearby bar or restaurant" every week, as well as "a few mixers that take place between different schools every quarter."

Located on the Southern California coast, life in Orange County is "fantastic." With its "gorgeous beaches" and sunny weather providing the perfect backdrop, "Students are always organizing outdoor activities (beach BBQs, intramural sports, etc)." There's "great food and nightlife in Irvine and Newport"; not to mention, the school is "close enough to L.A. that many people visit on the weekends." At the same time, the suburban atmosphere keeps things low-key; many mention that it's "very safe here."

Admissions

To apply to UC Irvine's Merage School of Business, students must submit an online application form, official transcripts from college, GMAT or GRE scores, two letters of recommendation, a résumé, and two essays. Qualified candidates will be invited to interview as a further requirement for admission. The current MBA class had an average GPA of 3.35 and average GMAT scores of 660 (with a middle 80 percent range of 600-720). Though the average work experience for entering students is five years, incoming students have prior professional experience ranging from zero to fifteen years.

FINANCIAL FACTS

Annual tuition (in-state/ out-of-state)	$37,946/$46,585
Cost of books	$2,400
Room & board (on/off-campus)	$12,473/$17,219

ADMISSIONS

Admissions Selectivity Rating	90
# of applications received	805
% applicants accepted	33
% acceptees attending	40
Average GMAT	660
Average GPA	3.35
TOEFL required of international students	Yes
Minimum TOEFL (paper/computer)	600
Application fee	$150
International application fee	$150
Early application deadline	11/1
Early notification date	12/1
Regular application deadline	2/1
Regular application notification	4/1
Application Deadline/Notification	
Round 1:	11/1 / 1/15
Round 2:	12/1 / 3/1
Round 3:	2/1 / 4/1
Round 4:	4/1 / 6/15
Deferment available	No
Transfer students accepted	No
Non-fall admissions	Yes
Need-blind admissions	Yes

EMPLOYMENT PROFILE

Career Rating		94
Percent employed 3 months after graduation		94
Average base starting salary		$76,736
Primary Source of Full-time Job Acceptances		

Grads Employed by Function	%	Avg. Salary
Marketing	(23%)	$76,631
Operations	(7%)	$91,250
Consulting	(18%)	$78,850
Management	(5%)	$81,333
Finance	(41%)	$75,848
HR	(2%)	
MIS	(4%)	

Top 5 Employers Hiring Grads
AT&T, Deloitte Consulting, Walt Disney Company, Southern California Edison, Experian

University of California—Los Angeles
UCLA Anderson School of Management

GENERAL INFORMATION

Type of school	Public
Affiliation	No Affiliation
Academic calendar	Quarters

SURVEY SAYS...

Students love Los Angeles, CA,
Friendly students, Good social scene,
Good peer network, Helpful alumni,
Happy students
Solid preparation in:
Entrepreneurial studies

STUDENTS

Enrollment of parent institution	41,341
Enrollment of MBA Program	1,615
% male/female	68/32
% out-of-state	28
% part-time	53
% underrepresented minority	8
% international	33
Average age at entry	29
Average years work experience at entry	6.0

ACADEMICS

Academic Experience Rating	96
Profs interesting rating	93
Profs accesible rating	93
Student/faculty ratio	11:1
% female faculty	20
% underrepresented minority faculty	12
% part-time faculty	40

Joint Degrees

MBA/JD, MBA/MD, MBA/DDS,
MBA/MPH, MBA/Master of Latin
American Studies, MBA/MURP,
MBA/Master of Computer Science,
MBA/MPP, MBA/MLIS, MBA/MN

Prominent Alumni

Mr. Jim Moffatt, Chairman and CEO;
Deloitte Consulting LLP; Ms. Susan
Wojcicki, Senior Vice President,
Advertising; Google Inc.; Mr.
Laurence D. Fink, Chairman & CEO;
BlackRock Inc.; Mr. Mitch Kupchak,
General Manager, Los Angeles
Lakers

Academics

UCLA's Anderson School of Management takes great pains to ensure the curriculum offered is "very practical" and that it continually reflects "emerging business trends." This success can partially be attributed to the fact that many classes "bring in renowned industry professionals to speak and give real world context to the course content." Though the majority of students find the coursework "challenging," they also say their classes are "rewarding" and issue assurance that "you will learn a lot."

Students speak glowingly of their "engaged" professors who are "all without a doubt incredibly intelligent and masters of their fields of study." Moreover they truly "understand the rigors and time challenges of an MBA program so they are very helpful in making sure we are successful." Additionally, these "outstanding" teachers "have a genuine concern that we learn; they ask for feedback a third- to half-way through the term to ensure that students are learning all the material and that the pace and style are well balanced." Another highly content student chimes in, "My professors have the kind of industry experience that make my jaw drop, they challenge me every day in class but at the end of the year I can go out with them." That camaraderie is "simply the best!"

Additionally, MBA candidates at UCLA Anderson are quick to note that the administration is "always available" and "very responsive to student suggestion and inquiry." A first-year student shares, "I feel as though I can meet with anybody at school." Perhaps more importantly, the administration is highly respected for being "transparent about [their] operations and strategies." Finally, a fellow first-year eloquently asserts, "The leadership team at Anderson is like the Showtime Lakers: just a set of all-stars that each brings something unique to the table."

Career and Placement

The opportunities for career placement and training at UCLA Anderson are plentiful. Students are happy to report that the school does "a great job of harnessing the formidable LA business community." Further, many deem the career service office to be "excellent." As one student on the brink of graduation gratefully shares, "They connected us with plenty of good companies. Interview preparation and resume/cover letter advice were also outstanding. [And they] prepared us well for the toughest interviews." Indeed, career services strives to offer "the best opportunity to land a top tier job markedly superior to the one we had before business school." This success also stems from "an institutionalized process whereby first year students have 'ACT Coaches" and a "Parker Career Management Series' which serves to spend months on interview and networking prep during the first and second quarters. Second year students spend countless hours helping to ensure first year students are engaged and will be successful in their job search."

ADMISSIONS CONTACT: ALEX LAWRENCE, ASSISTANT DEAN OF ADMISSIONS AND FINANCIAL AID
ADDRESS: 110 WESTWOOD PLAZA, GOLD HALL, SUITE B201,
LOS ANGELES, CA 90095-1481 • PHONE: 310-825-6944 • FAX: 310-825-8582
E-MAIL: MBA.ADMISSIONS@ANDERSON.UCLA.EDU • WEBSITE: WWW.ANDERSON.UCLA.EDU

Student Life and Environment

UCLA Anderson MBAs happily reveal that their program provides a "fantastic balance between school and social life." By and large, students love living in LA. And how can you not when "it's sunny all year?" Of course beyond weather, the city has "an impressive mix of large corporations and entrepreneurial ventures" ripe with internship opportunities. The school is continually hosting events which offer a great "mix of professional focus, student get-togethers, alumni networking and conferences." And one excited second-year even brags, "We are the first B-school to have a partnership with TED!" Overall, students embrace an "active lifestyle" which often means "hikes discussing case studies, beach visits with text books and a positive attitude across the school that mirrors the great weather."

Importantly, a congenial atmosphere permeates UCLA Anderson's campus. Across the board, students find their peers to be "extremely friendly and open." Fortunately, there "are no egos here." Instead, students approach everything with a "collaborative" mindset. And many truly appreciate that their fellow students "have incredibly different backgrounds, from all industries, countries and cultures and are willing to share and use that experience in their work and interactions."

Admissions

A top MBA program, competition for admission to UCLA Anderson is certainly stiff. Anderson is looking for candidates with strong communication skills who have a clear vision for their professional future. They want students who understand how they'll benefit from this particular MBA program. All applicants are required to have an undergraduate degree from an accredited 4-year university (or international equivalent). Additionally, they must submit GMAT (highly preferable) or GRE scores, TOEFL (for students who did not attend an English speaking university), no more than two letters of recommendation and two required essays. Work experience is recommended but not required. Finally, interviews will be conducted on an invitation only basis.

FINANCIAL FACTS

Annual tuition (in-state/ out-of-state)	$48,243/$54,530
Cost of books	$2,400
Room & board	$14,172
% of students receiving aid	69
% of first-year students receiving aid	68
% of students receiving grants	60
Average award package	$44,738
Average grant	$19,499
Average loan	$46,519
Average student loan debt	$71,995

ADMISSIONS

Admissions Selectivity Rating	**97**
# of applications received	3,335
% applicants accepted	23
% acceptees attending	48
Average GMAT	704
Range of GMAT	660–750
Average GPA	3.56
TOEFL required of international students	Yes
Minimum TOEFL (paper/computer)	560/220
Application fee	$200
International application fee	$200
Early application deadline	10/22
Early notification date	1/28
Regular application deadline	4/15
Regular application notification	6/3
Application Deadline/Notification	
Round 1:	10/22 / 1/28
Round 2:	1/7 / 4/2
Round 3:	4/15 / 6/3
Deferment available	No
Maximum length	
Transfer students accepted	No
Non-fall admissions	No
Need-blind admissions	Yes

EMPLOYMENT PROFILE

Career Rating	98	Grads Employed by Function	% Avg. Salary
Percent employed at graduation	72	Marketing	(28%) $101,721
Percent employed 3 months after graduation	86	Operations	(2%) $107,000
		Consulting	(19%) $121,396
Average base starting salary	$105,556	Management	(11%) $110,327
Primary Source of Full-time Job Acceptances		Finance	(31%) $99,016
School-facilitated activities	182(70%)	Other	(10%) $100,652
Graduate-facilitated activities	80(31%)	**Top 5 Employers Hiring Grads**	

Deloitte Consulting (10), Mattel Inc. (10), Bank of America Merrill Lynch (8), Amazon, Inc. (7), Amgen, Inc. (6)

UNIVERSITY OF CALIFORNIA—RIVERSIDE
A. GARY ANDERSON GRADUATE SCHOOL OF MANAGEMENT

GENERAL INFORMATION
Type of school	Public
Affiliation	No Affiliation
Academic calendar	Quarter

SURVEY SAYS...
Friendly students, Good social scene,
Smart classrooms
Solid preparation in:
Finance, Accounting, General
management

STUDENTS
Enrollment of parent institution	21,000
Enrollment of MBA Program	92
% male/female	49/51
% out-of-state	3
% part-time	1
% underrepresented minority	3
% international	75
Average age at entry	24
Average years work experience at entry	2.5

ACADEMICS
Academic Experience Rating	82
Profs interesting rating	83
Profs accesible rating	87
Student/faculty ratio	4:1
% female faculty	22
% underrepresented minority faculty	30
% part-time faculty	52

Academics

Combine the Southern California climate with a "fantastic school" offering "generous financial aid, and it's easy to understand why the A. Gary Anderson Graduate School of Management at UC—Riverside gets such high marks from students. One raves, "I am having the time of my life [and]...feel very privileged to be here." Many MBA candidates here are taking their first steps in the business world, as applicants are not required to have work experience—which can be a good or bad thing depending on who you talk to. Some feel that the program only offers a "surface-level understanding of business." Other students laud the "challenging" classes, bolstered by the "very accessible" professors who "care very much about their students' learning and understanding of the course material." However, some gripe that a few seem "more focused on research, and not curriculum."

The six components of an MBA from AGSM are the core courses, an internship, the communication workshop, the electives, a "capstone course," and a case project or thesis.

Though the core courses take up more time than any other single component, students are most enthusiastic about the "wide diversity of electives," which are all seminar size and designed to "encourage participative learning." One student explains, "I love coming to a small school like UCR's AGSM. You get real interaction with professors, and all of the students know each other, which allows for tighter bonds and networks." There are 10 areas of electives, and students are allowed to take up to nine courses from any area, such as accounting, entrepreneurial management, finance, general management, human resources management/organizational behavior, international management, management information systems, management science, marketing, and production and operations management.

Most students agree that "discussion is greatly encouraged" in class. A fair number of courses "require presentation with business formal attire" and some "even require group debate." One student notes, "It gives you some pressure, but it's fun." Some lament the feeling that the university "does not attach [enough] importance to our business school," and hope for this to change in the near future. Others, though conscious that the school is a "research-oriented university," wouldn't mind getting more "attention from some professors" who they find to be "mostly researchers and not lecturers."

Career and Placement

Aside from recent budget cuts, the thing that has most students at AGSM up in arms is the Career Resources Center. As one student says, "The school desperately needs a stronger Career Counseling Center designed just for the MBA students." Another adds, "I really think the school should begin to target the school's alumni more. There are many UCR MBAs in the industry and they could be a real resource and asset to the school." The MBA now has its own Career Services, which should help alleviate many of the students' concerns regarding "job placement," "internships," and "professional networking."

Student Life and Environment

In recent years, Riverside, California has undergone both something of a renaissance and an influx of people. Gone are the days of quiet orange groves, and in their place resides the veritable capital of the Inland Empire. Whether your tastes run to the great outdoors or to great shopping, students find "plenty of unique hangouts, interesting shopping, and a wide variety of eats to fit anyone's desires (and budget)." Some MBA students feel that they "lack social activities" within the program, though in many instances this could be blamed on the large amount of "homework" these students undertake. That said, as the university (and those that surround it) continue to grow, students can expect more avenues to their social outlets to open.

The school itself is housed in a 30,000-square-foot building that features "state-of-the-art research and teaching facilities." MBA students agree that their "computer lab is very nice" and relish that they, as MBAs, "have priority over all computers in the lab." Other students gripe that they're stuck in "a small building that consists of one lecture room and one classroom. Our school has suffered greatly from the previous budget cuts." Still, the building must have something going for it because "MBA students rarely venture onto the main campus at [UC Riverside], unless it's to go to the library or bookstore."

Students report that "most people are very nice, and it is easy to meet new people if you try." These "very laid-back and friendly" students have formed "a tight-knit community here because our graduate program is so small." "I pretty much know and am friends with every other MBA student," says one. Due to the proximity of students, there is "a level of competition between students during academic competitions and presentations," but most happily note that "it is healthy and in good fun."

Admissions

At AGSM, students from all undergraduate majors and levels of business experience are eligible for admission. In fact, more than 30 percent of all incoming students come from a background other than business and have little—if any—experience in the business world. According to the school, "There is no minimum GPA or GMAT requirement for MBA admission consideration." However, they also say "Satisfying minimal standards does not guarantee admission, since the number of qualified applicants far exceeds the number of places available," meaning that you'd best do your best. It is worth noting that because the school doesn't require prior work experience, all prospective MBAs must complete an internship "to ensure your success upon graduation."

FINANCIAL FACTS

Annual tuition (in-state/ out-of-state)	$11,220/$23,465
Fees	$26,275
Cost of books	$2,000
Room & board (on/off-campus)	$10,890/$15,045
% of students receiving aid	41
% of first-year students receiving aid	33
% of students receiving grants	31
Average award package	$22,848

ADMISSIONS

Admissions Selectivity Rating	81
# of applications received	403
% applicants accepted	53
% acceptees attending	43
Average GMAT	578
Range of GMAT	540–610
Average GPA	3.38
TOEFL required of international students	Yes
Minimum TOEFL (paper/computer)	550/213
Application fee	$100
International application fee	$125
Regular application deadline	9/1
Deferment available	No
Transfer students accepted	Yes
Transfer application policy: A maximum of 8 graduate units taken in residence may be transferred from qualifying institutions and courses.	
Non-fall admissions	Yes
Need-blind admissions	Yes

EMPLOYMENT PROFILE

Career Rating	78	Grads Employed by Function	% Avg. Salary
Percent employed at graduation	12	Marketing	(17%) $62,440
Percent employed 3 months after graduation	82	Operations	(42%) $40,536
		Consulting	(6%) $80,000
Average base starting salary	$56,745	Management	(17%) $6,995
		Finance	(12%) $52,500
		Other	(6%) $35,000

Top 5 Employers Hiring Grads
East West Bank (2), Ogilvy (2), GE Energy (1), HSBC (1), European Union (1)

University of Central Arkansas
College of Business

Academics

University of Central Arkansas operates two graduate business programs, including full-time and part-time MBA programs and a master of accountancy with an optional emphasis on international business. One testament to the quality of education at University of Central Arkansas (UCA), which one student refers to as a "research institute," is that many undergraduate students choose to return to the University for a graduate degree, directly out of college or many years later. A current student writes, "I attended UCA for my undergrad degree, and it is such a good fit for me that it was an easy decision to stay."

Before students can begin the MBA program at UCA, they must complete prerequisite coursework in accounting, economics, and finance. After they have completed the prerequisites, the MBA program consists of ten business courses. Students also have the option of pursuing an international specialization through an additional six credit hours in an approved elective or internship experiences related to international business. Focused on advanced general management principles, the MBA coursework is quite traditional, and some would like to see "more (as in any) online classes." In response, UCA is currently developing new online course work for 2012. A number of students say they'd like a more interactive business school experience and more "team-building skills/training." "I would like to see classroom materials tied to the real-world work experience through classroom discussions, applying the material or past occurrences of classmates or the professor. It would give me a better understanding of where and how the material is applicable," says a student.

When it comes to the teaching staff, student opinions are that they are "very good for the most part;" a current student assures us that most are "intelligent individuals whose diverse perspectives give me a well-rounded view of course materials." With an entering class of about 20 students each year, class sizes are small, and the "professional, excellent, and personable" instructors generally encourage students to add their personal experiences to academic material and "emphasize presentation skills." It follows that the professors are "great resources" and "open to helping students in any way they can, whether it's tutoring on difficult homework concepts or getting the student's foot in the door at a hiring corporation."

UCA is rapidly expanding its offerings and campus facilities, a common response from an administration that is "willing to work with the students on any type of problem." The College of Business is likewise on the up-and-up. A student writes, "The administration is in a transition to make the College of Business one of the best in the state. The transition is not complete, but it is well on its way." Case in point, a new business school building, including state-of-the-art case study classrooms, a student commons, a graduate student lounge with lockers, and a professional conference room opened in January 2010.

Career and Placement

The "affordable, quality education" offered here attracts a large part-time population of students who already have professional jobs, and the College of Business doesn't dedicate many resources to career planning and placement and seems content with remaining just "a great regional school." However, business students can use the UCA Career Services office, which offers resume writing assistance, campus interviews, current job listings, career fairs, and workshops for job seekers. Even so, those who'd like to start a new career after graduation say the business school could do more to "help with job placement and recruitment." After graduation, UCA students can keep networking with other alumni through the MBA Alumni Association.

Student Life and Environment

Located "right in the middle of Arkansas," UCA boasts a "laid back atmosphere" and a "beautiful" campus with "a lot of amenities," including a fantastic "new state-of-the-art building." "The campus is big enough to give a 'big-school' feel, but small enough to get to know many of the people one might see on a daily basis," says one student. On the larger campus, there are "a lot" of opportunities for students to get involved, "from academic clubs to sports teams to on-campus ministries. There is definitely a place for any student to get involved if they take the time to look at the opportunities available." However, some MBA students feel they are "left to fend for themselves," with few networking events or campus activities expressly for them.

Within the MBA program, "the students are divided between professionals and those who did their undergraduate work here"—the former group usually comprising younger, recent graduates. Those who did their undergraduate degree at UCA tend to feel more connected to the University than those who entered the University to pursue an MBA or master's degree. Both full-time and part-time students at UCA are all very busy, but the part-time students who attend classes primarily at night would especially "like more attention paid to 'non-traditional' students." As a result, "there is not much time for socializing." The surrounding town of Conway is a growing city of 50,000 in the heart of the Bible Belt, which offers modest recreational activities for students. Though UCA is located in a dry county, there are numerous local restaurants where students convene for food and drinks. However, students note that you have to travel over 30 miles to get a drink after class, which "can be frustrating when you need that stress reliever."

Admissions

To be considered for admission at UCA, students must submit a minimum GMAT score of 500 and a minimum undergraduate GPA of 2.7, or a 3.0 in the last sixty hours. Along with their application, students must submit a personal essay, two letters of recommendation, and a current resume. Last year's entering class had an average GMAT score of 540 and an average undergraduate GPA of 2.98. International students must have a TOEFL score of 550 on the paper version or 213 on the computerized version.

FINANCIAL FACTS

Annual tuition (in-state/ out-of-state)	$3,983/$410
Fees	$1,024
Cost of books	$1,000
Room & board (on/off-campus)	$5,180/$5,590

ADMISSIONS

Admissions Selectivity Rating	83
# of applications received	38
% applicants accepted	53
% acceptees attending	80
Average GMAT	540
Range of GMAT	460–690
Average GPA	2.98
TOEFL required of international students	Yes
Minimum TOEFL (paper/computer)	550/213
Application fee	$25
International application fee	$50
Regular application deadline	7/15
Deferment available	Yes
Maximum length of deferment	3 years
Transfer students accepted	Yes
Transfer application policy: A maximum of 6 graduate hours is transferrable from a accredited institution.	
Non-fall admissions	Yes
Need-blind admissions	Yes

EMPLOYMENT PROFILE

Career Rating	65	Top 5 Employers Hiring Grads
		Acxiom, Hewlett Packard

UNIVERSITY OF CENTRAL FLORIDA
COLLEGE OF BUSINESS ADMINISTRATION

GENERAL INFORMATION

Type of school	Public
Affiliation	No Affiliation
Academic calendar	Semester

SURVEY SAYS...
Friendly students
Solid preparation in:
Accounting, General management, Quantitative skills, Entrepreneurial studies

STUDENTS

Enrollment of parent institution	59,785
Enrollment of MBA Program	558
% male/female	57/43
% out-of-state	3
% part-time	49
% underrepresented minority	30
% international	8
Average age at entry	26

ACADEMICS

Academic Experience Rating	**79**
Profs interesting rating	81
Profs accesible rating	80
Student/faculty ratio	49:1
% female faculty	17
% underrepresented minority faculty	28
% part-time faculty	0

Joint Degrees
MBA/Master of Sport Business Management (21 months)

Prominent Alumni
Karen L. Hackett, CEO American Academy of Orthopedic Surgeons; Dr. R Glenn Hubbard, Dean, Columbia Business School; Cathleen H. Nash, Direct:Presidnet and Chief Executive Officer of the Compnay and the Bank, Citizens Republic Bancorp,Inc.; Steve Felkowitz, Chairman & CEO, Atico International; Jim Atchison, SeaWorld Parks & Enterntainment President and CEO

Academics

University of Central Florida is known for its great administration, making it arguably the "best-managed MBA." "The tuition is more than fair" at this state school, and UCF enjoys a reputation as "a high-quality education for an affordable price." Some students even use "state employee tuition waivers" to bypass tuition entirely. The program offers a "wide variety of business school options," such as "executive MBA, professional MBA, and lockstep MBA." UCF "draws a predominantly local student body," although "that is changing with the growing reputation of the school's MBA." "UCF's rapid growth and development of attracting experienced teaching talent is an indicator the MBA program here is a good place to be," as is its "involvement with the local business community." Students do wish the school offered "more opportunities for study abroad." The school could give students more "flexibility in selecting core classes" and could offer "a more specialized curriculum offered for marketing, finance, and other fields. The current curriculum is very generalized." The school's "unique cohort program" makes students take classes together and "helps in creating social networks."

The school's administration is a key strength, and it does "a great job providing us with all necessary information and support." "The administration is supportive and accessible, and they ensure students get the assistance needed." Students love the "ease with which students can handle things online via automated administrative services." "If I have a question, they are the first I ask and always get an immediate response," says one student. "This is the best administration I have seen in my life." "School administration is mostly automated via online services . . . and that is greatly appreciated!" However, the administration could work more on "building facilities." In particular, "the downtown campus is small; some of us have had to use a UCF-run building at a local community college campus."

Students also enjoy the faculty and classes where each "discussion is interesting; you never know who'll throw in a gem from their prior experience or contacts." The professors are "full of industry experience and really know how to project importance to their students." That said, "the school's professors could do a little better in preparing for classes. At times, it just seems that the effort is not there." Overall, though, the "extremely knowledgeable" professors "make the best out of the class lectures, so that students do not have to waste time teaching themselves at home (given most students have full-time jobs)." Professors tend to have real-life experience, and "they share stories of their industry experience, which really helps us become more connected with real-life situations." Why are the teachers of such high quality? One student suggests that "the MBA program cherry-picks the best professors from among the large pool of teaching talent at UCF, which is now the second-largest university in the United States."

Career and Placement

The UCF administration "does a fantastic job of tying students to careers" and "preparing you to succeed after graduation." "They continue to look for the best fit for every one of their students," drawing on their "deep connections with the local corporate community" to help "students become future leaders in the business community surrounding Orlando."

ADMISSIONS CONTACT: JUDY RYDER, DIRECTOR OF GRADUATE ADMISSIONS
ADDRESS: 36 WEST PINE STREET, ORLANDO, FL 32801
PHONE: 407-235-3917
E-MAIL: CBAGRAD@BUS.UCF.EDU • WEBSITE: WWW.BUS.UCF.EDU

The mean base salary for new graduates is about $47,600, and about 85 percent of students have accepted a job by graduation. Some employers who have recruited out of UCF recently include Lockheed Martin, Convergys, Morgan Stanley Smith Barney, NAVAIR, and A+Tutor U.

Student Life and Environment

Students at UCF are "all aspiring, young business-oriented people, who are eagerly seeking opportunity in life." "Most are very young, right out of undergraduate," although there are still "some older, experienced students that are able to contribute to class discussion from their experiences rather than classroom theory." Students of any age "want to learn and push themselves and gain the most out of the MBA program." "Everyone in the cohort is very supportive of each other," and "they like to compete, but at the same time to support each other!" "We all get along and frequently participate in trips and activities outside of school together," one student says. "UCF MBA students are very diverse . . . students often speak more than one foreign language and are well-travelled."

"Campus activities are abundant" for students who are able to squeeze them into their busy schedules. "There is always something to do. The school has really started to build a strong foundation of diehard UCF fans" thanks to "a new stadium and arena and ranked football and basketball teams." However, for most MBA students, "the focus has been on coursework and not necessarily on school-life issues." Many students have "a full-time career," leaving them with "little interaction with the campus outside of class time." "UCF is mostly a commuter school; this is especially true of the MBA students who have lives (work, families, etc.) outside of academics," one student explains.

Admissions

Applicants to the UCF College of Business MBA program must submit an online application to the UCF School of Graduate Studies. Additionally, applicants must submit official transcripts for each university or college previously attended, an official GMAT score report, a personal essay, a current resume, and letters of recommendation. The average GMAT score and undergrad GPA for last year's class were 570 and 3.55, respectively.

FINANCIAL FACTS

Annual tuition (in-state/ out-of-state)	$8,448/$27,480
Cost of books	$2,000
Room & board (on/off-campus)	$8,500/$14,000
% of students receiving aid	52
Average award package	$31,961
Average grant	$5,750
Average loan	$21,904
Average student loan debt	$27,514

ADMISSIONS

Admissions Selectivity Rating	78
# of applications received	414
% applicants accepted	66
% acceptees attending	74
Average GMAT	548
Range of GMAT	510–580
Average GPA	3.40
TOEFL required of international students	Yes
Minimum TOEFL (paper/computer)	575/233
Application fee	$30
International application fee	$30
Early application deadline	1/15
Early notification date	4/15
Regular application deadline	7/15
Deferment available	No
Transfer students accepted	No
Transfer application policy: Transfer applicants must be from a regionally or nationally accredited university. May transfer in up to 9 hours.	
Non-fall admissions	No
Need-blind admissions	Yes

EMPLOYMENT PROFILE

Career Rating	78	Grads Employed by Function% Avg. Salary	
Percent employed at graduation	12	Marketing	(3%)
Percent employed 3 months after graduation	52	Operations	(12%)
		Management	(15%)
Average base starting salary	$51,667	Finance	(9%)
Primary Source of Full-time Job Acceptances		Other	(12%)
School-facilitated activities	4(24%)	Top 5 Employers Hiring Grads	
Graduate-facilitated activities	13(76%)	Lockheed Martin(2), Disney (2), Chrysler (2), Grant Thornton (2), PricewaterhouseCooper (1)	

THE UNIVERSITY OF CHICAGO
BOOTH SCHOOL OF BUSINESS

GENERAL INFORMATION

Type of school	Private
Affiliation	No Affiliation
Academic calendar	Quarter

SURVEY SAYS...

Students love Chicago, IL, Good peer network, Happy students, Smart classrooms
Solid preparation in:
Finance, Accounting, Quantitative Skills

STUDENTS

Enrollment of parent institution	15,626

ACADEMICS

Academic Experience Rating	**95**
Profs interesting rating	84
Profs accesible rating	88
% female faculty	16
% part-time faculty	20

Joint Degrees

MBA/MA Area Studies and Business; MBA/MA International Relations and Business; MBA/JD Law and Business; MBA/MD Medicine and Business; MBA/MPP Public Policy Studies and Business; MBA/MA Social Service Administration and Business

Prominent Alumni

Mary Tolan, CEO, Accretive Health; Robert W. Lane, Chairman and CEO, Deere & Company; Joseph Neubauer, Chairman and CEO, ARAMARK Corp.; Joe Mansueto, CEO/Founder, Morningstar; Brady Dougan, CEO Investment Banking, Credit Suisse

Academics

"The emphasis on [students] learning the basics rather than some predigested goo" along with "an unbeatable faculty" are "what make the University of Chicago's Booth School of Business one of the best, especially in hard-core areas such as finance and accounting," students tell us. A "rigorous quantitative program that compels students to think critically and analytically" is the hallmark of a Chicago Booth MBA, although students hasten to add that Booth also "emphasizes persuasion, communication, and negotiation skills."

Chicago Booth offers a full-time, part-time evening, part-time weekend, and executive MBA program. All four tracks share "top-notch" faculty, wide-ranging academic options, and an approach that "doesn't chase new trends in business but instead relies on teaching sound fundamentals that can then be applied to any situation." The programs differ in some details; full-time students, for example, enjoy a student-enacted grade nondisclosure policy that creates a conducive environment for "teamwork and sharing of ideas." Students must also complete the Leadership Exploration and Development (LEAD) program, which "provides analytic frameworks for leadership that are very helpful in determining the best way to use [one's] strengths and where to improve." Part-timers enjoy "great flexibility," noting that "most classes have several sessions taught by the same professor during the same quarter, enabling students to make up class sessions if for some reason they cannot attend their normal session." Booth's weekend MBA and Executive MBAs have "students flying to Chicago from across the U.S. and world to attend classes," which "connects a much broader and more diverse group of people than other MBA programs can."

Chicago Booth's faculty includes Nobel laureates and cutting-edge researchers "who also excel in the classroom." One accounting student reports, "Both my corporate tax strategy professor and my M&A accounting professor consult for corporate and government clients, so they have intimate knowledge of how to apply what they teach in the real world." Booth is best known for its faculty in finance, economics, and accounting, but students note that the school should work to "increase awareness of its excellence in marketing, entrepreneurship, and general management disciplines." Many students also "do a one-term or full-year exchange program at a foreign business school," and "These international career development opportunities are a big part of the experience for many Booth students."

Career and Placement

The Booth Career Services Office doesn't have to work hard; as one student explains, "The network and doors that open up to a graduate from Chicago Booth are outstanding. Gaining an MBA from this school carries a lot of weight and in the job market no one will question your education." That doesn't mean that Career Services slacks off, however; on the contrary, it "is an excellent resource and deserves praise," and does a good job attracting recruiters in consulting, accounting, and finance including McKinsey & Company, Citigroup, The Boston Consulting Group, UBS, A.T. Kearney, Credit Suisse, Goldman Sachs, Bank of America/Merrill Lynch, and Booz and Company.

Chicago Booth also excels at "preparing career changers. You learn from the best faculty in the world to attain the skills you need to succeed in your given career. The alumni, and especially second-year students at the school, are available to answer any questions. Career Services does an excellent job of helping you identify your transferable skills to your new targeted career. . . . I would highly recommend the school for people looking to change careers."

ADMISSIONS CONTACT: KURT AHLM, DIRECTOR OF ADMISSIONS
ADDRESS: 5807 SOUTH WOODLAWN AVENUE, CHICAGO, IL 60637
PHONE: 773-702-7369 • FAX: 773-702-9085
E-MAIL: ADMISSIONS@CHICAGOBOOTH.EDU • WEBSITE: CHICAGOBOOTH.EDU

Student Life and Environment

"The social aspect of University of Chicago is often overlooked," students in the full-time program tell us, reporting that "There are all kinds of opportunities to get together with other students in social or more formal settings, including school-sponsored happy hours, etc." Although "MBAs here work as hard as students at any other b-school, we know how to have fun too." One student writes, "If anything, there are too many programs and opportunities to be involved. You need to carefully consider them all to properly juggle [your] schedule." And with "the great city of Chicago is at our doorstep," students don't have to look far to find a wide range of fun diversions.

The school is located on Chicago's South Side in the Hyde Park neighborhood, which "is too often made out to be a scary place when, in fact, it's not. There is a pretty unique mixture of socioeconomic groups here, so you can drive by a building with three poor families living in it and four blocks later be at a stop sign next to a million-dollar (or more) home. The fact is that it's on the South Side of Chicago so people automatically say, 'bad, scary neighborhood.'" Part-time students attend classes at the Gleacher Center, "a beautiful building" in downtown Chicago, just off the Magnificent Mile. For students whose activities keep them in the Hyde Park area, Booth's Charles M. Harper Center boasts a "winter garden," a "dramatic foyer in the center of the building" where "People can catch up, do work, or just relax for a moment."

Admissions

Admission to the Chicago Booth School of Business is extremely competitive. Admissions Officers scrutinize a wide array of qualifications, including academic record (quality of curriculum, scholarships, special honors, etc.), work experience (quality as well as quantity), and overall "fit"(interpersonal skills, unique experiences, philanthropic activity). Applicants must provide the Admissions Office with transcripts for all postsecondary academic work, an official GMAT score report, letters of recommendation, personal essays, and TOEFL/IELTS scores (for international students only). Interviews are required for all candidates. Applicants to the full-time program interview on a "by invitation only" basis.

FINANCIAL FACTS	
Annual tuition	$50,900
Fees	$714
Cost of books	$2,100
Room & board	$18,900
Average student loan debt	$79,539

ADMISSIONS	
Admissions Selectivity Rating	94
TOEFL required of	
international students	Yes
Minimum TOEFL	
(paper/computer)	600/250
Application fee	$200
International application fee	$200
Early application deadline	10/12
Early notification date	12/14
Regular application deadline	4/25
Regular application notification	5/16
Deferment available	No
Transfer students accepted	No
Non-fall admissions	No
Need-blind admissions	Yes

EMPLOYMENT PROFILE			
Career Rating	83	Grads Employed by Function% Avg. Salary	
Percent employed at graduation	76	Marketing	(7%) $93,939
Percent employed 3 months		Consulting	(27%)$117,363
after graduation	13	Management	(14%) $102,260
Average base starting salary	$108,045	Finance	(49%) $105,939
Primary Source of Full-time Job Acceptances		Other	(2%) $133,000
School-facilitated activities	398(83%)	Top 5 Employers Hiring Grads	
Graduate-facilitated activities	82(17%)	McKinsey & Company, Inc.(24), The Boston Consulting Group (19), Barclays PLC (16), Bain & Company, Inc. (15), Citigroup Inc. (13)	

University of Cincinnati
Carl H. Lindner College of Business

GENERAL INFORMATION

Type of school	Public
Affiliation	No Affiliation
Academic calendar	Semester

SURVEY SAYS...

Smart classrooms
Solid preparation in:
Teamwork

STUDENTS

Enrollment of parent institution	41,970
Enrollment of MBA Program	261
% male/female	68/32
% out-of-state	6
% part-time	58
% underrepresented minority	14
% international	27
Average age at entry	26
Average years work experience at entry	4.0

ACADEMICS

Academic Experience Rating	73
Profs interesting rating	75
Profs accesible rating	75
Student/faculty ratio	4:1
% female faculty	34
% underrepresented minority faculty	16
% part-time faculty	58

Joint Degrees

MBA/JD; MBA/MA in Arts Administration; MBA/MD - 5 years; MBA/Nursing; MBA/MS in Accounting, Information Systems, Marketing or Business Finance, Analytics; MBA/MA degree in Applied Economics; MBA in Finance and Taxation.

Prominent Alumni

Paul Polman, CEO, Unilever; John F. Barrett, President & CEO, Western-Southern Life; Myron E. Ullman, III, CEO, JCPenney; Oscar Robertson, Hall of Famer, Voted one of the 50 Greatest Players in NBA History; Richard E. Thornburgh, Vice-Chairman, Credit Suisse First Boston

Academics

Part of the University of Cincinnati business behemoth, the Carl H. Lindner College of Business MBA Program is "equally flexible as it is respected," offering both a part-time (completed in as little as 18 months) and a full-time option (completed in as little as twelve months), with classes held at its Clifton Heights and Blue Ash campuses, as well as online. The "affordable" school will even waive foundational courses if a student has an undergraduate business degree. "I needed a program that could adapt to my unpredictable work schedule while still challenging me as well as being known beyond this region," says a student.

The program focuses "heavily on project-team based work and less on outdated traditional classroom instruction/testing." "[It] has challenged me to think out of the box and I have gained a great deal of respect for the school and its faculty in the past year," says a student. Professors are "loaded with experience" and a "passion to teach" and "can relate that knowledge in class." All classes are put online as podcasts, which "is great if you have to work late or are traveling," and the school also uses programs like Aplia and Connect to supplement lectures.

The school administration is "always looking to grow and adapt to the changing economy. They're focused on building for the future." "At the end of the day you can find good people who will help you get what you need," says one student. The school is "very accommodating" to working professional's schedules, and "encourages students to be creative and find creative ways to challenge ourselves and change our communities." "As an MBA student at UC, I feel like I am an important part of the program. My ideas are heard; I am connected with my fellow students and faculty," says a student. "I was very skeptical at first but now I've realized what a brilliant business school it really is, and how relevant the courses are," says another.

Career and Placement

Students do wish that the UC name were a little further out there, in terms of getting recruiters to come to campus. "UC's business college sometimes seems to be like a well-kept secret," says one. Still, the university does a decent job of accessing "a great network of companies to interact with students and provide career opportunities." The school is fortunate to be located in a city with several Fortune 500-headquartered companies, so "the learning and employment opportunities are great."

Top employers hiring graduates are Apex Supply Chain, Ernst & Young, Procter & Gamble, Honda, and General Electric.

ADMISSIONS CONTACT: JASON DICKMAN, ASSOCIATE DIRECTOR, ADMISSIONS
ADDRESS: CARL H. LINDNER HALL, SUITE 606, P.O. BOX 210020, CINCINNATI, OH 45221-0020
PHONE: 513-556-7024 • FAX: 513-558-7006
E-MAIL: GRADUATE@UC.EDU • WEBSITE: WWW.BUSINESS.UC.EDU/MBA

Student Life and Environment

"Parking is easy" and the "beautiful" campus is small enough that you "don't ever feel rushed," though the location is in "a somewhat rough area of Cincinnati." The MBA students are "instantly put into groups that we meet with outside of class, led by a faculty member," so all students are connected to one another, and "are willing to give you a hand if you have questions or help work together through a particular topic."

Many day students are coming directly from undergrad (or just after), while students in the evening classes "have a little more age and more experience in the field." There are many clubs to help students relieve stress and have fun on and off campus, regardless of age, and everyone "is always doing something" whether it's "going to the school's sports games, hanging out in the courtyard, [or] just having fun." A great deal of UC students are commuters, and quite a few also attended the university for undergrad.

Admissions

The Admissions Committee requests the following from candidates seeking admission: an official GMAT score report; personal essay; sealed copies of official transcripts for all post-secondary schools previously attended; and letters of recommendation. An interview is optional but is considered of great import if conducted. Both GMAT scores and GPA are very important to the committee. The average GPA is 3.4, while the average GMAT score is 565.

FINANCIAL FACTS

Annual tuition (in-state/ out-of-state)	$28,329/$35,445
Fees	$2,490
Cost of books	$4,500
Room & board (on/off-campus)	$17,500/$19,000
% of students receiving aid	88
% of first-year students receiving aid	88
% of students receiving grants	56
Average award package	$15,291
Average grant	$8,215
Average loan	$20,276
Average student loan debt	$24,766

ADMISSIONS

Admissions Selectivity Rating	72
# of applications received	141
% applicants accepted	92
% acceptees attending	62
Average GMAT	565
Range of GMAT	530–620
Average GPA	3.40
TOEFL required of international students	Yes
Minimum TOEFL (paper/computer)	600/250
Application fee	$65
International application fee	$70
Application Deadline/Notification	
Round 1:	1/1 / 2/1
Round 2:	3/15 / 4/15
Round 3:	8/1 / 8/15
Deferment available	Yes
Maximum length of deferment	1 year
Transfer students accepted	Yes
Transfer application policy:	
Transferring from an AACSB accredited institution, no more than 16 credit hours, must have 3.0 in transferred class	
Non-fall admissions	Yes
Need-blind admissions	Yes

EMPLOYMENT PROFILE

Career Rating	81	Grads Employed by Function	% Avg. Salary
Percent employed at graduation	69	Marketing	(18%) $43,666
Percent employed 3 months after graduation	73	Operations	(18%) $68,400
		Consulting	(6%) $61,000
Average base starting salary	$56,671	Management	(3%) $70,000
Primary Source of Full-time Job Acceptances		Finance	(24%) $56,500
School-facilitated activities	7(20%)	MIS	(15%) $72,000
Graduate-facilitated activities	5(15%)	Other	(18%)
Unknown	22(65%)	**Top 5 Employers Hiring Grads**	

Top 5 Employers Hiring Grads
Apex Supply Chain (3), Ernst & Young (1), Procter & Gamble (1), Honda (1), General Electric (1)

UNIVERSITY OF CONNECTICUT
SCHOOL OF BUSINESS

GENERAL INFORMATION
Type of school   Public
Affiliation   No Affiliation
Academic calendar   Semester

SURVEY SAYS...
Friendly students, Smart classrooms
Solid preparation in:
Finance, Accounting, Teamwork

STUDENTS
Enrollment of parent
  institution   30,256
Enrollment of MBA Program   1,185
% male/female   67/33
% out-of-state   18
% part-time   92
% underrepresented minority   12
% international   49
Average age at entry   29
Average years work experience
  at entry   5.6

ACADEMICS
Academic Experience Rating   **89**
Profs interesting rating   80
Profs accesible rating   85
Student/faculty ratio   13:1
% female faculty   22
% underrepresented minority
  faculty   3
% part-time faculty   31

Joint Degrees
MBA/JD; MBA/MD; MBA/MSW;
MBA/MA International Studies;
MBA/Master of International
Management; MBA/PharmD. 4
years.

Prominent Alumni
John Y. Kim '86 MBA, CIO &
Executive Management Committee
Member, New York Life Insurance
Company; Lauralee E. Martin '79
MBA, CEO, Americas, Jones Lang
LaSalle Inc.; Denis J. Nayden '78
MBA, Managing Partner, Oak Hill
Capital Management; William S.
Simon Jr. '88 MBA, President &
CEO, Walmart US

Academics

A great place to develop real-world credentials, the University of Connecticut's MBA program teaches business fundamentals while maximizing students' access to practical learning experiences. UConn's full-time MBA curriculum was recently redesigned to give students a highly personalized MBA experience, while drawing on the program's traditional strengths. UConn is "highly-regarded in the areas of finance and risk analytics," but the first-year core covers all functional areas of business in an integrated fashion. In the second year, students develop an individualized plan of study, taking a range of classes within business concentrations like finance, marketing, or real estate, among others. In addition to an active internship program, "UConn's MBA program [is] unique in that it offers numerous experiential learning accelerators," which are practice-based programs, often operated in conjunction with a corporate partner. While first-year full-time MBA classes are held in Storrs, second-year courses are offered in Hartford, Stamford and Waterbury, so they can easily coordinate with the experiential learning centers. Examples of accelerator programs include: innovation, a student managed investment fund, and a Sustainable Community Outreach and Public Engagement program. A current student elaborates, "I've been able to complete three semester-long consulting projects for real companies and non-profits, and have participated in two study abroad programs." In addition to the full-time program, working professionals can complete the MBA part-time program in Waterbury, Hartford, or Stamford.

A relatively small program, the full-time MBA "intimate class size" makes it easier for UConn students to build relationships with both their teachers and classmates. With roughly 60–70 students in each full-time class, "Being part of this small cohort allows for personal attention and focused learning." In general, professors are "receptive to any type of question" in class, and many are "extremely motivated and genuinely interested in the academic success of their students." However, students admit that when it comes to teaching style, "professors run a wide gamut," including some highly-skilled instructors, and some professors who seem more focused on their own projects.

For Connecticut residents, "the price of attending a state school was more reasonable" than attending a similar, private institution. On the downside, "The effects of state budget cuts can be seen throughout UConn as a whole, as well as the business school." Currently, "UConn is undergoing a great deal of change under the leadership of a new Dean," and there have been some bumps in the road as the program changes course. However, optimistic students observe, "The dean and the MBA director are very responsive to students' concerns, and changes have been made and continue to be made to improve the value of the school."

Career and Placement

While UConn enjoys great "local brand recognition" and "very good connections in the state of Connecticut," many students are disappointed with their school's career center. Drawing the majority of its business contacts from the immediate region, many feel that the "career center perhaps needs to widen its focus," and try "digging deeper into Wall Street or Boston" to make contact with more recruiters. On the flipside, a current student counters, "I have had interviews with Covidien, Pitney Bowes, General Electric, and Travelers Insurance, and I know UConn has a strong presence when I see that I am competing in the second round interviews with students from Yale and Cornell."

ADMISSIONS CONTACT: MICHAEL DEOTTE, DIRECTOR
ADDRESS: 2100 HILLSIDE ROAD UNIT 1041, STORRS, CT 06269-1041
PHONE: 860-486-2872 • FAX: 860-486-5222
E-MAIL: UCONNMBA@BUSINESS.UCONN.EDU • WEBSITE: WWW.BUSINESS.UCONN.EDU

In a recent year, 58 percent of UConn graduates were working, negotiating a job offer, or pursuing further study within three months of graduation. By six months, that number had jumped to 71 percent of students. The mean salary for recent UConn grads was $95,120 in the previous year, with a high of $120,000. Companies hiring UConn graduates include AC Nielsen, Aetna, Atlantic Records, Barclays, CIGNA, Citigroup, CVS Caremark, Deloitte Consulting, ESPN, General Electric, Hasbro Hewitt, Hubbell, Inc, IBM, ING, Liberty Mutual, Nestle, Nasdaq, PepsiCo, Pitney Bowes, Prudential Financial, Siemens, Sun Products Corporation, Travelers, Webster Bank, and XL Global Insurance.

Student Life and Environment

On University of Connecticut's Storrs campus, "The School of Business is new and modern with all the requisite amenities," including an MBA lounge, comfortable classrooms, and lockers. While "dining hall food is unimpressive," "the Student Union is newer," boasting a larger food court with better options. Attracting a "diverse group from all over the world," almost 40 percent of University of Connecticut's full-time MBA candidates are international. A collaborative cohort environment, "team activities are an integrated part of our school culture," and students are generally "smart, cheerful, [and] enthusiastic."

For first-year students, "School days are treated similar to a nine to five job," with class in the morning and homework to complete in the evening. Within this small program, everyone knows everyone, and students "typically socialize with the entire MBA class in-between classes." On campus, "mixers with students are fairly regular" and "some people are very motivated and active in clubs and networking events." However, "the full-time MBA is comprised of mostly commuter students, so we do not generally stay on campus when we are not in class." Plus, the school's campus in Storrs is "out in the middle of nowhere"—affording a great view of the New England woods, but limiting the scope of extracurricular and recreational activities in the immediate vicinity. On that note, prospective students "should keep in mind that a car is all but required to participate in local internships over the summer."

Admissions

To be considered for UConn's MBA program, students must have at least two years of professional work experience, strong GMAT scores (usually between 580 and 660), and a solid undergraduate academic record. In recent years, the UConn incoming class had an average undergraduate GPA of 3.5 and an average GMAT score of 630. Full-time students had an average of five and a half years in the work force, while part-time students had eight years of professional experience.

FINANCIAL FACTS

Annual tuition (in-state/ out-of-state)	$10,782/$27,990
Fees	$2,084
Cost of books	$4,000
Room & board (on/off-campus)	$12,534/$13,500
% of students receiving aid	82
% of first-year students receiving aid	60
% of students receiving grants	42
Average award package	$30,624
Average grant	$16,802
Average loan	$22,000
Average student loan debt	$20,040

ADMISSIONS

Admissions Selectivity Rating	87
# of applications received	164
% applicants accepted	49
% acceptees attending	49
Average GMAT	654
Range of GMAT	630–690
Average GPA	3.48
TOEFL required of international students	Yes
Minimum TOEFL (paper/computer)	575/233
Application fee	$75
International application fee	$75
Regular application deadline	3/1
Deferment available	Yes
Maximum length of deferment	12 months
Transfer students accepted	No
Non-fall admissions	No
Need-blind admissions	Yes

EMPLOYMENT PROFILE

Career Rating	91	Grads Employed by Function	% Avg. Salary
Percent employed at graduation	63	Marketing	(16%) $70,000
Percent employed 3 months after graduation	90	Operations	(16%) $73,500
		Consulting	(24%)$86,667
Average base starting salary	$77,536	Management	(3%) $100,000
Primary Source of Full-time Job Acceptances		Finance	(32%) $83,700
School-facilitated activities	16(46%)	HR	(6%) $70,500
Graduate-facilitated activities	18(51%)	Other	(3%)
Unknown	1(3%)	**Top 5 Employers Hiring Grads**	
		The Hartford (3), Henkel (2), Booz Allen Hamilton (1), GE Capital (1), PricewaterhouseCoopers (1)	

UNIVERSITY OF DAYTON
SCHOOL OF BUSINESS ADMINISTRATION

GENERAL INFORMATION
Type of school   Private
Affiliation   Roman Catholic
Academic calendar   Semester

SURVEY SAYS...
Cutting-edge classes, Happy students, Smart classrooms
Solid preparation in:
Teamwork

STUDENTS
Enrollment of parent
institution   11,214
Enrollment of MBA Program   450
% male/female   62/38
% part-time   67
% underrepresented minority   10
% international   35
Average age at entry   27
Average years work experience
at entry   5.0

ACADEMICS
Academic Experience Rating   78
Profs interesting rating   81
Profs accesible rating   86
Student/faculty ratio   7:1
% female faculty   20
% underrepresented minority
faculty   5
% part-time faculty   8

Joint Degrees
Joint Juris of Doctor of Law (JD)
and Master of Business
Administration (MBA) 3-4 years
(combined JD and MBA degrees)

Prominent Alumni
Keith Hawk, Vice President, Lexis-Nexis; Phil Parker, President & CEO, Dayton Area Cham. of Commerce; Mike Turner, US Congressman, OH; Linda Berning, Berning Investments

Academics

Students tell us that UD's integrated curriculum "is one of...the program's biggest strengths. It is unlike what any school in the region is offering, and it results in a more thorough educational experience." The school's program typically include an emphasis on "new management techniques. The Toyota Way and Lean Manufacturing are very popular" here. Students also boast of UD's "Marianist identity and values, which leads to a great sense of family. Students, staff and faculty are really close to one another. People help each other a lot." As one MBA explains, "If I get a B, someone is asking me what they can do to help. If I get an A, someone is asking me if I can help them, and I always agree. We're a team, no doubt."

One student reports that he is "really impressed by all the opportunities UD provides its students with outside classes. Its entrepreneurship program is supported by out-of-class valuable experiences. For example, the Business Plan Competition...offers us the possibility to create a real business plan and to receive funds to implement it. I also heard finance students telling me that they can't believe that they are allowed to manage millions of dollars on behalf of UD at the Davis Center. I really like being able to turn my theoretical knowledge into practical experience at UD, because now, I feel more confident that I will be able to apply what I learned to real-life situations."

The University provides students with numerous chances to broaden their business resumes. One student reports that he is "really impressed by all the opportunities UD provides its students with outside classes.... For example, the Business Plan Competition offers...us the possibility to create a real business plan and to receive funds to implement it...I really like being able to turn my theoretical knowledge into practical experience at UD, because now, I feel more confident that I will be able to apply what I learned to real-life situation."

UD also offers a very popular five-year bachelor's in Accounting/MBA program in which University of Dayton undergraduates are "able to achieve 150 hours for the CPA exam and get an MBA degree." The school's "administration is good and getting better" and "cares about what the students think," professors are "passionate and well-prepared leaders who are engaging and challenging," and students enjoy "many opportunities to gain experience in your particular field, whether with student organizations, access to alumni, or career/academic development programs and workshops." With all that going for the school, it's no wonder students tell us that "UD's MBA program is probably one of the best-kept secrets in Ohio."

Career and Placement

MBAs at the University of Dayton are served by the Career Services Office, which assists undergraduates, graduates, and alumni in their development and placement needs. The office provides graduate students with the following services: career advisement; job search and résumé critiquing workshops, career fairs, online résumé referral, on-campus recruiting events, mock-interviews, and contact with the alumni career network. Students tell us that the school "has an excellent reputation and a great relationship with local/regional employers." Top employers of U Dayton MBAs include Wright Patterson Air Force Base, Emerson Climate Technologies, Fifth Third Bank, Reynolds & Reynolds, and LexisNexis. Other employers include AK Steel, AT&T, Greene Memorial Hospital, Honda, IBM, Kettering Medical Center, and Premier Health Partners.

ADMISSIONS CONTACT: JANICE GLYNN, DIRECTOR MBA PROGRAM
ADDRESS: 300 COLLEGE PARK AVENUE, DAYTON, OH 45469-2234
PHONE: 937-229-3733 • FAX: 937-229-3882
E-MAIL: MBA@UDAYTON.EDU • WEBSITE: BUSINESS.UDAYTON.EDU/MBA

Student Life and Environment

Students brag that UD is a collegial campus, the sort of place where "every time you pass someone, whether that be a student, professor, or even the custodial staff, a pleasant 'Hello, how is your day?' is exchanged. This allows for a comfort in the classroom that, in turn, allows for education beyond the text to flourish." This open dialogue is equally available to international students; writes one from France, "UD is reputed for taking care of its international students. I knew before my arrival here that faculty and staff would be very accessible and helpful, and that I would be individually recognized by them."

SBA accommodates "a lot of MBA social events and opportunities as well as seminars for career and professional skill development," while the university at large offers "plenty of activities organized by the students and university-sponsored events that give the students plenty of options to take a break and get away from school work for a while."

While "there is an overwhelming majority of Caucasian students" here, there are also "students from France, Germany, China, and various racial minorities as well. Age covers the vast spectrum from recent graduate to retired. Non-traditional students mix well with young professionals."

Admissions

All applications to the University of Dayton MBA program must include official transcripts for all postsecondary academic work, a completed application, and an official GMAT score report; the GMAT entrance requirement may be delayed for students with strong academic records, allowing them to enroll conditionally for one semester before submitting GMAT scores. A cover letter, current resume, and letters of recommendation from employers or professors are recommended but not required. International applicants must meet all of the above requirements and must also provide a translation of any non-English language transcripts and official scores for the TOEFL (minimum score of 550 paper exam, 213 computer exam, or 80 Internet-based exam required for unconditional admission. Alternatively, international students may submit an IELTS score of 6.5 or higher in lieu of the TOEFL requirement.

FINANCIAL FACTS

Annual tuition	$19,032
Fees	$75
Cost of books	$700
% of students receiving aid	50
% of students receiving grants	20
Average grant	$1,000

ADMISSIONS

Admissions Selectivity Rating	74
# of applications received	336
% applicants accepted	80
% acceptees attending	80
Average GMAT	550
Range of GMAT	500–580
Average GPA	3.22
TOEFL required of international students	Yes
Minimum TOEFL (paper/computer)	550/213
Application fee	$0
International application fee	$50
Deferment available	Yes
Maximum length of deferment	1 year
Transfer students accepted	Yes
Transfer application policy: Students may request up to 6 Semester hours of approved graduate transfer credit of course work of "B" or better graded quality completed in acceptable time frame.	
Non-fall admissions	Yes
Need-blind admissions	Yes

EMPLOYMENT PROFILE		
Career Rating	72	**Top 5 Employers Hiring Grads**
		Wright Patterson Air Force Base, Emerson Climate Technologies, Fifth Third Bank, Reynolds & Reynolds, LexisNexis

UNIVERSITY OF DENVER
DANIELS COLLEGE OF BUSINESS

Academics

The University of Denver's Daniels College of Business combines its focus on "values-based leadership," "sustainability," globalization, and "ethics," with its "strong reputation" and extensive "business network within the Denver community." The result is a well-balanced program which builds a community of "sharp, young professionals" who enjoy the school's status as "the best in the region."

As a private institution, students say "networking is better and class sizes are smaller." In addition to attracting a large number of students who hail from abroad, the school offers high-achieving undergraduates the opportunity to pursue their MBA in only one extra year of course work. Thus, the student body at Daniels College of Business tends to be divided between younger faces fresh out of their undergraduate studies and those working professionals looking to pursue an advanced degree in their field through the Daniels part-time Professional MBA program. One student characterizes the population thusly, "the [average] age range is 23–32 years old. Most have or are working for Fortune 1000 companies. The type of experience is diverse, ranging from Finance to Engineering to Medicine. All are in a similar situation of balancing work, school, and family." A Professional MBA adds, the "part-time program lets me work full-time while in school, so my career isn't put on pause."

Overall, the professors at the Daniels College of Business "are very knowledgeable in their areas." Many professors and staff "are world-class, with incredible business knowledge and experience outside of academia, as well as within academia." Although "some of the lectures may not be entirely interesting and difficult to stay focused on, it is easy to see the teachers really do enjoy their profession and want to see their students excel." Others say, "some of the professors are subpar;" however, as at any MBA program, it's all about seeking out leaders in your field as "many of [the professors] are excellent" and are quick to provide "mentoring opportunities." In addition, "the tenured faculty tends to be quite good."

The administration here is generally viewed as "average." Students say the top brass sets their sights high and "tries to empower their students to achieve big goals while supporting their communities, but they do very little to support their students to achieve this success...corporation/partnership with the school is very limited." However, the school has made some notable improvements in this area, investing in a new Corporate and Community Relations Program, through which they've signed on 80 companies as annual partners.

Career and Placement

With the school's focus on "networking, business plan deliverables, and connections with [the] Denver community," students here enjoy a competitive edge within the local business sector. In addition, Daniels has "a fabulous executive mentor program" and "one-of-a-kind class consulting opportunities with major companies like Newmont Mining and Deutsche Bank with an international component that includes projects in sustainability and social entrepreneurship."

Some students report that the "Career Center is not very helpful." The Center could "bring in more companies for career fairs [and] improve its offerings for people interested in entrepreneurship." Says one student, "Graduate recruitment is mostly focused on finance/accounting concentrations. If you are not interested in those areas, you really have to look outside of the companies that come to recruit." In 2011, 45 percent of full-time MBA graduates seeking employment had received a job offer prior to

ADMISSIONS CONTACT: DAVID COX, ASSISTANT DEAN FOR FULL TIME GRADUATE PROGRAMS
ADDRESS: 2101 S. UNIVERSITY BLVD. #255, RIFKIN CENTER FOR STUDENT SERVICES, DENVER, CO 80208
PHONE: 303-871-3416 • FAX: 303-871-4466
E-MAIL: DANIELS@DU.EDU • WEBSITE: WWW.DANIELS.DU.EDU

graduation with a mean base salary of $63,000. Consumer products, financial services, technology, and government were industries with strong draws with approximately 15 to 18 percent of the graduating class matriculating into these fields.

Student Life and Environment

Students at University of Denver Daniels College of Business "are highly-motivated, intelligent, fun people who are very diverse." This leads to "an energized environment and creates an atmosphere that is inspiring." When it comes to their academic camaraderie, students are "competitive in that we like to challenge each other. There is a high bar set, and everyone works to help each other." However, "they are also great friends."

Set at the foot of the Rocky Mountains, hometown Denver offers ample recreation and outdoor activities. This tends to attract students who are "physically active, outdoors-oriented, laid-back, interested in social and environmental responsibility, ethical and conscientious, caring and accepting." The atmosphere "is one of fun and appreciation for a good work/life balance (outdoor activities, skiing, mountain biking, etc) with [a] focus on new ideas, innovation, [and] sustainability, all within the framework of values-based leadership." In addition, the school hosts bimonthly happy hours, many of which are hosted by local companies. This is a good thing as many students here might be characterized as "bright people with a passion for business and a thirst for beer."

Admissions

Daniels seeks out students who embody its mission statement of ethical practice, thought leadership, and global impact. Admission is selective and officials consider each student's whole package including the candidate's personal, professional, and intellectual background. In 2011, the matriculating class had an average undergraduate GPA of 3.89 and an average GMAT of 602. Work experience is required for the professional MBA and executive MBA programs. The admission interview is an integral part of the Daniels selection process. Interviews are offered on an invitation only basis for the full-time program and required for the part-time and Executive MBA programs.

FINANCIAL FACTS

Annual tuition	$42,480
Fees	$785
Cost of books	$1,925
Room & board (on/off-campus)	$10,665
% of students receiving aid	75
% of first-year students receiving aid	79
% of students receiving grants	53
Average award package	$11,446
Average grant	$6,235
Average loan	$15,079

ADMISSIONS

Admissions Selectivity Rating	74
# of applications received	404
% applicants accepted	79
% acceptees attending	45
Average GMAT	599
Range of GMAT	550–660
Average GPA	3.19
TOEFL required of international students	Yes
Minimum TOEFL (paper/computer)	570/230
Application fee	$100
International application fee	$100
Early application deadline	11/15
Early notification date	12/15
Regular application deadline	3/15
Regular application notification	5/1
Application Deadline/Notification	
Round 1:	11/15 / 12/15
Round 2:	1/15 / 2/15
Round 3:	3/15 / 4/15
Round 4:	5/15 / 6/15
Deferment available	Yes
Maximum length of deferment	1 year
Transfer students accepted	Yes
Transfer application policy: 8 quarter hours (6 Semester hours) toward electives	
Non-fall admissions	Yes
Need-blind admissions	Yes

EMPLOYMENT PROFILE

Career Rating	88	**Grads Employed by Function% Avg. Salary**	
Percent employed at graduation	41	Marketing	(24%) $55,375
Percent employed 3 months after graduation	69	Operations	(6%)
		Consulting	(12%) $56,250
Average base starting salary	$61,609	Management	(9%)
Primary Source of Full-time Job Acceptances		Finance	(38%) $69,318
School-facilitated activities	27(73%)	MIS	(3%)
Graduate-facilitated activities	9(24%)	Other	(9%)
Unknown	1(3%)	**Top 5 Employers Hiring Grads**	

Top 5 Employers Hiring Grads
Panorama Consulting Solutions (3), Newmont Mining (2), Dish Network (2), Marsico Capital Management (1), Zayo Group (1)

UNIVERSITY OF FLORIDA
HOUGH GRADUATE SCHOOL OF BUSINESS

GENERAL INFORMATION

Type of school	Public
Affiliation	No Affiliation
Academic calendar	Semester

SURVEY SAYS...

Good social scene, Good peer network
Solid preparation in:
Marketing, Communication/interpersonal skills

STUDENTS

Enrollment of parent institution	49,589
Enrollment of MBA Program	876
% male/female	69/31
% out-of-state	34
% part-time	87
% underrepresented minority	18
% international	23
Average age at entry	28
Average years work experience at entry	4.9

ACADEMICS

Academic Experience Rating	95
Profs interesting rating	92
Profs accesible rating	86
Student/faculty ratio	10:1
% female faculty	19
% underrepresented minority faculty	11
% part-time faculty	2

Joint Degrees

MBA/JD (4 years); MBA/MS in Medical Sciences, Biotechnology; MBA/Ph.D in Medical Sciences, Biotechnology; MBA/B.S. in Industrial and Systems Engineering; MBA/Doctor of Pharmacy; MBA/PhD in Medical Sciences; MBA/MD; MBA/Master of Exercise and Sport Science (3 years)

Academics

No matter what your educational background, professional experience, or career goals, you're likely to find a fit at the University of Florida. This large university caters to a diverse student body, offering a slew of MBA and master's programs for business mavens at every stage of their professional development. Among the school's three full-time MBAs, there are two one-year programs and a traditional two-year program. The school also offers a professional MBA for working students and an executive MBA for advanced professionals. In both "convenient" part-time programs, students come to campus one weekend each month, and "Assignments are turned in electronically during the intervening month between classes." In addition to its campus-based programs, University of Florida offers one of the top-ranked distance MBAs in the country.

Across programs, the curriculum is well-balanced, designed to "teach students about fundamentals, as well as real-world applications of course materials." Emphasizing creative thinking, "The experience does not only provide students with skills; it expands their minds enormously and teaches the critical thinking and insightful and thoughtful analysis required of business leaders." Lessons are further augmented by the MBA executive speaker series, alumni mentoring programs, and ample group work outside the classroom. Within the full-time program, "Teamwork is a must, and we change up the teams so you work with different people which has been great to really meet new people."

Professors come in every flavor, from those who are "very current on events and management issues" to those who are "very quantitative and have you learn financial formulas." What they share is excellence. At this top-ranked business school, "The professors are not only accomplished, but are very good at relaying the required material in interesting and meaningful ways." At the same time, the curriculum is very challenging. Here, "academic expectations are intense" and, even for high-achieving students, "A's are definitely hard-earned." A satisfied student declares, "I have never felt so uncomfortable and out of league in my life. And, isn't that the point? An MBA should be difficult and enriching."

Despite the scope of the graduate programs, the school runs smoothly and students are amply supported. To the delight of many, administrative staffers "assist with all enrollment issues, tuition, and course arrangements for working professional students." A current student explains, "When we arrive in Gainesville for the first day of a new semester, our books and meal vouchers are waiting for us." While excellence and ease are the program's greatest strengths, the icing on the cake is the school's great value: "Scholarships combined with small class sizes and the resources of one of the nation's great research universities have combined to make the UF MBA the best value in the nation."

Career and Placement

The Graduate Business Career Services (GBCS) works exclusively with MBA candidates, helping them prepare for a career through individualized counseling, mock interviews, an active on-campus recruiting program, and corporate site visits. Career counselors also send out a bi-weekly email update with job listings, and maintain a database of alumni who are willing to serve as job contacts and advise current students. For part-time students who receive tuition assistance from their employers, Career Services are provided by an outside career consulting company; however, to avoid ethical conflicts, their participation in recruiting programs is limited. All MBA candidates may also use the school's university-wide Career Resource Center.

University of Florida has a "very strong alumni network," which is an enormous asset to professional students, as well as those looking to start a new career. UF alumni are represented at a wide range of companies, including AIG, Allstate, AOL, Bank of America, Ashland Chemical, Bell South, Blue Cross Blue Shield, Citicorp, Delta Airlines, Deloitte, Ericsson, EDS, Ernst & Young, FedEx, General Electric, Morgan Stanley, Nissan, Motorola, Proctor & Gamble, Siemens, Time Warner, Wachovia, Walt Disney World, Wells Fargo, and many more.

Student Life and Environment

Gator pride is alive and well at the University of Florida. On this lively campus, the student experience is "very reminiscent of undergraduate studies many years ago, despite everyone being older, more professional, and focused on academics now." "Social life is vibrant," there are numerous clubs and activities, and Gator sports are a huge draw. In the part-time programs (which meet on campus once a month), most students don't live within driving distance. However, almost everyone "stays overnight near campus on the weekends we attend class," and, during that time, "Everyone tends to eat together, attend basketball games together, party together, study together, etc."

In and around the business school, "Facilities are convenient, with food and coffee shops everywhere." Of particular note, "The library system is ample and well-integrated, and the newer libraries are great places to study or meet for group meetings." In addition, there are "excellent gym facilities" and plenty of "opportunities for activities such as intramural sports, museum/library lectures, and the arts." A medium-sized city, Gainesville is a "cozy college town" boasting a "'low cost-of-living" and plenty of recreational activities. And, don't forget, it's Florida, so the "weather is fantastic."

Admissions

The first step in the admissions process is to decide which of the many Florida MBA programs is the right fit for you and your career goals. You can only apply to one MBA program at a time; however, after reviewing an application, the admissions staff may recommend a student for another MBA program. For traditional full-time students, the average GMAT score is about 670. In the executive, online, and professional programs, the average GMAT score for entering students is about 600. All UF MBA programs admit students on a rolling basis.

Prominent Alumni
Mr. James M. Heaney, CFO, SeaWorld Parks and Entertainment, MBA 1988; Ms. Valerie Insignares, Senior Vice President, Chief Restaurant Operations Officer, Darden Restaurants, Inc., MBA 1999

FINANCIAL FACTS
Annual tuition (in-state/ out-of-state)	$11,954/$29,347
Fees	$500
Cost of books	$1,440
Room & board	$10,240
% of students receiving aid	85
% of first-year students receiving aid	86
% of students receiving grants	67
Average award package	$23,915
Average grant	$9,864
Average loan	$28,452
Average student loan debt	$14,191

ADMISSIONS
Admissions Selectivity Rating	96
# of applications received	217
% applicants accepted	24
% acceptees attending	40
Average GMAT	677
Range of GMAT	650–700
Average GPA	3.50
TOEFL required of international students	Yes
Minimum TOEFL (paper/computer)	600/250
Application fee	$30
International application fee	$30
Early application deadline	12/1
Regular application deadline	2/15
Deferment available	Yes
Maximum length of deferment	1 Year
Transfer students accepted	No
Non-fall admissions	Yes
Need-blind admissions	Yes

EMPLOYMENT PROFILE

Career Rating	92	**Grads Employed by Function% Avg. Salary**	
Percent employed at graduation	50	Marketing	(15%) $76,875
Percent employed 3 months after graduation	81	Operations	(8%) $69,750
		Consulting	(12%) $78,833
Average base starting salary	$73,975	Management	(6%) $57,333
Primary Source of Full-time Job Acceptances		Finance	(40%) $70,779
School-facilitated activities	33(52%)	HR	(2%)
Graduate-facilitated activities	27(43%)	MIS	(6%) $78,767
Unknown	3(5%)	Other	(12%) $75,000

Top 5 Employers Hiring Grads
Burger King Corporation (7), LNR Property, Inc. (5), CSX (3), ExxonMobil (2), Johnson & Johnson (2)

UNIVERSITY OF GEORGIA
TERRY COLLEGE OF BUSINESS

GENERAL INFORMATION
Type of school   Public
Affiliation   No Affiliation

SURVEY SAYS...
Students love Athens, GA, Good
social scene, Happy students, Smart
classrooms
Solid preparation in:
Operations

STUDENTS
Enrollment of parent institution	34,475
Enrollment of MBA Program	93
% male/female	72/28
% out-of-state	33
% underrepresented minority	12
% international	18
Average age at entry	28
Average years work experience at entry	3.8

ACADEMICS
Academic Experience Rating	**92**
Profs interesting rating	84
Profs accesible rating	83
Student/faculty ratio	1:1
% female faculty	28
% underrepresented minority faculty	17

Joint Degrees
JD/MBA, 4 years

Prominent Alumni
Daniel P. Amos, Chairman & CEO
of Aflac Incorporated; James W.
Barge, Executive Vice President &
CFO of Viacom Inc.; A.D. "Pete"
Correll, Chairman of Atlanta Equity
Investors, LLC; Retired as Chairman
and CEO of Georgia-Pacific
Corporation; Virginia C. Drosos,
Retired as Group President, Global
Beauty, Skin, Cosmetics and
Personal Care with Procter &
Gamble; M. Dougas Ivester,
President, Deer Run Investments
LLC; Retired Chairman of the Board
and CEO of The Coca-Cola Company

Academics

Located in beautiful Athens, Georgia, the Terry College of Business's "world class" MBA program offers a little bit of everything: a "strong alumni base," "phenomenal town, Southern charm, [low] cost of living, affordable tuition, and proximity to Atlanta." This "small program" allows for small class sizes and "provides better interaction with faculty" than many other MBA programs. That does not mean that there are not a "vast number of courses available to pick from." "I also liked its focus on leadership and the fact that Terry requires volunteer hours to graduate," one student says. There are "many scholarships and assistantships offered" for students who qualify. UGA is a merit "school that was focused on building well-rounded business leaders (plenty of field trips, business dinners, and golf outings.)" Explaining their decision to attend, one student says: "As a career changer, I was drawn to the fact UGA has an extremely dedicated career services team, a strong alumni network, and a great reputation with companies."

Perhaps due to its small size, the Terry College of Business has a "very personable administrative staff" and "down-to-earth admissions." "The commitment of the administration to improve and partner with the students is phenomenal," and both the administration and faculty are "very accessible." The small size of the program "offers absolute accessibility to any class and professor." The "knowledgeable and passionate" professors "are leaders in their field." "They teach skills that will be extremely useful in a work setting, and they utilize real-world business cases to prepare us for management roles." As with anything, "you can work as little or as much as you want, but at the end of the day you get out of it what you put into it." "The doors always seem to be open" at UGA, and the professors "encourage you to reach out to them with questions outside of class."

Career and Placement

Placement for UGA students is helped by the fact "that all the professors have had extensive real business experience beyond academia" and that the "MBA Director and admissions staff are excellent." "The career center does everything in their power to help you land a job," although "our career management center staff could provide students with a more well-rounded and customized career search." There are some issues with placement, such as the "small number of companies that recruit on campus," but that is directly related to "the program's small size." The most recent graduating class found an average mean base salary of about $81,000. Nearly 64 percent earned placement in the Southern region of the United States.

ADMISSIONS CONTACT: KERRY TERRELL, DIRECTOR, FULL-TIME MBA ADMISSIONS
ADDRESS: 358 BROOKS HALL, ATHENS, GA 30602-6264
PHONE: 706-542-5671 • FAX: 706-583-8277
E-MAIL: TERRYMBA@TERRY.UGA.EDU • WEBSITE: WWW.TERRY.UGA.EDU

Student Life and Environment

Students love Athens, declaring "this town is great!" "There is plenty to do" in town such as "live music, outdoor activities, intramural sports, good people, [and] great city events." In addition, this "great college town" is "nearby Atlanta." "We're close to a big city, yet far enough away to have a small town feel," one student explains.

The typical MBA student is "energetic, supportive, friendly, [and] ambitious," and students "have a diverse set of backgrounds and future ambitions." Although one student cautions that the student body is "not very diverse in the sense of ethnicity/Race." The students here "have personalities as well as brains," although at times they can be "fiercely competitive." "My fellow students roll up their sleeves without hesitation but are still willing to kick back when the work is done," one student says. While "the workload is demanding" students still are "left with enough time to get to know each other, and the town, outside of the academic setting." "We have a focus on academic work during the week and enjoy our weekends, especially during football season," a Financial student states. Students "all have fun together" and develop a "strong identity" as proud Bulldogs.

Admissions

UGA's strong reputation and small size—forty four students were enrolled last year—make it competitive to get into. The 2012 class had an average GPA of over 3.2 and an average GMAT of 637. The school looks most closely at applicants GPA, GRE or GMAT scores, work experience and interview. Because interpersonal skills are highly important to the program, a personal interview with admissions staff is mandatory prior to acceptance.

FINANCIAL FACTS

Annual tuition (in-state/ out-of-state)	$11,916/$29,626
Fees	$2,196
Cost of books	$1,800
Room & board	$14,700
% of students receiving aid	100
% of first-year students receiving aid	100
% of students receiving grants	35
Average award package	$28,544
Average grant	$6,149
Average loan	$21,645
Average student loan debt	$12,625

ADMISSIONS

Admissions Selectivity Rating	89
# of applications received	186
% applicants accepted	39
% acceptees attending	60
Average GMAT	637
Range of GMAT	590–680
Average GPA	3.21
TOEFL required of international students	Yes
Minimum TOEFL (paper/computer)	600/250
Application fee	$100
International application fee	$100
Application Deadline/Notification	
Round 1:	10/15 / 12/3
Round 2:	12/3 / 1/15
Round 3:	1/15 / 3/14
Round 4:	3/4 / 5/2
Deferment available	Yes
Maximum length of deferment	1 year
Transfer students accepted	No
Non-fall admissions	No
Need-blind admissions	Yes

EMPLOYMENT PROFILE

Career Rating	94	Grads Employed by Function% Avg. Salary	
Percent employed at graduation	66	Marketing	(27%) $76,424
Percent employed 3 months after graduation	87	Operations	(21%) $68,831
		Consulting	(9%) $90,000
Average base starting salary	$81,163	Management	(3%)
Primary Source of Full-time Job Acceptances		Finance	(30%) $96,667
School-facilitated activities	21(64%)	HR	(3%)
Graduate-facilitated activities	12(36%)	MIS	(3%)
		Other	(3%)

Top 5 Employers Hiring Grads
SunTrust Robinson Humphrey (2), GE Capital (1), Delta (1), Tyson Foods (1), Johnson & Johnson (1)

UNIVERSITY OF HARTFORD
BARNEY SCHOOL OF BUSINESS

GENERAL INFORMATION

Type of school	Private
Affiliation	No Affiliation

SURVEY SAYS...

Solid preparation in:
Accounting, General management, Operations, Communication/interpersonal skills, Presentation skills

STUDENTS

Enrollment of parent institution	6,992
Enrollment of MBA Program	323
% male/female	56/44
% out-of-state	17
% part-time	84
% underrepresented minority	32
% international	17
Average age at entry	33
Average years work experience at entry	0.0

ACADEMICS

Academic Experience Rating	**86**
Profs interesting rating	80
Profs accesible rating	84
Student/faculty ratio	10:1

Joint Degrees

E2M (MBA & ME Engineering)-
(self-paced)

Prominent Alumni

David Cordani, CEO, CIGNA Corporation; Patrick Tannock, President, XL Insurance Bermuda; Roger Klene, CEO, MOTT Corp.; Evaristo Stanziale, Founding Partner SCS Commodities Corp.; Richard Booth, Vice Chairman, AIG

Academics

University of Hartford's Barney School of Business has "a good reputation" and great "flexibility" for students to accommodate full-time work. "Unlike other schools I looked at, they put work first and are flexible with course scheduling and business travel," says one insurance student. "The class offerings accommodate full-time working hours" by having most classes at night. The School offers "a wide variety of electives (communication, marketing, psychology)" and "international classes," which are "awesome." Many students love the "GMAT waiver option" for applications, where there is "no GMAT requirement with three years of work experience." "For the working professional, this program is perfect," one student says, "In and out of classes at convenient times leaves time to do other activities and keep a good work/school-life balance."

One common complaint is the business school's administration. Although some students said, "the support/administrative staff, although understaffed, really go out of their way to help," many said, "the school is run very poorly, and administrators are very wasteful." "Parking is very impractical and insufficient," and classrooms need to "upgrade technology." "Bureaucracy is everywhere," and it's "a true example of Oscar Wilde's saying 'the bureaucracy is expanding to meet the expanding needs of the bureaucracy.'"

In contrast to the administration, "the professors are great" and "very accessible and approachable; if you have any issues, they will always make the time to work with you." "The greatest strength" of the program "is the quality and enthusiasm of the professors in the program as it relates to their disciplines." "The faculty is amazing. They really care, and do the best to foster a great learning environment" by being "clear and straightforward in their explanations." "Some professors are true gems," says a student. The school is unable to retain them because benefits and pay are much worse than state schools nearby." Most of the faculty members "have a strong background in the business world and keep up with the changing environment." "I think the business school could improve with regard to the classes that are offered," one student says. Overall, the professors and administration are "effective at creating a tremendous sense of community within the business school; it's a tight-knit group of ambitious individuals, who work across all facets of business in the area."

Career and Placement

Placement and career-counseling services are provided to Barney MBAs by the Career Services Office, which serves the entire undergraduate and graduate student body of the University. Services include resume and cover-letter writing workshops, seminars on networking and interviewing strategies, job banks, on-campus interviewing, and job fairs. However, students say "career services is ineffective and unhelpful, though as most students here already work full time, the school does not strongly emphasize placement, channeling its resources elsewhere." "I have not seen the mentoring program or any enrichment workshops since I have been a student for four years," one student says. "There are a lot of students who work in the insurance industry, since Hartford is the insurance capital of the world." Some prominent alumni from the Barney MBA program include Robert Saunders, CEO of Kaman Music Corp.; Roger Klene, CEO of MOTT Corp.; and Thomas Barnes, Chairman of the Board of The Barnes Group.

ADMISSIONS CONTACT: DAMIAN MIERNY, MANAGER, MBA PROGRAM
ADDRESS: 200 BLOOMFIELD AVENUE, CENTER FOR GRADUATE & ADULT SERVICES, CC231 WEST
HARTFORD, CT 06117
PHONE: 860-768-4444 • FAX: 860-768-4821
E-MAIL: ADMISSIONS@HARTFORD.EDU • WEBSITE: BARNEY.HARTFORD.EDU

Student Life and Environment

Students at University of Hartford are "hard working, competitive, friendly, and successful" and trying to "balancing full-time careers, families, and getting graduate degrees." "The average age in the MBA program is about 32. Almost everyone works full time in addition to going to class." The student body provides "very little networking value for where I am at in my career," one older student says. Students are "mostly highly driven individuals who are looking to advance their careers." "Most seem to be attending school because they get reimbursed by their companies." "I would say that half of the MBA students are good people, who want to advance their careers and bring a lot to the table," one student calculates. The school has "a diverse student population" ethnically. There are, for example, "a lot of students from India."

A "get in, get out" attitude pervades at Hartford, as most students work full time, and many commute. Thus, there is limited social life outside of class for most students, as they have families and work to attend to. "Student life is limited for commuting students but is very active for residents. There are many good restaurants and bars nearby, however the School is also very close to a dangerous neighborhood." "Most of us have full-time jobs [and] go to school after a long day at work," one student explains "The interaction is moderate, and the professors seem to understand we need to balance all of our life responsibilities with school."

Admissions

The Barney admissions office requires all MBA applicants to submit official transcripts from all previously attended post-secondary schools, two letters of recommendation, official GMAT results, a current resume, a letter of intent describing the applicant's academic and career goals, and a completed application. Applicants with at least three years of continuous work experience may apply for a GMAT waiver, as may applicants who have already successfully completed another master's program. Because space in each incoming class is limited, it greatly benefits applicants to apply as early as possible.

FINANCIAL FACTS

Annual tuition	$10,440
Cost of books	$750
% of students receiving aid	22
% of first-year students receiving aid	65
% of students receiving grants	9
Average award package	$15,555
Average grant	$5,423
Average loan	$16,165
Average student loan debt	$25,934

ADMISSIONS

Admissions Selectivity Rating	89
# of applications received	181
% applicants accepted	47
% acceptees attending	85
Average GMAT	540
Range of GMAT	480–720
Average GPA	3.60
TOEFL required of international students	Yes
Application fee	$45
International Deferment available	Yes
Maximum length of deferment	1 year
Transfer students accepted	Yes
Transfer application policy: Based on Individual Cases.	
Non-fall admissions	Yes
Need-blind admissions	No

UNIVERSITY OF HOUSTON
C.T. BAUER COLLEGE OF BUSINESS

GENERAL INFORMATION
Type of school	Public
Affiliation	No Affiliation
Academic calendar	Semester

SURVEY SAYS...
Students love Houston, TX, Friendly students, Good peer network, Cutting-edge classes
Solid preparation in:
Teamwork, Communication/ interpersonal skills

STUDENTS
Enrollment of parent institution	40,747
Enrollment of MBA Program	795
% male/female	59/41
% out-of-state	0
% part-time	80
% underrepresented minority	17
% international	31
Average age at entry	28
Average years work experience at entry	4.8

ACADEMICS
Academic Experience Rating	80
Profs interesting rating	83
Profs accesible rating	86
Student/faculty ratio	4:1
% female faculty	25
% underrepresented minority faculty	26
% part-time faculty	30

Joint Degrees
MBA/JD - 111 credits (3.5 to 6 years); MBA/MIE in Industrial Engineering - 72 credits (2 to 5 years); MBA/M.S. in Hospitality Management - 78 credits (3 to 5 years); MBA/MSW - 87 credits (3 to 5 years); MBA/Master's in Global Management - 66 credits (2.5 to 5 years)

Prominent Alumni
Mark Papa, Chairman and CEO, EOG Resources, Inc.; Karen Katz, President and CEO, Neiman Marcus Stores; Marvin Odum, President, Shell Oil Company

Academics

University of Houston's C.T. Bauer College of Business has a "great business school reputation," "excellent staff with great corporate experience, top notch facilities," and is "strategically located in the oil and gas state." Its location in Houston is a big draw for students, as "Houston is home to more Fortune-500 companies than any other U.S. city other than New York City," and "the Bauer College of Business is well known in the Houston area." Tuition is reasonable, and Bauer is known "for providing a quality education for an affordable price." The "part-time, evening schedule allows full-time work, and an MBA in 30 months," says one commercial construction student. "University of Houston is located in the heart of the energy hub of the world. It has some of the world's best energy courses and a first-of-its-kind energy research institute," and "many of the students and teachers have many years of experience in the oil and gas industry, finance industry, and other business-related industries."

"The business school itself is run very well and is very organized," and everyone on staff "is very nice, helpful, and willing to do anything to satisfy their students' experience at the College." "The admin staff is very supportive and treats each one of the MBA candidates as individuals instead of reciting the same old FAQ." The staff and professors are "very easy to access via email, phone, and meetings." "The campus is a bit old," though, so some buildings "could use some sprucing up." "Amazing and admirable" professors abound who "care a lot about the students," and most "have practical knowledge of business practices." "Many professors would like to see UH ranked at the top with the likes of UT and A&M, therefore, they work hard to make sure their students have every opportunity to do well," one student explains. A large number of professors "have a surprising amount of industry experience" and use their real-world experience to inform students and help with career prospects. "You know you can count on your professors for a helping hand if needed," one happy student says. "You feel the love." The School has "the best energy-focused MBA curriculum in the country," and the University offers students flexibility. "Bauer College of Business was appealing to me because of its focus in the part-time program, excellent course work, and flexibility to help diversify my MBA experience," a financial services student explains. "By allowing me to tailor my MBA to what my goals are, I take more exciting classes related to energy than your typical finance/accounting classes."

Career and Placement

Students at Houston feel confident nearing graduation as "effective career placement services [is an] outstanding strength of the University of Houston!" "There are workshops (resume building, interview skills, job-search strategies) available throughout each semester," as well as "company visits, seminars, and job fairs." "My experience with the Rockwell Career Center was exceptional," one student says. "I thank them for helping me to land an excellent job in the oil and gas industry that I will be starting right after graduation." Perhaps the biggest advantage of attending the University of Houston for business students is its location. "Houston is an economic epicenter of both energy and technology industries." One thing to note is that "it's much more difficult and stressful for full-time students to procure post-graduate employment, and internships are equally hard to come by" as compared to the larger part-time program.

ADMISSIONS CONTACT: DALIA PINEDA, DIRECTOR OF STUDENT SERVICES
ADDRESS: 334 MELCHER HALL, ROOM 330, HOUSTON, TX 77204-6021
PHONE: 713-743-0700 • FAX: 713-743-4807
E-MAIL: HOUSTONMBA@UH.EDU • WEBSITE: WWW.BAUER.UH.EDU/MBA

About 45 percent of graduates find employment in the petroleum and energy industry. The mean base salary for recent graduates is about $65,000, and 77 percent of graduates find employment within three months of graduation. Prominent alumni include Mark Papa, Chairman and CEO, EOG Resources, Inc.; Karen Katz, President and CEO, Neiman Marcus Stores; Marvin Odum, President, Shell Oil Company; Zhigang Wang, Deputy Director, General China National Petroleum Corporation; David McClanahan, President and CEO, CenterPoint Energy.

Student Life and Environment

The student body at the University of Houston is "diverse, intelligent, compassionate, constructive, and strong" with most students being "between 25 and 35." "Almost all have a career, and most are married or have family members that depend upon them," says one student. The University has "all kinds of students from commuters to international students." Students "come from all backgrounds, which gives the University much-needed diversity" and "enables discussions and an exchange of ideas from very different perspectives."

The University of Houston has an active campus, and there is plenty to do for students who stay on campus. However, most students in the business school are part-time and are "only on campus for class and the gym." "Since the school is a commuter school, most students only see each other during class time." "Most of the students are employed full time" and do not have much time to socialize. "Networking happens where you make it happen," such as at the "large atrium and the Starbucks area where we usually meet and network." Still, through classes, networking, and workgroups, the students bond. "My fellow classmates are my second family," one student says.

Admissions

The University of Houston requires GMAT scores, undergraduate GPA, personal statement, letters of recommendation, a resume, and a self-appraisal form. Work experience is not required, but it is factored heavily by the admissions board. Admitted students have an average of three years of professional experience. Since the University of Houston seeks a diverse student body, it understands that the strengths of students vary, and there is a range of GPAs and GMAT scores accepted. However, the average GPAs and GMAT scores for last year's class were 3.28 and 592 respectively.

FINANCIAL FACTS

Annual tuition (in-state/ out-of-state)	$11,354/$19,778
Fees	$5,645
Room & board (on/off-campus)	$11,102
% of students receiving aid	34
% of first-year students receiving aid	47
% of students receiving grants	9
Average award package	$11,462
Average grant	$6,716
Average loan	$19,184

ADMISSIONS

Admissions Selectivity Rating	80
# of applications received	417
% applicants accepted	62
% acceptees attending	68
Average GMAT	592
Range of GMAT	560–620
Average GPA	3.28
TOEFL required of international students	Yes
Minimum TOEFL (paper/computer)	603/250
Application fee	$75
International application fee	$150
Regular application deadline	6/1
Deferment available	Yes
Maximum length of deferment	1 year
Transfer students accepted	No
Non-fall admissions	Yes
Need-blind admissions	Yes

EMPLOYMENT PROFILE

Career Rating	87		
Percent employed at graduation	53		
Percent employed 3 months after graduation	77		
Average base starting salary	$65,172		

Primary Source of Full-time Job Acceptances

Grads Employed by Function	%	Avg. Salary
Marketing	(14%)	$55,896
Operations	(28%)	$68,460
Consulting	(14%)	$91,300
Management	(6%)	$51,000
Finance	(22%)	$55,188
MIS	(17%)	$63,687

Top 5 Employers Hiring Grads
Hewlett Packard, Baker Hughes, Deloitte, Waste Management, Entergy

UNIVERSITY OF HOUSTON—VICTORIA
SCHOOL OF BUSINESS ADMINISTRATION

GENERAL INFORMATION
Type of school	Public
Affiliation	No Affiliation

SURVEY SAYS...
Cutting-edge classes
Solid preparation in:
General management, Doing business in a global economy

STUDENTS
Enrollment of parent institution	4,569
Enrollment of MBA Program	1,139
% male/female	52/48
% out-of-state	5
% part-time	76
% underrepresented minority	75
% international	18
Average age at entry	35

ACADEMICS
Academic Experience Rating	**70**
Profs interesting rating	75
Profs accesible rating	80
% female faculty	31
% underrepresented minority faculty	91

Academics

The University of Houston—Victoria (UHV) School of Business Administration "has excellent accreditations and is also one of the most cost effective schools available." The "high-quality programs are convenient and affordable." UHV offers many different ways for students to earn their degree. One may enroll full-time or part-time, choose on-line courses or a traditional classroom setting, or a combination of both. With so many options and so much flexibility, many can take advantage of the opportunity to earn a graduate business degree. Students can choose from the Strategic MBA, which can be completed full-time in 16 months or part-time over the course of three years; the Global MBA, which can be completed full-time in 11-21 months and provides a specialized curriculum for students interested in international business; or the MS-Economic Development/Entrepreneurship, which takes nearly 24 months to complete on a part-time schedule. There is also a program designed especially for international students: the Fourth Year Bridge (Strategic or Global) MBA.

According to current students, "The education is great, challenging, and affordable," and the school's excellent reputation is well deserved. The professors at UHV are an excellent resource and are "very helpful, professional, [courteous], caring, fair, and highly knowledgeable in their areas of study." They understand what a suitable workload is for graduate students who most likely work full-time and may have a family besides. "While they show mercy they do push us to become the best that they can train us to be." Diversity exists both in the student body as well as in the faculty. This variety of experiences that come from a global classroom enriches all of the courses, especially those conducted in a classroom setting. "The professors are experts in their fields, and encourage real-world, practical applications of the concepts discussed in class." Students attest that "the quality of the curriculum is very high" and courses do a great job at staying relevant so that they "relate to current events around us."

The University of Houston—Victoria has auxiliary facilities at Sugar Land and Cinco Ranch. Courses at these locations, as well as at Victoria, include comprehensive coursework in economics, management, finance, marketing, and leadership. One student describes the courses as "very challenging," yet feels that "the academic experience is priceless." Administration at each facility is "helpful," and they "care about ensuring a quality educational experience for the students."

ADMISSIONS CONTACT: TRUDY WORTHAM
ADDRESS: OFFICE OF ADMISSIONS/RECORDS, 3007 N BEN WILSON ST VICTORIA, TX 77901
PHONE: 361-570-4848 • FAX: 361-580-5500
E-MAIL: ADMISSIONSANDREGISTRATION@UHV.EDU • WEBSITE: WWW.UHV.EDU

Career and Placement

Career services here are not so predominant as at other graduate schools. Rather than students hoping to land a new job after graduation, many are just looking for a "career boost," such as a promotion, to propel them upward at the job they already have. "Most students are currently employed in the professional field, and are married with children. They see the MBA program as a chance to improve their careers." Others, like this student comment, "It was suggested that I attend UH-Victoria by my manager."

Although the school provides the "best courses and professors," they tend to provide "less opportunities for graduate students in the job market." One student notes that the University provides fewer internship opportunities to graduate students than expected. Help is available for those who are looking for a new career, and "the campus always has career fairs and resume workshops." In addition, "the school sends out many emails with job, internship, and special training opportunities." However, students who are working full-time may find it hard to attend these events. An alumni network might better serve these students who could network on their own schedules. Regardless of what the career center provides to graduate students, students profess that just being a part of the program promotes continuous "opportunities to network and build professional relationships."

Student Life and Environment

Student life varies greatly, depending on where, when, and how classes are taken. Since taking classes online "doesn't leave much interaction," these students will miss some of the diversity and bonding experiences traditional classroom-learners experience. Fellow students are described as "very diverse," with a "wide variety of ages, experience levels, and backgrounds." They are also noted as being "very creative," and they do their best to "support each other in achieving goals."

UHV students are proud of their school. They take classes seriously and expect a high degree of professionalism from not only their professors and administration but from their fellow students as well. Therefore, it is not surprising that they are not only "friendly" but "great to work with." The busy life of most students allows for some activities outside of class but not many. Most commuters simply "attend class and get back home." Others are able to find time to "arrive early to talk and [to review] questions on class and mingle."

The Houston area is very conducive to jobs in the energy industry. Here, students are surrounded by "multinational global energy companies so "the location is perfect."

Admissions

Students enroll at the University of Houston—Victoria School of Business Administration from a wide range of ages, with the average age being 35. GMAT scores and undergraduate GPAs are required and hold the most weight in the admissions office. Letters of recommendation, essays, extracurricular activities, and work experience are not considered for enrollment.

ADMISSIONS	
Admissions Selectivity Rating	**67**
# of applications received	196
% applicants accepted	99
% acceptees attending	85
TOEFL required of international students	Yes
Minimum TOEFL (paper/computer)	550/213
Application fee	$0
International application fee	$0
Deferment available	Yes
Maximum length of deferment	1 year
Transfer students accepted	Yes
Transfer application policy: Graduate business students may transfer up to 6 hours of graduate-level business coursework from an AACSB-accredited program with the approval of the Assistant Dean.	
Non-fall admissions	Yes
Need-blind admissions	Yes

UNIVERSITY OF ILLINOIS—CHICAGO
LIAUTAUD GRADUATE SCHOOL OF BUSINESS

GENERAL INFORMATION

Type of school	Public
Affiliation	No Affiliation

SURVEY SAYS...
Students love Chicago, IL, Happy
students
Solid preparation in:
General management, Teamwork,
Entrepreneurial studies

STUDENTS

Enrollment of parent institution	27,512
Enrollment of MBA Program	257
% male/female	65/35
% out-of-state	37
% part-time	47
% underrepresented minority	20
% international	21
Average age at entry	28
Average years work experience at entry	4.0

ACADEMICS

Academic Experience Rating	85
Profs interesting rating	86
Profs accesible rating	78
Student/faculty ratio	13:1
% female faculty	33
% underrepresented minority faculty	33

Joint Degrees
MBA/Master of Science in
Accounting; MBA/Master of Public
Health; MBA/Master of Science
Nursing; MBA/Master of Arts in ;
MBAn/Master of Science in
Management Information Systems;
MBA/Doctor of Medicine;
MBA/Doctor of Pharmacy

Prominent Alumni
Martin Hughes, Chairman, CEO,
HUB International Ltd.; Vikki Pryor,
CEO, American Red Cross Greater
New York; Ray Roman, Exec. VP,
Leap Wireless International; Mary
Dillon, President and CEO, US
Cellular Corp.; Michael Fung, Sr. VP,
Chief Audit Exec, Walmart.

Academics

With its "incredibly affordable tuition and access to a Tier One research university," the MBA program at the Liautaud Graduate School of Business "provides the best value for the cost. It offers a top-quality education for a fraction of the cost of Northwestern or University of Chicago." The MBA candidates at the school value "the flexibility of an evening" or weekend program since many of them are "currently employed and trying to balance it all." They also rave about the business school's "strong" entrepreneurship department which "will soon put Liautaud on the map." Many highlight the "excellent programs like Technology Ventures Program on experience." Liautaud's many academic assets also include its Professional Topics courses, which are "two-hour courses that focus on current topics." One student explains, "I took 'Social Entrepreneurship' last fall, and it has been a major springboard for me. We had real practitioners visit class and we engaged with them, solving a business 'problem' of theirs throughout the course. It changed the way I thought a business needs to run."

Students across the board are quite satisfied with their professors who "are world-class researchers in their fields" and who "stand [out] for their passion for teaching and encouraging creativity." These "professors effectively prompt feedback from students, who often engage in constructive debate." Students consider themselves "lucky to have professors of diverse backgrounds." One particularly impressed student shares, "It's exciting when you turn on the TV and see your professor being interviewed about Al Capone's finances right on the History Channel. It's even more exciting when he integrates this topic into his classroom lecture." Students generally feel that the learning experience at the school is supported and enhanced by their classmates because "many work full-time at large companies and provide great experience[s] to discuss in class." One student notes, "I also appreciate that UIC requires prior work experience, so we are surrounded by other bright peers that can offer insight from their own experiences at work." While overall satisfied with their course work, professors, and peers, the students at Liautaud are less enamored with their facilities. These concerns were addressed when Douglas Hall opened in 2011. This fully-renovated building is designed for business education with state of the art technology resources.

Career and Placement

Advantageously situated next to "banker's row" in Chicago, the university's "proximity and connections to [the] Chicago Financial District" serve as a resource for Liautaud students. According to the school's website, the Liautaud Career Services Office provides a range of services for its students including "seminars, workshops, and online tools covering all aspects of the career development process." These workshops and tools focus on resume-building, career-mapping, personal branding, networking and salary negotiation. Students also have access to advising, employer contacts, online job postings and career fairs. The Career Services Office also provides special services for its international students including assistance with learning about U.S. protocol and business writing.

Some of the notable companies that have recruited and hired graduates of Liautaud include Abbott Laboratories, Caterpillar, Combined Insurance, Deloitte, James Hardic Building Products, PriceWaterhouseCoopers, Morningstar, Navigant Consulting, TransUnion, and Wells Fargo.

Student Life and Environment

The reputation of Liautaud's MBA program along with the allure of Chicago attracts students ranging "from helicopter pilots to surgeons, and consultants to bankers." The mix also includes "mid-career types [who] are attending classes part-time" and "students raised in India and China [who] are having their first U.S. experience at UIC."

One student proclaims, "These are down-to-earth people who are future entrepreneurs and the people that keep Chicago's small- to mid-size businesses going." Described as "competitive, bright, caring, social, and heartwarmingly nerdy," these students "group within their concentrations and have many opportunities to network outside of class." "There several active student organizations, including Net Impact and the MBAA" on campus.

Despite the many opportunities to socialize and network, it can sometimes be a challenge for Liautaud sudents to meet up in person. "All classes are held in the evenings so students have to make a deliberate effort to schedule time to get involved," observes one student. In addition, "most graduate students live off campus, and many have full-time jobs. This means that group collaboration occurs mostly online." Given its high population of commuters, students are pleased that "the campus itself is in a great spot for commuters from around Chicago, just west of downtown. And there are great places to eat nearby."

Admissions

All applicants to the MBA program at the Liautaud Graduate School of Business must submit an online application, an application fee, two copies of official transcripts for all post-secondary academic work, two letters of recommendation, a personal statement, resume, and official GMAT or GRE score. Students who are non-native speakers of English must also submit a TOEFL score. A minimum of a B average is required in at least the last 60 hours of undergraduate course work (though provisional acceptance may be extended to promising applicants who fail to meet this benchmark). For the best results, applicants' GMAT scores should be at or above the average GMAT scores of the incoming class. The school also places emphasis on professional work experience. After submitting their materials for review, qualified applicants will be invited to interview with the admissions committee.

FINANCIAL FACTS

Annual tuition (in-state/ out-of-state)	$19,766/$31,764
Fees	$3,750
Cost of books	$1,499
Room & board (on/off-campus)	$12,970
% of students receiving aid	60
% of first-year students receiving aid	52
% of students receiving grants	27
Average award package	$31,808
Average grant	$13,984
Average loan	$38,553

ADMISSIONS

Admissions Selectivity Rating	**82**
# of applications received	253
% applicants accepted	49
% acceptees attending	51
Average GMAT	570
Range of GMAT	520–610
Average GPA	3.25
TOEFL required of international students	Yes
Minimum TOEFL (paper/computer)	570/213
Application fee	$60
International application fee	$60
Regular application deadline	5/15
Regular application notification	3–4 weeks
Deferment available	Yes
Maximum length of deferment	1 year
Transfer students accepted	Yes

Transfer application policy: Applicants need to apply and be accepted to the Liautaud MBA Program. They can submit transcripts for previous coursework with a grade of B or better and a course description. The classes must be from an AACSB accredited institution. Maximum of 12 Semester hours may transfer.

Non-fall admissions	Yes
Need-blind admissions	Yes

EMPLOYMENT PROFILE

Career Rating	89	**Grads Employed by Function% Avg. Salary**	
Percent employed at graduation	10	Marketing	(22%) $85,000
Percent employed 3 months after graduation	60	Operations	(11%)
		Consulting	(22%) $85,000
Average base starting salary	$71,679	Management	(17%) $72,333
Primary Source of Full-time Job Acceptances		Finance	(11%)
School-facilitated activities	8(44%)	MIS	(6%)
Graduate-facilitated activities	7(39%)	Other	(11%)
Unknown	3(17%)	**Top 5 Employers Hiring Grads**	

Top 5 Employers Hiring Grads
James Hardie (2), Combined Insurance (2), HUB International (2), AON Hewitt (1), Deloitte Consulting (1)

UNIVERSITY OF ILLINOIS AT URBANA-CHAMPAIGN
COLLEGE OF BUSINESS

GENERAL INFORMATION
Type of school   Public
Affiliation   No Affiliation
Academic calendar   Semester

SURVEY SAYS...
Smart classrooms
Solid preparation in:
Finance, Teamwork

STUDENTS
Enrollment of parent
  institution   44,197
Enrollment of MBA Program   341
% male/female   70/30
% out-of-state   62
% part-time   30
% underrepresented minority   9
% international   43
Average age at entry   28
Average years work experience
  at entry   4.0

ACADEMICS
Academic Experience Rating   **95**
Profs interesting rating   91
Profs accesible rating   92
Student/faculty ratio   14:1
% female faculty   22
% underrepresented minority
  faculty   9
% part-time faculty   8

Joint Degrees
MBA/MA Architecture; MBA/MS
Electrical & Computer Engineering;
MBA/MS Civil and Environmental
Engineering; MBA/MS Electrical
Engineering; MBA/MS Industrial
Engineering; MBA/MS Mechanical
Engineering; MBA/MD Medicine;
MBA/MS Journalism; MBA/JD Law;
MBA/MS Human Resource
Education; MBA/ILIR; MBA/MS
Materials Science & Engineering.

Prominent Alumni
Mike Tokarz, Chairman, The Tokarz
Group; Tom Siebel, Founder,
Chairman & CEO, Siebel Systems,
Inc.; Jan Valentic, Senior VP
Marketing

Academics

The low in-state tuition and access to the resources of a large university have made the University of Illinois at Urbana-Champaign's MBA program a popular one. That means getting into popular courses can be difficult, especially highly desired electives seen as "much more interesting" than the sometimes "very elementary" basic business courses. These electives, which have "excellent professors and course material," is where UI shines. Students at UI are encouraged to tailor their MBA to their own career goals. In year two, students take sixteen credits of electives and sixteen credits towards a concentration in fields like marketing, finance, information technology, or general management. The "relentless coursework" —one student referred to it as "a proving ground" —is balanced by a "terrific staff" who "care about students doing well and make themselves available to everyone for additional support."

Developing not only your skills but also your ability to use those skills after school is a priority for many professors here. "Overall, the professors here take an interest in students beyond class work and will offer their support in a career search and personal learning and growth." Indeed, "the school provides ample opportunities for students to get as involved as they'd like. There are several out of the classroom opportunities to gain experience (case competitions, leadership roles, work experience, consulting)." That experience is not limited to working with business leaders in the region, either. "The international opportunities here for MBAs are outstanding. Every student is given the opportunity to do at least one global consulting project that includes travel to a foreign country. Some students are able to travel to two or more countries related to their studies."

Though professors here are almost universally praised, the administration "has a lot of room for improvement," especially with regard to "inefficient" communication with students – though others note that the administration is clearly "concerned about student needs." Overall, "in addition to peerless international immersion opportunities, the University of Illinois provides a close-knit, family-like atmosphere that is simply not matched by any other MBA program, public or private."

Career and Placement

The University of Illinois proves to be a draw in part because "it provides international opportunities that far exceed any other program" in the same price range. One student notes the school "gave me the chance to travel to five emerging economies and apply my media and consulting skill set to diverse clientele." Responding to student suggestions that the school improve its corporate ties in big cities, the MBA Career Services Organization has become part of a new college wide Business Career Services Organization aimed at increasing visibility for MBA students to companies that recruit at the college.

Prospects for graduates tend to be good. The media base salary for graduates of the Illinois MBA program is close to $90,000 annually, ranging from about $60,000 on the low end to $160,000 on the high end. General management and finance fields draw the highest number of graduates, about half of them taking jobs in the Midwest. The top hiring companies included AT&T, Cisco Systems, Ernst & Young, ExxonMobil, Hewitt Associates, LG, Peabody Energy, Procter & Gamble, Robert Bosch Corporation, and Sears Holdings Corporation.

ADMISSIONS CONTACT: JAQUILIN WILSON, DIRECTOR OF ADMISSIONS,
REWRITING AND ALUMNI RELATIONS
ADDRESS: 3019 BUSINESS INSTRUCTIONAL FACILITY, 515 E GREGORY, CHAMPAIGN, IL 61820
PHONE: 217-244-7602 • FAX: 217-333-1156
E-MAIL: MBA@ILLINOIS.EDU • WEBSITE: WWW.MBA.ILLINOIS.EDU

Student Life and Environment

With peers who tend to be "young professionals who generally are more likely to spend a night in studying class material than go out socially or network," and who represent a diverse range of places, ages and experiences—some 40 percent come from overseas—it may be surprising that students here are "are easy to engage, very involved and supportive in each others' learning." There is a high level of competition to do well, but students are not overly competitive with one another. "Students are more concerned about seeing success in everyone than putting others down so they can rise to the top." One student noted, "I was pleasantly surprised that everyone has been really collaborative and not cut throat. Everyone wants to see one another succeed."

Students here stay busy. If not immersed in studies, they are involved with extracurricular activities, networking, or simply enjoying what this college town has to offer. "It's been a great place to try new things, meet new people, and figure out what my strengths are." It's easy to find the time to wind down from the grind if you're so inclined, such as on "Thursday nights for Mug Club, when the class goes out to a different bar every week and celebrates the survival of another seven days." Clubs and students organizations are numerous. "I feel that Illinois strongly encourages students to take on new challenges," one student notes, "and I've gained a lot from this."

Admissions

Though recent classes had median GMAT score of 650, with an 80 percent range between 540 and 710, there are no minimum GMAT scores required for entry to the program. However, at least two years of work experience are strongly recommended. Most admitted to the program have more; the average student had about four years of professional experience prior to acceptance. You can learn more about the Illinois MBA by chatting online with one of the school's admissions officers, or attending an admissions event in your area.

FINANCIAL FACTS

Annual tuition (in-state/ out-of-state)	$19,975/$29,975
Fees	$3,506
Cost of books	$5,800
Room & board	$11,400

ADMISSIONS

Admissions Selectivity Rating	**92**
# of applications received	665
% applicants accepted	32
% acceptees attending	55
Average GMAT	650
Average GPA	3.20
TOEFL required of international students	Yes
Application fee	$75
International application fee	$90
Application Deadline/Notification	
Round 1:	11/1 / 1/4
Round 2:	1/15 / 3/8
Round 3:	3/15 /
Round 4:	5/1 /
Deferment available	Yes
Maximum length of deferment	1 year
Transfer students accepted	No
Non-fall admissions	No
Need-blind admissions	Yes

EMPLOYMENT PROFILE

Career Rating	89	Grads Employed by Function	% Avg. Salary
Percent employed at graduation	65	Marketing	(14%) $81,738
Percent employed 3 months after graduation	77	Operations	(8%) $86,600
		Consulting	(25%) $90,294
Average base starting salary	$87,818	Management	(23%) $91,083
Primary Source of Full-time Job Acceptances		Finance	(16%) $88,156
School-facilitated activities	(61%)	HR	(4%)
Graduate-facilitated activities	(39%)	MIS	(3%)
Unknown	(0%)	Other	(7%)

Top 5 Employers Hiring Grads
AT&T (3), State Farm (3), Allstate Insurance Company (2), Cognizant (2), Cymer (2)

THE UNIVERSITY OF IOWA
HENRY B. TIPPIE SCHOOL OF MANAGEMENT

GENERAL INFORMATION

Type of school	Public
Affiliation	No Affiliation
Academic calendar	Semester

SURVEY SAYS...

Good social scene, Helpful alumni
Solid preparation in:
Finance, Quantitative skills

STUDENTS

Enrollment of parent institution	31,498
Enrollment of MBA Program	1,085
% male/female	75/25
% out-of-state	55
% part-time	88
% underrepresented minority	12
% international	26
Average age at entry	28
Average years work experience at entry	4.3

ACADEMICS

Academic Experience Rating	**94**
Profs interesting rating	94
Profs accesible rating	87
Student/faculty ratio	13:1
% female faculty	24
% underrepresented minority faculty	14
% part-time faculty	39

Joint Degrees

Joint-degree MBA programs with Law, 4 years; Hospital and Health Administration, 2.5-3 years; Medicine, 5 years.

Prominent Alumni

Christopher Klein, CEO, Fortune Brands; Laura Desmond, CEO, Starcom MediaVest; Mark Buthman, CFO, Kimberly Clark; Jerre L. Stead, CEO and Chairman, IHS Inc.; Karen Alber, CIO, MillerCoors

Academics

While some students extol the "wonderful experiential learning," and the "breadth of courses unmatched by most other institutions" that are offered at the Henry B. Tippie School of Management at The University of Iowa, others praise its "small class sizes along with the unique Academy structure." The Academy structure requires students to select "one of three academies based on their interests: Finance, Marketing, [or] Strategic Innovation," the latter which encompasses both Strategic Management and Innovation and Supply Chain and Analytics tracks. In 2009 the school revamped its curriculum "two 16-week semesters to four eight-week modules. This allows students to take fewer classes at one time and focus all attention on the subject matter at hand."

Nevertheless, students generally laud the school's "high return on investment" and feel that "the greatest strengths of the University of Iowa are the [number] of opportunities that are available in academics, athletics, government, and volunteer work." They also highlight that "the Tippie School's Supplu Chain and Analytics courses and association with the John Pappajohn Entrepreneurial Center are outstanding resources whether you want to start or improve a business." The Entrepreneurial Center, in particular, is "a hidden gem" that "offers many business competition events throughout the year that provide funding for startups, access to successful entrepreneurs and business mentorship." Students also boast that "the school's Henry Fund"—a $3.1 million student managed investment fund—"has received the top honors for performance the past five years as well."

Classes at Tippie provide a "comfortable environment" where there is a "good mix of readings, lectures, simulations, and real-world applications" that helps to nurture "thought and healthy conversation." The small size of the program creates "opportunity for involvement, interviews, and faculty interactions" and "more personalized attention."

The students are also impressed by their "outstanding" and "top-notch" professors who are often "national experts [in] their subject area." These "approachable" professors "do a very good job getting to know the students and build a personal relationship with most." The school's administration also received kudos from the students who observe that "the administration and professors meet frequently to incorporate ideas that they have gained from other schools, their own insight, and feedback from students."

Career and Placement

Tippie students reveal, "We can do a little better with career services. As such, it is good but we have faced some challenges during the economic downturn." Another student says they feel "disappointed with the efforts given by the University of Iowa for career guidance." Other students offer a more positive view of the Career Services Office, saying that they "motivate you and they also are as demanding as our professors in doing things like mock interviews, networking events etc. Also there is a leadership course that offers help to prepare one to present in professional and personal setting[s]."

Although they long for "more geographically diverse recruiters" and feel that there needs to be more effort put into "attracting more companies to visit on campus," Tippie students have noticed some recent improvement in recruiting on campus. "During the past year we have begun attracting high-tech firms and investment banks due to the efforts of career services and alumni. We have recently had Amazon recruit on campus...and are seeking to expand Goldman-Sachs undergraduate recruitment to include MBAs. We are also seeing many mid-market investment banks and private equity groups recruit on campus."

ADMISSIONS CONTACT: JODI SCHAFER, DIRECTOR, MBA ADMISSIONS & FINANCIAL AID
ADDRESS: C432 POMERANTZ CENTER, TIPPIE SCHOOL OF MANAGEMENT, THE UNIVERSITY OF IOWA
IOWA CITY, IA 52242-1000
PHONE: 319-335-1039 • FAX: 319-335-3604
E-MAIL: TIPPIEMBA@UIOWA.EDU • WEBSITE: TIPPIE.UIOWA.EDU/FULLTIMEMBA

Student Life and Environment

Students are enthusiastic in their praise of Iowa City's "vibrant atmosphere which helps you both learn and relax." The city's "night-life is great and there are also a lot of hole-in-the-wall restaurants that provide a lot of diversity in dining." Iowa City also "has easy access to Chicago, Minneapolis, St. Louis, and Kansas City, and is 20 minutes from the airport for longer journeys."

Students count their school's "friendly atmosphere from admissions to faculty and students" as one of its strengths. When not immersed in their studies, students can participate in "lots of social activities as well as many school-related activities" including "company presentations and speaker sessions every fortnight." One student gushes, "The guest speakers are phenomenal—John Rice [Vice Chairman of General Electric], Fred Whyte [President of Stihl] and Clay Jones [CEO of Rockwell Collins]—are just a snapshot of the leaders that spoke at our school while I was a student." For the more athletically-inclined students, "the football atmosphere is awesome and something that should be experienced."

The school's "small community of students" is self-described as "classic Midwest[ern] people—hardworking, fairly narrow life experience, super friendly, outcome-oriented, family people." "There is a strong moral compass, and you do not have to be worried about being stabbed in the back by a fellow student for an A." These "very friendly, welcoming, and supportive" students who are "top-of-the-line performers" include "motorbike racers, go-cart racers, triathlon/marathon runners, musicians, math geeks, entrepreneurs, ex-military men, etc."

Admissions

Applicants to Tippie's MBA programs must submit an online application, official transcripts of post-secondary work, essays, a professional resume, contact information for three references, an official GMAT or GRE score report, an admissions interview, and a TOEFL or IELTS score for international students. The school also strongly encourages applicants "to have a minimum of two years full-time, post-baccalaureate work experience."

FINANCIAL FACTS

Annual tuition (in-state/ out-of-state)	$19,246/$35,314
Fees	$1,629
Cost of books	$1,000
Room & board	$10,500
% of students receiving aid	88
% of first-year students receiving aid	88
% of students receiving grants	83
Average award package	$39,262
Average grant	$9,260
Average loan	$22,976
Average student loan debt	$49,056

ADMISSIONS

Admissions Selectivity Rating	**92**
# of applications received	245
% applicants accepted	39
% acceptees attending	59
Average GMAT	665
Range of GMAT	640–700
Average GPA	3.35
TOEFL required of international students	Yes
Minimum TOEFL (paper/computer)	600/250
Application fee	$60
International application fee	$100
Early application deadline	12/1
Regular application deadline	7/30
Deferment available	Yes
Maximum length of deferment	1 year
Transfer students accepted	Yes
Transfer application policy: Maximum number of transferable credits is nine (from AACSB-accredited programs only)	
Non-fall admissions	No
Need-blind admissions	Yes

EMPLOYMENT PROFILE

Career Rating	**95**	**Grads Employed by Function**	**% Avg. Salary**
Percent employed at graduation	73	Marketing	(27%) $76,000
Percent employed 3 months after graduation	90	Operations	(14%) $79,717
		Consulting	(11%) $96,750
Average base starting salary	$80,737	Management	(3%)
Primary Source of Full-time Job Acceptances		Finance	(43%) $80,525
School-facilitated activities	25(58%)	Other	(3%)
Graduate-facilitated activities	18(42%)	**Top 5 Employers Hiring Grads**	
		Gavilon (2), Home Depot (2), Deloitte (1), Discover Financial Services (1), Hewlett Packard (1)	

UNIVERSITY OF KANSAS
SCHOOL OF BUSINESS

GENERAL INFORMATION

Type of school	Public
Affiliation	No Affiliation
Academic calendar	Semester

SURVEY SAYS...

Students love Lawrence, KS, Happy students
Solid preparation in:
Doing business in a global economy

STUDENTS

Enrollment of parent institution	27,939
Enrollment of MBA Program	278
% male/female	73/27
% out-of-state	25
% part-time	65
% international	20
Average age at entry	29
Average years work experience at entry	4.0

ACADEMICS

Academic Experience Rating	**84**
Profs interesting rating	81
Profs accesible rating	85
Student/faculty ratio	14:1
% female faculty	24
% underrepresented minority faculty	17
% part-time faculty	45

Joint Degrees

MBA/Master in Management with ESC Clermont Ferrand- 1 year; MBA/JD - 1 year; MBA/MA in Architecture- 1 year; MBA/Global Studies- 2.5 years; MBA/PharmD - 2 years; MBA/Architecture- 3 years MBA with concentration in Petroleum Management- 2 years

Academics

Students at the University of Kansas' School of Business describe their institution as "the best business school in the Midwest," and they have good reason to be so complimentary. "Positive, up-tempo, friendly, and lots of work," the Kansas program is "vastly under-rated" and a "truly wonderful" grad school experience. The students characterize the professors as "second to none" and are impressed with their academic and professional backgrounds." KU profs, who are "active in the business world within their fields," exhibit "a great blend of teaching skills and real-world experience."

Students are held to a high standard and are "expected to be well-prepared, well-read, and well-spoken in course discussions." The "fantastic" administration receives high praise as well. One MBA candidate reported that "if you want to try something different or want to attend a conference, they support you 100 percent of the time." Students also mention the administration's constant efforts "to improve facilities, encourage student involvement and input, and expand the faculty and curriculum."

On top of the full-time MBA offered at KU, the school also offers an evening-profession-al MBA, a Master's in Accounting, Master's in Finance, and several dual-degree MBAs, including a JD/MBA, MBA/MIM, MBA-PharmD, MBA/PM (petroleum management), as well as three international-themed dual degrees involving Latin American, European, and Asian studies. KU also has an extensive PhD program in which students can concen-trate in accounting, information systems, finance, marketing, decision sciences, and man-agement. KU's "focus on the global business environment" is a huge draw for many applicants, who feel that the school provides "an exceptional international business pro-gram for being in the middle of the United States and far from the coasts." Reasonable fees also are a major plus, and many students feel they're receiving a great deal of value for their money.

As one might expect from a school that focuses a great deal on international business, KU has an international program that allows students to obtain real-world experience in the global marketplace. The KU School of Business partners with the Center for International Business Education and Research to facilitate study abroad with an array of businesses across the globe. In the past few years students have traveled to India, China, Germany, France, Brazil, and Mexico as part of the program. With these types of experiences avail-able to students, it's no wonder they describe the KU program as a "good value for the money that offered many options in terms of international experience."

Career and Placement

On its website the school boasts that "KU Business alumni are chief officers and senior executives of dozens of *Fortune* 500 companies." Fortunately for KU students who aspire to such heights, Kansas City is home to many large corporations, including Sprint and Hallmark, and the metropolitan area has been named one of the "Top 20 Areas to Start and Grow a Company" by Inc.com. KU also has a second campus (Edwards Campus) located in nearby Overland Park, which was named one of the top 10 cities for doing business by Business Development Outlook.

Students give glowing reviews to the school's Career Services Department, which does a "fantastic job of preparing students for the job-search process and facilitating that process through two massive career fairs, many interview and resume workshops, one-on-one counseling, and more." One student says, "I already have a job waiting for me when I complete the master's program, thanks to the business school's Career Services, and KU's strong reputation in the region."

ADMISSIONS CONTACT: DEE STEINLE, ADMINISTRATIVE DIRECTOR OF MASTERS PROGRAMS
ADDRESS: 206 SUMMERFIELD HALL, 1300 SUNNYSIDE AVENUE, LAWRENCE, KS 66045
PHONE: 785-864-7500 • FAX: 785-864-5376
E-MAIL: BSCHOOLGRAD@KU.EDU • WEBSITE: WWW.BUSINESS.KU.EDU

Approximately 66 percent of Kansas students accepted job offers before graduating in a recent academic year, and by three months after graduation, that number had grown to 100 percent. The average salary for graduates was $67,139 (not including bonus). The majority of students accepted jobs in marketing and finance, although there were quite a few who went into operations and consulting. A range of companies recruit on campus, and the ones who hire graduates most frequently include Tradebot, MarketSphere, United Missouri Bank, and Sprint Nextel.

Student Life and Environment

KU students enjoy life on campus, which many describe as "great." The only complaint is that "there are really more things that I'd like to be able to participate in than I have time to do!" One student described life at KU as "filled with a variety of activities, including extracurriculars (Net Impact, Graduate Business Council), social events put on by MBA student organizations, working for the MBA Admissions Office, and of course, course work."

Although the majority of the class is "ambitious and concentrated on their future," students are also "very fun people." There is diversity among the MBA candidates, and the students "vary from people straight out of undergrad to people 35 years old, and they all have different goals and lifestyles, but they communicate well and make the classes enjoyable by opening up discussion without judging others." Some say their classmates "are the very best part about my experience in the KU MBA program." Overall, students are more than satisfied with their experiences at KU. As one student said, "I cannot thank KU enough for preparing me to excel in my future endeavors."

Admissions

Applications are accepted at anytime, up until posted application deadlines. In a recently admitted class, students' average undergraduate GPA was around 3.2, and the average GMAT was approximately 568. Students had an average of three years of work experience.

FINANCIAL FACTS

Annual tuition (in-state/ out-of-state)	$8,250/$19,300
Fees	$9,570
Cost of books	$2,000
Room & board	$9,500
% of students receiving aid	80
% of first-year students receiving aid	85
% of students receiving grants	30
Average grant	$8,000

ADMISSIONS

Admissions Selectivity Rating	89
# of applications received	146
% applicants accepted	32
% acceptees attending	52
Average GMAT	573
Range of GMAT	460–720
Average GPA	3.30
TOEFL required of international students	Yes
Minimum TOEFL (paper/computer)	53/20
Application fee	$65
International application fee	$65
Early application deadline	1/15
Regular application deadline	6/1
Deferment available	No
Transfer students accepted	Yes
Transfer application policy: Maximum number of transferable credit hours is six.	
Non-fall admissions	Yes
Need-blind admissions	Yes

EMPLOYMENT PROFILE

Career Rating	74	Grads Employed by Function% Avg. Salary	
Percent employed at graduation	40	Marketing	(25%)
Percent employed 3 months after graduation	53	Operations	(10%)
		Consulting	(5%)
Average base starting salary	$65,353	Finance	(35%)
Primary Source of Full-time Job Acceptances		MIS	(5%)
School-facilitated activities	8(18%)	Other	(20%)
Graduate-facilitated activities	13(30%)	Top 5 Employers Hiring Grads	
Unknown	23(52%)	Cerner (4), Associated Wholesale Grocers (1), Google (2), Sabre Holdings (1), Walmart (1)	

UNIVERSITY OF KENTUCKY
GATTON COLLEGE OF BUSINESS AND ECONOMICS

GENERAL INFORMATION
Type of school   Public
Affiliation   No Affiliation
Academic calendar   Semester

SURVEY SAYS...
Students love Lexington, KY, Friendly
students
Solid preparation in:
Teamwork

STUDENTS
Enrollment of parent
  institution   28,928
Enrollment of MBA Program   174
% male/female   70/30
% out-of-state   16
% part-time   56
% underrepresented minority   5
% international   10
Average age at entry   26
Average years work experience
  at entry   2.2

ACADEMICS
Academic Experience Rating   **79**
Profs interesting rating   77
Profs accesible rating   81
Student/faculty ratio   8:1
% female faculty   9
% underrepresented minority
  faculty   13
% part-time faculty   0

Joint Degrees
MBA/JD (4 years); BS
Engineering/MBA (5 years);
MD/MBA (5 years); PharmD/MBA (4
years); MBA/MA International
Relations (3 years)

Prominent Alumni
Paul Rooke, CEO, Lexmark
International; W. Rodney McMullen,
President, Kroger Company; Joseph
W. Craft, Chairman, President, &
CEO, Alliance Coal,LLC; Paul C.
Varga, Chairman, President, & CEO,
Brown-Forman Corporation; James
E. Rogers, Jr., Chairman, President
& CEO, Duke Energy Corporation

Academics

The Gatton College of Business and Economics at the University of Kentucky offers both a part-time MBA designed for the needs of local professionals and a full-time, 11-month immersion MBA. Many students in our survey identified the accelerated pace of the full-time program as a major attraction. It's "a quick program that offers a more intense learning experience along with the opportunity to work with executives at some of the largest world corporations" through "Project Connect, a partnership between the university and industry to provide practical education via projects" with regional businesses.

Students in both programs appreciate that Gatton "is recognized [as] the best graduate business school in the state," which "is very helpful in getting a job." "Good professors" and the "relatively low" tuition is also appealing, of course. The Gatton curriculum "is broken into modules such as new product development, mergers and acquisitions, supply chain management, and financial analysis," and "all tools and skills (finance, accounting, ops) are taught around the basis of these modules." The program "stays on top of the latest trends and technologies in business," another plus. This "very structured" program requires "a lot of group work." "The whole program is team-based, which is going to be helpful in the future," one student writes.

The Gatton MBA emphasizes new product development, supply chain management, and mergers and acquisitions. Cross-functional teams of five are created and work with companies on projects in each of the three areas of emphasis. This is complemented by professors who are generally "very good and have a fairly structured teaching style" and blend "theory and real-world experience." In recent years the school "has added many faculty with real-world experience and shaped the program and skill sets you learn around executives' requests for incoming employees. It is amazing how tailored this program is to real work experience." Part-timers appreciate how "the professors understand that their students are also working professionals and have other lives besides the classroom." As a result, "The course load has not been unbearable, but it keeps you busy."

Career and Placement

MBA students have access to comprehensive career services through Gatton College's Office of Career Services, including a career development course, which is required for one-year students and optional for part-time students. They also put on events in conjunction with the university-wide James W. Stackert Career Center, such as a large, two-day career fair each semester, employer information sessions, and campus interviews. To help students prepare for these events, MBA Career Services offers individualized coaching sessions on topics including: resume writing, job searching, networking, interviewing, salary negotiating, etiquette, and more.

Last year the average salary for a Gatton graduate was $55,926. Companies hiring Gatton MBAs include Aldi, Alltech, BB&T, Brown-Forman, Deloitte, Ernst & Young, Fifth Third, Goldman Sachs, Honda Motors, Humana, KPMG, Lexmark, Procter & Gamble, PricewaterhouseCoopers, Schneider Electric, Tempur-Pedic, Toyota, and Wright-Patterson Air Force Base.

ADMISSIONS CONTACT: BEVERLY KEMPER, MBA ACADEMIC COORDINATOR
ADDRESS: 145 GATTON COLLEGE OF BUSINESS AND ECONOMICS, LEXINGTON, KY 40506-0034
PHONE: 859-257-7722 • FAX: 859-323-9971
E-MAIL: KEMPER@UKY.EDU • WEBSITE: GATTON.UKY.EDU

Student Life and Environment

For full-time MBAs, "Life at UK is focused on school rather than extracurricular activities, largely because of the length and intensity of the program." Cramming two years' worth of learning into eleven months doesn't leave a lot of time for extracurriculars or socializing. Full-timers generally live in "nice...well-priced" housing located "relatively close" to campus, "which is nice considering we are all working with companies [on Project Connect projects] and we have to meet daily." The MBA group forms "a very strong community." On days we have class, nearly all students arrive 45 minutes to an hour early to socialize and visit" in the "dedicated MBA lounge...Professors will stop by as well." When time permits, students enjoy getting out and about in Lexington, an "exciting" and "excellent city" with "plenty to do."

Gatton full-timers don't have "as much work experience as [students at] some schools," but they are "hard workers and add a certain competitive edge in the classroom which I feel improves the overall experience. Outside of class, many of us commonly get together to socialize and even discuss business-related topics/concerns that arise in our workplaces and in the economy." The part-time student body includes a substantial number of "engineer-schooled and extremely goal-oriented" professionals.

Admissions

Applicants to the Gatton MBA program must submit the following materials: official transcripts for all undergraduate study (minimum GPA of 2.75 on a 4.0 scale required); an official score report for either the GMAT or the GRE; three letters of recommendation from individuals who can objectively assess the applicant's character and capabilities; a current resume; and a completed application. International applicants who do not hold undergraduate degrees from a U.S. institution must also submit an official score report for the TOEFL or the TWE. Gatton admits MBAs for the fall semester only. Among those accepted to the most recent class, the average GMAT score was 603 and the average undergraduate GPA was 3.34.

FINANCIAL FACTS

Annual tuition (in-state/ out-of-state)	$11,165/$22,237
Fees	$8,812
Cost of books	$2,500
Room & board (on/off-campus)	$8,250/$9,100
% of students receiving aid	29
% of first-year students receiving aid	29
% of students receiving grants	29
Average award package	$18,241
Average grant	$18,241
Average loan	$0
Average student loan debt	$0

ADMISSIONS

Admissions Selectivity Rating	76
# of applications received	206
% applicants accepted	80
% acceptees attending	78
Average GMAT	602
Range of GMAT	550–660
Average GPA	3.37
TOEFL required of international students	Yes
Minimum TOEFL (paper/computer)	550/213
Application fee	$65
International Early application deadline	4/1
Regular application deadline	5/11
Deferment available	Yes
Transfer students accepted	Yes
Transfer application policy: File must be completed and applicant is considered as a regular applicant only for Evening program	
Non-fall admissions	Yes
Need-blind admissions	Yes

EMPLOYMENT PROFILE

Career Rating	87	**Grads Employed by Function% Avg. Salary**	
Percent employed at graduation	55	Marketing	(25%) $50,857
Percent employed 3 months		Operations	(28%) $56,018
after graduation	78	Consulting	(5%)
Average base starting salary	$54,811	Management	(15%) $60,000
Primary Source of Full-time Job Acceptances		Finance	(8%) $46,667
School-facilitated activities	18(45%)	MIS	(7%) $59,000
Graduate-facilitated activities	16(40%)	Other	(12%) $48,375
Unknown	6(15%)	**Top 5 Employers Hiring Grads**	
		Big Ass Fans (3), Humana (1), Schneider Electric (1), Target (1), JP Morgan Chase (1)	

UNIVERSITY OF LOUISIANA—LAFAYETTE
B. I. MOODY III COLLEGE OF BUSINESS

Academics

University of Louisiana—Lafayette's strong regional reputation, convenient course schedule, and friendly staff make it a justifiably popular choice for ambitious local professionals. Although students may choose to take a full course load, this "MBA program caters to students who work full-time jobs" and attend classes in the evenings. According to the busy bees in the program, the "curriculum is challenging and relevant," consisting of core courses in advanced business fundamentals like accounting, management information systems, marketing, and finance, followed by two elective courses in a student's discipline of choice. In addition to the traditional program, the school operates a respected MBA in health care administration, which combines six specialized courses in that field with five core courses from the general MBA core.

Students are happy to report that the MBA at University of Louisiana—Lafayette is overseen by a team of "very knowledgeable" and "amazingly talented teachers." While "the faculty and staff have high expectations" for their students, they are always "willing to assist those who ask for help." Here, "Professors are very approachable," and the "school is small enough for teachers to get to know all students." "Presentations and teamwork" are a fixture in almost every class, and the varying professional backgrounds of MBA candidates help to foster "rich, insightful classroom discussions and activities." One student agrees, "With a lot of hands-on group projects, MBA students learn a great deal from working with other students from different backgrounds." Likewise, the school's staff and administration "wants students to succeed and ensures all needs for MBA students are met." In terms of improvement, students would also love to see "more diverse classes" offered, with newer topics like social media incorporated into the instruction.

For exacting business students, one of the most attractive aspects of a University of Louisiana education is the great return on investment. As a public school, "The tuition is very low considering the quality of education and the many great facilities." Students also note that the program is on the up-and-up, having "gained national recognition/honors in the last few years" and, under the vigilant leadership of the current administrators, constantly improving. Of particular note, the program director and the administrative assistant who oversee the program receive top marks from students. A current MBA declares, "Dr. Viguerie, and Mrs. Jan are AMAZING!!! They are in constant communication with anybody that has questions, and they actually encourage students to come to them with any and every question that they might have!" Similarly, "professors are a great support system"; they "really care about teaching the students and want to provide any help they can." In fact, professors "go out of their way to work with your work schedule should issues arise," making it easier to balance work, school, and family life.

ADMISSIONS CONTACT: DR. C. EDDIE PALMER, DEAN OF THE GRADUATE SCHOOL
ADDRESS: MARTIN HALL, ROOM #332, P. O. BOX 44610, LAFAYETTE, LA 70504-4610
PHONE: 337-482-6965 • FAX: 337-482-1333
E-MAIL: GRADSCHOOL@LOUISIANA.EDU • WEBSITE: MOODY.LOUISIANA.EDU

Career and Placement

Univeristy of Louisiana—Lafayette's MBA is geared toward working professionals (some of whom receive tuition assistance from their current employer), so very few MBA candidates are actively looking for a new job at graduation. Instead, most plan to leverage their education for a better position in their current company. As a result, professional development activities are somewhat limited on campus.

Those who are looking for a new job or hoping to switch careers after graduation can get help at the campus Career Services center. Though principally aimed at the undergraduate community, Career Services organizes campus career fairs, hosts on-campus interviews and recruiting sessions, offers professional-development seminars, and keeps an updated list of open positions in the area. In addition, the school has a "great alumni base" and an active MBA Association, both of which can assist with local networking.

Student Life and Environment

Although it draws the majority of its students from the local community, "There is a very diverse age range, as well as diversity in ethnicity and fields of interest" at University of Louisiana—Lafayette. Most students have at least a few years of professional experience before coming to the MBA program, and even recent college graduates are likely to be working full-time when they join the program. Though there is a considerable group of single students, many are "married and have children," often balancing family life alongside school and career. Striking a good balance, almost everyone here is "motivated and achievement oriented, while at the same time being extremely open and friendly."

Though many students are busy with work obligations and family life, others are "very conscientious and involved" in the campus community. In their free time, MBA students can participate in social and networking events put on by the MBA Association, or sign up for volunteer projects with other MBA candidates. Located in the "little city" of Lafayette, the overally environment is low-key and student-friendly. According to UL students, "Lafayette is a great college town," with ample outdoor activities, great Cajun and Creole restaurants, and plenty of live music and nightlife.

Admissions

To be considered for admission to the University of Louisiana—Lafayette's MBA program, students must have an undergraduate degree from an accredited university, with a grade point average of 2.75 or better. Prospective students are also required to submit GMAT scores, three letters of recommendation, a professional résumé, and a statement of purpose.

FINANCIAL FACTS

Annual tuition (in-state/ out-of-state)	$5,265/$13,887
Fees	$0
Cost of books	$1,200
Room & board (on/off-campus)	$5,700/$10,200
Average award package	$12,765
Average grant	$3,000

ADMISSIONS

Admissions Selectivity Rating	84
# of applications received	176
% applicants accepted	45
% acceptees attending	76
Average GMAT	508
Range of GMAT	450–560
Average GPA	3.23
TOEFL required of international students	Yes
Minimum TOEFL (paper/computer)	550/213
Application fee	$25
International application fee	$30
Regular application deadline	7/15
Deferment available	Yes
Maximum length of deferment	12 months
Transfer students accepted	Yes
Transfer application policy: Can transfer a maximum of 9 credit hours. Must apply through regular process. All transfer credits must be approved by MBA Director.	
Non-fall admissions	Yes
Need-blind admissions	Yes

UNIVERSITY OF LOUISVILLE
COLLEGE OF BUSINESS

GENERAL INFORMATION
Type of school | Public
Academic calendar | Year-round

SURVEY SAYS...
Cutting-edge classes
Solid preparation in:
General management, Teamwork,
Communication/interpersonal skills

STUDENTS
Enrollment of parent
  institution | 22,293
Enrollment of MBA Program | 259
% male/female | 73/28
% out-of-state | 35
% part-time | 85
% underrepresented minority | 8
% international | 13
Average age at entry | 28
Average years work experience
  at entry | 4.6

ACADEMICS
Academic Experience Rating | 90
Profs interesting rating | 89
Profs accesible rating | 91
Student/faculty ratio | 6:1
% female faculty | 24
% underrepresented minority
  faculty | 24
% part-time faculty | 2

Joint Degrees
Joint degree oppurtunities are available with all graduate and professional programs at U of L, including the Law, Engineering, and Medical schools. Program lengths vary in the partner schools but the program length of the MBA is not changed. Students must complete degree requirements of both programs to be awarded the joint degrees.

Prominent Alumni
David Jones, Founder/ Former Chairman, Humana; Terry Forcht, Owner, Forcht Group

Academics

The University of Louisville has some unique opportunities. For example, if you are looking for a paid internship "with established businesses," and one that "also includes an international trip," then UL's "accelerated" 13-month full-time MBA program may be for you. One student reports favorably on this, saying, "The internship pays for almost the entire tuition which is a big plus." But don't wait too long to apply because this "program seem[s] to be gaining in reputation."

The progression of classes for the MBA program is "well thought out with early classes setting the stage for later courses and everything nesting into a coherent business education." On the whole, students have a high opinion of their professors. "The faculty consists of many successful professionals turned educators. The program encourages strategic alignment and thinking across functions in a very creative way. The professors show what worked for them and what works for others all to arm students with a strong foundation of strategic thinking and creative solutions." Although not every faculty member receives glowing praise, some "outstanding" professors were noted in the Entrepreneurship program, as they "blend real-world experience with academia. The results are exciting and realistic. It makes learning the theories more meaningful." There is a genuine feeling of kinship among many since "the administration and faculty want us to succeed in the program and develop our business knowledge further. If we need to spend extra time to master a subject, we will, and it's simply because everyone cares enough to take the extra time to ensure we build solid foundations of knowledge."

Career and Placement

Louisville is described as "an excellent city" with "very useful resources," and the school receives accolades from students regarding its excellent location and proactive approach to helping place students in decent jobs. For students interested in pursuing professional opportunities locally, "this program offers a tremendous amount of resources for anyone [who] would like to start a business in the Louisville area. There are lots of introductions to angel investors and venture capitalists," and "focused and educational classes taught by actual entrepreneurs" are offered as well. The University of Louisville's career center provides resume assistance and interview training seminars and also helps with "any job searching needs or questions" students may have. Available internships are another advantage to helping one successfully find a job upon graduation. One student who profited from the experience explains, "The internship opportunity in this tough market is extremely beneficial. It was good practice to get several interview opportunities and now I work for a good company 15 minutes from UL." Additionally, "There are lots of amazing guest speakers that further expand the networking possibilities."

Student Life and Environment

At the University of Louisville, you will be surrounded by "lots of motivated individuals that aim to accomplish a lot in this life." There is a "wide age range" and classmates "come from many different cultures and education backgrounds." One student has the opinion that, "not a lot of people outside of Kentucky know about UL." But not all students share this perspective. Although some students do come from the Kentucky area, one will also encounter students "from all over, including Germany, India, and Mongolia." One Louisville native states, "It's great to be a part of such an interesting group of people with different backgrounds, beliefs, and experiences." Overall, students transcend a "high energy" with a "desire to learn, grow and develop."

There is definitely a "sports atmosphere" here and students make good use of the "very nice facilities including the "state-of-the-art gym." UL offers intramural programs and discounts to attend various campus sporting events. Taking advantage of these is not difficult. "Administration is helpful in providing opportunities to purchase tickets with ease."

Louisville also provides a "very friendly and involving" campus in an urban environment. The "locked-cohort style" makes getting to know one's classmates easy as it "ensures that students spend all two years with the same 26 individuals. This really bonds the class and leads to long-lasting friendships and networking opportunities."

Admissions

Students do not need to rush their applications into the University of Louisville College of Business. Rolling admissions are open for all MBA programs until July 1. But applying early does have a financial advantage. A $1,000 scholarship is available to Entrepreneurship MBA early admit students who meet the May 1 priority deadline. Student interviews, GMAT scores, and undergraduate GPAs are given the highest consideration for incoming students. College transcripts, personal statement, letters of recommendation, and resume are also required. Students average over six years of work experience before enrolling at UL and the average age of enrollees over the past several years has been 28. About 50 students make up the Professional MBA classes, about 40 attend the Entrepreneurship MBA classes, and about 35 are in the full-time MBA class.

FINANCIAL FACTS

Annual tuition	$32,000
Fees	$0
Cost of books	$1,500
Room & board	
(on/off-campus)	$10,500/$12,500
% of students receiving aid	52
% of first-year students	
receiving aid	31
% of students receiving grants	19
Average award package	$11,683
Average grant	$6,190
Average loan	$12,750
Average student loan debt	$16,282

ADMISSIONS

Admissions Selectivity Rating	87
# of applications received	359
% applicants accepted	46
% acceptees attending	91
Average GMAT	562
Range of GMAT	510–610
Average GPA	3.36
TOEFL required of	
international students	Yes
Minimum TOEFL	
(paper/computer)	550/213
Application fee	$50
International application fee	$50
Regular application deadline	7/1
Deferment available	Yes
Maximum length	
of deferment	case by case basis, generally one year
Transfer students accepted	Yes
Transfer application policy: Up to 9 credits are accepted (grade B or better) from an AACSB accredited MBA program, reviewed on a case by case basis.	
Non-fall admissions	Yes
Need-blind admissions	Yes

EMPLOYMENT PROFILE

Career Rating	93	Grads Employed by Function	% Avg. Salary
Percent employed at graduation	74	Marketing	(21%) $47,125
Percent employed 3 months		Operations	(26%) $55,600
after graduation	100	Finance	(26%) $38,600
Average base starting salary	$65,955	HR	(6%) $27,790
Primary Source of Full-time Job Acceptances		Other	(21%) $59,250
School-facilitated activities	7(39%)	**Top 5 Employers Hiring Grads**	
Graduate-facilitated activities	2(11%)	Humana (1), Kindred (1), Merrill Lynch (1),	
Unknown	9(50%)	Louisville Water Company (1), Alltech (1)	

UNIVERSITY OF MARYLAND, COLLEGE PARK
ROBERT H. SMITH SCHOOL OF BUSINESS

GENERAL INFORMATION

Type of school	Public
Affiliation	No Affiliation
Academic calendar	Semester

SURVEY SAYS...

Friendly students, Cutting-edge classes
Solid preparation in:
General management, Teamwork, Quantitative skills, Doing business in a global economy

STUDENTS

Enrollment of parent institution	37,248
Enrollment of MBA Program	1,049
% male/female	70/30
% out-of-state	30
% part-time	78
% underrepresented minority	10
% international	43
Average age at entry	28
Average years work experience at entry	5.0

ACADEMICS

Academic Experience Rating	**87**
Profs interesting rating	91
Profs accesible rating	79
Student/faculty ratio	5:1
% female faculty	30
% underrepresented minority faculty	24
% part-time faculty	25

Joint Degrees

MBA/MS - 66 credits (21 months to 5 years); MBA/JD - 108 credits (3 to 5 years); MBA/Master of Public Management - 66 credits (2.3 years to 5 years); MBA/Master of Social Work - 88 credits (2.3 to 5 years); MBA/MS in Nursing - 66 credits (3 - 5 years)

Academics

A large school with a commanding reputation in the Washington, D.C., and Baltimore metropolitan areas, the Robert H. Smith School of Business offers a wide range of MBA options to a diverse student body of more than 1,000 graduate students. Depending on their professional experience, work schedule, and academic objectives, students can apply to Smith's full-time MBA program, Executive MBA, Accelerated MBA, or the part-time Evening MBA or Weekend MBA, and the school does not require students to choose a track. The School also has numerous graduate assistant positions, which allow students to not only receive in-state tuition, but also include tuition remission, a stipend, and eligibility for State of Maryland healthcare.

While each program differs in terms of class schedules, enrollment, admissions requirements, overall length, and location, they share an emphasis on the global economy, the integration of technology, and business, marketing, and entrepreneurship, all with "a strong quantitative core." "My undergraduate is from a liberal arts school, so I chose Smith because it would develop my weaknesses," says a student. At the same time, real-world experience is paramount to a Smith education, and the School allows many opportunities for students to learn outside the classroom, such as case competitions, consulting projects, international teams, and "an excellent entrepreneurship center." In addition to the "numerous leadership positions and international experiences," the School has a special program called the Mayer Fund, where 12 selected MBA students from the entire school get to manage a $1.2 million endowment fund. There is a similar fund (Global Equity Fund) for part-time students. Adding to the School's dynamic atmosphere is its urban location (Smith maintains campuses in College Park, Washington, Baltimore, and Rockville.), which helps attract some top-notch students to join the school, and "it really shows in the class discussion."

Smith attracts a team of "world class" faculty members, who "incorporate the most pressing issues in their research into their classes and teach us the real-world implications." Fortunately, the classroom experience does not come second to the faculty's research interests; at Smith, professors "sincerely enjoy engaging with students on class topics" and "provide good independent-study projects" for students to pursue. Evening students tell us that Smith professors "are very good at holding the attention of the class, even late at night." Small class sizes "allow for ideal interaction and extraction of knowledge from professors and other students." Most Smith "professors have been very involved in both the Baltimore and Washington business communities" throughout their careers, adding an important practical dynamic to the classroom. In addition to their expertise, Smith professors "are also just great people to be around; very personable and approachable. They work as hard for us as we work for them."

Career and Placement

A large percentage of Smith's part-time students plan to stay at their current company after graduation. In fact, many are receiving tuition reimbursement for their studies. However, for students seeking a new position or career change after graduation, the Smith School of Business boasts "excellent job placement rates" and lots of deep ties in the local community. "Great companies recruit at Smith," says a student. Smith's Director of Career Services is "committed, focused, and approachable. He has been successful in his own consulting business, as well as his academic career and uses these skills to make strong employer connections at Smith." Students can also get highly individualized assistance from one of the office's professional staff members or take advantage of the numerous resources offered.

Recent companies that have recruited Smith grads include American Express Financial Advisors, Bank of America, Barclays Capital, Capital One, Chase Card Services, Citigroup, Deloitte Services, DuPont, Fannie Mae, FedEx, IBM, Intel Corporation, Lockheed Martin, Morgan Stanley, Motorola, The Washington Post, and The World Bank.

Student Life and Environment

Smith has MBA programs on four campuses in College Park, Rockville, Washington, and Baltimore, though the College Park location is primarily used for the full-time program. At each campus, you'll find a different range of resources and opportunities. The School's reputation and selective admissions draws a group of students who are "intelligent, well-informed, confident, hardworking, kind, and dependable," and "fellow classmates are interested in collaboration and learning rather than competition and sabotage." You'll also find a "diverse range of career backgrounds, and a high level of experience," though most "have rich business experience prior to business school."

In College Park, students are "heavily involved in clubs." Clubs are diverse and run events from professional development events to international celebrations and happy hours. The small class sizes also lead to "a very intimate environment where you get to know your fellow students very well." When it comes to having fun, students report a lively and social atmosphere among MBAs, including "great happy hours and frequent, memorable cultural and variety nights." Luckily, part-time students don't miss out on the fun; while their schedules leave little downtime, part-timers still find time for "happy hours after class, if we are still awake. We also have parties on weekends." While there aren't school-sponsored events specifically for kids, "many events are baby friendly."

Admissions

To apply to Smith, students must submit two official copies of their undergraduate transcripts, official GMAT scores, two letters of recommendation, and a set of personal essays. An undergraduate GPA of 2.8 is required. In the full-time program, the current entering class had GMAT scores ranging from 610–730, and an average undergraduate GPA of 3.3. The part-time class submitted GMAT scores between 500 and 690. Students have an average of 4.5 to 5 years of professional work experience before beginning the MBA program.

Prominent Alumni

Kevin Plank, CEO and Founder, Under Armour; Carly Fiorina, Head of Carly Fiorina Enterprises; Richard Shaeffer, Chairman, NYMEX Holdings; Bob Basham, Co-Founder, Outback; Albert P. Carey, Chief Executive Officer, PepsiCo

FINANCIAL FACTS

Annual tuition (in-state/ out-of-state)	$38,475/$45,765
Fees	$1,683
Cost of books	$1,500
Room & board	$15,000

ADMISSIONS

Admissions Selectivity Rating	87
# of applications received	661
% applicants accepted	44
% acceptees attending	39
Average GMAT	656
Range of GMAT	620–690
Average GPA	3.30
TOEFL required of international students	Yes
Minimum TOEFL (paper/computer)	600/250
Application fee	$75
International application fee	$75
Early application deadline	1/15
Early notification date	4/1
Regular application deadline	3/1
Regular application notification	5/1
Application Deadline/Notification	
Round 1:	11/1 / 1/15
Round 2:	12/15 / 2/15
Round 3:	1/15 / 4/1
Round 4:	3/1 / 5/1
Deferment available	Yes
Maximum length of deferment	1 year
Transfer students accepted	No
Non-fall admissions	No
Need-blind admissions	Yes

EMPLOYMENT PROFILE

		Grads Employed by Function	% Avg. Salary
Career Rating	93	Marketing	(20%) $89,313
Percent employed at graduation	68	Operations	(4%) $88,250
Percent employed 3 months after graduation	88	Consulting	(28%)$100,523
Average base starting salary	$92,938	Management	(11%) $96,667
Primary Source of Full-time Job Acceptances		Finance	(22%) $90,258
School-facilitated activities	42(48%)	HR	(3%) $83,000
Graduate-facilitated activities	19(22%)	MIS	(5%) $92,500
Unknown	26(30%)	Other	(6%) $87,400

Top 5 Employers Hiring Grads
Cognizant(7), Deloitte Consulting (7), Capital One (4), Computer Science Corporation (CSC) (4), PWC (3)

University of Massachusetts Amherst
Isenberg School of Management

Academics

For savvy business students, Isenberg School of Management unites convenience, quality, and cost. Any way you slice it, University of Massachusetts—Amherst is an "exceptional value," boasting a low in-state tuition, yet all the prestige and resources you'd expect from the UMass name. For students who participate in the school's full-time graduate assistantship program, the deal is even sweeter. A student enthuses, "The best business decision I've made so far is to get my MBA in the full-time program where all of my tuition and fees are waived and I get paid to be a research assistant!" A comprehensive 55-unit program, the full-time MBA at UMass is completed on the school's main campus over the course of two years. For those already in the workforce, Isenberg "caters to part-time students who have to work full-time" by offering a convenient part-time MBA, which can be completed in class at Holyoke, Shrewsbury, or online. In addition, UMass offers dual degree programs in many fields, including sports management, public policy and civil, environmental, industrial, and mechanical engineering.

Although the full-time MBA enrolls only 35 students each year, UMass is a large, public university. Therefore, it can be "hard to get a hold of the administrators because they're very busy." A student continues, "The administration has been nearly invisible, which is exactly how it should be—there have been no hassles over courses or deadlines." One exception: scheduling is often disorganized, and many students receive their "course schedule and textbook requirements sometimes just a week or two before classes begin"—creating lots of headaches at the beginning of the term. In 2011, the administration was reorganized under two Associate Deans, one dedicated to the Full-time MBA Program and one dedicated to the Part-time MBA Program. In contrast, the academic experience is surprisingly intimate, boasting small class sizes and "very supportive" professors. In the classroom, "Discussions are interesting and it's easy to participate," and professors "welcome discussion and feedback and are willing to let students run with ideas while still…keep[ing] us on track."

Uniting practical knowledge with academic savvy, "professors are very knowledgeable within their respective fields" and "very current" on industry trends. Students also get a taste of the real world through various experiential learning opportunities. After completing the core curriculum, students have "freedom to choose courses, practicum, and search for jobs." Among other offerings, the "Practicum" is a semester-long consulting project, which lets second-year students test their business acumen while working directly with for-profit and not-for-profit local businesses. A current student enthuses, "The end-of-program practicum project is extremely well put together, and is valuable for both real-world experience and resume-building."

Career Placement

Isenberg's MBA Career Management Office helps MBA candidates prepare for their career through a variety of services and networking programs. Among other offerings, the office operates a mandatory first-year Professional Seminar, which teaches full-time students how to self-assess in relation to the marketplace. It also focuses on practical life-long learning skills that will make graduates better leaders in their organizations. While "the career center is good if you have specific questions," students admit that, "you really need to go out there and work for yourself to get anywhere" with the job search. Among students, "We rely on each other to bring our personal networks into the program." Here, "people know what you are looking to do and keep their ears open for opportunities to pass along."

On campus, students have access to career fairs and networking events; however, MBA candidates would also like to see more upper-level recruiting at UMass. In fact, companies "often come to campus to recruit undergrads but have no interest in the MBAs." A student adds, "Since the program is so small there are no visits from recruiters. While the career center has been infinitely useful for me, it would be more beneficial if they could interest recruiters in the MBA class." In recent years, Isenberg graduates have taken jobs at Bose, Canon, EMC, General Electric, Hearts of Fire, Kaufman Bros., KPMG, MassMutual, PriceWaterhouseCoopers, and United Technologies Corp.

Student Life and Environment

Amherst, Massachusetts, is the quintessential college town, and students in the business program aren't immune to their lively surroundings. Here, the atmosphere is collegial and friendly, and "students are active in clubs, sports/healthy living, arts activities, and more." Moreover, "Being a small program affords the majority of us to continue to practice our leadership skills in clubs, which provides a semblance of running a business and gives us high visibility in the university, with alumni, and in the broader community."

With only 70 students in the full-time program, Isenberg is "truly a community." During the challenging first-year curriculum, "the class gets very close, works hard together, and works to help each other." In addition, "Second-years are very active in helping the first-years adjust to the work load." In their free time, MBA candidates get together for "hikes, pot-luck dinners, [or] ice skating," and many attend the "weekly Thursday Night Out event sponsored by the Graduate Business Association." On the school's satellite campuses, students rarely get involved in any activities beyond classes. Nonetheless, they "enjoy interacting with the other students," and tell us that, "the facilities function well for what we need to accomplish."

Admissions

Isenberg accepts students based on their demonstrated record of academic achievement, promise for success in graduate school, quality of professional experience, and clarity of career purpose. To be eligible for Isenberg's full-time or part-time programs, students must have at least three years of professional, post-undergraduate work experience. The school accepts either GMAT or GRE scores. The part-time program enrolls students three times a year; the full-time program begins once a year, in the fall.

Prominent Alumni

Eugene M. Isenberg, Chairman and CEO, Nabors Industries, Ltd.; John (Jack) F. Smith, Former Chairman & CEO, General Motors; Edward D. Shirley, President and CEO, Bacardi Ltd.; Anshu Jain, Co-Chairman & CEO Deutsche Bank; David Fubini, Senior Director of McKinsey & Company

FINANCIAL FACTS

Annual tuition (in-state/ out-of-state)	$2,640/$9,937
Fees	$10,695
Cost of books	$3,000
Room & board (on/off-campus)	$10,100/$11,500
% of students receiving grants	100
Average grant	$29,294
Average student loan debt	$20,447

ADMISSIONS

Admissions Selectivity Rating	96
# of applications received	229
% applicants accepted	25
% acceptees attending	60
Average GMAT	655
Range of GMAT	610–690
Average GPA	3.40
TOEFL required of international students	Yes
Minimum TOEFL (paper/computer)	600/100
Application fee	$75
International application fee	$75
Regular application deadline	12/1
Application Deadline/Notification	
Round 1:	12/1 /
Round 2:	2/1 /
Round 3:	4/1 /
Deferment available	Yes
Maximum length of deferment	1 year
Transfer students accepted	No
Non-fall admissions	No
Need-blind admissions	Yes

EMPLOYMENT PROFILE

Career Rating	93	Grads Employed by Function% Avg. Salary		
Percent employed at graduation	50	Marketing	(20%)	
Percent employed 3 months after graduation	95	Operations	(10%)	
Average base starting salary	$82,900	Consulting	(20%)	$115,000
Primary Source of Full-time Job Acceptances		Management	(32%)	
School-facilitated activities	9(47%)	Finance	(6%)	
Graduate-facilitated activities	6(32%)	HR	(6%)	
Unknown	4(21%)	MIS	(6%)	

Top 5 Employers Hiring Grads
United Technologies Corp. (3), EMC^2 Corporation (1), Google, Inc. (1), The Travelers (1), Cognizant, Inc. (1)

UNIVERSITY OF MASSACHUSETTS BOSTON
GRADUATE COLLEGE OF MANAGEMENT

GENERAL INFORMATION

Type of school	Public
Affiliation	No Affiliation
Academic calendar	Semesters

SURVEY SAYS...
Solid preparation in:
Teamwork, Communication/
interpersonal skills

STUDENTS

Enrollment of parent institution	15,454
Enrollment of MBA Program	531
% male/female	48/52
% out-of-state	52
% part-time	52
% underrepresented minority	26
% international	54
Average age at entry	27
Average years work experience at entry	7.4

ACADEMICS

Academic Experience Rating	86
Profs interesting rating	84
Profs accesible rating	85
Student/faculty ratio	4:1
% female faculty	27
% underrepresented minority faculty	38
% part-time faculty	20

Joint Degrees
MS in Accounting - 2 years; MS in Finance - 2 years; MS in International Management 2 years; MS in Information Technology 2 years

Prominent Alumni
Thomas M. Menino, Mayor, City of Boston; Joseph Abboud, Fashion Designer; George Kassas, Founder, Cedar Point Communications; Mark Atkins, CEO, Invention Machine; Joseph Kennedy, U.S. Congressman

Academics

The MBA program at the University of Massachusetts—Boston's College of Management (the only public MBA available in the area) combines strategically focused management curriculum with optional specializations, offering in-state residents one of "the best educational values in the Boston area." "The in state tuition is a lot more reasonable than all of the local private business schools," says one resident student. "My overall experience has been very positive and I recommend the program to anyone," says another.

"The classes are tailored to meet the needs of working students," and students with a related degree may even be eligible to waive some of the business core courses. Classes are "small and personal," and many MBA classes have a major case component that provides insight into corporate, non-profit and small business issues, while others use real-world projects and simulations. For students interested in specializing beyond just general management, the college offers fourteen specializations, including Accounting, Business Intelligence, and Entrepreneurship.

As most here are working professionals, students are all "committed to bettering themselves," and "group work is mandatory." The "diverse working backgrounds" that students bring to the table makes for "engaged classes with a lot of interaction with professors." As far as guidance goes, there is "definitely no hand holding," "you have to seek out advisors and course scheduling on your own," and "you have to keep your responsibilities in check." Luckily, "the professors are solid." Though some say they can be "hit and miss" with a "mix of teaching ability," overall the MBA professors 'know their material." The Chancellor gets high marks; students say that "given time he can turn this university in to the shining jewel of the UMass system."

Career and Placement

Many members of this "laid back community" are already employed for the most part (though around forty percent of students have only one year or less of professional experience), but "there are good on campus jobs available for full-time students to support their education." "If you plan on staying in the same field and going part time, it makes financial sense with return on investment," says one student who did just so. Another benefit is the "possibility of networking due to the college being in Boston." Students who are on the job hunt do wish that the school brought in "more potential employers for career fairs," or perhaps would start "a job board/portal exclusively for students."

Recent employers of UMass-Boston graduates include State Street Corporation, Bank of America, Ernst & Young, Fidelity Investments, and PriceWaterhouseCoopers.

ADMISSIONS CONTACT: WILLIAM KOEHLER, ASSISTANT DEAN
ADDRESS: 100 MORRISSEY BOULEVARD, MBA OFFICE, BOSTON, MA 02125-3393
PHONE: 617-287-7720 • FAX: 617-287-7725
E-MAIL: MBA@UMB.EDU • WEBSITE: WWW.MANAGEMENT.UMB.EDU

Student Life and Environment

It's a commuter school, so the community is less cohesive than others, but UMass Boston "has the most diverse campus imaginable" in "a beautiful location." Many students here are first generation immigrants and/or first generation college graduates (the program is "very diverse in race, age, nationality, socio economic class"), so "in many ways, it's the embodiment of the American Dream." This is truly "a working class of people with real world experience in both life and in the workplace." Unfortunately, the "campus design is a nightmare" and an extreme lack of parking is a daily headache.

The administration is "well in touch with day to day activities," and "there is constant information and updates" regarding lectures, opportunities, and the "many sports activities, clubs, and other events offered."

Admissions

To be eligible for the MBA program at UMass Boston's College of Management, prospective students must have an undergraduate degree from an accredited college or university, GMAT scores, three letters of recommendation, and completed essays. In addition to test scores and undergraduate record, the admissions department evaluates students based on their recommendations, personal essays, and interview with the admissions department.

FINANCIAL FACTS

Annual tuition (in-state/ out-of-state)	$2,590/$9,758
Fees	$6,753
Cost of books	$1,000
Room & board	$10,000
% of students receiving aid	65
% of first-year students receiving aid	55
% of students receiving grants	21
Average grant	$17,000
Average student loan debt	$13,000

ADMISSIONS

Admissions Selectivity Rating	82
# of applications received	411
% applicants accepted	52
% acceptees attending	66
Average GMAT	580
Range of GMAT	510–600
Average GPA	3.30
TOEFL required of international students	Yes
Minimum TOEFL (paper/computer)	600/250
Application fee	$60
International application fee	$100
Early application deadline	3/1
Early notification date	4/1
Regular application deadline	6/1
Regular application notification	7/1
Application Deadline/Notification	
Round 1:	3/1 / 4/1
Round 2:	6/1 / 7/1
Deferment available	Yes
Maximum length of deferment	1 Semester
Transfer students accepted	Yes
Transfer application policy: Same applicant procedure. Transfer credits and waivers will be considered.	
Non-fall admissions	Yes
Need-blind admissions	Yes

EMPLOYMENT PROFILE

Career Rating		93	Grads Employed by Function	% Avg. Salary
Percent employed at graduation		94	Marketing	(13%)
Percent employed 3 months after graduation		75	Operations	(20%)
			Consulting	(13%)
Average base starting salary		$74,257	Management	(13%)
Primary Source of Full-time Job Acceptances			Finance	(53%)
School-facilitated activities		1(100%)	MIS	(13%)
			Other	(%)

Top 5 Employers Hiring Grads
State Street Corporation (4), Bank of America (4), Ernst & Young (6), Fidelity Investments (2), PriceWaterhouseCoopers (2)

University of Massachusetts Dartmouth
Charlton College of Business

GENERAL INFORMATION
Type of school	Public
Affiliation	No Affiliation
Academic calendar	Sep - May

SURVEY SAYS...
Solid preparation in:
Marketing, General management,
Communication/interpersonal skills,
Doing business in a global economy

STUDENTS
Enrollment of MBA Program	250
% male/female	50/50
Average age at entry	26
Average years work experience at entry	6.0

ACADEMICS
Academic Experience Rating	83
Profs interesting rating	77
Profs accesible rating	81
% female faculty	10
% underrepresented minority faculty	16
% part-time faculty	0

Joint Degrees
JD/MBA in conjunction with
Southern New England School of
Law

Academics

The University of Massachusetts Dartmouth's Charlton College of Business goes the extra mile to make its MBA program as convenient as possible. The student body, largely made up of busy young professionals, appreciates the effort. Three locations (the main campus in North Dartmouth, Fall River, and Cape Cod Community College) make it easier for students to attend classes; "the ability to take online/blended courses" means they can sometimes skip the classroom entirely. An accommodating curriculum also helps; as one student explains, "I love the flexibility in the program. I can choose my classes in any order. Although it will be a four-year period before I finish in total, the slower pace is flexible and the option to take one course at a time is the only way I could have done it."

Cost is also a factor; students declare the UMD MBA "the least expensive AACSB-accredited business program in the area." Students also praise "a stellar international core of professors with a wide range of professional and academic experience," noting their instructors' "focus on group work and presentations," which they regard as "very realistic in the business world." They're less bullish on the administration, describing it as "disjointed." "The administration needs to work more diligently at ironing out some of the bureaucracy in the system," one student explains. "On more than one occasion, I have received multiple answers to the same question, depending on who I speak with."

Students also note "there is sometimes trouble with the offerings in certain concentrations." Class availability sometimes diminishes the convenience of the program; students wish the school would "rotate the elective course offerings and have courses available for all concentrations that are offered" in order to mitigate the problem. Even so, students' opinion of the program as a whole is favorable; one writes, "The overall academic experience is challenging and engaging, [leaving me] very optimistic about potential for more success after graduation."

Career and Placement

The MBA program at UMD utilizes the university's Career Resource Center, which serves all undergraduates, graduate students, and alumni. The office provides a battery of career services, including workshops in resume-writing, interviewing, and salary negotiation; online job and resume listings; and on-campus recruiting events, including job fairs. Efforts here are primarily directed toward the undergraduate population. One MBA explains, "The majority of MBA students are usually using the MBA program to advance in their current occupation, with many large local corporations paying their tuition. The CRC is available and encouraged to be utilized for students seeking employment after graduation." Some students are less than satisfied with the situation; "They need to build their network of companies up badly. In so doing, they need to get more companies to come on campus and recruit," one such student writes.

ADMISSIONS CONTACT: NANCY LUDWIN, MBA COORDINATOR
ADDRESS: 285 OLD WESTPORT ROAD, NORTH DARTMOUTH, MA 02747-2300
PHONE: 508-999-8543 • FAX: 508-999-8776
E-MAIL: GRADUATE@UMASSD.EDU • WEBSITE: WWW.UMASSD.EDU/CHARLTON

Student Life and Environment

The business school facility on UMD's main campus is of recent vintage; the ultramodern building, funded by a three million dollar grant from the Earle P. Charlton Family Trust, opened in 2004. Students speak highly of the main campus. They are less enthusiastic about the Fall River site, which one MBA complains "has broken windows" and "is in a scary area."

Students describe the UMD MBA program as "commuter-based," with students' involvement "mostly limited to evening courses, with little interaction on campus during the day unless attending a special lecture." "There's no mandatory participation" in extracurricular activities, "which is good for me," a typical student offers. That's because most here "are working full time and do not have time to get involved in other things outside of class."

The student body here "is a mixture of students that have just graduated from college and others who are working and raising a family." One reports, "Some are young—in their twenties—but there is a good mix of twenties, thirties, and forties. I'm 52 but feel comfortable in the environment." The program is "internationally diverse," with "people from all around the world. It is much more diverse than I would have expected," a locally based student observes. "The international students are extremely friendly and bright. I enjoy working with them on projects," one student notes.

Admissions

Applicants to the UMD MBA program must submit the following materials to the Admissions Committee: official transcripts from all post-secondary academic institutions attended (transcripts from institutions outside the US must be translated when not in English and evaluated by a Credit Evaluation service where the grading system deviates from the standard American four-point system); an official GMAT score report; two letters of recommendation, preferably one reflecting academic ability and one reflecting professional experience; a personal essay; and a current resume. International applicants must submit all the above plus an official score report for the TOEFL (minimum score 533 paper-based test, 200 computer-based test) and visa-related paperwork. Admissions are processed on a rolling basis, with decisions typically coming with a month after the completed application is received. International applicants must apply by March 1 for fall entry and by October 1 for spring entry.

FINANCIAL FACTS
Annual tuition (in-state/ out-of-state)	$12,150/$22,680

ADMISSIONS
Admissions Selectivity Rating	88
Average GMAT	500
Average GPA	3.40
TOEFL required of international students	Yes
Application fee	$60
International Deferment available	Yes
Maximum length of deferment	1 Semester
Need-blind admissions	Yes

UNIVERSITY OF MASSACHUSETTS LOWELL
ROBERT MANNING SCHOOL OF BUSINESS

GENERAL INFORMATION
Type of school   Public

SURVEY SAYS...
Cutting-edge classes
Solid preparation in:
Accounting, General management,
Operations

STUDENTS
Enrollment of parent
  institution   16,294
Enrollment of MBA Program   523
% male/female   52/48
% out-of-state   58
% part-time   87
% underrepresented minority   15
% international   41
Average age at entry   33
Average years work experience
  at entry   11.0

ACADEMICS
Academic Experience Rating   **80**
Profs interesting rating   80
Profs accesible rating   78
Student/faculty ratio   11:1
% female faculty   25
% underrepresented minority
  faculty   2
% part-time faculty   34

Joint Degrees
Master of Science in Innovation
and Technological Entrepreneurship
(MS ITE) is a UMass Lowell
PlusOne program. This means that
qualifying science and engineering
undergraduates may take 2 graduate courses in their senior year and
apply it to the MS ITE, and can then
complete the program in one additional year.

Academics

Providing a "good balance between reputation and affordability" to business grads in and around the northeast corner of Massachusetts, the University of Massachusetts— Robert Manning School of Business offers an MBA "tailored to meet the busy working person's schedules." With "evening classes," a "practical approach to tests and assign-ments," and, most conveniently of all, an "excellent online program" that "allows you to blend online with on-campus courses" (or even take all classes online, if you prefer), a Lowell MBA offers enough "freedom and flexibility" to suit its student body, which largely consists of professionals looking for a leg up to management positions.

The UML MBA commences with 12 hours of foundation courses in subjects traditional-ly covered in undergraduate business programs. Students who have completed equiva-lent undergraduate classes within the last five years and have earned at least a B may receive a waiver for some or all of these courses; alternately, students may attempt to place out of these classes through written exams. The curriculum also includes seven core courses in accounting, finance, analysis of customers and markets, MIS, operations, managing organization design and change, and strategy. The program concludes with three electives, which students may use to develop a concentration in accounting, finance, or information technology. They may also take an MBA in general business.

UML professors "are excellent and helpful," "not pretentious," and "demanding, which helps students do a better job." The school works hard on the service end; professors and administrators "are hands on, always follow up, and contact you regarding any ques-tions." That said, UML is a state school, so naturally "sometimes there is non-applicable red tape, like when I was asked for proof of immunizations even though I take all my classes online." All in all, students appreciate what they have here, reporting that "Administrators do the best they can on limited staff and resources." As one student sums up, "the campus lacks the glossy touch, but I guess most here would agree that it gives the best value for your money. You have to remember that you are paying less than a third of what you would have paid at any private college [and] you still get a highly accomplished and dedicated faculty [that] works hard to embed the right kind of morals and values into your brain. The course textbooks, HBR case studies, and other miscella-neous materials are mostly the same as the ones used by the Ivy Leagues. The discus-sions are intense, and many ideas are innovative. I really don't think therefore that there is anything lacking academically."

Career and Placement

The UML Career Services Office provides counseling and placement services to all undergraduates, graduates, and alumni of the university. The office organizes a variety of job fairs throughout the school year. It also provides mock interviews, counsels stu-dents on resume writing and job-search skills, schedules corporate information sessions on campus, and offers access to online job search engines such as MonsterTRAK. The office coordinates the efforts of the University Career Advisory Network, which is essen-tially an online community of alumni and current students. Employers who most fre-quently hire UMass Lowell MBAs include: Bank of America, TD Bank, Fidelity, Putnam Investments, Raytheon, Pfizer, Procter & Gamble, EMC, Cisco, US Air Force and U.S. Government.

ADMISSIONS CONTACT: GARY M. MUCICA, DIRECTOR, GRADUATE MANAGEMENT PROGRAMS
ADDRESS: ONE UNIVERSITY AVENUE, PA 303, LOWELL, MA 01854-2881
PHONE: 978-934-2848 • FAX: 978-934-4017
E-MAIL: KATHLEEN_ROURKE@UML.EDU • WEBSITE: WWW.UML.EDU/MBA

Student Life and Environment

Over the years, online course offerings at Lowell have steadily grown in popularity. Today, one MBA explains, "Students are commuters or online, so the experience is not intimate. You don't form personal relationships with mentors/instructors" to the extent that students do elsewhere. Connections can be made with effort, however. Some students report "great opportunities for building relationships with professional networks," and others note that "there are many clubs and organizations for students to join. The office of student activities does a great job in matching students with their activities." These options are only really pursued by the program's few full-time students or by part-timers who don't also hold demanding full-time jobs.

Most here don't fit those descriptions. They're "working professionals" who "have at least a few years of professional experience and are part-time students who work full-time jobs." Their experiences "help in discussions in the class, as most of the arguments given are very practical and time-tested, and there is a lot to learn from everyone's experiences."

Admissions

The MBA program at the University of Massachusetts Lowell admits new students for both the fall and spring terms and requires applicants to submit the following materials: an official transcript of undergraduate grades; an official GMAT score report; three letters of recommendation from "employment-related sources" demonstrating a minimum of two years of relevant work experience; a current resume; and a one-page essay describing academic and career objectives. Applicants must complete prerequisite courses in microeconomics and statistics prior to entering the program. According to the school's website, "An aptitude for management decision-making and demonstrated academic ability are the most important qualifications for admission." International students whose first language is not English must submit an official score report for the TOEFL. There is also a full-time one year accelerated program that requires no work experience of recent college graduates with a minimum 3.2 GPA and a GMAT score from non-UMass Lowell students.

FINANCIAL FACTS

Annual tuition (in-state/ out-of-state)	$1,637/$6,425
Fees	$9,592
Cost of books	$1,000
Room & board	$11,000
% of students receiving aid	27
% of first-year students receiving aid	8
% of students receiving grants	3

ADMISSIONS

Admissions Selectivity Rating	72
# of applications received	250
% applicants accepted	88
% acceptees attending	64
Average GMAT	570
Range of GMAT	510–600
Average GPA	3.16
TOEFL required of international students	Yes
Minimum TOEFL (paper/computer)	600/250
Application fee	$50
International application fee	$50
Deferment available	Yes
Maximum length of deferment	1 year
Transfer students accepted	Yes

Transfer application policy: Must be fron an AACSB accredited institution. Maximum of 12 transfer credits for the advance core courses, with a grade of a "B" or better earned in each of these courses.

Non-fall admissions	Yes
Need-blind admissions	Yes

EMPLOYMENT PROFILE			
Career Rating	73	Grads Employed by Function	% Avg. Salary
Percent employed at graduation	98	Marketing	(8%)
Percent employed 3 months after graduation	98	Operations	(28%)
		Management	(10%)
Average base starting salary	$68,475	Finance	(21%)
		MIS	(13%)
		Other	(12%)

UNIVERSITY OF MEMPHIS
FOGELMAN COLLEGE OF BUSINESS AND ECONOMICS

GENERAL INFORMATION

Type of school	Public
Affiliation	No Affiliation
Academic calendar	Semester

SURVEY SAYS...

Cutting-edge classes
Solid preparation in:
General management, Computer skills, Doing business in a global economy

STUDENTS

Enrollment of parent institution	22,421
Enrollment of MBA Program	410
% male/female	64/36
% out-of-state	75
% part-time	59
% underrepresented minority	27
% international	40
Average age at entry	30
Average years work experience at entry	4.0

ACADEMICS

Academic Experience Rating	78
Profs interesting rating	70
Profs accesible rating	80
% female faculty	27
% underrepresented minority faculty	23
% part-time faculty	17

Joint Degrees

MBA/JD: 54 credits (4 years);
EMBA Health Systems Pharmacy: 41 credits (17 months)

Academics

Fogelman College of Business and Economics at the University of Memphis is a no-nonsense professional MBA program designed for working people "from all walks of business life" who are looking to further their careers but who don't have a lot of time or energy to waste. The school has a solid reputation among locally-based businesses like FedEx. One student holds Memphis in such high regard that she has two degrees from there: "The University of Memphis is where I received my BBA in accounting. I liked my experience there, and I knew that an MBA from there would open many doors in the company that I work for."

Students say their "very knowledgeable" professors "present concepts completely" and help them relate the course material to practice. "Each of them has done extensive research in their field and [is] noted to be among the best in the country for their area of expertise." Another student says: "Every professor is interested in the development of each student into future managers and business leaders." The administration does not receive the same ringing endorsement, however. Some take issue with the allocation of funds in certain areas. One student was succinct and blunt: "Solid professors, good academic experience, but really bad administration that spends money" excessively.

Some students also have difficulty with course selection and enrollment; many required or desired classes are offered only once per semester under limited enrollment, and these courses "often conflict with each other." Since pretty much all of the courses take place in the evenings to accommodate the vast majority of students who have day jobs, there's very little leeway in terms of scheduling. But these night classes also give part-time and full-time students the opportunity to interact with each other through "small classes and heavy teamwork," something not found in a lot of MBA programs. "A lot of projects are team-based, so you get to know classmates very well." One student takes away warm feelings about the camaraderie he felt at the school: "I have a new set of best friends. I never thought it was possible after reaching age 40."

In keeping with the no-frills approach to the program, however, the facilities tend toward the sparse side. Several students expressed disdain for the academic buildings and equipment and spoke of the need for "more technology in the classroom." One student said the classrooms "need better seating. The desks were made for 4th graders."

Career and Placement

Some students say the program needs better ties to "big industries" to provide those students seeking out new or nonlocal careers with better job prospects. Fortunately for the students looking to stay in the area (and there are many), "There are several excellent companies in the area, also, that recruit heavily," and since the student body is, as one student puts it, "not nearly as competitive as I expected," everyone is "very supportive" and happy to help each other land available positions. Another boon to the school's local reputation is the recently formed partnership with the Leadership Academy. The partnership, known as the Community Internship, gives MBA students the chance to team with Leadership Academy fellows on projects designed to benefit the community.

ADMISSIONS CONTACT: MARK GILLENSON, DIRECTOR OF MASTERS PROGRAMS
ADDRESS: GRADUATE SCHOOL ADMINISTRATION BUILDING RM. 216, MEMPHIS, TN 38152-3370
PHONE: 901-678-2911 • FAX: 901-678-5023
E-MAIL: GRADSCH@MEMPHIS.EDU • WEBSITE: FCBE.MEMPHIS.EDU

Student Life and Environment

The school is located in the midtown area of Memphis, which "is great for students because there are a lot of social establishments nearby" offering "a lot of things for students to do recreationally." Of course, there are the well-traveled destinations like Graceland (check out Elvis' gaudy yellow and black rec room), Sun Studios, and the famous Beale Street, with its string of live-music joints and soul food. And the National Civil Rights Museum, located at the old Lorraine Motel where Martin Luther King, Jr., assassinated in 1968, is a haunting must-see for tourists and locals alike. Overall, "The University of Memphis, like the city of Memphis, is greatly underrated," one student says.

Since "Most graduate students work and commute," little time is left for a social life outside of the classroom, but there's a foundation for friendship and networking among the "outgoing" and "friendly" individuals that attend Fogelman. Though some think "The school could put more effort into organized activities for students outside of class," the "busy" nature of the student body doesn't lend itself to much free time anyway, so complaints are few. Everyone is in agreement over the variety of backgrounds provided by their classmates: "The graduate population is very diverse, which makes things more interesting." "You have a great opportunity to meet people from various backgrounds (educational and ethnic)," another student says.

Admissions

Admittance to the professional MBA program at the Fogelman College of Business and Economics is not terribly selective, and the admissions requirements are fairly standard. Applicants to the school's professional MBA program must submit the following materials: a completed application (either online or via mail); an official copy of undergraduate transcripts from all colleges and universities attended (even if you did not graduate); a copy of your current resume; a statement of personal interest; a 1,000-word essay answering one of the acceptable questions provided on the school's admissions website; two letters of recommendation; and an official GMAT or GRE score report. Interviews and previous work experience are optional. In addition to the above documents, international students whose primary language is not English must also provide an official score report for the TOEFL (minimum score: 550, paper-based test; 213, computer-based test).

FINANCIAL FACTS

Annual tuition (in-state/ out-of-state)	$5,155/$11,615
Fees	$420
Cost of books	$1,000

ADMISSIONS

Admissions Selectivity Rating	80
Average GMAT	575
Range of GMAT	500–650
Average GPA	3.16
TOEFL required of international students	Yes
Minimum TOEFL (paper/computer)	550/210
Application fee	$35
International application fee	$60
Regular application deadline	7/1
Deferment available	Yes
Maximum length of deferment	1 year
Transfer students accepted	Yes

Transfer application policy: Approved transfer credit may be accepted in the Fogelman Colletge for not more than 9 Semester hours of course credit toward a master's degree. Grades earned at another institution will not be computed in the University cumulative grade point average, nor will they be accepted for transfer, unless they are "B" (3.0) or better. No credit will be transferred unless it meets with the approval of the major advisor or program graduate coordinator.

Non-fall admissions	Yes
Need-blind admissions	No

EMPLOYMENT PROFILE

Career Rating	76	Grads Employed by Function	% Avg. Salary
Percent employed at graduation	79	Marketing	(44%) $70,500
Percent employed 3 months after graduation	16	Other	(56%) $90,500
Average base starting salary	$81,833	**Top 5 Employers Hiring Grads**	
		FedEx, Smith&Nephew	

UNIVERSITY OF MIAMI
SCHOOL OF BUSINESS ADMINISTRATION

GENERAL INFORMATION
Type of school	Private
Affiliation	No Affiliation
Academic calendar	August-May

SURVEY SAYS...
Good peer network, Cutting-edge classes, Happy students
Solid preparation in:
Teamwork

STUDENTS
Enrollment of parent institution	16,172
Enrollment of MBA Program	158
% male/female	65/35
% out-of-state	23
% part-time	0
% underrepresented minority	23
% international	39
Average age at entry	25
Average years work experience at entry	1.5

ACADEMICS
Academic Experience Rating	90
Profs interesting rating	91
Profs accesible rating	84
Student/faculty ratio	1:1
% female faculty	29
% underrepresented minority faculty	19
% part-time faculty	13

Joint Degrees
JD/MBA, can be completed within a period of 3.5 to 4 years; MD/MBA, can be completed in 5 years; BArch/MBA, can be completed in 5 years; JD/LLM/MBA, can be completed in 4 years

Prominent Alumni
Joseph Echevarria, CEO, Deloitte LLP; Raul Alvarez, Former President and COO, McDonald's Corporation; Gerald Cahill, Chairman Emeritas, Merrill Lynch & Co.; David H. Komansky, Chairman, CEO and President, Collective Brands Inc.

Academics

The University of Miami offers cultural diversity and a "strong connection to [the] Latin American business environment" as well as highly regarded "programs in leadership and international studies." "If you want to end up doing business in Lat Am, this is the school to go to." Students who arrive here uncertain of their career objectives can take comfort in the unusually broad range of options open to them. In addition to the expected full-time and executive MBA options, UM also offers an Executive MBA in health sector management and policy, an MD/MBA, and even a unique Spanish-language-only Global Executive MBA.

Each term gives students an intense six weeks of studies. Life is "very fast paced, especially with the four term scheduling, but this keeps the content fresh and the students interested." Weeklong breaks between terms provide "relief" from the "rigorous" schedule in which students can recharge and gear up for the next session.

Students esteem the school for its "high caliber students" and "exquisite professors," many of whom "come from [the] private sector and work as consultants to high profile companies." The "professors are always ready to help you," and the experience and expertise they have in regards to today's hottest, most relevant topics enables them to give students "only the best academic experience at UM." There are also "opportunities for students to work with faculty outside of [the] classroom on interesting research projects."

Motivated students and professors are backed by a committed administration that "is very well run and does a great job [of] listening to students and aiming to exceed their expectations." Other strengths mentioned by students include the school's location in Miami which provides "local business opportunities in a growing market," the "many computer labs available," the "international student body," "the variety of things to do" at UM, and the "strong alumni connection." "There is a strong focus on encouraging students to not only find careers within [an] organization, but to find their entrepreneurial spirit and start something on their own, or better yet with their classmates. The environment fosters great partnerships given all the teamwork exercises we do."

Although finding jobs after graduation in Latin America may not be a problem, students suggested that expanding career placement services to other parts of the world could stand improvement. "The career center also needs to focus on finding jobs for the international students."

Career and Placement

The Ziff Graduate Career Services Center has an array of services to help graduate students meet their career goals after graduation. Although the Career Center does not suit everyone's career needs, networking is an effective yet somewhat underutilized tool at the University of Miami. One student points out that not all students make the effort though. "There is a major trend for students to rely heavily on the career center without taking the initiative to reach out to Miami's strong alumni base, who for the most part is extremely receptive to current students." Another student agrees by saying that "one of the UM's greatest strengths is the alumni base who are always willing to help their fellow Canes."

Finding jobs locally does not seem to be a problem with the wide "array of networking opportunities" available. "Administration and professors work excellent[ly] with the local community and University alumni in setting up career opportunities." The Finance and Investment Banking club appears to be "extremely engaged in academic, organizational, [and] leadership activities." The group even "led initiatives to bring in local leaders to network with current students interested in finance."

Currently, "recruiting reflects Miami's strengths in real estate and tourism." Students seeking jobs in finance will probably do well here also. Students holding other degrees may have to work a little harder to find the right opportunity for them; however, the "school is broadening its hiring base by sponsoring trips for students to meet employers and interview."

Student Life and Environment

The University of Miami is attractive to MBA students for many reasons, including its prime location. Attending school in Miami "almost guarantees that family and friends (many you haven't heard from in years) will visit often." Altogether, the "12 months of warm weather," pleasant beaches, and the "great city" of Miami offer lots to do year round. The school's surroundings are an extension of the active life that students enjoy on campus. "Often classes and activities begin early in the morning and continue in social, networking events at night. The local community is intertwined into the UM experience." The "extremely friendly and close-knit" students often socialize together during the weekends, which "usually consist of fun time[s] at [the] beach or bars but always with classmates and people met through school."

The student body is both "ethnically and professionally" diverse. Although students may seem young, they are "very mature for their ages." Learning is a full-time experience with "great discussions [occurring] on breezeways, dining areas, and in and outside of classrooms." The atmosphere provides "great social circles" that can occur anywhere and help "build camaraderie outside of the classroom." There are "fun social events" both on and around campus, such as" "great food and leisure activities" and "daily activities...from gym and happy hours to projects and study groups."

Admissions

Applications are received and reviewed on a rolling basis until the class is full; students are encouraged to apply by the Round 3 application deadline. Students who wish to be considered for merit-based scholarships, fellowships, or graduate assistantship are advised to apply early, as they are limited and available for fall applicants only. Deadline for fall applicants is 8/01. The greatest factors used in determining admissions include GMAT and GRE scores as well as undergraduate GPA. Letters of recommendation, a personal essay, and a resume are also required along with the student application.

FINANCIAL FACTS

Annual tuition	$39,840
Fees	$516
Cost of books	$1,904
Room & board	
(on/off-campus)	$0/$17,520
% of students receiving aid	70
% of first-year students	
receiving aid	73
% of students receiving grants	62
Average award package	$39,093
Average grant	$22,553
Average loan	$37,615
Average student loan debt	$67,577

ADMISSIONS

Admissions Selectivity Rating	**87**
# of applications received	329
% applicants accepted	45
% acceptees attending	54
Average GMAT	632
Range of GMAT	590–675
Average GPA	3.28
TOEFL required of	
international students	Yes
Minimum TOEFL	
(paper/computer)	600/240
Application fee	$100
International application fee	$100
Early application deadline	10/1
Early notification date	12/1
Regular application deadline	12/1
Application Deadline/Notification	
Round 1:	12/1 /
Round 2:	2/1 /
Round 3:	3/15 /
Round 4:	5/1 /
Deferment available	Yes
Maximum length	
of deferment	1 year
Transfer students accepted	No
Non-fall admissions	No
Need-blind admissions	Yes

EMPLOYMENT PROFILE

Career Rating	87	**Grads Employed by Function% Avg. Salary**	
Percent employed at graduation	51	Marketing	(21%) $47,500
Percent employed 3 months		Operations	(3%) $65,000
after graduation	65	Consulting	(6%)$70,000
Average base starting salary	$62,613	Management	(12%) $49,295
Primary Source of Full-time Job Acceptances		Finance	(43%) $70,079
School-facilitated activities	18(55%)	Other	(15%) $65,000
Graduate-facilitated activities	15(45%)	**Top 5 Employers Hiring Grads**	
		Ernst & Young (3), Citigroup, Inc. (2), Burger King Corporation (2), PepisCo, Inc. (1), Booz Allen Hamilton (1)	

University of Michigan—Ann Arbor
Stephen M. Ross School of Business

GENERAL INFORMATION

Type of school   Public
Affiliation   No Affiliation
Academic calendar   Semester

SURVEY SAYS...

Good social scene, Good peer network, Cutting-edge classes, Happy students
Solid preparation in:
Teamwork, Environmental sustainability, Social responsibility

STUDENTS

Enrollment of parent
  institution   43,426
Average age at entry   28
Average years work experience
  at entry   5.0

ACADEMICS

Academic Experience Rating	**93**
Profs interesting rating	91
Profs accesible rating	88
Student/faculty ratio	8:1
% female faculty	26
% underrepresented minority faculty	24
% part-time faculty	28

Joint Degrees

MBA-JD; MBA-MD. Architecture Art and Design; Asian Studies; Chinese Asian Studies; Japanese Asian Studies; South Asia Asian Studies; Southeast Asia Education; Construction; Engineering and Management; Health Services Admin (Public Health); Industrial and Operations Engineering; Information Law; Management of Patient Care Services (Nursing); Manufacturing Engineering; Medicine (MD); Modern Middle Eastern and North African Studies; Music; Natural Resources and Environment (Erb); Naval Architecture and Marine Engineering; Public Health; Public Policy; Russian and Eastern European Studies; Social Work; Urban Planning

Academics

Armed with a "stellar reputation," extensive alumni network and offering great "flexibility in career concentration," it's no wonder that Michigan has such a well regarded MBA program. Students truly value the focus Ross has placed on both entrepreneurship and "hands-on" "action-based" learning. Indeed, there's a strong "emphasis on learning by doing, rather than lecture or case." Additionally, students appreciate that the school works diligently to foster a "collaborative culture." Moreover, the "general management curriculum" and "leadership development" ensures that students will leave Ross as effective, well-rounded business professionals.

While the "academic experience is surprisingly rigorous," students can rely on professors who "are heavily invested in our success and understanding." They are also very "accessible," "passionate" and "down to earth." A handful have even been deemed "rock stars that push students beyond the usual MBA platitudes and really transform your thinking." As a second-year student gushes, "The professors at Ross are amazing; they take the time to help with anything along their subject lines for class and for outside projects. Not only that but they are always more than happy to help you connect with their own contacts and other professors at the school."

By and large, the administration is held in high esteem as well. Students feel fortunate that "administrators continue to push an academic environment and curriculum that produces MBAs well-equipped to thrive in real world business settings." Even better, "the school is open to new ideas, courses, and course content, and courses are constantly under review." In the end, it's certainly easy to understand why these business students are so content!

Career and Placement

Considering the high "recognition of [the] Ross brand across the country and world," it's no surprise that career opportunities abound for Michigan MBAs. For starters, a strong alumni network means that "graduates are very accessible and interested in helping current students." Ross also manages to attract a high number of recruiters. As one appreciative second-year tells us, "The quality of companies that recruit here are...extremely diverse and of high quality." Ross Career Services also does a great job of helping advise and guide students in their search. Individual counseling sessions and career workshops are continually available. Moreover, the office helps student manage both the on-campus interview process as well as their personal outreach efforts.

Michigan MBAs can be found everywhere from New York and San Francisco to Chile, China and Russia. Employers who frequently hire Ross grads include Citigroup, Kraft Foods Inc., Target Corp., McKinsey & Co., Booz Allen Hamilton Inc., Bain and Company Inc., Johnson & Johnson, American Express Co., Amazon.com, Proctor & Gamble, Goldman Sachs Inc. and Deutsche Bank AG.

ADMISSIONS CONTACT: SOOJIN KWON, DIRECTOR OF ADMISSIONS
ADDRESS: 701 TAPPAN STREET, ANN ARBOR, MI 48109-1234
PHONE: 734-763-5796 • FAX: 734-763-7804
E-MAIL: ROSSMBA@UMICH.EDU • WEBSITE: WWW.BUS.UMICH.EDU

Student Life and Environment

Michigan MBA students strive to create a good work-life balance for themselves. And luckily, "Ross gives the freedom and flexibility to pursue what you want, whether that's academics, the job market, club activities, helping others, or having fun." Certainly, "what you get out of the experience is up to you, and between the collegial atmosphere and various sporting events in Michigan's rich history, it is highly enjoyable to be at Ross." Indeed, "life in Ann Arbor is highly social, whether it [involves] tailgating at football games, mingling at the weekly happy hour for business students, or catching up with friends at a local restaurant." And since Michigan is in a college town and not a booming metropolis, "you're constantly running into your fellow classmates, which is fantastic from a networking perspective. You can't help but hang out with classmates ALL THE TIME, which means they become your good friends instead of classmates."

Admissions

Admissions officers are on the lookout for candidates who will truly benefit from Ross' approach to business management. They seek applicants with keen intellectual ability who will bring strong interpersonal and leadership skills into the classroom. Due to the analytical rigor of the program, it is recommended that students have a working knowledge of college-level mathematics. However, a traditional business background is not necessary or required and there are no pre-requisite courses for admission.

Prominent Alumni

Stephen M. Ross, Chairman, CEO and Founder, The Related Companies

FINANCIAL FACTS

Annual tuition (in-state/ out-of-state)	$47,750/$52,750
Fees	$189
Cost of books	$7,858
Room & board	$12,478
% of students receiving aid	75
% of students receiving grants	37
Average award package	$53,469
Average grant	$24,175
Average loan	$48,372
Average student loan debt	$95,720

ADMISSIONS

Admissions Selectivity Rating	92
# of applications received	2,435
% applicants accepted	41
% acceptees attending	51
Average GMAT	703
Range of GMAT	650–750
Average GPA	3.40
TOEFL required of international students	Yes
Application fee	$200
International application fee	$200
Regular application deadline	3/4
Regular application notification	5/15
Application Deadline/Notification	
Round 1:	10/10 / 12/20
Round 2:	1/3 / 3/15
Round 3:	3/4 / 5/15
Deferment available	Yes
Maximum length of deferment	1 year
Transfer students accepted	Yes
Transfer application policy: Transfer applicants are welcome to apply, but no credits will transfer into our program.	
Non-fall admissions	No
Need-blind admissions	Yes

EMPLOYMENT PROFILE

Career Rating	95	Grads Employed by Function	% Avg. Salary
Percent employed at graduation	74	Marketing	(21%) $101,599
Percent employed 3 months after graduation	81	Operations	(3%) $104,378
		Consulting	(38%) $126,122
Average base starting salary	$111,047	Management	(9%) $107,200
Primary Source of Full-time Job Acceptances		Finance	(9%) $100,827
School-facilitated activities	255(62%)	Other	(6%) $99,418
Graduate-facilitated activities	151(37%)	Top 5 Employers Hiring Grads	
Unknown	2(1%)	Deloitte (29), Accenture Ltd (17), The Boston Consulting Group (16), Amazon (14), McKinsey Company (14)	

UNIVERSITY OF MICHIGAN—DEARBORN
COLLEGE OF BUSINESS

Academics

After comparing MBA programs, many students choose University of Michigan—Dearborn for the unbeatable triumvirate of "value, location, and name brand" its College of Business offers. The program is geared toward part-time students, and the combination of "evening and online MBA classes are perfect for professionals already in the workforce." Courses begin three times a year (in September, January, and May), and through the "flexible online program," students can take as many (or as few) classes as fit their schedule. Core courses cover all functional business areas and comprise more than half the 60 units of required course work; however, students with undergraduate business degrees may be eligible to waive core course work, thereby completing the program in less time. After the core, students can choose to take various electives, or complete a concentration in finance, international business, marketing, supply chain management, or accounting. But the program is definitely open to students of all undergraduate majors and all levels of Professional experience. The college has long maintained a strong local reputation (not to mention, it boasts the excellent University of Michigan name). Even so, students say things are always improving: "In the last few years, the program has become increasingly relevant and well-suited for graduate studies."

Just as they praise the college's dean, UMD students are pleased to report that the administration is "very accommodating and helpful," assisting students with everything from scheduling to academic advising. With a fairly large student body, it "can be difficult to get into popular classes, but the college has offered several options to help students get the classes they need." For students who take their classes on campus, the facilities are modern, and the school "provides the variety and excellence expected of a satellite campus of a world-class university." And, like the academic offerings, facilities are consistently improving. For example, the school opened a trading floor on campus in 2010, which helps bring real-world capacities to finance and accounting courses, in addition to being open for general use.

In terms of faculty, "There is a wide range of professor capability at this school." Many "are clearly experts in their fields," while others are less prepared for their important posts. On the whole, however, professors are "friendly and easily approachable" and "Lectures are well-organized, and there is plenty of opportunity provided for discussion on topics of current interest." With an average of 16 students in each classroom, "Small class sizes help the interaction between students and professors, as well as among our peers." If you'd like assistance outside of class, "Most of the professors will give you their home telephone number to reach them if you can't make office hours. They are as committed to us as we are to learning."

ADMISSIONS CONTACT: JOAN DOHERTY, GRADUATE ADMISSIONS COUNSELOR
ADDRESS: COLLEGE OF BUSINESS, 19000 HUBBARD DR., DEARBORN, MI 48126-2638
PHONE: 313-593-5460 • FAX: 313-271-9838
E-MAIL: GRADBUSINESS@UMD.UMICH.EDU • WEBSITE: WWW.COB.UMD.UMICH.EDU

Career and Placement

A large percentage of UMD students are already working full-time, and many receive tuition assistance from their employers. For those who are looking for a new job (or to make a career change), the College of Business's Career Planning and Placement Office assists graduate students with their job and internship search through resume critiques, online job and internship boards, and career fairs. On the Career Planning and Placement Office's website, students can get information about upcoming events and workshops, or peruse current job listings and links to local employment assistance. Students are often surprised to find that their professors can be a great way to get a foot in the door of the local job market. A current student attests, "They are quite supportive even when you're finished with their class—it is not uncommon for professors to help with networking or career searches."

Student Life and Environment

On this urban campus, most students are "working professionals" with a "few full-time students" added to the mix. While many are busy with work and family, this profession-al group takes their studies seriously, and most students are "eager to participate in class and highly focused on their academics." "Being a commuter university, there is not much networking outside of class," and clubs and extracurricular activities are limited. Still, some part-time students say they use "the library, health club, and all of the business offices" while others get together for "study groups outside of class time to prepare for exams or group projects."

For those who'd like a bit more camaraderie, the "COB has worked hard to improve student life," and many full-time MBA candidates say, "I have made friends that I expect to have the rest of my life." In addition, the larger university is home to over 9,083 students. There, "You will always find clubs sponsoring and advertising activities to try and get other students engaged." Campus facilities get good reviews, and recently, "A new food court and study lounge was added" to the business school area. "Research and technologies are top notch and on par with other major business schools," and "The College of Business has its own computer lab" with Internet access and printers.

Admissions

Applications to University of Michigan—Dearborn are accepted on a rolling basis; however, students are encouraged to apply by the priority deadline. Usually, once the university has received all of a student's application materials, an admissions decision will be made in just a few days. Most accepted applicants have a GMAT score in the high-500s and an undergraduate GPA of 3.5 on a 4.0 scale. At least two years of full-time work experience is required before entering the program.

FINANCIAL FACTS

Annual tuition (in-state/ out-of-state)	$13,413/$22,485
Fees	$598
Cost of books	$4,300
Room & board (on/off-campus)	$0/$7,000
% of students receiving aid	34
% of first-year students receiving aid	51
% of students receiving grants	4
Average award package	$17,723
Average grant	$5,963
Average loan	$20,500
Average student loan debt	$30,130

ADMISSIONS

Admissions Selectivity Rating	89
# of applications received	86
% applicants accepted	36
% acceptees attending	77
Average GMAT	577
Range of GMAT	535–590
Average GPA	3.50
TOEFL required of international students	Yes
Minimum TOEFL (paper/computer)	560/220
Application fee	$60
International application fee	$60
Regular application deadline	8/1
Deferment available	Yes
Maximum length of deferment	1 year
Transfer students accepted	Yes
Transfer application policy: Waivers will be given for courses equivalent to MBA core courses. Up to six credits of transfer may also be awarded for other MBA courses.	
Non-fall admissions	Yes
Need-blind admissions	Yes

UNIVERSITY OF MICHIGAN—FLINT
SCHOOL OF MANAGEMENT

GENERAL INFORMATION

Type of school	Public
Academic calendar	Semesters

SURVEY SAYS...

Cutting-edge classes
Solid preparation in:
Operations

STUDENTS

Enrollment of parent institution	8,289
Enrollment of MBA Program	183
% male/female	53/47
% out-of-state	53
% part-time	92
% underrepresented minority	0
% international	47
Average age at entry	30
Average years work experience at entry	5.0

ACADEMICS

Academic Experience Rating	85
Profs interesting rating	87
Profs accesible rating	88
Student/faculty ratio	7:1
% female faculty	17
% underrepresented minority faculty	28
% part-time faculty	25

Prominent Alumni

J. Donald Sheets II, VP and CFO, President America Area, Dow Corning Corp., MBA SOM; Robert J. Joubran, COO & Treasurer, Plantinum Equity LLC, BBA SOM; Michelle Goff, Senior VP & CFO, R. L. Polk & Co., BBA SOM; Cristin Reid English, President, Corp. Operations, Capital Bank Limited, MBA SOM; Robert J. Beltz, Vice President-Commercial Europe for U.S. Steel, MBA SOM

Academics

If you are looking for a "prestigious top school for management" that offers a great deal of "flexibility," then consider the University of Michigan—Flint School of Management. The MBA program is "very structured and organized." One student who is "a very busy mom, wife, and full-time employee," says, "I like that they take care of everything for me. I do not need to worry about what classes I am taking next, or how to obtain my books. The courses are relevant and … [can be taken] on campus [or] online. They encourage networking and are available when you need them." Other students agree, saying that the school is "well-managed" and "the time to complete the program was far less restrictive than others."

Coursework at UM–Flint is "a rigorous academic experience." "The pace is quick and the work is challenging; within the structure provided, there is plenty of room for self-expression." There are no easy grades here. "You earn an A, it's never handed to you." The faculty does a great job of providing students with the help and guidance they need to achieve that A. Faculty members "have an excellent grasp of the knowledge needed to convey difficult concepts. They encourage interaction among both students and other faculty." The content studied in the MBA program is "interesting and incredibly applicable." Also, "many fields and industries are represented in the classroom, not only in people from Michigan, but from all over the country and even some from different countries. My classmates have had a very positive impact on my learning experience."

Besides the traditional on-campus courses, students can opt for "NetPlus!," an innovative program that combines both online and in-class offerings. Students choosing the NetPlus! format work according to their own, flexible schedule, and are only required to attend on-campus classes once every six weeks. This enables students to "pursue an MBA while [they] travel for work." It also helps many who are juggling school with a demanding work schedule or long commute to campus. As one student sums it up, this "mixed-mode format was very appealing. It offered the best of both worlds (online and in-class)." Students also give the administration high marks. "The MBA program has a very strong administrative staff. They are friendly, listen well, and work very quickly."

Career and Placement

Students at UM–Flint have the support of "a strong career development office." Students benefit from the school's fine reputation with employers in Michigan and beyond. The Academic Advising & Career Center (AACC) at University of Michigan–Flint offers career guidance and counseling to undergraduates, alumni, and graduate students. The center hosts career fairs and offers advising services, however these services cater principally to undergraduates. One student points out that they can "receive daily emails from the career department listing campus visits and recruitment sessions from major companies." Unfortunately, not all students "take advantage of the office, though, and one must sign up for the service."

ADMISSIONS CONTACT: D. NICOL TAYLOR-VARGO, MBA, PROGRAM DIRECTOR
ADDRESS: SCHOOL OF MANAGEMENT, UM-FLINT, RIVERFRONT CENTER, 303 EAST KEARSLEY
STREET, FLINT, MI 48502-1950 • PHONE: 810-762-3160 • FAX: 810-762-3282
E-MAIL: SOM.MBA@UMFLINT.EDU • WEBSITE: MBA.UMFLINT.EDU

Student Life and Environment

A "very friendly campus environment" helps create the sentiment in which "it is always pleasant to be at school." Classmates are "highly experienced and educated." "They have different academic backgrounds, work environments, home settings, ages, genders, and [ethnicities]." This diversity in the graduate program "is one of its biggest strengths," says a student. "When having discussions in class or outside of class, the multiple frames of reference help me understand how different concepts could be used in real world settings. It's great that this program is able to intertwine theory and practice." Strong bonds are commonplace among graduate students here. One student is astounded at the ease in which friendships form, saying, "I've made more friends in the two years of my Graduate [degree] than I did in the four years of my Undergraduate degree."

The downtown location of UM–Flint offers convenience in "a great location and parking is included in your tuition." "The downtown area offers places to meet with classmates after class as well." A commuter notes that there are plenty of study spaces available "that are open 24 hours a day. So, for group projects class-mates and I are able to meet late in the evening, after class. This is fantastic, because so many of us have busy family and work lives. We don't have to take time off during the day to use the library, or find an off campus meeting location."

The program recently had a huge boost in technology and now students enjoy a new "state-of-the-art facility." They can now experience its finance lab and "there are many high tech study rooms, and a state of the art computer lab, research center, and student organization offices." But many students worry about the surrounding environment. Some "do not feel safe when walking to and from [their] car." "The university has a wonderful alert system that you can sign up for to get emails or alerts via text message regarding school closures or crimes," but "it's frightening to get a text about a mugging in broad daylight." UM-Flint public safety alerts include tips to remain safe on campus and officers are available 24/7 to escort students around campus and to their vehicles.

Admissions

Prospective students must submit GMAT scores, or GRE scores, undergraduate GPA, essay, letters of recommendation, as well as a resume to be considered for enrollment at the University of Michigan—Flint. The most weight in the admissions decision process is based on GRE or GMAT, and GPA scores. The Traditional MBA program starts classes twice a year. NetPlus! MBA enrolls students four times a year.

FINANCIAL FACTS

Annual tuition	$10,530
Fees	$412
Cost of books	$1,000
Room & board	$7,506
% of students receiving aid	40
% of first-year students receiving aid	63
% of students receiving grants	20
Average award package	$5,502
Average grant	$1,023
Average loan	$6,142
Average student loan debt	$28,178

ADMISSIONS

Admissions Selectivity Rating	85
# of applications received	105
% applicants accepted	47
% acceptees attending	84
Average GMAT	539
Range of GMAT	490–590
Average GPA	3.19
TOEFL required of international students	Yes
Minimum TOEFL (paper/computer)	500/173
Application fee	$55
International application fee	$55
Early application deadline	5/1
Deferment available	Yes
Maximum length of deferment	1 year
Transfer students accepted	Yes
Transfer application policy: AACSB accredited, "B" or better, grad level, 9 cr hrs only, not part of any other degree program	
Non-fall admissions	Yes
Need-blind admissions	Yes

UNIVERSITY OF MINNESOTA

Academics

MBA students at University of Minnesota's Carlson School of Management experience a "very positive, modern, and up-to-date learning environment." The school has a "great reputation" and is comfortably located in "close proximity to many Fortune 500 companies." U of M is "well known for experiential learning" through its four Enterprise programs. Student-managed teams in Brand, Funds, Consulting, and Ventures give students "the chance to work on consulting project[s] ranging from strategy to brand management for Fortune 500 companies." This unique opportunity for business students "is also great in providing what is effectively an in-class internship," and "helps students to gain real world experience and be able to hit the ground running right after their graduations."

Opinions on some professors vary, but "the vast majority" are considered "excellent." Students at the executive MBA level experience a nice relationship with their faculty saying professors "are more like trusted mentors." The camaraderie "leads to a stronger learning environment and experience." "The staff have been very helpful, and always put students first," a student explains. "They create an environment where I feel like I can talk to them whenever I need help." One student noted that the faculty is very responsive. They are "very open to comments and suggestions from students." The administration is "highly communicative and forward thinking with respect to integrating technology and new trends in business."

Students at Carlson's School of Management enjoy a "wide range of class options," as well as "great international learning opportunities." The school's full-time and part-time programs provide convenience and flexibility in a close-knit learning environment. The school community includes "a very diverse background of students, vice presidents, marketers, sales management, doctors, accountants and CFO's along with engineers." Students are deemed "competitive" yet "fun." Although Carlson has a strong reputation in Minnesota and the surrounding area, some would like to "improve national awareness," and see the school "climb in the school rankings," because the "top quality education here... is not reflected in the numbers."

Career and Placement

Finding a new job or a new career is not as daunting as it might seem thanks to a well-run and well-connected career placement center. "If you need a job in the Twin Cities area, there is an alumni network that will help out anybody with a Carlson MBA." The graduate school has a "great relationship with Fortune 500 companies. Additionally, the Medical Industry Leadership Institute provides students [with] a very advantageous preparation for the careers in the Medical Device industry and other healthcare careers." U of M also has a "strong connection with excellent local companies (Target, 3M, General Mills, Medtronic, [Best] Buy, Carlson Companies, Delta, etc.)."

The administration also provides "a number of resources and companies to help advance our careers," such as "interviewing skills, resume writing, as well as free courses on excel and outlook." "The biggest asset of the program though is how connected the faculty is with the business community."

One student was pleased to report a very positive experience with the program and career center when after only a couple of months, "I secured an internship through on-campus recruiting in a field completely new to me, at an expected (full-time) salary which is about 3 times what I earned before B-School." Some international students were not as quick to praise career services, saying, "Career opportunities for international students are very limited."

ADMISSIONS CONTACT: LINH GILLES, DIRECTOR ADMISSIONS AND RECRUITING
ADDRESS: 321 NINETEENTH AVENUE SOUTH, SUITE 1-110, MINNEAPOLIS, MN 55455
PHONE: 612-625-5555 • FAX: 612-626-7785
E-MAIL: MBA@UMN.EDU • WEBSITE: WWW.CARLSONSCHOOL.UMN.EDU

Student Life and Environment

For a small graduate school, Carlson has plenty to offer its students outside of the classroom. "It is easy to get involved in both the leadership and social activities of the school. There is a Leadership Advisory Board (LAB) of students who work closely with our administrative offices to make improvements based on results of student surveys. The board is open to anyone who applies and can make the time commitment." Other students agree. "The most difficult part of school is deciding what activities to be a part of." In addition to "a lot of formally organized student activities...informal connections and get-togethers also drive a lot of social life." "There are a variety of MBA happy hours, tailgating events, galas, etc. which are really great because they promote relationship building across students without requiring the involvement in a specific club or group. It's a great way to meet people with different interests and experiences."

University of Minnesota graduate students "are from diverse social, cultural, and professional backgrounds." They "are all goal-oriented and busy people, juggling families, work, school, and a social life." Those that can afford the luxury of socializing outside of class can be found "grabbing beers with classmates or playing ping-pong in the master's lounge." "There is also a professional student network that partners with the LAB to put on fun social events for students and their spouses. The alumni network also holds social events for students, alumni, and their spouses."

Admissions

Candidates will need to submit GMAT scores, undergraduate GPA, work experience, a personal statement, and professional references. All are highly factored into the decision process. An interview is also required. GPAs average 3.30 and average GMAT scores are 686. The Multicultural Affairs and Diversity Education (MADE) outreach program works jointly with several organizations to bring qualified minority candidates to the school. These organizations include the National Black MBA Association (NBMBAA), the National Society of Hispanic MBAs (NSHMBA), as well as the Asian MBA (AMBA).

FINANCIAL FACTS

Annual tuition (in-state/ out-of-state)	$30,262/$42,560
Fees	$2,098
Cost of books	$3,000
Room & board (on/off-campus)	$13,000/$15,000
% of students receiving aid	67
% of first-year students receiving aid	73
% of students receiving grants	67
Average award package	$42,207
Average grant	$18,702
Average loan	$35,015
Average student loan debt	$60,473

ADMISSIONS

Admissions Selectivity Rating	90
# of applications received	538
% applicants accepted	41
% acceptees attending	45
Average GMAT	686
Range of GMAT	650–718
Average GPA	3.30
TOEFL required of international students	Yes
Minimum TOEFL (paper/computer)	580/240
Application fee	$60
International application fee	$90
Application Deadline/Notification	
Round 1:	11/1 / 12/31
Round 2:	12/1 / 2/15
Round 3:	2/1 / 4/15
Round 4:	4/1 / 5/15
Deferment available	Yes
Maximum length of deferment	1 year
Transfer students accepted	No
Non-fall admissions	No
Need-blind admissions	Yes

EMPLOYMENT PROFILE

Career Rating	90	Grads Employed by Function	% Avg. Salary
Percent employed at graduation	63	Marketing	(44%) $95,352
Percent employed 3 months after graduation	88	Operations	(2%)
		Consulting	(18%) $102,500
Average base starting salary	$96,072	Management	(3%)
Primary Source of Full-time Job Acceptances		Finance	(23%) $95,273
School-facilitated activities	37(62%)	Other	(10%) $97,708
Graduate-facilitated activities	18(30%)	**Top 5 Employers Hiring Grads**	
Unknown	5(8%)	General Mills Inc. (9), 3M Company (5), Medtronic Inc. (5), Best Buy (3), Target Corporation (2)	

UNIVERSITY OF MISSISSIPPI
SCHOOL OF BUSINESS ADMINISTRATION

GENERAL INFORMATION
Type of school	Public
Affiliation	No Affiliation
Academic calendar	Semester

SURVEY SAYS...
Good social scene, Cutting-edge
classes
Solid preparation in:
Finance, Accounting, Teamwork,
Doing business in a global economy

STUDENTS
Enrollment of parent institution	21,000
Enrollment of MBA Program	128
% male/female	60/40
% out-of-state	45
% part-time	40
% underrepresented minority	12
% international	5
Average age at entry	24
Average years work experience at entry	1.0

ACADEMICS
Academic Experience Rating	**81**
Profs interesting rating	80
Profs accesible rating	74
Student/faculty ratio	7:1
% female faculty	30
% underrepresented minority faculty	15
% part-time faculty	0

Academics

The University of Mississippi—known affectionately as "Ole Miss" to its many students and supporters—offers students two MBA options. The first is an intensive, one-year full-time MBA, which does not require post-undergraduate professional experience for admission; the other is the two-year online MBA for working adults, which gives strong preference to students with at least two years of post-undergraduate business-related employment.

Ole Miss' one-year program runs 11 months, commencing in July and ending in May. The curriculum consists of 13 prescribed courses, taught cohort-style with an emphasis on "the integration of subjects into real business applications." Students warn that the program is intense. As one explains, "Overall, you have to be very serious if you want to be in a one-year program. Don't let the kind recruiters fool you: You are in for hell if you are not 100 percent committed...There is hardly any time to breathe. This is only for the extremely serious." Instructors "expect a lot out of us," and even "The administration is concerned with our performance and takes measures to continually monitor our progression through the classes. Overall, the academic experience is rigorous." One student concurs, "The program could use more breaks. Or, they could lengthen it to ease the stress."

The part-time MBA at Ole Miss is more flexible, using "alternate methods of delivering course content" through internet tools. The online program delivers the same MBA content and degree as the on campus program. In both the part-time and full-time program, "Professors all have business backgrounds and have been tenured for a long time, or they have short academic careers and long, successful business careers in the fields they teach." Instructors typically employ "real-world examples and tie your education from them into your own work experiences. Dictation seldom happens. Discussion of the assigned readings is the primary classroom focus."

Career and Placement

Ole Miss MBAs receive career support from the university's Career Center. Students report that many of the best career opportunities come via the alumni network, which is "very supportive. The Ole Miss 'brand' is well-respected in the Southeast." Employers that recruit on the Ole Miss campus include Axciom, Allstate, Bancorp South, FedEx, Harrah's, IBM, International Paper, Regions Bank, and the Tennessee Valley Authority.

Student Life and Environment

The swift pace of the full-time MBA program means that many students "study so much that it is hard to have a life. But when there are small breaks, the potential to have a great time is definitely there." First and foremost, is Ole Miss football and the requisite tailgate parties beforehand, but there's much more to the social scene than sports. The school "offers a wide variety of activities socially and academically that you can become involved in. This place has a lot of great traditions." Students appreciate the Ole Miss grounds, which one describes as "a walking campus that promotes and produces beautiful people!"

ADMISSIONS CONTACT: DR. JOHN HOLLEMAN, DIRECTOR OF MBA ADMINISTRATION
ADDRESS: 319 CONNER HALL, OXFORD, MS 38677
PHONE: 662-915-5483 • FAX: 662-915-7968
E-MAIL: JHOLLEMAN@BUS.OLEMISS.EDU • WEBSITE: WWW.OLEMISSBUSINESS.COM

Hometown Oxford is a small, Southern college town distinguished by the university and the residences of several famous writers, including John Grisham. The town has become a travel destination for many, not only for Ole Miss sporting events but also for festivals such as the Double Decker Arts Festival and conferences as the Faulkner & Yoknapatawpha Conference (named after the author William Faulkner, who made his home in Oxford, and the fictional county in which much of his work is set). The city of Memphis is just 70 miles to the north.

Full-timers at Ole Miss tend to be "very young. The majority are 22 years old. Some have had internships, but none have actually worked. It's very difficult to have a discussion about business if you've never been involved in one. The few students with work experience talk 95 percent of the time." The student community is close. As one student explains, "One thing about going through an MBA 'boot camp' like this is that you come together very quickly. Because you're all suffering together, people are very friendly and quick to help you out."

Admissions

All applicants to the full-time MBA program at Ole Miss must provide an official transcript of undergraduate work showing a minimum 3.0 GPA for the final 60 semesters hours of academic work; an official GMAT score report (the school lists 550 as the cut-off for "acceptable" scores); two letters of recommendation; and a 400-word personal statement of purpose. Students who have not completed prerequisite course work in undergraduate business disciplines will be required to complete such courses successfully before commencing work on their graduate degrees. International students must meet all of the above requirements and submit TOEFL scores (minimum acceptable score is 600). Applicants to the professional MBA program "with two or more years of post-baccalaureate degree professional work experience" receive "particular consideration" from the Admissions Committee. The professional MBA program is "very competitive."

FINANCIAL FACTS

Cost of books	$5,000

ADMISSIONS

Admissions Selectivity Rating	81
Average GMAT	570
Average GPA	3.65
TOEFL required of international students	Yes
Minimum TOEFL (paper/computer)	/600
Application fee	$40
International application fee	¢40
Regular application deadline	4/1
Deferment available	Yes
Maximum length of deferment	1 year
Transfer students accepted	No
Non-fall admissions	Yes
Need-blind admissions	Yes

UNIVERSITY OF MISSOURI—COLUMBIA
ROBERT J. TRULASKE, SR. COLLEGE OF BUSINESS

GENERAL INFORMATION

Type of school	Public
Affiliation	No Affiliation
Academic calendar	Semester

SURVEY SAYS...

Students love Columbia, MO, Good social scene, Happy students
Solid preparation in:
Teamwork, Communication/ interpersonal skills

STUDENTS

Enrollment of parent institution	34,748
Enrollment of MBA Program	195
% male/female	67/33
% out-of-state	40
% part-time	5
% underrepresented minority	7
% international	28
Average age at entry	26
Average years work experience at entry	3.0

ACADEMICS

Academic Experience Rating	91
Profs interesting rating	93
Profs accesible rating	82
Student/faculty ratio	5:1
% female faculty	26
% underrepresented minority faculty	15
% part-time faculty	19

Joint Degrees

MBA/Bachelors in Industrial Engineering (5 years); MBA/MS in Industrial Engineering (3 years); MBA/JD (4 years); MBA/Master of Health Administration (3 years)

Prominent Alumni

Stan Kroenke, Real Estate, Sports Teams, & Media; Ralph Babb, CEO, Comerica; Jon Hamm, Actor; Sheryl Crow, Singer; Jean McKenzie, EVP, Mattel & President of American Girl

Academics

The University of Missouri-Columbia, commonly referred to as "Mizzou," is the central and most populous campus in the four-school University of Missouri system. The Crosby MBA program, named after Gordon E. Crosby, Jr., the former USLIFE CEO who made a $10 million donation to the program in 2002, has been described as a "versatile program" where "current business issues and trends are the core of many classes." Mizzou has a "great combination of cutting edge curriculum and facilities for a bargain." Point in fact, both the benefits of in-state tuition and "excellent financial aid" make Mizzou a draw for in- and out-of-state residents alike. Mizzou's "well-ranked" business school also boasts "excellent dual-degree programs," such as a dual JD/MBA, a popular MHA/MBA and the five-year IMSE/MBA program, which according to one student, "allows me to get an education in both engineering and business while on the same campus."

Other program offerings within the Trulaske College of Business include degrees or concentrations in accounting, economics, healthcare administration, finance, international business, investment banking, leadership/management, marketing, marketing analytics, and non-profit management/public administration. The Mizzou campus itself also has the advantage of size. One chemical engineering student tells us, "The campus has a medical school, law school, and veterinary school, within a few blocks, making it ideal for entrepreneurship and innovation." All MBA candidates are required to take a course focused on experiential learning and to personally consult with small business owners.

Since Mizzou does offer such a "broad curriculum" and a large number of "resources available for students," the student body covers a wide range of experience, both professional and academic. One thankful student tells us Mizzou "allowed me to pursue my MBA without prior professional experience." Another student has indicated, "The students with work experience tend to come more from management and marketing backgrounds and have stronger skill sets than the 'straight-through' students." This dichotomy, while beneficial in many ways, has also prompted one concerned student to plead for the business school to "increase the number of students with work experience."

Career and Placement

The Crosby MBA Program Career Services provides a broad range of services, including resume-building workshops, on-campus interviews, counseling, and a mentoring program. Companies are often invited to Mizzou to present themselves and recruit worthy candidates. While some students comment that networking opportunities with alumni and top employers are lacking, and "there doesn't seem to be a push to attract companies outside the Midwest," global companies, such as AT&T, Deloitte, and Edward Jones, Cerner, and Chevron have all made frequent visits to the school. One student tells us, "I just had coffee with one of our alums working for a major consulting firm in Philadelphia and that was just the start of my alumni search." The MBA program also offers a variety of school-facilitated internship opportunities, and post-graduate job placement data suggests that Mizzou MBAs are not pigeonholed into one or two industries, but several, from manufacturing to non-profit and healthcare.

Student Life and Environment

Columbia is a "great college town," with an abundance of restaurants, bars, music, culture, parks, and related activities. Even though Mizzou enjoys a large campus at the center of town, downtown Columbia is just a few steps away, and there's always something to do. Students have described the Crosby MBA program as a "close-knit community of students who are very willing to help one another and a great learning community where there are a multitude of opportunities for students to get involved on campus." This "open and friendly" atmosphere has helped foster a business program that students laud for being "cooperative" and "less competitive" than similarly sized MBA programs.

The MBA Association at Mizzou holds "weekly happy hours and other social events," where students have the chance to "play numerous intramural sports and even participate on club teams." Prospective students may also be pleased to learn that the Association pays close attention to the diversity of its student body. Several Association members are also members of the National Association of Women MBAs, while others serve on the College of Business Diversity Committee.

Admissions

Applicants to the Crosby MBA program at The University of Missouri-Columbia are required to submit the following materials: GMAT or GRE scores, essay/personal statement, official undergraduate transcript, and an updated resume. Particularly close attention is paid to applicants' test scores, undergraduate GPA (3.5 is average), and personal statement. International applicants are required to submit TOEFL or IELTS scores, with a 550 minimum for written test, 213 for computer-based, and 79-80 for web-based. While substantive post-undergraduate work experience (three or more years) is strongly considered, it is not a requirement for admission. Prospective students with excellent educational backgrounds in technology, engineering, bio/life sciences, journalism, and social sciences are historically successful in the Crosby MBA Program. The school also offers substantive review modules in statistics, finance, and Microsoft Excel during orientation week before classes begin.

FINANCIAL FACTS

Annual tuition (in-state/out-of-state)	$10,110/$26,070
Fees	$3,600
Cost of books	$1,000
Room & board (on/off-campus)	$10,612/$10,612
% of students receiving aid	78
% of first-year students receiving aid	84
% of students receiving grants	77
Average award package	$21,749
Average grant	$21,233
Average loan	$15,976
Average student loan debt	$7,210

ADMISSIONS

Admissions Selectivity Rating	90
# of applications received	375
% applicants accepted	43
% acceptees attending	57
Average GMAT	658
Range of GMAT	640–690
Average GPA	3.50
TOEFL required of international students	Yes
Minimum TOEFL (paper/computer)	550/213
Application fee	$55
International application fee	$75
Application Deadline/Notification	
Round 1:	11/15 / 1/15
Round 2:	1/1 / 3/1
Round 3:	2/15 / 4/15
Round 4:	4/1 / 5/15
Deferment available	Yes
Maximum length of deferment	1 year
Transfer students accepted	Yes
Transfer application policy: Students may transfer 6 credit hours from an AACSB-accredited MBA program.	
Non-fall admissions	No
Need-blind admissions	Yes

EMPLOYMENT PROFILE

		Grads Employed by Function	% Avg. Salary
Career Rating	89		
Percent employed at graduation	80	Marketing	(27%) $62,129
Percent employed 3 months after graduation	84	Operations	(20%) $65,638
		Consulting	(20%)$55,143
Average base starting salary	$59,696	Finance	(23%) $50,357
Primary Source of Full-time Job Acceptances		Other	(10%) $66,050
School-facilitated activities	36(90%)	**Top 5 Employers Hiring Grads**	
Graduate-facilitated activities	4(10%)	Cerner (4), Edward Jones (3), Ascension Health (2), IBM (2), Epic (2)	

UNIVERSITY OF MISSOURI—KANSAS CITY
HENRY W. BLOCH SCHOOL OF BUSINESS AND PUBLIC ADMINISTRATION

GENERAL INFORMATION
Type of school	Public
Affiliation	No Affiliation
Academic calendar	Semester

SURVEY SAYS...
Solid preparation in:
Teamwork, Communication/interpersonal skills, Presentation skills

STUDENTS
Enrollment of parent institution	15,492
Enrollment of MBA Program	375
% male/female	61/39
% out-of-state	43
% part-time	63
% underrepresented minority	14
% international	10
Average age at entry	30
Average years work experience at entry	3.0

ACADEMICS
Academic Experience Rating	80
Profs interesting rating	79
Profs accesible rating	80
Student/faculty ratio	13:1
% female faculty	26
% underrepresented minority faculty	21
% part-time faculty	5

Joint Degrees
JD/MBA (81 law school credit hours + 42 MBA credit hours); JD/MPA (81 law school credit hours + 36-39 MPA credit hours)

Prominent Alumni
Gerald Kelly, CEO of Silpada Designs; Terry Dunn, President and CEO, Dunn Industries, Inc.; Bob Regnier, President, Bank of Blue Valley; Tom Holcom, President, Pioneer Financial Services, Inc.; Esther George, COO of Federal Reserve Bank of Kansas City

Academics

The "dynamic community" at the University of Missouri—Kansas City unites some of the brightest business minds in the region. Academically, the school's MBA is known for its "outstanding entrepreneurship and innovation program," which was developed to compliment the growing number of new ventures and technology companies in the local area. Kansas City, together with several other Midwestern cities, is sometimes dubbed the "Silicon Prairie," and "There is a feeling that everyone at the Henry W. Bloch School of Management is a part of a larger movement in Kansas City to be officially known as the entrepreneurship capital of the United States." Those ties to the community are a huge strength of the program, and students praise the "local business community and their willingness to contribute to classes and research." A current student shares, "My involvement with the UMKC Institute for Entrepreneurship and Innovation recently helped me win a business planning contest valued at $100,000. I now have the opportunity to connect with the leading business men and women in my city."

Aside from the school's noted strength in entrepreneurship, the MBA curriculum trains students in business fundamentals, beginning with 24 credit hours of core coursework in key topics like marketing, management, and economics. After completing the core, students take fifteen credits of electives, with the option of pursuing a concentration in entrepreneurship, finance, general management, international business, leading and managing people, management information systems, marketing, or supply chain and operations management. While the faculty includes some "world-class researchers," "UMKC is not as heavy on theory, but they are VERY strong on practical." Professional students can immediately take knowledge and skills back to the workplace, as coursework focuses on "activities applicable to real-world situations." Students explain that even their employers regard UMKC as "the best business school at preparing students for the job" in the Kansas City area.

On campus, "UMKC offers a big-city feel with a suburban community and attitude, meaning the faculty and students are down-to-earth and the quality of the education is up to Ivy League standards." Speaking of the Ivy League, students dole out praises for their experienced and well-educated faculty, saying instructors are "engaging, intelligent, and fair." Most have "great real world experience they can draw on," which makes their lectures more applicable. These professors ultimately serve as valuable "resources for future opportunities" as well. A student adds, "The Bloch School professors are a cut above the rest. They are always there when you need them, and [they] are practical in their project assignment." Convenience and affordability make the UMKC programs all the more attractive. "Most students are working while in the program," so they appreciate the school's flexible evening schedule, while the "affordable" in-state tuition is the icing on the cake.

ADMISSIONS CONTACT: W.C. VANCE, DIRECTOR OF ADMISSIONS
ADDRESS: 5100 ROCKHILL ROAD, KANSAS CITY, MO 64110
PHONE: 816-235-1111 • FAX: 816-235-5544
E-MAIL: ADMIT@UMKC.EDU • WEBSITE: WWW.BLOCH.UMKC.EDU

Career and Placement

Students generally start the Bloch MBA when their professional career is already underway. "Most work for large corporations and are participating in a tuition reimbursement program," in which they plan to remain with the same company after graduation. Other students join the program "to start a business as part of the Entrepreneurship initiative." While they are in the minority, students at the early stages of their careers also say they benefit from the school's strong, practical education. A current student details, "I chose UMKC because I honestly believed they would help me find myself and the career in which I would fit. I have not been let down. Each class I'm learning more about myself and what the future holds." No matter what their career goals, Bloch students benefit from "personal access to Kansas City's top business professionals," through faculty, speakers, and networking events.

The Bloch Career Network adviser plans career-related workshops and helps manage an online job board, though these resources are principally aimed at assisting undergraduates. MBA candidates can also access the Career Services Center at UMKC, which serves the entire school community. Among other services, they offer resume help, internship placements, career fairs, and campus recruiting for both undergraduate and graduate students.

Student Life and Environment

UMKC has specially designed their MBA program to appeal to local professionals. As a result, a majority of students are "married with children, or what you would consider 'nontraditional,'" though there is a small community of students who "come straight out of [their] undergraduate" schooling. The campus as a whole attracts students from "a large mix of careers," so you will share a classroom and a campus with "MBA students, engineers, lawyers, and MPA students." On the whole, Bloch business students are "highly intelligent, motivated and friendly."

Masters of time management, most students "take a balanced approach to life," splitting their time between career obligations, coursework, and personal life. There are "a lot of commuters" so there is "not a whole lot of socializing" between MBA students on campus. Most "people show up for their class and leave," though they occasionally linger in the "computer labs, study areas, and meeting with class team members." Home to almost over 14,000 students, UMKC's vibrant campus is located in the Rockhill area of Kansas City. In their free time, students can easily access the range of cultural, recreational, shopping, and dining options around town.

Admissions

In addition to GMAT scores and undergraduate transcripts, applicants for University of Missouri—Kansas City's evening MBA program must submit a one-page goals statement, a current resume, and information about their current employment, including any travel commitments. Applicants to the EMBA program are not required to take the GMAT, but they must have extensive upper-level work experience as evidenced by their resume, letters of recommendation, and personal statement. Applications are accepted year-round on a rolling basis.

FINANCIAL FACTS

Annual tuition (in-state/ out-of-state)	$5,522/$14,256
Fees	$888
Cost of books	$1,180
Room & board (on/off-campus)	$9,560/$8,320
% of students receiving aid	43
% of first-year students receiving aid	50
% of students receiving grants	12
Average award package	$17,209
Average grant	$4,947
Average loan	$18,657
Average student loan debt	$26,513

ADMISSIONS

Admissions Selectivity Rating	**81**
# of applications received	203
% applicants accepted	60
% acceptees attending	80
Average GMAT	546
Range of GMAT	500–600
Average GPA	3.34
TOEFL required of international students	Yes
Minimum TOEFL (paper/computer)	550/213
Application fee	$35
International application fee	$50
Regular application deadline	5/1
Deferment available	Yes
Maximum length of deferment	1 year
Transfer students accepted	Yes
Transfer application policy: We will accept up to 6 hours of grad credit from an AACSB accredited institution	
Non-fall admissions	Yes
Need-blind admissions	Yes

University of Missouri—St. Louis

College of Business Administration

GENERAL INFORMATION

Type of school	Public
Affiliation	No Affiliation
Academic calendar	Semester

SURVEY SAYS...

Solid preparation in:
General management,
Communication/interpersonal skills,
Presentation skills

STUDENTS

Enrollment of parent institution	16,719
Enrollment of MBA Program	487
% part-time	100
Average age at entry	28
Average years work experience at entry	3.4

ACADEMICS

Academic Experience Rating	76
Profs interesting rating	77
Profs accesible rating	75
Student/faculty ratio	11:1
% female faculty	30
% underrepresented minority faculty	9
% part-time faculty	30

Academics

The University of Missouri—St. Louis is a smart choice for local professionals who want to complete an MBA without interrupting their career. One of four "AASCB-accredited schools in the St. Louis area," UMSL offers several MBA options: the traditional evening MBA, the professional MBA, and the international MBA, offered in conjunction with partner universities overseas. For students in the evening program, "convenient class schedules" make UMSL a great choice (though evening students also say, "there is a great need for online course options" to provide greater flexibility). While classes in the evening program generally meet once a week, the professional MBA is a hybrid program, which combines weekend course work with online communication. As these options illustrate, the school's programs are principally geared toward "working professionals that attend UMSL and come to class and go home." However, the student body seems to be "shifting to younger students as they recognize the education level being received...surpasses the minimal cost to attend." On that note, USML is an excellent value. This school maintains a "good reputation in the St. Louis area for providing a good, quality business education," while also maintaining a "very affordable" tuition price.

The curriculum in both the evening and professional format provides training in the functional areas of business (though students in the evening program may also pursue an area of emphasis through elective course work). By all accounts, the administration is very "well-organized" and the curriculum is "up-to-date on trends and technology." At the same time, some students would like to see the core courses more ably synched. In some cases, "courses are repetitive," and students feel the MBA "should encompass a more general/integrated look at business and manage[ment]." Throughout the MBA, there is an emphasis on "combining the practical knowledge with the theoretical knowledge" in the classroom. At UMSL, "The professors are almost all professionals in their field," who "teach about real-world work experience and tie current events into the curriculum." Here, talented professors "make the course work interesting by providing practical knowledge in addition to theoretical knowledge, and truly being engaged in the industry." In fact, in the rare case that a teacher doesn't excel in the classroom, they nonetheless are experts in their fields. A student remembers, "There have been a few that were poor teachers but were good technically on the subject matter." Despite their real-world credentials, faculty "all seem to teach for the love of teaching versus for the pay," and they are "readily available outside of class and are always willing to help."

Career and Placement

Most UMSL programs are designed for working professionals who are looking to advance in their current position, rather than find a new job. However, for those seeking a career change, the UMSL Office of Career Services helps undergraduate and graduate students prepare for the job search through career counseling and job preparation workshops. The Office of Career Services also connects the university with local employers through networking events and job fairs. (At recent UMSL job fairs, numerous prominent companies attended, including Aflac Insurance, AT&T, Bank of America, Boeing, Commerce Bank, FedEx, Maxim Healthcare Services, Mutual of Omaha, Northwestern Mutual, Sherwin-Williams, St. Luke's Hospital, Target, Walgreens, and many more.) Through Career Services, students can also post their resume online, where it can be electronically matched with recruiting companies.

ADMISSIONS CONTACT: KARL KOTTEMANN, DIRECTOR, GRADUATE PROGRAMS
ADDRESS: ONE UNIVERSITY BOULEVARD, 350 JC PENNEY NORTH, ST. LOUIS, MO 63121-4499
PHONE: 314-516-5885 • FAX: 314-516-7202
E-MAIL: MBA@UMSL.EDU • WEBSITE: MBA.UMSL.EDU

Student Life and Environment

With a convenient evening or weekend schedule, UMSL attracts a lot of working professionals, who are "busy juggling work, school, and home responsibilities." While they have worries outside the classroom, this is a "hardworking" bunch, and "students are focused on doing well in their classes while also working a full-time job." When course work requires collaboration between classmates, students are "friendly and professional," and they "work well together in groups." By and large, "UMSL is a commuter school" and most people "are there to learn and leave."

As a part of the largest research university in the St. Louis area, UMSL has an "ethnically diverse" and active student body. As graduate business students, MBA candidates have access to numerous facilities on this 350-acre campus. For example, "The campus houses the largest Performing Arts Center in the Saint Louis Area. There are weekly and sometimes nightly events on campus, available for free or at a discount to UMSL students." Within the business school, however, students would like the administration to "upgrade our facilities and buildings." Located in suburban St. Louis, this school offers excellent access to the largest metropolitan center in Missouri. However, some students feel the campus is "set in a rough part of St. Louis," so there aren't many options for recreation or nightlife in the local area.

Admissions

The traditional (evening) MBA enrolls students three times a year, in the fall, spring, and summer terms. For the professional MBA and the international MBA, classes only start once a year, in the fall term. To apply, all programs require undergraduate transcripts, two letters of recommendation, and GMAT scores. Admission is selective, with only about 60 percent of applicants receiving an offer of admission. To be competitive, students should have a GMAT score of 500 or better, and an undergraduate GPA of at least 3.0. Promising students who fall short of these minimum standards may be considered for restricted admission.

FINANCIAL FACTS

Room & board	$10,300
% of students receiving aid	46
% of first-year students receiving aid	51
% of students receiving grants	20
Average award package	$12,741
Average grant	$7,390
Average loan	$14,527
Average student loan debt	$10,052

ADMISSIONS

Admissions Selectivity Rating	72
# of applications received	225
% applicants accepted	80
% acceptees attending	70
Average GMAT	513
Range of GMAT	490–540
Average GPA	3.36
TOEFL required of international students	Yes
Minimum TOEFL (paper/computer)	550/213
Application fee	$35
International application fee	$40
Regular application deadline	7/1
Deferment available	Yes
Maximum length of deferment	1 year
Transfer students accepted	Yes
Transfer application policy: Transcripts are evaluated for relevant course work. Maximum of nine hours of acceptable graduate credit allowed to transfer in.	
Non-fall admissions	Yes
Need-blind admissions	Yes

EMPLOYMENT PROFILE

Career Rating	71	Grads Employed by Function	% Avg. Salary
Average base starting salary	$57,200	Marketing	(100%) $45,000
Primary Source of Full-time Job Acceptances		Operations	(67%) $85,000
School-facilitated activities	17(23%)	Management	(88%) $68,600
Graduate-facilitated activities	58(77%)	Finance	(100%) $51,400
		HR	(100%) $39,000
		MIS	(83%) $48,600

UNIVERSITY OF NEVADA—LAS VEGAS
COLLEGE OF BUSINESS

GENERAL INFORMATION

Type of school   Public
Affiliation   No Affiliation
Academic calendar   Semesters

SURVEY SAYS...

Students love Las Vegas, NV, Good
social scene, Smart classrooms
Solid preparation in:
Teamwork

STUDENTS

Enrollment of parent
  institution   27,364
Enrollment of MBA Program   186
% male/female   100/0
% out-of-state   0
% part-time   100
% underrepresented minority   0
% international   0
Average age at entry   28
Average years work experience
  at entry   7.0

ACADEMICS

Academic Experience Rating   82
Profs interesting rating   76
Profs accesible rating   81
Student/faculty ratio   30:1
% female faculty   15
% underrepresented minority
  faculty   6
% part-time faculty   0

Joint Degrees

MS Hotel Administration/MBA 2.5
years; MS Management Information
Systems/MBA 2.5 years; JD/MBA 4
years full time/ 5 years part time;
MBA/DMD Dental Medicine

Prominent Alumni

Rossi Rolenkotter, President/CEO,
Las Vegas Convention and Visitors
Authority; Dave Rice, Head men's
basketball coach, UNLV; Darcy
Neighbors, Founder and CEO, CIM
Marketing Partners; Linda
Rheinberger, Owner, One Source
Realty and Management; Cass
Palmer, President/CEO United Way
of Southern Nevada

Academics

The College of Business at the University of Nevada—Las Vegas offers two MBA tracks. One is an evening MBA, which students can complete either full- or part-time, and the other is an Executive MBA, available only to those with experience. "For working students or students, who need to balance family life, this is the perfect environment." The evening program can be completed in two to four years, and students may opt to concentrate in one of the following fields: finance, service marketing, management information systems, or new venture management. Students must complete 48 credit hours, 33 of which are devoted to a core curriculum. An accelerated program is open to students in the evening program who have a minimum score of 600 on the GMAT. Students must also exceed the 50th percentile on both the verbal and quantitative skills portion of the GMAT. Another prerequisite for the Executive MBA is an undergraduate business degree from an AACSB-accredited university.

The Executive MBA is an 18-month program during which all students follow the same general course of study. Students should have seven years work experience prior to applying, and of those seven years, three must be in "a key decision-making role." Classes take place every Friday and Saturday from 8:30 a.m. to 5:30 p.m. There is an initial full-week intensive prior to the start of classes. UNLV also offers joint degrees. Students can pursue degrees in hotel administration, dental medicine, management information systems, and a JD/MBA. Students choose UNLV due to its "location, affordability, and flexibility." It's the "only school in the state with AACSB accreditation," and students say "UNLV has the best hotel program." Some wish UNLV offered an additional specialization, one which might help them better prepare for work in "green jobs."

"UNLV's best attribute is the willingness of its professors to help students. Because half the students work full-time, they are very flexible when it come to scheduling office hours or addressing questions through email." "Professors come prepared for lectures" and "treat MBA students like professionals." The curriculum is "well organized," and professors stay on top of pertinent issues. "I feel I have gotten a superb exposure to the current business environment from them." Professors are also equipped with bedside manner. They "are always friendly and willing to help further explain difficult topics." Students praise "the use of teamwork, in almost every aspect of class." As for the administration, they "promptly respond to requests by phone and email."

Career and Placement

The Career Services Center at UNLV serves only the University's graduate students, giving the students more direct attention. The office assists them in developing career goals and a career plan, as well as helping students market themselves and contact alumni for jobs. The office also acts as a liaison between students and local businesses. The Career Services Center maintains an online job database and organizes recruiting events for students on campus. Students say they like how close the school is "to the thousands of jobs that are on the Las Vegas strip." However, others worry UNLV needs to develop its image. "Our school needs to be perceived as competition by other learning institutions. Potential employers should know that UNLV produces analytical, top-notch graduates."

UNLV MBAs are hired by the gaming and engineering industries, as well as by the state and federal government. Nearly all students in a recent graduating class had found employment by graduation.

ADMISSIONS CONTACT: LISA DAVIS, MBA PROGRAMS RECRUITMENT DIRECTOR
ADDRESS: 4505 MARYLAND PARKWAY BOX 456031, LAS VEGAS, NV 89154-6031
PHONE: 702-895-3655 • FAX: 702-895-3632
E-MAIL: COBMBA@UNLV.EDU • WEBSITE: BUSINESS.UNLV.EDU

Student Life and Environment

"The atmosphere at UNLV is similar to a commuter school. Most students, even undergraduate, work full time and live off campus." Students "are business professionals in many different industries and are on average a few years out of undergrad." The average age is "late twenties." "They are a diverse group that come from a variety of backgrounds," "a mixing pot of international students and students from other states." Regardless of their differences, students seem to share "similar values and goals." They are "smart, outgoing, and welcome challenges." Students say they value their classmates' ability "to stimulate" their minds. They are also "great friends and very helpful."

Las Vegas is half an hour from the Hoover Dam, the Colorado River, and Lake Mead. There is skiing and hiking less than an hour northwest of the city. However, being in Las Vegas itself has its bonuses for business students. The "modern" campus is "very exciting considering it is only miles from the Las Vegas strip." The campus also regularly hosts a variety of entertainers and lecturers.

Admissions

The Admissions Committee requests the following from its applicants: official transcripts for all post-secondary institutions attended, an official score report for the GMAT, two letters of recommendation, a personal essay, and a resume. The GMAT score and the GPA are most important to the committee, as is work experience. An interview is required only of those seeking admission to the Executive MBA. The average GPA of entering students is 3.20 and the average GMAT score is approximately 600. All international students seeking admission are asked to supply financial certification documents.

FINANCIAL FACTS

Annual tuition	$8,736
Fees	$3,000
Cost of books	$2,400
Room & board	
(on/off-campus)	$10,000/$12,000
% of students receiving aid	57
% of students receiving grants	8
Average award package	$15,192
Average student loan debt	$30,701

ADMISSIONS

Admissions Selectivity Rating	86
# of applications received	137
% applicants accepted	52
% acceptees attending	82
Average GMAT	600
Range of GMAT	560–620
Average GPA	3.27
TOEFL required of	
international students	Yes
Minimum TOEFL	
(paper/computer)	550/213
Application fee	$60
International application fee	$95
Regular application deadline	6/1
Regular application notification	7/1
Deferment available	Yes
Maximum length	
of deferment	one Semester
Transfer students accepted	Yes
Transfer application policy: Must meet our admission deadlines and requirements. A total of 12 credits from an AACSB accredited school	
Non-fall admissions	Yes
Need-blind admissions	Yes

EMPLOYMENT PROFILE	
Career Rating	72
Average base starting salary	$71,794

UNIVERSITY OF NEVADA—RENO
COLLEGE OF BUSINESS

GENERAL INFORMATION
Type of school	Public
Affiliation	No Affiliation
Academic calendar	Semester

SURVEY SAYS...
Solid preparation in:
General management, Doing business in a global economy

STUDENTS
Enrollment of parent institution	18,004
Enrollment of MBA Program	250
% part-time	100
Average age at entry	30
Average years work experience at entry	6.0

ACADEMICS
Academic Experience Rating	**79**
Profs interesting rating	86
Profs accesible rating	80
Student/faculty ratio	30:1
% female faculty	24
% underrepresented minority faculty	20
% part-time faculty	32

Academics

One of the state's top MBA programs, the extremely affordable Nevada MBA program accommodates the needs of full and part time students by offering all evening courses so that students can complete a degree at their own pace without interrupting their professional career. A heavy emphasis on group projects, the ability to waive core course requirements if comparable courses have been completed, and "ideal" flexibility only further endear this program to those who come here. "I wouldn't be able to work and get my MBA nearly as easily without the setup we have here," says a student.

Students may also choose an "Area of Emphasis," in which they take nine elective credits that have an industry or functional emphasis. Current areas of emphasis include accounting, entrepreneurship, finance, and information technology (students can also pursue other areas of emphasis by taking graduate courses of their choice outside of CB).

Professors are "readily available outside the classroom and are knowledgeable about the subject that they are teaching," and "the adaptability and overall performance of the administrative staff and professors is admirable." The faculty "not only have academic experience, but are able to share real world knowledge that is invaluable to students working in such competitive business environments." Since most every student is also working while getting their degree, the intensity of the classes is tailored to allow for the busy professional and personal lives of students, and professors "understand if we have to miss a class for a particular reason." "I feel as though the coursework is challenging enough to get the message across, while still being understanding of the fact that we do have a life outside of school," says a student.

Career and Placement

The CB "encourages students to work with other students," which makes for a built-in networking as most students are working professionals. "I have heard of several job opportunities from fellow students," says one. Though the majority of those who attend Nevada are already employed, "many people are in the program to move to a new career path or because they want to advance from their current position." A good deal of engineers and tech-oriented people are seeking MBAs, so recruitment from companies like Microsoft occurs frequently, although a couple of students wish the school would "partner with companies to give students more job opportunities."

ADMISSIONS CONTACT: VICKI KRENTZ, COORDINATOR OF GRADUATE PROGRAMS
ADDRESS: MAILSTOP 0024, RENO, NV 89557
PHONE: 775-784-4912 • FAX: 775-784-1773
E-MAIL: VKRENTZ@UNR.EDU • WEBSITE: WWW.COBA.UNR.EDU/MBA

Student Life and Environment

This group (mostly in their twenties or thirties, and often married) is "friendly, supportive, team oriented, hardworking, [and] driven," yet "still incredibly personable." They understand "that the MBA program requires a different level of focus than under grad classes, and most of them seem to really embrace the challenge." The campus has several new buildings, and "the library and Student Union are great places to study and do group work." There is "a great sense of community" all around the campus, as seen by attendance at major sporting events and fine arts or other activities on campus, and "class diversity is great."

Being that this is a part-time program, the school does "a very good job of socializing information about clubs and other social gatherings." Reno itself has tons of "amazing" outdoor activities: it is within an hour of around twenty ski resorts and hiking trails (including Lake Tahoe), there's a river flowing through downtown for rafting, and there are "plenty of lakes to camp and fish." "It has the benefits of a big city in a small town," says a student.

Admissions

Two or more years of work experience, a minimum GPA of 2.75 on a 4.0 scale, and a GMAT score of at least 500 are required for admission to the College of Business at UNR. A resume, three letters of reference, and a two- to three-page personal statement concerning background and goals are also needed. A minimum TOEFL score of 550 paper-based, 213 computer-based, or 79 iBT (or an IELTS score of at least 7.0) is required from nonnative English speakers. The average GMAT score for those admitted in Fall of 2012 was 584, the average GPA was 3.2, and the average length of work experience was six years.

FINANCIAL FACTS

Room & board	$6,000
% of students receiving aid	10
Average award package	$7,000
Average student loan debt	$6,300

ADMISSIONS

Admissions Selectivity Rating	71
# of applications received	81
% applicants accepted	93
% acceptees attending	63
Average GMAT	584
Range of GMAT	530–590
Average GPA	3.20
TOEFL required of international students	Yes
Minimum TOEFL (paper/computer)	550/213
Application fee	$60
International application fee	$100
Regular application deadline	3/15
Deferment available	Yes
Maximum length of deferment	1 year
Transfer students accepted	Yes
Transfer application policy: The university's graduate school will only accept 9 transfer credits from another graduate program.	
Non-fall admissions	Yes
Need-blind admissions	No

EMPLOYMENT PROFILE

Career Rating	76	Grads Employed by Function	% Avg. Salary
Average base starting salary	$50,000	Marketing	(20%)
		Operations	(10%)
		Management	(10%)
		Finance	(25%)
		HR	(10%)
		MIS	(20%)
		Other	(5%)

University of New Hampshire
Paul T. Paul College of Business and Economics

GENERAL INFORMATION

Type of school	Public
Affiliation	No Affiliation
Academic calendar	Five Terms in one year

SURVEY SAYS...

Students love Durham, NH
Solid preparation in:
General management, Teamwork,
Communication/interpersonal skills,
Presentation skills, Computer skills

STUDENTS

Enrollment of parent institution	15,155
Enrollment of MBA Program	103
% male/female	69/31
% out-of-state	21
% part-time	57
% underrepresented minority	35
% international	6
Average age at entry	35
Average years work experience at entry	5.2

ACADEMICS

Academic Experience Rating	84
Profs interesting rating	77
Profs accesible rating	86
Student/faculty ratio	5:1
% female faculty	21
% underrepresented minority faculty	3
% part-time faculty	3

Joint Degrees

Combined JD and MBA in 3 1/2 years. JD comes from UNH Law School. Current UNH seniors can apply early admission to MS Accounting program and count one graduate course towards both degree requirements.

Academics

The Paul College of Business and Economics at the University of New Hampshire has all the bases covered. For those in a hurry to get an MBA, the school offers an intensive one-year full-time program. For young professionals looking for a leg up the corporate ladder, the school has a part-time evening program (offered on on the main campus, the Manchester campus, and online) that can be completed in two to six years. And for established managers lacking that all-important sheepskin, UNH has a nineteen-month Executive MBA program that meets on alternating Fridays and Saturdays in Portsmouth.

Students praise Whittemore's entrepreneurial track as "one of the best in the nation," touting the school's "reputation for developing business leaders in the field of entrepreneurship and venture capital." Professors earn high marks for "their 'real world' experience" and for being "very available and friendly." Students also see the school's "desirable location (proximity to Boston)" and affordability as great assets.

Full-time students warn that the workload can be overwhelming. "The schedule is so compressed that most time is spent on completing coursework and not on understanding," one writes. Another sees an upside; "You learn about yourself through group work and intense deadlines," he explains.

Career and Placement

In 2009, UNH rolled out a dedicated MBA career services program, which works in partnership with the university-at-large placement office, the University Advising and Career Center. Career staff work with business undergraduates, graduates, and alumni to forge career strategies, identify potential employers, and navigate the recruitment process. Students tell us that the school "could definitely improve in the area of career placement." One writes, "Career placement is not a priority for the school because we already have jobs for the most part. However, "it still should be offered to us because [some of us] are looking to leave our present situations. That is why we enrolled."

Recent employers of Paul College graduates include BAE Systems, Coastal Forest Products, Dartmouth Hitchcock, Newmarket International, Sikorsky, Sprague Energy, State Street, ThermoFisher, Wackenhut, and Windward Petroleum. About half of UNH MBAs enter the field of marketing (avg. mean base salary, of that group $48,750).

Student Life and Environment

Paul's MBAs proclaim that their peers are one of the school's greatest assets. Indeed, "the students bring a diversity of work experience and perspective to class." As one student shares, "Currently, I am in classes with military budget officer, a bank CFO, a manager of a vineyard, and many other interesting individuals."Importantly, there's also a sense of camaraderie and though, "homework can be demanding, the students band together and help each other out as much as possible."

Full-timers says that, despite the "heavy workload...we still find time to be social. There is strong support for UNH hockey team." For eMBAs, however, "life is not as rosy. I haven't skied once in the two years I have been enrolled because there is already not enough time to get the homework done as it is.... It would be great to partake in some of the entrepreneurial extracurriculars but there is just not enough bandwidth with the workload." Students attending the Manchester satellite campus report that "life at school is solely in the classroom."

ADMISSIONS CONTACT: REBECCA BARBOUR, DIRECTOR OF GRADUATE PROGRAMS
ADDRESS: 10 GARRISON AVENUE, DURHAM, NH 03824
PHONE: 603-862-1367 • FAX: 603-862-4468
E-MAIL: PAUL.GRAD@UNH.EDU • WEBSITE: WWW.MBA.UNH.EDU

Admissions

Applicants to the MBA program at UNH's Paul College must provide the Admissions Department with all of the following: official copies of transcripts for all postsecondary academic work; an official score report for the GMAT; three letters of reference focusing on the candidate's "strengths, weaknesses, and potential for academic and managerial success"; responses to essay questions, which the school deems a "crucial" aspect of the application; a current resume; and any evidence of leadership skills that the applicant wishes to provide. Applicants to the Executive MBA program must undergo an admissions interview. Applicants to other MBA programs may request an interview but are not required to do so. (It is, however, "strongly recommended" that applicants who have "one or more weak components in their profile" schedule an appointment.) Two years of work experience is "recommended but not required" for the full-time and part-time MBA programs; a minimum of five years of professional experience is required for the Executive MBA program. International applicants must meet all of the above requirements and must submit an official score report for the TOEFL (minimum required score: 550 paper-based test, 213 computer-based test).

Prominent Alumni

Ronald K. Noble, Secretary General, INTERPOL; Elisa Steele, EVP and CMO, Yahoo!; Garrett Ilg, President, SAP Japan; David Cote, Chairman/President/CEO of Honeywell; Elizabeth Hilpman, Owner, Barlow Partners

FINANCIAL FACTS

Annual tuition (in-state/ out-of-state)	$28,000/$42,000
Fees	$817
Cost of books	$2,400
Room & board (on/off-campus)	$10,160/$11,608
% of students receiving aid	78
% of first-year students receiving aid	78
% of students receiving grants	24
Average award package	$2,557
Average grant	$3,151
Average loan	$20,889
Average student loan debt	$24,234

ADMISSIONS

Admissions Selectivity Rating	86
# of applications received	280
% applicants accepted	49
% acceptees attending	81
Average GMAT	550
Range of GMAT	440–700
Average GPA	3.31
TOEFL required of international students	Yes
Minimum TOEFL (paper/computer)	550/213
Application fee	$60
International application fee	$60
Early application deadline	4/1
Regular application deadline	7/1
Application Deadline/Notification	
Round 1:	1/31 / 3/15
Round 2:	4/1 / 5/15
Round 3:	6/1 / 7/15
Deferment available	Yes
Maximum length of deferment	1 year
Transfer students accepted	Yes
Transfer application policy: A maximum of eight credits may be considered for transfer credit.	
Non-fall admissions	Yes
Need-blind admissions	Yes

EMPLOYMENT PROFILE

Career Rating	75	**Top 5 Employers Hiring Grads**
Percent employed at graduation	56	Sprague Energy (1), ThermoFisher (1), State Street (1), BAE (1), Dartmouth Hitchcock (1)
Percent employed 3 months after graduation	17	
Average base starting salary	$60,958	

THE UNIVERSITY OF NORTH CAROLINA AT CHAPEL HILL
KENAN-FLAGLER BUSINESS SCHOOL

GENERAL INFORMATION
Type of school	Public
Affiliation	No Affiliation
Academic calendar	Semester
	with modules

SURVEY SAYS...
Students love Chapel Hill, NC,
Friendly students, Good social scene,
Good peer network, Helpful alumni
Solid preparation in:
Teamwork, Environmental
sustainability, Social responsibility

STUDENTS
Enrollment of parent	
institution	23,000
Enrollment of MBA Program	580
% male/female	73/27
% out-of-state	77
% underrepresented minority	15
% international	33
Average age at entry	28
Average years work experience	
at entry	5.0

ACADEMICS
Academic Experience Rating	**91**
Profs interesting rating	93
Profs accesible rating	92
Student/faculty ratio	5:1
% female faculty	23
% underrepresented minority	
faculty	1
% part-time faculty	0

Joint Degrees
MBA/MD; MBA/JD; MBA/Master of
Regional Planning; MBA/Master of
Health Care Administration;
MBA/Master of Public Health;
MBA/Master of Science in
Information Science; MBA/Master of
Public Policy; MBA/PharmD.

Academics

The University of North Carolina at Chapel Hill's Kenan-Flagler Business School has been on the rise for years, and it continues its ascent thanks to a resoundingly happy student body, stellar alumni base, and good connections to growing industries such as consulting, healthcare, life sciences. The first semester of the two-year program is front-loaded to teach the core business skills, and then students can select from more than 125 elective courses as the year progresses. There are also two summer sessions prior to the start of the academic year, and most students participate in one or both of these sessions, enabling them "to start preparing for the recruiting process early."

The academic experience is "nothing short of fantastic." It is common for professors "to sit down with individual students for an hour or more to discuss classes and career goals." The "balanced curriculum" and focus on analytical skills, problem solving, and interpersonal skills give students a "fundamental skillset as a general manager." "I think the school is a powerhouse for teaching students practical skills to get them started on their post-MBA careers," says a student. UNC's outstanding merit scholarship program also attracts many students that are accepted to top 10 schools, ensuring "that the high end of the class can compete with anyone" in the workforce. People are "very kind to each other here," and "it really helps that the admissions office screens for team players with strong values."

The school is "run very well" ("I have been in all the classes I have wanted without problems," says a student) and is "very flexible in responding to students' demands." For example, in response to students' concern about too heavy a workload during the job search season, the administration "made a quick decision to change the course schedule and to increase support for students in their job search process."

Career and Placement

The career center "does a phenomenal job bring recruiters on campus and preparing students for the recruiting process," especially in "bringing in well-renowned firms, particularly in finance." "I have never heard of a school which is more supportive than Kenan-Flagler," says a student. Students say that the alumni base is smaller than other B-schools, but "closer and more willing to help current MBAs as a result". "The Carolina Blue mafia, as they are called, go out of their way to help UNC grads get jobs in the industry," says a student. "I don't think you can overstate the strength of our alumni network." Alumni generously work to create opportunities for UNC Kenan-Flagler students at their firms, in addition to "acting as mentors, helping us to perfect our interview skills by acting as sounding boards, and helping us network to find the best fit for us in terms of our career searches."

The Career Management Center has also taken significant initiatives in building a network with new companies like Amazon, Google and Roland Berger. They have also "increased their commitment to help international students find a job in the United States." Recent employers of UNC Kenan-Flager graduates include Deloitte Consulting, Johnson & Johnson, Bank of America, Barclays, and Ernst & Young.

Student Life and Environment

Chapel Hill is the quintessential college town and the MBA students take advantage of the great restaurants, nightlife, shopping, and athletics nearby. Every Thursday there are "endless socials that are extremely fun and inclusive" that bring together first and second years students and alumni, and it pays off in the rapport that results: "[Students] really take care of each other." "I have had classmates help me prepare for a job interview that they were also interviewing for." As a result of sufficient social networking opportunities, this "healthy mix of singles and students with families" all "know the faces and names of most of all the first and second year students." A "diverse and growing number of clubs and organizations" also allows students to pursue common interests. "Everyone is genuinely happy to come to school and is excited to learn," though some agree that "facilities could use a bit of a facelift. A lot of the decor and architecture is clearly from at least a decade ago."

Admissions

UNC Kenan-Flagler admits students who demonstrate leadership and organizational skills, communication ability, interpersonal skills, teamwork ability, analytic and problem-solving skills, drive and motivation, prior record of academic excellence, and strong career progression and commitment to career goals. Though no specific coursework is necessary, students must have knowledge of financial accounting, statistics, macroeconomics, and calculus. The average undergraduate GPA for the fall 2012 entering class was 3.34, and the average GMAT was 692.

Prominent Alumni

Rolf Hoffmann, SVP US Commercial Operations, Amgen, Inc.; Julian Robertson, Founder, Tiger Management, Hedge Fund; Brent Callinicos, VP, Treasurer & Chief Accountant, Google, Inc.; Gary Parr, Deputy Chairman, Lazard Freres and Co.

FINANCIAL FACTS

Annual tuition (in-state/ out-of-state)	$27,400/$48,681
Fees	$3,005
Cost of books	$2,400
Room & board	$21,938
% of students receiving aid	74
% of first-year students receiving aid	72
% of students receiving grants	51
Average award package	$47,717
Average grant	$21,532
Average loan	$45,090
Average student loan debt	$82,784

ADMISSIONS

Admissions Selectivity Rating	90
# of applications received	1,595
% applicants accepted	41
% acceptees attending	44
Average GMAT	692
Range of GMAT	660–720
Average GPA	3.34
TOEFL required of international students	Yes
Minimum TOEFL (paper/computer)	600/250
Application fee	$145
International application fee	$145
Early application deadline	10/19
Early notification date	12/10
Application Deadline/Notification	
Round 1:	10/19 / 12/10
Round 2:	12/7 / 2/4
Round 3:	1/11 / 3/18
Round 4:	3/15 / 4/29
Deferment available	Yes
Maximum length of deferment	1 year emergency only
Transfer students accepted	No
Non-fall admissions	No
Need-blind admissions	Yes

EMPLOYMENT PROFILE

Career Rating	98	**Grads Employed by Function% Avg. Salary**	
Percent employed at graduation	72	Marketing	(23%) $100,340
Percent employed 3 months		Operations	(3%) $95,300
after graduation	84	Consulting	(21%)$113,085
Average base starting salary	$102,170	Management	(9%) $99,575
Primary Source of Full-time Job Acceptances		Finance	(39%) $97,357
School-facilitated activities	122(57%)	HR	(1%) $95,333
Graduate-facilitated activities	52(24%)	MIS	(1%)
Unknown	41(19%)	Other	(2%) $117,500

Top 5 Employers Hiring Grads
Deloitte Consulting (14), Johnson & Johnson (11), Bank of America (9), Barclays (7), Ernst & Young (5)

THE UNIVERSITY OF NORTH CAROLINA AT CHARLOTTE
BELK COLLEGE OF BUSINESS

GENERAL INFORMATION

Type of school   Public
Affiliation   No Affiliation
Academic calendar   Semesters

SURVEY SAYS...

Students love Charlottesville, NC,
Happy students
Solid preparation in:
Quantitative skills

STUDENTS

Enrollment of parent
  institution   26,000
Enrollment of MBA Program   305
% part-time   74
Average age at entry   30
Average years work experience
  at entry   5.6

ACADEMICS

Academic Experience Rating   **78**
Profs interesting rating   81
Profs accesible rating   79
Student/faculty ratio   26:1
% female faculty   26
% underrepresented minority
  faculty   74
% part-time faculty   0

Joint Degrees

JD/MBA (4-5 years); MBA/MHA (3
years)

Prominent Alumni

Gene Johnson, retired Chairman &
CEO, Fairpoint Communications;
Robert Niblock, Chairman & CEO -
Lowe's Home Improvement; Kelley
Earnhardt, General Manager, JR
Motorsports; Robert Hull, CFO,
Lowe's Home Improvement; Bob
Qutub, CFO, MSCI, Inc.

Academics

Students at The University of North Carolina at Charlotte love the "proximity to the financial district in Charlotte," which is a "financial hub" with "Fortune 500 and other reputable companies throughout the region." "The flexibility of the program allows you to customize your concentrations, so they are relative to your strengths and what you would like to do in a future career," remarks one happy student. There is a "focus on banking, as there are a lot of BofA, Wells Fargo, and TIAA-CREF students," and the school has a particularly strong finance faculty. "The work piles up and is demanding," one student says, "however, I'm getting used to the pace, and I feel that the extra work I put in is appreciated and noticed." UNC Charlotte "is known for its diverse background and for its high expectation of students, which helps set up a two-way benchmark establishing goals for both the business school and the students."

Students are very happy with the "very hands on" and "extremely flexible" administration. There is a "strong commitment from administrators to help students succeed at scholastic and career goals," and "administrators will bend over backwards to help you in any way they can," such as "constantly making you aware of internships and available jobs." The administration is particularly quick at "answering questions or fixing problems." "I have not had an issue yet that they haven't fixed quickly," one student says. "Overall they are friendly, responsive, and knowledgeable." "The business school staff is very helpful and always available." Students do feel the administration should do more for students outside of normal weekday work hours. There are "not many 'after-work-hours' networking opportunities" and not enough "night/weekend class offerings for graduate studies."

Students are also proud of their professors, who "really care about their students" and whose "doors are always open." "My professors for the most part seem engaged, very intelligent, and reasonably demanding. The professors don't want cookie-cutter answers and encourage depth in responses." "A majority of the professors are top-notch," and the ones who aren't are "subject matter experts at worst." Although most professors "are really great," others "miss the mark and just teach the syllabus." "Like any academic institution, it's bureaucratic, but not so much." One student explains the school "is accessible, and you can always be pointed in the right direction."

Career and Placement

The administration at the Belk College of Business is the school's "primary strength." They put in extra work to help students network and intern to improve future job prospects. "They helped me to create an exchange program with a top MBA program in the UK, even though no previous relationship existed," says one student. "UNC Charlotte offers great mentoring and career placement," and its location in the financial hub of Charlotte is very helpful for students. The school has "close ties to the Charlotte business community" and a "reputation for placement." The school claims a mean base salary of $83,000 for new graduates. Some prominent alumni include Susan DeVore, president and CEO of Premier; John P. Derham Cato, Chairman of the Board, president, and CEO of The Cato Corporation; and Kelley Earnhardt, General Manager of JR Motorsports.

ADMISSIONS CONTACT: JEREMIAH NELSON, DIRECTOR OF GRADUATE STUDENT SERVICES
ADDRESS: 9201 UNIVERSITY CITY BOULEVARD, CHARLOTTE, NC 28223-0001
PHONE: 704-687-7566 • FAX: 704-687-2809
E-MAIL: MBA@UNCC.EDU • WEBSITE: WWW.MBA.UNCC.EDU

Student Life and Environment

Students are very impressed with the diversity at UNC Charlotte. "We have students from all races, all different types of work backgrounds, etc. It is very beneficial for class discussions because of all the different types of opinions that are voiced." There is everyone "from students straight out of undergrad school to workers who have been in the field 15 years, but everyone is friendly." "Students are heavily engaged in academics and current events." Still, "most are in their early 30s with careers and are married," and some students wish the school recruited younger students. Others enjoy the "experienced workers who see a benefit in taking time from their personal lives to invest in this program" and provide a "great mix of professionals from different industries."

Students do feel that the "social aspect of the school" is lacking. "I feel that there really isn't a strong connection with graduate students and campus life. There aren't many graduate-level activities and clubs, which is quite the opposite environment from what I am used to," explains one student. A stronger social aspect could also improve the "brand" and make it "even stronger in the surrounding areas." There could also be more "family involvement in the MBA program, such as weekend activities. This will allow spouses and children to feel good about their loved ones being away from home twice a week for two years." That said, "emphasis on student life has been increasing with the construction of the new Student Union and the fact that a new football program is coming to the school." "We know it's a business school," one student laments, "but a little less formality to actually make it fun and worthwhile would be great!"

Admissions

Students applying to the Belk College of Business are evaluated based on their undergraduate record, GMAT scores, resume, personal essays, and letters of recommendation. The average GMAT score for entering students is currently 588. Work experience is strongly recommended but not required. For fall 2012, the program began accepting the GRE with a minimum score of 151 on the quantitative and verbal sections.

FINANCIAL FACTS

Annual tuition (in-state/ out-of-state)	$11,349/$23,636

ADMISSIONS

Admissions Selectivity Rating	77
# of applications received	189
% applicants accepted	69
% acceptees attending	69
Average GMAT	585
Range of GMAT	540–620
Average GPA	3.39
TOEFL required of international students	Yes
Minimum TOEFL (paper/computer)	557/220
Application fee	$65
International application fee	$75
Early application deadline	1/15
Early notification date	3/15
Application Deadline/Notification	
Round 1:	1/15 / 3/15
Round 2:	3/1 / 5/1
Deferment available	Yes
Maximum length of deferment	1 year
Transfer students accepted	Yes

Transfer application policy: All students have to complete the graduate application materials and submit official test scores. With permission, it may be possible to transfer graduate level work from an AACSB-accredited university. This will be considered when the application materials are officially reviewed. At least 30 hours of graduate level coursework must be completed in residence at UNC Charlotte.

Non-fall admissions	Yes
Need-blind admissions	Yes

EMPLOYMENT PROFILE	
Career Rating	76
Average base starting salary	$83,000

THE UNIVERSITY OF NORTH CAROLINA AT GREENSBORO
JOSEPH M. BRYAN SCHOOL OF BUSINESS AND ECONOMICS

GENERAL INFORMATION

Type of school	Public
Affiliation	No Affiliation
Academic calendar	Semester

SURVEY SAYS...
Friendly students
Solid preparation in:
General management, Operations,
Quantitative skills, Computer skills,
Doing business in a global economy

STUDENTS

Enrollment of parent institution	18,172
Enrollment of MBA Program	172
% male/female	58/42
% out-of-state	37
% part-time	63
% underrepresented minority	26
% international	27
Average age at entry	25
Average years work experience at entry	2

ACADEMICS

Academic Experience Rating	**79**
Profs interesting rating	82
Profs accesible rating	85
Student/faculty ratio	6:1
% female faculty	34
% underrepresented minority faculty	26
% part-time faculty	5

Joint Degrees
MSN/MBA, 54 credits, 2-5 years;
MS Gerontology/MBA, 58 credits, 2-5 years

Prominent Alumni
Dan Carpenter, Vice President, Global Operations/Chief Technology Officer, Energizer Household Products; Jeff Kellan, Vice President, Global Distribution Operations, ToysRUs; Steve Strader, Senior Vice President, Retail Operations, AutoNation; Dean Priddy, Executive Vice President/CFO, RFMD; Greg Walker, Managing Director, JP Morgan Private Bank

Academics

The University of North Carolina at Greensboro Bryan School of Business and Economics offers its students a rigorous program filled with "great courses." The graduate program at this "prestigious" school is "challenging," but not necessarily overwhelming. Students agree that with dedication and the help of "a very supportive MBA Office," a degree here is very achievable. "The academic value is excellent!" exclaims a current student. "The degree can be attained in two-years, costs less than any comparable program in Central NC, and is very highly rated." High praise goes to the "fantastic student services and administration," which are "immensely effective in helping students [achieve] their goals." "The entire school administration shows a care for the student body and a strong desire for them to do well."

The faculty also receives glowing reports from students for being "well versed in their disciplines and very enthusiastic about teaching." They are also noted for being "very diverse" and "approachable and have the students' best interest in mind." One student agrees by saying, "I absolutely love the professors in the MBA program. They inspire me to want more out of myself. They aren't teaching us how to pass a test, they are teaching us how to survive and thrive in the world." Another student appreciates how "professors are effective at integrating recent business trends into the curriculum." The "classes are set up to ensure dialogue versus a monologue from the professor" which creates an "academically stimulating environment." The school as a whole does an excellent job helping students stay on track. Administrators "strive to facilitate each student mapping out a plan of study to match their particular career and life goals. Professors make themselves available throughout the entire program, not just during their class."

"Affordability" and a positive experience at UNCG's undergraduate school are both popular reasons for attending the graduate program here. One student sums this up saying, "I attended UNCG for my undergraduate studies and greatly appreciated the quality of my education, especially with respect to the price of tuition." Studying abroad is yet another draw to the school. "Our study abroad program is superb. We have a special course for MBA's in the spring to learn about business in a given country and then visit that country and make business contacts as part of the course."

Career and Placement

The school's location in Greensboro, North Carolina has "plenty of employers" and "provides for good job opportunities." Bryan's unique targeted recruiting service works to actively partner with local employers and in doing so promotes current students to employers with specific needs. There are several on-campus recruiting events and many of the MBA social events include alumni, who tremendously help in networking. "UNCG has a solid reputation in the oldest MBA program in the Triad. Many of the top companies in the area recruit from UNCG." Administration is very good about sending "email communication and announcements to students regarding activities, job fairs, and other announcements."

ADMISSIONS CONTACT: TUISHA FERNANDES, ASSOCIATE DIRECTOR
ADDRESS: PO BOX 26165, GREENSBORO, NC 27402-6165
PHONE: 336-334-5390 • FAX: 336-334-4209
E-MAIL: BRYANMBA@UNCG.EDU • WEBSITE: HTTP://BRYANMBA.UNCG.EDU

Student Life and Environment

A broad mix of students, both full-time and part-time, attend UNCG. One student put it this way: "The students in the Bryan MBA program come from a range of different backgrounds. My cohort alone represents seven different countries. This allows for different perspectives on international business and global issues. The students are friendly, but are focused on their studies and internships so there is limited social time."

The University of North Carolina at Greensboro has "great spirit" in a "nice little town" on a "safe campus." "The school is very much a community where professors, students, athletes, and non-students are frequently passing each other on campus." There are "nice buildings, classrooms, and facilities." "The gym is in great condition and the student union center has plenty of food options with space to sit and eat while studying." "There is plenty of off-campus housing." For those driving to campus, "Parking is easily accessible." Campus transportation is available and "runs rather late for those that commute or want to get off campus. There are plenty of restaurants nearby including a few on campus as well as downtown." "The city of Greensboro is wonderful and offers everything a graduate student could want."

Classmates "are all bright, motivated individuals" who are "very amiable and fun, great to work with in group assignments, and very dedicated to their education and work." Many "are working parents…who have chosen to reach for something more either within their chosen careers or in a new and exciting one." They "come from very diverse backgrounds, making in-class discussions very fruitful and enriching. Everyone is open to discussion and generally accepting of each other's differences in opinions." "Classes are all very discussion driven and students are very active in them and will debate respectfully. Everyone is willing to help each other." People here are very tolerant. "Race and sexual preference never are a problem at our school."

Admissions

Admission requirements include GMAT scores, which average 557; an essay; undergraduate GPA, which averages 3.32; three letters of recommendations, and a resume. Fellowships, scholarships, and graduate assistantships are available to help defray already low tuition costs. International students must also submit TOEFL or IELTS scores and an affidavit of financial support. Alternatively, the Bryan Prelude program enables students to take MBA courses before committing to a degree. To apply to Bryan Prelude, students must submit an application, undergraduate transcripts, a statement of purpose, and resume.

FINANCIAL FACTS

Annual tuition (in-state/ out-of-state)	$8,206/$21,655
Fees	$2,357
Cost of books	$1,300
Room & board (on/off-campus)	$9,174/$8,662
% of students receiving aid	58
% of first-year students receiving aid	71
% of students receiving grants	40
Average award package	$12,138
Average grant	$3,201
Average loan	$8,937

ADMISSIONS

Admissions Selectivity Rating	73
# of applications received	110
% applicants accepted	75
% acceptees attending	61
Average GMAT	557
Range of GMAT	502–607
Average GPA	3.32
TOEFL required of international students	Yes
Minimum TOEFL (paper/computer)	550/213
Application fee	$60
International application fee	$60
Early application deadline	3/1
Regular application deadline	7/1
Deferment available	Yes
Maximum length of deferment	1 Year
Transfer students accepted	Yes

Transfer application policy: They must be in good standing at a fellow AACSB Accredited MBA Program and may transfer no more than 12 Semester credit hours of approved coursework with grades of B or better.

Non-fall admissions	Yes
Need-blind admissions	Yes

EMPLOYMENT PROFILE

Career Rating	70	Grads Employed by Function	% Avg. Salary
Percent employed at graduation	53	Marketing	(11%) $28,000
Percent employed 3 months after graduation	84	Operations	(42%) $47,000
		Consulting	(5%) $65,000
Average base starting salary	$52,000	Finance	(11%) $69,000
Primary Source of Full-time Job Acceptances		Other	(5%) $55,000
School-facilitated activities	8(50%)		
Graduate-facilitated activities	8(50%)		

THE UNIVERSITY OF NORTH CAROLINA AT WILMINGTON
CAMERON SCHOOL OF BUSINESS

GENERAL INFORMATION

Type of school	Public
Affiliation	No Affiliation
Academic calendar	Semester

SURVEY SAYS...

Students love Wilmington, NC,
Cutting-edge classes
Solid preparation in:
Presentation skills

STUDENTS

Enrollment of MBA Program	122
% male/female	83/17
% out-of-state	27
% part-time	50
% underrepresented minority	3
% international	18
Average age at entry	31
Average years work experience at entry	7.0

ACADEMICS

Academic Experience Rating	**84**
Profs interesting rating	82
Profs accesible rating	85
Student/faculty ratio	15:1
% female faculty	16

Academics

Uniting a top-notch business faculty with an intimate campus atmosphere, getting an MBA at the University of North Carolina at Wilmington's Cameron School of Business is a "warm, rewarding experience." This small public school offers several graduate business programs, including the popular Professional MBA, as well as a full-time International MBA (conferred in conjunction with partner universities overseas.) For working professionals in the PMBA program, convenience is a key factor in their decision to attend UNCW. "The campus is conveniently located in the center of Wilmington" and all classes are held in the evenings or on the weekends. The school offers a "lock-step program where all students take the same classes together," and the curriculum spans two years(21 months if you were a business undergrad), with four courses per semester. While the course load is demanding (especially for those holding down a full-time job), "classes are...manageable" and professors are friendly, accessible, and "reasonable regarding student expectations."

With a competent administrative team at the helm, "The MBA program is well-designed and run," and many students say the "caliber of professors and course material has exceeded my expectations." Group work is encouraged, and through assignments, "You to learn to work with all different types of people—just like the real work force." Among many of the school's special programs, the Learning Alliance is a 15-month course through which "students are put into groups and assigned a local company" where they study and consult on business procedures. A student elaborates on the Learning Alliance: "Rather than just writing a marketing report based on a case study, an actual marketing project will be performed where students work with local businesses on their particular marketing needs." On the flipside, students would like the curriculum to include a broader international perspective, while others would like to see more specialized course offerings, as well as "more freedom to choose classes within the program."

UNCW students are impressed with the teaching staff, describing them as "highly educated with a lot of "hands-on" work experience." Drawing from a wide range of industries, Wilmington professors range "from economics teachers who have worked at the Fed for 30 years, to management teachers who have worked for large corporations in high positions globally, to significantly published authors and highly sought-after consultants." In the classroom, they are on top of their game; "Professors of UNCW exhibit strong, experienced leadership in preparing, teaching, and guiding students through the business program." Likewise, "The administration is very service-oriented and goes out of [its] way to make student administrative obstacles easy [to overcome]." "Affordability" is the cherry on top of the cake—here, in-state tuition runs less than 50 percent the price at comparable private schools.

ADMISSIONS CONTACT: KAREN BARNHILL, GRADUATE PROGRAMS ADMINISTRATOR
ADDRESS: 601 SOUTH COLLEGE ROAD, WILMINGTON, NC 28403-5680
PHONE: 910-962-3903 • FAX: 910-962-2184
E-MAIL: BARNHILLK@UNCW.EDU • WEBSITE: WWW.CSB.UNCW.EDU/GRADPROGRAMS

Career and Placement

The UNCW Career Center serves both the undergraduate and graduate student community, assisting with internships, as well as full-time and part-time job placements. The Career Center organizes annual career fairs and networking events on campus, and offers an online job board and resume posting service for UNCW students. However, the business school does not have graduate-specific resources for career planning, and students say, "There is very little discussion about various fields and ways in which to apply an MBA degree." At the same time, the school does provide opportunities for networking through speaker panels, alumni events, and special events for local executives.

For students who would like to make a career change after completing their MBA, career services at UNCW can be a disappointment. A current student admits, "UNCW needs to do a better job with attracting recruiters to hire their MBA students. With top-level faculty and a top-level business education, our MBA students should be given networking and interviewing opportunities with various businesses in different fields on a regular basis." On the other hand, students point out that, "So many people's employers are paying for their MBA education, they feel it is a violation of ethics to strongly encourage us to find new jobs."

Student Life and Environment

While they come from diverse professional and educational backgrounds ("from engineers to business students"), MBA candidates at UNCW are generally "Hard-working, funny, and willing to support and help others." Competitiveness is kept to a minimum, and within cohorts, "a tight-knit bond forms between classmates." On campus, business students have access to "quiet study lounges in each building" and a "well-equipped library;" however, the classroom experience could improve with the introduction of "more technology tools." In fact, some students think, "CSB could really use a new building" altogether.

In the professional MBA program, "Most all of the students are working professionals, so they are not involved in the day-to-day campus activities." However, graduate students do have access to the facilities and resources on the greater campus, and "about 10 percent use the gym facilities and library during non-class hours." Nonetheless, the atmosphere is friendly and social, boasting "that homey feeling of a small town where everyone knows and cares about everyone else." While they may not go out every weekend, "Most of the students belong to the MBA Association, and participate in social events with each other outside of class." Even in the classroom, the feeling is laid-back; "Because of the warm climate and laid back atmosphere, I believe some students have never worn footwear besides flip flops ever."

Admissions

At UNCW, the MBA Program Committee—a group of 5 faculty members—reviews applications and makes all admissions decisions. In recent years, the average incoming student had an undergraduate GPA of 3.05 and a GMAT score of about 555 (in most cases, the school only considers applicants with a GMAT or GRE equivalent of 500 or better.) Most years, the school accepts about 75 percent of applicants annually.

FINANCIAL FACTS

Annual tuition (in-state/ out-of-state)	$5,622/$11,244
Fees	$11,928
Cost of books	$1,000
Room & board	$13,690
% of students receiving aid	80
% of first-year students receiving aid	80
% of students receiving grants	40
Average award package	$20,000
Average grant	$2,000
Average loan	$20,000

ADMISSIONS

Admissions Selectivity Rating	**79**
# of applications received	92
% applicants accepted	77
% acceptees attending	87
Average GMAT	531
Range of GMAT	475–570
Average GPA	3.26
TOEFL required of international students	Yes
Minimum TOEFL (paper/computer)	550/217
Application fee	$60
International application fee	$60
Early application deadline	11/1
Regular application deadline	5/15
Deferment available	Yes
Maximum length of deferment	1 year
Transfer students accepted	No
Non-fall admissions	No

THE UNIVERSITY OF NORTH DAKOTA
COLLEGE OF BUSINESS AND PUBLIC ADMINISTRATION

GENERAL INFORMATION
Type of school   Public
Affiliation   No Affiliation

SURVEY SAYS...
Happy students
Solid preparation in:
General management, Computer
skills

STUDENTS
Enrollment of parent
  institution   15,250
Enrollment of MBA Program   116
% male/female   69/31
% out-of-state   28
% part-time   66
% underrepresented minority   23
% international   18
Average age at entry   28

ACADEMICS
Academic Experience Rating   76
Profs interesting rating   74
Profs accesible rating   84
Student/faculty ratio   3:1
% female faculty   26
% underrepresented minority
  faculty   21
% part-time faculty   0

Joint Degrees
JD/MBA, 81 JD credit hours and 27
MBA credit hours, 4 to 7 years.

Prominent Alumni
Neil Arnold, Executive Vice
President/CFO/Treasurer; Dave
Goodin, President and CEO; Randy
Newman, President/CEO/Chairman;
Major Gerald F. Perryman Jr., Vice
President/ISR/SBA; Steve Shirley,
President

Academics

The AACSB-accredited MBA program at the University of North Dakota is "focused on offering students the resources they need for a flourishing future." Classes are offered in the afternoon, evening, and long distance and "can easily be fit into your busy schedule." Many students earn their degrees remotely, through a "convenient online MBA program." The curriculum at UND focuses on business technology with an opportunity to concentrate in international business. Due to the unique location of the school in Grand Forks, the middle of a large agricultural zone, students are exposed to both rural and big-city business. They are pleased with the school's state-of-the-art facilities, including modern computer labs and a marketing research center.

Professors are "dedicated and caring." They "take interest in students and truly care about them." Students say they are helpful and knowledgeable, and the small classroom size allows for real relationships to develop. They are respectable of students' lives outside the classroom and help them balance school and life. Professors also "do a very good job connecting the real world to the classroom." Students believe this is due to their work involvement outside of school. Most professors "have great experiences prior to their professorships and do an excellent job of sharing them." "Professors are always accessible and have an open-door policy." Students say they are "great mentors and will be lifelong connections." "So far every one of them has been helpful and engaging."

"The administration is professional and very well organized. Overall, my academic experience at the University of North Dakota has been superior to any other university I have attended." Students also like "the online tutoring center and the outstanding tech support." Most students agree things run smoothly. Although one student suggests UND could improve "by offering more sections of classes taught during day hours, rather than focusing on night classes."

Career and Placement

"The greatest strength of the University is its commitment to its students. There is no doubt in my mind that UND does everything in its power to help its students succeed." Career services at UND assist both undergraduate and graduate students with internship and job placement. The office offers career counseling and hosts an annual career fair each fall. In the spring, it coordinates on-campus interview sessions. Some students wish there were a separate fair specifically for the College of Business and Public Administration. The three most popular career fields after graduation are manufacturing, the military, and financial services. "Life in Grand Forks is not as diversified as that in big cities. However, we have good social events and networks with the companies around the Midwest." The placement percentage for the business school (graduate and undergraduate) is 97.2 percent. UND alumni have high positions at some of the following companies: Bank of America, Coca-Cola, General Motors Defense, and Nodak Electric Cooperative.

ADMISSIONS CONTACT: MICHELLE GARSKE, ASSISTANT DIRECTOR OF GRADUATE PROGRAMS
ADDRESS: 293 CENTENNIAL DRIVE, STOP 8098, GRAND FORKS, ND 58202
PHONE: 701-777-2397 • FAX: 701-777-2019
E-MAIL: MBA@BUSINESS.UND.EDU • WEBSITE: BUSINESS.UND.EDU/MBA

Student Life and Environment

"Everyone I have met through the program has been very nice and good to work with," one student says. Students describe fellow students as "charismatic, dedicated, and intelligent," as well as "helpful" and "eager to learn." They enjoy working together and say they can learn a lot from each other. Most students seem to be commuters or involved in Internet courses; however, those who do live on campus have the option of living in the school's apartments and dormitories. Commuters remark on the location's convenience, but admit they do not really engage in life on campus. There is an MBA Student Association that organizes weekly discussions and other social activities for those who wish to participate. Also, "many activities and student organizations cross the line between undergraduate and graduate, so there is never a problem networking with students from a variety of disciplines." If students seek further recreation, the North Dakota Museum of Art is located right on the UND campus. Also, the school has a hockey team, which students "take pride in." They also mention that the "gym facility is outstanding."

Grand Forks is a city with a population of roughly 53,000 people. It sits on the western banks of the Red River of the North, just 75 miles south of Canada. An international student says North Dakota is "a safe and easygoing place where foreign students can easily concentrate on their studies and become familiar with American culture."

Admissions

The admissions committee requests the following from its applicants: official GMAT scores, undergraduate GPA, personal essay, and letters of recommendation. The most important factors are GPA and GMAT score. The graduate business program desires candidates with GPAs higher than 3.0 and GMAT scores more than 500. That being said, students who show promise may be admitted on a provisional basis if one score is high enough to balance out the other. GRE scores may be submitted in lieu of a GMAT score. The average GRE score is 1233. Admissions at UND College of Business are rolling.

FINANCIAL FACTS

Annual tuition (in-state/ out-of-state)	$6,388/$17,055
Fees	$1,616
Cost of books	$1,000
Room & board	$8,520
% of students receiving aid	50
% of first-year students receiving aid	46
% of students receiving grants	66
Average award package	$8,322
Average grant	$4,460
Average loan	$10,204

ADMISSIONS

Admissions Selectivity Rating	77
# of applications received	47
% applicants accepted	70
% acceptees attending	73
Average GMAT	553
Range of GMAT	450–710
Average GPA	3.35
TOEFL required of international students	Yes
Minimum TOEFL (paper/computer)	550/213
Application fee	$35
International application fee	$35
Early application deadline	3/15
Regular application deadline	7/15
Deferment available	Yes
Maximum length of deferment	Up to one Semester
Transfer students accepted	Yes
Transfer application policy: Up to nine credits of approved coursework can be transferred.	
Non-fall admissions	Yes
Need-blind admissions	Yes

UNIVERSITY OF NORTH FLORIDA
COGGIN COLLEGE OF BUSINESS

GENERAL INFORMATION
Type of school   Public
Affiliation   No Affiliation

SURVEY SAYS...
Good peer network, Cutting-edge
classes
Solid preparation in:
Computer skills

STUDENTS
Enrollment of parent
  institution   16,356
Enrollment of MBA Program   388
% male/female   57/43
% out-of-state   4
% part-time   71
% underrepresented minority   17
% international   27
Average age at entry   28
Average years work experience
  at entry   0.0

ACADEMICS
Academic Experience Rating   **83**
Profs interesting rating   82
Profs accesible rating   84
Student/faculty ratio   9:1
% female faculty   38
% underrepresented minority
  faculty   33

Joint Degrees
GlobalMBA - 63 hours

Prominent Alumni
John McCalpin, Senior Executive,
Accenture; Mark Vitner, Chief
Economist, Wachovia; Elaine
Johnson, Principal, Navigy; David
Hayes, Founder & CEO, Tempus
Software; Donna Harper, Founder &
CEO, SystemLogics Co., LLC

Academics

The Coggin College of Business at the University of North Florida has quite a bit to offer young business students and working professionals, many of whom describe UNF as "the best school in Jacksonville." "Location," "reputation," and an "amazing logistics program" are just some of the reasons many students offer for this. "I went here as an undergrad," one student tell us, "and had the best experience with the teachers and students. It was an easy decision to continue my education at UNF." While UNF is a relatively large university, many current MBA students laud the "small classes" at Coggin, particularly the "online opportunities" and "evening classes" for those students with full-time jobs. We are told time and again that many of Coggin's students are "motivated, hard-working professionals looking to advance their skills and knowledge."

Inside the classroom, as one student puts it, "professors are eager to facilitate learning." Another student majoring in information technology in higher education says, "I appreciated the emphasis on group and project work, which resulted in greater camaraderie and cohesion with my fellow classmates." However, in a considerate counterpoint, this student said some professors tend to "gloss over critical issues that I would think would be foundational in the curriculum of any business school today: ethics, social responsibility, and sustainability." While courses with a sustainability and green jobs focus are not currently offered at UNF, other efforts are made to broaden the school's reach in the business community, including hosting Women in Business networking events and various support groups for women, minorities, and international students.

Coggin enrolls about 380 students in its MBA program, and roughly 80 percent of the student body works full time while attending school, which explains UNF's abundance of evening, weekend, and hybrid course offerings. However, for those with more flexible schedules, students may take advantage of UNF's study abroad program, with partner universities in France, Germany, Poland, China and India. The traditional MBA program at UNF offers degrees and concentrations in accounting, construction management, e-business, economics, finance, international business, logistics, management applications, and sports management. In addition to the MBA program, UNF offers a unique GlobalMBA, a 63-hour program in which students earn a UNF MBA as well as a joint master's degree from the University of Warsaw and Cologne University of Applied Sciences. GlobalMBA participants join a cohort of about 40 students who spend a residency at Cologne University of Applied Sciences (Germany), University of Warsaw (Poland), Dongbei University of Finance & Economics (China) and UNF.

Career and Placement

Coggin enrolls about 380 students in its MBA program, and roughly 80 percent of the student body works full time while attending school, which explains UNF's abundance of evening, weekend, and hybrid course offerings. However, for those with more flexible schedules, students may take advantage of UNF's study abroad program, with partner universities in France, Germany, Poland, China and India. The traditional MBA program at UNF offers degrees and concentrations in accounting, construction management, e-business, economics, finance, international business, logistics, management applications, and sports management. In addition to the MBA program, UNF offers a unique GlobalMBA, a 63-hour program in which students earn a UNF MBA as well as a joint master's degree from the University of Warsaw and Cologne University of Applied Sciences. GlobalMBA participants join a cohort of about 40 students who spend a residency at Cologne University of Applied Sciences (Germany), University of Warsaw (Poland), Dongbei University of Finance & Economics (China) and UNF.

ADMISSIONS CONTACT: LILITH RICHARDSON, THE GRADUATE SCHOOL COORDINATOR
ADDRESS: 1 UNF DRIVE, JACKSONVILLE, FL 32224-7699
PHONE: 904-620-1360 • FAX: 904-620-1362
E-MAIL: L.RICHARDSON@UNF.EDU • WEBSITE: WWW.UNF.EDU/COGGIN

Student Life and Environment

Located in Jacksonville, a "great mid-sized city" that's "near the beach" and "surrounded by islands," UNF's "rapidly growing" 1,300-acre campus has been "designed for future expansion," which can only mean good things for this young university.

The Coggin Business School is mostly a school for "working adults" who "cannot afford to stop working for two years," and in many cases are "entrenched because they own homes." With this type of student body, one might not expect an abundance of social activities on campus, but they'd be wrong. "There are many clubs and activities on campus," one student informs us. "They have live concerts and movies for free . . . throughout the year. The new student union is very comfortable," and students can now enjoy wireless access from anywhere on campus. However, for such a young university as UNF, there is always room for improvement. One student explains that he "would like to see more green initiatives" on campus, like "green rooftops" and "water saving urinals" that can save up to "40,000 gallons of water each year."

Admissions

Applicants to the Coggin College of Business must submit the following materials for consideration: GMAT or GRE scores. For GMAT, score greater than 500, for GRE (after 7/1/11) is minimum 145 verbal and 150 quantitative and an official undergraduate transcript (undergrad GPA of 3.0 or higher). Letters of reference and personal statement should not be submitted because these will not be taken into account. International students are required to submit TOEFL scores, with 550 minimums of 550 paper, 213 computer and 80 internet. A limited number of small scholarships are offered on a first-come, first-served basis to students from Latin American countries, in addition to which these students receive a waiver on out-of-state tuition fees.

FINANCIAL FACTS

Annual tuition (in-state/ out-of-state)	$11,593/$24,983
Cost of books	$1,200
Room & board (on/off-campus)	$8,190/$8,842
% of students receiving aid	52
% of first-year students receiving aid	39
% of students receiving grants	17
Average award package	$14,263
Average grant	$3,926
Average loan	$15,721
Average student loan debt	$22,724

ADMISSIONS

Admissions Selectivity Rating	84
# of applications received	220
% applicants accepted	47
% acceptees attending	63
Average GMAT	561
Range of GMAT	520–580
Average GPA	3.21
TOEFL required of international students	Yes
Minimum TOEFL (paper/computer)	550/213
Application fee	$30
International application fee	$30
Regular application deadline	8/1
Deferment available	Yes
Maximum length of deferment	1 Semester
Transfer students accepted	Yes
Transfer application policy: On a case by case basis	
Non-fall admissions	Yes
Need-blind admissions	Yes

EMPLOYMENT PROFILE

		Grads Employed by Function	% Avg. Salary
Career Rating	66		
Percent employed at graduation	75	Operations	(25%) $39,000
Percent employed 3 months after graduation	25	Management	(13%) $40,000
		Finance	(38%) $52,667
Average base starting salary	$44,667	Other	(25%) $33,250
Primary Source of Full-time Job Acceptances		**Top 5 Employers Hiring Grads**	
School-facilitated activities	2(25%)	Deutsche Bank (10), CSX Transportation (6), KPMG (3), Deloitte (5), Ernst & Young (3)	

UNIVERSITY OF NORTHERN IOWA
COLLEGE OF BUSINESS ADMINISTRATION

Academics

The "AACSB accredited" University of Northern Iowa (UNI) College of Business Administration offers MBA students a "practical business curriculum that can be directly applied to the business world." The school's "facilities, staff, and real world projects" are appealing. Students are also "attracted by the course content and program length," which gives students the ability to "earn the MBA degree in 13 months." With its "great business school reputation," UNI offers students a "quality education at a minor cost for an MBA." This "cost-effective, flexible, [and] fast" MBA program is more compatible with the active lifestyles of most graduate students today.

The MBA program consists of "small classes" in a "focused yet fun learning atmosphere." Coursework is "intensive," but "fantastic professors" "are dedicated to students," and provide "a very positive academic experience." The faculty does a good job of "mixing strategies for big business with small business. Showing how the same strategy or methodology can apply to both but how differently it applies." They "want to integrate what we already have in business knowledge with what we are currently learning. It is a highly interactive atmosphere with professors who want you to [learn]."

Overall, the school receives strong marks in communication and organization to provide a unified MBA program. One student says, "I think they have a strong administrative and instruction staff with a common vision of where the program should go and the results they expect. I see common business concepts stressed which tie the individual courses together into a focused package."

"Administrative staff [is] wonderful here; they go beyond limits to help you in any kind of issues." There was advice offered to the registrar though, which "needs improvement on adjusting to the modules that the MBA operates on as opposed to the semester system that the rest of the school does."

Also appealing to students who want a more global experience are the short-term and semester-long study abroad programs available at UNI. A Hong Kong MBA can be obtained through the school's long-distance learning program. The classes take place in Hong Kong with "all classes taught by UNI professors" on-site. It is a "very compact program" and "intensive" option due to the "limited period of time professors can stay in Hong Kong (usually 3 weeks)"; however, "students can complete the program in one and half year[s], which is good."

Career and Placement

Locally, UNI is well known and their students are well received as potential employees. "Top employers of UNI MBA graduates include Viking Pump and John Deere." "Allen Hospital, part of the Iowa Health System, is also a top area employer." The Career Services Center at UNI's College of Business Administration offers student workshops, resume reviews, cover letter advice, and mock interviews to help hone their skills. Internet resources are also provided to assist in the job search. Recruiters visit the campus throughout the year, and the school also hosts the Fall Career Fair Day and the Spring Job and Internship Fair for job seekers. Top employers of UNI graduates include: Klaussner, Loparex, Progressive, Target Distribution, US Bank, and Venture Computer Systems. "Internship awareness and mentoring" was noted as areas where improvement is needed.

ADMISSIONS CONTACT: NANCY L. HOFFMAN, MBA PROGRAM ASSISTANT
ADDRESS: COLLEGE OF BUSINESS ADMINISTRATION, CURRIS BUSINESS BUILDING 325, CEDAR FALLS,
IA 50614-0123 • PHONE: 319-273-6243 • FAX: 319-273-6230 • E-MAIL: MBA@UNI.EDU
WEBSITE: WWW.CBA.UNI.EDU/DBWEB/PAGES/PROGRAMS/GRADUATE-BUS-ADMIN.CFM

Student Life and Environment

Students enjoy a "nice environment" at UNI's campus in Cedar Falls, Iowa. The town of Cedar Falls might be "kind of boring" by some student's standards; however, the lack of excitement helps keep distractions down to a minimum and encourages more "time to study." The school does provide "many clubs and student organizations" in which students can broaden their graduate school experience. Students say on-campus "housing is moderate [and] clean, but old." While taking breaks from their studies, students enjoy the opportunity "to support some athletic functions," and can also take part in attending seminars on campus. UNI is "absolutely fabulous at offering relevant seminars or workshops that students are invited to attend. They make for a well-rounded [education]."

The MBA program is made up of "a variety of mid-career professionals, small business owners, and international students, [who] bring diverse experiences to class discussions." Having a "very diverse range of viewpoints, age, nationalities, and backgrounds…enhances the learning experiences." Classmates are described as "highly-competent" "eager learners, competitive, yet very friendly." Some look forward to "driving in early to spend time with various teams, to work on project activity. Although the adult students already have an established life and home to go back to, I am seeing increasing [camaraderie] among students as teaming and bonding occurs." Not all students with families are able to adjust their class schedules to suit their needs. One student says, "The school does not support parents with small children. Daycare hours do not coincide with classroom hours."

Admissions

GMAT scores, a personal statement, undergraduate GPA, and previous work experience are all very important for enrollment consideration. Letters of recommendations and college transcripts are also required along with one's application to UNI's College of Business Administration. Communication skills are highly factored into the decision process, as well as the applicant's demonstrated leadership potential, intellectual capability, and academic success during undergraduate and graduate work. The average age of recent students is 32, the average undergraduate GPA is 3.3, and the average GMAT score is 611.

FINANCIAL FACTS

Annual tuition (in-state/ out-of-state)	$9,312/$18,582
Fees	$987
Cost of books	$2,000
Room & board	$7,600
% of students receiving aid	30
% of students receiving grants	18
Average loan	$14,054

ADMISSIONS

Admissions Selectivity Rating	**82**
# of applications received	64
% applicants accepted	52
% acceptees attending	52
Average GMAT	575
Range of GMAT	450–700
Average GPA	3.37
TOEFL required of international students	Yes
Minimum TOEFL (paper/computer)	600/250
Application fee	$50
International application fee	$50
Early application deadline	2/1
Regular application deadline	7/20
Deferment available	Yes
Maximum length of deferment	1 year
Transfer students accepted	Yes
Transfer application policy: Students may transfer up to 10 hours of AACSB-accredited, graduate credit	
Non-fall admissions	Yes
Need-blind admissions	Yes

University of Notre Dame
Mendoza College of Business

Academics

Students come to the University of Notre Dame to become part of the "Notre Dame family," and few leave disappointed; the MBA program at the Mendoza College of Business fosters a strong sense of community that, coupled with the campus-wide school spirit, quickly makes Notre Dame feel like home. Add "outstanding professor-student interaction" and "great potential for alumni networking" and you understand why student satisfaction levels are so high here.

The Mendoza MBA program "excels at providing an overall business understanding," students tell us. The school offers a two-year full-time program that "is perfect for non-business undergraduate majors to gain a well-rounded understanding of business fundamentals," as well as a one-year program for those with exceptionally strong business backgrounds. Students say, "Ethics is a hallmark of the school and it can be seen in every course," and "The school's reputation for producing ethical graduates is more important in recent years than ever before."

Mendoza implemented a modular curriculum a few years back, and "The 2007 class was the first to complete our entire course work under the current 'module' system. The module system will allow Notre Dame MBAs to be better prepared than were previous classes. Although "There was some negative press after the transition," "now that the transition is completed, Notre Dame will move quickly [back] up the rankings." The faculty here "is top-notch." Their research, publications, work experience, and generally great personalities inspire confidence in their ability to prepare [students] for the business world."

Career and Placement

"The majority of recruiting is Midwest-based" at Notre Dame, and while some complain about the dearth of New York finance-sector recruiters, most students feel that "the Career Office does a good job of locating companies from various regions." Mendoza MBAs recognize that "our small class size hinders our ability to get a large selection of companies from each region, but they are represented." However, "The situation is greatly improving, with some bulge-bracket and many middle-market banks already recruiting on campus. This will improve over time as the school moves toward its long-term mission of improving rank."

Of course, Notre Dame's storied alumni network helps with placement. Students tell us that "the Career Development Office recently made it easier for current MBA students to get in contact with alumni. Prior to this, it was a very prolonged process that involved Career Development responding to individual student's requests for alumni contact information in their respective field." These contacts can be invaluable. As one student reports, "The alumni of the school are always willing to go the extra mile for you. I have met with alumni from my hometown to get resume and career search advice." No wonder students brag that "becoming a member of the alumni network is worth more than the cost of tuition."

Companies recruiting Mendoza MBAs include: Avaya Systems, DaimlerChrysler, Deloitte Touche Tohmatsu, Ernst & Young, Ford Motor Company, GE, Hewlett-Packard, Honeywell, IBM, Intel, Johnson & Johnson, Kraft Foods, PricewaterhouseCoopers, SAP, Sandler O'Neill, Sprint, Textron Financial, The Gallup Organization, Western & Southern Life, and Whirlpool.

ADMISSIONS CONTACT: BRIAN LOHR, DIRECTOR OF ADMISSIONS
ADDRESS: 276 MENDOZA COLLEGE OF BUSINESS, NOTRE DAME, IN 46556-4656
PHONE: 574-631-8488 • FAX: 574-631-8800
E-MAIL: MBA.BUSINESS@ND.EDU • WEBSITE: BUSINESS.ND.EDU/MBA

Student Life and Environment

There's no doubt that Notre Dame is a very social campus, but the extent to which MBAs can partake in that social life depends on whether they're in their first or second year of the program. First year is "very difficult" with a massive workload. Many students "spend twice as much time on schoolwork" during their first year, and find it difficult to "juggle [classes] with career pursuits." Those who can carve out some leisure time agree that "Notre Dame has a culture that is contagious! It's not hard to keep yourself busy with a broad range of activities, whether it's class, a group meeting, intramural game, community-service event, or a football tailgate. There's never a dull moment." Football unites the campus and provides more than mere entertainment; it also "lures large corporations for networking events." Also, alumni return to campus for football games "for years after graduation and usually for life." Hometown South Bend is a small town, with only a "few good places to go out." The "students make up for it, though. We host a lot of social gatherings."

Mendoza MBAs benefit from "a strong esprit de corps" built on team projects and "an ethical foundation that is reinforced constantly so that it actually has an effect." Most are "married, with families and children." They represent "more diverse backgrounds than some of the 'big' schools back East, meaning we have folks from engineering, the public sector, and other nontraditional or non-business backgrounds. These are very sharp people who may have had the 'wrong' undergrad pedigree but are every bit as bright as those at any b-school anywhere."

Admissions

Applicants to Mendoza's two-year MBA program must provide the Admissions Department with all of the following: proof of an undergraduate degree from an accredited college or university; official transcript(s); GMAT scores; a current resume; three essays (topics provided by school); and two letters of recommendation. Transcripts and/or resume must demonstrate familiarity with basic quantitative processes and accounting methods. A background in statistics is strongly recommended. International students must also provide TOEFL scores and visa documentation. Applicants to the one-year program must present academic transcripts showing successful completion of six credit hours each of mathematics, accounting, and economics and three credit hours each of marketing and MIS. All applicants must have at least two years of meaningful work experience.

FINANCIAL FACTS

Annual tuition	$45,130
Fees	$3,150
Cost of books	$1,550
Room & board	$9,250
% of students receiving aid	87
% of first-year students receiving aid	88
% of students receiving grants	69
Average award package	$48,403
Average grant	$27,490
Average loan	$43.550
Average student loan debt	$57,969

ADMISSIONS

Admissions Selectivity Rating	92
# of applications received	835
% applicants accepted	35
% acceptees attending	41
Average GMAT	687
Range of GMAT	650–720
Average GPA	3.27
TOEFL required of international students	Yes
Minimum TOEFL (paper/computer)	600/250
Application fee	$175
International application fee	$175
Early application deadline	10/29
Early notification date	12/21
Regular application deadline	1/17
Regular application notification	3/1
Application Deadline/Notification	
Round 1:	10/29 / 12/21
Round 2:	1/7 / 3/1
Round 3:	2/25 / 4/12
Round 4:	4/1 / 5/17
Deferment available	Yes
Maximum length of deferment	1 year
Transfer students accepted	No
Non-fall admissions	Yes
Need-blind admissions	Yes

EMPLOYMENT PROFILE

Career Rating	97	**Grads Employed by Function% Avg. Salary**	
Percent employed at graduation	75	Marketing	(22%) $92,985
Percent employed 3 months after graduation	87	Operations	(4%) $92,800
		Consulting	(22%)$110,500
Average base starting salary	$98,623	Management	(12%) $105,313
Primary Source of Full-time Job Acceptances		Finance	(32%) $93,676
School-facilitated activities	98(65%)	HR	(1%)
Graduate-facilitated activities	35(23%)	Other	(7%) $92,571
Unknown	18(12%)	**Top 5 Employers Hiring Grads**	
		IBM (8), Deloitte (8), Ernst & Young (7), Bank of America (5), General Electric (4)	

University of Oklahoma
Michael F. Price College of Business

Academics

The Price College of Business at the University of Oklahoma is "fittingly identified with a legendary value investor," students tell us, justifying the claim by pointing out that the program "offers small class sizes and destination internship opportunities at a low cost with numerous financial aid opportunities." That sounds like value to us, too. A Price MBA "is very affordable for students in comparison to other graduate programs" and is an especially good value for those interested in careers in the energy and banking sectors. Students describe Price's concentrations in risk management and energy as "most sought after," with finance also drawing plenty of interest.

Price boasts "beautiful facilities," "professors who work their hardest for the students," and a "high diversity of concentration options" for a school of its size. Students may pursue the MBA either full-time (in a 16-month program) or part-time (in an evening program). Full-time students report that "a majority of our [first-year] courses take place in two-hour blocs between the hours of 9 A.M. and 1:30 P.M." while all classes after your first year are at night. "Full-time MBA students are essentially moved to part-time MBA students taking classes at night after your first three-quarters of a year. This is one huge disadvantage of such a small program."

Despite their dedication, Price professors earn mixed reviews. Some observe that the College of Business is located in "a research-based university," saying this explains why "many of the professors are not real effective teachers." One feels instruction would benefit from "a greater balance between real-world applications and textbook learning for some classes. Many of the professors seem to be fixated on tests as a method of learning and not enough on applications like cases, projects, etc." Students tell us that the problems are primarily isolated to the front end of the program. "[Intro] courses lack substance," they say, but fortunately, the teaching "gets much better as the program progresses." Students also approve of the "guest faculty and the seminars on current economic and financial challenges."

Career and Placement

At Price, the primary responsibility for career counseling and placement services falls to the MBA Student Support Center. The Center provides one-on-one mentoring, assistance with resume preparation and interviewing skills, and contacts with corporate recruiters. Students see the school's "ties to the energy industry" as a big asset and note that alumni connections in these industries are especially helpful. Finance is another strong suit. However, students warn that placement opportunities are minimal outside these areas. Some critics concede that "job placements were good here until the recession hit the economy." On the bright side, "there is a strong focus on finding internships for first-year students," although "the school expects students to do their fair share of the internship search as well."

Employers who hire Price MBAs include: ExxonMobil, Bank of Oklahoma, OGE, RiskMetrics, ConocoPhillips Company, Fujitsu, SBC, American Airlines, Devon Energy, Schlumberger, Shell, KPMG International, Halliburton, Raytheon, Mary Kay, BancFirst, Michelin, Ernst & Young, and Liquidnet.

ADMISSIONS CONTACT: GINA AMUNDSON, DIRECTOR OF GRADUATE PROGRAMS
ADDRESS: 1003 ASP AVENUE, PRICE HALL, SUITE 1040, NORMAN, OK 73019-4302
PHONE: 405-325-4107 • FAX: 405-325-7753
E-MAIL: OKLAHOMAMBA@OU.EDU • WEBSITE: PRICE.OU.EDU/MBA

Student Life and Environment

Price's "recently built" building "is one of the greatest strengths of the school," providing "exceptional classrooms equipped with all of the technological benefits to teach today's students." Grad students especially appreciate their dedicated lounge, where they have "lockers, a fridge, a microwave, coffee, tables for working on projects or homework, and couches for hanging out…or the occasional between-class nap."

Life on the OU campus offers "a good mix of study, extracurricular activities, and social events." MBAs have "a very active Graduate Business Association that sets up events ranging from networking, cultural diversity (the International Food Night is always popular), and community service (Relay for Life), to general social or special interest events (such as a Wine 101 night)." Norman "is a great college town," and "OU has so many great traditions that it's nearly impossible not to feel like you are a part of something bigger, something really special. Football season is always a hit, and game days are indescribably fun and special. Many MBA students choose to participate in tailgating and other various pre-game activities." The school "has a really rich fine-arts community as well, with a wonderful art museum right on campus and a performance center and music hall that boast numerous productions and performances throughout the year."

Admissions

Applicants to the Price MBA program must submit the following materials to the Office of Admissions and Records: an application for admission to the university; an official transcript from every undergraduate and graduate institution attended; and, for international applicants, a financial statement as well as an official TOEFL score report if English is not their first language. In addition, all applicants must also submit the following materials to the MBA Admissions Office: a completed supplemental application for graduate study in business; an official score report for the GMAT or GRE; a current resume; and a personal statement of career and educational goals. Two years of work experience is preferred but not required.

FINANCIAL FACTS

Annual tuition (in-state/ out-of-state)	$4,204/$15,667
Fees	$4,170
Cost of books	$1,200
Room & board	$11,170
Average grant	$0

ADMISSIONS

Admissions Selectivity Rating	79
# of applications received	117
% applicants accepted	73
% acceptees attending	71
Average GMAT	616
Range of GMAT	580–640
Average GPA	3.48
TOEFL required of international students	Yes
Minimum TOEFL (paper/computer)	600/250
Application fee	$40
International application fee	$90
Regular application deadline	6/1
Deferment available	Yes
Maximum length of deferment	1 year
Transfer students accepted	Yes
Transfer application policy: Students may transfer into our PT MBA program from other AACSB accredited institutions.	
Non-fall admissions	No
Need-blind admissions	Yes

EMPLOYMENT PROFILE

Career Rating	89	Grads Employed by Function	% Avg. Salary
Percent employed at graduation	64	Marketing	(3%) $0
Percent employed 3 months after graduation	80	Operations	(6%)
		Consulting	(29%) $57,417
Average base starting salary	$67,758	Management	(0%) $0
Primary Source of Full-time Job Acceptances		Finance	(31%) $56,812
School-facilitated activities	12(34%)	HR	(3%) $0
Graduate-facilitated activities	23(66%)	MIS	(3%) $0
		Other	(25%) $83,306

Top 5 Employers Hiring Grads
E&Y (3), AT&T (2), KPMG (1), Chesapeake Energy (1), Devon Energy (1)

UNIVERSITY OF OREGON
CHARLES H. LUNDQUIST COLLEGE OF BUSINESS

Academics

The University of Oregon's Charles H. Lundquist College of Business is a relatively small, green-oriented school offering an "excellent program in sustainable business practices," a particularly "strong entrepreneurship tract," and a top-ranked sports marketing and business program that, according to many students, is the "premier" program of its kind in the nation. As one very satisfied student puts it, "I would not have even looked at Oregon as an option if it weren't for its renowned sports business program." The Warsaw Sports Marketing program also offers its students the "opportunity to combine studies in corporate finance with the sports industry." One student working toward an MBA in sustainable business praises the school's "interdisciplinary nature" and its "ability to work directly with companies to consult on real world issues." However, based on the feedback we have received, the administration and faculty don't do a lot of hand holding when it comes to the students. While students "benefit from personal attention from the teaching staff in terms of advice on courses, career paths, and general resources," MBA candidates are expected to take full ownership of their studies and be proactive in their job search.

The role sustainability plays in Oregon's MBA program cannot be overstated. The College of Business's MBA in sustainable business was established in 2008, and its popularity has only grown since then. Many students come to Oregon specifically to earn their MBA at the school's relatively new Center for Sustainable Business Practices housed in the Lillis Business Complex, a LEED silver certified facility and one of the most environmentally friendly buildings of its kind in the country. "Business schools are a dime a dozen," says one sports business student, "I knew I wanted a school that offered a top-flight entrepreneurship focus, and the University of Oregon was tops on my list, but, beyond that, there is substantial value in being surrounded by students who are also staunchly interested in entrepreneurship."

In addition to Oregon's lauded programs in sports management, sustainability, and entrepreneurship, a number of dual-degree programs are also available, including a JD/MBA and MS/MBA with varying concentrations, as well as individual programs in finance, supply chain management, accounting, and media/entertainment. An Executive MBA program, which is located in Portland, is also offered. There are almost 200 students in the graduate business programs, with approximately 100 of them pursuing an MBA.

The age range of students is mid 20s to early 30s, and many in the program tend to arrive with at least a couple years of work experience, with backgrounds ranging from large corporations to small non-profit firms. Most students feel this helps provide students with a "well-rounded view of issues" that isn't disconnected from "real-world experiences." During students' second year of study, full-time MBA students also participate in a strategic planning project over the course of two terms. Through this experiential learning program, small student groups work as consultants to major Northwest businesses, including Adidas, Amazon, Hewlett Packard, and Intel.

Career and Placement

The Lundquist College of Business boasts four different centers, dedicated to sports marketing, security analysis, entrepreneurship, and business sustainability. Each of these centers aims to foster experiential learning to "provide [students with] opportunities to interface with the business community." Regarding the college's career services center, some students have told us that, while the "center is always willing to proofread a resume or cover letter," many would like to see "increased on-campus recruiting" from

ADMISSIONS CONTACT: HOLLY COBLE, ADMISSIONS COORDINATOR
ADDRESS: 1208 UNIVERSITY OF OREGON, 302 PETERSON HALL, EUGENE, OR 97403-1208
PHONE: 541-346-3306 • FAX: 541-346-0073
E-MAIL: INFO@OREGONMBA.COM • WEBSITE: WWW.OREGONMBA.COM

businesses, both local and national, and overall improvements in "career service offerings." The school does arrange for "periodic visits to regional business centers" in San Francisco, Portland, and Seattle, and there is regular shuttle service to career fairs in Portland for interested students. "MBA recruiting is essentially non-existent," one advertising and marketing student tells us. But with some 110 employers actively recruiting summer interns each year, a mean base salary of $61,140 for recently graduated MBAs, and nearly 70 percent of students having either received or accepted a job offer by graduation, U of O students appear to be pretty self-sufficient.

Student Life and Environment

"I work hard and play hard. I've never been so busy," says one first-year student. Situated in bucolic Eugene, Oregon, "a small and quirky town" just "two hours down the road from Portland," students assure us that while this is no "thriving city," "we all appreciate the surrounding natural beauty . . . and there are endless opportunities to stay fit and well." Despite Eugene's "laid-back culture," a microenterprise development student informs us, "When you're in the program you are BUSY, but it's a good kind of busy. You spend a lot of time working on group projects and participating in clubs." Many industry professionals and guest speakers are invited to speak at on-campus events "almost every night."

Eugene is also "an environmentally conscious town," which helps explain the draw and reputation of U of O's sustainability program. In short, few students have anything remotely negative to say about the area. The abundance of outdoor "recreational activities" and "local breweries" fills up much of the students' leisure time, although a good portion of MBA students have conveyed that many "don't have any downtime."

Admissions

All applicants to the Lundquist College of Business should first consider that all graduate business students are in full-time programs, and no part-time option is offered. Applicants are required to submit their GMAT scores (600 minimum), official undergrad transcript (minimum GPA of 3.0), essay/personal statement, at least two letters of reference, and a resume or summary of professional experience. Applicants with real-world business experience will be given particular attention. International applicants must submit TOEFL scores, with 600 minimum on the written test or 96 minimum on web-based. Interviews are a requirement for admission.

FINANCIAL FACTS

Annual tuition (in-state/out-of-state)	$20,888/$28,917
Fees	$1,300
Cost of books	$1,050
Room & board	$10,854
% of students receiving aid	86
% of first-year students receiving aid	83
% of students receiving grants	68
Average award package	$21,430
Average grant	$20,187
Average loan	$26,743
Average student loan debt	$38,222

ADMISSIONS

Admissions Selectivity Rating	80
# of applications received	119
% applicants accepted	56
% acceptees attending	58
Average GMAT	620
Range of GMAT	580–682
Average GPA	3.40
TOEFL required of international students	Yes
Minimum TOEFL (paper/computer)	600
Application fee	$50
International application fee	$50
Early application deadline	11/15
Early notification date	12/18
Regular application deadline	4/15
Regular application notification	5/18
Application Deadline/Notification	
Round 1:	11/15 / 12/18
Round 2:	2/15 / 3/15
Round 3:	3/15 / 4/15
Deferment available	Yes
Maximum length of deferment	1 year
Transfer students accepted	No
Non-fall admissions	Yes
Need-blind admissions	Yes

EMPLOYMENT PROFILE

Career Rating	77	**Grads Employed by Function% Avg. Salary**	
Percent employed at graduation	32	Marketing	(32%) $64,813
Percent employed 3 months after graduation	68	Operations	(4%) $45,000
		Consulting	(24%)$59,167
Average base starting salary	$61,140	Management	(12%) $50,667
Primary Source of Full-time Job Acceptances		Finance	(16%) $70,500
School-facilitated activities	13(36%)	Other	(12%) $58,667
Graduate-facilitated activities	18(50%)	**Top 5 Employers Hiring Grads**	
Unknown	5(14%)	Adidas (1), Cisco Systems (1), GMR Marketing (1), Pricewaterhouse Coopers (1), United Talent Agency (1)	

UNIVERSITY OF OTTAWA
TELFER SCHOOL OF MANAGEMENT

GENERAL INFORMATION

Type of school   Public

SURVEY SAYS...
Smart classrooms
Solid preparation in:
Teamwork

STUDENTS

Enrollment of parent institution	42,027
Enrollment of MBA Program	218
% male/female	56/44
% part-time	40
% international	19
Average age at entry	32
Average years work experience at entry	7.3

ACADEMICS

Academic Experience Rating	83
Profs interesting rating	80
Profs accesible rating	80
% female faculty	28
% underrepresented minority faculty	59

Joint Degrees

MBA/JD (MBA and Law) (40 months)

Prominent Alumni

Ian Telfer, Chairman of Goldcorp Inc.; Paul Desmarais, Chairman of the Executive Committee, Power Corp.; Robert Ashe, General Manager, Business Intelligence & Performance Management at IBM; Guy Laflamme, Senior Vice-President, Capital Experience, Communications and Marketing, National Capital Commission; Dominique DeCelles, Sr. Vice-president Active Cosmetics Division, L'Oreal Canada

Academics

Located in Ottawa, the capital of Canada, the Telfer School of Management offers "a great place for learning with such a dynamic environment." Students are drawn to the "triple accreditation" (AACSB, AMBA and EQUIS) and the fact that the school is "bilingual" meaning the "MBA [is] available in French." The program has a "strong focus on global environment," a "solid reputation relative to other schools in the area," and a "low cost of tuition." It's "location in the national capital region" offers many "connections with local industry and the federal government." Consequently, "a lot of government workers" attend the program. "Because of the triple accreditation the school has, we get a lot of international students," one student explains. "This allows us to work and interact with many diverse cultures that we would normally not be exposed to. In a global marketplace, this is invaluable and should serve me well."

The "dedicated professors" are "available and reliable" and a real "pillar of strength and wisdom." The majority of the faculty are "well versed in their areas" and "showcase some of the brightest in their respective fields." "There are some very knowledgeable professors at this school who go the extra mile to connect with students and," one happy student reports. The administration is also "available and courteous," making an overall "very well organized administrative support unit."

The MBA at University of Ottawa is an intensive "one-year program," which "means less time out of the workforce." Despite the short program, the program "still incorporates a large practical component (consulting project and international trip)." The school places students in teams "for the duration of the program" which lets students "combine our strengths to overcome our weaknesses." It is also worth noting that the University of Ottawa is "very good at supporting partners and acknowledging the toll of an MBA on families." One student sums up their experience succinctly: "I just have two words: 'NET AWESOME'!"

Career and Placement

Since the Telfer School of Management is "well connected to the local business community," many MBA students find work in Canada's capital. Seventeen percent of 2012 graduates found work in government. The average mean base salary for that class was a little over $77,500. Employers who most frequently hire Ottawa MBAs include Adobe Systems, Bank of Nova Scotia, Bank of Canada, Canada Mortgage and Housing Corporation (CMHC), Costco, Deloitte, L'Oréal, RBC Royal Bank, SwiftTrade Securities, TD Waterhouse Investment, and Xerox Canada.

ADMISSIONS CONTACT: DANIELLE CHARETTE, ACADEMIC SERVICE OFFICER
ADDRESS: 55 LAURIER AVENUE EAST, ROOM 4160, OTTAWA, ON K1N 6N5
PHONE: 613-562-5884 • FAX: 613-562-5164
E-MAIL: MBA@TELFER.UOTTAWA.CA • WEBSITE: WWW.TELFER.UOTTAWA.CA

FINANCIAL FACTS

Annual tuition (in-state/ out-of-state)	$20,954/$31,412
Fees	$1,829
Cost of books	$1,600
Room & board (on/off-campus)	$9,741/$8,215
Average grant	$5,984

ADMISSIONS

Admissions Selectivity Rating	84
# of applications received	253
% applicants accepted	51
% acceptees attending	69
Average GMAT	627
Range of GMAT	580–660
Average GPA	2.90
TOEFL required of international students	Yes
Minimum TOEFL (paper/computer)	600/250
Application fee	$100
International application fee	$100
Regular application deadline	4/1
Deferment available	No
Transfer students accepted	Yes
Transfer application policy: A maximum of 24 credits could be retained for graduate courses in management completed in a Canadian MBA program or AACSB accredited program.	
Non-fall admissions	No
Need-blind admissions	Yes

Student Life and Environment

Since the student body at University of Ottawa is "such a unique blend of local, national and international students that it is very hard to pinpoint what my fellow students are 'like'." However, most students are "friendly, outgoing, and helpful," and "the average age is late 20s, early thirties." Students get along well, perhaps thanks to "the program's approach to team work" which "facilities this positive environment."

As "Ottawa is in the heart of downtown Ottawa, Canada's capital city," there is plenty to do both on campus and off. "Day to day, there is freedom to do what you want," one student explains. "If you want to be very involved in the school, you can be. If you prefer to do your own thing, that's fine as well." As Canadians, "we celebrate winter (given the weather), and enjoy the summer." "Due primarily to its intensive, twelve-month nature," there may not be as much time for extracurricular activities as at other programs. As one student states, "the important thing to know going into this program, is that you are willing to give it your all for a full twelve months."

Admissions

The University of Ottawa requires GMAT scores, personal statement, undergraduate transcripts, two letters of recommendation, at least three years of work experience, and an interview. Last year's class had an average GPA of 2.9 and an average GMAT score of 627. As the program is bilingual, applicants can apply in either French or English but will need to establish proficiency in their desired language.

EMPLOYMENT PROFILE			
Career Rating	92	Grads Employed by Function% Avg. Salary	
Percent employed at graduation	54	Marketing	(11%)
Percent employed 3 months after graduation	83	Operations	(9%)
		Management	(24%)
Average base starting salary	$77,527	Finance	(11%)
Primary Source of Full-time Job Acceptances		HR	(7%)
		MIS	(7%)
		Other	(31%)

UNIVERSITY OF THE PACIFIC
EBERHARDT SCHOOL OF BUSINESS

GENERAL INFORMATION

Type of school	Private
Affiliation	Non-denominational, Methodist founded and affiliated
Academic calendar	Semester

SURVEY SAYS...

Friendly students, Good social scene, Smart classrooms
Solid preparation in:
Presentation skills, Entrepreneurial skills

STUDENTS

Enrollment of parent institution	6,652
Enrollment of MBA Program	41
% male/female	51/49
% part-time	0
% underrepresented minority	7
% international	29
Average age at entry	24
Average years work experience at entry	1.0

ACADEMICS

Academic Experience Rating	82
Profs interesting rating	77
Profs accesible rating	80
Student/faculty ratio	2:1
% female faculty	32
% underrepresented minority faculty	24
% part-time faculty	8

Joint Degrees

PharmD/MBA- 4 years; JD/MBA- 4 years; Peace Corps/MBA- 3 and 1/2 years

Prominent Alumni

A.G. Spanos, Real Estate Development; Pete Carroll, Coah, Seattle Seahawks; Dell Demps, General Manager, New Orleans Hornets, NBA; David Gerber, MGM/Columbia/20thCenturyFox - Film & TV Production; Dave Brubek, Jazz Composer/ Musician

Academics

Located in Stockton, California, University of the Pacific is a distinctive private college that boasts a "very high standing both academically and professionally throughout our local community and state." Ideal for early-career professionals, the school's full-time program allows students from a range of academic backgrounds "to obtain an MBA in a highly intensive and challenging program." Fast-paced and efficient, the first term is "an intensive phase 17-unit semester broken down into eight modules. This intensive phase allows students to learn the fundamentals necessary for a business degree and requires spending most of the students' time at school." During this time, students are placed "in a cohort . . . and share all required classes." Therefore, each entering class is incredibly tight-knit, creating a unique learning environment. A current student explains, "This cohort of students is a wide array of culturally- and educationally-diverse students coming from various countries and experience levels. These factors contribute to an intellectually challenging classroom experience [that] goes beyond traditional book- or case-based classes." In addition to traditional business students, the "MBA program offers joint programs with Pacific's PharmD and JD programs...having the interaction from the other schools is a great resource."

After the first term, Eberhardt School's MBA program follows a typical semester model, with a more "moderate workload." At that point, students can tailor their educational experiences by choosing electives in entrepreneurship, finance, healthcare management, sport management, or marketing. They also take advantage of "the unique opportunity to study abroad in another country," through the school's Global Business Competition, or specialize in international issues through the school's Master's International MBA Program in cooperation with the Peace Corps. Future finance mavens can also hone their skills through the school's $2.6 million Eberhardt Student Investment Fund. While University of the Pacific and the Eberhardt School boast many world-class opportunities, students are most impressed by the small and intimate feeling that pervades this intimate Northern California school. With a student-faculty ratio of 16 to 1, "The greatest strengths of this school are the small classroom sizes [and] the professors' willingness to help students and get to know them on a one-on-one basis." A current student agrees, "I have been pleased with the teacher's performance and one-on-one help outside of classrooms. Teachers really take the time to make sure students understand the material and frequently check to make sure everyone is on the same page." Another adds, "Students are always welcome to question or seek help from professors and the professors offer a more peer-to-peer interaction, rather than the typical student-teacher relationship, which further encourages a beneficial educational experience." In addition to their friendliness and accessibility, Pacific professors are strong class leaders. On the whole, students are "very impressed with the quality of the teaching," saying their professors are "professional and can apply the material to real-life situations."

Career and Placement

Career development is directly incorporated into the Eberhardt School's curriculum. Throughout the first term, students are required to take a weekly Career Development course to help them build a job search strategy and prepare for the professional world. Students are also required to complete a summer business internship, which offers the opportunity to build real-world skills and contacts. In addition, the Career Management Center hosts various on-campus recruiting events and interviews. Located a stone's throw away from the San Francisco Bay Area, the Silicon Valley and the state capital of Sacramento, "the network of contacts built from attending is excellent." The average student interviews with about seven different companies and receives two job offers by graduation. Recent employers of MBA graduates include Clorox, E & J Gallo, Blue Shield, FDIC, KPMG, Twitter, and William Sonoma.

Student Life and Environment

Pacific's enthusiastic students dole out praises for their diligent classmates, saying, "Fellow students are both driven and work as a team. Together, we hope to succeed and push past boundaries." Due to the intense cohort format, "each class that comes through is extremely close-knit and shares their experiences like a single unit." A current MBA candidate elaborates, "Students are very genuine and really look out for one another. Because we spend all week together, many students have found strong friendships and even business partners for future ventures." While the school draws a few students from further a field, "the MBA student population is predominantly local—though they may have originated from somewhere else."

Based in the mid-size city of Stockton, California, "The campus is like a world of its own within the community"—a place where students feel comfortable studying and relaxing. To burn off steam, MBA students can participate in "intramural sports like evening basketball and flag football that are played against other schools on campus." Thursdays are a popular night for gatherings, and "the MBAs also spend a lot of time together outside of campus at dinner and studying." Attracting a younger crowd, some say the school could "try to make more programs available for full-time working students and their families." One explains, "Being a father and husband, my time is very limited. There are several times that I would've liked to involve my wife and children in my school activities, but that seemed out of place."

Admissions

To be considered for admission to the Eberhardt School's MBA program, students must submit an acceptable GMAT score. Prospective students are evaluated based on their performance in prior coursework, recommendation letters, GMAT scores, and an admissions interview. Admissions decisions are made on a rolling basis, and a new cohort of students is admitted each fall.

FINANCIAL FACTS

Annual tuition (in-state/ out-of-state)	$37,800/$37,800
Fees	$520
Cost of books	$1,666
Room & board (on/off-campus)	$13,000/$15,000
% of students receiving aid	89
% of first-year students receiving aid	95
% of students receiving grants	66
Average award package	$31,691
Average grant	$21,229
Average loan	$19,658

ADMISSIONS

Admissions Selectivity Rating	79
# of applications received	110
% applicants accepted	56
% acceptees attending	31
Average GMAT	593
Range of GMAT	570–620
Average GPA	3.37
TOEFL required of international students	Yes
Minimum TOEFL (paper/computer)	550/213
Application fee	$0
International application fee	$0
Early application deadline	1/15
Regular application deadline	3/1
Application Deadline/Notification	
Round 1:	11/15 / 1/1
Round 2:	1/15 / 3/1
Round 3:	3/1 / 5/1
Deferment available	Yes
Maximum length of deferment	1 year
Transfer students accepted	Yes
Transfer application policy: Students may transfer up to two Advanced courses (not foundation level) from another AACSB accredited MBA Program. No more than 6 units of the 53 required units will be transferred. Transfers not accepted for Master of Accounting (MAcc Program)	
Non-fall admissions	No
Need-blind admissions	Yes

EMPLOYMENT PROFILE

		Grads Employed by Function% Avg. Salary	
Career Rating	86		
Percent employed at graduation	31	Marketing	(8%) $48,000
Percent employed 3 months after graduation	50	Operations	(8%)
		Consulting	(0%)
Average base starting salary	$66,675	Management	(31%) $63,750
Primary Source of Full-time Job Acceptances		Finance	(38%) $53,020
		Other	(15%) $116,000

Top 5 Employers Hiring Grads
Goldman Sachs (1), Deloitte (1), FDIC (1), E&J Gallo Winery (1), Blue Shield (1)

UNIVERSITY OF PENNSYLVANIA
WHARTON SCHOOL GRADUATE DIVISION

GENERAL INFORMATION

Type of school	Private
Affiliation	No Affiliation
Academic calendar	Semester

SURVEY SAYS...

Good social scene, Good peer network, Smart classrooms
Solid preparation in:
Finance, Accounting, Quantitative Skills

STUDENTS

Enrollment of parent institution	24,107
Enrollment of MBA Program	1,691
% part-time	0

ACADEMICS

Academic Experience Rating	98
Profs interesting rating	94
Profs accesible rating	84
% female faculty	20
% part-time faculty	24

Joint Degrees

MBA/JD (3 yr); MBA/MD; MBA/DMD; MBA/MSE; MBA/MArch; MBA/MA-Lauder; MBA/MA-SAIS at Johns Hopkins; MBA/MPA-Harvard's Kennedy School of Government; MBA/MSW; MBA/PhD; MBA/VMD; MBA/MSN; MBA/MA in Environmental Studies

Academics

The University of Pennsylvania's Wharton School, one of the premier MBA programs in the world, is best known for its "strong finance reputation," but the curriculum's "strong emphasis on quantitative analysis" extends "across many disciplines, not just finance but marketing, entrepreneurship, operations, international business, real estate, etc." as well. All areas present a "holistic program with a mix of case studies, traditional lecture formats, experiential learning opportunities, and strong co-curricular programs."

Students brag that Wharton "provides all the resources necessary for us to succeed, and then some," reporting that "the difficult part here is deciding between which resources— lectures, seminars, simulations, clubs, special events—one can fit into one's schedule." Writes one student, "The breadth and depth of the academic curriculum and the extracurricular activities is so huge that I would need at least six MBA years to experience 20 percent of it all." A heavy workload, described as "difficult for everyone but the most brilliant to manage," makes those choices even tougher. But what impresses students most here is the degree to which students themselves contribute to the learning experience. Wharton uses a "co-production model of learning" that "requires engagement from all participants in the Wharton community." One MBA observes, "Students sometimes add more value than assigned readings. Students make Wharton. 'Student-run' is an understatement." Another agrees, "The 'co-production model' is not just a buzz word; it really exists here."

Under the Wharton pedagogic system, "Classes build on each other. Professors are known to coordinate timing of discussing certain topics to ensure that the student has mastered the concept in another class." Much work here is done in teams. To promote cooperation and reduce competitiveness, Wharton policy currently forbids grade disclosure to recruiters. Students report that the policy "fosters an environment of helping at the school." Nondisclosure apparently has little impact on students' motivation to work. One notes, "The school has high expectations for each admit, and the overall performance of the students rises to that expectation."

Career and Placement

Wharton is a brand that pretty much sells itself, so it's no surprise that the school's career services are highly regarded and widely appreciated by students. Each year brings the following career placement services to the campus: over 200 employer information sessions; almost 300 recruiting companies; and, more than 5,000 job-board postings. Wharton's Career Management Services Office also offers resume review and distribution, mock interviews, internship placement, one-on-one counseling, and over 25 career treks both in and outside the U.S. No wonder students praise the "fantastic career opportunities and resources." About 55 percent of Wharton MBAs take jobs in the finance sector; 28 percent wind up in consulting; and seven percent find jobs in the marketing arena.

Student Life and Environment

Life at Wharton offers "an amazing number of choices in terms of classes, activities, clubs, etc." It's an atmosphere students tell us is filled with a constant stream of unique opportunities they wouldn't otherwise have. One student cites these personal examples: "At Wharton I have done a four-week study trip to greater China; a consulting project to an Israeli company that wanted to enter the U.S. market; a marketing consulting project for AOL for the mobile location-based services product; a leadership venture to Ecuador next spring to learn about teamwork through a mountain climbing expedition; dozens of fantastic speakers; and finally, some great parties." MBAs appreciate that their "partners are involved in almost all campus-related activities here." One reports, "My wife and one-year-old daughter enjoy going to activities every Wednesday and Friday with the Wharton Kids Club. This has proved to be very helpful in providing an environment where my wife can make lots of friends in a new city, and my daughter can play with other kids her own age."

Hometown Philadelphia "is underrated but still needs work." One Bay Area native notes, "I was worried about Philadelphia after living in San Francisco, but I have been pleasantly surprised by the depth of culture, fun, and good food." Wharton's new facility, Huntsman Hall, is "top-of-the-line" but MBAs gripe that "sharing the building with undergraduates leads to scarce group study rooms. Most students do not use the library because it is overrun with undergrads." Still, Wharton does most things right. You realize this when you ask students what most needs improving here and all they can think to mention is "full-size lockers for each student."

Admissions

Wharton is among the most selective MBA programs in the country. On average, the school receives between seven and 10 applications for each available slot. The school's website notes that "approximately 75 to 80 percent of all applicants are qualified for admission." Applicants are evaluated holistically by at least three members of the Admissions Committee. All prior academic experience, including graduate work and certifications, is considered. GMAT scores also figure into the decision. Quality of professional experiences, career choices, and stated goals for entering the program are all carefully reviewed. Committee members also look for evidence of leadership, interpersonal skills, entrepreneurial spirit, and good citizenship. International students must demonstrate competency in English through essays and interviews. Wharton offers three rounds of an admission each year; the first two rounds are equal with regard to a candidate's admissibility. The third round offers admission on a space-available basis and is generally more competitive.

FINANCIAL FACTS

Annual tuition	$57,026
Fees	$5,008
Cost of books	$5,222
Room & board	$25,744

ADMISSIONS

Admissions Selectivity Rating	99
# of applications received	6,408
Average GMAT	720
Range of GMAT	560–790
TOEFL required of international students	Yes
International application fee	$265
Application Deadline/Notification	
Round 1:	10/1 / 12/20
Round 2:	1/3 / 3/26
Round 3:	3/5 / 5/3
Deferment available	Yes
Maximum length of deferment	case by case for extenuating circumstances only
Transfer students accepted	No
Non-fall admissions	No
Need-blind admissions	Yes

EMPLOYMENT PROFILE

Career Rating	99	Grads Employed by Function	%	Avg. Salary
Percent employed at graduation	80	Marketing	(9%)	$106,468
Percent employed 3 months after graduation	92	Operations	(1%)	$114,167
		Consulting	(31%)	$127,811
Average base starting salary	$120,605	Management	(6%)	$109,086
Primary Source of Full-time Job Acceptances		Finance	(40%)	$121,087
School-facilitated activities	366(62%)	HR	(0%)	
Graduate-facilitated activities	221(38%)	Other	(13%)	$116,683
Unknown	0(%)	**Top 5 Employers Hiring Grads**		

Top 5 Employers Hiring Grads
McKinsey & Company (53), Boston Consulting Group (45), Bain & Company (25), Deloitte Consulting (16), Goldman Sachs (16)

UNIVERSITY OF PITTSBURGH
JOSEPH M. KATZ GRADUATE SCHOOL OF BUSINESS

GENERAL INFORMATION

Type of school	Public
Affiliation	No Affiliation
Academic calendar	August - April

SURVEY SAYS...

Students love Pittsburgh, PA, Smart classrooms
Solid preparation in:
Teamwork, Social responsibility

STUDENTS

Enrollment of parent institution	35,330
Enrollment of MBA Program	701
% male/female	71/29
% out-of-state	24
% part-time	76
% underrepresented minority	12
% international	41
Average age at entry	27
Average years work experience at entry	2.9

ACADEMICS

Academic Experience Rating	**93**
Profs interesting rating	87
Profs accesible rating	93
Student/faculty ratio	8:1
% female faculty	27
% underrepresented minority faculty	5
% part-time faculty	24

Joint Degrees

MBA-MS-Engineering in the following specialties: Bioengineering, Chemical and Petroleum Engineering, Civil and Environmental Engineering, Electrical and Computer Engineering, Industrial Engineering;, MBA/JD, MBA/Master of International Business, MBA/Master of Science in Management Information Systems, MBA/Master of Public and International Affairs, and MBA/Master of International Development.

Academics

Students are drawn to the University of Pittsburgh's Joseph M. Katz Graduate School of Business for its "value, location, course offerings, [and] study abroad program." In addition, many tout "the small class size, accessibility of the administration and faculty, and the collegial and collaborative environment, percent of matriculating students hailing from abroad." As one student says, "we have a very international class at Katz. In my first year, about 55 percent of the class hailed from outside the U.S., including China, Taiwan, India, and Europe." This is not surprising given the school's "dual-degree programs and international connections with universities abroad."

In 1960, Katz became the first business school to offer a one-year MBA program designed for students with a strong background in business or economics. Students continue to laud the "reputation of [the] finance department [and] reputation for placement in finance-related careers." In addition, the school offers a part-time program where working professionals can pursue an advanced degree in their field through evening classes. In the part-time program, "classes meet at night for three hours and some of the work can be a little tedious after you have put in a full day of work." The full-time, two-year MBA program focuses on providing students with a longer, more comprehensive introduction to all aspects of business management. The first-semester students "are focused on the core MBA classes." "Starting the second semester, students are able to start taking electives."

Overall, students say the faculty here "is adequate." Professors are "smart, engaged and come from diverse backgrounds—from prominent *Fortune* 500 companies to non-profits and start-up companies. They're generally very good at soft skills while maintaining a high level of skill in the more technical aspects of b-school." "The course offerings in certain departments are not extensive, particularly in marketing" and "adjunct professors are particularly weak." As is the case at many large research universities, others add a cautionary note saying, "professors are a mixed bag, ranging from excellent teachers who are extremely accessible, to…being so concerned with their research that they treat students like a nuisance." The administration however "is amazing." "I love the fact that the Dean knows students by name." "One can just walk into the Dean's office. The Dean and his staff at the MBA Programs Office interact with students all the time."

Career and Placement

In terms of job placement students here say, "the social networks…are priceless. I feel if I ever lost my current job, through my developed network I would be employed very quickly." In addition, "the network events and alumni database are particularly helpful." Most importantly, Katz has a long arm into the Pittsburgh community and the Pennsylvania region at large. However, students say "career services could be more involved in getting more companies on site for recruiting;" however they are quick to attribute any dip in recruiting opportunities to "the recession and difficult times as far as hiring and job availability in general."

In 2010, 70 percent of graduating Katz MBA students had received a job offer prior to graduation with a mean base salary of $71,328. Though by in large students accepted jobs in the surrounding Middle Atlantic region, an impressive 30.4 percent accepted jobs internationally. Financial services, manufacturing, consulting, and technology remain fields with big draws for Katz grads. Bayer, IBM, Deloitte & Touche, Crane Co., and Ford Motor Company were listed as the top five employers.

Student Life and Environment

Katz students are "a very diverse group." There is "a large percentage of foreign students as well as a large female population. The students also have a wide variety of work backgrounds and they bring this to classroom conversations." Overall, students describe themselves as "active, intelligent, ambitious, a good group of individuals with good overall work ethic." Those directly out of undergraduate tend to be "young and fun-loving individuals with an excitement to learn the tools and acquire the expertise to advance their business careers." Part-time and returning students "generally have work and family lives outside of school" and "are able to bring their own life experiences to group and project work" which "enhances the learning experience."

Life on campus is "both exciting and stressful. There are always plenty of opportunities for various activities within professional and social realms." One student jokes, "There are too many different activities, lectures, clubs, etc. to choose from. Something is always going on." Working professionals note, "being a full-time employee and part-time student is difficult." However, "this school tries to tailor courses to meet the needs of busy adults while still catering to full-time students as well."

Admissions

Applicants to the Joseph M. Katz Graduate School of Business are evaluated on their demonstrated leadership skills, record of accomplishment, previous academic performance, and analytical skills as well as their future potential as leaders in business. The average GPA for the matriculating class of 2010 was 3.4 with an average GMAT of 610. Evaluative interviews are required for admission. Last year, 97 percent of applicants to the full-time MBA program were interviewed. Interviews for part-time candidates are arranged by invitation and take place after the admissions committee's initial review of a candidate's application.

Prominent Alumni

Frank Gaoning Ning, CEO and Chairman of COFCO, Ltd. (China); Raymond William Smith, Chairman Verizon Ventures; Kevin Woods Sharer, Chair & CEO Amgen, Inc.; Robert Paserick, President, Boeing Shared Services Group; Jeffrey A. Davis, Senior Vice President and Treasurer, Wal-Mart Stores, Inc.

FINANCIAL FACTS

Annual tuition (in-state/ out-of-state)	$19,280/$26,118
Fees	$2,740
Cost of books	$1,132
Room & board (on/off-campus)	$16,052
% of students receiving grants	70
Average grant	$11,828

ADMISSIONS

Admissions Selectivity Rating	89
# of applications received	432
% applicants accepted	35
% acceptees attending	54
Average GMAT	608
Range of GMAT	580–660
Average GPA	3.20
TOEFL required of international students	Yes
Minimum TOEFL (paper/computer)	600
Application fee	$50
International application fee	$50
Application Deadline/Notification	
Round 1:	10/15 / 12/3
Round 2:	12/10 / 2/1
Round 3:	2/8 / 4/1
Round 4:	4/8 / 5/6
Deferment available	Yes
Maximum length of deferment	1 year
Transfer students accepted	Yes
Transfer application policy: Matching coursework, accepting up to one-third total credits from an AACSB MBA program, provided that credits were not used to complete a previous MBA degree.	
Non-fall admissions	No
Need-blind admissions	Yes

EMPLOYMENT PROFILE

Career Rating	92
Percent employed at graduation	69
Percent employed 3 months after graduation	88
Average base starting salary	$76,136

Primary Source of Full-time Job Acceptances

School-facilitated activities	34(52%)
Graduate-facilitated activities	26(39%)
Unknown	6(9%)

Grads Employed by Function% Avg. Salary

Marketing	(17%)	$65,069
Operations	(18%)	$77,800
Consulting	(27%)	$82,708
Management	(3%)	
Finance	(20%)	$71,654
HR	(3%)	
Other	(3%)	

Top 5 Employers Hiring Grads
Deloitte (8), Crane (5), SDLC Partners (3), PNC (2), IBM (2)

UNIVERSITY OF PORTLAND
PAMPLIN SCHOOL OF BUSINESS ADMINISTRATION

Academics

The Pamplin School of Business Administration at the University of Portland features some of the Pacific Northwest's top-notch faculty and a curriculum "integrating professional experience into academic concepts." The program administrator has made this "wonderfully run" program "extremely easy to do while working," as many do, and the university even offers some tuition discounts to those who are seeking Nonprofit Management degrees (a notable program here), as well as scholarships for international students. The school is part of JEBNET, Jesuit Education in Business Network, which is a network of 30 AACSB-accredited universities nationwide that share similarly "strong mission statements" and provide students the ability to transfer credits and complete their MBA at another university.

The "good atmosphere within the classroom" is built on the foundation of "some of the most engaged professors I have had," according to one student. They "seem to really enjoy what they are teaching and a majority do a great job engaging students," and "are just as invested in your academic and career advancement" as the individual themselves. "Most of [the] professors treat me as their family or friends, and I've learned a lot of practical things from my school," says a student. Varied experiential backgrounds help instructors to provide a well-rounded curriculum.

The school's Catholic ties result in "an ideals driven environment," one that also happens to be "understanding of students working while attending classes." Most of the students are able to "work with professors one on one" outside of class. "The staff is amazing and the professors are intense, but it's an MBA program, so what'd you expect?!" says one happy student.

Career and Placement

Pamplin has an excellent "reputation against other schools locally," so those who are looking for jobs within the area have a leg up. Many people here are getting degrees for advancement in their current jobs, but the school does a good job of recruiting for the handful that are looking. "If you are young [and] under 30...it's a good program because that is the age bracket that the recruiting companies pursue" at Pamplin. Since admission is rolling, students can begin immediately following their acceptance in the fall, spring, or summer, which is a huge advantage to working students.

ADMISSIONS CONTACT: MELISSA McCARTHY, MBA PROGRAM DIRECTOR
ADDRESS: 5000 N. WILLAMETTE BLVD., PORTLAND, OR 97203
PHONE: 503-943-7225 • FAX: 503-943-8041
E-MAIL: MBA-UP@UP.EDU • WEBSITE: BUSINESS.UP.EDU

Student Life and Environment

Pamplin has a "great facility, small class sizes," and a diverse student body that "is very professional and we are all in the same situation. We balance work, school, family, and friends." Students "tend to be younger than 30," have "3-5 years work experience at best," and are "career minded but not uptight." Many have careers in addition to school, which "makes relating easy," and the numerous nationalities of the student body beneficially "increases the world view of the program, as we are obviously moving towards a more world-based economy." Most of the students "like discussion and analysis," so one can learn "a lot of things not only from lecture, but [also from] my fellow students." Students work "in an incredibly tight cohort" and are "very, very supportive of one another's opinions and experiences."

The unique culture of the Pacific Northwest is reassuring to all who go here since many are regional locals, and the "gorgeous scenery" has more than a few fans. The UP campus itself "is breathtaking" and offers many "nice" transportation options.

Admissions

Applicants to the MBA program at the University of Portland must meet the following minimum requirements: an undergraduate GPA of at least 3.0; a GMAT score of at least 500; and an "admission index" of at least 1,100 under the formula [(undergraduate GPA x 200) + GMAT score]. Work experience, though strongly recommended, is not required; applicants with at least three years of post-baccalaureate professional experience are considered optimal candidates for the program. International students must score at least 570 on the TOEFL paper test or 230 on the computer-adaptive version of the TOEFL or a 7.0 on the IELTS exam. All applications to the University of Portland must include a completed application form, a resumé, a personal statement of goals, official transcripts for all post-secondary academic work, an official GMAT score report, and two letters of recommendation. International students must submit all of the above as well as an official TOEFL score report and a financial statement that indicates they will have adequate support throughout the duration of study. This is required before the I-20 form is issued to them.

FINANCIAL FACTS

Annual tuition	$27,810
Fees	$1,350
Cost of books	$1,200
Room & board	$12,000
% of students receiving aid	69
% of first-year students receiving aid	77
% of students receiving grants	28
Average award package	$14,403
Average grant	$4,283
Average loan	$18,067
Average student loan debt	$29,014

ADMISSIONS

Admissions Selectivity Rating	88
# of applications received	167
% applicants accepted	44
% acceptees attending	90
Average GMAT	536
Range of GMAT	470–580
Average GPA	3.61
TOEFL required of international students	Yes
Minimum TOEFL (paper/computer)	570/230
Application fee	$50
International application fee	$50
Deferment available	Yes
Maximum length of deferment	1 year
Transfer students accepted	Yes

Transfer application policy: 9 Semester hours of transfer credit from AACSB accredited program as long as the student received a B grade or higher in the course and the course has been taken within the last 5 years; or all credits in the Jesuit Transfer Agreement as long as the student has received a B grade in the course or higher

Non-fall admissions	Yes
Need-blind admissions	Yes

UNIVERSITY OF RHODE ISLAND
COLLEGE OF BUSINESS ADMINISTRATION

GENERAL INFORMATION
Type of school   Public
Affiliation   No Affiliation
Academic calendar   Semesters

SURVEY SAYS...
Solid preparation in:
Accounting, General management

STUDENTS
Enrollment of parent
   institution   15,900
Enrollment of MBA Program   186
% male/female   58/42
% out-of-state   25
% part-time   87
% underrepresented minority   8
% international   21
Average age at entry   28
Average years work experience
   at entry   0.0

ACADEMICS
Academic Experience Rating   78
Profs interesting rating   82
Profs accesible rating   77
% part-time faculty   0

Joint Degrees
MBA/Pharm.D - 7 years
MBA/Engineering - 5 years
MBA/Master of Oceanography - 16 months

Academics

The College of Business Administration at the University of Rhode Island has been providing MBAs to in-state and national students since 1961. With its emphasis on innovation and small class sizes, including the "flexibility of the program and the availability of the required classes," the school offers students a satisfying, affordable option for career advancement.

Students may complete a part-time MBA at the Providence campus – designed for individuals who want to pursue a degree while maintaining their personal and professional commitments – or the "unusual" One-Year MBA Program in Strategic Innovation at the main campus in Kingston. The One-Year MBA was recently redesigned to promote critical thinking, analytical skills, hands-on projects, and organization among students requiring them to gather and analyze data before making critical decisions; it has many fans among the students, who sing its praises. The program's administration also receives high marks. It is "absolutely top shelf, [is] always helpful, [and] always encouraging." When students have questions, the staff, "responds via email/phone within minutes."

"I have been pleasantly surprised with how well the professors are able to adapt the 'book knowledge' to the real world," says a student. URI has many part-time students, and "all of the faculty, staff, and students are very aware and understanding of the strains put on the work-school-life balance." Professors "try to accommodate the students' needs without taking away from their curriculum." To this point, "the classes to this point have not wasted anyone's valuable time and provide pertinent course work and projects." Most professors are "good, with interesting and applicable professional backgrounds."

Career and Placement

Most here choose to go the part-time evening route, and so are not looking for any sort of help in the placement department. Though recruitment is not a huge concern here, some wish that URI would make efforts to "grow stronger partnerships with local companies in an effort to allow students a true-to-life work environment for projects and course work." Administration and faculty are very helpful "in assisting students in positioning the right pats to succeed in the MBA program and future careers." The timescale of the One-Year MBA, in particular, is "really convenient for students who are eager to get back in the workforce and do not wish to spend more than a year returning to or continuing school."

Student Life and Environment

Students here are "bright, motivated individuals with a common goal towards career advancement." Most are just at the school to advance their careers, and appreciate the commonality of that goal. "I am a part-time student. I work full-time during the day and attend class at night. I am surrounded by individuals in the same situation," says one. There are plenty of "different ethnic backgrounds," and students are "very engaging in class, focused, cooperative, and willing to collaborate with others. "Many who go here are from the sciences or engineering [fields], as the school offers a joint MBA/Master's of Oceanography program.

Aside from the program redesign, the school also features updated facilities and technology, including wireless classrooms, a trading room, and a computer lab. Though the Providence campus is located centrally downtown, the Kingston campus has "no real town and therefore no public transportation" and luckily, the "commute to school is easy." Almost all the MBA students live off campus and rely on their vehicles to get to and from campus. However, the area is "beautiful," and "great for people who like outdoors activities (hiking, biking, running, surfing, sailing, etc.)"

Admissions

URI offers many components of its application online and encourages applicants to submit materials online whenever possible. Students may provide all of the following materials via the Internet: a current resume, a personal statement of purpose, and two letters of recommendation (applicants e-mail referees, who then send their recommendations directly to the school). Students must also provide the admissions office with official transcripts for all postsecondary academic work and an official score report for the GMAT – scores must be no more than five years old. International applicants must provide all the above plus an official TOEFL or IELTS score report (scores must be no more than two years old); the minimum required score for admission is 575 on the paper-based TOEFL, 91 on the Internet-based TOEFL, or 6.5 on the IELTS. The school notes that most accepted applicants have an undergraduate GPA of at least 3.0 and GMAT scores ranked in at least the 50th percentile, but allows that grades and test scores are not the sole criteria for admission. The school seeks candidates with demonstrated strength in quantitative skills, work experience ("valued," but not required, according to university materials), leadership potential, motivation, and communication skills.

FINANCIAL FACTS

Annual tuition (in-state/ out-of-state)	$16,178/$40,520
Fees	$4,500
Cost of books	$4,500
Average grant	$0
Average loan	$0

ADMISSIONS

Admissions Selectivity Rating	**75**
# of applications received	97
% applicants accepted	75
% acceptees attending	75
Average GMAT	562
Average GPA	3.28
TOEFL required of international students	Yes
Minimum TOEFL (paper/computer)	575/233
Application fee	$65
International application fee	$65
Regular application deadline	4/15
Deferment available	Yes
Maximum length of deferment	1 year
Transfer students accepted	Yes
Transfer application policy: Can take up to 20% of total credits from another AACSB accredited college/university.	
Non-fall admissions	Yes
Need-blind admissions	Yes

UNIVERSITY OF RICHMOND
ROBINS SCHOOL OF BUSINESS

GENERAL INFORMATION

Type of school	Private
Affiliation	No Affiliation
Academic calendar	Semester

SURVEY SAYS...

Good peer network
Solid preparation in:
General management, Doing
business in a global economy

STUDENTS

Enrollment of parent institution	4,361
Enrollment of MBA Program	115
% male/female	98/2
% out-of-state	0
% part-time	85
% underrepresented minority	2
% international	2
Average age at entry	29
Average years work experience at entry	6.0

ACADEMICS

Academic Experience Rating	**82**
Profs interesting rating	88
Profs accesible rating	84
Student/faculty ratio	7:1
% female faculty	20
% underrepresented minority faculty	5
% part-time faculty	22

Joint Degrees

Juris Doctor/Master of Business
Administration (24 months)

Prominent Alumni

David Beran, President & Chief
Operating Officer, Altria Group, Inc.;
R. Lewis Boggs, President, Property
Investment Advisors; Bruce Kay,
Vice President of Investor Relations,
Markel Corporation; Michael
Matthews, President & CEO, H&A
Architects and Engineers; Margaret
"Lyn" McDermid, Chief Information
Officer, Federal Reserve System

Academics

The MBA program at the University of Richmond is an engaging experience, which offers small classes and an interesting curriculum and boasts "top-tier faculty and staff." Students are challenged and rewarded here. The "amazing" professors "are quite accomplished" and "well-educated." Many students are pleased to discover that their professors are not just intellectually smart but are "great teachers" as well. "It is evident that the business school places teaching ability above research expertise when hiring faculty." "I feel fortunate to be in such a stimulating environment," a student explains. "I often leave class with a great sense of appreciation for the discussions I've had and the insight gained."

The administration as a whole won students' admiration for being "very responsive and engaged with the MBA program." "Whether I want to [meet] with the Dean, my professors, or the Program Director it is always easy to access those I need to speak with to resolve questions and concerns." Students are impressed that the administration and staff "know each student personally and really engage with us at every opportunity." "Part of that may be the small class size, which makes it a much more manageable experience and offers the opportunity to interact more on a personal level." One student feels "the personal attention that comes with [the small size] is the biggest strength of the program."

Equally appealing to students is the school's program of study. The convenience of having a program where adults do not "have to forego income and [can] attend in the evenings" gives many students the opportunities to apply their newfound skills to their jobs "on a daily basis," as it also makes the school a good option for those who may not otherwise be able to afford tuition. The program definitely requires a good amount of effort. One student suggests that the school might consider cutting down some of the required courses and offering more electives in their place, which would "allow students to more highly specialize in their chosen field of study."

Many students commented on the high caliber of fellow classmates that are "as motivated as I [am] to learn." "As a part-time program for working adults, the program does an exceptional job of promoting team work so that the students become a close-knit network of friends." There is also an added "international component" provided by several international students. This "real-world (vs. only theoretical cases in classroom) experience" is of great value to those wishing to expand their global knowledge.

Career and Placement

UR is situated in a "thriving business community that is strong in many realms, from finance (Harris Williams) to marketing (The Martin Agency)." The school's location draws many part-time MBA students who value the convenience of improving their education while working on the job. Sitting side-by-side with similar "top notch" students, "networking opportunities abound." In addition to fostering prospects with fellow students, the "administrative staff works hard to connect you with businesses and job opportunities." There are "many events with prominent speakers on campus," as well as "workshops, etc., outside of class to meet local business leaders." "The ability to network with alumni and the various panels and speakers that speak at the business school," create yet another layer of opportunities for graduate students. Still, some students feel that "the focus on job placement could stand to be improved. Graduate business students in search of employment advice or placement help must use the undergraduate career development center. Additionally, career fairs on campus tend to be focused on undergraduates."

ADMISSIONS CONTACT: DR. RICHARD S. COUGHLAN
ADDRESS: MBA OFFICE, ROBINS SCHOOL OF BUSINESS, UNIVERSITY OF RICHMOND, VA 23173
PHONE: 804-289-8553 • FAX: 804-287-1228
E-MAIL: MBA@RICHMOND.EDU • WEBSITE: BUSINESS.RICHMOND.EDU/MBA

Student Life and Environment

Due to the nature of the program, student life as a graduate student is very different from that of an undergrad. "As a part-time program, most of the students commute to campus; some international students do live on campus. The students are friends with one another and will regularly meet off-campus, however, 'life at school' does not apply to most." "The program is taught entirely in the evening, almost exclusively to students who are working full-time. This makes networking and family involvement difficult, but there are some efforts made by the university to help on this front. Recently, UR opened an MBA lounge where MBA's can mingle before and after class. Also, spouses are invited to events like the annual holiday party."

Commitments of graduate students outside of school, however busy they may be, do not seem to affect this "energetic, intelligent" student body from their group work or their class bonding experience. The opening residency is "fantastic for creating relationships with students in your class" and the students are "exceptionally hard working leaders in the local business community," and are all quite capable of "maximizing the value of their time." "Richmond is a great city to live in as a business student. The graduate business school is a relatively small community on campus (with the undergraduate population being much larger, and the law school population being significantly larger as well), but MBA students often socialize together off-campus."

Admissions

The University of Richmond Robins School of Business accepts applications up to 05/01 on a rolling basis. GMAT scores, which average 611, as well as undergraduate GPAs, which average 3.36, are strongly taken into consideration as well as previous work experience and resume, all of which are required with your application. Interviews are also important.

FINANCIAL FACTS

Cost of books	$1,200
% of students receiving aid	57
% of first-year students receiving aid	16
% of students receiving grants	23
Average award package	$20,335
Average grant	$13,080
Average loan	$22,660
Average student loan debt	$53,250

ADMISSIONS

Admissions Selectivity Rating	82
# of applications received	54
% applicants accepted	63
% acceptees attending	85
Average GMAT	604
Range of GMAT	550–653
Average GPA	3.21
TOEFL required of international students	Yes
Minimum TOEFL (paper/computer)	600/250
Application fee	$50
International application fee	$50
Regular application deadline	5/13
Regular application notification	5/20
Deferment available	Yes
Maximum length of deferment	1 Year
Transfer students accepted	Yes
Transfer application policy: Maximum of 8.0 hours of transfer credit accepted from other AACSB-accredited schools at the discretion of Program Director.	
Non-fall admissions	Yes
Need-blind admissions	Yes

UNIVERSITY OF ROCHESTER
WILLIAM E. SIMON GRADUATE SCHOOL OF BUSINESS ADMINISTRATION

GENERAL INFORMATION
Type of school   Private
Affiliation   No Affiliation
Academic calendar   Quarter

SURVEY SAYS...
Helpful alumni, Smart classrooms
Solid preparation in:
Finance, Teamwork,
Quantitative skills

STUDENTS
Enrollment of parent
  institution   10,510
Enrollment of MBA Program   569
% male/female   72/28
% part-time   48
% underrepresented minority   21
% international   53
Average age at entry   27
Average years work experience
  at entry   4.6

ACADEMICS
Academic Experience Rating   **92**
Profs interesting rating   91
Profs accesible rating   91
Student/faculty ratio   10:1
% female faculty   17
% underrepresented minority
  faculty   0
% part-time faculty   18

Joint Degrees
MBA/Master of Public Health, 3
years; MD/MBA, 5 years

Prominent Alumni
Douglas Petno, CEO, Commercial
Banking, JP Morgan Chase; Mark
Grier, Vice Chairman, Prudential
Insurance Co.; Jay Benet, Vice
Chairman/CFO- Travelers
Companies; Mark Ain, Founder and
Chairman/Kronos Incorporated;
Sandeep Pahwa, Vice
Chairman/Head of Investment
Banking, SE Asia, Barclays Capital

Academics

Founded in the 1960s under its already revered parent institution, the William E. Simon Graduate School of Business Administration is not only a "top school in the region," with "a strong faculty and course work and a solid reputation," it has gone on to stake its claim as a leading business school in the nation. Known for its "small size, economic-based academic framework, international diversity," "analytic curriculum," and "approachable faculty," "it is considered one of the best finance schools in the world."

Life at the Simon School "is very involved. Since the school is small, more responsibility is placed on students to fill leadership positions in clubs and student government. If somebody is looking to get involved both in[side] and out[side] the classroom, then Simon is definitely the place for them." Classes are "very intense." "Coupled with the clubs and job hunt, it can get overwhelming at times," says one overtaxed student. "Luckily we work in teams, so everyone is going through the same thing!" Others add, "Anyone who has been through the Simon MBA knows that what you receive in challenge and stress comes back two fold in confidence and business expertise."

Small class sizes at Simon "create phenomenal professor-student interaction" and are a consistent highlight for students. "By having a class of roughly 200 students you really have the opportunity to build relationships with all of your cohorts." Professors at Simon "are top-notch." Many operate on an "open-door policy, and even the most disguised professors are accessible." Others note, "The best teachers (tenured and otherwise) teach the core courses at Simon, which leaves us very well-prepared for our internships in the coming summer." In addition, the school boasts "three very well-reputed journals edited on campus (Journal of Financial Economics, the Journal of Monetary Economics, and the Journal of Accounting and Economics)."

The administration here "is 100 percent behind its students" and "is willing to do whatever is necessary to ensure all of its students are satisfied." "Our Dean [specifically] has impacted almost every student at our school. He is an amazing role model for all of the students and faculty." Succinctly put, "The overall academic experience is flawless at Simon; if you are seriously interested in receiving a top-notch education, I don't think you can consider any other university."

Career and Placement

Students say Simon's career center "has a great NYC recruiting program." Others feel "the school could do more to attract top employers." "Given that we are a small school, not many large firms are willing to devote a lot of resources to recruit on our campus." Alumni, however, "are very responsive." In fact, students feel that perhaps this provides an avenue which the school might tap into more heavily in the future; "I would like to see more alumni come to campus to share their experiences and help the school place talented students in great positions." Despite areas of needed improvement, students are quick to note that "it's a tough market right now"; "The career management office is still a work in progress—they need to diversify the job openings and provide international students more skills in networking and job search."

In 2010, 73.3 percent of full-time MBA graduates seeking employment received a job offer with a mean base salary of $72,744 for those who accepted positions within three months after graduation. Constellation Brands, The University of Rochester, Deloitte, Xerox Corporation, and Citigroup were the top five employers. Most students matriculated into the financial services, consulting, and consumer industries.

ADMISSIONS CONTACT: REBEKAH S. LEWIN, EXECUTIVE DIRECTOR OF ADMISSIONS AND ADMIN
ADDRESS: 305 SCHLEGEL HALL, ROCHESTER, NY 14627-0107
PHONE: 585-275-3533 • FAX: 585-271-3907
E-MAIL: ADMISSIONS@SIMON.ROCHESTER.EDU • WEBSITE: WWW.SIMON.ROCHESTER.EDU

Student Life and Environment

With over 40 percent of 2011's incoming class hailing from abroad, the student body at Simon is "very diverse, both in terms of work experience and ethnicity." "The culture mix is amazing, but also very rewarding to the b-school experience." Overall the student body reflects a mixture of younger students and returning executives which produces "a great bunch of students and professionals." With many students coming fresh out of undergraduate studies, "the mix is younger on average." The Executive MBA class "is close, and many socialize outside of class and study times. We have a wide variety of backgrounds, interests, ages, and cultures."

Overall, the atmosphere at Simon is "competitive yet very cooperative, [and] adaptive to the changing business environment." Although some may appear "to have a chip on their shoulder about attending Simon," [including] many wannabe investment bankers that have very little work experience," by in large students here are "intellectually curious, and very kind and helpful." Ambition and a hard-working attitude aren't hard to come by. Simon's students "are the most fascinating, motivated people you could hope to meet." "Every student is passionate about some area of business. I often find conversations taking place in the coffee shop about how what we are learning relates to the real world." "Many Simon students forgo the opportunity to have an internship over the summer and end up starting companies/practices with one another. It is a small school and the close-knit nature of the students reflects that."

Life at school is "extremely busy" with "lectures, study groups, assignments, networking, corporate presentations, alumni events, club activities, and recruitment events." In addition, "students are involved in clubs and activities and course work [...] with a lot of team-based assignments, ensuring that we build communications, teamwork and leadership skills." The town of Rochester "is somewhat small, but people are friendly and there is plenty to do." The "beautiful Ivy League-looking campus" boasts an "amazing library and resources" and "separate graduate study areas both in the business school and the library."

Admissions

Admission to Simon is extremely competitive. Students with exceptional GPAs, applicable test scores, and relevant leadership experience (including post-baccalaureate work and extracurricular activities) rise to the top of the pool. Applicants to the school's MBA program must submit the following: an online application, one required essay, undergraduate transcripts, one letter of recommendation, a current resume, an official GMAT report, and interview (if requested by the Admissions Committee). International students for whom English is not a primary language must submit an official score report for the TOEFL. This requirement is waived if students have studied for at least one full year in a college or university where English is the language of instruction.

FINANCIAL FACTS

Annual tuition	$47,220
Fees	$1,005
Cost of books	$1,935
Room & board	$12,980
% of students receiving aid	90
% of first-year students receiving aid	90
% of students receiving grants	86
Average award package	$35,496
Average grant	$21,144
Average loan	$36,640
Average student loan debt	$41,211

ADMISSIONS

Admissions Selectivity Rating	92
# of applications received	673
% applicants accepted	34
% acceptees attending	34
Average GMAT	680
Range of GMAT	660–710
Average GPA	3.45
TOEFL required of international students	Yes
Application fee	$150
International application fee	$150
Early application deadline	10/15
Early notification date	1/15
Application Deadline/Notification	
Round 1:	11/15 / 2/15
Round 2:	1/5 / 3/31
Round 3:	3/15 / 5/20
Round 4:	5/15 / 7/15
Deferment available	No
Transfer students accepted	Yes
Transfer application policy: No more than 9 credit hours, may not be core courses.	
Non-fall admissions	Yes
Need-blind admissions	Yes

EMPLOYMENT PROFILE

Career Rating	95	**Grads Employed by Function% Avg. Salary**	
Percent employed at graduation	65	Marketing	(18%) $87,331
Percent employed 3 months after graduation	92	Operations	(3%) $88,000
		Consulting	(33%)$85,171
Average base starting salary	$86,553	Management	(10%) $85,090
Primary Source of Full-time Job Acceptances		Finance	(33%) $88,662
School-facilitated activities	84(67%)	MIS	(4%) $83,526
Graduate-facilitated activities	42(33%)	**Top 5 Employers Hiring Grads**	
		Deloitte (9), University of Rochester (5), Liberty Mutual (3), M&T Bank (3), KPMG (3)	

UNIVERSITY OF SAN DIEGO
SCHOOL OF BUSINESS ADMINISTRATION

Academics

Students at the University of San Diego appreciate the "beautiful campus" that one student describes as, "the most stunning campus I have ever seen." Students also comment favorably on the warm Southern California weather. San Diego may be "the best city in the world," but the real selling point to prospective students lies in the strength of the MBA program. The program itself seems to be a perfect example of how to run an effective business. The cohort system "keeps incoming class sizes small," and ensures "that you become great friends with your classmates." This in turn "bolsters students' comfort to ask tough questions and push each other." Professors are "well rounded in business and academics," and "push students" to excel in their classes, making for "a very dynamic environment." Many of the faculty "bring vast amounts of real-world business experience to the classroom and teach well beyond the limitations of textbooks." They are "cordial" and "genuinely care for students' careers," and they understand "how to equip us in this job market." Administration is the glue that holds everything together. Administrators are "well organized" and "terrific in helping to guide your academic career."

In one student's opinion, classmates at USD "are not ... typical MBA student[s]. [They] come from a wide range of backgrounds and are not solely focused on making the most money possible. Most USD MBAs select USD based on a desire to serve society as a whole."

With "an emphasis on ethical leadership," students tend to see the bigger picture and see past using financial gain as the only tool for measuring a successful business. At USD they "focus on supply chain, social responsibility, and legal implications of business all within the same semester." This integration of materials follows "the schools' mission to develop socially responsible leaders with a global mindset."

USD students have many good things to say about the quality of the degree they receive. "The class choices are broad and cover all topics I was hoping to study in an MBA program," affirms one student. Another is pleased to report that the "overall academic experience has been positively life-changing." The "big emphasis on corporate social responsibility and community service" appeals to many students, but at least one student wishes "less of these classes were required so I could take more electives in my areas of interest."

Career and Placement

"USD has a job placement office dedicated solely to its MBA students. This office provides direct connections to regional, national, and international employment opportunities, internships, and contract projects." The career services personnel "are knowledgeable and dedicated recruiting professionals clear in their mission of providing every MBA student with the information and connections necessary to secure the career of their dreams." The majority of students appreciate the "stellar" career placement services staff. They do "an excellent job assisting MBA students find the right companies that will enable them to achieve their career goals." One student defends them in response to a few complaints from classmates: "The career services department for the MBA program offers as much support as a given student wishes to receive. It's true that they don't land the job for you, but they do offer you every tool available to find and land the job yourself." "The school is well integrated with the surrounding business community and alumni." The school provides "job fairs, recruiting events," and "a large network that includes Alumni and the professional world." Additionally, "the school makes teamwork an important part of the curriculum and as a result the students are eager to work together and help each other out." A student in the middle of a career transition explains that because of this group interaction, "I have gotten my foot in the door of four different companies by networking with my classmates." Companies recruiting on campus include: Cymer, Hewlett-Packard, California Bank & Trust, Jack in the Box, Qualcomm.

Student Life and Environment

USD offers "a very pleasant campus environment" in a convenient location that provides everything you need "in or nearby campus." "The library is amazing and provides a truly quiet and inspiring atmosphere for studies." Activities are plentiful. "There are clubs, internships, and competitions to match every major and interest," as well as "countless activities/events/speaking engagements each week that one can attend. Additionally, there are MBAR events which are nights out at local bars/clubs for MBA students which represent great social outings." The school is "close to the beach and downtown," and, "as a city, San Diego is unbeatable." Commuters will find that traffic "is not bad even during rush hour."

Classmates are "very busy due to balancing a full time career and family demands with an MBA program." Yet, they remain "active, social people who are extremely motivated to learn. Some are here to progress their careers and others to shift their focus entirely." Although they are competitive, they are also "very helpful and friendly. Everyone wants everyone else to succeed and the culture and community is very strong in that respect."

Admissions

Prospective students must hold an undergraduate degree from an accredited college with a GPA of 3.0 or better. GMAT scores, undergraduate academic performance, and work experience are all important factors in determining enrollment. Letters of recommendation, essays, and an interview are also required. Students may apply to more than one graduate program, but additional applications and associated fees apply. One set of transcripts can be used for both applications.

FINANCIAL FACTS

Annual tuition	$35,840
Fees	$270
Cost of books	$1,300
Room & board	
(on/off-campus)	$11,602/$10,980
% of students receiving aid	97
% of first-year students	
receiving aid	100
% of students receiving grants	91
Average award package	$26,336
Average grant	$9,375
Average loan	$39,204

ADMISSIONS

Admissions Selectivity Rating	79
# of applications received	141
% applicants accepted	56
% acceptees attending	24
Average GMAT	626
Range of GMAT	605–645
Average GPA	3.20
TOEFL required of	
international students	Yes
Minimum TOEFL	
(paper/computer)	580/237
Application fee	$80
International application fee	$80
Application Deadline/Notification	
Round 1:	11/15 / 1/15
Round 2:	1/15 / 3/15
Round 3:	3/15 / 5/15
Round 4:	5/15 / 7/15
Deferment available	Yes
Maximum length	
of deferment	1 year
Transfer students accepted	Yes
Transfer application policy: Only students in an affiliated "JESUIT MBA" program can be considered for transfer.	
Non-fall admissions	Yes
Need-blind admissions	Yes

EMPLOYMENT PROFILE		
Career Rating	89	**Top 5 Employers Hiring Grads**
		Cymer, Hewlett-Packard, California Bank & Trust, Jack in the Box, Qualcomm.

UNIVERSITY OF SAN FRANCISCO
MASAGUNG GRADUATE SCHOOL OF MANAGEMENT

GENERAL INFORMATION

Type of school	Private
Affiliation	Jesuit
Academic calendar	Semester

SURVEY SAYS...

Students love San Francisco, CA,
Friendly students, Good social scene,
Good peer network
Solid preparation in:
Teamwork, Doing business in a global economy, Entrepreneurial studies

STUDENTS

Enrollment of parent institution	10,017
Enrollment of MBA Program	215
% male/female	54/46
% out-of-state	30
% part-time	48
% underrepresented minority	25
% international	21
Average age at entry	30
Average years work experience at entry	5.0

ACADEMICS

Academic Experience Rating	79
Profs interesting rating	80
Profs accesible rating	86
Student/faculty ratio	11:1
% female faculty	28
% underrepresented minority faculty	32
% part-time faculty	41

Joint Degrees

DDS/MBA (in conjuction with UCSF School of Dentistry); JD/MBA; MAPS/MBA (Asia Pacific Studies); MSEM/MBA (Environmental Management); MSFA/MBA (Financial Analysis)

Academics

"A great emphasis on entrepreneurship and finance" is among the program strengths that draw MBAs to the University of San Francisco's School of Management, which offers a variety of MBA options are offered to suit all needs. USF's MBA is available in three program formats: a traditional two-year, full-time MBA, an accelerated one-year MBA, a part-time MBA, and an Executive MBA.

In all programs, USF's "strong connections with venture capitalists in the area" as well as "the technology and innovation of the Silicon Valley" help make entrepreneurship "such a strength" of this MBA program. The school's "international draw"—21 percent of students here are internationals—makes USF a great place for those interested in international business to learn and network. "I believe that anyone looking to get into international business would find USF a great fit," one student tells us. Each of USF's MBA programs maintains "small class sizes" that promote "personal relationships with professors," especially valuable since professors here "will get you business contacts." Each program embodies "the Jesuit approach toward a well-rounded education" and works at "ensuring ethics" throughout the curriculum.

Once core courses are completed, the USF curriculum is "taught in seven-week modules, which can be stressful. It's a tight workload within seven weeks, but it is also satisfying to have four classes done in seven weeks." The program places "an emphasis on group cooperation while nurturing individual growth."

Career and Placement

If you want to live and work in the Bay Area, USF will give you an edge in the local market. A staple in the community, USF has a strong alumni base and the school creates "good opportunities to network." Currently, USF graduates are employed at a range of prestigious companies, including Bank of the West, Gartner Consulting, Wells Fargo, Salesforce.com, Silicon Valley Bank, Credit Suisse, Blue Shield of CA, Pandora, Quantcast, Medivation.

For those pursuing new positions after graduation, USF Graduate Career Services hosts a variety of workshops, events, and individual advising sessions to help students with career planning and professional development. The department typically collaborates with student clubs for speakers and strongly encourages student participation at various business community events. Despite these services, students feel the office can do better. "The ability to bring in more big name companies or even jobs for the MBA students" is an area for improvement, one student writes, adding "I believe it is difficult because we have to compete with Stanford and Berkley, but USF MBA grads have a lot to offer and I believe being in San Francisco they should be marketing the MBA program much better to the job market."

ADDRESS: 101 HOWARD STREET, SAN FRANCISCO, CA 94105
PHONE: 415-422-2221 • FAX: 415-358-9112
E-MAIL: MANAGEMENT@USFCA.EDU • WEBSITE: WWW.USFCA.EDU/MBA

Student Life and Environment

USF's "wired campus" in "one of the most beautiful cities in the world" offers "good resources" to students. "We have easy access to study rooms, computers, technology, and food (very important)," one student reports. Students' involvement on campus depends on their program. Part timers here "are not very involved [with the program] outside the classroom," nor are students in the "intense" Executive MBA program, who happily report that the program "takes care of its students," a process that includes "catering all the food so you can concentrate on your classes."

Full timers, on the other hand, tell us that extracurricular life is "very active: a lot of clubs, good sport programs, a lot of speakers from Silicon Valley." There's also "Thirsty Thursday events, where students get together at local bars on Thursdays and have a drink." The event calendar is easy to track, as events "are summarized each week in an email from the VP of Marketing from the Graduate Business Association."

All here agree that San Francisco is an "excellent location" where there's "always something to do." There are "plenty of attractions nearby, including bars, parks, and museums. Students hang out with each other outside of school at these places." The MBA population is "a good mix of students in terms of background, gender, work experience" and include "many international students, students from across the U.S., married and single students, as well as students who come from all sorts of professional backgrounds."

Admissions

Admissions requirements vary among USF's various MBA programs. All require that applicants submit official transcripts for all post-secondary academic work. All but the Executive MBA require a GMAT or GRE score. At least two years of professional business experience is required for the Part-Time MBA program and two years of professional business experience is preferred for the Full-Time MBA program; the Executive MBA requires at least eight years of experience. Essays, letters of recommendation, and a current resume are required by all programs. International applicants may be required to demonstrate English proficiency through the TOEFL, IELTS, or PTE Academic. A Certification of Finances form is also required of all international students.

Prominent Alumni

Sheila Burke, The former Undersecretary of the Smithsonian; Heather Fong, The former San Francisco Police Chief; Paul Otellini, President and CEO of Intel Corporation; James Phelan, Former US Senator; Pete Rozelle, Former Commissioner of the National Football League

FINANCIAL FACTS

Annual tuition	$34,580
Fees	$200
Cost of books	$1,000
% of students receiving aid	59
% of first-year students receiving aid	53
% of students receiving grants	17
Average award package	$27,668
Average grant	$7,500
Average loan	$28,433
Average student loan debt	$70,845

ADMISSIONS

Admissions Selectivity Rating	77
# of applications received	364
% applicants accepted	58
% acceptees attending	46
Average GMAT	577
Range of GMAT	540–610
Average GPA	3.10
TOEFL required of international students	Yes
Minimum TOEFL (paper/computer)	600/250
Application fee	$55
International application fee	$55
Application Deadline/Notification	
Round 1:	12/5 / 1/16
Round 2:	2/6 / 3/20
Round 3:	5/1 / 6/12
Deferment available	Yes
Maximum length of deferment	1 year
Transfer students accepted	Yes
Transfer application policy: Students are eligible to transfer up to 6 credits when coming from another AACSB accredited program.	
Non-fall admissions	Yes
Need-blind admissions	Yes

EMPLOYMENT PROFILE

Career Rating	75
Percent employed at graduation	51
Average base starting salary	$69,353

Primary Source of Full-time Job Acceptances

School-facilitated activities	9(56%)
Graduate-facilitated activities	4(31%)
Unknown	2(13%)

Grads Employed by Function	%	Avg. Salary
Marketing	(41%)	$69,000
Operations	(6%)	$80,000
Consulting	(12%)	$87,000
Management	(6%)	$50,000
Finance	(6%)	$70,000
HR	(6%)	$55,000
Other	(24%)	$73,000

Top 5 Employers Hiring Grads
Bank of the West, Gartner Consulting, Wells Fargo, Salesforce.com, Silicon Valley Bank

UNIVERSITY OF SCRANTON
KANIA SCHOOL OF MANAGEMENT

Academics

Most of the learning at the University of Scranton is informed by the principle of *Cura Personalis*, which translates from the Latin to mean "Care for the Entire Person." What this essentially describes is a respect for and appreciation of another's unique needs, circumstances, and gifts. These Jesuit values add an element of social responsibility to the work students do at the Kania School of Management (KSOM). Being a Jesuit institution does not, however, mean that the program is in any way light or insufficient. The MBA program at Scranton is accredited by the AASCB and "has a great reputation." It simply means that in the process of achieving their goals, students can rely on each other for a sense of camaraderie and support. The program places an emphasis on globalization and the intersection of technology and business. "At KSOM the diversity of the learning environment mirrors the global and diverse business setting of today's world. It offers an environment which is collaborative, values different ideas, encourages discussion, and lets the students think about phenomena in a very creative manner."

"The school offers many classes every term," and in addition to the general MBA, students are invited to specialize in the following disciplines: accounting, finance, international business management, information systems, marketing, and operations management. There are also programs that allows students to jointly pursue both a BS and an MBA. In addition to the University of Scranton's reputation and "forward thinking" attitude, are a multitude of amenities. The Irwin E. Alperin Financial Center has a simulated trading floor where students can learn via market simulations. It even has an electronic ticker and news and data feeds. Also, the wireless system at Kania ensures 24-hour access to business applications and other online resources. The school prides itself on remaining "focused on what will be required of an MBA graduate in today's marketplace." Both a full-time and part-time track toward the MBA are offered at Kania, and those already in the workplace commend the "convenience" and "proximity" of the school. The Kania School of Management is described as an "excellent learning atmosphere," where "everyone is friendly and willing to help." "Professors are outstanding" and "provide critical insight." They are great at bringing real-world experience "into the four corners of a classroom." "They are all very well educated individuals, who take a lot of pride in teaching." Professors are also described as "accommodating to their students." As far as the administration is concerned, some say that "everything is smooth," while others complain of miscommunications with advisors and possible language barriers for international students.

Career and Placement

The Office of Career Services at the University of Scranton helps both graduate and undergraduate students find internships and full-time employment. They host workshops on various career-enhancing skills, as well as maintain an online job database. Still, students feel there are too "few job fairs," and that more of an effort needs to be made to assist students in finding "job opportunities after graduation." The Kania School of Management has "a very strong reputation" regionally. This means that students, who are up for jobs in Scranton usually get them. Of those students who responded to the poll, 95 percent had accepted employment three months after graduation. They were placed mainly in the Northeast and Middle Atlantic states. Some of the employers who hired graduates were Kraft Foods, Lowe's, PNC Bank, PricewaterhouseCoopers, and Sanofi Pasteur.

CAITLYN HOLLINGSHEAD, DIRECTOR, GRADUATE ADMISSIONS
ADDRESS: THE UNIVERSITY OF SCRANTON, OFFICE OF ADMISSIONS,
800 LINDEN STREET, SCRANTON, PA 18510-4631 • PHONE: 570-941-7600 • FAX: 570-941-5995
E-MAIL:CGCE@SCRANTON.EDU WEBSITE: SCRANTON.EDU/MBA

Student Life and Environment

"The overall environment at the University of Scranton is very inviting. The University is open to its students and has created a very comfortable environment to learn and grow as a person." Students are "supportive, understanding, mature, and family-like." They also tend to help each other out and share "similar goals." They abide by "the founding moral principle of respect and care to all people." "There are limitless offerings of activities." It seems "everyone is involved in the University and the overall community." Students span a wide range. "Some are five-year MBA program majors with little real-world work experience, while others are working adults expanding their professional backgrounds and career opportunities." The MBA Student Association "works to get all MBA students involved outside of the classroom. They have socials and presentations a few times a semester in order to get MBA students socializing."

The campus is located in downtown Scranton, in the northeastern part of Pennsylvania. It is situated in the Lackawanna River Valley and has a population of roughly 76,000 people. The school itself encompasses 58 acres and has been described by students as "scenic."

Admissions

The admissions committee requests the following from its applicants: Official GMAT scores, undergraduate GPA, personal essay, and letters of recommendation. Of those materials, GMAT score and GPA are of primary importance to the committee. Work experience will also be considered. Proficiency in English is an additional requirement. Admitted students had an average GPA of 3.2 and an average GMAT score of 510.

FINANCIAL FACTS

Annual tuition (in-state/ out-of-state)	$21,288
Fees	$2,500
Cost of books	$2,300
Room & board	$14,000
% of students receiving aid	43
% of first-year students receiving aid	50
% of students receiving grants	29
Average loan	$18,670
Average student loan debt	$14,419

ADMISSIONS

Admissions Selectivity Rating	**90**
# of applications received	346
% applicants accepted	14
% acceptees attending	45
Average GMAT	510
Average GPA	3.20
TOEFL required of international students	Yes
Minimum TOEFL (paper/computer)	500/61
International Deferment available	Yes
Maximum length of deferment	1 years
Transfer students accepted	Yes
Transfer application policy: A transfer from an AACSB-accredited Jesuit school, otherwise 6 credits max	
Non-fall admissions	Yes
Need-blind admissions	Yes

EMPLOYMENT PROFILE

Career Rating	86	Top 5 Employers Hiring Grads
Percent employed 3 months after graduation	93	Pricewaterhouse Coopers (6), Rasmussen College (4), Sanofi Pasteur (2), Bank of America (1), Deloitte (1)
Average base starting salary	$75,304	

UNIVERSITY OF SOUTH CAROLINA
MOORE SCHOOL OF BUSINESS

GENERAL INFORMATION

Type of school	Public
Affiliation	No Affiliation
Academic calendar	Semester

SURVEY SAYS...

Friendly students, Good social scene,
Good peer network, Helpful alumni
Solid preparation in:
Doing business in a global economy

STUDENTS

% male/female	72/28
% out-of-state	47
% part-time	70
% underrepresented minority	10
% international	16
Average age at entry	30
Average years work experience at entry	6.3

ACADEMICS

Academic Experience Rating	83
Profs interesting rating	88
Profs accesible rating	84
Student/faculty ratio	11:1
% female faculty	23
% underrepresented minority faculty	6
% part-time faculty	0

Joint Degrees

JD/IMBA (4 years); JD/MHR (3 years); JD/MACC (3 years); JD/MAECON (4 Years)

Prominent Alumni

Larry W. Kellner, Retired CEO/Chairman, Continental Airlines; Emory Wayne Rushton, Managing Director, Promontory Financial Group: Previously Senior Deputy Comptroller and Chief National Bank Examiner, U.S. Office of the Comptroller of the Currency; Charles S. Way, Chairman, the Beach Company [developer of Isle of Palms, Kiawah Island and other Low Country and Southeast prime real estate]

Academics

Widely considered "one of the top institutions to study international business," the Darla Moore School of Business at University of South Carolina offers an "alternative program to traditional business school" through its flagship international MBA (IMBA) program (although it does offer a professional MBA as well). The IMBA program exposes Moore's students to a combination of "international work experience, education, and opportunity to learn a new language while completing [an] MBA." The program's required core classes make lead to "well-rounded" students. In the IMBA program, "the first seven months are spent doing a year's worth of core classes. Students are very tightly woven to provide each other academic, mental, and social support. The next four (or 12) months are spent overseas learning another language…then a four to seven-month internship, internationally or domestically, followed by a year of electives (in Columbia or abroad)."

Supporting the unique structure of the program are the school's "extremely talented" and "stellar" professors who "truly bring a wealth of international experience into the classroom." These professors "teach worldwide and use cases, simulations, and other situations to help us get a better understanding of how our decisions interact instead of just reading text." They make "the most abstract material understandable." As a result, students develop "a deep understanding of business fundamentals." Particularly noteworthy is the Global Supply Chain and Operations Management department which "prepares students to manage supply chains in a global environment, and provides students with operations management knowledge and practical training that puts them at the same level [as] engineers currently working at *Fortune* 500 companies."

While generally pleased with the quality of their professors, students are a bit more critical of the business school's administration which "is new and has some kinks to work out." On a more positive note, students feel that the administration is "open to working with the students to improve the school community, which makes up for a lack of organization and gives students a chance to gain valuable leadership skills." One recent development that is generating a lot of excitement among the students is the new "green" "multimillion dollar business school building" which was designed with "input from everyone," including "undergrads, master's [students], PhD [students], [and] staff" and which all hope will "bring unbelievable opportunities for future students."

Career and Placement

The majority of students surveyed expressed the need to improve the Office of Career Management (OCM) which they suggested should "spend less time 'coaching' students and more time focusing on building relationships with employers" as well as "reach out to a more diverse company base including ones from a wider geographic range." They also point out that "the highly-touted internship experience has suffered in recent years—the result of a failure to maintain relationships with companies (specifically in Latin America)." Students realize that not all of the blame falls on the OCM and acknowledge that "classes are small and our alumni network is small as a result. We attract some *Fortune* 500 companies who recruit on campus, but because there aren't as many of us out there in leadership, sometimes it is harder for us to get our foot in the door with these companies and during the recession we were one of the first schools cut from recruiting trips as a result." One of the more optimistic students has hopes for a brighter future and observes, "The Office of Career Management has partnered this year with a new external company and I believe they are doing a good job at providing students with placement services in a difficult hiring environment."

ADMISSIONS CONTACT: SCOTT KING, DIRECTOR, ADMISSIONS-GRADUATE PROGRAMS
ADDRESS: 1705 COLLEGE STREET, COLUMBIA, SC 29208
PHONE: 803-777-4346 • FAX: 803-777-0414
E-MAIL: GRADINFO@MOORE.SC.EDU • WEBSITE: MOORE.SC.EDU

Student Life and Environment

The city of Columbia "is small but the student population makes going out fun" and "football is king." Despite its "good bar scene and nightlife," many of the students are "too busy during the core to enjoy the Columbia area. During your second year you have more of a chance, but it is a challenge to become involved in the community outside of the business school." The school campus provides "a lot of social and cultural activities" and has "everything from the normal Finance Club to Net Impact and even a Wine Society. We organize plenty of intramural teams and usually open them up to most people in the class."

The school attracts "a diverse set of students from Peace Corps volunteers to *Fortune* 500 company employees," to "Mormons with families" who all form a "very close-knit community." One student offers the more general observation that "half the students are more conservative and half are more liberal." While coming from a diverse set of backgrounds and experiences, "all are interested in new adventures and experiences particularly those having to do with learning aspects of other cultures and how their business practices differ from U.S. standards." "Overall, everyone is friendly and the atmosphere was one more of cooperation than competition."

Admissions

Applicants must submit an application, an application fee, official transcripts of post-secondary academic work, personal essays, letters of recommendation, and an official GMAT score report. International students must also submit TOEFL or IELTS scores unless they are graduates of an American college or university. Strong preference is shown for applicants with at least two years of work experience.

FINANCIAL FACTS

Annual tuition (in-state/ out-of-state)	$40,229/$68,805
Fees	$525
Cost of books	$2,000
Room & board (on/off-campus)	$15,000/$18,000
% of students receiving aid	61
% of first-year students receiving aid	59

ADMISSIONS

Admissions Selectivity Rating	82
# of applications received	
Average GMAT	633
TOEFL required of international students	Yes
Minimum TOEFL (paper/computer)	600/250
Application fee	$100
International application fee	$100
Early application deadline	11/15
Early notification date	1/15
Regular application deadline	5/1
Regular application notification	6/8
Application Deadline/Notification	
Round 1:	11/15 / 1/15
Round 2:	2/15 / 3/15
Round 3:	5/1 / 6/8
Deferment available	Yes
Maximum length of deferment	1 Year
Transfer students accepted	Yes
Transfer application policy: Can transfer up to a maximum of 12 credit hours (4 courses)	
Non-fall admissions	Yes
Need-blind admissions	Yes

EMPLOYMENT PROFILE

Career Rating	78	Grads Employed by Function	% Avg. Salary
Percent employed at graduation	53	Marketing	(30%) $78,650
Percent employed 3 months after graduation	30	Operations	(14%) $73,333
		Consulting	(14%) $60,492
Average base starting salary	$72,399	Management	(8%) $60,375
Primary Source of Full-time Job Acceptances		Finance	(34%) $76,071
School-facilitated activities	22(51%)	Other	(7%)
Graduate-facilitated activities	20(47%)	**Top 5 Employers Hiring Grads**	
Unknown	1(2%)	Bank of America (2), Exxonmobil (2), Wipro (3), Honeywell (1), Hewlett Packard (1)	

THE UNIVERSITY OF SOUTH DAKOTA
BEACOM SCHOOL OF BUSINESS

GENERAL INFORMATION

Type of school	Public
Affiliation	No Affiliation
Academic calendar	Semester

SURVEY SAYS...

Good peer network
Solid preparation in:
Finance, Communication/interpersonal skills, Quantitative skills

STUDENTS

Enrollment of parent institution	9,970
Enrollment of MBA Program	239
% male/female	70/30
% out-of-state	3
% part-time	84
% underrepresented minority	1
% international	2
Average age at entry	29
Average years work experience at entry	3.5

ACADEMICS

Academic Experience Rating	73
Profs interesting rating	76
Profs accesible rating	73
Student/faculty ratio	6:1
% female faculty	46
% underrepresented minority faculty	32
% part-time faculty	0

Joint Degrees

JD/MBA - approximately 3 years of full time study

Prominent Alumni

John Thune, US Senator from South Dakota

Academics

The University of South Dakota "has a very good reputation among business schools in the area." Indeed, it has the best reputation as "it is the only accredited school in the state," and students in South Dakota appreciate the quality education and proximity to home. "Tuition is extremely affordable" at the University of South Dakota, which allows students "to pursue an MBA without taking on added debt." "I attended USD for my undergraduate degree, and I was offered a traineeship position as part of the graduate program," a health services administration student explains. Students also "love the online MBA program," which is something of a rarity for MBA programs. "My research that led me to select USD indicated that it is one of the few online MBA programs that is accredited," says one student. The online program "is tough and challenging, yet possible to complete while working a full-time job."

The University of South Dakota "has great facilities. Many of the major buildings, including the business school and student center, have been built within the last couple years." The "solid administration" is always "only a phone call or email away." "IT help has great customer service and follow-up." However, some students feel "the University tries to be forward-looking but ends up relying on outdated logic and 'rules.' The University needs to evolve along with social attitudes and needs of its students." "USD routinely makes big changes or implementations without seeking any student feedback" and "seems to be focused mostly on undergraduate enrollment more than on investing in and improving current programs." Fortunately, the program has also been making some positive changes to the MBA. Previously, students noted that the school was "very flexible" with course schedules; today, administrators have reworked the program to allow more frequent course offerings.

"The faculty is the greatest strength at this school," providing great "human capital" for the school. "The professors at USD are a very diverse group of individuals" and "take a vested interest in the success of their students." "The professors are very professional and have an open-door policy. They strongly encourage anyone to stop by and ask questions or just talk," one student explains. Although other students caution that while "the professors that have been teaching for a while are amazing," many other teachers "with little to no real-world experience . . . have no idea how to teach" and rely too heavily on PowerPoint. The school boasts "small class sizes" which help students "get to know each other and their professors and actually develop friendships and relationships that help the learning environment."

Career and Placement

One of the Beacom School of Business's "greatest strengths is placement for internships and jobs." The school brings companies into the "business school to hold interviews for jobs." "I received an internship and a job with a top-four accounting firm," says one student. However, others say "the job fairs have the same 30 employers" that are mostly "accounting and insurance companies." The school needs to gain "more national contacts for employment of new graduates (more specifically in major commerce areas . . . like Chicago and New York)," and "there needs to be more variety in company types and in specific employers."

About 48 percent of students are in finance and accounting, and 38 percent of recent graduates found government employment. The average salary for new graduates is about $43,000. Some companies that have recruited out of the University of South Dakota include FDIC, Citi, and Sanford Health.

ADMISSIONS CONTACT: DR. ANGELINE LAVIN, MBA AND MPA PROGRAMS DIRECTOR
ADDRESS: 414 E. CLARK, SCHOOL OF BUSINESS, VERMILLION, SD 57069
PHONE: 866-890-1622 • FAX: 605-677-5058
E-MAIL: MBA@USD.EDU • WEBSITE: WWW.USD.EDU/MBA

Student Life and Environment

Students here "are diverse people of all different age groups" who are "intelligent, ambitious, outgoing, and friendly." "These people will be successful someday," boasts one student. "Most are young (early to mid-20s)" and "either just completed their undergrad or have a few years of work experience." Students work together and are "eager to help answer each other's questions and share how course topics relate to their jobs or past experiences." The school needs "more ethnic diversity" though, as the student body is predominantly white. "I wouldn't say ethnically diverse [students], but [they are] intellectually very diverse, with points of view that add to classroom discussion in a very productive manner," one student offers.

"The University of South Dakota is in the small town of Vermillion," a "very outdoor-oriented town" that provides "a small-town feel with a big-town university." It is the kind of town where "you see your friends on every corner." "Many students walk to class," although that can be a problem during the cold winters. "I've walked to class this year multiple times in sub-zero weather. It'd be great to have underground tunnels," one student says. "The city of Vermillion is very limiting," and there isn't much to do "if you don't hunt or fish." However, the actual campus is "very nice, especially for business students who get to enjoy a brand new building." Students did wish "housing officials [weren't so] anti-drinking". As one student puts it, "It's a college campus; get over it."

Admissions

The Beacom School of Business offers three types of MBA programs: on-campus, online, or hybrid (online and on-campus). All three require an undergraduate degree, GMAT scores, resume, statement of purpose, and two letters of recommendation. The average GMAT score for last year was 552.

FINANCIAL FACTS

Annual tuition (in-state/ out-of-state)	$6,494/$13,746
Fees	$5,826
Cost of books	$1,700
% of students receiving aid	57
% of first-year students receiving aid	56
% of students receiving grants	18
Average award package	$16,134
Average grant	$988
Average loan	$16,039

ADMISSIONS

Admissions Selectivity Rating	73
# of applications received	80
% applicants accepted	84
% acceptees attending	82
Average GMAT	534
Range of GMAT	480–590
Average GPA	3.34
TOEFL required of international students	Yes
Minimum TOEFL (paper/computer)	550/213
Application fee	$35
International application fee	$35
Regular application deadline	6/1
Deferment available	Yes
Maximum length of deferment	3 Semesters
Transfer students accepted	Yes
Transfer application policy: Maximum of 9 credit hours from an accredited institution may be transferred.	
Non-fall admissions	Yes
Need-blind admissions	Yes

EMPLOYMENT PROFILE

Career Rating		75
Percent employed at graduation		21
Percent employed 3 months after graduation		39
Primary Source of Full-time Job Acceptances		
School-facilitated activities	8(42%)	
Graduate-facilitated activities	7(37%)	
Unknown	4(21%)	

Grads Employed by Function% Avg. Salary		
Marketing	(21%)	$40,000
Consulting	(5%)	$50,500
Management	(21%)	
Finance	(33%)	$39,489
HR	(5%)	
MIS	(5%)	$42,000
Other	(10%)	

Top 5 Employers Hiring Grads
Avera McKennan (2), Target (1), POET (1), Eide Bailly (1), Wells Fargo (1)

University of Southern California
Marshall School of Business

Academics

Offering "international business learning opportunities not available elsewhere" as well as solid programs in entrepreneurship, real estate, marketing, and entertainment, the University of Southern California's Marshall School of Business excels in a broad range of areas. Best of all, perhaps, USC boasts "the most amazing alumni network in the nation," a huge asset when the time for job searches arrives. As one student explains, "I have never met another Trojan anywhere in the world who wasn't excited to meet another fellow Trojan!" "The Trojan Network is enormous and expansive, providing a lifetime equity of resources."

Marshall offers a two-year full-time program as well as a part-time evening MBA, an executive MBA, and a one-year international MBA (called the IBEAR MBA). The school "combines a rigorous curriculum" with "the personal attention of a private college." The MBA program here "has a strong emphasis on providing students an international perspective on business issues. It is more than just saying 'We think it is important that you consider other cultures.' At Marshall, it's mandatory that all students work on a consulting project for a company overseas and travel to that region through the PRIME program. As a result of PRIME and other programs, I've had meaningful work, educational, and fun experiences in Singapore, Thailand, Vietnam, and in Western Europe."

Marshall professors "are outstanding. They bring new research into the classroom and encourage students to actively participate in class." The faculty represents "a mixture of academics and recent career switchers from their fields in business...they do a very good job giving us a base to learn from." Course work is demanding; one student warns, "Marshall is much more difficult than I expected. I have nine years of work experience and consider myself a fairly bright individual. If I put in a decent amount of work and keep up with the reading, I can get a B-plus in our classes with relative ease, but it really is difficult to break the A barrier." Administrators "are committed to growth and innovation as an institution." As a result, "Chaos is inherent when new programs and classes are initiated.... This is a leading school's greatest challenge, and USC Marshall does everything in its power to attend to students' individual needs as well as meet their own goals and expectations."

Career and Placement

Marshall's Career Resources Center "has already made incredible changes" since bringing on a new director five years ago. "The resources and energy the career coaches bring to the students are head and shoulders above what students at [another prominent area business school] have. While I'm sure the CRC will continue to improve and bring in more high-profile companies, it is already a premier organization." Students praise the center's one-week winter inter-term program for first-years, through which "students learn how to fine tune their resume and interview skills. Additionally, they learn about networking, discover their inner interests, and come up with a value proposition. I believe this gives Marshall students a leg up in recruiting."

Companies most likely to employ Marshall MBAs include: Deloitte, Johnson & Johnson, Cisco, Booz, Toyota, Samsung, General Electric, IBM, Hewlett Packard, PriceWaterhouseCoopers, and Houlihan Lokey.

Student Life and Environment

Full-time students tell us that "there are numerous professional and social club opportunities in which to be involved at Marshall." Several point out that "being involved with the community is easy and fun due to the Challenge 4 Charity Club, which schedules regular volunteer days for junior achievement and hosts parties at popular LA night clubs where the entry fees are donated to the Special Olympics." One student adds, "With the numerous clubs and organizations, USC students are really only limited by the amount of time and energy they possess. Personally, I wanted to take a leadership role in the community, and have had the opportunity to do just that. That makes my schedule a little bit more hectic than normal, but that was a personal decision. Really, life at Marshall is as challenging as one has the ambition to make it." Throughout the program and the campus, students enjoy "a very communal atmosphere. Football season is amazing."

Los Angeles is a great hometown, "a fun and vibrant city" with "fabulous weather all year round." Students note that "living in LA requires a car" and tell us that there are "nice apartments by the ocean for a decent price" within a 20-minute commute of the campus. The city provides many opportunities "to spend time together outside of class." "There are parties or small get-togethers almost every weekend."

Admissions

The Marshall Admissions Office warns that its MBA programs are "highly selective," and that the Admissions Committee "carefully assesses each candidate on a number of dimensions, including prior academic, professional, and personal accomplishments." All applicants must provide the school with official transcripts for all postsecondary academic work, an official GMAT score report, an official TOEFL score report (for international students who have not previously attended an English-language undergraduate or graduate program), an online application, a current resume, three required essays (a fourth optional essay is available), and two letters of recommendation (at least one from a direct supervisor is preferred).

Prominent Alumni

Ronnie C. Chan, Chairman, Hang Lung Group Ltd.

FINANCIAL FACTS

Annual tuition	$48,515
Fees	$3,125
Cost of books	$1,344
Room & board	$15,900

ADMISSIONS

Admissions Selectivity Rating	95
# of applications received	1,794
% applicants accepted	30
% acceptees attending	41
Average GMAT	690
Range of GMAT	660–720
Average GPA	3.30
TOEFL required of international students	Yes
Minimum TOEFL (paper/computer)	600
Application fee	$150
International application fee	$150
Application Deadline/Notification	
Round 1:	11/1 / 2/1
Round 2:	1/15 / 4/1
Round 3:	3/15 / 5/15
Deferment available	No
Transfer students accepted	No
Non-fall admissions	No
Need-blind admissions	Yes

EMPLOYMENT PROFILE

Career Rating	95	Grads Employed by Function	% Avg. Salary
Percent employed at graduation	66	Marketing	(26%) $96,237
Percent employed 3 months after graduation	77	Consulting	(17%)$110,833
		Finance	(37%) $95,706
Average base starting salary	$97,921	Other	(20%) $88,842
Primary Source of Full-time Job Acceptances			
School-facilitated activities	56(51%)		
Graduate-facilitated activities	17(15%)		
Unknown	37(34%)		

University of Southern Maine

School of Business

GENERAL INFORMATION

Type of school	Public
Affiliation	No Affiliation
Academic calendar	Semester

SURVEY SAYS...

Students love Portland, ME, Good
social scene
Solid preparation in:
General management

STUDENTS

Enrollment of parent institution	9,382
Enrollment of MBA Program	135
% male/female	71/29
% out-of-state	0
% part-time	79
% underrepresented minority	0
% international	0
Average age at entry	30
Average years work experience at entry	5.1

ACADEMICS

Academic Experience Rating	81
Profs interesting rating	78
Profs accesible rating	81
Student/faculty ratio	17:1
% female faculty	24
% underrepresented minority faculty	0
% part-time faculty	0

Joint Degrees

3-2 Master of Business
Administration, 5.5-6 years; B.S.
and MBA MS in Nursing and MBA,
3-4 years; JD/MBA, 4-5 years;
Master of Public Health and MBA,
3-4 years

Academics

University of Southern Maine's MBA program distinguishes itself through strong academics, "relatively low cost," and a decidedly local focus. This "internationally accredited" program is the best choice for Portland-area professionals, offering "convenient class times" and an easily accessible location on the school's main campus. Busy students appreciate that "most professors offer very organized courses with defined expectations and outcomes." Despite efficiency, USM is "not an online school or a '3-week' MBA, but is a traditional business school with the rigors that come with it." The school augments the part-time program with a special 3-2 degree, through which business undergraduates can earn an MBA with just one additional year of full-time study.

With a strong background in the real world, "faculty is very professional, and topics covered are generally relevant and current." Students explain that "certain professors are more cutting edge and prepare you better for an innovative and sustainable professional culture than others, but the majority stay current and keep you up to date." Maine business plays a central role in the curriculum, and "the professors also do an excellent job using case studies from local companies." On that note, "USM has a lot of connections to the business community and works with them often, which helps create experience and visibility." While the program offers concentrations in accounting, finance, sustainability, or health management and policy, students would "absolutely love the school to offer targeted MBA courses (or someday concentrations) specific to some of Maine's fastest growing industries, such as biotechnology, medical devices, IT, etc." Students also note that "more interpersonal or organizational development classes could be offered as electives," along with a greater focus on entrepreneurship.

Drawing from the local business community, "the majority of USM MBA students study part time and are involved in diverse industry sectors, from food to music to finance to health care and to biotechnology." The varied experience among the student body "keeps business projects and case studies interesting, with diverse opinions and ideas to bring back to my own career." When it comes to staff and administrators, "some will do anything for students, while others will ignore their needs." In addition, students have noticed "political strife among the faculty and administration at the school." At the same time, "it's very easy to get into both required and popular classes" at University of Southern Maine, which distinguishes it from many other part-time business schools, and students are quick to point out that "the good side outweighs the bad by a large margin."

Career and Placement

Many of University of Southern Maine's graduate students are already working in the region, with plans to remain at their current companies after graduation. For those who'd like to make a career change, the School of Business Career Services and Internships Office operates an online job development website where current undergraduate and graduate students can search for open positions, take career assessments, and research companies and industries. The office offers resume and cover letter critiques, salary negotiation assistance, and individual career counseling. It also organizes a series of employer sessions, where students can meet with representatives from local companies. In addition to the services offered through the business school, there is a University-wide career fair every spring, which includes opportunities for MBA graduates.

Within the business school, the administration is eager to present new professional opportunities to its students. In addition to online resources, "Several times a week we get emails for job and intern openings." In fact, a current student shares, "I get more emails about job openings than anything else from USM. While I am employed, it's nice to see what other opportunities are available in the local market."

Student Life and Environment

On this Portland campus, students join the MBA program from a mix of industries, and encompass a "nice mix of ages, from 22 to 50." In the part-time program, "most MBA students live off campus, work full time, and take classes part time," which means they are rarely able to participate in extracurricular or social activities. "There really isn't that much to do as far as clubs and student organizations are concerned," and, unfortunately, "due to budget issues, the childcare and spouse programs had to be cut last year." However, unlike many part-time programs, "commuter MBA students do have opportunities to join clubs, workshops, and more" at USM. A current student assures us that "not many people stay on campus, but those who do have a great time" with their classmates. No matter what their involvement in campus life, "UMS MBA students are incredible friends, mentors, advisors, and team members."

Life at USM has recently made a big step up, as "new buildings were just added" to the business school campus, which "offer study areas and kitchen areas." On the greater campus, "the gym is excellent," and the range of "art and cultural events here are phenomenal." Off campus, "the city of Portland offers an amazing quality of life with affordable housing in the rural suburbs and a great, but safe, night life." With many wonderful restaurants and cafes near campus, "there is always a place to relax with your professors after class or meet with your teammates."

Admissions

Applications for University of Southern Maine's MBA program are accepted on a rolling basis, though prospective students who would like to be considered for a scholarship must apply early in the admissions cycle. Students are evaluated based on their undergraduate performance, potential for success in the program, and demonstrated leadership experience. For regular admission, prospective students must have a GMAT score of 500 or higher. The average GMAT for entering students is 570. Students may apply to the 3-2 program directly from high school or during their undergraduate studies at USM.

FINANCIAL FACTS

Annual tuition (in-state/ out-of-state)	$6,840/$18,468
Fees	$778
Cost of books	$1,200
Room & board (on/off-campus)	$11,230

ADMISSIONS

Admissions Selectivity Rating	82
# of applications received	57
% applicants accepted	60
% acceptees attending	85
Average GMAT	556
Range of GMAT	500–610
Average GPA	3.32
TOEFL required of international students	Yes
Minimum TOEFL (paper/computer)	550/213
Application fee	$65
International application fee	$65
Early application deadline	1/15
Regular application deadline	8/1
Deferment available	Yes
Maximum length of deferment	1 year
Transfer students accepted	Yes
Transfer application policy: A maximum of nine Semester hours of transfer credit may be accepted. Please see catalog. http://usm.maine.edu/catalogs	
Non-fall admissions	Yes
Need-blind admissions	Yes

THE UNIVERSITY OF TAMPA
JOHN H. SYKES COLLEGE OF BUSINESS

GENERAL INFORMATION

Type of school	Private
Affiliation	No Affiliation
Academic calendar	Semester

SURVEY SAYS...
Students love Tampa, FL
Solid preparation in:
Teamwork, Communication/interpersonal skills, Presentation skills

STUDENTS

Enrollment of parent institution	6,912
Enrollment of MBA Program	365
% male/female	57/43
% out-of-state	24
% part-time	17
% underrepresented minority	44
% international	30
Average age at entry	29
Average years work experience at entry	1.0

ACADEMICS

Academic Experience Rating	85
Profs interesting rating	84
Profs accesible rating	89
Student/faculty ratio	10:1
% female faculty	32
% underrepresented minority faculty	14
% part-time faculty	13

Joint Degrees
MS-ACC/MBA 16-30 months, MS-FIN/MBA 16-30 months, MS-MKT/MBA 16-30 months, MSN/MBA 16-30 months

Prominent Alumni
Dennis Zank, COO, Raymond James; John M. Barrett, President and CEO, First Citrus Bank; William N. Cantrell, President, Peoples Gas System; John Friedery, Senior VP, CFO, Ball Corporation; Karen Surplus, CFO, DNAprint Genomics, Inc.

Academics

The MBA program at the University of Tampa's John H. Sykes College of Business provides "a great, friendly place to study," with "small class sizes" that "enhance class interaction and active participation" and a "cheap tuition" that students can't help but appreciate. The school offers students three curricular options: a full-time program that can be completed in 16 months, a part-time program (with "a course schedule that is excellent for the working professional") that is typically completed in about three years, and a six-term Executive MBA program for business leaders ("the only true Saturday program in the area," one student tells us). Roughly one-third of the student body attends full time.

In all programs, students tout the curriculum, which "is outlined with a lower core, integrated core, and principal concentration that involves three electives. The program is flexible with the electives if you wanted to do a general MBA concentration." "Most of the classes require heavy interaction instead of just the instructor speaking," one MBA student writes, adding, "This leads to a lot of good insight and interesting conversations." Concentrations are available in entrepreneurship, finance, information systems management, international business, [innovation] management, marketing, and nonprofit management.

MBAs are just as sanguine about their instructors. UT Professors "are willing to give their personal cell phone numbers and adapt to office hours at the students availability." Their only complaint is that they feel some instructors aren't utilized "to their full potential. For example, for finance courses, it would be cool if students got a field trip to a trading floor somewhere in either Tampa, or anywhere in the U.S. Other more hands on activities like that for other majors too would be good." Still, students generally concur that; overall, "The academic experience is excellent. The school has built an environment that pushes the students to talk to each other, and ask each other for support." Administrators "focus on teamwork and building an environment that puts very little stress on the student." Students also appreciate how the administration "strives to remain cutting edge by preparing students as leaders in this new global marketplace." One student sums up, "The University of Tampa does an excellent job preparing you for the business world."

Career and Placement

UT's Office of Career Services provides Sykes MBAs with a battery of services, including assessment tests, workshops in business etiquette and business dress, one-on-one counseling, and job fairs. Students here praise "the professors' desire to help students obtain careers after graduation." Attendees of a recent on-campus career fair included ADP, Central Intelligence Agency, Chase Retirement Services, Deloitte, Franklin Templeton Investment, Geico, New York Life Insurance Company, Raymond James Financial, Syniverse Technologies Inc., Target Corporation, T. Rowe Price, The Nielsen Company, U.S. Department of State and USAA.

Student Life and Environment

UT students reap the benefits of "a beautiful campus and of course, warm weather and beaches" as well as a "business building that is top notch, with up-to-date facilities." MBAs enjoy access to "outstanding educational, professional and social events for future business leaders," including "numerous seminars in which well-known CEOs and entrepreneurs make presentations throughout the semester. This provides excellent networking opportunities." The MBA program hosts "numerous clubs and local activities advertised weekly," and students with the time to spare also enjoy "sporting events on and around campus."

Not all can. About one-third of students here attend full-time, and they generally reap the benefits of the gorgeous, lively campus. The rest are part-timers, typically working full time in addition to their class work; they have little time for anything other than school assignments. The school draws a diverse student body "with people from different cultures and countries" as well as different professional backgrounds. The school works hard to build cohorts that exploit these differences "so that everyone brings something to the table. We get along great and have in-depth discussions."

Students' wish list for quality of life improvements include more parking facilities. One writes, "Parking has always been an issue for this school. The student population is constantly growing, thereby requiring an increase in faculty and staff. Most of the area on campus is developed with various types of buildings (administrative, classrooms, residence halls, etc.) and although there are two parking garages it is sometimes difficult to find convenient parking." Some full-timers also feel that "Day care is needed as well as the introduction of family activities in order to get spouses and children more involved in students' lives. Many of us are so busy studying and doing assignments that our home life is highly affected."

Admissions

Admission to the full-time and part-time MBA programs at Sykes is based on undergraduate work; GMAT score (average score is 550); demonstration of proficiency in mathematics, computers, and written and oral communications skills; and professional experience. International students must demonstrate proficiency in English by scoring at least 577 on the written TOEFL, 230 on the computer-based TOEFL, 90 on the Internet-based TOEFL, or 7.0 on the IELTS. Admission to the Executive MBA program requires relevant work experience; applicants are required to have seven years of relevant work experience. Applicants to all programs must submit two letters of recommendation, a resume, and a personal statement.

FINANCIAL FACTS

Annual tuition	$8,560
Fees	$80
Cost of books	$800
Room & board	$9,116
% of students receiving aid	54
% of first-year students receiving aid	64
% of students receiving grants	5
Average award package	$15,776
Average grant	$8,172
Average loan	$13,246
Average student loan debt	$33,336

ADMISSIONS

Admissions Selectivity Rating	76
# of applications received	473
% applicants accepted	62
% acceptees attending	41
Average GMAT	550
Range of GMAT	480–600
Average GPA	3.40
TOEFL required of international students	Yes
Minimum TOEFL (paper/computer)	577/230
Application fee	$40
International application fee	$40
Early application deadline	6/1
Regular application deadline	7/15
Deferment available	Yes
Maximum length of deferment	1 year
Transfer students accepted	Yes
Transfer application policy: Up to 8 hrs. from an AACSB accredited school	
Non-fall admissions	Yes
Need-blind admissions	Yes

EMPLOYMENT PROFILE

Career Rating	86
Percent employed at graduation	41
Percent employed 3 months after graduation	61
Average base starting salary	$55,109

Primary Source of Full-time Job Acceptances

School-facilitated activities	12(19%)
Graduate-facilitated activities	34(53%)
Unknown	18(28%)

Grads Employed by Function	% Avg. Salary
Marketing	(7%) $47,500
Operations	(13%) $48,750
Management	(13%) $65,833
Finance	(27%) $65,833
HR	(7%) $37,500
MIS	(7%) $67,500
Other	(27%) $48,333

Top 5 Employers Hiring Grads
Citi (2), Bank of America (1), Price Waterhouse Cooper (1), The Hartford Insurance Group (1), United Way (1)

THE UNIVERSITY OF TENNESSEE AT CHATTANOOGA
COLLEGE OF BUSINESS

GENERAL INFORMATION
Type of school   Public
Affiliation   No Affiliation
Academic calendar   Semester

SURVEY SAYS...
Students love Chattanooga, TN
Solid preparation in:
Accounting, Computer skills

STUDENTS
Enrollment of parent
  institution   11,660
Enrollment of MBA Program   280
% male/female   59/41
% out-of-state   10
% part-time   75
% underrepresented minority   11
% international   2
Average age at entry   27
Average years work experience
  at entry   4.0

ACADEMICS
Academic Experience Rating   80
Profs interesting rating   80
Profs accesible rating   81
Student/faculty ratio   23:1
% female faculty   32
% underrepresented minority
  faculty   4
% part-time faculty   11

Prominent Alumni
General B. B. Bell, Four-Star
General in U. S. Army; The
Honorable Mercer Reynolds III

Academics

Celebrating its 50th anniversary in 2013, the University of Tennessee at Chattanooga offers students "quality academic programs in a great city." The school's focus on current events keeps students in the business school "really up-to-date" and "relevant" to "the global business world." The ability to "adapt to current business trends" allows students to obtain "the most realistic view of the business world today." A recently built Bloomberg lab is a "great resource" for MBA students. Classes push students to achieve both as individuals and as part of a team. "The required group project for almost every class is a great tool for honing group skills, communication, and offers networking opportunities."

Working students find the school's MBA schedule very accommodating. They note the flexible schedule and the administration's ability to adjust "to a changing business environment," as important factors in melding their work schedule and education schedule. Some students wish the workload was a little more challenging but others agree with this student's comment that "UTC not only challenges me to push my limits, but also does so in a way that I enjoy it and know it will be put to good use one day." Praise is given to the "very strong" finance department, which possesses several professors who are "an [asset] to the program" and also maintains strong working "relationships with local businesses." This is a major benefit for those entering the workforce. Another student notes the MBA program's strength of creating a well-rounded graduate saying, "I have acquired skills that help me in management, ethical decision making, strategy development, and presentation skills. I have become a better person and a better, more marketable employee as a result of my education at UTC."

On the whole, students in UTC's MBA program are satisfied with their professors, who "bring real work experience and examples to class." Professors have such "a love for their fields" that one student says they are "trying to sell students" on making their class your concentrations. The "real world experience" taught in these lessons creates engaging classes. "Many professors don't just teach from a textbook, they teach from experience." The "years of experience in their fields" definitely "show."

The administration functions efficiently. They keep "everything running very smoothly" and show a "dedicated commitment to the success of each executive MBA student." The "friendly" and "focused" students are "hard-working" and always "ready to take on a challenge." At least one student would like to see more focus on creating a sense of student "unity" within the MBA program. There was a "desperate" need for a new library, which has been answered. A new "state of the art" building is currently being built.

Career and Placement

Chattanooga is a good place to be these days. "The city is growing so much and attracting so many talented professionals." This growth can "only benefit the school." There is already a strong trend of "local businesses willing to partner with us." "The school has the greatest number of business resources and is located in a town known for entrepreneurship. The linkages between the school and the business community are strong and are continuously growing."

The school has several well-honed systems in place to assist students in their job pursuits. Annual reports, job postings, an annual career fair, and recruitment interview sessions help students prepare and search for their future career. The surrounding Chattanooga community "offers an excellent opportunity for connecting graduate students with local business executives."

ADMISSIONS CONTACT: BONNY CLARK, GRADUATE PROGRAM LIAISON
ADDRESS: GRADUATE SCHOOL, DEPARTMENT 5305, 615 MCCALLIE AVENUE, CHATTANOOGA, TN 37403
PHONE: 423-425-4667 • FAX: 423-425-5223
E-MAIL: BONNY-CLARK@UTC.EDU • WEBSITE: WWW.UTC.EDU/ACADEMIC/BUSINESS

Student Life and Environment

UTC has "a beautiful campus in a beautiful city," and "the school is well integrated with the local community." For some, student life "is very fulfilling on both an academic and a social level," yet others feel "there are no social activities or networking opportunities for graduate students outside of school." Many students work full-time and may have families, which keep them from fully utilizing the school's extracurricular activities. They "come to class and go home." One student notes, "Classes are offered around a working schedule, but outside of that not much is offered." A grad student who has attended some school activities and clubs still feels "left out" as the school seems to be more "focused on undergrads." Another student agrees, "There are no graduate student clubs or associations for business students." For those who can stay on campus a little longer, there is a "great," "new fitness center," which "is open to students, faculty and alumni."

Admissions

Gaining admittance to the UTC Graduate School is a prerequisite for applicants to the MBA program. Students must have a minimum 2.7 GPA and minimum 450 GMAT score for consideration. Applications are accepted on a rolling basis and due 30 days before the start of the semester. Official transcripts from one's universities are required as are GMAT scores, which average 509, and GPAs, which average 3.12. Work experience, although not mandatory, can prove to be advantageous in the admissions process. GRE scores may be submitted in lieu of GMAT scores. International students whose first language is not English must submit an official score report for the TOEFL (minimum grade required: 550, paper-based; 213, computer-based; 79 Internet-based) or the IELTS (minimum score 6.0).

FINANCIAL FACTS

% of students receiving aid	54
% of first-year students receiving aid	76
% of students receiving grants	10
Average award package	$16,920
Average grant	$7,747
Average loan	$19,164
Average student loan debt	$30,613

ADMISSIONS

Admissions Selectivity Rating	80
# of applications received	164
% applicants accepted	57
% acceptees attending	80
Average GMAT	492
Range of GMAT	450–570
Average GPA	3.29
TOEFL required of international students	Yes
Minimum TOEFL (paper/computer)	550/213
Application fee	$30
International application fee	$35
Deferment available	Yes
Maximum length of deferment	1 year
Transfer students accepted	Yes

Transfer application policy: Students can transfer up to six hours from an AACSB accredited school. All transfer courses are subject to department approval.

Non-fall admissions	Yes
Need-blind admissions	Yes

EMPLOYMENT PROFILE

Career Rating	68	Top 5 Employers Hiring Grads
		Blue Cross Blue Shield, Unum, TVA, Decosimo and Company, Volkswagen

THE UNIVERSITY OF TENNESSEE AT KNOXVILLE
COLLEGE OF BUSINESS ADMINISTRATION

GENERAL INFORMATION
Type of school   Public
Affiliation   No Affiliation
Academic calendar   Semester

SURVEY SAYS...
Good social scene, Cutting-edge
classes, Happy students, Smart
classrooms
Solid preparation in:
Teamwork, Presentation skills,
Computer skills

STUDENTS
Enrollment of parent
  institution   25,418
Enrollment of MBA Program   149
% male/female   72/28
% part-time   0
% underrepresented minority   17
% international   8
Average age at entry   26
Average years work experience
  at entry   3.0

ACADEMICS
Academic Experience Rating   **84**
Profs interesting rating   84
Profs accesible rating   81
Student/faculty ratio   5:1
% female faculty   37
% underrepresented minority
  faculty   3

Joint Degrees
MBA/MS Business Analytics - 2
years; JD/MBA, 4years;
MBA/Masters in Engineering, 2
years + 6 week summer session;
MBA/MS Sport Managment, 2
years; MBA/ Masters in Agricultural
Economics, 2 years; MBA/ PharmD,
5 years

Prominent Alumni
Ralph Heath, VP & COO, Lockheed
Martin Aeronautics; Kiran Patel,
CFO, Solectron; Kevin Clayton,
President & CEO, Clayton Homes;
Bob Hall, CEO, Jewelry Television by
ACN; James Gower, President &
CEO, Rigel Pharmaceuticals

Academics

You'll be glad for the opportunity to join "an institution steeped in tradition and pride" and to "get an excellent education at an affordable price from professors who care, in an environment that promotes a full student life," but you'll have to work for it. Packing a full MBA program (including a required internship) into an intense three semesters is a challenge, but it is one students welcome thanks to educators who "are passionate about teaching their subject matter. There is not the overwhelming emphasis present in the classroom that they are 'too busy' to teach or help students that need it outside of class." The key is in making the subject matter engaging and interesting. "They have real world experience that they apply to the classroom, and they are very informed in all areas of business." These "very engaging" professors "have a great sense of humor, which makes the material 100 times more interesting."

Notably, "the professors all have lengthy experience working in industry prior to teaching, so the lessons are very well grounded in what actually takes place outside of academia." Even more important, these educators "continue to remain active in their previous fields, so they continue to infuse current lessons learned from industry into their classes." This means "they teach you skills that you can use in the real world." Those skills come through an education Knoxville students can tailor to suit their own needs, choosing to either focus on a single concentration or to pursue a dual major. Supply chain management "is the program's flagship area of study," but majors in areas like engineering, sports management or business analytics, and academic concentrations in entrepreneurship and innovation, finance, operations management, and marketing are all on the agenda.

While "there have been a few communication issues between the professors and staff," by and large students praise the accessibility of their teachers and the work of the administration. "The administration works hard to make everything easy for potential and current students," while professors "are very easy to contact and very willing to help." Indeed, "faculty and staff are always available to talk about our career paths and advise us for the future." None of it comes easily—in the classroom, students "are challenged and expected to give maximum effort in order to succeed" —but students wouldn't have it any other way. One student sums it up: "Overall, this program has been a great academic experience and I learn something new about myself and my leadership skills every day."

Career and Placement

Connections and opportunities abound. "The program emphasizes career placement and devotes a lot of time to teaching business skills needed for effective job search and interviewing." The staff can be "instrumental in making professional connections." The program here provides "a lot of networking opportunities in the southeast." In addition, the faculty "are very active in helping find internships as well as providing interview prep and resume writing assistance. They provide a lot of networking lunches, dinners, and other opportunities as well as interesting speakers like the CEO of Walmart."

Most students find placement in the South (about 50 percent) and the Midwest (about 20 percent), with 40 percent of graduates taking jobs in logistics or operations. In recent years, graduating UTK students reported a mean base salary of about $75,000, with a salary range between $33,000 and $100,000.

ADMISSIONS CONTACT: DONNA POTTS, DIRECTOR OF ADMISSIONS, MBA PROGRAM
ADDRESS: 504 HASLAM BUSINESS BUILDING, KNOXVILLE, TN 37996-4150
PHONE: 865-974-5033 • FAX: 865-974-3826
E-MAIL: MBA@UTK.EDU • WEBSITE: MBA.UTK.EDU

Student Life and Environment

Expect a "positive, high energy atmosphere" here driven by a "very friendly and helpful" student population. In part because "we take a lot of classes in a short period of time, which always keeps us on our toes," students here are quick to support one another. "Everyone is very friendly and willing to help in any way they can." The "fun college town" offers plenty to do, with football being one of the biggest draws, while the "very diverse academic and professional backgrounds (of your classmates) adds to the collective learning." That diversity may be surprising to some. Between 25 and 30 percent of the class is from Europe and Asia, adding a broad mix of viewpoints to the "fast-paced and enjoyable" Knoxville culture.

"There is a very professional culture amongst my classmates that has proven to be quite contagious," but don't mistake that as meaning students don't know how to have fun. "It is not uncommon for a group of more than 20 MBA students to go out together on weekends or attend a cookout together. Overall, everyone gets along very well." Students find that their classmates are "fun to work with in class as well as great to be around outside of class. Everyone has very different backgrounds and stories, which makes our class diverse and interesting."

Admissions

A completed application form, undergraduate transcripts, a GMAT score report, two letters of recommendation, and four personal essays are required when applying for University of Tennessee at Knoxville's MBA program. A personal interview is also recommended. Students from the United States are required to have a minimum GPA of 2.7 to be eligible for the program, while international candidates must have the equivalent GPA of 3.0 on a 4.0 scale. Incoming students tend to be high performers; in recent years, they had an average undergraduate GPA of 3.4, an average GMAT score of 606, and average work experience totaling three years.

FINANCIAL FACTS

Annual tuition (in-state/ out-of-state)	$21,280/$39,768
Fees	$1,000
Cost of books	$3,500
Room & board (on/off-campus)	$10,000/$15,000
% of students receiving aid	75
% of first-year students receiving aid	75
% of students receiving grants	16
Average award package	$19,585
Average grant	$8,000
Average loan	$25,174
Average student loan debt	$36,754

ADMISSIONS

Admissions Selectivity Rating	80
# of applications received	148
% applicants accepted	69
% acceptees attending	75
Average GMAT	608
Range of GMAT	570–640
Average GPA	3.40
TOEFL required of international students	Yes
Minimum TOEFL (paper/computer)	600/250
Application fee	$60
International application fee	$60
Early application deadline	2/1
Regular application deadline	2/1
Deferment available	No
Transfer students accepted	No
Non-fall admissions	No
Need-blind admissions	Yes

EMPLOYMENT PROFILE

Career Rating	92	Grads Employed by Function	%	Avg. Salary
Percent employed at graduation	62	Marketing	(20%)	$60,000
Percent employed 3 months after graduation	80	Operations	(43%)	$84,500
		Consulting	(16%)	$107,500
Average base starting salary	$78,029	Finance	(14%)	$71,000
Primary Source of Full-time Job Acceptances		Other	(11%)	$74,125
School-facilitated activities	21(48%)	Top 5 Employers Hiring Grads		
Graduate-facilitated activities	23(52%)	Deloitte (4), Ernst & Young (3), Scripps Network Interactive (3), Caterpillar (2), CROSSMARK (2)		

THE UNIVERSITY OF TENNESSEE AT MARTIN
COLLEGE OF BUSINESS AND GLOBAL AFFAIRS

GENERAL INFORMATION

Type of school	Public
Affiliation	No Affiliation
Academic calendar	Semester

SURVEY SAYS...
Happy students
Solid preparation in:
General management, Teamwork

STUDENTS

Enrollment of parent institution	8,000
Enrollment of MBA Program	97
% male/female	67/33
% out-of-state	0
% part-time	55
% underrepresented minority	9
% international	6
Average age at entry	24
Average years work experience at entry	2.0

ACADEMICS

Academic Experience Rating	81
Profs interesting rating	76
Profs accesible rating	75
Student/faculty ratio	4:1
% female faculty	31
% underrepresented minority faculty	13
% part-time faculty	7

Academics

Offering part-time and full-time MBA options, as well as an online degree, University of Tennessee at Martin is a friendly, flexible, and low-key place to get a quality business education. On campus, the character of the MBA is largely defined by the fact that "UT Martin is a small campus and small school," which encourages relationships and networking within the College of Business. One of the many goals of the MBA curriculum includes developing strong communication and teamwork skills, and "The program requires regular engagement with faculty and fellow students" through both classes and group projects. A current student enthuses, "I love that my professors know my name and connect with me on a level deeper than just academics." The regular MBA curriculum is focused on the principles of general management, kicking off with a series of core courses in accounting, management, economics, and other key areas, followed by electives. Within the business school, "All professors are good, some are excellent," including strong faculty in finance, management, and other areas.

When students analyze the costs and benefits of pursuing an MBA, the numbers come out in favor of a UT Martin degree. At this state-run school, "The tuition cost is extremely low for an AACSB-accredited degree." Plus, many recent graduates are "offered a graduate assistant position," which helps cover the cost of their education in exchange for working with a UT professor. Convenience and flexibility are also key factors for local professionals. The school offers a flexible program in Martin, which can be completed either full-time or part-time. MBA candidates "go to school at night," while maintaining full-time employment during the day. "The classes are typically 3 to 2.5 hours long" making it possible to work, attend class, and head home for dinner. While MBA students have a lot on their plate, "Academically it is appropriately rigorous, but not too overwhelming for a working adult."

In addition to its traditional program, University of Tennessee—Martin operates a 20-month fully online MBA for working professionals, whose schedules require the "flexibility of online classes." This program is principally directed at finance and banking professionals, though coursework covers all important business areas, from marketing to ethics. In the online program, students "usually watch recorded lectures and attend live meetings with the professor and the class once a week." In contrast to the campus program, the online curriculum is entirely "cohort-based," which means students complete the core "one class at a time" and in tandem with the same group of students throughout the program. While they do not benefit from face-to-face networking, online students "regularly work with students in workgroups from all around the US using video chat, email, and other collaboration tools." Students describe the experience as "relaxed but challenging," and that, "The professors are willing to go above and beyond to keep the students engaged." When it comes to running the online group, the "Administration is absolutely excellent," and they help to "keep us on track" throughout the course of the year-and-a-half program.

Career and Placement

Outside of Memphis, UT Martin's College of Business offers the only AASCB-accredited MBA program in West Tennessee. Even though the campus is located in the small town of Martin, students benefit from the strong University of Tennessee brand name, as well as the extensive alumni network across the many UT campuses.

ADMISSIONS CONTACT: KEVIN HAMMOND, COLLEGE OF BUSINESS & GLOBAL AFFAIRS GRADUATE PROG
ADDRESS: 109 BUSINESS ADMINISTRATION BUILDING, MARTIN, TN 38238-5015
PHONE: 731-881-7208 • FAX: 731-587-7241
E-MAIL: BAGRAD@UTM.EDU • WEBSITE: WWW.UTM.EDU/MBA

There is a university-wide Career Employment and Placement Services at the Student Success Center. This office typically assists undergraduate students in making career choices and applying for jobs. However, it does also have regional job opportunities for MBA graduates.

Student Life and Environment

UT Martin's traditional MBA programs attract ambitious professionals from the local region. On campus, there is "a good mix of 20-somethings who are just out of undergraduate work, and career progressives in their 30s who are taking the next steps for success." In addition to locals, the student body includes "a large percentage of international students," which adds an interesting cultural dimension to the campus culture and "leads to even greater discussion in class." Students on the main campus in Martin, Tennessee, have all the benefits of life in a small college town, which offers a relaxed and affordable environment for work and study. While they have access to the many clubs, organizations, and activities on the larger UT Martin campus, "As a graduate student, its pretty much just class and nothing else." A current student says, "My only extracurricular involvement is serving as a chapter adviser for my fraternity."

Though they may not meet face-to-face, online students still benefit from contact with their classmates—a group of "successful, intelligent, dependable, helpful, working professionals." Coming from Tennessee, as well as the greater United States, students in the online program have "very diverse work experience" and make great contributions to their cohort.

Admissions

University of Tennessee Martin determines a prospective student's admissions eligibility based on an index number, which is calculated using their GMAT score and GPA. To be accepted to the program unconditionally, students must achieve a score of at least 1050 when their cumulative undergraduate GPA is multiplied by 200 then added to their GMAT score. Students with extensive professional experience may be considered with a slightly lower index number, and those who do not meet published admissions standards may still be eligible for conditional acceptance to the program.

FINANCIAL FACTS

Annual tuition (in-state/ out-of-state)	$10,044/$27,135
Cost of books	$1,000
Room & board (on/off-campus)	$1,110

ADMISSIONS

Admissions Selectivity Rating	81
# of applications received	32
% applicants accepted	53
% acceptees attending	94
Average GMAT	491
Range of GMAT	430–540
Average GPA	3.27
TOEFL required of international students	Yes
Minimum TOEFL (paper/computer)	525
Application fee	$30
Deferment available	Yes
Transfer students accepted	Yes
Transfer application policy: Transfer coursework must be from regionally accredited institution. See graduate section of the current catalog for further specifics.	
Non-fall admissions	Yes
Need-blind admissions	No

THE UNIVERSITY OF TEXAS AT ARLINGTON
COLLEGE OF BUSINESS

GENERAL INFORMATION
Type of school	Public
Affiliation	No Affiliation
Academic calendar	Semester

SURVEY SAYS...
Good peer network, Cutting-edge classes, Smart classrooms
Solid preparation in:
Teamwork, Communication/interpersonal skills, Presentation skills

STUDENTS
Enrollment of parent institution	33,239
Enrollment of MBA Program	881
% male/female	54/46
% part-time	66
% underrepresented minority	28
% international	35
Average age at entry	31
Average years work experience at entry	5.0

ACADEMICS
Academic Experience Rating	77
Profs interesting rating	78
Profs accesible rating	79
Student/faculty ratio	20:1
% female faculty	16
% underrepresented minority faculty	5
% part-time faculty	38

Joint Degrees
May combine any two degrees (usually MBA and specialized program) or a business degree with others, such as Engineering, Architecture, Science, Nursing. Can obtain second degree with as few as 18 additional hours. May pursue MBA at UTA with MIM at Thunderbird, the American Graduate School, or international management, with reduced requirements.

Academics

The University of Texas at Arlington is "a highly recognized" business program that is "a good value for the dollar" with "strong alumni," "a good reputation, and is fully AACSB accredited." Many students enjoy the "cohort format of the program," which allows students to grow and learn together. A real strength of the MBA program is how it "caters to people who have a full-time job. Almost all classes start about 7:00 p.m. so that commuters have time to get to class." Commuters can face some problems as "parking is horrendous, and it is extremely expensive." One student claims "I pay over $100 and still have to walk half a mile or more to class."

"The College of Business at UTA is at the cutting edge of the business world," one student says. "Our professors and administrators are always looking for the most innovative ideas or technologies, and the students get to research them and learn that not only the proven facts work, but also new ones." The campus is "very clean and very well organized" and "undergoing massive renovations to improve the quality of the campus. The overall appeal of the University should increase dramatically" once the renovations are done.

"The professors here are great," and the faculty is a real strength of the program. "Professors are tough, but they know well what they teach" and "have real-life work experience in what they are teaching." "The teaching styles have been diverse, but effective, and the professors are always interested in helping students succeed." One student says, "Ninety-five percent of the faculty is truly passionate about teaching students," although another says, "The majority of them are old-school professors, teaching from the book." Students who like to know where they stand academically may get slightly frustrated as "finding out grades is next to impossible," and you "very rarely know where you stand in class grade-wise until grades are posted."

"The administration must be the best in Texas," as they are "very helpful and there to answer any questions you have." "I liked the fact that it had two different programs to choose from: the cohort and the flexible," one student explains. Another student says the administration "even tailored a 'hybrid' program for me based on my situation." The career center "needs to bring in more companies" though, and "UTA should focus less on recruiting international students and more on recruiting U.S. students from other states."

Career and Placement

University of Texas at Arlington is "recognized by companies" around the country and has a good placement track record. UTA's brand is especially recognized in its region, and the "close proximity to Dallas" and Fort Worth gives students opportunities to establish connections with local businesses for when they graduate. "The school has established a very good rapport with businesses around the metroplex that easily absorb fresh graduates!" Some students did feel the school could do more to "partner with local, national, and international businesses." One caveat to note is that "members of the professional cohort MBA program" study on another campus, and "its students are not informed of the main campus job fairs or placement services."

Some prominent alumnae include John Goolsby, the retired CEO of Howard Hughes Corporation; Roy Williams, retired Chief Scout Exec. of Boy Scouts America; and Jackie Fouse, Sr. VP, CFO & Corp Strategy of Bunge, Ltd.

ADMISSIONS CONTACT: MELANIE WOODARD McGEE, DIRECTOR OF MBA PROGRAMS
ADDRESS: BOX 19376, ARLINGTON, TX 76019
PHONE: 817-272-0658 • FAX: 817-272-5799
E-MAIL: MWMCGEE@UTA.EDU • WEBSITE: WWW.UTA.EDU/GRADBIZ

Student Life and Environment

"As the program is designed for working individuals, a large majority work," and most of the students are "less than 30 years old." Life on the UTA campus is "very casual and relaxed," although there is "practically no life at school other than to attend classes." "The campus is well designed to provide plenty of areas for students to gather and be respected." Graduate students "mostly all work full time" between jobs, classes, and studying. "We're very removed from the 'social' side of the University," one student explains. If there is one area that students really wish the school could improve on, it is "adding a football team," as "this is Texas, and nobody respects a college in Texas that doesn't have a football team."

UTA "has an extremely diverse makeup that includes students from all over the world," and "everyone of all races gets along very well." Although some students feel that despite the "very diverse" makeup, the student body is "segregated." In addition to racial and international diversity, the school sports "working professionals, working students, and non-working" students. Working students come "from the defense, pharmaceuticals, information technology, transportation, construction, and other service industries," and "we really teach each other, lending experience and hard-learned career knowledge to fellow classmates."

Admissions

UT Arlington carefully considers both quantitative and qualitative factors in every admissions decision. Although not required, professional experience after earning a bachelor's degree is factored heavily alongside GMAT scores, GPA, personal essay, and letters of recommendation. Average GMAT and GPA scores for last year's class were 550 and 3.25 respectively.

Prominent Alumni

Gen. Tommy Franks, U.S. Army (ret.); John Goolsby, President CEO (ret.) - Howard Hughes Corporation; Roy Williams, Chief Scot Exec. (ret.) - Boy Scouts America

FINANCIAL FACTS

Annual tuition (in-state/ out-of-state)	$11,424/$19,848
Cost of books	$1,160
Room & board (on/off-campus)	$7,708
% of students receiving aid	20
Average award package	$8,500
Average grant	$1,000
Average loan	$8,585
Average student loan debt	$23,475

ADMISSIONS

Admissions Selectivity Rating	77
# of applications received	1,212
% applicants accepted	56
% acceptees attending	44
Average GMAT	550
Range of GMAT	470–620
Average GPA	3.25
TOEFL required of international students	Yes
Minimum TOEFL (paper/computer)	550/213
Application fee	$40
International application fee	$70
Regular application deadline	6/15
Deferment available	Yes
Maximum length of deferment	1 year
Transfer students accepted	Yes
Transfer application policy: Maximum number of transferable credits is nine. Grades 'B' or better from an AACSB accredited university.	
Non-fall admissions	Yes
Need-blind admissions	Yes

THE UNIVERSITY OF TEXAS AT AUSTIN
McCOMBS SCHOOL OF BUSINESS

GENERAL INFORMATION
Type of school	Public
Academic calendar	Semester

SURVEY SAYS...
Students love Austin, TX, Good social scene
Solid preparation in:
Communication/interpersonal skills

STUDENTS
Enrollment of parent institution	52,186
Enrollment of MBA Program	1,036
% male/female	69/31
% out-of-state	41
% part-time	51
% underrepresented minority	9
% international	25
Average age at entry	28
Average years work experience at entry	5.0

ACADEMICS
Academic Experience Rating	97
Profs interesting rating	96
Profs accesible rating	96
Student/faculty ratio	4:1
% female faculty	19
% underrepresented minority faculty	16
% part-time faculty	15

Joint Degrees
MBA/Doctor of Jurisprudence; MBA/Master of Mechanical Engineering; MBA/Master of Science in Nursing; MBA/Master of Arts in Public Affairs; MBA/Master of Arts (Advertising); MBA/Master of Arts (Asian Studies); MBA/Master of Arts (Communication Studies); MBA/Master of Arts (Journalism); MBA/Master of Arts (Latin American Studies); MBA/Master of Arts (Middle Eastern Studies); MBA/Master of Arts (Radio-Television-Film); MBA/Master of Arts (Russian, East European, and Eurasian Studies); MBA/Master of Global Policy Studies; MBA/Master of Arts in Energy and Earth Resources

Academics

The University of Texas at Austin is "well-known for academic excellence in many aspects, such as accounting, entrepreneurial, IT management, marketing, and energy finance." The School's "good entrepreneurial track [record]" and "reasonable cost of living" in "one of the most fun cities in the United States" makes it attractive to students across the nation. "Austin provides a great environment for business school students" as it is "a hotbed of entrepreneurial activity." "Some highlights of McCombs include the "Marketing Fellows organization in academics" and the "commitment to development of the top energy reputation among business schools." Students have "a great deal of freedom in which classes we take," and there is a "collaborative, yet competitive team-based atmosphere" where "students support each other." Academics are "very rigorous," and the "workload is pretty high, but people help each other." "It's intense but not insane," one student explains. "The course work is very intense for a semester and then frees up a bit." Overall, the Texas MBA "is a very rigorous program academically, yet students still find time to have fun." The School gives students the "ability to personalize your degree and supplement it with courses from other UT graduate programs."

The "administration does a good job of running things," "supporting the students," and improving "the overall academic experience." "Students have incredible freedom to start new programs with very few restrictions from administration," one student explains. The "administration is very involved with the MBA program," although it can be "a bit disorganized" and "disconnected from students." "The MBA program office is great and easy to work with; the only difficulties arise when we have to deal with the UT bureaucracy." "The UT campus in general is beautiful, but the business school buildings need some serious attention," and "the food available for the business school building is average at best." "I know you want to keep the revenues in house, but get us some real grub!" one student laments.

Students love their professors, who are "very accessible and knowledgeable" and "have had practical work experience that makes them that much better." "Ninety-five percent of the instructors are very engaging, accessible, intelligent, inspiring, and passionate about the material they teach." This "excellent" faculty is a "good mix of academics with a strong history of research and practitioners who have real-world knowledge," such as "leading researchers and ex-CEOs." "Class content is nicely divided up between theory, case, and simulation." One student says, "It has been more challenging than I could have ever imagined, but after going through this, I know I will be prepared for anything."

Career and Placement

McCombs has an "enthusiastic alumni base" and "strong employer connections," which help provide excellent career placement for its graduates. "Career services is one of the best in the nation," one student boasts. The "health of the Texas economy" in general offers "solid post-graduation job opportunities." "Texas is the place to be in terms of oil and gas and renewable," says one government and public policy student. McCombs' Investment Fund, Venture Fellows program, MBA+, and the Venture Labs Investment Competition are all excellent opportunities for hands-on learning" that the school provides to help students eventually find careers.

ADMISSIONS CONTACT: RODRIGO MALTA, DIRECTOR OF ADMISSION, MBA PROGRAMS
ADDRESS: ADMISSIONS, MBA PROGRAM OFFICE, 2110 DPEEDWAY, STOP B6004, AUSTIN, TX 78712
PHONE: 512-471-7698 • FAX: 512-471-4131
E-MAIL: TEXASMBA@MCCOMBS.UTEXAS.EDU • WEBSITE: WWW.MCCOMBS.UTEXAS.EDU/MBA/FULL-TIME

The school claims that 89 percent of students have job offers at graduation, and 93 percent find employment within three months of graduation. Some prominent alumni include Jim Mulva, President & CEO of Conoco Phillips; William Johnson, Chairman, President & CEO of Heinz; and Sara Martinez Tucker, President & CEO of the Hispanic Scholarship Fund. Hewlett Packard, Dell, Advanced Micro Devices (AMD), Bank of America, and Deloitte Consulting are a handful of the many companies that recruit McCombs MBA graduates.

Student Life and Environment

The students at McCombs are "intelligent, clever, extremely hard working—the epitome of go-getters." Students "consistently beat top schools (including Ivy League) at National Case Competitions." "My classmates are from so many different backgrounds that it is impossible to characterize them," one student says. The student body is somewhat more "liberal" than your average business school, although it strikes "a good balance of conservative Texans and generally smart people who are open to social chemistry." "The culture really sets University of Texas at Austin apart," and students here are "very diverse and very competitive, but always willing to help." "Everyone is willing to help one another; it's not dog eat dog." "Everyone is very social, but this is NOT a party school," one student says. "I'm constantly in awe of the breadth and depth of the intelligence and experience that my peers have to offer. The School is also located in one of the most dynamic and interesting cities in the country. "I love Austin; it's a fantastic place to go to school," says one student. "While I'm very busy with school activities, our class always finds ways to socialize and enjoy Austin." Another student says, "Austin is the greatest city in the United States. I am going to miss it dearly."

Admissions

The McCombs School of Business only accepts online applications. A completed application must include a resume detailing work history (Two years of post-baccalaureate work experience is strongly recommended.), personal essays, official copies of transcripts for all postsecondary academic work, letters of recommendation, and an official score report for the GMAT. The average undergraduate GPA and GMAT scores for the most recent class were about 3.4 and 692 respectively.

Prominent Alumni

Jim Mulva, President & CEO/Conoco Phillips; William Johnson, Chairman, President & CEO/Heinz; Don Evans, former Secretary of Commerce/U.S. Gov't.; Sara Martinez Tucker, President & CEO/ Hispanic Scholarship Fund; Gerard Arpey, Chairman, President & CEO/American Airlines

FINANCIAL FACTS

Annual tuition (in-state/ out-of-state)	$33,296/$48,832
Cost of books	$1,504
Room & board	$16,500
% of students receiving aid	71
% of students receiving grants	26
Average award package	$50,870
Average grant	$11,090
Average student loan debt	$80,589

ADMISSIONS

Admissions Selectivity Rating	96
# of applications received	1,900
% applicants accepted	29
% acceptees attending	43
Average GMAT	692
Range of GMAT	660–720
Average GPA	3.40
TOEFL required of international students	Yes
Minimum TOEFL (paper/computer)	620/260
Application fee	$175
International application fee	$175
Application Deadline/Notification	
Round 1:	10/16 / 12/14
Round 2:	12/4 / 2/15
Round 3:	1/23 / 3/29
Round 4:	3/26 / 5/10
Deferment available	Yes
Maximum length of deferment	1 year
Transfer students accepted	No
Non-fall admissions	No
Need-blind admissions	Yes

EMPLOYMENT PROFILE

Career Rating	97	**Grads Employed by Function% Avg. Salary**	
Percent employed at graduation	81	Marketing	(21%) $99,702
Percent employed 3 months after graduation	93	Operations	(9%) $104,559
		Consulting	(27%)$121,648
Average base starting salary	$105,112	Management	(9%) $94,259
Primary Source of Full-time Job Acceptances		Finance	(32%) $98,005
School-facilitated activities	155(74%)	HR	(1%)
Graduate-facilitated activities	46(22%)	MIS	(1%)
Unknown	10(5%)	Other	(2%) $107,667

Top 5 Employers Hiring Grads
Deloitte Consulting (20), Dell (8), PepsiCo (7), Pricewaterhouse Coopers (7), JPMorgan Chase (6)

The University of Texas at Dallas
Naveen Jindal School of Management

GENERAL INFORMATION

Type of school	Public
Affiliation	No Affiliation
Academic calendar	Semester

SURVEY SAYS...

Smart classrooms
Solid preparation in:
Doing business in a global economy

STUDENTS

Enrollment of parent institution	19,727
Enrollment of MBA Program	1,107
% male/female	61/39
% out-of-state	10
% part-time	89
% underrepresented minority	5
% international	45
Average age at entry	26
Average years work experience at entry	4.0

ACADEMICS

Academic Experience Rating	97
Profs interesting rating	93
Profs accesible rating	89
Student/faculty ratio	37:1
% female faculty	25
% underrepresented minority faculty	5
% part-time faculty	22

Joint Degrees

MS in Electrical Engineering/MBA - 3 years; MD/MBA - 4 years

Prominent Alumni

Dr. Dipak Jain, Former Dean/Kellogg School of Management; Michael S. Gilliland, President, CEO/Sabre; Charles Davidson, President, CEO/Noble Oil; Linnet Deily, Former Ambassador/WTO; David Holmberg, President, CEO/Jo-Ann Stores Inc.

Academics

The University of Texas at Dallas is "one of the fast growing schools" with a "good reputation in the Southwest area," offering "a variety of concentration areas, as well as MS degrees within those areas." Unlike most MBA programs, UT Dallas's full-time, cohort-based MBA's "duration is only 16 months." "UT Dallas is a great bargain for an MBA program, factoring in national rank, prestige, and tuition prices," one student declares. UT Dallas is "ranked in the top 50," yet has "reasonable tuition" and is "a quarter of the price of SMU (the other good option in Dallas)." The Jindal School has a "rigorous curriculum," "flexible scheduling," "higher than average test scores, and top tier faculty." The city of Dallas is a huge plus for business students, as the "DFW Metro area [is] where many Fortune-500 companies base their headquarters," which provides "many opportunities for graduates."

The professors at UT Dallas "are very attentive and interested in their students learning," which is evidenced by how readily they "make themselves available for extra instruction outside of class." The faculty strikes a balance "between professors with an academic background and real-world background," giving students the best of both worlds. "They seem to have a genuine interest in teaching the courses" and "are very enthusiastic about what they teach, and this is very motivating." Professors at UT Dallas work hard to "encourage debates and arguments to explore other opinions in the classroom." However, some students say too many of the professors are "boring academics" who teach with "an unnecessary emphasis on working in groups or giving presentations." While not small, the class sizes are "manageable" and "have a small-school feel" where "you are able to really know each and every student in the class and develop close relationships beyond just a name."

Students are mostly happy with the school administration, calling it "extremely helpful" and "very interested in the experience of its students." The Jindal School "administrators are extremely caring and always make themselves accessible," one student says, "whether it be for school or non-school issues. Many times, they go above and beyond expectations just to help us in our lives, both career and personal." "When emailing various offices and professors, I always got a swift and helpful response," says another. However, "online registration and notification of critical deadlines" could be "communicated [more] effectively and thoroughly," and there are always "long lines at bursar's, financial aid, and advising" offices. Students with cars beware that "parking is a nightmare." The School's problems may be improving, though. As one student says, "We are still an up-and-coming university, so all the kinks may not be worked out, but we are heading in the right direction. I'm excited to be a part of this university, and I know it has a very bright future." According to university officials, newly approved construction projects will add 1,700 parking spaces in the near future.

Career and Placement

UT Dallas provides many services to help students' career prospects, such as "frequent workshops and seminars," which "help students find the right job after (or during) the program." It doesn't hurt that the school is located in Dallas where "lots of companies . . . are interested in hiring graduates." "The Dallas business community is among the most vibrant in the United States, and I wanted to stay close to this when I graduate," says one consulting student about his decision to attend UT Dallas. The school could do more to "improve in developing further relationships with the large companies in the Dallas/Fort Worth area" and "improve on job prospects of students." "Maybe it's the

ADMISSIONS CONTACT: LISA SHATZ, DIRECTOR - FULL-TIME (COHORT) MBA PROGRAM
ADDRESS: UT DALLAS—SCHOOL OF MANAGEMENT, 800 WEST CAMPBELL ROAD, SM 21
RICHARDSON, TX 75080-3021 • PHONE: 972-883-6191 • FAX: 972-883-4095
E-MAIL: LISA.SHATZ@UTDALLAS.EDU • WEBSITE: SOM.UTDALLAS.EDU/GRADUATE/MBA/FULLTIMEMBA

economy, but we haven't seen many prominent recruitments on campus," says one student. "[We are] pretty much on our own."

Other students say that although placement may not be as strong as it could be, the school is "on the right track." UT Dallas is "still a relatively young full-time MBA program that is growing its alumni base," but it is "building a strong reputation and connections to the Dallas business community." The school claims an average base salary of about $70,000 for recent graduates, and almost 88 percent find placement in the Southwest. Some companies that recruit from UT Dallas include Richards Group, JP Morgan, Sunquest, Bank of America, and Capital One.

Student Life and Environment

Students at UT Dallas are "smart, ambitious, driven" and "usually foreign, married, or just out of undergrad." One student says, "Fifty to seventy-five percent of each of my classes comprises Asian and Asia-Indian students." "The diverse student population helps expose us to many different types of people, opinions, and experiences." "Most of the students are friendly and conservative." In addition to ethnic diversity, there is a "good mix of working students with families and singles coming straight in from undergrad programs." "I have classmates from diverse backgrounds, experience, age, culture, ethnicity, and countries," explains one student. "It's fun." The "team-oriented approach allows us to connect closely to each other." As for life on campus, the school is "very safe," and UT Dallas "tries to bring students together with different activities for people with similar interests." "I can definitely say that the social offerings and opportunities are very high and also very popular" one student explains. "Graduate students may not have the time/want of such extracurricular activities; however, they are available if wanted."

Admissions

UT Dallas admissions standards are high. Currently, admission to the full-time MBA (cohort) program is particularly competitive, admitting just about 25 percent of applicants. Admissions rates and requirements depend on the program to which you are applying. The entering class had an average GMAT score of 668 and an average undergraduate GPA of 3.6. In addition to transcripts and test scores, students are required to submit personal essays and recommendation letters.

FINANCIAL FACTS

Annual tuition (in-state/ out-of-state)	$14,258/$28,118
Fees	$3,800
Cost of books	$2,000
Room & board	$7,500
% of students receiving aid	76
% of first-year students receiving aid	76
% of students receiving grants	76
Average award package	$10,904
Average grant	$7,872
Average loan	$0

ADMISSIONS

Admissions Selectivity Rating	97
# of applications received	370
% applicants accepted	26
% acceptees attending	65
Average GMAT	669
Range of GMAT	650–700
Average GPA	3.50
TOEFL required of international students	Yes
Minimum TOEFL (paper/computer)	550/213
Application fee	$100
International application fee	$150
Early application deadline	1/15
Early notification date	3/1
Regular application deadline	5/1
Regular application notification	6/15
Application Deadline/Notification	
Round 1:	1/15 / 3/1
Round 2:	3/1 / 4/15
Round 3:	6/1 / 6/15
Round 4:	7/1 / 7/15
Deferment available	Yes
Maximum length of deferment	1 year
Transfer students accepted	Yes
Transfer application policy: Full-Time (Cohort) MBA accepts 6 hours if they qualify. PMBA accepts 12 if they qualify.	
Non-fall admissions	Yes
Need-blind admissions	Yes

EMPLOYMENT PROFILE

Career Rating	90	Grads Employed by Function	% Avg. Salary
Percent employed at graduation	50	Marketing	(23%) $71,875
Percent employed 3 months after graduation	39	Operations	(17%) $73,640
		Consulting	(31%) $82,855
Average base starting salary	$78,107	Finance	(6%)
Primary Source of Full-time Job Acceptances		MIS	(9%) $78,167
School-facilitated activities	28(65%)	Other	(14%) $86,400
Graduate-facilitated activities	12(28%)	**Top 5 Employers Hiring Grads**	
Unknown	3(7%)	7 Eleven (4), Ericsson (3), Deloitte (3), Alcatel - Lucent (3), E & Y (1)	

THE UNIVERSITY OF TEXAS—PAN AMERICAN
COLLEGE OF BUSINESS ADMINISTRATION

GENERAL INFORMATION

Type of school	Public
Affiliation	No Affiliation
Academic calendar	Semester

SURVEY SAYS...

Students love Edinburg, TX, Friendly
students, Happy students
Solid preparation in:
Finance, General management,
Operations

STUDENTS

Enrollment of parent institution	17,500
Enrollment of MBA Program	186
% male/female	68/32
% part-time	69
% underrepresented minority	75
% international	15
Average age at entry	31
Average years work experience at entry	2.0

ACADEMICS

Academic Experience Rating	80
Profs interesting rating	81
Profs accesible rating	75
Student/faculty ratio	27:1
% female faculty	30
% part-time faculty	0

Academics

The University of Texas – Pan American offers two tracks to an MBA, one through evening courses and another via online classes. Both are accredited by the American Assembly of Collegiate Schools of Business (AACSB). Students with an undergraduate degree in business can complete the evening program in just two years. Further specialization is offered upon completion of nine extra credit hours in one of the following disciplines: accounting, economics, finance, management, management information systems, and marketing.

Students agree that UTPA "offers quality education at an affordable cost." It's "close to the border" with a big focus on Latin American business. Class sizes are small. "You aren't only a number, but you have an identity." Students say professors know their names and are "dedicated" to their professions. They are also well versed in the material, and at the same time, "open to debate." The program's director "is always available and knows everyone in the program personally." She "demands the best of her instructors and makes changes if they are not providing the quality of work she expects." This results in classes that "are interesting and interactive. Everyone is given the chance to speak and have an opinion." "Each and every professor is knowledgeable in their field of study, and they are accessible." Professors respond "promptly to emails," "even late at night and on weekends." One student says, "I have enjoyed every class, and I utilize the knowledge gained on a daily basis." Students feel challenged, yet supported. "Every MBA class I have taken has required numerous case study reviews and numerous team projects. We have reviewed approximately 50-60 case studies of different subject matter in a year. These have been instrumental." Students "work well together, both in and out of the classroom environment." "Everyone is willing to contribute."

As far as the administration is concerned, "they do the best they can with what they have. Improvements can always be made." Students say, "The number of elective classes needs to be improved." They'd like to see more variety and perhaps different times for classes. Also, some feel frustrated when classes that are offered get cancelled. However, "for the most part, everything runs smoothly."

Career and Placement

The career office at UTPA serves both graduate and undergraduate students. CARIR, or the Center for Advisement, Recruitment, Internships, and Retention, offers career counseling and job-related assistance. However, most students feel that the "career center needs a lot of improvement." They would like to see "more efforts for career placement." One student believes that there are "no internships" readily available to students, and that it is "hard to be placed after graduation." However, both regional and national job databases do exist. Students can access them through their UTPA accounts. The office also hosts workshops on resume writing, networking, and other helpful career strategies. The following are just some organizations that hire UTPA graduates: Proctor and Gamble, Texas Instruments, Boeing Ernest and Young, and Northrop Grunman.

ADMISSIONS CONTACT: DR. ANGELICA C. CORTES, DIRECTOR OF MBA PROGRAM
ADDRESS: 1201 WEST UNIVERSITY DRIVE, EDINBURG, TX 78539-2999
PHONE: 956-381-3313 • FAX: 956-381-2970
E-MAIL: MBAPROG@UTPA.EDU • WEBSITE: WWW.COBA.UTPA.EDU/MBA

Student Life and Environment

Students describe fellow students as "the type of people who go the extra mile for anybody." They are "smart," "extremely friendly," and "always willing to lend a helping hand." The student body at UTPA is "honest," "mature," and "easy to talk to." UTPA "has a great cultural feel." "One of my classes has students from India, Mexico, Texas, China, Japan, Taiwan, Turkey, France, Romania, and I'm sure I've missed a couple others." Students are "very open to new cultures" and "create a learning environment that is conducive to expanding one's ideas." Another student says, "We are all like one big family." Students "keep in touch even when the final days of a course are over."

The University of Texas is located in Edinburg, Texas, where the cost of living is low and the "weather is good." UTPA is "far south of the northern snow." The gym "is brand new," and has "very good equipment." There are "movie nights when new releases come out for free" and other "events, from poker tournaments to trips to Europe." Some students "work full time" and have families, so their "time on campus is spent in the classroom during the week and in the library on the weekends." However, "a good portion of students don't have kids and often enjoy hanging out with each other on the weekends." There are also collaborative projects every semester, so even when students don't have time to socialize, they are still creating friendships through schoolwork.

Admissions

Applicants seeking admission to the College of Business are asked to submit the following materials to the Admissions Committee: sealed copies of official transcripts sent directly from all post-secondary institutions previously attended; official GMAT scores; three letters of recommendation; a current resume; a personal essay answering five specific questions; and the general application for the UPTA Graduate School. The most important criteria are the GMAT score and GPA. The committee will also consider extracurricular activities and work experience. Most applicants average two years work experience. The average GPA of accepted students is 3.0, and the average GMAT score is 450. Roughly one in two applicants is admitted.

FINANCIAL FACTS

Annual tuition (in-state/out-of-state)	$2,797/$8,900
Fees	$314
Cost of books	$1,500
Average grant	$10,000
Average loan	$6,000

ADMISSIONS

Admissions Selectivity Rating	79
# of applications received	78
% applicants accepted	47
% acceptees attending	73
Average GMAT	450
Range of GMAT	380–555
Average GPA	3.00
TOEFL required of international students	Yes
Minimum TOEFL (paper/computer)	500/173
Application fee	$50
International application fee	$50
Early application deadline	12/1
Regular application deadline	8/1
Deferment available	Yes
Maximum length of deferment	One Semester
Transfer students accepted	Yes
Transfer application policy: Accept max. 3 courses	
Non-fall admissions	Yes
Need-blind admissions	Yes

THE UNIVERSITY OF TEXAS AT SAN ANTONIO
COLLEGE OF BUSINESS

GENERAL INFORMATION

Type of school	Public
Affiliation	No Affiliation
Academic calendar	Semester

SURVEY SAYS...
Students love San Antonio, TX
Solid preparation in:
Finance, Quantitative skills

STUDENTS

Enrollment of parent institution	30,474
Enrollment of MBA Program	255
% male/female	72/28
% part-time	62
% underrepresented minority	31
% international	6
Average age at entry	29
Average years work experience at entry	5.5

ACADEMICS

Academic Experience Rating	**88**
Profs interesting rating	87
Profs accesible rating	88
Student/faculty ratio	25:1
% female faculty	32
% underrepresented minority faculty	49
% part-time faculty	7

Prominent Alumni
Gilbert Gonzalez, US Depart Ag. Undersecretary for Rural Dev; Ernest Bromley, President & CEO of Bromley & Associates; Jeanie Wyatt, CEO of South Texas Money Management

Academics

The University of Texas at San Antonio, or simply UTSA, is a school "developing rapidly in the UT system, and the College of Business is one of the top business schools in the South." With a "high reputation" for top-notch "finance and marketing courses," "generous scholarships," and "great professors," UTSA benefits greatly from the "UT name" and is a place where students are encouraged to "develop their own career paths." A good portion of students also mention that UTSA is a "conveniently located" and "relatively inexpensive" option for MBA students. One student with a concentration in supply chain/operations management tells us, "[my] coworkers graduated from UTSA and [gave it a] good recommendation."

Like a lot of large business schools, UTSA MBA candidates have both praise and criticism for their faculty. According to one student, of the 109 faculty members currently working in the business school, all are "excellent, with outstanding academic knowledge and contributions." But another student says, "Professors are quick to tell you they are only here for the research money and that they don't like teaching students . . . Professors are quick to judge and often make discouraging comments about the students who struggle." Given the feedback we have received, the consensus seems to be that "this school has really tried to attract great faculty and support them in teaching." In turn, while UTSA continues to grow in both size and reputation within the UT system, there is a balance of "great" professors, who infuse their courses with a "heavy research aspect," and others who "don't have any business teaching."

The College of Business at UTSA offers a flexible MBA (students can attend part time or full time). Students can choose a general MBA (no concentration) or an MBA in a variety of 11 concentrations. Additional degree options include an Executive MBA (designed for seasoned executives, professional, and entrepreneurs), an MBA in international business (full-time, cohort program), a Ph.D. in business administration, and a Ph.D. in applied statistics. Discipline based Master's programs include a master of arts in economics; master of science degrees in applied statistics, finance, finance with real estate concentration, information technology, information technology with infrastructure assurance concentration, and management of technology—all of which are 33-credit hour programs. UTSA also offers a master of accountancy degree, which is 30 credit hours. In addition to the school's vast academic arsenal, the College of Business offers international immersion programs in Brazil, the Canary Islands, Chile, China, Finland, Italy, Morocco, Singapore, Spain and Vietnam. In short, UTSA MBA candidates have "attended programs all over the world."

Career and Placement

Based on recent feedback from students, it's apparent that UTSA has made improvements in recent years to its Career Services office, as well as to the school's recruitment events, where students are offered abundant "opportunities to meet with national and international companies." According to one student, "I find there to be many strong relationships between employers and the business school. Most of the professors and counseling staff seem well connected and ready to help students network. I would admit though, that many of the opportunities are either local or regional." "There are good companies that recruit and sponsor events." Regional companies, such as Valero, Ernst & Young, Deloitte, and KPMG, just to name a few, have actively recruited UTSA students in the past, but data also indicate many graduates end up finding work outside Texas and the Southwest region at large. One student, who works part time as a teaching assistant says, "There are so many opportunities for students to attend amazing workshops

ADMISSIONS CONTACT: MONICA RODRIGUEZ, MANAGER OF GRADUATE ADMISSIONS
ADDRESS: ONE UTSA CIRCLE, SAN ANTONIO, TX 78249-0603
PHONE: 210-458-4330 • FAX: 210-458-4332
E-MAIL: GRADUATESTUDIES@UTSA.EDU • WEBSITE: BUSINESS.UTSA.EDU/GRADUATE

and certifications and hear interesting business speakers for free," all in addition to the College of Business's popular internship and faculty-led study abroad programs. "I think at other bigger-named schools," the same student continues, "it would be hard to be a name instead of a number and more challenging to get all the services and support that this program provides."

Student Life and Environment

The MBA program at UTSA is mostly geared toward the working professional, which would explain why "most of the MBA classes are at night." While this has obvious benefits for those with full-time jobs, "they could offer more classes during the day." "They are trying to change that," one student reminds us. "The staff and faculty really try to provide time for us to network and force us into groups so that we can connect." We are told there is "an excellent diversity of students" in the UTSA MBA program, many of whom describe their fellow students as "very kind and creative," "studious," "rich [with] work experience and a spirit of teamwork."

There is no shortage of activities on UTSA's campus. The library has been described to us as "one of the nicest in the country right now," although the "stacks are a bit dreary, but the aesthetics don't limit the selection." There is also a top-rated rec center, and the "food on campus is great, with recent additions, such as Chili's, Subway, Pita-Grill" and various other cuisine choices for all tastes.

Admissions

Applicants to the MBA program at The University of Texas at San Antonio are required to submit the following: GMAT scores, essay/personal statement, and an official undergraduate transcript. Letter of reference, resume, proof of state residency, and a list of extracurricular activities are all optional, but encouraged, if relevant to an applicant's planned course of study. Admissions will pay particularly close attention to GMAT scores and undergraduate GPA. Incoming students had an average of 600 and 3.2 respectively. International candidates are required to submit TOEFL scores (550 minimum for written test, 213 minimum for computer-based test).

FINANCIAL FACTS

Annual tuition (in-state/ out-of-state)	$4,671/$17,307
Fees	$1,907

ADMISSIONS

Admissions Selectivity Rating	86
# of applications received	187
% applicants accepted	46
% acceptees attending	70
Average GMAT	585
Range of GMAT	550–620
Average GPA	3.20
TOEFL required of international students	Yes
Minimum TOEFL (paper/computer)	550/213
Application fee	$45
International application fee	$80
Regular application deadline	7/1
Deferment available	Yes
Maximum length of deferment	2 terms
Transfer students accepted	Yes
Transfer application policy: Please refer to Current Graduate Catalog.	
Non-fall admissions	Yes
Need-blind admissions	Yes

EMPLOYMENT PROFILE

Career Rating	77	Grads Employed by Function	% Avg. Salary
Percent employed at graduation	69	Marketing	(16%) $47,000
Percent employed 3 months after graduation	6	Consulting	(26%) $67,400
		Management	(16%) $54,167
Average base starting salary	$56,026	Finance	(21%) $49,000
Primary Source of Full-time Job Acceptances		Other	(21%) $57,000
School-facilitated activities	8 (33%)		
Graduate-facilitated activities	16 (67%)		

THE UNIVERSITY OF TOLEDO

COLLEGE OF BUSINESS AND INNOVATION

GENERAL INFORMATION

Type of school	Public
Affiliation	No Affiliation
Academic calendar	Semester

SURVEY SAYS...

Smart classrooms
Solid preparation in:
General management, Doing business in a global economy

STUDENTS

Enrollment of parent institution	21,500
Enrollment of MBA Program	403
% male/female	61/39
% out-of-state	12
% part-time	74
% underrepresented minority	56
% international	30
Average age at entry	28
Average years work experience at entry	5.0

ACADEMICS

Academic Experience Rating	79
Profs interesting rating	77
Profs accesible rating	77
Student/faculty ratio	10:1
% female faculty	36
% underrepresented minority faculty	3
% part-time faculty	4

Joint Degrees

JD/MBA - 3-4 years, MD/MBA - 4-5 years, MPH/MBA- 20 months - 24 months

Prominent Alumni

Edward Kinsey, Co-Founder, Ariba, Inc.; Ora Alleman, VP, National City Bank; Michael Durik, Executive VP, The Limited Stores, Inc.; Marvin Herb, CEO Coca-Cola Bottling Company; Julie Higgins, Exective VP, The Trust Company of Toledo

Academics

Offering a "good education at a very competitive price with convenient scheduling," the College of Business and Innovation at The University of Toledo fits the needs of area businesspeople in search of a quality MBA. One student explains, "The program is very accommodating toward people who work full-time. The majority of classes are taught at night, so I have been able to continue to work full-time while taking one or two classes at night." And, with a "low cost of living and low tuition fees when compared to other business schools," a UT MBA isn't a wallet buster.

UT distinguishes its MBA program with a number of cutting-edge concentrations. Students here may specialize in CRM and marketing intelligence, human resource management, information systems, operations and supply chain management, and professional sales as well as in the more traditional areas of administration, finance, international business, and marketing. Still, students warn that despite this apparent variety of choices, "The grad-level courses are fairly limited, [with] not enough variety/electives available to really customize our education. Classes are usually only offered once per semester at one specific time, so time conflicts between class and work schedules are quite common."

Students agree that "the greatest strengths of the UT MBA program come from its people. Overall, students are helpful, and it is easy to make connections through classmates. Professors follow a 40-40-20 rule with their time: 40 percent on research, 40 percent on preparing for classes, and 20 percent on advising students. This allows teachers to be student-centric." One student adds, "Receiving individual attention is a norm, be it in the Advising Office or from a professor."

Career and Placement

MBA students at Toledo may choose from an assortment of career support options. The school coordinates both academic graduate assistantships and corporate assistantships with employers like ProMedica Health System, Therma-Tru Doors, SSOE, Mercy Medical, Paramount Medical, and Goodwill. The school also sponsors regular networking events at which current students can meet and greet alumni. Finally, the Business Career Programs Office organizes on-campus recruiting, conducts mock interviews, performs resume reviews, provides counseling services, and manages a biannual Business Career Fair that brings more than 90 recruiters to campus.

Recent employers of UT MBAs include Calphalon, Chrysler, Dana Corp., DTE Energy, Ernst & Young, GM Powertrain, KeyBank, Heartland Information Systems, Hickory Farms, National City Corporation, Owens Corning, Owens Illinois, and Pilkington.

Student Life and Environment

"Life at UT is comfortable," students assure us. One praises, "Classrooms are clustered centrally so travel time between classes is quick. Most buildings have a computer lab, and the library has many quiet places to study. The fitness center is one of the largest I've seen for a college, and workouts are great. There aren't too many students crowding resources, so long lines are never a problem." If there's one area that needs help, students tell us it's the traffic and parking. One student warns, "There's an extreme lack of parking available.... On days/nights when a major event such as a basketball or football game is going on, the school allows outsiders (nonstudents) to park on campus for a fee. This usually keeps students from being able to go to class as there's so much spillover of vehicles sometimes that parking in grass or restricted areas is common. I've had to turn

ADMISSIONS CONTACT: KARI DILWORTH, GRADUATE PROGRAMS COORDINATOR
ADDRESS: 2801 W. BANCROFT ST., MS 103, TOLEDO, OH 43606-3390
PHONE: 419-530-2087 • FAX: 419-530-5353
E-MAIL: KARI.DILWORTH@UTOLEDO.EDU • WEBSITE: WWW.UTOLEDO.EDU/BUSINESS/MBA

around and go home, missing class, due to not being able to park or to get through traffic in a timely manner to park." To top it off, "The traffic situation on campus is horrendous."

Most students attend UT's MBA program on a part-time basis, arriving after a full day of work. Consequently, they have little time or inclination to participate in activities other than classes and group projects. Full-time students tell us that "there are many organizations to be involved in if you choose to. There are also department social functions quite frequently that are highly advertised." As for evenings and weekends, they are "what you make of them. Most people settle for simply just going to house parties or campus bars, which grows old fast. The downtown area offers good times, but most of that area is dead."

Toledo MBAs "come from diverse backgrounds, including majors, universities, religions, and ethnicity." While they "are competitive in their pursuit of high-quality jobs," they also enjoy "an atmosphere of mutual respect and teamwork between students in the program. Students are very comfortable approaching other students for help in their studies. In exchange, it is expected that every student pulls his or her own weight on the many team-based assignments." About one in three students originates from outside the United States, "providing a unique and interesting perspective on major business topics of the day."

Admissions

Applicants to the MBA program at UT must submit the following materials: a completed application; official copies of transcripts from each undergraduate and graduate institution attended; three letters of recommendation; and an official score report for the GMAT. In addition to the above, all international applicants must submit a financial statement and supporting documents. International applicants from countries in which English is not the primary language must submit an official score report for the TOEFL. Students are encouraged to complete their applications online.

FINANCIAL FACTS

Annual tuition (in-state/ out-of-state)	$12,096/$21,984
Fees	$1,190
Cost of books	$1,200
Room & board (on/off-campus)	$0/$5,830
Average grant	$17,646
Average loan	$18,500

ADMISSIONS

Admissions Selectivity Rating	**72**
# of applications received	175
% applicants accepted	95
% acceptees attending	98
Average GMAT	525
Range of GMAT	450–680
Average GPA	3.20
TOEFL required of international students	Yes
Minimum TOEFL (paper/computer)	550/213
Application fee	$45
International application fee	$75
Deferment available	Yes
Maximum length of deferment	1 Semester
Transfer students accepted	Yes
Transfer application policy: Maximum 9 credit hours with at least a B from an AACSB-accredited school.	
Non-fall admissions	Yes
Need-blind admissions	Yes

EMPLOYMENT PROFILE	
Career Rating	77
Percent employed at graduation	37
Percent employed 3 months after graduation	84

THE UNIVERSITY OF TULSA
COLLINS COLLEGE OF BUSINESS

GENERAL INFORMATION

Type of school	Private
Affiliation	No Affiliation
Academic calendar	Spring, Summer, Fall Semesters

SURVEY SAYS...

Friendly students
Solid preparation in:
Teamwork, General management,
Communication/interpersonal skills

STUDENTS

Enrollment of parent institution	4,165
Enrollment of MBA Program	83
% male/female	50/50
% out-of-state	31
% part-time	25
% underrepresented minority	8
% international	23
Average age at entry	25
Average years work experience at entry	3.0

ACADEMICS

Academic Experience Rating	**81**
Profs interesting rating	84
Profs accesible rating	80
Student/faculty ratio	9:1
% female faculty	28
% underrepresented minority faculty	10
% part-time faculty	10

Joint Degrees

MBA/MSF: 61 hours MSF/MS
Applied Mathematics: 54 hours
JD/MBA: 109 hours JD/MSF: 109
hours

Prominent Alumni

Doug McMillon, President and
CEO, Wal-Mart International; Chet
Cadieux, CEO, Quiktrip Corporation;
Joe Moeller, President and COO
(Retired), Koch Industries; Bob
Prince, Co-CIO, Bridgewater
Associates; Robyn Ewing, CAO,
Williams

Academics

The University of Tulsa operates a rigorous and contemporary MBA program within the context of a small, friendly, private school environment. With a "low student-to-professor ratio," class sizes are uniformly small, and "you really get a chance to develop relationships with the faculty and other students." In the classroom, the teaching staff gets top marks for experience: "Many of them are leaders in their fields and have remained very current and relevant to the vast changes we are seeing economically and globally." They are also excellent educators, and "although classes are difficult and grades are competitive, the professors are able to drive home the overall picture of what we are studying and why." Most importantly, TU is a thoroughly supportive environment, so it's easy to stay on the right track academically. If a student needs extra help (or just wants to chat), "Professors are all readily available outside of class and genuinely interested in the well-being of each student." In addition, staff and advisors "work with students to ensure that we follow the right path, are able to do what we want and need to do, and succeed in all areas of our academic lives." A current student adds, "I have had a great experience in regards to the administration, especially the graduate advisor. She has been instrumental in helping me navigate course loads."

Although TU is a small school, the MBA program is constantly working to remain on the cutting edge. With an eye towards industry trends, administrators "recently revamped the course work to reflect what companies stated that they were looking for in MBA grads, and they also are constantly injecting anything current into the courses, seminars, and lectures." A current student observes, administrators "are constantly seeking outside input from various companies and individuals so that their students are as best prepared upon graduation as they can be." To offer one example, business ethics has been heavily introduced into the curriculum, which students say is "refreshing and relevant." In addition, the school recently redesigned the academic calendar from semesters to quarters. While they admit that, "the new MBA program still has some kinks to work out," students appreciate the fact that they can now "take a wider variety of courses." In addition to course work, TU students have the opportunity to participate in co-curricular activities on and off campus. A particularly popular offering, "the Friends of Finance organization, brings in CEOs, presidents of *Fortune* 500 companies, etc., to speak to the business students, and also offers a special session afterwards for students to ask the speaker questions one-on-one."

Career and Placement

With a "strong reputation in the energy industry" and a "prestigious reputation" in the area, TU students are well-positioned to find a choice position after graduating from the MBA program. For assistance with the career planning and placement process, "TU has a Business Career Center that is entirely focused on job placement for business students." Through the Business Center, students have access to myriad services, including resume and cover letter revisions, mock interviews, salary information, career workshops, and various online resources and job boards. In addition, "The events and workshops...allow students to have one-on-one time with executives of *Fortune* 500 companies." Recently, TU graduates have taken jobs at organizations including Bank of Oklahoma, ConocoPhillips, Deloitte Consulting, DHL, GE, Grant Thornton, Honeywell International, IBM, Level 3 Communications, PriceWaterhouseCoopers, Toyota, Trammel Crow, and the U.S. Government.

ADMISSIONS CONTACT: PATRICIA DEBOLT, MARKETING AND RECRUITING
ADDRESS: 800 SOUTH TUCKER DRIVE, HELM 215, TULSA, OK 74104-9700
PHONE: 918-631-2242 • FAX: 918-631-2142
E-MAIL: GRADUATE-BUSINESS@UTULSA.EDU • WEBSITE: WWW.UTULSA.EDU/GRAD-BUSINESS

Student Life and Environment

Drawing "a good mix of working professionals and recent graduates," TU students come from "a diverse background ethnically, academically, and professionally." Through group work and class discussions, "the diverse professional backgrounds of many of the students...lends itself to a very enriching atmosphere." Since the majority of students are "full-time working professionals or graduate student assistants that are taking classes part time," students admit that, "There isn't much time to take part in social or community activities." Nonetheless, the school offers plenty of opportunities for TU students to get together socially. For example, "graduate student luncheons take place every month where all graduate students are invited to eat and mingle." In addition, "there are many opportunities to meet other graduate students and employers at company panel sessions, etiquette dinners, and meet-and-greet times off campus."

Located on the edge of downtown Tulsa, "The campus is not large, but it is very beautiful and has all of the amenities of a larger university, just on a smaller scale." Looking to the future, the school's administration is "continually improving the campus;" For example, "Over the past three to four years they have built suite-style dormitories for student housing," in an effort to promote "a more united student body, and a better overall...experience." In addition, "The fitness facility is first class" and many students make use of the well-stocked library. The surrounding area is home to many students, and they "feel very safe walking to class in the evening."

Admissions

The Graduate Business Programs office at University of Tulsa accepts applications on a rolling basis. All students are automatically considered for merit-based scholarships (more than 80 percent of current students receive some form of merit-based aid). Students may also apply to the graduate assistantship program, through which they receive a full-tuition scholarship in exchange for 20 hours of work each week on campus. In recent years, the entering class had an average undergraduate GPA of 3.5 and an average of two years professional work experience before entering the program.

FINANCIAL FACTS

Annual tuition	$1,035 per credit hour
Cost of books	$1,600
Room & board (on/off-campus)	$5,524/$4,300
% of first-year students receiving aid	88
% of students receiving grants	89
Average grant	$18,583

ADMISSIONS

Admissions Selectivity Rating	71
# of applications received	53
% applicants accepted	96
% acceptees attending	69
Average GMAT	581
Range of GMAT	530–630
Average GPA	3.37
TOEFL required of international students	Yes
Minimum TOEFL (paper/computer)	575/232
Application fee	$40
International application fee	$40
Early application deadline	2/1
Regular application deadline	7/1
Deferment available	Yes
Maximum length of deferment	1 year from start term indicated on application
Transfer students accepted	Yes
Transfer application policy: Upon transcript review, up to 6 credit hours of related course work may be transferred from another AACSB accredited university.	
Non-fall admissions	Yes PT only
Need-blind admissions	Yes

EMPLOYMENT PROFILE

		Grads Employed by Function	% Avg. Salary
Career Rating	87		
Percent employed at graduation	80	Marketing	(20%) $75,667
Percent employed 3 months after graduation	100	Operations	(5%) $60,000
		Consulting	(10%)$57,500
Average base starting salary	$58,202	Finance	(55%) $51,380
Primary Source of Full-time Job Acceptances		MIS	(5%) $60,000
School-facilitated activities	5(25%)	Other	(5%)
Graduate-facilitated activities	1(5%)	**Top 5 Employers Hiring Grads**	
Unknown	14(70%)	National Oilwell Varco (1), Occidental Petroleum (1), Ernst and Young (1), Phillips 66 (1), Verizon Communications (1)	

UNIVERSITY OF UTAH
DAVID ECCLES SCHOOL OF BUSINESS

GENERAL INFORMATION
Type of school   Public
Affiliation   No Affiliation
Academic calendar   Semester

SURVEY SAYS...
Students love Salt Lake City, UT
Solid preparation in:
General management, Teamwork

STUDENTS
Enrollment of parent
  institution   32,388
Enrollment of MBA Program   602
% male/female   81/19
% out-of-state   25
% part-time   76
% underrepresented minority   9
% international   6
Average age at entry   29
Average years work experience
  at entry   4.5

ACADEMICS
Academic Experience Rating   85
Profs interesting rating   90
Profs accesible rating   82
Student/faculty ratio   6:1
% female faculty   23
% underrepresented minority
  faculty   9
% part-time faculty   46

Joint Degrees
MBA/MS (Bioengineering,
Mechanical Eng., Chemical Eng.,
Electrical Eng., Computer Science) 2
years; MBA/JD 4 years; MBA/Master
of Health Administration, 2 years;
MBA/Master of Architecture, 3-4
years, depending on undergraduate
degree

Prominent Alumni
J. Willard Marriot, II, Executive
Chairman, Marriott International;
Robert A. McDonald, Chair and
CEO, Procter and Gamble; Norm
Wesley, Former Chair and CEO,
Fortune Brands; Geoffrey Wooley,
Founding Partner, Dominion
Ventures

Academics

Ask a Utahan about her state's flagship university and chances are good she'll pull from a litany of the school's selling points, including "a great medical school [known for] cancer research and the treatment center; a great business school; and strong athletics traditions." "An outstanding research school," the university's prestige is well known in the Beehive State and widely regarded as well-earned. Students in the Eccles MBA programs are no outliers in this regard; they enthusiastically praise both their program and the university that hosts it.

There are strong synergies between the Eccles School of Business and the university at large. The university's offerings in healthcare, international studies, and engineering all impact a business program that has "a strong reputation for innovation and technology commercialization" and provides "opportunities in the life science industry." Eccles' greatest strength is in entrepreneurship, with a program that creates "a great niche for entrepreneurs who want to team up with engineers and the life sciences." Highlights of the entrepreneurship program include the Utah Entrepreneur Challenge, which the university sponsors; the student-run Venture Development Fund; the Lassonde New Venture Center, a "great experience that allows business students to partner with researchers on campus to commercialize technology"; and Gangplank, "a club that connect[s] aspiring students to successful entrepreneurs."

Eccles offers a full-time MBA, a Professional MBA (part-time) that "caters to working professionals," and an Executive MBA; the last is "the top-ranked EMBA program in the region," with a student body numbering over 100. All programs benefit from "terrific professors" who "bring real-world experience and insight to class." The program is rigorous, with "material taught in class [that] is the same that is taught at Harvard, Georgetown, University of Chicago, etc., because that was where our professors were recruited from." Administrators are "very hands-on to ensure that the education is of quality and that the experience of the MBA courses is exciting and relevant."

Career and Placement

The Office of Career Services for Graduate Business Students works in conjunction with the university's Career Services Office to provide counseling and career placement services including career fairs and on-campus recruiting events. Student feedback on the service is mixed. Its harshest critics dismiss it as "poor, especially if you're not in accounting or finance." Others note that the office has "taken many steps this year to improve [services] for the future," but still has further to go. And others still report that with the arrival of a new dean in 2009, "alumni connections have been greatly improved" and the administration has grown more "supportive and informative, especially on career-related matters as well as courses offered at school. They are also very enthusiastic about connecting students with activities outside classrooms, such as company visits and networking events."

Employers who most frequently hire Utah MBAs include Comcast, ATK, GE Capital, Boart Longyear, Omniture, American Express, and the federal government. Nearly 40 percent of Eccles MBAs find work in finance and accounting after leaving the program.

ADMISSIONS CONTACT: GRADUATE ADMISSIONS
ADDRESS: 1645 EAST CAMPUS CENTER DRIVE, ROOM 101, SALT LAKE CITY, UT 84112-9301
PHONE: 801-581-7785 • FAX: 801-581-3666
E-MAIL: MASTERSINFO@BUSINESS.UTAH.EDU • WEBSITE: WWW.BUSINESS.UTAH.EDU

Student Life and Environment

Eccles "is located on a hillside overlooking Salt Lake City" that is "located 15 minutes from world-class skiing (winter time) and mountain biking (summer time). The campus is in a great setting," and students try to take the opportunity to enjoy both the surroundings and campus life. UU fans are "rabid," one student informs us. "The school is confident and walks tall." In short, "the overall environment is excellent" at UU. "The school provides all the resources we need. The campus is excellent; the library is a really comfortable place to study; and most of [the] classrooms at DESB have outlets for every student, access to internet and technology needed to do presentations, etc."

The MBA program "is very supportive of students who have kids," and "there have been family-friendly tailgate parties where students can bring their families and mingle with alumni." The program also offers "some good activities for single students as well as families," including sporting events, mixers, and outings.

Eccles "is making efforts to be more internationally diverse," but "the school needs to encourage more diversity of opinions as well." The student body reflects Utah's conservative and Mormon population, though there are plenty of students from many other states, cultures, and religious backgrounds at the business school.

Admissions

The Eccles admissions committee requires applicants to provide the following: an undergraduate transcript demonstrating a GPA of at least 3.0 (students failing to meet this requirement may gain entry based on evaluation of their performance during the final two years of undergraduate work); proof of successful completion of a college-level statistics course; GMAT scores (minimum 50th percentile score in math required); two recommendations, submitted online; responses to essay questions; and a resume. International students whose first language is not English must take the TOEFL. Two years of post-undergraduate professional experience are strongly encouraged but not required. The school reports that it administers "several privately-donated scholarships reserved for underrepresented groups and [designed] to help us build the gender, ethnic, and geographic diversity of our student body."

FINANCIAL FACTS

Annual tuition (in-state/ out-of-state)	$45,000/$75,000
Fees	$900
Cost of books	$2,400
Room & board (on/off-campus)	$9,200/$12,000
% of students receiving aid	100
% of first-year students receiving aid	100
% of students receiving grants	70
Average award package	$23,538
Average grant	$8,000

ADMISSIONS

Admissions Selectivity Rating	83
# of applications received	153
% applicants accepted	57
% acceptees attending	59
Average GMAT	601
Range of GMAT	560–640
Average GPA	3.43
TOEFL required of international students	Yes
Minimum TOEFL (paper/computer)	600
Application fee	$55
International application fee	$65
Application Deadline/Notification	
Round 1:	11/1 / 12/13
Round 2:	12/1 / 1/14
Round 3:	2/1 / 3/15
Round 4:	4/1 / 5/13
Deferment available	Yes
Maximum length of deferment	1 Term
Transfer students accepted	Yes
Transfer application policy: In special circumstances, up to 6 credit hours may be transferred into the program from another AACSB program.	
Non-fall admissions	No
Need-blind admissions	Yes

EMPLOYMENT PROFILE

Career Rating	77	**Grads Employed by Function**	**% Avg. Salary**
Percent employed at graduation	74	Marketing	(29%) $80,938
Percent employed 3 months after graduation	15	Operations	(33%) $65,013
		Finance	(19%) $68,375
Average base starting salary	$69,362	HR	(2%) $86,400
Primary Source of Full-time Job Acceptances		MIS	(4%) $81,000
School-facilitated activities	25(64%)	Other	(13%) $58,625
Graduate-facilitated activities	14(36%)	**Top 5 Employers Hiring Grads**	

Instructure (2), Ford Motor Company (1), Extra Space Storage (2), Adobe (1), Proctor and Gamble (1)

UNIVERSITY OF VERMONT
SCHOOL OF BUSINESS ADMINISTRATION

GENERAL INFORMATION

Type of school   Public
Affiliation   No Affiliation
Academic calendar   12 month

SURVEY SAYS...

Students love Burlington, VT
Solid preparation in:
Operations

STUDENTS

Enrollment of parent
  institution   13,488
Enrollment of MBA Program   54
% male/female   50/50
% international   50
Average age at entry   27
Average years work experience
  at entry   4.3

ACADEMICS

Academic Experience Rating   78
Profs interesting rating   76
Profs accesible rating   76
Student/faculty ratio   5:1
% female faculty   53
% underrepresented minority
  faculty   13
% part-time faculty   0

Prominent Alumni

Doug Goldsmith, Earth Turbines,
CFO & VP, Finance & Admin; Corp.
Finance; John Paul "Jack" Barnes,
President, Banking; Bernhard
Kindelbacher, Head of Strategy,
Lufthansa Cargo; Daria Kim, Head
of Treasury, SeverStal, Moscow;
Carrie Teffner, CFO, Pet Smart; Briar
Alpert, CEO & President, Biotek
Instruments

Academics

Professors at UVM will go the extra mile as well. "They always make themselves available," says one student, "and are willing to meet outside of office hours." Some are "amazing leaders and role models." Naturally, as with almost any intense business program, students tell us "some are better and more dedicated than others," but as one candid student conveys, "The majority of the salient lessons I learned have come from other students in the business school."

Many students "work in green [industries] or have a green conscience component to their employment," so an undertone of environmental awareness and social responsibility permeates this school, no matter the discipline or course of study. The bottom line is "everyone is friendly, punctual, and dedicated to their work," and while a competitive streak is present here like almost any other graduate business program, most students actively contribute to class discussions, making for an "intelligent and relevant" MBA program.

In fall 2014, the University of Vermont will launch a new Sustainable Entrepreneurship MBA (SEMBA) program. The SEMBA program consists of a curriculum based on knowing (classroom learning), doing (project-driven learning), and being (value alignment, self-knowledge, and reflection). Sustainability will be built into the foundation of the program. The SEMBA curriculum will begin by teaching students how to start a sustainable enterprise, how to manage the enterprise as it grows, and then how to invest in its sustainability—its long-term viability. The program design includes teaching from a set of common business cases on a same enterprise that will allow the discussion of sustainability from different perspectives; business cases will draw upon the experiences of business leaders and entrepreneurs who will serve as guest speakers and co-teachers,and a number of courses will be offered by faculty from UVM's Gund Institute and the Rubenstein School of Natural Resources and by the faculty of the Vermont Law School. The program will be delivered on a twelve-month calendar. It is a full-time, lock-step program and consists of 45 credits divided into five modules, including the 3-credit hands-on practicum during the summer.

Applications for fall 2014 will be due January 1 and more information on the SEMBA curriculum and faculty can be found on the website (www.uvm.edu/business/mba).

Career and Placement

Career Services at UVM School of Business offers resume and cover letter assistance, job interview prep, and a recruiting database, as well as regular career fairs and networking events. One student tells us, "UVM has a close connection with many Vermont businesses," which would help explain why many graduating MBAs remain in Vermont or elsewhere in the Northeast. As the only AACSB-accredited program in the state, UVM MBA students have a virtual corner on the local market.

ADMISSIONS CONTACT: AMELIA COLEMAN, GRADUATE PROGRAMS COORDINATOR
ADDRESS: 332 KALKIN HALL, 55 COLCHESTER AVENUE, BURLINGTON, VT 05405
PHONE: 802-656-4119 • FAX: 802-656-4078
E-MAIL: MBA@UVM.EDU • WEBSITE: WWW.UVM.EDU/BUSINESS/MBA

Student Life and Environment

There's little doubt that those who live in Burlington are there because they love the area and its laid back lifestyle. Described by students as "a great place to live and work," both full- and part-time students have few negative if any things to say about their beloved city.

There is a student association that organizes group activities, and "1st Thursdays" give students regular occasion to "meet downtown for a drink and conversation."

Admissions

At the University of Vermont's graduate business program, there is no minimum GMAT score or undergraduate GPA required for admission. However, test scores and one's official undergrad transcript will be considered—in the admissions decision. Applicants should also submit at least two letters of reference and an essay/personal statement. GRE scores, if current, and an updated resume are also advisable. International applicants are required to submit TOEFL scores, with a minimum of 550 on the written test, 213 on computer-based, or 80 on web-based. They may also submit official scores from IELTS, with a minimum band score of 6.5. If a student has attended a U.S. institution for three or more years, UVM may waive the requirement for TOEFL/IELTS scores, determined on a case-by-case basis.

ADMISSIONS	
Admissions Selectivity Rating	**77**
TOEFL required of international students	Yes
Minimum TOEFL (paper/computer)	550/213
Application fee	$40
International application fee	$40
Early application deadline	1/1
Regular application deadline	1/1
Deferment available	Yes
Maximum length of deferment	1 year
Transfer students accepted	No
Transfer application policy: No transfer credit accepted	
Non-fall admissions	No
Need-blind admissions	Yes

UNIVERSITY OF VIRGINIA
DARDEN GRADUATE SCHOOL OF BUSINESS ADMINISTRATION

GENERAL INFORMATION

Type of school	Public
Academic calendar	Semester

SURVEY SAYS...
Good peer network, Helpful alumni, Smart classrooms
Solid preparation in:
Finance, General management

STUDENTS

Enrollment of parent institution	21,049
Enrollment of MBA Program	658
% male/female	71/29
% part-time	0
% underrepresented minority	18
% international	27
Average age at entry	27
Average years work experience at entry	4.0

ACADEMICS

Academic Experience Rating	96
Profs interesting rating	95
Profs accesible rating	96
Student/faculty ratio	7:1
% female faculty	22
% underrepresented minority faculty	14
% part-time faculty	30

Joint Degrees
MBA/JD, 4 years; MBA/MA in East Asian Studies, 3 years; MBA/MA in Government or Foreign Affairs, 3 years; MBA/ME, 3 years; MBA/MSN, 3 years; MBA/PhD, 4 years; MBA/MD, 5 years; MBA/MPH, 3 years; MBA/MPP, 3 years; MBA/MEd, 3 years

Prominent Alumni
Ms. Susan Sobbott, President, American Express OPEN; Ms. Martina Hund-Mejean, Chief Financial Officer, MasterCard World Wide; Mr. Bruce R. Thompson, Chief Financial Officer, Bank of America; Mr. Thomas J. Baltimore, Jr., President, RLJ Development, LLC.

Academics

Offering a unique, challenging, and spirited MBA program, the Darden School of Business at the University of Virginia distinguishes itself through "the outstanding reputation of the faculty and students, the rigorous and exciting case method, and the broad focus on general management that the school offers." Hailed as "one of the toughest programs in the world," the hallmark of a Darden education is the case-based curriculum—an intensive, discussion-based teaching method with an emphasis "on experiential learning in a collaborative environment and through teamwork." Sounds fun, but students warn that "the first-year curriculum is rigorous, and the case method demands students be prepared and take leadership positions." Not to mention that curricular requirements are incredibly time consuming. First-year students typically spend the day at school: Classes run from 8:00 A.M. to 2:00 P.M. and related activities can run until 10:00 P.M.

It's a challenge, but a Darden education is well worth the effort as "you really gain mastery of the material." Encouraging a lively and interactive classroom environment, the school's savvy professors "are outstanding at leading a case conversation and covering all of the key learning points." A second-year student raves, "The faculty at Darden has revolutionized my life. They have challenged me to think differently, to go deeper to find solutions to complex problems and stimulate my mind each day." Darden really distinguishes itself in its commitment to the student experience: "Professors at Darden are there because they want to teach. Students are the priority, not research." A current student enthuses, "Professors have enormous levels of experience and are ridiculously available outside class. I've gone in unscheduled and been able to spend over an hour working on an issue—the professor just made the time."

Teamwork is integral to the Darden experience, and each new student is assigned to a learning team of five or six students with whom they prepare for class each day. Working together, students say that Darden's "intense and competitive" academic atmosphere is counterbalanced by the fact that "Darden has an extremely helpful and collegial environment." In this stimulating campus setting, "The common thread running through the student body is a general sense of appreciation for the atmosphere, enthusiasm toward the learning experience, and a desire to collaborate with the learning experience through student-led review sessions, informal help sessions, etc."

Career and Placement

Students say "the Career Development Center has improved to a great extent," bringing a "record number of recruiters and companies on grounds this [past] fall." The center offers a variety of services to MBA students, including Career Discovery Forums, individual career consultations, a professional development series, and workshops and special events. Through the Career Development Center, students also have access to the Darden Networking Partnership, a database of nearly 2,000 alumni who have volunteered to help fellow grads in career searches.

Last year, 85 percent of graduates seeking employment had received a job offer by graduation, and 91 percent had received a job offer within three months of graduation. Finance was the most popular career choice, drawing 43 percent of students; consulting drew 20 percent. Among the top recruiters were: A.T. Kearney, Booz Allen Hamilton, Deloitte Touche Tohmatsu, The Boston Consulting Group, Everest, General Mills, Johnson & Johnson, Kraft Foods, Bank of America, Citigroup, Merrill Lynch, McKinsey & Company, Bain and Company, Standard and Poor's, UTC, Progressive, Danaher Corp., Mass Mutual Financial Group, Goldman Sachs, DuPont, General Electric, JPMorgan Chase, The McGraw-Hill Companies, Centex, Target, Dell, EDS, Intel, and Sprint Nextel.

ADMISSIONS CONTACT: SARA E. NEHER, ASSISTANT DEAN OF MBA ADMISSIONS
ADDRESS: P.O. BOX 6550, CHARLOTTESVILLE, VA 22906
PHONE: 434-924-7281 • FAX: 434-243-5033
E-MAIL: DARDEN@VIRGINIA.EDU • WEBSITE: WWW.DARDEN.VIRGINIA.EDU

Student Life and Environment

For those who thrive under pressure, Darden is an ideal environment as "The rhythm is extremely hectic, but the atmosphere is jovial, and there is a real palpable energy and excitement about learning in the place." In fact, Darden students seem to take a masochistic pleasure in the hectic pace of life where "Sleep is a rare commodity." In the hearty words of one first-year student: "Although the workload seems unbearable at times, and I have to schedule phone calls with my spouse, I really wouldn't trade this experience for any other." While acknowledging the rigors of the workload, students continually emphasize the kindness of the Darden community, where "Everything from the computer services to the dining hall is done for the students and with their best interests at heart."

When it comes to extracurricular activities, students reassure us that "even with the demanding workload students are very active in clubs, social events, MBA case competitions, and the community." They also manage to sneak in a moment of socializing during the daily First Coffee, "a break between classes in which you can catch up with classmates in other sections, friends, or professors. Everyone in the Darden community comes by for a cup of joe (partners and children included at times)." When it's time to relax, "Saturdays during the fall are a time for attending football games, the Chili Cook-Off, or the International Food Festival." Another favorite is "the Thursday Night Drinking Club where the majority of students meet up at a different bar every Thursday." An ideal college town, "Charlottesville is a great place to live; it has a really low cost of living without sacrificing culture."

Admissions

Darden evaluates a student's readiness for business school in three broad areas: academics, professional experience, and personal qualities and characteristics. These competencies are measured through the applicant's undergraduate record, GMAT scores, resume and work experience, letters of recommendation, and admissions essays. In addition, interviews are required and are considered an important part of the application. While there are no minimum requirements for admission, last year's entering class had a mean GMAT of 701. The mean GPA was 3.38.

FINANCIAL FACTS

Annual tuition (in-state/ out-of-state)	$44,609/$48,937
Fees	$2,391
Cost of books	$3,000
Room & board	$18,500
% of students receiving aid	76
% of first-year students receiving aid	69
% of students receiving grants	30
Average award package	$56,086
Average grant	$30,779
Average loan	$51,997
Average student loan debt	$90,949

ADMISSIONS

Admissions Selectivity Rating	**96**
# of applications received	2,269
% applicants accepted	26
% acceptees attending	54
Average GMAT	701
Average GPA	3.40
TOEFL required of international students	Yes
Minimum TOEFL (paper/computer)	650/270
Application fee	$215
International application fee	$215
Application Deadline/Notification	
Round 1:	10/17 / 12/21
Round 2:	1/12 / 3/28
Round 3:	4/4 / 5/16
Deferment available	No
Transfer students accepted	No
Non-fall admissions	No
Need-blind admissions	Yes

EMPLOYMENT PROFILE

Career Rating	**97**	**Grads Employed by Function**	**%**	**Avg. Salary**
Percent employed at graduation	83	Marketing	(15%)	$96,685
Percent employed 3 months after graduation	92	Consulting	(18%)	$124,325
		Management	(27%)	$99,621
Average base starting salary	$104,478	Finance	(32%)	$99,555
Primary Source of Full-time Job Acceptances		Other	(2%)	
School-facilitated activities	203(77%)	**Top 5 Employers Hiring Grads**		
Graduate-facilitated activities	42(16%)	Microsoft Corp. (10), Bank of America (10), Amazon.com, Inc. (8), Accenture (7), Bain & Company, Inc. (7)		

UNIVERSITY OF WASHINGTON
MICHAEL G. FOSTER SCHOOL OF BUSINESS

GENERAL INFORMATION

Type of school	Public
Affiliation	No Affiliation
Academic calendar	Quarter

SURVEY SAYS...

Students love Seattle, WA, Good peer network, Helpful alumni
Solid preparation in:
Marketing, Finance, Teamwork

STUDENTS

Enrollment of parent institution	42,570
Enrollment of MBA Program	535
% male/female	58/42
% out-of-state	53
% part-time	64
% underrepresented minority	6
% international	25
Average age at entry	29
Average years work experience at entry	6.2

ACADEMICS

Academic Experience Rating	91
Profs interesting rating	92
Profs accesible rating	87
Student/faculty ratio	5:1
% female faculty	38
% underrepresented minority faculty	24
% part-time faculty	36

Joint Degrees

JD/MBA - 4 years; MBA/MAIS - 3 years; MBA/MHA Health Administration - 3 years; MBA/MPA - 3 years; Others by arrangement

Prominent Alumni

William Ayer, Former CEO, Alaska Airlines; Dan Nordstrom, Former CEO, Nordstrom.com; Charles Lillis, Former CEO, Media One Group; Gary Neale, Chairman, Nisource; Yoshihiko Miyauchi, CEO, Orix

Academics

The Foster School of Business at the University of Washington draws on its Seattle locale to inform the focus of its program. The curriculum emphasizes a global perspective (especially as it pertains to countries in the Pacific Rim), and there is an overall focus on technology reflecting UW's proximity to such tech heavyweights as Microsoft and Amazon ("Think tons of Microsoft alums"). There are also numerous opportunities to learn about entrepreneurship, in keeping with the city's relaxed and independent vibe. In fact, many students choose UW for its "entrepreneurship and technology focus." This plays out in case studies, projects, and real-world examples drawn from these areas during core courses, as well as in areas of concentration.

Those core courses comprise about half of the Foster MBA program. Foundation subjects such as accounting, finance, ethics, and marketing are included in the required core. Toward the end of the first year, each student can begin talking electives, which allow closer exploration of areas available for concentration in the second year of the program. Students say, "All classes require a good bit of teamwork." "The level of involvement is left up to individuals, but most take part in a lot of the activities." Most students take an internship between their first and second years and return for the second year to specialize in fields such as entrepreneurship and innovation, international business, e-commerce, or marketing.

Washington's MBA students are happy with the quality of teaching, as well as the support from the university's administration. "UW has excellent professors who value teaching and helping students learn. That means everything!" The "mix of case and lecture method and small class size" also are helpful, as are professors who "go beyond to make sure that students get all the education they want." That same student adds, "I haven't met more dedicated professors than the professors at UW." Another MBA candidate says, "The core professors are superstars—far and away the best instructors I've ever had in my life." The evening MBA program is also well staffed: The "Evening program generally is taught by full-time established professors who are very good at their fields, and have made themselves available via e-mail if 'in person' is not convenient for working students."

Career and Placement

MBA Career Services in the University of Washington program offers network events, career-evaluation tools, a mentorship program with local business leaders, an online jobs data base, and personal career counseling. They "excel at connecting students with alums and other business leaders in the community and elsewhere. They stress the importance of networking and help students to establish a network." The center boasts "great connections to the Seattle business community," and "relationships with world-class companies like Microsoft, Starbucks, [and] Amazon.com." "In most cases, students are extremely successful in landing desirable internships and jobs."

Students also say there's room for improvement: "UW could improve getting access to companies and jobs outside the Pacific Northwest," one student says, and others' comments echo his opinion. However, the career center now subsidizes travel to other regions for interviews and career treks.

AT&T Wireless, Alaska Airlines, Hewlett-Packard, Intel, Microsoft, Hitachi Consulting, Samsung, Starbucks, Tektronix, and Wells Fargo are among the companies that recruit on campus.

ADMISSIONS CONTACT: ERIN ERNST, DIRECTOR OF ADMISSIONS
ADDRESS: 110 MACKENZIE HALL, BOX 353200, SEATTLE, WA 98195-3200
PHONE: 206-543-4661 • FAX: 206-616-7351
E-MAIL: MBA@U.WASHINGTON.EDU • WEBSITE: WWW.FOSTER.WASHINGTON.EDU/MBA

Student Life and Environment

Students find much to like about their classmates, the lifestyle, and the opportunities offered at the University of Washington. "UW has a collaborative, rigorous, and challenging academic environment, plus a sense of work/life balance that many schools do not have," says one student. "When I visited [before enrolling], I met several students, faculty, and staff, who all impressed me with their intelligence, enthusiasm, kindness, and humor. I knew that this was the type of community I wanted to be a part of."

"Smart people without the attitude," is how another MBA candidate described his classmates. Another says, "One of the greatest things about the MBA program is that there were activities and clubs for my wife. Some of these activities were social, while others were community-related." But improving the "quality of child care or providing child care for all students" is area that needs to be addressed, student agree. One area that doesn't need improvement are the facilities; the business school's new state-of-the-art building opened in the Fall of 2010.

Admissions

Those making admissions decisions for the Foster MBA program look for leadership potential, tech skills, communicative ability, and intellectual ability. They evaluate quantitative and language skills through transcripts, GMAT scores, GPAs, and, if needed, TOEFL scores. UW does not have minimum GMAT score or GPA requirement. "If a student is lacking in one area but strong in others, he or she may still be admitted," the school says on its website. For the most recent class admitted, the average GMAT score was 670, and the average GPA was 3.38. These students averaged six years of work experience.

FINANCIAL FACTS

Annual tuition (in-state/out-of-state)	$26,532/$39,081
Fees	$1,089
Cost of books	$1,608
Room & board	$18,416
% of students receiving aid	73
% of first-year students receiving aid	76
% of students receiving grants	54
Average award package	$35,148
Average grant	$9,145
Average loan	$21,200
Average student loan debt	$40,015

ADMISSIONS

Admissions Selectivity Rating	90
# of applications received	523
% applicants accepted	43
% acceptees attending	57
Average GMAT	670
Range of GMAT	620–730
Average GPA	3.37
TOEFL required of international students	Yes
Minimum TOEFL (paper/computer)	600/250
Application fee	$75
International application fee	$75
Early application deadline	10/15
Early notification date	12/15
Regular application deadline	3/15
Regular application notification	5/15
Application Deadline/Notification	
Round 1:	10/15 / 12/15
Round 2:	11/15 / 1/14
Round 3:	1/20 / 3/30
Round 4:	3/15 / 5/13
Deferment available	No
Transfer students accepted	Yes
Transfer application policy: Transfer applicants should apply as any other new student. The status of a transfer student is determined on a case by case basis, depending on the work completed at another school.	
Non-fall admissions	No
Need-blind admissions	Yes

EMPLOYMENT PROFILE

		Grads Employed by Function	% Avg. Salary
Career Rating	98	Marketing	(38%) $98,541
Percent employed at graduation	81	Operations	(4%) $90,533
Percent employed 3 months after graduation	97	Consulting	(21%)$97,438
Average base starting salary	$96,814	Management	(9%) $111,571
Primary Source of Full-time Job Acceptances		Finance	(20%) $92,867
School-facilitated activities	54(68%)	HR	(3%) $90,000
Graduate-facilitated activities	25(31%)	MIS	(1%) $90,000
		Other	(4%) $75,187

Top 5 Employers Hiring Grads
Amazon.com, Microsoft, PricewaterhouseCoopers, T-Mobile, Intel

University of West Georgia
Richards College of Business

GENERAL INFORMATION

Type of school	Public
Affiliation	No Affiliation
Academic calendar	Semester

SURVEY SAYS...

Students love Carrollton, GA, Happy
students, Smart classrooms
Solid preparation in:
General management

STUDENTS

Enrollment of parent institution	11,769
Enrollment of MBA Program	109
% male/female	61/39
% out-of-state	29
% part-time	72
% underrepresented minority	55
% international	35
Average age at entry	30

ACADEMICS

Academic Experience Rating	**81**
Profs interesting rating	83
Profs accesible rating	88
Student/faculty ratio	2:1
% female faculty	28
% underrepresented minority faculty	21
% part-time faculty	0

Academics

The Richards College of Business at the University of West Georgia offers an "affordable," highly accredited business program via evening or web classes that are "great for working students." Students can work out their own "flexible schedule" by enrolling in MBA courses at the main campus in Carrollton, Newnan and Douglasville. Since many people are here purely to get ahead in their current careers, the environment is often "very work intensive and challenging," but the "integrity" of the student body and the tremendous support provided by the school makes UWG an excellent fit for the needs and goals of its students.

Professors here are what one student calls "the best I have ever had the pleasure to work with," and are "very knowledgeable, willing to help, and very understanding of needs that come up, be it work, family, etc." There is great diversity among instructors, and the various backgrounds – both educational and geographic – prove to be "a winning formula for our team and the MBA program." The terrific professor to student ratio feeds into the idea of a "big school with a cozy feeling of being small."

The online MBA program is administered by the University of Georgia system, and is "tops." "Not only do I get to interact with very intelligent, driven students from all over the world, but I am able to learn from top notch professors from various University of Georgia System universities," says one student. Professors at UWG are "great to work with," and students have "always been able to get help" when it is needed. "I have professors from several different schools in my program, and have seen an overall high quality in both the teaching and the support of the students," says one.

The school's "very fair" administration is "very competent and addresses issues timely and thoroughly," and "helps students to get the best out of their stay in the school." "My school understands that there is life beyond school hours and is flexible in both schedules and demands," says a student of the "around-the-clock assistance" provided. Together, the administration and professors have "created an excellent and dynamic learning environment." "My overall academic experience has been excellent, I wouldn't have picked any other school," says a student.

Career and Placement

The diversity of both the student body and the professors" is one of the program's greatest preparatory measures for the real world, and the perspectives they bring to classes "are very practical and apply directly to career fields." The University of West Georgia is close to metropolitan Atlanta, so "many business are recruiting our graduates." "For a business school to be close to many major companies in the Atlanta area is great." Still, some students feel that "better career-oriented speakers or guests would be nice."

Student Life and Environment

"My fellow students are diverse in demographics and background," according to one student, "but are very friendly and encouraging." People come to UWG of "all ages, ethnicities, income levels, married, singles, and many nationals." Most students who go to UWG are local and commute, and since the MBA program is still relatively small, "life at UWG is very much like a community" where "you know everyone in your classes, semester after semester." "It's kind of like high school, without all the drama. We all meet up early/late in the library to study, etc.," says a student. The generally pleasant mood is also helped by the fact that the location is great: there is "no heavy downtown traffic," and "campus is beautiful and well-kept."

There is definitely "a feeling of inclusion amongst the body," even though students at UWG are mostly working students who "show up for class and leave afterward." They also adopt an attitude of "'let's get it done soon and right.'" Despite this, "there is a lot of teamwork." "Being an older student, I have had to rely heavily on the younger students and they have been a saving grace for me!" says one student. "We are all in the program for the same reason, so everyone is willing to help!" A very significant portion of the student body is international; many recently completed their undergraduate degrees (often at UWG), but some have long been out of school. Mostly, students "are getting an MBA to advance their career."

Admissions

Students are considered for admission to UWG based mainly on an admissions index number, which is calculated using a student's undergraduate GPA and GMAT scores. To be considered for admission, the analytical writing section of the GMAT must be 3.0 or higher and the total GMAT score must be 450 or more. An applicant must have a minimum of at least 950 points based on the formula: 200 x undergraduate GPA (4.0 system) + GMAT; or at least 1000 points based on the formula: 200 x upper division GPA (4.0 system) + GMAT. At the same time, students are also evaluated based on their letters of recommendation (three are required), and a current resume. Applicants to the Georgia WebMBA are also required to have two years professional work experience.

FINANCIAL FACTS

Annual tuition (in-state/ out-of-state)	$6,072/$24,192
Fees	$1,858
Cost of books	$1,300
Room & board (on/off-campus)	$8,582
% of students receiving aid	83
% of first-year students receiving aid	86
% of students receiving grants	26
Average award package	$19,918
Average grant	$927
Average loan	$13,092
Average student loan debt	$28,222

ADMISSIONS

Admissions Selectivity Rating	75
# of applications received	74
% applicants accepted	62
% acceptees attending	76
Average GMAT	469
Range of GMAT	415–525
Average GPA	3.16
TOEFL required of international students	Yes
Minimum TOEFL (paper/computer)	550/213
Application fee	$40
International application fee	$40
Regular application deadline	7/15
Deferment available	Yes
Maximum length of deferment	1year without reapplying
Transfer students accepted	Yes
Transfer application policy: A maximum of 6 Semester hours of graduate credit may be transferred from another accredited institution. See catalog for more information.	
Non-fall admissions	Yes
Need-blind admissions	Yes

UNIVERSITY OF WISCONSIN—MADISON
SCHOOL OF BUSINESS

GENERAL INFORMATION

Type of school	Public
Affiliation	No Affiliation
Academic calendar	Semester

SURVEY SAYS...

Students love Madison, WI, Friendly students, Good social scene, Happy students, Smart classrooms
Solid preparation in:
Marketing

STUDENTS

Enrollment of parent institution	42,595
Enrollment of MBA Program	351
% male/female	72/28
% out-of-state	68
% part-time	42
% underrepresented minority	20
% international	18
Average age at entry	29
Average years work experience at entry	5.2

ACADEMICS

Academic Experience Rating	**97**
Profs interesting rating	92
Profs accesible rating	88
Student/faculty ratio	3:1
% female faculty	27
% underrepresented minority faculty	2
% part-time faculty	20

Joint Degrees

JD/MBA - 4 years

Prominent Alumni

Thomas J. Falk, Chairman & CEO, Kimberly-Clark; John Morgridge, Chairman Emeritus, Cisco Systems; John Oros, Managing Director of J.C. Flowers & Co. LLC; Tadashi Okamura, Chairman Emeritus, Toshiba Corporation; Steve Bennett, Retired CEO, Intuit

Academics

The University of Wisconsin—Madison offers a unique and challenging MBA program, well suited to highly-focused students with clear career goals. Whereas most MBA programs require a wide array of course work in general management topics, the Wisconsin MBA curriculum is designed around career specializations, through which students focus their studies on a single business area such as real estate, brand management, or marketing research. Through their career specialization, students work within the business school's Centers for Expertise, which "ensure that students have lots of exposure to alumni, specific industry news, and professionals at various levels." A current student explains, "I chose the University of Wisconsin because they have a specialized program in marketing research that would give me the specialized skill set to continue in this field."

While career specializations are the hallmark of the Wisconsin MBA curriculum, "The program emphasizes strong learning within a specific discipline while allowing flexibility to learn cross-functional skills." Before beginning their studies within a specific center, students must complete the general management core curriculum, which provides a solid foundation in management essentials. Students comment that "The specified 'center' does make it difficult at times to expand into other departments." Throughout the curriculum, applied learning is an important component of the Wisconsin MBA, and students participate in live business projects for a wide range of companies. For example, students may conduct market research for leading companies, manage stock portfolios, or manage a portfolio of real estate securities.

The business school draws a team of top-notch faculty "committed to up-to-date teaching styles and topics." Student input here is valued. "Feedback is taken from the students at the end of every semester and the recommended changes are implemented for the next incoming class," says one MBA. "It's a constantly evolving and improving program that is viewed as a collaborative effort between the administration and students." On the whole, "Wisconsin represents a culture of collaboration and teamwork," and students reassure us that "when students compete, there is a general collegiate respect for one another." Another major perk of a Wisconsin MBA education is its public school price tag, made better by the fact that through assistantships "The tuition is covered, benefits are covered, and you get a stipend." A student exclaims, "You might find it hard to catch your breath, but it's a great way to avoid loans."

Career and Placement

Starting at Orientation and through the first months of their MBA, students receive plenty of help to initiate their internship search, including instruction on resume writing, interviewing, researching companies and more. After that, students have access to the Career Center's Internet database as well as one-on-one career advising with professional counselors. However, the program's unique in-depth focus is what really makes the difference in career placement. A current student explains, "Access to corporate recruiters is unprecedented since we have a program which consists of specializations, rather than a generic MBA. You get put on a niche career track right away, so recruiters know exactly what they're getting during interviews."

With strong ties in the region, 60 percent of students take jobs in the Midwest. However, for those looking to expand their horizons, students reassure us that "last year and the current year, we have been utilizing our alumni and board member connections to send a significant number of finance students out to New York for positions with bulge bracket firms." Currently, the top 5 recruiters at UW are: Johnson & Johnson, Procter & Gamble, General Mills, State of Wisconsin Investment Board, Cisco Systems, Inc.

ADMISSIONS CONTACT: MARIA REIS, ASSISTANT DIRECTOR, MBA ADMISSIONS & RECRUITING
ADDRESS: 2450 GRAINGER HALL, 975 UNIVERSITY AVENUE, MADISON, WI 53706
PHONE: 800-390-8043 • FAX: 608-265-4192
E-MAIL: MBA@BUS.WISC.EDU • WEBSITE: WWW.BUS.WISC.EDU/MBA

Student Life and Environment

When they aren't hitting the books, Wisconsin MBA students say there are "plenty of activities to become involved in, such as fundraising events, guest lecturers and social get-togethers." Even if you aren't into extracurricular activities, it's easy to get to know your classmates, because "In addition to clubs, classes, and social events, most students are well connected with the other students in their centers." Most Wisconsin MBAs maintain a balanced perspective on life, work, and studies. A current student elaborates, "The students in the business school are very serious about their studies and put in long, dedicated hours to get things done. Then they go party. It takes a mature kind of mindset to be able to effectively balance the two." Another chimes in, "It's not uncommon to work on group projects until two or three in the morning."

At this famous university, the business school is located "in the middle of campus with the 42,000 other students, so there is a constant buzz of activity." The consummate college town, students love Madison, "a city with a thriving arts and cultural scene, and plenty of opportunities for recreation and entertainment." Since the business school is close to downtown, "you get the undergraduate as well as the professional demographic all within seven blocks." With so many entertainment options, it's no surprise that "most of the MBA students go out every Thursday night for a beverage—a great way to get to know everyone."

Admissions

The University of Wisconsin—Madison seeks students from diverse personal, professional, and cultural backgrounds, who have demonstrated success in business and management. Last year's class had an average GMAT score of 675 and average work experience of 5 years. In addition to their academic and professional achievements, Wisconsin looks for students who demonstrate intellectual curiosity, motivation, leadership, communication skills, and analytical ability. An applicant's fit with their chosen career specialization, academic record, standardized test scores, and work experience are among the most important factors in an admissions decision.

FINANCIAL FACTS

Annual tuition (in-state/ out-of-state)	$14,184/$26,678
Fees	$1,111
Cost of books	$1,190
Room & board	$9,790
% of students receiving aid	81
% of first-year students receiving aid	81
% of students receiving grants	81
Average award package	$28,175
Average grant	$28,175

ADMISSIONS

Admissions Selectivity Rating	96
# of applications received	434
% applicants accepted	33
% acceptees attending	66
Average GMAT	675
Range of GMAT	640–710
Average GPA	3.33
TOEFL required of international students	Yes
Minimum TOEFL (paper/computer)	600/250
Application fee	$56
International application fee	$56
Regular application deadline	4/26
Regular application notification	5/31
Application Deadline/Notification	
Round 1:	11/5 / 12/14
Round 2:	2/4 / 3/11
Round 3:	3/15 / 4/30
Round 4:	4/26 / 5/31
Deferment available	Yes
Maximum length of deferment	1 year
Transfer students accepted	No
Non-fall admissions	No
Need-blind admissions	Yes

EMPLOYMENT PROFILE

Career Rating	96	Grads Employed by Function	% Avg. Salary
Percent employed at graduation	70	Marketing	(42%) $93,008
Percent employed 3 months after graduation	86	Operations	(11%) $94,175
		Consulting	(4%) $83,667
Average base starting salary	$91,625	Management	(7%) $91,617
Primary Source of Full-time Job Acceptances		Finance	(23%) $94,541
School-facilitated activities	73(75%)	HR	(7%) $88,824
Graduate-facilitated activities	24(25%)	MIS	(1%)
		Other	(5%) $65,000

Top 5 Employers Hiring Grads
Procter & Gamble (5), Target (5), Johnson & Johnson (4), General Mills (3), Kimberly-Clark (3)

UNIVERSITY OF WISCONSIN—MILWAUKEE
SHELDON B. LUBAR SCHOOL OF BUSINESS

GENERAL INFORMATION
Type of school   Public
Affiliation   No Affiliation
Academic calendar   Semester

SURVEY SAYS...
Students love Milwaukee, WI

STUDENTS
Enrollment of parent institution	29,768
Enrollment of MBA Program	257
% male/female	70/30
% part-time	82
% underrepresented minority	7
% international	7
Average age at entry	28
Average years work experience at entry	5

ACADEMICS
Academic Experience Rating	**83**
Profs interesting rating	77
Profs accesible rating	79
Student/faculty ratio	3:1
% female faculty	25
% underrepresented minority faculty	28
% part-time faculty	17

Joint Degrees
Master of Human Resources and Labor Relations - 2-7 years; Master Of Public Administration, Non-Profit Management - 2-7 years; MBA/MS Nursing - 3-7 years; MS-MIS.MBA - 3-7 years

Prominent Alumni
Steve Davis, Chairman and CEO, Bob Evans Farms, Inc.; Mark Doll, Sr. VP and CIO, Northwestern Mutual; Jacquelyn Frederick, President and CEO, The Blood Center of Wisconsin; John Heppner, President, Master Lock; Keith Nosbusch, Chairman, President, and CEO, Rockwell Automation

Academics

The University of Wisconsin – Milwaukee Sheldon B. Lubar School of Business offers graduate students a "variety of classes" in a "convenient location." Students have "variety and flexibility" in choosing a part-time or full-time program. The MBA degree can be completed at the main campus in Milwaukee. The Lubar School's campus is located on Milwaukee's lovely east side, a few blocks from Lake Michigan. Classes generally take place in the evening, with the exception of a few courses scheduled on Saturdays or in a hybrid online format. Students in the Executive MBA program will meet over a 17-month period on alternating Fridays and Saturdays for a series of five 10-week sessions.

The graduate programs at Lubar do "an excellent job to prepare the business leaders and managers of tomorrow." Besides the core courses in management, students may also pursue an elective in cost management and ERP, e-business, entrepreneurship, financial strategy, global strategy, HR management, IT management, innovation management, investment management, leadership, manufacturing and service operations, managing change, health care management, supply chain management, marketing, or nonprofit management. The programs on the whole offer concrete "academic challenges." There is also a "good business community in Milwaukee" that students are able to take advantage of both during the program and after graduation.

Faculty at UWM consists of "strong professors with a business aptitude." They "do a great job in lecture explaining the material." One student comments about undergraduate teachers at a different university who "were intelligent about the subject matter, but could not teach at all." However, this same student avows, "The teachers at UW-Milwaukee really know how to teach." Having professors with direct experience of the business topics that they teach is deemed important to many students. "Most of the professors have been in the business world so they are able to provide practical examples during discussions." It was also noted that there are "some exceptional professors, dedicated to student learning and outcomes."

When asked about their school, UWM students "have nothing but good things to say about the administration, professors and [their] overall experience." Of course, there is always room for improvement. There were some suggestions regarding class offerings such as the addition of "online classes." Another student would like to see "more school spirit" on campus, especially at sporting events where it seems to be lacking.

Career and Placement

While most MBA students are employed full-time, UWM provides students at the Lubar School of Business with an array of programs and services to assist in job placement after graduation. There are career fairs, a resume referral service program that helps match students with the appropriate employers, a confidential alumni database placement service for employers to locate prospective candidates, on-campus recruiting services, and internships. Advisors are also available for mock interview sessions; job postings; help with resume design, cover letter writing, and interviewing; as well as scheduling on-campus interviews online via the e-Recruiting system. Recent top employers of Lubar graduates include US Bank, Kohler Company, Rockwell Automation, and Aurora Health Care. Other recent employers include Ernst & Young, Miller Brewing Company, Stark Investments, Cobalt Corp., and Wells Fargo. However, students did note the school's need of "getting more companies to recruit" on their list of improvements.

ADMISSIONS CONTACT: MATT JENSEN, MBA/MS PROGRAM MANAGER
ADDRESS: PO BOX 742, MILWAUKEE, WI 53201-0742
PHONE: 414-229-5403 • FAX: 414-229-2372
E-MAIL: MBA-MS@UWM.EDU • WEBSITE: WWW.UWM.EDU/BUSINESS

Student Life and Environment

Life at the University of Wisconsin – Milwaukee is "busy," though "great." For students looking for more ways to be involved, there is an abundance of professional business student organizations from which to choose. Although, many students are "not super involved" due to schedules that keep them away from campus, some manage to find the time for extracurricular activities. Although one student points out, there are "lots of activities for undergrads, not necessarily so for grads."

Students at UWM fall into a wide range of ages but the average student age is 28. The students are "professional, hard-working, [and] friendly," and most "look to be [in their] mid 30's" and seem to "fall within a large range from 'Just graduated from College' to 'Mid-level managers.'" Students at UWM are "intelligent" and "down to earth." Working on team projects is a good way to get to know this "dynamic" group of students and is usually a rewarding experience since everyone is so "willing to learn." One student explains, "Everyone has been really great to work with. Whenever I've been in teams, everyone has pulled their weight and set a target of an A grade."

Admissions

Prospective candidates should send completed applications online to the UW-Milwaukee Graduate School website for review and recommendation. All applicants must submit a completed application form, an official GMAT score, one official copy of transcripts for all undergraduate work, and a personal statement. Letters of recommendation will also be considered. Students must achieve a minimum undergraduate GPA of 2.75 and have a GMAT score "that indicates a high probability of success in graduate school" to be considered for "admission in good standing." Applicants who fail to meet these minimum requirements may be granted "admission on probation" status. International students must meet all of the above requirements and must also submit an official TOEFL score report. Previous work experience is not necessary upon enrollment. Admissions are accepted on a rolling basis, and students in programs other than the EMBA or CO-20 MBA may start in any semester.

FINANCIAL FACTS

Annual tuition (in-state/ out-of-state)	$11,739/$23,887
Cost of books	$900
Room & board (on/off-campus)	$9,000/$10,000
% of students receiving aid	30
% of first-year students receiving aid	50
% of students receiving grants	8
Average award package	$16,078
Average grant	$13,265
Average loan	$14,037
Average student loan debt	$21,056

ADMISSIONS

Admissions Selectivity Rating	82
# of applications received	141
% applicants accepted	50
% acceptees attending	61
Average GMAT	559
Range of GMAT	500–610
Average GPA	3.20
TOEFL required of international students	Yes
Minimum TOEFL (paper/computer)	550/79
Application fee	$56
International application fee	$96
Application Deadline/Notification	
Round 1:	8/1
Round 2:	1/1
Round 3:	5/1
Deferment available	Yes
Maximum length of deferment	1 year
Transfer students accepted	Yes
Transfer application policy: The application process is the same for all applicants.	
Non-fall admissions	Yes
Need-blind admissions	Yes

EMPLOYMENT PROFILE

Career Rating	65	Grads Employed by Function	% Avg. Salary
Percent employed at graduation	63	Marketing	(2%) $46,500
Percent employed 3 months after graduation	98	Management	(40%) $63,845
		Finance	(35%) $57,091
Average base starting salary	$71,782	MIS	(13%) $69,750
		Other	(10%) $51,000

Top 5 Employers Hiring Grads
Kohler Co., Rockwell Automation, GE Healthcare, U.S. Bank Corp.

UNIVERSITY OF WISCONSIN—WHITEWATER
COLLEGE OF BUSINESS AND ECONOMICS

GENERAL INFORMATION

Type of school	Public
Affiliation	No Affiliation
Academic calendar	Semester

SURVEY SAYS...
Solid preparation in:
Marketing, General management,
Doing business in a global economy,
Social responsibility

STUDENTS

Enrollment of parent institution	10,720
Enrollment of MBA Program	570
% male/female	55/45
% out-of-state	10
% part-time	85
% underrepresented minority	1
% international	28
Average age at entry	34
Average years work experience at entry	5.0

ACADEMICS

Academic Experience Rating	74
Profs interesting rating	77
Profs accesible rating	84
Student/faculty ratio	28:1
% female faculty	29
% underrepresented minority faculty	22
% part-time faculty	0

Academics

The University of Wisconsin-Whitewater offers "a great business school" for "anyone on a budget." One current student tells us, "I chose UW-Whitewater for my MBA because of the school's reputation, and they have the courses I want to be able to specialize in marketing." Adopting a two-pronged approach, UW-Whitewater offers students either a traditional in-class MBA or an online-only option, full- or part-time, both at "an affordable price compared to other AACSB-accredited programs." The online program in particular was recently ranked in U.S. News & World Report as one the country's top-25 online MBA programs, and students can complete the program in one year with the proper prerequisites. Whatever one's time commitment or location, there are "two types of grad students" at UW-Whitewater: "The MBA students and MPA (master's of accountancy) students," both of whom can now take advantage of Hyland Hall, the school's new "state-of-the-art" business building, which has "changed the school 100 percent" for the better. What's more, MBA or MPA students getting their degree online—many of whom have "never stepped foot on campus"—enjoy the convenience of things "like chat groups [that] are not live meetings." According to one online student who lives in Japan, "When you are doing an online degree many students are in different time zones and have difficulty making meetings." Another online student, a self-proclaimed "full-time career woman and mother" shares with us that the online program "fits my lifestyle."

While UW-Whitewater "isn't as famous as UW-Madison," the school does boast "one of the best accounting master's programs in the nation," and according to many a student, "well-experienced" professors who are "accessible," "have high credentials," and "make themselves readily available outside of the classroom." As one pleasantly surprised student puts it, "I thought that a lot of my professors did not have real-world experience, but a majority of them have 20+ years." "However," one full-time student offers, "a few should not be in the teaching career because of a lack of understanding."

There is no typical graduate student at UW-Whitewater; it's more of "a mix of students who are older and seeking greater academic qualifications, as well as those students . . . starting an MBA right after undergraduate" work. To add to this already diverse make-up, MBA students have a wide array of concentrations from which to choose, including finance, human resources management, international business, IT management, marketing, technology and training, and operations and supply chain management. Study-abroad programs are also available in France, Czech Republic, Mexico, Netherlands, Russia, Sweden, England, Switzerland, and Australia. The University also offers support services for international and minority students. "While I cannot say that UW-Whitewater is just as good as the expensive schools," one student tells us, "I would recommend this school over and over again to anyone considering an MBA."

Career and Placement

The University's Career Services Office offers "numerous programs and presentations" for students, including career counseling, career groups, a resource center and classes, resume and cover letter workshops, career fairs, interview prep, online job postings, on-campus interviews, and related resources. The career office is much more a resource for those students who attend classes on campus, while online-only students may feel left out for obvious reasons. However, one student reminds us, "There are so many ways to participate and always e-mails coming out for job openings and career fairs." But in terms of servicing this growing community of online students, the "Career Services Office seems lost as to how to help students search for jobs and how to help them connect with employers." For those students on campus, other improvement needs are cited,

ADMISSIONS CONTACT: JOHN D. CHENOWETH, ASSOCIATE DEAN
ADDRESS: 800 WEST MAIN STREET, WHITEWATER, WI 53190
PHONE: 262-472-1945 • FAX: 262-472-4863
E-MAIL: GRADBUS@UWW.EDU • WEBSITE: WWW.UWW.EDU

such as a "better mentoring program" and attracting a more diverse set of employers to the school's job fairs, besides Target and Walgreens. All the same, with a mean base salary of $54,000 for recently graduated full-time students, newly minted MBAs from UW-Whitewater aren't doing too badly these days.

Student Life and Environment

There's no two ways to cut it, "Whitewater is remote," but several students assure us that they've "enjoyed living in a small town," which can provide the quiet and seclusion many people need while earning their graduate degree. However, with few local employment opportunities, one student tells us, "No one really stays in Whitewater after graduation." Located "about an hour from the capital" of Madison, and not too far from Milwaukee either (from which several students hail), "the town itself is lacking in many ways," with "only one grocery store . . . and one or two clothing stores. Students must travel 30 minutes to a city that has a satisfactory place to shop." Several on-campus clubs and organizations allow students to get involved and apply their new skills and knowledge, but for the most part, UW-Whitewater is a school for commuters or those with full-time day jobs (85 percent of students attend part-time). "Convenience," above all else, is what UW-Whitewater students cite time and again about their school. Commuters have little trouble managing their class schedules, and online-only students praise the fact that they can "take classes from anywhere in the world." There is definitely "a lot of variety" in terms of classes and concentrations, although some students would like to see more "weekend classes for working professionals."

Admissions

With a mostly part-time student body of working professionals and online-only students, undergraduate GPAs and GMAT scores (both required for all applicants) tend to cover a wide range. The average undergrad GPA for MBA students is 3.2, and the average GMAT score is 479. However, those applicants with lower than average numbers in either category should not feel deterred, as optional materials like letters of reference, resume/work experience, and extracurricular activities can potentially shift the scales in one's favor. International applicants must submit TOEFL scores, with a minimum of 550 on the written test or 213 on the computer-based test.

FINANCIAL FACTS

Annual tuition (in-state/ out-of-state)	$8,730/$18,214
Cost of books	$2,800
Room & board (on/off-campus)	$3,700
Average grant	$500
Average loan	$0

ADMISSIONS

Admissions Selectivity Rating	**72**
# of applications received	183
% applicants accepted	83
% acceptees attending	86
Range of GMAT	300–700
Average GPA	3.20
TOEFL required of international students	Yes
Minimum TOEFL (paper/computer)	550/213
Application fee	$56
Deferment available	Yes
Maximum length of deferment	1 year
Transfer students accepted	Yes
Transfer application policy: They must meet the same requirements as a non-transfer student. Nine credits may be transferred into the program.	
Non-fall admissions	Yes
Need-blind admissions	Yes

VALPARAISO UNIVERSITY
COLLEGE OF BUSINESS

GENERAL INFORMATION
Type of school | Private
Affiliation | Lutheran

SURVEY SAYS...
Solid preparation in:
General management,
Communication/interpersonal skills,
Presentation skills

STUDENTS
Enrollment of parent
  institution | 4,100
Enrollment of MBA Program | 66
% male/female | 50/50
% out-of-state | 44
% part-time | 76
% underrepresented minority | 25
% international | 19
Average age at entry | 30
Average years work experience
  at entry | 8.0

ACADEMICS
Academic Experience Rating | **90**
Profs interesting rating | 88
Profs accesible rating | 88
Student/faculty ratio | 2:1
% female faculty | 25
% underrepresented minority
  faculty | 15
% part-time faculty | 5

Joint Degrees
Juris Doctorate/Master of Business
Administration 4 years

Prominent Alumni
Rachel Saxon, President, Horizon
Trust & Investment Management;
Joan Fischmann, AVP, Chicago
Federal Reserve Bank; Jay Jorbin,
Director of International Finance,
Walgreens; Paul Stark, Manager of
Logistics & Planning, ArcelorMittal;
Jeff Perry, Global Risk Manager,
Kellogg

Academics

Lutheran-run Valparaiso University offers "strong academic programs with an emphasis on values-based leadership and sustainability," thereby creating MBAs who are "well-equipped to be the leaders of the future green economy," students report. It's a big deal; Valpo's "commitment to moral and ethical standing" is frequently cited by students when asked to explain why they chose to attend this northwest Indiana university. Convenience, especially for the part-time students who make up about half the MBA student body, is another factor. Valpo offers evening classes and "the integration of online class options," through which live on-campus classes are broadcast over the Internet (allowing those participating remotely to participate in class). Valpo's online software also allows students to collaborate on group projects remotely.

Valpo's MBA program is small and relatively new. It is also innovative, particularly in its scheduling. Valpo's eight-week bloc system creates six different entry dates during the academic year and allows a pick-and-choose approach that accommodates both fast-trackers and those who need take a little more time to complete the degree. The Valpo MBA entails 14 core courses and six elective, or "enhancement" courses; the latter run the gamut from business reporting to brand management to e-commerce. Students who lack adequate undergraduate training in business are required to complete a series of foundation courses in addition to their core and enhancement work.

The small size of the MBA program and a "low student-to-professor ratio" mean plenty of "individual attention from professors," which students appreciate. "Access to mentors and extra projects is excellent" here, and students report that "it's easy to get into the classes you want" (although class selection, due to the size of the program, is limited). Professors bring "real-world experience" to the classroom to "provide real-world examples that we can immediately implement at work." Administrators are "constantly looking to improve the available programs. They seek student input [on] topics [ranging from]…new courses offered to the overall strategic plan of the university."

Career and Placement

Valpo's MBA program is only a decade old. Students admit that "the word has not spread about Valpo," and the business community is just beginning to catch on to this new source of talented recruits. However, with the power of the Valparaiso name behind it and the strength of the MBA curriculum, students know it's just a matter of time before their program begins to draw its rightful share of attention from recruiters.

Many Valpo students are already employed when they begin their MBA and plan to continue at their current companies after graduation. However, those who are looking for new positions have access to the Valparaiso University Career Center. The Career Center serves the school's graduate and undergraduate community and offers a variety of professional development workshops and career counseling, an annual campus career fair, and a job search database.

ADMISSIONS CONTACT: CINDY A. SCANLAN, ASSISTANT DIRECTOR MBA
ADDRESS: 104 URSCHEL HALL, 1909 CHAPEL DRIVE, VALPARAISO, IN 46383
PHONE: 800-599-0840 • FAX: 219-464-5789
E-MAIL: MBA@VALPO.EDU • WEBSITE: WWW.VALPO.EDU/MBA

Student Life and Environment

Valpo MBAs are primarily part-time students. Part-timers range from 22 to 54 years old and have, on average, almost seven years of professional experience coming into the program. They typically "exhibit strong leadership skills with an emphasis on integrity, fairness, honesty and trust." Full-timers tend to be younger, less experienced, and less likely to be valued class partners. "Those students who have been in the workforce following undergrad are good learning partners. Those straight from undergrad tend to be detrimental to the learning experience," one MBA opines. International students make up 1 percent of the part-time student body and 3 percent of the full-time population.

There is "little to do" in the small town of Valparaiso, so most students who live on campus "stay in on the weekends either to study or talk with friends." On campus, there are athletic events and multicultural events weekly for our enjoyment," and the program "encourages interaction with fellow students outside the classroom throughout the week." For those seeking big city entertainment, Chicago is only 50 miles to the northwest—you can't get much more "big city" than that! On the other hand, part-timers are typically too busy for any of that.

Admissions

Admissions decisions are made on a rolling basis with six different entry dates offered during the year (thanks to the program's eight-week course schedule). Valparaiso makes admissions decisions holistically, assessing a combination of undergraduate and postgraduate academic performance, applicable professional experience, letters of recommendation, GMAT scores (working professionals can apply for a GMAT waiver), and a one-page personal statement describing the applicant's goals in order to determine the candidate's potential to benefit, and to benefit from, a Valpo MBA. In addition to the qualifications listed above, international students whose first language is not English must submit an official score report for the TOEFL or IELTS. All international students must submit an Affidavit of Financial Support.

FINANCIAL FACTS

Annual tuition	$36,348
Fees	$498
Cost of books	$1,200
Room & board	$13,500
Average grant	$0

ADMISSIONS

Admissions Selectivity Rating	**89**
# of applications received	62
Average GMAT	527
Range of GMAT	480–560
Average GPA	3.30
TOEFL required of international students	Yes
Minimum TOEFL (paper/computer)	577/233
Application fee	$30
International application fee	$50
Early application deadline	6/28
Early notification date	7/12
Regular application deadline	7/26
Regular application notification	8/9
Deferment available	Yes
Maximum length of deferment	1 year
Transfer students accepted	Yes
Transfer application policy: Students must meet admission requirements. Up to 6 credit hours from another AACSB-accredited institution, subject to approval.	
Non-fall admissions	Yes
Need-blind admissions	Yes

EMPLOYMENT PROFILE

Career Rating	66	**Grads Employed by Function% Avg. Salary**	
Percent employed at graduation	67	Finance	(25%) $55,000
Average base starting salary	$44,014	Other	(75%) $58,667
Primary Source of Full-time Job Acceptances		**Top 5 Employers Hiring Grads**	
Graduate-facilitated activities	10(42%)	Northern Illinois University (1), Teach for	
Unknown	14(58%)	America (1), UGN (1), Silgan (1)	

VANDERBILT UNIVERSITY
OWEN GRADUATE SCHOOL OF MANAGEMENT

GENERAL INFORMATION
Type of school   Private
Affiliation   No Affiliation
Academic calendar 7-week modules

SURVEY SAYS...
Good social scene, Good peer net-work, Helpful alumni, Happy students
Solid preparation in:
Communication/interpersonal skills, Social responsibility

STUDENTS
Enrollment of parent
  institution   12,859
Enrollment of MBA Program   162
% male/female   64/36
% part-time   0
% underrepresented minority   15
% international   20
Average age at entry   28
Average years work experience
  at entry   4.5

ACADEMICS
Academic Experience Rating   **96**
Profs interesting rating   95
Profs accesible rating   95
Student/faculty ratio   10:1
% female faculty   1
% underrepresented minority
  faculty   1
% part-time faculty   1

Joint Degrees
MBA/JD, 4 years; MBA/MD, 5 years; MBA/MDIV, 4 years; MBA/PhD Medicine or MBA/PhD Engineering, 3 years after the start of core courses at Owen; MBA/BA or MBA/BS, 5 years

Prominent Alumni
David Farr, CEO, Emerson Electric; David Ingram, Chairman & President, Ingram Entertainment; Adena Friedman, Carlyle Group, Chief Financial Officer; Doug Parker, Chairman, President & CEO, U.S. Airlines; Josue Gomes de Silva, President, Coteminas (Brazil)

Academics

Students are drawn to Vanderbilt University's Owen Graduate School of Management for its "outstanding reputation, world-class professors, impressive network of alumni, prestigious program, [and] competitive employment rates upon graduation." However, above and beyond the prestige of attending a top university, students universally cite the "small school size" as the "number one" draw. The tight-knit community "gives Owen a big advantage when it comes to administration and classes." As one student attests, "There has never been a class that I was not able to take, with the professor I wanted to take it with. Furthermore, it is very easy to get access to the world-class faculty here. I have great experiences working for hours one-on-one with celebrity professors [that] it might be impossible to even get into class with at a different institution. I was particularly impressed by the school's ability to have classes taught by Senators, Congressmen, and *Fortune* 500 CEOs."

Owen has a great reputation for energizing "a sense of camaraderie between the students as well as between the students and faculty." Though course work is "a very challenging and demanding experience," "students are very driven to excel, but do so while supporting one another." The academic atmosphere is "competitive, while maintaining a sense of camaraderie." All students "have a strong sense of honor." In essence, Owen "gives back a multiple of your effort." Due to the small class sizes, students benefit from individual attention. "You really get to know everyone in your class which helps to develop a strong network for your professional career." This sense of camaraderie pays off down the line when it comes to seeking out a career; "Given the small size of the student body, alumni are very receptive when you reach out for networking and advice."

Owens's MBA program "is known for its strong performance in the finance sector," as well as "one of the best healthcare MBA programs in the country." The school "is efficiently run, and the professors are accessible, social, and are willing to help in any way they can." Overall, the academic experience here "is extremely pleasant." Garnering equal praise as that attributed to professors, the school administrators are "fantastic and accessible." "Both the Dean and other administrators are more than willing to meet with students to address concerns."

Career and Placement

From the top brass to those working in career management, "the school is extremely well-organized and unfailingly prepared." Owen's Career Management Center "has beefed up efforts significantly given the recession." That said, students are always hoping to "increase the volume of on-campus recruiting." Others add, it's "easy to navigate a wide range of social and cultural activities balanced by dozens of neighboring market leaders in diverse industries that allows insights into career tracks and opportunities. The alumni community, stretched all over the world, is very generous with [its] time and insight, too."

In 2011, 87 percent of full-time MBA graduates seeking employment had received a job offer within three months of graduation. For those who accepted positions, the mean base salary was $91,653. Pharmaceutical/Biotechnology/Healthcare, Financial Services, and consumer products are the industries attracting the majority of recent Owen graduates with General Electric, Goldman Sachs, and Johnson and Johnson listed as the top five employers in 2009.

Student Life and Environment

By in large, students at Owen embrace the age-old, "work hard, play hard approach." Students "are competitive academically but not to the point [that] they are unwilling to help or that they don't have a social life." The Owen culture "embraces diversity but we are collaborative in our social, personal, and professional discourse. We work hard and intelligently and moreover, [we] take advantage of Nashville-based social outlets to reduce stress and activate an intense sense of camaraderie." A nostalgic second year adds, "I have developed friendships in business school at Owen that are just as strong as the friendships I had in college. It's important to have such a welcoming atmosphere like the one at Owen so that you can balance your life as well as possible while in business school."

Nashville "is a great city." As one resident confesses, "I'm from the north and was very reticent to move below the Mason Dixon line. I'm convinced Nashville is a diamond in the [rough]—a city that has yet to be discovered and appreciated for its great food, live music, and expanding economy." Every Thursday night, "students...and the faculty mingle at a social for several hours. The relationships we are building with each other and the teachers are a vital part of our education." In addition, "the city has plenty of options for outdoor activities, music, food, bars, and sports." However, students lament, "there is no on-campus housing for post-graduate students," and a "bigger library with more study rooms would be great!"

Admissions

With an incoming class size of approximately 175 students each year, the Vanderbilt MBA program is one of the world's most selective. Admission to the full-time MBA program is highly competitive. Admissions officers seek out an "exceptionally talented and diverse group of students who are willing and able to grow, prosper, and contribute in an environment that is academically rigorous, professionally rewarding, and personally enriching." In selecting candidates for admission, incoming students are evaluated for their academic aptitude and interest, experience and goals, and personal qualities and potential. The class which entered in fall of 2011 had an average GPA of 3.4 and an average GMAT of 695.

FINANCIAL FACTS

Annual tuition	$43,902
Fees	$828
Cost of books	$1,788
Room & board	$9,192
% of students receiving aid	77
% of first-year students receiving aid	82
% of students receiving grants	71
Average award package	$47,074
Average grant	$18,557
Average loan	$44,644
Average student loan debt	$87,587

ADMISSIONS

Admissions Selectivity Rating	96
# of applications received	1,014
% applicants accepted	33
% acceptees attending	49
Average GMAT	695
Range of GMAT	640–760
Average GPA	3.40
TOEFL required of international students	Yes
Early application deadline	10/3
Early notification date	11/22
Regular application deadline	11/28
Regular application notification	1/20
Application Deadline/Notification	
Round 1:	10/3 / 11/22
Round 2:	11/28 / 1/20
Round 3:	1/16 / 3/9
Round 4:	3/5 / 4/19
Deferment available	Yes
Maximum length of deferment	1 year
Transfer students accepted	No
Non-fall admissions	No
Need-blind admissions	Yes

EMPLOYMENT PROFILE

Career Rating	97
Percent employed at graduation	67
Percent employed 3 months after graduation	83
Average base starting salary	$91,653

Primary Source of Full-time Job Acceptances

School-facilitated activities	108(71%)
Graduate-facilitated activities	32(21%)
Unknown	12(8%)

Grads Employed by Function% Avg. Salary

Marketing	(19%)	$88,226
Operations	(7%)	$86,286
Consulting	(19%)	$105,632
Management	(11%)	$84,909
Finance	(28%)	$89,968
HR	(10%)	$94,250
Other	(6%)	$75,875

Top 5 Employers Hiring Grads

Deloitte (7), Bank of America Merrill Lynch (5), General Electric (4), Goldman, Sachs & Co. (4), Johnson & Johnson (4)

VILLANOVA UNIVERSITY
SCHOOL OF BUSINESS

GENERAL INFORMATION
Type of school	Private
Affiliation	Roman Catholic
Academic calendar	Semester

SURVEY SAYS...
Good peer network, Cutting-edge classes
Solid preparation in:
Teamwork, Communication/interpersonal skills, Presentation skills

STUDENTS
Enrollment of parent institution	10,626
% male/female	68/32
% part-time	100
Average age at entry	27
Average years work experience at entry	5

ACADEMICS
Academic Experience Rating	89
Profs interesting rating	85
Profs accesible rating	91
Student/faculty ratio	4:1
% female faculty	34
% underrepresented minority faculty	17
% part-time faculty	34

Joint Degrees
The Villanova School of Business and the Villanova School of Law offers the JD/MBA: 24–36 months. In addition, VSB offers a MAC to MBA and MSF to MBA program

Prominent Alumni
Beth Mazzeo, COO, Bloomberg; Christopher T. Gheysen, President & CEO, WaWa; Robert F. Moran, President and COO, PetSmart; Robert J. McCarthy, COO, Marriott International, Inc.; Thomas Quindlen, President & CEO, GE Capital Corporate Finance

Academics

For Philly professionals, the Villanova MBA is a smart choice, providing "solid academic rigor while allowing a degree of flexibility needed for working professionals." Widely known as the "best part-time program offered in the area," the MBA is offered on two urban campuses and in two distinct formats. Busy students with demanding jobs will appreciate the Flex MBA, which can be started any semester and allows students to complete coursework in three to five years of study. In the Flex MBA, "You can really move at your own pace based on work/life balance, financial readiness, and learning style." Those looking for maximum efficiency will likely prefer the cohort-based Fast Track program, which allows you to complete the MBA in two years while maintaining full-time employment. In addition to praising the speedy degree, Fast Track students say "the cohort environment is incredibly beneficial with regards to networking."

For students in either track, the MBA begins with core coursework, including accounting, economics, and management. After completing the core, students choose electives from a "large variety of course offerings," and have the option of tailoring their degree by pursuing a specialization in finance, health care management, international business, corporate management, or marketing, or by pursuing a real-estate concentration through the Daniel M. DiLella Center for Real Estate. "Elective courses are outstanding," and include special "opportunities for international travel and learning" through the overseas programs; recent trips have taken students to business capitals like Dubai and Milan. Villanova doesn't stop there: In addition to coursework, students must complete a consulting project with a local nonprofit company, and another with a global corporation. (Note that "the Fast Track curriculum includes a one-week international trip" as a part of the Strategic Management for Global Organizations class, though overseas programs are optional for Flex Track students.) Finally, "The Leadership Development classes that bookend the program are especially valuable in group work and networking for MBA students."

The faculty comprises both academics and career professionals, so "Some core courses have more academic-oriented professors while some have professors with substantial work experience." While students might prefer one type of professor to the other, all agree that it's "a good balance" among the faculty. Just as important, most professors are accessible, friendly, and "really want to help students maximize their potential." A student adds, "So far, I have nothing but good things to say about the teaching quality at Villanova. I've never had a problem reaching a teacher outside of class, and I've never had a professor that I didn't understand." That said, The Villanova curriculum was recently revamped, and students mention that, "There have definitely been some serious kinks in the administrative side of the program." Fortunately, "the staff encourages and actually listens to student feedback," so problems rarely persist.

ADMISSIONS CONTACT: MEREDITH LOCKYER, MANAGER, RECRUITMENT & ADMISSIONS
ADDRESS: OFFICE OF GRADUATE AND EXECUTIVE PROGRAMS, VILLANOVA SCHOOL OF BUSINESS,
1074 BARTLEY HALL, VILLANOVA, PA 19085 • PHONE: 610-519-4336 • FAX: 610-519-6273
E-MAIL: GRADBUSINESS@VILLANOVA.EDU • WEBSITE: WWW.GRADBUSINESS.VILLANOVA.EDU

FINANCIAL FACTS

Annual tuition	$855–1,000 per credit
Cost of books	$860

ADMISSIONS

Admissions Selectivity Rating	90
% acceptees attending	86
Average GMAT	610
Average GPA	3.3
TOEFL required of international students	Yes
Minimum TOEFL (paper/computer)	550/213
Application fee	$50
International application fee	$50
Regular application deadline	6/30
Deferment available	Yes
Maximum length of deferment	up to one year
Transfer students accepted	Yes
Transfer application policy: Up to nine credits from AACSB accredited MBA Programs	
Non-fall admissions	Yes
Need-blind admissions	Yes

Career and Placement

As a part-time program, Villanova isn't focused on job placement as much as on preparing students to excel in their current field. Certainly, the Villanova MBA will help you "to improve your career options and ultimately to get a better job"; for most Villanova students, however, that better job is something they are pursuing at their current company, rather than through a career search. As such, the MBA program doesn't offer many recruitment or networking opportunities for graduate students.

Those looking to make a career change generally "have to create their own opportunities through networking sites such as LinkedIn, or postings on job sites." Fortunately, students note an improvement is already in process: "There is a new graduate career placement person who has been very diligent in working with students for positions after their MBA." In addition, the school offers a number of career-related resources, including corporate information sessions, career coaching, and online resources, and students can also reach out to Villanova's "strong alumni network."

Student Life and Environment

Given the inherent struggle of maintaining a full-time job while pursuing a graduate degree, it's no surprise that Villanova students are generally "engaged and hardworking," though they are a "friendly and collaborative" bunch, too. A huge benefit academically and socially, students at Villanova are "very diverse in terms of academic background, work experience, life experience, ethnicity, interests, and age." Here, you'll share a classroom (and chat over drinks) with "early- to mid-career professionals across a wide-range of industry sectors, ranging from healthcare to energy to financial services."

At Villanova, "most students work all day and then attend class at night," which makes for an incredibly busy schedule. Fortunately, that doesn't mean MBAs never socialize. While some students spend little time at school or with their MBA colleagues, others forge meaningful friendships in the program. "After class, a lot of the students go to the bar together," and the school schedules various events, including "regular casual happy hours, resume and LinkedIn profile counseling, lectures, [and] fundraisers," at both Villanova campuses. One student enthuses, "The networking opportunities that the program has provided me have far exceeded what I expected, especially in a part-time program. I have made a lot of friends who I expect will be lifelong contacts."

Admissions

For both the Flex Track and the Fast Track MBAs, students submit official academic transcripts, GMAT scores, two recommendations, a professional résumé, answers to two essay questions, and, for international students, the TOEFL. The current class has a GMAT range (for the middle 80 percent) of 570–700, an average undergraduate GPA of 3.3, and about six years of work experience before entering the program.

VIRGINIA COMMONWEALTH UNIVERSITY
SCHOOL OF BUSINESS

GENERAL INFORMATION
Type of school   Public
Affiliation   No Affiliation
Academic calendar   Semester

SURVEY SAYS...
Smart classrooms
Solid preparation in:
General management

STUDENTS
Enrollment of parent
  institution   31,963
Enrollment of MBA Program   180
% male/female   72/28
% part-time   72
% international   10
Average age at entry   28
Average years work experience
  at entry   3.5

ACADEMICS
Academic Experience Rating   82
Profs interesting rating   77
Profs accesible rating   84
Student/faculty ratio   20:1
% female faculty   15
% underrepresented minority
  faculty   5
% part-time faculty   24

Joint Degrees
Pharm.D./MBA - 5 years;
MBA/MSIS - 3 years; MBA/MEd
Sport Leadership - 2 years

Academics

With a "low tuition rate," "flexibility in class choice and time," and a reputation as "an up-and-coming school," the School of Business at Virginia Commonwealth University has numerous assets with which to lure potential MBAs. One VCU student tells us that he "explored other local options, such as the University of Richmond, and found that the quality of faculty, reputation for excellent, well-balanced instruction and the reasonable cost made VCU the more attractive option." Most who choose the VCU MBA feel the same way.

VCU's Richmond location is a major asset, students agree. Richmond is home to a number of major corporate headquarters, and MBAs report that this creates excellent networking opportunities. VCU's solid reputation with regional employers helps translate those opportunities into positive results. Many of these same employers feed the VCU MBA program with young managers looking for a leg up in their careers, many of who plan to stay with their companies post-graduation (in fact, quite a few attend on their employer's dime). Several students cite "support of the community businesses and government" as one of VCU's main selling points.

The VCU MBA program offers "a wide variety of MBA concentrations," including business analytics, global business, human capital, managing innovation, real estate, and supply chain management. "Excellent" professors seek "to teach the students how to think outside of the box" and often succeed, according to the MBAs we surveyed. Administrators are "flexible...they're pretty good about allowing substitute courses, etc." They also have a vision for the future. As one student puts it, "the school's momentum is its strength. A great effort has been undergoing since the new [business school facility] was built." "Programs have been redesigned to [meet] the needs in today's economy and business world. The courses are actually based on everyday life...which adds both to the attractiveness of the courses and their usefulness also."

Career and Placement

The Career Center at the VCU School of Business serves all undergraduate and graduate students in the School of Business. The office provides a wide range of counseling, skills development, and placement services. Area businesses also contact the School of Business directly to post internship and career opportunities available to MBA students. Students can stay up-to-date on such notifications by subscribing to the School of Business Listserv. About 75 percent of VCU's MBA students attend part-time; nearly all work part-time or full-time, many for companies with whom they intend to remain after graduation. One student who sought, and found, a post-MBA position through the Center tells us that the "Career Services Center is excellent. I was given the opportunity to go to two career fairs on campus in the fall of 2009. I also took advantage of the bus ride to the MBA Career Quest career fair at the University at Maryland, College Park. The Career Services Center also got me two interviews on campus with federal government agencies. I was offered both positions!"

ADMISSIONS CONTACT: JANA P. MCQUAID, ASSOCIATE DEAN, MASTERS PROGRAMS
ADDRESS: 301 WEST MAIN STREET, PO BOX 844000, RICHMOND, VA 23284-4000
PHONE: 804-828-4622 • FAX: 804-828-7174
E-MAIL: GSIB@VCU.EDU • WEBSITE: WWW.BUSINESS.VCU.EDU/GRADUATE

Student Life and Environment

The VCU School of Business recently moved into a "state-of-the-art…newly built" facility that "provides a comfortable, well-designed environment, including all of the technological amenities one would expect of a top-tier business school." While many crow about "all the high technology installed" here, some are just as impressed that "the parking deck is located right next to [the] business school building." Despite the convenience, many students here tell us that "parking is quite the issue unless you purchase a parking pass."

VCU's "convenient" campus location is "equidistant from downtown Richmond and the more college-town environment of 'the Fan' district." Life on campus "is very diverse, with an established art school and up-and-coming business and engineering schools. The student life reflects the characteristics one might find in each of these three schools." The MBA program hosts "many clubs and organized meetings" that help "academic and social communication and activities occur seamlessly." Not everyone is fully engaged; "there is a very small group of students who are full-time and involved," with many others attending part-time while working at part-time or full-time jobs. The latter group has little time to participate in extracurriculars.

The VCU MBA program "is geared to part-time students, full-time employees. Most [students] are reimbursed for classes by their employers." These "friendly" and "professional" students "from diverse backgrounds" "take their academic studies seriously, as they are quite competitive. They're sociable and are very professional in their manners and their interactions with each other."

Admissions

Applicants to all MBA programs at VCU must submit a completed application, one copy of official transcripts for all post-secondary academic work, an official GMAT score report, a resume, a personal statement, and three letters of recommendation. International applicants whose first language is not English must also provide proof of English proficiency (the school accepts both the TOEFL and the IELTS and evidence of sufficient financial support to cover the cost of attending and expenses while at VCU. VCU admits students for the fall, spring, and summer semesters.

FINANCIAL FACTS

Annual tuition (in-state/ out-of-state)	$8,616/$17,883
Fees	$2,289
Cost of books	$2,500
Room & board (on/off-campus)	$10,000/$12,000
% of students receiving aid	40
% of first-year students receiving aid	59
% of students receiving grants	17
Average award package	$12,758
Average grant	$5,719
Average loan	$15,847
Average student loan debt	$29,067

ADMISSIONS

Admissions Selectivity Rating	77
# of applications received	86
% applicants accepted	59
% acceptees attending	59
Average GMAT	528
Range of GMAT	505–570
Average GPA	3.25
TOEFL required of international students	Yes
Minimum TOEFL (paper/computer)	600/250
Application fee	$50
International application fee	$50
Regular application deadline	7/1
Regular application notification	7/15
Deferment available	Yes
Maximum length of deferment	1 year
Transfer students accepted	Yes

Transfer application policy: Students who were admitted to and completed coursework at other AACSB accredited institutions may apply to VCU and seek transfer of up to six Semester hours of work toward the VCU graduate degree. Students must have earned no less than a "B" in each class to be transferred. The decision to transfer courses is left to the discretion of the Associate Dean of Masters Programs in Business.

Non-fall admissions	Yes
Need-blind admissions	Yes

VIRGINIA POLYTECHNIC INSTITUTE AND STATE UNIVERSITY
PAMPLIN COLLEGE OF BUSINESS

GENERAL INFORMATION

Type of school   Public
Affiliation   No Affiliation

SURVEY SAYS...
Students love Blacksburg, VA,
Friendly students, Good social scene
Solid preparation in:
Finance, Communication/
interpersonal skills

STUDENTS

Enrollment of parent institution	31,087
Enrollment of MBA Program	316
% male/female	68/32
% out-of-state	66
% part-time	47
% underrepresented minority	2
% international	48
Average age at entry	26
Average years work experience at entry	2.0

ACADEMICS

Academic Experience Rating	84
Profs interesting rating	80
Profs accesible rating	83
Student/faculty ratio	27:1
% female faculty	25
% underrepresented minority faculty	18
% part-time faculty	11

Joint Degrees
MBA/Master of International Management (33 Semester hours in the Pamplin MBA Program and 30 trimester hours at Thunderbird). l'Institute National des Telecommunications (INT) in France

Prominent Alumni
John Ritzert, Attorney/Private Practice; Mark Krivoruchka, Sr. VP/Human Resources; Todd Rowley, Sr. VP/Banking; Kurt Barkley, Managing Director/Investment Banking; Angela Parrish, Client MGR/Consulting

Academics

The Pamplin College of Business at Virginia Polytechnic Institute offers a number of MBA programs in an intimate atmosphere and at a reasonable cost. Virginia Tech has a full-time MBA, a part-time MBA, a Professional MBA, and an Executive MBA, though they are each at different locations. The school also offers four dual-degree programs: Masters of Industrial and Systems Engineering/MBA, Masters of Civil Engineering/MBA, Masters of Building Construction/MBA, and Masters of International Business/MBA in partnership with either the Thunderbird School of Global Management in Arizona or Telecom Ecole de Management in France. Students in the full-time MBA program take one year of foundation classes and specialize in one of the following areas their second year: Finance, Organizational Management & Strategy, General Marketing, and Information Technology. Students can also "design a custom curriculum, which incorporates the MBA core materials and is tailored to their specific career goals."

Students are very happy with the program overall. They "love how small the classes are" because they gain tons of "hands-on learning" experience, "know all of their classmates personally," and easily "interact with the faculty and administration." Students say their professors are "incredibly up to date on what's going on in the world" and make sure students understand the practical application of classroom material. "The big picture is crucial to success in class," one student explains, "If you aren't working on how this applies to the larger context of the professional world, you're missing out." Professors are "always willing to speak with students, and often the conversations are incredibly engaging beyond just the coursework. Professors also provide connections to leading business people and alumni who can offer advice, mentorship, and their own network to you." The administration "works hard to make the program successful" and is "always willing to hear what's going on," including student ideas "on how we can integrate some of the latest trends into courses." One student says that recently, "blogging and the importance of social media branding has been diversified beyond marketing into a job search course," which was "something that came from student interest."

Career and Placement

Virginia Tech's MBA Career Services office does everything it can to make sure students are prepared for the job search and to land the jobs they want. The office offers personalized career counseling, workshops, talks, and "corporate visits." Additionally, students can participate in career fairs and mentoring programs. "The alumni network of Virginia Tech is amazing," which means lots of chances for "networking." Students who graduated last year were hired at many prestigious companies, including Pricewaterhouse Coopers, Deloitte, Capital One Bank, Nielson, Ernst & Young, and Accenture.

Student Life and Environment

Virginia Tech's various MBA programs are offered at three different campuses in Virginia, with the full-time MBA located in Blacksburg. Of the atmosphere at Blacksburg, students say it's "a campus with heart," and the "sense of community is very strong." "We are passionate about serving the community," one student says, "and you see the passion for life every day." Students are constantly planning projects to help those in Haiti or Africa, but they also care about those closer to home. "If you miss a class," your peers "will not only notice, but give you call to make sure you're all right." The "very active MBA Association" brings "professional, social, and service opportunities to the students within the MBA program." Students "get together often for social events and spend a significant amount of the day in study groups." The rest of the University offers a lot of activities, including clubs and sporting events.

Nearly fifty percent of students at Virginia Tech are international students, and their American peers really appreciate that the program is "very ethnically diverse." "Look around the room of a Virginia Tech MBA class," and you'll see "people from countries around the world, and not just in the 'we're trying to meet our quotas' sense." For the most part, everyone really "meshes," and the small class sizes and rigorous curriculum means everyone "gets to know each other very well both inside and outside the classroom." Students are "very outgoing and intelligent" and "competitive," yet "down-to-earth." There's a lot of school pride. One student describes Virginia Tech as "one of the most highly spirited universities that I have ever experienced." Another simply says, "my fellow students are the kind of people I hope to work with in the real world."

Admissions

Virginia Tech does not have an admissions quota, but instead selects students who will "enhance the classroom environment." While each of Virginia Tech's MBA programs have different requirements, all students must submit two letters of recommendation and a resume, and sit for an interview. Not all programs require previous work experience, but an applicant's professional background is certainly considered when relevant. Last year's entering full-time MBA class had an average GMAT score of 624 and an average undergraduate GPA of 3.46. International students whose primary language is not English must take the TOEFL, and the admissions office is looking for students who achieve 100 on the Internet-based portion, 235 on the computer-based portion, and 600 on the paper-based portion, though it will consider students who do not reach these standards.

FINANCIAL FACTS

Annual tuition (in-state/out-of-state)	$10,677/$20,926
Fees	$5,636
Cost of books	$8,340
Room & board	$8,820
% of students receiving aid	94
% of first-year students receiving aid	78
% of students receiving grants	81
Average award package	$22,975
Average grant	$13,857
Average loan	$17,310
Average student loan debt	$34,375

ADMISSIONS

Admissions Selectivity Rating	85
# of applications received	173
% applicants accepted	52
% acceptees attending	54
Average GMAT	627
Range of GMAT	610–650
Average GPA	3.46
TOEFL required of international students	Yes
Minimum TOEFL (paper/computer)	550/213
Application fee	$65
International application fee	$65
Early application deadline	12/1
Early notification date	12/15
Deferment available	Yes
Maximum length of deferment	1 year
Transfer students accepted	No
Non-fall admissions	No
Need-blind admissions	Yes

EMPLOYMENT PROFILE

Career Rating	87	Grads Employed by Function	% Avg. Salary
Percent employed at graduation	53	Marketing	(12%) $65,333
Percent employed 3 months after graduation	66	Operations	(12%) $64,000
		Consulting	(20%) $81,200
Average base starting salary	$67,392	Management	(8%) $60,000
Primary Source of Full-time Job Acceptances		Finance	(20%) $65,000
School-facilitated activities	17(68%)	MIS	(12%) $70,667
Graduate-facilitated activities	8(32%)	Other	(16%) $55,405

Top 5 Employers Hiring Grads
PWC (3), Ernst & Young (1), Deloitte (1), KPMG (1), Capitol One (1)

WAKE FOREST UNIVERSITY
SCHOOLS OF BUSINESS

GENERAL INFORMATION
Type of school	Private
Affiliation	No Affiliation
Academic calendar	Semester

SURVEY SAYS...
Friendly students, Smart classrooms
Solid preparation in:
Finance, Teamwork, Quantitative skills

STUDENTS
Enrollment of parent institution	7,079
Enrollment of MBA Program	356
% male/female	77/23
% out-of-state	69
% part-time	66
% underrepresented minority	13
% international	23
Average age at entry	28
Average years work experience at entry	4.5

ACADEMICS
Academic Experience Rating	88
Profs interesting rating	86
Profs accesible rating	89
Student/faculty ratio	6:1
% female faculty	30
% underrepresented minority faculty	12
% part-time faculty	41

Joint Degrees
JD/MBA (Law/MBA) – 4 years
MD/MBA (Medicine/MBA) – 5 years
PhD/MBA (Graduate School of Arts & Sciences/MBA) – 5 years
MSA/MBA (Accountancy/MBA) – 6 years

Prominent Alumni
Charles W. Ergen, Founder, Chairman, President & CEO, EchoStar Corporation; Donald E. Flow, Chairman & CEO, Flow Automotive Companies; Warren A. Stephens, Chairman, President & CEO, Stephens, Inc.; Eric C. Wiseman, Chairman, President & CEO, VF Corporation

Academics

The Wake Forest University Schools of Business offers "a first-rate education delivered in a small school atmosphere that is conducive to high levels of interaction between students and the faculty." Students universally laud the "personal touch" the graduate business program employs with its "commitment to academic excellence, strong faculty, [and] small class size that enables plenty of interaction among students and faculty."

Academics at Wake Forest follow a holistic approach. The integrated curriculum helps students learn to analyze and solve problems by understanding the many components of a solution. Course content follows suit and is organized around a strong first-year core which includes essentials such as international business management, financial management, macroeconomics, operations management, and quantitative methods. In their second year students choose a career concentration within the broader areas of consulting/general management, finance, entrepreneurship, marketing, operations management, health, or an individually-designed concentration. As one student attests, "The workload...is generally much more intense than what most students expect coming into the school and in comparison to students at similar schools. However, this intense and well-rounded education has already proven beneficial in my summer internship and in job interviews."

The administration is "easily accessible and from faculty to staff, everyone is friendly. Student voices can be heard." When it comes to professors, at Wake Forest it's a first name, open-door policy; "All of my professors are engaged in my success. The level of dedication is a defining factor that sets Wake Forest apart," says one student. In addition, the "Dean has fantastic visions for the school." Dean of Business Steve Reinemund, former chairman and CEO of PepsiCo, believes that by developing passionate business leaders who are ready to succeed in the marketplace the School's overall goal—to impact the marketplace in positive ways and to get results with integrity—will be achieved.

Career and Placement

Wake Forest alumni "are very open to mentoring and helping with [students] job search." However, some current MBA students feel "Career Development needs to better prepare students for the internship and job search...clubs could have more activities that connect students with potential employers." In addition, current students would like to see more "diversity of companies that come to campus." Right now, "the focus is primarily on the Southeast, but they are taking strides to move to a more national scope." However, others note that the Career Management Center has already been making strides to improve; "For example, a dedicated mentoring program and alumni outreach program has been developed and is being implemented."

In 2011, 100 percent of full-time MBA students seeking employment received a job offer within three months after graduation with those accepting jobs averaging a mean base salary of $82,035. Bank of America, Ernst & Young, FedEx, Hanesbrands Inc., and Lowe's Co. were the top five employers of 2009 grads with financial services and consumer products being industries with the biggest draw.

ADMISSIONS CONTACT: STACY POINDEXTER OWEN, DIRECTOR OF GRADUATE BUSINESS ADMISSIONS
ADDRESS: 1834 WAKE FOREST ROAD, WORRELL PROFESSIONAL CENTER, ROOM 3208
WINSTON-SALEM, NC 27106 UNITED STATES • PHONE: 336-758-5422 • FAX: 336-758-5830
E-MAIL: BUSADMISSIONS@WFU.EDU • WEBSITE: WWW.BUSINESS.WFU.EDU

Student Life and Environment

Wake Forest MBAs are "outgoing, dedicated, hard workers who are easy to get along with and fun to be around." There are countless student activities and the academic work is rigorous, but students love the atmosphere and enjoy getting together to debate key topics of the day or cheer on the Demon Deacons at a basketball game. "We are a tight-knit group. Everyone knows everyone for the most part. The week can get pretty busy, but a lot of us play intramurals or pickup games during the week." Fridays are the time "when we all go out and blow off some steam. Students, even ones on different teams, will help each other out."

Life on campus "is fast-paced and exciting." The workload is pretty demanding, but there is time for fun." "The student government "puts on lots of social events that bring most people out to socialize." There are "tons of clubs, activities, both athletic, cultural, and community oriented," and "the town of Winston-Salem also has plenty of dining venues." The typical day at Wake "ranges from all-nighter's in the study room with your learning team to happy-hour events in the courtyard where students cut loose, to Alive at 5 concerts in downtown. It very much is a work hard play hard atmosphere," which "prepares you well for the future." "Quality of life is part of what makes Wake Forest such a great place to be." In essence, Wake Forest's Full-Time MBA Program is full of "brilliant, type-A achievers you can get along with." There is "a prevailing atmosphere of collaboration and support." There is also excitement about the upcoming fall 2013 completion of Farrell Hall, the future state-of-the-art home of the School of Business.

Admissions

The Wake Forest University Schools of Business "seeks individuals who have demonstrated achievement through academic course work, professional experience, and community involvement." Admissions Counselors "look for leadership ability, motivation, focus, enthusiasm, strong values, and teamwork skills in its prospective students." Postgraduate work is extremely important to the admissions process. All full-time MBA applicants must have at least 24 months of full-time, post-graduate work experience prior to the August of their application year. Through the Wachovia Scholars Program, the Wake Forest University Schools of Business offer scholarships to full-time students from underrepresented minority groups. These scholarships include a full-tuition waiver, stipend and an international summer study trip. The average GPA for the 2011 entering class was 3.2 with a mean GMAT score of 651.

FINANCIAL FACTS

Annual tuition	$38,988
Fees	$626
Cost of books	$2,000
Room & board	$10,000
% of students receiving aid	88
% of first-year students receiving aid	92
% of students receiving grants	70
Average award package	$40,686
Average grant	$17,585
Average loan	$43,780
Average student loan debt	$49,689

ADMISSIONS

Admissions Selectivity Rating	88
# of applications received	335
% applicants accepted	41
% acceptees attending	46
Average GMAT	651
Range of GMAT	630–683
Average GPA	3.20
TOEFL required of international students	Yes
Minimum TOEFL (paper/computer)	600/250
Application fee	$100
International application fee	$100
Early application deadline	11/1
Early notification date	12/1
Regular application deadline	4/15
Deferment available	No
Transfer students accepted	No
Non-fall admissions	No
Need-blind admissions	Yes

EMPLOYMENT PROFILE

Career Rating	94	Grads Employed by Function	% Avg. Salary
Percent employed at graduation	70	Marketing	(29%) $79,300
Percent employed 3 months after graduation	93	Operations	(9%) $77,500
		Consulting	(19%) $91,750
Average base starting salary	$82,035	Management	(8%) $77,333
Primary Source of Full-time Job Acceptances		Finance	(27%) $81,833
School-facilitated activities	29 (56%)	HR	(2%)
Graduate-facilitated activities	13 (25%)	MIS	(4%)
Unknown	10 (19%)	Other	(2%)

Top 5 Employers Hiring Grads
Bank of America (4), Ernst & Young (4), FedEx (3), Hanesbrands Inc. (3), Lowe's Cos. (3)

WASHBURN UNIVERSITY
SCHOOL OF BUSINESS

Academics

For Topeka professionals, the MBA at Washburn University's School of Business has a lot of selling points, among them its "location, reputation, cost, and appealing schedule for full-time workers." An "amazing value," this public school offers "lower tuition" than many business programs, yet maintains its standing as "one of the best business schools in [the] Midwest." No matter what your schedule and educational goals, Washburn makes it possible to complete a graduate degree without disrupting your career. "There are traditional day classes, as well as an abundance of night-class options," which gives busy professionals the opportunity to "work full-time and get a world-class MBA" simultaneously. Those who want to complete the program more quickly can enroll in more classes, taking up to a full course load. The school also offers a JD/MBA dual degree through which six hours of credit from the law school can be applied to the MBA.

As a true "teaching institution," Washburn's classroom experience is greatly enhanced by the fact that Washburn professors "love to teach and share what they know." They are also "skillful at encouraging students to lead the class," which makes coursework "interesting and engaging" across disciplines. The school boasts small class sizes and an excellent teacher-student ratio, so it's "easier to interact with professors and fellow students." "Accessible" professors keep regular office hours, and many "love collaborating with students on research or outside projects." In fact, "Professors tend to form relationships with promising students, offering assistance whenever asked." The student-oriented faculty is complemented by a "very friendly and cooperative staff" and administration; however, students warn that, "Outside of the School of Business, it can be difficult to get various tasks accomplished (i.e., financial aid, registrar issues, etc.)"

Washburn's curriculum is divided into nine foundation-level courses and eight upper-level business classes, followed by two advanced elective courses; students with an undergraduate degree in business can waive many or all of the foundational courses. Covering finance, quantitative methods, marketing, international business, strategy, and information systems, the Washburn curriculum is more academic than experiential. Through the school's professors come from "diverse backgrounds," contributing a great deal of "real world experience" to the academic environment, many students would like to see the school "provide opportunities for students to branch out, gain experience, and even earn credit through non-traditional routes." Students also note the general "lack of electives" makes it harder to specialize in a specific business discipline. Not to mention, most elective courses aren't offered every semester. A current MBA candidate notes, "I would love to have had the opportunity to engage in more specialized elective courses, aside from the general course requirements."

ADMISSIONS CONTACT: DR. ROBERT J. BONCELLA, MBA DIRECTOR
ADDRESS: SCHOOL OF BUSINESS, WASHBURN UNIVERSITY, TOPEKA, KS 66621
PHONE: 785-670-1308 • FAX: 785-670-1063
E-MAIL: MBA@WASHBURN.EDU • WEBSITE: WWW.WASHBURN.EDU/BUSINESS/MBA

Career and Placement

The Washburn MBA is an ideal program for "full-time workers that would like to grow in their company or look for upper-level positions." Classes are geared toward improving your business knowledge and skill set, and many students hope to leverage their education into a better job at their company or in their field. However, the school offers few on-campus recruitment programs, networking, or interviewing opportunities for students considering a career change. A student says, "I would expect more head-hunting from surrounding companies, but that just does not happen."

MBA candidates hoping to find a new gig after graduation can get assistance from the campus Career Services office. They offer career counseling services and host career fairs on campus that are open to undergraduates, graduate students, and alumni; recent career fairs were attended by local employers like Payless ShoeSource, CBW Bank, Cintas Corporation, and the City of Topeka. Prospective MBA candidates should note, however, that the majority of the opportunities offered through Career Services are geared toward undergraduates. As a result "most of the 'opportunities' that are presented to MBA students do not actually fit the ambitions of such individuals."

Student Life and Environment

Located in the heart of Topeka, "Washburn is a physically small institution, spanning just a few city blocks in each direction." The intimacy of the campus contributes to the close-knit feeling among the student body. With a limited enrollment of fewer than sixty students, it's an intimate atmosphere; a current student attests, "It feels like I know everyone in the MBA program." Students come to Washburn from "from diverse backgrounds and cultures," as well as from a range of professional backgrounds. In addition to locals, the school has "a great international student presence, as well, which adds a more worldly perspective to classroom discussions and reports."

Although the program was specifically designed to accommodate working professionals, there are also a handful of full-time students at Washburn. During the daylight hours, full-timers "study as a group in the library and participate in activities on campus," from sports to student clubs. Specifically aimed at graduate business students, the MBA Association is often involved in "inviting guest speakers and gathering MBA students in activities" around campus. Here, part-time students don't feel left out of campus life: "Unlike some institutions, though, Washburn is "alive" almost all hours of the day, due to its course flexibility."

Admissions

To be considered for admission at Washburn's MBA program, students must have an undergraduate GPA or 2.75 or better and a minimum GMAT score of 450, and those numbers must combine to meet a minimum "admissions index" number (which means that a higher GPA can offset a lower GMAT score and vice versa, though neither number can be excessively low). Students are also required to submit two letters of recommendation from former professors or employers. Applications are received and processed on a rolling basis.

FINANCIAL FACTS

Room & board	
(on/off-campus)	$11,500

ADMISSIONS

Admissions Selectivity Rating	70
# of applications received	20
% applicants accepted	100
% acceptees attending	100
Average GMAT	497
Range of GMAT	465–530
Average GPA	3.26
TOEFL required of	
international students	Yes
Minimum TOEFL	
(paper/computer)	550/213
Application fee	$40
International application fee	$110
Deferment available	Yes
Maximum length	
of deferment	One Semester
Transfer students accepted	Yes
Transfer application policy: Meet WU MBA Admission Requirements and we will accept up to nine hours from an AACSB Accredited Graduate Program.	
Non-fall admissions	Yes
Need-blind admissions	Yes

WASHINGTON UNIVERSITY IN ST. LOUIS
JOHN M. OLIN SCHOOL OF BUSINESS

Academics

Washington University's stellar MBA program "has a reputation for academic excellence without a hyper-competitive atmosphere." The small class sizes really allow for a "community based learning experience, [both] in and out of the classroom." Additionally, Olin affords students a "large degree of flexibility in course selection" and many "credits can be electives." Ultimately, this "provides students with a lot of freedom to design their own path." Further, most MBA candidates highlight both the finance and entrepreneurship programs as especially strong.

Just as essential, Olin manages to attract (and retain) "very friendly and smart" professors who are quite "approachable and...willing to spend time talking with you and discussing about current trends in business." Indeed, they "are generally very interested in individuals outside of their presence in the classroom, and they are even willing to share contacts with past students if a connection can be made."

For the most part, students have had positive interactions with the administration as well. A second-year shares, "The administration and staff [are] very engaging and willing to help out wherever possible...Every challenge I have faced was resolved within a week." A content peer chimes in, "The school's administration and faculty met and exceeded my expectations. They strive to make the program an individualized experience: one where you feel as though you, as an individual, have the potential to bring significant value to the program, the classroom, and the Olin community." Finally, a first-year student succinctly summarizes, "The overall academic experience has been phenomenal."

Career and Placement

When it comes to the job market, Olin MBAs are definitely competitive applicants (as evidenced by "very high post graduation employment rates"). Indeed, Wash U. "has a great reputation with a number of outstanding companies that hire for...general corporate management, finance, and operations." Additionally, as one marketing student proudly reveals, there's a "strong recruiting presence for brand management" as well. Many students are also "extremely impressed by [the] career services office." The counselors available provide fantastic, personalized advice tailored to each student's individual skill-sets and professional interests.

While you can definitely find a smattering of Wash U. MBAs scattered about the country, the majority of graduates finds jobs within the Midwest. Employers that frequently hire Wash. U. students include Citigroup, First National Bank of Omaha, IBM, Microsoft, Proctor & Gamble, Wells Fargo, Johnson & Johnson, Emerson, and Nestle Purina Pet Care.

ADMISSIONS CONTACT: EVAN BOUFFIDES, DIRECTOR OF MBA ADMISSIONS AND FINANCIAL AID
ADDRESS: 1 BROOKINGS DR., CAMPUS BOX 1133, ST. LOUIS, MO 63130
PHONE: 314-935-7301 • FAX: 314-935-6309
E-MAIL: MBA@WUSTL.EDU • WEBSITE: WWW.OLIN.WUSTL.EDU

Student Life and Environment

MBA candidates find Olin to be a "very inclusive" program, replete with "friendly" students who are definitely "open to building relationships." A first-year supports this notion stating, "As a small program, I can honestly say I knew everyone in my class by the end of the first semester and had the opportunity to work with a diverse team." And a second-year quickly follows up, "We know that our success requires teamwork and collaboration, so we are all sure to respect each other and help out where we can." Further, "We have insanely diverse backgrounds and experiences that lead to fun and engaging in-classroom and outside classroom discussion. We are passionate, but not cut-throat competitive."

Additionally, you can be assured that "there's never a dull moment" at Olin. To begin with, "you have so many ways to explore all of your interests and meet incredible thinkers and business leaders." Indeed, "there are events nearly every day of the week to attend. Workshops, fairs, club events, social events, etc can quickly fill up our schedules." Beyond the campus, students can readily take advantage of St. Louis, "a fantastic city [in which] to be a student. There are a ton of free museums and activities to take part in on the weekend, and the city as a whole is experiencing a renaissance right now. [And] because rents are cheap, it's possible to have a fantastic apartment or house on a student budget."

Admissions

Naturally, gaining admission to Olin is no cakewalk. The admissions committee truly wants to create a diverse class of students. Therefore, they do their utmost to select applicants from varying backgrounds. Moreover, they certainly take a holistic approach, considering experience, academic ability and leadership potential. The school offers six different application rounds (though from April 1st onward it operates on a rolling basis). If Olin is high on your list, we recommend applying as early as possible.

FINANCIAL FACTS

Annual tuition	$47,800
Fees	$1,100
Cost of books	$2,400
Room & board (on/off-campus)	$0/$16,800

ADMISSIONS

Admissions Selectivity Rating	94
# of applications received	1,289
% applicants accepted	34
% acceptees attending	32
Average GMAT	698
Range of GMAT	670–730
Average GPA	3.43
TOEFL required of international students	No
Application fee	$0
International application fee	$0
Application Deadline/Notification	
Round 1:	11/15 / 1/15
Round 2:	1/4 / 3/31
Round 3:	2/15 / 4/15
Round 4:	4/1 / 6/1
Deferment available	Yes
Maximum length of deferment	If approved - 1 year
Transfer students accepted	Yes
Transfer application policy: With approval, up to 9 credits from an AACSB-accredited graduate program.	
Non-fall admissions	No
Need-blind admissions	Yes

EMPLOYMENT PROFILE

Career Rating	98	Grads Employed by Function	% Avg. Salary
Percent employed at graduation	79	Marketing	(29%) $91,800
Percent employed 3 months after graduation	96	Operations	(6%) $85,000
		Consulting	(25%) $103,217
Average base starting salary	$94,762	Management	(7%) $93,000
Primary Source of Full-time Job Acceptances		Finance	(26%) $91,300
School-facilitated activities	55(57%)	HR	(1%)
Graduate-facilitated activities	37(39%)	Other	(5%) $88,467
Unknown	4(4%)	**Top 5 Employers Hiring Grads**	
		Citi (5), Deloitte Consulting (4), Lumeris Healthcare (4), Emerson (3), Kimberly-Clark (3)	

WAYNE STATE UNIVERSITY
SCHOOL OF BUSINESS ADMINISTRATION

Academics

Asked why they chose the School of Business Administration at Wayne State, most MBAs cite the affordability and convenience of the program. The school offers classes at its 203-acre main campus in Midtown Detroit, the Oakland Center in Farmington Hills and online; students extol these "convenient campus locations to choose from" and appreciate that "every MBA course can be taken at your choice of the two campuses or online." Evening classes and "a very flexible online class schedule" further help to facilitate the busy schedules of WSU MBAs, the great majority of whom work full-time while pursuing their degrees.

A "good finance" program and a strong local alumni network are among the other assets cited by students here. MBAs also point out that "WSU is an urban research-centered school," so "if you were interested in being a researcher, there are some great opportunities here." The downtown campus is "set in an urban environment" that "helps students get an education above and beyond classroom lectures," and because some adjunct "professors who teach the MBA classes work for local companies," participation in the program "is great for networking," not only with instructors but also with working classmates. Professors, students tell us, "have a nice mix of textbook-to-real world experience and knowledge... many published works and a few were either a CEO or high-ranking executive at a successful company. They challenge us to become better students but make themselves available to assist us in accomplishing our goals."

On the downside, some instructors have not yet figured out how to maximize the online course format even as it grows more popular with students. "Though some professors structure their in-class and online courses very, very well, this is not the norm at this school," one student explains. In many cases, "all we get are three to four-hour lectures, a talking head, and PowerPoint. The professors generally record their in-class lectures so we can't hear the students' questions," which students describe as "very annoying. It makes it hard to stay interested and focused." Some here also feel that the curriculum could use some revamping to place "more emphasis on core subjects and less on electives. Currently there is a 50/50 split."

Career and Placement

Dedicated solely to students in the School of Business Administration, the Career Planning and Placement Office offers career counseling and professional development assistance to undergraduate and graduate students, as well as alumni of Wayne State. The center hosts a variety of on-campus interviews, career days, and meet-and-greet events. The center also offers career counseling services and comprehensive online resources. The school is well-integrated into the Detroit community; "In the Detroit area Wayne State business, medical, and law school alumni can be found in all industries and are happy to help fellow Wayne State alumni," one student reports.

A vast majority of Wayne State students are already working in a full-time, professional capacity when they begin their MBA. Therefore, many students are more focused on progressing in their current job, rather than making a career change or finding new positions.

ADMISSIONS CONTACT: AMBER CONWAY, DIRECTOR, GRADUATE PROGRAMS OFFICE
ADDRESS: GRADUATE PROGRAMS OFFICE, 5201 CASS, ROOM 103, DETROIT, MI 48202
PHONE: 313-577-4511 • FAX: 313-577-5299
E-MAIL: GRADBUSINESS@WAYNE.EDU • WEBSITE: WWW.BUSINESS.WAYNE.EDU

Student Life and Environment

WSU has an "urban Detroit campus" and so must live with "the city's poor reputation" for poverty-related crime. Public safety "is better on campus than the surrounding areas, but many people need to park or walk to surrounding areas and have issues." While "the school is not responsible" for the city's crime rate, some here feel that "perhaps it could take measures to make the campus area very safe. This could include more police, security, and surveillance cameras." However, the university does have its own police department. Others are philosophical on the matter. "Until the auto industry rebounds, this urban Detroit campus will always have problems with the occasional stranger on campus. They don't pose any immediate threat, however it can be an unnerving experience for some people," one student observes. Students also note that "there are not a lot of healthy eating options around campus, and the rest of the restaurants are hit or miss."

"There aren't a lot of graduate-targeted activities or clubs" at either of the two WSU MBA locations, "but most students are much too busy for such endeavors anyway. The student body, which "has got to be one of the most diverse student populations in the country," is a "mixed group of working adults and international students, mostly aged 25 to 35." Students have "varying levels of work experience, although there are few who have management experience."

Admissions

The Wayne State University MBA program is predominately part-time, with nearly 1,000 students enrolled. Minimum qualifications for admission include a score of at least 450 on the GMAT and an undergraduate GPA of at least 2.75. The average entering student performs somewhat better: the median GMAT score among entering students is 485, while the median GPA is 3.2.The admissions committee also evaluates a student's leadership potential and professional experience when making an admissions decision. Students may apply for admission in the fall, winter, or spring/summer semesters. International applicants must present an excellent academic record, demonstrate proficiency in English, and show sufficient means to cover tuition, supplies, and living expenses while enrolled in the program.

FINANCIAL FACTS

Annual tuition (in-state/ out-of-state)	$14,843/$30,299
Fees	$1,367
Cost of books	$1,122
Room & board (on/off-campus)	$9,026/$8,813
% of students receiving aid	43
% of first-year students receiving aid	61
% of students receiving grants	13
Average award package	$15,546
Average grant	$4,455
Average loan	$18,537
Average student loan debt	$32,842

ADMISSIONS

Admissions Selectivity Rating	87
# of applications received	454
% applicants accepted	31
% acceptees attending	68
Average GMAT	488
Range of GMAT	415–550
Average GPA	3.20
TOEFL required of international students	Yes
Minimum TOEFL (paper/computer)	550/213
Application fee	$50
International application fee	$50
Regular application deadline	8/1
Deferment available	Yes
Maximum length of deferment	one Semester
Transfer students accepted	Yes
Transfer application policy: Must meet admission standards and a maximum of 6 credits are accepted. Students with a non-business undergraduate degree may only petition to transfer credit from an AACSB accredited MBA program.	
Non-fall admissions	Yes
Need-blind admissions	No

EMPLOYMENT PROFILE

Career Rating	64	**Grads Employed by Function%**	**Avg. Salary**
Average base starting salary	$53,000	Marketing	(9%)
Primary Source of Full-time Job Acceptances		Operations	(3%) $65,000
School-facilitated activities	13(40%)	Consulting	(3%)
Graduate-facilitated activities	1(3%)	Management	(3%) $35,000
Unknown	18(56%)	Finance	(44%) $59,000
		MIS	(9%) $54,000
		Other	(6%) $87,500

Top 5 Employers Hiring Grads
Deloitte (2), General Motors (2), Plante Moran (2)

WEBER STATE UNIVERSITY
JOHN B. GODDARD SCHOOL OF BUSINESS AND ECONOMICS

GENERAL INFORMATION
Type of school	Public
Affiliation	No Affiliation

SURVEY SAYS...
Students love Ogden, UT, Happy students, Smart classrooms
Solid preparation in:
General management

STUDENTS
Enrollment of parent institution	25,000
Enrollment of MBA Program	212
% part-time	100
Average age at entry	31
Average years work experience at entry	4.7

ACADEMICS
Academic Experience Rating	80
Profs interesting rating	81
Profs accesible rating	75
Student/faculty ratio	9:1
% female faculty	16
% underrepresented minority faculty	0
% part-time faculty	32

Joint Degrees
MBA-Master of Health Administration combined degree program, length varies from 60 - 72 credit hours dependent upon undergraduate degree (business or non-business).

Academics

Designed specifically for working professionals, the MBA program at Weber State University in Utah offers one of the most flexible degree tracks around, allowing students to switch between full-time and part-time study at any time. With eight-week courses taught one night per week, the Goddard School requires a "relatively low financial and time investment" and is "challenging enough to teach...something useful while recognizing that most students work full time," according to one student. "The experience is just want I wanted it to be: practical."

Registration is "simple," and "classes are scheduled to accommodate program progress without being in a cohort." There are six class blocks per year, and students can take a block off or take multiple classes in a block, and "can also take courses in any order as long as you have the prerequisites." The quality of instruction and the depth of professors' knowledge are "high," and teachers "bring a lot of outside experience to the table." The material they use is up to date and relevant, and if students "have questions or need additional help outside class, they are available." "They treat us like the working adults we are," says a student.

The administration is "very focused on the success of the students," are "very responsive," and "seem to have an honest desire to help students." The course schedules are released early, and individuals in the administration put in "consistent effort on their part to make clear where their offices are, what their respective roles are, and how best they can be contacted."

Career and Placement

Practically everyone who attends Goddard is working during the day, so recruitment and job placement is not a major concern for students, who are for the most part looking to further their existing careers. "The career personnel do more networking for the students than the students do on their own." Still, "the career counselor is the most connected job resource in the state" for those who are on the hunt, and the school "does an amazing job" of communicating "great and diverse" job opportunities to students. "We get weekly emails with links to [jobs]," says one.

Student Life and Environment

The program "caters to students who are working full-time and have families and who cannot take advantage of the student life offered," so "the majority are working and not involved in the many activities." The MBA program is at an extended campus, which lacks housing but does have its own clubs, programs, "bookstore, snacks, ample parking, nice library, and allows MBA students a dedicated, well-furnished classroom for study lab," as well as providing "an inviting environment for students to participate" should they so choose.

"The environment is great for a working professional and a terrific value for anyone wanting to further their career with an MBA," says a student of the "commuter" school, which is populated by mainly men. "I have been impressed with the professional nature of the students and their desire to do well in the program." Many interactions occur online, and students (who are accustomed to the working world) do their part. "I have yet to work in a group where I felt somebody did not pull their weight."

Admissions

To apply to the John B. Goddard MBA Program, students must possess a bachelor's degree from an accredited university. The primary criteria for selection are the student's undergraduate record and GMAT performance. Current students have a median GMAT score of 550 and an average GPA of 3.29 on a 4.0 scale. Other factors, such as work experience and professional progression, are also considered by the admissions committee. Each application is evaluated individually for the applicant's ability to succeed, potential for success, and possible strengths to contribute to the program. International applicants whose first language is not English must demonstrate English proficiency through testing; they must also have their undergraduate transcripts translated by a recognized service. Applications should be submitted online.

FINANCIAL FACTS

Annual tuition (in-state/ out-of-state)	$13,415/$26,775
Fees	$1,210
Cost of books	$1,200
Room & board	$6,700
% of students receiving grants	5
Average grant	$3,500

ADMISSIONS

Admissions Selectivity Rating	**77**
# of applications received	118
% applicants accepted	74
% acceptees attending	94
Average GMAT	558
Range of GMAT	510–610
Average GPA	3.29
TOEFL required of international students	Yes
Minimum TOEFL (paper/computer)	550/213
Application fee	$60
International application fee	$95
Regular application deadline	5/2
Regular application notification	5/20
Application Deadline/Notification	
Round 1:	9/26 / 10/10
Round 2:	11/1 / 11/15
Round 3:	3/28 / 4/18
Round 4:	5/2 / 5/20
Deferment available	Yes
Maximum length of deferment	1 year
Transfer students accepted	Yes
Transfer application policy: Full application required. Transfer credits from AACSB-accredited programs accepted, no more than one-third of degree total; from non-AACSB-accredited programs on a case-by-case basis.	
Non-fall admissions	Yes
Need-blind admissions	Yes

WEST VIRGINIA UNIVERSITY
COLLEGE OF BUSINESS AND ECONOMICS

GENERAL INFORMATION
Type of school   Public
Affiliation   No Affiliation
Academic calendar   Semester

SURVEY SAYS...
Cutting-edge classes, Smart
classrooms
Solid preparation in:
Finance, General management,
Teamwork

STUDENTS
Enrollment of parent institution	28,113
Enrollment of MBA Program	55
% male/female	67/33
% part-time	0
% underrepresented minority	18
% international	18
Average age at entry	23
Average years work experience at entry	2.3

ACADEMICS
Academic Experience Rating	89
Profs interesting rating	90
Profs accesible rating	89
Student/faculty ratio	17:1
% female faculty	18
% underrepresented minority faculty	2
% part-time faculty	6

Joint Degrees
MBA/JD, 3 years

Prominent Alumni
John Chambers, CEO, Cisco
Systems; Glen Hiner, CEO, Owens
Corning; Homer Hickam, Author;
Ray Lane, Frm. Pres & COO, Oracle;
Jerry West, GM, LA Lakers

Academics

The College of Business and Economics at West Virginia University "has a well-known business program with top professors," and this earns it "prestige within the state," students in this growing MBA program tell us. Full-time students love the one-year accelerated program that gets them in and out quickly, while those in the Executive MBA program love the convenience of being able to attend in one of nine satellite sites scattered about the Mountain State.

Students in both programs praise "the curriculum design," noting that "the sequence of courses is good, giving a good foundation in business: economics, accounting, marketing, finance, and operations." They appreciate that the WVU MBA program "teaches skills instead of memorization" and that administrators are always looking for ways to improve the curriculum. "There have been some significant improvements to make the program have a more global focus on business education," one impressed student reports.

WVU's full-time MBA is a 48 credit-hour program presented over a 14-month period. All domestic students are required to participate in an international trip to China, Poland, Italy, German, or the Czech Republic. The curriculum interweaves business themes and skills, building toward culminating coursework in planning and strategy. Students in the full-time program do not specialize in an area of concentration; however, WVU also offers an MBA in Finance, which can be completed in 12 months by students with substantial academic or professional experience in the field and in two years by students lacking such experience. Students in the EMBA program tell us that the program "provides students with one of the most diverse faculty groups in the country" and that "The diverse background of each faculty member provides students with a unique view of real life business experiences." (Students in the full-time program share this assessment of the faculty.)

All students here point out that "Students not only focus on textbook examples, they get to participate in business experiences such as the Washington Campus and study-abroad programs to Italy, Czech Republic, Mexico, Germany, and China." These elements, they say, make for an "exceptional academic experience" and elevate the WVU MBA "a notch above the rest."

At the end of the day, the class sessions are very unique and productive based on multiple views from professionals working in various industries.

Career and Placement

The College of Business and Economics at WVU has its own dedicated Center for Career Development to serve business undergraduates and graduate students. The office provides counseling services, workshops, seminars, and on-campus recruiting events. Students tell us that the office seems geared mostly toward the needs of undergraduates. One writes that the office "is not geared well for MBA students. It is good for MSIR and MPA students. Even if they are for MBA students, the positions are only for entry level such as internships, leadership programs, etc." While students feel that "the career development center tries to give us information," they also feel that "it looks like they are working without any direction."

ADMISSIONS CONTACT: GARY INSCH, DIRECTOR OF GRADUATE PROGRAMS
ADDRESS: P.O. BOX 6027, MORGANTOWN, WV 26506-6025
PHONE: 304-293-7812 • FAX: 304-293-8905
E-MAIL: MBA@WVU.EDU • WEBSITE: WWW.BE.WVU.EDU

Student Life and Environment

WVU's full-time MBA program is attended by "a mix of professionals going back for MBAs and current college students." The program calls for a lot of group work; students tell us that "Groups are very diverse, hardworking professionals that can appreciate the opinion of others.... The people in each group end up being the people you call for advice or to go out to dinner after class or on the weekend!" Some here, however, complain that the quality of students admitted to the full-time program needs to improve. One writes: "The class atmosphere is not that intellectually-motivating. Out of an entering class of 65 students, ten are very good and others are below average."

EMBA students may attend classes at the main campus in Morgantown or at any of nine satellite sites in Beckley, Charleston, Elkins, Keyser, Lewisburg, Martinsburg, Moorefield, Parkersburg, or Wheeling. One student calls these options "a blessing. The rural location where I live would not permit an economical pursuit of such a degree by traveling to the main campus for each class. The fact that classes are streamed to the distant location and the technology provides two-way communication and interaction is terrific!"

Admissions

Applicants to the MBA program must submit a completed application (paper or online), official transcripts for all postsecondary academic work, an official GMAT score report, and a resume. Letters of recommendation and a statement of purpose are optional. In addition, international students must submit an official TOEFL or IELTS score report (minimum score: 580, paper-and-pencil test; 237, computer-based test; 92, Internet-based test; or 6.5 IELTS). All students must have full use of a laptop PC that meets prescribed minimum software, memory, and processor-speed requirements; contact the school or visit the website for details. Applicants to the EMBA program must have at least two years of "significant work experience." For applicants with less than five years experience, GPA and GMAT figure most heavily in the admissions decision. Professional experience, especially managerial experience, is the greater factor for applicants with at least five years of experience.

FINANCIAL FACTS

Annual tuition (in-state/ out-of-state)	$11,776/$32,080
Cost of books	$1,800
Room & board	$9,080
Average grant	$0
Average loan	$0

ADMISSIONS

Admissions Selectivity Rating	85
# of applications received	172
% applicants accepted	47
% acceptees attending	68
Average GMAT	536
Range of GMAT	450–630
Average GPA	3.43
TOEFL required of international students	Yes
Minimum TOEFL (paper/computer)	580/237
Application fee	$60
International application fee	$60
Early application deadline	10/15
Early notification date	10/30
Regular application deadline	3/1
Regular application notification	3/15
Deferment available	Yes
Maximum length of deferment	1 year
Transfer students accepted	Yes
Transfer application policy: Applicants request transfer credits and the admission committee reviews the request.	
Non-fall admissions	Yes
Need-blind admissions	Yes

WESTERN CAROLINA UNIVERSITY
COLLEGE OF BUSINESS

GENERAL INFORMATION
Type of school   Public
Affiliation   No Affiliation
Academic calendar   Semester

SURVEY SAYS...
Solid preparation in:
Finance, General management

STUDENTS
Enrollment of parent
  institution   9,608
Enrollment of MBA Program   98
% male/female   52/48
% out-of-state   24
% part-time   70
% underrepresented minority   10
% international   10
Average age at entry   30
Average years work experience
  at entry   5.0

ACADEMICS
Academic Experience Rating   76
Profs interesting rating   80
Profs accesible rating   75
Student/faculty ratio   7:1
% female faculty   23
% underrepresented minority
  faculty   7
% part-time faculty   23

Prominent Alumni
Dr. David Ellis, Pardee Hospital;
Carolyne Pelton, BB&T Corporate
Banking - Senior Vice President;
Wendy Cagle, Small Business
Technology and Development
Center; David Kemper, President -
Kemper Strategies; Matthew
Hutcherson, Regional Director for
Mountain Bizworks

Academics

Located in a gorgeous, unique region of the Mid-Atlantic, the College of Business at Western Carolina University has worked hard to distinguish itself from other MBA programs, and has built a "reputation for not being an 'assembly-line' program." Students are encouraged to think for themselves and become effectively "better equipped to deal with future challenges." The small size of the school means that each student "has good learning opportunities" and "gets a lot of attention" from the "excellent, accessible professors with relevant professional experience." All in all, WCU offers a "quality MBA program with experienced, grounded faculty at a great price."

Although the school is based in Cullowhee—"an exceptional environment"—almost all of the MBA courses are held in Asheville. The school is very "oriented towards face-to-face classes" in Asheville and uses very little "new technology" (such as videoconferencing and electronic communications) for its courses. Professors and administrators "do a decent job of being available, considering that the main campus is over an hour away from our location." Both are "eager to tailoring course material to how students actually learn," and the professors "are very knowledgeable and have a lot of professional experience." The program heads and assistants are also "readily available and helpful with any questions that may arise."

The program's core courses are about mastering management in applied settings; students form small work groups and are trained to deal with real-world problems Through the school's new MBA curriculum, developed in collaboration with faculty, recent graduates, and local employers, students learn and often perform the functions of chief officers in marketing, research and development, information technology, operations, legal affairs, finance, and the chief executive office.

Career and Placement

The fact that there are no online classes makes for "great networking opportunities." "Group projects help us network and the Graduate Business Students' Association is great," says a student. The "schedule flexibility for full-time employed students" is a great perk of the WCU program, as is the option for a 16-month "speedy graduation—in three semesters and a summer!" Although most students here are not looking for new jobs, students place great value on the real world applicability provided by the program design, which is "most beneficial to understanding the different aspects of the C-suite" and shows "how the different aspects work together to create a functioning business through real world examples."

ADMISSIONS CONTACT: DR. STEVE HA, DIRECTOR OF MBA PROGRAM
ADDRESS: 104D FORSYTH, CULLOWHEE, NC 28723
PHONE: 828-227-3008 • FAX: 828-227-7414
E-MAIL: IHA@WCU.EDU • WEBSITE: MBA.WCU.EDU

Student Life and Environment

WCU really strives to create "a friendly, but competitive learning environment and the bonds you create with other students are very close." This "challenging and competitive" group is "very, very cooperative," "conscientious, mature, eager to learn, committed, and friendly." The student body tends to be a bit younger but still brings plenty of experience to bear. "As an older student, I am impressed and astonished by how astute the students are," says a student. "They are very helpful and supportive. I genuinely like them." Some "are Cherokee tribal members, some are from other local area businesses, and some are students continuing straight from school"; many are also "employees at the nearby casino. Though most students commute, there are enough distractions for those who want them, as Asheville is "a mid-sized city with plenty of activities in the area."

Admissions

Applicants to the MBA program at Western Carolina University must submit official copies of transcripts for all post-secondary academic work, an official score report for the GMAT or GRE, three letters of recommendation, a goal statement, and a resume. A minimum GMAT score of 450 and a minimum undergraduate GPA of 3.0 are generally required. Graduates of institutions in which the language of instruction is not English must also submit official score reports for the TOEFL and achieve a minimum score of 79–80 on the Internet-based test, 550 on the paper test, or 213 on the computer test. International applications are due by July 15 for the fall semester and by November 15 for the spring semester.

FINANCIAL FACTS

Annual tuition (in-state/ out-of-state)	$3,794/$13,379
Fees	$2,528
Cost of books	$947
Room & board (on/off-campus)	$8,749

ADMISSIONS

Admissions Selectivity Rating	**72**
# of applications received	45
% applicants accepted	89
% acceptees attending	78
Average GMAT	531
Range of GMAT	480–590
Average GPA	3.25
TOEFL required of international students	Yes
Minimum TOEFL (paper/computer)	550/213
Application fee	$50
International application fee	$50
Early application deadline	3/1
Deferment available	Yes
Maximum length of deferment	1 year
Transfer students accepted	Yes
Transfer application policy: Up to 6 hours of graduate credit may be transferred from an AACSB institution	
Non-fall admissions	Yes
Need-blind admissions	Yes

WESTERN MICHIGAN UNIVERSITY
HAWORTH COLLEGE OF BUSINESS

GENERAL INFORMATION

Type of school	Public
Affiliation	No Affiliation
Academic calendar	Semester

SURVEY SAYS...

Happy students, Students love
Kalamazoo, MI
Solid preparation in:
General management, Teamwork,
Presentation skills

STUDENTS

Enrollment of parent institution	24,598
Enrollment of MBA Program	381
% male/female	65/35
% out-of-state	1
% part-time	100
% underrepresented minority	9
% international	12
Average age at entry	28

ACADEMICS

Academic Experience Rating	**80**
Profs interesting rating	77
Profs accesible rating	77
% female faculty	25
% underrepresented minority faculty	31
% part-time faculty	0

Academics

Word of mouth plays a big part in many students' decision to attend the Graduate College at the University of Western Michigan with "great recommendations from family and friends." One student was even referred to the school by a CEO. Most students seem quite happy with their choice. They also like that the school "is nationally accredited," and ranked as a "top 100 school."

The graduate program at Western "is primarily a 'night school.' Most students work full-time jobs and take two classes a semester." "Classes are all from 6-9 at night spread across 3 campuses. The MBA program is targeted at working people who want to pursue an MBA." Students find the program adaptable. One student agrees, saying, "I also like the ability to earn a specialization within my MBA program - I have some flexibility to change my curriculum if my interests change." The school also offers several online, weekend, and condensed-hybrid format courses.

While some classes are clearly more challenging than others, the workload is manageable for most students. "Academics are easy when you show up to class, pay attention, and do the work." The program also provides students with an "excellent emphasis on international business." This "global outlook" is "important in today's workforce."

Although not all the professors receive the same high praise, several do get excellent reviews. Considered "stellar" to "amazing people," these "teachers bring a great attitude and very effective teaching style[s]" to class. One student says, "Every semester I have entered into a new classroom and thought, 'Wow, this is my most favorite professor ever.' Now I'm struggling with which one is my favorite because there are so many and each one has helped me with situations that I will eventually face in my future." While one student claims to be "challenged to constantly find a way to incorporate what I am learning into my career," another student suggests, "WMU employs too many career educators, and I would like more real world applications of the materials we are learning." Class sizes are mostly adequate for sufficient student/teacher communication, usually "limited to 30 students so you get to interact quite a bit with the professors."

Career and Placement

The Career Services Center at WMU offers preparation services for graduate students at the Graduate College by way of resume, interviewing, and cover letter writing assistance. Students report satisfaction in their fellow peers' abilities of building "networking opportunities with fellow students." Simply going to class offers students "a great chance to meet people in my area." A student says, "It is amazing to me how much of an opportunity there is to network with international students from all around the globe here at Western Michigan University." Professors also do a good job in the classroom by teaching students "to grasp the knowledge of the subject and to incorporate that with their career fields." From one student's observations, professors "are willing to work with each student individually to help them make the right choices regarding career changes.... They also help with job placement and career fields."

The location of the school's main campus, "in a great city, Kalamazoo," also allows students a direct "community connection with local Fortune 500 companies." "The business school and WMU in general have a great relationship with what is a growing and vibrant city."

ADMISSIONS CONTACT: SATISH DESHPANDE, ASSOCIATE DEAN FOR OPERATIONS & GRADUATE PROGRAMS
ADDRESS: 2320 SCHNEIDER HALL, MS #5480, KALAMAZOO, MI 49008-5480
PHONE: 269-387-5133 • FAX: 269-387-5045
E-MAIL: MBA-ADVISING@WMICH.EDU • WEBSITE: WWW.WMICH.EDU/MBA

Student Life and Environment

Student life outside the classroom is "what you make it." "The school has many different social functions and sporting events to give student's the full college experience." Unfortunately, "Family life for a lot of us limits the student involvement in clubs and activities." For the most part, though, students seem to get more out of [their] degree then just what they learn in class." At WNU, students come from many different cultures and backgrounds. "Western Michigan University is an international melting pot in the heart of west Michigan." One student attests, "Classmates are from as far away as China, India, and the Ukraine…. This opportunity to meet and collaborate with such a diverse student body is setting the stage for my ability to expand my professional network in the global economy."

Students in the graduate program as a whole are described as, "very team and school focused. "MBA students are largely uninvolved with campus as they are working full-time, commuting, and already established within their communities/workplaces." For example, one student recently "started an MBA social club to help build a greater sense of community." Overall, "People have a lot of school spirit and are very social. It is a fun school to go to."

Students make many positive remarks regarding UWM's Business School campus. "The campus is laid out well." The "landscaping is meticulous. The buildings are modern." However, another student says that as a commuter, "the parking is expensive and not that great." "WMU is in between a Big 10 school and a little private school; it has a great campus that is only becoming greater with reconstruction of more 'Green' space. The university is listening to the student population with regards to better housing, better food quality, and becoming green."

Admissions

Students with lower test scores and/or not so attractive grade point averages will take comfort in knowing that it is still possible to "get in with a lower GPA and GMAT score." These two scores are the only requirements along with the application; however, a personal statement and letters of recommendation can also be sent in for consideration.

FINANCIAL FACTS

Annual tuition (in-state/ out-of-state)	$11,510/$24,378
Fees	$844
Cost of books	$1,665
Room & board (on/off-campus)	$8,414/$8,006
% of students receiving aid	37
% of first-year students receiving aid	6
% of students receiving grants	9
Average award package	$16,650
Average grant	$6,302
Average loan	$17,520
Average student loan debt	$30,045

ADMISSIONS

Admissions Selectivity Rating	78
# of applications received	228
% applicants accepted	106
% acceptees attending	79
Average GMAT	526
Range of GMAT	480–570
TOEFL required of international students	Yes
Minimum TOEFL (paper/computer)	550/213
Application fee	$40
International application fee	$100
Deferment available	Yes
Maximum length of deferment	One Year
Transfer students accepted	Yes
Transfer application policy: Students transferring from an AACSB accredited MBA program may transfer six credit hours of work from their prior MBA program providing they have at least a 3.0 in the transfer course work and an overall gpa of 3.0 from the transfer institution.	
Non-fall admissions	Yes
Need-blind admissions	Yes

WICHITA STATE UNIVERSITY
BARTON SCHOOL OF BUSINESS

GENERAL INFORMATION
Type of school	Public
Affiliation	No Affiliation
Academic calendar	Semester

SURVEY SAYS...
Friendly students, Happy students,
Smart classrooms

STUDENTS
Enrollment of parent institution	15,000
Enrollment of MBA Program	240
% male/female	92/8
% out-of-state	30
% part-time	91
% international	80
Average age at entry	27
Average years work experience at entry	3.0

ACADEMICS
Academic Experience Rating	**80**
Profs interesting rating	73
Profs accesible rating	79
Student/faculty ratio	4:1
% female faculty	3
% underrepresented minority faculty	21

Academics

At the W. Frank Barton School of Business at Wichita State University, students benefit from a traditional, management-based MBA program that offers a broad range of course work in accounting, economics, finance, management, and marketing. Depending on a student's academic background (those who studied business as an undergraduate may be able to waive some requirements), the MBA is comprised of 36 to 51 credit hours, beginning with a core curriculum that covers business fundamentals. Throughout the core curriculum, particular attention is given to understanding the organization as an integrated system. Later, students may choose an area of concentration, taking up to 9 credit hours of electives in finance, entrepreneurship, Business analytics and information management, or health care administration.

The school offers a fast-paced executive MBA program for high-level professionals, as well as a traditional MBA program. Whether enrolled in the accelerated or traditional program, a majority of students work full-time while attending school in the evenings. In fact, "Most of them are professionals with aircraft industries in the Wichita area," which means a double dose of work and responsibility. However, the school is aware of its students' special needs and "is very adept at offering programs that fit the schedules of its students." On top of that, students reassure us that the workload is manageable—"substantial at times, but for the most part, the average workload is within the expected output of a graduate program."

Reporting on the great classroom experience, WSU students generally describe their professors as "candid, well-spoken, knowledgeable, prepared, and fun." Unfortunately, students admit that a few staff members don't deserve such rave reviews. "There are some professors' classes I wish I could get a refund on, simply because the professors seem to be there only to earn a paycheck or a boosted ego," grumbles one student. In addition to their professors, classmates form an essential part of the learning experience at WSU. Drawing "a mix of mid-career business people and young business students," Wichita State students enjoy the fact that "everyone is very opinionated, which makes for great class discussions."

The "only AACSB-accredited school in the Wichita area," WSU is an excellent match for those who work or wish to start a career in the region, and WSU promotes a great deal of "community involvement with local businesses and entrepreneurs." Students appreciate the fact that "the school brings in wonderful special speakers and has a good reputation in the community." For example, "Recently, the CEOs of Wal-Mart and PepsiCo visited the business school." Beyond Kansas, the school also runs an "international project with Berlin School of Economics, where students taking the advanced strategic management course go to Berlin, Germany for one week and do the project there in conjunction with Berlin students."

Career and Placement

The Career Services office at Wichita State University serves the school's undergraduate and graduate community, including the business school. Through Career Services, students have access to career counseling, an online job database, and an alumni database. The office also hosts several campus career fairs and on-campus interviews.

ADMISSIONS CONTACT: ANGELA R. JONES, DIRECTOR OF MBA PROGRAM
ADDRESS: 1845 FAIRMOUNT, WICHITA, KS 67260-0048
PHONE: 316-978-3230 • FAX: 316-978-3767
E-MAIL: MBA@WICHITA.EDU • WEBSITE: WICHITA.EDU/MBA

At Wichita State, "Many students seem to be earning their MBAs in order to receive a raise or progress upward with their current employers," with a number of them also receiving tuition assistance. For those looking for a position with a new company after graduation, major employers in Wichita include Bank of America, Boeing, Bombardier Aerospace Learjet, Cargill Meat Solutions, Cessna Aircraft Company, The Coleman Company, Hawker Beechcraft, INTRUST Bank, Koch Industries, Spirit AeroSystems, Via Christi Health Systems, and York International.

Student Life and Environment

Those looking for a close-knit and community-oriented business school may be disappointed by "commuter-school" Wichita State. While they get a great business education, students admit that "the opportunities for networking are not particularly strong, as most students are too busy with work and families to attend mixers or be involved on campus." On the other hand, the atmosphere is pleasantly casual and friendly, and the community is "very diverse with local, national, and international students." A current student shares: "Even though we come from very different backgrounds and experiences, everyone seems to be incredibly open-minded and accepting to all students in the program."

The university provides plenty of extracurricular and recreational opportunities. In fact, students assure us that "if you want to do an activity and you look for one, you can find one." A case in point: One student who went from part-time to full-time status in his second year tells us, "I was surprised when I concentrated life to studies...I learned a lot that I missed when I was working in my first year." Off campus, Wichita is a pleasant, low-cost, medium-sized city with plenty of cultural, financial, shopping, performing arts, festivals, and entertainment options for graduate students.

Admissions

To be considered for admissions at Wichita State University, students must possess a four-year degree from an accredited college or university and be proficient in word processing, spreadsheet, and presentation software. Admissions decisions are made by evaluating the following: official GMAT scores, undergraduate transcript, an applicant's personal goals statement, two letters of recommendation, and a current resume. For the traditional MBA, career experience is a plus in an application package but is not required. Applicants to the executive MBA must have at least five years of relevant post-graduate work experience. Students may apply for entry in the spring and fall semesters.

FINANCIAL FACTS

Annual tuition (in-state/ out-of-state)	$5,180/$14,412
Fees	$1,267
Cost of books	$2,000
Room & board (on/off-campus)	$5,280
% of students receiving aid	44
% of first-year students receiving aid	38
% of students receiving grants	14
Average award package	$9,454
Average grant	$2,067
Average loan	$11,672

ADMISSIONS

Admissions Selectivity Rating	83
# of applications received	69
% applicants accepted	68
% acceptees attending	98
Average GMAT	565
Range of GMAT	N/A–N/A
Average GPA	3.70
TOEFL required of international students	Yes
Minimum TOEFL (paper/computer)	570/230
Application fee	$50
International application fee	$65
Regular application deadline	7/1
Deferment available	Yes
Maximum length of deferment	1 year
Transfer students accepted	Yes
Transfer application policy: Only AACSB accredited classes may be transferred in.	
Non-fall admissions	Yes
Need-blind admissions	Yes

WILFRID LAURIER UNIVERSITY
SCHOOL OF BUSINESS & ECONOMICS

GENERAL INFORMATION
Type of school	Public
Affiliation	No Affiliation

SURVEY SAYS...
Good peer network

STUDENTS
Enrollment of parent institution	15,000
Enrollment of MBA Program	500
% male/female	60/40
% part-time	80
% international	10
Average age at entry	28
Average years work experience at entry	6.0

ACADEMICS
Academic Experience Rating	74
Profs interesting rating	70
Profs accesible rating	75
% female faculty	36

Joint Degrees
MBA-CMA: approximately 3.3 years part time. MBA-CFA: approximately 3.3 years part time.

Academics

As Canada's largest full classroom-contact MBA program, there is something for everyone at the School of Business & Economics at Wilfrid Laurier University. Whether you want to take courses during the week, during the weekend, during the day, at night, on a part-time basis, on a full-time basis, at the Waterloo campus, or at the satellite campus in Toronto, chances are there is going to be an MBA format option at Laurier that suits your needs. In addition, the school's many MBA options cater to students from all professional and academic backgrounds. At Laurier, business executives have the opportunity to get a high-speed degree though the school's accelerated MBA program, while students with no previous work experience may apply to the "co-op" program, designed to help business newcomers develop their managerial and organizational skills. In addition, many students come to Laurier because it offers "the ability to get a professional designation (i.e., CMA, CFA) along with the MBA" through several joint-degree programs.

No matter how, when, or where they pursue an MBA, Laurier students appreciate the school's commitment to the case-based learning method, which "requires that you understand both the theory and then apply them in real-world situations." Emphasizing practical competence over strict academic theory, "The Laurier experience builds your thinking skills and allows you to attack complex problems from many angles." Discussion and debate are fundamental to the program, and "Almost all courses include a group work component which promotes the teamwork abilities within each student." This interaction is an undeniable asset to the MBA education, since many "Students are already at the manager/director level in their careers." A current student praises the professors, saying, "Not only do they contribute to the learning experience due to their vast work experiences, but they are very willing to help out both within the classroom and outside of it (networking)."

The core curriculum takes an "integrated" approach to business topics, which "allows you to cement concepts since you are dealing with them in multiple courses at the same time." After completing the core, students can tailor their education through a concentration in a number of fields (such as finance, accounting, brand communication management, supply chain management, or international business to name a few) by completing at least four courses in that subject area. They may also add breadth to their education through one of the school's international programs in Europe and Asia, or through the school's ample list of special seminars.

At the top of their field, Laurier professors are an excellent "mix of tenured professors and recognized, practicing professionals." Most "are PhDs and have recent/relevant consulting or real business experience." Friendly, down to earth, and well run, administrators at Laurier "communicate frequently with students and have always responded to questions very quickly."

Career and Placement

Career Services for the School of Business & Economics Graduate Programs provides assistance to MBA and MABE students and alumni. Their services include one-on-one career counseling and specialized workshops on topics such as resume writing, networking, interviewing, and cocktail and dining etiquette. Career Services also hosts special events, such as executive recruiter panels.

MAUREEN FERRARO OR AARON MILLER, MBA MARKETING COORDINATORS
ADDRESS: 75 UNIVERSITY AVENUE WEST, WATERLOO, ON N2L 3C5 CANADA
PHONE: 519-884-0710 • FAX: 519-886-6978
E-MAIL: MFERRARO@WLU.CA • WEBSITE: WWW.LAURIERMBA.CA

FINANCIAL FACTS	
Annual tuition	$25,000
Fees	$1,000
Cost of books	$3,000

ADMISSIONS	
Admissions Selectivity Rating	**85**
Average GMAT	620
Range of GMAT	550–750
Average GPA	3.20
TOEFL required of international students	Yes
Minimum TOEFL (paper/computer)	573
Application fee	$125
International application fee	$125
Deferment available	No
Transfer students accepted	No
Non-fall admissions	Yes
Need-blind admissions	Yes

Students agree that their school enjoys a great reputation in Canada, telling us that "employers love Laurier MBA students because they are much better educated and friendlier to work with." The following companies are among the extensive list of organizations recently recruiting Laurier MBAs: Accenture, American Express Canada, Bank of Canada, Canada Revenue Agency, CIBC World Markets, CPP Investment Board, Dell Canada, Deloitte Touche Tohmatsu, FedEx Canada, GE Canada, General Mills Canada, General Motors Canada, IBM Canada, The Loyalty Group, Managerial Design, Manulife Financial, National Bank Financial, Proctor & Gamble, Raytheon Canada, RLG International, Scotiabank Group, and TD Securities.

Student Life and Environment

With such a large and diverse student population, it's hard to summarize life at Laurier. Not surprisingly, there is something of a split between students who attend the program part-time and those who chose to pursue their studies full-time. There are two campuses in the Wilfrid Laurier University MBA program. One is on the Waterloo-based university campus and the other is a satellite campus right in downtown Toronto. Part-timers attending school at the Toronto MBA campus sometimes feel a little cut off from the main campus. However, Toronto students are required to participate in MBA events and competitions at the Waterloo campus.

In both locations, the majority of students are "mature with an established career and family life." For most, "Life happens off campus," and students admit that there isn't much enthusiasm for campus activities or after-hours socializing. "Social activities with the satellite or main campus are limited due to work/family commitments in addition to academic demands," explains a current MBA candidate.

With many personal and professional commitments, most students at Laurier are talented multitaskers, who "are very good at balancing personal, work, and school life." However, they warn that the many group assignments, homework, and classes can make it difficult to juggle your educational, professional, and personal life. A student laments, "You have to be tough skinned to do an MBA on a part-time basis at WLU."

Admissions

To be considered for admission to Wilfrid Laurier University's MBA program, students must possess a 4-year, undergraduate degree or equivalent (in any field of study) with at least a B average (73%) in the last 10 half-credit courses taken. Except for the MBA with co-op option (for which no work experience is required), applicants must have at least 2 years of full-time work experience to apply for an MBA at Laurier. Students must also submit a GMAT score of at least 550. In addition to test scores and transcripts, students must send three letters of recommendation from professional and academic references 1. to apply to the full-time or any of the part-time MBA Programs at Laurier. It is mandatory for students applying to the Co-op option to provide a 600+ GMAT score..

WILLAMETTE UNIVERSITY
ATKINSON GRADUATE SCHOOL OF MANAGEMENT

GENERAL INFORMATION

Type of school	Private
Affiliation	Methodist
Academic calendar	Semester

SURVEY SAYS...

Cutting-edge classes
Solid preparation in:
Marketing, Teamwork, Presentation
skills, Social responsibility

STUDENTS

Enrollment of parent	
institution	2,500
Enrollment of MBA Program	207
% male/female	60/40
% out-of-state	68
% underrepresented minority	16
% international	35
Average age at entry	25
Average years work experience	
at entry	1.5

ACADEMICS

Academic Experience Rating	82
Profs interesting rating	85
Profs accesible rating	79
Student/faculty ratio	7:1
% female faculty	28
% underrepresented minority	
faculty	12
% part-time faculty	50

Joint Degrees

MBA/JD - Joint Degree in
Management and Law - 4 Years

Prominent Alumni

Michael Woolfolk, Senior Currency
Strategist, The Bank of New York;
Ronald Silveira, Vice President,
Universal Studios Digital Services;
Punit Renjen, CEO, Deloitte
Consulting; Sandy Baruah,
President & CEO, Detroit Regional
Chamber; Jai Desai, CEO, Universal
Consulting India, Pvt., Ltd.

Academics

With a unique focus on young professionals, Willamette's friendly but rigorous MBA is a great way to get your feet wet in the business world. While most MBA programs require work experience before matriculation, this program is "specifically geared toward the early career or career change MBA." In fact, many Willamette students have never held a professional position. The focus on early career students does not mean that the curriculum is a cake walk. On the contrary, this "very fast-paced, intense program" is more like a crash course for future business leaders. "Active participation and discussion is strongly emphasized in most classes," and the "very well-thought out curriculum for first-year students," is augmented by excellent elective courses in the second year. Attracting a surprisingly "idealistic" business school crowd, many students also choose Willamette because of its unusual areas of concentration, especially it's "reputation for non-profit, government, and social entrepreneurship excellence." The school has also invested in its operations, systems, and analysis offerings, with analytical and decision-making tools like SAP introduced in first-year coursework.

While Willamette students may begin the program with very little career experience, they won't leave that way. Experiential learning is key to the curriculum, helping "students with all levels of experience gain that edge usually gained through lots of years in corporate jobs." For example, through Willamette's required Practical Application for Careers and Enterprises (PACE) program, students are "placed in an eight-person team for the year to do consulting work for a non-profit or government organization." Practical applications take center stage in the classroom, as well. "Accomplished professionals" in their fields, professors "definitely bring expertise and know-how with a clear distinction between theory and real world practices." In addition to attending lectures, students "work on a lot of case studies," which prepare them "with the skills to analyze a situation from many different points of view." In addition, "There is also a lot of stress placed on teamwork and presentation skills," staples of a successful business career.

Bringing both warmth and enthusiasm to the classroom, "Most professors really make you love their courses, even if you're not an innate financier or marketer." With a clear focus on the student, "They are approachable and flexible if you require out of class time for assistance." A student agrees, "The learning environment at Willamette is incredibly unique in that it is more intimate than most business schools. Professors are very accessible and truly invested in helping students understand course material." Adds another, "Rarely do I write an e-mail to any of my professors without receiving a reply (and usually a solution to my problem) by the next day."

Career and Placement

In addition to the ample experiential education included in the Willamette curriculum, the Career Management Office offers recruiting programs, resume revisions and interview preparation services, company site visits, peer advisors, networking events, and career counseling. On the Willamette campus, "There are many activities and events that provide students with the opportunity to network with alumni and other professionals," though some would like to see those efforts expanded, especially when it comes to the alumni network. When it comes to career placement, one of the biggest obstacles is that "WU is still relatively unknown beyond the Northwest region"—though, fortunately, the school does enjoy an "incredible reputation in the Northwest" and strong ties in Portland, Seattle and Salem.

In recent years, 80 to 85 percent of Willamette graduates had a job offer within three months of graduation, and 90 to 100 percent had received an offer within six months, with salaries ranging from about $40,000 to $100,000 annually. A third of graduates chose to pursue careers in non-profit or government organizations. Willamette graduates were hired by companies including Hewlett Packard Company, Americorps, U.S. Fish and Wildlife, SENTECH Inc, LinkedIn, Amazon, Daimler, Aramco, Intel and Nike.

Student Life and Environment

The life of a frazzled Willamette business student is comprised of "lots of classes, preparations, [and] project meetings, blended with a coffee mug at The Bistro (the university's student-managed coffee shop.)" With so much on their plates, "Free time can sometimes be scarce." Fortunately, "Social activities like Thursday Night Out, the small size of the class, along with the design of the class schedule, allow us not only to get to know all of our classmates but also to maintain the family atmosphere that characterizes Atkinson." Drawing a large international population, the MBA program is "extremely ethnically diverse and that brings a high level of intercultural experience to the students." For over-achievers (of which you'll meet a few), "There are many ways to be involved in more than just class: associations, peer advisor positions, TA positions, etc."

Set in Oregon, "The campus is gorgeous," with "a river crossing the university and many green areas." "Being in Oregon you always have things to do outside of the town like the beach, mountains, forests, trails, and hikes" and there are "lots of bars nearby" in downtown Salem. Savvy business students also point out that despite the private school tuition, "the low cost of living made Willamette University cheaper by thousands per year."

Admissions

While the GMAT is the typical exam required for business school entry, Willamette also accepts the General GRE. In recent years, the mean GMAT score and GPA for incoming Willamette students was 583 and 3.3, respectively. For the MBA for Career Change program, students must have at least two years of work experience, whereas there are no minimum work requirements for the Early Career MBA. All students must have a personal interview with the admissions staff.

FINANCIAL FACTS

Annual tuition	$33,126
Fees	$80
Cost of books	$1,200
Room & board (on/off-campus)	$12,000/$11,000
% of students receiving aid	89
% of first-year students receiving aid	89
% of students receiving grants	75
Average award package	$31,676
Average grant	$10,000
Average loan	$20,000
Average student loan debt	$34,932

ADMISSIONS

Admissions Selectivity Rating	80
# of applications received	272
% applicants accepted	61
% acceptees attending	64
Average GMAT	592
Range of GMAT	530–650
Average GPA	3.20
TOEFL required of international students	Yes
Minimum TOEFL (paper/computer)	570/230
Application fee	$100
International application fee	$100
Early application deadline	3/15
Regular application deadline	5/1
Application Deadline/Notification	
Round 1:	12/15 /
Round 2:	2/1 /
Round 3:	3/15 /
Round 4:	5/1 /
Deferment available	Yes
Maximum length of deferment	1 year
Transfer students accepted	Yes
Transfer application policy: may transfer up to six Semester credits of MBA course work from an AACSB accredited MBA program to the Willamette Early Career and Career Change MBA program with the approval of the Dean. Students who have completed an entire first year of an AACSB accredited MBA program or a NASPAA accredited MPA program may be eligible to transfer up to 27 Semester credits of course work.	
Non-fall admissions	No
Need-blind admissions	Yes

EMPLOYMENT PROFILE

Career Rating		88	Grads Employed by Function	%	Avg. Salary
Percent employed at graduation		40	Marketing	(13%)	$58,386
Percent employed 3 months after graduation		82	Operations	(8%)	$48,070
			Consulting	(10%)	$64,840
Average base starting salary		$56,127	Finance	(38%)	$58,456
Primary Source of Full-time Job Acceptances			HR	(8%)	$48,216
School-facilitated activities	32(48%)		MIS	(4%)	$75,000
Graduate-facilitated activities	34(52%)		Other	(19%)	$48,027

Top 5 Employers Hiring Grads
Intel (5), Avanade (4), Nike (2), PWC (2), Aramco (2)

WILLIAM PATERSON UNIVERSITY
CHRISTOS M. COTSAKOS COLLEGE OF BUSINESS

GENERAL INFORMATION

Type of school	Public
Affiliation	No Affiliation
Academic calendar	Semester

SURVEY SAYS...
Solid preparation in:
General management, Operations

STUDENTS

Enrollment of parent institution	11,423
Enrollment of MBA Program	100
% male/female	50/50
% part-time	74
% underrepresented minority	15
% international	27

ACADEMICS

Academic Experience Rating	**70**
Profs interesting rating	73
Profs accesible rating	72
Student/faculty ratio	4:1
% female faculty	18
% underrepresented minority faculty	29
% part-time faculty	25

Academics

A New Jersey institution with an accredited MBA program, William Paterson University provides a "good academic atmosphere" for business professionals. At this largely local school, the faculty comprises "very intelligent" business experts who have "valuable real-world experience to bring into the classroom." Eager to engage their students, WPU professors initiate "challenging discussions and clearly bring their experiences with them to the classroom." While the teaching staff boasts solid academic credentials, students say, "some are better teachers than others." For the best experience, a student says, "there are quite a few topnotch professors, and once you learn who they are, try to take as many classes with them as possible."

At William Paterson, MBA coursework is divided into three phases: the lower core, the upper core, and electives. Students with advanced business experience or an undergraduate business degree may be able to place out of lower core courses, though they are required to complete at least 30 credits. Currently, the school offers MBA concentrations in accounting, marketing, entrepreneurship, and finance. They also operate a unique program in music management (one of two music management programs in the country), which capitalizes on the school's prime location near New York City. No matter what your field of interest, "professors promote teamwork" throughout the curriculum and soft skills are promoted alongside technical ability.

Principally catering to local professionals, William Paterson does its best to meet the needs and schedules of its busy student body. Of particular note, all courses are taught at night so that students may continue with work and personal obligations during the day. In addition, there is a culture of support within the school community. A current MBA tells us "this is my first year back after ten years, and the school administration and professors have made coming back a smooth experience." With just over 100 students in the MBA program, "class sizes are typically small (15 or so students)," and the "intimate setting" is ideal for promoting camaraderie and fostering individual talents. For additional assistance, the majority of professors are also "willing and eager to answer questions outside the classroom."

While professors are well regarded, "the administration, on the other hand, has virtually no connection to its students." Additionally, there are administrative and scheduling glitches throughout the MBA. For example, it is "difficult to graduate on time as there is a limit to class offerings and restrictions on virtually every lower-core course offering." Even so, William Paterson is constantly improving its programs and appears to be on the up-and-up. As the school gains more exposure, students would like to see "more full-time faculty to assist in the growing MBA program." If the positive changes continue, William Paterson's "MBA program may become one of the absolute best in the region."

ADMISSIONS CONTACT: TINU ADENRIAN, ASSISTANT DIRECTOR
ADDRESS: 300 POMPTON ROAD, WAYNE, NJ 07470
PHONE: 973-720-2237
E-MAIL: GRADUATE@WPUNJ.EDU • WEBSITE: WWW.WPUNJ.EDU/COB

Career and Placement

William Paterson's MBA program is specially designed for working professionals, rather than full-time students. While few MBA candidates are actively looking for a new position after graduation, the business school maintains an online job board, where MBA candidates can browse career opportunities in the area. Registered employers can also use the site to view student resumes. Because William Paterson is located within commuting distance of New York, students can apply for jobs locally and in the city, which is a definite advantage for those looking for big name employers or music industry contacts. Frequent alumni reunions on the William Paterson campus help graduates keep an ongoing network within the school community.

Beyond the business school, William Paterson graduate students and alumni can get additional job development assistance at the Career Development and Gloria S. Williams Advisement Center. Here MBA candidates may schedule an appointment for individual career counseling or a resume revision. However, the majority of the Center's services, including job fairs, are directed at the undergraduate community.

Student Life and Environment

William Paterson attracts professionals from across New Jersey, and there is a "diverse population of students." While the school community is "mostly young and ambitious," students "span a broad age range," from early professionals to seasoned managers. Across the board, students are "eager to learn" and bring enthusiasm to the classroom.

The Cotsakos School of Business is located in a newly constructed building at William Paterson's Valley Road campus, which is located just a few miles from the main University. Although there are campus housing options for graduate students, few students in the business program take advantage of them. With a class of working professionals, "the school is primarily a commuter school." In fact, for most MBA candidates, "life consists of the classroom experience" and little else. On the greater University campus, "activities are offered, but the MBA program isn't heavily involved."

Admissions

To be considered for admission to William Paterson's MBA program, students must submit official transcripts from undergraduate work, GMAT scores, and a personal essay. Eligible students must have a GMAT score of 500 or better, or a combination of a GMAT score of at least 450 and a GPA higher than 2.75. Students with a terminal degree in any field or an undergraduate GPA of 3.75 or better may be eligible to waive the GMAT. In lieu of test scores, these students must submit letters of recommendation and a writing sample.

FINANCIAL FACTS

Annual tuition (in-state/ out-of-state)	$8,997/$15,369
Fees	$2,469
% of students receiving aid	34
% of first-year students receiving aid	49
% of students receiving grants	10
Average award package	$11,596
Average grant	$11,153
Average loan	$11,029
Average student loan debt	$25,475

ADMISSIONS

Admissions Selectivity Rating	68
# of applications received	77
% applicants accepted	48
% acceptees attending	70
Average GPA	3.50
TOEFL required of international students	Yes
Minimum TOEFL (paper/computer)	550/213
Application fee	$50
International application fee	$50
Deferment available	Yes
Maximum length of deferment	1 year
Transfer students accepted	Yes
Transfer application policy: Maximum of 6 credits transferable; requires grade of B or better.	
Non-fall admissions	Yes
Need-blind admissions	Yes

WORCESTER POLYTECHNIC INSTITUTE
SCHOOL OF BUSINESS

GENERAL INFORMATION
Type of school   Private
Affiliation   No Affiliation
Academic calendar   Semester

SURVEY SAYS...
Cutting-edge classes
Solid preparation in:
General management, Operations,
Doing business in a global economy

STUDENTS
Enrollment of parent
  institution   5,575
Enrollment of MBA Program   201
% male/female   67/33
% part-time   90
% underrepresented minority   10
% international   62
Average age at entry   30
Average years work experience
  at entry   7.0

ACADEMICS
Academic Experience Rating   88
Profs interesting rating   89
Profs accesible rating   87
Student/faculty ratio   13:1
% female faculty   40
% underrepresented minority
  faculty   5
% part-time faculty   30

Joint Degrees
Dual MS/MBA — 3 yrs. Dual
BS/MS in Management — 5 yrs.
Students can then apply the MS
credits towards the MBA after 2
years of work experience.

Prominent Alumni
Paul Allaire, Chairman and CEO
Xerox Corporation; Judith Nitsch,
President, Judith Nitsch
Engineering, Inc.; Windle Priem,
President and CEO, Korn/Ferry
International; Stephen Rubin,
President and CEO, Intellution, Inc.;
Ronald Zarella, President, GM North
America

Academics

Offering "more of a technical leadership program than a traditional MBA," the School of Business at Worcester Polytechnic Institute unites a broad-based degree in business essentials with highly specialized instruction in technology and technology management to fit the needs of graduate-level biz-savvy technophiles. Students appreciate the value of this approach; "The technology focus is great, considering where the business world is headed," one MBA observes. Another explains that the program "works very well in the intersection of business and technology, teaching us how to create and extract maximum value" from that nexus.

WPI's 48-credit hour program features ten highly-integrated required courses; two major projects; and four electives. All coursework is taught from a technological perspective and practical applications to business theory are emphasized. Students tailor their education via electives in cutting-edge fields such as information security management, process design, or technological innovation. In addition to electives offered through the business school, WPI students can enroll in graduate-level electives in other departments, including computer science, biomedical engineering, and electrical engineering. Students may study on campus, online, or switch back and forth between the two formats, an arrangement they love. "You can take classes online or portions of it online in case you are away on business and can't make the class one night," creating a "high amount of schedule[ing] flexibility."

WPI is committed to keeping up with the Data Age, with "courses updated frequently" and online course delivery "allowing for larger numbers of students to take classes, so I have never been closed out of a class." It isn't just all-tech, all-the-time at WPI; professors "express strong concerns with teaching us the importance of ethics applied in business management." Course work, students warn, "is fairly extensive, averaging about three to six hours per week per credit for reading and homework," but "professors are fair in their grading and flexible to accommodate working student schedules," which helps. Administrators "operate the program seamlessly," another plus.

Career and Placement

A high percentage of WPI students work full time, many receiving tuition reimbursement from their current company while pursuing the MBA. Therefore, most will continue at the same company after completing the WPI program. However, those considering a career change can receive support and guidance through the university's Career Development Center, which serves the undergraduate, graduate, and alumni population. The CDC offers career counseling, workshops, and assessments, and maintains contact with regional employers and WPI alumni. The CDC also hosts several annual campus career fairs. Students appreciate "the way [WPI] fosters and enables networking opportunities and works with the students toward their career goals."

Employers who most frequently hire WPI MBAs include: BAE Systems, EMC, Fidelity, GE, Intel, Raytheon, Staples, Teradyne, and Textron.

Student Life and Environment

WPI occupies "a small urban campus with excellent access," making it easy for busy part-time students to zip in and zip out for classes, group meetings, etc. Students tell us that the library and student center are excellent resources; both "are well-staffed, clean, and contain useful equipment and products to support the learning environment." The program "offers a variety of activities and events throughout the year. These events range from academic to social to career-driven to special interests." To the extent that time permits, students "are not only actively engaged in school-related activities, but also go out of their way to actively participate in building a better world for the future. From holding forums on solar energy to fundraising for the community, WPI is always active in working to improve life for everyone [else]." Even the program's many distance-learning-only participants are surprised by their level of engagement. "It is not what I expected...it is very interactive. I love chat sessions most."

WPI MBAs tend to be "technical people in the stage of their careers [where they are ready] to transit[ion] from [a] professional role to [a] managerial position." There are "multiple nationalities represented" among the students, most of whom "have a good comprehension of English."

Admissions

The MBA program at Worcester Polytechnic Institute accepts students whose academic and professional record demonstrates the ability to excel in a challenging, technology-focused graduate program. Students are analyzed on the basis of their academic and professional performance, as well as their career goals and personal statement. In addition, all applicants must have demonstrated capacity to succeed in a technology-driven management program; therefore, a minimum of three semesters of college-level math or two semesters of college-level calculus are a prerequisite of the program. To apply, students must submit undergraduate transcripts, official GMAT or GRE scores, three letters of recommendation, and a completed application form. Applicants whose native language is not English and who have not earned degrees from English-language institutions must submit an official score report for the TOEFL or IELTS. WPI recruits underrepresented minorities through the Society of Hispanic Professional Engineers and the Society of Women Engineers, and maintains offices of diversity to increase recruitment among these groups.

FINANCIAL FACTS

Annual tuition	$29,736
Fees	$55
Cost of books	$1,100
Room & board	$8,100
% of students receiving aid	65
% of first-year students receiving aid	75
% of students receiving grants	4
Average award package	$4,800
Average grant	$24,780
Average loan	$18,000

ADMISSIONS

Admissions Selectivity Rating	89
# of applications received	119
% applicants accepted	45
% acceptees attending	87
Average GMAT	604
Range of GMAT	570–640
Average GPA	3.32
TOEFL required of international students	Yes
Minimum TOEFL (paper/computer)	563/223
Application fee	$70
International application fee	$70
Application Deadline/Notification	
Round 1:	11/30 / 1/15
Round 2:	2/1 / 3/30
Round 3:	3/15 / 4/30
Round 4:	4/15 / 5/15
Deferment available	Yes
Maximum length of deferment	1 year
Transfer students accepted	Yes
Transfer application policy: Accepted transfer applicants may transfer in up to 9 prior graduate-level credits toward the WPI MBA, provided those credits were not applied toward another earned degree.	
Non-fall admissions	Yes
Need-blind admissions	Yes

EMPLOYMENT PROFILE

		Grads Employed by Function	% Avg. Salary
Career Rating	95		
Percent employed at graduation	80	Marketing	(20%) $71,000
Percent employed 3 months after graduation	100	Operations	(14%) $74,000
		Consulting	(20%) $76,000
Average base starting salary	$75,520	Management	(16%) $81,111
Primary Source of Full-time Job Acceptances		MIS	(30%) $78,800
School-facilitated activities	38(76%)	**Top 5 Employers Hiring Grads**	
Graduate-facilitated activities	12(24%)	EMC (3), United Technologies Corp. (3), Fidelity (2), General Electric (2), Staples (2)	

WRIGHT STATE UNIVERSITY
RAJ SOIN COLLEGE OF BUSINESS

GENERAL INFORMATION
Type of school   Public
Affiliation   No Affiliation
Academic calendar   Semester

SURVEY SAYS...
Solid preparation in:
General management,
Social responsibility

STUDENTS
Enrollment of parent institution	17,789
Enrollment of MBA Program	449
% male/female	58/42
% out-of-state	7
% part-time	77
% underrepresented minority	11
% international	22
Average age at entry	30
Average years work experience at entry	6.0

ACADEMICS
Academic Experience Rating	**79**
Profs interesting rating	80
Profs accesible rating	85
Student/faculty ratio	10:1
% female faculty	24
% underrepresented minority faculty	1
% part-time faculty	15

Joint Degrees
MBA/MS Nursing (3 - 5 years);
MBA/MS Social & Applied
Economics (2-3 years); MBA/MD (4
years)

Prominent Alumni
William Pohlman, Pohlman &
Talmadge, Partner; Bradley Mayer,
President Finance & IT, Speedway
LLC; Gary McCullough, President &
CEO, Career Education, Corp;
Richard P. Davis, Founder Flagship
Financial Service, (Retired); Thomas
Duncan, CFO Premier Health
Partners

Academics

Wright State University's Raj Soin College of Business offers a "great education for a low price." In addition to a traditional full-time MBA, Wright state offers cohort MBA programs that meet in the evenings or on the weekends to accommodate the needs of working students. The weekend program is held at three different campuses in the Dayton area to maximize convenience. The majority of students attend part time, and they appreciate that they can get a "great" education without "sacrificing too much of their work life," and that the school is "very commuter friendly." Students at other part-time MBA programs often complain about their ability to get into classes, but at Wright State, "picking and choosing classes online is very easy and convenient," and there are always "many seats available."

The academic program at Wright State provides an in-depth, multi-disciplinary understanding of business, while emphasizing ethics and sustainability and a global perspective. Some students are required to take foundation courses, though students who took similar classes as undergraduates and did well in them may be exempt. After that, students take eight core courses, such as Analysis of Global Economic Conditions, Leading Teams and Organizations, and Legal and Ethical Decision Making to gain a deeper understanding of business. Students can then choose a concentration in one of seven areas, including Economics, Finance, International Business, and Project Management to further specialize in their fields of interest. Wright University's study-abroad program is designed for working professionals and part-time students, which is rare. Trips to China and Paris are offered during Spring Break, and students have the opportunity to take classes and meet with international business leaders while learning more about global markets and economic issues.

Classes at Wright State "foster innovation and creativity." "Lectures and discussions revolve around real-world experiences," and professors create "safe spaces where students and their point of view is respected." The workload is "challenging," but "manageable," which is another bonus for working students. Most professors are "top-notch" and "passionate" and "provide students with the skills and knowledge needed to succeed in the real world," though there are some who "make students wish that tenure was eliminated." Overall, however, dedicated professors are one of the many aspects of life at Wright State that help students "become well-rounded business professionals." "This school is on the rise," one student says, "and is poised to be a leader not only in the country, but the world."

Career and Placement

Many Wright State students are already employed and are receiving tuition assistance from their current employers, so lots of students in the program aren't hoping to score a new job after graduation. Those who are, however, will benefit from Wright State's Career Services center, which actively works with local companies to determine their staffing needs. The Center hosts recruiting and networking events, as well as onsite interviews, and it provides personal career counseling. "Professors, administrative staff, and alumni are always willing to help any student in the job hunt" as well. Some students would like to see Wright State put more effort into its career services for business students and increase alumni networking opportunities.

ADMISSIONS CONTACT: MICHAEL EVANS, DIRECTOR, MBA PROGRAMS
ADDRESS: 100 RIKE HALL, 3640 COLONEL GLENN HIGHWAY, DAYTON, OH 45435-0001
PHONE: 937-775-2437 • FAX: 937-775-3545
E-MAIL: RSCOB-ADMIN@WRIGHT.EDU • WEBSITE: WWW.WRIGHT.EDU/BUSINESS

Student Life and Environment

"Wright State University attracts students that are truly interested in their education." Students are "extremely hard-working and motivated, dedicated, and passionate about improving their breadth of knowledge and applying this to make a difference." The student body is a "mix of those just out of college undergraduate studies, students with a few years of experience, and students who have been in the workplace for a long time," and "many are pursuing a second or third master's degree." The student body at Wright State is also "very diverse." One student says, "You can meet hardworking students of all colors, nationalities, genders, ages, etc., in your classes." You're guaranteed to hear "different perspectives on issues," and students report that being exposed to "different viewpoints and life experiences enhances their learning experience."

Since the majority of students work full time and have demanding home lives, many of them don't have the opportunity to socialize with their peers. "I just drive to class after work and go to school and go home," one student explains. An upside of this is "the majority understand what each other are going through and are willing to help." Though many do disappear after class, one student says, "The lobby in the business school is always full with students socializing and working on school-related activities and projects." There are many business-oriented clubs, such as those dedicated to accounting and finance, as well as all kinds of organizations and intramural teams offered by Wright State University, should students find themselves with some free time.

Admissions

Students at Wright State University have an average of five years of work experience, but students are accepted with much less. Applicants must submit GMAT scores, a resume (required for the full-time MBA program), and three references; letters of recommendation are not required. Students who already have completed a master's degree in another discipline do not need to take the GMAT. The admission office ranks students according to an admissions index (College GPA X 200 + GMAT Score) and requires a minimum of 1,100 points for acceptance, though many students score much higher. The average undergraduate GPA for last year's incoming class was 3.15. The average GMAT score was 500. International students must submit a translated transcript where necessary, and if their primary language is not English, they must also take the TOEFL.

FINANCIAL FACTS

Annual tuition (in-state/ out-of-state)	$12,240/$20,792
Fees	$0
Cost of books	$2,400
Room & board	$10,000
% of students receiving aid	15
% of first-year students receiving aid	20
% of students receiving grants	15
Average award package	$17,899
Average grant	$5,102
Average loan	$9,282
Average student loan debt	$36,006

ADMISSIONS

Admissions Selectivity Rating	77
# of applications received	356
% applicants accepted	55
% acceptees attending	70
Average GMAT	478
Range of GMAT	420–540
Average GPA	3.19
TOEFL required of international students	Yes
Minimum TOEFL (paper/computer)	550/213
Application fee	$40
International application fee	$40
Early application deadline	4/15
Early notification date	5/1
Regular application deadline	7/1
Regular application notification	8/1
Deferment available	Yes
Maximum length of deferment	1 year
Transfer students accepted	Yes
Transfer application policy: They must meet WSU admissions requirements. Can transfer up to 15 credit hours with department approval.	
Non-fall admissions	Yes
Need-blind admissions	Yes

EMPLOYMENT PROFILE

Career Rating	76	Grads Employed by Function	% Avg. Salary
Percent employed 3 months after graduation	30	Consulting	(20%)$55,000
		Finance	(60%) $55,000
Average base starting salary	$51,272	Other	(20%) $49,000
Primary Source of Full-time Job Acceptances		**Top 5 Employers Hiring Grads**	
School-facilitated activities	8(19%)	Wright Patterson Air Force Base (>10), Lexis-	
Graduate-facilitated activities	13(32%)	Nexis (>10), Premier Health Partners (>5),	
Unknown	20(49%)	CareSource (>5), Teradata (>5)	

XAVIER UNIVERSITY
WILLIAMS COLLEGE OF BUSINESS

Academics

The Williams College of Business at Cincinnati's Xavier University offers multiple MBA programs across the main and satellite campuses, as well as five different study abroad locations as part of the school's International MBA program. The school "definitely caters to part time students": small classes take place at night and create an "atmosphere [that] is intimate," and the school works to provide great diversity in the MBA curriculum. Beyond the usual in concentrations like Health, Finance, and Management, they continue to add areas such as Business Intelligence and International Business in an effort to be "constantly improving." In addition, Xavier's roots in the Jesuit learning experience are "a remarkable approach to education."

"Excellent" professors and "efficient and understanding" administrators "put the student first." Most are working in the field or maintain contact with the business community, "therefore, the material is constantly evolving." Teaching is important here, but "Xavier still manages to keep on the cutting edge in terms of research." The faculty is "great, somewhat crazy, and always thoughtful," "highly analytical and intelligent, outgoing, and fun," and "very attentive to students' needs and business expectations." The students are as "strong contributors to the classroom as the professors."

Most professors have office hours outside of the standard nine-to-five, and the MBA office has later evening hours, "making it easy for part time students to reach someone after work." Administrative communication is "stellar." "Within the first week of class, the administration knew me by first name from our MBA orientation," says a student. "I feel I am valued."

Career and Placement

Though the school is completely "well respected in the Cincinnati area" and has "a strong alumni base," many admit that "Xavier needs a more national presence." "Right now it's mostly Cincy-based financial services companies that show up to the career fairs," says one student of the region, which has a high concentration of marketing and management companies. "Many *Fortune* companies located in the city don't directly recruit from my school, however they do send their current employees to get their MBA at my school," explains a student. Still, the school's star is on the rise, and "many of the big companies in the area recognize it as a leader."

Recent top employers of Xavier graduates are Procter & Gamble, Fidelity Investments, The Kroger Company, Fifth Third Bank, and General Electric.

ADMISSIONS CONTACT: ANNA MARIE WHELAN, ASSOCIATE DIRECTOR, MBA PROGRAMS
ADDRESS: 3800 VICTORY PARKWAY, CINCINNATI, OH 45207-1221
PHONE: 513-745-3525 • FAX: 513-745-2929
E-MAIL: XUMBA@XAVIER.EDU • WEBSITE: WWW.XAVIER.EDU/MBA

Student Life and Environment

Most students in the MBA are part-time and working, though a recently added full-time program has changed the dynamics of the school somewhat (in a good way). Students are "a mix of quirky and straight-laced" ("ages range from early twenties to mid fifties") which "creates an eclectic atmosphere" in which everyone is "very friendly and willing to help others."

"Fine new facilities aid in the learning process" and are "beautiful, plus they are wired with technology", such as the Bloomberg trading center. Clubs and social gatherings take place in the "bustling" great lobby of the business college every night, and Xavier offers "a host of amenities" so commuting students can "easily pack up a bag and spend the day at the College of Business interacting with fellow classmates, studying on my own, and more." Students don't even have to stray far from the building, as "the library is across the street, there are restaurants within walking distance, [and] private study rooms and computer labs in the building." "It really is my home away from home," says a student.

Admissions

To be considered for admission to Xavier's graduate programs, students must have a GPA of at least 2.5 from their undergraduate studies—though, on average, entering students had a 3.29 GPA, on a 4.0 scale. Students must also have a minimum GMAT score of 470. Letters of recommendation are optional, but are recommended for students whose test scores or GPA fall below the average applicant. Previous career experience is not a requirement of the program; however, it is highly recommended.

Prominent Alumni

George Schaefer, President/CEO Fifth Third Bancorp; Robert J. Kohlhepp, Vice Chairman, Cintas Corporation; John Lechleiter, President & CEO, Eli Lilly & Company; Carlos Alcantara, President/CEO Chalaco; Mary Jean Ryan, F.S.M. MEA., President and CEO SSM Health Care

FINANCIAL FACTS

Annual tuition	$13,320
Fees	$6
Cost of books	$1,000
% of students receiving aid	28
% of students receiving grants	42
Average award package	$14,393
Average grant	$530
Average loan	$17,667
Average student loan debt	$30,750

ADMISSIONS

Admissions Selectivity Rating	81
# of applications received	345
% applicants accepted	53
% acceptees attending	58
Average GMAT	514
Range of GMAT	500–610
Average GPA	3.29
TOEFL required of international students	Yes
Minimum TOEFL (paper/computer)	550/213
Application fee	$0
International application fee	$0
Deferment available	Yes
Maximum length of deferment	1 year
Transfer students accepted	Yes

Transfer application policy: 6 hours of core curriculum from AACSB accredited programs only. Up to 18 hours of core curriculum from AACSB accredited Jesuit MBA Network Schools.

Non-fall admissions	Yes
Need-blind admissions	Yes

EMPLOYMENT PROFILE

Career Rating	74	Grads Employed by Function	% Avg. Salary
		Marketing	(21%) $71,036
		Operations	(4%) $46,750
		Consulting	(9%) $76,829
		Management	(10%) $64,125
		Finance	(27%) $74,292
		HR	(3%) $60,500
		MIS	(6%) $109,467
		Other	(18%) $65,142

Top 5 Employers Hiring Grads
Procter & Gamble (7), Fidelity Investments (5), The Kroger Company (2), Fifth Third Bank (7), General Electric (5)

YALE UNIVERSITY
SCHOOL OF MANAGEMENT

GENERAL INFORMATION
Type of school | Private
Affiliation | No Affiliation
Academic calendar | Semester

SURVEY SAYS...
Friendly students, Good social scene, Good peer network, Cutting-edge classes
Solid preparation in:
General management, Teamwork, Doing business in a global economy, Environmental sustainability, Social responsibility

STUDENTS
Enrollment of parent
institution | 11,906
Enrollment of MBA Program | 494
% male/female | 65/35
% international | 28
Average age at entry | 28
Average years work experience
at entry | 5.3

ACADEMICS
Academic Experience Rating | **99**
Profs interesting rating | 97
Profs accesible rating | 95
% female faculty | 17

Joint Degrees
Four-year MBA/JD (4 years); Three-year Accelerated Integrated MBA/JD (3 years); MBA/MD (5 years) MBA/MARCH (4 yrs); MBA/MFA (4 yrs); MBA/MDIV or MAR (3 yrs); MBA/MEM or MF (3 yrs); MBA/MPH (3 yrs); MBA/PhD; MBA/MA in International Relations

Prominent Alumni
Timothy Collins, CEO & Senior Managing Director, Ripplewood Holding; Jane Mendillo, President & CEO, Harvard Management Company; Indra Nooyi, Chairman and CEO, PepsiCo Inc.; Fred Terrell, Vice Chairman, Credit Suisse; John Thornton, Non-Executive Chairman, HSBC.

Academics

Yale is one of the world's most respected universities, so it is no surprise that the "world-renowned" "brand of Yale" is a huge draw for students. The School of Management has Yale's characteristic "academic rigor" coupled with a "low faculty to student ratio" and an "international focus." SOM students can take advantage of the entirety of Yale University, taking "elective courses anywhere across the university - anything from bankruptcy at the law school to art or film studies." Located in New Haven, Connecticut, Yale can also boast a close "proximity to NY and Boston." "There was a unique combination of intelligence and humility at SOM that I didn't find anywhere else," one student says of their decision to attend. The SOM is "non-traditional" and puts "emphasis on educating leaders for both business AND society." "The business world itself does not function in a vacuum, so it is important to understand how business fits in with the greater societal landscape," elaborates one student.

"The school is on an upward trajectory in terms of academic programming," and the "administration is very productive, approachable, and helpful." As one would expect at Yale, "the academic experience is unparalleled," and the "professors are leaders in their fields." Students take a "core curriculum" which engenders a close community and "a spirit for learning and risk-taking." However, the program is "flexible" and students are able to "dictate our curriculum." "The professors are committed to partnering with students to make sure they learn the material," although some say that "the University often puts up bureaucratic roadblocks."

Students at the SOM are "very diverse in their interests," but "everyone understands that what they want to do." "I felt I 'found my people,'" an Environmental Non-Profit student says. "Smart, ambitious, mission-driven, inclusive, diverse, concerned with the world, who want to make a difference and appreciate that the principles of good leadership and management transcend sectors."

Career and Placement

"The Career Development Office is a mixed bag" at Yale. "Career services is always available to help, but because of the small size there are just fewer opportunities," one student says. However, another declares that "the CDO staff is incredibly personable, has many individual meetings with students, and not only connects students with jobs, but acts as a sort of therapy for students trying to figure out their calling." One "growing sector for Yale" is Technology "with people heading to Google, Apple, Amazon, Palantir, and others" in recent years.

In 2012, the average mean base salary was over $104,000 and 89 percent of graduates had job offers by three months after graduation. Nearly one-fourth of students found work in Consulting and another fourth found work in Financial Services. Barclays, Boston Consulting Group, Bain & Company, Goldman Sachs, and Amazon.com were among the companies where SOM graduates landed.

ADMISSIONS CONTACT: BRUCE DELMONICO, DIRECTOR OF ADMISSIONS
ADDRESS: 135 PROSPECT STREET, P.O. BOX 208200, NEW HAVEN, CT 06520-8200
PHONE: 203-432-5635
E-MAIL: MBA.ADMISSIONS@YALE.EDU • WEBSITE: WWW.MBA.YALE.EDU

Student Life and Environment

Students at SOM's "close-knit community" are "collaborative, genuine, and incredibly smart." "The difference between Yale and other b-schools is that we have a unique ethos amongst the students; one of social awareness, and generosity of spirit and camaraderie," explains a Non-Profit Consulting student. "The flavor of the school…is very familial, congenial, and fun-filled." Because "it's a relatively small school" most students find that "you become friends with just about everyone very quickly, which makes for a very tight community." "Yale SOM is heavily integrated with 'greater Yale' both academically and socially" and both New York City and Boston are fairly short trips away. "There's a student club for just about any interest" although Yale's demanding program combined "with too many exciting activities and opportunities to take advantage of" means that prioritizing can be "a difficult job." "At any given hour of any given day there are multiple talks/lectures I'd die to attend, so opportunities are overwhelming," one student explains.

Admissions

The extremely high quality of the School of Management means lots of competition. However, Yale looks to create a student body with a diversity of backgrounds, experiences, and voices. The average undergraduate GPA for the 2012 class was 3.55 and the average GMAT was 717. In addition to traditional metrics, Yale admissions are decided by academic potential, personal values, professional accomplishment, and personal interviews.

FINANCIAL FACTS

Annual tuition	$55,050
Fees	$1,480
Cost of books	$900
Room & board (on/off-campus)	$14,760
% of students receiving aid	66
Average grant	$18,933
Average loan	$54,648
Average student loan debt	$95,235

ADMISSIONS

Admissions Selectivity Rating	99
# of applications received	2,554
% applicants accepted	21
% acceptees attending	46
Average GMAT	717
Range GMAT	700–740
Average GPA	3.55
TOEFL required of international students	No
Application fee	$225
Deadline/Notification	
Round 1:	9/25 / 12/9
Round 2:	1/9 / 4/4
Round 3:	4/24 / 5/22
Deferment available	No
Transfer students accepted	No
Non-fall admissions	No
Need-blind admissions	Yes

EMPLOYMENT PROFILE

Career Rating	98	Grads Employed by Function	% Avg. Salary
Percent employed at graduation	67	Marketing	(11%) $102,500
Percent employed 3 months after graduation	86	Operations	(5%) $98,416
		Consulting	(35%) $113,121
Average base starting salary	$104,147	Management	(11%) $96,500
Primary Source of Full-time Job Acceptances		Finance	(35%) $98,994
School-facilitated activities	(69%)	HR	(1%)
Graduate-facilitated activities	(26%)	Other	(2%) $102,000
Unknown	(5%)	**Top 5 Employers Hiring Grads**	

Top 5 Employers Hiring Grads: Barclays, PricewaterhouseCoopers, Boston Consulting Group, Amazon.com, Bain & Company, Goldman Sachs

Part III-B
Business School Data
Listings

ARKANSAS STATE UNIVERSITY
COLLEGE OF BUSINESS

ADMISSIONS CONTACT: DR. THOMAS WHEELER, DEAN, GRADUATE SCHOOL
ADDRESS: PO BOX 60, STATE UNIVERSITY, AR 72467
PHONE: 870-972-3029 • FAX: 870-972-3857
E-MAIL: GRADSCH@CHOCTAW.ASTATE.EDU • WEBSITE: BUSINESS.ASTATE.EDU

GENERAL INFORMATION

Type of school: Public Academic calendar: Semester

STUDENTS

Enrollment of MBA Program: 104 Average years work experience at entry: 0.0

ACADEMICS

Student/faculty ratio: 25:1 % female faculty: 24 % underrepresented minority faculty: 1

FINANCIAL FACTS

Annual tuition (in-state/out-of-state): $1,488/ $3,744 Cost of books: $2,100 Room & board: $3,500 Average grant: $6,427 Average loan: $0

ADMISSIONS

Admissions Selectivity Rating: 63

# of applications received: 53 % applicants accepted: 85 % acceptees attending: 80 TOEFL required of international students: Yes Minimum TOEFL: 550

Deferment available: No Transfer students accepted: No Non-fall admissions: No Need-blind admissions: No

ASHRIDGE (UNITED KINGDOM)
ASHRIDGE BUSINESS SCHOOL

ADMISSIONS CONTACT: JULIET HARRY, ADMISSIONS OFFICER
ADDRESS: ASHRIDGE, BERKHAMSTED, HERTFORDSHIRE, HP41NS UNITED KINGDOM OF GREAT BRITAIN AND NORTHERN IRELAND
PHONE: +44 (0)1442 841120
E-MAIL: ADMISSIONS@ASHRIDGE.ORG.UK • WEBSITE: WWW.ASHRIDGE.ORG.UK

GENERAL INFORMATION

Type of school: Private

STUDENTS

Enrollment of MBA Program: 67 % male/female: 60/40 % part-time: 67 % international: 92 Average age at entry: 35 Average years work experience at entry: 11.0

ACADEMICS

% female faculty: 40

FINANCIAL FACTS

Annual tuition: $49,420 Cost of books: $800 Room & board: (on/off-campus) $12,558/$16,100 % of students receiving aid: 30 % of first-year students receiving aid: 30 % of students receiving grants: 30 Average award package: $100,000 Average grant: $10,000

ADMISSIONS

Admissions Selectivity Rating: 78

# of applications received: 76 % applicants accepted: 67 % acceptees attending: 43 Average GMAT: 620 Range of GMAT: 550–750 TOEFL required of international students: Yes Minimum TOEFL (paper/computer): 600/250 Application fee: $0 International Application fee: $0

Deferment available: Yes Maximum length of deferment: 12 months Transfer students accepted: No Non-fall admissions: Yes Need-blind admissions: Yes

EMPLOYMENT PROFILE

Percent employed at graduation: 59 Percent employed 3 months after graduation: 59 Average base starting salary: $82,777

Primary Source of Full-time Job Acceptances

School-facilitated activities: 7(32%) Graduate-facilitated activities: 6(27%) Unknown: 9(41%)

Grads Employed by Function	......%	Avg. Salary
Consulting:	(40%)	$87,000
Management:	(5%)	$129,000
MIS:	(5%)	
Other:	(23%)	$67,000

Top 5 Employers Hiring Grads (number of hires in last class)
Coca Cola (1), Roland Berger Strategy Consulting (1), Aston Martin (1), British Telecom (1), Johnsons Controls (1)

ASIAN INSTITUTE OF MANAGEMENT (PHILIPPINES)
ASIAN INSTITUTE OF MANAGEMENT

ADMISSIONS CONTACT: MR. REY REYES, EXECUTIVE MANAGING DIRECTOR
ADDRESS: GROUND FLR. EUGENIO LOPEZ FOUNDATION BLDG., JOSEPH R. MCMICKING CAMPUS, ASIAN INSTITUTE OF MANAGEMENT, 123 PASEO DE ROXAS, MAKATI CITY, 01260 PHILIPPINES
PHONE: +63 2 8937631 • FAX: +63 2 8937631
E-MAIL: ADMISSIONS@AIM.EDU • WEBSITE: WWW.AIM.EDU

GENERAL INFORMATION

Type of school: Private Academic calendar: Sep. to Dec. of following year

STUDENTS

Enrollment of parent institution: 393 Enrollment of MBA Program: 140 % male/female: 72/28 % out-of-state: 72 % part-time: 0 % international: 72 Average age at entry: 26 Average years work experience at entry: 4.2

ACADEMICS

Student/faculty ratio: 3:1 % female faculty: 28 % part-time faculty: 33

FINANCIAL FACTS

Annual tuition (in-state/out-of-state): $16,130 Cost of books: $8,000 Room & board: $4,100 % of students receiving grants: 10

ADMISSIONS

Admissions Selectivity Rating: 89

# of applications received: 468 **% applicants accepted:** 45 **% acceptees attending:** 67 **Average GMAT:** 656 **Range of GMAT:** 680–640 **TOEFL required of international students:** No **International Early application deadline:** 4/30 **Early notification date:** 3/22 **Regular application deadline:** 8/5 **Regular application notification:** 10/1

Deferment available: Yes **Maximum length of deferment:** After 1 year **Transfer students accepted:** No **Non-fall admissions:** No **Need-blind admissions:** No

EMPLOYMENT PROFILE

Percent employed at graduation: 13 **Percent employed 3 months after graduation:** 32

Top 5 Employers Hiring Grads (number of hires in last class)
Cognizant India (9), Citibank (3), BPI (2), Renoir (2), JP Morgan (2)

ASTON UNIVERSITY
ASTON BUSINESS SCHOOL

ADDRESS: ASTON TRIANGLE, BIRMINGHAM B4 7ET,
PHONE: 011-44 (0) 121 204 3100 • FAX:
E-MAIL: ABSPG@ASTON.AC.UK • WEBSITE: WWW.ABS.ASTON.AC.UK

GENERAL INFORMATION

Type of school: Private

STUDENTS

Average years work experience at entry: 0.0

FINANCIAL FACTS

Annual tuition: $35,608

ADMISSIONS

Admissions Selectivity Rating: 60*

TOEFL required of international students: No **Regular application deadline:** 7/1

BARRY UNIVERSITY
ANDREAS SCHOOL OF BUSINESS

ADMISSIONS CONTACT: GUSTAVO CORDEIRO, MARKETING COORDINATOR
ADDRESS: GRADUATE ADMISSIONS, 11300 NE 2ND AVENUE, MIAMI SHORES, FL 33161-6695
PHONE: (305) 899-3100 • FAX: (305) 892-6412
E-MAIL: ADMISSIONS@MAIL.BARRY.EDU • WEBSITE: WWW.BARRY.EDU/BUSINESS

GENERAL INFORMATION

Type of school: Private **Academic calendar:** All year

STUDENTS

Enrollment of MBA Program: 119 **% part-time:** 100 **Average age at entry:** 29 **Average years work experience at entry:** 3.9

ACADEMICS

Student/faculty ratio: 7:1 **% female faculty:** 47 **% underrepresented minority faculty:** 47 **% part-time faculty:** 0

FINANCIAL FACTS

Annual tuition: $17,150 **Cost of books:** $1,500 **Room & board: (on/off-campus)** $15,000 **% of students receiving aid:** 55 **% of first-year students receiving aid:** 52 **% of students receiving grants:** 29 **Average award package:** $25,308 **Average grant:** $7,719 **Average loan:** $28,219 **Average student loan debt:** $28,137

ADMISSIONS

Admissions Selectivity Rating: 83

# of applications received: 213 **% applicants accepted:** 31 **% acceptees attending:** 40 **Average GMAT:** 460 **Range of GMAT:** 400–450 **Average GPA:** 3.64 **TOEFL required of international students:** Yes **Minimum TOEFL (paper/computer):** 550/213 **Application fee:** $30 **International Application fee:** $30

Deferment available: Yes **Maximum length of deferment:** 1 year **Transfer students accepted:** Yes **Transfer application policy:** Up to six transfer credits (2 graduate classes) from an AACSB-accredited institution. Restrictions include (but not limited to): 1. All transfer credits must be a B (3.0) or better and courses must be directly parallel to required or elective courses in the MBA program. If the credits originate from a business program, that program must be accredited by AACSB International. 2. Graduate credits are not transferable if they were previously applied to a graduate degree that was awarded to the applicant. 3. No graduate credit will be allowed for correspondence or extension work. 4. Students may not transfer credits after they have entered the program. **Non-fall admissions:** Yes **Need-blind admissions:** Yes

EMPLOYMENT PROFILE

Percent employed at graduation: 20 **Percent employed 3 months after graduation:** 20 **Average base starting salary:** $75,700

Primary Source of Full-time Job Acceptances

School-facilitated activities: 0(0%) **Graduate-facilitated activities:** 6(33%) **Unknown:** 12(67%)

Top 5 Employers Hiring Grads (number of hires in last class)
Kony Solutions (1), South Florida Regional Extention Center (1), Telcome Argentina USA (1), Saudi Telecom Company (1), Lotificaciones Las Haciendes, SA (1)

BILKENT UNIVERSITY
FACULTY OF BUSINESS ADMINISTRATION

ADMISSIONS CONTACT: ILHAM CIPIL, MBA COORDINATOR
ADDRESS: BILKENT UNIVERSITY FACULTY OF BUSINESS ADMINISTRATION, MA-209 TEL:+90 312 2902817 CANKAYA BILKENT, ANKARA, NA 06800 TURKEY
PHONE: +90 312 2902817 • FAX: +90 312 2664958
E-MAIL: MBACOORDINATOR@BILKENT.EDU.TR
WEBSITE: WWW.MAN.BILKENT.EDU.TR

GENERAL INFORMATION

Type of school: Private

STUDENTS

Enrollment of MBA Program: 36 **% male/female:** 66/34 **% international:** 3 **Average age at entry:** 25 **Average years work experience at entry:** 27.0

FINANCIAL FACTS

Annual tuition (in-state/out-of-state): Room & board: (on/off-campus) % of students receiving aid: 15 % of first-year students receiving aid: 15 % of students receiving grants: 30

ADMISSIONS

Admissions Selectivity Rating: 60*

Average GMAT: 614 **TOEFL required of international students:** Yes **Minimum TOEFL:** 213

Application Deadline/Notification:

Round 1: 1/5

Round 2: 5/6

Deferment available: No **Transfer students accepted:** Yes **Transfer application policy:** The transfer applicant should contact the MBA Coordinator for the required materials and deadlines. **Non-fall admissions:** No **Need-blind admissions:** Yes

BIRMINGHAM-SOUTHERN COLLEGE

ADMISSIONS CONTACT: BRENDA D. DURHAM, DIRECTOR OF MPPM ADMISSION
ADDRESS: 900 ARKADELPHIA ROAD, BOX 549052, BIRMINGHAM, AL 35254
PHONE: 205-226-4803 • FAX: 205-226-4843
E-MAIL: GRADUATE@BSC.EDU • WEBSITE: WWW.BSC.EDU/MPPM

GENERAL INFORMATION

Type of school: Private t

STUDENTS

Enrollment of parent institution: 1,400 **Enrollment of MBA Program:** 68 % male/female: 52/48 **Average age at entry:** 37 **Average years work experience at entry:** 15.0

ACADEMICS

Student/faculty ratio: 20:1 **% female faculty:** 29

FINANCIAL FACTS

Annual tuition (in-state/out-of-state): $13,825/ $13,825 **Fees:** $300 **Cost of books:** $800

ADMISSIONS

Admissions Selectivity Rating: 60*

# of applications received: 15 **TOEFL required of international students:** Yes **Minimum TOEFL (paper/computer):** 600/213 **Application fee:** $25

Deferment available: Yes **Maximum length of deferment:** 1 year **Transfer students accepted:** Yes **Transfer application policy:** May transfer up to 6 graduate hours with a grade of B or better. Transfer coursework must be comparable to BSC-MPPM coursework and be approved by the Dean of Business Programs. **Non-fall admissions:** Yes **Need-blind admissions:** Yes

BOISE STATE UNIVERSITY
COLLEGE OF BUSINESS AND ECONOMICS

ADMISSIONS CONTACT: J. RENEE ANCHUSTEGUI, DIRECTOR, PROFESSIONAL MBA, MSA, MSAT
ADDRESS: BUSINESS GRADUATE STUDIES, 1910 UNIVERSITY DRIVE MS1600, BOISE, ID 83725-1600
PHONE: 208-426-3116 • FAX:
E-MAIL: GRADUATEBUSINESS@BOISESTATE.EDU
WEBSITE: COBE.BOISESTATE.EDU/GRADUATE

GENERAL INFORMATION

Type of school: Public **Academic calendar:** Semester

STUDENTS

Enrollment of parent institution: 18,447 **Enrollment of MBA Program:** 190 % male/female: 74/26 % out-of-state: 20 % part-time: 34 % underrepresented minority: 4 % international: 7 **Average age at entry:** 35 **Average years work experience at entry:** 11.8

ACADEMICS

Student/faculty ratio: 23:1 **% female faculty:** 20 **% underrepresented minority faculty:** 7 **% part-time faculty:** 2

FINANCIAL FACTS

Annual tuition (in-state/out-of-state): $0/ $8,576 **Fees:** $6,898 **Cost of books:** $3,000 **Room & board:** (on/off-campus) $6,800/$7,200 % of students receiving aid: 70 % of first-year students receiving aid: 23 % of students receiving grants: 22 **Average award package:** $16,700 **Average grant:** $19,492 **Average loan:** $14,599 **Average student loan debt:** $12,000

ADMISSIONS

Admissions Selectivity Rating: 83

# of applications received: 130 **% applicants accepted:** 55 % **acceptees attending:** 66 **Average GMAT:** 579 **Range of GMAT:** 510–665 **Average GPA:** 3.32 **TOEFL required of international students:** Yes **Minimum TOEFL (paper/computer):** 587/240 **Application fee:** $55 **International Application fee:** $55 **Early application deadline:** 2/1 **Early notification date:** 3/15 **Regular application deadline:** 6/1 **Regular application notification:** 7/15

Deferment available: Yes **Maximum length of deferment:** 1 year **Transfer students accepted:** Yes **Transfer application policy:** Limit of up to 1/3 of total credits required to completed the degree at Boise State. Must receive grade of B or above from an AACSB accredited institution for transfer consideration. **Non-fall admissions:** Yes **Need-blind admissions:** Yes

EMPLOYMENT PROFILE

Percent employed at graduation: 78 **Percent employed 3 months after graduation:** 95 **Average base starting salary:** $73,077

Primary Source of Full-time Job Acceptances

School-facilitated activities: 3(15%) **Graduate-facilitated activities:** 8(40%) **Unknown:** 9(45%)

Grads Employed by Function ......% Avg. Salary

Marketing: ....(5%) $70,000

Operations: ....(10%) $61,667

Consulting: ....(5%) $69,000

Management: ....(15%) $63,000

Finance:.......................................(30%) $48,000

HR: ....(5%) $53,000

MIS: ....(10%) $100,000

Other: ....(10%) $46,000

Top 5 Employers Hiring Grads (number of hires in last class)

Micron Technology (4), Northwest Mutual (2), Wells Fargo (2), Scentsy (2)

BRADLEY UNIVERSITY
FOSTER COLLEGE OF BUSINESS ADMINISTRATION

ADMISSIONS CONTACT: SUSANNAH GAWOR, DIRECTOR OF MBA PROGRAM
ADDRESS: 1501 WEST BRADLEY AVENUE, PEORIA, IL 61625
PHONE: 309-677-2253 • FAX: 309-677-3374
E-MAIL: MBA@BRADLEY.EDU • WEBSITE: WWW.BRADLEY.EDU/FCBA

GENERAL INFORMATION

Type of school: Private **Academic calendar:** Semester

STUDENTS

Enrollment of parent institution: 5,914 **Enrollment of MBA Program:** 99 % **part-time:** 65 **Average age at entry:** 30 **Average years work experience at entry:** 3.8

ACADEMICS

Student/faculty ratio: 2:1 % female faculty: 29 % underrepresented minority faculty: 0 % part-time faculty: 5

FINANCIAL FACTS

Annual tuition (in-state/out-of-state): $710/ $710 **Fees:** $50 **Cost of books:** $1,000 **Room & board: (on/off-campus)** /$8,200 **Average award package:** $6,435

ADMISSIONS

Admissions Selectivity Rating: 72

# of applications received: 41 % applicants accepted: 90 % acceptees attending: 76 **Average GMAT:** 543 **Range of GMAT:** 500–605 **Average GPA:** 3.45 **TOEFL required of international students:** Yes **Minimum TOEFL (paper/computer):** 550/213 **International Application fee:** $50 **Early application deadline:** 3/1 **Early notification date:** 4/1

Deferment available: Yes **Maximum length of deferment:** 1 Semester **Transfer students accepted:** Yes **Transfer application policy:** No more than 9 hours of credit from another AACSB-accredited school can transfer to Bradley MBA program. **Non-fall admissions:** Yes **Need-blind admissions:** Yes

CALIFORNIA STATE UNIVERISTY, LOS ANGELES
COLLEGE OF BUSINESS AND ECONOMICS

ADMISSIONS CONTACT: EDWARD HSIEH, ASSOCIATE DEAN
ADDRESS: COLLEGE OF BUSINESS AND ECONOMICS, 5151 STATE UNIVERSITY DRIVE, LOS ANGELES, CA 90032
PHONE: (323) 343-2800 • FAX: (323) 343-5462
E-MAIL: MBACBE@CALSTATELA.EDU • WEBSITE: CBE.CALSTATELA.EDU

GENERAL INFORMATION

Type of school: Public **Academic calendar:** 2012-2013

STUDENTS

Enrollment of parent institution: 21,755 **Enrollment of MBA Program:** **Average age at entry:** 27 **Average years work experience at entry:** 3.0

ACADEMICS

Student/faculty ratio: 15:1 % female faculty: 30 % underrepresented minority faculty: 37 % part-time faculty: 10

FINANCIAL FACTS

Annual tuition (in-state/out-of-state): $7,600/ $13,600 **Fees:** $4,080 **Cost of books:** $1,800 **Room & board: (on/off-campus)** $12,000/$17,000

ADMISSIONS

Admissions Selectivity Rating: 80

# of applications received: 135 % applicants accepted: 45 % acceptees attending: 34 **Average GMAT:** 550 **Range of GMAT:** 510–570 **Average GPA:** 3.25 **TOEFL required of international students:** Yes **Minimum TOEFL (paper/computer):** 550/213 **Application fee:** $55 **International Application fee:** $55 **Regular application deadline:** 4/26

Deferment available: No **Transfer students accepted:** Yes **Transfer application policy:** At most 13 units (3 courses) can be transfered. **Non-fall admissions:** Yes **Need-blind admissions:** No

CALIFORNIA STATE UNIVERSITY, SACRAMENTO
COLLEGE OF BUSINESS ADMINISTRATION

ADMISSIONS CONTACT: JEANIE WILLIAMS, GRADUATE PROGRAMS COORDINATOR
ADDRESS: 6000 J STREET, TAHOE HALL ROOM 1035, SACRAMENTO, CA 95819-6088
PHONE: 916-278-6772 • FAX: 916-278-4233
E-MAIL: CBAGRAD@CSUS.EDU • WEBSITE: WWW.CBA.CSUS.EDU

GENERAL INFORMATION

Type of school: Public **Academic calendar:** Semester

STUDENTS

Enrollment of parent institution: 23,280 **Enrollment of MBA Program:** 492 **Average age at entry:** 27 **Average years work experience at entry:** 4.5

ACADEMICS

% female faculty: 33

FINANCIAL FACTS

Annual tuition (in-state/out-of-state): $25,000/ $37,276 **Cost of books:** $2,500 **Room & board: (on/off-campus)** $8,435/$8,435

ADMISSIONS

Admissions Selectivity Rating: 84

# of applications received: 215 % applicants accepted: 52 % acceptees attending: 67 Average GMAT: 570 Range of GMAT: 440–740 Average GPA: 3.19 TOEFL required of international students: Yes Minimum TOEFL (paper/computer): 510/180 Application fee: $55 International Application fee: $55 Regular application deadline: 4/1 Regular application notification: 5/30

Deferment available: No Transfer students accepted: Yes Transfer application policy: We accept up to 6 units of transfer coursework from other AACSB accredited institutions. Non-fall admissions: Yes Need-blind admissions: Yes

CALIFORNIA STATE UNIVERSITY, STANISLAUS
COLLEGE OF BUSINESS ADMINISTRATION

Address: , Turlock, CA 95382
Phone: (209) 667-3070 or 1-800-300-7420
E-mail: Outreach_Help_Desk@csustan.edu
Website: www.csustan.edu/cba

GENERAL INFORMATION

Type of school: Public

STUDENTS

Enrollment of parent institution: 9,246 Enrollment of MBA Program: 158 % male/female: 55/45 % part-time: 32 % underrepresented minority: 16 % international: 11 Average age at entry: 28

FINANCIAL FACTS

Annual tuition (in-state/out-of-state):$11,160 Fees: $7,848 Cost of books: $1,700 Room & board: (on/off-campus) $8,368/$10,598

ADMISSIONS

Admissions Selectivity Rating: 60*

# of applications received: 68 % applicants accepted: 81 Average GMAT: 500 TOEFL required of international students: Yes Minimum TOEFL (paper/computer): 550/213 Application fee: $55 International Application fee: $55

Deferment available: No Transfer students accepted: Yes Transfer application policy: Proespective students may only transfer nine units of coursework into a graduate degree. Non-fall admissions: Yes

CANISIUS COLLEGE
RICHARD J. WEHLE SCHOOL OF BUSINESS

Admissions Contact: Laura McEwen, Director, Graduate Business Programs
Address: Canisius College, 2001 Main St, Bagen Hall 201, Buffalo, NY 14208-1098
Phone: 716-888-2140 • Fax: 716-888-2145
E-mail: gradbiz@canisius.edu • Website: www.canisius.edu/mba

GENERAL INFORMATION

Type of school: Private Academic calendar: Semester

STUDENTS

Enrollment of parent institution: 4,908 Enrollment of MBA Program: 311 % male/female: 97/3 % out-of-state: 10 % part-time: 93 % international: 0 Average age at entry: 26

ACADEMICS

% female faculty: 20 % underrepresented minority faculty: 10

FINANCIAL FACTS

Annual tuition (in-state/out-of-state): $25,992/ Cost of books: $500 Room & board: (on/off-campus) $11,820 Average grant: $0 Average loan: $0

ADMISSIONS

Admissions Selectivity Rating: 60*

TOEFL required of international students: Yes Minimum TOEFL (paper/computer): 500/200

Deferment available: Yes Maximum length of deferment: 1 year Transfer students accepted: Yes Transfer application policy: Case-by-case basis. Non-fall admissions: Yes Need-blind admissions: No

CLARION UNIVERSITY
COLLEGE OF BUSINESS ADMINISTRATION

Admissions Contact: Dr. Brenda Ponsford, Director of MBA Program
Address: 302 Still Hall, Clarion University, 840 Wood Street, Clarion, PA 16214
Phone: 814-393-2605 • Fax: 814-393-1910
E-mail: mba@clarion.edu • Website: www.clarion.edu/1077

GENERAL INFORMATION

Type of school: Public Academic calendar: Semester

STUDENTS

Enrollment of parent institution: 7,315 Enrollment of MBA Program: 108 % male/female: 90/10 % out-of-state: 7 % part-time: 76 % underrepresented minority: 0 % international: 0 Average age at entry: 32 Average years work experience at entry: 6.1

ACADEMICS

Student/faculty ratio: 0:1 % female faculty: 18 % underrepresented minority faculty: 23

FINANCIAL FACTS

Cost of books: $3,500 **Average award package:** $0 **Average grant:** $0 **Average loan:** $0

ADMISSIONS

Admissions Selectivity Rating: 69

# of applications received: 113 % applicants accepted: 99 % acceptees attending: 96 **Average GMAT:** 532 **TOEFL required of international students:** Yes **Minimum TOEFL (paper/computer):** 550/213 **Application fee:** $30 **International Application fee:** $30

Deferment available: Yes **Maximum length of deferment:** 1 year **Transfer students accepted:** Yes **Transfer application policy:** May transfer up to six approved credits as electives. **Non-fall admissions:** Yes **Need-blind admissions:** Yes

CLARK ATLANTA UNIVERSITY
SCHOOL OF BUSINESS ADMINISTRATION

ADMISSIONS CONTACT: LORRI SADDLER RICE, DIRECTOR OF ADMISSIONS
ADDRESS: 223 JAMES P. BRAWLEY DRIVE, ATLANTA, GA 30314
PHONE: 404-880-8447 • FAX: 404-880-6159
E-MAIL: LRICE@CAU.EDU • WEBSITE: WWW.SBUS.CAU.EDU

GENERAL INFORMATION

Type of school: Private **Academic calendar:** Semester

STUDENTS

Enrollment of parent institution: 5,000 **Enrollment of MBA Program:** 120 % male/female: 38/62 % part-time: 10 % underrepresented minority: 90 % international: 10 **Average age at entry:** 28 **Average years work experience at entry:** 5.0

ACADEMICS

Student/faculty ratio: 111 % female faculty: 39 % underrepresented minority faculty: 92 % part-time faculty: 22

FINANCIAL FACTS

Annual tuition (in-state/out-of-state): $19,127/ **Fees:** $550 **Cost of books:** $800 **Room & board:** (on/off-campus) /$4,875 % of students receiving aid: 95 % of first-year students receiving aid: 95 % of students receiving grants: 95 **Average award package:** $32,000 **Average grant:** $32,000 **Average loan:** $32,000 **Average student loan debt:** $65,000

ADMISSIONS

Admissions Selectivity Rating: 72

# of applications received: 134 % applicants accepted: 67 % acceptees attending: 69 **Average GMAT:** 430 **Range of GMAT:** 340–520 **Average GPA:** 3.00 **TOEFL required of international students:** Yes **Minimum TOEFL (paper/computer):** 175/ **International Application fee:** $55 **Regular application deadline:** 4/1

Deferment available: Yes **Maximum length of deferment:** 1 year **Transfer students accepted:** Yes **Transfer application policy:** We will accept up to 6 credit hours earned while enrolled in an accredited MBA program. **Non-fall admissions:** No **Need-blind admissions:** No

EMPLOYMENT PROFILE

Percent employed at graduation: 25 **Percent employed 3 months after graduation:** 2 **Average base starting salary:** $82,500

Primary Source of Full-time Job Acceptances

School-facilitated activities: 7(25%) **Graduate-facilitated activities:** 15(50%) Unknown: 7(25%)

Grads Employed by Function ......% Avg. Salary

Marketing:	(52%)	$80,000
Operations:	(7%)	$75,000
Finance:	(30%)	$82,000
HR:	(7%)	$75,000
Other:	(4%)	$50,000

Top 5 Employers Hiring Grads (number of hires in last class)
Chevron/Texaco, Coca Cola, American Express, Union Pacific, Delta Airlines

CLEVELAND STATE UNIVERSITY
MONTE AHUJA COLLEGE OF BUSINESS

ADMISSIONS CONTACT: RONALD MICKLER JR., ASSISTANT DIRECTOR GRADUATE BUSINESS
ADDRESS: 2121 EUCLID AVENUE, BU 219, CLEVELAND, OH 44115
PHONE: 216-687-3730 • FAX: 216-687-5311
E-MAIL: CBACSU@CSUOHIO.EDU • WEBSITE: WWW.CSUOHIO.EDU/BUSINESS/MBA/

GENERAL INFORMATION

Type of school: Public **Academic calendar:** Semester

STUDENTS

Enrollment of parent institution: 16,900 **Enrollment of MBA Program:** 766 % male/female: 57/43 % out-of-state: 38 % part-time: 71 % underrepresented minority: 18 % international: 29 **Average age at entry:** 26 **Average years work experience at entry:** 3.9

ACADEMICS

Student/faculty ratio: 28:1 % female faculty: 25 % underrepresented minority faculty: 16 % part-time faculty: 17

FINANCIAL FACTS

Annual tuition (in-state/out-of-state): $14,222/ $26,865 **Fees:** $53 **Cost of books:** $1,500 **Room & board:** (on/off-campus) $12,000/$12,000 % of students receiving aid: 4 % of first-year students receiving aid: 8 % of students receiving grants: 1 **Average award package:** $22,000 **Average grant:** $1,500 **Average loan:** $0 **Average student loan debt:** $26,397

ADMISSIONS

Admissions Selectivity Rating: 74

# of applications received: 573 % applicants accepted: 69 % acceptees attending: 57 **Average GMAT:** 449 **Range of GMAT:** 460–590 **Average GPA:** 3.14 **TOEFL required of international students:** Yes **Minimum TOEFL (paper/computer):** 550/213 **Application fee:** $30 **International Application fee:** $30 **Regular application deadline:** 7/1

Deferment available: Yes **Maximum length of deferment:** 12 months **Transfer students accepted:** Yes **Transfer application policy:** Must be in good academic standing **Non-fall admissions:** Yes **Need-blind admissions:** Yes

EMPLOYMENT PROFILE

Percent employed at graduation: 50 **Percent employed 3 months after graduation:** 66 **Average base starting salary:** $62,500

Primary Source of Full-time Job Acceptances

School-facilitated activities: 34(49%) **Graduate-facilitated activities:** 27(39%) **Unknown:** 8(12%)

Grads Employed by Function ......% Avg. Salary

Marketing:	(17%)	
Management:	(29%)	$58,772
Finance:	(17%)	$60,625
HR:	(12%)	$37,742
Other:	(25%)	$67,013

Top 5 Employers Hiring Grads (number of hires in last class)

Key Bank (2), Cleveland Clinic (2), Lubrizol (2), Sherwin Williams (2), Progressive Insurance (2)

COASTAL CAROLINA UNIVERSITY
WALL COLLEGE OF BUSINESS

ADMISSIONS CONTACT: DR. JAMES O. LUKEN, ASSOC. PROVOST/DIR. OF GRADUATE STUDIES
ADDRESS: P.O. BOX 261954, CONWAY, SC 29528-6054
PHONE: 843-349-2394
E-MAIL: GRADUATE@COASTAL.EDU • WEBSITE: WWW.COASTAL.EDU/GRADUATE

GENERAL INFORMATION

Type of school: Public

STUDENTS

Enrollment of parent institution: 9,084 **Enrollment of MBA Program:** 54 **% male/female:** 68/32 **% out-of-state:** 67 **% part-time:** 43 **% underrepresented minority:** 14 **% international:** 14 **Average age at entry:** 24 **Average years work experience at entry:** 5.0

ACADEMICS

Student/faculty ratio: 6:1 **% female faculty:** 56 **% underrepresented minority faculty:** 11 **% part-time faculty:** 0

FINANCIAL FACTS

Annual tuition (in-state/out-of-state): $12,480/ $19,080 **Fees:** $80 **Cost of books:** $3,094 **Room & board: (on/off-campus)** /$7,964 **% of students receiving aid:** 90 **% of first-year students receiving aid:** 91 **% of students receiving grants:** 35 **Average award package:** $15,393 **Average grant:** $7,368 **Average loan:** $15,172 **Average student loan debt:** $43,206

ADMISSIONS

Admissions Selectivity Rating: 70

# of applications received: 45 **% applicants accepted:** 89 **% acceptees attending:** 60 **Average GMAT:** 490 **Range of GMAT:** 450–540 **Average GPA:** 3.41 **TOEFL required of international stu-**

dents: Yes **Minimum TOEFL (paper/computer):** 575/ **Application fee:** $45 **International Application fee:** $45

Deferment available: Yes **Maximum length of deferment:** 1 Semester **Transfer students accepted:** Yes **Transfer application policy:** All course work must be 3.0 or higher. 6 hours - maximum transfer. **Non-fall admissions:** Yes **Need-blind admissions:** Yes

COLORADO STATE UNIVERSITY - PUEBLO
MALIK AND SEEME HASAN SCHOOL OF BUSINESS

ADMISSIONS CONTACT: JOE MARSHALL, DIRECTOR OF ADMISSIONS
ADDRESS: 2200 BONFORTE BLVD, PUEBLO, CO 81001
PHONE: 719-549-2461 • FAX: 719-549-2419
E-MAIL: INFO@COLOSTATE-PUEBLO.EDU • WEBSITE: HSB.COLOSTATE-PUEBLO.EDU

GENERAL INFORMATION

Type of school: Public **Academic calendar:** students may begin at any time

STUDENTS

Enrollment of parent institution: 5,100 **Enrollment of MBA Program:** 109 **% male/female:** 76/24 **% out-of-state:** 33 **% part-time:** 37 **% underrepresented minority:** 19 **% international:** 32 **Average age at entry:** 28 **Average years work experience at entry:**

ACADEMICS

Student/faculty ratio: 11:1 **% female faculty:** 17 **% underrepresented minority faculty:** 50

ADMISSIONS

Admissions Selectivity Rating: 74

# of applications received: 56 **% applicants accepted:** 88 **% acceptees attending:** 100 **Average GMAT:** 440 **Range of GMAT:** 400–680 **Average GPA:** 3.30 **TOEFL required of international students:** Yes **Minimum TOEFL (paper/computer):** 550/213 **Application fee:** $35 **International Application fee:** $35

Deferment available: No **Transfer students accepted:** Yes **Transfer application policy:** Students may transfer up to 9 credit hours of approved graduate courses. **Non-fall admissions:** Yes **Need-blind admissions:** Yes

COLUMBUS STATE UNIVERSITY
TURNER COLLEGE OF BUSINESS AND COMPUTER SCIENCE

ADMISSIONS CONTACT: BETHANY YANDELL, TURNER COLLEGE RECRUITER
ADDRESS: 4225 UNIVERSITY AVE., COLUMBUS, GA 31907
PHONE: 706-507-8800 OR 706-507-8186
E-MAIL: YANDELL_BETHANY@COLUMBUSSTATE.EDU • WEBSITE: COBCS.COLUMBUSSTATE.EDU/

GENERAL INFORMATION

Type of school: Public

STUDENTS

Enrollment of parent institution: 8,307 Enrollment of MBA Program: 100 % male/female: 65/35 % out-of-state: 59 % part-time: 83 % underrepresented minority: 35 % international: 41 Average age at entry: 33 Average years work experience at entry: 4.0

ACADEMICS

Student/faculty ratio: 30:1 % female faculty: 18 % underrepresented minority faculty: 0 % part-time faculty: 0

FINANCIAL FACTS

Annual tuition (in-state/out-of-state): $2,070/ $8,271 Fees: $835 Cost of books: $600 Room & board: (on/off-campus) % of students receiving aid: 47 % of first-year students receiving aid: 47 % of students receiving grants: 11 Average award package: $499,653 Average grant: $16,074 Average loan: $477,829 Average student loan debt: $42,189

ADMISSIONS

Admissions Selectivity Rating: 76

# of applications received: 93 % applicants accepted: 56 % -acceptees attending: 62 Average GMAT: 485 Range of GMAT: 430–550 Average GPA: 3.11 TOEFL required of international students: Yes Minimum TOEFL (paper/computer): 550/213 Application fee: $40 International Application fee: $40 Regular application deadline: 6/30

Deferment available: Yes Maximum length of deferment: 1 year Transfer students accepted: Yes Transfer application policy: No more than 6 Semester hours may be transferred. Non-fall admissions: Yes Need-blind admissions: Yes

CONCORDIA UNIVERSITY
JOHN MOLSON SCHOOL OF BUSINESS

ADMISSIONS CONTACT: MARIE LYSTER, GRADUATE RECRUITMENT OFFICER
ADDRESS: 1450 RUE GUY, MB 6.201 (6TH FLOOR), MONTREAL, QC H3H 0A1 CANADA
PHONE: 514-848-2424 EXT 2708 • FAX: 514-848-2816
E-MAIL: GRADPROGRAMS@JMSB.CONCORDIA.CA
WEBSITE: JOHNMOLSON.CONCORDIA.CA

GENERAL INFORMATION

Type of school: Public Academic calendar: Trimester

STUDENTS

Enrollment of parent institution: 45,954 Enrollment of MBA Program: 322 % male/female: 67/33 % part-time: 69 Average age at entry: 29 Average years work experience at entry: 5.8

ACADEMICS

Student/faculty ratio: 12:1 % female faculty: 28 % underrepresented minority faculty: 0 % part-time faculty: 39

FINANCIAL FACTS

Annual tuition (in-state/out-of-state): $1,626/ $14,801 Fees: $990 Cost of books: $4,000 Room & board: (on/off-campus) $5,000/$10,750 Average award package: $9,000 Average grant: $8,111 Average loan: $8,000

ADMISSIONS

Admissions Selectivity Rating: 88

# of applications received: 325 % applicants accepted: 42 % acceptees attending: 58 Average GMAT: 626 Average GPA: 3.34 TOEFL required of international students: Yes Minimum TOEFL (paper/computer): 577/233 Application fee: $100 International Application fee: $100

Application Deadline/Notification:

Round 1: 6/1
Round 2: 10/1
Round 3: 2/15

Deferment available: Yes Maximum length of deferment: 1 year Transfer students accepted: Yes Transfer application policy: Applicants may be eligible for advanced standing Non-fall admissions: Yes Need-blind admissions: Yes

EMPLOYMENT PROFILE

Percent employed 3 months after graduation: 76 Average base starting salary: $79,071

Top 5 Employers Hiring Grads (number of hires in last class)

Bombardier, Deloitte Consulting, BMO, Ericsson Canada, Amazon.com

CRANFIELD UNIVERSITY
CRANFIELD SCHOOL OF MANAGEMENT

ADMISSIONS CONTACT: HELEN KNIGHT, ADMISSIONS EXECUTIVE
ADDRESS: CRANFIELD SCHOOL OF MANAGEMENT, CRANFIELD, BEDFORD, MK43 0AL
PHONE: 0044-1234-754432 • FAX: 0044-1234-752439
E-MAIL: MBAADMISSIONS@CRANFIELD.AC.UK
WEBSITE: WWW.CRANFIELDMBA.INFO

GENERAL INFORMATION

Type of school: Public Academic calendar: Year Long

STUDENTS

Enrollment of MBA Program: 284 % male/female: 78/22 % part-time: 48 % international: 90 Average age at entry: 31 Average years work experience at entry: 7.0

ACADEMICS

Student/faculty ratio: 3:1 % female faculty: 25

FINANCIAL FACTS

Annual tuition (in-state/out-of-state): $53,082/ $53,082 Cost of books: $1,078 Room & board: (on/off-campus) $9,973/$9,973 % of students receiving aid: 64 % of first-year students receiving aid: 64 % of students receiving grants: 64 Average grant: $12,733

ADMISSIONS

Admissions Selectivity Rating: 88

# of applications received: 446 % applicants accepted: 50 % acceptees attending: 67 Average GMAT: 680 Range of GMAT: 640–710 TOEFL required of international students: Yes Minimum TOEFL (paper/computer): 600/250 Application fee: $0 International Application fee: $0

Deferment available: Yes Maximum length of deferment: 2 years

Transfer students accepted: No Non-fall admissions: No Need-blind admissions: Yes

EMPLOYMENT PROFILE

Percent employed at graduation: 47 **Percent employed 3 months after graduation:** 49

Primary Source of Full-time Job Acceptances

School-facilitated activities: 26(22%) **Graduate-facilitated activities:** 54(45%) **Unknown:** 39(33%)

Grads Employed by Function ......% Avg. Salary

Marketing: ....(9%) $107,025
Operations: ....(6%) $94,448
Consulting: ....(16%) $99,919
Management: ....(18%) $92,172
Finance:.......................................(8%) $72,330
MIS: ....(5%) $98,217
Other: ....(25%) $91,590

Top 5 Employers Hiring Grads (number of hires in last class)

Brambles Ltd., Newcastle Science City, CHEP, HCL Technologies, Rolls-Royce

CREIGHTON UNIVERSITY
COLLEGE OF BUSINESS ADMINISTRATION

ADMISSIONS CONTACT: GAIL HAFER, COORDINATOR OF GRADUATE BUSINESS PROGRAMS
ADDRESS: COLLEGE OF BUSINESS ADMINISTRATION, ROOM 212C, 2500 CALIFORNIA PLAZA, OMAHA, NE 68178
PHONE: 402-280-2853 • FAX: 402-280-2172
E-MAIL: COBAGRAD@CREIGHTON.EDU • WEBSITE: COBWEB.CREIGHTON.EDU

GENERAL INFORMATION

Type of school: Private

STUDENTS

Enrollment of parent institution: 6,723 **Enrollment of MBA Program:** 118 **% male/female:** 58/42 **% part-time:** 84 **% underrepresented minority:** 1 **% international:** 31 **Average age at entry:** 25 **Average years work experience at entry:** 3.0

ACADEMICS

Student/faculty ratio: 2:1 **% female faculty:** 10 **% part-time faculty:** 35

FINANCIAL FACTS

Annual tuition (in-state/out-of-state): $10,206/ **Fees:** $764 **Cost of books:** $1,600 **Room & board: (on/off-campus)** $7,000/$6,000 **% of students receiving aid:** 15 **% of first-year students receiving aid:** 8 **Average award package:** $19,653 **Average grant:** $0 **Average loan:** $0

ADMISSIONS

Admissions Selectivity Rating: 72

# of applications received: 24 **% applicants accepted:** 96 **% acceptees attending:** 78 **Average GMAT:** 570 **Average GPA:** 3.40 **TOEFL required of international students:** Yes **Minimum TOEFL**

(paper/computer): 550/213 **International Application fee:** $40 **Early application deadline:** 3/1

Deferment available: Yes **Maximum length of deferment:** 1 year **Transfer students accepted:** Yes **Transfer application policy:** Maximum of 6 hours considered for transfer from AACSB accredited institution, unless student transferring from another AACSB accredited Jesuit institution in which case more than six hours may be considered for transfer. **Non-fall admissions:** Yes **Need-blind admissions:** No

DEPAUL UNIVERSITY
KELLSTADT GRADUATE SCHOOL OF BUSINESS

ADMISSIONS CONTACT: ROBERT RYAN, ASSISTANT DEAN AND DIRECTOR
ADDRESS: 1 EAST JACKSON BLVD, SUITE 7900, CHICAGO, IL 60604
PHONE: 312-362-8810 • FAX: 312-362-6677
E-MAIL: KGSB@DEPAUL.EDU • WEBSITE: KELLSTADT.DEPAUL.EDU

GENERAL INFORMATION

Type of school: Private **Academic calendar:** quarter

STUDENTS

Enrollment of parent institution: 25,398 **Enrollment of MBA Program:** 1,328 **% male/female:** 80/20 **% out-of-state:** 3 **% part-time:** 36 **% underrepresented minority:** 9 **% international:** 5 **Average age at entry:** 28 **Average years work experience at entry:** 4.0

ACADEMICS

Student/faculty ratio: 13:1 **% female faculty:** 25 **% underrepresented minority faculty:** 14 **% part-time faculty:** 41

FINANCIAL FACTS

Annual tuition (in-state/out-of-state): Fees: $363 **Cost of books:** $1,134 **Room & board: (on/off-campus)** $13,130/$13,130 **% of students receiving aid:** 61 **% of first-year students receiving aid:** 69 **% of students receiving grants:** 33 **Average award package:** $32,362 **Average grant:** $19,939 **Average loan:** $30,521 **Average student loan debt:** $51,891

ADMISSIONS

Admissions Selectivity Rating: 82

# of applications received: 660 **% applicants accepted:** 55 **% acceptees attending:** 69 **Average GMAT:** 573 **Range of GMAT:** 530–630 **Average GPA:** 3.11 **TOEFL required of international students:** Yes **Minimum TOEFL (paper/computer):** 550/213 **International Application fee:** $60 **Regular application deadline:** 7/1

Application Deadline/Notification:

Round 1: ....:........................2/1
Round 2: 4/1
Round 3: 7/1

Deferment available: Yes **Maximum length of deferment:** 1 year **Transfer students accepted:** Yes **Transfer application policy:** Must apply like any other applicant. **Non-fall admissions:** Yes **Need-blind admissions:** Yes

EMPLOYMENT PROFILE

Percent employed at graduation: 67 **Percent employed 3 months after graduation:** 18 **Average base starting salary:** $70,488

Primary Source of Full-time Job Acceptances

School-facilitated activities: 19(58%) **Graduate-facilitated activities:** 14(42%) **Unknown:** 0(0%)

Grads Employed by Function ......% Avg. Salary

Marketing: ....(11%) $74,204

Operations: ....(2%) $64,700

Consulting: ....(3%) $59,333

Finance:..(14%) $72,286

HR: ....(2%) $57,250

Top 5 Employers Hiring Grads (number of hires in last class)

Sears (2), Kellogg's (2), Garret Popcorn (2), Nestle/Purina (1), Credit Suisse (1)

DRAKE UNIVERSITY
COLLEGE OF BUSINESS AND PUBLIC ADMINISTRATION

ADMISSIONS CONTACT: DANETTE KENNE, DIRECTOR OF GRADUATE PROGRAMS
ADDRESS: 2507 UNIVERSITY AVENUE, ALIBER HALL, SUITE 211, DES MOINES, IA 50311
PHONE: 515-271-2188 • FAX: 515-271-2187
E-MAIL: CBPA.GRADPROGRAMS@DRAKE.EDU
WEBSITE: WWW.CBPA.DRAKE.EDU/ASPX/PROGRAMS/PROGRAMDETAIL.ASPX?ID=6

GENERAL INFORMATION

Type of school: Private **Academic calendar:** Semester

STUDENTS

Enrollment of parent institution: 5,617 **Enrollment of MBA Program:** 167 **% male/female:** 20/80 **% part-time:** 97 **Average age at entry:** 28 **Average years work experience at entry:** 0.0

ACADEMICS

Student/faculty ratio: 19:1 **% female faculty:** 19 **% underrepresented minority faculty:** 5 **% part-time faculty:** 10

FINANCIAL FACTS

Annual tuition (in-state/out-of-state): $9,400/ **Fees:** $412 **Cost of books:** $800 **Room & board: (on/off-campus)** $7,350 **Average grant:** $0 **Average loan:** $0

ADMISSIONS

Admissions Selectivity Rating: 65

# of applications received: 98 **% applicants accepted:** 61 **% acceptees attending:** 65 **TOEFL required of international students:** Yes **Minimum TOEFL (paper/computer):** 550/213 **International Application fee:** $25 **Early application deadline:** 3/6 **Regular application deadline:** 7/6

Deferment available: Yes **Maximum length of deferment:** one term **Transfer students accepted:** Yes **Transfer application policy:** Case by case evaluation **Non-fall admissions:** Yes **Need-blind admissions:** Yes

EASTERN ILLINOIS UNIVERSITY
LUMPKIN COLLEGE OF BUSINESS AND APPLIED SCIENCES

ADMISSIONS CONTACT: DR. JOHN R. WILLEMS, COORDINATOR, GRADUATE BUSINESS STUDIES
ADDRESS: 600 LINCOLN AVENUE, 4025 LUMPKIN HALL, CHARLESTON, IL 61920-3099
PHONE: 217-581-3028 • FAX: 217-581-6642
E-MAIL: MBA@EIU.EDU • WEBSITE: WWW.EIU.EDU/~MBA

GENERAL INFORMATION

Type of school: Public **Academic calendar:** FA, SP, SU

STUDENTS

Enrollment of parent institution: 12,000 **Enrollment of MBA Program:** 128 **% male/female:** 61/39 **% out-of-state:** 3 **% part-time:** 47 **% underrepresented minority:** 7 **% international:** 8 **Average age at entry:** 28 **Average years work experience at entry:** 5.0

ACADEMICS

Student/faculty ratio: 23:1 **% female faculty:** 23 **% underrepresented minority faculty:** 31

FINANCIAL FACTS

Annual tuition (in-state/out-of-state): $7,887/ $23,661 **Fees:** $2,330 **Cost of books:** $325 **Room & board: (on/off-campus)** $7,626/$8,000 **% of students receiving aid:** 18 **% of first-year students receiving aid:** 30 **% of students receiving grants:** 18 **Average grant:** $7,560

ADMISSIONS

Admissions Selectivity Rating: 77

# of applications received: 98 **% applicants accepted:** 63 **% acceptees attending:** 89 **Average GMAT:** 510 **Range of GMAT:** 450–545 **Average GPA:** 3.25 **TOEFL required of international students:** Yes **Minimum TOEFL (paper/computer):** 550/ **Application fee:** $30 **International Application fee:** $30 **Early application deadline:** 3/12 **Early notification date:** 4/15

Deferment available: Yes **Maximum length of deferment:** 1 academic year **Transfer students accepted:** Yes **Transfer application policy:** Maximum of 9 Semester hours at grade of B or better. **Non-fall admissions:** Yes **Need-blind admissions:** Yes

EMPORIA STATE UNIVERSITY
EMPORIA STATE UNIVERSITY

ADMISSIONS CONTACT: MARY SEWELL, ADMINISTRATIVE SPECIALIST
ADDRESS: 1200 COMMERCIAL STREET, CAMPUS BOX 4003, EMPORIA, KS 66801
PHONE: 620-341-5403 • FAX: 620-341-5909
E-MAIL: MSEWELL@EMPORIA.EDU • WEBSITE: WWW.EMPORIA.EDU

GENERAL INFORMATION

Type of school: Public **Academic calendar:** Semester and Summer

STUDENTS

Enrollment of parent institution: 6,404 **Enrollment of MBA Program:** 117 **% male/female:** 50/50 **% out-of-state:** 2 **% part-time:** 28 **% underrepresented minority:** 2 **% international:** 57 **Average age at entry:** 26

ACADEMICS

Student/faculty ratio: 7:1 **% female faculty:** 13 **% underrepresented minority faculty:** 0 **% part-time faculty:** 0

FINANCIAL FACTS

Annual tuition (in-state/out-of-state): $3,976/ $12,028 **Fees:** $842 **Cost of books:** $1,000 **Room & board: (on/off-campus)** $7,090/$5,620

ADMISSIONS

Admissions Selectivity Rating: 69

# of applications received: 70 **% applicants accepted:** 96 **% acceptees attending:** 60 **Average GMAT:** 526 **Range of GMAT:** 490–540 **Average GPA:** 3.42 **TOEFL required of international students:** No **Minimum TOEFL (paper/computer):** 550/213 **Application fee:** $40 **International Application fee:** $75

Deferment available: Yes **Maximum length of deferment:** 1 year **Transfer students accepted:** Yes **Non-fall admissions:** Yes **Need-blind admissions:** Yes

EMPLOYMENT PROFILE

Percent employed at graduation: 29 **Percent employed 3 months after graduation:** 54 **Average base starting salary:** $42,500

Primary Source of Full-time Job Acceptances

School-facilitated activities: 3(23%)

Grads Employed by Function ......% Avg. Salary

Management: ....(4%)

Finance:...(38%) $40,000

MIS: ....(4%) $45,000

Top 5 Employers Hiring Grads (number of hires in last class)

Koch Industries (1), Grant Thornton (2), Emporia State University (2), BKD, LLP (1), CBIZ Accounting Tax & Advisory Services, LLC (1)

FAIRLEIGH DICKINSON UNIVERSITY
SILBERMAN COLLEGE OF BUSINESS

ADMISSIONS CONTACT: SUSAN BROOMAN, DIRECTOR OF GRADUATE RECRUITMENT & MARKETING
ADDRESS: FAIRLEIGH DICKINSON UNIVERSITY GRADUATE ADMISSIONS, COLLEGE AT FLORHAM 285 MADISON AVENUE (M-RIO-01), MADISON, NJ 07940
PHONE: 973-443-8905 • FAX: 973-443-8088
E-MAIL: GRAD@FDU.EDU • WEBSITE: WWW.FDU.EDU

GENERAL INFORMATION

Type of school: Private

STUDENTS

Enrollment of parent institution: 12,247 **Enrollment of MBA Program:** 704 **% male/female:** 60/41 **% out-of-state:** 39 **% part-time:** 51 **% underrepresented minority:** 18 **% international:** 28 **Average age at entry:** 29

ACADEMICS

Student/faculty ratio: 20:1 **% female faculty:** 21 **% underrepresented minority faculty:** 41 **% part-time faculty:** 15

FINANCIAL FACTS

Annual tuition (in-state/out-of-state): $20,340/ $20,340 **Fees:** $225 **Cost of books:** $1,200 **Room & board: (on/off-campus) % of students receiving aid:** 75 **% of students receiving grants:** 25 **Average award package:** $13,500 **Average grant:** $5,225 **Average loan:** $14,670

ADMISSIONS

Admissions Selectivity Rating: 67

# of applications received: 642 **% applicants accepted:** 57 **% acceptees attending:** 34 **Average GPA:** 3.40 **TOEFL required of international students:** Yes **Minimum TOEFL (paper/computer):** 550/213 **Application fee:** $40 **International Application fee:** $40

Deferment available: Yes **Maximum length of deferment:** N/A **Transfer students accepted:** Yes **Transfer application policy:** Foundation courses can be waived by meeting FDU waiver policy. 6 graduate level credits can be transferred from other AACSB schools. **Non-fall admissions:** Yes **Need-blind admissions:** Yes

EMPLOYMENT PROFILE

Top 5 Employers Hiring Grads (number of hires in last class)

Johnson & Johnson, ADP, Verizon, Credit Suisse, Deloitte

FLORIDA ATLANTIC UNIVERSITY
COLLEGE OF BUSINESS

ADMISSIONS CONTACT: TIFFANY NICHOLSON, ASSOCIATE DIRECTOR OF ACADEMIC SUPPORT SERVICES
ADDRESS: 132 FLEMING WEST, 777 GLADES ROAD, BOCA RATON, FL 33431
PHONE: 561-297-2786 • FAX: 561-297-1315
E-MAIL: MBA@FAU.EDU • WEBSITE: WWW.BUSINESS.FAU.EDU

GENERAL INFORMATION

Type of school: Public **Academic calendar:** Semesters

STUDENTS

Enrollment of parent institution: 27,021 **Enrollment of MBA Program:** 599 **% male/female:** 57/43 **% out-of-state:** 11 **% part-time:** 63 **% underrepresented minority:** 27 **% international:** 6 **Average age at entry:** 32 **Average years work experience at entry:** 6.5

ACADEMICS

Student/faculty ratio: 12:1 **% female faculty:** 36 **% underrepresented minority faculty:** 20 **% part-time faculty:** 13

FINANCIAL FACTS

Annual tuition (in-state/out-of-state): $4,867/ $16,486 **Fees:** $849 **Cost of books:** $1,100 **Room & board: (on/off-campus)** $9,000/$12,000

ADMISSIONS

Admissions Selectivity Rating: 84

# of applications received: 486 **% applicants accepted:** 49 **% acceptees attending:** 73 **Average GMAT:** 550 **Range of GMAT:**

510–605 **Average GPA:** 3.20 **TOEFL required of international students:** Yes **Minimum TOEFL (paper/computer):** 600/250 **Application fee:** $30 **International Application fee:** $30 **Regular application deadline:** 7/1

Deferment available: Yes **Maximum length of deferment:** Up to 1 year **Transfer students accepted:** Yes **Transfer application policy:** We allow the transfer of up to 6 Semester credit hours from an AACSB accredited graduate program. Credits must be no more than 7 years old. **Non-fall admissions:** Yes **Need-blind admissions:** Yes

EMPLOYMENT PROFILE

Percent employed at graduation: 40 **Percent employed 3 months after graduation:** 32 **Average base starting salary:** $77,380

Grads Employed by Function ......% Avg. Salary

Marketing: ....(14%) $80,000
Operations: ....(9%) $100,000
Consulting: ....(0%)
Management: ....(36%) $70,500
Finance:......................................(27%) $72,500
HR: ....(0%)
MIS: ....(9%) $65,000
Other: ....(5%) $120,000

Top 5 Employers Hiring Grads (number of hires in last class)
IBM (1), LexisNexis (1), Lilly (1), Ryder Systems (1), FBI (1)

GEORGE MASON UNIVERSITY
SCHOOL OF MANAGEMENT

ADMISSIONS CONTACT: ANGEL BURGOS, MBA DIRECTOR
ADDRESS: 4400 UNIVERSITY DRIVE, MSN 5A2, ENTERPRISE HALL, ROOM 28, FAIRFAX, VA 22030
PHONE: (703) 993-2136 • FAX: 703-993-1778
E-MAIL: MBA@GMU.EDU • WEBSITE: WWW.SOM.GMU.EDU

GENERAL INFORMATION

Type of school: Public **Academic calendar:** Semester

STUDENTS

Enrollment of parent institution: 30,714 **Enrollment of MBA Program:** 342 **% male/female:** 54/46 **% part-time:** 88 **% international:** 28 **Average age at entry:** 29 **Average years work experience at entry:** 5.0

FINANCIAL FACTS

Annual tuition (in-state/out-of-state): $14,496/ $26,112 **Fees:** $0 **Cost of books:** $1,000

ADMISSIONS

Admissions Selectivity Rating: 84

# of applications received: 296 **% applicants accepted:** 49 **% acceptees attending:** 68 **Average GMAT:** 580 **Average GPA:** 3.20 **TOEFL required of international students:** Yes **Minimum TOEFL (paper/computer):** 650/250 **Application fee:** $60 **International Application fee:** $60 **Early application deadline:** 3/15 **Early notification date:** 4/15 **Regular application deadline:** 4/15 **Regular application notification:** 5/15

Application Deadline/Notification:
Round 1:.......................................3/154/15
Round 2:.......................................4/155/15

Deferment available: No **Transfer students accepted:** No **Non-fall admissions:** Yes **Need-blind admissions:** Yes

GEORGIA COLLEGE & STATE UNIVERSITY
THE J. WHITNEY BUNTING COLLEGE OF BUSINESS

ADMISSIONS CONTACT: KATE MARSHALL, GRADUATE ADMISSIONS COORDINATOR
ADDRESS: GC&SU CAMPUS BOX 107, MILLEDGEVILLE, GA 31061
PHONE: 478-445-6289 • FAX: 478-445-1336
E-MAIL: GRADADMIT@GCSU.EDU • WEBSITE: MBA.GCSU.EDU

GENERAL INFORMATION

Type of school: Public **Academic calendar:** Semester

STUDENTS

Enrollment of parent institution: 6,444 **Enrollment of MBA Program:** 105 **% male/female:** 38/62 **% out-of-state:** 15 **% part-time:** 88 **% underrepresented minority:** 46 **% international:** 15 **Average age at entry:** 40 **Average years work experience at entry:** 0.0

ACADEMICS

Student/faculty ratio: 18:1 **% female faculty:** 35 **% underrepresented minority faculty:** 28 **% part-time faculty:** 0

FINANCIAL FACTS

Annual tuition (in-state/out-of-state): $4,950/ $17,946 **Fees:** $1,984 **Cost of books:** $1,350 **Room & board: (on/off-campus)** $8,976/$9,970

ADMISSIONS

Admissions Selectivity Rating: 86

# of applications received: 79 **% applicants accepted:** 41 **% acceptees attending:** 78 **Average GMAT:** 520 **Range of GMAT:** 460–580 **Average GPA:** 3.27 **TOEFL required of international students:** No **Minimum TOEFL (paper/computer):** 550/213 **Application fee:** $35 **International Application fee:** $0

Deferment available: Yes **Maximum length of deferment:** 1 year **Transfer students accepted:** Yes **Transfer application policy:** Must meet regular admission requirements. Maximum of nine Semester hours are transferable if equivalent to GC&SU curriculum and from an AACSB-accredited school. **Non-fall admissions:** Yes **Need-blind admissions:** Yes

EMPLOYMENT PROFILE

Percent employed at graduation: 36 **Percent employed 3 months after graduation:** 71

Top 5 Employers Hiring Grads (number of hires in last class)
Boy Scouts of America (2), AT&T (1), Geico Insurance (1), Pacesetter Steel (1), Georgia Military College (1)

HENDERSON STATE UNIVERSITY
SCHOOL OF BUSINESS ADMINISTRATION

ADMISSIONS CONTACT: MISSIE BELL, GRADUATE SCHOOL ADMINISTRATIVE ASSISTANT
ADDRESS: 1100 HENDERSON STREET, BOX 7802, ARKADELPHIA,
 AR 71999-0001
PHONE: (870) 230-5126 • FAX: (870) 230-5479
E-MAIL: GRAD@HSU.EDU • WEBSITE: WWW.HSU.EDU/SCHOOLOFBUSINESS/

GENERAL INFORMATION
Type of school: Public

STUDENTS
Enrollment of parent institution: 3,754 Enrollment of MBA Program: 45 % male/female: 50/50 % out-of-state: 5 % part-time: 25 % underrepresented minority: 10 % international: 20 Average years work experience at entry: 0.0

ACADEMICS
Student/faculty ratio: 6:1 % female faculty: 38 % underrepresented minority faculty: 0 % part-time faculty: 0

FINANCIAL FACTS
Annual tuition (in-state/out-of-state): $2,916/ $5,832 Fees: $411 Room & board: (on/off-campus) $3,874/$3,874

ADMISSIONS
Admissions Selectivity Rating: 68

# of applications received: 19 % applicants accepted: 100 % acceptees attending: 32 Average GMAT: 450 Range of GMAT: 390–670 Average GPA: 3.00 TOEFL required of international students: Yes Minimum TOEFL (paper/computer): 550/213 Application fee: $40 International Application fee: $40

Deferment available: No Transfer students accepted: Yes Transfer application policy: 6 hours from an accredited university. Non-fall admissions: Yes Need-blind admissions: Yes

IE UNIVERSITY
IE BUSINESS SCHOOL

ADMISSIONS CONTACT: JULIAN TRIGO, ADMISSIONS DIRECTOR
ADDRESS: MARIA DE MOLINA, 11, 13, 15, MADRID, 28006 SPAIN
PHONE: 34915689610
E-MAIL: ADIMISIONSS@IE.EDU • WEBSITE: WWW.IE.EDU

GENERAL INFORMATION
Type of school: Private Academic calendar: November - December

STUDENTS
Enrollment of parent institution: 2,160 Enrollment of MBA Program: 400 % male/female: 69/31 % part-time: 0 % international: 88 Average age at entry: 29 Average years work experience at entry: 5.2

ACADEMICS
% female faculty: 33

FINANCIAL FACTS
Annual tuition (in-state/out-of-state): $75,800/ $75,800 Fees: $1,500 Cost of books: $2,500 Room & board: $25,000

% of students receiving aid: 40 % of first-year students receiving aid: 40 % of students receiving grants: 35 Average award package: $19,000 Average grant: $18,000 Average loan: $20,000

ADMISSIONS
Admissions Selectivity Rating: 94

# of applications received: 2,366 % applicants accepted: 33 % acceptees attending: 52 Average GMAT: 680 Range of GMAT: 610–760 Average GPA: 3.30 TOEFL required of international students: Yes Minimum TOEFL (paper/computer): 600/250

Deferment available: Yes Maximum length of deferment: 3 intakes Transfer students accepted: No Non-fall admissions: Yes Need-blind admissions: Yes

EMPLOYMENT PROFILE
Percent employed at graduation: 30 Percent employed 3 months after graduation: 92

Primary Source of Full-time Job Acceptances

School-facilitated activities: (43%) Graduate-facilitated activities: (58%) Unknown: (%)

Grads Employed by Function ......% Avg. Salary

Marketing:	(18%)
Operations:	(4%)
Consulting:	(24%)
Management:	(21%)
Finance:	(17%)
MIS:	(3%)
Other:	(13%)

Top 5 Employers Hiring Grads (number of hires in last class)
Johnson&Johnson (11), Altair Management Consultants (8), BCG (6), Accenture (5), PWC (3)

INCAE
INCAE BUSINESS SCHOOL

ADMISSIONS CONTACT: RYAN FRAZEE, DIRECTOR OF ADMISSIONS AND RECRUITMENT
ADDRESS: 2 KM OESTE DEL VIVERO PROCESA NÂ°1, LA GARITA, ALAJUELA, COSTA RICA
E-MAIL: RYAN.FRAZEE@INCAE.EDU • WEBSITE: WWW.INCAE.EDU

GENERAL INFORMATION
Type of school: Private Academic calendar: Modules

STUDENTS
Enrollment of parent institution: 172 Enrollment of MBA Program: 172 % male/female: 65/35 % part-time: 0 % international: 33 Average age at entry: 27 Average years work experience at entry: 4.2

ACADEMICS
Student/faculty ratio: 8:1 % female faculty: 75 % underrepresented minority faculty: 83 % part-time faculty: 0

FINANCIAL FACTS
Annual tuition (in-state/out-of-state): $37,150/ Fees: $1,655 Cost of books: $2,564 Room & board: (on/off-campus) $11,556 % of

first-year students receiving aid: 85 **Average award package:**
$5,900 **Average grant:** $4,700 **Average loan:** $2,200

ADMISSIONS

Admissions Selectivity Rating: 73

# of applications received: 345 **% applicants accepted:** 80 %
acceptees attending: 62 **Average GMAT:** 602 **Range of GMAT:**
570–620 **TOEFL required of international students:** Yes **Minimum
TOEFL (paper/computer):** 600/250 **Regular application deadline:**
7/15

Deferment available: Yes **Maximum length of deferment:** 9999
Transfer students accepted: No **Non-fall admissions:** No **Need-
blind admissions:** No

EMPLOYMENT PROFILE

Average base starting salary: $53,000

INDIANA UNIVERSITY NORTHWEST
SCHOOL OF BUSINESS AND ECONOMICS

*ADMISSIONS CONTACT: JOHN GIBSON, DIRECTOR, GRADUATE/UNDERGRADUATE
PROGRAMS IN B*
ADDRESS: 3400, BROADWAY, GARY, IN 46408-1197
PHONE: 219-980-6635 • FAX: 219-980-6916
E-MAIL: JAGIBSON@IUN.EDU • WEBSITE: WWW.IUN.EDU/~BUSNW

GENERAL INFORMATION

Type of school: Public **Academic calendar:** Semester

STUDENTS

Enrollment of parent institution: 4,300 **Enrollment of MBA
Program:** 115 **% male/female:** 100/0 **% out-of-state:** 0 **% part-
time:** 99 **% underrepresented minority:** 0 **% international:** 0
Average age at entry: 35 **Average years work experience at entry:**
0.0

ACADEMICS

Student/faculty ratio: 10:1 **% female faculty:** 26 **% underrepresented minority faculty:** 37

FINANCIAL FACTS

Annual tuition (in-state/out-of-state): $4,300/ $10,000 **Cost of
books:** $999 **Room & board: (on/off-campus)** **% of students
receiving grants:** 1 **Average grant:** $999 **Average loan:** $999

ADMISSIONS

Admissions Selectivity Rating: 72

# of applications received: 50 **% applicants accepted:** 70 %
acceptees attending: 100 **Average GMAT:** 470 **TOEFL required of
international students:** Yes **Minimum TOEFL (paper/computer):**
550/213 **Application fee:** $25 **International Application fee:** $55

Application Deadline/Notification:

Round 1: 1/11/5
Round 2: 5/15/5
Round 3: 8/18/15

Deferment available: Yes **Maximum length of deferment:** 1 year
Transfer students accepted: Yes **Transfer application policy:** Must
be a student in Good Standing from an accredtied institution. Up to
six credit hours may transfer in if the grade is 'B' or beter. **Non-fall
admissions:** Yes **Need-blind admissions:** Yes

EMPLOYMENT PROFILE

Average base starting salary: $60,000

Primary Source of Full-time Job Acceptances

School-facilitated activities: (25%) **Graduate-facilitated activities:**
(65%) Unknown: (10%)

INDIANA UNIVERSITY—PURDUE
UNIVERSITY AT FORT WAYNE
SCHOOL OF BUSINESS AND MANAGEMENT

ADMISSIONS CONTACT: SANDY FRANKE, SECRETARY, MBA PROGRAM
*ADDRESS: NEFF 366, 2101 COLISEUM BOULEVARD EAST, FORT WAYNE, IN
46805-1499*
PHONE: 260-481-6498
E-MAIL: EMAIL@SCHOOL.EDU • WEBSITE: WWW.IPFW.EDU/BMS/MBA1.HTM

GENERAL INFORMATION

Type of school: Public **Academic calendar:** Semester

STUDENTS

Enrollment of parent institution: 10,749 **Enrollment of MBA
Program:** 191 **% male/female:** 65/35 **% part-time:** 91 **Average age
at entry:** 32 **Average years work experience at entry:** 0.0

ACADEMICS

Student/faculty ratio: 1:1

ADMISSIONS

Admissions Selectivity Rating: 63

# of applications received: 45 **% applicants accepted:** 91 %
acceptees attending: 95 **TOEFL required of international students:**
No **Application fee:** $1 **Regular application deadline:** 7/15 **Regular
application notification:** 1/1

Deferment available: Yes **Maximum length of deferment:** 1
Transfer students accepted: No **Non-fall admissions:** Yes **Need-
blind admissions:** No

Instituto Tecnologico y de Estudios Superiores de Monterrey (ITESM)
EGADE, Monterrey Campus

Admissions Contact: Lic. Olga Renée De La Torre, Academic Services Director
Address: Av. Fundadores y Rufino Tamayo, Col. Valle Oriente, San Pedro Garza GarcÃ?a, NL 66269 Mexico
Phone: 011-52-818-625-6204 • Fax: 818-625-6208
E-mail: admisiones.egade@itesm.mx • Website: www.egade.itesm.mx

GENERAL INFORMATION

Type of school: Private **Academic calendar:** Quarter

STUDENTS

Enrollment of parent institution: 19,358 **Enrollment of MBA Program:** 597 **% male/female:** 79/21 **% part-time:** 90 **% underrepresented minority:** 0 **% international:** 66 **Average age at entry:** 28 **Average years work experience at entry:** 5.0

ACADEMICS

Student/faculty ratio: 14:1 **% female faculty:** 25 **% part-time faculty:** 39

FINANCIAL FACTS

Annual tuition (in-state/out-of-state): $17,500/ **Cost of books:** $780 **Room & board: (on/off-campus)** $7,800/$6,400 **% of students receiving aid:** 26 **% of first-year students receiving aid:** 24 **% of students receiving grants:** 23 **Average grant:** $11,375 **Average loan:** $8,750

ADMISSIONS

Admissions Selectivity Rating: 80

# of applications received: 199 **% applicants accepted:** 73 **% acceptees attending:** 74 **Average GMAT:** 615 **Average GPA:** 3.50 **TOEFL required of international students:** No **International Application fee:** $115 **Regular application deadline:** 5/1 **Regular application notification:** 6/1

Deferment available: Yes **Maximum length of deferment:** 1 year **Transfer students accepted:** Yes **Transfer application policy:** The applicant has to fulfill all of the admission requisites **Non-fall admissions:** Yes **Need-blind admissions:** No

EMPLOYMENT PROFILE

Grads Employed by Function ......% Avg. Salary

Marketing: ....(12%)
Operations: ....(25%)
Finance:.......................................(38%)
Other: ....(19%)

Iowa State University
College of Business

Admissions Contact: Amy Hutter, Director, MBA Recruitment & Marketing
Address: 1360 Gerdin Business Building, Ames, IA 50011
Phone: 515-294-8118 • Fax: 515-294-2446
E-mail: busgrad@iastate.edu • Website: www.bus.iastate.edu/mba

GENERAL INFORMATION

Type of school: Public **Academic calendar:** Semester

STUDENTS

Enrollment of parent institution: 26,380 **Enrollment of MBA Program:** 94 **% male/female:** 62/38 **% out-of-state:** 8 **% part-time:** 62 **% international:** 31 **Average age at entry:** 26 **Average years work experience at entry:** 3.0

ACADEMICS

Student/faculty ratio: 4:1 **% female faculty:** 9 **% underrepresented minority faculty:** 12 **% part-time faculty:** 9

FINANCIAL FACTS

Annual tuition (in-state/out-of-state): $7,718/ $18,132 **Fees:** $930 **Cost of books:** $1,000 **Room & board: (on/off-campus)** $10,200/$10,200 **% of students receiving aid:** 50 **% of first-year students receiving aid:** 50 **Average award package:** $8,120 **Average grant:** $1 **Average loan:** $1

ADMISSIONS

Admissions Selectivity Rating: 78

# of applications received: 210 **% applicants accepted:** 69 **% acceptees attending:** 65 **Average GMAT:** 595 **Average GPA:** 3.41 **TOEFL required of international students:** Yes **Minimum TOEFL (paper/computer):** 600/250 **Application fee:** $30 **International Application fee:** $70

Deferment available: Yes **Maximum length of deferment:** 1 year **Transfer students accepted:** No **Non-fall admissions:** Yes **Need-blind admissions:** Yes

EMPLOYMENT PROFILE

Percent employed at graduation: 75 **Percent employed 3 months after graduation:** 94 **Average base starting salary:** $57,848

Primary Source of Full-time Job Acceptances
School-facilitated activities: 23(69%) **Graduate-facilitated activities:** 12(31%) **Unknown:** 35(10%)

Grads Employed by Function ......% Avg. Salary

Marketing: ....(11%) $61,667
Operations: ....(33%) $53,000
Consulting: ....(6%) $68,000
Management: ....(14%) $43,500
Finance:..(21%) $51,800
HR: ....(3%)
MIS: ....(12%) $74,500

JACKSONVILLE STATE UNIVERSITY
COLLEGE OF COMMERCE AND BUSINESS
ADMINISTRATION

ADMISSIONS CONTACT: DR. JEAN PUGLIESE, ASSOCIATE DEAN
ADDRESS: 700 PELHAM ROAD N, JACKSONVILLE, AL 36265
PHONE: 256-782-5329 • FAX: 256-782-5321
E-MAIL: PUGLIESE@JSU.EDU • WEBSITE: WWW.JSU.EDU

GENERAL INFORMATION

Type of school: Public

STUDENTS

Enrollment of parent institution: 9,100 **Enrollment of MBA Program:** 65 % **male/female:** 45/55 % **out-of-state:** 10 % **part-time:** 70 % **underrepresented minority:** 10 % **international:** 75 **Average age at entry:** 28 **Average years work experience at entry:** 3.0

ACADEMICS

Student/faculty ratio: 15:1 % **female faculty:** 33 % **underrepresented minority faculty:** 0 % **part-time faculty:** 0

FINANCIAL FACTS

Annual tuition (in-state/out-of-state): $6,048/ $12,096 **Cost of books:** $2,000 **Room & board: (on/off-campus)** $4,000/$10,000 **Average award package:** $18,000 **Average grant:** $1,000 **Average loan:** $10,000

ADMISSIONS

Admissions Selectivity Rating: 69

# of applications received: 37 % **applicants accepted:** 89 % **acceptees attending:** 61 **Average GMAT:** 477 **Range of GMAT:** 410–560 **Average GPA:** 3.18 **TOEFL required of international students:** Yes **Minimum TOEFL (paper/computer):** 500/173 **Application fee:** $30 **International Application fee:** $30 **Regular application deadline:** 7/1

Deferment available: No **Transfer students accepted:** Yes **Transfer application policy:** 6 hrs. of approved courses with grade of A or B. Must be from AACSB-International accredited institution. **Non-fall admissions:** Yes **Need-blind admissions:** Yes

JAMES MADISON UNIVERSITY
COLLEGE OF BUSINESS

ADMISSIONS CONTACT: KRISTA D. DOFFLEMYER, ADMINISTRATIVE ASSISTANT
ADDRESS: ZANE SHOWKER HALL, MSC 0206, ROOM 616, HARRISONBURG, VA 22807
PHONE: 540-568-3253 • FAX: 540-568-3587
E-MAIL: MBA@JMU.EDU • WEBSITE: WWW.JMU.EDU/COB/MBA

GENERAL INFORMATION

Type of school: Public **Academic calendar:** Aug-July

STUDENTS

Enrollment of parent institution: 18,971 **Enrollment of MBA Program:** 67 % **male/female:** 69/31 % **out-of-state:** 18 % **part-time:** 75 % **underrepresented minority:** 0 % **international:** 29

Average age at entry: 30 **Average years work experience at entry:** 6.0

ACADEMICS

Student/faculty ratio: 15:1 % **female faculty:** 33 % **underrepresented minority faculty:** 17 % **part-time faculty:** 8

FINANCIAL FACTS

Annual tuition (in-state/out-of-state): $7,320/ $21,360 **Cost of books:** $5,676 **Room & board: (on/off-campus)** % **of students receiving aid:** 79 % **of first-year students receiving aid:** 76 % **of students receiving grants:** 46 **Average award package:** $6,117 **Average grant:** $6,907 **Average loan:** $16,505 **Average student loan debt:** $13,623

ADMISSIONS

Admissions Selectivity Rating: 77

# of applications received: 60 % **applicants accepted:** 78 % **acceptees attending:** 77 **Average GMAT:** 560 **Range of GMAT:** 530–760 **Average GPA:** 3.30 **TOEFL required of international students:** Yes **Minimum TOEFL (paper/computer):** 570/250 **Application fee:** $55 **International Application fee:** $55 **Early application deadline:** 3/1 **Regular application deadline:** 7/1

Deferment available: Yes **Maximum length of deferment:** 1 year **Transfer students accepted:** Yes **Transfer application policy:** Can transfer up to 9 credit hours from another AACSB accredited MBA program. **Non-fall admissions:** No **Need-blind admissions:** No

EMPLOYMENT PROFILE

Average base starting salary: $75,000

KANSAS STATE UNIVERSITY
COLLEGE OF BUSINESS ADMINISTRATION

ADMISSIONS CONTACT: LYNN WAUGH, GRADUATE STUDIES ASSISTANT
ADDRESS: 107 CALVIN HALL, MANHATTAN, KS 66506-0501
PHONE: 785-532-7190 • FAX: 785-532-7809
E-MAIL: GRADBUSINESS@KSU.EDU • WEBSITE: WWW.CBA.KSU.EDU

GENERAL INFORMATION

Type of school: Public **Academic calendar:** Semesters

STUDENTS

Enrollment of MBA Program: 91 % **male/female:** 70/30 % **out-of-state:** 4 % **part-time:** 18 % **underrepresented minority:** 9 % **international:** 22 **Average age at entry:** 24 **Average years work experience at entry:** 2.0

ACADEMICS

Student/faculty ratio: 5:1 % **female faculty:** 22 % **underrepresented minority faculty:** 4 % **part-time faculty:** 100

FINANCIAL FACTS

Annual tuition (in-state/out-of-state): $6,855/ $19,340 **Fees:** $666 **Cost of books:** $1,000 **Room & board: (on/off-campus)** $5,000/$6,000 % **of students receiving aid:** 18 % **of first-year students receiving aid:** 12 **Average grant:** $2,500 **Average loan:** $3,000

ADMISSIONS

Admissions Selectivity Rating: 92

# of applications received: 86 **% applicants accepted:** 40 % **acceptees attending:** 100 **Average GMAT:** 565 **Range of GMAT:** 500–660 **Average GPA:** 3.40 **TOEFL required of international students:** Yes **Minimum TOEFL (paper/computer):** 550/213 **Application fee:** $60 **International Application fee:** $60 **Early application deadline:** 2/1 **Early notification date:** 4/15 **Regular application deadline:** 6/1 **Regular application notification:** 7/15

Deferment available: Yes **Maximum length of deferment:** 1 year **Transfer students accepted:** Yes **Transfer application policy:** Up to 9 graduate credit hours from an AACSB accredited institution for courses that are part of the K-State MBA program will be accepted **Non-fall admissions:** No **Need-blind admissions:** Yes

EMPLOYMENT PROFILE

Average base starting salary: $42,000

Grads Employed by Function	...%	Avg. Salary
Marketing:	(8%)	$42,000
Consulting:	(22%)	$42,000
Finance:	(30%)	$46,000
HR:	(8%)	$52,000
MIS:	(8%)	$55,000

LA SALLE UNIVERSITY
SCHOOL OF BUSINESS ADMINISTRATION

ADMISSIONS CONTACT: KATHY BAGNELL, DIRECTOR, MARKETING AND GRADUATE ENROLLMENT
ADDRESS: 1900 WEST OLNEY AVENUE, PHILADELPHIA, PA 19141
PHONE: 215-951-1057 • FAX: 215-951-1886
E-MAIL: EMAIL@SCHOOL.EDU
WEBSITE: WWW.LASALLE.EDU/ACADEM/SBA/GRAD/INDEX.SHTML

GENERAL INFORMATION

Type of school: Private **Academic calendar:** Trimester

STUDENTS

Enrollment of parent institution: 5,408 **Enrollment of MBA Program:** 687 **% male/female:** 59/41 **% part-time:** 90 **% underrepresented minority:** 12 **% international:** 11 **Average age at entry:** 32 **Average years work experience at entry:** 0.0

ACADEMICS

% part-time faculty: 31

FINANCIAL FACTS

Annual tuition (in-state/out-of-state): $12,800/ **Fees:** $85

ADMISSIONS

Admissions Selectivity Rating: 64

# of applications received: 142 **% applicants accepted:** 85 % **acceptees attending:** 89 **TOEFL required of international students:** Yes **Minimum TOEFL (paper/computer):** 550/ **Regular application deadline:** 8/14

Deferment available: Yes **Maximum length of deferment:** 99999 **Transfer students accepted:** No **Non-fall admissions:** Yes **Need-blind admissions:** No

LEHIGH UNIVERSITY
COLLEGE OF BUSINESS AND ECONOMICS

ADMISSIONS CONTACT: JEN GIORDANO, DIRECTOR OF RECRUITMENT AND ADMISSIONS
ADDRESS: 621 TAYLOR STREET, BETHLEHEM, PA 18015
PHONE: 610-758-3418 • FAX: 610-758-5283
E-MAIL: MBA.ADMISSIONS@LEHIGH.EDU • WEBSITE: WWW.LEHIGH.EDU/MBA

GENERAL INFORMATION

Type of school: Private **Academic calendar:** Semester

STUDENTS

Enrollment of MBA Program: 244 **% male/female:** 72/28 **% part-time:** 90 **% underrepresented minority:** 4 **% international:** 52 **Average age at entry:** 31 **Average years work experience at entry:** 8.0

FINANCIAL FACTS

Annual tuition (in-state/out-of-state): $17,100/ $17,100 **Fees:** $0 **Cost of books:** $1,300 **Room & board: (on/off-campus)** /$10,800 **Average loan:** $0

ADMISSIONS

Admissions Selectivity Rating: 78

# of applications received: 122 **% applicants accepted:** 76 % **acceptees attending:** 86 **Average GMAT:** 628 **Range of GMAT:** 580–640 **Average GPA:** 3.33 **TOEFL required of international students:** Yes **Minimum TOEFL (paper/computer):** 600/250 **International Application fee:** $100 **Regular application deadline:** 5/1

Deferment available: Yes **Maximum length of deferment:** 1 year **Transfer students accepted:** Yes **Transfer application policy:** Six credits from an AACSB accredited school **Non-fall admissions:** Yes **Need-blind admissions:** Yes

LOUISIANA STATE UNIVERSITY-SHREVEPORT
COLLEGE OF BUSINESS ADMINISTRATION

ADMISSIONS CONTACT: SUSAN WOOD, MBA DIRECTOR
ADDRESS: ONE UNIVERSITY PLACE, SHREVEPORT, LA 71115
PHONE: 318-797-5213 • FAX: 318-797-5017
E-MAIL: SWOOD@PILOT.LSUS.EDU • WEBSITE: WWW.LSUS.EDU/BA/MBA/

GENERAL INFORMATION

Type of school: Public **Academic calendar:** Semester

STUDENTS

Enrollment of parent institution: 4,237 **Enrollment of MBA Program:** 150 **% male/female:** 47/53 **% part-time:** 93 **% underrepresented minority:** 10 **% international:** 5 **Average years work experience at entry:** 0.0

ACADEMICS

Student/faculty ratio: 20:1 % part-time faculty: 0

FINANCIAL FACTS

Annual tuition (in-state/out-of-state): $3,245/ $9,420 % of students receiving aid: 60

ADMISSIONS

Admissions Selectivity Rating: 64

# of applications received: 70 % applicants accepted: 71 % acceptees attending: 80 TOEFL required of international students: Yes Minimum TOEFL (paper/computer): 550/ Application fee: $10 Regular application deadline: 6/30

Deferment available: No Transfer students accepted: No Non-fall admissions: Yes Need-blind admissions: No

EMPLOYMENT PROFILE

Average base starting salary: $40,000

LOUISIANA TECH UNIVERSITY
COLLEGE OF BUSINESS

ADMISSIONS CONTACT: DR. DOUG AMYX, ASSOCIATE DEAN OF GRADUATE STUDIES
ADDRESS: PO BOX 10318, RUSTON, LA 71272
PHONE: 318-257-4528 • FAX: 318-257-4253
E-MAIL: SSTRICK@LATECH.EDU • WEBSITE: WWW.BUSINESS.LATECH.EDU

GENERAL INFORMATION

Type of school: Public Academic calendar: Quarter

STUDENTS

Enrollment of parent institution: 11,804 Enrollment of MBA Program: 57 % male/female: 68/32 % underrepresented minority: 5 Average age at entry: 0 Average years work experience at entry: 0.0

ACADEMICS

Student/faculty ratio: 25:1 % female faculty: 21

FINANCIAL FACTS

Annual tuition (in-state/out-of-state): $5,368/ $9,700 Fees: $1,500 Cost of books: $1,100 Room & board: (on/off-campus) $8,880/$8,880

ADMISSIONS

Admissions Selectivity Rating: 77

# of applications received: 48 % applicants accepted: 60 % acceptees attending: 72 Average GMAT: 460 Range of GMAT: 460–560 Average GPA: 3.24 TOEFL required of international students: Yes Minimum TOEFL (paper/computer): 550/213 Application fee: $40 International Application fee: $40 Regular application deadline: 8/1

Deferment available: Yes Maximum length of deferment: 1 year Transfer students accepted: Yes Transfer application policy: Can only transfer 6 graduate hours from the university in which you are coming from. Non-fall admissions: Yes Need-blind admissions: No

MARSHALL UNIVERSITY
LEWIS COLLEGE OF BUSINESS

ADMISSIONS CONTACT: DR. MICHAEL A. NEWSOME, MBA DIRECTOR
ADDRESS: CORBY HALL 217, 400 HAL GREER BOULEVARD, HUNTINGTON, WV 25755-2305
PHONE: 304-696-2613 • FAX: 304-696-3661
E-MAIL: EMAIL@SCHOOL.EDU • WEBSITE: LCOB.MARSHALL.EDU/

GENERAL INFORMATION

Type of school: Public Academic calendar: Semesters

STUDENTS

Enrollment of MBA Program: 80 % male/female: 40/60 % underrepresented minority: 15 % international: 30 Average years work experience at entry: 2.0

ACADEMICS

Student/faculty ratio: 5:1 % female faculty: 10 % underrepresented minority faculty: 10 % part-time faculty: 25

FINANCIAL FACTS

Annual tuition (in-state/out-of-state): $2,020/ $5,653 Fees: $1,100 Cost of books: $1,000 Room & board: (on/off-campus) /$4,000 % of students receiving aid: 50 % of first-year students receiving aid: 50

ADMISSIONS

Admissions Selectivity Rating: 74

# of applications received: 100 % applicants accepted: 84 % acceptees attending: 95 Average GMAT: 530 Average GPA: 3.50 TOEFL required of international students: Yes Minimum TOEFL (paper/computer): 525/195 Application fee: $40 International Application fee: $25

Deferment available: No Transfer students accepted: Yes Transfer application policy: When a student's Plan of Study is approved, credit may be transferred with the approval of the Graduate Dean. The work must have been completed at another regionally accredited graduate institution and must be appropriate to the student's program. Grades earned must be at the grade level of B or better, and acceptable to the advisor and the Graduate Dean. A maximum of 12 hours will be accepted, provided that they meet time limitation requirements. Graduate credit transferred from other institutions will not become part of the Marshall University grade point average and will simply meet credit hour requirements toward graduation. Non-fall admissions: Yes Need-blind admissions: No

EMPLOYMENT PROFILE

Average base starting salary: $50,000

McMaster University
DeGroote School of Business

Admissions Contact: Steven Walker/Denise Anderson/Caitlin Rivero, Administrators, Recruiting & MBA Admissions
Address: 4350 South Service Rd, RJC 316, Burlington, ON L7L 5R8 Canada
Phone: (905) 525-9140 ext. 27024 • Fax: (905) 634-4985
E-mail: mbainfo@mcmaster.ca • Website: www.degroote.mcmaster.ca

GENERAL INFORMATION

Type of school: Public **Academic calendar:** September to May

STUDENTS

Enrollment of MBA Program: 482 **% part-time:** 32 **% international:** 10 **Average age at entry:** 27 **Average years work experience at entry:** 3.0

ACADEMICS

% female faculty: 16 **% part-time faculty:** 1

FINANCIAL FACTS

Annual tuition (in-state/out-of-state): $25,440/ **Fees:** $790 **Cost of books:** $1,000 **Room & board:** (on/off-campus) **% of students receiving grants:** 20 **Average grant:** $3,000

ADMISSIONS

Admissions Selectivity Rating: 85

# of applications received: 512 **% applicants accepted:** 56 **% acceptees attending:** 67 **Average GMAT:** 623 **Range of GMAT:** n/a–n/a **Average GPA:** 3.48 **TOEFL required of international students:** Yes **Minimum TOEFL (paper/computer):** 600/250 **Application fee:** $150 **International Application fee:** $150 **Regular application deadline:** 6/1

Deferment available: No **Transfer students accepted:** Yes **Transfer application policy:** An application must be submitted and will be reviewed on a case-by-case basis **Non-fall admissions:** Yes **Need-blind admissions:** Yes

EMPLOYMENT PROFILE

Percent employed at graduation: 73 **Percent employed 3 months after graduation:** 27 **Average base starting salary:** $66,022

Primary Source of Full-time Job Acceptances

School-facilitated activities: 36(72%) **Graduate-facilitated activities:** 14(28%) Unknown: 0(0%)

Grads Employed by Function ......% Avg. Salary

Marketing:	(21%)	$57,855
Consulting:	(8%)	$65,624
Management:	(10%)	$70,546
Finance:	(41%)	$69,690
Other:	(20%)	$66,790

Top 5 Employers Hiring Grads (number of hires in last class)

Scotiabank/Scotia Capital (6), CIBC (4), TD Bank/TD Financial /TD Securities (4), KPMG (3), GlaxoSmithKline Consumer Healthcare (2)

McNeese State University
MBA Program

Admissions Contact: Tammy Pettis, University Admissions
Address: Box 92495, Lake Charles, LA 70609-2495
Phone: 337-475-5145 • Fax: 337-475-5189
E-mail: info@mcneese.edu
Website: www.mcneese.edu/colleges/business/mba

GENERAL INFORMATION

Type of school: Public **Academic calendar:** Semester

STUDENTS

Enrollment of parent institution: 8,423 **Enrollment of MBA Program:** 98 **% male/female:** 68/32 **% out-of-state:** 3 **% part-time:** 64 **% underrepresented minority:** 1 **% international:** 36 **Average age at entry:** 30 **Average years work experience at entry:** 0.0

ACADEMICS

Student/faculty ratio: 16:1 **% female faculty:** 1 **% underrepresented minority faculty:** 45

FINANCIAL FACTS

Annual tuition (in-state/out-of-state): $3,097/ $9,163 **Cost of books:** $1,200 **Room & board:** (on/off-campus) $4,380/$3,600 **% of students receiving aid:** 0 **% of first-year students receiving aid:** 0 **% of students receiving grants:** 0 **Average grant:** $0 **Average loan:** $0

ADMISSIONS

Admissions Selectivity Rating: 69

# of applications received: 36 **% applicants accepted:** 97 **% acceptees attending:** 51 **Average GMAT:** 480 **Range of GMAT:** 250–690 **Average GPA:** 3.60 **TOEFL required of international students:** Yes **Minimum TOEFL (paper/computer):** 550/213 **Application fee:** $20 **International Application fee:** $30

Deferment available: Yes **Maximum length of deferment:** 1 year **Transfer students accepted:** Yes **Transfer application policy:** No more than 6 hours from AACSB Accredited School **Non-fall admissions:** Yes **Need-blind admissions:** Yes

Michigan State University
The Eli Broad Graduate School of Management

Admissions Contact: Paul North, Director, MBA Admissions and Marketing
Address: Full-Time MBA Program, 215 Eppley Center, East Lansing, MI 48824-1121
Phone: 517-355-7604 • Fax: 517-353-1649
E-mail: mba@msu.edu • Website: mba.msu.edu

GENERAL INFORMATION

Type of school: Public **Academic calendar:** Semester

STUDENTS

Enrollment of parent institution: 47,131 **Enrollment of MBA Program:** 246 **% male/female:** 80/20 **% part-time:** 0 **% underrepre-**

sented minority: 12 % international: 33 **Average age at entry:** 28 **Average years work experience at entry:** 4.0

FINANCIAL FACTS

Annual tuition (in-state/out-of-state): $24,900/ $39,500 **Fees:** $35 **Cost of books:** $1,500 **Room & board: (on/off-campus)** $10,737/$10,737 **Average award package:** $27,575 **Average grant:** $7,840

ADMISSIONS

Admissions Selectivity Rating: 90

# of applications received: 508 **% applicants accepted:** 36 % **acceptees attending:** 50 **Average GMAT:** 638 **Average GPA:** 3.30 **TOEFL required of international students:** Yes **Minimum TOEFL (paper/computer):** 600/250 **Application fee:** $85 **International Application fee:** $85

Application Deadline/Notification:

Round 1:..11/112/15

Round 2:..1/93/29

Round 3: 3/14/18

Round 4: 4/165/23

Deferment available: No **Transfer students accepted:** No **Non-fall admissions:** No **Need-blind admissions:** Yes

EMPLOYMENT PROFILE

Percent employed at graduation: 67 **Percent employed 3 months after graduation:** 7 **Average base starting salary:** $88,672

Primary Source of Full-time Job Acceptances

School-facilitated activities: 53(73%) **Graduate-facilitated activities:** 20(27%) Unknown: 0(0%)

Grads Employed by Function ......% Avg. Salary

Marketing: ....(15%) $86,800

Operations: ....(40%) $87,500

Consulting: ....(4%) $110,000

Management: ....(0%)

Finance:...(31%) $81,500

HR: ....(10%) $80,100

MIS: ....(0%)

Other: ....(0%)

Top 5 Employers Hiring Grads (number of hires in last class)

Cummins (4), Deloitte Consulting (3), General Motors (3), Intel (3), Sears (3)

MIDDLE TENNESSEE STATE UNIVERSITY
JENNINGS A. JONES COLLEGE OF BUSINESS

ADMISSIONS CONTACT: TROY A. FESTERVAND, DIRECTOR, GRADUATE BUSINESS STUDIES
ADDRESS: PO BOX 290 BAS N222, MURFREESBORO, TN 37132
PHONE: 615-898-2368 • FAX: 615-904-8491
E-MAIL: GBS@MTSU.EDU
WEBSITE: WWW.MTSU.EDU/~GRADUATE/PROGRAMS/BUAD.HTM

GENERAL INFORMATION

Type of school: Public

STUDENTS

Enrollment of MBA Program: 410 **% male/female:** 64/36 **% underrepresented minority:** 22 **Average age at entry:** 26 **Average years work experience at entry:** 0.0

ACADEMICS

Student/faculty ratio: 20:1 **% part-time faculty:** 0

FINANCIAL FACTS

Annual tuition (in-state/out-of-state): $3,250/ $6,100 **Fees:** $300 **Cost of books:** $1,000 **Room & board: (on/off-campus)** $2,500/$2,500 **Average grant:** $0 **Average loan:** $0

ADMISSIONS

Admissions Selectivity Rating: 68

# of applications received: 325 **% applicants accepted:** 93 **Average GMAT:** 490 **Average GPA:** 3.20 **TOEFL required of international students:** Yes **Minimum TOEFL (paper/computer):** 525/197 **Application fee:** $25 **International Application fee:** $30 **Regular application deadline:** 7/1 **Regular application notification:** 8/1

Deferment available: Yes **Maximum length of deferment:** varies **Transfer students accepted:** Yes **Transfer application policy:** Depends on courses and programs **Non-fall admissions:** Yes **Need-blind admissions:** No

MISSISSIPPI STATE UNIVERSITY
COLLEGE OF BUSINESS

ADMISSIONS CONTACT: DR. BARBARA SPENCER, DIRECTOR OF GRADUATE STUDIES IN BUSINESS
ADDRESS: P.O.DRAWER 5288, MISSISSIPPI STATE, MS 39762
PHONE: 662-325-1891 • FAX: 662-325-8161
E-MAIL: GSB@COBILAN.MSSTATE.EDU
WEBSITE: WWW.BUSINESS.MSSTATE.EDU/GSB/

GENERAL INFORMATION

Type of school: Public **Academic calendar:** Semester

STUDENTS

Enrollment of parent institution: 17,824 **Enrollment of MBA Program:** 75 **% male/female:** 71/29 **% out-of-state:** 26 **% part-time:** 44 **% underrepresented minority:** 10 **% international:** 10 **Average age at entry:** 27

ACADEMICS

Student/faculty ratio: 4:1 % female faculty: 28 % underrepresented minority faculty: 13 % part-time faculty: 19

FINANCIAL FACTS

Annual tuition (in-state/out-of-state): $7,726/ $18,754 Fees: $0 Cost of books: $1,500 Room & board: (on/off-campus) $14,073/$14,073 % of students receiving aid: 66 % of first-year students receiving aid: 75 % of students receiving grants: 47 Average award package: $15,793 Average grant: $3,880 Average loan: $10,887 Average student loan debt: $11,067

ADMISSIONS

Admissions Selectivity Rating: 74

# of applications received: 156 % applicants accepted: 71 % acceptees attending: 68 Average GMAT: 521 Range of GMAT: 460–560 Average GPA: 3.42 TOEFL required of international students: Yes Minimum TOEFL (paper/computer): 575/233 Application fee: $30 International Application fee: $30 Regular application deadline: 7/1

Deferment available: Yes Maximum length of deferment: 1 year Transfer students accepted: Yes Transfer application policy: 6 hours of transfer credit from accredited institutions. Non-fall admissions: Yes Need-blind admissions: Yes

MISSOURI STATE UNIVERSITY
COLLEGE OF BUSINESS

ADMISSIONS CONTACT: MICHAEL EDWARDS, COORDINATOR, GRADUATE ADMISSIONS
ADDRESS: 901 S. NATIONAL AVENUE, SPRINGFIELD, MO 65897
PHONE: 417-836-5616 • FAX: 417-836-6636
E-MAIL: GRADUATECOLLEGE@MISSOURISTATE.EDU
WEBSITE: WWW.MBA.MISSOURISTATE.EDU

GENERAL INFORMATION

Type of school: Public Academic calendar: 16 week fa/sp Semesters; 8 week summer

STUDENTS

Enrollment of parent institution: 21,059 Enrollment of MBA Program: 368 % male/female: 49/51 % out-of-state: 5 % part-time: 34 % international: 59 Average age at entry: 26 Average years work experience at entry: 2.0

ACADEMICS

Student/faculty ratio: 28:1 % female faculty: 17 % underrepresented minority faculty: 4

FINANCIAL FACTS

Annual tuition (in-state/out-of-state): $4,896/ $9,432 Fees: $788 Cost of books: $1,000 Room & board: (on/off-campus) $7,302/$8,582

ADMISSIONS

Admissions Selectivity Rating: 73

# of applications received: 210 % applicants accepted: 80 % acceptees attending: 71 Average GMAT: 500 Range of GMAT: 470–560 Average GPA: 3.40 TOEFL required of international stu-

dents: Yes Minimum TOEFL (paper/computer): 550/213 Application fee: $35 International Application fee: $50

Deferment available: Yes Maximum length of deferment: 1 Semester Transfer students accepted: Yes Transfer application policy: With advisor permission Non-fall admissions: Yes Need-blind admissions: No

MORGAN STATE UNIVERSITY
EARL GRAVES SCHOOL OF BUSINESS AND MANAGEMENT

DIRECTOR OF GRADUATE ADMISSIONS
ADDRESS: 1700 EAST COLD SPRING LANE, BALTIMORE, MD 21251
WEBSITE: WWW.MORGAN.EDU/ACADEMICS/SBM/ACADEMIC/SBM.HTM

GENERAL INFORMATION

Type of school: Public Academic calendar: Semester

STUDENTS

Enrollment of parent institution: 5,900 Enrollment of MBA Program: 103 % part-time: 100 Average years work experience at entry: 0.0

ACADEMICS

Student/faculty ratio: 12:1 % part-time faculty: 9

FINANCIAL FACTS

Room & board: (on/off-campus) $2,990

ADMISSIONS

Admissions Selectivity Rating: 60*

# of applications received: 0 TOEFL required of international students: Yes Minimum TOEFL (paper/computer): 600/ Application fee: $20

Deferment available: Yes Maximum length of deferment: n/a Transfer students accepted: No Non-fall admissions: No Need-blind admissions: No

MURRAY STATE UNIVERSITY
COLLEGE OF BUSINESS AND PUBLIC AFFAIRS

ADMISSIONS CONTACT: DR. GERRY NKOMBO MUUKA, ASSISTANT DEAN AND MBA DIRECTOR
ADDRESS: 109 BUSINESS BUILDING, GRADUATE ADMISSIONS OFFICE, SPARKS HALL, MURRAY, KY 42071
PHONE: 270-762-6970 • FAX: 270-762-3482
E-MAIL: CBPA@MURRAYSTATE.EDU
WEBSITE: WWW.MURSUKY.EDU/QACD/CBPA/MBA/INDEX.HTM

GENERAL INFORMATION

Type of school: Public Academic calendar: Semester

STUDENTS

Enrollment of parent institution: 9,000 Enrollment of MBA Program: 160 % part-time: 53 Average age at entry: 31 Average years work experience at entry: 0.0

ACADEMICS

Student/faculty ratio: 20:1

FINANCIAL FACTS

Annual tuition (in-state/out-of-state): $4,185/ $11,700 **Room & board:** (on/off-campus) $3,800

ADMISSIONS

Admissions Selectivity Rating: 64

# of applications received: 121 % applicants accepted: 75 % acceptees attending: 52 TOEFL required of international students: Yes Minimum TOEFL (paper/computer): 525/ Application fee: $25

Deferment available: Yes Maximum length of deferment: 0

Transfer students accepted: Yes Transfer application policy: none

Non-fall admissions: Yes Need-blind admissions: No

NANYANG TECHNOLOGICAL UNIVERSITY
NANYANG BUSINESS SCHOOL

ADMISSIONS CONTACT: ASSOCIATE PROFESSOR OOI LEE LEE, DIRECTOR (MBA)
ADDRESS: THE NANYANG MBA, NANYANG BUSINESS SCHOOL, NANYANG AVENUE, BLK S3, B3A, SINGAPORE, 639798 SINGAPORE
PHONE: 011-65-67906183 • FAX: 011-65-67913561
E-MAIL: NBSMBA@NTU.EDU.SG • WEBSITE: WWW.NANYANGMBA.NTU.EDU.SG

GENERAL INFORMATION

Type of school: Public

STUDENTS

Enrollment of parent institution: 28,949 Enrollment of MBA Program: 282 % male/female: 72/28 % part-time: 34 % international: 81 Average age at entry: 31 Average years work experience at entry: 7.0

ACADEMICS

Student/faculty ratio: 2:1 % female faculty: 27 % part-time faculty: 7

FINANCIAL FACTS

Annual tuition (in-state/out-of-state):$19,000 Cost of books: $5,000 Room & board: (on/off-campus) $7,000/$10,000 % of students receiving grants: 9 Average grant: $17,300

ADMISSIONS

Admissions Selectivity Rating: 90

# of applications received: 904 % applicants accepted: 30 % acceptees attending: 62 Average GMAT: 652 Range of GMAT: 610–690 TOEFL required of international students: Yes Minimum TOEFL (paper/computer): 600/250 Application fee: $35 International Application fee: $35 Early application deadline: 12/31 Early notification date: 1/31 Regular application deadline: 3/31 Regular application notification: 4/30

Deferment available: Yes Maximum length of deferment: 1 year Transfer students accepted: Yes Transfer application policy: Reviewed on a case-by-case basis Non-fall admissions: Yes

EMPLOYMENT PROFILE

Percent employed at graduation: 51 Percent employed 3 months after graduation: 40 Average base starting salary: $57,797

Primary Source of Full-time Job Acceptances

School-facilitated activities: 45(76%) Graduate-facilitated activities: 14(24%) Unknown: 0(0%)

Grads Employed by Function ......% Avg. Salary

Marketing:	(15%)
Operations:	(12%)
Consulting:	(6%)
Management:	(4%)
Finance:	(57%)
MIS:	(2%)
Other:	(4%)

Top 5 Employers Hiring Grads (number of hires in last class)

Cisco Systems (2), OCBC Bank (2), PricewaterhouseCoopers (2), ABN Amro Bank (1), Bain & Company (1)

NATIONAL CHENGCHI UNIVERSITY
COLLEGE OF COMMERCE

ADMISSIONS CONTACT: 29393091 EXT. 65406, PUBLICE RELATIONS SPECIALIST
ADDRESS: RM. 406, YI-XIAN BUILDING,, 64, ZHI-NAN ROAD, SEC. 2, TAIPEI, 11605 TAIWAN
PHONE: 886-2-29393091 EXT. 65406 • FAX: 886-2-29387882
E-MAIL: IMBA@NCCU.EDU.TW
WEBSITE: HTTP://WWW.COMMERCE.NCCU.EDU.TW/INDEX.PHP?LANG=EN

GENERAL INFORMATION

Type of school: Public

STUDENTS

Average age at entry: 31 Average years work experience at entry: 6.0

ADMISSIONS

Admissions Selectivity Rating: 60*

# of applications received: 152 % applicants accepted: 39 TOEFL required of international students: No Regular application deadline: 12/22 Regular application notification: 4/8

Deferment available: Yes Maximum length of deferment: 2 years Transfer students accepted: No Non-fall admissions: No Need-blind admissions: Yes

Nicholls State University
College of Business Administration

Admissions Contact: Becky LeBlanc-Durocher, Director of Admissions
Address: PO Box 2004, Thibodaux, LA 70310
Phone: 877-642-4655 • Fax: 985-448-4929
E-mail: esai-bl@nicholls.edu • Website: www.nicholls.edu

GENERAL INFORMATION

Type of school: Public **Academic calendar:** Semester

STUDENTS

Enrollment of parent institution: 7,482 **Enrollment of MBA Program:** 116 **% male/female:** 49/51 **% out-of-state:** 1 **% part-time:** 59 **% underrepresented minority:** 6 **% international:** 12 **Average years work experience at entry:** 0.0

ACADEMICS

Student/faculty ratio: 15:1 **% female faculty:** 19 **% part-time faculty:** 0

FINANCIAL FACTS

Annual tuition (in-state/out-of-state): $3,075/ $8,523 **Cost of books:** $2,000 **Room & board:** (on/off-campus) $4,584 **% of students receiving aid:** 20 **Average grant:** $4,000 **Average loan:** $0

ADMISSIONS

Admissions Selectivity Rating: 68

# of applications received: 70 **% applicants accepted:** 99 **% acceptees attending:** 57 **Average GMAT:** 486 **Average GPA:** 3.10 **TOEFL required of international students:** Yes **Minimum TOEFL (paper/computer):** 550/213 **Application fee:** $20 **International Application fee:** $30 **Regular application deadline:** 7/1

Deferment available: Yes **Maximum length of deferment:** 1 Semester **Transfer students accepted:** Yes **Transfer application policy:** Maximum of 9 approved hours may be transferred from an accredited institution. **Non-fall admissions:** Yes **Need-blind admissions:** Yes

North Dakota State University
College of Business Administration

Admissions Contact: Paul Brown, MBA Director
Address: PO Box 5137, Fargo, ND 58018
E-mail: Paul.Brown@ndsu.edux • Website: www.ndsu.edu/cba/

GENERAL INFORMATION

Type of school: Public **Academic calendar:**

STUDENTS

Enrollment of MBA Program: 537 **% male/female:** 60/40 **% part-time:** 89 **% international:** 8 **Average age at entry:** 29 **Average years work experience at entry:** 0.0

ACADEMICS

Student/faculty ratio: 19:1 **% part-time faculty:** 28

FINANCIAL FACTS

Annual tuition (in-state/out-of-state): $4,600/ $10,800 **Fees:** $340

ADMISSIONS

Admissions Selectivity Rating: 63

# of applications received: 162 **% applicants accepted:** 90 **% acceptees attending:** 80 **TOEFL required of international students:** Yes **Minimum TOEFL (paper/computer):** 550/ **Application fee:** $35 **Regular application deadline:** 7/15

Deferment available: Yes **Transfer students accepted:** No **Non-fall admissions:** Yes **Need-blind admissions:** No

Northern Illinois University, College of Business
MBA Programs

Admissions Contact: Mona Salmon, Assistant Director
Address: Barsema 203, Dekalb, IL 60115
Phone: 866-648-6221 • Fax: 815-753-1668
E-mail: mba@niu.edu • Website: www.cob.niu.edu/mbaprograms

GENERAL INFORMATION

Type of school: Public

STUDENTS

Enrollment of parent institution: 25,000 **Enrollment of MBA Program:** 528 **% male/female:** 100/0 **% part-time:** 99 **% underrepresented minority:** 0 **Average age at entry:** 32 **Average years work experience at entry:** 9.0

ACADEMICS

Student/faculty ratio: 24:1 **% female faculty:** 19 **% underrepresented minority faculty:** 4

FINANCIAL FACTS

Annual tuition (in-state/out-of-state): $8,154/ $11,538 **Cost of books:** $750 **Average grant:** $0

ADMISSIONS

Admissions Selectivity Rating: 70

# of applications received: 262 **% applicants accepted:** 97 **% acceptees attending:** 70 **Average GMAT:** 550 **Average GPA:** 3.20 **TOEFL required of international students:** Yes **Minimum TOEFL (paper/computer):** 550/213 **Application fee:** $30 **Regular application deadline:** 6/1

Deferment available: Yes **Maximum length of deferment:** 24 months **Transfer students accepted:** Yes **Transfer application policy:** For the Evening MBA a limit of 9-Semester-hours accepted for phase two credit from AACSB-accredited schools only. **Non-fall admissions:** Yes **Need-blind admissions:** Yes

NORTHERN MICHIGAN UNIVERSITY
WALKER L. CISLER COLLEGE OF BUSINESS

ADMISSIONS CONTACT: GERRI DANIELS, DIRECTOR
ADDRESS: 1401 PRESQUE ISLE AVENUE, MARQUETTE, MI 49855
PHONE: 1-800-682-9797 • FAX: 906.227.1747
E-MAIL: ADMISSIONS@NMU.EDU • WEBSITE: WWW.NMU.EDU/BUSINESS

GENERAL INFORMATION
Type of school: Public

ACADEMICS
Student/faculty ratio: 15:1 **% female faculty:** 33 **% underrepresented minority faculty:** 0

FINANCIAL FACTS
Annual tuition (in-state/out-of-state): $8,640/ $8,640 **Fees:** $308 **Room & board: (on/off-campus)** $8,026

ADMISSIONS
Admissions Selectivity Rating: 60*

TOEFL required of international students: Yes **Minimum TOEFL (paper/computer):** 500/173 **Application fee:** $50 **International Application fee:** $50

Deferment available: Yes **Maximum length of deferment:** 1 year **Transfer students accepted:** Yes **Transfer application policy:** Transfer Credit More than 50 percent of the minimum credits for graduate degrees must be Northern Michigan University credits. To be accepted the following must occur: 1. The student must be in good standing in the college or university from which credit is transferred.   2. Courses to be transferred must carry a grade of B or better.   3. Courses to be transferred must be appropriate to the graduate program as determined by the program adviser.   4. Credit must have been earned within the past seven years.   5. Official transcripts must have been received by the College of Graduate Studies before transfer credit can be awarded.   6. All transfer credit must be reviewed by the student's adviser and approved by the Dean of Graduate Studies. The necessary documentation must be provided by the student.   7. Transfer grades will not be used in calculating the grade-point average required for graduation. The transfer credit form, available from the College of Graduate Studies Web site at www.nmu.edu/graduate_studies, is to be completed by the adviser and submitted to the College of Graduate Studies. This form will be used by the adviser and department to signify approval of the appropriateness of all courses. **Non-fall admissions:** Yes **Need-blind admissions:** Yes

NYENRODE BUSINESS UNIVERSITEIT
NYENRODE BUSINESS UNIVERSITEIT

ADMISSIONS CONTACT: VICTORIA BRESSERS, HEAD OF ADMISSIONS
ADDRESS: P.O. BOX 130, BREUKELEN, 3620 AC, NETHERLANDS
PHONE: 00 31 346 291 291 • FAX: 00 31 346 291 450
E-MAIL: INFO@NYENRODE.NL • WEBSITE: WWW.NYENRODE.NL

GENERAL INFORMATION
Type of school: Private

STUDENTS
Enrollment of MBA Program: 55 **% male/female:** 77/23 **% part-time:** 45 **% international:** 90 **Average age at entry:** 31 **Average years work experience at entry:** 7.0

ACADEMICS
Student/faculty ratio: 4:1 **% female faculty:** 16 **% part-time faculty:** 58

FINANCIAL FACTS
Annual tuition (in-state/out-of-state): $44,311/ **Cost of books:** $1,597 **Room & board: (on/off-campus)** $15,000 **% of first-year students receiving aid:** 20

ADMISSIONS
Admissions Selectivity Rating: 60*

# of applications received: 103 **% applicants accepted:** 29 **Average GMAT:** 560 **TOEFL required of international students:** Yes **Minimum TOEFL (paper/computer):** 600/250 **Application fee:** $80 **International Early application deadline:** 5/31 **Regular application deadline:** 8/31

Deferment available: Yes **Maximum length of deferment:** 2 years **Transfer students accepted:** No **Non-fall admissions:** No **Need-blind admissions:** No

EMPLOYMENT PROFILE
Average base starting salary: $50,000

Primary Source of Full-time Job Acceptances

School-facilitated activities: 4(%) **Graduate-facilitated activities:** 0(%) **Unknown:** 18(%)

Grads Employed by Function	......% Avg. Salary
Marketing:	(15%)
Consulting:	(31%)
Management:	(8%)
Finance:	(31%)
HR:	(15%)

OAKLAND UNIVERSITY
SCHOOL OF BUSINESS ADMINSTRATION

ADMISSIONS CONTACT: PAUL M. TRUMBULL, COORDINATOR OF GRADUATE BUSINESS PROGRAMS
ADDRESS: 238 ELLIOTT HALL, ROCHESTER, MI 48309-4493
PHONE: 248-370-3287 • FAX: 248-370-4964
E-MAIL: GBP@LISTS.OAKLAND.EDU • WEBSITE: WWW.OAKLAND.EDU/SBA

GENERAL INFORMATION

Type of school: Public **Academic calendar:** Semester

STUDENTS

Enrollment of parent institution: 19,379 **Enrollment of MBA Program:** 284 **% out-of-state:** 5 **% underrepresented minority:** 13 **% international:** 6 **Average age at entry:** 28 **Average years work experience at entry:** 7.0

ACADEMICS

Student/faculty ratio: 19:1 **% female faculty:** 19 **% underrepresented minority faculty:** 5 **% part-time faculty:** 22

FINANCIAL FACTS

Annual tuition (in-state/out-of-state): $10,998/ $18,970 **Cost of books:** $1,290 **Room & board: (on/off-campus)** $7,986/$8,400

ADMISSIONS

Admissions Selectivity Rating: 60*

Average GMAT: 535 **Average GPA:** 3.23 **TOEFL required of international students:** Yes **Minimum TOEFL (paper/computer):** 550/213 **Regular application deadline:** 8/1

Deferment available: Yes **Maximum length of deferment:** 1 year **Transfer students accepted:** Yes **Transfer application policy:** Up to nine credits of relevant course work may be transfered(3.0 or better) **Non-fall admissions:** Yes **Need-blind admissions:** Yes

EMPLOYMENT PROFILE

Percent employed 3 months after graduation: 91 **Average base starting salary:** $78,625

OHIO UNIVERSITY
COLLEGE OF BUSINESS

ADMISSIONS CONTACT: JAN ROSS, ASSISTANT DEAN, GRADUATE PROGRAM
ADDRESS: 514 COPELAND HALL, ATHENS, OH 45701
PHONE: 740-593-4320 • FAX: 740-593-1388
E-MAIL: ROSSJ@OHIO.EDU • WEBSITE: WWW.COB.OHIOU.EDU/GRAD/

GENERAL INFORMATION

Type of school: Public **Academic calendar:** Quarters

STUDENTS

Enrollment of parent institution: 19,000 **Enrollment of MBA Program:** 119 **% male/female:** 68/32 **% out-of-state:** 67 **% part-time:** 64 **% underrepresented minority:** 12 **% international:** 16 **Average age at entry:** 25 **Average years work experience at entry:** 1.5

ACADEMICS

Student/faculty ratio: 4:1 **% female faculty:** 25 **% underrepresented minority faculty:** 10

FINANCIAL FACTS

Annual tuition (in-state/out-of-state): $12,675/ $25,995 **Fees:** $5,000 **Cost of books:** $4,000 **Room & board: (on/off-campus)** $10,000/$10,000 **% of students receiving aid:** 70 **% of first-year students receiving aid:** 70 **Average award package:** $15,000 **Average grant:** $8,000 **Average loan:** $15,000

ADMISSIONS

Admissions Selectivity Rating: 89

# of applications received: 180 **% applicants accepted:** 32 **% acceptees attending:** 75 **Average GMAT:** 562 **Range of GMAT:** 480–670 **Average GPA:** 3.30 **TOEFL required of international students:** Yes **Minimum TOEFL (paper/computer):** 600/250 **Application fee:** $50 **International Application fee:** $50 **Regular application deadline:** 2/1 **Regular application notification:** 4/1

Deferment available: Yes **Maximum length of deferment:** 1 year **Transfer students accepted:** No **Non-fall admissions:** Yes **Need-blind admissions:** Yes

EMPLOYMENT PROFILE

Percent employed at graduation: 58 **Average base starting salary:** $56,350

Primary Source of Full-time Job Acceptances

School-facilitated activities: 13(25%) **Graduate-facilitated activities:** 14(25%) **Unknown:** 27(50%)

Grads Employed by Function	%	Avg. Salary
Marketing:	(53%)	$56,350
Operations:	(14%)	$56,350
Consulting:	(3%)	$56,350
Management:	(19%)	$56,350
Finance:	(11%)	$56,350
HR:	(0%)	
MIS:	(0%)	

Top 5 Employers Hiring Grads (number of hires in last class)
Deloitte & Touche (2), Ernst & Young (1), KPMG (1)

OKLAHOMA STATE UNIVERSITY
SPEARS SCHOOL OF BUSINESS

ADMISSIONS CONTACT: JANICE ANALLA, ASSISTANT DIRECTOR, GRADUATE PROGRAMS
ADDRESS: OKLAHOMA STATE UNIVERSITY, 102 GUNDERSEN HALL, STILLWATER, OK 74078-4022
PHONE: 405-744-2951 • FAX: 405-744-7474
E-MAIL: SPEARSMASTERS@OKSTATE.EDU • WEBSITE: SPEARS.OKSTATE.EDU/MBA/

GENERAL INFORMATION

Type of school: Public **Academic calendar:** Semester

STUDENTS

Enrollment of MBA Program: 534 **% male/female:** 61/39 **% part-time:** 77 **% international:** 17 **Average age at entry:** 27

ACADEMICS

Student/faculty ratio: 25:1 % female faculty: 18 % underrepresented minority faculty: 2 % part-time faculty: 0

FINANCIAL FACTS

Annual tuition (in-state/out-of-state): $4,026/ $15,652 Fees: $2,466 Cost of books: $730 Room & board: (on/off-campus) $7,650

ADMISSIONS

Admissions Selectivity Rating: 74

# of applications received: 256 % applicants accepted: 82 % acceptees attending: 80 Average GMAT: 559 Range of GMAT: 510–603 Average GPA: 3.31 TOEFL required of international students: Yes Minimum TOEFL (paper/computer): 575/233 Application fee: $40 International Application fee: $75 Regular application deadline: 7/1

Deferment available: Yes Maximum length of deferment: 1 yr. Transfer students accepted: Yes Transfer application policy: They must be a student in good standing at an AACSB accredited university. Non-fall admissions: Yes Need-blind admissions: Yes

EMPLOYMENT PROFILE

Percent employed at graduation: 67 Percent employed 3 months after graduation: 29 Average base starting salary: $52,855

Primary Source of Full-time Job Acceptances

School-facilitated activities: 17(55%) Graduate-facilitated activities: 10(32%) Unknown: 4(13%)

Grads Employed by Function	% Avg. Salary
Marketing:	(20%) $48,250
Operations:	(0%) $0
Consulting:	(0%) $0
Management:	(35%) $62,429
Finance:	(45%) $47,456

THE OPEN UNIVERSITY
THE OPEN UNIVERSITY BUSINESS SCHOOL

ADMISSIONS CONTACT: STUDENT REGISTRATION & ENQUIRY SERVICE,
ADDRESS: THE OPEN UNIVERSITY BUSINESS SCHOOL, THE OPEN UNIVERSITYPO BOX 197, MILTON KEYNES, MK7 6BJ UNITED KINGDOM OF GREAT BRITAIN AND NORTHERN IRELAND
PHONE: +44 8700100311 • FAX: +44 1908 654806
E-MAIL: OUBS-ILGEN@OPEN.AC.UK • WEBSITE: WWW.OPEN.AC.UK/OUBS/

GENERAL INFORMATION

Type of school: Public Academic calendar: Rolling May & November intakes

STUDENTS

Enrollment of parent institution: 5,500 Enrollment of MBA Program: 2,000 % male/female: 65/35 % part-time: 100 Average age at entry: 37 Average years work experience at entry: 14.0

ACADEMICS

Student/faculty ratio: 16:1 % part-time faculty: 413

FINANCIAL FACTS

Annual tuition (in-state/out-of-state): $19,880/ Room & board: (on/off-campus) % of students receiving aid: 0 % of first-year students receiving aid: 0 % of students receiving grants: 0 Average award package: $0 Average grant: $0 Average loan: $0 Average student loan debt: $0

ADMISSIONS

Admissions Selectivity Rating: 62

# of applications received: 2,000 % applicants accepted: 100 % acceptees attending: 100 Range of GMAT: n/a–n/a TOEFL required of international students: No

Deferment available: No Transfer students accepted: No Non-fall admissions: Yes Need-blind admissions: Yes

OREGON STATE UNIVERSITY
COLLEGE OF BUSINESS

ADMISSIONS CONTACT: DAVID BALDRIDGE, DIRECTOR FOR BUSINESS MASTER'S PROGRAMS
ADDRESS: 200 BEXELL HALL, COLLEGE OF BUSINESS, CORVALLIS, OR 97331
PHONE: 541-737-5510 • FAX: 541-737-6033
E-MAIL: OSUMBA@BUS.OREGONSTATE.EDU
WEBSITE: BUSINESS.OREGONSTATE.EDU/MBA/PROSPECTIVE-GRADUATE-STUDENTS

GENERAL INFORMATION

Type of school: Public Academic calendar: Quarter

STUDENTS

Enrollment of parent institution: 26,393 Enrollment of MBA Program: 144 % male/female: 52/48 % out-of-state: 6 % part-time: 25 % underrepresented minority: 7 % international: 65 Average age at entry: 27 Average years work experience at entry:

ACADEMICS

Student/faculty ratio: 2:1 % female faculty: 18 % underrepresented minority faculty: 20 % part-time faculty: 2

FINANCIAL FACTS

Annual tuition (in-state/out-of-state): $18,360/ $29,106 Fees: $493 Cost of books: $1,602 Room & board: (on/off-campus) $9,444/$9,444 Average loan: $0

ADMISSIONS

Admissions Selectivity Rating: 70

# of applications received: 79 % applicants accepted: 99 % acceptees attending: 95 Average GMAT: 554 Range of GMAT: 530–580 TOEFL required of international students: Yes Minimum TOEFL (paper/computer): 575/233 Application fee: $60 International Application fee: $60 Regular application deadline: 8/1

Deferment available: No Transfer students accepted: Yes Transfer application policy: Up to 15 credits of approved coursework (AACSB-accredited) Non-fall admissions: Yes Need-blind admissions: Yes

EMPLOYMENT PROFILE

Average base starting salary: $54,950

Grads Employed by Function ......% Avg. Salary

Marketing: ....(1%) $45,000

Operations: ....(1%) $60,000

Management: ....(1%) $30,000

Finance:......................................(7%) $57,000

MIS: ....(2%) $52,500

Other: ....(1%) $45,000

PACE UNIVERSITY
LUBIN SCHOOL OF BUSINESS

ADMISSIONS CONTACT: SUSAN FORD-GOLDSCHEIN, DIRECTOR OF GRADUATE ADMISSION
ADDRESS: ONE PACE PLAZA, NEW YORK, NY 10038
PHONE: 212-346-1531 • FAX: 212-346-1585
E-MAIL: GRADNYC@PACE.EDU • WEBSITE: WWW.PACE.EDU/LUBIN/

GENERAL INFORMATION

Type of school: Private **Academic calendar:** Semester

STUDENTS

Enrollment of parent institution: 12,772 **Enrollment of MBA Program:** 539 **% male/female:** 50/50 **% out-of-state:** 14 **% part-time:** 71 **% underrepresented minority:** 20 **% international:** 46 **Average age at entry:** 26 **Average years work experience at entry:** 2.0

ACADEMICS

Student/faculty ratio: 23:1 **% female faculty:** 20 **% underrepresented minority faculty:** 25 **% part-time faculty:** 34

FINANCIAL FACTS

Annual tuition (in-state/out-of-state): $31,050/ $31,050 **Fees:** $982 **Cost of books:** $3,025 **Room & board: (on/off-campus)** $12,310/$20,704 **% of students receiving aid:** 60 **% of first-year students receiving aid:** 89 **% of students receiving grants:** 42 **Average award package:** $22,490 **Average grant:** $12,958 **Average loan:** $23,312 **Average student loan debt:** $42,404

ADMISSIONS

Admissions Selectivity Rating: 82

# of applications received: 694 **% applicants accepted:** 46 **% acceptees attending:** 48 **Average GMAT:** 559 **Range of GMAT:** 520–590 **Average GPA:** 3.24 **TOEFL required of international students:** Yes **Minimum TOEFL (paper/computer):** 600/230 **Application fee:** $70 **International Application fee:** $70 **Regular application deadline:** 8/1

Deferment available: Yes **Maximum length of deferment:** one academic year **Transfer students accepted:** Yes **Transfer application policy:** maximum of 6 credits **Non-fall admissions:** Yes **Need-blind admissions:** Yes

EMPLOYMENT PROFILE

Percent employed at graduation: 49 **Percent employed 3 months after graduation:** 25 **Average base starting salary:** $63,700

Primary Source of Full-time Job Acceptances

School-facilitated activities: 24(42%) **Graduate-facilitated activities:** 11(19%) Unknown: 22(39%)

Grads Employed by Function ......% Avg. Salary

Marketing: ....(7%) $42,600

Operations: ....(2%) $0

Consulting: ....(0%) $0

Management: ....(7%) $110,000

Finance:......................................(72%) $60,400

HR: ....(2%) $44,000

Other: ....(11%) $107,500

Top 5 Employers Hiring Grads (number of hires in last class)

Ernst & Young (9), PricewaterhouseCoopers (6), Morgan Stanley (4), KPMG (2), Goldman Sachs (2)

PENN STATE UNIVERSITY—
GREAT VALLEY CAMPUS
SCHOOL OF GRADUATE PROFESSIONAL STUDIES

ADMISSIONS CONTACT: SUSAN HALDEMAN, GRADUATE ENROLLMENT COORDINATOR
ADDRESS: 30 EAST SWEDESFORD ROAD, MALVERN, PA 19355
PHONE: 610-648-3248 • FAX: 610-725-5296
E-MAIL: GVMBA@PSU.EDU • WEBSITE: WWW.GV.PSU.EDU

GENERAL INFORMATION

Type of school: Public **Academic calendar:** Semester

STUDENTS

Enrollment of parent institution: 2,000 **Enrollment of MBA Program:** 340 **% part-time:** 97 **Average age at entry:** 31 **Average years work experience at entry:** 8.0

ACADEMICS

Student/faculty ratio: 18:1 **% female faculty:** 40 **% underrepresented minority faculty:** 5 **% part-time faculty:** 20

FINANCIAL FACTS

Annual tuition (in-state/out-of-state): $16,752/ $27,312 **Fees:** $600 **Cost of books:** $4,872 **Room & board: (on/off-campus)** $0/$20,000 **% of students receiving aid:** 60 **% of first-year students receiving aid:** 50 **% of students receiving grants:** 1 **Average award package:** $4,500 **Average grant:** $15,000 **Average loan:** $4,500 **Average student loan debt:** $8,000

ADMISSIONS

Admissions Selectivity Rating: 74

# of applications received: 115 **% applicants accepted:** 72 **% acceptees attending:** 71 **Average GMAT:** 522 **Average GPA:** 3.23 **TOEFL required of international students:** Yes **Minimum TOEFL (paper/computer):** 550/230 **Application fee:** $60 **International Application fee:** $60

Deferment available: Yes **Maximum length of deferment:** 1 year **Transfer students accepted:** Yes **Transfer application policy:** Transfer applicants are encouraged and should submit all application materials, including official transcripts of courses already taken and course descriptions. **Non-fall admissions:** Yes **Need-blind admissions:** Yes

EMPLOYMENT PROFILE

Grads Employed by Function	% Avg. Salary
Marketing:	(6%)
Operations:	(8%)
Consulting:	(5%)
Management:	(10%)
Finance:	(10%)
HR:	(4%)
MIS:	(7%)
Other:	(11%)

PENNSYLVANIA STATE UNIVERSITY, HARRISBURG CAMPUS
SCHOOL OF BUSINESS ADMINISTRATION

ADMISSIONS CONTACT: ROBERT COFFMAN, JR., DIRECTOR OF ENROLLMENT SERVICES
ADDRESS: 777 WEST HARRISBURG PIKE, UNIVERSITY PARK, PA 17057
PHONE: 717-948-6250 • FAX: 717-948-6325
E-MAIL: HBGADMIT@PSU.EDU
WEBSITE: WWW.HBG.PSU.EDU/PROGRAMS/GRADUATE/BUSINESSADMIN./PHP

GENERAL INFORMATION
Type of school: Public **Academic calendar:** Semester

STUDENTS
Enrollment of parent institution: 4,700 **Enrollment of MBA Program:** 196 **% male/female:** 98/2 **% out-of-state:** 18 **% part-time:** 91 **% international:** 2 **Average age at entry:** 29 **Average years work experience at entry:** 3.0

ACADEMICS
Student/faculty ratio: 7:1 **% part-time faculty:** 0

FINANCIAL FACTS
Average grant: $6,000

ADMISSIONS
Admissions Selectivity Rating: 60*
# of applications received: 22 **Average GMAT:** 558 **Average GPA:** 3.26 **TOEFL required of international students:** Yes **Minimum TOEFL (paper/computer):** 550/213 **Application fee:** $65 **International Application fee:** $65 **Regular application deadline:** 7/18
Deferment available: Yes **Maximum length of deferment:** 3 years **Transfer students accepted:** Yes **Transfer application policy:** 10 credits max will transfer **Non-fall admissions:** Yes **Need-blind admissions:** Yes

PURDUE UNIVERSITY CALUMET
SCHOOL OF MANAGEMENT

ADMISSIONS CONTACT: PAUL MCGRATH, COORDINATOR, GRADUATE MANAGEMENT PROGRAMS
ADDRESS: SCHOOL OF MANAGEMENT, PURDUE UNIVERSITY CALUMET, HAMMOND, IN 46323-2094
PHONE: 219-989-2425 • FAX: 219-989-3158
E-MAIL: PMCGRAT@CALUMET.PURDUE.EDU • WEBSITE: WWW.CALUMET.PURDUE.EDU

GENERAL INFORMATION
Type of school: Public **Academic calendar:** Semester

STUDENTS
Enrollment of parent institution: 9,500 **Enrollment of MBA Program:** 213 **% male/female:** 100/0 **% out-of-state:** 0 **% part-time:** 96 **% underrepresented minority:** 0 **% international:** 0 **Average age at entry:** 28 **Average years work experience at entry:** 5.0

ACADEMICS
Student/faculty ratio: 10:1 **% female faculty:** 43 **% underrepresented minority faculty:** 24 **% part-time faculty:** 5

FINANCIAL FACTS
Annual tuition (in-state/out-of-state): $4,325/ $9,322 **Cost of books:** $6,000 **Room & board: (on/off-campus)** % of students receiving aid: 0 **% of first-year students receiving aid:** 0 **% of students receiving grants:** 0 **Average grant:** $0 **Average loan:** $0

ADMISSIONS
Admissions Selectivity Rating: 72
# of applications received: 102 **% applicants accepted:** 93 **% acceptees attending:** 98 **Average GMAT:** 538 **Average GPA:** 3.20 **TOEFL required of international students:** Yes **Minimum TOEFL (paper/computer):** 550/213 **Application fee:** $55 **International Application fee:** $55 **Regular application deadline:** 8/1 **Regular application notification:** 8/1
Deferment available: Yes **Maximum length of deferment:** 1 year **Transfer students accepted:** Yes **Transfer application policy:** Six Semester hours of B or better coursework, evaluated for equivalence by the Graduate Admissions Committee **Non-fall admissions:** Yes **Need-blind admissions:** Yes

EMPLOYMENT PROFILE
Average base starting salary: $37,000

QUEEN'S UNIVERSITY
QUEEN'S SCHOOL OF BUSINESS

ADMISSIONS CONTACT: 613-533-2302, PROGRAM MANAGER
ADDRESS: GOODES HALL, QUEEN'S UNIVERSITY, SUITE 338, KINGSTON, ON K7L 3N6 CANADA
PHONE: 613-533-2302 • FAX: 613-533-6281
E-MAIL: QUEENSMBA@BUSINESS.QUEENSU.CA • WEBSITE: WWW.QUEENSMBA.COM

GENERAL INFORMATION

Type of school: Public **Academic calendar:** 12 months starting in January

STUDENTS

Enrollment of parent institution: 23,865 **Enrollment of MBA Program:** 75 **% male/female:** 80/20 **% international:** 45 **Average age at entry:** 28 **Average years work experience at entry:** 4.5

FINANCIAL FACTS

Annual tuition (in-state/out-of-state): $73,350/ $83,130 **Room & board: (on/off-campus)** $26,406/$26,406

ADMISSIONS

Admissions Selectivity Rating: 60*

Average GMAT: 660 **Range of GMAT:** 580–770 **TOEFL required of international students:** Yes **Minimum TOEFL (paper/computer):** 600/100 **Application fee:** $0 **International Application fee:** $0

Application Deadline/Notification:
Round 1: 5/31
Round 2: 7/12
Round 3: 9/13
Round 4: 11/15

Deferment available: Yes **Maximum length of deferment:** 1 year **Transfer students accepted:** No **Non-fall admissions:** Yes **Need-blind admissions:** Yes

RIDER UNIVERSITY
COLLEGE OF BUSINESS ADMINSTRATION

ADMISSIONS CONTACT: JAMIE MITCHELL, DIRECTOR, GRADUATE ADMISSIONS
ADDRESS: PJ CIAMBELLI HALL, 2083 LAWRENCEVILLE ROAD, LAWRENCEVILLE, NJ 08648-3099
PHONE: 609-896-5036 • FAX: 609-895-5680
E-MAIL: GRADADM@RIDER.EDU • WEBSITE: WWW.RIDER.EDU/CBA

GENERAL INFORMATION

Type of school: Private **Academic calendar:** Semester

STUDENTS

Enrollment of parent institution: 5,636 **Enrollment of MBA Program:** 186 **% male/female:** 51/49 **% out-of-state:** 7 **% part-time:** 67 **% underrepresented minority:** 59 **% international:** 25 **Average age at entry:** 31 **Average years work experience at entry:**

ACADEMICS

Student/faculty ratio: 6:1 **% female faculty:** 35 **% underrepresented minority faculty:** 26 **% part-time faculty:** 32

FINANCIAL FACTS

Cost of books: $4,240

ADMISSIONS

Admissions Selectivity Rating: 73

# of applications received: 101 **% applicants accepted:** 71 **% acceptees attending:** 69 **Average GMAT:** 490 **Range of GMAT:** 410–530 **Average GPA:** 3.22 **TOEFL required of international students:** Yes **Minimum TOEFL (paper/computer):** 585/240 **International Application fee:** $50 **Regular application deadline:** 8/1

Application Deadline/Notification:
Round 1: 8/1
Round 2: 12/1
Round 3: 5/1

Deferment available: Yes **Maximum length of deferment:** 1 year **Transfer students accepted:** Yes **Transfer application policy:** Each case is evaluated individually. No more than 24 transferred credits against 51 required maximum. Maximum of 6 credits against 30 in the advance portion. **Non-fall admissions:** Yes **Need-blind admissions:** Yes

ROCKHURST UNIVERSITY
HELZBERG SCHOOL OF MANAGEMENT

ADMISSIONS CONTACT: MICHELLE HOLTMAN, DIRECTOR MBA ADMISSION
ADDRESS: MASSMAN HALL, 1100 ROCKHURST ROAD, KANSAS CITY, MO 64110
PHONE: 816-501-4632 • FAX: 816-501-4241
E-MAIL: MBA@ROCKHURST.EDU • WEBSITE: WWW.ROCKHURST.EDU/HELZBERG

GENERAL INFORMATION

Type of school: Private **Academic calendar:** Standard

STUDENTS

Enrollment of parent institution: 2,808 **Enrollment of MBA Program:** 163 **% male/female:** 77/23 **% out-of-state:** 58 **% part-time:** 71 **% underrepresented minority:** 6 **% international:** 0 **Average age at entry:** 26 **Average years work experience at entry:**

ACADEMICS

Student/faculty ratio: 10:1 **% female faculty:** 18 **% underrepresented minority faculty:** 10 **% part-time faculty:** 25

FINANCIAL FACTS

Annual tuition (in-state/out-of-state): $10,350/ $10,350 **Fees:** $450 **Cost of books:** $1,631 **Room & board: (on/off-campus)** $10,000

ADMISSIONS

Admissions Selectivity Rating: 73

# of applications received: 97 **% applicants accepted:** 90 **% acceptees attending:** 80 **Average GMAT:** 524 **Range of GMAT:** 470–580 **Average GPA:** 3.94 **TOEFL required of international students:** Yes **Minimum TOEFL (paper/computer):** 550/213 **Application fee:** $0 **International Application fee:** $0

Deferment available: Yes **Maximum length of deferment:** two terms **Transfer students accepted:** Yes **Transfer application policy:** All credits transfer seamlessly for transfer students from universities that participate in the Jesuit Transfer Agreement (JTA). Transfer students from non-JTA universities may transfer up to 9 credit hours. **Non-fall admissions:** Yes **Need-blind admissions:** Yes

SAINT MARY'S UNIVERSITY OF MINNESOTA
GRADUATE SCHOOL OF BUSINESS AND TECHNOLOGY

ADMISSIONS CONTACT: YASIN ALSAIDI, DIRECTOR OF ADMISSIONS
ADDRESS: 2500 PARK AVENUE, MINNEAPOLIS, MN 55404-4403
PHONE: 612-728-5100 • FAX: 612-728-5121
E-MAIL: TC-ADMISSION@SMUMN.EDU
WEBSITE: HTTP://WWW.SMUMN.EDU/GRADUATE-HOME/AREAS-OF-STUDY/ GRADUATE-SCHOOL-OF-BUSINESS-TECHNOLOGY

GENERAL INFORMATION
Type of school: Private

STUDENTS
Enrollment of parent institution: 5,688 **Enrollment of MBA Program:** 233 **% male/female:** 57/43 **% out-of-state:** 2 **% part-time:** 31 **% underrepresented minority:** 23 **% international:** 24 **Average age at entry:** 30

FINANCIAL FACTS
Annual tuition (in-state/out-of-state): $8,280/ $8,280 **Fees:** $0

ADMISSIONS
Admissions Selectivity Rating: 62

# of applications received: 41 **% applicants accepted:** 100 **% acceptees attending:** 88 **TOEFL required of international students:** Yes **Minimum TOEFL (paper/computer):** 550/213

Deferment available: Yes **Maximum length of deferment:** 1 year **Transfer students accepted:** Yes **Transfer application policy:** May transfer up to six graduate credits from another regionally accredited institution. **Non-fall admissions:** Yes **Need-blind admissions:** Yes

SAINT MARY'S UNIVERSITY, CANADA
SOBEY SCHOOL OF BUSINESS

ADMISSIONS CONTACT: LEAH RAY, MANAGING DIRECTOR, MBA PROGRAM
ADDRESS: 923 ROBIE STREET, HALIFAX, NS B3H 3C3 CANADA
PHONE: 902-420-5002 • FAX: 902-420-5119
E-MAIL: MBA@SMU.CA • WEBSITE: WWW.SOBEY.SMU.CA

GENERAL INFORMATION
Type of school: Private **Academic calendar:** Semester

STUDENTS
Enrollment of parent institution: 8,000 **Enrollment of MBA Program:** 82 **% male/female:** 40/60 **% out-of-state:** 60 **%**

part-time: 68 **% international:** 40 **Average age at entry:** 27 **Average years work experience at entry:** 5.0

ACADEMICS
Student/faculty ratio: 25:1

FINANCIAL FACTS
Annual tuition (in-state/out-of-state): $9,235/ **Fees:** $480 **Cost of books:** $1,000 **Room & board: (on/off-campus)** **% of students receiving grants:** 50 **Average grant:** $2,500

ADMISSIONS
Admissions Selectivity Rating: 83

# of applications received: 114 **% applicants accepted:** 64 **% acceptees attending:** 78 **Average GMAT:** 600 **Range of GMAT:** 550–720 **Average GPA:** 3.30 **TOEFL required of international students:** Yes **Minimum TOEFL (paper/computer):** 580/237 **International Application fee:** $70 **Early application deadline:** 1/31 **Regular application deadline:** 6/15

Deferment available: No **Transfer students accepted:** Yes **Transfer application policy:** Must submit full application & suppporting documents as we evaluate on a case by case basis. **Non-fall admissions:** No **Need-blind admissions:** Yes

SALISBURY UNIVERSITY
FRANKLIN P. PERDUE SCHOOL OF BUSINESS

MBA DIRECTOR
ADDRESS: 1101 CAMDEN AVENUE, SALISBURY, MD 21801-6837
PHONE: 410-548-5564 • FAX: 410-548-2908
E-MAIL: MBA@SALISBURY.EDU • WEBSITE: MBA.SALISBURY.EDU

GENERAL INFORMATION
Type of school: Public **Academic calendar:** Semester

STUDENTS
Enrollment of parent institution: 7,000 **Enrollment of MBA Program:** 73 **% male/female:** 58/42 **% part-time:** 56 **% underrepresented minority:** 1 **% international:** 12 **Average age at entry:** 26 **Average years work experience at entry:** 1.5

ACADEMICS
Student/faculty ratio: 25:1 **% female faculty:** 4 **% underrepresented minority faculty:** 0 **% part-time faculty:** 0

FINANCIAL FACTS
Annual tuition (in-state/out-of-state): $9,180/ $19,244 **Fees:** $1,870 **Cost of books:** $1,100 **Room & board: (on/off-campus)** /$8,500 **Average grant:** $9,680

ADMISSIONS
Admissions Selectivity Rating: 83

# of applications received: 50 **% applicants accepted:** 70 **% acceptees attending:** 100 **Average GMAT:** 550 **Range of GMAT:** 490–750 **Average GPA:** 3.40 **TOEFL required of international students:** Yes **Minimum TOEFL (paper/computer):** 550/ **Application fee:** $45 **International Application fee:** $45 **Early application deadline:** 3/1 **Early notification date:** 4/1 **Regular application deadline:** 3/1 **Regular application notification:** 4/1

Deferment available: No Transfer students accepted: No Non-fall admissions: No Need-blind admissions: Yes

EMPLOYMENT PROFILE

Percent employed at graduation: 61

SAM HOUSTON STATE UNIVERSITY
COLLEGE OF BUSINESS ADMINISTRATION

ADMISSIONS CONTACT: DR. LEROY ASHORN, ASSOCIATE DEAN
ADDRESS: PO BOX 2056, HUNTSVILLE, TX 77341-2056
PHONE: 936-294-1239 • FAX: 936-294-3612
E-MAIL: BUSGRAD@SHSU.EDU • WEBSITE: COBA.SHSU.EDU/

GENERAL INFORMATION

Type of school: Public Academic calendar: September 1 to August 31

STUDENTS

Enrollment of parent institution: 17,580 Enrollment of MBA Program: 360 % male/female: 65/35 % out-of-state: 10 % part-time: 68 % underrepresented minority: 10 % international: 15 Average years work experience at entry: 0.0

ACADEMICS

Student/faculty ratio: 23:1 % female faculty: 33 % underrepresented minority faculty: 10

FINANCIAL FACTS

Annual tuition (in-state/out-of-state): $8,994/ $18,471 Cost of books: $1,350

ADMISSIONS

Admissions Selectivity Rating: 73

# of applications received: 219 % applicants accepted: 73 % acceptees attending: 57 Average GMAT: 504 Range of GMAT: 460–540 Average GPA: 3.35 TOEFL required of international students: Yes Minimum TOEFL (paper/computer): 550/213 Application fee: $40 International Application fee: $75 Regular application deadline: 8/1

Deferment available: Yes Maximum length of deferment: 1 year Transfer students accepted: Yes Transfer application policy: Accept up to six Semester hours from accredited universities Non-fall admissions: Yes Need-blind admissions: Yes

SAMFORD UNIVERSITY
SAMFORD UNIVERSITY BROCK SCHOOL OF BUSINESS

ADMISSIONS CONTACT: MR. LARRON C. HARPER, DIRECTOR OF GRADUATE PROGRAMS
ADDRESS: DBH 413, BROCK SCHOOL OF BUSINESS, 800 LAKESHORE DR., BIRMINGHAM, AL 35229
PHONE: 205-726-2040 • FAX: 205-726-4555
E-MAIL: LCHARPER@SAMFORD.EDU • WEBSITE: WWW.SAMFORD.EDU/MBA

GENERAL INFORMATION

Type of school: Private Academic calendar: Two sixteen week Semesters, one ten week

STUDENTS

Enrollment of parent institution: 4,700 Enrollment of MBA Program: 130 % male/female: 100/0 % part-time: 100 % underrepresented minority: 0 Average age at entry: 26 Average years work experience at entry: 5.0

ACADEMICS

Student/faculty ratio: 12:1 % female faculty: 25 % underrepresented minority faculty: 8 % part-time faculty: 4

ADMISSIONS

Admissions Selectivity Rating: 75

# of applications received: 86 % applicants accepted: 72 % acceptees attending: 95 Average GMAT: 570 Range of GMAT: 510–600 TOEFL required of international students: No Application fee: $25 International Application fee: $25

Deferment available: Yes Maximum length of deferment: one-year Transfer students accepted: Yes Transfer application policy: must submit complete application and meet admissions deadlines. Limited number of credits may transfer Non-fall admissions: Yes Need-blind admissions: Yes

SOUTHEASTERN LOUISIANA UNIVERSITY
COLLEGE OF BUSINESS

ADMISSIONS CONTACT: SANDRA MEYERS, GRADUATE ADMISSIONS ANALYST
ADDRESS: SLU 10752, HAMMOND, LA 70402
PHONE: 800-222-7358 • FAX: 985-549-5882
E-MAIL: ADMISSIONS@SELU.EDU
WEBSITE: WWW.SELU.EDU/ACAD_RESEARCH/COLLEGES/BUS/INDEX.HTML

GENERAL INFORMATION

Type of school: Public Academic calendar: Semester

STUDENTS

Enrollment of parent institution: 15,414 Enrollment of MBA Program: 77 % male/female: 62/38 % out-of-state: 3 % part-time: 27 % underrepresented minority: 13 % international: 12 Average age at entry: 25

ACADEMICS

Student/faculty ratio: 5:1 % female faculty: 13 % underrepresented minority faculty: 7 % part-time faculty: 0

FINANCIAL FACTS

Annual tuition (in-state/out-of-state): $3,977/ $12,002 Fees: $1,111 Cost of books: $1,200 Room & board: (on/off-campus) $7,190/$8,328 Average student loan debt: $14,195

ADMISSIONS

Admissions Selectivity Rating: 82

# of applications received: 82 % applicants accepted: 45 % acceptees attending: 62 Average GMAT: 501 Range of GMAT: 468–560 Average GPA: 3.13 TOEFL required of international students: Yes Minimum TOEFL (paper/computer): 525/ Application fee: $20 International Application fee: $30 Regular application deadline: 7/15

Deferment available: Yes Maximum length of deferment: 1 year Transfer students accepted: Yes Transfer application policy: Must earn 12 hours of graduate credit at Southeastern before applying for any transfer credit from another university. That university must be an accredited institution that regularly grants the master's degree or an equivalent foreign institution. The student must be eligible for readmission to the institution from which the credits are to be transferred and must have earned a minumun grade of "B" in each course to be transferred. No more than one-third of the hours required for graduation may be transferred. Non-fall admissions: Yes Need-blind admissions: Yes

SOUTHERN UTAH UNIVERSITY
SOUTHERN UTAH UNIVERSITY SCHOOL OF BUSINESS

ADMISSIONS CONTACT: CHRISTINE PROCTOR, ASSOCIATE DIRECTOR OF ADMISSIONS
ADDRESS: SOUTHERN UTAH UNIVERSITY, 351 W. UNIVERSITY BLVD., CEDAR CITY, UT 84720
PHONE: 435-586-7742 • FAX: 435-865-8223
E-MAIL: PROCTOR@SUU.EDU • WEBSITE: SUU.EDU/BUSINESS/

GENERAL INFORMATION

Type of school: Public Academic calendar: Semester

STUDENTS

Enrollment of MBA Program: 63 % male/female: 86/14 % part-time: 33 % underrepresented minority: 14 Average age at entry: 27

ACADEMICS

Student/faculty ratio: 5:1 % female faculty: 8 % underrepresented minority faculty: 8 % part-time faculty: 8

FINANCIAL FACTS

Annual tuition (in-state/out-of-state): $9,048/ $29,986 Fees: $540 Cost of books: $1,600 Room & board: (on/off-campus) $6,189/$7,500 % of students receiving aid: 32 % of first-year students receiving aid: 36 % of students receiving grants: 17 Average grant: $7,750 Average loan: $11,099

ADMISSIONS

Admissions Selectivity Rating: 73

# of applications received: 42 % applicants accepted: 74 % acceptees attending: 71 Average GMAT: 420 Range of GMAT: 300–580 Average GPA: 3.66 TOEFL required of international students: Yes Minimum TOEFL (paper/computer): 550/213 Application fee: $50 International Application fee: $50 Early application deadline: 3/1 Regular application deadline: 3/1

Deferment available: Yes Maximum length of deferment: Two years Transfer students accepted: Yes Non-fall admissions: Yes Need-blind admissions: Yes

EMPLOYMENT PROFILE

Percent employed 3 months after graduation: 92 Average base starting salary: $42,293

Primary Source of Full-time Job Acceptances

School-facilitated activities: (%) Graduate-facilitated activities: (%) Unknown: 50(100%)

Grads Employed by Function	%	Avg. Salary
Marketing:	(2%)	$47,500
Operations:	(2%)	$47,500
Management:	(24%)	$47,272
Finance:	(39%)	$44,111
HR:	(4%)	$42,500
MIS:	(2%)	$37,500
Other:	(26%)	$34,500

Top 5 Employers Hiring Grads (number of hires in last class)

Southern Utah University (6), Boeing (3), First Equity Holdings (2), Hafen, Buckner, Everett & Graff (2),

ST. CLOUD STATE UNIVERSITY
HERBERGER COLLEGE OF BUSINESS

ADMISSIONS CONTACT: GRADUATE STUDIES OFFICE—ANNETTE DAY, GRADUATE ADMISSIONS MANAGER
ADDRESS: 720 4TH AVE. SOUTH, AS-121, ST. CLOUD, MN 56301-4498
PHONE: 320-308-2112 • FAX: 320-308-3986
E-MAIL: GRADUATESTUDIES@STCLOUDSTATE.EDU
WEBSITE: WWW.STCLOUDSTATE.EDU/MBA/

GENERAL INFORMATION

Type of school: Public Academic calendar: Semester

STUDENTS

Enrollment of parent institution: 16,334 Enrollment of MBA Program: 166 % male/female: 71/29 % out-of-state: 18 % part-time: 75 % underrepresented minority: 10 % international: 48 Average age at entry: 28 Average years work experience at entry: 5.0

ACADEMICS

Student/faculty ratio: 25:1 % female faculty: 27 % underrepresented minority faculty: 20 % part-time faculty: 8

FINANCIAL FACTS

Annual tuition (in-state/out-of-state): $14,292/ $14,292 Fees: $165 Cost of books: $1,800 Room & board: (on/off-campus) Average grant: $0 Average loan: $0

ADMISSIONS

Admissions Selectivity Rating: 83

% acceptees attending: 48 Average GMAT: 525 Range of GMAT: 470–700 Average GPA: 3.30 TOEFL required of international students: Yes Minimum TOEFL (paper/computer): 550/213 Application fee: $35 International Application fee: $35 Early application deadline: 4/15 Early notification date: 6/15

Deferment available: Yes Maximum length of deferment: 2 yr Transfer students accepted: No Non-fall admissions: Yes Need-blind admissions: No

EMPLOYMENT PROFILE

Average base starting salary: $38,000

ST. JOHN FISHER COLLEGE
BITTNER SCHOOL OF BUSINESS

ADMISSIONS CONTACT: MR. JOSE PERALES, DIRECTOR OF TRANSFER/GRADUATE ADMISSIONS
ADDRESS: 3690 EAST AVENUE, SKALNY WELCOME CENTER, ROCHESTER, NY 14618
PHONE: 585.385.8161 • FAX: 585.385.8344
E-MAIL: GRAD@SJFC.EDU
WEBSITE: WWW.SJFC.EDU/ACADEMICS/BITTNER/ABOUT/INDEX.DOT

GENERAL INFORMATION

Type of school: Private Academic calendar: Semester

STUDENTS

Enrollment of parent institution: 3,987 Enrollment of MBA Program: 148 % male/female: 61/39 % out-of-state: 4 % part-time: 66 % underrepresented minority: 14 % international: 0 Average age at entry: 29

ACADEMICS

Student/faculty ratio: 15:1 % female faculty: 11 % underrepresented minority faculty: 0 % part-time faculty: 42

FINANCIAL FACTS

Annual tuition (in-state/out-of-state): Cost of books: $900 Room & board: (on/off-campus) % of students receiving aid: 80 % of first-year students receiving aid: 87 % of students receiving grants: 47 Average award package: $14,057 Average grant: $4,347 Average loan: $18,157

ADMISSIONS

Admissions Selectivity Rating: 74

# of applications received: 97 % applicants accepted: 74 % acceptees attending: 67 Average GMAT: 502 Range of GMAT: 400–600 Average GPA: 3.41 TOEFL required of international students: Yes Minimum TOEFL (paper/computer): 575/233 Application fee: $30 International Application fee: $30

Deferment available: Yes Maximum length of deferment: One Semester Transfer students accepted: Yes Transfer application

policy: Students can request transfer credit for graduate course work taken at accredited institutions. These credits must have been taken in an appropriate graduate program related to MBA graduate program of study. Only courses with a grade of "B" or better will be considered and the course must have been taken within 7 years prior to beginning graduate study at Fisher. A maximum of 9 credits may be permitted as transfer credit. Non-fall admissions: Yes Need-blind admissions: Yes

STEPHEN F. AUSTIN STATE UNIVERSITY
NELSON RUSCHE COLLEGE OF BUSINESS

ADMISSIONS CONTACT: MICHAEL D. STROUP, MBA DIRECTOR
ADDRESS: PO BOX 13004, SFA STATION, STEPHEN F. AUSTIN STATE UNIVERSITY, NACOGDOCHES, TX 75962-3004
PHONE: 936-468-3101 • FAX: 936-468-1560
E-MAIL: MBA@SFASU.EDU • WEBSITE: WWW.COB.SFASU.EDU

GENERAL INFORMATION

Type of school: Public

STUDENTS

Enrollment of parent institution: 10,000 Enrollment of MBA Program: 45 % male/female: 60/40 % out-of-state: 5 % part-time: 50 % underrepresented minority: 25 % international: 15 Average age at entry: 25 Average years work experience at entry: 3.0

ACADEMICS

Student/faculty ratio: 10:1 % female faculty: 30 % underrepresented minority faculty: 10 % part-time faculty: 0

FINANCIAL FACTS

Annual tuition (in-state/out-of-state): $1,134/ $7,236 Fees: $126 Cost of books: $1,000 Room & board: (on/off-campus) $5,000/$6,500 % of students receiving aid: 15 % of first-year students receiving aid: 5 % of students receiving grants: 0 Average award package: $3,500 Average grant: $3,500

ADMISSIONS

Admissions Selectivity Rating: 60*

# of applications received: 60 Average GMAT: 510 Range of GMAT: 290–660 Average GPA: 3.00 TOEFL required of international students: Yes Minimum TOEFL (paper/computer): 550/213 Application fee: $25 International Application fee: $50 Early application deadline: 7/1 Early notification date: 8/1 Regular application deadline: 8/1 Regular application notification: 8/15

Deferment available: Yes Maximum length of deferment: 1 year Transfer students accepted: Yes Transfer application policy: Applicant may transfer in 6 hours graduate credit from an AACSB - International Accredited school. Non-fall admissions: Yes Need-blind admissions: Yes

EMPLOYMENT PROFILE

Average base starting salary: $52,000

Grads Employed by Function ......% Avg. Salary

Marketing: ....(25%) $45,000

Consulting: ....(20%) $45,000

Management: ....(15%) $65,000

TENNESSEE STATE UNIVERSITY
TENNESSEE STATE UNIVERSITY

ADMISSIONS CONTACT: SHARON THACH, COORDINATOR, MBA
ADDRESS: 330 10TH AVENUE NORTH, SUITE K, NASHVILLE, TN 37203
PHONE: 615-963-7133 • FAX: 615-963-7139
E-MAIL: MBA@TNSTATE.EDU • WEBSITE: WWW.COB.TNSTATE.EDU

GENERAL INFORMATION

Type of school: Public **Academic calendar:** Semesters (3)

STUDENTS

Enrollment of MBA Program: 102 **% part-time:** 80 **% international:** 20

ACADEMICS

Student/faculty ratio: 12:1 **% female faculty:** 15 **% part-time faculty:** 0

FINANCIAL FACTS

Annual tuition (in-state/out-of-state): $15,000/ $360,000 **Cost of books:** $2,000 **% of students receiving aid:** 10 **% of students receiving grants:** 5

ADMISSIONS

Admissions Selectivity Rating: 60*

Average GMAT: 510 **Average GPA:** 3.20 **TOEFL required of international students:** Yes **Minimum TOEFL (paper/computer):** 500/173 **Application fee:** $25

Application Deadline/Notification:

Round 1: 7/1

Round 2: 11/1

Round 3: 4/1

Deferment available: Yes **Maximum length of deferment:** 1 year **Transfer students accepted:** Yes **Transfer application policy:** Non AACSB on appeal 12 credits from AACSB college **Non-fall admissions:** No **Need-blind admissions:** Yes

TENNESSEE TECH UNIVERSITY
COLLEGE OF BUSINESS

ADDRESS: BOX 5023 TTU, 1105 N. PEACHTREE JH 112, COOKEVILLE, TN 38505
PHONE: 931-372-3600 • FAX: 931-372-6544
E-MAIL: MBASTUDIES@TNTECH.EDU • WEBSITE: WWW.TNTECH.EDU/MBA/

GENERAL INFORMATION

Type of school: Public **Academic calendar:** Semester

STUDENTS

Enrollment of parent institution: 11,469 **Enrollment of MBA Program:** 188 **% male/female:** 67/33 **% out-of-state:** 7 **% part-time:** 70 **% underrepresented minority:** 4 **% international:** 5 **Average age at entry:** 28 **Average years work experience at entry:** 4.0

ACADEMICS

Student/faculty ratio: 25:1 **% female faculty:** 27 **% underrepresented minority faculty:** 17 **% part-time faculty:** 0

FINANCIAL FACTS

Cost of books: $1,500 **Room & board: (on/off-campus)** $7,760/$10,800 **% of students receiving aid:** 50 **% of first-year students receiving aid:** 45 **% of students receiving grants:** 25

ADMISSIONS

Admissions Selectivity Rating: 76

# of applications received: 151 **% applicants accepted:** 70 **% acceptees attending:** 72 **Average GMAT:** 533 **Range of GMAT:** 490–590 **Average GPA:** 3.35 **TOEFL required of international students:** Yes **Minimum TOEFL (paper/computer):** 550/213 **Application fee:** $25 **International Application fee:** $30

Deferment available: Yes **Maximum length of deferment:** 1 year **Transfer students accepted:** Yes **Transfer application policy:** TTU will transfer 9 hours or less from an AACSB accredited school. Student must satisfy admission requirements. **Non-fall admissions:** Yes **Need-blind admissions:** Yes

EMPLOYMENT PROFILE

Top 5 Employers Hiring Grads (number of hires in last class)

Nissan, FedEx, Tennessee Valley Authority, HCA Corporation, Asurion

TEXAS A&M UNIVERSITY-COMMERCE
COLLEGE OF BUSINESS AND TECHNOLOGY

ADMISSIONS CONTACT: VICKY TURNER, GRADUATE ADMISSIONS
ADDRESS: P O BOX 3011, COMMERCE, TX 75429
PHONE: 903-886-5167 • FAX: 903-886-5165
E-MAIL: GRADUATE_SCHOOL@TAMU-COMMERCE.EDU
WEBSITE: WWW.TAMU-COMMERCE.EDU/GRADUATEPROGRAMS

GENERAL INFORMATION

Type of school: Public **Academic calendar:** Semester

STUDENTS

Enrollment of parent institution: 8,875 **Enrollment of MBA Program:** 489 **% male/female:** 56/44 **% part-time:** 61 **% underrepresented minority:** 53 **% international:** 23 **Average age at entry:** 22 **Average years work experience at entry:** 0.0

ACADEMICS

Student/faculty ratio: 27:1 **% female faculty:** 10 **% underrepresented minority faculty:** 10 **% part-time faculty:** 20

FINANCIAL FACTS

Annual tuition (in-state/out-of-state): $7,000/ $18,000 **Cost of books:** $1,000 **Room & board: (on/off-campus)** $2,950/$2,200

ADMISSIONS

Admissions Selectivity Rating: 75

# of applications received: 1,215 % applicants accepted: 60 % acceptees attending: 65 Average GMAT: 460 Range of GMAT: 380–620 Average GPA: 3.00 TOEFL required of international students: Yes Minimum TOEFL (paper/computer): 500/173 Application fee: $35 International Application fee: $50 Early application deadline: 1/1 Regular application deadline: 6/1

Deferment available: Yes Maximum length of deferment: 2 Semesters Transfer students accepted: Yes Transfer application policy: Students can transfer up to 9 SH for the 30-33 HR. Non-fall admissions: Yes Need-blind admissions: No

UNION GRADUATE COLLEGE
SCHOOL OF MANAGEMENT

ADMISSIONS CONTACT: ERIN WHEELER, DIRECTOR OF STUDENT RECRUITMENT
ADDRESS: 80 NOTT TERRACE, SCHENECTADY, NY 12308
PHONE: 518-631-9850 • FAX: 518-631-9901
E-MAIL: INFO@UNIONGRADUATECOLLEGE.EDU
WEBSITE: WWW.UNIONGRADUATECOLLEGE.EDU

GENERAL INFORMATION

Type of school: Private

STUDENTS

Enrollment of parent institution: 756 Enrollment of MBA Program: 247 % male/female: 56/44 % out-of-state: 5 % part-time: 44 % underrepresented minority: 9 % international: 4 Average age at entry: 25 Average years work experience at entry: 2.0

ACADEMICS

Student/faculty ratio: 15:1 % female faculty: 22 % underrepresented minority faculty: 11 % part-time faculty: 75

FINANCIAL FACTS

Annual tuition (in-state/out-of-state): $25,400/ $25,400 Fees: $125 Cost of books: $1,200 Room & board: (on/off-campus) /$8,800 Average award package: $19,435 Average grant: $3,866 Average loan: $21,368 Average student loan debt: $56,000

ADMISSIONS

Admissions Selectivity Rating: 72

# of applications received: 91 % applicants accepted: 96 % acceptees attending: 94 Average GMAT: 560 Range of GMAT: 510–590 Average GPA: 3.33 TOEFL required of international students: Yes Minimum TOEFL (paper/computer): 550/213 Application fee: $60 International Application fee: $60

Deferment available: Yes Maximum length of deferment: 1 year Transfer students accepted: Yes Transfer application policy: Will accepted up to 8 transfer courses. Non-fall admissions: Yes Need-blind admissions: Yes

EMPLOYMENT PROFILE

Percent employed at graduation: 70 Percent employed 3 months after graduation: 86 Average base starting salary: $48,000

Grads Employed by Function ......% Avg. Salary

Marketing:	(13%)
Operations:	(13%)
Consulting:	(2%)
Management:	(11%)
Finance:	(29%)
HR:	(8%)
MIS:	(8%)
Other:	(16%)

Top 5 Employers Hiring Grads (number of hires in last class)

General Electric, Albany Medical Center

UNIVERSITÉ LAVAL
FACULTÉ DES SCIENCES DE L'ADMINISTRATION

ADDRESS: PAVILLON PALASIS PRINCE, 2325 RUE DE LA TERRASSE, QUÉBEC, QC
G1V 0A6 CANADA
PHONE: 418-656-3080 • FAX: 418-656-5216
E-MAIL: REG@REG.ULAVAL.CA • WEBSITE: WWW.FSA.ULAVAL.CA

GENERAL INFORMATION

Type of school: Public Academic calendar: Semester

STUDENTS

Enrollment of parent institution: 40,690 Enrollment of MBA Program: 110 % male/female: 58/42 % part-time: 54 % international: 25 Average age at entry: 28 Average years work experience at entry: 4.0

ACADEMICS

Student/faculty ratio: 25:1 % female faculty: 36 % part-time faculty: 0

FINANCIAL FACTS

Annual tuition (in-state/out-of-state): $2,233/ $12,157 Room & board: (on/off-campus) $3,500/$9,200

ADMISSIONS

Admissions Selectivity Rating: 68

# of applications received: 1,305 % applicants accepted: 52 % acceptees attending: 45 Average GPA: 3.22 TOEFL required of international students: Yes Minimum TOEFL (paper/computer): 550/213 Application fee: $64 International Application fee: $64 Early application deadline: 3/1 Regular application deadline: 3/1

Deferment available: Yes Maximum length of deferment: 1 year Transfer students accepted: No Non-fall admissions: Yes Need-blind admissions: No

EMPLOYMENT PROFILE

Percent employed at graduation: 46 Percent employed 3 months after graduation: 66

Top 5 Employers Hiring Grads (number of hires in last class)

Desjardins, Université Laval, Quebec government, Genivar, Arcelot Mittal

UNIVERSITY COLLEGE DUBLIN
MICHAEL SMURFIT GRADUATE SCHOOL OF BUSINESS

ADMISSIONS CONTACT: ELAINE MCAREE, ADMISSIONS MANAGER
ADDRESS: CARYSFORT AVENUE, BLACKROCK, DUBLIN, IRELAND
PHONE: 00353 1 7168862 • FAX: 00353 1 7168981
E-MAIL: MBA@UCD.IE • WEBSITE: WWW.SMURFITSCHOOL.IE

GENERAL INFORMATION
Type of school: Public Academic calendar: Sept-Aug

STUDENTS
Enrollment of MBA Program: 126 % male/female: 75/25 % part-time: 63 % international: 40

ACADEMICS
Student/faculty ratio: 2:1 % female faculty: 30

FINANCIAL FACTS
Annual tuition (in-state/out-of-state):$29,500 Fees: $29,500 Cost of books: $1,000 Room & board: (on/off-campus) $5,000/$5,500 Average award package: $14,750

ADMISSIONS
Admissions Selectivity Rating: 87

# of applications received: 363 % applicants accepted: 48 % acceptees attending: 73 Average GMAT: 630 TOEFL required of international students: Yes Minimum TOEFL (paper/computer): 600/250 International Early application deadline: 12/15 Early notification date: 1/15 Regular application deadline: 7/10 Regular application notification: 7/20

Application Deadline/Notification:

Round 1: 3/27
Round 2: 5/15
Round 3: 7/10

Deferment available: Yes Maximum length of deferment: 1 year Transfer students accepted: Yes Transfer application policy: Credit is may be awarded on the basis of ECTS (European Credit Transfer System) equivalency from accredited business schools only. Non-fall admissions: No Need-blind admissions: Yes

UNIVERSITY OF ALABAMA IN HUNTSVILLE
COLLEGE OF BUSINESS ADMINISTRATION

ADMISSIONS CONTACT: DR. DAVID BERKOWITZ, ASSOCIATE DEAN FOR GRADUATE PROGRAMS
ADDRESS: BAB 368, HUNTSVILLE, AL 35899
PHONE: 256-824-6681 • FAX: 256-824-7571
E-MAIL: GRADBIZ@UAH.EDU • WEBSITE: WWW.UAH.EDU

GENERAL INFORMATION
Type of school: Public Academic calendar: Semester

STUDENTS
Enrollment of MBA Program: 59 % male/female: 61/39 % part-time: 61 % international: 15 Average age at entry: 29 Average years work experience at entry: 5.0

ACADEMICS
Student/faculty ratio: 9:1 % female faculty: 22 % underrepresented minority faculty: 47 % part-time faculty: 39

FINANCIAL FACTS
Annual tuition (in-state/out-of-state): $10,671/ $25,518 Fees: $17 Cost of books: $1,700 Room & board: (on/off-campus) $9,410 % of students receiving aid: 12 % of first-year students receiving aid: 1 Average grant: $0 Average loan: $0

ADMISSIONS
Admissions Selectivity Rating: 73

# of applications received: 70 % applicants accepted: 87 % acceptees attending: 97 Average GMAT: 556 Range of GMAT: 480–570 Average GPA: 3.23 TOEFL required of international students: Yes Application fee: $40 International Application fee: $50

Application Deadline/Notification:

Round 1: 7/18
Round 2: 11/30
Round 3: 4/30

Deferment available: No Transfer students accepted: Yes Transfer application policy: transfer credit evaluated by program advisor Non-fall admissions: Yes Need-blind admissions: Yes

EMPLOYMENT PROFILE
Grads Employed by Function ......% Avg. Salary
Marketing: ....(%) $60,000
Top 5 Employers Hiring Grads (number of hires in last class)
RedStone Arsenal, Boeing, ADTRAN, NASA, SAIC

UNIVERSITY OF ALASKA ANCHORAGE
COLLEGE OF BUSINESS AND PUBLIC POLICY

ADMISSIONS CONTACT: AL KASTAR, DIRECTOR OF ADMISSIONS
ADDRESS: PO BOX 141629, ANCHORAGE, AK 99514-1629
PHONE: 907-786-1480 • FAX: 907-786-4888
E-MAIL: AYADMIT@UAA.ALASKA.EDU
WEBSITE: HTTP://WWW.CBPP.UAA.ALASKA.EDU/BUSADMIN.ASP

GENERAL INFORMATION
Type of school: Public Academic calendar: Sep - May

STUDENTS
Enrollment of MBA Program: 143 % male/female: 43/57 % out-of-state: 28 % part-time: 66 % underrepresented minority: 33 % international: 9

ACADEMICS
Student/faculty ratio: 28:1 % female faculty: 6 % underrepresented minority faculty: 39

FINANCIAL FACTS

Annual tuition (in-state/out-of-state): $5,688/ $11,628 **Fees:** $590
Cost of books: $900 **Room & board: (on/off-campus)** $8,980

ADMISSIONS

Admissions Selectivity Rating: 66

# of applications received: 79 % **applicants accepted:** 76 %
acceptees attending: 78 **Average GPA:** 3.06 **TOEFL required of
international students:** Yes **Minimum TOEFL (paper/computer):**
550/80 **Application fee:** $60

Deferment available: Yes **Maximum length of deferment:** 1 year
Transfer students accepted: Yes **Transfer application policy:**
Applicants must meet all UAA and MBA admissions requirements.
Up to 9 Semester credits not previously used to obtain any other
degree or certificate may be transferred to UAA from a regionally
accredited institution and accepted toward a graduate degree or certificate. **Non-fall admissions:** Yes **Need-blind admissions:** Yes

UNIVERSITY OF ALASKA FAIRBANKS
SCHOOL OF MANAGEMENT

ADMISSIONS CONTACT: NANCY DIX, DIRECTOR
ADDRESS: P.O. BOX 757480, FAIRBANKS, AK 99775
PHONE: 907-474-7500 • FAX: 907-474-5379
E-MAIL: ADMISSIONS@UAF.EDU • WEBSITE: WWW.UAFSOM.COM/GPMBA.HTML

GENERAL INFORMATION

Type of school: Public

STUDENTS

Enrollment of parent institution: 5,025 **Enrollment of MBA
Program:** 30 **Average age at entry:** 32 **Average years work experience at entry:** 10.3

ACADEMICS

Student/faculty ratio: 3:1 % **female faculty:** 30 % **underrepresented minority faculty:** 20

FINANCIAL FACTS

Annual tuition (in-state/out-of-state): $4,824/ $9,846 **Fees:** $670
Cost of books: $1,076 **Room & board: (on/off-campus)**
$6,030/$10,413 **Average grant:** $16,928 **Average loan:** $6,083
Average student loan debt: $12,166

ADMISSIONS

Admissions Selectivity Rating: 60*

% acceptees attending: 92 **Average GMAT:** 547 **Average GPA:** 3.51
TOEFL required of international students: Yes **Minimum TOEFL
(paper/computer):** 550/213 **Application fee:** $50 **International
Application fee:** $50 **Regular application deadline:** 8/1 **Regular
application notification:** 8/1

Deferment available: Yes **Maximum length of deferment:** 1 year
Transfer students accepted: Yes **Transfer application policy:** We
take up to 3 courses. **Non-fall admissions:** Yes **Need-blind admissions:** Yes

UNIVERSITY OF ARKANSAS AT LITTLE ROCK
COLLEGE OF BUSINESS

*ADMISSIONS CONTACT: DR. SONYA PREMEAUX, ASSOCIATE DEAN FOR GRADUATE
STUDIES*
ADDRESS: 2801 SOUTH UNIVERSITY AVENUE, LITTLE ROCK, AR 72204
PHONE: 501-569-3356 • FAX: 501-569-8898
WEBSITE: UALR.EDU/COB

GENERAL INFORMATION

Type of school: Public **Academic calendar:** Semester

STUDENTS

Enrollment of parent institution: 9,925 **Enrollment of MBA
Program:** 225 % **male/female:** 58/42 % **out-of-state:** 1 % **part-
time:** 87 % **underrepresented minority:** 8 % **international:** 15
Average age at entry: 29 **Average years work experience at entry:**
0.0

ACADEMICS

% part-time faculty: 19

FINANCIAL FACTS

Annual tuition (in-state/out-of-state): $30,500/ $30,500

ADMISSIONS

Admissions Selectivity Rating: 65

# of applications received: 87 % **applicants accepted:** 66 %
acceptees attending: 74 **TOEFL required of international students:**
Yes **Minimum TOEFL (paper):** 550

Deferment available: Yes **Maximum length of deferment:** text
marker **Transfer students accepted:** No **Non-fall admissions:** No
Need-blind admissions: No

EMPLOYMENT PROFILE

Average base starting salary: $40,000

UNIVERSITY OF BALTIMORE
MERRICK SCHOOL OF BUSINESS

ADMISSIONS CONTACT: DEAN DREIBELBIS, ASSISTANT DIRECTOR OF ADMISSIONS
ADDRESS: 1420 NORTH CHARLES STREET, BALTIMORE, MD 21201
PHONE: 888-664-0125 • FAX: 410-837-4774
E-MAIL: MBA@TOWSON.UBALT.EDU • WEBSITE: WWW.UBTOWSONMBA.COM

GENERAL INFORMATION

Type of school: Public **Academic calendar:** Semester

STUDENTS

Enrollment of parent institution: 5,240 **Enrollment of MBA
Program:** 518 % **male/female:** 58/42 % **out-of-state:** 17 % **part-
time:** 77 % **underrepresented minority:** 15 % **international:** 37

Average age at entry: 30 **Average years work experience at entry:** 4.0

ACADEMICS

Student/faculty ratio: 15:1 % female faculty: 30 % underrepresented minority faculty: 34

FINANCIAL FACTS

Cost of books: $900

ADMISSIONS

Admissions Selectivity Rating: 84

# of applications received: 434 % applicants accepted: 44 % acceptees attending: 81 **Average GMAT:** 525 **Range of GMAT:** 480–535 **Average GPA:** 3.15 **TOEFL required of international students:** Yes **Minimum TOEFL (paper/computer):** 550/213 **Application fee:** $30 **International Application fee:** $30

Deferment available: Yes **Maximum length of deferment:** 1 year **Transfer students accepted:** Yes **Transfer application policy:** Maximun 6 credits accepted in transfer. Must be from an AACSB accredited MBA program. **Non-fall admissions:** Yes **Need-blind admissions:** Yes

UNIVERSITY OF CENTRAL MISSOURI
HARMON COLLEGE OF BUSINESS ADMINISTRATION

ADMISSIONS CONTACT: LAURIE DELAP, ADMISSIONS EVALUATOR, GRADUATE SCHOOL
ADDRESS: WARD EDWARDS 1800, WARRENSBURG, MO 64093
PHONE: 660-543-4328 • FAX: 660-543-4778
E-MAIL: DELAP@UCMO.EDU • WEBSITE: WWW.UCMO.EDU/MBA

GENERAL INFORMATION

Type of school: Public **Academic calendar:** Semester

STUDENTS

Enrollment of parent institution: 10,980 **Enrollment of MBA Program:** 66 **% male/female:** 63/37 **% out-of-state:** 39 **% part-time:** 30 **% underrepresented minority:** 6 **% international:** 28 **Average age at entry:** 26 **Average years work experience at entry:** 2.0

ACADEMICS

Student/faculty ratio: 2:1 % female faculty: 30 % underrepresented minority faculty: 3 % part-time faculty: 0

FINANCIAL FACTS

Annual tuition (in-state/out-of-state): $5,904/ $11,808 **Fees:** $604 **Cost of books:** $1,200 **Room & board: (on/off-campus)** $6,000/$6,000 **% of students receiving aid:** 60 **% of students receiving grants:** 35 **Average grant:** $4,500

ADMISSIONS

Admissions Selectivity Rating: 80

# of applications received: 93 % applicants accepted: 55 % acceptees attending: 71 **Average GMAT:** 517 **Range of GMAT:** 450–560 **Average GPA:** 3.37 **TOEFL required of international students:** Yes **Minimum TOEFL (paper/computer):** 550/213 **Application

fee: $30 International Application fee: $50

Deferment available: Yes **Maximum length of deferment:** 2 Semesters **Transfer students accepted:** Yes **Transfer application policy:** A maximum of 9 hours may be transferred and a "B" or higher is required for each transferred course. **Non-fall admissions:** Yes **Need-blind admissions:** Yes

UNIVERSITY OF COLORADO AT BOULDER
LEEDS SCHOOL OF BUSINESS

ADMISSIONS CONTACT: ANNE SANDOE, DIRECTOR OF MBA PROGRAMS
ADDRESS: 995 REGENT DRIVE, 419 UCB, BOULDER, CO 80309-0419
PHONE: 303-492-8397 • FAX: 303-492-1727
E-MAIL: LEEDSMBA@COLORADO.EDU • WEBSITE: LEEDS.COLORADO.EDU/MBA

GENERAL INFORMATION

Type of school: Public **Academic calendar:** Semester

STUDENTS

Enrollment of parent institution: 30,000 **Enrollment of MBA Program:** 282 **% male/female:** 75/25 **% out-of-state:** 54 **% part-time:** 0 **% underrepresented minority:** 14 **% international:** 23 **Average age at entry:** 29 **Average years work experience at entry:** 5.0

ACADEMICS

% female faculty: 28 % underrepresented minority faculty: 20 % part-time faculty: 28

FINANCIAL FACTS

Annual tuition (in-state/out-of-state): $15,282/ $29,898 **Fees:** $1,436 **Cost of books:** $1,998 **Room & board: (on/off-campus)** /$17,388 **% of students receiving grants:** 25 **Average grant:** $2,726 **Average student loan debt:** $26,517

ADMISSIONS

Admissions Selectivity Rating: 80

# of applications received: 299 % applicants accepted: 62 % acceptees attending: 45 **Average GMAT:** 630 **Range of GMAT:** 590–670 **Average GPA:** 3.32 **TOEFL required of international students:** Yes **Minimum TOEFL (paper/computer):** 600/250 **Application fee:** $70 **International Application fee:** $70 **Early application deadline:** 11/15 **Early notification date:** 2/15 **Regular application deadline:** 4/1 **Regular application notification:** 6/15

Application Deadline/Notification:

Round 1: 11/152/15
Round 2: 1/154/15
Round 3: 4/16/15

Deferment available: Yes **Maximum length of deferment:** for 1 year **Transfer students accepted:** No **Non-fall admissions:** No **Need-blind admissions:** Yes

EMPLOYMENT PROFILE

Percent employed at graduation: 50 **Percent employed 3 months after graduation:** 18 **Average base starting salary:** $76,750

Primary Source of Full-time Job Acceptances

School-facilitated activities: 25(41%) **Graduate-facilitated activities:** 20(33%) Unknown: 16(26%)

Grads Employed by Function ......% Avg. Salary

Marketing: ....(33%) $69,059

Operations: ....(7%)

Consulting: ....(12%) $93,143

Management: ....(7%)

Finance:...(28%) $77,563

HR: ....(3%)

MIS: ....(0%)

Other: ....(12%) $8,500

Top 5 Employers Hiring Grads (number of hires in last class)

Covidien (3), Datalogix (3), Deloitte Consulting (2), Level 3 (2), UDR (2)

UNIVERSITY OF COLORADO AT COLORADO SPRINGS
GRADUATE SCHOOL OF BUSNIESS ADMINISTRATION

ADMISSIONS CONTACT: JOLENE SCHAULAND, MBA ADMISSIONS COORDINATOR ADDRESS: GRADUATE SCHOOL OF BUSINESS ADMINISTRATION, 1420 AUSTIN BLUFFS PARKWAY, COLORADO SPRINGS, CO 80918 PHONE: 719-255-3122 • FAX: 719-255-3100 E-MAIL: MBACRED@UCCS.EDU • WEBSITE: WWW.UCCS.EDU/MBA

GENERAL INFORMATION

Type of school: Public **Academic calendar:** Semester

STUDENTS

Enrollment of MBA Program: 346 **% part-time:** 100 **Average age at entry:** 31 **Average years work experience at entry:** 5.0

ACADEMICS

Student/faculty ratio: 10:1 **% female faculty:** 11 **% underrepresented minority faculty:** 1 **% part-time faculty:** 11

ADMISSIONS

Admissions Selectivity Rating: 74

# of applications received: 94 **% applicants accepted:** 78 **% acceptees attending:** 73 **Average GMAT:** 540 **Range of GMAT:** 500–580 **Average GPA:** 3.25 **TOEFL required of international students:** Yes **Minimum TOEFL (paper/computer):** 550/213 **Application fee:** $60 **International Application fee:** $75

Application Deadline/Notification:

Round 1: 6/1

Round 2: 11/1

Round 3: 4/1

Deferment available: Yes **Maximum length of deferment:** 1 year

Transfer students accepted: Yes **Transfer application policy:** Students may transfer up to a maximum of 6 credit credit hours from another AACSB-accredited school. All potential transfer courses must be approved by the program director and members of the graduate faculty. **Non-fall admissions:** Yes **Need-blind admissions:** Yes

UNIVERSITY OF COLORADO DENVER
BUSINESS SCHOOL

ADMISSIONS CONTACT: SHELLY TOWNLEY, DIRECTOR OF GRADUATE ADMISSIONS ADDRESS: CAMPUS BOX 165, PO BOX 173364, DENVER, CO 80217-3364 PHONE: 303-315-8200 • FAX: 303-315-8199 E-MAIL: GRAD.BUSINESS@UCDENVER.EDU. WEBSITE: WWW.BUSINESS.CUDENVER.EDU

GENERAL INFORMATION

Type of school: Public **Academic calendar:** Semester

STUDENTS

Enrollment of parent institution: 19,089 **Enrollment of MBA Program:** 790 **% male/female:** 63/37 **% out-of-state:** 48 **% part-time:** 67 **% underrepresented minority:** 7 **% international:** 7 **Average age at entry:** 28 **Average years work experience at entry:** 0.0

ACADEMICS

Student/faculty ratio: 35:1

FINANCIAL FACTS

Annual tuition (in-state/out-of-state): $7,844/ $18,638 **Fees:** $594 **Cost of books:** $1,700 **Room & board (on/off-campus)** $9,950/$8,110 **% of students receiving aid:** 61 **% of first-year students receiving aid:** 24 **% of students receiving grants:** 22 **Average award package:** $7,380 **Average grant:** $4,640 **Average loan:** $6,696 **Average student loan debt:** $33,815

ADMISSIONS

Admissions Selectivity Rating: 75

# of applications received: 265 **% applicants accepted:** 72 **% acceptees attending:** 77 **Average GMAT:** 547 **Range of GMAT:** 500–590 **Average GPA:** 3.16 **TOEFL required of international students:** Yes **Minimum TOEFL (paper/computer):** 525/197 **Application fee:** $50 **International Application fee:** $75 **Regular application deadline:** 6/1

Deferment available: Yes **Maximum length of deferment:** 1 year **Transfer students accepted:** Yes **Transfer application policy:** Varies by student and program **Non-fall admissions:** Yes **Need-blind admissions:** Yes

EMPLOYMENT PROFILE

Average base starting salary: $57,903

Grads Employed by Function ......% Avg. Salary

Marketing: ....(%) $61,250

Management: ....(%) $62,143

Finance:..(%) $50,625

UNIVERSITY OF DELAWARE
ALFRED LERNER COLLEGE OF BUSINESS & ECONOMICS

ADMISSIONS CONTACT: DENISE WATERS, DIRECTOR RECRUITMENT & ADMISSIONS
ADDRESS: 103 ALFRED LERNER HALL, NEWARK, DE 19716
PHONE: 302-831-2221 • FAX: 302-831-3329
E-MAIL: MBAPROGRAM@UDEL.EDU • WEBSITE: SITES.UDEL.EDU/GRADBIZ/

GENERAL INFORMATION

Type of school: Public **Academic calendar:** Semester

STUDENTS

Enrollment of parent institution: 20,000 **Enrollment of MBA Program:** 348 **% male/female:** 51/49 **% out-of-state:** 81 **% part-time:** 71 **% underrepresented minority:** 8 **% international:** 69 **Average age at entry:** 32 **Average years work experience at entry:** 5.0

ACADEMICS

Student/faculty ratio: 18:1 **% female faculty:** 21 **% underrepresented minority faculty:** 4 **% part-time faculty:** 34

FINANCIAL FACTS

Annual tuition (in-state/out-of-state): $13,620/ $27,240 **Fees:** $850 **Cost of books:** $2,000 **Room & board: (on/off-campus)** $9,500/$11,000 **% of students receiving aid:** 37 **% of first-year students receiving aid:** 30 **Average award package:** $29,495

ADMISSIONS

Admissions Selectivity Rating: 84

# of applications received: 240 **% applicants accepted:** 40 **% acceptees attending:** 42 **Average GMAT:** 570 **Average GPA:** 3.10 **TOEFL required of international students:** Yes **Minimum TOEFL (paper/computer):** 600/260 **Application fee:** $75 **International Application fee:** $75 **Early application deadline:** 2/1 **Regular application deadline:** 6/1

Deferment available: Yes **Maximum length of deferment:** One academic year **Transfer students accepted:** Yes **Transfer application policy:** Up to nine Semester hours of graduate credit earned at another AACSB accredited institution may be accepted toward the University of Delaware MBA degree. The courses must have completed with grades of "B" or better and within five years of the date of the requested transfer. Only those credits earned at an American Academy of Collegiate Schools of Business (AACSB) accredited institution are transferable and only after the candidate has completed at least nine credit hours as a matriculated MBA Program student at the University of Delaware. The student must submit a written request for credit evaluation and a waiver examination may be required. (Only the credits — not the grades — are transferable. **Non-fall admissions:** Yes **Need-blind admissions:** Yes

EMPLOYMENT PROFILE

Percent employed at graduation: 64 **Percent employed 3 months after graduation:** 29 **Average base starting salary:** $73,000

Primary Source of Full-time Job Acceptances

School-facilitated activities: 15(43%) **Graduate-facilitated activities:** 6(17%) **Unknown:** 14(40%)

Grads Employed by Function ......% Avg. Salary

Marketing: ....(20%) $73,000

Consulting: ....(20%) $61,000

Finance:..(40%) $58,000

MIS: ....(20%) $66,000

Top 5 Employers Hiring Grads (number of hires in last class)

Ashland (2), J.P.Morgan (6), DuPont (4), Siegfried (2), AAA (6)

UNIVERSITY OF DETROIT MERCY
COLLEGE OF BUSINESS ADMINISTRATION

ADMISSIONS CONTACT: STEVEN CODDINGTON, ASSISTANT DIRECTOR OF ADMISSIONS
ADDRESS: 4001 W. MCNICHOLS ROAD, DETROIT, MI 48221-3038
PHONE: 313-993-1245 • FAX: 313-993-3326
E-MAIL: ADMISSIONS@UDMERCY.EDU • WEBSITE: WWW.BUSINESS.UDMERCY.EDU

GENERAL INFORMATION

Type of school: Private **Academic calendar:** Semester

STUDENTS

Enrollment of parent institution: 5,550 **Enrollment of MBA Program:** 200 **Average age at entry:** 29 **Average years work experience at entry:** 5.0

ACADEMICS

Student/faculty ratio: 30:1 **% female faculty:** 17 **% underrepresented minority faculty:** 13 **% part-time faculty:** 26

FINANCIAL FACTS

Annual tuition (in-state/out-of-state): $11,970/ **Fees:** $570 **Cost of books:** $1,200 **Room & board: (on/off-campus)** $4,125 **Average grant:** $40,000 **Average loan:** $18,500

ADMISSIONS

Admissions Selectivity Rating: 60*

Average GMAT: 541 **Range of GMAT:** 410–720 **Average GPA:** 3.35 **TOEFL required of international students:** No

Application Deadline/Notification:

Round 1: 8/15

Round 2: 12/15

Round 3: 4/15

Round 4: 5/15

Deferment available: Yes **Maximum length of deferment:** 2 years **Transfer students accepted:** Yes **Transfer application policy:** Must submit transcripts and a GMAT for MBA program. GMAT can be waived. See website for conditions. **Non-fall admissions:** Yes **Need-blind admissions:** No

EMPLOYMENT PROFILE

Average base starting salary: $57,000

Top 5 Employers Hiring Grads (number of hires in last class)
Chrysler, Ford Motor, Bank One, Comerica, Henry Ford Health systems

UNIVERSITY OF HAWAII AT MANOA
SHIDLER COLLEGE OF BUSINESS

ADMISSIONS CONTACT: MICHELLE GARCIA, MBA ADMISSIONS DIRECTOR
ADDRESS: 2404 MAILE WAY, G202, HONOLULU, HI 96822
PHONE: 808-956-8266 • FAX: 808-956-9890
E-MAIL: MBA@HAWAII.EDU • WEBSITE: WWW.SHIDLER.HAWAII.EDU

GENERAL INFORMATION

Type of school: Public **Academic calendar:** Semester

STUDENTS

Enrollment of parent institution: 50,000 **Enrollment of MBA Program:** 75 **% male/female:** 69/31 **% out-of-state:** 56 **% part-time:** 40 **% underrepresented minority:** 58 **% international:** 18 **Average age at entry:** 28 **Average years work experience at entry:** 5.0

ACADEMICS

Student/faculty ratio: 25:1 **% female faculty:** 5 **% underrepresented minority faculty:** 10 **% part-time faculty:** 22

FINANCIAL FACTS

Annual tuition (in-state/out-of-state): $6,456/ $9,912 **Fees:** $300 **Cost of books:** $1,200 **Room & board: (on/off-campus)** $13,517/$13,517

ADMISSIONS

Admissions Selectivity Rating: 88

# of applications received: 224 **% applicants accepted:** 46 **% acceptees attending:** 73 **Average GMAT:** 628 **Range of GMAT:** 590–670 **Average GPA:** 3.30 **TOEFL required of international students:** Yes **Minimum TOEFL (paper/computer):** 600/250 **Application fee:** $60 **International Application fee:** $60 **Early application deadline:** 3/1 **Early notification date:** 5/1 **Regular application deadline:** 5/1 **Regular application notification:** 7/1

Application Deadline/Notification:

Round 1: 11/151/15
Round 2: 1/153/15
Round 3: 3/15/1
Round 4: 5/17/1

Deferment available: No **Transfer students accepted:** Yes **Transfer application policy:** Credits may be transferred into the Part-time MBA program from other AACSB-accredited business schools, from other University of Hawaii graduate programs, or by petition as follows: Nine credits of coursework may be transferred into the PT MBA program. Transfer credit is appropriate for both Core classes(upon approval) and electives. Due to the cohort nature of the program, FT MBA's may not transfer in any credits. **Non-fall admissions:** No **Need-blind admissions:** Yes

UNIVERSITY OF HOUSTON— CLEAR LAKE
SCHOOL OF BUSINESS

ADMISSIONS CONTACT: JANICE SAURWEIN, INTERIM REGISTRAR/DIRECTOR, ACADEMIC RECORDS
ADDRESS: 2700 BAY AREA BLVD, HOUSTON, TX 77058-1098
PHONE: 281-283-2500 • FAX: 281-283-2522
E-MAIL: ADMISSIONS@UHCL.EDU • WEBSITE: WWW.UHCL.EDU

GENERAL INFORMATION

Type of school: Public **Academic calendar:** Semester

STUDENTS

Enrollment of parent institution: 7,288 **Enrollment of MBA Program:** 368 **% male/female:** 55/45 **% out-of-state:** 10 **% part-time:** 62 **% underrepresented minority:** 23 **% international:** 15 **Average age at entry:** 30 **Average years work experience at entry:** 5.0

ACADEMICS

Student/faculty ratio: 18:1 **% female faculty:** 31 **% underrepresented minority faculty:** 19 **% part-time faculty:** 0

FINANCIAL FACTS

Annual tuition (in-state/out-of-state): $3,600/ $13,608 **Fees:** $9,504 **Cost of books:** $1,800 **Room & board: (on/off-campus)** $12,836/$12,836 **% of students receiving aid:** 20 **Average award package:** $8,300 **Average grant:** $1,000 **Average loan:** $8,000 **Average student loan debt:** $26,916

ADMISSIONS

Admissions Selectivity Rating: 70

# of applications received: 148 **% applicants accepted:** 80 **% acceptees attending:** 42 **Average GMAT:** 507 **Range of GMAT:** 460–570 **Average GPA:** 2.86 **TOEFL required of international students:** Yes **Minimum TOEFL (paper/computer):** 550/213 **Application fee:** $35 **International Application fee:** $75 **Regular application deadline:** 8/1

Deferment available: Yes **Maximum length of deferment:** 12 months **Transfer students accepted:** Yes **Transfer application policy:** Final 24 Semester hours earned at UHCL-BUS **Non-fall admissions:** Yes **Need-blind admissions:** Yes

UNIVERSITY OF LONDON
LONDON BUSINESS SCHOOL

ADMISSIONS CONTACT: CAROLINE CHUKWUMANOEL CALISTE, CLIENT SERVICES OFFICER
ADDRESS: REGENT'S PARK, LONDON NW1 4SA, UNITED KINGDOM OF GREAT BRITAIN AND NORTHERN IRELAND
PHONE: +44 (0)20 7000 7500 • FAX: +44 (0)20 7000 7501
E-MAIL: MBAINFO@LONDON.EDU • WEBSITE: WWW.LONDON.EDU

GENERAL INFORMATION
Type of school: Public **Academic calendar:** August - July

STUDENTS
Average age at entry: 28

FINANCIAL FACTS
Annual tuition (in-state/out-of-state): **Cost of books:** $345 **Room & board: (on/off-campus)** /$22,500 **% of students receiving grants:** 30 **Average award package:** $76,250 **Average loan:** $62,245 **Average student loan debt:** $65,500

ADMISSIONS
Admissions Selectivity Rating: 60*

# of applications received: 2,765 **Average GMAT:** 697 **Range of GMAT:** 600–790 **TOEFL required of international students:** Yes

Application Deadline/Notification:

Round 1: 10/7 12/17
Round 2: 1/6 3/26
Round 3: 3/35 21
Round 4: 4/21 7/5

Deferment available: No **Transfer students accepted:** No **Non-fall admissions:** No **Need-blind admissions:** Yes

EMPLOYMENT PROFILE
Percent employed 3 months after graduation: 81 **Average base starting salary:** $108,212

Primary Source of Full-time Job Acceptances

School-facilitated activities: (77%) **Graduate-facilitated activities:** (23%) **Unknown:** (%)

Top 5 Employers Hiring Grads (number of hires in last class)

McKinsey & Company (21), Credit Suisse (9), The Boston Consulting Group (10), Barclays Group (11), Booz & Company (7)

UNIVERSITY OF MAINE
MAINE BUSINESS SCHOOL

ADMISSIONS CONTACT: CAROL L. MANDZIK, MANAGER OF MBA PROGRAMS
ADDRESS: 5723 DP CORBETT BUSINESS BUILDING, ORONO, ME 04469-5723
PHONE: 207-581-1971 • FAX: 207-581-1930
E-MAIL: CAROL.MANDZIK@MAINE.EDU • WEBSITE: WWW.UMAINE.EDU/BUSINESS

GENERAL INFORMATION
Type of school: Public **Academic calendar:** Semester

STUDENTS
Enrollment of parent institution: 10,901 **Enrollment of MBA Program:** 54 **% male/female:** 87/13 **% out-of-state:** 18 **% part-time:** 30 **% underrepresented minority:** 1 **% international:** 1 **Average age at entry:** 27 **Average years work experience at entry:** 7.0

ACADEMICS
Student/faculty ratio: 7:1 **% female faculty:** 31 **% underrepresented minority faculty:** 1 **% part-time faculty:** 5

FINANCIAL FACTS
Annual tuition (in-state/out-of-state): $7,524/ $21,636 **Fees:** $1,102 **Cost of books:** $800 **Room & board: (on/off-campus)** $10,466/$10,466 **% of students receiving aid:** 80 **% of students receiving grants:** 55 **Average grant:** $5,000

ADMISSIONS
Admissions Selectivity Rating: 81

# of applications received: 38 **% applicants accepted:** 58 **% acceptees attending:** 50 **Average GMAT:** 572 **Range of GMAT:** 490–640 **Average GPA:** 3.69 **TOEFL required of international students:** No **Minimum TOEFL (paper/computer):** 550/213 **Application fee:** $65 **International Application fee:** $65 **Early application deadline:** 1/15 **Early notification date:** 1/20 **Regular application deadline:** 6/1 **Regular application notification:** 7/1

Deferment available: Yes **Maximum length of deferment:** 1 year **Transfer students accepted:** Yes **Transfer application policy:** A maximum of 6 hours accepted from accredited schools **Non-fall admissions:** Yes **Need-blind admissions:** Yes

UNIVERSITY OF MANITOBA
I.H. ASPER SCHOOL OF BUSINESS

ADMISSIONS CONTACT: EWA MORPHY, GRADUATE PROGRAM MANAGER
ADDRESS: 324 DRAKE CENTER, WINNIPEG, MB R3T 5V4 CANADA
PHONE: 204-474-8448 • FAX: 204-474-7544
E-MAIL: ASPERMBA@UMANITOBA.CA • WEBSITE: WWW.UMANITOBA.CA/ASPER

GENERAL INFORMATION
Type of school: Public **Academic calendar:** Term based

STUDENTS
Enrollment of parent institution: 27,000 **Enrollment of MBA Program:** 160 **% male/female:** 60/40 **% part-time:** 75 **% international:** 9 **Average age at entry:** 30 **Average years work experience at entry:** 5.5

ACADEMICS
Student/faculty ratio: 30:1 **% female faculty:** 18 **% underrepresented minority faculty:** 32 **% part-time faculty:** 24

FINANCIAL FACTS
Annual tuition (in-state/out-of-state): $23,000/ $32,000 **Cost of books:** $3,000 **Room & board: (on/off-campus)** $6,000/$14,000 **Average grant:** $2,000

ADMISSIONS
Admissions Selectivity Rating: 83

# of applications received: 155 **Average GMAT:** 582 **Range of GMAT:** 500–720 **Average GPA:** 3.00 **TOEFL required of international students:** Yes **Minimum TOEFL (paper/computer):** 550/213 **Application fee:** $100 **International Application fee:** $100 **Regular application deadline:** 5/1

Deferment available: No **Transfer students accepted:** Yes **Transfer application policy:** To earn an Asper MBA, at least half of the courses must be completed at Asper School of Business **Non-fall admissions:** Yes

EMPLOYMENT PROFILE

Percent employed at graduation: 75 **Percent employed 3 months after graduation:** 85 **Average base starting salary:** $80,000

Grads Employed by Function ......% Avg. Salary
Marketing: ....(5%)

UNIVERSITY OF MINNESOTA DULUTH

LABOVITZ SCHOOL OF BUSINESS AND ECONOMICS

ADMISSIONS CONTACT: CARLEE WILLIAMS, DGS ASSISTANT
ADDRESS: 385 LSBE, 1318 KIRBY DRIVE, DULUTH, MN 55812
PHONE: 218-726-7757 • FAX: 218-726-7578
E-MAIL: UMDGRAD@UMN.EDU • WEBSITE: HTTP://Z.UMN.EDU/MBA/

GENERAL INFORMATION

Type of school: Public **Academic calendar:** Semester

STUDENTS

Enrollment of parent institution: 12,000 **Enrollment of MBA Program:** % **part-time:** 100 **Average age at entry:** 33 **Average years work experience at entry:** 8.0

ACADEMICS

Student/faculty ratio: 20:1 % **female faculty:** 23

FINANCIAL FACTS

Annual tuition (in-state/out-of-state): **Cost of books:** $1,000 **Room & board: (on/off-campus)** /$6,000

ADMISSIONS

Admissions Selectivity Rating: 68

# of applications received: 80 % **applicants accepted:** 96 **Average GMAT:** 585 **Range of GMAT:** 470–680 **Average GPA:** 3.35 **TOEFL required of international students:** Yes **Minimum TOEFL (paper/computer):** 550/213 **Application fee:** $75 **International Application fee:** $95 **Regular application deadline:** 7/15 **Regular application notification:** 9/1

Application Deadline/Notification:
Round 1: 7/158/31
Round 2: 11/112/31
Round 3: 5/15/30

Deferment available: Yes **Maximum length of deferment:** 1 year without reapp **Transfer students accepted:** Yes **Transfer application policy:** No more than 12 graduate credits can be transferred into program. **Non-fall admissions:** Yes **Need-blind admissions:** Yes

UNIVERSITY OF NEBRASKA AT OMAHA

COLLEGE OF BUSINESS ADMINISTRATION

ADMISSIONS CONTACT: LEX KACZMAREK, DIRECTOR, MBA PROGRAM
ADDRESS: 6708 PINE STREET, OMAHA, NE 68182-0048
PHONE: 402-554-2303 • FAX: 402-554-3747
E-MAIL: MBA@UNOMAHA.EDU • WEBSITE: CBA.UNOMAHA.EDU/MBA

GENERAL INFORMATION

Type of school: Public **Academic calendar:** Semester

STUDENTS

Enrollment of parent institution: 14,712 **Enrollment of MBA Program:** 276 % **male/female:** 69/31 % **out-of-state:** 19 % **part-time:** 83 % **underrepresented minority:** 6 % **international:** 21 **Average age at entry:** 26 **Average years work experience at entry:** 4.0

ACADEMICS

Student/faculty ratio: 9:1 % **female faculty:** 30 % **underrepresented minority faculty:** 6 % **part-time faculty:** 19

FINANCIAL FACTS

Annual tuition (in-state/out-of-state): $0/ $0 **Fees:** $0 **Cost of books:** $0 **Room & board: (on/off-campus)** $8,500/$9,000 % **of students receiving aid:** 3 % **of first-year students receiving aid:** 4 % **of students receiving grants:** 3 **Average grant:** $11,732

ADMISSIONS

Admissions Selectivity Rating: 83

# of applications received: 67 **Average GMAT:** 575 **Range of GMAT:** 530–610 **Average GPA:** 3.43 **TOEFL required of international students:** Yes **Minimum TOEFL (paper/computer):** 550/213 **Application fee:** $45 **International Application fee:** $45 **Regular application deadline:** 7/1

Deferment available: Yes **Maximum length of deferment:** 1 year **Transfer students accepted:** Yes **Transfer application policy:** A maximum of nine hours of transfer credit may be accepted from another accredited (AACSB) institution. **Non-fall admissions:** Yes **Need-blind admissions:** Yes

UNIVERSITY OF NEBRASKA— LINCOLN

COLLEGE OF BUSINESS ADMINISTRATION

ADMISSIONS CONTACT: STEPHANIE OSTERTHUN, ON-CAMPUS MBA PROGRAM COORDINATOR/ADVISOR
ADDRESS: CBA 139, LINCOLN, NE 68588-0405
PHONE: 402-472-2338 • FAX: 402-472-5997
E-MAIL: CBAGRAD@UNL.EDU • WEBSITE: WWW.CBA.UNL.EDU

GENERAL INFORMATION

Type of school: Public **Academic calendar:** Semester

STUDENTS

Enrollment of parent institution: 24,207 **Enrollment of MBA Program:** 269 **% male/female:** 75/25 **% out-of-state:** 38 **% part-time:** 71 **% underrepresented minority:** 6 **% international:** 13 **Average age at entry:** 28 **Average years work experience at entry:** 2.7

ACADEMICS

Student/faculty ratio: 6:1 **% female faculty:** 25 **% underrepresented minority faculty:** 16 **% part-time faculty:** 16

FINANCIAL FACTS

Annual tuition (in-state/out-of-state): $6,345/ $17,109 **Fees:** $1,280 **Cost of books:** $1,032 **Room & board: (on/off-campus)** $9,722/$9,248 **% of students receiving aid:** 27 **% of first-year students receiving aid:** 38 **% of students receiving grants:** 12 **Average award package:** $12,821 **Average grant:** $5,861 **Average loan:** $12,294 **Average student loan debt:** $27,796

ADMISSIONS

Admissions Selectivity Rating: 82

# of applications received: 119 **% applicants accepted:** 61 **% acceptees attending:** 60 **Average GMAT:** 620 **Range of GMAT:** 600–650 **Average GPA:** 3.39 **TOEFL required of international students:** Yes **Minimum TOEFL (paper/computer):** 550/213 **Application fee:** $50 **International Application fee:** $50 **Early application deadline:** 3/1 **Regular application deadline:** 6/15

Deferment available: Yes **Maximum length of deferment:** 1 year **Transfer students accepted:** Yes **Transfer application policy:** 12 credit hours may be accepted from an AACSB accredited institution if approved by the MBA Committee **Non-fall admissions:** Yes **Need-blind admissions:** Yes

EMPLOYMENT PROFILE

Average base starting salary: $65,873

Grads Employed by Function	%	Avg. Salary
Marketing:	(14%)	$51,667
Operations:	(20%)	$66,600
Consulting:	(9%)	$42,500
Management:	(15%)	$72,760
Finance:	(8%)	$98,000
HR:	(1%)	
MIS:	(2%)	$59,500
Other:	(10%)	$45,000

Top 5 Employers Hiring Grads (number of hires in last class)
Cerner Corporation (2), IBM (2), Sandhills Publishing (2), Union Pacific Railroad (2)

UNIVERSITY OF NEW MEXICO

ROBERT O. ANDERSON GRADUATE SCHOOL OF MANAGEMENT

ADMISSIONS CONTACT: MEGAN CONNER, MANAGER, ACADEMIC ADVISEMENT
ADDRESS: THE UNIVERSITY OF NEW MEXICO, MSC05 3090, 1 UNIVERSITY OF NEW MEXICO, ALBUQUERQUE, NM 87131
PHONE: 505-277-3290 • FAX: 505-277-8436
E-MAIL: MCONNER@MGT.UNM.EDU • WEBSITE: WWW.MGT.UNM.EDU/

GENERAL INFORMATION

Type of school: Public **Academic calendar:** Semester

STUDENTS

Enrollment of parent institution: 36,722 **Enrollment of MBA Program:** 479 **% male/female:** 55/45 **% out-of-state:** 8 **% part-time:** 44 **% underrepresented minority:** 43 **% international:** 8 **Average age at entry:** 28 **Average years work experience at entry:**

ACADEMICS

Student/faculty ratio: 17:1 **% female faculty:** 27 **% underrepresented minority faculty:** 35 **% part-time faculty:** 39

FINANCIAL FACTS

Annual tuition (in-state/out-of-state): $10,401/ $25,171 **Fees:** $1,256 **Cost of books:** $1,080 **Room & board: (on/off-campus)** $8,068/$8,518 **% of students receiving aid:** 70 **% of first-year students receiving aid:** 69 **% of students receiving grants:** 43 **Average award package:** $12,710 **Average grant:** $5,171 **Average loan:** $14,105

ADMISSIONS

Admissions Selectivity Rating: 79

# of applications received: 284 **% applicants accepted:** 68 **% acceptees attending:** 79 **Average GMAT:** 554 **Range of GMAT:** 510–600 **Average GPA:** 3.49 **TOEFL required of international students:** Yes **Minimum TOEFL (paper/computer):** 550/213 **Application fee:** $50 **International Application fee:** $50 **Regular application deadline:** 4/1

Deferment available: Yes **Maximum length of deferment:** 1 Year **Transfer students accepted:** Yes **Transfer application policy:** Up to 12 credit hours may transfer **Non-fall admissions:** Yes **Need-blind admissions:** Yes

EMPLOYMENT PROFILE

Percent employed at graduation: 12 **Average base starting salary:** $51,434

Primary Source of Full-time Job Acceptances
School-facilitated activities: 15(21%) **Graduate-facilitated activities:** 42(60%) Unknown: 13(19%)

Grads Employed by Function ......% Avg. Salary

Marketing: ....(10%) $40,833

Operations: ....(1%)

Consulting: ....(4%) $58,000

Finance:...(33%) $50,363

HR: ....(3%) $42,500

MIS: ....(13%) $52,544

Other: ....(36%) $51,507

Top 5 Employers Hiring Grads (number of hires in last class)

Sandia National Laboratories (16), University of New Mexico (4), USDA Forest Service (2), KPMG (2), Thornburg Investments (1)

UNIVERSITY OF NEW ORLEANS
COLLEGE OF BUSINESS ADMINSTRATION

DIRECTOR OF ADMISSIONS
ADDRESS: ADMIN BLDG RM 103, 2000 LAKESHORE DRIVE, NEW ORLEANS, LA 70148
PHONE: 504-280-6595 • FAX: 504-280-5522
E-MAIL: ADMISSIONS@UNO.EDU • WEBSITE: WWW.UNO.EDU

GENERAL INFORMATION

Type of school: Public **Academic calendar:** Semester

STUDENTS

Enrollment of parent institution: 10,903 **Enrollment of MBA Program:** 384 **% male/female:** 70/30 % **out-of-state:** 19 % **part-time:** 40 % **underrepresented minority:** 15 % **international:** 13 **Average age at entry:** 29

ACADEMICS

Student/faculty ratio: 24:1 **% female faculty:** 25 % **underrepresented minority faculty:** 20 % **part-time faculty:** 3

FINANCIAL FACTS

Annual tuition (in-state/out-of-state): $4,644/ $16,168 **Fees:** $4,467 **Cost of books:** $1,300 **Room & board: (on/off-campus)** $11,793/$11,793 **% of students receiving aid:** 47 % **of first-year students receiving aid:** 54 % **of students receiving grants:** 8 **Average award package:** $13,504 **Average grant:** $2,643 **Average loan:** $14,663

ADMISSIONS

Admissions Selectivity Rating: 80

# of applications received: 274 **% applicants accepted:** 44 % **acceptees attending:** 85 **Average GMAT:** 481 **Range of GMAT:** 440–540 **TOEFL required of international students:** Yes **Minimum TOEFL (paper/computer):** 550/213 **Application fee:** $50 **International Application fee:** $50 **Early application deadline:** 7/1 **Regular application deadline:** 8/1

Deferment available: Yes **Maximum length of deferment:** 1 Semester **Transfer students accepted:** Yes **Transfer application policy:** maximum number of credit hours transferrable = 12 **Non-fall admissions:** Yes **Need-blind admissions:** Yes

THE UNIVERSITY OF NEW SOUTH WALES (UNSW)
AGSM MBA PROGRAMS

ADMISSIONS CONTACT: RECRUITMENT & ADMISSIONS,
ADDRESS: AGSM BUILDING, UNSW, SYDNEY NSW, 02052 AUSTRALIA
PHONE: 0061 2 99319490 • FAX: 0061 2 99319205
E-MAIL: ADMISSIONS@AGSM.EDU.AU
WEBSITE: WWW.AGSM.EDU.AU/FUTURELEADERS

GENERAL INFORMATION

Type of school: Public

STUDENTS

Enrollment of MBA Program: % male/female: 81/19 % part-time: 0 % international: 56 **Average age at entry:** 29 **Average years work experience at entry:** 7.0

ACADEMICS

Student/faculty ratio: 4:1 **% female faculty:** 36 % **underrepresented minority faculty:** 0 % **part-time faculty:** 6

FINANCIAL FACTS

Annual tuition (in-state/out-of-state): $46,170/ $46,170 **Cost of books:** $2,000 **Room & board: (on/off-campus)** /$20,000

ADMISSIONS

Admissions Selectivity Rating: 90

Average GMAT: 664 **Range of GMAT:** 620–700 **Average GPA:** 3.00 **TOEFL required of international students:** No **Minimum TOEFL (paper/computer):** 577/ **Application fee:** $50 **International Application fee:** $50

Application Deadline/Notification:

Round 1: 6/16/30

Round 2: 8/18/31

Round 3: 10/310/31

Deferment available: Yes **Maximum length of deferment:** 1 year **Transfer students accepted:** Yes **Transfer application policy:** Transfer applicants must submit a completed application and meet all entry requirements; entry is January each year only; recognition of prior learning may be offered only for core courses correlations. **Non-fall admissions:** No **Need-blind admissions:** Yes

EMPLOYMENT PROFILE

Percent employed 3 months after graduation: 3 **Average base starting salary:** $116,411

Grads Employed by Function ......% Avg. Salary

Marketing: ....:....................(9%) $104,500

Consulting: ....(35%) $109,923

Management: ....(13%) $81,190

Finance:...(17%) $92,821

Other: ....(4%) $78,413

Top 5 Employers Hiring Grads (number of hires in last class)

ABN AMRO, American Express (Brazil), Australian Stock Exchange, Australian Campus Network, Bain & Company

UNIVERSITY OF NORTH TEXAS
COLLEGE OF BUSINESS

ADMISSIONS CONTACT: STACY SCHIED OR BRANDI EVERETT, GRADUATE ACADEMIC ADVISORS
ADDRESS: P.O. BOX 311160, DENTON, TX 76203
PHONE: 940-369-8977 • FAX: 940-369-8978
E-MAIL: MBACOB@UNT.EDU • WEBSITE: WWW.COB.UNT.EDU

·GENERAL INFORMATION

Type of school: Public **Academic calendar:** Semester

STUDENTS

Enrollment of parent institution: 35,778 **Enrollment of MBA Program:** 338 **% male/female:** 43/57 **% part-time:** 67 **% underrepresented minority:** 27 **% international:** 34 **Average age at entry:** 28 **Average years work experience at entry:** 2.3

ACADEMICS

Student/faculty ratio: 7:1 **% female faculty:** 22 **% underrepresented minority faculty:** 10 **% part-time faculty:** 0

FINANCIAL FACTS

Annual tuition (in-state/out-of-state): $7,863/ $17,340 **Fees:** $2,189 **Cost of books:** $1,000 **Room & board: (on/off-campus)** $11,166/$17,100

ADMISSIONS

Admissions Selectivity Rating: 76

# of applications received: 229 **% applicants accepted:** 69 **% acceptees attending:** 83 **Average GMAT:** 515 **Range of GMAT:** 460–560 **Average GPA:** 3.35 **TOEFL required of international students:** Yes **Minimum TOEFL (paper/computer):** 550/213 **Application fee:** $60 **International Application fee:** $95 **Regular application deadline:** 7/15

Deferment available: Yes **Maximum length of deferment:** Three Semesters **Transfer students accepted:** Yes **Transfer application policy:** Transfer applicants must meet the same university application deadline. Only six to nine hours may transfer into our program. These hours will be determined by the departmental advisor. **Non-fall admissions:** Yes **Need-blind admissions:** Yes

UNIVERSITY OF QUEENSLAND
UQ BUSINESS SCHOOL

ADMISSIONS CONTACT: THE MANAGER, STUDENT ADMIN,
ADDRESS: UQ BUSINESS SCHOOL, THE UNIVERSITY OF QUEENSLAND, ST LUCIA, Q 04072 AUSTRALIA
PHONE: 011-617-3365 6475 • FAX: 011-617-3365 6988
E-MAIL: POSTGRAD_ENQUIRIES@BUSINESS.UQ.EDU.AU
WEBSITE: WWW.BUSINESS.UQ.EDU.AU

GENERAL INFORMATION

Type of school: Private

STUDENTS

Average years work experience at entry: 0.0

FINANCIAL FACTS

Annual tuition (in-state/out-of-state): $17,050/

ADMISSIONS

Admissions Selectivity Rating: 60*

TOEFL required of international students: No **Regular application deadline:** 1/30 **Regular application notification:** 1/30

UNIVERSITY OF SOUTH ALABAMA
MITCHELL COLLEGE OF BUSINESS

ADMISSIONS CONTACT: OFFICE OF ADMISSIONS,
ADDRESS: MEISLER HALL SUITE 2500, MOBILE, AL 36688-0002
PHONE: 251-460-6141 • FAX: 251-460-7876
E-MAIL: ADMISS@USOUTHAL.EDU • WEBSITE: MCOB.SOUTHALABAMA.EDU/

GENERAL INFORMATION

Type of school: Public

STUDENTS

Enrollment of parent institution: 13,500 **Enrollment of MBA Program:** 135 **% male/female:** 55/45 **% out-of-state:** 0 **% part-time:** 0 **% underrepresented minority:** 55 **% international:** 10 **Average age at entry:** 28 **Average years work experience at entry:** 0.0

ACADEMICS

Student/faculty ratio: 31:1 **% female faculty:** 21 **% underrepresented minority faculty:** 10 **% part-time faculty:** 0

FINANCIAL FACTS

Annual tuition (in-state/out-of-state): $4,008/ $8,016 **Fees:** $2,460 **Cost of books:** $1,200 **Room & board: (on/off-campus)** $4,750/$7,200 **Average grant:** $0 **Average loan:** $0

ADMISSIONS

Admissions Selectivity Rating: 74

# of applications received: 80 **% applicants accepted:** 78 **% acceptees attending:** 73 **Average GMAT:** 550 **Average GPA:** 3.40 **TOEFL required of international students:** Yes **Minimum TOEFL (paper/computer):** 525/ **Application fee:** $25 **International Application fee:** $25 **Regular application deadline:** 7/15 **Regular application notification:** 7/25

Deferment available: No **Transfer students accepted:** Yes **Transfer application policy:** May transfer in up to 9 credits toward degeree. **Non-fall admissions:** No **Need-blind admissions:** Yes

UNIVERSITY OF SOUTH FLORIDA
COLLEGE OF BUSINESS

ADMISSIONS CONTACT: IRENE HURST, DIRECTOR OF MBA PROGRAMS
ADDRESS: 4202 E. FOWLER AVE.   BSN 3403, LOC BSN 103, TAMPA, FL 33620
PHONE: 813-974-3335 • FAX: 813-974-4518
E-MAIL: MBA@COBA.USF.EDU • WEBSITE: BUSINESS.USF.EDU

GENERAL INFORMATION

Type of school: Public **Academic calendar:** Semester

STUDENTS

Enrollment of parent institution: 47,854 **Enrollment of MBA Program:** 269 % male/female: 87/13 % out-of-state: 5 % part-time: 61 % underrepresented minority: 7 % international: 11 **Average age at entry:** 29 **Average years work experience at entry:** 8.0

ACADEMICS

Student/faculty ratio: 5:1 % female faculty: 14 % underrepresented minority faculty: 26 % part-time faculty: 0

FINANCIAL FACTS

Annual tuition (in-state/out-of-state): $10,410/ $20,600 **Fees:** $37 **Cost of books:** $2,500 **Room & board: (on/off-campus)** $10,500/$11,000 % of students receiving aid: 40 % of students receiving grants: 8 **Average award package:** $6,870 **Average grant:** $2,000 **Average student loan debt:** $36,873

ADMISSIONS

Admissions Selectivity Rating: 72

# of applications received: 162 % applicants accepted: 82 % acceptees attending: 71 **Average GMAT:** 547 **Range of GMAT:** 500–580 **Average GPA:** 3.21 **TOEFL required of international students:** Yes **Minimum TOEFL (paper/computer):** 550/213 **Application fee:** $30 **International Application fee:** $30

Deferment available: Yes **Maximum length of deferment:** 1 year **Transfer students accepted:** Yes **Transfer application policy:** 12 credits from an AACSB University with grades of B or better. **Non-fall admissions:** Yes **Need-blind admissions:** Yes

EMPLOYMENT PROFILE

Percent employed at graduation: 10 **Percent employed 3 months after graduation:** 10 **Average base starting salary:** $59,167

Primary Source of Full-time Job Acceptances

School-facilitated activities: 4(40%) **Graduate-facilitated activities:** 2(20%) Unknown: 4(40%)

Grads Employed by Function	% Avg. Salary
Marketing:	(%)
Operations:	(0%)
Consulting:	(10%)
Management:	(10%)
Finance:	(20%) $41,500
HR:	(0%)
MIS:	(10%)
Other:	(50%) $68,000

Top 5 Employers Hiring Grads (number of hires in last class)
Gerdau (2), Ernst&Young (1), Harkness & Associates (1), Citi (2), Ecleptic (1)

UNIVERSITY OF SOUTH FLORIDA ST. PETERSBURG
COLLEGE OF BUSINESS

ADDRESS: 140 SEVENTH AVENUE SOUTH, BAY 104, ST. PETERSBURG, FL 33701
PHONE: 727-873-4142 • FAX: 727-873-4525
E-MAIL: ADMISSIONS@STPT.USF.EDU • WEBSITE: WWW.STPT.USF.EDU

GENERAL INFORMATION

Type of school: Public

STUDENTS

Enrollment of parent institution: 0 **Enrollment of MBA Program:** 162 % male/female: 100/0 % out-of-state: 0 % part-time: 100 % underrepresented minority: 0 % international: 0 **Average age at entry:** 29 **Average years work experience at entry:** 4.0

ACADEMICS

Student/faculty ratio: 9:1 % female faculty: 39 % underrepresented minority faculty: 6 % part-time faculty: 11

ADMISSIONS

Admissions Selectivity Rating: 83

# of applications received: 75 % applicants accepted: 59 % acceptees attending: 82 **Average GMAT:** 568 **Range of GMAT:** 530–590 **Average GPA:** 3.44 **TOEFL required of international students:** No **Minimum TOEFL (paper/computer):** 550/213 **Application fee:** $30 **International Application fee:** $30 **Regular application deadline:** 7/1 **Regular application notification:** 7/8

Deferment available: Yes **Maximum length of deferment:** 1 year **Transfer students accepted:** Yes **Transfer application policy:** Students who meet our admission criteria may import up to two courses (6 credit hours) from any AACSB accredit business school. Courses require MBA Director approval **Non-fall admissions:** Yes **Need-blind admissions:** Yes

UNIVERSITY OF SOUTHERN INDIANA
COLLEGE OF BUSINESS

ADMISSIONS CONTACT: DR. WESLEY DURHAM, INTERIM DIRECTOR OF GRADUATE STUDIES
ADDRESS: 8600 UNIVERSITY BOULVARD, ROBERT D. ORR CENTER 1063, EVANSVILLE, IN 47712
PHONE: 812-465-7015 • FAX: 812-228-5018
E-MAIL: GSSR@USI.EDU • WEBSITE: BUSINESS.USI.EDU

GENERAL INFORMATION

Type of school: Public **Academic calendar:** Semester

STUDENTS

Enrollment of parent institution: 10,467 Enrollment of MBA Program: 86 % male/female: 67/33 % out-of-state: 8 % part-time: 86 % underrepresented minority: 17 % international: 17 Average age at entry: 28 Average years work experience at entry: 7.0

ACADEMICS

Student/faculty ratio: 21:1 % female faculty: 6 % underrepresented minority faculty: 22 % part-time faculty: 0

FINANCIAL FACTS

Annual tuition (in-state/out-of-state): $5,292/ $10,458 Fees: $240 Cost of books: $1,200 Room & board: (on/off-campus) $7,600/$9,640 % of students receiving aid: 24 % of first-year students receiving aid: 34 % of students receiving grants: 8 Average award package: $8,733 Average grant: $5,310 Average loan: $10,445

ADMISSIONS

Admissions Selectivity Rating: 72

# of applications received: 40 % applicants accepted: 90 % acceptees attending: 89 Average GMAT: 534 Range of GMAT: 498–575 Average GPA: 3.33 TOEFL required of international students: Yes Minimum TOEFL (paper/computer): 550/213 Application fee: $40 International Application fee: $40

Deferment available: No Transfer students accepted: Yes Transfer application policy: Twelve accepted hours can be transferred into the program Non-fall admissions: Yes Need-blind admissions: Yes

THE UNIVERSITY OF SOUTHERN MISSISSIPPI
COLLEGE OF BUSINESS

ADMISSIONS CONTACT: GABRIEL MCPHEARSON, ASSISTANT TO THE DIRECTOR
ADDRESS: 118 COLLEGE DRIVE #5096, HATTIESBURG, MS 39406-5096
PHONE: 601-266-4653 • FAX: 601-266-5814
E-MAIL: MBA@USM.EDU • WEBSITE: WWW.USM.EDU/MBA

GENERAL INFORMATION

Type of school: Public Academic calendar: Semester

STUDENTS

Enrollment of parent institution: 15,030 Enrollment of MBA Program: 93 % male/female: 58/42 % out-of-state: 24 % part-time: 59 % underrepresented minority: 8 % international: 8 Average age at entry: 27 Average years work experience at entry: 0.0

ACADEMICS

Student/faculty ratio: 30:1 % female faculty: 25 % underrepresented minority faculty: 15 % part-time faculty: 0

FINANCIAL FACTS

Annual tuition (in-state/out-of-state): $4,312/ $4,312 Fees: $0 Cost of books: $1,600 Room & board: (on/off-campus) $5,800/$7,600 % of students receiving aid: 75 % of students receiving grants: 25 Average grant: $8,690 Average loan: $2,000

ADMISSIONS

Admissions Selectivity Rating: 80

# of applications received: 73 % applicants accepted: 56 % acceptees attending: 76 Average GMAT: 508 Range of GMAT: 450–560 Average GPA: 3.36 TOEFL required of international students: Yes Minimum TOEFL (paper/computer): 550/213 Application fee: $25 International Application fee: $25 Regular application deadline: 7/15

Deferment available: Yes Maximum length of deferment: 2 Semesters Transfer students accepted: Yes Transfer application policy: They must fully apply to the program and can only transfer a total of 6 hours of graduate courses from other accredited institutions. The coursework must be graded (i.e., not pass/fail.) Non-fall admissions: Yes Need-blind admissions: Yes

EMPLOYMENT PROFILE

Average base starting salary: $43,179

Grads Employed by Function	%	Avg. Salary
Marketing:	(15%)	$35,000
Operations:	(7%)	$48,600
Management:	(23%)	$37,301
Finance:	(15%)	$35,056
Other:	(31%)	$58,375

Top 5 Employers Hiring Grads (number of hires in last class)
Cintas, Frito Lay, Walgreen's, Sherman Williams Co., AmSouth Bank

UNIVERSITY OF ST. GALLEN (SWITZERLAND)
UNIVERSITY OF ST. GALLEN

ADMISSIONS CONTACT: PEGGY VAN DER WALLEN, ADMISSIONS MANAGER
ADDRESS: BLUMENBERGPLATZ 9, ST. GALLEN, CH 09000 SWITZERLAND
PHONE: 41712247355 • FAX: 41712242473
E-MAIL: MBA@UNISG.CH • WEBSITE: WWW.MBA.UNISG.CH

GENERAL INFORMATION

Type of school: Public

FINANCIAL FACTS

Annual tuition: $56,000 Room & board: $22,000

ADMISSIONS

Admissions Selectivity Rating: 60*

TOEFL required of international students: No Minimum TOEFL (paper/computer): 600/250 Application fee: $0 International Application fee: $0

Application Deadline/Notification:

Round 1: 12/112/15

Round 2: 2/12/15

Round 3: 4/14/15

Round 4: 6/16/15

Deferment available: Yes **Transfer students accepted:** No **Non-fall admissions:** No **Need-blind admissions:** No

UNIVERSITY OF STRATHCLYDE, GLASGOW

UNIVERSITY OF STRATHCLYDE GRADUATE SCHOOL OF BUSINESS

ADMISSIONS CONTACT: 141-553- 6118, LUCY REYNOLDS
ADDRESS: 199 CATHEDRAL STREET, GLASGOW, G4 0QU
PHONE: 141-553-6118 • FAX: 141-553-6162
E-MAIL: ADMISSIONS@GSB.STRATH.AC.UK • WEBSITE: WWW.GSB.STRATH.AC.UK

GENERAL INFORMATION

Type of school: Private

STUDENTS

Enrollment of MBA Program: 107 % male/female: 86/14 % part-time: 37 % underrepresented minority: 88 % international: 84 **Average age at entry:** 32 **Average years work experience at entry:** 9.0

ACADEMICS

Student/faculty ratio: 4:1 % female faculty: 11 % part-time faculty: 2

FINANCIAL FACTS

Annual tuition (in-state/out-of-state): $0/ **Fees:** $31,600 **Cost of books:** $150 **Room & board: (on/off-campus)** $13,500/$15,300 **Average loan:** $0

ADMISSIONS

Admissions Selectivity Rating: 71

# of applications received: 280 % applicants accepted: 90 % acceptees attending: 42 **Average GMAT:** 560 **Average GPA:** 3.40 **TOEFL required of international students:** Yes **Minimum TOEFL (paper/computer):** 600/250 **International Application fee:** $0

Deferment available: Yes **Maximum length of deferment:** 2 years **Transfer students accepted:** No **Non-fall admissions:** Yes

EMPLOYMENT PROFILE

Average base starting salary: $124,000

Grads Employed by Function ......% Avg. Salary

Marketing: ....(5%) $85,500

Consulting: ....(10%) $142,000

Finance:...(13%) $130,000

Other: ....(41%) $95,000

Top 5 Employers Hiring Grads (number of hires in last class)

Mott McDonald (4), BT (3), RBoS (1), Standard Life (1), Prince and Princess of Wales Hospice (1)

THE UNIVERSITY OF TEXAS AT EL PASO

COLLEGE OF BUSINESS ADMINISTRATION

ADMISSIONS CONTACT: LAURA URIBARRI, ASSISTANT DEAN OF MBA PROGRAMS
ADDRESS: COLLEGE OF BUSINESS ADMINISTRATION,RM 102, 500 W UNIVERSITY AVENUE, EL PASO, TX 79968
PHONE: 915-747-7726 • FAX: 915-532-8213
E-MAIL: MBA@UTEP.EDU • WEBSITE: WWW.MBA.UTEP.EDU

GENERAL INFORMATION

Type of school: Public **Academic calendar:** Semester

STUDENTS

Enrollment of parent institution: 22,740 **Enrollment of MBA Program:** 261 % male/female: 66/35 % out-of-state: 2 % part-time: 18 % underrepresented minority: 58 % international: 15 **Average age at entry:** 34 **Average years work experience at entry:** 12.0

ACADEMICS

Student/faculty ratio: 4:1 % female faculty: 27 % underrepresented minority faculty: 54 % part-time faculty: 8

FINANCIAL FACTS

Annual tuition (in-state/out-of-state): $5,952/ $14,376 **Fees:** $7,080 **Cost of books:** $1,600 **Room & board: (on/off-campus)** $8,924/$11,490 % of students receiving grants: 12 **Average grant:** $8,275 **Average loan:** $12,224 **Average student loan debt:** $24,448

ADMISSIONS

Admissions Selectivity Rating: 69

# of applications received: 101 % applicants accepted: 93 % acceptees attending: 84 **Average GMAT:** 479 **Range of GMAT:** 440–515 **Average GPA:** 3.03 **TOEFL required of international students:** Yes **Minimum TOEFL (paper/computer):** 600/250 **Application fee:** $45 **International Application fee:** $80 **Regular application deadline:** 7/15

Deferment available: Yes **Maximum length of deferment:** 1 yr for US Applicants **Transfer students accepted:** Yes **Transfer application policy:** Limited transfer credits allowed. Must be from AACSB accredited institution and receive approval from Associate Dean for transfer courses to be considered. **Non-fall admissions:** Yes **Need-blind admissions:** Yes

EMPLOYMENT PROFILE

Percent employed at graduation: 21 **Percent employed 3 months after graduation:** 73 **Average base starting salary:** $66,836

Grads Employed by Function ......% Avg. Salary

Marketing: ....(2%) $65,667

Operations: ....(2%) $71,000

Management: ....(4%) $62,400

Other: ....(1%) $85,000

Top 5 Employers Hiring Grads (number of hires in last class)

Dean Foods (1), Lockheed Martin (2), Federal Reserve Bank of New York (1), DeWalt (1), Market Scout Group (1)

THE UNIVERSITY OF TEXAS AT TYLER
COLLEGE OF BUSINESS AND TECHNOLOGY

ADMISSIONS CONTACT: DR. MARY FISCHER, ASSOCIATE DEAN
ADDRESS: 3900 UNIVERSITY BOULEVARD, TYLER, TX 75799
PHONE: 903-566-7433 • FAX: 903-566-7372
E-MAIL: MFISCHER@UTTYLER.EDU • WEBSITE: WWW.UTTYLER.EDU/CBT

GENERAL INFORMATION

Type of school: Public **Academic calendar:** Semester

STUDENTS

Enrollment of parent institution: 6,150 **Enrollment of MBA Program:** 189 **% part-time:** 99 **Average age at entry:** 3 **Average years work experience at entry:** 0.0

ACADEMICS

Student/faculty ratio: 20:1 **% female faculty:** 45 **% underrepresented minority faculty:** 33 **% part-time faculty:** 12

FINANCIAL FACTS

Cost of books: $975

ADMISSIONS

Admissions Selectivity Rating: 74

# of applications received: 110 **% applicants accepted:** 76 **% acceptees attending:** 100 **Average GMAT:** 513 **Average GPA:** 3.11 **TOEFL required of international students:** Yes **Minimum TOEFL (paper/computer):** 550/213 **Application fee:** $25 **International Application fee:** $50

Deferment available: Yes **Maximum length of deferment:** 12 months **Transfer students accepted:** No **Non-fall admissions:** Yes **Need-blind admissions:** Yes

UNIVERSITY OF TORONTO
JOSEPH L. ROTMAN SCHOOL OF MANAGEMENT

ADMISSIONS CONTACT: CHERYL MILLINGTON, DIRECTOR OF MBA RECRUITING AND ADMISSIONS
ADDRESS: 105 ST. GEORGE STREET, TORONTO, ON M5S 3E6 CANADA
PHONE: 416-978-3499 • FAX: 416-978-5812
E-MAIL: MBA@ROTMAN.UTORONTO.CA • WEBSITE: WWW.ROTMAN.UTORONTO.CA

GENERAL INFORMATION

Type of school: Public **Academic calendar:** Sept-May

STUDENTS

Enrollment of parent institution: 70,000 **Enrollment of MBA Program:** 366 **% male/female:** 72/28 **% part-time:** 28 **% international:** 37 **Average age at entry:** 27 **Average years work experience at entry:** 4.7

ACADEMICS

Student/faculty ratio: 7:1 **% female faculty:** 24 **% part-time faculty:** 15

FINANCIAL FACTS

Annual tuition (in-state/out-of-state): $30,820/ **Fees:** $1,078 **Cost of books:** $5,000 **Room & board: (on/off-campus)** $10,000/$10,000 **% of students receiving aid:** 70 **% of first-year students receiving aid:** 70 **% of students receiving grants:** 20 **Average grant:** $8,000 **Average loan:** $20,000

ADMISSIONS

Admissions Selectivity Rating: 96

# of applications received: 1,100 **Average GMAT:** 660 **Range of GMAT:** 550–780 **Average GPA:** 3.40 **TOEFL required of international students:** Yes **Minimum TOEFL (paper/computer):** 600/250 **Application fee:** $150 **International Application fee:** $150 **Regular application deadline:** 4/30 **Regular application notification:** 7/1 **Application Deadline/Notification:**

Round 1: 11/151/15

Round 2: 1/153/15

Round 3: 4/307/1

Deferment available: Yes **Maximum length of deferment:** 1 year **Transfer students accepted:** No **Non-fall admissions:** No **Need-blind admissions:** Yes

EMPLOYMENT PROFILE

Percent employed 3 months after graduation: 93 **Average base starting salary:** $83,067

Primary Source of Full-time Job Acceptances

School-facilitated activities: (60%) **Graduate-facilitated activities:** (40%) **Unknown:** (%)

Grads Employed by Function ......% Avg. Salary

Marketing: ....(8%) $78,000

Operations: ....(2%) $68,300

Consulting: ....(23%) $103,000

Management: ....(10%) $80,000

Finance: ....(23%) $77,600

Other: ....(34%)

Top 5 Employers Hiring Grads (number of hires in last class)

CIBC (19), RBC Financial Group (12), Deloitte (11), BMO Financial Group (9), Scotiabank (7)

University of Warwick
Warwick Business School

ADMISSIONS CONTACT: EMMA SHAW, MBA ADMISSIONS OFFICE
ADDRESS: WARWICK BUSINESS SCHOOL, COVENTRY, CV4 7AL
PHONE: 011-44 (0)24 7652 4100 • FAX:
E-MAIL: WARWICKMBA@WBS.AC.UK • WEBSITE: WWW.WBS.AC.UK

GENERAL INFORMATION

Type of school: Public Academic calendar: Trimester

STUDENTS

Enrollment of parent institution: 16,000 Enrollment of MBA Program: 575 % male/female: 73/27 % part-time: 90 % international: 91 Average age at entry: 30 Average years work experience at entry: 6.0

ACADEMICS

Student/faculty ratio: 4:1 % female faculty: 39

FINANCIAL FACTS

Annual tuition (in-state/out-of-state): $47,931/ $47,931 Cost of books: $1,000 Room & board: (on/off-campus) $13,000/$13,000 % of students receiving aid: 25 % of students receiving grants: 25 Average award package: $24,000 Average grant: $24,000 Average loan: $0

ADMISSIONS

Admissions Selectivity Rating: 88

# of applications received: 249 % applicants accepted: 39 % acceptees attending: 57 Average GMAT: 647 Range of GMAT: 560–720 TOEFL required of international students: Yes Regular application deadline: 7/31

Deferment available: Yes Maximum length of deferment: 12 months Transfer students accepted: No Non-fall admissions: No Need-blind admissions: Yes

EMPLOYMENT PROFILE

Percent employed 3 months after graduation: 96

Primary Source of Full-time Job Acceptances

School-facilitated activities: (36%) Graduate-facilitated activities: (44%) Unknown: (20%)

Grads Employed by Function	% Avg. Salary
Marketing:	(20%)
Operations:	(8%)
Consulting:	(12%)
Management:	(22%)
Finance:	(10%)
HR:	(6%)
MIS:	(4%)
Other:	(2%)

Top 5 Employers Hiring Grads (number of hires in last class)

Deloitte, Accenture, Johnson & Johnson, Pepsico, Proctor & Gamble

University of West Florida
College of Business

ADMISSIONS CONTACT: GRADUATE ADMISSIONS OFFICE, GRADUATE ADMISSIONS OFFICERS
ADDRESS: 11000 UNIVERSITY PKWY, BLDG 18, PENSACOLA, FL 32514
PHONE: 850-474-2230 • FAX: 850-474-3360
E-MAIL: ADMISSIONS@UWF.EDU • WEBSITE: UWF.EDU/MBA

GENERAL INFORMATION

Type of school: Public

STUDENTS

Enrollment of MBA Program: 178 % male/female: 60/40 % out-of-state: 80 % part-time: 90 % international: 80 Average age at entry: 29 Average years work experience at entry: 0.0

ACADEMICS

Student/faculty ratio: 25:1 % female faculty: 13 % underrepresented minority faculty: 13 % part-time faculty: 28

FINANCIAL FACTS

Annual tuition (in-state/out-of-state): $8,325/ $30,093 Cost of books: $1,000 Room & board: (on/off-campus) Average grant: $1,400

ADMISSIONS

Admissions Selectivity Rating: 84

# of applications received: 71 % applicants accepted: 49 % acceptees attending: 80 Average GMAT: 537 Range of GMAT: 460–600 Average GPA: 3.36 TOEFL required of international students: Yes Minimum TOEFL (paper/computer): 550/213 Application fee: $30 International Application fee: $30 Regular application deadline: 6/1

Deferment available: Yes Maximum length of deferment: 1 year Transfer students accepted: Yes Transfer application policy: Student can transfer in no more than 6 credit hours from an AACSB Accredited School. Student must meet the minimum GMAT score of 450. Non-fall admissions: Yes

University of Wisconsin—Eau Claire
University of Wisconsin - Eau Claire College of Business

ADMISSIONS CONTACT: MS. JAN STEWART, MBA PROGRAM ASSOCIATE
ADDRESS: 105 GARFIELD AVENUE, EAU CLAIRE, WI 54702-4004
PHONE: 715-836-4733 • FAX: 715-836-2409
E-MAIL: ADMISSIONS@UWEC.EDU •
WEBSITE: HTTP://WWW.UWEC.EDU/COB/GRADUATE/INDEX.HTM

GENERAL INFORMATION

Type of school: Public Academic calendar: Semester

STUDENTS

Enrollment of parent institution: 10,500 Enrollment of MBA Program: 130 % male/female: 55/45 % out-of-state: 80 % part-time: 90 % underrepresented minority: 5 % international: 80 Average age at entry: 28 **Average years work experience at entry:** 7.0

ACADEMICS

Student/faculty ratio: 5:1 % female faculty: 30 % part-time faculty: 0

FINANCIAL FACTS

Annual tuition (in-state/out-of-state): $8,186/ $18,276 **Cost of books:** $1,000 **Room & board: (on/off-campus)** $5,630 **Average grant:** $0 **Average loan:** $0

ADMISSIONS

Admissions Selectivity Rating: 60*

# of applications received: 0 **Average GMAT:** 540 **Average GPA:** 3.25 **TOEFL required of international students:** Yes **Minimum TOEFL (paper/computer):** 550/213 **Application fee:** $56 **International Application fee:** $56

Deferment available: Yes **Maximum length of deferment:** 1 year **Transfer students accepted:** Yes **Transfer application policy:** Transfer credits are accepted from other AACSB accredited schools. **Non-fall admissions:** Yes **Need-blind admissions:** Yes

EMPLOYMENT PROFILE

Grads Employed by Function ......% Avg. Salary

Marketing:	(20%)
Operations:	(10%)
Management:	(30%)
MIS:	(10%)

UNIVERSITY OF WISCONSIN— LA CROSSE
COLLEGE OF BUSINESS ADMINISTRATION

ADMISSIONS CONTACT: KATHY KIEFER, DIRECTOR
ADDRESS: 1725 STATE STREET, LA CROSSE, WI 54601
PHONE: 608-785-8939 • FAX: 608-785-6695
E-MAIL: ADMISSIONS@UWLAX.EDU • WEBSITE: WWW.UWLAX.EDU

GENERAL INFORMATION

Type of school: Public **Academic calendar:** Semester

STUDENTS

Enrollment of parent institution: 9,198 **Enrollment of MBA Program:** 68 **Average age at entry:** 26 **Average years work experience at entry:** 3.0

ACADEMICS

Student/faculty ratio: 30:1 % female faculty: 28 % underrepresented minority faculty: 22

FINANCIAL FACTS

Annual tuition (in-state/out-of-state): $8,592/ $18,362 **Cost of books:** $600 **Room & board: (on/off-campus)** $8,000/$8,000 **Average grant:** $0 **Average loan:** $0

ADMISSIONS

Admissions Selectivity Rating: 73

# of applications received: 56 % applicants accepted: 79 % acceptees attending: 84 **Average GMAT:** 515 **Average GPA:** 3.05 **TOEFL required of international students:** Yes **Minimum TOEFL (paper/computer):** 550/213 **Application fee:** $56

Deferment available: Yes **Maximum length of deferment:** rolling **Transfer students accepted:** Yes **Transfer application policy:** Maximum of nine credits may be transferrable. **Non-fall admissions:** Yes **Need-blind admissions:** Yes

UNIVERSITY OF WISCONSIN— OSHKOSH
COLLEGE OF BUSINESS ADMINSTRATION

ADMISSIONS CONTACT: LYNN GRANCORBITZ, MBA PROGRAM ASSISTANT DIRECTOR AND ADVISOR
ADDRESS: 800 ALGOMA BLVD., OSHKOSH, WI 54901
PHONE: 800-633-1430 • FAX: 920-424-7413
E-MAIL: MBA@UWOSH.EDU
WEBSITE: WWW.UWOSH.EDU/COLLEGES/COBA/ASSETS/GRAD/INDEX.PHP

GENERAL INFORMATION

Type of school: Public **Academic calendar:** Semester

STUDENTS

Enrollment of parent institution: 10,528 **Enrollment of MBA Program:** 525 % male/female: 55/45 % out-of-state: 2 % part-time: 95 % underrepresented minority: 2 % international: 3 **Average age at entry:** 32 **Average years work experience at entry:** 5.0

ACADEMICS

Student/faculty ratio: 11:1 % female faculty: 15 % underrepresented minority faculty: 5

FINANCIAL FACTS

Annual tuition (in-state/out-of-state): $4,664/ $13,622 **Room & board: (on/off-campus)** % of students receiving aid: 5 % of first-year students receiving aid: 5 % of students receiving grants: 0

ADMISSIONS

Admissions Selectivity Rating: 72

# of applications received: 115 % applicants accepted: 90 % acceptees attending: 93 **Average GMAT:** 540 **Range of GMAT:** 470–610 **Average GPA:** 3.10 **TOEFL required of international students:** Yes **Minimum TOEFL (paper/computer):** 550/ **Application fee:** $45 **International Application fee:** $45 **Regular application deadline:** 7/1

Deferment available: Yes **Maximum length of deferment:** 3 years **Transfer students accepted:** Yes **Transfer application policy:** Accept up to 9 credits from an AACSB accredited MBA program. **Non-fall admissions:** Yes **Need-blind admissions:** No

EMPLOYMENT PROFILE

Percent employed at graduation: 30 **Percent employed 3 months after graduation:** 50

Primary Source of Full-time Job Acceptances Graduate-facilitated activities: 100(100%)

University of Wisconsin— Parkside

School of Business and Technology

ADMISSIONS CONTACT: DIRK BALDWIN, ASSOCIATE DEAN
ADDRESS: 900 WOOD ROAD, BOX 2000, KENOSHA, WI 53141-2000
PHONE: 262-595-2046 • FAX: 262-595-2680
E-MAIL: GRADPROGRAMS.SBT@UWP.EDU
WEBSITE: WWW.UWP.EDU/DEPARTMENTS/BUSINESS

GENERAL INFORMATION

Type of school: Public **Academic calendar:** Semester

STUDENTS

Enrollment of parent institution: 5,000 **Enrollment of MBA Program:** 82 % **male/female:** 64/36 % **out-of-state:** 57 % **part-time:** 83 % **underrepresented minority:** 21 % **international:** 57 **Average age at entry:** 28 **Average years work experience at entry:** 3.0

ACADEMICS

Student/faculty ratio: 6:1 % **female faculty:** 35 % **underrepresented minority faculty:** 30

FINANCIAL FACTS

Annual tuition (in-state/out-of-state): $7,414/ $17,759 **Fees:** $277 **Cost of books:** $600 **Room & board: (on/off-campus)** **Average grant:** $0 **Average loan:** $0

ADMISSIONS

Admissions Selectivity Rating: 71

# of applications received: 34 % **applicants accepted:** 94 % **acceptees attending:** 78 **Average GMAT:** 521 **Range of GMAT:** 440–615 **Average GPA:** 3.18 **TOEFL required of international students:** Yes **Minimum TOEFL (paper/computer):** 550/213 **Application fee:** $56 **International Application fee:** $56 **Early application deadline:** 3/1 **Regular application deadline:** 8/1

Deferment available: Yes **Maximum length of deferment:** 12 mo **Transfer students accepted:** Yes **Transfer application policy:** Must be accepted and max of 12 credits in transfer **Non-fall admissions:** Yes **Need-blind admissions:** Yes

University of Wyoming

College of Business

ADMISSIONS CONTACT: TERRI L. RITTENBURG, DIRECTOR OF MBA PROGRAM
ADDRESS: P.O. BOX 3275, LARAMIE, WY 82071
PHONE: 307-766-2449 • FAX: 307-766-4028
E-MAIL: MBA@UWYO.EDU • WEBSITE: BUSINESS.UWYO.EDU/MBA

GENERAL INFORMATION

Type of school: Public **Academic calendar:** Semester

STUDENTS

Enrollment of parent institution: 11,904 **Enrollment of MBA Program:** 63 % **male/female:** 64/36 % **part-time:** 48 % **underrepresented minority:** 0 % **international:** 18 **Average age at entry:** 28 **Average years work experience at entry:** 0.0

ACADEMICS

Student/faculty ratio: 3:1

FINANCIAL FACTS

Annual tuition (in-state/out-of-state): $2,988/ $8,676 **Fees:** $246 **Cost of books:** $300 **Room & board: (on/off-campus)** $6,212 % **of students receiving aid:** 0 % **of first-year students receiving aid:** 0 **Average grant:** $0 **Average loan:** $0

ADMISSIONS

Admissions Selectivity Rating: 60*

# of applications received: 0 % **acceptees attending:** 0 **Average GMAT:** 558 **Average GPA:** 3.20 **TOEFL required of international students:** Yes **Minimum TOEFL (paper/computer):** 525/197 **Application fee:** $40 **International Application fee:** $0 **Early application deadline:** 2/1 **Regular application deadline:** 2/1

Deferment available: Yes **Maximum length of deferment:** 1 year **Transfer students accepted:** Yes **Transfer application policy:** Maximum number of transferable credits is nine with a minimum grade of B from an AACSB-accredited school. **Non-fall admissions:** No **Need-blind admissions:** Yes

EMPLOYMENT PROFILE

Average base starting salary: $38,878

Utah State University

Jon M. Huntsman School of Business

ADMISSIONS CONTACT: SCHOOL OF GRADUATE STUDIES, ADMISSIONS OFFICER
ADDRESS: 0900 OLD MAIN HILL, LOGAN, UT 84322-0900
PHONE: (435) 797-1190 • FAX: (435) 797-1192
E-MAIL: APRIL.FAWSON@USU.EDU • WEBSITE: WWW.HUNTSMAN.USU.EDU

GENERAL INFORMATION

Type of school: Public **Academic calendar:** Semester

STUDENTS

Enrollment of parent institution: 28,994 **Enrollment of MBA Program:** 234 % **male/female:** 71/29 % **out-of-state:** 15 % **part-time:** 69 % **underrepresented minority:** 5 % **international:** 18 **Average age at entry:** 28 **Average years work experience at entry:** 7.9

ACADEMICS

Student/faculty ratio: 3:1 % **female faculty:** 19 % **underrepresented minority faculty:** 6 % **part-time faculty:** 0

FINANCIAL FACTS

Annual tuition (in-state/out-of-state): $21,686/ $35,179 **Cost of books:** $1,800 **Room & board: (on/off-campus)** $5,000/$5,000 % **of students receiving aid:** 20 % **of first-year students receiving aid:** 20 % **of students receiving grants:** 20 **Average award package:** $6,000 **Average grant:** $2,800 **Average loan:** $4,000 **Average student loan debt:** $13,000

ADMISSIONS

Admissions Selectivity Rating: 78

# of applications received: 211 % **applicants accepted:** 67 % **acceptees attending:** 86 **Average GMAT:** 532 **Range of GMAT:** 488–574 **Average GPA:** 3.42 **TOEFL required of international stu-**

dents: Yes **Minimum TOEFL (paper/computer):** 550/213 **Application fee:** $55 **International Application fee:** $55

Application Deadline/Notification:

Round 1: 12/11/15

Round 2: 2/13/1

Round 3: 3/14/1

Round 4: 4/15/1

Deferment available: Yes **Maximum length of deferment:** 1 year **Transfer students accepted:** Yes **Transfer application policy:** Classes to be transferred are reviewed and approved on an individual basis to ensure that equivalent course content is covered. **Non-fall admissions:** No **Need-blind admissions:** Yes

EMPLOYMENT PROFILE

Percent employed 3 months after graduation: 81 **Average base starting salary:** $55,889

Grads Employed by Function ......% Avg. Salary

Marketing: ....(27%) $50,012

Operations: ....(9%) $54,025

Consulting: ....(0%)

Management: ....(15%) $54,383

Finance:...(29%) $57,000

HR: ....(10%) $57,500

MIS: ....(5%) $63,250

Other: ....(5%) $95,000

Top 5 Employers Hiring Grads (number of hires in last class)

Harris Research Inc. (2), Goldman Sachs (1), Honeywell Inc. (1), Monsanto Corp. (1), Hewlett Packard (1)

VALDOSTA STATE UNIVERSITY
LANGDALE COLLEGE OF BUSINESS ADMINISTRATION

ADMISSIONS CONTACT: JUDY TOMBERLIN, GRADUATE SCHOOL
ADDRESS: 903 N. PATTERSON STREET, VALDOSTA, GA 31698-0005
PHONE: (229) 333-5696 • FAX: (229) 245-3853
E-MAIL: MBA@VALDOSTA.EDU • WEBSITE: WWW.VALDOSTA.EDU/LCOBA/GRAD/

GENERAL INFORMATION

Type of school: Public **Academic calendar:** Semester

STUDENTS

Enrollment of parent institution: 10,500 **Enrollment of MBA Program:** 31 % **male/female:** 50/50 % **part-time:** 100 % **underrepresented minority:** 0 % **international:** 8 **Average age at entry:** 30 **Average years work experience at entry:** 8.0

ACADEMICS

Student/faculty ratio: 3:1 % **female faculty:** 20 % **underrepresented minority faculty:** 0 % **part-time faculty:** 0

FINANCIAL FACTS

Annual tuition (in-state/out-of-state): $3,766/ $12,544 **Fees:** $708 **Cost of books:** $800 **Room & board: (on/off-campus)** $2,684/$2,684 **Average grant:** $1,000 **Average loan:** $8,966

ADMISSIONS

Admissions Selectivity Rating: 86

# of applications received: 21 % **applicants accepted:** 48 % **acceptees attending:** 80 **Average GMAT:** 534 **Range of GMAT:** 500–640 **Average GPA:** 3.30 **TOEFL required of international students:** Yes **Minimum TOEFL (paper/computer):** 550/213 **Application fee:** $25

Deferment available: Yes **Maximum length of deferment:** One Semester **Transfer students accepted:** Yes **Transfer application policy:** Maximum of 6 hours transfered from AACSB institution. **Non-fall admissions:** Yes **Need-blind admissions:** Yes

VLERICK LEUVEN GENT MANAGEMENT SCHOOL
VLERICK LEUVEN GENT MANAGEMENT SCHOOL

ADMISSIONS CONTACT: YOLANDA HABETS, PROGRAMME MANAGER
ADDRESS: VLAMINGENSTRAAT 83, 3000 LEUVEN, BELGIUM., REEP 1, 9000 GENT, BELGIUM, LEUVEN, VB 03000 BELGIUM
PHONE: + 32 16 24 88 86 • FAX: + 32 16 24 88 11
E-MAIL: MBA@VLERICK.BE • WEBSITE: WWW.VLERICK.COM

GENERAL INFORMATION

Type of school: Public

STUDENTS

Enrollment of parent institution: 30,000 **Enrollment of MBA Program:** 320 % **male/female:** 75/25 % **out-of-state:** 90 % **part-time:** 55 % **international:** 90 **Average age at entry:** 30 **Average years work experience at entry:** 6.0

ACADEMICS

Student/faculty ratio: 4:1 % **female faculty:** 25 % **underrepresented minority faculty:** 100 % **part-time faculty:** 0

FINANCIAL FACTS

Annual tuition (in-state/out-of-state): $42/ $42 **Cost of books:** $0 **Room & board: (on/off-campus)** $12,000/$12,000 % **of students receiving aid:** 10 % **of first-year students receiving aid:** 10 % **of students receiving grants:** 10 **Average award package:** $630,000 **Average grant:** $15,000 **Average loan:** $22,000 **Average student loan debt:** $12,500

ADMISSIONS

Admissions Selectivity Rating: 90

# of applications received: 600 % **applicants accepted:** 34 % **acceptees attending:** 43 **Average GMAT:** 660 **Range of GMAT:** 600–700 **Average GPA:** 3.50 **TOEFL required of international students:** Yes **Minimum TOEFL:** 255 **Application fee:** $50 **International Application fee:** $50 **Early application deadline:** 3/31 **Early notification date:** 4/14 **Regular application deadline:** 6/30 **Regular application notification:** 7/14

Application Deadline/Notification:

Round 1: 1/222/1

Round 2: 3/244/1

Round 3: 6/307/14

Deferment available: Yes **Maximum length of deferment:** 1 year **Transfer students accepted:** No **Non-fall admissions:** No **Need-blind admissions:** Yes

EMPLOYMENT PROFILE

Percent employed at graduation: 50 **Percent employed 3 months after graduation:** 90 **Average base starting salary:** $120,000

Primary Source of Full-time Job Acceptances

School-facilitated activities: 25(45%) **Graduate-facilitated activities:** 15(30%) **Unknown:** 14(25%)

Grads Employed by Function ......% Avg. Salary

Marketing: ....(10%) $120,000

Consulting: ....(15%) $120,000

Management: ....(10%) $120,000

Finance:......................................(15%) $120,000

Top 5 Employers Hiring Grads (number of hires in last class)

Bechtel (1), Inbev (1), Belgacom (1), ING Bank (1), US Foreign Service (1)

WASHINGTON STATE UNIVERSITY
COLLEGE OF BUSINESS

ADMISSIONS CONTACT: MITCH SWANGER, RECRUITMENT AND ADMISSIONS COORDINATOR
ADDRESS: PO BOX 644710, PULLMAN, WA 99164-4710
PHONE: 509-335-7617 • FAX: 509-335-4735
E-MAIL: MBA@WSU.EDU • WEBSITE: WWW.MBA.WSU.EDU

GENERAL INFORMATION

Type of school: Public **Academic calendar:** Semester

STUDENTS

Enrollment of parent institution: 18,000

ACADEMICS

Student/faculty ratio: 25:1

FINANCIAL FACTS

Cost of books: $1,104

ADMISSIONS

Admissions Selectivity Rating: 60*

TOEFL required of international students: Yes **Minimum TOEFL (paper/computer):** 580/237 **Application fee:** $75 **International Early application deadline:** 1/10 **Early notification date:** 3/30 **Regular application deadline:** 1/10 **Regular application notification:** 3/30

Deferment available: No **Transfer students accepted:** Yes **Transfer application policy:** Transfer students will only be able to apply 6 credits of elective coursework to the WSU MBA on a case-by-case basis. **Non-fall admissions:** Yes **Need-blind admissions:** Yes

WESTERN ILLINOIS UNIVERSITY
COLLEGE OF BUSINESS AND TECHNOLOGY

DIRECTOR OF MBA PROGRAM
ADDRESS: 1 UNIVERSITY CIRCLE, 115 SHERMAN HALL, MACOMB, IL 61455
PHONE: 309-298-3157 • FAX: 309-298-3111
E-MAIL: ADMISSIONS@WIU.EDU • WEBSITE: WWW.WIU.EDU/USERS/MICOBTD/

GENERAL INFORMATION

Type of school: Public **Academic calendar:** Semester

STUDENTS

Enrollment of parent institution: 13,000 **Enrollment of MBA Program:** 111 **% male/female:** 52/48 **% part-time:** 55 **% underrepresented minority:** 2 **% international:** 26 **Average years work experience at entry:**

ACADEMICS

Student/faculty ratio: 24:1 **% female faculty:** 29 **% underrepresented minority faculty:** 15 **% part-time faculty:** 7

FINANCIAL FACTS

Annual tuition (in-state/out-of-state): $5,696/ $11,392 **Fees:** $1,453 **Cost of books:** $1,150 **Room & board: (on/off-campus)** $7,210/$9,000 **% of students receiving aid:** 17 **% of first-year students receiving aid:** 37 **% of students receiving grants:** 20 **Average grant:** $4,696

ADMISSIONS

Admissions Selectivity Rating: 71

# of applications received: 47 **% applicants accepted:** 89 **% acceptees attending:** 64 **Average GMAT:** 549 **Range of GMAT:** 500–600 **Average GPA:** 3.26 **TOEFL required of international students:** Yes **Minimum TOEFL (paper/computer):** 550/ **Application fee:** $30

Deferment available: Yes **Maximum length of deferment:** 1 **Transfer students accepted:** No **Non-fall admissions:** Yes **Need-blind admissions:** No

WESTERN NEW ENGLAND UNIVERSITY
COLLEGE OF BUSINESS

ADMISSIONS CONTACT: MATTHEW FOX, DIRECTOR OF RECRUITING AND MARKETING
ADDRESS: 1215 WILBRAHAM RD, SPRINGFIELD, MA 01119
PHONE: 413-782-1517 • FAX: 413-782-1777
E-MAIL: STUDY@WNE.EDU • WEBSITE: WWW.WNE.EDU

GENERAL INFORMATION

Type of school: Private **Academic calendar:** Four 11-week terms

FINANCIAL FACTS

Annual tuition (in-state/out-of-state): $25,560/ $25,560 **Fees:** $0 **Cost of books:** $3,100 **Room & board: (on/off-campus)** $8,000/$8,000

ADMISSIONS

Admissions Selectivity Rating: 60*

TOEFL required of international students: Yes **Minimum TOEFL (paper/computer):** 550/213 **Application fee:** $30 **International Application fee:** $30

Deferment available: Yes **Maximum length of deferment:** 1 year **Transfer students accepted:** Yes **Transfer application policy:** The College will consider up to 12 credits from an AACSB accredited program. **Non-fall admissions:** Yes **Need-blind admissions:** Yes

WESTERN WASHINGTON UNIVERSITY
COLLEGE OF BUSINESS AND ECONOMICS

ADMISSIONS CONTACT: DANIEL PURDY, MBA PROGRAM ASSOCIATE DIRECTOR
ADDRESS: 516 HIGH ST., PARKS HALL 419, BELLINGHAM, WA 98225-9072
PHONE: 360-650-3825 • FAX: 360-650-4844
E-MAIL: DANIEL.PURDY@WWU.EDU • WEBSITE: WWW.CBE.WWU.EDU/MBA

GENERAL INFORMATION

Type of school: Public **Academic calendar:** Fall through Spring - Quarter System

STUDENTS

Enrollment of parent institution: 14,979 **Enrollment of MBA Program:** 97 **% male/female:** 53/47 **% out-of-state:** 16 **% part-time:** 40 **% underrepresented minority:** 22 **% international:** 7 **Average age at entry:** 29 **Average years work experience at entry:** 6.0

ACADEMICS

Student/faculty ratio: 2:1 **% female faculty:** 21 **% underrepresented minority faculty:** 20 **% part-time faculty:** 9

FINANCIAL FACTS

Annual tuition (in-state/out-of-state): $7,344/ $17,190 **Fees:** $846 **Cost of books:** $1,000 **Room & board: (on/off-campus)** $11,000 **% of students receiving aid:** 18 **% of first-year students receiving aid:** 11 **Average award package:** $170,500

ADMISSIONS

Admissions Selectivity Rating: 75

# of applications received: 116 **% applicants accepted:** 77 **% acceptees attending:** 70 **Average GMAT:** 575 **Range of GMAT:** 458–690 **Average GPA:** 3.29 **TOEFL required of international students:** Yes **Minimum TOEFL (paper/computer):** 567/227 **Application fee:** $50 **International Application fee:** $50 **Early application deadline:** 2/15 **Regular application deadline:** 5/1

Deferment available: Yes **Maximum length of deferment:** 1 year, fee required **Transfer students accepted:** Yes **Transfer application policy:** Transfer maximum of 9 quarter (six Semester) credits; graded with a b, 3.0, or better; taken no more than three years prior to a student's quarter of admission; be acceptable to the granting institution for its master's degree; and meet the requirements and conditions of approved courses offered by WWU. **Non-fall admissions:** Yes **Need-blind admissions:** Yes

WIDENER UNIVERSITY
SCHOOL OF BUSINESS ADMINISTRATION

ADMISSIONS CONTACT: ANN SELTZER, GRADUATE ENROLLMENT PROCESS ADMINISTRATOR
ADDRESS: 1 UNIVERSITY PLACE, CHESTER, PA 19013
PHONE: 610-499-4305 • FAX: 610-499-4615
E-MAIL: SBAGRADV@MAIL.WIDENER.EDU • WEBSITE: WWW.WIDENER.EDU

GENERAL INFORMATION

Type of school: Private **Academic calendar:** Semester

STUDENTS

Enrollment of MBA Program: 105 **% male/female:** 40/60 **% part-time:** 90 **% international:** 10 **Average age at entry:** 29 **Average years work experience at entry:** 7.0

ACADEMICS

Student/faculty ratio: 6:1 **% female faculty:** 39 **% underrepresented minority faculty:** 5 **% part-time faculty:** 27

FINANCIAL FACTS

Annual tuition (in-state/out-of-state): $21,600/ **Fees:** $200 **Cost of books:** $850 **Room & board: (on/off-campus)** /$7,650 **% of students receiving aid:** 9 **% of first-year students receiving aid:** 3 **% of students receiving grants:** 5 **Average award package:** $19,174 **Average grant:** $9,660 **Average loan:** $15,283

ADMISSIONS

Admissions Selectivity Rating: 84

# of applications received: 130 **% applicants accepted:** 45 **% acceptees attending:** 85 **Average GMAT:** 533 **Range of GMAT:** 450–540 **Average GPA:** 3.20 **TOEFL required of international students:** Yes **Minimum TOEFL (paper/computer):** 550/213 **Regular application deadline:** 5/1

Deferment available: Yes **Maximum length of deferment:** 1 year **Transfer students accepted:** Yes **Transfer application policy:** Students may transfer all foundation level courses from other institutions. Up to 6 credits of core or elective courses may be transferred from AACSB accredited programs. **Non-fall admissions:** Yes **Need-blind admissions:** Yes

WINTHROP UNIVERSITY
COLLEGE OF BUSINESS ADMINISTRATION

ADMISSIONS CONTACT: PEGGY HAGER, DIRECTOR OF GRADUATE PROGRAMS
ADDRESS: 213 THURMOND BUILDING, ROCK HILL, SC 29733
PHONE: 803-323-2409 • FAX: 803-323-2539
E-MAIL: MBAOFFICE@WINTHROP.EDU • WEBSITE: WWW.WINTHROP.EDU/CBA/MBA

GENERAL INFORMATION
Type of school: Public **Academic calendar:** Semester

STUDENTS
Enrollment of parent institution: 6,249 **Enrollment of MBA Program:** 168 **% male/female:** 64/36 **% out-of-state:** 41 **% part-time:** 57 **% underrepresented minority:** 38 **% international:** 26 **Average age at entry:** 29 **Average years work experience at entry:** 5.0

ACADEMICS
Student/faculty ratio: 4:1 **% female faculty:** 40 **% underrepresented minority faculty:** 12 **% part-time faculty:** 8

FINANCIAL FACTS
Cost of books: $1,400

ADMISSIONS
Admissions Selectivity Rating: 69

# of applications received: 102 **% applicants accepted:** 90 **% acceptees attending:** 70 **Average GMAT:** 470 **Range of GMAT:** 400–550 **Average GPA:** 3.20 **TOEFL required of international students:** Yes **Minimum TOEFL (paper/computer):** 550/ **Application fee:** $50 **International Application fee:** $50 **Regular application deadline:** 7/15

Deferment available: Yes **Maximum length of deferment:** 1 year **Transfer students accepted:** Yes **Transfer application policy:** 9 graduate Semester hours of approved coursework may be transferred **Non-fall admissions:** Yes **Need-blind admissions:** Yes

YOUNGSTOWN STATE UNIVERSITY
WILLIAMSON COLLEGE OF BUSINESS ADMINISTRATION

ADMISSIONS CONTACT: SUE DAVIS, INTERIM DIRECTOR
ADDRESS: ONE UNIVERSITY PLAZA, YOUNGSTOWN, OH 44555
PHONE: 330-742-2000 • FAX: 330-742-1658
E-MAIL: ENROLL@YSU.EDU • WEBSITE: WWW.WCBA.YSU.EDU

GENERAL INFORMATION
Type of school: Public

STUDENTS
Average years work experience at entry: 0.0

FINANCIAL FACTS
Annual tuition (in-state/out-of-state): $5,670/ $8,520

ADMISSIONS
Admissions Selectivity Rating: 60*
TOEFL required of international students: No

SCHOOL SAYS . . .

In this section you'll find schools with extended listings describing Admissions, curriculum, internships, and much more. This is your chance to get in-depth information on programs that interest you. The Princeton Review charges each school a small fee to be listed, and the editorial responsibility is solely that of the university.

AMERICAN UNIVERSITY
Kogod School of Business

AT A GLANCE
American University's Kogod School of Business is committed to the belief that profit and purpose are not at odds. Kogod is recognized for program excellence and innovation by prestigious business and academic organizations worldwide. The school is accredited by The Association to Advance Collegiate Schools of Business (AACSB International), which represents the highest standard of achievement for business schools worldwide.

Dedicated to providing an interdisciplinary business education, Kogod offers market-driven graduate degree programs. The MBA program combines a high-quality business education with the top-rated programs of other American University (AU) professional schools to ensure a fully integrated learning experience. Kogod's global network of alumni and Students are driven to make a difference within organizations and the world at large.

CAMPUS AND LOCATION
The Kogod School of Business is situated on American University's beautiful, 84-acre campus in one of the most desirable residential neighborhoods of Northwest Washington, DC. Getting to campus is simple; AU is located on the metro, along with several bus routes.

PROGRAMS AND CURRICULUM
Kogod's Full-Time MBA program is built around an integrated core curriculum, designed to build foundation analytical skills, as well as conceptual and critical thinking abilities in strategic thinking and decision making.

The Professional MBA program is designed specifically for the working professional seeking to advance their career. The program's carefully sequenced courses build on knowledge in all areas of business, while reinforcing problem solving and critical thinking skills. Students attend class only one night a week and complete the program in 27 months, over seven consecutive semesters.

At Kogod, education takes on real-world relevancy through close collaboration with corporations, nonprofits, and government organizations. This market-driven approach is reflected in our MBA hands-on consulting projects, co-curricular opportunities, scholarly research, and career development.

The MBA core curriculum consists of carefully sequenced and designed to build upon foundation coursework in economics, accounting, and quantitative methods. The program is balanced by elective courses that allow Students the opportunity to concentrate coursework around a particular career path or take courses from the other AU graduate schools.

Kogod's graduate programs in Finance, Accounting, Taxation, Sustainability Management, Marketing, and Real Estate provide advanced training from real-world professionals and thought leaders. Students gain expertise in their chosen field through a combination of classroom, practical, and career management experience. Kogod leverages its connections within each industry to help Students broaden their knowledge about career options, current industry trends, and the general industry landscape.

COST AND EXPENSES
Full-Time MBA and Graduate degree program tuition (2012-2013 academic year):

Cost per credit hours: $1,261

12-17 credit hours: $16,507 per semesterr

Professional MBA program Tuition:

Flat Rate for Total Program: $71,400. This includes tuition, program fees, international module, textbooks, software, and light meals on class days. Tuition is paid in seven semester installments on August 1 for the fall semester, December 1 for the spring semester, and May 1 for the summer semester.

FACULTY
The Kogod Faculty is composed of internationally recognized scholars, outstanding lecturers, researchers, and advisors, all of whom are committed to the highest standards of teaching. Most importantly, they bring real-world business challenges into the classroom for Students to solve. Many Faculty are currently serving as consultants to major corporations and governments, or actively engaged in research.

STUDENTS
At Kogod we believe education should extend beyond the classroom. Hands-on experiences enhance leadership ability, communication skills, and self-confidence. K-LAB (Kogod Leadership and Applied Business) allows Students to learn valuable professional skills in real-world settings and includes options to participate in graduate study abroad, the annual case competition, graduate clubs, and community volunteer programs.

ADMISSIONS
The application process for the Kogod School of Business is an electronic process. Complete the online application at http://kogod.american.edu/apply.

Kogod application requirements include the following:

° A bachelors degree from a regionally accredited college or university.
° Official GMAT score or GRE
° International Students: TOEFL or IELTS score
° Personal statement
° Resume
° Two letters of recommendation
° $100 application fee
° Interview with a member of the Graduate Admissions Committee. (Interview invitations are extended to selected applicants after a preliminary review of the completed application).

SPECIAL PROGRAMS
Kogod offers an extensive set of interdisciplinary programs that include three dual-degree programs: LLM/MBA, JD/MBA, and the MA/MBA.

Kogod Students are encouraged to have an international experience to broaden their perspectives and inform their decision making. To facilitate this, Kogod offers quality short-term, summer, and semester abroad opportunities for graduate Students.

The Kogod Center for Business Communication understands that all successful business people are by definition successful communicators. The Center helps Students develop their academic and professional writing, public speaking, and team presentation skills. Through the Center, Students receive individual coaching from season communications specialists.

ADDITIONAL INFORMATION
American University
Kogod School of Business
Attn: Graduate Admissions
4400 Massachusetts Avenue N.W.
Washington, DC 20016
Telephone: 202-885-1913
Fax: 202-885-1078
E-mail: kogodgrad@american.edu
Website: kogod.american.edu

BABSON COLLEGE
F.W. Olin Graduate School of Business

AT A GLANCE

At Babson's F.W. Olin Graduate School or Business, we believe that entrepreneurship is applicable-and crucial-in organizations of all types and sizes, in established businesses as well as new ventures. Babson is the only business school that has developed and advanced an innovative teaching method, Entrepreneurial Thought and Action(r). Unlike most business schools that teach entrepreneurship as a discrete, siloed subject, Babson incorporates Entrepreneurial Thought and Action(r) across all disciplines. In fact, Babson's MBA program has been ranked number one in the country for entrepreneurship for 20 consecutive years by U.S. News & World Report, as well as by the Princeton Review.

Building off the classroom curriculum are the Signature Learning Experiences (SLEs). These experiences reinforce and expand classroom learning through hands-on activities that require graduate Students to put theories into practice. To supplement, there is a wide array of elective courses for deeper experiential and field-based learning. Students can customize their portfolio of electives to meet their career aspirations.

CAMPUS AND LOCATION

Babson College has three campus locations-Wellesley, MA, Boston, MA and San Francisco CA. Main campus: Wellesley, MA; elective courses offered at Boston campus; Fast Track program offered at San Francisco campus.

DEGREES OFFERED

Babson offers Master of Business Administration and Master of Science degrees.

ACADEMIC PROGRAMS

With four programs, the Babson MBA allows you to choose the program that best suits your lifestyle and objectives. With the unified curriculum across all programs, Students will take the same core courses with the same Faculty and can choose from a common set of electives.

One-Year Program Suited for those with a strong academic foundation in business and a career-track that demands an accelerated, full-time MBA experience.

Two-Year Program Ideal for individuals who need a comprehensive business focus to redirect their careers and want a full-time campus experience.

Evening Program Ideal for working professionals who seek a part-time MBA program that allows flexibility to accommodate professional or personal demands.

Fast Track Program Favorable to working professionals seeking a part-time MBA that allows for increased flexibility through a blend of web-based and face to face sessions.

MS Programs

Masters of Science in Accounting: he program prepares graduates for public accounting careers in a dynamic global profession. Graduates gain technical accounting knowledge while developing skills immediately applicable to one's career.

Masters of Science in Management in Entrepreneurial Leadership: A 9-month Master's program that prepares leaders who both assess and act their way into new opportunities that create value for themselves, their organizations, and the wider society.

FACILITIES

Babson Students have access to extensive business resources. From the Horn Library, to the Academic Centers and Institutes on campus, that are designed to provide Students with real-life experience. For more information on these centers, go to:

EXPENSES AND FINANCIAL AID

Tuition for the 2013-2014 academic year:

One-Year Program: $69,888

Two-Year Program: $58,884 for the first year of the Two-Year program. Estimated tuition for the second year of the program is $37,200.

Evening Program: $1,498 per credit

Fast Track Program: $78,200

MSA Program: $1,498 per credit

MSM Program: Program begins Fall 2014. Tuition to be determined.

Merit awards for the One-Year and Two-Year programs include Fellowships and Scholarships, , Forté Foundation Fellowships, Women's Leadership Awards, President's and Dean's Scholarships, and several awards based on entrepreneurial accomplishments.

FACULTY

Babson's Faculty is an internationally and professionally diverse group. The Faculty includes seasoned corporate executives, visionary entrepreneurs, and academic thought leaders.

STUDENTS

The graduate student population reflects the global landscape as it is today-diverse, respectful of international perspective, fast paced, and forward thinking. Students are pursuing their graduate degrees with varying focuses: switching careers, advancing careers, refining organizational impact in the near term, and poising themselves for continued growth with their employer in the long term. Babson Students represent a variety of geographic and professional backgrounds, but their desire to become entrepreneurial leaders is the common thread.

ADMISSIONS

Students are admitted to the program based on a careful evaluation of academic records, professional qualifications, GMAT or GRE scores, and personal attributes. Interviews are required for admission to all programs. International Students must submit TOEFL or IELTS results and official English translations of all academic documents.

Application deadlines and decision dates for all programs may be found at:

http://www.babson.edu/mbadeadlines

For more information, contact:

Telephone: 781-239-4317; 800-488-4512 (toll-free within the U.S.)

E-mail: gradAdmissions@babson.edu

Website: www.babson.edu/graduate

SPECIAL PROGRAMS

Babson provides many on and off campus opportunities for you to connect and learn from one another, as well as collaborate and get involved. Here are just a few of the graduate clubs and organizations: Babson Entrepreneurship Forum, Asian Business Forum, Babson Association of Women MBAs, Babson Consulting Group, Babson Marketing Club, Babson Energy and Environmental Club and Net Impact.

In addition to clubs and organization, Babson offers a variety of opportunities to analyze a real-time organizational opportunity and create value-added solutions. Through experiential learning, Students enhance their classroom learning through real world experience, team dynamic skill building, and career insight.

BAYLOR UNIVERSITY
Hankamer School of Business

AT A GLANCE

Where you choose to attain your MBA is an important decision. Baylor University can be a valuable partner on your journey in achieving your highest personal and professional potential. Baylor offers MBA Students the exceptional resources of a premier institution recognized worldwide for academic quality, superior teaching, and a reputation for graduating persons of both competence and character.

Small classes set the stage for an integrated learning experience that balances leading-edge business theory with practical, hands-on, real-world challenges.

CAMPUS AND LOCATION

Chartered in 1845, Baylor University is the oldest, continually operating university in Texas. Baylor has grown to a 735-acre campus with 15,000 Students. With an area population of 229,000, Baylor is centrally located in Waco, Texas, within 150 miles of four major metropolitan cities: Dallas, Houston, Austin and San Antonio.

GRADUATE BUSINESS DEGREES OFFERED

Master of Business Administration (MBA)
Executive MBA Program in Dallas (EMBA)
Executive MBA Program in Austin (EMBA)
MBA/Master of Science in Information Systems (MBA/MSIS)
Juris Doctorate/MBA (JD/MBA)
MBA/Master of Engineering (MBA/ME)
MBA/Master of Social Work (MBA/MSW)
MBA/Master of Divinity (MBA/MDIV)

FACILITIES

The Hankamer School of Business features seminar-style classrooms, a 75-seat videoconferencing room, and the Graduate Center that maximizes discussion and interaction between Students and Faculty. With Baylor's wireless data network, AirBear, Students can connect their notebook computers to the Internet from any location on campus, unencumbered by a physical network connection.

EXPENSES AND FINANCIAL AID

More than half of the MBA Students receive some form of merit-based scholarships or graduate assistantship awards. Merit-based scholarships or assistantships are awarded ranging from 50 to 100 percent tuition remission. Additionally, Students can earn a stipend in exchange for working 10 hours per week for a professor in the Business School.

Tuition and Fees for 2012-2013

Tuition is $32,574 per academic year (fall and spring)

Estimated student fees for an academic year are $3,500.

FACULTY

Baylor MBA Students can expect a personalized and integrative educational experience administered by a highly supportive academic community. The MBA Faculty is accessible, involved, and intent on your success. Your relationship with Faculty members will help you sharpen your ambitions and form a solid basis upon which to develop the business acumen to succeed.

All professors teaching in the MBA are active in their professional fields, are business consultants, and are well published.

STUDENT BODY

MBA Student Profile-Fall 2011
Total number of full-time MBA Students enrolled: 100

Number of Applications Received: 180
Number of Applications Accepted: 71
Entered in 2012: 52
Average GMAT: 628
Average age: 25
Percent male/female: 65/35%
Average work experience: 26 months
Average class size: 15 Students

ADMISSIONS

Admission to Baylor Business is competitive. We're looking for individuals with professional work experience, outstanding scholarship, a commitment to community service, and a motivation to pursue an intense graduate business program. MBA candidates should have strong analytical capabilities and communication skills.

SPECIAL PROGRAMS

The adage is true: The best way to learn something is through practice. It is the concept behind both the corporate-alliance practicum known as Focus Firm and the "Practicum in Portfolio Management" finance class.

In the Focus Firm project, Students research, critically assess and recommend viable solutions to an identified business dilemma for an actual business. See www.baylor.edu/mba/focusfirm.

In the portfolio management class, Students manage a live fund valued at more than $5 million. See www.baylor.edu/business/financial_markets.

ADDITIONAL INFORMATION

Baylor Business-Our commitment to the personal as well as professional development of our Students is distinctive. Values-based guidance of Faculty mentors and innovative program design allow you to take your career-and your life-wherever you want to go. Baylor's graduate business programs provide the comprehensive learning experience you need to achieve your career objectives, within the context of greater personal development goals designed to serve you for life.

CAREER SERVICES AND PLACEMENT

MBA Students take two career development courses which address critical areas such as self-assessment, job-search strategies and resume development, as well as provide valuable instruction on appropriate interviewing behavior, negotiating successfully and accepting a job offer in a professional manner.

A pivotal function of Career Management is matching our graduates with the perfect job opportunity. To accomplish this objective, each MBA develops a personalized plan of action based on his or her unique qualifications, talent, experience and vocational leanings.

Internships present opportunities to apply the management theory learned in the first year of your MBA program to the marketplace within a large or small corporation. At the same time, internship employers have an opportunity to discover an outstanding candidate with a proven record of expertise. Experience gained through internships aids both Students and employers by providing each with what they need: the skills and expertise to get the job done.

All MBA Students are required to participate in one off-campus educational experience in conjunction with their Career Development courses. Students will meet with corporate leaders of top financial companies to gain a greater understanding of how the financial services industry operates today. The one-week trip will be held in the fall semester only. Students will take the trip in the first fall semester of their MBA degree plan.

BELMONT UNIVERSITY
The Jack C. Massey Graduate School of Business

AT A GLANCE

The Massey Graduate School provides graduate business programs (MBA and MACC) to working and aspiring professionals in the Nashville area. All classes are offered in a weeknight, evening format.

AT A GLANCE

The Jack C. Massey Graduate School of Business was founded in 1986 through a gift from one of the country's most successful entrepreneurs. Mr. Massey remains as the only U.S. businessperson to ever take three different private companies (i.e., Kentucky Fried Chicken, HCA, and Winners Corp.) public to the New York Stock Exchange. The School was created to offer graduate business programs to Nashville area working professionals and offers a part-time and full-time MBA, as well as a healthcare MBA and a Masters of Accountancy program-each in a weeknight, evening format on the Belmont University campus. Belmont is the only private university in Tennessee to maintain AACSB International accreditation in business and accounting. Massey's part-time MBA program was 9th in BusinessWeek's most recent regional (south) ranking of part-time MBA programs, and Fortune Magazine has identified Belmont as one of the top five universities in the United States at which to study entrepreneurship.

CAMPUS AND LOCATION

As an academic unit within Belmont University, The Massey Graduate School is located in the heart of Nashville, Tennessee, a rare place combining big-city charisma and small-town charm. Known internationally as "music city," Nashville is also a hotbed for entrepreneurship, healthcare, and international trade. Belmont University, a host campus for the 2008 U.S. Presidential Debates, is located on a 62-acre campus and maintains a total enrollment of ~6,000 Students.

DEGREES OFFERED

The Massey Graduate School offers two degree programs:

The Master of Business Administration (MBA) degree requires 34 credits, with 15 specialty tracks across accounting, entrepreneurship, finance, healthcare management, marketing, music business and business negotiation. The MBA is offered in three formats: (1) a part-time "Professional MBA" version designed for working professionals with prior business experience and (2) a full-time "Accelerated MBA" version for individuals with little to no business work experience and (3) a part-time "Healthcare MBA" (42 credits)-for experienced individuals from the healthcare industry. Classes for all three programs are offered Monday-Thursday evenings throughout the year.

The Master of Accountancy (MACC) degree requires 30 credits and is designed to prepare Students to meet the 150 hour CPA requirement, and a Becker CPA Review program is also available. MACC classes are offered year-round, Monday-Thursday evenings.

PROGRAMS AND CURRICULUM

The Massey Graduate School resides within the College of Business Administration, which also includes the Center for Entrepreneurship, the Kennedy Center for Business Ethics, Center for International Business, and the Center for Executive Education, each of which houses additional learning opportunities for Students. A Summer Accounting Institute option for aspiring MACC Students offers non-business undergraduates a fast-track opportunity to begin their graduate accounting course work, while a Summer Business Institute offers a similar option for those non-business majors preparing for the MBA program.

All graduate Students complete a brief study-abroad experience course as part of their degree requirements. Trips are scheduled between terms and

typically last 8-10 days. Destination options for 2013-14 include Argentina, Belgium, Brazil, China, France, Germany, Italy, the Netherlands, South Africa, Spain, and Turkey.

The curriculum is designed with 2-credit hour courses instead of the traditional 3-credit format. This gives Massey Students a greater breadth of curriculum in the core business/accounting offerings, while also assuring a greater number of electives for matching to a particular student career plan. All Students also complete a required entrepreneurship course, as well as preparation in business ethics.

Massey alumni appreciate the existence of the "Massey Passport" program that provides a lifetime option for graduates to return to campus and attend graduate business classes for free on a space-available basis.

FACILITIES

All classes are held in the Jack C. Massey Business Center, which includes a variety of high-tech classrooms, computer labs, a finance trading center, and student support offices. Graduate Students also have a separate computer lab workspace, as well as a well-equipped study area.

EXPENSES AND FINANCIAL AID

Tuition charges per course for 2013-2014 are calculated at $2,780 for all MBA Students and $2,150 for all MACC Students. There are a limited number of scholarship opportunities (e.g., merit, financial need, minority status), as well as graduate assistant opportunities.

FACULTY

Over 90 percent of graduate Faculty are doctorally-qualified and full-time professors, while the remaining minority are full-time business executives. Continuing Faculty are hired on the basis of their academic and professional preparation, as well as a demonstrated commitment to high-quality instruction.

STUDENTS

The typical Massey Professional MBA student has 6 years of business experience, is 29 years old, and works full-time, while completing the degree program in 2 years. The typical Accelerated MBA student has less than 2 years of business experience, is 23-24 years old, and is focused full-time on completing the degree program in 1 year. MACC Students also tend to be somewhat younger as a group, with less business experience and are preparing to sit for the CPA exam. Many MACCs are full-time graduate Students.

ADMISSIONS

All applicants are required to complete the GMAT or GRE test, submit a personal essay and two recommendations, submit transcripts from all undergraduate coursework, and have completed a minimum of two years of business experience. The experience requirement is waived for MACC and Accelerated MBA applicants. A personal interview is required of all graduate applicants. Testing may be waived for physicians who are board-certified.

SPECIAL PROGRAMS

Massey graduate Students who complete elective coursework (2 courses) in business negotiation and mediation are eligible for listing as an "Approved Rule 31 Mediator" by the Supreme Court of the State of Tennessee. And other certifications such as Six Sigma green and black belt status are also available..

CAREER SERVICES AND PLACEMENT

The Massey School has a dedicated Career Development Center that provides comprehensive career services to graduate business Students and alumni. Career Services are a lifetime benefit for alumni of The Massey School.

CLARK UNIVERSITY
Graduate School of Management

950 Main Street
Worcester, MA 01610
www.clarku.edu/gsom
Admissions Contact:
Phone: 508-793-7373

Email: gradAdmissions@clarku.edu

FAST FACTS
° Accredited by AACSB International

° Named a Princeton Review Best Business School

° Ranked in top 16 MBA programs for 'green business'

Accredited by AACSB International, Clark GSOM ranks among the most prestigious business schools in the world. We offer Students the highest quality curriculum, educational resources, and opportunities.

Our professors include some of the most highly regarded and groundbreaking researchers in fields from leadership to finance to corporate social responsibility. They have years of industry experience, are widely published, love to teach, and bring innovative ideas to the classroom.

Living and studying in Worcester, Massachusetts - the second largest city in New England - offers several distinct advantages, including easy access to exciting job and internship opportunities. What's more, from Clark's historic, tree-lined campus, you can get to Boston and some of the country's most beautiful beaches and mountains in less than an hour and to New York City in just three hours.

GSOM partners with a Clark's renowned International Development, Community, and Environment (IDCE) department, allowing student to develop cross-sector skills sought by forward thinking nonprofit organizations and corporations worldwide.

ACADEMIC PROGRAMS
Master of Business Administration (MBA)
Master of Science in Finance (MSF)
Master of Science in Accounting (MSA)
MBA/MA in Community Development & Planning
MBA/MS in Environmental Science & Policy
MBA/MSA
MBA/MSF

MBA

The MBA program is a maximum of 17 course units (51 credits) and a minimum of 12 course units (36 credits) depending on the academic background of the student (up to 5 course units can be waived based on prior coursework). Full-time Students typically complete the program in 2 years although Students with course waivers may finish in 1.5 years.

The MBA program offers eight concentrations.

Six classic concentrations: Accounting; Finance; Global Business; Information Systems; Management; Marketing

Two new concentrations:

Social Change - Demand is surging for professionals who understand the socio-political forces that shape communities and businesses. Students take elective courses mainly offered in IDCE in subject areas including social entrepreneurship, community development, and international development.

Sustainability - Couples the principles of environmental sustainability with the business strategies and fundamentals necessary to achieve responsible management at both the local and global level.

Courses include Eco-Entrepreneurship, Energy Management, Sustainability Marketing, and Sustainability Consulting Projects.

The MSA program is 10-course units (30 credits) plus 2 foundation course units (which are both eligible to be waived based on prior coursework). Full-time Students can complete the program in 1 year.

The program is Level 1 approved by the Board of Public Accountancy meaning graduates have automatically fulfilled the education requirement to sit for the CPA exam, for which they are well-prepared.

MSF

The MSF program is 10 course units (30 credits) and Students typically complete the program in 3 semesters and graduate in December.

The program is heavily quantitative and prepares Students for a variety of careers in the finance field. Clark GSOM is one of the only schools in the US to partner with the Chartered Alternative Investment Analyst Association and one of a handful offering courses on hedge funds.

Dual Degrees Offered in GSOM:

Gain the breadth of an MBA and the depth of an MS and stand out to employers with an MBA/MSA or MBA/MSF. These programs are 23 course units (69 credits) and 5 of those course units are eligible to be waived based on prior coursework. Students typically take 3 years to complete the dual degree programs.

Dual Degrees Offered in conjunction with IDCE:

MBA/MS in Environmental Science & Policy

MBA/MA in Community Development & Planning

Earn two world class degrees in three years. These dual degrees are 24 course units (72 credits) and 5 of those units are eligible to be waived based on prior coursework.

EXPENSES AND FINANCIAL AID
2013-2014 tuition
MBA: $3860 per course unit
MS: $4150 per course unit
Dual degrees with IDCE: $4380 per course unit
Clark GSOM offers generous merit-based scholarships ranging from 25 percent to 100 percent of tuition.

STUDENT BODY

Clark GSOM is proud to welcome a diverse student population who represent the multinational nature of business today. About 50 percent of full-time Students are international from more than 20 countries. Students come from a wide variety of industry and functional backgrounds, from large multinational corporations and small family-run enterprises, and at different stages in their careers including some who come straight from undergrad. This multiplicity of experiences and backgrounds benefits our Students as they learn first-hand how to manage in a diverse community.

CAREER SERVICES
Experience the difference at the Stevenish Career Management Center where successful corporate recruiters have 'crossed over' to university career services.

With three decades of corporate recruiting and HR expertise, we create successful relationships with employers looking to hire talented, resourceful business professionals. Our real-world, real-life approach to career planning and job searching provides Students with the optimal skillset to achieve their goals.

DUQUESNE UNIVERSITY
Donahue School of Business

AT A GLANCE

The Donahue Graduate School of Business at Duquesne University in Pittsburgh, Pennsylvania, prepares responsible leaders who are capable of transforming organizations, communities and the world. We challenge our Students to reach their full potential, reflecting our university's century-long commitment to ethics and service, excellence and innovation. Among the graduate business schools accredited by AACSB-International, Duquesne was among the first 100 endorsers of the Principles for Responsible Management Education (PRME). The Donahue School ranks among the Global Top 25 on the Aspen Institute's Beyond Grey Pinstripes for integrating social and environmental stewardship into the full-time MBA and was cited among the top three graduate business schools for ethics by the Academy of Management Learning and Education.

RESEARCH FACILITIES

Gumberg Library brings over 200 world class e-research databases to Students' fingertips. The university library itself houses over 710,500 volumes, more than 19,000 journal titles, and an extensive microprint and audiovisual center. Other library facilities include an online card catalog and a CD-ROM center that gives Students access to hundreds of additional periodicals not physically housed in the library.

The Donahue School also operates independent centers including an Investment Center, the Beard Institute, the Chrysler Corporation Small Business Development Center, the Center for Competitive Workforce Development and the Center for International Regulatory Assistance.

The Investment Center offers access to syndicated databases and sophisticated analytical tools in a classroom setting that mimics worldwide trading operations with real-time data feeds for stocks, bonds, international markets, futures, options and other securities. Students have regular access to historical and current data from Boomberg(r), Reuters(r), Morningstar(r), Ibbotson(r), Compustat(r), CSI(r) and KLD(r) and Trucost. Adjacent technology labs offer state-of-the-art software for enterprise resource planning (ERP), networking, modeling and computing.

The Beard Institute focuses on the importance of business ethics, responsible financial management and sustainability in the global marketplace and offers educational programing and resources.

FINANCIAL AID

Full-time MBA Sustainability and Macc Programs: All applicants are considered for merit scholarships, research fellowships and graduate assistantships based on the strength of application materials.

Evening MBA and MS-ISM programs: A limited number of graduate assistantships, which provide up to 9 credits of tuition remission each semester and a monthly cash stipend, are available on a merit basis to high potential Students who take the equivalent of a full-time course load (8 or more credits) in evening classes.

COST OF STUDY

The MBA Sustainability program is billed in three equal installments. Tuition for 2013-14 is $15,125 per semester and fees are $1,236 per semester, totaling $49,083 for the three semester program. Tuition and fees do not include airfare, incidentals or some meals for the mandatory international study trip.

The evening MBA, MAcc and MS-ISM programs are billed on a per credit basis. Tuition for the 2013-14 academic year is $1,009 per credit and the university fee is an additional $96 per credit.

LIVING AND HOUSING COSTS

Although space is limited, graduate housing is available on campus. Furnished and unfurnished studio, one and two bedroom apartments on campus can be rented at annual rates ranging from $13,140 to $24,255. Most graduate Students prefer off-campus housing, which is abundant and affordable. The University's Office of Residence Life assists Students in finding off-campus housing in Pittsburgh's many residential communities.

STUDENT BODY

The Donahue School student body of approximately 350 Students is diverse. Duquesne actively recruits and enrolls Students from Africa, Asia, Europe, and Latin America, bringing an international dimension to every classroom. Evening Students make up about 85 percent of the study body. Many work at Pittsburgh's multi-national and regional firms and bring real-world issues to the classroom experience. The daytime MBA Sustainability Students, over half of whom hail from outside the region, take their core courses as a cohort during the day. They bring a broad range of geographic, ethnic, educational and professional backgrounds to their studies and field work. MAcc Students also take daytime classes as a cohort. Evening and daytime student interface regularly for idea cafes with corporate partners, symposia, case competitions, speaker events, intramural sports, and student organizations such as Net Impact and the Donahue Business Society.

LOCATION

Long noted as one of the world's great business centers, Pittsburgh combines the features of big-city living with many of the charms and personal characteristics of a much smaller town. Consistently ranked among the most livable cities for its safe neighborhoods and living standards, Pittsburgh has a large concentration of corporate headquarters, a strong civic identity and a sense of pride in its rebirth as a modern urban community. Students from Duquesne and neighboring universities participate in a wide variety of cultural, social, recreational and sporting activities in Western Pennsylvania.

APPLYING

Required application materials for all programs: on-line biographical application form, official transcripts and GMAT scores, two professional references/ratings, personal essays (questions vary by program), and a resume or vitae. TOEFL scores are required for international Students who completed their undergraduate degrees in a language other than English.

The full-time MBA Sustainability admits one cohort per academic year. Early decision applications are accepted from September through February 1, and rolling admission continues until July 1. Scholarships, fellowships and graduate assistantships are granted on a merit basis, and all applicants are considered based on the strength of application materials. http://mba.sustainability.duq.edu.

The evening MBA program accepts new Students in Fall and Spring and Summer. Application deadlines are July 1 for Fall enrollment, November 1 for Spring Admissions and April 1 for Summer Admissions. A separate application is required for candidates interested in graduate assistantships. www.duq.edu/mba

The MAcc program accepts early admission applications from September through February 1 and offers rolling Admissions until July 1. Graduate assistantships are granted on a merit basis, and all applicants are considered based on the strength of application materials. www.duq.edu/macc

The MS-ISM program accepts early admission applications from September through February 1 and offers rolling Admissions until July 1. Graduate assistantships are granted on a merit basis, and all applicants are considered based on the strength of application materials. Deadlines are July 1 for Fall admission. www.duq.edu/msism

FAIRFIELD UNIVERSITY
Charles F. Dolan School of Business

AT A GLANCE

Fairfield University was founded in 1942 by the Jesuits, a Roman Catholic order renowned for its 450-year-old tradition of excellence in education and service to others. This Jesuit tradition inspires a commitment to educating the whole person for a life of leadership in a constantly changing world. Fairfield University welcomes students of all faiths and beliefs who value its mission of scholarship and social justice, and it values the diversity the students bring to the university community. Faculty members are known and respected for their accessibility to students as mentors and advisors.

CAMPUS AND LOCATION

Set on 200 acres of woods and rolling lawns with views of nearby Long Island Sound, Fairfield's campus is a beautiful setting for study and personal growth. The beaches of the Sound offer recreation, while the woods and trails of Southern New England offer hiking, biking and other outdoor activities. Metro North railroad, also in town, enables students to travel into New York City for all the diverse cultural and career opportunities. Further, Fairfield County itself is a Mecca for small and large corporations, with one of the largest concentrations of Fortune 500 companies in the nation.

DEGREES OFFERED

Programs

The MBA (36-54 credits, depending on waivers)

The MBA program has three components: core courses, breadth courses, and concentration courses. The core courses are functional courses, designed to provide fundamental tools and functional area competencies for students who either did not major in a business discipline as undergraduates or took only a portion of the functional courses that comprise the MBA core. The core courses are prerequisites to the breadth of the MBA program. Certain core courses MAY be waived, based on review of the individual's undergraduate academic background.

Core Courses - 18 credits

AC 400	Introduction to Accounting
FI 400	Principles of Finance
MG 400	Organizational Behavior
MK 400	Marketing Management
OM 400	Integrated Business Processes
QA 400	Applied Business Statistics

The breadth courses are specially designed by each department to provide students with in-depth coverage of an important disciplinary topic that will enable the students to become more competent (and competitive) managers. Regardless of one's intended area of concentration, all MBA students must complete the breadth classes.

Breadth Courses - 18 credits

AC 500	Accounting for Decision-Making
FI 500	Shareholders Value
IS 500	Information Systems
MG 500	Leadership
MG 503	Legal and Ethical Environment of Business
MK 500	Customer Value

Concentration Courses - 12 credits

Four courses are required from one of the following concentrations (Accounting, Accounting Information Systems, Entrepreneurship, Finance, Human Resource Management, ISOM, General Management, International Business, Marketing or Taxation).

In addition, each student has one free elective (any 500 level course - 3 credits), as well as the Capstone course in global competitive strategy (MG 584 - 3 credits).

The Master of Science in Finance (30 credits)

The MS in Finance provides unique opportunities for individuals who want to enhance their career opportunities in the areas of investments, corporate finance, or banking. The program consists of ten 3-credit courses (7 required and 3 electives) and is especially useful for those who want to pursue advanced certification, such as the CFA, CFM or CFP. Applicants must have completed at least an undergraduate degree and have an adequate background in micro- and macroeconomics, financial accounting, and statistics.

Master of Science in Accounting (30 credits)

The MS in Accounting is designed to provide students who have obtained a B.S. degree in Accounting advanced studies in the discipline, as well as the requisite extra credits to enable students to meet the 150 hours to sit for the uniform CPA exam. The MSA is a one-year, full-time program, which the students begin immediately following Commencement in May. Courses are taken over the summer, then during the following fall and spring academic semesters. In addition to needing an undergraduate degree in accounting, applicants must have adequate background in micro- and macroeconomics, statistics and college-level mathematics.

Certificate Programs for Advanced Study (15 credits)

The Certificate Programs for Advanced Study are appropriate for working professionals who have already earned a graduate degree. Such individuals may need to either further their knowledge within their area of expertise or acquire knowledge from another discipline in order to adequately perform their duties and/or advance within their organizations. These programs enable such students to focus their studies on courses within a specific discipline.

Financial Aid: Student Loan programs available.

Graduate Assistantships available on a competitive basis.

Student Body: approximately even split on gender; approximately 40% attend on a full-time basis (3 or more classes a semester).

ADMISSIONS

Mark Ligas, PhD

Associate Dean

Director of Graduate Programs

www.fairfield.edu/mba

INDIANA UNIVERSITY OF PENNSYLVANIA

Eberly College of Business and Information Technology

AT A GLANCE

The Eberly College of Business and Information Technology MBA program (accredited by AACSB International), with its global strategy focus and highly international student and Faculty composition, is designed to sharpen Students' managerial, analytical, and decision-making skills so that they can compete in today's global environment. The Eberly MBA program has a long tradition of providing cost-effective preparation for a successful career in business. IUP is consistently ranked among the best institutions in the region for cost, and academic quality by a wide variety of sources such as The Princeton Review's Best Business Schools; Kiplinger's Personal Finance Magazine; Barron's Best Buys in College Education; Forbes Magazine's America's Best Colleges, The New York Times; Money magazine; Entrepreneur Magazine and U.S. News and World Report.

CAMPUS AND LOCATION

Indiana University of Pennsylvania enrolls 15,100 Students from across the nation and around the globe. Located in the heart of Indiana, Pa. (70 miles Northeast of Pittsburgh, PA), IUP's main campus has grown from twelve acres and one building in 1875, to 354 acres and 75 major buildings now. In recent years, IUP has been replaced more than a dozen residential and academic buildings to enhance the campus's living-learning environment. The small town atmosphere of Indiana PA brings the double advantage of low cost of living as well as safe and friendly living environments to the Students. Proximity to the city of Pittsburgh brings the connections with major businesses and corporations of the area to enhance internship and career building connections.

DEGREES OFFERED

Eberly College offers a full-time, on-campus MBA program for young professionals and recent college graduates that can be completed in 12 months. In addition, an executive MBA program for experienced working professionals is available at IUP's off-campus sites in the Monroeville, Northpointe (Pittsburgh) and Johnstown area. In a partnership with PES Institutions, Bangalore, India we also offer the IUP MBA program at PES campus in Bangalore. The college also offers bachelor's degrees in accounting, entrepreneurship and small business management, finance, general management, human resource management, supply chain management, international business, management information systems, and marketing.

The MBA

The Eberly MBA is a 36-credit, integrated, general management program with an option to complete concentrations/specializations (nine/twelve additional credits) in Finance, Human Resource Management, International Business, Marketing, Professional Accountancy or Supply Chain Management. The MBA courses focus on business applications and current analytical tools and techniques and strongly emphasize information technology utilization in managerial problem solving. A variety of elective courses are available in each of the concentration areas. Opportunities are available for internships with local, national, and international organizations.

FACILITIES

A state-of-the-art, $12-million facility houses the MBA classrooms. The Eberly complex is a beautiful, four-story facility that offer a spacious atrium for student interaction and studying, complete wireless access, a café, a 450-seat auditorium, and a 24-hour computing lab operation. Students of the Eberly College study in one of the most technologically advanced business schools in the country. The Eberly complex houses more than 600 computer workstations; more than 20 file servers; nine computing labs, including a financial trading room; digital production studio; wireless technology throughout the campus; and online access to comprehensive business periodicals and journals databases. The college also houses a Small Business Institute and a Small Business Incubator where

MBA Students can gain business consulting and entrepreneurship experience. The Financial Trading Room in Eberly offers Students databases and related software to conduct financial analysis and learn valuation techniques, arbitrage techniques, and portfolio risk-management strategies. Eberly also offers the Bloomberg Professional service software system, an industry-grade comprehensive data-monitoring and analytical tool used to train Students to study real-time movements in global markets. Marketing department of the college houses the Consumer Neuroscience lab for research in the field of buyer behavior in which MBA Students can participate as research assistants.

EXPENSES AND FINANCIAL AID

Tuition, Pennsylvania residents, 2012-2013: $416/credit
Tuition, non-Pennsylvania residents, 2012-2013: $624/credit

Miscellaneous fees (for 9 credits/semester) are approximately $1,085 (residents) and $1,479 (non-residents)/semester. On-campus housing costs: from $2,230/semester (double room) to $3,169/semester (single room); [Tuition/Fees/Housing Costs are subject to change every academic year]

More than 30 percent of full-time MBA Students receive graduate assistantships on a competitive basis that include a full- or partial-tuition waiver and a stipend. International Students are eligible to compete for partial-tuition waiver during the first semester of study. Travel support scholarships are available for Students to do summer study abroad program in our Bangalore, India, MBA Program.

FACULTY

Eberly MBA courses are taught by Faculty members who have doctoral degrees in their fields of specialization and extensive research and publication track records. Their international backgrounds and/or exposure, experience in industry, and current research projects bring an ideal blend of theory and practice to the MBA courses. Eberly Faculty members serve as editors on nine national/international journals.

STUDENTS

Eberly provides Students with an opportunity to learn with a diverse group of individuals. More than half the Students are from 30 countries other than the U.S., 26 percent have previous business work experience, and 6 percent are currently working full-time in professional careers. Eberly College takes great pride in the activities and initiatives of its College of Business Student Advisory Council and the members of its 14 student organizations. Eberly College of Business Graduate Business Students Association provides MBA Students professional development opportunities including participation in regional and national case competitions, company visits, career-fair visits and group visits to professional and business organizations in New York, Chicago and Washington, DC.

ADMISSIONS

Requirements for admission include a completed undergraduate degree in any field with a superior academic track record from an accredited college/university, GMAT scores, academic/professional letters of recommendation, and the applicant's career goal statement and resume. The GMAT score of admitted candidates range from 450-720 with an average GMAT of 520; the average undergraduate grade point average is 3.2. GRE scores are accepted as a substitute for GMAT. International applicants must also submit an official TOEFL score report with a minimum score of 76 (iBT Score) or IELTS minimum score of 6.0 and an affidavit of financial support indicating availability of sufficient funds to study in the U.S. For information and a complete application packet, visit www.iup.edu/mba ; contact Dr. Krish Krishnan, Eberly College MBA Program, 301 Eberly College of Business and Information Technology, IUP, 664 Pratt Drive, Indiana, PA 15705; or e-mail iup-mba@iup.edu or Krishnan@iup.edu; Telephone: 1-724-357-2522 Fax: 1-724-357-6232.

LOYOLA UNIVERSITY—CHICAGO
Quinlan School of Business

AT A GLANCE
At Loyola University Chicago's Quinlan School of Business, we provide an excellent Faculty, diversity of Students, the vast resources of a great university, and individualized attention to create a superb learning environment. By studying with us, you will enhance your ability to think critically, solve problems, work in a team environment, think strategically about technology, and effectively communicate your ideas. Consistent with 450 years of Jesuit education, we emphasize the foundation necessary to make ethical decisions in today's complex business environment.

CAMPUS AND LOCATION
The Quinlan School of Business is located adjacent to Chicago's Magnificent Mile at Loyola's Water Tower Campus. Chicago is home to the Chicago Board of Trade, Chicago Board Options Exchange, and Chicago Mercantile Exchange, making the city one of the largest financial trading centers in the world. Many national and multinational companies in a broad range of industries are headquartered in Chicago. As a result, job opportunities at major firms abound throughout the Chicago area, in fields as diverse as manufacturing, retailing, health care, and consulting.

Campus resources include a student center, conference rooms, computer labs, libraries, Faculty and administrative offices, food services, a wellness center, and an exercise facility.

The Business Career Services office staff assists Quinlan School of Business Students in making satisfying and informed career decisions, setting appropriate goals, and creating opportunities to help meet those goals. In addition, internship opportunities are available for Students needing to build their resumes and those considering a career change.

ACADEMIC PROGRAMS
At Loyola University Chicago's Quinlan School of Business, we help prepare graduate Students for the global demands of business by routinely including international considerations in all our courses and by offering courses that singularly focus on the international dimensions of a topic. Students whose career goals demand an intensive grounding in international business can take advantage of our innovative study abroad programs. We offer two-week courses at a number of international locations including our campuses in Beijing and Rome. Each course focuses on topical international issues. Both part-time and full-time Students have the opportunity to attend.

Additionally, graduate business Students can attend overseas programs through the AJCU (the Association of Jesuit Colleges and Universities).

TUITION AND HOUSING
Tuition for 2012-2013 is $4,011 per course for both full- and part-time Students. A wide variety of housing options are available both on and off campus. Many full-time Students live within walking distance of the Quinlan Graduate School of Business. Other Students choose to live in housing located on the Water Tower Campus. The estimated cost of room and board for 12 months is $14,500.

FINANCIAL AID
Graduate scholarship positions, providing tuition support and monetary stipends, are available through the Quinlan GSB. Merit scholarships are also available. All Students are automatically considered for the merit scholarship upon admission.

FACULTY
The Loyola University Chicago Quinlan School of Business Faculty is strongly committed to teaching as well as research. Because 88 percent of the Faculty members are full time and 91 percent of those have a PhD or equivalent degree, classes are taught by experienced, highly trained leaders in their fields. Quinlan also augments regular Faculty with practicing managers and consultants who teach classes in special topics, such as emerging technologies and negotiations.

As leaders in their fields, many Faculty members have important industry and community ties in such areas as financial and policy studies, consulting, and marketing and communications. In the classroom, they offer a scholarly approach gained through research as well as practical business experience.

Our Faculty's dedication to research invigorates the MBA experience by developing new ideas that can be applied in the classroom. The Faculty is involved in an impressive range of research projects in all major areas of business and is also widely published.

STUDENT ORGANIZATIONS AND ACTIVITIES
Being an active member of a student organization enriches the overall Quinlan GSB experience with friendships, leadership experiences, professional growth, industry-specific knowledge, and connections with alumni. Potential employers see our Students' commitment to the program and to a balance between their academic and social lives.

Quinlan School of Business Student Organizations:

- Association of Loyola Entrepreneurs
- Economics Forum
- Graduate Marketing Association
- Graduate Women in Business
- Human Resource Student Association
- Investment Banking & Financial Markets Association
- LUC Net Impact
- Quinlan Consulting Group
- Quinlan Graduate Advisory Council
- Quinlan Graduate Business Student Association
- Quinlan Graduate International Club (Quinlan GIC)

ADMISSIONS
A rolling Admissions policy allows the flexibility to enroll in any of the four quarters during the academic year. Prospective Students should apply well in advance of the quarter in which they plan to enter. Applications are accepted until July 15 for the fall quarter; October 1 for the winter quarter; January 15 for the spring quarter; and April 1 for the summer quarter.

Admission decisions are based on demonstrated interest, aptitude, and capacity for business study, as indicated by the previous academic record, GMAT or GRE scores, a written statement of purpose, letters of recommendation, and professional experience. Our average admitted student's undergraduate GPA is 3.2, average GMAT score is 550, and average work experience is three to five years.

Loyola welcomes applications from international Students who have completed a four-year bachelor's degree or its equivalent.

For more information:

http://luc.edu/quinlan/mba/

LOYOLA UNIVERSITY—NEW ORLEANS

Joseph A. Butt, S.J. College of Business

AT A GLANCE

The Master of Business Administration Program at Loyola University New Orleans is designed for ambitious working executives seeking to bolster their career by obtaining the skills needed to lead complex organizations. The coursework is demanding and analytically rigorous, based on internationally-proven standards of performance excellence. The curriculum is purposefully designed using a "horizontal" and "systems-based" approach to leadership education, which is in sharp contrast to traditional "silo" curricula designed to produce functional specialists. The program's advanced approach is highly valued by elite organizations competing in internationally competitive industries. Students are encouraged to obtain professional certifications by the American Society for Quality (Six Sigma) and Project Management Institute (PMP or CAPM), while receiving training in Malcolm Baldrige Award Architecture design and assessment. Such validations of commitment to professional excellence are more desired by many of the nation's highest performing organizations than the MBA degree itself.

In addition, the program includes a renowned, hands-on entrepreneurship track through which a university-sponsored Angel Fund raises money for real startup businesses. Students specializing in entrepreneurship have practical experience in creating and evaluating funding proposals for a new business, as well as creating business plans for implementation.

The program has a strong ethical content based on Jesuit/Catholic commitment to social justice. A core belief of the program is that social justice is best served through the creation of companies who hire employees and treat them well, as well as creating innovative products that satisfy customers and make the world a better place.

PLACEMENT

The program boasts a very high, virtually 100 percent, recent placement rate at professional jobs. Recent graduates have been employed by several Fortune 500 companies, including General Electric, General Motors, Symetra, and Shell, while Students not changing employers almost universally report of promotions and advances at work. The content of the program, especially certifications by outside professional groups, is highly valued in a competitive job market. Coursework focuses on real projects with real organizations with real applications.

CAMPUS AND LOCATION

Loyola University New Orleans is located five miles from the Central Business District on historic St. Charles Avenue in the heart of one of the most beautiful neighborhoods. New Orleans has been rated by several sources as one of the most active and growing business climates, especially for startups and high tech companies. The city has emerged from the devastation of Katrina with a can-do spirit ideal for ambitious young executives and entrepreneurs.

DEGREES OFFERED

Loyola University New Orleans offers a traditional MBA program that can be taken at a full-time or part-time basis. Additionally, a JD/MBA program is offered in coordination with the College of Law and an MBA/MPS program in coordination with the Loyola Pastoral Studies.

ACADEMIC PROGRAMS

Loyola's MBA program is designed for working professionals. Most Students complete the MBA program in two years. The program is intentionally designed to be small with highly selected and screened applicants, who are capable of fostering the values upon which the program is based.

Minimum requirements for graduation are 27 hours of "core" classes, 6 hours of elective classes, and a 3 hour "Capstone" business plan project, for a total of 36 hours, although many Students opt to take additional coursework. Students who have not completed undergraduate coursework in fundamental business topics from an AACSB-accredited business school may be required to take as many as 18 credit hours of preparatory classes.

Classes are offered exclusively in the evenings to allow Students to apply the concepts taught in the coursework to organizations. Students not employed in New Orleans on arrival will be placed in organizations or assigned to our award-winning Small Business Development Center. Outside-class experiences are essential to the mastery of concepts taught in class. Both are required for success.

No classes are taught online, as our experience dictates that learning is a dialogue and the internet is largely a monologue.

FACILITIES

Loyola offers the typical wi-fi connections throughout campus and has a computer lab dedicated for business Students. With the addition of the Carlos M. Ayala Stock Trading room, Students in the College of Business have access to state-of-the-art technological resources for increased educational experience.

Loyola's Monroe Library offers the latest in online technology, as well as traditional book and periodical references. Students and Faculty have online computer network access at each table and study carrel, allowing more than 700 simultaneous computer links to millions of resources across the globe. The library has been ranked one of ten best nationwide by the Princeton Review since 2006.

EXPENSES AND FINANCIAL AID

The current MBA tuition is $1005 per credit hour. For Additional Information about tuition and financial aid, please visit http://www.business.loyno.edu/mba/tuition-fees-financial-aid.

ADMISSION

The MBA application process is housed online via http://www.business.loyno.edu/mba/apply-now, where applicants complete the required forms, upload a current resume and personal statement, and email a formal request and instructions to two recommenders. Applicants must also submit an application fee, official transcripts, and an official score report for the GMAT or GRE. Work experience, though not required, is strongly recommended. A minimum 500 GMAT or 300 GRE score is required for consideration.

International Students requiring an F-1 or J-1 visa must provide verification of English proficiency and an affidavit demonstrating sufficient financial resources to support themselves during their tenure at the university in addition to the general application materials.

MISSOURI STATE UNIVERSITY
College of Business

AT A GLANCE

The College of Business (COB) at Missouri State University is the largest AACSB-accredited public college of business in the state of Missouri and in the Midwest region with over 4,700 Students. Meeting rigorous AACSB International (Association to Advance Collegiate Schools of Business) accreditation standards means that the College and the University have committed the necessary resources to achieve and maintain a high quality, nationally-competitive program. AACSB accreditation also ensures that COB graduate Students will be taught by terminally-degreed Faculty who are actively publishing in their disciplines. Educational value in this program is defined by a high quality, culturally-diverse program in a safe, inviting campus community situated in Springfield, Missouri.

CAMPUS AND LOCATION

The Missouri State University campus is located in the heart of Springfield, Missouri, near attractions like Hammons Field (home of St. Louis Cardinals' AA affiliate, the Springfield Cardinals) and the resurgent downtown district. Updated campus amenities include a recently expanded library, a University Recreation Center and continuously updated open-access computer labs.

DEGREES OFFERED

The College of Business at Missouri State includes seven academic departments: Accounting, Computer Information Systems, Fashion and Interior Design, Finance and General Business, Technology and Construction Management, Management, and Marketing, offering 29 undergraduate programs.

COB has five graduate programs, including the Master of Accountancy, Master of Business Administration, Master of Science in Computer Information Systems, Master of Health Administration, and Master of Project Management.

PROGRAMS AND CURRICULUM

The Missouri State MBA program (mba.missouristate.edu) has an important strength-flexibility. Along with integrating a variety of courses offered by seven departments in the College of Business, the MBA program allows Students an opportunity to tailor their degree to meet their career needs. Apart from the 24 credits required, Students choose an area of concentration (9 credits) to help focus their MBA degree. This flexibility gives MBA Students the opportunity to structure an MBA degree to match their interests. If needed, Missouri State's program provides a solid foundation of prerequisite graduate-level courses that prepare Students for the advanced topics covered in the core MBA program. Students with appropriate prior academic preparation in business will be able to complete the 33 credit program in one calendar year. A part-time, online MBA is now available, as well.

Students also have access to a professional student group, the MBA Association, launched in Spring 2012. The MBA Association provides professional development and networking opportunities for all MBA candidates.

The Master of Accountancy (http://www.missouristate.edu/soa/Graduate/) program is designed to fulfill the education needs of professional accountants. The mission of the program is to offer graduate Students the opportunity to enhance their business common body of knowledge and specialized accounting knowledge beyond the foundational undergraduate level.

The MS CIS Program (http://mscis.missouristate.edu/) is an accelerated course of study leading to a Master of Science in Computer Information Systems degree. Developed exclusively for Information Technology professionals with three or more years of work experience, the program enables Students to earn an accredited MS CIS degree in just 23 months without interrupting their careers.

The Master of Health Administration (http://mha.missouristate.edu/) degree includes a number of health management and policy courses contributed by Public Health, Economics & Political Science in addition to courses taught by business Faculty. The program is designed for Students holding undergraduate degrees who wish to further their careers in the administration of health organizations.

FACILITIES

COB is housed in David D. Glass Hall, an 185,000 square foot state-of-the-art building containing classrooms, four computer classrooms and four computer labs supplied with the latest technological equipment. Newly added, the COB Student Study Lounge, which features lounge chairs and couches, individual and group study areas, as well as wireless internet access.

EXPENSES AND FINANCIAL AID

Tuition for the 2013-14 academic year is $279 per credit hour for Missouri residents. Out-of-state resident tuition is $526 per credit hour. Graduate assistantships are available, which waive the base cost of tuition and provide a stipend. Assistantships are awarded on a competitive basis and require the student to work 20 hours per week.

FACULTY

The College of Business employs 118 Faculty. A total of 95 percent of the full-time Faculty hold doctorates. Many Faculty have received state and national recognition for accomplishments in teaching and research.

STUDENT BODY

Our graduate student population includes working professionals and traditional Students plus Students from South America, Africa, Europe, and Asia. Such diversity offers the opportunity for Students to share a broad perspective on global business events. International Students make up approximately 40 percent of the graduate student population and represent 32 countries from around the world.

ADMISSIONS

Admission requirements for the various COB graduate programs vary. For specific admission information, visit our website at www.business.missouristate.edu.

ADVISEMENT

Students in the College of Business are advised by nationally-recognized staff, both at the undergraduate and graduate (MBA) levels. Each advisor holds an MBA (or is a candidate for the MBA) and maintains Master Advisor certification each year. Advisors in the College are active in the state and national associations and also contribute to the learning community on-campus.

CAREER SERVICES AND PLACEMENT

Students are assisted in their career search by the Career Services office located within the College of Business in Glass Hall, Room 103. Resume preparation assistance, enhancement of interviewing techniques, and internship placement assistance are some of the services provided. Each fall, over 100 firms visit the College of Business during the annual COB Career Fair and/or participate in ongoing campus recruiting.

NORTH CAROLINA STATE UNIVERSITY
Jenkins Graduate School of Management

AT A GLANCE

At NC State's Jenkins Graduate School of Management, we've created an MBA with focus. The NC State MBA Program will help you develop a keen understanding of general business and management principles. And your concentrated study of a technology-oriented business process or function will give you an edge in the marketplace.

The NC State MBA offers a full-time program, a professional program with campuses in Raleigh and RTP for working professionals, and a professional online program.

Our focus on outstanding MBA education is illustrated by a reputation for excellence in technology management, an innovative Faculty with cutting-edge teaching and research, quality Students from diverse backgrounds, and unmatched value in management education.

CAMPUS AND LOCATION

NC State was founded in 1887 as a land-grant institution that has become one of the nation's leading research universities. Located in the Research Triangle, a world-renowned center of research, industry, and technology, the Poole College of Management is housed on the 2,110-acre main campus of NC State, which lies just west of downtown Raleigh, the state capital. NC State comprises eleven colleges and schools, serving a total student population of over 30,000.

DEGREES OFFERED

MBA-Master of Business Administration

Full-time (55 credit hours) and professional (39 credit hours) programs. Concentrations/Areas of Emphasis: Biosciences Management, Entrepreneurship & Technology Commercialization, Financial Management, Marketing Management, Product Innovation Management, Services Management, and Supply Chain Management

ACADEMIC PROGRAMS

The NC State MBA curriculum was designed to prepare Students for management careers and to provide unique offerings of technology-oriented courses and concentrations/areas of emphasis.

Our areas of emphasis will give you an opportunity to focus your studies on a specialized technology process or critical business function. Each area of emphasis includes some required courses and a choice among electives in that field, and most require Students to complete a semester-long team project by working closely with a corporate client to solve a relevant business problem.

No matter what your background, you will be surrounded by classmates with a wide range of experience. In some of the technical courses, you will work on projects with Students from NC State's highly regarded graduate programs in computer science, engineering, design, and the sciences.

FACILITIES

The College of Management is located in Nelson Hall, which houses classrooms, computer labs, and the offices of the Faculty members and Students. Classrooms have been completely remodeled with tiered seating, laptop connections, and complete multimedia facilities. Nelson Hall is also wireless accessible. We also have a campus in Research Triangle Park, which is convenient to many of our working professionals.

EXPENSES AND FINANCIAL AID

The estimated total tuition beginning in the 2013-2014 school year is $39,954 for North Carolina residents in the full-time program and $65,600 for non-residents in the full-time program. Estimated total expenses for Students in the professional program is $36,000-47,076.

Graduate assistantships are available to full-time Students. Graduate assistantships cover full or partial tuition, health insurance, and a monthly stipend. Grants and loan programs are available through the Graduate School and the University's Financial Aid Office.

FACULTY

The College of Management has built a Faculty rich in technology-related business expertise, management experience and practical research. Our professors also have a passion for teaching and a commitment to working closely with industry to solve real-world problems. Our Faculty excel in both traditional scholarly pursuits and practical, corporate-sponsored research. We are home to a number of extensively published scholars, and editors and editorial board members of prestigious research journals.

STUDENTS

Almost all MBA Students have professional work experience, many in high-technology industries, such as telecommunications or software and others in industries, such as health care or financial services. A technical background is not essential for the MBA, but all Students must be willing to learn about technology and the management challenges it creates.

The average full-time MBA student has four years of work experience. The age range of Students is between 22 and 45. Women comprise approximately 35 percent of each entering class; members of minority groups, approximately eight percent; and international Students, 32 percent.

ADMISSIONS

Admission to the MBA program is highly competitive. Applicants need to demonstrate the following personal accomplishments and attributes:

1. Strong intellectual performance and academic promise, evidenced by previous undergraduate and graduate work as well as GMAT scores

2. An employment history demonstrating management potential

3. Leadership skills, maturity, creativity, initiative and teamwork orientation

4. A desire and willingness to learn about technology and the management challenges it creates

MBA Students must have a baccalaureate degree from an accredited college or university. Admissions decisions are based on previous academic performance, GMAT or GRE scores (those with graduate degrees should contact the MBA office for information on waivers), essays, letters of reference, and previous work experience. Applicants whose native language is other than English, regardless of citizenship, must also submit TOEFL or IELTS scores (professional program applicants may qualify for a waiver and should inquire with the MBA office). Interviews are required for applicants for both the full-time and professional MBA programs.

SPECIAL PROGRAMS

The NC State MBA Program now offers dual masters degrees in Accounting, Biomanufacturing, Global Innovation Management, Industrial Engineering, Law, Microbial Biotechnology, and Veterinary Medicine.

CAREER SERVICES AND PLACEMENT

MBA Students have access to a wide range of programs and services to enhance their marketability, including career counseling and workshops on resume writing, cover letters, interviewing, and job search strategies. In addition to on-campus recruiting for permanent jobs and internships, the Career Resource Center maintains an online resume referral and job posting service, hosts job fairs, and maintains a library of information about career opportunities with specific companies.

RENSSELAER POLYTECHNIC INSTITUTE
Lally School of Management

AT A GLANCE

The Lally School of Management and Technology was founded in 1963 as an integral part of Rensselaer Polytechnic Institute. Building on Rensselaer's heritage of more than 175 years of leadership in science and engineering, the Lally School develops technologically-savvy, entrepreneurial business leaders who can initiate and guide innovation for commercial success. All programs enable the next generation of business leaders to combine their passion for technology with the management ability to succeed in today's challenging global marketplace.

CAMPUS AND LOCATION

Rensselaer's 275-acre campus is a blend of modern style and classic design. Built into a hillside, it overlooks the Hudson River and the city of Troy, which is experiencing a rebirth as an emerging hotbed of startups, restaurants and artist galleries.

The area offers a relaxed lifestyle with many cultural and recreational opportunities, with easy access to both the high-energy metropolitan centers of the Northeast—Boston, New York City, and Montreal, Canada—and the quiet beauty of the neighboring Adirondack Mountains.

Rensselaer is committed to a campus culture and engaging student experience where students can learn and grow in an environment that encourages discovery, creativity, innovation, and diversity.

DEGREES OFFERED

- MBA - Full time program - 12 months to 22 months to complete.
- MS Business Analytics
- MS Management
- MS Financial Engineering and Risk Analytics
- MS Supply Chain Management
- MS Technology Commercialization and Entrepreneurship
- PhD research program.
- Rensselaer's Hartford CT campus—Education for Working Professionals, including Lally's part-time MBA and MS and Executive MBA programs.

ACADEMIC PROGRAMS

The Lally MBA program prepares business leaders with the skills and thinking that are essential for meeting the day-to-day, real-world challenges of running a business within the evolving dynamics of the global economy. Through experiential hands-on instruction, students acquire an overall understanding of the new sources of value creation brought about by the convergence of globalization and the information technology (IT) revolution.

The curriculum enables students to gain critical expertise in launching, running, and growing a successful business: creating and managing an enterprise; value creation, managing networks, and driving innovation; developing innovative products and services; formulating and executing competitive business strategies; and managing the business implications of emerging technologies. Courses focus on critical business issues in today's global marketplace and integrate all discrete business functions, from finance and operations to global marketing and supply chain management. Key modules include global business, decision models, social responsibility and business ethics, and succeeding in knowledge-intensive organizations.

FACILITIES

The Lally School of Management and Technology is located in one of Rensselaer's most historic buildings, now a technology-intensive center for teaching and research.

The facility features four large classrooms with facilities that are computer-interactive, and set up for videoconferencing. The building also includes fully networked faculty and staff offices, wireless access, a computer study hall, student and faculty lounges, a centrally located student services suite, and a food service concession.

EXPENSES AND FINANCIAL AID

Full-time graduate tuition for the 2012–13 academic year is $43,350. Other costs (estimated living expenses, insurance, etc.) are projected to be about $15,840. Therefore, the cost of attendance for full-time graduate study is approximately $59,190 per year. Part-time study and cohort programs are priced separately.

Upon application to the Lally School for the full time graduate programs, students are automatically considered for financial aid. Financial aid is competitive and granted based on merit.

Financing options include:

Federal Stafford Loans – contact the Rensselaer Financial Aid Office at 518-276-6813.

FACULTY

Lally's faculty are scholars of significant standing and deep experience in a wide range of business contexts. They are research-oriented and focus on advancing business through using the basic disciplines of economics, behavioral science, and analytical methods.

Our clinical faculty strive to exploit their experience and professional expertise to turn theory into practice. They bring real world business experiences into the Lally learning environment.

ADMISSIONS

The Lally School of Management & Technology attracts candidates who clearly articulate and act on their personal and professional goals. Accepted candidates share a strong entrepreneurial spirit and are confident about their analytical and quantitative skills. Required items include completion of the online Rensselaer graduate application, essays, resume, transcripts, letters of recommendation, and a GMAT score. The TOEFL is required for international applicants.

CAREER SERVICES AND PLACEMENT

The Lally School Career Resource Center provides extensive career resources including workshops, mock interview sessions, and career counseling. Lally's industry partners work with us to influence curriculum to meet the most current demands in an ever-changing workplace; provide meaningful internship and co-op experiences for students; and create industry programs that become the platform for cutting-edge faculty research.

RICE UNIVERSITY
Jesse H. Jones Graduate School of Business

AT A GLANCE

Rice University aspires to path-breaking research, excellence in teaching and contributions to the enhancement of our world. As the university's business school, The Jesse H. Jones Graduate School of Business adheres to those same values to cultivate a diverse community of learning and discovery.

More specifically, the Jones School develops principled, innovative thought leaders in global communities. Through a combination of rigorous curriculum, elite Faculty and impressive facilities, Students receive an outstanding business school experience. The result is innovative leadership that engages the entrepreneurial spirit and impacts business on a global level.

The Jones School is one of the world's best teaching and research universities, offering Full-Time MBA, MBA for Executives, and MBA for Professionals and PhD programs. Business concentrations highlight the school's strengths while allowing full-time MBA Students to focus on areas of interest.

Additional Information is available through our website at www.business.rice.edu

CAMPUS AND LOCATION

Rice University is located on a beautiful wooded 300-acre campus in central Houston, minutes from the downtown business district and the city's world-class theater district. The campus is located across the street from the renowned Texas Medical Center and within walking distance to the museum district, Houston Zoological Gardens, and Hermann Park.

DEGREES OFFERED

A Rice MBA is available three distinct programs (Full-Time, MBA for Professionals and MBA for Executives) designed to accommodate Students at every stage of their career. Also available are an MBA/Masters in Engineering with the George R. Brown College of Engineering at Rice; an MBA/MS with Rice's Weiss School of Natural Sciences ; and an MBA/MD in conjunction with Baylor College of Medicine. The Jones School also offers a PhD in Management to develop business school Faculty.

ACADEMIC PROGRAMS

Every course offers unparalleled opportunity to work one-on-one with an accessible, involved, and energetic Faculty. The Jones School Faculty maintains an important balance between teaching and research, believing that current industry knowledge is as critical as textbooks to your education.

A comprehensive core curriculum focuses on managerial and leadership skills, ethics, information technology, and communication skills in addition to the functional areas. Students take elective credit hours, which allow them to custom design their curriculum to suit career goals.

FACILITIES

McNair Hall is the 167,000-square-foot home of the Jones School. It offers a state-of-the-El Paso finance center; the Business Information Center (BIC); tiered classrooms; behavior research and observation room for marketing research and interviews; a 450-seat auditorium; and a career planning center. Fully loaded laptops are provided to all Students, and the Jones School is equipped to make sophisticated use of electronic access.

EXPENSES AND FINANCIAL AID

Application fee: $125

Tuition: $48,500 for the 2013-2014 academic year for the Full-Time program. The total two-year tuition for the MBA for Professionals program for Students beginning in fall 2013 is $95,500 (evenings) or $98,000 (weekends). The total two-year tuition for the MBA for Executives program for Students beginning in fall 2013 is $109,000.

Financial Aid: Over 85 percent of Students attending the Full-Time MBA program receive merit-based scholarships. Rice University's Office of Student Financial Services also administers a variety of federally and privately funded loan programs.

FACULTY

The Jones School's Faculty is consistently recognized for their knowledge, research, teaching ability, and student focus. Each member of the Jones Faculty maintains a balance between teaching and research, ensuring that Students receive the most current, leading-edge education.

STUDENTS

The Jones School attracts Students both nationally and internationally. In fact, 29 percent of first year Students hail from outside the United States and an additional 24 percent are from outside of Texas. A variety of student organizations are available and many sponsor guest speakers, visit area businesses, and take on special projects. In addition, weekly corporate-sponsored "partios"-parties on the Jones School patio-provide relaxation and opportunities to network and bond with fellow Students.

ADMISSION

The Jones School considers each aspect of the application when making Admissions decision. The application requirements include: GMAT; TOEFL or PTE for some international applicants; transcripts from educational institutions; resume; confidential evaluations; essays; interview (invitation only); completed application form and application fee.

Academic Background: A four-year undergraduate degree from an accredited college or university is required for U.S. applicants. International applicants must have an undergraduate degree equivalent to a four-year U.S. degree. Undergraduate and graduate GPAs, test scores, choice of major, electives, course load, and grade patterns are all considered.

Leadership Potential: Demonstrated leadership and management experiences, both on the job and through extracurricular activities, will help us assess leadership potential. We look for individuals with at least two years of professional work experience.

Confidential Evaluations: Evaluations from employers provide perspective on potential student capabilities, enabling us to assess your qualifications more accurately.

Essays: Essays articulating career goals, work experience, and reasons for choosing the Rice MBA program are a crucial component of the application process. These essays are designed to convey intangibles such as reasons for pursuing an MBA; benefits of academic, professional and personal opportunities; and personal expectations of the Jones School experience.

CAREER SERVICES

The Career Management Center (CMC) is housed within the Jones School building and works only with Rice MBA Students and alumni. The CMC serves to support each student's development of a career plan throughout their two years at the Jones School. From day one of immersion to graduation, the CMC works individually with Students to ensure they develop the strategy, job search skills, and networking opportunities that will help them succeed in the MBA job market.

UNIVERSITY OF CALIFORNIA—RIVERSIDE

A. Gary Anderson Graduate School of Management

AT A GLANCE

The A. Gary Anderson Graduate School of Management (AGSM) is all about growth. We are the school of choice for Students, recruiters, and Faculty members who wish to focus on how to identify and evaluate growth opportunities, how to launch and develop, as well as manage and sustain those opportunities. AGSM faces the important growth markets of the future along the Pacific Rim, in Asia, and in South America. All of the growth industries of the future are in our backyard: biotechnology, nanotechnology, information technology, communications, and health care services. AGSM is also about personal growth; we challenge our Students to grow as individuals, as leaders, as managers, and as contributors to community. We invite you to come grow with us.

CAMPUS AND LOCATION

The 1,200-acre Riverside campus of the University of California is conveniently located some 50 miles east of Los Angeles, within easy driving distance of most of the major cultural and recreational offerings in southern California. Enrollment at UCR is approximately 18,500, nearly 16 percent graduate Students. The campus, with modern classroom buildings, beautiful commons, and 161-foot Carillon Tower, is designed to support the academic and research programs as part of its assigned mission in the University of California system. A city of 250,000, Riverside has several major shopping malls, a symphony orchestra, an opera association, two community theaters, an art center, and many restaurants in proximity to the campus.

PROGRAMS AND CURRICULUM

AGSM oversees all graduate programs, including the MBA, PhD in business administration and Master of Professional Accountancy (MPAc). The MBA curriculum balances the art and science of management, with an emphasis on managing through information, and recognizes the global context of management. The program stresses the essential interdependencies that exist across functional areas, emphasizing the development of superior management skills as well as theoretical foundations.

The PhD program is an academic program that will provide candidates with the chance to do intensive research in the field of business. It is built upon an interdisciplinary theme with collaborations from other departments at UCR, including economics, sociology, psychology and statistics.

The Master of Professional Accountancy (MPAc) program will fill the growing demand for qualified certified public accountants (CPAs), especially with a California law effective for years after 2013 that will require 150 semester hours (or 225 quarter hours) of applicable college credit.

FACILITIES

The University library is the focal point of research and study at UCR. The collection includes more than 2.5 million bound volumes, 89,811 print and electronic serial subscriptions, and 2.2 million microforms.

The graduate programs are housed in Anderson Hall. All Students have access to the latest computing equipment, including PC platforms and powerful UNIX workstations.

EXPENSES AND FINANCIAL AID

Several kinds of financial assistance are available. These include fellowships, teaching assistantships, and research assistantships. Applicants indicate interest in support on the application form. Student loans may be applied for through the UCR Financial Aid office.

FACULTY

The A. Gary Anderson Graduate School of Management has a renowned, multi-cultural Faculty, representing excellence in their respective areas. Faculty members have doctorates from world-class universities and publish research in top journals in their fields. Faculty members also have industry and consulting experience and teach in executive programs and workshops.

STUDENTS

Diverse backgrounds and experiences are characteristic of Students in the AGSM graduate programs. The average age of Students is 24. Approximately 52 percent are women, and 10 percent are members of minority groups. Approximately 70 percent of AGSM's MBA Students are international Students. The International Services Center provides special assistance to international Students and their dependants. The diverse student population helps create a dynamic learning experience which enhances the overall experience and the intellectual environment at AGSM.

ADMISSIONS

Admission is open to eligible Students from all undergraduate majors. Admission is based on several criteria, including the quality of previous academic work as measured by GPA for the last two years of undergraduate work, scores on the Graduate Management Admission Test (GMAT) or Graduate Records Examination (GRE), letters of recommendation, and potential for success in the program. Each graduate program has additional admission requirements pertaining to each degree.

Applications are only accepted for the PhD and MPAc for fall quarter only; and applications are accepted for the fall and spring quarters for the MBA. The fall application deadline for International Students is May 1; for domestic Students, June 1 (priority consideration). The spring application deadline for International Students is October 1, and for domestic Students (priority consideration) December 1. Deadlines are subject to change.

For further information, go to http://www.agsm.ucr.edu

SPECIAL PROGRAMS
Global Focus

Most of AGSM's required courses include a global perspective, with recognition of the international issues that affect each functional area. In addition, electives in many of the functional areas provide opportunities for in-depth studies of international topics.

CAREER SERVICES AND PLACEMENT

A full range of internship and career planning services is offered through the AGSM Career Center. The center is staffed by professional counselors to address the specific career needs of graduate business Students. Services available include on-campus interviews, career seminars and resume writing workshops, mock interviews, and individual counseling.

UNIVERSITY OF COLORADO BOULDER

AT A GLANCE

Robust curriculum, inspired instruction, dynamic environment, supportive community.

Whether you're pursuing an MBA or MS degree to advance your career, broaden your skill set, or change course, the Leeds School of Business serves as a foundation for professional and personal development. The supportive Leeds community encourages you to embrace the entrepreneurial spirit, create change, and act on new ideas. We offer Students the opportunity to pursue a Leeds MBA degree as a member of the full-time program, which provides an immersive experience, or the part-time program, designed specifically for working professionals. Both programs take two years to complete, share Faculty and staff, and provide Students with a strong business foundation. We also offer four different MS programs in specialized fields - MS in Finance, MS in Real Estate, MS in Supply Chain Management, and MS in Data Analytics for Students who want to develop depth and expertise in a single specific area.

CAMPUS AND LOCATION

Leeds offers a highly individualized academic experience with approximately 300 MBA and Master's Students in its full-time, part-time MBA and MS programs. As a premiere research university, the University of Colorado Boulder provides broad resources with the latest in engineering and technology innovation and a beautiful campus setting with breathtaking mountain views. The Boulder-Denver business corridor is an epicenter for start-up and venture activity, new and emerging industries, and is a national hub for telecommunications, high tech, and bio tech companies.

DEGREES OFFERED

Leeds MBA programs offer a general management foundation and the ability to customize with a functional area of expertise in marketing, finance, management, or systems. Students may combine this breadth and depth of study with one of our nationally recognized specialties in entrepreneurship, real estate and sustainability. We also offer four MS programs in finance, real estate, data analytics, and supply chain management, each providing in-depth education in a single area of emphasis.

PROGRAMS AND CURRICULUM

Leeds has dual degree programs with eight other graduate departments at the University of Colorado Boulder (See Form J). Aside from dual degree options, Students may take up to four graduate school electives outside of the MBA curriculum. Two full-semester study abroad opportunities are available with Instituto de Empressa in Madrid, Spain and the Indian Institute of Management, Calcutta.

FACILITIES

Leeds' Koelbel Building is a LEED (Leadership in Energy & Environmental Design) certified showcase of environmental stewardship and state-of-the-art classroom technology. The Koelbel Building offers spacious classrooms, an information commons, team rooms, corporate interviewing suites, community space, and breathtaking mountain views.

EXPENSES AND FINANCIAL AID

As a public institution, the University of Colorado offers comparatively low tuition rates. US citizens and permanent residents who are not Colorado residents can establish residency during the first year of the program and qualify for in-state tuition for the second year of the program. In addition, merit fellowships are awarded to outstanding candidates. Need-based awards are available and require applicants to file a Free Application for Federal Student Aid (FAFSA) form.

FACULTY

Leeds Faculty are leading scholars and business practitioners who integrate their research into the curriculum and their teaching. The Faculty actively partner with local entrepreneurs and CEOs to generate hands-on learning experiences and challenge Students to develop and apply new problem-solving skills.

STUDENTS

Students come to Leeds from a wide variety of professional backgrounds, undergraduate institutions and majors, and from different parts of the globe. They choose Leeds for the high level of interaction with Faculty, rigorous academic programs, exposure to entrepreneurship and innovation, involvement in emerging industries, quality of life, and return on investment.

ADMISSIONS

The Admissions process, while selective, is designed to be personal and holistic. Applications are reviewed with a variety of criteria in mind including educational background, GMAT or GRE test scores, professional work experience, letters of recommendation, essays, and, in some cases, personal interviews.

SPECIAL PROGRAMS

Eight dual degree options are available through the Leeds School of Business: JD/MBA, MBA/MS in Telecommunications, MBA/MS in Computer Science, MBA/MS in Environmental Studies, MBA/MA or MFA in Fine Arts, MBA/MA in Theatre and Dance, MBA/MA in Germanic and Slavic Languages, MBA/MA in Anthropology.

CAREER SERVICES AND PLACEMENT

The Career Connections Office at Leeds takes a proactive role in preparing incoming Master's program Students to strategize about short and long term goals that lead to internships and permanent placement. Our Centers of Excellence in Entrepreneurship and Real Estate also play a significant part in the networking process for Students interested in smaller companies and start-up ventures, or real estate development.

UNIVERSITY OF CONNECTICUT
School of Business

AT A GLANCE

Educating business leaders for over 130 years, the University of Connecticut (UConn) is ranked among the top 3 percent of business schools worldwide according to BloombergBusinessweek, Forbes, and U.S. News & World Report. UConn's MBA Program offers a comprehensive state-of-the-art business education that empowers business leaders to anticipate and effectively manage the challenges within today's dynamic and complex world of business. UConn's competitive advantages include a completely individualized plan of study based on the candidate's ultimate career goals, as well as the integration of award-winning innovative experiential learning opportunities that radically challenge a student's intellect, enhance skill sets and prepare individuals for success in life as well as in the competitive world of business.

CAMPUS AND LOCATION

UConn has grown in recent years from a strong regional school to a prominent national academic institution with over 29,000 Students and 190,000 alumni. The University's span of 4,300+ acres includes ten schools and colleges at its main campus in Storrs, separate Schools of Law and Social Work in Hartford, five regional campuses throughout the state and Schools of Medicine and Dental Medicine at the UConn Health Center in Farmington. Right in the middle of Fortune 500 territory, the state capital and metropolitan area of Hartford is 30 minutes away, Boston is a 90 minute drive, and New York City is a 3-hour drive.

DEGREES OFFERED

The UConn School of Business offers a traditional full-time MBA degree, as well as part-time and Executive MBA programs. UConn also offers MS degrees in Accounting (online), Financial Risk Management (FRM), and Business Analytics & Project Management (BAPM), as well as a variety of dual-degree programs including MBA/JD, MBA/MD, MBA/PharmD, MBA/MA in International Studies, MBA/MS in Nursing. A post graduate Advance Business Certificate is also offered in various business disciplines.

ACADEMIC PROGRAMS

The full-time, 2-year MBA program at UConn offers Students a practical, comprehensive business education that truly integrates basic business fundamentals with innovative experiential learning. This carefully blended curriculum guarantees the highly desirable real-world experience that today's global businesses demand.

The curriculum includes fundamental business courses with a yearlong capstone project-the Application of Core Teaching (ACT), an Internship Milestone, experiential learning opportunities and customized areas of specialization based on individual career goals and objectives.

FACILITIES

UConn Students study in state-of-the-art research and learning facilities. Classrooms and meeting spaces are outfitted with broad multimedia capability reflecting the School's commitment to meet the demands of the information era.

EXPENSES AND FINANCIAL AID

2012-2013 tuition and fees for the full-time MBA program for the academic year (two semesters) are $12,866 for Connecticut residents and $30,074 for non-residents. Housing and living costs vary among candidates, but are approximately $7,250 for graduate resident housing and $5,200 for meals. Additional costs include required health insurance, textbooks, mobile computer, laundry and incidentals.

Financial aid is available in the form of loans and scholarships. Most financial aid is awarded on the basis of established need, primarily determined through an analysis of an applicant's Free Application for Federal Student Aid (FAFSA). The School of Business also offers a limited number of merit-based graduate/teaching assistantships and scholarships. More information is available through UConn's Financial Aid Office at 860-486-2819 or www.financialaid.uconn.edu.

FACULTY

UConn's Faculty offer a wealth of academic and business experience to Students. Over 96 percent of them have earned a PhD or the highest degree in their field. Most are actively involved in scholarly activities that enable them to stay current in and contribute to their fields of knowledge, as well as to bring a balanced perspective between theory and practice into the classroom.

STUDENT BODY

UConn MBA Students come from a wide variety of undergraduate institutions, both domestic and international. Their undergraduate degrees represent majors in many diverse areas - from engineering and English, sciences and fine arts, to business and economics. In a typical class of Students, 35 percent are women, the average age is 28, and approximately 35 percent are international Students. Friendliness and informality characterize student life at the main campus. Social and professional organizations, including the Graduate Business Association (GBA), offer a variety of activities to satisfy the needs of Students.

ADMISSIONS

Admission to UConn's MBA Program is very competitive. The minimum requirements for admission include two years of postgraduate professional work experience; a minimum 3.0 GPA on a 4.0 scale, or the equivalent, from a four-year accredited institution; and a total GMAT score of at least 600. For international Students whose native language is not English, a TOEFL score of at least 233 (computer-based) is required. The application deadline for international applicants is January 31 and for domestic applicants, March 1.

SPECIAL PROGRAMS

Essential to UConn's MBA Program curriculum is the incorporation of innovative experiential learning accelerators. These unique practice-based initiatives integrate traditional teaching and classroom instruction with high-profile practical applications to close the gap between theory and practice. UConn MBA experiential learning accelerators include the SS&C Technologies Financial Accelerator, Connecticut Innovation Accelerator, $2M Student Managed Fund, International Business Accelerator and SCOPE (sustainable community outreach and public engagement.)

ADDITIONAL INFORMATION

The UConn School of Business is nationally accredited by AACSB International - The Association to Advance Collegiate Schools of Business - and is a member of the Graduate Management Admissions Council (GMAC), the European Foundation for Management Development (EFMD), and the MBA Roundtable. UConn is also accredited by the New England Association of Schools & Colleges (NEASC).

CAREER SERVICES AND PLACEMENT

UConn's career planning activities begin during orientation and continue throughout the MBA program. Primary recruiters include Aetna, Cigna, CVS, Deloitte, Ernst & Young, General Electric, Gerber Technologies, Hartford Financial Services, IBM, Nike, Philips, PricewaterhouseCoopers, The Hartford, United Technologies Corp., Wachovia, ESPN, and UBS. For the class of 2013, the average salary offer was $96,555 with sign-on bonuses ranging up to $15,000.

UNIVERSITY OF HOUSTON—VICTORIA
School of Business Administration

AT A GLANCE

Quality - The University of Houston-Victoria School of Business Adminis-tration is accredited by AACSB International, the hallmark of excellence in management education. The business school has been ranked number one for the Greatest Opportunity for Minority Students, serving Students from nearly 25 countries by award winning Faculty from over 12 countries.

Value - The school has been named nationally as one of the "Top 25 Ranked Best Buys" in distance learning by GetEducated.com for the past five years and UHV consistently ranks in the top four best value Texas Universities for affordability.

Convenience - Face to face evening courses are offered at multiple loca-tions. Students may choose face to face and online courses and create a sched-ule to fit around their professional life. UHV is considered a national leader in distance education and online course delivery and the MBA has been of-fered completely online since 1999. The convenient program formats allow Students to continue their education part time in conjunction with a full time career or accelerate degree completion as a full time student.

CAMPUS AND LOCATION

Business programs are offered at three locations listed below. The main cam-pus is in Victoria, TX and the teaching centers in Sugar Land and Katy are approximately 20 miles from downtown Houston and the energy corridor.

University of Houston-Victoria
3007 North Ben Wilson
Victoria, Texas 77901
University of Houston Sugar Land
14000 University Boulevard
Sugar Land, Texas 77479
University of Houston System Cinco Ranch
4242 South Mason Road
Katy, Texas 77450

DEGREES OFFERED

Graduate Programs

Strategic MBA and Global MBA
° Accounting
° Finance
° General Business
° International Business (except Global MBA)
° Management
° Marketing
° Economic Development
° Entrepreneurship

Fourth year Bridge MBA and Global MBA

   This program is designed for Students holding a three year bachelors degree from outside the US.

Master of Science in Economic Development and Entrepreneurship

   This 36 credit hour online program is ideal for entrepreneurs and those work-ing in the economic development field of attracting and growing businesses.

FACILITIES

University of Houston-Victoria, Victoria, Texas

University of Houston Sugar Land, Sugar Land, Texas

University of Houston System-Cinco Ranch, Katy, Texas

EXPENSES AND FINANCIAL AID

As of August 2012, tuition and fees for Texas residents are $1140 per 3 credit hour graduate course. Non residents pay $2193 per course in tuition and fees. The UHV School of Business Administration has been named one of the "Top 25 Ranked Best Buys" in distance learning by GetEducated.com for the past five years.

UHV offers scholarships, grants and loan options, as well as payment plans to assist Students with funding their education. A limited number of gradu-ate assistantships and fellowships are also available.

FACULTY

Business programs are taught by Faculty from over 12 countries, with PhDs from schools such as University of Texas-Austin, Arizona State, Indiana University, Michigan State, University of Illinois, Georgia State, and Syra-cuse. Most importantly, Faculty are dedicated teachers who are responsive and accessible to Students, and are active researchers with publications in leading journals in their fields.

ADMISSIONS

The individual attention for which UHV School of Business Administra-tion is known begins with the admission process. Admission requirements for the MBA program include the following:

° An overall GPA of 2.5 or a GPA of 2.5 based on your last 60 hours of course work.

° A GMAT score of 450. Students may enroll in up to 12 hours without their official GMAT scores on file. For those Students who qualify, a GMAT waiver is available.

° International Students need a TOEFL score of 550 (written), 213 (com-puter based), or 79 (IBT).

° Online application with no application fee.

° Admissions decisions are made promptly and early application is encour-aged but not required.

SPECIAL PROGRAMS

In addition to the Strategic MBA, UHV offers a Global MBA and a Master of Science in Economic Development and Entrepreneurship. The MS-EDE is the only program of its kind, combining traditional economic de-velopment (attracting businesses) with entrepreneurship (starting busi-nesses). The 36-hour curriculum may be completed part-time in 2 years, and is available entirely online.

UNIVERSITY OF ROCHESTER
Simon School of Business

AT A GLANCE

The William E. Simon School of Business at the University of Rochester in Rochester, New York offers an integrated, cross-functional approach to management, using economics as both the framework and common language of business. Programs offered are Full-Time MBA and MS programs, Executive MBA, Accelerated Professional MBA, Part-Time Flexible MBA and Part-Time MS programs.

The school is accredited by the AACSB-The Association to Advance Collegiate Schools of Business since 1966.

CAMPUS AND LOCATION

The Simon School is situated on the River Campus of the University of Rochester, near the banks of the Genesee River, and three miles from downtown Rochester, New York. The Simon School is one of seven schools and colleges within the University of Rochester.

DEGREES OFFERED
Full-Time Study

The flagship two-year MBA degree requires 67 hours of study and a 3.0 grade-point average. There are two entrance dates, August or January. A new One-Year MBA option is tailored for career builders who are looking to stay within their industry or market and want a shorter term of study.

Accelerated Professional MBA

The PMBA is a partial lock-step, class cohort system in which teams of Students take their nine core courses together in a structured program. Then 11 electives are required to complete the desired concentrations. Continuing at two classes per quarter, cohort members typically complete their degrees in 2.5 years.

Part-Time Study

Applicants to the Part-Time Flexible MBA Program may matriculate in any quarter. They may also take up to four classes before matriculating to the program.

Executive MBA Program

The program offers candidates the same curriculum, resources and Faculty as the full-time program without career interruption. Classes meet every other Friday/Saturday for two academic years in Rochester, New York. The Simon School also offers a program in Bern, Switzerland. (22 months).

MS Programs

Ten Master of Science programs are offered: Accountancy, Business Analytics, Finance, Information Systems Management, Management, Manufacturing Management, Marketing, Medical Management, Pricing, and Service Management. Each MS degree is offered on a full-time or part-time basis.

Academic Programs General

The Simon School's MBA programs are designed to train individuals to solve management problems as team members in a study-team structure. The curriculum emphasizes learning the principles of economics and effective decision making through a mix of lecture, case study, and project courses. Nine core courses are required. A three-credit course over three quarters in business communications is required of all full-time Students. Eleven elective courses are required.

FACILITIES

The following is a description of Simon School facilities:

Schlegel Hall is a four-story classroom and student services building. The building contains nine theatre-style classrooms, which seat 35 to 100 Students, and 21 rooms for group study. Classrooms are equipped with state-of-the-art audio and visual technology.

Carol G. Simon Hall houses the school's administration, Faculty and PhD Students. Carol G. Simon Hall is linked to Schlegel and Gleason Halls by the Florescue-von Manstein Plaza and is also connected to it by a tunnel. The building contains more than 75 offices, several conference rooms, and a variety of lounge spaces for Faculty and staff.

James S. Gleason Hall is the 38,000-square-foot classroom building linked to Schlegel Hall. Gleason Hall houses five classrooms, up to 16 study rooms, and a significantly expanded Career Management Center suite, including eight dedicated interview rooms.

EXPENSES AND FINANCIAL AID

In addition to the $150 application fee, tuition is $48,007 per year, for 2012-2013. The cost of books and supplies averages $1,935 a year, and living expenses (rent, food supplies, personal expenses, and health insurance) were estimated at approximately $18,170 for the 2012-2013 academic year. Both US and international applicants are eligible for merit awards.

STUDENT BODY

Each August, approximately 350 full-time Students enter the Simon community. Another 40 Students join their classmates in January. August entrants complete the first-year core courses during the fall and winter quarters; the majority of January entrants complete core courses during the winter, spring, and summer quarters. Within each cohort, Students are assigned to a study team of four or five members. Each team always includes representatives from at least three countries.

In the MBA and MS Classes of 2013, 25 countries are represented. For the MBA class, prior full-time work experience averages 4.8 years, and the average age is 28. Women comprise 23 percent of the class. Nineteen percent of Simon Students are members of American minority groups.

ADMISSIONS

A Simon School Admissions Committee reads each application individually and evaluates recommendations, teamwork, and communication skills, the nature and scope of prior work experience, the undergraduate academic record, and GMAT or GRE scores. All undergraduate majors are represented in the program.

SPECIAL PROGRAMS

During the one-week Orientation Program, Students participate in self-assessment exercises, personal selling and communication skills instruction, corporate leadership training, and one-on-one career counseling. In addition, Students have the opportunity to participate in the Vision Partnership Program, designed to foster relationships between our Students and the business community. It is a unique opportunity for Students to work as a multi-disciplinary team and build experience by tackling real-world problems and challenges.

ADDITIONAL INFORMATION

Year after year, the Simon School consistently ranks high on the lists of top b-school programs. These rankings include: Bloomberg Businessweek, U.S. News & World Report, Financial Times of London and Forbes.

CAREER SERVICES AND PLACEMENT

The Career Management Center team works diligently to develop new and enhance existing corporate partnerships to provide a wide range of career opportunities for both summer internships and full-time career positions.

The Career Management Center's staff offers a targeted, personalized approach to assist Students in identifying, initiating, and implementing highly effective career search plans.

THE UNIVERSITY OF TULSA
College of Business Administration

AT A GLANCE
The University of Tulsa's College of Business Administration has graduated skilled and inspired business professionals since 1935. In 2008, the college was renamed the Collins College of Business in honor of the visionary leadership of Tulsa businessman and Board of Trustees Chair, Fulton Collins. Today, as business evolves under the forces of globalization and technology, we pride ourselves on keeping pace with a variety of programs that prepare Students for success in the business world.

CAMPUS AND LOCATION
Founded in 1894, The University of Tulsa is a private, doctoral-granting university located in Tulsa, OK. The university has an earned reputation for exceptional academics, with one in every ten undergraduate Students being a National Merit Scholar. Student life abounds the campus of 4,100 Students with over 40 Registered Student Organizations, 5 IFC fraternities and 6 NPC sororities. We are the nation's smallest university to participate in the NCAA's Division IA, and one in ten Students is participating in intercollegiate athletics. Located just 10 minutes from downtown Tulsa, Students enjoy all of the amenities of the city.

DEGREES OFFERED
Master of Business Administration (MBA)

Full Time MBA: Partnering with Business

MBA for Working Professionals

Master of Accountancy (MAcc)

Master of Science in Finance (MSF)

Concentrations: Corporate Finance, Investments and Portfolio Management, Risk Management

Online Master of Energy Business (MEB)

The following dual programs are also available:

MBA/MSF

MSF/MS Applied Mathematics

Juris Doctor/MBA

Juris Doctor/MSF

PROGRAMS AND CURRICULUM
STUDENT INVESTMENT FUND: Students are able to apply financial theories and models by making investment decisions and managing a real portfolio of financial assets in excess of $2.5M.

STUDY ABROAD: The Center for Global Education provides oversight for TU's academic programs abroad, managing 11 reciprocal exchange partnerships with universities in Austria, Australia, China, Finland, France, Germany, England, Switzerland and New Zealand.

WILLIAMS RISK MANAGEMENT CENTER: This learning laboratory allows Students to participate in controlled financial scenarios where they make informed business decisions using Bloomberg terminals, extensive financial databases and computer software.

GOVERNORS CUP: The Donald W. Reynolds state-wide Governor's Cup business plan competition is designed to encourage Students to act upon their ideas and talents. Our graduate teams won top honors in both the 2012 and 2013 competitions.

INTERNSHIPS: Internships may be available to provide you with the relevant work experience you need to make the next step toward your ultimate career goal.

FACILITIES
The Williams Student Services Center, located in Helmerich Hall, home of the Collins College of Business, provides graduate Students the ability to consult their academic advisor, enroll for classes, or research and strategize career opportunities with the Assistant Dean of the Business Career Center, all in the same suite. Campus amenities include on-campus luxury apartments, wireless internet access, eateries, a post office, McFarlin Library, Collins Fitness Center and Case Tennis Center.

EXPENSES AND FINANCIAL AID
2013-2014 Tuition is $1,087 per credit hour for all domestic and international Students. Student fees are $5 per credit hour.

More than 90 percent of our graduate business Students receive merit-based financial assistance, either through scholarships, graduate assistantships or company-tuition reimbursement. All financial award application deadlines are February 1; financial award applicants are required to submit a FAFSA.

FACULTY
With an 11:1 student-to-Faculty ratio, Students are never a "number" to our professors. We have 30 full-time Faculty members teaching at the graduate level. Passionate, approachable, and accessible, they are able to combine academic theory with real world experience.

ADMISSIONS
Students applying to a Collins College of Business Graduate Program must submit the following documents:

° Application (available online)

° $40.00 fee

° Transcripts from ALL institutions of higher education

° Acceptable GMAT score (GRE acceptable for MSF program ONLY)

° Three professional reference letters

° Résumé

International Applicants must also submit:

° Acceptable TOEFL score (575 paper, 232 computer, 90 internet), or

Acceptable IELTS score (6.5)

° Confirmation of Financial Resources

ADDITIONAL INFORMATION
The Collins College of Business has been accredited by AACSB International since 1949. This accreditation is important to you because it provides assurance that the university and Faculty are producing relevant research and remaining current with issues in business. Many companies are now requiring employees to attend AACSB accredited schools in order to participate in tuition reimbursement programs.

CAREER SERVICES AND PLACEMENT
Career services are an integral component of our graduate business programs; more than 200 companies turn to The University of Tulsa annually to hire our graduates. The Collins College of Business Assistant Dean of the Business Career Center works one-on-one with Students to research and strategize career opportunities. These services are available to all business Students and may include mentorship and internship opportunities.

WILLAMETTE UNIVERSITY
Atkinson Graduate School of Management

AT A GLANCE

As a national leader in experiential learning, the Willamette MBA builds the knowledge, experience and professional career management skills needed for successful careers in business, government and not-for-profit organizations. Programs include the Early Career/Career Change MBA for Students preparing for their first professional position, career change or advancement; and the MBA for Professionals for experienced Students seeking career enhancement or advancement. All Willamette MBA programs emphasize hands-on learning and are accredited by AACSB International—the global hallmark of excellence in business education.

CAMPUS AND LOCATION

Our location offers an excellent quality of life, friendly people, mild climate and the recreational resources of the beautiful Pacific Northwest. Professionally, the Portland-Salem area provides convenient access to a multitude of businesses (including Northwest legends Nike and Intel) and a number of government and not-for-profit organizations.

Willamette MBA Students are an active community who benefit from a vibrant recreational and social life. Students can ski the Cascade Mountains, enjoy Oregon's Pacific Coast, windsurf in the Columbia River Gorge, hike forested areas, participate in student activities and professional organizations, and enjoy the big city opportunities of Portland.

Willamette's campus is spacious and beautiful, and located across the street from the Oregon State Capitol near downtown Salem.

PROGRAMS AND CURRICULUM

The MBA for Professionals allows individuals with three or more years of professional work experience to complete their MBA while employed. The program is 24 months long, and features experiential learning and convenient evening classes. Students immediately apply what they learn to their job and accelerate their career.

The Early Career/Career Change MBA is specifically designed for Students seeking career entry, change or advancement. The program emphasizes learning-by-doing, and does not require previous work experience. From the first day of class Students apply what they learn to real organizations and develop the tools they need to manage, lead and succeed <http://www.willamette.edu/mba/full-time/curriculum/index.html>. In just 21 months, Early Career/Career Change MBA Students learn the core principles of management and strategic decision-making, refine their career interests, build a resume of respected professional experience, and develop in-depth expertise in one or more career areas of interest:

Accounting
Entrepreneurship
Finance
Global Management
Human Resources
Marketing
Operations, Analysis & Systems
Organizational Analysis
Public & Not-for-Profit Management
Sustainability Management

FACILITIES

The Salem campus includes two libraries, recreational and fitness facilities, dining centers, student center, concert hall, art museum, and more. The Portland Center is conveniently located in the Pearl District with easy access to public transportation and public parking. All facilities offer wireless access to the Internet, email, network software and printing services.

EXPENSES AND FINANCIAL AID

2013-2014 tuition for the Early Career/Career Change MBA is $34,782 for the two semester academic year. Merit-based scholarships, Federal Stafford Loans and Federal Graduate Plus Loans are available to eligible Students. 2013-2014 tuition for the MBA for Professionals is $66,600 (total cost) for the six semester program. MBA for Professionals tuition includes the cost of books and fees. Merit-based scholarships, Federal Stafford Loans and Federal Graduate Plus Loans are available to eligible Students.

FACULTY

Willamette MBA Faculty are award winning teachers, scholars and mentors. They believe that great MBA teaching emphasizes the importance of an integrated understanding of management decision-making and the practical application of what you learn to real organizations. They are also easily accessible and dedicated to the success of their Students and alumni.

STUDENTS

Our Students are described by their references as energetic, creative, ethical, exceptional, friendly, mature, hard working, insightful, professional, reliable, team-players and leaders. Early Career/Career Change Students come from around the world and across the U.S. The average student is 25 years old, has zero to five years of work experience, and is utilizing the MBA to prepare for career entry or career change. MBA for Professionals Students have three or more years of work experience and are preparing for career advancement and enhancement. The average student is 33 years old and employed while completing their MBA. Students represent a wide variety of businesses and organizations from the Portland/Salem metropolitan areas.

ADMISSION

Applicants for the Early Career and Career Change MBA program should visit http://www.willamette.edu/mba/full-time/index.html for information. Applicants for the MBA for Professionals program should visit http://www.willamette.edu/mba/professionals/index.html for information.

SPECIAL PROGRAMS:

The Willamette Early Career/Career Change MBA builds your professional experience through internships, consulting projects with client organizations, and innovative elective courses. Students have the opportunity to learn SAP and other analytical tools, manage the student investment fund, participate as a member of an angel investing group, start their own entrepreneurial venture, and apply the tools of marketing, human resources, accounting, operations, sustainability, ethics, strategy and finance to real organizations through class projects and internships.

ADDITIONAL INFO

The Early Career/Career Change MBA offers a unique opportunity to use an MBA to start or change your professional career.

CAREER

An outstanding program of career services supports the goals of Willamette MBA Students. Services include the best practices of career management, workshops, internships, networking, employment connections and interviews, individual counseling, mentoring, career and networking fairs, peer advisors and student professional organizations.

Nearly 100 percent of Early Career/Career Change Students participate in an internship. A sample of internship employers includes Columbia Sportswear, Hewlett Packard, Merrill Lynch, Intel, Microsoft, Nike, Tektronix, Habitat for Humanity, Mercy Corps Northwest, and State of Oregon.

DECODING DEGREES

Many business programs offer a number of degrees, including joint- or combined-degree programs with other departments (or with other schools) that you can earn along with your MBA. You'll find the abbreviations for these degrees in the individual school profiles, but we thought we'd give you a little help in figuring out exactly what they are.

AGSIM	American Graduate School of International Management Social Service Administration		MA	Master of Arts
			MAB	Master of Agribusiness
APC	Advanced Professional Certificate		MAcc	Master of Accountancy (or Accounting)
BA	Bachelor of Arts		MAAE	Master of Arts in Applied Economics
BASC	Bachelor in Engineering		MAEcon	Master of Arts in Economics
BBA	Bachelor of Business Administration		MAg	Master of Agriculture
BPA	Bachelor of Public Affairs		MAIB	Master of Arts in International Business
BS	Bachelor of Science		MAIS	Master of Accounting and Information Systems
BSB	Bachelor of Science in Business			
BSBA	Bachelor of Science in Business Administration		MALL	Master of Arts in Language Learning
			MAPS	Master of Asian Pacific Studies
CIS	Computer Information Systems (or Sciences)		MAR	Master of Arts in Religion
			MArch	Master of Architecture
DBA	Doctor of Business Administration		MAS	Master of Actuarial Science
DDS	Doctor of Dental Surgery		MBA	Master of Business Administration
DMD	Doctor of Dental Medicine		MBE	Master of Business Education
DO	Doctor of Osteopathic Medicine		MBI	Master of Business Informatics
DPS	Doctor of Professional Studies		MBS	Master of Business Studies
EdD	Doctor of Education		MD	Doctor of Medicine
EDM	Executive Doctor of Management		MDIV	Master of Divinity
EMBA	Executive MBA		ME	Master of Engineering
EMIB	Executive Master of International Business		MECOM	Master of Electronic Commerce
EMPA	Executive Master of Public Administration		MEd	Master of Educational Leadership/ Master of Education
EMS	Executive Master of Science			
EMSM	Executive Master of Science in Management		MEM	Master of Engineering and Management
			MEng	Master of Engineering
EMSMOT	Executive Master of Science in Management of Technology		MF	Master of Forestry
			MFA	Master of Fine Arts
EMST	Executive Master of Science in Taxation		MHA	Master of Health Administration
GDPA	Graduate Diploma in Accounting		MHR	Master of Human Resources
GEMBA	Global Executive Master of Business Administration		MHRM	Master of Human Resources Management
HRIM	Hotel, Restaurants and Institutional Management		MIA	Master of International Affairs
			MIAS	Master of International and Area Studies
IAMBA	Information Age Master of Business Administration		MIB	Master of International Business
IMBA	International MBA		MIE	Master of Industrial Engineering
IPD	Interdisciplinary Product Development		MILR	Master of Industrial and Labor Relations
JD	Juris Doctorate		MIM	Master of International Management
LLB	Bachelor of Law		MIS	Management Information Systems

MISM	Master of Information Systems Management	MSIM	Master of Science in Industrial Management
MLAS	Master of Liberal Arts and Science	MSIMC	Master of Science in Integrated Marketing Communications
MMIS	Master of Management Information Systems	MSIR	Master of Science in Industrial Relations
MMR	Master of Marketing Research	MSIS	Master of Science in Information Systems
MMS	Master of Management Science	MSISE	Master of Science in Industrial and Systems Engineering
MNO	Master of Nonprofit Organizations		
MOD	Master of Science in Organizational Development	MSISM	Master of Science in Information Systems Management
MPA	Master of Public Administration	MSIT	Master of Science in Information Technology
MPAcc	Master of Professional Accounting		
MPH	Master of Public Health	MSITM	Master of Science in Information Technology Management
MPIA Affairs	Master of Public and International	MSM	Master of Science in Management
MPL	Master of Planning	MSMIS	Master of Science in Management Information Systems
MPP	Master of Public Policy		
MRED	Master of Real Estate Development	MSMOT	Master of Science in Management of Technology
MS	Master of Science	MSN	Master of Science in Nursing
MSA	Master of Science in Accountancy (or Accounting)	MSOD	Master of Science in Organization Development
MSAIS	Master of Science in Accounting Information Systems	MSpAd	Master of Sports Administration
		MSRE	Master of Science in Real Estate
MSAT	Master of Science in Accountancy, Taxation	MSS	Master of Social Science
		MSSA	Master of Science in Social Administration
MSB	Master of Science in Business	MST	Master of Science in Taxation
MSBA	Master of Science in Business Administration	MSTM	Master of Science in Telecommunications Management
MSE	Master of Science in Engineering		
MSEC	Master of Science in Electronic Commerce	MSW	Master of Social Work
		MTAX	Master of Taxation
MSF	Master of Science in Finance	MTLM	Master of Transportation and Logistics Management
MSFA	Master of Science in Financial Analysis		
MSFS	Master of Science in Foreign Services	NEMBA	National Executive Master of Business Administration
MSG	Master of Science in Gerontology		
MSGFA	Master of Science in Global Financial Analysis	PharmD	Doctor of Pharmacy
		PhD	Doctor of Philosophy
MSHA	Master of Science in Health Administration	SM	Master of Science
MSHFID	Master of Science in Human Factors in Information Design	TSM	Telecommunications Systems Management
MSIAM	Master of Science in Information Age Marketing	VMD	Doctor of Veterinary Medicine
MSIB Business	Master of Science in International		
MSIE	Master of Science in Industrial Engineering		

INDEX

ALPHABETICAL INDEX

INDEX BY LOCATION

INTERNATIONAL

INDEX BY COST

INDEX BY MBA CONCENTRATION

ENTREPRENEURSHIP

FINANCE

HEALTHCARE ADMINISTRATION

HUMAN RESOURCES

INTERNATIONAL BUSINESS

LEADERSHIP

MARKETING

NON-PROFIT MANAGEMENT

REAL ESTATE

SUPPLY CHAIN MANAGEMENT

NOTES

NOTES

NOTES

Notes

NOTES

NOTES